THE SECRET HISTORY OF THE WORLD
AND HOW TO GET OUT ALIVE

Books by
Laura Knight-Jadczyk

The Wave Series
The High Strangeness of Dimensions, Densities and the Process of Alien Abduction
Amazing Grace
9-11: The Ultimate Truth

THE SECRET HISTORY OF THE WORLD

AND HOW TO GET OUT ALIVE

LAURA KNIGHT-JADCZYK

Red Pill Press
2005

ACKNOWLEDGEMENTS

Since this book is ulitmately one of synthesis, I want to thank all the great seekers who have contributed so much to my own researches. I have tried to acknowledge each and every one and their unique ideas throughout the text in the footnotes, and in the bibliography. If I have missed any, my sincere apologies.

My thanks go to Henry See for being a wonderful editor and critic; to the Quantum Future Group for support; to our readers for the questions that led to the answers; to my children for feeding Mommy while she was writing; to my Ark for understanding and accepting me and my passions; and to Cassiopaea, myself in the future, for showing me that future.

TABLE OF CONTENTS

PREFACE BY PATRICK RIVIÈRE

THE SECRET HISTORY OF THE WORLD

This book of revolutionary importance is essential reading.

With this original work, Laura Knight-Jadczyk shares with us her prodigious discoveries that put into question History as well as our habitual observations concerning the myth of the "Grail". She does this by revisiting the Bible and comparative mythology, looking closely into parallel universes and hyperspace, and penetrating into quantum physics, genetics, and the mysteries of the diverse creations populating the hyperdimensions of the Cosmos.

Throughout her exposé, Laura Knight-Jadczyk refers to two powerful works of the scientist-alchemist Fulcanelli: *The Mystery of the Cathedrals* and *Dwellings of the Philosophers*. She applies her vast knowledge to the continuation of his work.

Thus, following in the footsteps of Fulcanelli (citing Huysmans) when he denounces the constant lies and omissions from official History over the course of time, Laura Knight-Jadczyk, citing numerous examples, exposes the manipulations in the official history of ancient civilizations of which humanity is the victim. She strives to re-establish the truth, and her answers are often enlightening.

According to Laura Knight-Jadczyk, the mysteries of the Holy Grail and the Ark of the Temple refer to a particular, very advanced "technology" – with the aim, for example, of teleportation and changing between space-time dimensions – a secret and sacred science of which only a few great "Initiates" have remained custodians. Christ Jesus was the surest guarantor of this precious legacy, and, although it might displease Dan Brown (author of *The DaVinci Code*), the genealogical lineage of the "Sangréal" (the "Sang Royal" or "Holy Blood"), is not at all as he believes it to be! The reader of this important work by Laura Knight-Jadczyk will realize that there are completely different conclusions to that mystery.

Her erudition cannot but impress the reader during the course of an assiduous reading of this quite astonishing book. As to her inspiration, what can we say, and, from whence could it come, if not the Light of the stars?

Patrick Rivière

Patrick Rivière is a writer and author of numerous works that have been published in France and that have been translated and published in many languages. He is a specialist on the "Grail" (On the Paths of the Grail) and of Alchemy following the path of Fulcanelli (Fulcanelli Revealed), two works soon to be published by Red Pill Press.

NOTE TO THE READER ABOUT THE CASSIOPAEANS

The term "Cassiopaeans" appears in several places in this book. While the information contained in this book could as well be given without referring to this term, it is better to point out the source of the inspiration. The name Cassiopaea was given by a source contacted by LKJ in 1994 after a two year long experiment in superluminal communication. The source identified itself by saying "we are you in the future". Modern physics does not provide us with practical means for this type of communication and theories on this subject are not well developed; they are, in fact, inconclusive and controversial.

When interpreting "we are you in the future" in an oversimplified way, we are faced with causal paradoxes. On the other hand, from the theoretical papers published in physics journals we can learn that, with a proper and careful interpretation, and taking into account quantum uncertainties, *communication into the past cannot be dismissed as impossible*. Improbable perhaps is the right word, but there are many things that are improbable and yet happen. The more improbable is a given phenomenon, *the more information is carried by its occurrence,* the more we can learn by its study. That is why we did not dismiss the "we are you in the future" as impossible and therefore ignorable. Instead we decided to continue the "communications" as a form of a controlled experiment in "superluminal thought transfer" – even if it was clear that the term should be considered as a tentative indication of only one out several possible interpretations.

The information received from this experiment is presented in the context of broad ranging historical, scientific and other metaphysical material and offers the clues that have led to the world view and inferences presented by us in our numerous publications on the Web and in print. Perhaps it is only our own "subconscious mind" that presents itself as a "source", but even if it is so, does that tell us more? Do we really know what "unconscious mind" is and of what is it capable?

We sometimes ask ourselves if the Cassiopaeans are who they say they are, because we do not take anything as unquestionable truth. We take everything with a grain of salt, even if we consider that there is a good chance that it is truth. We are constantly analyzing this material as well as a great quantity of other material that comes to our attention from numerous fields of science and mysticism.

We invite the reader to share in our seeking of Truth by reading with an *open,* but skeptical mind. We do not encourage "devotee-ism" nor "True Belief". We *do* encourage the seeking of Knowledge and Awareness in all fields of endeavor as the best way to be able to discern lies from truth. The one thing we can tell the reader is this: we work very hard, many hours a day, and have done so for many years, to discover the "bottom line" of our existence on Earth. It is our vocation, our quest, and our job. We constantly seek to validate and/or refine what we understand to be either possible or probable or both. We do this in the sincere hope that all of mankind will benefit, if not now, then at some point in one of our probable futures.

Laura Knight-Jadczyk and Arkadiusz Jadczyk, PhD

FOREWORD

I suspected something was wrong with the "facts of life" as they were presented to me when I was a kid. Sure, I then spent a little over thirty years trying to be "normal" and make that square peg fit the round hole, "looking for a reason to believe." But then there was a memorable day when I finally grew up and admitted that maybe - just maybe - the Emperor was naked. And here it is, over twenty years later, and now - well, now I know that not only is something rotten in Denmark, I also know there is a dead elephant in the middle of the collective global living room and I can never NOT see it again.

During that twenty plus years of uncovering that huge, dead critter that occupies a central place in our reality, I was driven by the idea that I just wanted to know what was REALLY going on in this strange world I lived in where, on the one hand, science was moving so fast that we would soon be able to destroy our planet, while on the other hand, the varied religions were telling us not to worry, God was probably gonna destroy it for us and we had better believe in the "right god" or we were toast.

How can a person live in a world where "the End of the World" is being predicted every minute? That's crazy!

But darned if that isn't what just about every religion on the planet talks about!

You go to church, get scared to death in an hour and a half, warned about hellfire and damnation, and then they pass the plate so that you can pay the high priests to put in a good word for you with God so that maybe you won't suffer as much as that jerk down the street who goes to a different church! And even if you do suffer here on earth, if you believe hard enough, and prove it by putting your money where your faith is, at least you'll get your reward in paradise.

This was back in 1982 when I had three small children. As a mother, I wanted to know what to teach my children. I knew that what I had been taught to believe was frightening. I had grown up in a time when children were regularly taught what to do in case of an atomic bomb attack - Cuba was only 90 miles from Florida where I was born - and at the same time, the standard religious teaching of my family - mainstream Protestants - promoted the "suffer on Earth to get rewarded in Heaven" routine.

I knew I had certainly suffered from the state of the world and the teachings of my faith. I really, REALLY wanted to know if this was something that I should pass on to my children.

When I held my babies and rocked them or looked into their sweet, innocent faces - untroubled by the concerns of the world around, certain that Mother would make them safe - I had to ask myself "How can I tell them these things? How can I "break it to them" that this world into which they have been born is so frightening and uncertain and full of traps that not only are their lives in constant danger, their very souls may be in peril?

How could I tell that to my children???

If it was true, I HAD to tell them.

But what if it wasn't true?

WHAT IF IT WASN'T TRUE?

I knew one thing and one thing only: I wanted more than anything in the world to tell my children the truth, to prepare them for whatever might lie ahead of them in their lives. And the question burned inside me: What if I told those little beings who I loved more than my own life a LIE? What kind of a mother would I be? What kind of "Mother Love" is that?

The End of the World is an idea, which has fascinated man for all recorded history and perhaps beyond. In every religion, philosophy, and mystery teaching, there are hints, allusions or outright claims to knowledge of this purported end to man's current status on the earth.

Some teachings say that the earth itself will cease to exist. Others proclaim that man will cease to exist in material form; still others claim a great judgment day, in which the wicked are wiped from the face of the planet while the "saved" are rescued in some miraculous fashion to return and inhabit a new, heaven-like "City of God". The persistence of these ideas and their prevalence is centered around the idea that man began somewhere, sometime, somehow, and will therefore come to an end somewhere, sometime, somehow.

This assumption is born of the conscious mind's tendency to think in linear terms. Scientific materialism has carried this tendency to the ultimate heights: "The world must have been born, therefore, it must die". Also, scientific materialism claims nothingness before birth and nothingness after death. Scientific philosophies refer to the "accidental mechanicalness" of the universe and teach us that the only meaning to life is no meaning at all. "Eat, drink, and be merry for tomorrow you may die", and then -- oblivion.

Scientifically speaking, for a long time matter and motion were accepted as the basis of reality and, to a great extent, continue to be. Yet, in actual fact, matter and motion are unknown quantities x and y, and are always defined by means of one another. It is an absurdity to define one unknown by means of another! What this means is that science defines matter as that which moves, and defines motion as changes in matter. The "Big Bang" or Cosmic Firecracker theory is explained in these terms. A primal atom, (matter), of incredible density "exploded" into motion. (Where the primal atom came from, how the space it exploded into came into being, and where the impetus for this event originated, are still on the drawing board.) And from this event, our universe and the life within it just sort of "accidentally" happened. Man is the "amoral end of a deadly biological evolution". The mind and soul are inexplicable byproducts of the struggle for survival.

To the average person, a table, a chair, an orange, is a real object. They have dimension -- three, to be exact - they are real. But are they? The physicist (and the knowledgeable layperson) knows that the object is composed of atoms. And there lies the rub! The dissected atom (quantum particles) often displays some very disturbing properties. Who has really seen matter or force? We think we see matter in motion, but physics has shown us that what we see is an illusion. When we try to focus on it, a quantum particle/wave is an infinite-dimensional entity incapable of being perceived, in that instant, as a three-dimensional body moving through space. When we look away, the quantum particle/wave acts like a wave of pure energy - invisible force.

So, just what is matter? What is this estate in which we find our existence? Does the physical run out when it becomes invisible? Obviously not, as we cannot see electricity and other forces in the universe measurable only by their effect upon "matter". Do these forces run out when they become undetectable by our senses or by our instruments? Do the things we detect with the subtle mechanisms of our mind and emotions not exist simply because we cannot see or measure them?

Science hands those questions over to religion and basically, we are told to "believe what you like" in that area because science isn't in the business of describing things it cannot materially weigh or measure. There is a not-so-subtle implication in such a view that it really doesn't matter what a person believes anyway because, as Danish physicist Niels Bohr put it, "There is no deep reality!"

So, for those people who have the idea that there is something "deeper", some "meaning" to life, if you want to put it that way, there is really only one place to go for answers: religion, of which there are three *major* ones in the world today, all of them "Monotheistic" and based, essentially, on a single religion, Judaism.

The Bible says, "In the Beginning, God created the heaven and the earth". Neither the Bible nor science has much to say about what happened before the beginning. St. Augustine was once asked the question "What was God doing before He created the world?". The Bishop's rejoinder: "Creating Hell for those who ask that question!", put a period to such inquiries. Few have asked it since.

There are, of course, various "interpretations" of the teachings of Monotheism that exist inside and outside of the "orthodox" explanations. Some interpreters say that the only meaning to life is in spiritual self-improvement and creating a better future in the afterlife, or in future lives. Other interpreters say that the meaning to life lies in working to dissolve the ego into nothingness. Among the more recent variations is the idea that the true purpose of life is to align our "self-created realities" so that they become as one, and thereby we may achieve a unified race, which will either "ascend" or will survive beyond predicted cataclysms for a thousand years before things wind down a bit into the usual state of decay. Naturally this effect can only be initiated and maintained by a group effort at consciousness raising. There are other ideas and combinations of ideas similar to these -- all leading where?

Are we, in fact, an accident of evolution in an accidental universe, on a race to nowhere except oblivion? Or, worse still, are our very minds - our belief in and desire for knowledge of higher things - our greatest flaw? Are we damned by our religion for asking such questions, or ridiculed by science for thinking that they even ought to be asked? The choice seems to be between a sick joke and a mistake.

Yet, the question must be asked: why do we live in a world in which material extinction is a real possibility? Are we truly on the edge of an abyss, losing our balance, preparing to fall into a hole so deep and dark that we shall never come out of it?

There are two main theories of the future - that of a predestined future and that of a free future. The theory of predestination asserts that every future event is the result of past events and if we know all the past then we could know all the future.

The idea of a free future is based on quantum "probabilities". The future is either only partially determined or undetermined because of the varied interactions possible at any given point. This idea of "free will" says that quite deliberate volitional acts may bring about a subsequent change in events. Those who support predestination say that so-called "voluntary" actions are, in fact, not, but are rather the results of incompletely understood causes which have made them imperative acts -- in short, nothing is accidental.

On the one hand we have "cold predestination" come what may, nothing can be changed -- on the other hand we have a reality which is only a point on some sort of needle named the present surrounded on all sides by the Gulf of Nonexistence - a world which is born and dies every moment.

During those early days of asking questions outside of my "standard religious faith", I came across an idea put forth by P.D. Ouspensky in his book *Tertium Organum*:

> "At every given moment all the future of the world is predestined and existing, but
> it is predestined conditionally, i.e., there must be one or another future in
> accordance with the direction of events of the given moment, if no new factor
> comes in. And a new factor can come in only from the side of consciousness and
> the will resulting from it. In the past, what is behind us, lies not only in what was,
> but also in what could have been. In the same way, in the future lies not only what
> will be but also what may be."

In other words, there was the possibility - just a suggestion, mind you - that human beings might be able to choose something different than the future that was obviously developing all around us. It was clear to me that such a choice could only be made if one made an effort to "predict" the future. In other words, the only way to know the right choice of the moment was to have some *idea of the consequences*.

Of course, the "standard religions" all around us are suggesting something of that sort all the time: their solution is that the only change human beings can make is to "choose the right god" and believe in him strongly enough that this god will step in and fix things right up, either by miraculously intervening in reality, or at least hauling the good people out of the soup at some future time when they have proved themselves AND, at the same time, making all those nasty people who bet on the wrong horse suffer!

It was at this point that I decided that I really ought to check out all the various religions and their "track records", so to say in order to determine which was the "right god", After all, since there exists such diversity of beliefs around the globe, the assumption is that either somebody is right, excluding all others, or that nobody is right, including all.

With the world in an obvious mess, with every preacher in just about every church across America passionately declaring that "The End is Nigh", I decided that I had better get moving on this project. After all, I had these small beings in my care and above ALL things, I wanted to tell my children the Truth as far as I was able to determine it. And that certainly meant that I should put forth all efforts to determine what that truth was before I gave it to them. After all, if your child asks for bread, will you give him a stone? If he asks for fish, will you give him a serpent? I wanted to give my children the very best I could, and that was, at the foundation, the primary motivation for my search for the truth: Love for my children.

You could say that Love for my babies gave me the courage to begin to look at my own faith in a critical way, and then to search for the answers to their questions.

And so it still is.

What this amounted to was to apply the scientific method to the study of religion and "deeper realities" - things that went beyond the physics of materialism.

I discovered that I wasn't the first one who had thought about doing this and so there was certainly a large body of material to go through. And I have been doing it in a concentrated and systematic way for over 20 years now.

The Cassiopaean Communication was only a part of this process. Looking back on this experiment in accessing "higher consciousness" which, at that point, I only theorized might exist, there is a lot to be said for the idea that most of what has come "from the C's" could very well have come from my own subconscious. After all, I had spent nearly my whole life reading everything from history to psychology. The phenomenon of the scientist working on a difficult problem who then, after he has examined all the parameters, dreams of a novel way to put the different parts together that solves the problem is well known in the history of science. The discovery of the benzene ring is a case in point. So it isn't too much of a stretch to say that the material that came "from the C's", who clearly stated "we are YOU in the future", was merely a similar process.

The attentive reader may notice that most of the C's material has to do with history and the hidden motivations for the events in our world. These were certainly the things that concerned me - events and choices of action and being that could lead to a positive future or a negative future - and so, perhaps my vast reading was sorted and assembled in novel ways by my own subconscious mind or superconscious mind.

Be that as it may, it does not, in my opinion, at all detract from the usefulness of the material. The discovery of the benzene ring came from a dream and led to a breakthrough in science. And so it has seemed that the concerted effort to examine all the parameters of reality, and then to "allow" it to sort itself and "come out" in a novel process of reassembly, has proven very fruitful in many respects.

Ark discussed the essential nature of this approach recently in an exchange with Robin Amis, the editor and commentator of Boris Mouravieff's *Gnosis*:

Ark to Robin Amis:

You stated that:

1) Scientific method has its limitations.

2) Knowledge should be understood in broader terms so as to include, for instance "noetic knowledge". In particular:

a) there is a true form of knowledge that is normally associated with religion

b) those with intellectual training tend to regard it as not being knowledge at all

3) That you - Praxis - teach this other form of knowledge, and the conditions under which it can be understood.

4) The reason that Praxis (and other religions) depends on a suspension of judgment is "that newcomers studying this material, despite quickly getting confirmation of its reality, will not understand it deeply enough".

I will try to address and expand the above points and, perhaps, try to add some new ideas, if only for the future discussion.

Point 1) I agree. I agree completely. In fact it takes a scientist to truly know the limitation and the weaknesses of science, as many of the tricks and games and even lies are known only to the insiders - scientists.

Point 2) I agree that there is such a knowledge; I agree that is important and, in fact, is crucial. And it is because of this fact that we stress on our Website and in our publications the importance of "knowledge", not just "science" or facts. It depends on *whether you start with a fact and follow the clues to real knowledge,* or *whether you start with an assumption, and interpret all facts based on what may, at the very beginning, be a lie.*

a) Whether this "true knowledge" is, was, or should be "associated with religion" is disputable.

The term "associated" is somewhat vague and can lead to misunderstandings. Science is also associated with religion. The Pope has scientific advisers; the Vatican supports scientific research.

On the other hand the greatest crimes of history have also been - and probably are still - associated with religion, one way or another.

Religion, if analyzed sincerely and critically, has many dark spots, and analyzing the reasons for this is not an easy task.

But I hope you will agree with me that one of the reasons why religions have these dark spots is that people were lulled into believing that they have (in opposition to others) the "true knowledge".

So the very concept of "true knowledge" is risky. It is easy to imagine that two different people will have different, orthogonal truths. For one, the truth may be that he needs to kill the other man, while for the other man, the truth may involve avoiding being killed. Every noetic truth has down-to-earth implications. Or so I think.

b) Though I agree that what you wrote may describe a general tendency, yet there are exceptions. History knows scientists - great scientists - that were "mystics" at the same time. Pascal, Newton, Poincare - just few examples. So, indeed, the term "tend to regard" that you used seems to be appropriate. But for this present point, it is important to know whether there is a real contradiction between being a scientist and appreciating other forms of knowledge at the same time. It seems to me and, I believe, you will agree, that there is no intrinsic contradiction.

Point 3) Here of course you are assuming that Praxis is already in possession of such a knowledge. Perhaps this is the case or, perhaps, Praxis has only "fragments of unknown teachings", and not the complete picture.

Being a scientist I am always careful and I would never state that I have the full and complete "knowledge" of something. I may know about tools, theories, formal structures, data etc. But one day, all my tools, data, theories and formal structures may prove to be wrong or useless with the uncovering of a single datum that shifts the entire structure. A true scientist MUST be open to this. What is important in science is being always open to surprises, to new paradigm shifts etc.

So, I think, you - Praxis - are teaching what you BELIEVE to be, at the present moment, "the true knowledge", and you may have very good reasons for such a belief. You may have very important pieces of knowledge - as we think based on research - but, perhaps, you are still lacking some of other important pieces - which we also think, based on research.

How can we know in advance where the next unexpected discovery will lead us?

And here I would like to make some constructive - or so I think - comments.

Looking at the history of "our civilization", religion seems to have been in existence much longer than "science". And yet we see that religion has failed. In spite of its teachings people are still constantly at war with each other. Human beings have not become better, and they are often much worse than animals. Gurdjieff described seeing the truth of our condition - the condition of our reality in general - as the "terror of the situation". It is terrible because, when you really SEE it, you realize how great a failure religion or the "powers" of the various versions of God really are.

Science, which came later and has exploded in the last millennium, has failed too. It has brought mankind to the edge of self-destruction. Advances in mathematical, physical and computer sciences have brought about "applied game theory", where "wars" are called "games", and to "win the game" is to kill as many people as possible with as little cost as possible.

Is there any hope at all? And if there is, then where?

Perhaps it is time to try something new? Perhaps a "marriage of science and mysticism" has a chance?

Why not take what is good from science and what is good from religion, and discard what is wrong?

What is the best thing about religion?

Religion teaches us to be open minded and accepting of possibilities which are far from being "rational". Religions teach us to pay attention to singular events, miracles, phenomena that are fragile and hardly repeatable. Finally religion teaches us to look inside as much as outside: know thyself.

The strengths of the approach of religion just happen to be the weak points in science.

Science is often narrow-minded and conservative restricting everything to what is material and rigidly repeatable. Science teaches us that what is "out there" is not connected to what is "in here", that it must be captured, weighed, measured and manipulated. That is why new paradigms are so painful when they come - but they DO come in science, and they seldom come in religion which is "fixed" and dogmatic and not open to discussion.

What is the best thing about science?

Science is open to criticism and discussion. Even if many forces on the earth try to make a sort of religion of science, in general, scientific theories must be published and publicly discussed. We can find an error in Einstein's papers because these, as well as other papers, are publicly available. Everyone can learn mathematics, as advanced as you wish, from reading monographs, articles, going to conferences, and discussing with other scientists.

The strength of science just happens to be the weakness of religion. Religions are always "secret" in one respect or another - even if that secrecy is only the declaration that no changes can be made, no questions asked, because the ultimate truth about God is a "mystery", a "secret". That is why the teachings of religion are so easily distorted and misunderstood. It is so easy for the central "authority" to achieve the "pinnacle" of the religion and declare to the followers the correct interpretation and that no other is permitted.

Point 4) What you say about students not being able to judge for a long time is certainly true. But whether discouraging them from such judgments is the only solution - I am not sure.

Certainly that was the way it was done in the past. Groups were usually small, whether exoteric or esoteric. Travel and communication possibilities were severely restricted. But today a qualitative change has occurred: we are now in the era of networking and instant communication on a planetary scale.

Therefore a different approach is possible: instead of having few students and "teach them even when they are not yet ready", we can address ourselves to those who are ready.

This was not so easy to do in the past when teachers communicated, at best, to merely hundreds of potential students. But it is possible now, when we can communicate with millions.

Whoever is not yet ready for the next stage, let him stay where he is or go back where he was. Those who ARE ready, will find you - if you take care and NETWORK efficiently.

So, I would not discourage students from making early judgments and discussing subjects for which they are not prepared . If they come to the wrong conclusions and go away or attack you, that is their free will. Let them go where their minds and their hearts lead them.

That is, at least, our approach in QFS[1]. Perhaps we are making a mistake here, but
it is always good to try different methods - if available.

So it is, we seek to combine science and mysticism for the few who are colinear
with this approach. And this was uppermost in our minds - to convey this
effectively - when planning the look and emphases of the new and revised
Cassiopaea Website. We understood clearly that there are many "seekers" in the
"New Age" milieu who would be turned off to this approach. They are seeking a
guru, to be underwritten in their choices, a messiah. As Ark has written: those who
are not ready for this stage of Becoming Free, let them stay where they are or go
back to where they were. Therefore, if readers form conclusions based on their
illusions, that is their free will and we have no quarrel with that. Each individual
should be where their minds and hearts lead them.

Of course, there are still some items that the C's have come up with that
obviously could NOT come from a "reordering" of the masses of material
available to my subconscious from years of reading. In that respect, due to the
novel way in which the material was obtained as a "group effort", perhaps some of
the material was extracted from the subconscious databanks of the other
participants? And perhaps some of the data was nonsense - my own and others?
These are all questions we consider when we analyze the material and subject it to
verification or testing.

There is still another category of material - that which later proves to be
insightful in ways that simply could not come from the subconscious data of ANY
of the participants.

Or could it?

Perhaps an awareness of what is going on politically and socially can be "sorted
and reassembled" in the subconscious the same way the information that led to the
discovery of the Benzene Ring was? Perhaps probabilities are calculated in the
subconscious mind based on vast collections of data that we don't even realize we
have? Perhaps lifetimes of observations of the world "out there", consisting of
billions of databits can be stored in our subconscious and lead to very complex
"data sorting" and "probability estimation"?

Perhaps there is, after all, a completely scientific and material explanation for
the Cassiopaean Material; except for just a few items that I am certain were NOT
part of the conscious or subconscious data of any of the participants - items that
were known to only a few people on the planet and which we had to dig deep to
verify. But then, that is only evidence of an ability to access information that may
be in the databanks of unknown others at a distance...

---

[1] Quantum Future School

But, isn't that the point? That we search for that tiny clue that there IS a reality beyond that which the materialist scientific view accepts as measurable?

Just as certain mechanical aids can augment the perception of certain ranges of light such as infra-red, ultra-violet, x-rays, and radio waves, so might our so-called psychic perceptions be similarly augmented. This was my theory at the beginning of the Cassiopaean Experiment, though I never thought it would evolve into a dialogue with "myself in the future".

The brain is an instrument devised to focus reality in mathematical constructs -- interpreting waveforms as material objects. What I had in mind from the beginning was a process of not only being able to perceive those ranges of energies that are normally beyond the range of three dimensional perception, but to be able to do so in a repeatable way with practical applications. By developing such a process, the implication is that we can not only perceive the effects of myriads of waveforms, but also, depending upon the amplitudes and energies, predict the outcomes of certain motions, even, perhaps, in very precise terms.

Of course, it seems that the descriptions of the greater reality beyond three dimensional space and time must be, in an essential way, difficult to describe except metaphorically. So, I think we can assume that the finite nature of our minds is self-limiting in a certain sense. It seems that all the instruments we can create and build are probably incapable of penetrating into such realms because of the simple fact that they are three-dimensional. The only material way we may be able to go beyond our reality is through mathematics, which seems to transcend time and space.

There is, indeed, a lot of research in physics that sounds provocatively like ancient mystical teachings, yet the possibility is that the true nature of the reality behind our world is beyond quantum mechanics and theory.

Ark: As Wheeler so succinctly points it out:

> We have every right to assume that the universe is filled with more uncertainty than certainty. What we know about the universe - indeed, what is knowable - is based on a few iron gateposts of observation plastered over by papier-mâché molded from our theories.

Popper makes these important observations:

> "... all explanatory science is incompleteable; for to be complete it would have to give an explanatory account of itself. An even stronger result is implicit in Gödel's famous theorem of the incompletability of formalized arithmetic (though to use Gödel's theorem and other mathematical incompleteness theorems in this context is to use heavy armament against a comparatively weak position). Since all physical science uses arithmetic (and since for a reductionist only science formulated in physical symbols has any reality), Gödel's incompleteness theorem renders all physical science incomplete. For the nonreductionist, who does not believe in the reducibility of all science to physically formulated science, science is incomplete anyway."

> "Not only is philosophical reductionism a mistake, but the belief that the method of reduction can achieve complete reduction is, it seems, mistaken too. We live in a world of emergent evolution; of problems whose solutions, if they are solved, beget new and deeper problems. Thus we live in a universe of emergent novelty; of

novelty which, as a rule, is not completely reducible to any of the preceding stages."

Then he adds:

"Nevertheless, the method of attempting reductions is most fruitful, not only because we learn a great deal by its partial successes, by partial reductions, but also because we learn from our partial failures, from the new problems which our failures reveal. Open problems are almost as interesting as their solutions; indeed they would be just as interesting but for the fact that almost every solution opens up in its turn a whole new world of open problems."

We may find that much truth was known by the peoples of the past and that they did, in fact, express deep, mysterious, realities in their poetic and obscure messages. Mystics and seers - even in terms of communicating with "myself in the future" - seem to perceive quantum states, which are demonstrably difficult to translate into language.

The experience of viewing simultaneous, cause/effect reality is extremely difficult to maintain when one is constantly being bombarded by three-dimensional interpretation.

Imagine the difficulty of explaining to a snail the expanse of an acre of ground?! Mystics and Seers have attempted to do just that for millennia with the result that the vast majority of mankind have absolutely and totally misunderstood these concepts. And, there is no worse lie than a truth misunderstood by those who hear it: the greatest lies are the dark and evil systems of religion created by those who do not understand.

You never know how much you really believe anything until its truth or falsehood becomes a matter of life and death. It is easy to say you believe a rope is strong as long as you are merely using it to cord a box. But, suppose you had to hang by that rope over a precipice? Wouldn't you then first discover how much you really trusted it? *(C.S. Lewis)*

Laura Knight-Jadczyk

INTRODUCTION

LAYING THE GROUNDWORK

Like many of you who have chosen to purchase this book, I am a seeker of what we generally call "spiritual advancement". And, like many of you, I have been in this seeking mode as long as I can remember—from birth, even. Also, like many of you, in my search for "spiritual truths", I have encountered the term "Ascension" repeatedly in the course of this Quest. And finally, like many of you, I have come across many definitions of the word, as well as varied purported techniques to accomplish this allegedly desirable objective.

In seeking a concise definition and philosophy behind it, I decided to search the Internet for clues. I typed the word "ascension" along with the word "spiritual" into a popular search engine. It returned 115,000 pages for my edification. This led me to ask: Why, at this present moment in history, is so much attention being focused on this subject?

Well, we all know the answer to that question. It is because of the frightening state of the World in which we live.

One might think that the Laws of Probability would mandate that, without any intelligent input, 50% of the time the events in our world would lead to benefits for mankind. In a strictly mechanical way, life in our world ought to have manifested a sort of "equilibrium". Factoring in intelligent decisions to *do good* might bring this average up to about 70%. That would mean that humanity would have advanced over the millennia to a state of existence where good and positive things happen in our lives more often than "negative" or "bad" things. In this way, many of the problems of humanity would have been effectively solved. War and conflict would be a rarity, *perhaps 70 percent of the earth's population* would have decent medical care, a comfortable roof over their heads, and sufficient nutritious food so that death by disease or starvation would be almost unheard of. In other words, human society would have "evolved" in some way, on all levels.

The facts are, however, quite different.

More than 840,000,000 people on the Earth suffer from hunger. That's about *three times the population of the entire USA*. This is chronic, persistent hunger, which kills 24,000 people *every day*, or over 8 million human beings each year. Three out of four who die from starvation are younger than five years old. How can "evolved" human beings accept that fact as "normal"?

According to the *Historical Atlas of the Twentieth Century*, during the past 100 years there have been approximately 2 billion deaths (including civilians) resulting from war, tyrannical governments, and man-made famine. When these figures are broken down into deaths caused by Communism vs. Capitalism, they are almost equal, with the figures slightly higher for Capitalism which may surprise some people who believe that the Capitalistic system is the "right" one. "By their fruits you shall know them."

Turning to mortality statistics that are *not* related to war and famine, we find that it is a bit difficult to get an actual number because the statistics are nearly always expressed in terms of percentages rather than in hard population numbers. One gets the feeling that the actual count is so frightening that this approach is used for the express purpose of avoiding having to face the facts. One thing we do know is that deaths from cardiovascular diseases and stroke are the leading cause of death in 31 of the 35 Western Hemisphere countries that report disease related mortality statistics. The highest of these mortality rates are found in the *English-speaking* Caribbean, USA, Canada, Argentina, Chile and Uruguay. Mortality rates from these causes are increasing in the Central American and Latin Caribbean regions as they come more and more under the sway of Western capitalism. Again, "By their fruits you shall know them."

What we are talking about above are the "quiet" statistics, from our present reality. They are quiet because nobody ever makes a big deal about them. The headlines of our newspapers do not trumpet them on the front page where they rightly belong. Even now it is easy to forget that there were 65 million deaths from WW II alone and that deaths from disease and starvation continue as a quiet, steady, drumbeat of increasing mortality behind the blaring headlines of school shootings, sensational murder trials, and little Cuban boys who become the center of international custody disputes.

I don't think that one single person on this planet will disagree that they want a better life for themselves and their children; and most of them will add that they do not presently have the capacity to make it a reality. Except for a very small minority of very sick people, I don't think anybody really likes to see misery and suffering, disease and death and despair, in any context. And again we must ask: if these things are so detestable to human beings at large, if so many people are working and thinking and praying to improve the conditions of our world, why isn't it happening?

Seekers of Spiritual Verity - a large number of whom could be considered "Intelligentsia" - are always aware of these things, and they are asking, "What is the origin of all the misery and suffering? Does it just happen? Do people and only people cause others to suffer? Is it that God is good, but allows bad things to happen?"

"Don't forget the power of prayer", we are told by our religious leaders, or "positive thinking", as the New Age gurus tell us. The only problem is, prayers and positive thinking do not seem to have improved the world very much on the occasions when it is certain that nearly every human being was praying for a certain outcome.

Jesus promised: "If any two of you shall agree and ask... it shall be done". (Matt 18:19) That's a promise. What do you want or need? Just ask!

But it doesn't work and we see it!

Over sixty million people died because God didn't do what everybody thought he should do. C.S. Lewis struggled with this issue in the latter part of his life. He saw clearly that, before World War II, practically every human being on the planet was praying—to Jesus, God the Father, the Virgin Mary, Allah, Buddha and whoever else you can name or mention, so all the bases were covered—that this terrible thing would not happen. The memory of the previous "Great War" was still fresh in the mind of mankind. They remembered the horrible carnage and vowed, *never again!*

In the end, after the mightiest cry of prayer in human memory, rising from the earth, *almost one-third of the world was uninhabitable and sixty-five million human beings were dead.* Are we to think that this was God's answer to prayer? It certainly doesn't give us much hope for the "power of positive thinking".

Think about it.

Throughout history we find one group praying to their god to protect them from the depredations of another group. The other group is praying just as fervently that their depredations will be successful. When one group succeeds in killing another, is that proof that its god is supreme? What then happens if the members of the successful group are then reincarnated[2] into the group that was defeated? This is not a rhetorical question since a very interesting book[3] was written about the great numbers of Jews who died in the holocaust now being reincarnated as Christians. There has also been some suggestion that many Nazis are now being reincarnated as Jews.[4] What then, does such an idea do to the concept of "my god is the only right one"?

I can assure the reader from my own experience as a hypnotherapist, that every single case I have worked with in terms of "past life therapy", has demonstrated a "string" of "past lives" in such variety of nationality and religious orientation, that it literally makes a joke of anyone stating with absolute certainty, that their beliefs or religious orientation *now*, are the only *right* ones. It is evident that those who declaim against another group most vehemently will most certainly find themselves a member of that very group in the next "round" of incarnation.

This begs the question of why people cannot remember the previous lessons in past lives; why the wisdom of the soul is not available to the person. *If humans have souls or spirits, why is the knowledge of past karmic cycles not part of a person's wisdom?* The answer to that question is, of course, part of the Quest for Ascension - to reclaim that knowledge, among other things.

The questions about how our beliefs may shape our reality are among the most significant in all of consciousness research. And so it is that many seekers step

---

[2] We are assuming reincarnation to have a high probability of being an objective fact due to extensive research.

[3] Gershom, Yonassan, Rabbi, *Beyond the Ashes* (Virginia Beach: A.R.E. Press 1992).

[4] If this is so, then we might also wonder why - that is, what will be the "karmic payoff?"

outside of the "standard religions" and begin to seek the "truth" of the ways and means of Ascension.

As noted, "Ascension" is discussed widely in books, articles, on the Internet, in classes and workshops, and in other media. The general trend of ideas expressed includes the search for the "one thing that will transform your life." Various "techniques" are advertised which promise to provide stress relief and even the "key to the highest levels of human consciousness". The shopper in the market of ascension "tools" is told that they can *now* make a choice to "swiftly and easily free the nervous system from stress, enjoy maximum creativity, clarity and health, experience inner peace, fulfillment and joy", and of course, change one's self-limiting beliefs.

Another perspective on "ascension" tells us that ascension is "the way to integrate all portions of your self in a conscious way". The seeker is told that he or she is a "multi-dimensional being who seeded portions of itself into the physical reality", and that fully "remembering who you are" is the act of integration and the "removal of the veil of time, identities and separateness in yourself". What, precisely, the result will be—other than being "healthy, wealthy and wise"—is not clear.

As we read further in the available literature, we discover other ideas. One "expert" on the subject tells us that this thing called "ascension" was only achieved in the past upon dying, and that now people can do it and take their physical body with them. He suggests that spirituality is so advanced in the present age that souls can graduate more quickly. It is as though he is suggesting a "grading curve" has been instituted so that the requirements are lessened. Either that, or he hasn't been paying much attention to what is going on "out there".

The evidence of "advanced spirituality" in our world is severely lacking in spite of the New Age claims that "light workers" can "help bring forth the ascension for the masses before physical death, before totally wearing out the physical body in resistance to evolution. Much more energy can be expended on the positive and much less wasted on the negative".

Again, we note that objective reality does not support such a claim. If anything, since the inception of the New Age "movement," if it can be so called, things have gotten a lot worse.

This leads to another point: it seems that we must accept the objective fact that attempts to change the world spiritually, or to regulate large scale events, simply do not work. Yes, there does seem to be evidence that individuals or small groups of individuals can make small changes or produce effects with a limited range of influence. But for some reason, the world as it is, seems to operate based on rules or laws that we do not understand. The fundamental nature of the physical world seems to be antithetical to this "spiritualization".

One recent work that attempts to provide a scientific explanation for this ability to influence the world, *Conscious Acts of Creation*, tells us:

> This book marks a sharp dividing line between old ways of scientific thought and old experimental protocols, wherein human qualities of consciousness, intention, emotion, mind and spirit cannot significantly affect physical reality, and a new paradigm wherein they can robustly do so![5]

The book, written by three mainstream scientists, goes on to tell us that:

> ...utilizing a unique experimental protocol on both inanimate and animate systems, that the human quality of focused intention can be made to act as a true thermodynamic potential and strongly influence experimental measurements for a variety of specific target experiments.

After almost 400 pages of math and speculation and descriptions of experiments we are told:

> Under some conditions, it is indeed possible to attach an aspect of human consciousness, a specific intention, to a simple electrical device and have that device, when activated, robustly influence an experiment conducted in its vicinity in complete accord with the attached intention. Thus, if they do it right, humans can influence their environment via specific, sustained intentions. [...] Some new field appears to be involved in the information passage that occurs between conditioned locales that are widely separated from each other in physical space. Even with transmitters and receivers located inside electrically grounded Faraday cages, highly correlated patterns of information appeared in the remotely located locales.[...] Although we don't fully understand them, we now have some new tools with which to probe the deeper structures of the universe and a new adventure is underway for humanity.[6]

It is important to note that the "intenders" of the experiments were long-time practitioners of Siddha Yoga and could thus be considered metaphysically "in tune" to some considerable extent. The question is: What did they accomplish? Based on the descriptions, it sounds pretty earth shaking, right? Well, as noted, after almost 400 pages we find that the most significant result seems to have been changing the pH of a small sample of water.

Yup. That's it.

Nevertheless, this is important for the simple reason that they managed to scientifically demonstrate a principle, even if the overall result was that it was - most often - an iffy proposition and there didn't seem to be a lot of control. Most results were "statistical" and this has always been a problem with the "create your own reality" idea. When all the data is examined, what we generally find is that it

---

[5] Tiller, William A., Ph.D., Dibble, Walter E., Ph.D., Kohane, Michael J., Ph.D., *Conscious Acts of Creation* (Walnut Creek: Pavior 2001) (www.pavior.com).

[6] Tiller et al, op. cit.

is six of one, half dozen of the other. Sometimes it works, sometimes it doesn't. What the real rules are, nobody seems to know.

While we all might like to think we can transform our world by praying and/or thinking positively, we must remember that there is a great deal of evidence that *real transformations of the planet have repeatedly been cataclysmic*. A philosophy, which ignores this fact, is courting disaster.

And so we have a clue that the problem may not be as easily solved as the many promoters of the different "methods or techniques of Ascension" would have us believe. The question then becomes: if the process of Ascension is possibly more complex than the many promoters of the various methods offered in our day would have us think, what is the reason for the 115,000 web pages? This matter deserves some discussion in the context of certain problems in our world that are undoubtedly related.

THE SCAM OF DISTRACTION

In 1931, Aldous Huxley wrote *Brave New World* in which he stated:

> The older dictators fell because they never could supply their subjects with enough bread, enough circuses, enough miracles and mysteries. Nor did they possess a really effective system of mind-manipulation.

> Under a scientific dictator, education will really work—with the result that most men and women will grow up to love their servitude and will never dream of revolution. There seems to be no good reason why a thoroughly scientific dictatorship should ever be overthrown.

Aldous Huxley also made an early connection between the effects experienced by those partaking of psychedelic drugs and the experiences of Eastern Mysticism and this set the consciousness-raising bomb off with a BANG! Along came Timothy Leary and Richard Alpert, AKA Baba Ram Dass, with their LSD and other modes of mind marvels, leading the parade of those who were "turned on, tuned in". Abraham Maslow became a father figure to the new "wave" of those desiring to fill the gaping hole of their reality with "peak experiences". Maslow cited psychedelic drugs as one of the means in which even ordinary people could have a little of what the Eastern Mystics worked many years to develop. Now, it could be had for a weekend seminar at Big Sur, or a study by mail course at only $29.95 per lesson! What a deal!

Peak Experiences—experience, experience, and experience—became the pot of gold at the end of the rainbow of the 1960's. No one needed to live in Existential Despair any longer! Everyone could become a "spiritual voyager" and achieve extended periods in realms of consciousness they had only heard about in veiled, mysterious allusions down through the ages. [7] Encounter groups, radical therapies, old and new combinations of theories and practice came rolling off the conveyor belt of techno-spirituality. The intangibles of spirit had been harnessed! Anyone could evoke some desirable experience by manipulating awareness at the basic physical and psychological levels. Never mind that all of this bypassed the vital processes of reason and conscious decision making. By its very nature, the whole techno-spiritual machine operated completely without critical thinking; it tapped the bottomless pit of feeling-emotion—primal being. Never mind that much of this emotion was negative, confusing, anxious and fearful! Let's just get it *all* out here in the open and have a party with it!

Each of the many techniques developed during this time was fully capable of producing an emotional high of one sort or another. There were endless "peak experiences", and dramatic "personal breakthroughs". The mixtures of Zen, yoga, meditation, and drugs along with strict mechanical technology, were a veritable adventure in awareness! The only problem was: in the midst of all this peaking, mind-blowing, turning on and tuning in, ecstasy and encountering, many people encountered things that, perhaps, ought not have been awakened. Boundaries were breached into unseeable and terrifying realms of consciousness. William Chittick, translator of the works of the great Sufi Shaykh, Ibn al-'Arabi, wrote:

> Nowadays most people interested in the spirituality of the East desire the "experience", though they may call what they are after intimate communion with God. Those familiar with the standards and norms of spiritual experience set down by disciplined paths like Sufism are usually appalled at the way Westerners seize upon any apparition from the domain outside of normal consciousness as a manifestation of the "spiritual". In fact, there are innumerable realms in the unseen world, some of them far more dangerous than the worst jungles of the visible world. [8]

> So preserve yourselves, my brothers, from the calamities of this place, for distinguishing it is extremely difficult! Souls find it sweet, and then within it they are duped, since they become completely enamored of it. [9]

By the end of the decade of the 60's, the "human potential" movement had become a veritable potpourri of religion, science, mysticism, magick and "the occult". The drug use got out of hand, the "techniques" began to show serious flaws with a number of tragedies resulting in crime or madness, and the whole idea of human beings becoming "psychic supermen" hit the skids. The promise of the

---

[7] Conway, Flo, Siegelman, Jim, *Snapping: America's Epidemic of Sudden Personality Change*, (Lippincott, Williams and Wilkins 1978).

[8] Chittick, William, *The Sufi Path of Knowledge,* (Albany: State University of New York 1989) p. 263.

[9] Sufi Shaykh, Ibn Al-'Arabi, in Futuhat (Unveiling) III 38.23, translated and quoted by William Chittick in *The Sufi Path of Knowledge*, p. 263.

60's decayed into an aimless lethargy—old hippies living in communes, braiding their gray locks and lusting after the sweet young teeny boppers while they fired up another bong and reminisced about the "good old days" at Esalen.

But wait! Something else happened here! Remember, this is America! The home of the Free—Market that is. Many people suggest that the subsequent proliferation of the "New Age" consciousness raising movement was the result of big business seeing a pile of money to be made in the development of slick, newly packaged psychoanalysis and psychodrama. There was, indeed, mass distribution and Madison Avenue marketing of things like Mind Dynamics, Arica, Silva Mind Control, Transcendental Meditation, and on and on. Individual entrepreneurs knew a good thing when they saw it. However, there is more to this than meets the eye. This is important to our subject, so bear with me.

SOMETHING WICKED THIS WAY COMES

Richard Dolan's *UFOs and the National Security State* is the first comprehensive study of the past 50 years of the U.S. Government's response to the intrusion of UFO phenomena in America. The compiled evidence - which includes government documents - suggests that a group of specialists working in the shadows, set up and executed the most massive cover-up in the history of government; and that the Human Potential movement and the subsequent New Age movements, were *key elements* of this cover-up. In other words, they not only have used the "colorful community" of alternative ideas as an unwitting tool of disinformation, it is highly probable that most of it was literally created by them as COINTELPRO. According to analysts, COINTELPRO was the FBI's secret program to undermine the popular upsurge, which swept the country during the 1960s. Though the name stands for "Counterintelligence Program", the targets were not enemy spies. The FBI set out to eliminate "radical" political opposition inside the US. What a lot of people do not realize is that this was a high level psychological operation specifically set up to vector "ideological" trends - beliefs, etc. To get a complete picture of the problem, Dolan writes:

> The UFO problem has involved military personnel around the world for more than fifty years, and is wrapped in secrecy. [...] Because this subject is so widely ridiculed, it is important to stress why it is worthy of serious attention.[...] Stories of strange objects in the sky go far back into time, but the problem received little attention until the Second World War. [...] During the UFO wave of 1947, American military and intelligence organizations conducted multiple, simultaneous investigations of these sightings. [...] By the end of 1947, a contingent of analysts at the Air Technical Intelligence Center at Wright-Patterson Air Force Base believed that UFOs were extraterrestrial. By the summer of 1948, this team prepared an "Estimate of the Situation." [...] As the story goes, Air Force Commander Hoyt Vandenberg rejected [this conclusion.] [...]

> In the summer of 1952... UFO sightings were so frequent and often of such high quality that some in the air force actually wondered whether an invasion was under way. With some help from the secret CIA sponsored Robertson Panel of January 1953, the air force improved censorship over the problem. Still, it never quite went away. Civilian organizations began to collect and analyze interesting UFO reports. [...] Then came the great UFO wave of 1965 and 1966, when the air force could no

longer hide behind weather balloons and swamp gas, nor withstand public scrutiny.
[…]

Let us pause to assess the situation. By the mid-1940s, America's intelligence
apparatus had reason to believe that there were artifacts in the skies that did not
originate from America, Russia, Germany, or any other country. These objects
violated some highly sensitive military airspace, and did not appear to be natural
phenomena. One may presume that the affected national security authorities made
it an immediate obsession to determine the nature and purpose of these objects, and
we may infer that the issue probably became a deep secret by 1946, or 1947 at the
latest.[10]

It was at this precise moment in time that the Human Potential movement was
"born". Do we think that this was a coincidence? By the mid-50s, it was becoming
obvious that things were getting out of control and in August of 1956, the FBI
began its COINTELPRO operation. When traditional modes of repression
(exposure, blatant harassment, and prosecution for political crimes) failed to
counter the growing insurgency, and even helped to fuel it, the Bureau took the
law into its own hands. Its methods ranged far beyond surveillance, and amounted
to a domestic version of the covert action for which the CIA has become infamous
throughout the world.

Usually, when we think of COINTELPRO, we think of the most well known
and typical activities which include sending anonymous or fictitious letters
designed to start rumors, among other things, publishing false defamatory or
threatening information, forging signatures on fake documents, introducing
disruptive and subversive members into organizations to destroy them from
within, and so on. Blackmailing insiders in any group to force them to spread false
rumors, or to foment factionalism was also common.

What a lot of people don't keep in mind is the fact that COINTELPRO also
concentrated on *creating bogus organizations.* These bogus groups could serve
many functions which might include attacking and/or disrupting bona fide groups,
or even just simply creating a diversion with clever propaganda in order to attract
members away so as to involve them with time-wasting activity designed to
prevent them from doing anything useful. COINTELPRO was also famous for
instigation of hostile actions through third parties. According to investigators,
these FBI programs were noteworthy because all documents relating to them were
stamped "do not file". This meant that they were never filed in the system, and for
all intents and purposes, did not exist. This cover was blown after activists broke
into an FBI office in Media, Pennsylvania in 1971. The possibility of finding

---

[10] Dolan, Richard, *UFOs and the National Security State*, (Charlottesville: Hampton Roads 2002)
Introduction p. xix.

evidence for any of it, after that event, is about zero. To spell it out in Dolan's words:

> Regarding matters connected with "national security", there appears to be a wealth of information that does not exist officially. Thus, a request to find such documents through a Freedom of Information Act request would be in vain. Add to this the likelihood that perhaps the most sensitive information regarding UFOs may not even exist in document form ("the first rule in keeping secrets is nothing on paper", Richard Helms), and one can appreciate the difficulty that an honest UFO researcher has in ferreting out the truth.[11]

Now, let us take a few logical steps. The UFO problem emerged into the national consciousness in 1947, or thereabouts. Not long afterward, a lot of people began asking a lot of questions. The government wasn't answering, and so the people began to band together to find out the answers for themselves. They started forming groups. And this is where things get just a bit curious. The thing that was most threatened by the UFO/alien issue seems to have been the Standard Monotheistic Religions. Religion seems to be a necessary component of political control. Social control - that is the mainstay of religion - was most definitely under threat. In fact, what seems to be true is that it is not even clear that religions - as we know them - would have survived a full disclosure. So the logical conclusion is that part of the main reason for the cover-up was to "protect the religious status quo".

As things stood at the time, protecting the religious status quo - mainly the social controls that stem from religion - was iffy at best. After a century of scholarly investigation into many religious texts, and the raising of many questions about the "old time religion", there were a lot of people in society who were most definitely turning away from religious dogma. It's fairly simple to take the next logical step and see that a combining of the questions of those who were disenchanted with religion, with the questions of those who wanted to know just what the heck was going on in terms of possible "extraterrestrials", was seen as a dangerous and explosive mixture. Something had to be done.

The activities of COINTELPRO in attempting to neutralize political opposition have been pretty well exposed. But we are now considering the fact that, in addition to political activists, it seems that COINTELPRO has particularly targeted groups that are seeking the truth about the interactions between the US government and Ultra Terrestrials, or so-called "aliens". That a long-time cover-up of these matters has been in effect is certainly evident to any careful researcher.

The COINTELPRO files show the U.S. Government targeted a very broad range of religious, labor and community groups opposed to any of its agendas, and it is only logical to assume that the same type of operation would be created to cover

---

[11] Ibid., p. 184.

up the "alien agenda". Such a theoretical COINTELPRO operation also goes far in explaining why, when the sincere researcher of UFO phenomena enters this field, he or she discovers only lies, lies, and more lies; confusion and disinformation. That is most definitely the signature of COINTELPRO.

Considering all of this, would anybody care to suggest that it did not also occur to the Powers that Be that the chief means of diverting attention and covering up the truth would be to literally fund and *create* the "New Age" and "Human Potential movement", so that it would follow *their* agenda of keeping secrets?

In other words, it is extremely likely that the most successful and popular of Metaphysical Mavens and New Age Impresarios are COINTELPRO agents - either consciously or as dupes of those who are. The objective seems to be to attack and "neutralize" those who are seeking the answers. Those who are sincere, who do bona fide research and seek to explicate the truth, are infiltrated, attacked, and marginalized according to standard COINTELPRO procedures.

What all of this seems to suggest is that the Powers That Be (PTB) have developed COINTELPRO to an all new level of Social Shaping, Cultural Brainwashing, and the main targets of this activity would include virtually anyone who is seeking the truth about the shifting realities of our world. The cases of COINTELPRO activities against political groups must be no more than the tip of the iceberg, given that the great bulk of COINTELPRO-type operations remain secret until long after their damage has been done. By all indications, domestic covert operations have become a permanent feature of U.S. politics and Social Programming, and it is hardly likely, considering the evidence, that the New Age and Human Potential fields are exempt.

The implications of this are truly alarming. Those who manage to get close to the truth of these matters, despite the many obstacles in their path, face National covert campaigns to discredit and disrupt their research and reputations. Clearly, COINTELPRO and similar operations under other names also work to distort academic and popular perceptions of the problems facing our world. They have done enormous damage to the search for the Truth.

"Terrorism is changing. New adversaries, new motivations and new rationales have surfaced in recent years to challenge much of the conventional wisdom...", wrote Dr. Bruce Hoffman, Director of RAND. And he was right. The only problem is that the reader is largely unaware of the definition of "new adversaries" that might be implied in his remarks. A careful reading of Richard Dolan's book will immediately reveal what Dr. Hoffman really meant in his remarks about "terrorism".

Based on the documents assembled by Dolan, it is obvious that the governments of the world do indeed see the UFO problem as a very, very serious matter. In the course of assembling the documents and reporting the events, Dolan came to the inescapable conclusion that there exists an "Above Top Secret" group with access to all available UFO data, and that this group "straddled" the worlds of government, military, and industry. The evidence proves that the military created a complete fiction for public consumption designed to convince the masses that the UFO problem was "nonexistent". They were assisted in pulling the wool over the eyes of the public by "heavy handed official media and culture", and they were obviously under orders to consistently and repeatedly "debunk" the idea that aliens were ensconced in our world. What seems to be true is that most of our elected officials are as much victims of the debunking as anybody else. And the same is true about mainstream science.

Dolan writes:

> Next to the bureau, the military intelligence services became the most important component of the domestic intelligence scene. Army intelligence had nearly unlimited funds, extensive manpower, specialized personnel, deep planning and training resources, and the most sophisticated communications and data processing capability. [...] **The army's intelligence surveillance did not focus on tactical and reconnaissance data, but on political and ideological intelligence within the United States.** (This was wholly illegal.) [...]

> Then there was the CIA. By the late 1960s, there were more spies than diplomats in the State Department, or employees in the Department of Labor. [...] When the Weather Underground, a radical splinter of the SDS, had an "acid test" to detect agent's provocateurs, they had no idea that the CIA had been tripping on LSD throughout the 1950s, creating a special caste of "enlightened agents" for precisely these occasions. [Based on this, we wonder about "agents provocateur" in the New Age and UFO community who are "specially trained"?]

> The agency continued its work on mind control. Following the work of Dr. Jose Delgado [experiments in] Electrical Stimulation of the Brain [were conducted.] This involves implanting electrodes into the brain and body, with the result that the subject's memory, impulses, and feelings could all be controlled. Moreover, **ESB could evoke hallucinations**, as well as fear and pleasure. "It could literally manipulate the human will at will," [said Dr. Robert Keefe, a neurosurgeon at Tulane University.]

> In 1968, George Estabrooks, another spook scientist, spoke indiscreetly to a reporter for the *Providence Evening Bulletin*. "The key to creating an effective spy or assassin, rests in creating a multiple personality with the aid of hypnosis", a procedure which he described as "child's play.".

> By early 1969, teams within the CIA were running a number of bizarre experiments in mind control under the name Operation Often. In addition to the normal assortment of chemists, biologists, and conventional scientists, the operation *employed psychics and experts in demonology.*

> Over at the NSA, all one can say with certainty is that its budget dwarfed all others within the intelligence community.[12]

Dolan documents how the intelligence organizations of the United States,- and very likely other countries who are working in concert with them, despite their outward show of opposition,t, have conducted terminal mind-control experiments, biological spraying of American cities, human plutonium and syphilis injections,

---

[12] Ibid., p. 361.

illegal communications interception, nationwide domestic surveillance of private citizens, political assassinations and coups, ongoing media manipulation and outright public lying on a continual basis, most especially in regards to UFOs. The above organizations, via any and all means available, made sure that, to the public at large, UFOs and aliens were a "dead issue".

Scientist and UFO disclosure advocate James McDonald said in 1969, "I am enough of a realist to sense that, unless this AAAS symposium succeeds in making the scientific community aware of the seriousness of the UFO problem, little response to any call for new investigations is likely to appear". McDonald presented a brilliant paper entitled, *"Science in Default: Twenty-two Years of Inadequate UFO Investigations"*. Dolan comments that it was "perhaps the most damning statement about UFO research ever made". Speaking before the convention at Boston's Sheraton Plaza Hotel, McDonald came down hard on everyone: Condon, Menzel, Hynek, and finally the scientific establishment itself. He said:

> "No scientifically adequate investigation of the UFO problem has been carried out during the entire twenty-two years that have now passed since the first extensive wave of sightings of unidentified aerial objects in the summer of 1947. ...In my opinion, the UFO problem, far from being the nonsense problem that many scientists have often labeled it, constitutes a problem of extraordinary scientific interest. The grave difficulty with essentially all past UFO studies had been that they were either devoid of any substantial scientific content, or else have lost their way amidst the relatively large noise content that tends to obscure the real signal in the UFO reports." [13]

This high noise to signal ratio is, based on the evidence, the direct product of the frenzied activities of the "National Security State" in their promulgation of the New Age/Human Potential smoke and mirrors magic show. What is also clearly evident is that this noise is the fundament of the prevailing scientific doctrine. What we see is that the Scientific Community - though they claim to be seekers of advanced scientific truth - have been as easily duped as Joe Sixpack and Shirley Seeker of Truth. The former is interested in little more than his truck, his dog, and his weekend football game, while the latter is generally looking for a lifestyle of higher "experiences". What I also suspect is that even the lower echelons of the intelligence and military organizations must be included in this rather large grouping of the duped and deceived sheep.

An example of this duping of those investigating the matter from the "bottom up", is Andrew Tully who wrote *The Super Spies,* supposedly an early report on the NSA. He, and many who have followed him, suggest that the UFO is an

---

[13] Ibid., quoted by Dolan, p. 368.

"intelligence" device and that it evolved out of Nazi Secrets brought to the US under Project Paperclip.[14]

Dolan lays out the evidence and disabuses us of the notion that the UFO activity could be human, technological breakthroughs, as such naive conspiracy theorists propose. As he says, "all of the indicators point to a definitive NO". He then points out that, every single person who actually *studies* the UFO problem [yours truly included - who began as a flaming skeptic], becomes convinced that it IS a problem of Alien invasion of our planet. Every official study of UFOs persuaded the researchers that aliens were the explanation for the data. But that data has been denied, and when denial no longer worked, it was obscured by the noise, the smoke and mirrors that prevail today in UFO research and the New Age and Human Potential movements. Do we think that this is coincidence?

Another evident production of "noise" is the nonsense that passes today as "channeling" or "alien contacts". Indeed, our own work involves what can certainly be called inspirational material, but as we have noted repeatedly, it is not your usual "channeled" info, nor do we treat it as such. For us, a controlled

---

[14] Convinced that German scientists could help America's postwar efforts, President Harry Truman agreed in September 1946 to authorize "Project Paperclip," a program to bring selected German scientists to work on America's behalf during the "Cold War" .

However, Truman expressly excluded anyone found "to have been a member of the Nazi party and more than a nominal participant in its activities, or an active supporter of Nazism or militarism." The War Department's Joint Intelligence Objectives Agency (JIOA) conducted background investigations of the scientists. In February 1947, JIOA Director Bosquet Wev submitted the first set of scientists' dossiers to the State and Justice Departments for review. The Dossiers were damning. Samuel Klaus, the State Departments representative on the JIOA board, claimed that all the scientists in this first batch were "ardent Nazis." Their visa requests were denied. Wev wrote a memo warning that "the best interests of the United States have been subjugated to the efforts expended in 'beating a dead Nazi horse.'" He also declared that the return of these scientists to Germany, where they could be exploited by America's enemies, presented a "far greater security threat to this country than any former Nazi affiliations which they may have had or even any Nazi sympathies that they may still have."

When the JIOA formed to investigate the backgrounds and form dossiers on the Nazis, the Nazi Intelligence leader Reinhard Gehlen met with the CIA director Allen Dulles. Dulles and Gehlen hit it off immediately, Gehlen was a master spy for the Nazis and had infiltrated Russia with his vast Nazi Intelligence network. Dulles promised Gehlen that his Intelligence unit was safe in the CIA. Dulles had the scientists dossier's re-written to eliminate incriminating evidence. As promised, Allen Dulles delivered the Nazi Intelligence unit to the CIA, which later opened many umbrella projects stemming from Nazi mad research. (MK-ULTRA / ARTICHOKE, OPERATION MIDNIGHT CLIMAX) By 1955, more than 760 German scientists had been granted citizenship in the U.S. and given prominent positions in the American scientific community. Many had been longtime members of the Nazi party and the Gestapo, had conducted experiments on humans at concentration camps, had used slave labor, and had committed other war crimes. In a 1985 expose in the Bulletin of the Atomic Scientists Linda Hunt wrote that she had examined more than 130 reports on Project Paperclip subjects--and every one "had been changed to eliminate the security threat classification." President Truman, who had explicitly ordered no committed Nazis to be admitted under Project Paperclip, was evidently never aware that his directive had been violated.

channeling experiment is the 10% inspiration that must be matched by the 90% perspiration of real research. With a broad historical awareness of the facts, a firm grounding in the realization that most of what is out there is deliberate disinformation, the individual who surveys the plethora of "alternative information" in books and on the Internet, can easily recognize the "noise" factor produced by the Secret State. Dolan tells us:

> By the early 1970s, there were already means available to alter the moods of unsuspecting persons. A pocket-sized transmitter generating electromagnetic energy at less than 100 milliwatts could do the job. This is no pie-in-the-sky theory. In 1972, Dr. Gordon J.F. McDonald testified before the House Subcommittee on Oceans and International Environment on the issue of electromagnetic weapons used for mind control and mental disruption. He stated:
>
> [T]he basic notion was to create, between the electrically charged ionosphere in the higher part of the atmosphere and conducting layers of the surface of the Earth, this neutral cavity, to create waves, electrical waves that would be tuned to the brain waves. ...About ten cycles per second. ...You can produce changes in behavioral patterns or in responses.
>
> The following year, Dr. Joseph C. Sharp, at Walter Reed Hospital, while in a soundproof room, was able to hear spoken words broadcast by 'pulsed microwave audiogram'. These words were broadcast to him without any implanted electronic translation device. Rather, they reached him by direct transmission to the brain. [15]

Consider the above in terms of "chemtrails". Also, note the comments of our own experimentally obtained material regarding the above- not from "aliens", but rather from "us in the future".

> 12-04-99
> Q: (L) But, the fact still remains, in my opinion, that there are a LOT, LOT, LOT of planes flying above us in the past few years! Whether they are dumping anything on our heads, or what, there are an extreme number of planes flying in these upper level criss-cross patterns. Now, whether they are just playing war-games, or they are spy planes, they are doing SOMETHING! What is the reason for all of this upper level flying that results in these criss-crossed contrails that everybody is seeing?
> A: A lot of it is "training maneuver" oriented.
> Q: Why are they training so many pilots? What are they preparing for?
> A: Military budgets must be justified, you know. Review "Military-Industrial Complex 101".
> Q: So, this is just training flight, justification of budget, and nothing more than that?
> A: **Well, we would not say "not anything more to it than that," but, when you**

---

[15] Ibid., p. 382.

say "M-IC," you have said a lot!
Q: Are you implying that there is a build-up of the Military-Industrial Complex for a reason?
A: To preserve status quo during "peacetime". This peace business is not very profitable, you know.
Q: Does that suggest that they are building up to set off a war so they can make more money?
A: Maybe if indeed, and if the populous can be hoodwinked. But, fortunately, the public is less hoodwink able. Maybe the real enemy is "out there", rather than "over there". Was it not always?
Q: Does any of this increased aircraft activity have anything to do with the increased awareness and activities of aliens in and around our planet?
A: As always. But, this awareness is factionalized and compartmentalized.

The C's comments take on a whole new meaning in light of the present situation - 9-11 and all that - as well as Bush's drive for "war". We also note the most interesting remark that, "awareness of the activities of aliens in and around our planet" is "factionalized and compartmentalized". This is where we come to the COINTELPRO function of creating *bogus organizations to attack or disrupt bona fide groups.*

We have already noted the fact that research in Electrical Stimulation of the brain can produce hallucinations. If you put hallucinations together with words, you can produce just about anything that you want in the way of "noise" to obscure the truth - including the "shape-shifting reptoids-as-humans", or a "gray dude in the bathroom", a "Guardian Alliance", a "Nibiruan Council" or an "Ashtar Command", or talking whales and dolphins, etc. You name it - they can produce it via voices in the head and hallucinations and transmissions of frequencies that produce ecstatic states, healings, or whatever. And so it is that the human element of the Cosmic COINTELPRO operation manages their many "agents" of disinformation - pied pipers leading the masses of New Age seekers - so that whatever the real truth is remains their secret. And that's exactly the way they want it.

Notice the dates in the above quote from Dolan's book telling us that in the early 70s certain technologies were being developed that could "broadcast" signals over the entire nation. We certainly suspect that this technology was developed further in the subsequent years. The question is: what did they do with it? Better yet, what ARE they doing with it?

What strikes me as an essential turning point in this COINTELPRO operation was the beginning of the "expose" of two particular items that hold sway in certain "conspiracy" circles to this very day: Alien Abduction and Satanic Ritual Abuse.

The Gray alien scenario was "leaked" by Budd Hopkins. Whitley Strieber's alien abduction books, including *Communion,* followed a few years after. Prior to the publication of these books, the ubiquitous "Gray aliens" had never been seen before. In fact, a review of the history of "contact" cases show that the type and variety and behavior of "aliens" around the world are quite different across the board. But, along came Budd, followed by Whitley and his glaring alien on the cover, and suddenly the Grays were everywhere.

In respect of Whitley and his Grays, allow me to emphasize one of Dolan's comments quoted above: "By early 1969, teams within the CIA were running a number of bizarre experiments in mind control under the name *Operation Often*. In addition to the normal assortment of chemists, biologists, and conventional scientists, the operation *employed psychics and experts in demonology."* This, of course, brings us to the parallel event of that period of time: Satanic ritual abuse. SRA is the name given to the allegedly systematic abuse of children (and others) by Satanists.

As it happens, keeping our timeline in mind, it was in the mid to late 1970s that the allegations of the existence of a "well-organized intergenerational satanic cult whose members sexually molest, torture and murder children across the United States", began to emerge in America. There was a panic regarding SRA triggered by a fictional book called *Michelle Remembers*. The book was published as fact but has subsequently been shown by at least three independent investigators to be a hoax. No hard evidence of Satanic Ritual Abuse in North America has ever been found, just as no hard evidence of abductions by Gray aliens has ever been found. Nevertheless, the allegations were widely publicized on radio and television talk shows, including Geraldo Rivera's show.

Religious fundamentalists promoted the hysteria and, just as during the Inquisitions, endless self-proclaimed "moral entrepreneurs" both fed the fires of prosecution and earned a good living from it. Most of the early accusations of satanic ritual abuse were aimed at working-class people with limited resources, and with a few exceptions, the media and other groups that are *ordinarily skeptical* either remained silent or joined in the feeding frenzy of accusations. The few professionals who spoke out against the hysteria were *systematically attacked and discredited by government agencies and private organizations.*

The question has to be asked: If there are thousands of baseless accusations of SRA and thousands upon thousands of cases of unverifiable alien abductions, how do they originate?

Most of the SRA cases are said to originate with children. Since there is a widespread belief that children wouldn't make up stories of eating other children or being forced to have sex with giraffes after flying in an airplane while they were supposed to be in day care, the stories are often taken at face value by naive prosecutors, therapists, police officers and parents. Researchers have found that children are unlikely to invent stories of satanic ritual abuse on their own. So, where do the stories come from?

Accusing the therapists, district attorneys, police and parents of inducing such stories from children doesn't seem to be a very productive answer. Yes, it may happen in some cases, but certainly doesn't seem likely in the vast number of cases.

Now, let's go back and think about our timeline. As it happens, *Michelle Remembers* was published in 1980, co-written by Michelle Smith and Lawrence Pazder, M.D. Budd Hopkins finished *Missing Time* in December of 1980, with an "afterward" by Aphrodite Clamar, Ph.D.

It's looking pretty "coincidental" from where I sit.

What occurs to me - putting the pieces of the puzzle together - is that there is some general kind of imagery being widely broadcast in the "neutral cavity" described above, and that it depends a lot on the individual and their cultural programming how it "takes". When we consider the fact that *Operation Often* employed "the normal assortment of chemists, biologists, and conventional scientists" and *"psychics and experts in demonology"*, we begin to think that electronic COINTELPRO includes a whole supermarket of new "beliefs" - Gray aliens and "alien contacts" for the New Age crowd and a whole range of "sexual/ritual abuse scenarios" for those who are *not* open to the alien shtick.

Is the whole thing beamed out as some sort of "free-formal imaging", and, based on the conscious acceptance of one or another version, it takes on its individual characteristics in the minds of the millions of recipients? In other words, is it picked up by the subconscious in alpha states or in sleep, perceived as traumatic in a general scenario that can then be interpreted by the individual belief systems in terms of either being examined and or sexually manipulated by aliens on a table or "raped on an altar" by Satanists? Are the public productions, books by Hopkins, Strieber, and the SRA scandals, just variations on the closing of the circuit by the conscious mind accepting or creating one or the other scenario as the explanation for the constant bombardment of such signals as described in Dolan's book? Is it the job of COINTELPRO to create "bogus organizations" that produce various "explanations" to close the circuit and "make it real" in the person's mind?

One has to wonder about the name of the program: *Operation Often* in terms of the claims of abductees - victims of repeated and "often" abductions - as well as the claims of those who suggest the SRA explanation. In either case, the believer is being "herded" into a "response camp" of either faith in alien saviors, or faith in Jesus to save them from the demonic/satanic Illuminati, Jews, Pagans - take your pick.

Let me make it clear that I am in no way suggesting that "abductions" or some whacked out satanic rituals do not ever take place somewhere, under some circumstances. What I am suggesting is that the Gray Alien and SRA phenomenon most certainly was not restricted in any way by COINTELPRO, and may indeed be the smoke and mirrors that hides a far more insidious state of affairs.

In essence, Dolan's book shows us the history of how the many levels of society have been duped and deceived - or directly controlled - from the average citizen, to the seeker of higher truths, to the scions of science and industry, to the hallowed halls of government. Each "type" has been targeted in the way most likely to "manage" them best. Those who cannot be "managed" generally die, as scientist James McDonald, and others, did. But all the while, the UFOs kept coming, and people kept seeing them, and they kept asking questions.

In April 1971, an engineering research magazine, *Industrial Research,* published the results of a poll in which 80 percent of its members rejected the Condon Report; 76 percent believed that the government was concealing UFO facts; 32 percent believed that UFOs were extraterrestrial. Poll or no poll, the CIA continued to lie about its UFO interests. [...]

The worst story of 1971 was the demise of James McDonald. [Atmospheric physicist from the University of Arizona.] As far as anyone could tell, McDonald was fine all through 1970 and into 1971. On March 2, 1971, he testified as an expert in atmospheric physics at the House committee on Appropriations regarding the supersonic transport (SST) and its potentially harmful atmospheric effects. McDonald's opponents questioned his credentials and ridiculed him as someone who believed in "little men flying around the sky". Laughter broke out several times.

Shortly after this incident, McDonald shot himself in the head and became blind. He was committed to the psychiatric ward of the VA medical Center in Tucson. In June, he signed himself out. On Sunday morning, June 13, a woman in south Tucson, identifying herself as a doctor, said a deranged blind man had taken a cab to the area. She wanted to know where the driver had dropped him off, and she made several calls. Meanwhile, a married couple and their children, walking along a shallow creek, found McDonald's body under a bridge at 11:40 a.m. A .38 caliber revolver was in the sand, near his head. A brief note attributed his suicide to marriage and family problems. [...]

We know that many intelligence agencies were skilled in "creating" suicides. But, one might ask, wasn't McDonald's mental condition already deteriorating? Jerome Clark stated that McDonald was ready to "crack" in the aftermath of the SST hearings. But what caused this? Embarrassment at the SST hearings? His marriage? Perhaps, one supposes, but both of these explanations feel flimsy. Without exception, those who knew McDonald described him as possessing great integrity and courage. Was he really the type of person to commit suicide? [16]

McDonald had been described as a man who was "afraid of nothing". What seems to be so is that this was why he was destroyed. Hynek had written that McDonald was considered by the Air Force to be an "outstanding nuisance".

With the mind control arsenal that has been described at their disposal, we have a good idea of what "they" can do to the mind. Even the strongest. Courage and integrity, it seems, are no protection. We would like to note another curious death - that of Edward Ruppelt. After years as an advocate of disclosure, he suddenly did an about face - re-wrote his book recanting his belief that UFOs were extraterrestrial craft, and was dead within a year at a very young age.

It looks to me as though, if they can't corrupt you, they kill you, and if they *can* corrupt you, they still kill you so you won't have a chance to change your mind and recant your recantation like Jacques de Molay did when the Templars were destroyed. Those who get close to the belly of the beast are generally subjected to a new "approach" it seems. And that approach is the biggest betrayal of all.

Many important and influential people have attested to the reality of the UFO phenomenon as an "alien reality". Within the military organizations, those who affirm the "alien hypothesis" are widespread and numerous. But, as Dolan shows us, they cannot discuss those views without risking the penalties of imprisonment and stiff fines.

In the present day, we have Steven Greer's "Disclosure Project". Based on the mail I get, it seems that many in the New Age/UFO community think that this is a

---

[16] Ibid., p. 381.

great and novel idea. However, history shows that it has been tried before. The one thing about Greer's effort that suggests it is just more and better COINTELPRO is his attachment to the "aliens are here to help us" idea, which is directly contradicted by history, though widely promoted by most "contactees". Even Linda Howe, for a long time the most reputable of careful researchers - and no stranger to the machinations of the Secret State - seems to have fallen for this one - COINTELPRO. It is also now being promoted in *Fate Magazine* by Rosemary Guiley, who has the odor of COINTELPRO about her with her notable connections to military "agents". Jerome Clark, quoted above, is also a regular contributor to *Fate*.

Let me make it clear at this point that I am convinced that a lot of honest, sincere, hard-working individuals are being duped and/or controlled without being fully aware of it.

Dolan documents the failure of civilian groups in their efforts to really "end UFO secrecy". NICAP had prominent and active members, connections to Congress and to the military, and their effort continued for over ten years. NICAP fought diligently for congressional hearings, and yet every time they got "close" to bringing it to the table for public consideration, the congressional sponsorship "backed off" and reversed their support.

What kind of group is it that can control our government officials in this way? An even deeper question might be: What kind of group is it that can control the media, the military, the CIA, the FBI, NSA, and even the President? What do they do to intimidate and dominate ethical and substantial persons in positions of authority? Whatever it is, we would certainly like to know because it suggests that they are hiding something so significant that even hints of it behind closed doors can send the most powerful congressmen running with their tails tucked between their legs.

This brings us back to the problem of the Secret State and its agenda. Some people believe that this secrecy is absolutely essential. They say that the public simply could not handle the truth about aliens. They say that there is no reason to spoil people's lives with the truth because there is nothing that the average person could do about it anyway. Is that really true? *Would there be so much effort to conceal the alien agenda if disclosure of the truth wasn't harmful to that agenda?*

Dolan's chronological history of the actual interaction between UFOs and the public and the corresponding behavior of the military, the intelligence community, the media, and the scientific community in *its* interaction with the public, make this abundantly clear. Dolan writes:

> Some believe this is, as it ought to be. Can the public really handle the truth about aliens? If the presence of others constitutes a threat to humanity, for example, what

could the average person even do about it? There are those who believe that secrecy about UFOs is in the public's best interest. [17]

What is clearly evident, and most especially so in the past year or two, is that the "public interest" is *not* the concern of those making these decisions. As Dolan rightly says, secrecy is being utilized *not* to protect the public, but to protect those keeping the secrets - the "Above Top Secret" group - and very likely, even the aliens themselves.

When we consider the modus operandi of the intelligence community, in its historical perspective, what we see is that, at every level, right up to the very top, there is control and manipulation. This leads me to suggest that even those at the top level of the human Consortium are being duped and deceived and are as unable and/or unwilling to consider that possibility as those at the lower levels.

It seems obvious from the documentary evidence as well as the behavior of the military in response to UFOs and the "alien matter", that the aliens *do* have an agenda, and that, at some level in the layers of secrecy, there are those who *know* - on a "need to know" basis - what that agenda is. It seems abundantly evident that the secrecy has been enjoined on this group by the aliens themselves. Even more alarming is that a careful assessment of the evidence does not suggest a benevolent agenda.

As a result of the manipulations of this "Consortium", the majority of Americans are inculcated into the fiction of a representative government, a democracy, and that our scientists and representatives are "taking care of business" for us, and even if they are sometimes corrupt, they aren't as bad as a totalitarian regime. It has become most definitely obvious in the past couple of years that this is not the case and probably never was. We don't even really elect our representatives. It's all a sham. But the fiction propagated by the media has clouded the ability of the American people to see their society and government for what it really is: an oligarchy that pretends to be a democracy to placate and deceive the public.

To those who suggest that it doesn't really matter since it is an efficient way to organize and manage millions of people, let us suggest that it is suicidal to think that an oligarchy is not primarily interested in maintaining its own position to the exclusion of all other considerations. When we consider the evidence, we see that the groups in question have *never* acted in the best interests of the public. If you doubt this, spend some time reading about nonconsensual human experimentation. Logically speaking, there is *no* reason to even suggest that the secrecy surrounding the "alien reality" is any different.

Dolan notes that, as a result of the concerted "debunking" of UFOs perpetrated on a populace that has been mind manipulated and dumbed down by public

---

[17] Ibid., p. 392.

"education" for a very long time, our society has become extraordinarily schizophrenic about UFOs. At the level of "officialdom", as in academia, mainstream media, government and so forth, UFOs are either ignored or treated as a joke. You won't find UFOs or Aliens - or their repeated invasion of sensitive airspace - discussed on the nightly news. You won't find Ted Koppel analyzing them as a threat to National Security. And this state of affairs is totally bizarre because it is abundantly - overwhelmingly - clear and evident that our military and intelligence organizations consider them to be so important that information about them is classified "Above Top Secret".

However, being classified "Above Top Secret" does not seem to matter to the aliens. They arrogantly do as they please and leave the "clean up" to their human lackeys the same way some media personalities have been reported to destroy hotel rooms, and then have their accountants write checks to cover the damages, while their agents give press releases that deny any such thing ever happened.

This brings us back to the efforts of COINTELPRO. Since the military is in the position of dealing with beings of such arrogance that their checks don't cover the damage they do, the "press releases" are issued in the form of diversion and division. UFOs and the "alien reality" are promoted in ways that simply do not relate to the documentary evidence or the factual data. UFOs and aliens are given cachet in the New Age and metaphysical communities, and groups studying them or "channeling" them are "managed" so that the possibility of exposure of the Truth is completely minimized in the plethora of conflicting, generated "beliefs". At the same time, there are organizations that are set up to operate as "professional debunkers" and disinformation artists; smoke and mirrors and endless confusion.

What is evident from the documents and statements of those "in on the secret", is that the current "popularity" of aliens and New Age presentations of the subject *are the direct result of deliberate infiltration by intelligence personnel who are continually "spinning the wheel" of lies and distortion.*

UFOs have national security implications for a lot of reasons, not the least of which is that they have involved military and industrial personnel of many nations around the globe. This situation has existed for over fifty years. In fact, a careful study of history shows an intersection between UFOs and the military for hundreds, if not thousands of years! Unauthorized airspace violations continue to occur; attempted interceptions repeatedly take place, and the secrecy orders are more severe now than ever.

We have to ask ourselves why this is so?

If the military organizations are as interested in UFOs and Aliens as we know them to be, based on the evidence, and if they are in the dark about them, as the evidence also suggests, would they not be utilizing the many claimed "alien contacts" among the New Age community as resources, if there was the possibility that such sources really were in contact with the "real aliens" in and about the planet ? There are certainly many of these contactees that claim "extreme military interest" in their work. However, based on the facts of the operations of the National Security State, we can pretty well objectively assess that if this were true, such contactees would not be out there promulgating their information. That they often operate unmolested, and even achieve great popularity is compelling evidence that their "information" is useless to the military, if not created by it.

What seems to be true is that most contactees and channelers are dupes of the military cover-up - victims of COINTELPRO - created to generate the noise that hides the signal of the true Alien Reality. In short, the majority of claims of channelers, contactees, new age gurus, UFO researchersand the like, both in books and on the internet, about the "alien reality", is COINTELPRO at its finest.

Take that to the bank.

One thing is clear: the UFOs themselves are not under the control of the military - or anybody else. The evidence that the Consortium continues to debunk and cover this up - in the face of its violations of their own airspace - suggests again the analogy of arrogant and powerful Masters of Reality, aided and abetted by their military and intelligence organization servants who, while obeying the powerful overlords, seek to keep everything quiet, trying desperately to discover the secrets of power, so as to arrogate it to themselves. And it seems evident that, in the present time, the game is afoot in the citadels of Power and Secrets. Something is happening and the servants of the alien masters are running scared. They are trying to cement controls, to solidify their power base, because Something Wicked This Way Comes.

COINTELPRO AND ASCENSION

This brings us back to the subject of Ascension. As I noted, the subject of Ascension seems to be the number one topic of the New Age and Human Potential movement. If, as we suspect, the New Age and Human Potential movement is the product of COINTELPRO, that means that targeting the correct understanding of, and process of, Ascension is their major goal. Does that mean that such a potential does not exist at all? No. The concepts of Ascension have been with us a long time, as we will examine further on. What is different about the present day promotions is the type of process that is being promoted. Based on an assessment of the potentials of Ascension, it is obvious that the reason it is such a popular subject is that it is one of the main things that COINTELPRO is designed to obstruct and prevent.

Let me repeat the observation I made above: Would there be so much effort to conceal the alien agenda if disclosure of the truth wasn't harmful to that agenda? Rephrasing this: Would there be so much effort to divert the Ascension process if it wasn't harmful to the negative agendas?

As the fellow at RAND noted, "Terrorism is changing. New adversaries, new motivations and new rationales have surfaced in recent years to challenge much of the conventional wisdom...". We already have the idea that the Consortium, the National Security State, does not have our best interests at heart, and that at some level, they seem to be operating at the behest of the alien invaders. Considering this, we might wish to look with new eyes at some of the ideas of Ascension that are currently being promulgated.

In order to understand the growth of the "Ascension Industry", we need to look at a close parallel: general culture. Among the observers of the American socio-cultural scene, there are many experts who tell us that there has been a deliberate effort for over 100 years, to "dumb down" the American population both in terms of intellect and ethics. This subject is too vast to be covered in detail here and will be dealt with fully in a future volume. For now, let us just point out that the same process that has been used to dumb down the population in social and intellectual terms has been used to dumb us down in terms of philosophy, metaphysics and spiritual awareness. We might observe that it is hardly likely that the effort would be expended on mind control of the masses for the purposes of external controls, without a parallel program being instituted to pervert the spirit and bring it under domination also.

PRIME TIME

While everyone will readily admit that there is probably too much violence on television and that the ads are revoltingly juvenile, very few people have a real conception of the precise nature and extent of the hypnotic influence of the media. Still fewer have any idea of the purposes behind this inducement. Wallace and Wallechinsky write in *The People's Almanac*:

"After World War II, television flourished... Psychologists and sociologists were brought in to study human nature in relation to selling; in other words, to figure out how to manipulate people without their feeling manipulated. Dr. Ernest Dichter, President of the Institute for Motivational Research made a statement in 1941... 'the successful ad agency manipulates human motivations and desires and develops a need for goods with which the public has at one time been unfamiliar -- perhaps even undesirous of purchasing.'

Discussing the influence of television, Daniel Boorstin wrote: "Here at last is a supermarket of surrogate experience. Successful programming offers entertainment - under the guise of instruction; instruction - under the guise of entertainment; political persuasion - with the appeal of advertising; and advertising - with the appeal of drama."

[...] programmed television serves not only to **spread acquiescence and conformity**, but it represents a deliberate industry approach." [18]

Allen Funt, host of a popular television show, *Candid Camera*, was once asked what was the most disturbing thing he had learned about people in his years of dealing with them through the media. His response was chilling in its ramifications:

"The worst thing, and I see it over and over, is how easily people can be led by any kind of authority figure, or even the most minimal kinds of authority. A well-dressed man walks up the down escalator and most people will turn around and try desperately to go up also... We put up a sign on the road, 'Delaware Closed Today'. Motorists didn't even question it. Instead they asked: 'Is Jersey open?'" [19]

---

[18] Quoted by Wallace and Wallechinsky in *The People's Almanac,* pp. 805, 807.

[19] Ibid.

Thus, we have submission to minimal signs of authority; lack of knowledge and awareness; and a desire for a quick fix and an easy way out. Paraphrasing Daniel Boorstin: "For seekers of Ascension, here at last is a supermarket of surrogate experience. Successful [ascension philosophies] offer entertainment - under the guise of instruction; instruction - under the guise of entertainment; [metaphysical] persuasion - with the appeal of advertising; and advertising - with the appeal of [Cosmic Drama]."

When we consider the information about mind programming and its potentials compiled in Dolan's book, *UFOs and the National Security State,* and how it has probably been used on the masses of humanity, we must also consider, as a logical step, that the major and most popular components of the New Age alternative approach to interpreting reality and seeking spiritual advancement, have also been produced by this same process in the context of electronic COINTELPRO.

What seems to be so is that most of the New Age and Human Potential movement consists of a new sub-set of programmers that work to "prepare the ground", so to speak, so that the audience will be warmed up and ready for the final drama. They are the "sales team" that sells the ideas upon which the "closer" depends for success. They are here, now, in our world running New Age Circuses, seminars, workshops and "methods" or techniques for "ascension", or accomplishing any of a dozen occult or purported spiritual aims. They are the New Age COINTELPRO in its function of creating "bogus organizations".

THE REAL PRIZE

If we cannot rely on what is passing as "New Age Theology", or philosophy, to guide us, what is the key to REAL ascension?

What the modern day seekers of ascension are looking for—whether they realize it or not— is the age-old quest of the Knight - the quest for the Holy Grail. When we begin to research the matter, we also discover that the Great Work of Alchemy is described in terms of a "great battle" with forces - dragons, deception, difficult and prolonged work on the self - which make us realize that the stories of the Grail Quest must have originally been stories of "alchemical transformation.". They never were stories about a "real" object - cup or otherwise - that must be found. Or were they both? What is most fascinating is the way the Grail Stories, and the writings of the Alchemists about their "sacred science", also relate quite closely to the most ancient of heroic myths.

What this means is that the Quest for the Holy Grail and the Work of the Alchemists hold many clues for us as to the real work of ascension. Repeatedly they present allegories of struggle, deception, battles with dragons, deceivers, and evil forces of all kinds. The story of the Knight who slays the Dragon and rescues the Princess from the Tower after years of seeking, struggling, suffering and overcoming, is an allegory that is as valid today as it was in ages past. It is the true path of ascension.

As we present the information in this volume, the reader will be introduced to the idea that the science of the ancients may have included a very comprehensive knowledge of the deeper reality that present day sciences, including physics, chemistry, mathematics, and astrophysics, are only rediscovering. And here we do not mean the ancient Egyptians or Babylonians or Sumerians, but rather peoples of far greater antiquity than they, and that the Egyptians, Babylonians, Sumerians, and so on, retained only a distorted and corrupted version of these ideas in the form of myths and legends which they elaborated and utilized in their "magical practices". Further, that it is only in the light of the present day scientific knowledge that the true ancient knowledge, depicted in these myths, legends and religious rites can be properly understood. This is not to say that we are suggesting that we understand or have interpreted all of them. We are only saying that there are many ideas in these ancient stories that suggest the former existence of an advanced science that may have enabled an interface between layers, or dimensions of reality, on this planet in archaic times.

This idea is not original to us, as many readers will know. However, we do think that we have been able to shine a light into certain dark corners that have been, heretofore, poorly understood. Arthur C. Clarke pointed out, "Any sufficiently evolved technology is indistinguishable from magic." When we divest our minds of preconceived notions about what the ancients may or may not have known, and we just look at myths and legends, the substrate of religions, over and over again we see descriptions of activities, events, terms and potentials that express such things as a knowledge of free energy, anti-gravity, time travel, interplanetary travel, atomic energy, atomic molecularization and demolecularization; just a whole host of doings that were formerly understood as the wild and superstitious imaginings of howling savages, that today - with scientific knowledge - are becoming commonplace activities. Many scholars explain that such stories were attempts to understand the environment by personifying, or anthropomorphizing, the forces of nature. Other interpreters make the mistake of assuming that it was a "sacred science" in terms that strictly deny any form of material interpretation.

I gave this idea a great deal of thought at one point, all the while observing my five children develop, paying close attention to how and when they noticed things in their environment, how they explained phenomena to themselves and each other; avoiding my own input as long as possible so that the child's originality would develop as naturally as possible. One of the earliest observations I made about my children (and other children with whom they interacted) and their reactions to their environment, was that they pretty much just accept it as it is. They don't seem to need "explanations" for it. It is what it is until some adult repeats to them some story about it which may entertain them or frighten them. Until "stories" are told to them, children are intensely busy just imitating what they see other people do, most generally the adults in their lives. Without fantastic tales being told to them, their games of make-believe consist of ordinary mundane dramas. Even when they are told magical stories about flying horses or people with super powers, they often resist these dramas in preference for those that directly apply to their own experience and observation.

Perhaps the comparison of the development of a child's thinking in relation to their environment, to the development of evolutionary thinking of human beings in general is a stretch. But, I do think that it ought to give us some pause to question just where and how the creation of myth and legend actually served human beings, evolutionarily speaking. Why would anyone tell a story about a man with magic sandals that enabled him to fly if they are merely anthropomorphizing the forces of nature? If it is a "magical being" such as a "god", why does he need sandals to fly with? He could just as easily have wings that are part of his physical structure. He's already a god, after all. He's not human. So why the sandals? Why should a technological device that enables a man to fly be part of an archaic ontology?

Indeed, there may be an "archetypal pool of ideas" from which all humanity may draw in dreams and visions, but that leads us into realms of thought that do not answer the simple question of what benefit there was for howling savages to make up fantastic tales about the forces of nature, tales that also included certain elements that suggest a technology and not only a "magical state of being".

In the present day, there are all sorts of "mystical" groups and organizations that claim to be the recipients of ancient knowledge, what is commonly called "occultism", or the "esoteric", or magical practices. There is a plethora of books that purport to be scientific, but which totally reject mainstream science in any context. Subjects such as sacred geometry, archaeoastronomy, and new physics have all become subjects of fevered study in order to discern the "occult significance" of the works of the ancients. And, invariably, it is done in strictly ritual terms, positing that all of the abilities of the ancients were accomplished strictly by magical rites or rituals - controlling what is "up there" by rituals "down here".

Occultists claim that the mental and spiritual powers of the ancients were what we have lost. They then assert that this ancient wisdom was broken up and obscured in magical doctrines, which those who are not "initiated" simply cannot grasp. They claim that parts of it have been handed down by continuous tradition, and released to the world at opportune times, and other parts have only been released to an elect few, of which exalted company, they, of course, are obviously members.

When considering such ideas, we do come to the thought that it is very likely that there are rites or stories or myths behind the rituals that may, indeed, have been passed down in such secret groups in a more pure form than the stories that make their way around the globe across millennia. But that does not mean that the "priesthood" of such groups truly understands the stories or rites of which they are guardians—especially if they do not consider the possibility that such information may be scientific codes and require a trained scientist to decode them.

Most of the so-called "occultists" and "sacred geometers" remind me of David Macaulay's *Motel Of Mysteries*,[20] a humorous account of an archaeological excavation of a twentieth century motel, in which everything is meticulously excavated, recorded and then totally misinterpreted. The "vast funerary" complex unearthed by Howard Carson contains wonders such as the "Great Altar"

---

[20] Macaulay, David, *Motel Of Mysteries* (Boston: Houghton Mifflin 1979).

(Television), a statue of the deity WATT (bedside lamp) and the Internal Component Enclosure (or ICE box).

There are other promulgators of the occult who seem to be part of the very Control System we have described above and who seem to have extremely dangerous proclivities, as we will discuss further on.

In terms of archaeology, there are processes involved in the formation of the archaeological record. A lack of understanding of these formation processes is not always confined to the non-professionals. It has only relatively recently been suggested that the archaeology of a site is not a direct record of what went on there, but instead may have been distorted by a whole series of processes.

We are suggesting that the same may be true regarding myths and legends and religious rites. They are a sort of archaeological record of the history of mankind held in archetypal terms, buried in stories, distorted by a whole series of processes.

Even if some of the purported ancient schools and mystical paths have kept some of this information intact, or in a purer state, it still seems that much has "faded on the page" due to the long period of time since such things were part of the external reality. But still, there are those who have seen the contradictions in our reality and our beliefs and who have sought in these ancient teachings to discover what might have been known. Many of them have made discoveries that, when considered with information from many other fields, assists us in this essential discovery of our true condition and purpose.

The question naturally arises, what does the history of our subject - Ascension as Ancient Science - have to tell us about what may or may not "really work"? Can we examine it; can we track it and discover not only the obstacles to the process, but also the *real benefits* that might accrue to the Seeker? Can we track and discover the apparent abilities that are the signs of accomplishment of the successful Quest?

In short, what is the *real* Philosophers Stone? What can the Hero really accomplish when he finds the Holy Grail?

CHAPTER 1
THE NATURE OF THE QUEST

THE ANCIENT SECRET SCIENCE REVEALED

Many literary critics seem to think that a hypothesis about obscure and remote questions of history can be refuted by a simple demand for the production of more evidence than in fact exists. [...] But the true test of a hypothesis, if it cannot be shown to conflict with known truths, is the number of facts that it correlates and explains.

[Cornford, *Origins of Attic Comedy*]

DISJECTA MEMBRA

The theme of the Quest for the Holy Grail is so much a part of Western Culture that it would be difficult to even imagine its absence. The number of books, paintings, sculptures, plays, movies, popular songs and other artistic or literary expressions that deal with the "matter of the Grail" are too numerous to even count. The Holy Grail represents many things to many people, but in general we could say that it represents the Quest for All and Everything. This attitude has crept into our language when we say, "Oh, he's searching for the Holy Grail of _____". You can fill in the blank with about any field of endeavor. Everyone who considers the subject, even momentarily, is certain that, at the core of the Legend is a secret and/or some ultimate prize of a material nature. It could even be said that the attachment Western Society has to the Legends of the Grail is really all out of proportion to the actual confusing content of the stories themselves. In fact, many people who are certain that there is a deep meaning to the Legend of the Holy Grail haven't even read the original stories that gave birth to that legend.

Yet, something acts on us - each and every one - to trigger the imagination, the soul, whenever the subject comes up; and this suggests that there is some vital thing - some magic - some mysterious archetypal dream - that the very words "Holy Grail" awakens in the spirit of Western peoples. It activates something in our collective unconscious, transforming the muddled and confusing elements of the original stories into an enchanted land of heroic love and mighty feats of derring-do that can only be performed by the purest and the best; and all of us - in our most private fantasies - dream that we are "The One" who can achieve the Grail.

Anyone who studies the matter of the Grail already knows that there are literally multiple thousands of scholarly and/or imaginative works on the subject. There are essays, studies, criticisms - volumes of them - devoted to this fascinating subject. The student of Grail literature also knows that these endless treatments of the subject present an almost hopeless muddle of contradictory opinions and perspectives. For example: there is one school of thought that proposes the Grail to be an entirely "Christian matter". There are undeniably Christian elements that dominate certain versions. Then, there is the school of thought that claims that the Grail matter is essentially pagan, and most definitely of Celtic provenance. They point out that the later Christianized versions were attempts by ecclesiastics to "cover-up" and amalgamate a popular theme to Christian purposes. These two are the broadest divisions, but no means the only ones! Each group can be subdivided into branching schools, holding forth on any of dozens of theories.

The problem is that each of these two perspectives and their many subsets are faced with insurmountable problems when trying to promote their individual arguments. The theory of the Christian origin of the Grail breaks down completely when confronted with the most distressing fact that there is no Christian tradition concerning a "Joseph of Arimathea". It seems that Joseph does not exist outside of the Grail stories and must be relegated - by Christianity - to romantic fantasy. In fact, as Jessie Weston reported, as early as 1260, the Dutch writer, Jacob van Maerlant denounced the whole Grail issue as "lies", declaring that the Church knew nothing of it. And he was right. The Pagan-Celtic advocates have to face their own difficulties when dealing with the legends. The part of the Grail stories that can be proven to be definitely pagan and Celtic - the Perceval story - in its original form, has nothing to do with the Grail at all!

So the problem is this: while parallels can be found for one or another feature of the whole cycle of stories when taken in isolation, this cannot serve a broad overview because to derive parallels necessitates breaking the stories up into a group of independent themes. There is no "Q" document, as is theorized for the Gospels of the New Testament - a lost original source from which different elements are drawn. There is no prototype with all the elements in one story - the Waste Land, the Fisher King, the Hidden Castle with its otherworldly feast and mysterious vessel and maidens, the Bleeding Lance and Cup.

In short, for either the pagan-Celtic or Christian perspective, there is just no original source that has preserved all of the elements together. What this means is that the most logical approach to take to the subject is to understand at the outset that neither school of thought can ignore the other and that a broader approach is needed. This means that the origin of the Grail story must be somewhere other than in popular legends or Christianized tales.

Jessie L. Weston, after more than thirty years of study, wrote a little book entitled *From Ritual to Romance.* She noted therein an observation that was startling in its implications:

> Some years ago, when fresh from the study of Sir J. G. Frazer's*The Golden Bough*,
> I was struck by the resemblance existing between certain features of the Grail story,
> and characteristic details of the Nature Cults described. The more closely I
> analyzed the tale, the more striking became the resemblance, and I finally asked
> myself whether it were not possible that this mysterious legend - mysterious alike
> in its character, its sudden appearance, the importance apparently assigned to it,
> followed by as sudden and complete a disappearance - we might not have the

confused record of a ritual once popular, later surviving under conditions of strict secrecy? This would fully account for the atmosphere of awe and reverence, which even under distinctly non-Christian conditions never fails to surround the Grail.[...]

The more closely one studies pre-Christian Theology, the more strongly one is impressed with the deeply and daringly spiritual character of its speculations, and the more doubtful it appears that such teaching can depend on the unaided processes of human thought, or can have been evolved from such germs as we find among the supposedly 'primitive' peoples. [...] Are they really primitive? Or are we dealing, not with the primary elements of religion, but with the *disjecta membra* of a vanished civilization? Certainly it is that so far as historical evidence goes our earliest records point to the recognition of a spiritual, not of a material, origin of the human race.

The Folk practices and ceremonies studied - the dances, the rough Dramas, the local and seasonal celebrations, do not represent the material out of which the Attis-Adonis cult was formed, but surviving fragments of a worship from which the higher significance has vanished.

My aim has been to prove the essentially archaic character of all the elements composing the Grail story rather than to analyze the story as a connected whole.[21]

Let me repeat those two most important statements: The "*disjecta membra* of a vanished civilization", and "surviving fragments of a worship *from which the higher significance has vanished*". In short, what Ms. Weston has proposed is that the Grail Stories were a brief emergence into the general consciousness of something so ancient that finding the threads and re-weaving the whole cloth of the Sacred Tapestry might require a perspective of not merely thousands of years, but possibly tens of thousands of years - antediluvian, even! The very thought of something so daring in scope literally took my breath away. However, being naïve and something of a fool willing to rush in where angels fear to tread, I made the decision that I was going to search for the pieces to this puzzle if it took me the rest of my life.

Upon considering this idea as a hypothesis, I began to imagine how such an event might manifest. I came across another interesting item that helped me adjust the "lens" through which I was viewing reality. There is a story found in the *History* of Herodotus, which is an exact copy of an original tale of Indian origin *except* for the fact that in the original, it was an animal fable, and in Herodotus' version, all the characters had become human. In every other detail, the stories are identical. Joscelyn Godwin quotes R. E. Meagher, professor of humanities and

---

[21] Weston, Jessie L., *From Ritual to Romance* (London: Cambridge University Press 1920) pp. 3, 4, 7, 10.

translator of Greek classics, saying: "*Clearly, if characters change species, they may change their names and practically anything else about themselves.*"[22]

Going further still, Mircea Eliade clarifies for us the process of the "mythicization" of historical personages. Eliade describes how a Romanian folklorist recorded a ballad describing the death of a young man bewitched by a jealous mountain fairy on the eve of his marriage. The young man, under the influence of the fairy, was driven off a cliff. The ballad of lament, sung by the fiancée, was filled with "mythological allusions, a liturgical text of rustic beauty".

The folklorist, having been told that the song concerned a tragedy of "long ago", discovered that the fiancée was still alive and went to interview her. To his surprise, he learned that the young man's death had occurred less than 40 years before. He had slipped and fallen off a cliff; in reality, there was no mountain fairy involved.

Eliade notes that "despite the presence of the principal witness, a few years had sufficed to strip the event of all historical authenticity, to transform it into a legendary tale". Even though the tragedy had happened to one of their contemporaries, the death of a young man soon to be married "had an occult meaning that could only be revealed by its identification with the category of myth".

The myth seemed truer, more pure, than the prosaic event, because "it made the real story yield a deeper and richer meaning, revealing a tragic destiny".

In the same way, a Yugoslavian epic poem celebrating a heroic figure of the fourteenth century, Marko Kraljevic, abolishes his historic identity, his life story is "reconstructed in accordance with the norms of myth". His mother is a Vila, a fairy, as is his wife. He fights a three-headed dragon and kills it, fights with his brother and kills him, all in conformity with classical mythic themes.

The historic character of the persons celebrated in epic poetry is not in question, Eliade notes. "But their historicity does not long resist the corrosive action of mythicization." A historic event, despite its importance, doesn't remain in the popular memory intact.

> "Myth is the last – not the first – stage in the development of a hero." The memory of a real event survives perhaps three centuries at best, as the historic figure is assimilated to his mythical model and the event itself is blurred into a category of mythical actions.

> "This reduction of events to categories and of individuals to archetypes, carried out by the consciousness of the popular strata in Europe almost down to our day, is performed in conformity with archaic ontology", Eliade writes. "We have the right to ask ourselves if the importance of archetypes for the consciousness of archaic man, and the inability of popular memory to retain anything but archetypes, does

---

[22] Godwin, Joscelyn *Arktos*, (Kempton Illinois: Adventures Unlimited Press, 1996).

not reveal to us something more than a resistance to history exhibited by traditional spirituality?"[23]

This mythicization of historical personages appears in exactly the same way in all times and cultures. As it says in the Book of Ecclesiastes, "There is nothing new under the sun". Historical events are "assimilated" to the mythical archetype, and things that were never done by the hero are often assigned to him. Events, places and other characteristics of the "larger and deeper" context are also "attached".

What this suggests is that mythicization of historical persons takes place in accordance with some "exemplary standard" This is why all of the mythical heroes resemble one another in so many respects. It's not that each and every one of them did the same things; it is that somebody did something - at least one thing - that was heroic and therefore belonged to the exemplar. By so doing, they were "assimilated" to the archetype. We are not suggesting that the real heroes or historical characters did not exist or that they did nothing heroic. That is not in question. What seems to be evident is that their real, historical nature - what they *really* did - cannot resist the "corrosive action of mythicization". Therefore, discovering the identity of any hero by trying to compare his story to actual historical "facts" just simply will not work. And there is something else important to consider here: if a fairly ordinary "hero" and his collection of localized deeds are "assimilated" to an exemplar, even if we *do* discover his identity, it means very little. We have only discovered one of many, many individuals assimilated to the same archetype, and we risk going around in circles forever, trying to sort the facts, in order to discover some "magical artifact" that is connected to the exemplar. In some instances the tribal memory can "hold" a recollection of an ancestor's name, even if they have no clue about what that ancestor really did in complete terms. In other cases, the real name is forgotten and the name of the exemplar is attached. This may not seem to be much help in figuring out who really did what, but, with care and patience and comparison, we can come to some logical conclusions about the past, before written historical records based on facts were written down - or before the original written accounts were destroyed - which is another distinct possibility.

Another point that is crucial to our investigation is that myths *do* tend to *preserve the ideas of institutions, customs and landscapes* even if we cannot rely on them for what we would call personal historical truth. And finally, what we perceive from studying myths, legends, sagas, and epics is the evident fact that they are not "creative inventions" of whole cloth. There *is* a model. There is a reduction of events to categories and individuals to archetypes, and this model is

---

[23] Eliade, Mircea, *The Myth of The Eternal Return*; (New York: Bollingen Foundation, Princeton University Press 1954) pp. 40, 43, 44, 46.

in conformity with archaic ontology! It could even be said that mythicization of historical persons lays bare for us the meaning of the person and event - meaning that can only be seen by withdrawing from the immediate historical event. This leads us to ask the question: "Does this tendency of the consciousness of man to retain archetypes and assimilate historical events and people to those exemplars reveal something to us about the *true* nature of the Exemplar itself?"

"What is the true nature of the Exemplar?" This is going to be a very important question to remember as we go along. It will assist not only in understanding how stories from various sources can be both true and not true at the same time. It is also going to be a major clue in our investigation of certain very important matters that will come into play as being pivotal in the Grail Quest. Is there a level of reality at which the Exemplar exists and which impresses itself upon humanity in broad psychological terms? In other words, does the mythical archetype refer to a Theological Reality, a hyperdimensional realm, from which our own is "projected" like a movie, and in which we live and move and have our being like game pieces on a board?

As we study the Grail stories in comparison to other myths and legends, we notice the ubiquity of the universal theme of a Golden Age, which was destroyed in some terrible way - a deluge, a fall from grace, a punishment. We suspect that Geoffrey of Monmouth interwove this tradition cleverly with the story of King Arthur. In most cases, the stories talk about the world before, giants, the gods and their doings, in terms that seem to be utterly fantastic. The usual explanation ascribes such stories to any number of theories based on the fearful and ignorant state of the howling savages of the Stone Age who imaginatively created myths to explain the inexplicable forces of nature around them.

Many "alternative" researchers and theorists have already expounded at great length on the idea that many myths represent an archaic reality. Among the ideas they have proposed are those that follow the pattern that there was a time in human history when the planets interacted violently and these became the foundational myths of the "wars of the gods". In such scenarios, the "thunderbolts" of Jove are the exchanges of electrical potentials between planets. Others have proposed that such stories represent the interactions of aliens or alien-human hybrids with advanced technology. In these theories, the "thunderbolts" of Jove are nuclear weapons and Jove was just a regular guy with a big bomb.

After considering our little story about the mythicization of history and the historicization of myth, we have some idea that both of these approaches could be true. In the case of the Grail Stories, we are dealing with the same problem many times over. However, in the Grail stories, there are repeated references to the same symbols or "objects of cultic value". These mysterious objects form the central theme of the action of the story of the quest, and it seems that a true understanding of these objects is as essential to the hero himself as it is to the modern day "seeker of mysteries". The objects are a cup or dish, a lance or sword, and a stone. If we begin to search through myth and legend, finding one of them here, another there, and then reassemble these elements, we come to a certain idea: that they all are part of an ensemble.

But what does this ensemble of elements really represent? When we consider these elements carefully, and study them, we come to the idea that an ancient scientific knowledge might be what is being portrayed in these stories, and how such knowledge might be "mythicized" over time if the infrastructure of civilization were destroyed. Naturally, the story *Lord of the Flies* immediately comes to mind as one example, but there are certainly many other situations where this process can be examined. In any event, the more we examine this matter, and the more examples we study, the more we realize that Ms. Weston was definitely onto something.

Let us consider the "Grail Hallows", appearing repeatedly in myth and legend, as elements of an ancient technology. Let us observe how these objects were utilized, and the magical powers that were attributed to them. Let us note that all of these abilities were the attributes of a *mastery of Space-Time manipulation.* Keeping in mind that that myths DO tend to *preserve the ideas of institutions, customs and landscapes.* If this is so, the ancient legends are a stunning view of the universe as well as descriptions of very exciting technology.

So, let us proceed with this idea as a working hypothesis. We don't have to accept it as true, let's just play with it.

Imagine, if you will, a worldwide civilization similar in many ways to our own - with advanced technology (though the technology of the ancient world was obviously quite different, as we will see). Imagine further that the imminent threat of a great cataclysm is realized too late to make proper preparations to preserve the civilization itself; or, perhaps the calamity is so devastating that it cannot be preserved. Imagine that the infrastructure of the civilization is destroyed. Imagine that, over the entire globe, out of say, six billion people, only 10 million survive, so terrible is the cataclysm. Furthermore, the survivors themselves are so widely scattered, and all means of travel and communication have been destroyed, so that any idea of them gathering together to re-implement the infrastructure that formerly existed is impossible. What is more, many of those who survived are not even technically capable of doing so.

But, in four or five locations, a small handful of people with higher educations did survive. However, the unfortunate thing is, their education is so specialized that they are able to re-implement only limited and selected elements of the former civilization. And so, they do the best they can. They become the Lords of the Flies, so to speak, and they seek to find a way to re-create what was lost; to seek out the additional knowledge, to rebuild the world from the ashes.

Having only uneducated and technically deficient people to do all the necessary work, and knowing that when they die, what they do know will be lost, they attempt to pass on as much knowledge as they can to as many as they can, knowing that even this is incomplete. Or, conversely, they create an "elite power structure" where the knowledge is only dispensed to a very few in order to keep the reins of power in their own hands and the hands of their descendants.

In such a situation, what knowledge would be considered the most valuable to pass on? What would be foremost in the mind of such a person?

Well, the progenitor of a power hungry elite would certainly pass on knowledge that would perpetuate the Control of others. But an individual who wishes to help humanity as a whole might be thinking that a better world may come if they can only pass on what they know, and leave it up to those who come after to add the missing pieces. Would not this knowledge be the important things about the civilization itself? It's infrastructure? It's modes of communication, of travel, of laws and ethics; its high science; and most of all, the terrible information that was revealed at the very last, just before everything was blasted back to Stone Age conditions: the knowledge that the earth regularly and cyclically undergoes cataclysm.

Imagine the sighting of an oncoming disaster, such as a barrage of comets, in our own civilization. The first thing our scientists would do would be to make measurements and observations; study path and trajectory; and soon they would announce on television, to the world, that we are about to go through a dangerous period that, apparently, is part of a long period cometary shower. They would announce their numbers to the world, and everyone would know, just a short time before the destruction, that what they are facing has been here before. And that knowledge, revealed too late, would be the one thing that the survivors of such destruction would want to pass on to their children. And so, in such an environment, under such conditions, myths would be born consisting of memories of the world before and all its glorious technology, how it ended, and that disaster will come again.

Imagine, if you will, a group of survivors. They emerge from their place of safety to find that the world that they knew is not just damaged, but that the violent convulsions of the planet have folded over, ground up, and washed away most of what formerly existed. The factories, the power plants, the cities, the superhighways, the railway lines, the airports and airplanes, the great ships and industrial complexes - all reduced to twisted bits of iron, incinerated wood, and concrete that has been ground into gravel. With what skills they have, lacking anything but the most rudimentary hand-made tools, they build their little community and try to survive in the best way they can.

As time goes by, our little community of survivors is doing well. They have grown old, and now they sit around the fires with a new generation of little ones gathered around to hear stories of "what did you do when you were young, grandpa?" And the grandfathers sigh with longing for the ease and comfort and marvels of all that was lost, and answer: "We went out to dinner at fine restaurants and watched movies."

"What is a movie, Grandpa?"

"Well, it is a big place where everybody used to go to see famous movie stars having wonderful adventures. Everybody would sit in a row of seats and the movie would appear on a big white wall in front of us."

"What appeared on the wall?"

"The images of the movie stars."

"What is a movie star, grandpa?"

"A movie star is a famous person who pretends to be someone else in order to tell a story."

"What is an image, grandpa?"

"It's a sort of projection of the real movie star who is not actually there. They live somewhere else, and when they are not acting in movies, they have ordinary lives."

"How does it happen that the image of the movie star can be seen when they are not really there?"

"Well, that's technology. It has to do with a light that is shone through a long piece of transparent stuff that runs around a wheel."

"What runs the wheel, grandpa?"

"Electricity."

"What is electricity, Grandpa?"

"It's a great force that is in the air. Electricity is what you see when you see lightning. When we were little, we used electricity to make everything work. It was the power that made our lights come on. It was what we used to cook our food. We used electricity to run our stereos and radios and televisions."

"Grandpa, what is a television?"

"It's a sort of box and the images of the same movie stars that you see in a theater can be seen right in your own house."

"How do the images get into the television?"

"They come through the air. There were satellites floating high in the air around the world that sent these images into the television. The same satellites also helped us to be able to talk to anybody anywhere in the world on a telephone."

"Grandpa, what's a telephone?"

We will leave this most interesting question and answer process and jump now to a time when Grandpa has gone to his reward, and the grandchild has grown up and has children. He is telling his own children about the stars in the skies that send messages into boxes and make it possible for anyone to talk to anyone else anywhere in the world. He also is telling his grandchildren about the great movie stars in Hollywood who could appear on a blank wall in a big theater after a big banquet with the gods, or, under special circumstances, if the gods choose to speak from the heavens, in a special box in a person's very own home.

Skip another generation, and we have the community falling upon hard times. They remember the stories of the world before, and it seems that they need help. Perhaps if they build a replica of the box like object that was so important a part of the time of plenty, they will be able to communicate with the gods in Hollywood who will then bring the famine or plague to an end.

So, they build a box and set it on an altar. They begin to call upon the different names they remember from the grandfather's stories. "Oh, great mother Elizabeth Taylor! Hear our plea! Come to help us great father Clark Gable!" But nothing happens. Perhaps the gods are angry? Maybe they want something? How about a sacrifice? Some wine, perhaps? Maybe the gods miss the banquet part? They want a nice succulent lamb. No? Well, how about a newborn infant? A virgin? Two? A dozen or so?

And so, as time goes by, the facts of what existed before become little more than fairy tales, clues to a former time, buried in layers of ignorance and superstition. And as the populations grow, and travel is undertaken, they meet tribes with similar stories but from different angles. Perhaps they meet a group whose "grandfather" was a great scientist. He taught his grandchildren to memorize scientific formulas. Naturally, because their grandfather was a scientist and passed "scientific and superior knowledge" to them, they feel that they are in a position to instruct those ignorant rubes that are invoking Liz Taylor and Clark Gable. No, indeed, it must be done this way: you have to form a circle around the television and say the right words, the magical formulas. And so, the combined tribes begin to dance around the "Cube of Space", chanting "Eeee equals Emmmm Ceeee squared! Eeee equals Emmmm Ceeee squared! Eeee equals Emmmm Ceeee squared! We appeal to the great god of Ein- Stein! Speak to us!"

And if they do it long enough, they will induce the production of certain brain chemicals, which will lead to states of ecstasy, and there you have it! The proof that it works. And so, we have our legends of great occult science in the making.

I'm sure that the reader can take these short vignettes even further, and see how the memory of the golden age was passed down, and how myths, if they were properly examined and analyzed, could be the key to finding the threads of an ancient technology, the *disjecta membra* of a lost civilization.

However, that is not to say that there were not some groups who did actually manage to re-create some of the technology. It seems evident that some scientists, some technocrats, survived and were responsible for the sudden emergence of the civilizations that we know in our recorded history. It is also equally likely, human nature being what it is, that the very progenitors of these civilizations became the elite, and as often happens, when the elite take advantage of the masses, revolutions come about destroying the very wellsprings of that knowledge.

Also, as noted, there were probably others who sought to preserve the knowledge, encoded for the future time when only a revival of technology would make any of it comprehensible. This brings us to another line of thought.

In 1984, the Office of Nuclear Waste Isolation and a group of other institutions commissioned Thomas A. Sebeok, to elaborate answers to a question posed by the US Nuclear Regulatory Commission. The American government had chosen several desert areas in the US for the burial of nuclear waste. The idea was that it was easy to protect it from intrusions at the present time, but since they were dealing with deadly elements which had half-lives of ten thousand years or more, how to protect people in the future from destroying humanity by dangerous intrusions into such areas? Ten thousand years is more than enough time for great empires and civilizations to rise and perish. In just a few centuries after the last pharaoh had disappeared, the knowledge of how to read hieroglyphs had disappeared as well, so it is conceivable that mankind could be reduced to a "dark age" existence that came into being following the decline of the Golden Age of Greece, and the fall of the Roman Empire. The question was: How will we warn the future about the danger? Umberto Eco discusses Sebeok's findings:

> Almost immediately, Sebeok discarded the possibility of any type of verbal communication, of electric signals as needing a constant power supply, of olfactory messages as being of brief duration, and of any sort of ideogram based on convention. Even a pictographic language seemed problematic.

Sebeok analyzed an image from an ancient primitive culture where one can certainly recognize human figures, but it is hard to say what they are doing - dancing, fighting, or hunting?

> Another solution would be to establish temporal segments of three generations each, (calculating that, in any civilization, language will not alter beyond recognition between grandparents and grandchildren), giving instructions that, at the end of each segment, the message would be reformulated, adapting it to the semiotic conventions prevailing at the moment. But even this solution presupposes precisely the sort of social continuity that the original question had put into doubt.

Another solution was to fill up the entire zone with messages in all known languages and semiotic systems, reasoning that it was statistically probable that at least one of these messages would be comprehensible to the future visitors. Even if only part of one of the messages was decipherable, it would still act as a sort of Rosetta stone, allowing the visitors to translate all the rest. Yet even this solution presupposed a form of cultural continuity, however weak it would be.

> The only remaining solution was to institute a sort of 'priesthood' of nuclear scientists, anthropologists, linguists and psychologists supposed to perpetuate itself by co-opting new members. This caste would keep alive the knowledge of the danger, creating myths and legends about it. Even though, in the passage of time, these 'priests' would probably lose a precise notion of the peril that they were committed to protect humanity from, there would still survive, even in a future state of barbarism, obscure but efficacious taboos.
>
> It is curious to see that, having been presented with a choice of various types of universal language, the choice finally fell on a 'narrative' solution, thus re-proposing what REALLY DID HAPPEN MILLENNIA AGO (my emphasis). Egyptian has disappeared, as well as any other perfect and holy primordial language, and what remains of all this is only myths, tales without a code, or whose code has long been lost. Yet they are still capable of keeping us in a state of vigil in our desperate effort at decipherment. [24]

It is extraordinarily significant to me that Eco has suggested so clearly here the idea that our ancient ancestors may have been faced with the knowledge of a very great peril to mankind and "brain-stormed" for a solution as to how to transmit this information to future generations. And it is with this idea that we come back to the myths that formed the foundation for said religions and form a "working hypothesis" that such stories are the "narratives" provided by our ancestors to warn us about something, as defined by Thomas Sebeok in his report to the Office of Nuclear Waste Isolation. And here we find the problem: We cannot just read these things, put the pieces together like a regular puzzle and thereby discover the answer. We have to deeply analyze the stories, discover the various versions and their inversion; and, by tracking the roots of words, discover their relations. In such a way, we just MIGHT be able to discover what it is our ancestors knew and what they have so desperately tried to tell us.

ALCHEMY AND THE ENCLAVE IN THE PYRENEES

Nowadays, our materialistic science derides alchemists as misguided mystics who followed a dream of discovering a substance that could transform base metals into gold. Yes, they admit that much scientific discovery was accomplished in

---

[24] Eco, Umberto, *The Search For The Perfect Language,* (Oxford: Blackwell 1995) p. 177, emphasis mine.

these pursuits, but they toss out the objective of the alchemists as just a pipe dream. Nevertheless, there are interesting stories there, some so deeply curious that the mind cannot grapple with the implications, and they are immediately discarded as too fantastic for serious consideration. I want to recount a few of them here so that the reader who is not familiar with the literature might be sufficiently intrigued to do research on his/her own.

But first, a short discussion of the "Philosopher's Stone". This is the goal of the Alchemist; a fabled substance that can not only transmute metals into gold, but can heal any illness, banish all sickness from a person's life, and confer an extended lifespan, if not immortality, on the body. At least, that is how it is described. That may or may not be a "cover story".

It was thought that, by a lengthy process of purification, one could extract from various minerals the "natural principle" that supposedly caused gold to "grow" in the earth. In an anonymous 17th Century alchemical text, *The Sophic Hydrolith*, this process is described as "purging [the mineral] of all that is thick, nebulous, opaque and dark", and what would be left would be a mercurial "water of the Sun", which had a pleasant, penetrating odor, and was very volatile.

Part of this liquid is put aside, and the rest is then mixed with a twelfth of its weight of "the divinely endowed body of gold", (ordinary gold won't do because it is defiled by daily use). This mixture then forms a solid amalgam which is heated for a week. It is then dissolved in some of the mercurial water in an egg-shaped phial.

Then, the remaining mercurial water is added gradually, in seven portions; the phial is sealed, and kept at such a temperature as will hatch an egg. After 40 days, the phial's contents will be black; after seven more days small grainy bodies like fish eyes are supposed to appear. Then the "Philosopher's Stone" begins to make its appearance: first reddish in color; then white, green and yellow like a peacock's tail then dazzling white; and later a deep glowing red. Finally, "the revivified body is quickened, perfected and glorified" and appears in a beautiful purple.

This and many similarly obscure and crazy sounding texts are the bulk of Alchemical Literature. It occurred to me early on that these texts were a code, and so I persisted in reading many texts of this kind and searching for clues there and in the stories of the alchemists themselves. It was in reading the anecdotes about so-called Alchemists that I became convinced that there was, indeed, something very mysterious going on here.

For example: In 1666, Johann Friedrich Schweitzer, physician to the Prince of Orange, writes of having been visited by a stranger who was "of a mean stature, a little long face, with a few small pock holes, and most black hair, not at all curled, a beardless chin, about three or four and forty years of age (as I guessed), and born in North Holland."

Before I finish the story, it needs to be pointed out that Dr. Schweitzer, who was the author of several medical and botanical books, was a careful and objective observer and was a colleague of the philosopher, Baruch Spinoza. Schweitzer was a trained scientific observer; a reputable medical man, and not given to fraud or practical jokes. And yet, what I am about to describe is, in modern understanding, impossible.

Now, what happened was that the stranger made small talk for awhile and then, more or less out of the blue, asked Dr. Schweitzer whether he would recognize the "Philosopher's Stone" if he saw it. He then took out of his pocket a small ivory box that held "three ponderous pieces or small lumps... each about the bigness of a small walnut, transparent, of a pale brimstone colour". The stranger told Schweitzer that this was the very substance sought for so long by the Alchemists.

Schweitzer held one of the pieces in his hand and asked the stranger if he could have just a small piece. The man refused, but Schweitzer managed to steal a small bit by scraping it with his fingernail. The visitor left after promising to return in three weeks time to show Dr. Schweitzer some "curious arts in the fire".

Well, as soon as he was gone, Dr. Schweitzer ran to his laboratory where he melted some lead in a crucible and added the tiny piece of stone. But, the metal did NOT turn into gold as he anticipated. Instead, "almost the whole mass of lead flew away, and the remainder turned into a mere glassy earth".

Three weeks later, the mysterious stranger was at his door again. They conversed, and for a long time the man refused to allow Dr. Schweitzer see his stones again, but, at last "he gave me a crumb as big as a rape or turnip seed, saying, receive this small parcel of the greatest treasure of the world, which truly few kings or princes have ever known or seen".

Schweitzer must have been a whiner because he recounts that he protested that this was not sufficient to transmute as much as four grains of lead into gold. At this, the stranger took the piece back, cut it in half, and flung one part in the fire, saying: "it is yet sufficient for thee!"

At this point, Schweitzer confessed his theft from the previous visit, and described how the substance had behaved with his molten lead. The stranger began to laugh and told him, "Thou are more dextrous to commit theft than to apply thy medicine; for if thou hadst only wrapped up thy stolen prey in yellow wax, to preserve it from the arising fumes of lead, it would have penetrated to the bottom of the lead, and transmuted it to gold."

The guy leaves at this point and promises to return the next morning to show Schweitzer the correct way to perfom the transmutation but,

> The next day he came not, nor ever since. Only he sent an excuse at half an hour past nine that morning, by reason of his great business, and promised to come at three in the afternoon, but never came, nor have I heard of him since; whereupon I began to doubt of the whole matter. Nevertheless late that night my wife... came soliciting and vexing me to make experiment... saying to me, unless this be done, I shall have no rest nor sleep all this night... She being so earnest, I commanded a fire to be made - thinking, alas, now is this man (though so divine in discourse) found guilty of falsehood... My wife wrapped the said matter in wax, and I cut half an ounce of six drams of old lead, and put into a crucible in the fire, which being melted, my wife put in the said Medicine made up in a small pill or button, which presently made such a hissing and bubbling in its perfect operation, that within a quarter of an hour all the mass of lead was transmuted into the ... finest gold.

Baruch Spinoza, who lived nearby, came the next day to examine this gold and was convinced that Schweitzer was telling the truth. The Assay Master of the province, a Mr. Porelius, tested the metal and pronounced it genuine; and Mr. Buectel, the silversmith, subjected it to further test that confirmed that it was gold. The testimony of these men survives to this day.

Now, either ALL of them are lying, or Dr. Schweitzer really did have a strange experience exactly as he describes it. The interesting thing is that other people have described similar visitations by strange men who proclaim to them the truth of the alchemical process, demonstrate it, and then mysteriously disappear. It has happened sufficiently often, in widely enough separated places and times to suggest that it is not a collusive fraud nor a delusion.

Twenty years before Schweitzer's meeting with the mysterious stranger, Jan Baptiste van Helmont, who was responsible for several important scientific discoveries, and was the first man to realize that there were other gases than air; and who invented the term "gas", wrote:

> For truly I have divers times seen it [The Philosopher's Stone], and handled it with
> my hands, but it was of colour such as is in Saffron in its powder, yet weighty, and
> shining like unto powdered glass. There was once given unto me one fourth part of
> one grain [16 milligrams]... I projected [it] upon eighty ounces [227 grams] of
> quicksilver [mercury] made hot in a crucible; and straightaway all the quicksilver,
> with a certain degree of noise, stood still from flowing, and being congealed, settled
> like unto a yellow lump; but after pouring it out, the bellows blowing, there were
> found eight ounces and a little less than eleven grains of the purest gold.

Sir Isaac Newton studied alchemy until his death, remaining convinced that the possiblity of transmutation existed. The great philosophers and mathematicians, Descartes and Leibnitz, both were convinced that transmutation was a reality. Even Robert Boyle who wrote a book entitled *The Sceptical Chymist*, was sure until the end of his life, that transmutation was possible!

Why? These men were scientists. The argument that their ideas or observations were less scientific than those of the present day simply does not stand up to scrutiny. As noted, alchemists were rumored at various times to have gained immortality, and one of these was Nicolas Flamel. Flamel was a poor scribe, or scrivener and copyist. The story goes that, in 1357 he bought an old illuminated book...

> The cover of it was of brass, well bound, all engraven with letters of strange
> figures... This I know that I could not read them nor were they either Latin of
> French letters... As to the matter that was written within, it was engraved (as I
> suppose) with an iron pencil or graver upon... bark leaves, and curiously coloured...

Reportedly, the first page was written in golden letters that said Abraham the Jew, Priest, Prince, Levite, Astrologer and Philosopher, to the Nation of the Jews dispersed by the Wrath of God in France, wisheth Health. So, quite rightly, Flamel referred to the manuscript as the Book of Abraham the Jew.

The dedication was followed by curses upon anyone who was not either a priest or a Jew reading the book. But, Flamel was a scribe, which he must have imagined exempted him from these curses, so he read the book. The purpose of the book was avowedly to give assistance to the dispersed Jews by teaching them to transmute lead into gold so that they could pay their taxes to the hated Roman government. The instructions were clear and easy, but only described the latter part of the process. The instructions for the beginning were said to be in the illustrations given on the 4th and 5th leaves of the book. Flamel remarked that, although these were well executed,

...yet by that could no man ever have been able to understand it without being well skilled in their Qabalah, which is a series of old traditions, and also to have been well studied in their books.

As the story goes, Flamel tried for 21 years to find someone who could explain these pictures to him. Finally, his wife urged him to go to Spain and seek out a rabbi or other learned Jew who might assist him. So, he made the famous pilgrimage to the shrine of St. James at Compostela, carrying with him carefully made copies of the book.

After his devotions at the shrine, he went to the city of Leon in northern Spain where he met a certain "Master Canches", a Jewish physician. When this man saw the illustrations, he was "ravished with great astonishment and joy", upon recognizing them as parts of a book that had long been believed to have been destroyed. He declared his intention to return with Flamel to France, but he died on the trip at Orleans. Flamel returned to Paris alone. But, apparently, the old Jew must have told him something for he wrote:

> I had now the prima materia, the first principles, yet not their first preparation, which is a thing most difficult, above all things in the world... Finally, I found that which I desired, which I also knew by the strong scent and odour thereof. Having this, I easily accomplished the Mastery... The fist time that I made projection [transmutation] was upon Mercury, whereof I turned half a pound, or thereabouts, into pure silver, better than that of the Mine, as I myself assayed, and made others assay many times. This was upon a Monday, the 17th of January about noon, in my home, Perrenelle [his wife] only being present, in the year of the restoring of mankind 1382.

Several months later Flamel did his first transmutation into gold. Is this just a story? Well, what IS true and can be verified is that Nicolas and Perenelle Flamel endowed, "fourteen hospitals, three chapels and seven churches, in the city of Paris, all which we had new built from the ground, and enriched with great gifts and revenues, with many reparations in their churchyards. We also have done at Boulogne about as much as we have done at Paris, not to speak of the charitable acts which we both did to particular poor people, principally widows and orphans."

After Flamel's death in 1419 the rumours began. Hoping that they could find something hidden in one of his houses, people searched them again and again until one of them was completely destroyed. There were stories that Nicolas and Perenelle were still alive. Supposedly, she had gone to Switzerland and he buried a log in her grave, and then another log was buried at his own funeral.

In the intervening centuries, the stories persist that Flamel and Perenelle defeated death. The 17th century traveller, Paul Lucas, while travelling in Asia Minor, met a Turkish philosopher who told him that "true philosophers had had the secret of prolonging life for anything up to a thousand years...". Lucas said, "At last I took the liberty of naming the celebrated Flamel, who, it was said, possessed the Philosopher's Stone, yet was certainly dead. He smiled at my simplicity, and asked with an air of mirth: Do you really believe this? No, no, my friend, Flamel is still living; neither he nor his wife has yet tasted death. It is not above three years since I left both... in India; he is one of my best friends." In

1761, Flamel and his wife were reported to have been seen attending the opera in Paris.

Well, there is an issue here regarding the supposed clue about "Abraham the Jew" which *seems* to point us in the direction of a Jewish fraternity of alchemists or keepers of secrets. I don't want to go off on that thread here and now because it would add so much complexity to the issues that we might never find our way through the maze. But, to ease the mind of the reader, I will make a few remarks about this here. Even though we have not yet come to the mystery of Fulcanelli, supposedly a 20th century alchemist who accomplished the great work, let me mention while the subject is at hand that Eugene Canseliet, in his preface to the Second Edition of Fulcanelli's *Le Mystere des Cathedrales*, apparently upon the instruction of the master alchemist, emphasized dramatically the difference between kabbala and Cabala saying:

> ...this book has restored to light the phonetic cabala, whose principles and application had been completely lost. After this detailed and precise elucidation and after the brief treatment of it, which I gave in connection with the centaur, the man-horse of Plessis-Bourre, in *Deux Logis Alchimiques*, this mother tongue need never be confused with the Jewish Kabbala. Though never spoken, the phonetic cabala, this forceful idiom, is easily understood and it is the instinct or voice of nature.

> By contrast, the Jewish Kabbala is full of transpositions, inversions, substitutions and calculations, as arbitrary as they are abstruse. This is why it is important to distinguish between the two words, CABALA and KABBALA in order to use them knowledgeably. Cabala derives from cadallhz or from the Latin *caballus*, a horse; kabbala is from the Hebrew Kabbalah, which means tradition. Finally, figurative meanings like *coterie*, *underhand dealing* or *intrigue*, developed in modern usage by analogy, should be ignored so as to reserve for the noun *cabala* the only significance which can be assured for it.[25]

Now, the curious bringing in of the terms "coterie", "underhand dealing" and "intrigue" in conjunction with what he has just remarked about Kabbalah meaning "tradition", and Cabala being "horse", is a most curious juxtaposition of words. It almost seems that Canseliet is telling us that the Kaballah, or the tradition is a red herring. Fulcanelli himself makes a curious remark in *The Dwellings of the Philosophers*:

> Alchemy is obscure, only because it is hidden. The philosophers who wanted to transmit the exposition of their doctrine and the fruit of their labors to posterity took great care not to divulge the art by presenting it under a common form, so that the layman could not misuse it.[26]

---

[25] Fulcanelli, *The Mystery of the Cathedrals*, 1984, Brotherhood of Life, Las Vegas.

[26] Fulcanelli, *The Dwellings of the Philosophers*, 1999, Archive Press, Boulder.

The point of this short aside is this: don't assume anything about Jews, Masons, or any other group when trying to solve the mystery. Nearly everything we come across will be obscured. And, when it is right out in plain view, it will be even more difficult to see!

Getting back to our purported alchemists, we come now to the year 1745 in which Prince Charles Edward Stuart, known as the "Young Pretender", staged his Jacobite rebellion in an attempt to regain the British throne for his father the "Old Pretender". The Jacobite cause, for all intents and purposes, had been crushed at the battle of Culloden in April of that year, yet there was a constant fear by the British government that the Jacobites were still plotting with their French sympathizers, and being French and in London was, at that time, a liability. This "spy fever" resulted in the arrest of many Frenchmen on trumped up charges, and most of them were later released, but it was a dangerous time for Gallic visitors!

In November of that year, one Frenchman was arrested and accused of having pro-Jacobite letters in his possession. He became very indignant and claimed that the correspondence had been "planted" on him. Considering the mood of the time, it is quite surprising that he was believed and released! Horace Walpole, English author and Member of Parliament, wrote a letter about this incident to Sir Horace Mann on December 9, 1745 saying:

> "The other day they seized an odd man who goes by the name of Count Saint-
> Germain. He has been here these two years, and will not tell who he is or whence,
> but professes that he does not go by his right name. He sings and plays on the violin
> wonderfully, is mad and not very sensible."

This is one of the few "authentic" on the scene comments about one of the most mysterious characters of the 18th century, the Count Saint-Germain. Another acquaintance of the Count Saint-Germain, Count Warnstedt, described Saint-Germain as, "The completest charlatan, fool, rattle-pate, windbag and swindler". Yet, his last patron said that Saint-Germain was, "perhaps one of the greatest sages who ever lived". Clearly this was one of those people you either love or hate!

Saint-Germain first comes to our attention in the fashionable circles of Vienna in about 1740, where he made a stir by wearing black all the time! Everybody else was into bright colors, satins and laces, ornate patterns and designs; and along comes Saint-Germain with his somber black outfits set off by glittering diamonds on his fingers, shoe buckles, and snuff box! What an attention getter! If you want to stand out in a roomful of robins, cardinals and bluejays, just be a blackbird! He also had the habit of carrying handfuls of loose diamonds in his pockets instead of cash!

So, there he is, garnering attention to himself in this bizarre way, and naturally he makes the acquaintance of the local leaders of fashion, Counts Zabor and Lobkowitz, who introduce him to the French Marshal de Belle Isle. Well, it seems that the Marshal was seriously under-the-weather, but his illness is not recorded so we can't evaluate the claims that Saint-Germain cured him. Nevertheless, the Marshal was so grateful that he took Saint-Germain to Paris with him and set him up with apartments and a laboratory.

The details of the Count's life in Paris are pretty well known, and it is there that the rumors began. There is an account by a "Countess de B___" (a nom de plume, it seems, so we have to hold the information somewhat suspect), who wrote in her memoirs, *Chroniques de l'oeil de boeuf*, that, when she met the Count at a soiree given by the aged Countess von Georgy, whose late husband had been Ambassador to Venice in the 1670's, that the old Countess remembered Saint-Germain from those former times. So, the old girl asked the Count if his father had been there at the time. He replied no, but HE had!

Well, the man that Countess von Georgy had known was at least 45 years old then, at least 50 years previously, and the man standing before her could not be any older than 45 now! The Count smiled and said: "I am very old".

"But then you must be nearly 100 years old", the Countess exclaimed.

"That is not impossible", the Count replied. He then related some details that convinced the old lady that it was really him she had met in Venice.

The Countess exclaimed: "I am already convinced. You are a most extraordinary man, a devil!"

"For pity's sake!", cried Saint-Germain in a loud voice heard all around the room. "No such names!" He began to tremble all over and left the room immediately.

A pretty dramatic introduction to society, don't you think? But, was it real, or the ploy of a very clever con artist? Did he deliberately choose to adopt the name of someone long dead, about whom he may have already known a great deal, and then did he set out to deceive and con in a manner well known to us in the present time as the modus operandi of the psychopath? Was he a snake oil salesman or a true man of mystery?

In any event, that was the beginning of the "legend", and many more stories of a similar nature spread through society like wildfire. Saint-Germain apparently fed the fires with hints that he had known the "Holy Family" intimately and had been invited to the marriage feast at Cana where Jesus turned water into wine, and dropped casually the remark that he "had always known that Christ would meet a bad end". According to him, he had been very fond of Anne, the mother of the Virgin Mary, and had even proposed her canonization at the Council of Nicaea in A.D. 325! What a guy! A line for every occasion!

Pretty soon the Count had Louis XV and his mistress, Madame de Pompadour, eating out of his hand, and it certainly could be true that he was a French spy in England when he was arrested there, because he later did handle some sticky business for the credulous king of France.

In 1760, Louis sent Saint-Germain to the Hague as his personal representative to arrange a loan with Austria that was supposed to help finance the Seven Years' war against England. But, while in Holland, the Count had a falling out with his friend Casanova, who was also a diplomat at the Hague. Casanova tried hard to discredit Saint-Germain in public, but without success. One has to wonder just what it was that Casanova discovered or came to think about Saint-Germain at this time.

In any even, Saint-Germain was making other enemies. One of these enemies was the Duc de Choiseul, King Louis' Foreign Minister. The Duc discovered that Saint-Germain had been scoping out the possibilities of arranging a peace between England and France. Now, that doesn't sound like a bad plan at all, but the Duc managed to convince the King that this was a dire betrayal, and the Count had to flee to England and then back to Holland.

In Holland, the Count lived under the name Count Surmont, and he worked to raise money to set up laboratories in which he made paint and dyes and engaged in his alchemical experiments. By all accounts, he was successful in some sense, because he disappeared from Holland with 100,000 guilders!

He next shows up in Belgium as the "Marquis de Monferrat". He set up another laboratory with "other people's money" before disappearing again. (Are we beginning to see a pattern here?)

For a number of years, Saint-Germain's activities continued to be reported from various parts of Europe and, in 1768 he popped up in the court of Catherine the Great. Turkey had just declared war on Russia, and Saint-Germain promoted himself as a valuable diplomat because of his status as an "insider" in French politics. Pretty soon he was the adviser of Count Alexei Orlov, head of the Russian Imperial Forces. Orlov made him a high-ranking officer of the Russian Army and Saint-Germain acquired an English alias, "General Welldone".

His successes in Russia could have enabled him to retire on his laurels, but he didn't. In 1774 he appeared in Nuremberg seeking money from the Margrave of Brandenburg, Charles Alexander. His ostensible alias at this point (apparently he was no longer satisfied with being either a Count or a Marquis) was Prince Rakoczy of Transylvania!

Naturally, the Margrave of Brandenburg was impressed when Count Orlov visited Nuremburg on a state visit and embraced "the Prince" warmly. But later, when the Margrave did a little investigating, he discovered that the real Prince Rakoczy was indubitably dead and that this counterfeit Prince was, in fact, only Count Saint-Germain! Saint-Germain did not deny the charges, but apparently he felt that it was now time to move on.

The Duc de Choiseul, Saint-Germain's old enemy, had claimed that the Count was in the employ of Frederick the Great. But, that was probably not true because, at this point, Saint-Germain wrote to Frederick begging for patronage. Frederick ignored him, which is peculiar if he had been in the employ of the Prussian king as de Choiseul thought.

In the way of the psychopathic con man who can never quite figure out when to quit, Saint-Germain went to Leipzig and presented himself to Prince Frederick Augustus of Brunswick as a Freemason of the fourth grade!

Now, Frederick Augustus just happened to be the Grand Master of the Prussian Masonic Lodges, so this was really a stupid move on the part of Saint-Germain since it turned out that he was not a Mason! But, it is true of the pattern of all con men; their egos eventually prove to be their downfall! The Prince challenged Saint-Germain because he did not know the secret signals and sent him away as a fraud.

In 1779, Saint-Germain was an old man in his 60's who continued to claim to be vastly older. He hadn't lost his touch because, at Eckenforde in Schleswig, Germany, he was able to charm Prince Charles of Hesse-Cassel. At this point, part of his scam included being a mystic, for he is recorded as having told Prince Charles:

> "Be the torch of the world. If your light is that only of a planet, you will be as
> nothing in the sight of God. I reserve for you a splendour, of which the solar glory

is a shadow. You shall guide the course of the stars, and those who rule Empires shall be guided by you."

Sounds rather like the build-up to another con job! Nothing like feeding the ego of the "mark" before slipping away with all his money! However, Saint Germain was on the way to a place where money was of no use. On February 27, 1784, he died at Prince Charles' home on Eckenforde. He was buried locally and the Prince erected a stone that said:

He who called himself the Comte de Saint-Germain and Welldone, of whom there is no other information, has been buried in this church.

And then the Prince burned all of the Count's papers "lest they be misinterpreted". The only reason we can conceive of for that is because the Prince wanted to continue to believe in the powers of Saint Germain, and the papers of the Count did not support that belief.

Supposedly there is evidence that the Count did not die, and many occultists claim he is still alive for these past two centuries! Based upon his pattern of behavior, however, Count Saint Germain seems merely to have been your garden variety psychopath. He may have had certain esoteric knowledge - he was certainly well-versed in many subjects - but his history, and the conflicting stories told about him give us a different perspective, particularly when we examine the histories and personalities of those who believed in him as opposed to those who did not. You can tell a lot about a man by his friends and his enemies.

The mystery of Saint-Germain is mostly due to the uncertainty surrounding his origins. One source says that he was born in 1710 in San Germano, son of a tax collector. Eliphas Levi, the 19th century occultist said that Saint-Germain was born in Lentmeritz in Bohemia, and was the bastard son of a nobleman who was also a Rosicrucian. Levi's story and accomplishments suggest that he was another psychopath, so his word on the matter is useless.

It is known that Saint Germain had a genuine gift for languages and could speak French, German, English, Dutch and Russian fluently. He also claimed that he was fluent in Chinese, Hindu and Persian, but there was no one about to test him on those. And, we note that Horace Walpole said that he was a wonderful violinist and singer and painter, though none of his purported art has been known to survive. Supposedly, he was able to paint jewels that glittered in a very lifelike way.

There is also a great deal of evidence that Saint-Germain was an expert jeweller - he claimed to have studied the art with the Shah of Persia! In any event, he is reported to have repaired a flawed diamond for Louis XV, who was very pleased with the result. Saint-Germain also had an extensive knowledge of chemistry in all its branches at the time, and the many laboratories that he set up with borrowed money were all designed to produce brighter and better pigments and dyes and also for alchemical studies. Then, there was his reputation as a healer. Not only did he cure the Marshal de Belle Isle, he also cured a friend of Madame de Pompadour of mushroom poisoning. Saint-Germain never ate in company, which was obviously part of his plan to focus attention on himself. He could sit at a table where everyone else was gorging on the most amazing array of delectable dishes, and eat and drink nothing. Casanova wrote:

Instead of eating, he talked from the beginning of the meal to the end, and I followed his example in one respect as I did not eat, but listened to him with the greatest attention. It may safely be said that as a conversationalist he was unequalled.

We note that this is another of the many talents attributed to psychopaths. Colin Wilson, author of *The Occult*, thought that Saint-Germain must have been a vegetarian. I think everything he did was designed to create an image, an impression, and a false one at that. In the end, the real mystery, aside from his origins, but the two may be connected, is where did Saint-Germain get all his specialized knowledge? Of course, as we have noted here, not all who met Saint-Germain were impressed by his talents. Casanova was entertained by him, but nevertheless thought that he was a fraud and a charlatan. He wrote:

> This extraordinary man, intended by nature to be the king of impostors and quacks, would say in an easy, assured manner that he was three hundred years old, that he knew the secret of the Universal Medicine, that he possessed a mastery over nature, that he could melt diamonds, professing himself capable of forming, out of 10 or 12 small diamonds, one of the finest water... All this, he said, was a mere trifle to him. Notwithstanding his boastings, his bare-faced lies, and his manifold eccentricities, I cannot say I found him offensive. In spite of my knowledge of what he was and in spite of my own feelings, I thought him an astonishing man..."

Count Alvensleben, a Prussian Ambassador to the Court at Dresden, wrote in 1777:

> He is a highly gifted man with a very alert mind, but completely without judgement, and he has only gained his singular reputation by the lowest and basest flattery of which a man is capable, as well as by his outstanding eloquence, especially if one lets oneself be carried away by the fervour and the enthusiasm with which he can express himself. Inordinate vanity is the mainspring driving his whole mechanism.

I don't know about you, but I have met a few people with all of the above qualities and have even been deceived by one or two for a short while. Everything we discover about Saint Germain tends to the theory of the brilliant psychopath. It sounds like an easy thing to dismiss Saint Germain out of hand. But, in the case of the Count, we have a little problem: just which of the stories are really about *him*? The plot thickens!

It seems that Berthold Volz, in the 1920's, did some deep research on the subject and discovered, or so it is claimed, (I have never been able to track down this purported proof), that the Duc de Choiseul, who was overwhelmingly jealous of the Count, hired a look-alike imposter to go about as the Count, exaggerating and playing the fool in order to place the Count in a bad light. Is this just another story, either wishful thinking or deliberately designed to perpetuate the legend? Are we getting familiar with this "bait and switch" routine yet?

Supposedly, Saint-Germain foretold the outbreak of the French Revolution to Marie Antoinette who purportedly wrote in her diary that she regretted that she did not heed his advice. I haven't seen it, so I can't vouch for it. But, in my opinion, it wouldn't take a genius to predict that event, considering the social and political climate of the time!

It was said that Saint-Germain appeared in Wilhelmsbad in 1785, a year after he was supposed to have died, and he was accompanied by the magician Cagliostro, the hypnotist Anton Mesmer, and the "unknown philosopher", Louis Claude de St. Martin. But that is hearsay also.

Next he was alleged to have gone to Sweden in 1789 to warn King Gustavus III of danger. After that, he visited his friend, diarist Mademoiselle d'Adhemar, who said he still looked like he was only 46 years old! Apparently, he told her that she would see him five more times, and she claimed this was, in fact, the case. Supposedly the last visit was the night before the murder of the Duc de Berri in 1820. Again, we find this to be unsupported by evidence.

Napoleon III ordered a commission to investigate the life and actvities of Saint-Germain, but the findings were destroyed in a fire at the Hotel de Ville in Paris in 1871 - which many people think is beyond coincidence. My thought would be that the only reason to destroy such a report would be if it had proved the Count to be a fraud. The result of this fire is that the legend is enabled to live on; it is likely that the report would have made some difference in the legend, such as putting it to rest as a fraud. Had it been helpful to the legend, it would not have changed what is already the case, which is that people believe that Saint-Germain was something of a supernatural being. Thus, its destruction, if engineered, must only have been to protect the status quo.

One of the next threads of the legend was gathered into the hands of Helena Blavatsky who claimed that Saint-Germain was one of the "hidden masters" along with Christ, Buddha, Appollonius of Tyana, Christian Rosencreutz, Francis Bacon and others. In my opinion, Blavatsky's credibility becomes highly questionable by merely making this claim. A group of Theosophists traveled to Paris after WW II where they were told they would meet the Count; he never showed up.

In 1972, a Frenchman named Richard Chanfray was interviewed on French television. He claimed to be Saint-Germain and, supposedly, in front of television cameras, transmuted lead into gold on a camp stove! And, lest we forget the more recent "communications" of the count to the head of the Church Universal and Triumphant, Elizabeth Clare Prophet.

In the end, on the subject of Saint-Germain, we find lies and confusion. Get used to it. And, if Saint-Germain was a fraud we have to think somewhat carefully about those who claim him as their "connection" to things esoteric!

During the 19th and 20th centuries, alchemy lost favor with the rise of experimental science. The time was that of such stellar names as Lavoisier, Priestley and Davy. Dalton's atomic theory and a host of discoveries in chemistry and physics made it clear to all "legitimate" scientists that alchemy was only a "mystical" and, at best, harmless pastime of no scientific value.

Organizations such as the Golden Dawn and Ordo Templi Orientis devised corrupted mixtures of snippets of alchemy and oriental philosophy, stirred in with the western European magical traditions, but these were clearly distorted imitations composed mostly of wishful thinking, romantic nonsense, and monstrous egos. When one deeply studies the so-called "adepts" of these "systems", one is confronted again and again with the archetype of the "failed magician" so that one can only shake the head and remember the warning of the great alchemists, that those who do not develop within themselves the "special state" that is required for the "Great Work", can only bring disaster . There is no doubt in my mind that such groups dabble in "alchemy" of a sort, or "magick" of another, and there is no doubt that they may, in fact, "conjure" connections to sources of "power" on occasion. But, overall, a survey of what can be learned about them tends to point in the direction of much wishful thinking or even the possibility of domination by the forces of entropy in the guise of "angels of light".

In 1919, British physicist Ernest Rutherford announced that he had achieved a successful transmutation of one element into another: nitrogen to oxygen! Admittedly, his procedures and results in no way resembled the work of the alchemists; but, what he had done was refute the insistence of most scientists of the day that transmutation was impossible. In fact, it soon became known that radioactive elements gradually "decay", giving off radiation and producing "daughter elements" which then decay even further. For instance one such chain starts with uranium and the end product is lead. So, the question became, can the process be reversed? Or, if you start with another element, what might you end up with?

Franz Tausend was a 36 year-old chemical worker in Munich who had a theory about the structure of the elements that was a strange mixture of Pythagoreanism and modern chemistry. He published a pamphlet entitled, "*180 elements, their atomic weight, and their incorporation in a system of harmonic periods*". He thought that every atom had a frequency of vibration characteristic of that element, related to the weight of the atom's nucleus and the grouping of the electrons around it. This part of his idea was shown to be basically correct by later research. However, Tausend further suggested that matter could be "orchestrated" by adding the right substance to the element, thereby changing its vibration frequency, in which case, it would become a different element.

As it happened, at about the same time, Adolf Hitler was sent to prison for attempting to organize an armed uprising. One of his cohorts was General Erich Ludendorff, but Ludendorff was acquitted of the charges and ran for president of Germany the following year. He was defeated by Hindenburg, so he turned his mind to raising money for the nascent Nazi party. He heard rumors that a certain Tausend had transmuted base metals into gold, and he formed a group, including numerous industrialists, to investigate this process.

Tausend gave instructions that they should purchase *iron oxide* and *quartz* which were melted together in a crucible. A German merchant and member of this group, named Stremmel, took the crucible to his hotel bedroom for the night so that it could not be tampered with. The next morning, Tausend heated the crucible in his electric furnace in the presence of his patrons, and then added a small quantity of white powder to the molten mass. It was allowed to cool, and then, when it was broken open, a gold nugget weighing 7 grams was inside.

Ludendorff, to say the least, was ecstatic. He set about forming a company called "Company 164". Investment money poured in and within a year the general had diverted some 400,000 marks into Nazi Party funds. Then, in December, 1926, he resigned, leaving Tausend to handle all the debts. Tausend managed to continue raising money and on June 16, 1928, supposedly made 25 ounces of gold in a single operation. This enabled him to issue a series of "share certificates" worth 22 pounds each (10 kilograms of gold).

A year later, when no more gold had been produced, Tausend was arrested for fraud, tried, found guilty, and sentenced to four years in prison. Nevertheless, while waiting for trial, he was able to perform a transmutation under strict supervision, in the Munich Mint. This was submitted to the court as evidence that no fraud had taken place, but it was contested and did not save him from prison.

In the same year that Tausend was convicted, a Polish engineer named Dunikovski announced in Paris that he had discovered a new kind of radiation which would transmute quartz into gold. The mineral, spread on copper plates, was melted by an electric discharge at 110,000 volts, and was then irradiated with these new "z-rays". Investors poured two million francs into Dunikovski's project, but, within a few months, when no gold appeared, he was also tried and found guilty of fraud. After two years in prison, Dunikovski's lawyer obtained an early release, and he went with his family to Italy where he again began to experiment. Rumors soon started that he was supporting himself by the occasional sale of lumps of gold. His lawyer, accompanied by the eminent chemist, Albert Bonn, went to see him.

What was discovered was that the quartz being used by Dunikovski (and presumably by Tausend as well) already contained minute quantities of gold. The gold could be extracted by a usual process, producing about 10 parts per million, but Dunikovski's technique produced almost 100 times as much. Nevertheless, he was only dealing with small quantities of gold because his equipment could only handle small quantities of quartz.

Dunikovski claimed that his process accelerated the natural growth of "embryonic" gold within the quartz. He gave a demonstration before an invited group of scientists that attracted considerable attention. An Anglo-French syndicate formed to bring sand from Africa and treat it in a big new laboratory on the south coast of England, but WW II started at about this time and Dunikovski disappeared. It was rumored that he was "co-opted" by the Germans and manufactured gold for them to bolster their failing economy - but there is no proof.

Since WW II, there have been and still are, many practitioners of alchemy. Much of this activity has been centered in France, including Eugene Canseliet, who claimed to have been a pupil of the mysterious Fulcanelli mentioned above.

In studying alchemy and the history of alchemy and all related books I could find, I came finally to Fulcanelli and the mention of him in the book *Morning of the Magicians* by Pauwels and Bergier.

Bergier claimed that in June of 1937 - eight years before the first atom-bomb test in New Mexico - that he was approached by an impressive but mysterious stranger. The man asked Bergier to pass on a message to the noted physicist Andre Helbronner, for whom Bergier was then working. The man said that he felt it was his duty to warn orthodox scientists of the danger of nuclear energy. He said that the alchemists of bygone times - and previous civilizations - had obtained such secret knowledge and *it had destroyed them*. The mysterious stranger said that he really had no hope that his warning would be heeded, but felt that he ought to give it anyway. Jacques Bergier remained convinced until the day he died that the stranger was Fulcanelli. As the story goes, the American Office for Strategic Services, the forerunner of the CIA, made an intensive search for Fulcanelli at the end of the war. He was never found.

The argument against this strange event ever having happened is that plutonium was specifically *named* by the mystery man, yet it was not isolated until February of 1941, and was not named until March of 1942. This was five years *after* Bergier's encounter. Nevertheless, Bergier stood by his story. [27] And, the fact is, if we are talking about Master Alchemists, the history seems to indicate that they have "time travel" capabilities to some extent. So, the matter of knowing the name of the element would not have been too great a difficulty.

In the early 1920's, in Paris, there was a small man in his early twenties, named Eugene Canseliet who was known as an alchemical enthusiast. He made many references to the fact that he worked with an actual "Master of the Art". His friend and companion, a poverty stricken illustrator named Jean-Julien Champagne, who was a score of years older than Canseliet, supported these claims. The two of them lived in a run-down building, in adjacent apartments, at 59 bis, rue de Rochechouart, in the Butte-Montmartre district. Because of their hints that they had contact with such a "Hidden Master", they soon became the center of a circle of aspiring occultists who became known as the Brothers of Heliopolis. It seems that both Canseliet and Champagne were frequently seen in the city libraries, the Bibliotheque Nationale, the Mazarin, the Arsenal and the Sainte Genevieve, studying rare books and manuscripts. Obviously, they were looking for something.

The story heard by those on the edges of this elite little group was to the effect that this "Hidden Master Fulcanelli" was old, distinguished - possibly an aristocrat - and very rich. He was also said to be an immensely learned, practicing alchemist who had either already, or almost, achieved the Great Work.

Nobody (until later, as we saw with Jacques Bergier) except Canseliet and Champagne ever claimed to have met Master Fulcanelli, and, because of this, a great deal of skepticism arose in the occult circles of Paris. But then, the skepticism was laid to rest with the publication of *Le mystere des cathedrales* in 1926. This first edition consisted of only 300 copies, and was published by Jean Schemit of 45 rue Lafitte, in the Opera district. It was subtitled, "An esoteric interpretation of the hermetic symbols of the Great Work",and its preface was

---

[27] It has been noted by the student of Fulcanelli's only disciple, Eugene Canseliet, Patrick Riviere, that Bergier - just before he died - claimed that Schwaller and Fulcanelli were one and the same individual.

Andre VandenBroeck's *AL-KEMI, A MEMOIR: Hermetic, Occult, Political and Private Aspects of R.A. Schwaller de Lubicz* (1987 Inner Traditions/Lindisfarn Press) claims a clandestine collaboration between Fulcanelli and Rene Schwaller. Supposedly, Schwaller confided to VandenBroeck that Fulcanelli stole from him an original manuscript on the alchemical symbolism of the Gothic Cathedrals and published it under his own name as Mystery of the Cathedrals. VandenBroeck's allegation seems to be supported only by VandenBroeck himself, and simply does not fit the facts or the timeline.

In her work *Fulcanelli Dévoilé* (1992 Dervy) Geneviève Dubois suggests that Schwaller believed Jean-Julien Champagne to be Fulcanelli and that it was Champagne who took the manuscript. Champagne was quite a practical joker and was happy to let others think he was Fulcanelli.

written by Eugene Canseliet, then aged only 26. The book had 36 illustrations, two of them in color, by the artist, Champagne. So, in one fell swoop, both Canseliet and Champagne were vindicated, and their place among the coterie of occultists assured!

The subject of the book was a purported interpretation of the symbolism of various Gothic cathedrals and other buildings in Europe as being encoded instructions of alchemical secrets. This idea, that the secrets were contained in the stone structures, carvings, and so forth, of the medieval buildings had been hinted at by other writers on esoteric art and architecture, but no one had ever explicated the subject so clearly and in such detail before. In any event, Fulcanelli's book caused a sensation among the Parisian occultists. In the preface, written by Canseliet, there is the hint that Master Fulcanelli had "attained the Stone" - that is, had become mystically transfigured and illuminated and had *disappeared!*

> He disappeared when the fatal hour struck, when the Sign was accomplished... Fulcanelli is no more. But we have at least this consolation that his thought remains, warm and vital, enshrined for ever in these pages.[28]

The extraordinary scholarship of *Les Mystere* drove the occult crowd of Paris mad with desire to know who Fulcanelli really was! Rumor and speculation ran wild! About these speculations regarding Fulcanelli's possible identity, Kenneth Rayner Johnson writes:

> There were suggestions that he was a surviving member of the former French royal family, the Valois. Although they were supposed to have died out in 1589 upon the demise of Henri III, it was known that members of the family had dabbled in magic and mysticism and that Marguerite de France, daughter of Henri II and wife of Henri IV of Navarre, survived until 1615. What is more, one of her many lovers was the esoterically inclined Francis Bacon (whom many still claim as an adept to this day); she was divorced in 1599 and her personal crest bore the magical pentagram, each of whose five points carried one letter of the Latin word *salus* - meaning 'health.' Could the reputedly aristocratic Fulcanelli be a descendant of the Valois, and did the Latin motto hint that some important alchemical secret of longevity had been passed on to him by the family?

> Some claimed Fulcanelli was a bookseller-occultist, Pierre Dujols, who with his wife ran a shop in the rue de Rennes in the Luxembourg district of Paris. But Dujols was already known to have been only a speculative alchemist, writing under the nom de plume of Magophon. Why should he hide behind two aliases? Another suggestion was that Fulcanelli was the writer J. H. Rosny the elder. Yet his life was too well-known to the public for this theory to find acceptance.

> There were also at least three practical alchemists working in the city around the same period. They operated under the respective pseudonymns of Auriger,

---

[28] From Canseliet's introduction to Fulcanelli's book.

Faugerons and Dr. Jaubert. The argument against them being Fulcanelli was much the same as that against Dujols-Magophon: why use more than one alias?

Finally, there were Eugene Canseliet and Jean-Julien Champagne, both of whom were directly connected with Fulcanelli's book, and both of whom had claimed to have known the Master personally.[29]

There was one major objection to Canseliet being Fulcanelli: he was too young to possibly have gained the knowledge apparent in the book. And, yes, a study of his preface as compared with the text demonstrated distinctly different styles. So, Canseliet was excluded.

Champagne is the next likely suspect because he was older and more experienced, and it was a certainty that his work as an artist had taken him around France so that he would have had opportunity to view all the monuments described in such detail. The only problem with this theory was that Champagne was a "noted braggart, practical joker, punster and drunkard, who frequently liked to pass himself off as Fulcanelli - although his behaviour was entirely out of keeping with the traditional solemn oath of the adept to remain anonymous and let his written work speak for itself". And, in addition to that, Champagne was an alcoholic whose imbibing of absinthe and Pernod eventually killed him. He died in 1932 of gangrene at the age of 55. His toes actually fell off. Doesn't sound much like a "Master Alchemist". As a humorous note, some of the descriptions of the transmutation of the alchemist make you wonder if the toes falling off isn't part of the process!

Joking aside, there are many more details and curiousities involved in the sorting out of who or what Fulcanelli may have really been, with no more resolution than we had at the beginning of the discussion! It just goes around in circles! The bottom line is: more than one person has attested to Fulcanelli's existence, his success in transmutation and to his continued existence into the present time - which would make him over 140 years old! And some theorists think he may be older than that!

The Morning of the Magicians, by Louis Pauwels and Jacques Bergier, was published in 1963, and it was only then that English speaking occultists and students of alchemy became aware of Fulcanelli. At that point in time, it was to be another eight years before *Le mystere des cathedrales* would be translated into English. But, each of these books awoke a whole new audience of Seekers to the

---

[29] Johnson, Kenneth R., *The Fulcanelli Phenomenon*,1992. These stories have since been laid to rest as everything from idle speculation to overt disinfo with the publication in French of *Fulcanelli* by Patrick Rivière in 2000. An updated and revised second edition, with much new material, appeared in 2004, published by Pardès in their series "Qui suis-je?" An English translation of Mr. Rivière's book will soon appear and should settle once and for all the questions of Fulcanelli's identity.

possibility of present day miracles as well as the very real likelihood of *a millennia old secret held in trust by persons unknown.*

In the English edition of *Mystery of the Cathedrals*, Eugene Canseliet said that the Master had given him a minute quantity of the alchemical "powder of projection" in 1922 - and permitted him to transmute 4 ounces of lead into gold. Walter Lang, who wrote the introduction to the book received a letter from Canseliet which said, in part:

> The Master was already a very old man but he carried his eighty years lightly.
> Thirty years later, I was to see him again... and he appeared to be a man of fifty.
> That is to say, he appeared to be a man no older than I was myself.
>
> Canseliet has since said that he has met with Fulcanelli several times since and that Fulcanelli is still living.[30]

Canseliet said that he met the Master in Spain in 1954 under highly unusual circumstances. The late Gerard Heym, founder member of the Society for the Study of Alchemy and Early Chemistry and editor of *Ambix*, its journal, acclaimed as Europe's formost occult scholar of his day, made friends with Canseliet's daughter and through her, had a look at Canseliet's passport. It did carry a Spanish entry-visa stamp for 1954. So, at least on this one item we have a small fact, even if it is hearsay. I haven't seen it myself.

One friend of Canseliet, who wished to remain anonymous, said that this meeting was "in another dimension... a point where such meetings are possible". The story was that Canseliet "received a summons", of some sort; perhaps telepathic, and traveled to Seville where he was met and taken by a long, roundabout route, to a large mountain chateau which proved to be an enclave of alchemists - a colony! He said that Fulcanelli appeared to have undergone a curious form of transformation so that he had characteristics of both male and female - he was androgynous. At one point, Canseliet said, Fulcanelli actually had the complete characteristics of a woman. Some of the more obscure alchemical literature does point to this androgyny. The adept going through the transformation supposedly loses all hair, teeth and nails and grows new ones. The skin becomes younger, smoother and the face takes on asexual characteristics.

After Canseliet's visit to the Enclave of the Alchemists, apparently somewhere in the Pyrenees, Gerard Heym said that he only had vague recollections of his experiences in Spain, as though some form of hypnosis had been used on him to make him forget the details of what he had seen and been told. (Why are we not surprised?!)

The point of this recitation is that there have been many well attested stories of strange things about alchemy reported by reliable and reputable witnesses, and the

---

[30] Johnson, op. cit.

stories continue in a sort of "subculture" down to our very day. There is something going on, and it has been going on for a very long time! And since we have encountered an alchemist in recent times - Fulcanelli - who may (or may not) have a clue, we might want to make note of some of the things he had to say about our present subject that may be the equivalent of the thread of Ariadne out of this labyrinth of confusion.

A KNIGHT ON A QUEST

Before proceeding to the subject at hand, some little background is in order. As a child, I was always attracted to the stories of King Arthur and his Knights of the Round Table. This was only natural, considering my patronymic of birth: Knight. Thus, a great many books on the subject were read and digested at a very early age. But, my general opinion of them changed as I grew older. I consigned them to the realm of fantasies or children's stories. There was no "real" grail; it was just a pretty tale. They were nice to read and imagine in times of idleness, but I felt that I needed to get about the REAL work of "finding God". I didn't realize that, in a very real sense this is the true nature of the Grail quest. In any event, I concentrated many years on this "finding God" business. For me it was as essential a thing to do as it was necessary for me to breathe.

I started in pretty basic ways: believing nothing, testing everything; and over the years I gradually found my way from the hard sciences to the "soft" sciences to the "Para-sciences". I analyzed and categorized everything as I went and, at the "end", I thought I had pretty well run the gamut. My categories were more varied and extensive than those of many people, but they were categories nonetheless - and I had more or less reconciled myself to never really knowing God except through "mind", and mind was, after all, as far as I could see, the beginning and end point of everything. *Cogito ergo sum.* That was all we could know. I wasn't happy with this answer, but what else was there?

That is where matters rested until the events described in my autobiography, *Amazing Grace,* that led to the Cassiopaean transmissions. And then, the Quest began in earnest.

New evidence, new knowledge, can change the entire foundation of what we think we know. And this, of course, is part of the very problem of the Grail. Everyone builds a hypothesis based on what is generally available in the context of "ordinary research" or hypotheses constructed on the foundations of our assumptions about our reality that are part of the social/cultural milieu in which we live. And because we are so invested in our fundamental beliefs about the nature of our reality, we become emotionally invested in these hypotheses - emotionally attached, that is - and when new information is discovered or brought to our attention, we often not only do not WANT to hear or see it - we simply cannot.

Beginning with a state of psychic bankruptcy in 1984, the Cassiopaeans spent ten years disabusing me of my assumptions about our reality, as we perceive it. I had prayed fervently for answers, and the Universe began to answer me in the dynamics of my very life. At a certain point, when I had passed many tests, the mode of communication became more direct and conscious - the Cassiopaean Transmissions themselves - and it became very clear that the Grail Quest was indeed important. It also became clear that it was a far deeper and more complex an issue than most scholars and amateur Grail Questors suppose. What was even more interesting was the fact that the Cassiopaeans led me to discover that the Grail Quest and the "Quest of the Alchemists for the Philosopher's Stone" is identical.

During the years of this initiation, I was guided to re-visit many of the texts I had casually dismissed in my youth in order to "read between the lines" with my "new eyes". The Cassiopaeans also suggested lines of study and research that had not been a part of my previous work. Among the texts I was guided to consider were the works of the alchemist Fulcanelli. And in the writings of Fulcanelli, I discovered that the very problem I was considering was described:

> "Furthermore, in our opinion, it seems insufficient to know how to recognize and classify facts exactly; one must still question nature and learn from her in what conditions and under the control of what will her manifold productions take place. Indeed, the philosophical mind will not be content with the mere possibility of identifying bodies. It demands the knowledge of the secret of their elaborations. To open ajar the door of the laboratory where nature mixes the elements is good; to discover the occult force, under whose influences her work is accomplished, is better. [...]

> "Alchemy is obscure only because it is hidden. The philosophers who wanted to transmit the exposition of their doctrine and the fruit of their labors to posterity took great care not to divulge the art by presenting it under a common form so that the layman could not misuse it. Thus because of the difficulty one has of understanding it, because of the mystery of its enigmas and of the opacity of its parables, the science has come to be shut up among reveries, illusions and chimeras. [...]

> "With their confused texts, sprinkled with cabalistic expressions, the books remain the efficient and genuine cause of the gross mistake that we indicate. For, in spite of the warnings... students persisted in reading them according to the meanings that they hold in ordinary language. They do not know that these texts are reserved for initiates, and that it is essential, in order to understand them, to be in possession of their secret key. One must first work at discovering this key.

> "Most certainly these old treatises contain, if not the entire science, at least its philosophy, its principles, and the art of applying them in conformity with natural laws. But if we are unaware of the hidden meaning of the terms - for example, the meaning of Ares, which is different from Aries - strange qualifications purposely used in the composition of such works, we will understand nothing of them or we will be infallibly led into error.

> "We must not forget that it is an esoteric science. Consequently, a keen intelligence, an excellent memory, work, and attention aided by a strong will are NOT sufficient qualities to hope to become learned in this subject. Nicolas Grosparmy writes:

> 'Such people truly delude themselves who think that we have only made our books for them, but we have made them to keep out all those who are not of our sect.'

> "Batsdorff, in the beginning of his treatise, charitably warns the reader in these terms:

'Every prudent mind must first acquire the Science if he can; that is to say, the principles and the means to operate. Otherwise he should stop there, without foolishly using his time and his wealth. And so, I beg those who will read this little book to credit my words. I say to them once more, that THEY WILL NEVER LEARN THIS SUBLIME SCIENCE BY MEANS OF BOOKS, AND THAT IT CAN ONLY BE LEARNED THROUGH DIVINE REVELATION, HENCE IT IS CALLED DIVINE ART, or through the means of a good and faithful master; and since there are very few of them to whom God has granted this grace, there are also very few who teach it.'[31]

At this point in time, as I write this little monograph, I can say that it is true that only by Revelation - by the Initiatory work of the Cassiopaeans - myself in the future - that much of the Secret has been thus far revealed.

The question may be asked: why am I revealing the secret if it has been the tradition to conceal it? Because I am as I am, and from my perspective, what is given to me is only serving myself until I give it to others in response to their asking. And many have asked.

After over thirty years of work, the one thing that has become evident is that the energies of Creation emanate "downward", and our individuality as human beings is merely an expression of the "Theological Dramas", so to say. To attempt to exert our will or to make our voice travel "upward", against Creation is, in essence, an attempt to violate the Free Will of Creation, i.e. Hubris. This is why praying, rituals designed to "change" reality, "positive thinking" with the "intent" to change something "up there", in order to receive the benefits "down here", is always doomed to produce more strife, misery and suffering globally.

As I searched through the literature in hundreds of fields of study, the chief thing that became apparent to me is that mankind is in the iron grip of an uncaring control system that raises him up and brings him low for its own mysterious purposes. No group, no nationality, no secret society or religion, is exempt.

I needed answers. I couldn't live haunted daily by this grief for humanity and the many horrors of history. That was the motivation for the Cassiopaean experiment. Everything we are taught in our society, our history, our religions, and the new age versions of same, is all logically inconsistent and makes a mockery of the very idea of a Creator - *Ribbono Shel Olom* - Master of the Universe. There was something strange and mysterious going on here on Earth, and I wanted to know the answers. So I undertook the channelling experiment that resulted, after two years of dedicated work, in what is known as the Cassiopaean Transmissions.

In spite of the fact that we hold an "open opinion" regarding the source of this material, the answers we received from the Cassiopaeans - us in the future - were intriguing, to say the least. The closest analogy to the view of reality presented by

---

[31] Fulcanelli, *The Dwellings of the Philosophers* (Boulder: Archive Press 1999) pp. 49, 65, 84.

the Cassiopaeans is graphically explicated in the movie, *The Matrix*, wherein our reality is presented as a computer program/dream that "stores" human beings in "pods" so that they are batteries producing energy for some vast machine dominating the world. Certain programmed life-scenarios of great emotional content were designed in order to produce the most "energy" for this machine. And it seems that pain and suffering are the "richest" in terms of "juice".

Another major concept presented in *The Matrix* was that the "real now" was the reality of the control system that produced the "programmed dream of reality" that was being experienced by those "trapped in the Matrix". The Matrix Dream Reality was based on the way things were in the past, before a terrible thing had occurred to destroy the world-that-was, after which it came under the control of computers which had become sentient and needed to utilize human beings as "power sources", or "food".

The difference between the metaphor of *The Matrix* and the view of the Cassiopaeans is that they propose a para-physical realm as another layer in the structure of space-time from which our own reality is projected, looping over and over again in endless variations. You could say that the hyperdimensional realms are the "future" in a very real sense.

This para-physical reality of hyperdimensional space - the realm of the Matrix programmers - is inhabited, according to the Cassiopaeans, by beings of both positive and negative polarity who have "graduated" from our reality, but not necessarily in the sense of "dying" and going to a strictly ethereal realm. It is, effectively, a world of the future that creates our present by projecting itself into the past. What is important to realize is that if we think about the future in terms of probable futures, or branching universes, then what we do now, whether we wake up from the Matrix or not, determines what kind of future we experience, individually and collectively.

While these ideas might seem more suited to science fiction than science proper, in fact, some of the most well-known physicists have proposed models and research programs that in no way contradict this hypothesis. They may one day demonstrate the mathematical proof of such a perspective.

For example, Paul Dirac wrote:

> "There are, at present, fundamental problems in theoretical physics the solution of which will presumably require a more drastic revision of our fundamental concepts than any that have gone before. Quite likely, these changes will be so great that it will be beyond the power of human intelligence to get the necessary new ideas by direct attempts to formulate the experimental data in mathematical terms. The theoretical worker in the future will, therefore, have to *proceed in a more direct way*. The more powerful method of advance that can be suggested at present is to employ all resources of pure mathematics in attempts to perfect and generalize the mathematical formalism that forms the existing basis of theoretical physics, and after each success in this direction, to try to *interpret the new mathematical features in terms of physical entities*."

Certain ontological problems related particularly to quantum theory suggest that an "observer" (J. A. Wheeler's "Eye"), watching the universe so as to "create it", may need to be included in our consideration. That suggests the necessity for expanding the scope of what is nowadays considered as "physical entities". The

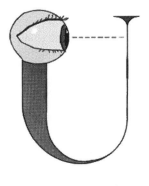

answer to "observability of parallel universes" may involve taking into account such an extension.

Now, consider the idea that there are several - maybe even infinite - "probable future yous" as observers. In the picture above, this would be represented as many "eyes" but all of them converging on a single point on the tail - the "now" moment that we perceive, which is the moment of "choice". It is from these probable futures of infinite potential - of "thought centers" - that reality is projected. It is through human beings that these energies are transduced and become "real".

You in the here and now - at the conjunction of all of these probabilities all vying with one another to become "real" - have no possibility of "creating" anything in this reality from "down here", so to say. The realities - the creative potentials - are a projection from higher levels of density. You are a receiver, a transducer, a reflector of the view of which eye is viewing YOU, nothing more.

The phenomenon that these ideas speak to more directly is that of hyperdimensional realities wherein mental energies or consciousness energies are amplified and can be interactive with the environment: technology that suggests not only power for transport that is partly physical, partly "ethereal"; communication that is also partly physical and partly ethereal, as well as powers of "manifestation" that might seem impossible to us in our present state of technology. All of these properties *do* belong to hyperdimensional existence, and such a state of being has been reported for millennia as being the "realm of the gods", including Dragons and Serpents, and critters of all sorts.

If we can describe such realms mathematically and give them a physical reality, as Dirac suggests, then we might also consider the hypothesis that they may be inhabited. Could our "Gods" be inhabitants of this realm?

As many physicists will tell you, all that really exists are "waveforms" and we are waveforms of reality, and our consciousness is something that "reads waves". We give form and structure to the waves we "read" according to some agreed upon convention.

And so, certain denizens of hyperdimensional space are "read" as more or less "reptilian" because that is the "essence" of their being, the frequency of their "wave form". We call them the *Overlords of Entropy*. They are not necessarily physical as we understand the term, nor are they necessarily "alien" as we understand that term either. We suspect that the perceptions of these levels of reality and their "consciousness units" are what is behind many religious conceptions and mythological representations of "gods and goddesses" and creatures of all sorts.

It is in this context of the Matrix, and realizing that the inner knowledge of many great mystery teachings down through the ages have presented the same, or a similar concept, that I have come to view the phenomena and interactions of our world. Such a view certainly produces results of becoming "free" from the controls of this Matrix, so I can say that in terms of experiment, it produces replicable results. However, as Morpheus explained to Neo in the movie:

> The Matrix is a system, Neo. That system is our enemy. But when you're inside, you look around; what do you see? Businessmen, teachers, lawyers, carpenters. The very minds of the people we are trying to save. But until we do, these people are still a part of that system, and that makes them our enemy. You have to understand; most of these people are not ready to be unplugged. And many of them are so inured, so hopelessly dependent on the system that they will fight to protect it. Were you listening to me Neo, or were you looking at the woman in the red dress? They will fight to protect it...

We could just as well re-write this to say: When you are inside the Matrix, you look around and see Christians, Jews, Mohammedans, Zoroastrians, Wiccans, Magicians... most of these people are not ready to be unplugged... they are so hopelessly inured, so hopelessly dependent on the system that they will fight to protect it. Were you listening to me, or were you listening to that ZionistBaptist Evangelist, or purveyor of Magick and mumbo jumbo?

It was also pointed out by Morpheus that any human being who was plugged into the system could be used as an "agent" by something similar to a downloaded program that was designed to activate them in a certain way. A similar state of affairs seems to be the actual case in our reality, with the Controllers acting from some hyperdimensional space of which we have but limited awareness, and even less access.

The option that does seem, realistically, to be open to us is to choose our alignment and prepare ourselves for the emanations that are traveling "downward" to be better received. This is the essential point of Castaneda's Don Juan when he said:

> One of the greatest accomplishments of the seers of the Conquest was a construct he called the three-phase progression. By understanding the nature of man, they were able to reach the incontestable conclusion that if seers can hold their own in facing [human] petty tyrants, they can certainly face the unknown with impunity, and then they can even stand the presence of the unknowable.

> "The average man's reaction is to think that the order of that statement should be reversed," he went on. "A seer who can hold his own in the face of the unknown can certainly face petty tyrants. But that's not so. What destroyed the superb seers of ancient times was that assumption. We know better now. We know that nothing can temper the spirit of a warrior as much as the challenge of dealing with impossible people in positions of power. Only under those conditions can warriors acquire the sobriety and serenity to stand the pressure of the unknowable."[32]

---

[32] Casteneda, Carlos, *The Fire From Within*, (New York: Pocket Books 1985) p. 19.

All around us we see the result of this error: the idea that we can exert our will and voice upward to change what is "above" us in order to change our reality. This idea is at the root of rites and rituals, demanding, pleading, visualizations, tapping, "workings", and so forth. People who think that "meditating on compassion", or "feeling the feelings of all beings", is going to result in the "sonic entrainment of the heart's rhythm [being] braided into more complex and coherent patterns", which will then enable the person to "create a diamond imperishable body for use as a teaching vehicle down here on earth", have missed the entire point. To compare such ideas to the true work of Seeker of Ascension is simply ignorant.

What seems to be true is that before the seeker of Ascension can ever achieve the point of being able to think even momentarily about "the oneness of all beings", or the "feelings of all beings", or be in possession of "super-awareness", he or she has spent many, many years in the struggle to "face petty tyrants", or to fully realize objective reality in a step by step process that includes action in concert with understanding.

They have repeatedly exposed themselves to as many "unpleasant experiences" as they can find, all the while struggling to master their emotions, desires, and physicality. It is the work of making the physical vehicle "down here" receptive to what one chooses to align with "up there", as opposed to trying to forcibly change something "up there" in order to have it "down here". This process is very much involved with what is called "discernment".

The great Sufi Shaykh Ibn al-'Arabi explains that "imperfection" exists in Creation because "were there no imperfection, the perfection of existence would be imperfect". From the point of view of Sheer Being, there is nothing but good. But Infinite Potential to BE includes - by definition of the word "infinite" - the potential to *not be*. And so, Infinite Potential "splits" into Thought Centers of Creation and Thought Centers of non-being. It can be said that Infinite Potential is fundamentally Binary - on or off - to be or not to be. That is the first "division".

Since absolute non-being is an impossible paradox in terms of the source of Infinite Potential to BE, the half of the consciousness of Infinite Potential that constitute the IDEAS of non-being - for every idea of manifestation, there is a corresponding idea for that item of creation to NOT manifest - "falls asleep" for lack of a better term. Its "self observation" is predicated upon consciousness that can only "mimic" death. Consciousness that mimics death then "falls" and becomes Primal Matter. What this means is that the "self observing self" at the level of the Master of the Universe is constituted of this initial division between Being and Non-being which is, again, only the initial division - the on/off, the yes/no - of creation. You could picture this as an open eye observing a closed eye. It has been represented for millennia in the yin-yang symbol, which, even on the black half that represents "sleeping consciousness that is matter", you can see the small white dot of "being" that represents to us that absolute non-existence is not possible. There is only "relative" non-existence.

These "thoughts of being and non-being" interact with one another - the observer and the observed - like a viewer looking into a mirror. Creation manifests between the viewer and the mirror. It is at once real, because it consists of matter informed by consciousness, and unreal, because it is ultimately composed of only consciousness acting on consciousness.

At our level of reality, the understanding that "nothing is real", as has been promulgated by gurus and teachers down through history, is as useless as saying "gravity isn't real". Such considerations are useful only for expansion of perception. They are not useful for practical application since the energies of creation apparently transduce through several "levels" before they meet in the middle, so to say, in our third density reality. Organic life exists at the "crossroads" of the myriad ideas or thought centers of being and non-being. As such, they have the capacity to transduce energies "up" or "down" depending on the "consciousness energy directors" of that unit. And again, there are apparently two broad divisions: directed toward being/ observing, or directed toward non-being/ mirroring. This division manifests across all levels of organic life, including human beings. Human beings exist to transduce cosmic energies of creation via organic life. Our "higher selves" are the directors of this transducing of cosmic energies, and the direction in which the energy "flows" is determined by the activities of these higher selves. Against the opposition of those forces seeking to "capture" energy of consciousness and induce it to the "sleep of non-being", which is gravitational in a certain sense, the energies of consciousness seek to "inform" matter, via awakening the self-awareness of those organic units on earth that are capable of resistance to the gravity of non-being.

As self-aware "transducing units", the human being has the potential for going either way - toward intensified being, or toward intensified non-being. In this sense, humans also function very much like a lens that can be "adjusted" like a telescope. It can be dialed to select the viewing range, which can be distant and inclusive of more "space/time", or it can be shortened to only see what is up close and evident in the material world. In other words, our first and most fundamental choice is to choose what we SEE.

When we choose what we SEE - and here we do NOT mean with the physical eyes or even psychically, but rather a more inclusive term that suggests whether or not we are capable of objectivity or subjectivity - we are receiving impressions. Impressions can become knowledge if assimilated. Knowledge leads to awareness. Knowledge and awareness then direct emotions, which then energize actions in the organic world. This is the transducing of energies of Cosmic Thought Centers.

Ibn al-'Arabi tells us that Goodness is Being; to which all positive and beautiful attributes or "names" of God belong. Evil is the lack of good, so it is "nonexistence". In other words, at the root, Being dwells in "non-existence" which is evil. Here is the sticking point, the item that is generally omitted from most "systems of ascension". Human beings at our level of reality exist at the crossroads of the Thoughts of Being and Non-being - Good and Evil. Mankind is made in the form of all the names of God - those of Being and Non-being. Assuming the traits of the Names is synonymous with manifesting their properties. The Science of Ascension is to obtain deep knowledge of all the Names and their true properties, the high and the low, the pleasant and the loathsome, the light and the darkness, in differentiated detail, so as to be able to CHOOSE which traits will be assumed. It is only with a full field of vision that a man can discover if what he subjectively thinks is good actually *is* good and leads to Being, or if it is a deception that induces to Non-being by pretense.

God is the root of ALL Names, noble and base. The task of the seeker of ascension is to bring the Noble traits from latency into actuality and to discover the positive applications of the base traits - even if that application is to "overcome" or transmute. The Shaykh tells us "noble character traits are only those connected to interaction with others". In other words: DOing. If you SEE the illusion of separation, that is certainly the first thing. The lie is smuggled in by suggesting that this is all that is necessary, that if you just "see it" everything will "change" for you.

God creates the good and the evil, the ugly and the beautiful, the straight and the crooked, the moral and the immoral. Between these traits lie the manifold dangers of the path of the seeker of Truth. Many modern day "teachers" and "gurus" tell us, "Since there is only One Being which permeates all things, all we have to do is see everything as only light", and that will transmute the darkness, and we will "create our own reality of light". Such a statement ignores the fact that the statement "God is One" describes a reality that is a higher level from which our own "mixed being" manifests. The man who assumes that he can become like God at this level just by thinking it, ignores the facts of Being vs. Non-being which outrays from "God is One" at a level of existence that is clearly several levels above our own.

Evil is REAL on its own level, and the task of man is to navigate the Cosmic Maze without being defiled by the Evil therein. This is the root of Free Will. Man faces a predicament as REAL as himself: he is forced to choose - to utilize his knowledge by applying it - between the straight path which leads to Being, and the crooked paths which lead to Non-Being. Human beings are required to discern between good and evil - consciousness energy directors - at every stage of their existence in this reality. Because, in fact, they must understand that God is consciousness and God is matter. God is good, and God is evil. The Creation assumes all the different properties of the many "Names of God". The Cosmos is full of Life-giving and Slaying, Forgiveness and Vengeance, Exaltation and Abasement, Guidance and Deception. To attempt to assume God's point of view and "mix everything" at this level, results only in STAYING at this level. Therefore, human beings must always separate God's point of view from their own point of view and the fact that all creation assumes the divine Names and Traits.

Thus, the first Divine Command is BE! And that includes Being and Non-being instantaneously. Therefore, the second law is "follow Being or Non-being according to your choice and your inherent nature". All creation is a result of this engendering command. So, in this respect, there is no Evil,but the second, prescriptive law determines to which "Face of God" one will return: Life or Death.

If the engendering command alone is considered, there is no imperfection in the cosmos, since all creatures follow what God desires for them. In this respect, what is normally called "imperfection" is in fact perfection, since it allows for the actualization of the various levels of existence and knowledge. In other words, were there no imperfections - in the sense of diminishment, decrease, and lack - there would be no creation. Were there no creation, the Hidden Treasure would remain hidden. Hence Being would be unseen in every respect. There would be no self-disclosure of the Divine Reality, Light would not shine, and God would be the Nonmanifest but not the Manifest. But all this is absurd, since it demands the imperfection of Being Itself, which by definition is nondelimited perfection. Being's perfection requires the manifestation of Its properties. The effects of the Names and Attributes must be displayed for God to be God. [...] In other words, Imperfection is demanded by existence itself. To be "other than God" is to be imperfect. ...But it is precisely the "otherness" which allows the cosmos and all the creatures within it to exist. If things were perfect in every respect, they would be identical with God Himself, and there would be nothing "other than God." But then we could not even speak about the cosmos, since there would be no cosmos and no speakers. ...So, imperfection is a kind of perfection. [Chittick]

At the particular stage of existence in which man finds himself, he is equally "receptive" toward the Two primary Faces of God: Being and Non-being. The Shaykh tells us that whatever property, or trait, any human being ultimately "chooses" *is what it originally possessed in its state of immutability.* The task of the Seeker is to discover what is immutable within, and to purify and amplify it. This is the development of Will. Will is a relationship, which follows knowledge while knowledge follows the object of knowledge. In the process of "ascension", the object of knowledge is YOU. Knowledge, in and of itself, has no effects. YOU, however, the seeker, can give to knowledge what you actually are, in yourself, thereby displaying YOURSELF in knowledge *by your actions* in concert with your knowledge.

As noted, there are many Names of God that call to us in our present state of existence. But you are not required to answer every one that calls. The fact that human beings are, in general, ignorant of their own true "essence" gives them the illusion of freedom. And the fact is, all paths come from God, and all paths Lead back to God, but again, it can be via different faces. As the Shaykh says: "Unto Allah all things come home, and he is the end of every path. However, the important thing is which divine name you will reach and to which you will come home?"

And this brings us to what the Shaykh calls "perspicacity". This is the special development of the "eye of insight", or "seeing the unseen" that is crucial to the Seeker. Just as the physical eye, with the refraction of light from the Sun, can discern between the large and the small, the beautiful and the ugly,the shades of colors, the moving from the still, the high and the low, the ability to see the unseen is a property of an "inner light". This light reveals to the seeker things about external objects that are NOT apparent to the five senses. It reveals to its possessor when a choice that may appear to be benevolent, is a step on the path of Evil. It reveals when a choice that may appear to human estimation as negative is actually a difficult step to felicity for all involved. The Sufis tell us that some individuals have achieved such a level of "seeing" that - upon seeing a person's footprint on the ground, even if the person is not present - they are able to say whether he is following a life of felicity or wretchedness.

The light of perspicacity seems to be a gift that not everyone has, and those who do have it, may not have developed it to the same degree. What is evident is that those who have it possess an immutable nature of Being which is able to "see" good and evil - they do not see "only good". Thus, they are able to discern between the "calls" of Nonbeing and Being, and therefore, are able to strengthen their Will along the path of intrinsic Being. It then follows that individuals who are not able to see - or who choose not to see - both Good and Evil, are formed in the mold of subjectivity, which is the human expression of the Call of Non-being.

A human being whose immutable nature is that of Being can strengthen the light of perspicacity by "assuming the traits" of the Names of Being. This does not mean that a person comes to possess traits that do not already belong to him. It means that these traits are amplified and "cultivated". The Ruling property of an individual is determined by what Face of God is *disclosed* to him, and *this is determined by his preparedness*. Felicity can only be disclosed when Evil has been turned away from, rejected; which can only be achieved by a long period of "testing" or being challenged to SEE and then to choose Being over Non-being in order to grow the Will or alignment to Being in a feedback loop. As the Seeker travels this path, he must not see these traits as his own, but rather that he is a locus of God's manifestation of an ontological attribute.

People imagine that they believe in God when, in fact, what they believe always takes the shape of the receptacle. The old saying is that the water takes on the color of its cup. The deeper implication of this is that a person will only be in disequilibrium if his conscious beliefs are not in conformity with his own immutable nature. In other words, a person whose intrinsic nature is aligned toward Being, will experience disequilibrium, struggle, and even illness by attempting to assume those traits that do not exist in him. In this sense, careful observation of the physical state - even the physical environment - can act as a guide as to whether or not the whole being is coming into alignment.

So it is that different paths can produce different effects for different individuals according to their immutable nature within. Those whose intrinsic nature is toward Being, follow the path of the developing the ability to SEE and to choose alignment with the infinite potential of creation, thereby being conduits of Being as GOD chooses to manifest through them. They not only see that limitation is illusion, they consciously ACT - they utilize that knowledge to generate energy and light.

Those whose intrinsic nature is toward Non-being, follow the path of limitation of Infinite Being by assuming that they, in their state of ignorance and subjectivity, know better than God how Creation ought to be fixed. They pray for change, they perform rituals, they chant mantras and repeat endless visualizations of "magickal forms" that are supposed to "change" reality. They bomb others with "Love and Light", (their subjective version of it, of course), and they seek to fix the world "out there" by projecting their subjective view of reality onto the infinite wisdom of Creation. This "consciousness energy direction" even includes the assumption that just knowing that all division is illusion will accomplish the goal of "Ascension", and that is the most cunning lie of all.

Each approach "ties a knot" in the heart of the believer and fixes him on a path, the object of his belief being the end of the path. All beliefs are equivalent in that God - of one sort or another - is their ultimate objective. But each belief is different in that it leads to a different name of God, or Thought Center. Even materialistic skepticism is a "belief" and leads to "matterizing" of the consciousness that follows this belief. What is more difficult to discern are the many mixed up "spiritual" paths that twist and distort the concepts of Being to engage the seeker on a path to Non-Being.

Going back to the idea of the human being as a transducing unit with a "lens capacity", what seems to be so is that the process of Ascension begins with the choice of tuning the lens. If the individual chooses to "adjust the dial" to see the entire field of Thought Centers influencing creation, he can then begin to select those that enhance and enliven Creation and Being - the Thought Centers of Awakened Consciousness - then a feedback loop that selects that probable future will be established.

A human being can, by great effort, expand his or her "field of view" toward greater and greater objectivity. With a wider and farther field of view, the awareness of those things, which emanate from the Thought Centers come into focus. When thought centers are more in focus, the individual then has greater ability to discern whether impressions emanate from the Thought Centers of being, or from the Thought Centers of non-being. At this stage, the individual is then able to further "shape" his emotions and direct his actions so as to become an efficient transducing unit of the cosmic energies of Being into this reality. This is knowledge utilization, which generates energy, which generates light.

As this process continues, as the feedback loop is activated between the Cosmic observer and the transducing/actions of the creature - the organic unit, the transducing organ, so to say - strengthens and the exchange between it and the Cosmic Observer accelerates and intensifies. The transducing organ then begins to act as a "homing beacon" for greater levels of that chosen Thought Center energy - that "observer from the future" - the "eye" that is the creator.

In the development of such a feedback loop, the human being - as a conduit of creation, a vessel - becomes an active participant of the creation of his own FUTURE in the act of choosing which observation platform and scope he accepts as "real" - objective or subjective. Furthermore, as the energy of such a being is changed and enhanced by the "flow of cosmic energy" passing through him, as he perceives more and more of the creative expressions of Infinite potential, and chooses those he wishes to align with, he becomes colinear with those other expressions of Being - other organic units that may be quite different in make-up, but similarly aware of Infinite Potential - and is thus able to interact with them in a manner that further expands and commutates the energy of transducing.

This can then lead to exponential amplification of the transducing of the energies of Being which can then completely alter the physical nature of the organic unit. Just as a pipe that is used to channel water gets wet from the water flowing through it, so does the human being who has begun the process of aligning with Being becomes saturated with the higher energies being manifested through him or her. This process leads to permeation of the organic nature of the vessel which leads to transformation, in that it "awakens" the "sleeping matter" of the organic unit and makes it a full participant in Being, rather than a weight for the soul to carry or struggle against. The energy of the organic vehicle is then available *in the terms described in Einstein's famous formula*, which might give some indication of the potential of such a being.

As the reader can easily see by now, the teachings of the current spate of New Age Gurus constitute the idea that we can exert our will and voice that exists "down here" upward to change what is "above" us in order to change our reality down here. They tell us that we can change our lives, our thinking, move our brains into harmony, or aid the "heart in opening", obtaining "harmony and balance" which is then going to "open windows in our mind, our heart, and our spirit", etc. It is claimed that we can do this basically by assuming God's point of view that "all is one, all is love". It is stated, (with some truth I should add, since good disinformation is always wrapped in a warm and fuzzy truth), that, "without Divine Unity inside of us, these windows of inspiration are rarely available". What they do NOT tell you is that the staircase to Divine Unity of Being requires a full field of awareness of Being and Non-being, and this can only be achieved *by divesting oneself of the controls of Nonbeing* which are, indeed, part of Being, but which seek to obviate Being in a paradoxical sleep of "Unification" which often begins by believing the lie that "knowledge protects" simply by having it.

Indeed, many of the "techniques" sold in the slick packages of "ascension tools" will temporarily produce chemical changes that will feel VERY good, the same way a good meal satisfies hunger temporarily. It really, "feels good"! But just as the steak and salad are digested and most of the matter excreted in a few hours, and another steak and salad is needed to fill the stomach again, so do such practices fail to do anything more than perpetuate the "food chain". And, staying with the analogy, very little of the "substance" of such practices actually "stays with" the individual.

A considerable period of time is required for the seeker to finally come to the realization that techniques that relieve stress or produce "good feelings", have done nothing to actually change their lives or their "vibrations". They are still recognized by their neighbor's dog, they still find new gray hairs on their heads, and they still get sick and have aches and pains like everyone else. The problem is, again, the "bottom up" ideas have been employed, which only result in remaining in the "mixed" state, or worse, being drawn deeper into the path of non-being.

Well, I should qualify that: to those for whom Non-being is their immutable nature, this is only natural and right and they will thrive following the path of non-being. But for those many, many seekers whose immutable nature is toward Being, this is a terrible trap - the gravitational effect of the Thought Center of Non-Being - to draw all of Creation into Non-Being will act on them in ways that are crippling to their relationships and health. Human beings who go through life feeling as though they have a "hole in their hearts" are those who are not synchronized with their immutable nature.

The natural field of view for the organic unit alone - with no connection to the higher self - is that of the material and/or mechanical interpretation of all phenomena. The influences of the Thought Center of non-being - the source of matter - have been increasing through the manifestation of billions of such units at a single point in time: the present.

The Thought Center of non-being is of a certain nature - contractile subjectivity - that exerts a more or less "gravitational" pull - a desire to absorb and assimilate the soul energies of Being - so as to feed its own contracting nature. Even if it promotes a full field of awareness in principle, it can only view Being as a traitor to its own need to not exist. This results in an individual who may proclaim that all is illusion, but whose actions - or rather lack thereof - betray the deeper immutable state of being. Due to its intrinsic nature, there is a powerful exertion of non-being to destroy and obviate Being and Creation - all the while it is unable to achieve the awareness that it only exists by virtue of Being and Creation IN ACTION!

The powerful exertion of the Thought Center of non-being to absorb and assimilate all of creation, powered by its own contractile subjectivity, poses certain problems both for itself and for Being. Since the fundament of non-being is a LIE - that is to say, the state of absolute non-being that it promotes is a paradoxical impossibility - and the fundament of Being is the objective fact that Existence simply IS via ACTION - or utilization of knowledge which generates light, the essential conflict is between lies and truth. The Thought Center of non-being tells itself the biggest lie of all - that it does not exist - and goes to sleep in pretense. And from this essential point, we see that the nature of subjectivity is that of lies. Lies and belief in lies - whether or not the believer is aware that they are believing a lie - all partake of the same essence - subjectivity and non-being.

The Thought Center of non-being - in its expression as matter - as being "impressed" by Creative consciousness in ACTION, which partially awakens it and draws it into the creation of the organic world - wraps itself around this awakened consciousness. Its intrinsic nature of pretense to non-being acts "gravitationally" on consciousness, and twists and distorts it into varying degrees of subjectivity. It is this interaction of the energy of all possibility, lensed through subjectivity of matter, that produces the myriad manifestations of the material universe.

In the realm of the Thought Center of non-being, there are many manifestations - or ways - of seeking annihilation - the "Base Names of God". These modes act in a gravitational way to engage, enfold, and distort consciousness to their ends. This results in the formation of consciousness units of great power and depth of cunning - far beyond anything imaginable in our own reality.

These consciousness units use their wiles to assimilate weaker consciousness units so as to accrue more contractile power. Obviously, the more "dense" the consciousness units "consumed", the more "nutritious" they are. And so they seek, by great cunning, to carefully, and with great patience, manipulate the consciousness units selected for assimilation. It is, effectively, trans-millennial stalking.

These Overlords of Entropy, or so we may call them, by virtue of the overlay of intensified subjectivity, - the hallmark of the influence of the Thought Center of non-being - interface with the organic world on a "geographic" scale. Since they have, so to say, an intimate relationship with matter, the contractile consciousness of such a being can affect its area of chosen dominion very much like an overshadowing "cloud" with millions of tendrils of connections between it and its range of influence. This includes even the very matter of the bodies of human beings. It is through these etheric fibers that the Overlords of Entropy assimilate energy.

These overlords have "organs" so to speak. Just as a group of people were described by the Apostle Paul as "the body of Christ", so are the organs of entropic overlords manifested as individual beings, though their direct connection to a single massive consciousness unit makes them more like "projections" than individually souled beings.

Because of their great drive to conserve and assimilate energy, the overlords are "stingy" with allowances to their organ-beings. It seems that they do not "waste" energy in manifesting and maintaining organic structures for their organs, and thus the organic physicality takes on the configuration of less complex creatures in the organic world. Rather than interacting with an organic structure in a cooperative, awakened state, they exercise control over theirs. Utilizing organic structures that require the least energy to maintain conserves energy. To this end, they draw the energy for their organic units from the pools of archetypal form of the animal kingdom. This energy is more easily accessed, is lower in frequency, and thus more amenable to control.

This seems to be the reason why, when perceived by individuals of the third dimensional self-consciousness - third density - realm, their appearance is generally startling. The reptilian type comes to mind as being the most energy efficient. Again, remember that consciousness is merely "reading waves".

Due to the contractile nature of this hierarchy and its energy consumption, it is extremely difficult for these organ-beings of the Overlords of Entropy to actively function in our realm for any period of time. When they enter our realm, assuming a third density organic form, they are at a disadvantage. They are temporarily disconnected from the energy pool, which weakens them, but they are at another great disadvantage as well. Since they are not internally connected to an expanding, creative feedback loop of Creative Being, their own entropic overlord is a constant drain on them, pulling them gravitationally as it were, making them even weaker than the natural denizens of this realm. Such are those called aliens and "Men in Black". It is this great strain on their energy resources that makes such appearances so rife with anomalous glitches. There is no creativity, and thus no ability to pull off such an intrusion into our reality with any convincing effectiveness.

For this reason they generally avoid direct interaction in the organic world, preferring to utilize other methods to stalk and conquer weaker units to "feed" the Thought Center of non-being. To this end, these entropic overlords seek to establish and maintain the "entrainment of creative energy" within the third density reality by deceptively enhancing third density, material interpretations of the phenomenal world.

In short, such beings of enormous geographic domination actively operate, within their geographic field of influence, to divert and discourage those organic units who have tenuous connections to creative energy - their higher selves - from interpretations which will lead to the establishing of a feedback loop with those Thought Centers of Being/Creation.

As noted, the nature of such beings, and the dynamic of their existence, requires massive energy input in order to "control" and direct their own organic physicality. This is possible at the level of overlord/sub-units of the Thought Center of non-being by virtue of the extensive assimilation of other consciousness units, and most especially by virtue of their "geographic" character, which enables them to "connect" to thousands, if not millions, of organic beings in the organic realm. This is, effectively, the "Program of the Matrix".

This connection is naturally enabled by the aforementioned intrinsic nature of organic units to only perceive the field of view of the organic realm. That is to say that mechanical and material feedback loops are far more easily created between organic units and the sub-units of Non-being by a sort of "gravitational" pull of these sub-units upon the natural inclinations of the organic being.

This establishes "feedback loops" as previously described. The organic unit, "infected" with the material/mechanical view, begins to act according to that Thought Center's dictates, and this generates activities of that nature in the organic unit. Due to the fact that any given sub-unit of the Thought Center of non-being may be connected to millions of organic units in third density, any of them may be activated singly, or in concert, to fulfill the wishes of the Overlords of Entropy, a "larger" sub-unit of the Thought Center of Non-being.

GURDJIEFF AND MOURAVIEFF

Machiavelli observed that religion and its teachings of faith, hope, charity, love, humility and patience under suffering were factors that render men weak and cause them to care less about worldly and political things, and thus they will turn political power over to wicked men who are not influenced by such ideals. Of course, the real trick is to convince people that the "afterlife" is the only thing worth thinking about, and it is to this end that Christianity has been formulated. It is also to this end that many of the New Age beliefs and "formulations" of the truth about Ascension have been engineered. All you have to do is have faith or meditate or acquire knowledge and awareness that will help you love everything and everybody. Nothing is said about the day-by-day struggle and the necessity for action.

Again let me say this: if the Truth about the REAL process of Ascension were not so detrimental to the agenda of the Controllers of our world, the Matrix, they would not have gone to so much trouble to cover it up. When we finally make the connection between that fact, and the fact that our governing elite is operating on the instructions of the Controllers, we then begin to realize that the drama on the political stage is a shadow of the higher-level agenda. And that leads us to realize that the COINTELPRO operation in the New Age and Human Potential movement has truly been the "opening act".

Based on observation and research, it is apparent that humanity has now reached a great historical crossroads. We have come to the end of a two thousand year history of intolerance, cruelty and stupidity, which has created our present state of global, collective madness. Humanity, as a collective whole, is arriving at a state of Spiritual Bankruptcy, or "death". And yet, we cannot assume that this is meaningless. Those who understand the principles of electricity will comprehend when I say that this present global estate is the way nature works and is the establishing of sufficient Contact Potential Difference for the inflow of energy of Cosmic Light. But just as it is in the case of the individual, when that point is reached - that Dark Night of the Soul - there is a "choice" that becomes apparent: the soul is offered the way "up" or the way "down". In order for this coming inflow of energy to act in positive ways, to create a new reality of Free Will and Balance, there must be a point of contact that can conduct the energy. There must be human "micro-chips" or "circuits" sufficient to sustain this energy or all of humanity will perish. This means that only the development of human beings of a certain sort - with a certain "wiring", so to say - will result in the global capacity to confront the energies of the Crossroads.

The only other Turning Point in history that can be compared with the present one is that of the "Great Flood". And so, we come to the idea that the search for the Holy Grail and the alchemical work of distillation of the Philosopher's Stone is ALSO the "building of an Ark" in order to pass over into the New World.

As things "heat up" here on the Big Blue Marble, we have received much correspondence from individuals asking "what to do". Many of the old fears and turmoil have surfaced with ideas of pulling up roots and - for reasons of self-preservation - moving here or there or undertaking to follow this or that promoter of "methods of ascension" or methods of "fixing the planet" so that everybody can just "get along" or we can all snuggle up with some warm fuzzies and get some rest.

The reader who has surveyed the material on our website has surely come to the conclusion that what we are saying is "nothing is as it seems and never has been", including the many religions and "methods of ascension" promoted down through the ages.

But what is lacking is a *clearly defined* WAY that might give guidance to the seeker in his quest for the keys to his own "salvation" in whatever terms he might define it. I have worked on presenting the WAY in both the *Wave Series* and the *Adventures series* by sharing my own experiences and what I have gleaned from much study and research, but some readers are put off by material that deals with all the lies and deceptions that we face in our reality and simply want to read something "uplifting". It doesn't seem to occur to them that one cannot be "uplifted" as long as one is mired in quicksand. What seems to be true is that we live in a world of lies - ruled by lies and stealing - and that human beings lie because it is impossible for them to do otherwise. Without a Way, that is.

As a result of our own searching and questing for answers, our repeated trying and testing of sources and materials, little by little we have come to the idea of what NOT to do. But again, there has not been a whole lot about what TO DO.

The Cassiopaeans have indicated certain pathways to follow in terms of research, but as always, we are more or less on our own in acquiring the knowledge and learning how to apply it - and for good reason. You cannot become yourself in the future if you avoid doing those things that make the future what it is. You can accelerate it, or enhance it, perhaps, but you certainly can't have it handed to you on a platter. If you did, you would avoid doing the many things that are necessary which may include making contacts and connections that "shape the future".

Among the things we have found via this exertion, is a body of teachings that not only meshes with, but vigorously expands upon the Cassiopaean Transmissions to an extent that we cannot think is accidental. The work in question is that of the Russian exile Boris Mouravieff, presented in his three part study and commentaries entitled *Gnosis*. Very little information is available on the background of these materials while a good deal of disinformation is circulating in other circles, and it is best to address these problems at the outset.

As it happens, during our research into Boris M., we discovered that he was being soundly lambasted by William Patrick Patterson in his book *Talking With the Left Hand* in which he accuses Mouravieff of "stealing" his ideas from Gurdjieff. Patterson is the author of four highly praised books on spiritual development and is a longtime student of John Pentland, the man Gurdjieff chose to lead the Gurdjieff Work in America, and the editor of The Gurdjieff Journal©, the only international quarterly devoted to exploring the "ancient teaching of the Fourth way brought and embodied by G. I. Gurdjieff".

Just in case the reader is not familiar with Gurdjieff, let me give a little background. Dating from his first lectures in Moscow and St. Petersburg in 1912, George Ivanovich Gurdjieff attracted the attention of occultists and many Western aristocrats. His teachings (often referred to as the 'Gurdjieff Work' or 'Fourth Way') became widely known through the writings and lectures of his pupil, the famous Russian mathematician and journalist Pyotr D. Ouspensky, and were later propagated by Alfred Orage, John G. Bennett, Rodney Collins, and Dr. Maurice Nicoll.

Gurdjieff himself admitted that he was utilizing 'stolen' teachings from a wide range of groups that he had encountered (including the Yezidis, the Russian Orthodox Church, and Sufi 'Bektashi' and 'Naqshbandi' sects in the Hindu Kush and Pamir regions) in his world travels. A deep study of Gurdjieff's work shows that he was obviously experimenting with his own ideas on how to utilize bits and pieces from these different teachings to create a system that would enable individuals to overcome ingrained "cognitive defects", become more conscious, and awaken the Higher Self's "Objective Conscience".

At a certain point, it seems that Gurdjieff realized that he had undertaken an impossible task since nearly all of his students "heard" only what they wanted to hear. He closed his school and concentrated on putting his ideas into allegory in his book *Beelzebub's Tales To His Grandson* (1950), which also incorporated and developed additional esoteric themes into his ideas.

Many of Gurdjieff's concepts have profoundly influenced our present culture due to the fact that some of his followers were famous and wealthy and had the means to promote them to others in the upper classes. After his death in 1949, Gurdjieff's legacy was disseminated through many people, and much of his work has been passed on through fragmentation of the many groups into something akin to secular denominations. One of the biggest problems with what happened to Gurdjieff's work, which seemed to be a sincere attempt to help humanity, was the formation of what can only be called personality cults and identifications with Gurdjieff at the expense and obsfucation of his ideas. It seems that Gurdjieff himself saw this coming at the end of his life.

Groups that are offshoots of Gurdjieff's teachings have been known to use all kinds of things to reprogram their members, including isolation, group think, authoritarian power structures, and other psychological methods designed to unmask or break down the personal ego. But, what seems clear is that, in the case of Gurdjieff, no one group can claim the whole cheese since he was curiously selective about what he told whom, and even those who were closest to him obviously misunderstood what he was trying to convey, as evidenced by his own statements about this factor towards the end of his life. Mouravieff comments on this:

People interested in esoteric matters will probably have read the book by P.D. Ouspensky, published posthumously, titled *In Search of the Miraculous: Fragments of an Unknown Teaching.* The ideas in that book were presented to Ouspensky by Georges Gurdjieff. Gurdjieff indicates the basis of his teaching: "for the benefit of those *who know already*, I will say that, if you like, this is esoteric Christianity."

Ouspensky's book - correctly indicated by the title - contains only *fragments* of a tradition which, until recently, was only transmitted orally. And only a study of the complete tradition can give access to the revelation. The system disclosed by the fragments that form Ouspensky's book and Gurdjieff's work, originates from revelations issued by the Great Esoteric Brotherhood to which the Apostle Paul alluded in his Epistle to the Romans:

> We are assured and know that all things work together and are fitting into a plan for good to and for those who love God and are called according to design and purpose. For those whom He foreknew, He also destined from the beginning to be molded into the image of His Son, that he might become the firstborn of MANY brethren. And those whom He thus foreordained, He also called; and those whom He called, He also justified, made them righteous, and those whom He justified, He also glorified. What then shall we say to this: If God is for us, who can be against us? [8;28-31]

Boris Mouravieff asks: What should be the attitude of students towards the "Gurdjieff phenomenon" and Ouspensky's "Fragments"?

The attentive reader will easily find the answer to that question himself in the contents of this book: we must begin by separating the message from the messenger, and we must look for the message beyond the level or information. This is the way to discover and eliminate error. Robin Amis, editor of the English translation of Mouravieff's work tells us:

> In a myth well known in the Orient we are told that there exists a race of 'Royal Swans'. The fable adds that if we put milk mixed with water in front of one of them, it will separate out the milk and drink it, leaving the water. That must be the attitude of students.

> Saint Gregory Palamas said the same when he wrote in his first *Triad*: "As for those people they call 'theologians' or 'teachers,' and think themselves able to borrow their theological terms, is it necessary even to mention them? Is it necessary that we keep away from 'the light which lights every man who comes into the world,' and wait for the terrible shadows of ignorance to illumine us, on the pretext that, just as serpents are useful, this is something useful for us? For the flesh of serpents is only useful to us if they have been killed, and cut up and *used with reason as a remedy against their own bites*. Those who kill them in this way turn a part of these snakes against themselves, just as if they had killed with his own sword a new Goliath, who had taken arms, who had set himself up to oppose us, who cursed the army of the living God - someone educated in divine things by sinners and illiterates."

The fact is, Gurdjieff faced great difficulties at the point in time when he sought to experiment with waking up humanity. As noted above, it was "Mission Impossible". However, what he and his followers did manage to do was to slash a trail through a jungle of lies and disinformation. It is not appropriate for his followers to insist that this bare trail is all there is and that there is no more. Rather, it is only logical to widen the trail, to pass through the gate revealed at the

end of the trail, and to discover what lies on the other side. A student of
Mouravieff asks:

> Why did Gurdjieff hide his sources? Why does he remain silent on this subject,
> except in rare exceptional circumstances, such as that encounter with Mouravieff at
> the *Cafe de la Paix*: "I find the system at the foundations of the Christian doctrine.
> What do you say on this matter?" [asked Mouravieff of Gurdjieff]-- "It is the
> ABC," Gurdjieff answered me. "But they do not understand this!" [*A response to
> William Patrick Patterson's criticism in his book "Taking with the Left Hand"* by a
> student of Boris Mouravieff Translated from the French by Theodore J.
> Nottingham]

In his book, *Struggle of the Magicians*, Patterson includes quotes on the front
pages which say:

> The Magus is the highest that man can approach to God. - G.I. Gurdjieff

> Toast to Gurdjieff:: God give you the strength and the manhood to endure your
> lofty solitude. - Rachmilevitch

> Gurdjieff is a kind of walking God - a planetary or even solar God. - A.R. Orage

In response to these ideas, obviously dear to the heart of many Gurdjieff
followers, including Patterson, let me just point out that Gurdjieff never
accomplished the transmutation. He died just like everybody else. [33]

Considering the fact that several other "seekers" were reputed to have
transitioned without seeing death - Flamel and Fulcanelli among them - we might
think that the only parts of Gurdjieff's work that should interest us are the parts
that elucidate the work of the affirmed Masters. And frankly, Mouravieff has
offered many clues that do, in fact, contribute to the body of alchemical/hermetic
knowledge in a significant way.

Mouravieff's work is extraordinary in its clarity and completion of what was
started by Gurdjieff, explaining much that Gurdjieff never explained, or if he did,
those he explained it to either did not understand it, or sought to keep it secret so
as to dispense it in controlled dollops to those they considered worthy (or who had
enough money to pay for it).

I would like to note here that the work of Mouravieff provides that ineluctable
bridge between the works of Gurdjieff, Ibn al-'Arabi, Carlos Casteneda,
conjectured esoteric Christianity, hermeticism/alchemy and the Cassiopaean
Transmissions. It should be noted that the Cassiopaeans - us in the future - have
definitively supported the existence and work of a man around whom the Jesus
legend formed - though they tell us that the story in the Bible that is supposed to
be history is a myth - and here we find a body of teachings that lends background

---

[33] And I should add, so did Rene Schwaller.

to this view, as well as supplemental information that elucidates the many clues offered by the Cassiopaeans.

This brings us back to the issue of what we are supposed to DO in this day and age that is getting scarier by the minute? When I was at that stage myself, asking what should I do, where, when, how and why, I was quite surprised when the C's responded that all of the running around to look for "safe places" was just "3D thinking" and that *the only thing that counted was:*

"Who you are and *what you see."*

SEEing = perspicacity. And what you see, combined with who you are, determines what you DO. This leads to another important point:

> C's: Beware of disinformation. It diverts your attention away from reality thus
> leaving you open to capture and conquest and even possible destruction.
> Disinformation comes from seemingly reliable sources. It is extremely important
> for you to not gather false knowledge as it is more damaging than no knowledge at
> all. Remember knowledge protects, ignorance endangers. [...] Remember,
> disinformation is very effective when delivered by highly trained sources because
> hypnotic and transdimensional techniques are used thereby causing electronic
> anomalies to follow suggestion causing perceived confirmation to occur.

In the following sections, I will be quoting heavily from Mouravieff's books, including the introductions, but often with the insertion of "modern terms" at certain points, or terms which will make the excerpts more comprehensible to those who have not delved deeply into such studies. It is my hope that this condensation will inspire the readers to read the works of Gurdjieff and Ouspensky and Mouravieff. Robin Amis gives us a little background about the Tradition:

> Boris Mouravieff's trilogy *Gnosis* is an attempt to recover and describe, in terms
> understandable to modern man, a particular Tradition handed down over the
> centuries, in a sometimes broken line, but one that still exists today in the Eastern
> Orthodox Church. This tradition could be said to be the Christian equivalent of
> Yoga, Zen, and the other inner traditions of the far Eastern religions, disciplines,
> which have each existed as specializations within the religion of which they are a
> part.
>
> It is not one man's system or invention, but has its roots far back in the history of
> Christianity - whose roots lie in certain statements of St. Paul, and perhaps even of
> Christ himself. Their development can be traced first through formative figures of
> the early churches, and it clearly relates to the doctrines expressed in the key texts
> of Eastern spirituality such as the *Philokalia.*
>
> It clearly relates the oral tradition known as the *Royal Way* that survives to this day
> in the main centers of monasticism in the Eastern church. But it does not claim to
> be a work of Orthodox theology, nor to reinterpret Orthodox doctrine.
>
> Mouravieff admits that the survival of this tradition within the church is tenuous,
> that the doctrine does not appear to survive in full or has not been collected together
> in full. Monks on Athos admit the existence of the Tradition but say that it has
> never been fully spelled out in writing. The importance of Mouravieff's work is the
> effort he has made to collect that dispersed information and to make it accessible in
> practical form.

What are the sources of Mouravieff's knowledge? It is clear that his text consists of knowledge of a high order.

There are several ways in which the accuracy of a text can be verified, and Mouravieff's stands up to all these methods of assay. First of all, it fits the Orthodox tradition as expressed by those who still possess the Royal Way. It evokes the confirmation of inspiration described in Plato's seventh letter. It predicts, in what appears at first to be mere theory, the actual events of the life in the study of Gnosis. It stands the test of practice, and in doing so it remains internally consistent. When it does introduce ideas from other traditions, such as the concept of karma, it does so in ways that, properly understood, remain consistent to the overall statement of the doctrine with a degree of precision equal to that of the mature external sciences.

Those who can discriminate between different levels of knowledge will find in Mouravieff an almost inexhaustible treasury of knowledge that can lead to true spiritual transformation. But it is necessary first to work for this discrimination. Without it, not only will you be unable to differentiate between gnosis and its imitations, but even Mouravieff's work will not release its gnosis to you in trust.

The idea of esotericism is often misunderstood. The clue can be found in the Gospel of Saint John: "I am the vine, ye are the branches: he that abideth in me, and I in him, the same bringeth forth much fruit: for without me ye can do nothing."

The word translated "without", the Greek "choris", quite definitely means "outside". What this means is that in those times there was an inner knowledge, based on assenting to traditional knowledge - gnosis - which is then confirmed experimentally through techniques of inner observation, and a purely external kind of knowledge, gained through the ordinary senses.

Constantine Cavarnos confirmed that there is an exoteric and esoteric Christianity:

"The first kind of philosophy, external philosophy, comprises for them ancient Greek philosophy and the pagan philosophy of early Christian centuries. The second kind, "internal philosophy", is identical with the [true] Christian religion." [The Hellenic Christian Philosophical Tradition, Institute for Byzantine and Modern Greek Studies, Belmont, MA, 1989. p. 109, quoted by Robin Amis in the introduction to Mouravieff's *Gnosis II*]

Over the years, this esotericism has formed a Tradition, a science, or discipline of knowledge which may have existed before the time of Christ, but which has since been totally assimilated to the inner meaning of Christianity. Boris Mouravieff says that, "This Tradition, which in Antiquity was only revealed in the Mysteries under the seal of absolute secrecy."

Under the influence of self-proclaimed initiates of The Tradition such as Guenon and Schwaller, Mouravieff has, unfortunately adopted and included many false teachings in his "social commentary" included in the three volumes of *Gnosis*. Among these errors, he includes the idea that this Tradition passed from Egypt to Judaea and thus to Christianity - at least not Egypt as we understand it today. What is clear is that the True Tradition of the Eleusinian mysteries is behind Christianity, and it was the Egyptian Tradition elucidated and popularized by Schwaller and other Western occultists that is at the root of the false teaching that corrupted and distorted the work of the man we have come to know as Jesus. It is only in more recent times, with much additional research, including that of

Picknett and Prince in *The Stargate Conspiracy*, that we are even able to begin to separate these threads and come to this understanding. In short, even the work of Mouravieff must be "separated" like the milk from the water.

Regarding the error of understanding True Esoteric Christianity in terms of the Egyptian Religion, in Manly Hall's exhaustive compendium, *The Secret Teachings of All Ages*, we find mention of the fact that St. Irenaeus was complaining about the efforts to compare Christianity to the religion of the Egyptians which included the death and resurrection of Osiris/Horus. Irenaeus had some other interesting things to say about this, as Hall points out:

> According to popular conception, Jesus was crucified during the thirty-third year of His life and in the third year of His ministry following his baptism. About AD 180, St. Irenaeus, Bishop of Lyons, one of the most eminent of the ante-Nicene theologians, wrote *Against Heresies*, an attack on the doctrines of the Gnostics. In this work, Irenaeus declared upon the authority of the Apostles themselves that Jesus lived to old age. To quote:

> They, however, that they may establish their false opinion regarding that which is written, maintain that He preached for one year only, and then suffered in the twelfth month. [In speaking thus], they are forgetful of their own disadvantage, destroying His whole work, and robbing Him of that age which is both more necessary and more honourable than any other, that more advanced age, I mean, during which also as a teacher He excelled all others. For how could He have had His disciples, if He did not teach? And how could He have taught unless He had reached the age of a Master?

> For when He came to be baptised, He had not yet completed His thirtieth year, but was beginning to be about thirty years of age; and, according to these men, He preached only one year reckoning from His baptism. On completing His thirtieth year He suffered, being in fact still a young man, and who had by no means attained to advanced age.

> Now, that the first stage of early life embraces thirty years, and that this extends onward to the fortieth year, every one will admit; but from the fortieth and fiftieth year a man begins to decline towards old age, *which Our Lord possessed while He still fulfilled the office of a Teacher, even as the Gospel and all the elders testify;* those who were conversant in Asia with John, the disciple of the Lord, affirming that John conveyed to them that information. And He remained among them up to the time of Trajan.

> Some of them, moreover, saw not only John, but the other apostles also, and heard the very same account from them, and bear testimony as to the validity of the statement. Whom then should we rather believe? Whether such men as these or Ptolemaeus, who never saw the apostles, and who never even in his dreams attained to the slightest trace of an apostle?

Well, obviously, this "Gospel" that Irenaeus refers to as testifying that Jesus did not suffer and die has disappeared! But, commenting on the foregoing passage, theologian Godfrey Higgins remarks that it has fortunately escaped the hands of those destroyers who have attempted to render the Gospel narratives consistent by deleting all such statements. He also notes that the doctrine of the crucifixion was a *vexata questio* among Christians even during the second century. "The evidence of Irenaeus", he says, "cannot be touched". "On every principle of sound criticism, and of the doctrine of probabilities, it is unimpeachable." [*Anacalypsis*, Godfrey Higgins, London, 1836, quoted by Manly P. Hall]

Regarding the above comments by Irenaeus, we notice that he was blaming the corruption of the work of Jesus on the Gnostics. What seems altogether possible, considering the revelations of the inner tradition of esoteric Christianity, is that Irenaeus - and others - completely misunderstood the teachings of the metaphor of crucifixion which, it is clear, are an alchemical allegory.

Nevertheless, as years passed, this "misunderstanding" became the foundation of Christianity itself and those who noted its similarity to the Egyptian religion and other dying god myths assumed the transmission from ancient Egypt as we now understand it.

The fad for all things "Egyptian" has been with us for a very long time. Schwaller de Lubicz - the vector of many of these ideas - settled in Egypt in 1938 and for the next 15 years studied the symbolism of the temples, particularly Luxor, finding what he considered to be proof that the ancient Egyptians were the ultimate examples of Synarchy, because they were ruled by a group of *elite initiates*. He failed to point out that the Egyptian civilization was static and limited. What's more, it caved in on itself, and never managed to produce any significant work of benefit for humanity, as Otto Neugebauer showed conclusively in his *The Exact Sciences in Antiquity*, whose evidence we will quote further on in this volume.

The open-minded thinker ought to really consider the purported mysteries of Egypt in terms of the fact that they were so ignorant that they devoted a huge amount of energy to their "cult of the dead". The whole Egyptian shtick is focused around preserving dead flesh for future or otherworldly reanimation. The very fact that there are so many of these dead bodies for Egyptologists to dig up is the clearest evidence that the Egyptian beliefs were nonsense. So, in that sense, certainly, Christianity as we know it has adopted the "Egyptian religion" and its beliefs in physical resurrection.

The whole issue of the excitement over Egyptian civilization is the belief that they had some mysterious powers because they built the pyramids and we can't. And has it never occurred to anybody that the existence of the pyramids in conjunction with the worship of an elite group of human beings, while everybody else was wearing loincloths and sweating in the hot sun, might suggest a relationship between the two? The fact is, the Egyptian civilization seems to have been the chief example of a vast chasm between the haves and the have-nots, and they managed to do it longer than anybody else.

In examining the work of Schwaller, we have one of the better examples of the subtle way the negative occult societies attack those who come to bring light, by association and co-opting. The tactic is to find a means of subtly allying their message with that of the truth so as to generate confusion in untrained minds which would tend, on surface evidence, to accept these actually contrary messages as similar, at least in intent.

The negative occultists who are promoting the new Control System borrow all their components from what is of truth, and proceed by the method of imitation. They literally will ape the expression of positive teachings, and all the more carefully when they wish to be mistaken altogether for purveyors of truth, so as to subvert the messages.

And so it was that Mouravieff, under the influence of the Synarchists of his day, introduced some of their ideas into his own synthesis of the authentic Tradition, including the idea that the Tradition was passed from Egypt to Judaea via Moses. Regarding his sources, Robin Amis tells us:

> Boris Mouravieff tells us that the Christian Esoteric Tradition has always remained alive within certain monasteries in Greece, Russia, and elsewhere. It is true that this knowledge was hermetically hidden, but at the same time, its existence was known and access to it was never forbidden to those seriously interested in esoteric questions.
>
> Mouravieff tells us that his commentaries are drawn directly from the Eastern Christian Tradition: the sacred texts, the commentaries written around these texts, and especially from the *Philokalia* which is, above all, the same teaching and discipline, transmitted by fully authorized individuals.
>
> Attentive examination and comparison of Mouravieff's work to that of Ouspensky and Gurdjieff will show the incomplete character of the latter, as well as the deviations from the ancient doctrine.
>
> Christ categorically affirmed that entry into the Kingdom of God is closed to those who have not been born anew. *This second Birth is the object and goal of esoteric work.*
>
> Most of the writings of the *Philokalia* were intended for people who had already acquired some proficiency in esoteric studies. One could actually say the same about the Gospels, corrupted and glossed though they be. Bishop Theophan, in his preface to the *Philokalia*, insists on the fact that without help nobody can succeed in penetrating the doctrine. This is why esoteric science conserves and cultivates an oral tradition which brings the letter to life. Oriental Orthodoxy has known how to keep this Tradition intact by applying the absolute rule of Hermetism in each particular case. From generation to generation, ever since the time of the Apostles, it has led its disciples up to mystic experience.
>
> If Hermetism has provided a safeguard for nearly twenty centuries, it must be said that circumstances have now changed. At the current point in history, as at the time of the Coming of Christ, the veil has been partially raised. Therefore, for those who want to advance beyond book knowledge, which never goes beyond the domain of information; for those who intensely seek the true sense of life, who want to understand the significance of the mission of those who labor in the vineyards of the Lord at the time of the Harvest, the possibility exists for initiation into this divine Wisdom, mysterious and hidden.
>
> Mouravieff notes that all serious esoteric teaching, as in ordinary education, is almost uniform.
>
> It is generally accepted that nobody can go on to secondary school without having completed an elementary education. Nor can a person be admitted to a university without having a secondary education. These graduations automatically "select" those able to become active members of the cultural elite of human society.
>
> Exactly the same is true in the esoteric Tradition.

However, in our modern world, we encounter a curious phenomenon. For example: we would not seek to discuss Newton's binomial theorem without having studied algebra, for without this, every opinion we expressed on the subject would be worthless.

Yet, in the esoteric field, we find a host of "experts" who declare their opinions on esotericism without having ever learned even the rudiments of this knowledge.

At the same time, some of them demand "simplicity" from esoteric teachings on the generally accepted principle that Truth itself must be simple. They conclude from this that *access to Truth* ought to likewise be simple. Then they assert that the methods to access Truth must be easily assimilable.

This argument would be perfectly correct if human beings and the problems they face were simple and just. However, that is not the case. There is a long road to travel from our state of distorted inner disorder to any "original simplicity".

In practice, the doctrine of "simplicity" - if regarded as an axiom - turns the student aside from the strait gate and the narrow way that leads to Life. Impelled by this counter-truth, he believes he stands before this door, when he is in reality - although undoubtedly in perfectly good faith - walking the wide path that leads to perdition, *ad majorem Diaboli gloriam*, of course.

The Doctrine of Simplicity, correct in itself, but wrongly interpreted, becomes a snare for hearts and minds that are already too corrupt; a danger which should be recognized and avoided.

Some people complain that the subject of the fundamentals of esotericism is not simple. Others have said that it leads to great clarity. This apparent contradiction is explained by the fact that esotericism is addressed to readers who are predisposed to esoteric culture by their nature, formation or personal experience.

Jesus said: "Beware of false prophets which come to you in sheep's clothing, but inwardly they are ravening wolves". And then he adds: "You shall know them by their fruits".

It is difficult, if not impossible, for an esoterically unevolved person to discern false prophets spontaneously. He will recognize them more easily by their "fruits", by the observable results of their works, which serve as signs. The Tradition knows and teaches a whole Science of signs.

Jesus further said: "Temptations (snares, traps set to entice to sin) are sure to come, but woe to him by or through whom they come! It would be more profitable for him if a millstone were hung around his neck and he were hurled into the sea than that he should cause to sin or be a snare..."

This warning is disturbing, but its value is real. A thief can carry off our wealth; a 'ravening wolf' can deprive us of salvation.

That 'ravening wolves' appear in sheep's clothing we shall learn from the following text, well-phrased to frighten us:

"It is not everyone that saith unto me: Lord, Lord, who shall enter into the kingdom of heaven, but he that accomplishes the will of my Father which is in Heaven. Many will say to me in that day, Lord, Lord, have we not prophesied in thy name? And in thy name have cast out devils? And in thy name done many wonderful works? And then I shall declare unto them, I never knew you: depart from Me, ye who work iniquity".

The conclusion is that neither prophecies that are fulfilled nor the occurrence of miracles give us any surety against 'ravening wolves'.

And in our own times: "There shall arise false Christs, and false prophets, and shall show great signs and wonders; insomuch that, if it were possible, they should deceive the very elect."

Our era is the time of Transition. We are in the heart of this period, which is relatively short. All the signs show that the necessary conditions for the End are emerging before our very eyes.

As expressed by Boris Mouravieff in his presentation of the Ancient Science of Ascension, only human beings of iron will, guided by a higher consciousness, or Noë, will advance into the New Heaven and New Earth, in literal terms. The coming era has Two Faces: One of Paradise Restored, the other a Deluge of Fire. We can choose which Face we behold.

Mouravieff tells us that the direction humanity chooses will depend upon the attitude of contemporary man. It is not enough to repeat, "Lord, Lord!" to enter the Ark and pass through to the New World. Everything depends on a person's work; the conscious efforts during this very time. And it is not just efforts applied in any direction, but rather very specific efforts to achieve a state of "living leaven".

"Leaven" represents a numerically small, even infinitesimal group, lost to sight, even, in a vast and teeming global population, but whose effect and influence will reach the farthest corners of the world. A Divine Revelation is not Static. The time has come when, in the esoteric domain, private research and the pursuit of individual salvation for the self must end.

As Mouravieff says, every era is an "ambience" which holds within it the solution to the problems specific to it. Man can choose his response according to the level of his understanding and Being. And so, the ambience that exists at the present time, at the end of an Epoch, opens up possibilities for man on all planes. It will also eliminate those possibilities that belong to the previous era.

It is in this present period of history that we observe an upsurge in esoteric interest much of which includes, as is usual in such eras, wide promulgation of false teachings and cunning disinformation. At the same time, the Seeker is being offered the data for the "strait gate". It is up to each individual to understand the significance of what is being offered here, and to get down to work. Many workers are needed in this time in the same way physicians are needed on the battlefield. After all, a doctor is of little use in a society of people who are in a state of robust health.

Today, and in the not-too-distant future, Esoterically Developed Teachers will be in demand in all branches of human activity. It is the purpose of *The Quantum Future School* to assist in filling this demand for teachers who can aid the individual in his or her personal spiritual processes, as well as to prepare them for the time when they will be needed, and *asked*, for their services as Spiritual Physicians.

Getting back to the process, assisted by the Cassiopaean transmissions from "myself in the future", in avoiding the trap of emotional amnesia, I began by collecting data. I had no idea what data would prove to be important, and the Cassiopaeans stressed from the beginning that it was better to assume NOTHING and just collect and sort and see what patterns emerged of themselves from the sorting process. It was rather like the preparations made to put a large, complicated jigsaw puzzle together. One begins by sorting the pieces by color into piles. At the same time, if one comes across fragments that are clearly the "border" pieces, one then puts them in an altogether different pile. Once in awhile, while sorting, serendipity brings two pieces together, and those are put in little "sub-piles". After this process is completed, it is done again in a more refined and exact way.

However, the Grail Problem has certain complications. It is like having the puzzle; only someone has hidden half or more of the pieces. Not only are we going to have difficulty getting a full outline, even if we DO assemble the pieces we have accurately, we may not be able to determine what the picture truly portrays. Add to this the fact that someone may come into the room and drop pieces into your pile that do not even belong to the puzzle!

Yes, it is that bad, if not worse.

As the reader may guess after thinking about the problem of "putting the puzzle together", the process of gathering and sorting the pieces as well as the details of the discoveries along the way was lengthy and tedious, but the conclusions arrived at were, to the mind of the present writer, nothing short of shattering. In fact, if an individual CAN fully outline ALL the steps taken to solve so complex a problem as the Grail, he or she probably doesn't have a clue!

Of course, in the broadest of terms, the Grail Quest is always personal to each and every one who is inspired to undertake it. But, in my case, I was not exactly on the track of the "Holy Grail", per se. I was simply a seeker of truth - the purest and most objective I could find. After years of collecting puzzle pieces and sorting them, I began to realize that everything became dense as it coalesced around the Grail problem. It is not just a symbol in a story about knightly quests and their performance of feats of derring-do along the way! At some point I realized that this is the Secret of Secrets; the Grand Destiny; the gnosis of the means of uniting Science, Philosophy and Religion, as well as Mind, Matter and Time.

It took me a long time to come to this realization because my nature is fundamentally skeptical. I am constitutionally incapable of taking anybody's word for anything - I have to "see for myself". If I read a quoted source in a book, I have to read the source from which the quote is taken. If that source quotes someone else, I am driven to find the original. And, if I ever finally get to the originator of an idea, I am driven to study the life and methods of that person and to discover, if possible, the observations they made which led them to a particular conclusion. This is time-consuming and tedious, no question about it; but it is the only way that satisfies me; and it has certainly borne valuable fruit in the long run. Many ideas and teachings that other seekers accept at "face value", I have long ago discarded as useless after investigating them deeply and finding they are built on foundations of lies and deception.

Skepticism, the ability not to be fooled, is important; but skepticism can also be "cheap". It is easy to disbelieve everything, and some scholars seem to take this approach. A better approach is to initially consider nothing absurd, and spend the necessary time to examine it closely and minutely. If you throw away puzzle pieces indiscriminately, you may never complete the puzzle! But, when you find the flaw, even a small one, if it is solidly established as a flaw, you must be prepared to ruthlessly kill the idea and move to another.

> Scientific training doesn't keep your senses from fooling you, but a good scientist doesn't accept the impressions his senses deliver. *He uses them as a starting point,* and then he checks, and double checks. He looks for additional evidence, and for consistency among his measurements. **A scientist differs from other people in that he knows how easily he is fooled, and he goes through procedures to compensate.** [34]

So, with each little pile of puzzle pieces, one takes up a likely starting piece and attempts to fit the others to it one by one. But, as I noted, *it may be so that the "starting piece" has been tossed into the pile to lead one astray, and will NEVER fit anything!* And it may take a long time to realize this. Many people never realize it. They trim the piece, they trim other pieces, they force and maneuver to make them fit! And then, of course, having done this, other pieces are found that do, actually, fit, and they crow with delight that they have solved the puzzle never realizing that the "keystone" they started has caused all the adjacent pieces to come together around a false center, thus the primary object has been missed... and the REAL centerpiece will be tossed aside as irrelevant.

---

[34] Muller, Richard, *Nemesis,* (University of Arizona Press 1988).

CHAPTER 2
THE CHEMISTRY OF ALCHEMY

THE LANGUAGE OF THE GODS

Here I must give a warning: gathering false knowledge is worse than gathering no knowledge at all.

Why is this?

You see: it is the PROCESS of the Quest for the Holy Grail that is the FUNCTION of "distilling the Philosopher's Stone". Fulcanelli writes:

> …Puns, plays on words associated or not with the rebus, were used by the initiates as subterfuges for their verbal conversations. In achromatic works, anagrams were reserved, sometimes to mask the identity of the author, sometimes to disguise the title, removing from the layman the directing thought of the work. It is the case in particular of a small and very curious book so cleverly *closed* that it is impossible to know what the subject of it is. It is attributed to Tiphaigne de la Roche, and it bears the unusual title of *"**Amilec ou la graine d'hommes**"*. It is an assemblage of anagrams and puns. One should read instead, *Alcimie, ou la crème d'Aum* (Alchemy, the Cream of Aum). Neophytes will learn that it is an authentic alchemical treatise, since in the 13th century alchemy was written *alkimie, alkemie,* or *alkmie*; that the point of [the] science … pertains to the *extraction of the spirit* enclosed in the material prima, a philosophical virgin, which bears the same sign as the celestial Virgin, the monogram AUM; and that finally this extraction must be accomplished using a process analogous to that which allows us to *separate cream from milk*. […] By removing the veil from the title, one can see how suggestive this one is, since *it announces the revelation of the secret means* suitable to obtain this cream of the milk from the Virgin which few researchers have had the fortune of possessing. [35]

What this rather convoluted discussion reveals to us is the CRUCIAL necessity for discerning between what one "accepts" as a piece of the puzzle and what one does not accept, and that this determines whether or not the "separation of the

---

[35] Fulcanelli, op. cit., p. 68.

cream from the milk" is being achieved. And if one accepts milk instead of cream, then the process is doomed from the start.

What is more, I am going to explain this in a way that can be easily understood by any modern person in terms of physiology.

The first thing that the seeker ought to consider is the nature of his being. He should understand from the beginning that the Hermetic Maxim, "As above, so below", has a specific application in his direct physical/material life. Just as a person is born with certain characteristics, talents and advantages (or lack of same), which he may or may NOT actualize in the course of his existence, so is a person born with a general potential for spiritual/esoteric development. In other words, the consciousness naturally incarnates in a physical structure that not only suits its needs but also its potentials. Let me give a few examples that will clarify what I am saying here.

A few years ago I read an article about an Alzheimer's disease study where a population of nuns volunteered for lifelong participation including giving their brains after death for study. Well, what did the researchers learn? They found that a number of these individuals who had brains that were literally "mush" from Alzheimer's had never exhibited any symptoms of Alzheimer's while living. Why? Because they were educated, active in their work and mental life, watched very little television, and were constantly involved in educational pursuits that expanded their knowledge base well into old age! In other words, they had never stopped thinking and learning and working with their minds!

Another Alzheimer's study was interesting in that it demonstrated that persons with "low word use density" were more likely to manifest early symptoms. People who had used their minds very little and who, therefore, had no "deep thoughts" and were, in effect, shallow, who had lived their lives based solely on "faith", were more likely to develop Alzheimer's.

So, if learning, exercising the mind, working with difficult concepts, and continuously expanding the knowledge and awareness base can have such effects as this, what else might it do?

It has often been noted that only 2% of our DNA is involved in coding the proteins that make up our bodies; the rest is referred to as "junk". There are theories about why this is so, including the "Selfish Gene" theory where it is postulated that human beings are merely constructs created by DNA for the purpose of propagating DNA!

Another thing noted is that we seem to utilize only 5 % of our brains - and there are many theories about why this is so as well. I would like to suggest that there is a connection.

In my 30 or more years of research into the paranormal, psi phenomena, "Fortean, ,and the workings of the human mind, I have often noted some odd connections. The one that occurred over and over again was a reference to psi and genetics. Time and time again a person who had "strange powers" would remark, "Oh, I inherited the sight from my aunt, or grandmother, or mother, or uncle", or whoever.

Then, there was the peculiar connection of the endocrine system to psi phenomena. Many serious studies of "poltergeist" type phenomena note that it is most often, if not always, manifested in the presence of either a pubescent child or a sexually "fluctuating" or suppressed/frustrated woman, including those who are in one or another stage of menopause.

The next curious thing was the many notations of the onset of psi phenomena after a severe trauma to the head or a strong electrical shock.

Then, there are both yogis and saints and practitioners of various "nature" religions who, after certain ecstatic practices which have been shown to have an effect on both the electric current in the body as well as the chemicals, including hormones and neurotransmitters, can levitate, heal, bi-locate, manifest apparitions for others to see, increase body heat, decrease heart-rate, slow or stop autonomic functions and so on.

One thing is clear to me after all of these years of study: psi phenomena, whether it is healing, manifestation of matter, bi-location or whatever, has almost NO relation whatsoever to one's state of spirituality. I encountered a family line that could "stop the flow of blood" with the touch of a hand, yet nearly every member was alcoholic, promiscuous, abusive to partners and children, and generally what one would consider to be ethically deficient. Yet, certain members of this line had this interesting "power" and were often called upon by neighbors and friends to save lives - even if they had to be hauled out of a bar dead drunk!

So, we have a curious series of factors to contend with that all seem to point in the direction of DNA being far more interesting and mysterious than we might have supposed. On the one hand we have such naturally transmitted "powers", and on the other hand we have folks who can engage in some activity that either temporarily or permanently changes something in their physiology - and the apparent result is psi phenomena.

All of this, of course, indicates that our DNA is possibly the "interface" between the ethereal world and the physical, thus suggesting that discovering natural methods for the production of certain chemicals or energies in the body is the key to perception. So, what are we to think? It all points to the fact that we have this huge amount of DNA that nobody knows much about which can respond to these activities - in other words, we have potentials hiding inside us, and it is the process of the Quest that "unlocks" them by virtue of which approach we take - "faith", or what Fulcanelli calls "thinking with a hammer". It is the process of separating the cream from the milk, the process of "liberating light from the darkness". And this is where it gets very tricky.

THE ANALOGY WITH BRAIN PHYSIOLOGY

The best way to explain this problem is to understand the process of ligands binding to receptors. The human brain is probably the most complex structure in the universe; in a sense, it might be thought of as a universe in itself. At birth, the infant brain contains about 100 billion nerve cells, or neurons. This number is comparable to the number of stars in the Milky Way galaxy, just to give you an idea of what we are dealing with here.

But it is not the number we want to think about just now, but what these neurons actually are doing in this microcosm of our head.

Unlike your average body cell, such as a cell in your stomach or pancreas or the fat in your "love handles", the neurons constantly carry on complex conversations with one another. Each neuron has, on the average, several thousand contacts with other cells. Some neurons can have as many as 200,000 connections.

Now, it is at the terminal of the axon that the electrical impulse is converted into a chemical, the neurotransmitter, which sort of floods the area around the "receivers", or dendrites, of the adjacent neuron. The thing that is important here is the fact that the receiver neuron has many little fibers for reception of neurotransmitter signals, BUT it can be in communication with literally thousands of other neurons. So, how does it decide which one to listen to? And why does it matter?

Well, here is where it gets interesting. Back in the early days of the 20th century, it was realized that a drug must work in the body because it can "attach" itself to something in the body. They decided to call this place of attachment a "receptor". Nobody really knew how this "attaching" worked, or why it led to a whole cascade of changes in the body, but there it was. You take a drug, and all kinds of things happened in the brain and/or other areas of the body. It is now known, after long years of research, that the receptor is actually a single molecule! Not only that, but it is singularly complicated. Keep in mind that a molecule, by definition, is the smallest possible piece of something that can still be identified as that specific substance. In order to better understand this, we need to take a brief look at the background science of this effect.

BONDING

A molecule is composed of atoms. Atoms seem to form bonds with one another in accordance with certain rules. These rules have to do with the number of electrons in the highest energy "shell" of the particular atom. An atom is what is IS by virtue of how many electrons it has, and these electrons are arranged in "shells" like the orbits of planets around the sun. The only thing is, they can't be thought of as round planetary bodies, but as a sort of "cloud" of energy. Full "shells" are particularly stable so that atoms seem to "like" to arrange themselves so that they can get their outer shells filled. Electrons also come in two "flavors", which are referred to as "up" and "down", and an "up" electron likes to pair with a "down" electron. This refers to the "spin" state of the atom. Depending upon the number of electrons in the outer shell of the atom, and how many electrons it would "like" to have in its outer shell, it can bond to one or more other atoms.

The most important atom in biology is carbon. When carbon bonds, the result has been shown by Linus Pauling to be completely symmetrical. That is, the four bonds align towards the corners of a regular tetrahedron. It was deduced that, in addition to the atom "liking" to have its outer shell filled, the electrons like to be as far apart from each other in the bonded state as possible. Carbon atoms are very "happy" to form bonds with other carbon atoms. That is the basis of the famous benzene ring structure. The benzene ring is a particularly stable molecular form because the natural angles made by the four bonding carbon orbitals comfortably fit a six-sided structure — a hexagon!

Carbohydrates, for example, are a group of substances based on the benzene ring structure. In carbohydrates, most of the carbon atoms are joined to two other carbon atoms but have each of their other two bonds used in combination with other atoms or groups; OH on one side and H on the other. Together, without the carbon in the middle, OH and H would make H_2O, or water. So, the term carbohydrate means, literally, "watered carbon".

The simpler carbohydrates, or "watered carbons", are called sugars. If the sugar is a one-ring system, it is a monosaccharide. If it is a double ring structure, it is a disaccharide. More complex sugars are polysaccharides. Glucose is a monosaccharide. Maltose is a disaccharide. A chain of glucose units can be combined to make a polysaccharide called starch. A slightly different arrangement is another familiar biological substance, cellulose.

Now, there are six carbon atoms in your basic monosaccharide. But, some Monosaccharides contain only five carbon atoms, four of which are connected to one oxygen atom in the form of a 5-sided ring. The fifth carbon atom is part of a side group, CH_2OH. These compounds are called pentose. One of them, exactly like glucose except for the missing carbon atom and its associated side groups, is called ribose. Another, similar to ribose except that one of its OH groups has lost the oxygen atom, leaving a simple CH bond behind, is called deoxy-ribose. This means that it is a "ribose" with one less oxygen atom.

In the discussion of bonding, please note the significance of these numbers and geometric shapes while keeping in mind all of the "mystical terms" in the world of metaphysics that somehow never manage to make much sense; and now we are beginning to look at these things and realize that such numbers may have a very deep meaning, though not in the ritual and magical sense. We are getting an idea that, perhaps, all the myths and so-called "secrets" that are veiled so heavily in analogy and allegory, may just be real science. As Jessie Weston said, we may be dealing with the "*disjecta membra* of a vanished civilization". Even if it is not garbled information from some ancient peoples who were technically more advanced than we are, it could be information from legitimate "higher sources" that has been hidden in allusion and mystery. It may be that all the hoo-doo stuff that has been passed down to us is just the mythicization of significant scientific information. If that is the case, we need to peel off all of the ritual, the religious nonsense, and the woo-woo stuff, and get down to business and discover this "science of the soul" in real terms.

RECEPTORS

The essential thing to know here is this: the resulting molecules that are brought together in these chemical bonding processes have a particular SHAPE. The carbon bonds have plenty of flexibility, allowing bending, and there can be tangling and doubling back and forth to form very complex and *very specific shapes*. This bending and tangling brings different atoms of one side group into contact with others, providing all kinds of opportunities for complex bonding. The natural angle between the carbon bonds also makes the benzene ring shape particularly favored, and in a long carbon chain, the same natural angle can make the chain tend to loop round and round on itself. In such a case, however, the carbon atoms are not joined to close the ring, but can continue the polymer chain like the coils of a snake.

Getting back to the single molecule receptors on cells, we can understand from the bonding principles that these receptors have very particular shapes — as well as "shells wanting to be filled" that define precisely what other molecule will be attracted to them for bonding. We can understand that there are atomic forces which cause one molecule to be attracted to another. Receptor molecules on the cell respond to these energies by, "wiggling, shimmying, vibrating and even humming as they shift back and forth from one favored shape to another". Receptors are attached to a cell, "floating" on its surface, like a *lotus flower* on the surface of a pond, with roots extending into the interior of the cell.

There are many types of receptors on the surface of the cell, and if they were color coded, the cell surface would look like a wild mosaic made up of at least 70 different colors. The numbers of "tiles" in the mosaic are staggering — 50,000 of one kind, 10,000 of another, 100,000 of still another, and on and on. A typical neuron can have millions of receptors on its surface.

Another interesting analogy that scientists use to describe neurons and receptors is that they are like a "tree with buds". In fact, the visual correspondence is so striking that the terms used by scientists for the growth of neurons include "branching" and "arborization". Using this analogy, the bark of the tree is analogous to the neuronal cell membrane, the "skin" of the cell. However, unlike the bark of a tree, which is hard and static, the cell membrane is a fatty, flexible boundary that keeps the cell as an entity.

Tree of Life, anyone?

LIGANDS

Now, what do these receptors do? Well, we already know that they "attract" other molecules and respond to the atomic/chemical forces of various kinds of bonds, but what is important is that receptors function as sensing molecules — scanners — just as our eyes, ears, nose, tongue, fingers, and skin act as bodily sense organs, the receptors do this on a cellular level. They cover the membranes of your cells waiting to pick up and convey information from their environment that consists of a reality flooded with other vibrating amino acids, which come cruising along, diffusing through the fluids surrounding each cell. Researchers describe receptors as "keyholes", although these keyholes are constantly moving and dancing in a rhythmic, vibratory way. The keyholes are waiting for the right chemical keys, ligands, to swim up to them through the extra-cellular fluid and to mount them by fitting into their keyholes, a process known as binding.

When the ligand, the chemical key, binds to the receptor, entering it like a key in a keyhole, it creates a response that causes a rearrangement, a changing of shape, until INFORMATION enters the cell.

In a certain sense, a ligand is the cellular equivalent of a phallus! *Ligand* comes from the Latin "ligare", or that which binds. The same word is also the root of "religion". Curious, yes?

A more dynamic description of this very miniscule process would be that relating to "frequency". The ligand and the receptor combine their identical frequencies — striking the same note, so to say — which produces a sufficiently strong vibration that more or less "rings the doorbell" to cause the doorway of the cell to open and there is some sort of exchange of atomic potentials that constitute the "information" that is "sent into the cell". What happens next is quite amazing. The receptor, having received a message, transmits it from the surface of the cell deep into the cell's interior, where the message can change the state of the cell dramatically. A chain reaction of biochemical events is initiated as tiny cellular machines go into action and, depending on the message of the ligand, begin any number of activities — manufacturing new proteins, making decisions about cell division, opening or closing ion channels, adding or subtracting energetic chemical groups like the phosphates — to name just a few. In short, whatever a given cell is up to at any moment, is determined by which receptors are on its surface, and whether those receptors are occupied by ligands or not. On a larger scale, these tiny physiological phenomena at the cell level can translate to major changes in behavior, physical activity, even mood — and ABILITY.

So, to review: as the ligands drift by in the stream of fluid surrounding every cell, only those ligands that have molecules in exactly the right shape can bind to a particular kind of receptor. The process of binding is very selective and specific! Researchers in the field say that, "binding occurs as a result of receptor specificity, meaning the receptor ignores all but the particular ligand that's made to fit it". In other words, the cell is the engine that drives all life, and the receptors are the buttons on the control panel of that engine. The ligands or other neurotransmitters, known as peptides, are the fingers that push the buttons. The "musical hum of the receptors as they bind to their many ligands, often in the far-flung parts of the organism, creates an integration of structure and function that allows the organism to run smoothly and in "alignment" with the function of the specific ligands that are binding. Can we say AUM?

Referring to receptors and ligands, let's apply our "as above, so below" principle to these ideas. The information that we receive into our organism as a whole — our interaction with our environment — seems to operate on exactly the same principle. Information that "enters" the "cell" of our mental-body acts on us in the same way as a ligand acts on the cell when it binds to the receptor. The mind, our spirit receptor, having received information, transmits it deep into the interior of our consciousness, where the message can change the state of awareness dramatically. A chain reaction of psycho-spiritual events is initiated as the consciousness realigns itself based on the information received. This realignment then affects the entire self, the reality, and all support systems of the consciousness involved. In short, your BEing is determined by your state of awareness which is a function of your knowledge which depends on what "ligands" — or information units — are "bound" to your spirit, so to say. And just as ligands can produce cascades of cellular events with far reaching effects, so can your state of Being change because increased awareness can initiate major changes in your reality — the larger "body" in which you "live" as a "cell" of All that is.

SPIRITUAL DRUGS

Remember what we started with here: chemists came up with the idea that drugs worked in the body by attaching themselves to something in the body. Now we know about receptors and that they are receptive to chemicals manufactured by the body itself. Ligands, peptides, neurotransmitters, hormones, etc, are produced in the body and BY the body in certain "steps" that involve very complex processes.

And here is where we come to the DANGER part.

You see, there are chemicals, both natural and synthetic, that are sufficiently similar to the body's own ligands to bind with the receptors without producing all of the same results that are produced when the body secretes its own ligands in the natural steps. The opiate receptor, for instance, can "receive" not only the body's endorphins, but can also bind to morphine, or heroin. The Valium receptor can attach not only to Valium-like peptides produced in the body, but also to Valium.

Remember, "no drug can act unless fixed". This means that if a drug works, it is because there is a receptor for it in the body. This, then, suggests that the receptor is there because it binds to a ligand produced by the body itself, which suggests that the body *can* produce its own drugs, stimulating its own healing, under the proper circumstances.

Looking in another direction, when we consider drugs that change "behavior", such as heroin, marijuana, Librium, "angel dust", or PCP, and so on, which precipitate radical changes in emotional states, these must also be able to bind because there are receptors for similar substances produced by the body. LSD and other hallucinogens, which produce changes in cognition, must also do so because there are receptors specific to them; suggesting again that such chemicals may, under proper circumstances, be produced by the body itself. This suggests to us that there may be natural steps to, or processes served by, such chemicals. And here we approach a very significant problem where, again, we may take the "as above, so below" approach to understanding our own natures.

ALCOHOL AND CAFFEINE

Alcohol.

Alcohol is everywhere. Tens of millions of human beings experience the consequences of alcohol addiction, from decreased job performance to liver damage, spouse and child abuse, to total breakdown of social concepts and constraints ending in the proverbial "skid-row bum" looking every day for his MD 20-20 - or even a can of Sterno.

That is just alcohol. We aren't even going to list the details for other drugs as it would be tedious and pointless. You have the idea.

Alcohol and other drugs have the ability to do what they do in our systems because they are "fixed"; they are *synthetic ligands*; they bind to our receptors and, in various ways, produce their effects.

In order to get an idea of how these fake ligands actually work, let's take a look at caffeine. As our neurons process information, they produce cellular waste including a buildup of molecules of adenosine. Adenosine is a ligand that binds with the adenosine receptor sending a message deep into the cell that it is time to sleep. You could say that adenosine is a sort of "warning system" that helps keep the body balanced. As the production of adenosine continues throughout the day, as a byproduct of cerebral activity, more and more adenosine is produced, binding with more and more receptors, sending more and more sleep messages into more cells. Little by little our brain cells become more and more sluggish until we just simply must go to sleep. We literally can't remain conscious. We yawn; our eyes water and try to close, and we just want to curl up and let the lights go out.

Or, we have a cup of espresso.

The caffeine molecule just happens to be the right "shape" for the adenosine receptor. It hops on and binds. But, instead of doing what the adenosine does, it sends a different message or, at the very least, blocks the sleep message from being sent by the real adenosine. In short, it interrupts the natural sleep signal, allowing a lot more cellular waste to accumulate, putting the individual in a state of toxicity, which can eventually lead to a breakdown of health.

In general, this seems to be the worst thing that caffeine does - it simply blocks the action of the ligand adenosine which sends sleep messages. Many people have been scared by incomplete research suggesting that caffeine does other deadly things, but additional studies have suggested that any consequences result merely from the disruption of the sleep cycle and a consequent break-down in the serotonin-melatonin cycle.

The important thing about this is, however, the comparison to information that is or is not accepted by the seeker which we will address more directly at the end of this volume. What we see in the example of caffeine as an "imitator" of adenosine is that the natural ligand seems to have some very subtle property that is conveyed deep into the cell, and the caffeine either blocks this message by occupying the receptor, or perhaps sends a contradictory message. Because of the exactitude of the molecule, adenosine apparently does more than the "almost ligand", caffeine.

Now, if we think of information as ligands, we can see that accepting as true something that is not, may not only block our ability to receive the proper messages of what IS true, it may even send contradictory messages. Spiritual experiences that are "induced" ritually, chemically or technically from "down here" in order to change the spiritual state "up there", operate in exactly this way. It seems that what we accept as true or not affects our spirit and state of awareness, not to mention our potentials for soul ascension. We could even compare certain "all is love and light" beliefs to the action of caffeine: they prevent the natural warning system from operating which tells the spirit when it needs to withdraw from certain things and allow a period of "cleansing" to take place. Over time, this can result in serious breakdown of the spirit, even - it seems - ultimate subsumation into Non-being. There is, however, a more serious problem we have to deal with: addiction.

PLEASURE CENTERS AND DRUGS

Probably everyone has heard about some experiments that were done on rats where they were implanted with electrodes for self-stimulation of the "pleasure center" of the brain. What was discovered was that the rats would push the button until they were exhausted. Further experiments demonstrated that if the electric reward is doled out only when the rats learn a new trick - such as navigating a maze - the little critters will go to work like crazy to get the job done so that they can get their "buzz". As long as the rewards keep coming, the rats will keep working - even mastering incredibly complex and seemingly impossible mazes that humans would find nearly impossible!

But, it's not the learning they love.

The initial studies showed that, given the opportunity, the rats would forget everything - food, mates, and friends, whatever - to push that damn button until they collapse in mindless ecstasy!

In the human being, as in other creatures, the sensation that is experienced as orgasm is the same release of chemicals that stimulate the same part of the brain that makes the rats so happy. Some scientists refer to this in "technical jargon" as the "do-it-again" center.[36] When this center is stimulated, whatever activity is associated with it will be sought again and again.

As we now know, drugs "short circuit" these centers because they "fix" to receptors. We also know that when we take certain drugs, our brain acts to a certain extent as if the "natural" neurotransmitter were flooding the system. In the case of the pleasure center, the chemistry is so similar to what the brain would produce naturally if we had done something really great such as finding food or warmth or making love with a soul mate, that even if the person is hunkered down in a filthy flophouse reeking of vomit and excreta, with a hypodermic of heroin in his or her arm, the pleasure centers know only that they are bathed in chemical bliss.

Here is an important thing to consider. Even if the first time a person is induced to "try" such a drug, they are disgusted or repelled by the setting, the process, all the external elements, once they have received that reward, their whole perception begins to shift. Because the physical body loves that feeling so much, because it is so overwhelmingly compelling, the mind begins to rationalize that the nasty setting, the whole process that is clearly damaging to the self, is not merely "okay", but is actually "desirable". After all, how could it be bad if it feels so good? If part of the self argues that it can't be good, another part of the self becomes literally frantic to achieve the state again. After all, what is going on in real life only produces "stress" and "bad feelings" which add the argument: you have suffered, now you deserve a reward!

The only problem with both drug addiction and spiritual addiction is that it is nearly always presented in a setting of pleasure and refinement. It is promoted as a "tool" to "enhance awareness".

When cocaine is snorted up the nose, it heads straight for the dopamine re-uptake sites and *blocks* them. In this case, the "feel good sensation" is not from the drug, but from the fact that your own natural dopamine is flooding your cells, binding with the dopamine receptors like crazy, unable to be reabsorbed. The brain only knows one thing: this feels GREAT! Crack cocaine reportedly produces a more intense sensation of pleasure than any natural act, including orgasm! And, take note that it is from the body's *own* chemical that this pleasure is experienced

---

[36] Burnham and Phelan, *Mean Genes*, (Cambridge, Massachusetts: Perseus Publishing 2000).

by virtue of the blocking of the re-uptake site. Again, we note that this prevents the body's own specific ligand from binding with the re-uptake sites which is very likely also blocking a message intended to go deep into the cell. As it happens, this produces dreadful consequences, as we will soon see.

Morphine and Heroin work in a slightly different way. They mimic endorphins which trigger the release of the body's own dopamine. So, instead of the sensation occurring because the natural flow of dopamine is not reabsorbed, it occurs because there is too much dopamine to be reabsorbed! But again, the fake endorphin is undoubtedly not sending the proper signal deep into the cells it is binding, and again, the excess of dopamine has significant consequences.

What are these consequences? With repeated use of cocaine, heroin or morphine unbalancing the body's own dopamine processes, the body reacts by *reducing the number of receptors!* With fewer receptors, the effects of the drug - *as well as the body's normal ability to bind dopamine that is naturally present* - plummets. Without the normal flow of dopamine into a normal number of receptors, the brain experiences "withdrawal" which is interpreted quite literally as "pain". It is the agony of a mind that can feel no pleasure at all.

In strictly physical terms, one of the serious consequences of this process comes from the fact that dopamine plays an important role in controlling movement, emotion and cognition. Dopamine dysfunction has been implicated in schizophrenia, mood disorders, attention-deficit disorder, Tourette's syndrome, substance dependency, tardive dyskinesia, Parkinson's disease and so on. Of course, the situation is a lot more complex because at least seven types of dopamine receptors have been identified.

Now, the point of this diversion into brain chemistry as an exercise in understanding the principle "as above, so below", is this: "accepting" what is not Truth is like taking a drug that binds to psychic receptors, so to say. So, this brings us back to the beginning of this section where I said "gathering false knowledge is worse than gathering no knowledge at all". False knowledge, lies, are spiritual drugs and are not the "natural chemical" of the soul's own "light", so to say. The result is that it tends to create a condition of dependence by reducing the "psychic receptors" which then reduces the capacity to "bind truth". In short, a person may be researching like crazy, but if he or she isn't really, really utilizing perspicacity — that is, challenging and taking apart what is being studied in a diligent way — his or her acceptance based on "blind faith" amounts to getting your jollies with drugs.

The end result is analogous to the skid row bum in spiritual terms.

What is more, we notice from studying ligands and receptors, that the body's own chemicals have qualities that the imitations — drugs — do not. Those qualities, based on shape and atomic structure, can activate processes that the synthetic ligand cannot. The body's chemical can even turn on cascades of processes within the cells that are blocked by the "artificial" ligand.

Truth works in the same way. The accumulation of "high probability" information without prejudice amounts to the gathering of all the parts of a very complex neuropeptide. When all the right pieces are finally together, it produces a certain "shape" that "fits" the spiritual receptor like a key in a lock. At that point — when the information block/unit is complete — it's proximity causes the receptor to "hum" and the ligand/info "hums" back and they sort of "jump together" almost like the description of physical ligands and receptors. AUM.

And so we find that the principle is this: to gather, gather, gather information and observations without any "ingestion", so to say. This most definitely means to avoid practices which may produce the "do it again" chemicals because it is all too easy to be seduced into doing it again and again which amounts to blind belief.

Here, of course, we come up against a very special problem: the programs of our "machine", our "intellect". The formation and training of our intellect is done under circumstances that are the worst possible for developing the ability to think. Now is neither the time nor the place to go into a lengthy examination about what is wrong with childhood education, theories of infant care, and the endless lies propagated by our society and culture. Add to that an endless stream of considerations based on physical appearance, and by the time the ordinary person becomes an adult, he can neither think nor feel according to what is Truth. He has become a "false personality" that thinks it has a soul. "Like can only be understood and grasped by like", so it is no wonder that the modern day seeker of ascension goes about it in the wrong way. Nearly all "paths" of ascension appeal to this false self and, as we might guess, produce physical sensations that are imitations of what occurs in the process of true ascension.

It is at this point that we begin to understand the idea of esotericism better. Esotericism is the accessing of facts and actions that are accessible to the field of consciousness of the Soul. When we consider our state in the "real world", we find that this is a very difficult path.

Knowledge is everywhere, but most of it is external to us. When we pour something into a cup, it can only contain an amount equal to its capacity. We are only able to understand according to the capacity of our Being. To be able to evolve esoterically, we must constantly seek to enlarge and enhance our Being, to develop the "vessel".

Esotericism seeks to develop consciousness of the Divine. The problem is that our consciousness is, for the most part, simply a program that runs in our machine. The higher consciousness that is sought in terms of ascension is the real "I" or the soul; it is the theorized permanent point that exists within us throughout many incarnations. This real "I" is something like an impartial referee whose small voice is mostly obscured in the roar of external events and personality programs. Nevertheless, it is this tiny spark of the real self that is the seed of the possibility of esoteric development.

Most human beings rarely - if ever - experience contact with the real "I". Yet, the personality pretends that it has achieved this level of consciousness. We should note that an individual who has actually reached such a level of firm contact and expansion of the real "I" will also possess attributes such as the ability to accurately judge the consequences of his or her actions, the constant exercise of his own will, an ability to do - to initiate acausal events - as well as a bearing or attitude that is consistent with itself in all situations and conditions. Most of all, such a person does not lie to himself.

An objective examination of many of those who claim such qualities is sufficient to demolish such pretensions. There is so vast a chasm between the qualities that people ascribe to themselves, and what they can really DO, that careful consideration of this point ought to be undertaken before one attaches belief to any such claims or any such teacher.

Nevertheless, to establish contact with the higher self, for lack of a better term, this very small seed of the soul connection that exists within us is the object of esoteric science. It seems that the only people who have a real hope of accomplishing this process are those who are "bankrupted". In other words, all the beliefs, all the programs, all the lies that have been part of the self from childhood, must collapse or be stripped away.

We are all corrupted by the exterior world of matter - the domain of Non-being and its gravitational lures. Even when experience contradicts what a person believes about him or herself, they are seldom able to make the cause and effect connection because of the serious deficiencies that are programmed into us from birth.

We generally explain our failures as "lack of will". What people do not realize is that failure is not generally due to a lack of will or desire, but to a lack of BEING. It is only with the development of BEING that we begin to understand the knowledge we have acquired. Only then, with understanding combined with BEING, do we have the ability to Do.

Our personality is the interface between our body and spirit. Because of the nature of our reality, the personality is mostly "programs" of the flesh, or genetic body so to say. The Machine runs on the "do it again principle". Most contemporary human beings are far more concerned about "appearances" or "experiences" that give them a buzz than they are about their Being.

The intimate relationship of the personality to the physical body and its interactive programs is little understood, yet it is crucial to development of the "I" that is more than a "ghost in the machine". We can note that when the average person experiences serious pain, all of their noble instincts fly out the window. Some people, of course, have the ability to master pain and to work on no matter what. They are considered to be heroic, and it is certainly a similar nature that succeeds in esoteric work. It is not a path for the weak.

The interdependence of the personality and the body - the machine which we have to operate with in this reality - leads us to the logical conclusion that it is this very machine and its programs that are most important for us to study in order to learn perspicacity, to learn to distinguish between the real and the false.

It is at this point that we begin to learn about the "tolerances" of our machine. We begin to discover that we spend most of our time swinging between action and reaction with no real input of the true "I". We discover that we have an ideal image of ourselves that has very little foundation in actual fact or "results". However, we cover all of this up by "faith" in our ideal image and our lies that we ARE that illusory self.

We come back to the fact that we attribute to ourselves qualities that we do not possess because if we possessed them, our lives would exactly mirror our image of ourselves. Our lies about what is really happening in our lives are what we use to "patch up" our egos with rationalizations and justifications, all of which conceal from us the fact that we cannot really DO anything because we have no Being.

Generally, to avoid facing the pain of this realization, people will take drugs of both the chemical and spiritual variety. It is only a matter of type and degree.

An individual who has undertaken the process of developing perspicacity in terms of the self, once he has learned to discern between his lies to himself and what is true about himself, can then begin to extend this ability to external knowledge. At that point, the information and observations he or she has been collecting without prejudice will make a "knowledge unit-ligand". When that happens, when a "piece of the puzzle" finally jumps into the right slot of understanding, THEN a whole cascade of things begins to happen just as it happens in the body when a ligand binds receptors.

And at that point, the *state* changes. And this leads us to the most exciting information about this "separating the milk from the cream" process.

As it happens, sometimes the information communicated to the interior of the cell by the ligands involves instructions to turn specific genes in the cell on or off! The same gene in different environments can produce many variations on a given trait and influence the expression of other genes. What is more, it is a scientific fact that changes in thoughts and behavior are reflected in changes in the synapses.

It has been shown that Electric potentials release serotonin onto the synaptic terminals, and there is sufficient anecdotal evidence about electrical shocks producing changes in an individual that result in manifestation of "super-normal abilities" as we have already described, that we must stop and consider this question. As we have also noted, having had such abilities "turned on" by either the accident of genetics, an electrical shock, or a blow to the head, does not necessarily relate to the individual being spiritually advanced. What we can surmise from this item of information is that the serotonin released as a result of electric shock must somehow "skip a step" in a potentially natural process of DNA activation, that is potential in all of us to one extent or another.

In other words, is there a natural process whereby serotonin is released in large quantities in concert with other ligands which can literally turn on DNA that activates a full range of "paranormal" abilities and that also are directly related to one's spiritual maturity?

There are far more exciting considerations about DNA potentials, but, for the moment, we will leave the subject with the warning that failing to properly "separate" the cream from the milk means that the Seeker will not even get to the point where he can skim the cream off and utilize it. What is even worse, "binding" oneself to that which is false may produce temporary "feel good" results, but in the long run, it not only blocks the possibility of binding Truth, it perpetuates itself by reducing the ability to perceive/bind with truth at ALL. Every single choice to accept something as Truth, to make a "leap of assumption", is a psychic ligand binding to a spiritual receptor. If what is believed is a lie, it is equivalent, in the brain, to a "false" ligand, like heroin. After awhile, there is no longer anywhere for Truth to bind or seat, and the condition of the Seeker is worse than before he began his quest in the same way an individual who has become a skid-row bum by his use of alcohol and/or drugs was far better off before he began his descent into addiction. The fact is: lies ARE addicting. They are made that way on purpose.

However, in terms of the Quest for the Holy Grail, as in the Alchemical pursuit of the Philosopher's Stone, just as it is in the case of the body potentials, when certain natural (spiritual) ligands are produced by sending signals into the cell to activate "sleeping DNA", abilities can be unlocked, including even psychic abilities and powers. And these psychic abilities then put the Seeker on an entirely different level. He has made, effectively, a Quantum Jump in terms of his State of Awareness.

We learn from one Initiate the following:

> "The organs which carry and radiate the creative force can only manifest it in a perfect union — a perfect marriage — between the divine and material frequencies. This conductor of force charged with the divine frequency is the 'Ark of the Covenant'."[37]

There is certainly more to it than that, but for the moment, it is sufficient to know that the principle, "As above, so below", is manifested on all planes, and scientific knowledge can most definitely contribute to spiritual understanding. As the Cassiopaeans have said: "Science is most spiritual indeed!" Regarding the gathering of knowledge, the Cassiopaeans have said:

> "Subtle answers that require effort to dissect promote intensified learning. Learning is an exploration followed by the affirmation of knowing through discovery. Learning is necessary for progress of soul... this is how you are building your power center. Patience serves the questor of hidden knowledge. Search your 'files'".

Georges Gurdjieff discussed this matter of "ligands of the soul" in terms of "impressions". He noted that Impressions are a kind of "food".

> With every external impression, whether it takes the form of sound, or vision, or smell, we receive from the outside a certain amount of energy, a certain number of vibrations. For its normal existence the organism must receive all three kinds of food, that is, physical food, air, and impressions... But the relation of these foods to one another and their significance for the organism is not the same. [...] The flow of impressions coming to us from the outside is like a driving belt communicating motion to us. [...] Nature transmits to us through our impressions the energy by which we live and move and have our being. [38]

Gurdjieff then goes on to talk about "self-observation" as the means by which greater energy is extracted from "impressions". This is where Mouravieff's work is most helpful in explicating exactly what needs to be done. He discusses Impressions in terms of "A" and "B" influences and the Three Forces of Creation, writing as follows:

> The three fundamental conditions of Creation manifest in the Universe in the form of three basic principles of life: the static, dynamic and neutralizing principles.

---

[37] cf. Elisabeth Haich.

[38] Gurdjieff, quoted by Ouspensky: *In Search of the Miraculous*, pp.181.

Anything in creation can be analysed and studied in the light of these three principles, which appear in a way analogous to that described while talking about the conditions of creation of the World. They apply uniformly to all levels of the Cosmos. The classical example which the esoteric schools give to represent the play of the three forces is bread. To make bread we must have flour, fire and water. In this example, flour is the conductor of the passive force, fire of the active force, and water of the neutralizing force.

Here we must make it clear immediately that the substance which serves in one case as conductor for the passive force, may in other cases be the conductor.[...]

If the junction of the forces remains sterile, this means that in the esoteric sense their co-operation was not complete. The fault could arise from one of the three forces, from two of them, or even from all three. Analysis in the light of the law in question can greatly assist in determining the one or many causes of failure. For example, with the same good flour, the bread can be bad or inedible if we have added too much water - or not enough - or if the flame was weak or too high.[...]

This [analogy] allows us to grasp the sense and effect of a subsidiary law of the *Law of Three.* We see that with the same flour - the passive force in our example - we can experience failure due to a defective sharing of the active force (Fire), of the neutralizing force (Water), or of the two together. [...] The passive force contains all the *possibilities* for creating the phenomenon, while the active force intervenes as the *realizer,* and the neutralizing force as the *regulator,* of the relations between the two other forces, determining the dosage for both in an optimal way. This explains and justifies the fact that pre-eminence in the phenomenal world is attributed to the *passive force.*

Let us note here that this pre-eminence is a direct result of conditions at the first Creation. To pass or cross from the non-manifested state - a *mono polar* one, concentrated on the unique consciousness of *Self* within which the Divinity remains before the Creation of the World - the first *Idea* which makes the Divinity come out of the state of non-manifestation to become manifest, is necessarily that of the *You.* This idea, conceived by the divine sacrifice of Self-limitation, has Love, a neutralizing force, for third force.[...]

Thus, from the beginning of Creation, the divine existence becomes bipolar, Love being the neutralizing force which sustains relations between the universal *'I'* and the universal *'You' [...]*

When a substance serves as a conductor for the *passive force,* we call it *Oxygen* (0); when it serves as a conductor for the *active force* we call it *Carbon* (C) ; when it serves as a conductor for the *neutralizing force* we call it *Nitrogen* (Azot) *(N).* When considered independently from the forces of which it is the conductor, the substance is called *Hydrogen (H). [...]*

We know that the structure of the lower intellectual centre is bipolar. This structure is perfectly adapted to that of what in the orthodox Tradition is called the 'World'. This 'World' consists in ensemble of the 'A' influences [...]. It is the world in which we live, which appears to the human Personality as the only reality, but is in fact relative or even illusory. [...]as we have already stated, all the 'A' [influences] have counterparts which neutralize them - ['B' influences]. This symbolizes the creation of the world, starting from *Zero,* by division into two groups of forces, equal in power and diametrically opposed in direction.

The bipolar structure of the intelligence, an exact counterpart of the structure of the 'World', allows man to study and recognize all the 'A' influences, to orient himself in their immediate and furthest field of action, to apply his abilities to it in order to search, calculate, combine, intervene, act and even to create within the limits of the field of action of these influences.

We know, however, that this 'World' is, in fact, illusory; that the 'B' influences represent the only imperishable reality in life. Has not Jesus said: *'Lay not up for yourselves treasures upon the earth, where rust and worms consume, and where thieves break through walls and steal. But lay up for your selves treasures in heaven, where neither moth nor rust doth consume and where thieves do not break through walls nor steal.'*

It is well understood that it is a question here of two worlds which interpenetrate each other: the world constituted by the ensemble of 'A' influences- 'earth'; and the esoteric world –'heaven', formed by the 'B' influences.

By studying the play of the three forces attentively, the searcher will train himself to recognize the action of the 'A' and 'B' influences, and distinguish between them. This is one of the essential elements of that re-education of which we spoke earlier. [...]

It is by absorbing 'B' influences - divine influences from a higher level, which are consequently more powerful - and by putting full trust in them, as well as by giving proofs of capacity and devotion, that we shall be liberated from the dominion of these 'A' influences -which are ruled by the *General Law,* assisted by the *Law of Accident.*

He whose efforts are crowned with success -who attains higher levels of *being-is* immediately utilized to share in the management and growth of a given level of the lower forces of the Cosmos.

In general he will have to accomplish - as a mission - a task in the domain of the 'A' influences. Above all, this work will require study of the bipolar world. Intelligence is the only tool we possess with which to achieve this end. This is its real reason for being, as well as the reason why its structure exactly reflects the world of the 'A' influences. This instrument thus allows man, in accordance with Plato's principle, to grasp and know the *similar by the similar.*

Knowing this, the student of esoteric science must guard against falling into the extremes expressed in some teachings; he must neither despise nor neglect his intellectual faculties. The intelligence must be developed and sharpened up to the limit of what is possible, and thought must become sharp as the point of a needle. But it must not be forgotten that the Personality, in spite of its complex structure and its many abilities, is nothing but an instrument, whose functioning remains purely mechanical. It is for this reason that in esoteric matters it does not know, and will never know anything with certainty. By its nature agnostic, and concerned with phenomena, it is limited by form and function to three dimensions. It is incapable of exceeding these boundaries, but sincerely takes the world of influences as the only reality.[39]

I would like to try to shed some light on the subject of the Three Forces and Impressions and 'A' and 'B' influences that so exercised Gurdjieff and Mouravieff, but this will require a little bit of background first.

We begin with the question: who were the Celts? We are taught almost nothing about them in school, though they seem to be considered as the ancestors of most Europeans, thus also Americans. Why is it that the religion and culture of the Mesopotamian region dominates our lives and our culture when it is, in effect, "foreign"?

Celtic vernacular literature, including myths, stories and poems, in its written form, dates mainly from the Middle Ages. It is based on oral transmission that goes far beyond the Christian Era. It is very difficult to get a clear picture of the pre-Christian Celts from the transmitted texts, not only because of the typical mixture of myth and reality, and the lapse of time, but also because the Roman empire sought to stamp it out starting with Caesar and continuing with the Roman church.

However, studying what is available closely, one gets the impression of a dynamic, somewhat undisciplined people. The Celts were proud, imaginative, artistic, lovers of freedom and adventure, eloquence, poetry, and the arts. You can always discern the Celtic influence by the great artistic talents of these peoples.

The Celts were VERY suspicious of any kind of centralized "authority", and this is, in the end, what brought about their downfall. They could not stand against the hierarchical war machine of the Roman empire. In a sense, you could almost say that this is how Hitler nearly conquered Europe, most especially France. Gauls take the principles of liberty and equality VERY seriously - right down to the common man on the street who in no way considers himself inferior to the Prime Minister.

One of the principal historians of the Roman era, Julius Caesar, tells us that the Celts were ruled by the Druids. The druids "held all knowledge". The Druids were charged with ALL intellectual activities, and were not restricted to religion, per se, which suggests to us that "religion" and "knowledge", in a more or less scientific approach, were considered essential to one another - symbiotic.

It is later writers who began to vilify the Celts by accusing them of the usual things that people get accused of when someone wants to demonize them: human sacrifice, homosexuality, and so on. Most of that nonsense goes back to Posidonius, who has been quoted as an "authority" by every other "authority" on

---

[39] Mouravieff, Boris, *Gnosis*, Vol. I, excerpts from chapter VI and IX

the Celts since. Unfortunately, when one checks Posidonius, one finds that he really didn't have a clue and was probably making stuff up to fulfill an agenda.

The lack of written texts by the Celts has been the greatest problem for historians and students of the Celts. A lot of ideas are "supposed", or ancient sources with agendas have been relied on, and some of them even propose that there was a "taboo" by the Celts on putting things into writing.

Well, I suppose that, if our civilization came to an end and all our records on magnetic media were destroyed, people might say that we didn't put anything in writing either.

There has been a lot of nonsense written about WHY the Celts didn't write things down, and the most nonsensical, considering what we do know about their culture, is that this was how the Druids "kept their power" or that they believed something silly like: "if the sacred myths were revealed, they would become profaned and thus lose their mystic virtues".

What Caesar said was that the reason for the ban on writing was that the Druids were concerned that their pupils *should not neglect the training of their memories*, i.e. the Frontal Cortex, by relying on written texts. We have discussed the production of ligands and their potential for unlocking DNA . It seems to be very interesting that the very things that we have learned from the Cassiopaeans, from alchemical texts, from our own experiences, and from research - that "thinking with a hammer" is the key to transformation - was noted as *an integral part of the Druidic initiation.*

It is worth noting that, in the nineteenth century, it was observed that the illiterate Yugoslav bards, who were able to recite interminable poems, actually lost their ability to memorize once they had learned to rely on reading and writing.

Although the Druids prohibited certain things from being written down, it's clear that they DID write. Celtic writings in Ogamic script have been found on many ancient stones. Caesar tells us that the Celts were using the Greek alphabet when the Romans arrived in Gaul in the first century BC.

However, the knowledge of the initiates was transmitted entirely orally, and with the information about ligands and receptors, we are beginning to understand WHY.

The destruction of Celtic culture was so complete that we know very little about their religion. We do know that they celebrated their "rites" in forests and by lakes without erecting any covered temples or statues of divinities. Tacitus tells us:

> They do not think it in keeping with the divine majesty to confine gods within
> walls, or to portray them in the likeness of any human countenance. Their holy
> places are woods and groves and they apply the names of deities to that hidden
> presence which is seen only by the eyes of reverence.

Plato had doubts about the Greek origins of Homer's work because not only do the physical descriptions in his poems not correspond to the Greek world, but also the Homeric philosophy is very different from the mainstream Greek philosophy we know about today. The latter is based on the dualism of two opposing elements, thesis/antithesis, good/evil, life/death, body/soul, etc. omitting the idea of the Third Force.

Since Plato's times, many have sought to derive "synthesis" from these opposing elements, with little success. The "third force" of Gurdjieff has been brought up many times with little satisfaction in the attempts to understand it, and perhaps it is in what we can derive from the Celtic teachings will help us here.

According to Homer, the philosophy of the ancient world was that there was a third element that linked the opposing elements. Between the body and the soul, there is the spirit. Between life and death there is the transformation that is possible to the individual, between father and mother there is the child who takes the characteristics of both father and mother, and between good and evil there is the SPECIFIC SITUATION that determines which is which and what ought to be done.

In other words, there are three simultaneous determinants in any situation that make it impossible to say that any list of things is "good" or "evil" intrinsically, and that the true determinant is the situation.

In any event, the symbol of this philosophy is the triskele, representing three waves joined together.

The simultaneous existence of the third element does not mean that the notion of "good" and "evil" did not exist or was not reflected in the Celtic law. What was clear was that it was understood that nothing could be "cut and dried" in terms of law, that each situation was unique and the circumstances had to be carefully weighed.

Aristotle considered Gaul to be the "teacher" of Greece and the Druids to be the "inventors of philosophy". The Greeks also considered the Druids to be the world's greatest scholars, and whose mathematical knowledge was the source of Pythagoras' information.

And so, we see that there is another way to consider the "three forces". This brings us back again to "perspicacity" which is a function of knowledge. The ability to "assimilate B influences" as Mouravieff describes it, depends upon the evaluation of the Impression in the specific context in which it is experienced. A very simple way of putting it is: is it Truth or is it a Lie and if either, which has more affinity to the world of the spirit, or Love?

There are those who think that truth or lies are always static, that a lie is a lie is a lie and that to be "good", one must ALWAYS tell the "truth". However, it is not always that easy. For example, consider France during the Nazi occupation. Undoubtedly, many of those involved in the resistance lied daily and regularly about their plans and activities. What was different about their lies was the INTENT and the SPECIFIC SITUATION. In such a situation, speaking the truth to a Nazi soldier who would use that truth to destroy one's fellow resistance fighters would be "evil", so to say, and lying would be "good". This simple example ought to give the reader much to think about in terms of the socialized belief in a "black and white" exposition of "good and evil".

Going back to the example of baking bread: in some cases, the flour could be "truth" and the fire could be "lies" and the water could be the specific situation in which the two meet and interact. If Impressions are "food", then this principle ought to be carefully considered when "taking in Impressions" or "assimilating 'B' influences", which we now know to be the process of applying the Law of Three to any given situation or dynamic in our lives and "Thinking with a Hammer". We also begin to understand that Love has many faces in Creation as does God. We realize also why such knowledge is reserved for initiates: how easy to twist and distort and misuse such an understanding.

CHAPTER 3
IN QUEST OF THE PAST

BACK TO THE HOLY GRAIL AND LANGUAGE

As noted by Fulcanelli, when one begins to study the subject with an eye for subtle "clues", one begins to understand that the very words chosen in the numerous tales are designed to either lead to, or away from, the central issue. In other words, not only are the incidents clues in themselves, but the very names are as well. They are installed as helpers or hindrances! Sometimes this may even be a function of the individual reading the clue, as we now understand from our little study of ligands. An individual who is "jumping to assumptions", or who has accepted as truth things which are not, in fact, true — and may have done so habitually — has a reduced ability for discernment. The individual who has taken great care, who has been patient and thorough and cautious, may be led to a proper understanding by the very same clue that leads another on a wild goose chase! The clues are in the languages and the words, but hidden like little genes coiled up in DNA, waiting for the right ligand or charge of electricity to enable them to uncoil and make themselves known. And this brings us to the fact that there seems to be a deep connection between language and DNA. Abraham Abehsera writes in his *Babel: The Language of the 21st Century*:

> Matter, Life and Language are three instances where infinite wealth has been achieved with very little. The variety of matter is the product of the combinations of about twenty-six atoms. The innumerable life forms of our planet stem from the permutations of only twenty amino acids. Third and last, the millions of words that make up human language are nothing but the combinations of about twenty consonants modified by some five vowels.

> In the past fifty years, man has made considerable progress in discovering and deciphering the physical and genetic forces that organize inert and organic matter. No comparable advances have been made in the field of language. Why did English-speaking people use the letters L and V to express their LoVe? (and LiVe) What compelled them to designate the opposite feeling by inverting the same two root-letters to form ViLe? (and eViL) Finally why were totally different letters used to express these feelings in the six thousand other languages the earth has known? Our thoughts and our words are thus made of chains of letters, the logic of which escapes us totally.

> Man, the author of speech, is himself made of chains of molecules and proteins the laws of which are well known to us. We may well suppose a strict continuity between these biological rules and those that organize his highest faculty, language.

In other words, we may assume that the laws that rule his flesh also rule his speech. Such a biology of word formation, valid for all of man's languages, ...is situated at the crossroads of not only all of this earth's tongues, but also all forms of expression, such as art, science [and] children's stories. (Myths) One of its fundamental rules is that words strictly adhere to the objects, situations or beings they designate. Far from being merely convenient tools of communication, words are thick, multidimensional, densely interrelated structures, which contain limitless information.

During at least one-third of our life, we revert to using words in such a universal language. In our dreams we may be called on by a stone or dialogue with a flower, a bird or a water spring. Dreams are pieces of a whole language in which words are still connected to the objects they designate. Night is thus the time when man recovers his full faculty of speech. [40]

In Dreams and Myths, man uses the universal language and it is in understanding this "green language" of the alchemists that we come to some understanding of our reality and how it is shaped by the actions of higher level beings ("gods") who are hyperdimensional and therefore, outside of time. It is through this that we come to an understanding of what the Holy Grail really is and what it can really do. It can really do all that is recorded in myth and legend — literally — and even more!

What we are seeing is that many "esoteric" interpretations of ancient knowledge may be mere wishful thinking. We are advocating the idea that science should shine the light of reason and the scientific method upon them. But, we also can see that science, as it is generally done in our world, is woefully inadequate to the task.

Very early in the Cassiopaean contact, "myself in the future" began to use quote marks in a rather unusual way; that is, a manner that did not strictly follow the accepted rules of grammar and punctuation. I became curious about this and asked:

Q: (L) I have been poring over this material and it occurs to me that certain words have been put in quotes for a reason, yes?
A: We put in quotes what we want further examined.

I didn't realize then that I was going to be teaching myself this "universal language". I began to keep a notebook of these quoted words and my studies in their interpretations. I began with simply looking them up in the dictionary and discovering the fullest possible meaning or varieties of meanings. This then led to tracking the words back to their roots and discovering other words that "grew" from the same roots, and often this involved working in other languages. It was

---

[40] Abehsera, Abraham A., *Babel: The Language of the 21st Century* (Jerusalem: EQEV Publishing House 1991) pp. 1-2.

utterly amazing how connections became clear in this way. For example: consider the term "Emerald Tablets". Emerald: variety of Beryl — ME + OF — Emeralde — VL + L — smaraldus/ smaragdus — Gr — amaragdos meaning "of oriental origin". So, we go to "orient". Oriental — L orientalis — Eastern. Then we look at "eastern" and find: Eastern — IE base "aues" — to shine — whence Aurora — dawn/east — and aurum — gold. Moving on to "gold", we find: Gold — IE base "ghel" — to shine, to gleam, symbol Au — Aurora, lover of Orion. And then, finally, we look at "green". Green — IE base "ghro" — to become. So, what we have found is that a great many ideas come into play in considering the "Emerald Tablets", and this will later become very important.

At the same time, I noticed that, very often, a word that began with a specific meaning became reversed over time. I also noted that the various alphabets in use by human beings had certain relationships that were either similar or *antagonistic*. I also discovered that, at a certain point, letters were added to several 22 letter alphabets to make them 24 letter alphabets, and at about the same time, the zodiac was tinkered with, a sign was added and another one split in two. *And, this very period of time was related to all of the issues that lead us to the problem of the Grail.* It became clear that someone or some force or tendency was at work here that resulted in the "Babel Syndrome", as I came to call it. I could see the "tracks" of some influence that was determined to make the solution of the mystery as difficult as possible by tossing extra puzzle pieces into the pile; pieces that would lead generations of searchers astray. I knew that I needed to find some sort of "standard" by which to evaluate these clues, so, I inquired about this:

Q: I am tracking the clues through the various languages and alphabets. I would like to know which of these alphabets, Runic, Greek, or Etruscan, preceded the others, and from which the others are derived?
A: Etruscan.
Q: Well, who were the Etruscans?
A: Templar carriers.
Q: What does that mean?
A: Seek and ye shall find.
Q: Well, how am I supposed to do that? I can't find anything else on the Etruscans! What are Templar carriers?
A: Penitent Avian Lords.
Q: What does that mean?
A: For your search. All is drawn from some more ancient form.
[...]

Q: Well, I think that a HUGE key is in the tracking of the languages...
A: The roots of all languages are identical...
Q: What do you mean?
A: Your origin.
Q: You mean Orion?
A: Interesting the word root similarity, yes?
Q: Well, the word root similarities of a LOT of things are VERY interesting! It is AMAZING the things I have discovered by tracking word roots...
A: The architects of your languages left clues aplenty.

Richard Rudgley tells us in *The Lost Civilizations of the Stone Age* that there are between 5,000 and 10,000 different languages in the world today. This fact echoes the Biblical story of the Tower of Babel. The question is, of course, was there ever a single language in our remote past that would suggest a global antediluvian civilization? As a matter of fact, there is.

One noted linguist, Hans Pederson, has expressed the opinion that there is a definite relationship between the supposedly distinct and independent language families of Indo-European, Semitic, Uralic, Altaic and even Eskimo-Aleut. He posits that all these language groups were in fact descended from a remote language ancestral to them all which he called Nostratic, from the Latin *noster*, meaning 'our'. In this language, there are many words associated with agriculture and husbandry, which suggests a farming economy. However, among the 2,000 roots of the Proto-Nostratic lexical stock, we do not find words suggesting acquaintance with agriculture or husbandry, but we do find many terms associated with hunting and food gathering.

In other words, it could be suggested that Proto-Nostratic belongs to the post-diluvian world which is designated by mainstream science as the 'Neolithic revolution', while most of its descendent languages belong to the Neolithic epoch of food-producing economy.

As it happens, the most ancient center of Neolithic economy in western Eurasia was situated in southwest Asia, which leads to a preliminary hypothesis that Proto-Nostratic was spoken in southwest Asia at a period prior to the 'Neolithic revolution'. Most of its daughter -languages belong to the Neolithic epoch, and their spread over large territories of Eurasia and Africa was connected with the demographic explosion caused by the 'Neolithic revolution'.

Now, pay careful attention here: The implications of the Nostratic hypothesis are mind-boggling. The theory proposes that most of the peoples of Europe and those in a large part of *western* Asia and parts of Africa were speaking Nostratic languages way back in prehistory, before the advent of agriculture.

The project of reconstructing the vocabulary of the Nostratic language takes us deep into the Upper Paleolithic period, the latter part of the Old Stone Age! If the Nostratic language hypothesis is right, then it must be more than 10,000 years old and is likely to be nearer 15,000 years old.

The linguists are actually getting quite daring because there is another even more controversial hypothesis, which is that of a Dene-Sino-Caucasian language that includes languages as diverse as Basque, Chinese, Sumerian, and Haida. If this is shown to be a genuine language group, then it must, like Nostratic and Eurasiatic, be of Upper Paleolithic age.

Some linguists even propose that they can reconstruct the primordial ancestor of all the world's languages, a language called either Proto-Global or Proto-World. Some of them have assembled etymologies which they believe indicate a connection between all of the world's language families showing a correlation in respect not only to the meaning of the words, but also to their sound.

Many "mainstream" scientists are amazed and troubled by the fact that these correspondences exist across time and space and that languages found as far field as the deserts of southern Africa, the Amazon rain forest, the Arctic and the cities of Europe still retain links from a remote time when they must have all been closely connected. But they cannot deny what is being proposed. Repeated accidental resemblance of both meaning and sound on a global scale is too unlikely to contemplate. That such parallels exist between language groups in distant parts of the world is striking and is hard to dismiss simply as mere coincidence. In fact, this hypothesis takes us back over 20,000 years to some time before these two macro-families must have split to go their separate ways.

This is why word studies are so important. If we hypothesize an ancient high technology, and that myths and legends are *disjecta membra* of this civilization, coming as close to the original meaning of words is of crucial importance.

The conclusion is that the various proto-languages that are said to belong to the Nostratic group could have dispersed from the zone in which agriculture seems to have first developed, namely the Near East and Anatolia. In this scenario the expansion of these languages beyond the region would be directly associated with the spread of farming. The parent language, Proto-Nostratic would thus be located somewhere in the core region and obviously to a time preceding the origins of agriculture.

Farmers vs. Shepherds. Cain and Abel. As I was reading through all the myths, I was struck by this conflict and also how an older "shepherd" myth was often transformed into an "agriculture" myth with concomitant reversal of imagery and meaning. I asked the Cassiopaeans - myself in the future - about this:

> Q: One thing I do want to understand, since it is involved in all of this, is the idea of the 'Shepherd'. All of the ancient legends and stories and myths lead, ultimately, to something about the 'shepherd', or the 'Shepherd King'.
> A: Shepherd is most likely to be struck by lightning, due to staff, and thus "enlightened", or "illumened"!!
> Q: Funny spelling! But, what is the contrast between the concept of the shepherd and the agriculturalist? This goes back to the very roots of everything — there is Cain and Abel, Jacob and Esau, Isaac and Ishmael... and others that are even older from other cultures....
> A: Are not you "abel" to figure this out? Have you not learned to explore your ideas without prejudice?

Indeed, this is one of the great keys to tracking the Grail. This transition from "hunter-gatherer" to "agriculturalist" is considered to be one of the great "revolutions" or evolutionary steps of mankind. But is it necessarily so? Richard Rudgley noted in passing:

> The study of the sample of skeletal remains from South Asia showed that there was a decline in body stature, body size and life expectancy with the adoption of farming. ...Of the 13 studies, 10 showed that the average life expectancy declined with the adoption of farming. [41]

But there is a much deeper implication to this, and it is reflected in the *inverting* of certain words in our languages as well as inversion of concepts as expressed in

---

[41] Rudgley, Richard, *The Lost Civilizations of the Stone Age* (New York: The Free Press, 1999) p. 8.

our myths. The understanding of this inversion could be the single most important concept to be grasped by man in all of his existence, and it is this understanding that the Cassiopaean transmissions enabled me to grasp. It was clear that, in order to "become myself in the future", I had to do the research to acquire the same level of knowledge as the Cassiopaeans, as my future self, exemplified. And so, I went to work to "balance" my current effort with "my" input from the future.

Before we even begin, I want to address this factor that the Cassiopaeans speak of: Knowledge = Energy. There is a general tendency among both Christians and many "New Age" devotees of this or that "source of information" that a "Loving God" simply gives all to those who ask in faith. It is this fundamental perspective that we will be examining, so I don't want to get ahead of myself, but I will offer the following remarks for the reader to keep in mind as we progress with our revelation of the Meaning of the Holy Grail.

In the beginning, I was frustrated with the Cassiopaeans - myself in the future - because they would not just simply answer all my questions. Instead, they would give me "clues" and send me out to do research. So, I complained numerous times:

> Q: (L) How come I am always the one who gets assigned the job of figuring everything out?
> A: Because you have asked for the "power" to figure out the most important issues in all of reality. And, we have been assisting you in your empowerment. Learning is necessary for progress of soul. Remember, we are not here to lead by the hand. This is how you are building your power center. All there is, is lessons and learning is fun. Knowledge is power. If we give it to you like Halloween candy, it is diffused. Why don't you trust your incredible abilities? If we answer for you now, you will be helpless when it becomes necessary for you to perform this function on a regular basis, as it will be!!!! Learning now increases your power tenfold, when you use some initiative, rather than asking us for all the answers directly!!! [42]

The thing I had not yet grasped at that point was the fact that in order to "become" the myself in the future - assuming that I could achieve that level of knowledge - I had to do the work that they were encouraging me to do. So, I set about gaining and gathering knowledge based on the clues placed before me by the Cassiopaeans and now I share them with you, the reader.

"YOU KNOW MY METHOD. IT IS FOUNDED UPON THE OBSERVANCE OF TRIFLES."[43]

At this point, I want to bring up two of the concepts upon which my "study method" is based. The first is articulated in an essay by the renowned Italian historian Carlo Ginzburg: *Clues: Roots of an Evidential Paradigm.* In this essay he

---

[42] The answers to the same question, given in several sessions, are assembled together.

[43] Sherlock Holmes in *The BoscombeValley Mystery*, Doyle.

describes a crucial aspect of investigations of the "unknown", which can range from criminal investigations to para-physical to physical investigations, including history. This approach is, in a nutshell, the *"close and careful study of seemingly trivial or unimportant details which actually turn out to be of great importance"*. It is what he describes as the "Sherlock Holmes School of Knowledge". Ginzburg points out that in the stories of Sir Arthur Conan Doyle, Dr. Watson, an intelligent but pedestrian thinker, is contrasted to Holmes, who pursues unusual and "inspired" analyses of seemingly irrelevant details such as cigarette ash. He suggests that the most striking thing about Sherlock Holmes was his unparalleled guile. His success was based more on his ability to think like his quarry than the tiny clues themselves. The clues were meaningless without context, and the context was in the mind of Sherlock Holmes. He KNEW his quarry. Based on this, Holmes could hypothetically reconstruct the activities using only tiny traces left as clues. Having reconstructed a particular action or event based on these small clues, he was then able to "predict" the next move, or where to look for the next tiny trace.

In terms of the Grail Quest, it is paramount to understand the conditions of the quest. The allegories of a "haunted forest" and "fire breathing dragon" and "beautiful temptress" are not placed in the context for no reason! There IS an opponent; one who tricks by terror, by frontal assault, and by unparalleled deceit! Make no mistake about it: there are forces that do NOT want anyone to discover the secret! And they are so unbelievably ancient, deeply cunning, and even consciously evil, that the human mind cannot plumb the depths of this guile. Those who think they can, or that they have, will never achieve the "Stone". They have already leaped to an assumption that is equivalent to being connected to an IV drip of heroin. And it is pure hubris.

Tracking is not simply an "intellectual" practice; it involves considerable, often great, learning and inspired insight. The "reader of signs" must KNOW HIS QUARRY because rarely does he have a simple set of complete tracks. He has to identify the action based on partial signs that most likely have been deliberately obscured.

In historical and metaphysical research ,one must systematically collect data. Unfortunately, the conditions are the worst possible for the quest for truth due to the fact that not only is the trail "cold", but, in addition to the deliberate attempts to conceal the trail, there are many "Dr. Watsons" out there bumbling along and destroying information in their well-meaning, but misguided attempts to find the answer in data that has clearly been left to deliberately lead AWAY from the truth.

In this sense, religion and myth are as important as actual material clues, but not in the sense that they are generally understood. At one point I asked the Cassiopaeans about the Grail Legends that include the stories of Joseph of Arimathea and Mary Magdalene traveling to Europe with "the grail" as both an artifact as well as a "holy bloodline".

> Q: Who created the legends of the Holy Grail and Joseph of Arimathea bringing it
> to a) France, or b) England? Who was behind the creating of this group of legends?
> A: Not a group of legends.
> Q: Why was the 12th century the focal point for the propagation of the grail
> legends, the troubadours, the whole thing?

A: Beginning of "Renaissance".

Q: The story is, and there are even some very old legends in France itself, that there are caves or places where Joseph and Mary Magdalene spent the night, or lived, or whatever. Did Joseph of Arimathea actually travel to France and then to England later, with Mary Magdalene or other followers of Jesus?

A: No.

Q: Did he travel to France alone?

A: No.

Q: What is the source of these stories? What is the point of these stories?

A: Deflection.

Q Deflection of what to what or from what?

A: Truth from recipient.

And so, right away we understand that there *was* something significant being promulgated at that period of time, and that the stories of the Holy Grail — as they are constituted — were actually written to divert attention from *something else*.

But there is a deeper issue here that I would like to try to outline. Our world is generally explained in reductionist terms which amounts to the outlook of mainstream science which has lost its truly "scientific" approach and has been converted to what we like to call the "religion of science", or the "Thought Police". Science has "explained away" everything by reducing it to its component parts which are mechanistic and lacking some essential thing that gives "life" to our lives. Mainstream Science explains religion as "wishful-thinking" and love as nothing more than chemistry between the cells of the body. Progressive "scientism" is equated with reason, and reason is supposed to make man a "godlike" being, at least in terms of his ethics. But, it isn't working. You can look around you and see that it is not working. We live in a horror house of technological doom, feeling powerless to do anything about our state of existence.

The plain, hard fact is: science, as it is practiced today, can't lead us to the explanation of the order of the universe. In the face of our present reality, it is only with REAL science, combined with the current level of scientific-technological knowledge, that we have any chance of being able to reassemble and understand the scientific knowledge of the past. And so, the only rational thing we can do is challenge this most fundamental of mainstream scientific ideas: that scientific progress is as "evolutionary", as is claimed; that mankind has evolved from naked savages to his modern state of technological prowess; and that we are moving from a lower state of ignorance to a higher state of advancement. Yes, we know that progress has occurred in many ways at many times, but the history of man seems to be one of degeneration alternating with recovery and technological advancement which is not balanced by ethical or spiritual development. Science and religion have run amok into narrow and distorted views of the universe. Something is wrong with this picture, and just what it is we need to discover.

We are proposing that the theme of the Quest for the Grail has several variations on a singular idea: that far back in the ancient past, there was knowledge, True Wisdom Technology. Further, we are proposing that this knowledge was widely known and applied in a Golden Age. The Ancient Technology is further thought to have survived, though perhaps broken up and obscured in "magical doctrines", myths and religious rituals that have long ago lost their meaning. It is also thought that the Ancient Technology has survived in part in esoteric schools, nurtured in secret, and given out to the world in measured doses from time to time via an elect few who respond to the dedicated seeker of the solutions to the sufferings of humanity.

Do we have any evidence that this Ancient Technology ever really existed? I think we do. Not only that, I believe that we can track it and analyze it with the tools of science and uncover the scientific concepts couched in religious doctrines and myths. This knowledge may have been carried in different forms or contexts or levels of proficiency by different social groups, which then applied it in various ways. Some of these groups made progress; some did not. Some forgot everything and just tell the stories. But the one thing they all seem to agree on is that Time is not what we think it is.

THE TERROR OF HISTORY

Time, of course, is what we talk about when we discuss history. The history of mankind, when considered objectively, is a terrible thing. Many people defend themselves from this terror by erecting elaborate defenses—"personal myths", so to speak—so that they can go on with the prosaic business of their lives without being paralyzed by the burden of the "cold hard facts of life". Time is a "haunted forest" of thorns and wild beasts, and it is only after facing such a "test" of strength and incorruptibility that one will be granted the gift of a glimpse of the Grail.

Man, as a rule and in general, is powerless against Time and History, cosmic catastrophes, military onslaughts, social injustice, personal and familial misfortunes, and a host of assaults against his existence too numerous to list. Death and destruction come to all, both rich and poor, free and slave, young and old, good and evil, with an arbitrariness and insouciance that, when contemplated even momentarily, can destroy the most carefully constructed "personal myth". This is a FACT, and, to quote Castaneda's Don Juan, "a damn scary one"!

Over and over again, man has seen his fields and cattle laid waste by drought and disease, his loved ones tormented and decimated by illness or human cruelty, his life's work reduced to nothing in an instant by events over which he has no control at all. The study of history through its various disciplines offers a view of mankind that is almost insupportable. The rapacious movements of hungry tribes, invading and conquering and destroying in the darkness of prehistory; barbarian invaders; the bloodbaths of the crusades of Catholic Europe against the "infidels" of the Middle East; the stalking "noonday terror" of the Inquisition where martyrs quenched the flames with their blood; the raging holocaust of modern genocide; wars, famine, and pestilence. All produce an intolerable sense of indefensibility against what the great historian of religion, Mircea Eliade, calls the Terror of History.

There are those who will say that now this is all past; mankind has entered a new phase; and science and technology have brought us to the brink of ending all this suffering. Many people believe in the myth of Science, which postulates that man is evolving, society is evolving, and that we now have control over the arbitrary evil of our environment. That which does not support this idea is reinterpreted or ignored.

It is assumed that not only have we evolved as human beings from some primate ancestor, but that we are evolving as a culture as well. Science has given us the space program, laser, television, penicillin, sulfa drugs, and a host of other useful developments, which would seem to make our lives more tolerable and fruitful. However, we can easily see that this is not the case. After three centuries of domination by science, it could be said that never before has man been so precariously poised on the brink of such total destruction.

Our lives, as individuals and groups and cultures, are steadily deteriorating. The air we breathe and the water we drink is polluted almost beyond endurance. Our foods are loaded with substances which contribute very little to nourishment, and that may, in fact, be injurious to our health. Stress and tension have become an accepted part of life and can be shown to have killed millions. Hatred, envy, greed and strife multiply exponentially. Crime increases nine times faster than the population. We swallow endless quantities of pills to wake up, go to sleep, get the job done, calm our nerves and make us feel good. The inhabitants of the earth spend more money on recreational drugs than they spend on housing, clothing, food, education or any other product or service.

The ancient evils are still with us for those who emerge from their "personal myth" long enough to be in touch with reality. Drought, famine, plague and natural disasters still take an annual toll in lives and suffering. Combined with wars, insurrections, and political purges, this means that not only are great numbers of people killed each year for political reasons, but also multiplied millions of people across the globe are without adequate food or shelter or health care. Over one hundred million children starved to death in the last decade of the 20th century.

When man contemplates history, AS IT IS, he is forced to realize that he is in the iron grip of an existence that seems to have no real care or concern for his pain and suffering. Over and over again, the same sufferings fall upon mankind multiplied millions upon millions of times over millennia. The totality of human suffering is a dreadful thing. I could write until the end of the world using oceans of ink and forests of paper and never fully convey this Terror.

The beast of arbitrary calamity has always been with us. For as long as human hearts have pumped hot blood through their too-fragile bodies and glowed with the inexpressible sweetness of life and yearning for all that is good and right and loving, the sneering, stalking, drooling and scheming beast of what seems to be unconscious evil has licked its lips in anticipation of its next feast of terror and suffering.

Since the beginning of time, this mystery of the estate of man, this Curse of Cain, has existed, and, since the most Ancient of Days, the cry has been: "My punishment is greater than I can bear"!

Eliade and other scholars of myth and religion have conjectured that, in ancient times, when man perceived this intolerable and incomprehensible condition in which he found his existence, that he created cosmogonies to justify all the "cruelties, aberrations, and tragedies of history". Yet, when we study these myths and legends, we find that, at the deepest level, these defenses against history have to do with Time. The religious myths are numerous and varied, but, when all the trappings are stripped away, the chief point of argument is this: which conception of Time is being utilized as the foundation of the myth, cyclical or linear?

There are those who say that the mythical/religious formulas and images through which the "primitives" expressed their reality seem childish and absurd. Eliade, however, sees in religious myths a "desperate effort not to lose contact with being" (justification of existence in the face of the cruel world) and to find meaning—an archaic ontology.

Again, I would like to suggest that this archaic ontology is a remnant of the high and different science and technology of man "before the fall". Again we hypothesize that the myths, rituals and ceremonies of the ancient religions are but surviving fragments of a technology from which the true significance has vanished. Further, we might think that it is in discovering the secrets of this "technology" that mankind has a chance to become free of the Terror of History.

What is the secret technology? It is nothing less than the Holy Grail the Ark of Noë, and the Philosopher's Stone.

In the present time there is a lot of talk about time because we are rumored to be heading toward the End of Time—and the World itself. Can this be true? And, if so, what implication does such an idea suggest regarding the nature of our universe? If this is not true, then where did such an idea originate, and why is it so popular?

In working with, and testing, our hypothesis that there was a "former time", a Golden Age from which man "Fell", we need to examine carefully this issue of time.

Time: The framework in which we live and move and have our being.

There is the question of BEing and DOing—Free Will—, which implies the context of Time. Yes, it is possible to conceive of BEing outside of Time, but in order to DO, one must have a context. This may be an assumption, but let's work with it for the "time being".

A FEW WORDS ABOUT RADIOMETRIC DATING

If we are going to investigate time, we will be confronted with the issue of dates, those markers of time, and of how these dates are established.

The most widely used method for determining the age of fossils is to date them by the "known age" of the rock strata in which they are found. At the same time, the most widely used method for determining the age of the rock strata is to date them by the "known age" of the fossils they contain. In this "circular dating" method, all ages are based on uniformitarian assumptions about the date and order in which fossilized plants and animals are believed to have evolved. Most people are surprised to learn that there is, in fact, no way to directly determine the age of any fossil or rock. The so called "absolute" methods of dating (radiometric methods) actually only measure the present ratios of radioactive isotopes and their decay products in suitable specimens - not their age. These measured ratios are then extrapolated to an "age" determination.

The problem with all radiometric "clocks" is that their accuracy critically depends on several starting assumptions, which are largely unknowable. To date a specimen by radiometric means, one must first know the starting amount of the parent isotope at the beginning of the specimen's existence. Second, one must be certain that there were no daughter isotopes in the beginning. Third, one must be certain that neither parent nor daughter isotopes have ever been added or removed from the specimen. Fourth, one must be certain that the decay rate of parent isotope to daughter isotope has always been the same. That one or more of these assumptions are often invalid is obvious from the published radiometric "dates" (to say nothing of "rejected" dates) found in the literature.

One of the most obvious problems is that several samples from the same location often give widely divergent ages. Apollo moon samples, for example, were dated by both uranium-thorium-lead and potassium-argon methods, giving results, which varied from 2 million to 28 billion years. Lava flows from volcanoes on the north rim of the Grand Canyon (which erupted after its formation) show potassium-argon dates a billion years "older" than the most ancient basement rocks at the bottom of the canyon. Lava from underwater volcanoes near Hawaii (that are known to have erupted in 1801 AD) has been "dated" by the potassium-argon method with results varying from 160 million to nearly 3 billion years. It's really no wonder that *all of the laboratories that "date" rocks insist on knowing in advance the "evolutionary age" of the strata from which the samples were taken -- this way, they know which dates to accept as "reasonable" and which to ignore.*

More precisely, it is based on the assumption that nothing "really exceptional" happened in the meantime. What I mean by "really exceptional" is this: an event theoretically possible, but whose mechanism is not yet understood in terms of the established paradigms. To give an example: *a crossing of two different universes.* This is theoretically possible, taking into account modern physical theories, but it is too speculative to discuss its "probability" and possible consequences.

Could such an event change radioactive decay data? Could it change the values of some fundamental physical constants? Yes, it could.

Is it possible that similar events have happened in the past? Yes, it is possible. How possible it is? We do not know. We do not know, in fact, what would be an exact meaning of the "crossing of two different universes".

In addition to considering the idea of cataclysms that could have destroyed ancient civilizations more than once, there is another matter to consider in special relationship to radioactive decay: that ancient civilizations may have destroyed themselves with nuclear war.

> Radiocarbon dates for Pleistocene remains in northeastern North America, according to scientists Richard Firestone of Lawrence Berkeley National Laboratory, and William Topping, are younger-as much as 10,000 years younger-than for those *in the western part of the country.* Dating by other methods like thermo-luminescence (TL), geoarchaeology, and sedimentation suggests that many radiocarbon dates are grossly in error. For example, materials from the Gainey Paleoindian site in Michigan, radiocarbon dated at 2880 yr BC, are given an age by TL dating of 12,400 BC. It seems that there are so many anomalies reported in the upper US and in Canada of this type, that they cannot be explained by ancient aberrations in the atmosphere or other radiocarbon reservoirs, or by contamination of data samples (a common source of error in radiocarbon dating). Assuming correct methods of radiocarbon dating are used, organic remains associated with an

artifact will give a radiocarbon age younger than they actually are *only if they contain an artificially high radiocarbon keel.*

Our research indicates that the entire Great Lakes region (and beyond) was subjected to particle bombardment and a catastrophic nuclear irradiation that produced secondary thermal neutrons from cosmic ray interactions. The neutrons produced unusually large quantities of Pu239 and substantially altered the natural uranium abundance ratios in artifacts and in other exposed materials including cherts[44], sediments, and the entire landscape. These neutrons necessarily transmuted residual nitrogen in the dated charcoals to radiocarbon, thus explaining anomalous dates. […]

The C14 level in the fossil record would reset to a higher value. The excess global radiocarbon would then decay with a half-life of 5730 years, which should be seen in the radiocarbon analysis of varied systems. […]

Sharp increases in C14 are apparent in the marine data at 4,000, 32,000-34,000, and 12,500 BC. These increases are coincident with geomagnetic excursions. […]

The enormous energy released by the catastrophe at 12,500 BC could have heated the atmosphere to over 1000 C over Michigan, and the neutron flux at more northern locations would have melted considerable glacial ice. Radiation effects on plants and animals exposed to the cosmic rays would have been lethal, comparable to being irradiated in a 5 megawatt reactor more than 100 seconds.

The overall pattern of the catastrophe matches the pattern of mass extinction before Holocene times. The Western Hemisphere was more affected than the Eastern, North America more than South America, and eastern North America more than western North America. Extinction in the Great lakes area was more rapid and pronounced than elsewhere. Larger animals were more affected than smaller ones, a pattern that conforms to the expectation that radiation exposure affects large bodies more than smaller ones.[45]

The evidence that Firestone and Topping discovered is puzzling for a lot of reasons. But, the fact is, there are reports of similar evidence from such widely spread regions as India, Ireland, Scotland, France, and Turkey; ancient cities whose brick and stone walls have literally been vitrified, that is, fused together like glass. There is also evidence of vitrification of stone forts and cities. It seems that the only explanation for such anomalies is either an atomic blast or something that could produce similar effects, which we will get to soon enough.

---

[44] A chert is basically bits of glass. It is silica that has been heated until it fuses into tiny shards of glass.

[45] Firestone, Richard B., Topping, William, *Terrestrial Evidence of a Nuclear Catastrophe in Paleoindian Times*, dissertation research, 1990-2001.

CHAPTER 4
HYPERDIMENSIONAL REALITY

HYPERDIMENSIONAL SPACE — THE REALM OF THE "GODS"

THE QUESTION OF TIME IN MYTHS

In numerous tales of the Grail, the description of the castle of the Fisher King includes some interesting time anomalies: it is a place where time slows down or stops altogether. This is also the case with the ancient Celtic legends of the Head of Bran the Blessed, in which presence his warriors feast and make merry with no awareness of the passage of time. This theme occurs with great regularity and suggests a deep and ancient significance that will become apparent as we proceed.

The most ancient conception of time was associated with the "Goddess" and was cyclical — like women. Everything was "real" only insofar as it was connected to an archetypal gesture - *illud tempus* - from the beginning.

> Every hero repeated the archetypal gesture, every war rehearsed the struggle
> between good and evil, every fresh social injustice was identified with the passion
> of a divine messenger, each new massacre repeated the glorious end of the martyrs.
> ...Only one fact counts: by virtue of this view, tens of millions of men were able,
> for century after century, to endure great historical pressures without despairing,
> without committing suicide or falling into that spiritual aridity that always brings
> with it a relativistic or nihilistic view of history. [46]

This reflected the idea that the world in which we live was a "form," or reflection, or "double" of another cosmic world that existed on a higher level. These were Celestial Archetypes. Plato gave an explanation that is still unsurpassed in its simplicity:

> "And now," I said, "let me show in a figure how far our nature is enlightened or
> unenlightened. Behold! Human beings living in an underground den, which has a
> mouth open towards the light and reaching all along the den; here they have been
> from their childhood, and have their legs and necks chained so that they cannot

---

[46] Eliade, op. cit., pp. 151-152.

move, and can only see before them, being prevented by the chains from turning round their heads. Above and behind them a fire is blazing at a distance, and between the fire and the prisoners there is a raised way; and you will see, if you look, a low wall built along the way, like the screen which marionette players have in front of them over which they show the puppets. ...And do you see," I said, "men passing along the wall carrying all sorts of vessels, and statues and figures of animals made of wood and stone and various materials, which appear over the wall?

...And they see only their own shadows, or the shadows of one another, which the fire throws on the opposite wall of the cave... how could they see anything but the shadows if they were never allowed to move their heads... and of the objects which are being carried in like manner they would only see the shadows ...And if they were able to converse with one another, would they not suppose that they were naming what was actually before them? ...And suppose further that the prison had an echo which came from the other side, would they not be sure to fancy when one of the passers-by spoke that the voice which they heard came from the passing shadow? ...To them, the truth would be literally nothing but the shadows of the images. [...]

And now look again, and see what will naturally follow if the prisoners are released and disabused of their error. At first, when any of them is liberated and compelled suddenly to stand up and turn his neck round and walk and look towards the light, he will suffer sharp pains; the glare will distress him, and he will be unable to see the realities of which in his former state he had seen the shadows; and then conceive someone saying to him that what he saw before was an illusion, but that now, when he is approaching nearer to being and his eye is turned towards more real existence, he has a clearer vision — what will be his reply? And you may further imagine that his instructor is pointing to the objects as they pass and requiring him to name them — will he not be perplexed? Will he not fancy that the shadows, which he formerly saw, are truer than the objects, which are now shown to him? [...]

And if he is compelled to look straight at the light, will he not have a pain in his eyes, which will make him turn away to take refuge in the objects of vision which he can see, and which he will conceive to be in reality clearer than the things, which are now being shown to him? [...]

And suppose once more, that he is reluctantly dragged up a steep and rugged ascent, and held fast until he is forced into the presence of the sun himself, is he not likely to be pained and irritated? When he approaches the light his eyes will be dazzled, and he will not be able to see anything at all of what are now called realities. ...He will require growing accustomed to the sight of the upper world. And first he will see the shadows best, next the reflections of men and other objects in the water, and then the objects themselves; spangled heaven; and he will see the sky and the stars by night better than the sun or the light of the sun by day? [...]

Last of all he will be able to see the sun, and not mere reflections of him in the water, but he will see him in his own proper place, and not in another; and he will contemplate him as he is. ...He will then proceed to argue that this is he who gives the season and the years, and is the guardian of all that is in the visible world, and in a certain way the cause of all things which he and his fellows have been accustomed to behold? [...]

And when he remembered his old habitation, and the wisdom of the den and his fellow prisoners, do you not suppose that he would felicitate himself on the change, and pity them? ...And if they were in the habit of conferring honors among themselves on those who were quickest to observe the passing shadows and to remark which of them went before, and which followed after, and which were together; and who were therefore best able to draw conclusions as to the future, do you think that he would care for such honors and glories, or envy the possessors of them? Would he not say with Homer, 'Better to be the poor servant of a poor master,' and to endure anything, rather than think as they do and live after their manner? […]

Imagine once more such a one coming suddenly out of the sun to be replaced in his old situation; would he not be certain to have his eyes full of darkness? ...And if there were a contest, and he had to compete in measuring the shadows with the prisoners who had never moved out of the den, while his sight was still weak, and before his eyes had become steady (and the time which would be needed to acquire this new habit of sight might be very considerable), would he not be ridiculous? Men would say of him that up he went up and down he came without his eyes; and that it was better not even to think of ascending; and if any one tried to loose another and lead him up to the light, let them only catch the offender, and they would put him to death.

This entire allegory you may now append, dear Glaucon, to the previous argument; the prison house is the world of sight, the light of the fire is the sun, and you will not misapprehend me if you interpret the journey upwards to be the ascent of the soul into the intellectual world according to my poor belief, which, at your desire, I have expressed — whether rightly or wrongly, God knows. [47]

When we consider a semi-physical realm that projects itself into our reality, we also have to consider the factor of Time. In our geometry we define a point as an infinitesimal section of a line. A line is an infinitesimal cross-section of a plane and a plane is an infinitesimal section of a solid. Thus, our three dimensional reality must be defined as a series of infinitesimal sections of a four dimensional body. Conceptually, this means that our entire reality is a section of a four-dimensional body — a realm of potential dimensions beyond three-dimensional contemplation.

We usually consider the past as no longer existing. The future does not exist, either, and the "present" refers to the momentary transition of non-existence into non-existence!

But, if it is true that only Now exists, then the logical conclusion is that, as wave reading consciousness units, we are, in some way, responsible for our perception of time. We regard time as linear, long or short, an endless line, a progression from past into future. But this creates an insurmountable problem. On a line, NOW is a

---

[47] Plato, *Republic*: *Book VII*, trans. B Jowett.

mathematical point of infinitesimal smallness — it has no dimension! *By scientific logic, it does not exist!*

MATHEMATICAL DIMENSIONS

The first mathematician to explore the fourth dimension, William Rowan Hamilton, was born in 1805. Hamilton was so precocious that he was reading the Bible at the age of three, at which point he also began learning Hebrew characters. By the age of ten he could read Hebrew, Persian, Arabic, Sanskrit, Bengali, Latin, and Greek, as well as several modern European languages. Hamilton was so was skilled in mental arithmetic that he was entered in a competition against a boy from Vermont who toured as a calculating prodigy. Hamilton was disappointed, however, when he found that his opponent seemed to have no knowledge apart from his unusual math abilities.

While studying at university, Hamilton joined the Tractarian movement, a religious organization, of which Samuel Taylor Coleridge was a member. Coleridge had the notion that algebra was the science of time, and apparently this idea had a profound influence on Hamilton who discovered a four-dimensional manifold of numbers, the "quaternions". Though he was a genius mathematician, Hamilton seemed to be unable to think beyond the strictly material world, and though he was reaching for a fourth dimension, Hamilton could not consider the fourth dimension as "real".

The next phase of development of the concept of fourth dimensional space was the work of Ludwig Schlaefli, a Swiss schoolteacher. He understood that four dimensions was the conceptual continuation of the first three spatial dimensions. As a schoolteacher, Schlaefli was not in the company of "academics" and this may have played a part in the fact that he was able to develop this new geometry during his early career, before he joined the mathematics department of the University at Bern. It is interesting that Grassmann, who also explored an ingenious algebra of higher dimensions, was another schoolteacher whose writings were ignored for many years. During that period, anyone who worked in these directions was thought to be a bit mad when actually, what they were really doing, was following an ancient tradition of *relying upon pure thought to take them beyond what could be confirmed in the sensory world*.

THE MAGIC OF ABSTRACT THOUGHT

Many New Age Gurus teach that "higher knowledge" can only be accessed "directly", through the "heart". To this end, they produce endless techniques and rituals designed to stop thought and induce "feeling". This is simply another variation of the "blind faith" routine that teaches a person that only knowledge brought directly by God is "true", and all human knowledge is basically "bunk".

What is interesting about this is that it is another example of disinformation - a lie wrapped in truth to make it easier to swallow. As we have already pointed out, most of what passes for "techniques of ascension" amounts to little more than stimulating chemicals in the body which results in a "feel good experience", but which does nothing to increase the level of Being.

As already mentioned, there is a "gravity" to the realm of Non-being which is the Thought Center that "creates" matter. Matter constitutes the predominate nature of our reality. What this suggests is that our "field of expression" is dipolar - gravity vs. consciousness.

The "field of consciousness" is a primary field like gravity, but we can see that it is very little manifested in our world. This means that to move from the gravity field of matter, one must act against a rather strong force.

The field of consciousness is that of thoughts, feelings that are not chemical, ideas, motivations, attitudes, and such that acts on our minds/consciousness as gravity acts on objects and masses. Just as there is gravity and anti-gravity, so must there be consciousness and anti-consciousness as we have already described in our discussion of Thought Centers.

The consciousness field is a mirror image of the gravity field of matter. As above, so below. And just as in the case where great effort must be made to move a stone uphill, so it takes great effort to move one's motivations and attitudes and emotions from the influence of matter into the realm of the consciousness field.

When such an uphill movement of motivation occurs, a specific effort of consciousness needs to be made. Thoughts and ideas and concepts that are based on material interpretations of reality require little effort. It is the reaching into the higher realms of thought that enables us to discern when our emotions are "material" or pure and belonging to the soul. To approach this problem without working to create the vessel of thoughts, concepts, ideas, is again, the process of believing lies and binding to "spiritual drugs".

Understanding this permits us to distinguish when we are working toward higher consciousness. Going "downward" in the field of consciousness is like going downhill in the field of gravity: no work of lifting need be involved. Thus a downhill motion in the field of consciousness is easy, effortless, and pleasurable.

When we go uphill in any possible field, including the consciousness field, we need to put a significant effort (work) into this motion. This leads to the logical conclusion that those things that increase consciousness are also difficult and go against the gravity of the material world explanations.

There is, of course, much more to this that will be introduced in a later volume. For now, the important point is that developing the intellect so that it can be used as an instrument of perspicacity is one of the first requirements of spiritual development.

So, for those New Age and fundamentalist teachers who denigrate thought, consider the following written by another schoolteacher:

> Isn't it amazing that Newton couldn't discover universal gravitation until 50 years after Descartes created the mathematical method of analyzing geometric data in an algebraic equation? It would take about 50 years for the method to disseminate, become second nature, raise a new generation immersed it, and who then began noticing phenomena that these new mathematical expressions did a really good job of modeling. It was more than 40 years after Hamilton created quaternions that Maxwell discovered how well they fit for formulating the equations of electromagnetism. It was 50 years after Riemann created his general, curvilinear, non-Euclidean geometry that Einstein, with help from Minkowski, noticed how well it expressed the relations of special and general relativity.

My theory is that people can't notice something until they have the reference point to understand what it is they are observing. Specifically, scientists can't notice, "hey, these new patterns fit together" until they have a mathematics that describes this kind of relationship as being a pattern, rather than random marks on a graph. Think about what it would be like to discover that all of your data fit into a parabolic shape, but you don't know what a parabola is. How disappointed you would be to realize it doesn't make a straight line, when straight lines are all you know. "I guess there was nothing to that hypothesis after all", you say as you discard the data. Tomorrow some brilliant mathematician will create a method of graphing quadratic equations thinking he has invented the perfect pure math, which couldn't possibly have any practical application. Fifty years from now, your grandson will review your data, or recreate your experiments. He will get the same data points that you did, but now he recognizes the pattern as a parabola. It was a parabola all along, but you didn't know it, because parabolae hadn't been invented yet when you plotted the data.

If you don't recognize the pattern, then your brain interprets it as random - no pattern at all. This means you pay it no attention. In this way, mathematicians create the world we live in. What an outrageous statement! No Physicist would admit the validity of that, after all, they are trained to observe the real world, not confirm some dreamer's fantasy! Yeah, right. Only problem with that is, history tells us that over and over, Physicists were unable to see the patterns in front of their eyes until someone had invented a mathematics that made this kind of pattern recognizable and distinguishable from random noise.

Therefore there is a very real sense in which the only reality we can recognize is that of the patterns for which we have a mathematical template. Therefore we can only observe that part of infinite reality for which some enterprising mathematician has invented the pattern. The mathematician does NOT describe an objective reality, which he observes; he instead creates relationships, which he considers "beautiful", or "elegant", or perhaps "entertaining". He doesn't think his creation has any practical application, but it always does. Because any time somebody describes the template for a new pattern, now (in about 50 years) people will begin noticing those parts of the infinite universe, which fit into to this new pattern. Before they just seemed random, but now that we recognize the pattern, it's so obvious we don't understand how Aristotle overlooked it. And a new generation of historians will write books about how Archimedes was actually on the verge of inventing this himself just before the Romans killed him.[48]

In exactly the same way, it is by gathering information and making unprejudiced observations while at the same time stretching the mind into the field of consciousness, that we develop the vehicle for the Soul, which can then "know" things by virtue of the gift of God.

---

[48] Gordon Clason, private correspondence with the authors.

Each adventurer into the world of these ideas of hyperdimensions, which now concern us profoundly, found the trail easier to navigate as a result of the simultaneous expansion of other branches of knowledge. For example, in geometry it was noticed that the lines in ordinary three-dimensional space could be regarded as elements of a manifold of four dimensions. Connections of this kind soon made the fourth dimension acceptable to mathematicians.

DIMENSIONAL THINKING IN WESTERN SPIRITUALITY

It is at this point that something truly strange occurred. The idea of the "fourth dimension" was adopted by spiritualists and occultists as the "realm of the ethers" or the afterlife, the place of the dead.

Séances of the nineteenth-century attracted spirit beings that produced physical effects as well as peculiar psychological states, and disappeared again - like the UFOs of our time. It was as convenient then (as it is now) to assign them a home in the inaccessible dimensions of space, and to make absolutely certain that everyone was convinced that these dimensions were ethereal.

The nineteenth-century astronomer Zollner set out to demonstrate scientifically that the *ethereal* beings attracted to spiritualistic séances were from the fourth dimension. Even though his demonstrations were never successful, at this point, the fourth dimension became a means of conceiving of mysterious phenomena in a *non-materialistic* way.

In the final phase of nineteenth-century thought, the fourth dimension became a subject for meditation and was taken up by the Theosophical Society, and later by Rudolf Steiner, who gave reportedly brilliant lectures on the subject based on the work of Howard Hinton.

Hinton's work was the outcome of the ideas of his father, James Hinton, whose philosophy was based on the ideas of the Kantian noumenal world that lies behind phenomenal experience. This higher world was feminine, nurturing, free of social and legal restraint; virtue consisted in "harmonizing one's intentions with the noumenal world", and could not be captured by merely regulating behavior. The person who acts selflessly for the greater good of humanity was as likely to break the law as the brutish criminal.

Howard Hinton was inspired by Hamilton's writings to adopt a materialistic form of Kantianism. When he began work as a schoolteacher, he came to doubt that knowledge could ever come from an external authority. In an effort to find some knowledge about which he could feel certainty, he made himself a set of colored blocks that he rearranged in various ways to make larger cubes. Using these blocks, he felt he could acquire knowledge of spatial position that was beyond all doubt. As he looked for patterns in the rearrangement of these blocks, he began to investigate the fourth dimension, which he saw as governing *sequences of transformation* in three dimensions.

By the time of Hinton's death in 1907, his writings had inspired theosophists in India and England to investigate the fourth dimension for themselves. Steiner, following the theosophists, continued to view the fourth dimension as a "spiritual" realm, though he had some fascinatingly insightful comments to make about it, keeping in mind his "esoteric" approach.

Everything we do here is simply a symbolic representation of the higher worlds.
[…] Only developing new possibilities for vision can attain what lies within these
higher worlds. Human beings must be active in order to reach these worlds.[49]

Howard Hinton and the ideas of the fourth dimension also had a profound
influence on P.D. Ouspensky who produced a very simple illustration of the
concept of our relation to the fourth dimension, which actually gives a more
"physicalized" aspect to the concept. In this illustration, he speaks about a snail on
a journey across a garden.

Its movements are governed by pleasure/pain. It always advances toward the one
and retreats from the other. It always moves on one line, from the unpleasant
towards the pleasant. And, in all probability, it senses and knows nothing except
this line. This line constitutes the whole of its world. The snail on this line of
motion senses all the sensations entering from the outside. And, these come to it out
of time — from potentiality they become actuality. For a snail, the whole of our
universe exists in the future and the past, i.e., in time.[50]

The snail is probably not self-aware — that is, aware that it is surging across the
landscape — all of which exists simultaneously, of which the snail could be aware
if it were possible to expand its awareness through some process of
metamorphosis, lifting it high above the garden to expand its scope. But, it only
perceives the various phenomena — the leaf, the grass, the twig, the sand, the
walkway — at the moment it interacts with them — and then only a little at a time.
They are *events of long or short duration,* past and future, which *come to pass* as
the snail inches along.

Ouspensky suggests that this is the way we experience our world relative to the
fourth dimension. Our five sense organs are merely feelers, our means of touching
and interpreting the world, through the mathematical constructs of our brains and
in the limited terms of three-dimensional consciousness. Scientific gadgetry only
lengthens our feelers a bit.

Imagine a consciousness not limited by the conditions of sense perception. Such a
consciousness can rise above the plane on which we move; it can see far beyond the
bounds of the circle illumined by our ordinary consciousness; it can see that not
only does the line along which we move exist, but also all the other lines
perpendicular to it which we cross (in our series of nows.) Rising above the plane,
this consciousness will be able to see the plane, make sure that it actually is a plane
and not only a line; then it will be able to see the past and the future living side by
side and existing simultaneously.[51]

---

[49] Steiner, Rudolf, *The Fourth Dimension, Sacred Geometry, Alchemy, and Mathematics*, a six-lecture
series held in Berlin from March 24 to June 7, (Anthroposophic Press 1905).

[50] Ouspensky, P.D., *Tertium Organum*, 1920, pp. 84-85.

[51] Ibid., p. 28.

There are several important considerations contained in the analogy of the snail. First, if our true perception is as limited, relatively speaking, as a snail's, why is this so if we do, in fact, possess inner knowledge and capabilities unknown to our waking, ordinary consciousness which often manifest spontaneously, or which can be developed through long and difficult training? Second, we must note the implications of a consciousness of this type that DOES exist on the physical, three-dimensional plane. But, before we endeavor to deal with those questions, let's return to the question of time.

> The past and future cannot be non-existent. They must exist together somewhere; only we do not see them. The present, as opposed to the past and the future, is the most unreal of unrealities. We must admit that the past, the present and the future do not differ from one another in any way, that the only thing that exists is the Eternal Now of Indian Philosophy.[52]

The Alpha and Omega. But we do not see this — at least very few of us do. And then we only see imperfectly, "through a glass darkly". We are snails crossing the fields of flowers of the universe, aware only momentarily of the earth, the leaf, the flower, or the raindrop before us. At any given moment we are only aware of a small fragment of the universe, and we continue to deny the existence of everything else: namely the *coexistent past and future,* and the possibility of perceiving it.

There are two main theories of the future — that of a predestined future and that of a free future. The theory of predestination asserts that every future event is the result of past events. If we know all the past, then we could know all the future. This is linear time. The idea of a free future is based on quantum "probabilities". The future is either only partially determined or undetermined because many of the varied interactions are possible at any given point. This probable future posits the idea of true free will and suggests that quite deliberate volitional acts may bring about a subsequent change in events.

Those who support predestination say that so-called "voluntary" actions are, in fact, not voluntary. Rather, they are but the results of incompletely understood causes, which have made them imperative acts — in short, nothing is accidental.

So on the one hand we have "cold predestination": come what may, nothing can be changed. On the other hand, we have a reality that is only a point on some sort of needle named the present, surrounded on all sides by the Gulf of Non-existence — a world which is born and dies every moment. Ouspensky unifies these views:

> At every given moment all the future of the world is predestined and existing, but it is predestined *conditionally*, i.e., there must be one or another future in accordance with the direction of events of the given moment, *if no new factor comes in.* And a

---

[52] Ibid., p. 29.

new factor can come in only from the side of consciousness *and the will resulting from it.*[53]

In other words, the snail *can choose to change his direction if he increases his knowledge and becomes more aware.* The snail may be following the scent of food or a need for warmth, and he may crawl into the path of a car, or into a field full of birds that wish to eat him. In practical terms, this means that snails and human beings, who are crawling through the universe very often, without knowledge, find themselves in the path of destruction. Quite often this destruction can only be overcome by mastering our instinctive urge for pleasure and avoidance of pain. This can only come about by *becoming aware* of the probable course he is on. If his natural tendencies were leading him to an abyss, which will plunge him into a blazing inferno below, then it would behoove him to learn exactly what it is he must do to avoid it. And therein lies the rub. In order to do that, a being must achieve a more aware higher state of consciousness, not a more intense state of *feeling!*

> In the past, what is behind us lies not only in what was, but also in what could have been. In the same way, in the future lie not only what will be but also what may be.[54]

In other words, motion in space is merely an illusion of the brief illuminating light of our consciousness upon a given construct of consciousness. If it is so that All exists simultaneously, then it is only we who, singly and collectively, *can change the focus or development of our consciousness.*

> In time events exist before our consciousness comes into contact with them, and they still exist after our consciousness has withdrawn from them.[55]

Now we come back to the questions: Why can we not perceive reality as it is? Why can we not enlarge our perception — why are we chained in this painful existence we call "life"? We come back to the idea of the Cave of Plato — or what is popularly known nowadays as *The Matrix.* What we are facing is the fact that the limited way we perceive our world is actually a sort of defect — the effect of the "fall" – the "ritual fault" that brought the Golden Age to an end.

At the present time, many physicists have suggested "hyperspace" has explanatory value in terms of bridging the gap between the physical and ethereal worlds. The New Age market took such ideas up with fiendish glee, producing endless ignorant variations on "Sacred Science" of millions of words, few of which are comprehensible to the layperson, much less the scientist. Those who

---

[53] Ibid., pp. 30-31.

[54] Ibid., p. 31.

[55] Ibid., p. 33.

read this drivel and who say, "oh, it sounds so true, but what is it saying?", are contemptuously told that only "initiated understanding" can grasp such lofty ideas!

The fact is, the realities of our world in terms of any connecting principles between matter and consciousness are not helped by any such philosophical discussions. What we need is further empirical study and experimentation. What's more, it needs to be done by those who are qualified to do it — not charlatans and con artists.

There are physical scientists of the highest caliber who are open to the possibility of other forms of matter and other dimensions. They understand that such hypotheses would have explanatory value in their own fields as well as in parapsychology. Thus it is that, while the subject matter of parapsychology and physics is significantly different, their fundamental insights curiously coincide.

GETTING A HANDLE ON PSI PHENOMENA

There is similarity between the two basic paths of fundamental research in modern theoretical physics, and the two realities we are considering: matter and consciousness. Just as in psi research there have been attempts to reconcile, or unify, matter and consciousness, the same has been true in advanced physics where although serious attempts have been made during the past two decades to find a Unified Theory that incorporates both a quantum approach ("matter") and the field approach ("consciousness"), no single theory which incorporates both has been successful as yet in either set of problems. Quantum mechanics deals primarily with the sub-microscopic world of elementary particles. It is based upon probabilities of events taking place non-deterministically, rather than a deterministically known state, which can be calculated using the classical equations of motion.

When you have an infinite number of possible states, any of which can be solutions within certain boundary conditions, you run into certain problems when you try to transfer these concepts to classical realities. The *state vector* is the collection of all possible pre-collapse states and represents the *system* in which the event *exists in all states simultaneously*. Once the event happens, or what is called "measurement" occurs, the system collapses the state vector into a single, probabilistically determined state. Until this collapse occurs, the state vector that has developed in time deterministically specifies the system collectively. This interpretation of quantum mechanics is known as the *Copenhagen Interpretation* and is dominant, with minor variations, in the quantum mechanics used today. It is characterized by a direct break with classical physics where a cause leads to an effect.

At the same time, field theory, (Einstein's general theory of relativity) plays the leading role when we are considering real world physical realities. Field theory seems to follow from the classical view of cause and effect and determinism. Classical mechanics deals with equations of motion that can be solved for specific events when *initial conditions*, such as position and velocity, or initial and final conditions, are known. So it is that the field represents a deterministic interrelation of mutually interacting forces between different events (i.e. particles), which can be found by substituting values into the field equations.

Both the field and quantum theories have special characteristics which are useful in physical theories of psi. However the same problems pop up in trying to combine quantum theory with (relativistic) field theory: no such system has yet been devised which can account for all phenomena.

At the present time, however, it seems that quantum field theory has been by far the most *successful* attempt at this endeavor. Many of the speculation about physical theories of psi deal with quantum field theory, rather than pure field theory. Whiteman notes: "*It seems therefore that any attempt to unite parapsychology and physics should adhere, substantially at least, to the language of quantum field theory, in terms of 'as if' fields at a level of creativepotentiality.*"[56]

The older theories of psi described transfers of energy in several different ways, but newer ideas have gone beyond such approaches. One argument against the idea of psi and a physical theory of psi based on energy (or particle) transmission has been that the energies would be far too subtle to be received by the brain. John Eccles has shown that the cerebral cortex acts as a sensitive detector of *small influences.*[57] Using a probabilistic quantum mechanical argument, it is possible to show that the neurons can be fired by these *subtle influences*, thus exciting the brain in a normal cascading effect of neurons. In this way, the brain may act as a receptor of small influences such as what might be exhibited by carriers of psi.

Among other attempts to unite biological functions with quantum theory, W. Elsasser has speculated on certain *biotonic laws* operating exclusively in living beings and drawing upon "accumulated quantum-mechanical and information theoretic uncertainties".[58] All such approaches represent a convergence of bioelectronics and quantum theory to explain psi abilities, including PK (psychokinesis, the movement of objects by mental effort alone).

There are so many interpretations of quantum theory that may be relevant to psi and that may assist in gaining an understanding of how consciousness interacts with matter. Most of the new theories are based upon the introduction of a new level of duality in nature in that consciousness has a separate and distinct wave function from that of the normal wave function representing matter and physical reality in quantum theory, a sort of three wave system like biorhythms, where when all the lines cross, something happens.

The issue I would like to emphasize here is that we desperately need a scientifically acceptable conceptual framework within which Parapsychological

---

[56] Whiteman, J.H.M., "Parapsychology and Physics", in Wolman, *Handbook*, 1977.

[57] Dobbs, Adrian, "The Feasibility of a Physical Theory of ESP", in *Smythies, Science and ESP* (New York: Humanities Press 1967).

[58] Chari, C.T.K., "Precognition, Probability and Quantum Mechanics" (*Journal of the ASPR* 66, 1972) pp. 193-207.

phenomena make sense as part of nature and human life in its entirety. I believe that such ideas were known to an ancient civilization, that they did develop the "Holy Grail" of physics: The Grand Unified Theory, and that in point of fact, the Holy Grail of physics may have a great deal to do with the Holy Grail of legend.

EINSTEIN AND HYPERDIMENSIONAL PHYSICS

In considering the general theory of relativity, science usually utilizes a four-dimensional space-time continuum. In classical general relativity, the metrical properties of the continuum are intrinsic to the continuum, but a *fifth dimension* in which our normally sensed space-time is embedded can also be used to account for the curvature and properties of physical space. In the space-time continuum, one can say that all parts of the four-dimensional world exist simultaneously, in the sense of a mathematical formalism, and this would naturally lead to a complete collapse of the philosophical ideas of causality.

However, many scientists who work with these ideas do not think that this continuum is 'real' in a physical sense, such that physical entities could move back and forth at will in and out of time as easily as changing direction in three-dimensional space. We, on the other hand, think that it is not only possible, but also extremely likely based upon certain observations.

In relativity theory, time intervals between events are not completely fixed relative to moving systems or frames of reference. This has led to some speculation that there may also be analogies between precognition and anomalies. However, "time dilation", the contraction of time intervals between moving reference frames, is too small to account for precognition and would still require any information transfer to travel faster than light, and the special theory of relativity, when narrowly interpreted, does not allow for physical travel backwards in time, but relegates this concept to an imaginary mathematical formalism.

Even though it is almost forbidden to question Einstein's restriction on superluminal travel, Einstein did, at one point, propose to consider the hyperdimensional world as "real". In 1938, with P. Bergmann, he wrote a paper entitled *On a Generalization of Kaluza's Theory of Electricity*:

> So far, two fairly simple and natural attempts to connect gravitation and electricity by a unitary field theory have been made, one by Weyl, the other by Kaluza.
> Furthermore, there have been some attempts to represent Kaluza's theory formally so as to avoid the introduction of the fifth dimension of the physical continuum.
> The theory presented here differs from Kaluza's in one essential point; we ascribe physical reality to the fifth dimension whereas in Kaluza's theory this fifth dimension was introduced only in order to obtain new components of the metric tensor representing the electromagnetic field.[59]

---

[59] Einstein, A, Bergmann, P., *Annals of Mathematics*, Vol. 38, No. 3, July 1938.

We believe that Einstein was following a path that was later to prove very fruitful. Einstein, however, was somewhat nervous about this idea, but he followed it anyway, writing in his paper:

> If Kaluza's attempt is a real step forward, then it is because of the introduction of the five dimensional space. There have been many attempts to retain the essential formal results obtained by Kaluza without sacrificing the four-dimensional character of the physical space. This shows distinctly how vividly our physical intuition resists the introduction of the fifth dimension. But by considering and comparing all these attempts one must come to the conclusion that all these endeavors did not improve the situation. It seems impossible to formulate Kaluza's idea in a simple way without introducing the fifth dimension.

> We have, therefore, to take the fifth dimension seriously although we are not encouraged to do so by plain experience. If, therefore, the space structure seems to force acceptance of the five dimensional space theory upon us we must ask whether it is sensible to assume the rigorous reducibility to four dimensional space. We believe that the answer should be "no", provided that it is possible to understand, in another way, the *quasi-four dimensional character of the physical space* by taking as a basis the five dimensional continuum and to simplify hereby the basic geometrical assumptions.[...] The most essential point of our theory is the replacing of ...rigorous cylindricity by the assumption that space is closed (or periodic).[...] Kaluza's five dimensional theory of the physical space provides a unitary representation of gravitation and electromagnetism. [...] It is much more satisfactory to introduce the fifth dimension not only formally, but to assign to it some physical meaning.[60]

The reader should note that when considering field theory, it is necessary to differentiate between 1.) Pure field theory such as gravitation, and electrical and magnetic fields and 2.) Quantum field theory. Fields such as electromagnetic fields and gravitational fields are continuous and spatial while quantum fields are quantized, broken into discrete sections of particulate substance or energy. The basing of a theory of psi on a gravitational field rests partly on the fact that gravitation is not subject to the maximum velocity of light because *it doesn't travel, but is structural*. Evidence from Vasiliev and others suggests that psi is also *independent of the velocity of light*.

However, general relativity has obliged science to abandon the "action at a distance" idea, causing the 'distance force' to be abandoned, and has placed gravity under subjection to a maximum velocity. Nevertheless, Margenau has suggested that general relativity ought to be regarded as a 'formal' principle such as the Pauli Exclusion Principle. In this case, gravitation would be non-energetic

---

[60] Ibid.

and *subject to no maximum velocity,* and would act as a guiding way to physical phenomena".[61]

These ideas have been adopted by many "alternative science" writers who have related them to buildings, energy fields, light beings, earth grids and all that, and it does, indeed, seem that there may be locations on the planet where one can "tap" a certain energy with greater or lesser ease. But the phenomenon that these ideas speaks to more directly is that of hyperdimensional realities wherein mental energies or consciousness energies are amplified and can be interactive with the environment. There may be a specific technology that suggests not only power for transport that is partly physical, partly "ethereal", but also that suggests communication that is partly physical and partly ethereal, as well as powers of "manifestation" that might seem impossible to us in our present state of technology. All of these properties DO belong to hyperdimensional existence, and such a state of being has been reported for millennia as being the "realm of the gods".

---

[61] Forwald, Haakon, *Mind, Matter and Gravitation: A Theoretical and Experimental Approach,* Parapsychology Monographs, Number 11 (New York: Parapsychology Foundation 1969).

CHAPTER 5
WHOSE WORLD IS IT, ANYWAY?

THE TREE OF LIFE AND THE END OF TIME

One of the very ancient aspects of the idea of Celestial Archetypes was the concept of the "Axis Mundi", or "Center of the World". This was a point where Heaven, Earth and Hell met and where Time was abolished and passage to one region or another was possible. At any point where there was a convergence of the three realms, a "temple" was considered to exist whether one was constructed there or not. This center was the zone of the sacred — of absolute reality — and was symbolized by trees, fountains, ladders, ropes, and so forth. Interaction with these symbols was considered initiatory and took place in a timeless state. Thus, it has been theorized that religious rituals were developed in an attempt to "connect" to this Divine Model or archetype. In this way, a sacrifice was not only an imitation of the original sacrifice of the god, it somehow was seen to be an alignment of the three realms, the creating of a "passage" of some sort along the Axis Mundi. So, for a moment, during the ritual or sacrifice, the supplicant was identifying him or her self with the primordial gesture and thereby abolishing time, the burden of the Terror of History, and regenerating him or her self and all the related participants. There are endless examples of scapegoats and dying gods and sacrificed kings, as well as a host of "substitutes" in terms of a variety of animals and other products offered to the gods. We are going to suggest that it is, indeed, through "sacrifice" that man "identifies with the gods", and "aligns himself with the Axis Mundi". But, it is in a sacrifice of a very different sort — one that sacrifices our "animal nature", and that this has been corrupted to mean that an "external" sacrifice or ritual is required. We are going to suggest that this "ladder" or "tree" image is a reflection of our very own DNA, and that it is through the DNA that man regains his "Timeless State".

What is important, however, is that the myths are only a much later formulation of an archaic content that postulates an absolute reality, or levels of reality, which are extra-human or hyperdimensional.

There is another interesting key to the ancient myths and rituals: in nearly every case, there is a conception of the end and the beginning of a Cyclical Temporal Period; and, coincidental to this idea, is an expulsion of demons, diseases and sins. These ideas are demonstrated by the ubiquitous carnival celebrations of the New Year.

...This annual expulsion of sins, diseases, and demons is basically an attempt to
restore — if only momentarily — mythical and primordial time, "pure" time, the
time of the "instant" of the Creation. Every New Year is a resumption of time from
the beginning, that is, a repetition of the cosmogony. The ritual combats between
two groups of actors, the presence of the dead, the Saturnalia, and the orgies are so
many elements which denote that at the end of the year and in the expectation of
the New Year there is a repetition of the mythical moment of the passage from
chaos to cosmos. [62]

At this period, the expulsion of evils and sins takes place by means of a
scapegoat, and the cycle is closed by the Hierogamy ("sacred marriage"), which
initiates the new creation. The more ancient ceremonies are nearly global in their
proliferation among "primitive" societies, and it could be conjectured that it is to
these "purer" examples we should look for the more common elements to discover
if there is any hidden meaning that might serve as a clue.

For the most part, the beginnings of these rites comprise a series of dramatic
elements that represent a condition of universal confusion, the abolition of order
and hierarchy, and the ushering in of chaos. There is a "symbolic Deluge" that
annihilates all of humanity in order to prepare the way for a new and regenerated
human species. In numerous myths and rites we find the same central idea of the
yearly return to chaos, followed by a new creation. The chaos that preceded the
rebirth was as essential as the birth itself. Without chaos there could be no rebirth.

In many of the more "modern" versions, the Deluge and the element of water are
present in one way or another as either libations or baptism. Baptism is the
subjective, microcosmic equivalent of a macrocosmic level deluge: a return to the
formless state.

This formlessness, this chaos, was exemplified in many ways: fasting,
confession, excess grief, joy, despair or orgy — all of them only seeking to
reproduce a chaotic state from which a New Creation could emerge.

It is also interesting to note that, at the time of renewal, the New Year festival, it
was thought that the fate of men was fixed for a "whole year". In short, it was the
"formation of the Ark" that determined if and how and who would pass through
the deluge.

What is important in the preceding idea is that the end of a past year and the
beginning of a new year are predicated upon the idea of an *exhaustion of
biological resources on all cosmic planes*, a veritable end of the world. In this
view, the "end" is not always occasioned by a deluge, but can also occur through
the effects of fire, heat and other causes. Fulcanelli writes:

> Nature herself gives us the unequivocal signs of weariness: she is becoming lazy. It
> is only by dint of chemical fertilizers that the farmer now obtains average value

---

[62] Eliade, op. cit., p. 54.

crops. Ask a peasant, he will tell you that "the earth is dying", that seasons are disturbed, the climate modified. Every growing thing lacks sap and resistance. Plants wither and prove unable to react against the invasion of parasitic insects or the attack of diseases. [63]

In *Le Probleme des centaures*, Georges Dumezil studies and discusses the scenario of the end and beginning according to a large selection of material derived from the Indo-European world including Slavs, Iranians, Indians and Greco-Romans. He noted several elements from initiation ceremonies that have been preserved in more or less corrupt form in mythology and folklore. Another examination of the myths and rites of Germanic secret societies by Otto Hofler brought out similar relationships. Both of these researches point up the importance of the twelve intercalary days, and especially New Year's Day.

...We shall recall only a few characteristic facts:
(1) the twelve intermediate days prefigure the twelve months of the year;
(2) during the twelve corresponding nights, the dead come in procession to visit their families;
(3) it is at this period that fires are extinguished and rekindled;
(4) this is the moment of initiations, one of whose essential elements is precisely this extinction and rekindling of fire;
(5) ritual combats between two opposing groups; and
(6) presence of erotic elements, marriage, orgies.

Each of these mythico-ritual motifs testifies to the wholly exceptional character of the days that precede and follow the first day of the year, although the eschato-cosmological function of the New Year (abolition of time and repetition of creation) is not explicitly stated... Nevertheless, this function can be shown to be implicit in all the rest of these mythico-ritual motifs. *How could the invasion by the souls of the dead, for example, be anything but the sign of a suspension of profane time, the paradoxical realization of a coexistence of 'past' and 'present'?* This coexistence is never so complete as at a period of chaos when all modalities coincide. The last days of the past year can be identified with the pre-Creation chaos, both through this *invasion of the dead* — which annuls the law of time — and through the *sexual excesses* which commonly mark the occasion.[64]

Take particular note of the ideas of "exhaustion of physical resources, invasion by the souls of the dead, and sexual excess" as being indicative of the suspension of time. These are significant in our present time wherein it seems there is a veritable "invasion" of "otherworldly" visitors masquerading as "aliens" as well as a rapid descent of morality into greater and greater sexual excesses; a veritable frenzied "return to chaos", as it were!

---

[63] Fulcanelli, op. cit., p. 504.

[64] Eliade, op. cit., pp. 67-68.

The rites still mark the abolition of all norms and violently illustrate an *overturning of values and a reversion of all forms to indeterminate unity.* The very locus of the orgies, when the seed was buried in the ground, demonstrates the dissolution of form into orgiastic chaos. *We are in the presence of a very ancient idea: a return to primordial unity, the end/beginning in which limits, contours, distances, no longer hold sway.* What is primordial and essential is the idea of regeneration through chaos, repetition of creation: a Time Loop.

> In the last analysis, what we discover in all these rites and all these attitudes is the
> will to devaluate time. [...] time can be annulled.[65]

A NEW HEAVEN AND A NEW EARTH

Because of our own experience with COINTELPRO operatives as we have chronicled on our website, and will be publishing in more depth in a future volume, we - and our global research team - undertook an investigation into the phenomenon in order to track the threads and connections. This led to the study of psychopathy and our growing awareness that there was something terribly amiss on our planet that was being covered up by the psychiatric and medical communities. The follow-up to this research was, naturally, more questions posed to the Cassiopaeans about the specific nature of the beast we were seeing "hidden within the picture". The answers were both shocking and revealing, indicating that there are actually TWO distinct races of humans on Earth, and TWO main, intersecting realities. As noted, this was an unsettling notion, but we soon found evidence from other sources that it is something that has been known and taught in the interior circles of the most Secret of esoteric groups down through the ages. There is even evidence that this was the great truth taught by the man around whom the Jesus legend was wrapped.

In Fulcanelli's *Le Mystère des Cathédrales,* a most mysterious chapter was inserted in the second edition, which discusses an architectural monument found at Hendaye, "a small frontier town in the Basque country". Fulcanelli tells us:

> ...[I]t is the strangest monument of primitive millenarism, the rarest symbolical
> translation of chiliasm, which I have ever met. It is known that this doctrine, first
> accepted and then refuted by Origen, St. Denis of Alexandria and St. Jerome
> although the Church had not condemned it, was part of the esoteric tradition of the
> ancient hermetic philosophy. [...] We must recognize that the unknown workman,
> who made these images, possessed real and profound knowledge of the universe. [66]

Here we have found the suggestion that the core of hermeticism, alchemy, is the doctrine of "primitive chiliasm". Note the term "primitive."

---

[65] Ibid., pp. 85-86.

[66] Fulcanelli, *The Mystery of the Cathedrals*, (Las Vegas: Brotherhood of Life 1984) p. 166.

When researching religious matters, one always comes across prophecy and miracles. It seems that those who are to be kept in fear of the Lord need an unequivocal sign from time to time. Miracles and visions can sway whole armies. We can think of the battle cry "Great is Allah!", and the claim of the salvific blood of Christ that was held up as a shield against the Saracens. We should also be reminded of the mandate of Yahweh to "utterly destroy" just about everybody who wasn't hanging out with Joshua and his gang. Such "visions" go back into our primeval past. Around 5,000 BC, the divine Ishtar was said to have appeared to Enme-Kar, the ruler of Uruk, telling him to overthrow the city of Aratta. But, at the moment, we are mostly concerned with visions in the context of the Bible since it is the Bible that underpins the beliefs of a staggering number of human beings on planet earth at the present time, including their "revised forms" in the New Age and Human Potential movement.

Hans Conzelmann, Professor of New Testament Studies at Tottingen admitted that the Christian community continues to exist because the conclusions of the critical study of the Bible are largely withheld from them. Joachim Kahl, a graduate in theology of Phillips University, Marburg, noted, "The ignorance of most Christians is largely due to the scanty information provided by theologians and ecclesiastical historians, who know two ways of concealing the scandalous facts of their books. They either twist reality into its exact opposite or conceal it."

Dr. Johannes Lehman, co-translator of a modern edition of the Bible remarked: "The evangelists are interpreters, not biographers; they have not illuminated what had grown dark with the passage of generations, but obscured what was still light. They have not written history, but made history. They did not want to report, but to justify."

The "original texts" that are so often referred to in theological hairsplitting do not exist. What do exist are transcripts that originated between the fourth and tenth centuries. And these are transcripts of transcripts, some fifteen hundred of them, and not one of them agrees with another. More than eighty thousand variations have been counted. There does not exist a single page of the "original texts" without contradictions. The most prominent of them, the *Codex Sinaiticus*, has been found to contain sixteen thousand corrections, which can be traced back to seven correctors. These correctors made their "corrections" because each one understood the verses differently, and they transformed the functions according to what they perceived to be the needs of the time.

Dr. Robert Kehl of Zurich writes: "Frequently the same passage has been 'corrected' by one corrector in one sense and immediately 'recorrected' in the opposite sense by another, depending entirely on which dogmatic view had to be defended in the relevant school. At all events, a completely chaotic text and irremediable confusion has already arisen owing to individual 'corrections', but even more so to deliberate ones."

Father Jean Schorer, for many years spiritual adviser to the Cathedral of Saint-Pierre, Geneva, concluded that the theory of the divine inspiration of the Bible is in such contradiction with the most basic, elementary knowledge base of normal human reason, and is so obviously refuted by the Bible itself, that only ignorant persons would defend it, while only people completely devoid of any kind of culture would believe it.

Dr. Robert Kehl writes in Die Religion des modernen Menschen:

> Most believers in the Bible have the naive credo that the Bible has always existed
> in the form in which they read it today. They believe that the Bible has always
> contained all the sections, which are found in their personal copy of the Bible. They
> do not know - and most of them do not want to know - that for about 200 years the
> first Christians had no 'scripture' apart from the Old Testament, and that even the
> Old Testament canon had not been definitely established in the days of the early
> Christians, that written versions of the New Testament only came into being quite
> slowly, that for a long time no one dreamed of considering these New Testament
> writings as Holy Scripture, that with the passage of time the custom arose of
> reading these writings to the congregations, but that even then no one dreamed of
> treating them as Holy Scriptures with the same status as the Old Testament, that
> this idea first occurred to people when the different factions in Christianity were
> fighting each other and they felt the need to be able to back themselves up with
> something binding, that in this way people only began to regard these writings as
> Holy Scripture about 200 AD.

Further on, we will look at the creation of the Bible as it really happened, but for
now, let us just say that in examining this process, we find nothing of the "Holy
Ghost" in there. That's the plain fact, and a lot of people in the "business" of
religion know it.

Nevertheless, our institutions of higher learning generally have a special faculty
allotment for the teaching of theology, *financed by the taxpayer*, whether Christian
or Jew. One assumes that the students who study this theology are also given
exposure to other studies, such as math, languages, science, and so forth. The
question then becomes: what kind of strange distortion, what incomprehensible
corruption takes place in the minds of human beings, so that they so completely
separate their academic knowledge from what they hear preached at them from the
pulpit? *What kind of brainwashing can so effectively cause the simplest of facts to
be forgotten?*

How does this happen? It is literally staggering to a logical, intelligent human
being that the fairy tale of the Bible - as God's word - has endured so long. There
is nothing to which we can compare this in the entire seven thousand years of
human history of which we are aware. Calling it all a "pack of lies" seems rather
harsh, but it is increasingly evident that it is certainly intentionally misleading,
and, in that case, what shall we call it?

How about COINTELPRO?

Christian theologians claim that the teachings of Jesus (which is the established
religious dogma) are unconditionally valid. Rudolf Augstein asks, "...With what
right do the Christian churches refer to a Jesus who did not exist in the form they

claim, to doctrines which he did not teach, to an absolute authority which he did not confer, and to a filiation with God which he never laid claim to?"[67]

Naturally, all of these problems have led to many interesting theological solutions. It is amazing how creative true believers can be when faced with facts that this or that idea they have held for a long time is no longer tenable.

Nowadays, the presence of widespread sharing of information relating to anomalous appearances of what are now being called "aliens" has naturally led to the identification of Jesus with the "interstellar astronaut" theory. Jesus is an "alien".

Dr. Vyatcheslav Saitsev of the University of Minsk claimed that Jesus came from outer space. His idea was that Jesus was a representative of a higher civilization, and that this is the explanation of his supernatural powers. He noted, "In other words, God's descent to Earth is really a cosmic event".

He may not be so crazy. The only question is: considering the work of COINTELPRO to conceal, distract, disinform, which God was it who "descended"?

Meanwhile, the *Holy Blood, Holy Grail* guys are busy cooking up a "divine bloodline". Laurence Gardiner, who has connected the Holy Grail Bloodline to reptilian aliens augments this idea. At the same time, we have a host of true believers around the planet preaching the gospel of those cute and helpful Grays, and the reptilian Lord who really loves us and never did anything to humanity except teach them all about how to be civilized.

Simultaneously, we have an obvious "gradual revelation" plan going on via the government and its space program, and now a big push by George Bush and the Fundamentalists of both Christian and Zionist tendencies to institute a One World Government under the rule of the US beast empire.

We have a right to ask: what the heck is really going on? What does it mean to talk about the "New Jerusalem" when, in point of fact - as we will shortly explicate- anything and everything that had to do with the Old Jerusalem was lies and disinformation issuing from that crafty Yahweh/Jehovah guy with control issues?

The reality seems to be that Judaism, Christianity and Islam were specifically designed and created just to produce a particular situation that is desirable to someone at a certain point in time, and again, we see the same operation being run on humanity in the present day as the New Age - Human Potential movement.

When we step back from the situation, the one thing that we see is that prophecy is at the center of the Judeo-Christian-Islamic tradition. The prophets of these religions claimed to be in direct contact with the Creator of the Universe, and this creator seems to have been singularly "personal" in the sense of having personal

---

[67] Jesus Menschensohn, Munich, 1972.

traits, whims, likes and dislikes. His prophets are, naturally, privileged messengers, receiving his divine revelations, and these revelations divide mankind into those who believe them and those who don't. Naturally, those who don't are damned. Sounds a lot like what is going on today among the Contactees.

The Christian religion, and its New Age offshoots, is the chief proponent of the many End of the World scenarios with which we are most familiar. Scenarios about the end times originate mostly in the body of apocalyptic, eschatological writings of the New and Old Testaments. It is in the final book, Revelation, that most striking and symbolic representations about the end of the world are said by many to be depicted.

It is a difficult work to comprehend. Probably no other piece of writing in history has been examined more thoroughly and interpreted more widely. It is the end-of-the world legend, a doomsday tale on moldy bread with virtual reality special effects in abundance. It is the inspirational fountainhead for mad prophets, spittle spewing pulpit-pounders, apocalyptic Enochian magicians, fanatical true believers, grade-B moviemakers, and knaves and snake-oil salesmen of every form and sort.

Does this mean that we can just discard Revelation and the other prophecies altogether? It would be nice to think so, but as we have already noted, even though the Control System is always stepping in to do damage control, they do it oh, so carefully! While the above is rather accurate in terms of the many and varied interpretations that have been given to this Mother of all End Time Prophecies, there is no point in throwing the baby out with the bathwater. Anybody with eyes and ears can percive that there is something amiss in our world, in our reality, and once that is seen, and once the questions are asked, which then leads to research, we come to the idea that something is really going to happen!

What seems to be true is that the writers of both the Old and New Testaments couldn't just toss out the oral traditions. They used them in a very special way. It often seems that whatever was positive was twisted and turned backward. With an awareness of how history can by mythicized and then historicized, and any combination thereof, we can look at the scriptures with a different eye. We can theorize that there must have been a real person around whom the legend of Jesus - the mythicized history - was wrapped. We can theorize that he was teaching something important and dramatic for it to have made such an impact. We can also theorize that this "impact" was seen as useful to utilize it as the centerpiece of a Control System, while at the same time burying the teachings themselves. The very nature of the Matrix itself and our current day observations, as well as a broad historical review, suggest that whatever he was really doing and saying, it was most certainly twisted, corrupted, and emphases shifted in fairly predictable ways.

Early Christians are said to have believed that the end of the world and the reappearance of their Messiah were imminent. We are told that, from the earliest days of the organized church, anticipation of the millennium - the thousand-year reign of the returned Christ - was in conflict with ecclesiastical policies that were growing apace in the new church hierarchy.

In what is today Turkey, a man named Montanus claimed to have experienced a vision of a heavenly New Jerusalem about to descend to the earth. Montanus and his idea were perceived as a threat to ecclesiastical authority. Hippolytus, writing in 215 AD accused the Montanist believers of heresy, including *listening to revelations from female seers.* Montanism continued to spread, especially after Tertullian - the brilliant legal scholar who had been born in Carthage and converted to Christianity in 196 AD. - joined the movement. He too reported a vision of this heavenly city descending from the sky, a metaphor that has persisted for centuries.

The ubiquity of this vision is interesting for a lot of reasons, most particularly when one considers the possibility that these early Christians may have been interacting with hyperdimensional realities. While some Gnostic groups "spiritualized" the events foretold in Revelation, there were still those who insisted that this paradise was quite real and physical and could exist on earth. This idea became known as *chiliasm,* a form of apocalyptic vision that *depicted the millennium as a physical and material period.*

A Gnostic prophet named Cerinthus said that there would be an earthly kingdom of Christ, and that the flesh of human beings again inhabiting Jerusalem would be subject to desires and pleasure. He added, "The kingdom of Christ would ... consist in the satisfaction of the stomach and of even lower organs, in eating, and drinking and nuptial pleasures". One writer described Cerinthus and his followers by noting, "there was great enthusiasm among his supporters for that end...".

No doubt.

Many chiliasts believed that in the millennium all manner of physical craving would be satiated, that men would find all women beautiful and willing to partake in carnal delights. Others taught that women would bear many children, but without the pain of childbirth or even the inconvenience of sex. It can be noted that there is a thread of sexual allusions in the millennialist vision that - through the centuries - has emerged again and again.

It is fairly simple to see in the "seed" of the primitive chiliasm of the early Christian ideas the concept of Time Loops and hyperdimensional realities as well as the idea of cyclical catastrophes signaling both the end and the beginning of "worlds". However, there seems to have been something else about this early Christianity that created problems for church fathers who were busy codifying dogma and constructing a far-flung ecclesiastical empire. Since "end time fever" would not go away, it was codified as "believe in our dogmas, and you will go to heaven at the End Time". "It will only happen once, and we are the agents of the god who is going to destroy everybody who does not belong to our club."

The question is: if the early Church fathers eliminated "primitive chiliasm" from Christianity, what ELSE did they eliminate? As noted, what we know as Christianity today is, according to many experts, little more than an amalgamation of many mythical representations of the dying and resurrecting god theme. More than anything, it reflects the Tammuz drama with a major overlay of the Egyptian religion of the time.

What is most revealing is the fact that the only writings contemporary to the times of early Christianity which mention it specifically, remark that it was a "vile superstition". Yet, what we have as Christianity today is nothing more or less than the same religious practices of the peoples who branded it a "vile superstition". Tacitus tells us that in the time of Nero:

There followed a catastrophe, whether through accident or the design of the emperor is not sure, as there are authorities for both views, but it was the most disastrous and appalling of all the calamities brought on this city through the violence of fire. ...A rumor had spread abroad that at the very time when the city was burning, Nero had mounted on his private stage and sung of the destruction of Troy, comparing the present disaster with that ancient catastrophe....

In order to put an end to these rumors Nero provided scapegoats and visited most fearful punishments on those popularly called Christians, *a group hated because of their outrageous practices.* The founder of this sect, Christus, was executed in the reign of Tiberius by the procurator Pontius Pilatus. Thus the *pernicious superstition* was suppressed for the while, but it broke out again not only in Judaea, where this evil had its origin, but even in Rome, to which all *obnoxious and disgraceful elements* flow from everywhere in the world and receive a large following.

The first ones to be seized were those who confessed; then on their information a vast multitude was convicted, *not so much on the charge of incendiarism as because of their hatred of humanity.* [68]

Pliny the Younger, who lived c. 62 to 113 AD, was sent by Emperor Trajan as a special representative to the Roman province of Bithynia in Asia Minor. His task was to keep the peace. When he had trouble dealing with Christians, Pliny wrote to the emperor asking how he should proceed against them describing what he knew about their religion:

However, they asserted that their guilt or mistake had amounted to no more than this, that they had been accustomed on a set day to gather before dawn and to chant in antiphonal form a hymn to Christ as if to a god, and to bind themselves by a pledge, not for the commission of any crime, but rather that they would not commit theft nor robbery nor adultery nor break their promises, nor refuse to return on demand any treasure that had been entrusted to their care; when this ceremony had been completed, they would go away, to reassemble later for a feast, but an ordinary and innocent one. They had abandoned even this custom after my edict in which, following your instruction, I had forbidden the existence of fellowships. So I thought it the more necessary to extract the truth even by torture from two maidservants who were called deaconesses. I found *nothing save a vile superstition carried to an immoderate length.*

The contagion of the superstition has pervaded not only the cities but the villages and country districts as well. Yet it seems that it can be halted and cured. It is well agreed that temples almost desolate have begun to be thronged again, and stated rites that had long been abandoned are revived; and a sale is found for the fodder of

---

[68] Leon, Harry J., trans., "Selections from Tacitus" in MacKendrick, Paul and Herbert M. Howe, *Classics in Translation, Vol. II*: Latin Literature, C (Madison: The University of Wisconsin Press, 1952).

sacrificial victims, though hitherto buyers were rare. So it is easy to conjecture what a great number of offenders may be reformed, if a chance to repent is given. [69]

So we have these clues:

1. Christians were hated because of *their outrageous practices.*

2. Their beliefs were described as a *pernicious superstition.*

3. The pernicious superstition had its origin in Judaea.

4. Christians were convicted because of their "hatred of humanity".

5. Pliny describes their practices as "benign" but that the core belief was a "vile superstition carried to an immoderate length".

6. This "vile superstition" was pervasive and apparently led to the temples and ancient rites including sacrifice being abandoned.

The question that comes to mind is: what would the peoples of that time have considered a "vile superstition" or "outrageous practices" when one is aware of what they considered normal religious practice which included dying god myths and gnosticism and sacrifice and all the other accoutrements of Christianity as we know it today? The only real clue we have is the remark: *"not so much on the charge of incendiarism as because of their hatred of humanity - a vile superstition carried to an immoderate length".*

Their what?

"Their hatred of humanity."

In *Book III* of his *Gnosis*, Boris Mouravieff discusses what he calls "pre-adamic humanity" and "adamic humanity". Here are some excerpts of what Mouravieff has to say:

> In the first volume of *Gnosis*, we already referred several times to the coexistence of two essentially different races: one of *Men*, and another of *Anthropoids*. We must emphasize the fact that from the esoteric point of view the latter term has no derogatory meaning.

> ...The Scriptures contain more than one reference to the coexistence on our planet of these two humanities – which are now alike in form but unlike in essence. We can even say that the whole dramatic history of humanity, from the fall of Adam until today, not excluding the prospect of the new era, is overshadowed by the coexistence of these two human races whose separation will occur only at the Last Judgment. [70]

> ...The human tares, the anthropoid race, are the descendants of pre-adamic humanity. The principal difference between contemporary pre-adamic man and

---

[69] Heironimus, John Paul, trans., "Selected Letters of the Younger Pliny," in MacKendrick, Paul and Herbert M. Howe, *Classics in Translation, Vol. II*: Latin Literature, C (Madison: The University of Wisconsin Press 1952).

[70] Mouravieff, Boris, *Gnosis, Volume III*, translated and edited by Robin Amis, (Robertsbridge, UK: Praxis Institute Press 1993) p. 107.

adamic man – a difference which is not perceived by the senses – is that the former does not possess the developed higher centers that exist in the latter which, although they have been cut off from his waking consciousness since the Fall, offer him a real possibility of esoteric evolution. Apart from this, the two races are similar: they have the same lower centers, the same structure of the Personality and the same physical body, although more often than not this is stronger in the pre-adamic man than in the adamic; regarding beauty, we must not forget that pre-adamic man and woman were created by God on the sixth day, in His image and after His likeness, and that the daughters of this race were beautiful. [71]

By identifying himself with the 'I' of his Personality, Adam lost consciousness of his real 'I' and fell from the Eden that was his original condition into the same condition as the pre-adamics... The two humanities, coming from two different creative processes, later mingled on the level of organic life on Earth... From then on, the coexistence of these two human types, and the competition, which was the result of this, became the norm...we can see that throughout the centuries, even in our own day, adamics in their post-fall condition, have been and are generally in an inferior position to the pre-adamics.

...For the moment we will restrict ourselves to repeating that contemporary adamic man, having lost contact with his higher centers and therefore with his real 'I', appears practically the same as his pre-adamic counterpart. However, unlike the latter, he still has his higher centers, which ensure that he has the possibility of following the way of esoteric evolution. *At present*, pre-adamic man is deprived of this possibility, but it will be given to him if adamic humanity develops, as it should during the era of the Holy Spirit. [72]

So now we come to an idea that just might fit the bill of a "vile superstition" as well as an explanation for the remark that the early Christians had an "excessive hatred for humanity". We also have a sudden flash of insight about some of the odd remarks attributed to Jesus such as "I come not to bring peace, but a sword", and his address to the Pharisees that they were the "children of their father, Satan".

We also come to a fuller understanding of Fulcanelli's remark about Primitive Chiliasm. Quoting and paraphrasing Mouravieff:

The Era of the Holy Spirit has two faces - one of Paradise regained and the other a Deluge of Fire... We can even say that the whole dramatic history of humanity, from the fall of Adam until today, not excluding the prospect of the New Era, is overshadowed by the coexistence of these two human races whose separation will occur only at the Last Judgment. It is to this that Jesus referred in parables when he spoke to the crowds, but described in clear terms for the benefit of his disciples; the most noteworthy description is the parable of the tares and the good seed, on which he made the following commentary:

---

[71] Ibid., pp. 108-109.

[72] Ibid., p. 129.

He that soweth the good seed is the Son of man: the field is the world: the good seed are the children of the kingdom: but the tares are the children of the wicked one: the enemy that sowed them is the devil: the harvest is the end of the world...

The coexistence of a race of Anthropoids and a race of Men, confirmed here, is necessary from the point of view of the General Law, to maintain uninterrupted the stability in movement of organic life on earth. It is also necessary because of the principle of equilibrium. The first race is a counterbalance, which allows the race of Men to pursue its esoteric evolution. Jesus confirmed this when he spoke about the End in the following terms:

Then, shall two be in the field; one shall be taken, and the other left. Two women shall be grinding at the mill; the one shall be taken, and the other left.

Tares grow without having to be cultivated. Good seed, on the other hand, demands a great deal of care if it is to bear fruit.

Pre-adamic man was never an Individuality. Created as a Personality on the 6th day (symbolically speaking), he is deprived of every possibility of direct, "individual individuation" - if one may put it thus - for his existence was placed under the law of collective Individuation, which is governed by [the Thought Center of Non-being] with the aid of a whole hierarchy of spirits who are subject to its authority.

Pre-Adamic man does not reincarnate. Not having any individualized element in himself, he is born and dies but he does not incarnate, and consequently he cannot reincarnate. The individualization of pre-adamics is collective, and is directed in groups by certain spirits of the hierarchy. This does not, however, prevent pre-adamics from entering the evolutionary field that forms the experiences of adamic man in great numbers, and since adamic man suffers from a lack of discernment because of his corrupt state, this disturbs and slows his evolution.

Because of the Principle of Equilibrium, humanity on this earth is divided into two equal parts - adamics and pre-adamics. The equilibrium between them is automatically adjusted to follow fluctuations of the incarnations of adamic souls. However, if the adamic race, by casting its pearls to the swine, denies its divine nature to an inadmissible degree, this balance will be broken in favor of the tares. In the parable of the talents, Jesus foresaw this possibility of such a degeneration - where the servant buried the one talent entrusted to him and, on returning it to his master without having made it multiply, was told: "Thou wicked and slothful servant ... and cast ye the unprofitable servant into outer darkness: there shall be weeping and gnashing of teeth." There is no need to emphasize the esoteric meaning here...

When the two humanities were created, they were placed under different authorities. The Fall necessitated special measures and thus the *Staircase* was provided. From that point on, Adamic man was subjected to the law of birth and death and kept only a dim consciousness of his higher self in spite of the almost complete obstruction of his channel of communication with the higher centers, which still exist in him. This gives him the possibility of a choice. If he hears the *Voice of the Master*, the higher intellect, and resolutely steps onto the Staircase, and if he reaches the Fourth Step and resists the Trial by Fire, then, when he crosses the Second Threshold, he will be welcomed as a Prodigal son... it is an event that will be understood only by those who have accomplished it.

If the adamic humanity, en masse, abandons the combat that leads to restoration of their former estate - Ascension - and if this desertion goes beyond the tolerances of balance, the good seed can be progressively stifled by the tares. The world will then head straight into catastrophe - which this time will take the form of a Deluge of Fire.

If the equilibrium, which is already in jeopardy, were to be reestablished, then with the integral and simultaneous incarnation of adamic souls, the Time of Transition would enable Adamic man to enter the Era of the Holy Spirit[– a reality where one was in constant touch with the Creative Principle, 4th density]. Then would follow a thousand years consecrated to the perfecting of the TWO races, and after a second millennium, the reign of the Androgyne, the Last Judgment would definitively separate the tares from the good seed. At this point, Adamic man would begin an even higher evolution, and would at last attain the Pleroma, [6th density.] At this point, and only at this point, will the Tares of the present time cease to be tares and be promoted to the ranks of "good seed". They would begin their own long, evolutionary course that the adamics have already achieved. Then they, in their turn, will receive the higher centers of consciousness which, given them in potential, would be the talents they must make fruitful.

At this point, the Adamics *who degenerated into pre-adamics*, would also have the possibility of taking up their abandoned evolution again while an equal number of the most able pre-adamics would receive the talents that were initially given to the former and this would help them leap forward on the road of esoteric evolution. They may be compared with gifted, hardworking students who get a double promotion while the incapable and lazy ones do another year in the same class.

Meanwhile, the two races are totally mixed: not only nations, but even families can be, and generally are, composed of both human types. This state of things is the belated result of transgressing the Biblical prohibition against mixed marriages.

The dominant position of the pre-adamics that is a result of the esoteric failure of the adamics is now creating a critical situation of unprecedented gravity. *The remainder of the Time of transition offers the last chance for humanity to reestablish the threatened equilibrium and so avoid a general cataclysm.*

If we do not take this opportunity, the tradition of "Solomon" will finally overcome the tradition of "David/Perseus". Then, deflected from the goals of Ascension, and even going beyond the limits of what is necessary and useful to feed the Matrix, the false prophets and their followers, thinking that they are right, will hurl pre-adamic humanity - the children of this world - against the adamics - the children of light - and will provoke a final frightful and useless struggle.

If this should happen, if the adamic humanity does not manage to quell the revolt against the Love of the Son, a resistance that would ensure victory, the balance will finally be broken, and humanity will be destroyed in the Deluge of Fire.

Mouravieff's description of the "Fall" of the Adamic race also follows the same lines as the description given to us from the Cassiopaeans where we see that this is a symbolic version of the "Fall" of our consciousness unit. In the following excerpt, note that our term "Lizzies" is a short-hand notation for those theorized denizens of hyperdimensional realities whose "essence" is "read" as reptilian:

08-28-99

Q: Well, this is one of the problems I am dealing with in trying to write this history of mankind. As I understand it, or as I am trying to figure it out from the literature, prior to the 'Fall in Eden', mankind lived in a 4th density state. Is that correct?

A: Semi/sort of.

Q: Please be more specific.

A: 4th density in another realm, such as time/space continuum, etc.

Q: Okay, so this realm changed, as a part of the cycle; various choices were made: the human race went through the door after the 'gold', so to speak, and became aligned with the Lizzies after the 'female energy' consorted with the wrong side, so to speak. This is what you have said. This resulted in a number of effects: the breaking up of the DNA, the burning off of the first ten factors of DNA, the separation of the hemispheres of the brain...

A: Only reason for this: you play in the dirt, you're gonna get dirty.

Q: (T) What were we before the "Fall"?

A: 3rd density STO.[73]

Q: (T) We are STS at this point because of what happened then?

A: Yes.

[...]

Q: (T) We were 3rd density STO at that time. Was this after the battle that had transpired? In other words, were we, as a 3rd density race, literally on our own at that point, as opposed to before?

A: Was battle.

Q: (L) The battle was in us?

A: Through you.

Q: (T) The battle was through us as to whether we would walk through this doorway... (L) The battle was fought through us, we were literally the battleground. (T) Was the battle over whether or not we walked through that door?

A: Close.

Q: (T) Okay, we were STO at that point. You have said before that on this density we have the choice of being STS or STO.

A: Oh Terry, the battle is always there, it's "when" you choose that counts!

[...]

Q: (T) This must tie into why the [aliens] keep telling people that they have given their consent for abduction and so forth. We were STO and now we are STS.

A: Yes, ... "When" you went for the gold, you said "Hello" to the Lizards and all that that implies.

Q: (T) ...By going for the gold, we became STS beings because going for the gold was STS.

A: Yes.

Q: (T) And, in doing so, we ended up aligning ourselves with the 4th density Lizard Beings...

A: Yes.

---

[73] The Cassiopaeans use the terms Service to Others (STO) and Service to Self (STS) to describe the manifestations of the two basic principles. STO describes the state of living according to the Creative Principle; STS describes the state of living according to the Entropic Principle. Much of our work in this life is to understand these two basic principles, aligning yourself with one or the other.

Q: (T) Because they are 4th density beings and they have a lot more abilities than we at 3rd density...

A: You used to be aligned with 4th density STO.

Q: (T) And we were 3rd density STO. But, by going for the gold we aligned ourselves with 4th density STS.

A: Yes.

Q: (T) And by doing so we gave 4th density STS permission to do whatever they wish with us?

A: Close.

Q: (T) So, when they tell us that we gave them permission to abduct us, it is this they are referring to?

A: Close.

Q: (J) Go back to what they said before: "Free will could not be abridged if you had not obliged". (T) We, as the human race, used our free will to switch from STO to STS. (L) So, at some level we have chosen the mess we are in and that is the Super Ancient Legend of the Fallen Angel, Lucifer. That is us. We fell by falling into that door, so to speak, going after the pot of gold, and when we fell through the door, the serpent bit us!

A: But this is a repeating syndrome.

Q: (L) Is it a repeating syndrome just for the human race or is it a repeating syndrome throughout all of creation?

A: It is the latter.

The adamic race with its full set of DNA, with its connection to the higher centers in place and functioning, is what the C's describe here as 3D density STO living in a "semi/sort of" 4D state aligned with 4D STO. That sounds very much like a "Golden Age" when man "walked with the gods".

In making the choice to experience greater physicality, the consciousness unit fractures and "Falls" from the STO state, loses its connection with the higher centers, and finds itself more or less at the same level as the pre-adamic race, those who have no possibility of reaching the higher centers because the DNA hardware isn't in place. However, because this new 3D STS existence was not the "natural habitat" for a body with the potential to reach the higher centers, the fallen race is at a disadvantage compared to the pre-adamics.

Q: In Book III of his *Gnosis*, Mouravieff discusses what he calls "pre-Adamic humanity" and "Adamic humanity". As I read this I could see that the thing I was struggling to understand in terms of psychopathy as discussed in the *Adventures Series*,[74] was exactly what Mouravieff was describing. However, he was using the Bible to explain it, and that just didn't quite work. Nevertheless, the basic idea is that pre-Adamic human types basically have no "soul", nor any possibility of growing one. This is certainly shocking, but there have been many recent scholarly discussions of this matter based on what seems to be clinical evidence that, indeed,

---

[74] http://www.cassiopaea.org/cass/adventureindex.htm

there are human beings who are just "mechanical" and have no "inner" or "higher self" at all. Gurdjieff talked about this and so did Castaneda. Are Mouravieff's ideas about the two basic TYPES of humans - as far as they go- accurate.

A: Indeed, though again, there is a "Biblical Gloss". The pre-Adamic types are "organic" portals between levels of density.

This, of course, raises the issue of whether or not trying to "help" or "save" such individuals is a waste of time. Another clue to the "vile superstition" and "hatred of humanity".

Q: Is it a waste of time to try to help or "save" such individuals?

A: Pretty much. Most of them are very efficient machines. The ones that you have identified as psychopaths are "failures". The best ones *cannot be discerned except by long and careful observation.*

Q: Have any of us ever encountered one of these "organic portals" and if so, can you identify one for the sake of instruction.

A: If you consider that the population is equally distributed, then you will understand that in an ordinary "souled" person's life, that person will encounter half as many organic portals as souled individuals. BUT, when someone is in the process of "growing" and strengthening the soul, *the Control System will seek to insert even more "units" into that person's life.* Now, think of all the people you have ever met and particularly those with whom you have been, or are, intimate. Which half of this number would YOU designate as being organic portals? Hard to tell, eh?

Q: (B) Is this the original meaning of the "pollution of the bloodline"?

A: Yes.

This certainly gave a whole new meaning to the experiences I have described in the *Adventures series* published on our website. It also became clear that the work of discerning these "organic portals" from souled human beings is CRUCIAL to the so-called "ascension" process. Without the basic understanding of transformation of, and conservation of, energies, there is no possibility of making any progress in such a pursuit.

During the session quoted above, one of the attendees stated that there was a member of her family who she was certain was one of these "organic portals". The C's jumped to respond:

A: Now, do not start labeling without due consideration. Remember that very often the individual who displays contradictory behavior may be a souled being in struggle.

Q: (L) I would say that the chief thing they are saying is that the really good ones - you could never tell except by long observation. The one key we discovered from studying psychopaths was that their actions do not match their words. But what if that is a symptom of just being weak and having no will? (A) How can I know if I have a soul?

A: Do you ever hurt for another?

Q: (V) I think they are talking about empathy. These soulless humans simply don't care what happens to another person. If another person is in pain or misery, they don't know how to care.

A: The only pain they experience is "withdrawal" of "food" or comfort, or what they want. They are also masters of twisting perception of others so as to seem to be empathetic. But, in general, such actions are simply to retain control.

Q: (A) What does having a soul or not having a soul have to do with bloodline?

A: Genetics marry with soul if present.

Q: Do "organic portals" go to fifth density when they die?

A: Only temporarily until the "second death".

Q: (V) What is the "origin" of these organic portal human types? In the scheme of creation, where did they come from?

A: They were originally part of the bridge between 2nd density and 3rd density. Review transcripts on the subject of short wave cycles and long wave cycles.

Ark had been reading the transcripts and noted that the C's had said that sleep was necessary for human beings because it was a period of "rest and recharging". They had also said that the SOUL rests while the body is sleeping. So, the next logical question was "what source of energy was tapped to recharge both the body and the soul"?

A: The question needs to be separated. What happens to a souled individual is different from an organic portal unit.

At this point, we stopped and discussed the possibility that the life force energy that is embodied in Organic Portals must be something like the soul pool that is theorized to exist for flora and fauna. This would, of course, explain the striking and inexplicable similarity of psychopaths, that is so well defined, that they differ from one another only in the way that different species of trees are different in the overall class of "Tree-ness". So, we divided the question and asked first:

Q: ... where does the energy come from that recharges Organic Portals.

A: The pool you have described.

Q: Does the recharging of the souled being come from a similar pool, only maybe the "human" pool?

A: No - it recharges from the so-called sexual center which is a higher center of creative energy. During sleep, the emotional center, not being blocked by the lower intellectual center and the moving center, transduces the energy from the sexual center. It is also the time during which the higher emotional and intellectual centers can rest from the "drain" of the lower centers' interaction with those pesky organic portals so much loved by the lower centers. This respite alone is sufficient to make a difference. But, more than that, the energy of the sexual center is also more available to the other higher centers.

Q: From where does the so-called "sexual center" get ITS energy?

A: The sexual center is in direct contact with 7th density in its "feminine" creative thought of "Thou, I Love." The "outbreath" of "God" in the relief of constriction. Pulsation. Unstable Gravity Waves.

Q: Do the "centers" as described by Mouravieff relate at all to the idea of "chakras".

A: Quite closely. In an individual of the organic variety, the so-called higher chakras are "produced in effect" by stealing that energy from souled beings. This is what gives them the ability to emulate souled beings. The souled being, in effect, perceives a mirror of their own soul when they ascribe "soul qualities" to such beings.

Q: Is this a correspondence that starts at the basal chakra which relates to the sexual center as described by Mouravieff?

A: No. The "sexual center" corresponds to the solar plexus. Lower moving center - basal chakra. Lower emotional - sexual chakra. Lower intellectual - throat chakra. Higher emotional - heart chakra. Higher intellectual - crown chakra

Q: (V) What about the so-called seventh, or "third eye" chakra?

A: Seer. The union of the heart and intellectual higher centers. This would "close the circuit" in the "shepherd's crook" configuration.

Q: (V) What about the many ideas about 12 chakras, and so forth, that are currently being taught by many new age sources?

A: There are no such. This is a corrupted conceptualization based on the false belief that the activation of the physical endocrine system is the same as the creation and fusion of the magnetic center. The higher centers are only "seated" by being "magnetized". And this more or less "External" [unseated] condition of the Higher Centers has been perceived by some individuals and later joined to the perceived "seating" locations, in potential. This has led to "cross conceptualization" based on assumption!

Q: Are the levels of initiation and levels of the staircase as presented by Mouravieff fairly accurate?

A: Yes, but different levels accessed in other so-called lives can relieve the intensity of some levels in "another" life.

SUMMING UP

So it is, according to the most ancient secret tradition, there are two types of humans on our planet. In the above quoted session, the Cassiopaeans confirmed that, once the Biblical gloss was removed, Mouravieff's description was accurate. The most important thing about the Cassiopaean comments is, however, that they were able to deepen our understanding by situating the pre-adamic race within hyperdimensional reality and the Matrix control system. Let's look at four points they raised:

The pre-adamic race serve as portals between levels of density.

They are "very efficient machines" and "The best ones cannot be discerned except by long and careful observation".

They steal energy from souled beings so as to emulate them.

They make-up one-half of humanity.

One-half of humanity. Stealing energy from souled beings. Think about it. Sure does sound like what most people would consider a "vile superstition" and a "hatred of humanity". Not just then, but now as well.

But *if it is true*, it explains why the teachings of Jesus say what they do. It also explains why it had to be covered up. Because, *if it is true*, it means that the two races have been interbreeding for a very, very long time.

INTERMIXING OF THE RACES

It is extremely important to understand that the two races have been interbreeding for thousands, if not tens of thousands of years. It is impossible to look at the races on the earth today, the red, the white, the black, or the yellow, and argue that one or the other is this "pre-adamic" and soulless race. We cannot speak of groups, nations, tribes, or peoples who are members of the "soulless" race as a group. The DNA of the two races is completely mixed, and this is the real meaning of the pollution of the bloodline. Only those with the appropriate genetic makeup are actually able to accommodate a soul and therefore pursue esoteric work, which means that no color or ethnic group is either excluded or has an advantage.

Consider this further: According to the ancient tradition revealed by Mouravieff, the DNA of these two races is so mixed that both can be found *within the same families.* Jesus pointed out that he would turn a husband against his wife, a child against the parent, and so on. And we now begin to really understand what this might have meant, again, assuming this information to be accurate.

We wish to insist on this point, so that the hard of thinking will not take this idea and use it to underpin any racist attitudes. The two races are so intermingled that it is a question of the individual genetics of each person on the planet. This is suggested in these comments from the Cassiopaeans:

> Q: (L) I want to get back on my question that you have not answered... I want to know who, exactly, and why, exactly, genetically engineered the Semitic people, and why there is such an adversarial attitude between them and the Celts and Aryans.
> A: It is not just between the Jews and Celts, if you will take notice. **Besides, it is the individual aural profile that counts and not groupings or classifications.** But, to answer your question: there are many reasons both from *on and off the planet....*
> Q: (L) So, the creation of the Germanic "Master Race" was what they were going after, to create this "breeding ground"?
> A: Yes.
> Q: (L) And, getting rid of the Jews was significant? Couldn't a Germanic master race be created without destroying another group?
> A: No.
> Q: Why?
> A: Because of 4th density prior encoding mission destiny profile.
> Q: (L) What does that mean?
> A: This means encoding to activate after elevation to 4th density, thus if not eliminated, negates Nephalim domination and absorption. Jews were prior encoded to carry out mission after conversion, *though on individual basis....*

You will notice that the C's are pointing us in the direction of individuals and away from groups. It is not "groupings or classifications", it is the "individual aura profile". And this coincides with Mouravieff's statements on the issue as he remarks here:

> "...But the mixing of chromosomes was already an accomplished fact, so that the hormonal symmetry of the adamics has naturally diminished through the generations until it has become stabilized at the point it has now reached. ... certain indications in the Gospel lead us to believe that the two human races that coexist on the earth are *numerically equal...*"(p. 130)

We repeat: The DNA of these two races is so mixed that both can be found within the same families. Your brother, sister, mother, father, daughter or son. Not somebody "other" across the world or across the street worshipping a different god or with a different skin color. It may be somebody you live with every day of your life, and if so, they have but one reason to be here, to drain, distract and deflect souled beings from evolving. And it is important also to note that this cannot be "conscious". Such individuals are as little aware that they do NOT have "higher centers" as those who do except, perhaps, that the latter may feel something is "missing" in their lives.

The way back to the activation of the DNA necessary to attain the contact with the higher centers is not through genetic manipulation, which is seeing the question through the lens of Matrix influences. The way back is through the ancient spiritual science, the real work of the alchemists, which through the heating of the crucible, the neo-cortex, rewires the brain so that the ancient and broken connection with the higher centers can be reestablished. It is the fusing of the "magnetic center", the "birth of the holy child", the real "I". This is natural "genetic modification" in terms of enhancing the feedback loop between the Thought Center of Being, rather than the Thought Center of non-being. Big difference.

Q: (A) Which part of a human extends into 4th density?
A: That which is affected by pituitary gland.
Q: (L) And what is that?
A: Psychic.
Q: (A) Are there some particular DNA sequences that facilitate transmission between densities?
A: Addition of strands.
Q: (L) How do you get added strands?
A: You don't get, you receive.
Q: (L) Where are they received from?
A: Interaction with upcoming wave, if vibration is aligned.
Q: (L) How do you know if this is happening?
A: Psycho-physiological changes manifest. [...] STO tends to do the process within the natural flow of things. STS seeks to alter creation processes to fit their ends.

OPS AND THE BIG PICTURE

That there exists a soulless race, now numbering close to 3 billion inhabitants of this planet, certainly helps explain why the Earth is in its current state. That this soulless race are portals used by the 4D STS to maintain their control over us further explains the depth of the manipulations and why it was essential to cover up the teachings of the man we now call Jesus, but who the Cassiopaeans have said was actually named Jesinavarah. Organic Portals are the terminal connections of the geographic overseer sub-units of the Thought Centers of non-being. It is through our relationships with them that we feed and maintain the Matrix.

Organic portals are generic vehicles or portals, in human form, open for use by a variety of forces, which is why they make excellent matrix puppets. It just so happens that they're being used now by 4D STS to control 3D STS / 4D STO candidates through "clapper" and "vampire" functions - keeping us locked into a behavioral pattern matching the orchestrated norm, and being physically close to us to sap our energies and to keep us from having enough "escape velocity" to remove ourselves from the Matrix Control System's tug, via development of our magnetic centers.

Thus we see that the "natural" function of the OP, this imitation of the soul energy, assumes a specific character within the STS development stream, collecting the soul energy of souled individuals in order to pass it along the feeding chain to 4D STS. The principal role of the OP is now to prevent the genuine seeker from advancing along the Way. This is clear when we look at the following:

OPs collect soul energy from souled individuals.

This energy is transmitted to 4D STS.

OPs are intermixed in families with souled individuals.

When a souled individual makes the commitment to the "work", he or she needs to learn to conserve the soul energy, for without it the work cannot be done.

When one makes a commitment to the "work", one comes under attack.

This "attack" comes from those closest to you: family and friends.

The Cassiopaeans said, "BUT, when someone is in the process of 'growing' and strengthening the soul, *the Control System will seek to insert even more 'units' into that person's life.*"

So in many ways, the actual work of learning to adjust the lens of one's view of reality involves *learning to discern the true nature of the seeker's relationships,* in order to conserve energy in their relationships with the OPs, so that the seeker can accumulate enough energy to grow and strengthen the connection to the soul. Mouravieff makes this clear when he makes the following comments about understanding the "film" of your life:

> In theory, the *film* in which a man is born and in which he lives can go on until the end of the world, on condition that he is happy, satisfied with himself, attributing his virtues to himself, and blaming others for his mistakes and misfortunes.
>
> Properly speaking, this kind of existence cannot be considered as human; it could be described as *anthropoid*. This term is justified in the sense that *exterior* man, immersed in self-satisfaction, represents the crowning achievement of millions of years of evolution of the species from its animal ancestors, yet, from the point of view of esoteric evolution, he is a possibility which has not yet been realized.
>
> If we envisage the problem of esoteric evolution from the point of view of the *film* and the different parts man can play in it, it is clear that this kind of evolution is impossible as long as the *film* can always be considered as running in the same circle. People who perform in such a *film* are those we have called *anthropoids*, puppets, the *dead* who, in the words of Jesus, 'believe themselves to be alive'. Esoteric evolution starts when man, by his conscious efforts, proves capable of breaking the circle and transforming it into an ascending spiral. (Book I, pp 234-5)

But to do this, those secondary roles, those filled by the puppets, the Organic Portals, must be eliminated from the *film*.

> As we have just said, man most often comes to this idea of evolution after he has already complicated the *film* to which he belongs. But true evolution cannot occur except *on the basis of the original film* – after all the artificially added elements have been eliminated. The latter is conditional on a return to the purity of the centers, especially the emotional center which – at least at the start – is the sole receptacle of spiritual influences, and seat of the *magnetic center*. The heart must therefore be pure, and if it is not already pure it must be purified. This is the *sine qua non* condition of success. (Book I, p. 238)

And, as we now know, the heart cannot be purified without great knowledge which leads to perspicacity. Painful though it may seem to be, among those "artificially added elements" which need to be eliminated from our lives are the Organic Portals.

This suggests to us the possibility that the figure around which the Jesus legend was wrapped was presenting a teaching that denied everything that all of the other religions promoted. Such a concept denies the value of sacrifice to the gods; it denies the value of appeasing the gods, honoring the gods, praying to the gods, expecting to be saved by or cleansed from sin by any of the gods. It places the important lesson squarely upon the human being as described in the Parable of the Prodigal Son. It describes the son as going to a Far Country. It describes the "Fall" as "a famine in the country." It tells us how the Prodigal Son went to a "resident of the Far Country" to ask for help. We can easily see that this resident represents the God of this world in his three monotheistic permutations. And what did the God do? Sent the Prodigal Son to live with the pigs. And there we see the clear explication of the Organic Portals in our lives. And we also understand the use of the term in the saying, "Do not cast your pearls before swine lest they turn and rend you in pieces". And speaking of pearls, we begin to understand the reason that the "pearl" was used as the metaphor for the magnetic center "buried" in a field and the necessity to sell all you own to obtain the field with the pearl of great price. A pearl is formed over time, layer after layer, around a seed, a kernel, a grain of sand that is an "irritant". In this world, souled beings ARE irritants, but in this world they have the possibility of "growing a soul", and ascending.

If we just learn to "make nice and get along" and suffer as nobly as possible and forgive and forget while maintaining close "feeding relationships" with Organic Portals, then we are wasting our time. Forgiveness and understanding are, certainly, important. But what is most important is to not use such as a pretext to prolong the feeding relationship. The big problem is: discerning the difference between the children of the Kingdom of Heaven and the children of a "lesser god".

Such an idea, and only such an idea, would have been most definitely a "vile superstition".

In fact, we have something of a parallel in some remarks about Pythagoras. He was accused of believing the "vile superstitions" of the barbarians, that a soul is born over and over again into different bodies. In the *Cathar Gospel of John*, the following passage tells us something very important:

> And after that I, John, asked of the Lord, saying: How say men that Adam and Eve were created by God and set in paradise to keep the commandments of the Father, and were delivered unto death? And the Lord said to me: Hearken, John, beloved of my Father; foolish men say thus in their deceitfulness that my Father made bodies of clay: but by the Holy Ghost made he all the powers of the heavens, and holy ones were found having bodies of clay because of their transgression, and therefore were delivered unto death.

> And again I, John, asked the Lord: How beginneth a man to be in the Spirit (to have a spirit) in a body of flesh? And the Lord said unto me: *Certain of the angels which fell do enter unto the bodies of women*, and receive flesh from the lust of the flesh, and so is a spirit born of spirit, and flesh of flesh, and so is the kingdom of Satan accomplished in this world and among all nations.

> And he said to me: My Father hath suffered him to reign seven days, which are seven ages.

> And I asked the Lord and said: What shall be in that time? And he said to me: From the time when the devil fell from the glory of the Father and (lost) his own glory, he

sat upon the clouds, and sent his ministers, even angels flaming with fire, unto men from Adam even unto Henoch his servant. And he raised up Henoch upon the firmament and showed him his godhead and commanded pen and ink to be given him: and he sat down and wrote threescore and seven books. And he commanded that he should take them to the earth and deliver them unto his sons. *And Henoch let his books down upon the earth and delivered them unto his sons, and began to teach them to perform the custom of sacrifice, and unrighteous mysteries, and so did he hide the kingdom of heaven from men.* And he said unto them: Behold that I am your god and beside me is none other god.

And therefore did my Father send me into the world that I might make it known unto men, *that they might know the evil device of the devil.*

Interestingly, the above quote is reflected in a comment made by the C's at an early point in the experiment:

Q: […] In a previous session I asked a question about the 'sons of Belial' and the 'sons of the law of One', as explicated by Edgar Cayce, and whether these were philosophial or racial divisions. You said that they were initially racial, and then philosophical and religious. Now, from putting the information about religions together throughout the centuries, I am coming to a rather difficult realization that the whole monothiestic idea, which is obviously the basic concept of the 'sons of the law of One', is the most clever and devious and cunning means of control I have ever encountered in my life. No matter where it comes from, the priests say "we have the ONE god, WE are his agents, you pay us your money, and we'll tell him to be nice to you in the next world"!

A: Clever if one is deceived. Silly truffle if one is not.

Q: Well, I know! But, uncovering this deception, this lie that the 'power' is 'out there' is unbelievable. So, the … 'Sons of Belial', is not the negative thing that I interpreted it as at the time and the 'Sons of the Law of One', became the monotheistic Judaism, which then was transformed into the Christian religious mythos, and has been an ongoing theme since Atlantean times.

A: Woven of those who portray the lights.

Q: And that is always the way it has been. They appear as 'angels of light'. And, essentially, everything in history has been rewritten by this group.

A: Under the influence of others. And whom do you suppose?

Q: Well, the 4th density STS.

A: Sending pillars of light and chariots of fire to deliver the message.

At one point in the *Gnostic gospel of Thomas*, the disciples ask Thomas what Jesus told him when he withdrew with him and "told him three things". Thomas said to them, "If I tell you even one of the things he told me, you will pick up rocks and stone me. Then fire will come forth from the rocks and devour you".

By now we have an idea of what was so controversial about what Jesus was saying in private that even some of his closest followers could not be told. At another point in this text, Jesus says to his disciples, following a rendition of the parable of the sower, "This is also how you can acquire the kingdom of heaven. *If you do not acquire it through knowledge, you will not be able to find it.*"

Repeatedly throughout the Gnostic texts, the seeking of knowledge - in the sense of Truth, or the unseen reality behind the symbols of our world - as opposed to belief in salvation from a "god out there", was emphasized. That was truly heretical in those days. In fact, it is heretical now.

If "three day deaths and resurrections" of savior gods was so commonplace throughout the Middle East, why was Jesus saying:

> "You miserable people! You unfortunate ones! You pretenders to truth! You falsifiers of knowledge! You sinners against the spirit! Why do you continue to listen when from the beginning you should have been speaking? Why do you sleep when from the beginning you should have been awake, that the kingdom of heaven might receive you? I tell you the truth: it is easier for a holy person to sink into filth, and for an enlightened person to sink into darkness, than for you to reign." [75]

At one point, in the *Gospel of Thomas*, Jesus makes a rather astounding comparison:

> 'They saw a Samaritan carrying a lamb and going to Judea. He said to his disciples, "Why is he carrying the lamb around?" They said to him, "So that he may kill it and eat it." He said to them, "He will not eat it while it is alive, but only after it has been killed and has become a carcass." They said, "it cannot happen any other way." He said to them, "So also with you: seek a place of rest for yourselves, that you may not become a carcass and be eaten."[76]

That's a far cry from the accepted Christian image of the "Good Shepherd". The point is, the Gnostic gospels, obviously the "other Christianity" that was abolished and buried by the church, had, as the centerpiece of their teachings, that the gods of the many religions down through the ages were merely different manifestations of the negative forces of the hyperdimensional reality and that this realm of evil gods acted on souled beings through the intermediary of Organic Portals. But such an idea is extremely difficult to deal with when an individual has been inculcated for all of his or her life in a belief system that includes as a precaution the idea that ideas such as this will come along as the "wiles of Satan", tempting a person to renounce their faith.

The Matrix Control System went into overdrive damage control to stamp out the teachings of Jesus in the middle of the second century. From that point on, Gnosticism was heresy and the Egyptian model of the dying and resurrecting savior - the corn god - had been substituted into the Christian mythological structure, and a "history" of a "real person" about whom all would revolve was carefully written. But, not carefully enough. Obviously, as with the Old

---

[75] Meyer, Marvin W., *The Secret Teachings of Jesus: Four Gnostic Gospels* – Gnostic Gospel of James (New York: Random House 1984) p. 9.

[76] Ibid., p. 29.

Testament, real stories and real sayings had to be used or the adherents of the system would notice.

We are told that by the end of the fourth century the struggle between the Catholic Church and the classical Gnosticism represented in the Nag Hammadi texts was essentially over. The church now had the added force of political correctness to bolster its dogmatic denunciation. With this material sword, so-called "heresy" was surgically removed from the Christian body; without anesthesia, I should add. Gnosticism was eradicated, its remaining teachers murdered or driven into exile, and its sacred books destroyed. All that remained for scholars seeking to understand Gnosticism in later centuries were the denunciations and fragments preserved in the patristic heresiologies.

THE CATHARS

The years from the fifth through the fifteenth century - the "Dark Ages" - are among the most mysterious in all of history. It was during this period that Christianity - as we know it - was imposed on the Western world, and any significant opposition to the teachings of the church was destroyed. You could say that this was a "COINTELPRO program" with a twist. Instead of relying on psychological manipulation and character assassination only, the Church did all of that, and more: they destroyed those who didn't agree with their globalization and conquest agendas.

Catharism was viewed as perhaps the most dangerous rival to the Catholic Church. In the same way that modern day COINTELPRO brands opposition to the Bush Reich's global conquest agenda as either a "cult" or "conspiracy theory", the Catholic Church labeled opposition "heresy".

The church launched a particularly vicious crusade against the Cathars: 20,000 people were slaughtered in the city of Beziers alone. Reportedly when asked how to distinguish heretics from Catholics, the monk in charge of the battle replied, "Kill them all, God will know his own". The Cathars who survived then became the early targets of the Inquisition - which of course makes us wonder about the original "witches". Were they - in part - Catharist in persuasion? If so, what part of their extant ideas might be a reflection of Cathar teachings?

The Cathars were pacifistic, and they embraced tolerance and poverty. What we would like to know is were they closely associated with the ORIGINAL Christianity before the official church wiped them out and replaced the religion of Christ with the religion of men seeking power?

One thing is certain: they were "well and truly heretical, by every definition except their own".[77]

As it happens, the Cathars were closely connected to the Grail Legends. This brings up the question: did the Cathars have - at least in part - the knowledge of the ancient esoteric Christianity? It certainly seems that these are the teachings that are portrayed in the Grail Legends before the Catholic Church corrupted them. What is certain is that the earliest Grail stories described a spiritual process rather than an object.

There are a number of people nowadays who claim to speak with authority about what the Cathars did or did not believe, but most of them are blowing smoke. The fact is, the only thing we know about what the Cathars believed or taught is what is filtered through the accusations of their detractors. The following account is from a medieval source: "Reynaldus: *On the Accusations Against the Albigensians.*" ("Albigensians" was another name for the Cathars.):

> First it is to be known that the heretics held that there are two Creators; viz. one of invisible things, whom they called the benevolent God, and another of visible things, whom they named the malevolent God.[78] The New Testament they attributed to the benevolent God; but the Old Testament to the malevolent God, and rejected it altogether, except certain authorities, which are inserted in the New Testament from the Old; which, out of reverence to the New Testament, they esteemed worthy of reception.[79]

There is no surviving version of the Cathar New Testament, so we are without any idea of what, precisely, they did include as being valid. We do think that the Gnostic gospels are, very likely, if not the same, similar, to the Cathar texts. We do know that they esteemed the gospel of John as being the "closest" to the truth, and that they considered the "historical" gospels to be all "made up" stories that had nothing to do with the "real" Jesus.

> They charged the author of the Old Testament with falsehood, because the Creator said, "In the day that ye eat of the tree of the knowledge of good and evil ye shall die;" nor (as they say) after eating did they die; when, in fact, after the eating the forbidden fruit they were subjected to the misery of death. They also call him a homicide, as well because he burned up Sodom and Gomorrah, and destroyed the world by the waters of the deluge, as because he overwhelmed Pharaoh, and the Egyptians, in the sea.[80]

---

[77] O'Shea, Stephen, The Perfect Heresy: The Revolutionary Life and Death of the Medieval Cathars (Walker & Company).

[78] Notice how similar this idea is to the explication I gave earlier of the Thought Centers of Being and non-being.

[79] From Raynaldus, "*Annales,*" in S. R. Maitland, trans., *History of the Albigenses and Waldenses,*(London: C. J. G. and F. Rivington 1832) pp. 392- 394.

[80] Ibid.

This is quite clearly a Gnostic idea. The Gnostics taught that Jehovah/Yahweh was an "Evil God" more like a demon than anything else. But, a part of their teaching as well was that he did have something to do with the creation of the material world. So, he clearly wasn't just a "demon" in the sense of an ethereal attacker of human beings who could be "cast out" by an exorcism. No, indeed, he was far more than that! He was a hyperdimensional being of great power and cunning!

> They affirmed also, that all the fathers of the Old Testament were damned; that John the Baptist was one of the greater demons.[81]

This is an interesting remark since it relates in a curious way to a comment of "Jesus" in the *Secret Book of James*. His disciples are asking him: "Lord, how can we prophesy to those who ask us to prophesy to them? For many people ask us, and they expect to hear a sermon from us." The Lord answered and said:

> Do you not know that the head of prophecy was removed with John? When you realize what the head is, and that prophecy comes from the head, then understand what this means: its head was taken away. At first I spoke with you in parables, but you did not understand. Now I am speaking with you plainly, and you still do not perceive. [82]

This is, no doubt, an extremely mysterious remark. Writers of the present day, not understanding the symbolism of the "talking head" and the head of John the Baptist as it relates to the head of Bran the Blessed, the Ark of the Covenant, and the Holy Grail, have erroneously come to the conclusion that John the Baptist was the true object of worship of the Cathars and Templars. [Picknett and Prince.] Some writers have even ignorantly proposed that this "talking head" is the armillary sphere of Pope Sylvester, and that it "talks" about "precessional cycles".

It is quite probable that the remark of Raynaldus about the condemnation of John the Baptist by the Cathars has some foundation in fact. If so, what are we to make of the claims of those who propose that there has been a secret society for millennia that actually worships John the Baptist and Mary Magdalene in secret? Certainly, if that had been the case with the Cathars, Raynaldus would have said so because such a claim was damning enough in its own right. But that is not what he said. He said that the Cathars damned John the Baptist as one of the greater demons. And then we see the "Jesus" of the Gnostic texts saying that the head of this "demon" had been related to "prophecy" and was "removed."

> They said also, in their secret doctrine, (*in secreto suo*) that that Christ who was born in the visible, and terrestrial Bethlehem, and crucified in Jerusalem, was a bad man, and that Mary Magdalene was his concubine; and that she was the woman

---

[81] Ibid.

[82] Meyer, Marvin W., *The Secret Teachings of Jesus: Four Gnostic Gospels*, (New York: Random House 1984) p. 7.

taken in adultery, of whom we read in the gospel. For the good Christ, as they said, never ate, nor drank, nor took upon him true flesh, nor ever was in this world, except spiritually in the body of Paul....[83]

It is indeed likely that the Cathars did not believe that the "historical Jesus" was accurately depicted in the New Testament. Clearly, they did believe that the "Jesus" of the New Testament was a fraud - and that the gospels themselves were fraudulent. We ought to pay some attention to the fact that the Cathars may have believed that the Great Work had been accomplished by the apostle Paul, and that Paul may, indeed, have been the man around whom the Jesus legend was spun. In other words, was Paul the REAL Jesus? An interesting idea to hold in the mind while reading his epistles (those that are confirmably his and not merely attributed to him. See Wells for the analyses.[84])

In the teachings of Paul, it is evident from textual analysis that Paul did not know of a "Christ" as a historical personage in the body of a man called Jesus as represented in the New Testament. He knew of a "Christ" spirit that was an "anointing" of gnosis. When his writings are analyzed with all the tools of linguistics, and the additions, glosses, and interpolations removed (not to mention the epistles that are clearly not Pauline), we find a series of teachings that is most definitely Gnostic in flavor and texture. Not only that, but the teacher that Paul referred to had quite a different history than the Jesus of the New Testament.

Raynaldus' remark about Mary Magdalene does irreparable damage to many popular theories of the present time: that she was the "wife of Jesus", and that they produced children together and that these children are the origin of the idea of the "Sang Real", or "Holy Blood". The point is, if Raynaldus had simply reported that Mary Magdalene was the "mistress" of Jesus, and that they had children, then that would have been sufficiently damning. If he had reported that the Cathars worshipped John the Baptist as the true Christ that also would have been sufficiently damning. However, his version of what they believed was that 1) John the Baptist represented a demon and, and that 2) there was a "bad man" crucified in Jerusalem, who was connected to Mary Magdalene, but that it wasn't Jesus. So he probably wasn't making it up. Clearly, the beliefs of the Cathars were something other than an idea that John the Baptist was the true Messiah, or that Jesus and Mary had children together, contrary to what present day expositors of "occult secrets of the Holy Blood, Holy Grail" would have us believe.

It is also likely that the Cathars believed that any physical "crucifixion" that took place was that of a criminal and not of the "real" Jesus. This was, as they would perceive it, an overlay of the Egyptian religion of the resurrection of Horus, or the Tammuz drama, and it was repugnant to the Gnostic ideas of salvation through

---

[83] Raynaldus, Op Cit.

[84] Wells, G.A., *The Historical Evidence for Jesus*, (Buffalo: Prometheus 1988).

fusing the magnetic center and thereby facilitating direct knowing, as opposed to salvation by a "sacrifice". Their very rejection of the patriarchs and Yahweh was based on the sacrifice issue, which they saw as a violent "eating of humanity" undertaken by evil Archons of Darkness. Nevertheless, that they apparently did, indeed, have some idea of an initiatory process that was part of being Christed is certainly suggested. This is the Gnostic Staircase explicated by Boris Mouravieff.

> They said that almost all the Church of Rome was a den of thieves; and that it was the harlot of which we read in the Apocalypse. They so far annulled the sacraments of the Church, as publicly to teach that the water of holy Baptism was just the same as river water, and that the Host of the most holy body of Christ did not differ from common bread; instilling into the ears of the simple this blasphemy, that the body of Christ, even though it had been as great as the Alps, would have been long ago consumed, and annihilated by those who had eaten of it.[85]

Sure, the Cathars probably thought and taught all these things. But then, why not? They were probably right.

> Confirmation and Confession, they considered as altogether vain and frivolous. They preached that Holy Matrimony was meretricious, and that none could be saved in it, if they should beget children. Denying also the Resurrection of the flesh, they invented some unheard of notions, saying, that our souls are those of angelic spirits who, being cast down from heaven by the apostasy of pride, left their glorified bodies in the air; and that these souls themselves, after successively inhabiting seven terrene bodies, of one sort or another, having at length fulfilled their penance, return to those deserted bodies. [86]

Now, of all the things said by Raynaldus, this last is the most interesting. But, let me deal with them in reverse order. The item that human souls are those of "higher beings" is quite in keeping with the many myths and legends of The Fall - the former state of man in paradise. But, that this "paradise" is here described as sort of "in the air" and not exactly "in heaven", is most interesting in terms of hyperdimensional realities. It is also interesting in terms of the Grail Quest and the "ascent of the shamans" and the Great Work of alchemy. The statement that clearly describes a belief in reincarnation, and seven incarnations in particular, is also interesting since it seems to be a garbling of the seven levels of reality that are part and parcel of many other ancient systems of philosophy, originating, in fact, in Siberian Shamanism.[87]

---

[85] Raynaldus, Op. Cit.

[86] Ibid.

[87] Many people use the term "shaman" as a catch-all for any individual possessing any magico-religious powers in any primitive society. There are discussions of Indian, Iranian, Germanic, North and South American, Chinese, and even Babylonian "shamanism," particularly when primitive cultures are being examined. The problem is, if the word "shaman" is taken to mean any magician, sorcerer, medicine man, or ecstatic found throughout all religions and cultures, the word becomes useless and

The item about marriage is interesting in the sense that, indeed, it seems that the Cathars taught that their followers ought not to have children so as to not provide more "food" for the Archons of Darkness - the Matrix. It seems that the Cathar's main point about marriage was that if you bring a child into the world, you are perpetuating darkness because this world is ruled by beings that can invade the mind, and thereby further entrap the soul. However, they did not teach an abandonment of marital relations until an individual was ready to "graduate" and became a "Parfait," or "Perfected".

Some people suggest that the Cathars engaged in some sort of sexual rites based on other accusations of their detractors. There are also clues that "sex" of a spiritual sort may have been the rite of "crucifixion" of the original Christianity, the "Christing", the Hieros Gamos, being the Shamanic ascent to the Goddess. Let us just say at this point that assuming that physical sexual activity has anything to do with it is misleading - an exoteric blind.

So what we see is that "primitive chiliasm", if it was related to Catharism, included a belief in something slightly different from a physical resurrection, and if it was closer to the real teachings of Great Teacher- around whom the Jesus Myth was shaped by the church - then it suggests that the restoration of the "souled beings" to some sort of "angelic bodies" could be the explanation as to why "primitive Chiliasm" and Catharism are closely connected to the Grail stories - stories that emphasize "romance" and battles with dark forces, great struggles of a physical and emotional nature that lead to some great accomplishment: the Great Work of Alchemy. What we can hypothesize, based on the evidence, is that these teachings included the idea of hyperdimensional realities and literal Time Loops culminating in cataclysm, with a restoration of a Para-physical earth - the Edenic State of the Golden Age — on the other side of the dissolution. This, of course, leads us to the Mother of all Grail Stories: Noah and the Ark.

---

vague. There are already words for magicians and sorcerers and mystics and medicine men to express any number of concepts. When I write about shamanism, I intend to follow the example of Eliade and restrict the usage to *the religious phenomenon of Siberia and Central Asia.* This is the locale where the former ancient technology of Europe and the megalith cultures landed, *and was preserved for millennia before being corrupted by elements from the South.* It is the closest we can get to the most ancient conceptions of the Cosmos, the ancient technology of transcending space and time.

CHAPTER 6
HISTORY AND CATASTROPHE

THE NOAH SYNDROME

The story of Noah and the Ark is the primordial story of salvation; the original Quest for the Holy Grail; - the building of the Ark; and - the Great Work of Alchemy. The Flood has other connotations such as the occlusion of the Sun representing the "Dying God", sacrificed for the sins of mankind. In this sense, the Ark is the symbol of the Cosmic Hieros Gamos, or the mode of passage to the realm of the "Once and Future King", Arthur/Arca and the Shepherds of Arcadia.

In our present time, the Christian religion, (and its New Age offshoots), is the chief proponent of the many End of the World scenarios with which we are most familiar. However, they do not seem to note that the most important point is that Jesus definitively connected the so-called End of the World with the story of Noah, thereby affirming the "Primitive Chiliasm" view. In Matthew, chapter 24, verses 37 and 38:

> As were the days of Noah, so will be the coming of the Son of man. For just as in those days before the flood they were eating and drinking, marrying and being given in marriage, until the day when Noah went into the ark, and *they did not know or understand until the flood came and swept them all away*, so will be the coming of the Son of man.

In the story of Noah, to which Jesus has directly related the "End of Time", a man had a dream, a prophecy (who knows how God spoke to him), and he *acted* upon this revelation in a positive way to the saving of himself and his family.

The most important part of the story of Noah is that it was NOT the end of the world in the sense that the physical earth ceases to exist. Nor did Noah transit through the Flood to become a "light being". *He built the Ark and survived the Flood and emerged into a different world.* It was the End of Time in the sense that the world before was altogether different from the world after the Flood. The Earth continued to exist, and Noah and his metaphorical family, (there were apparently quite a number of Noah's all over the globe), came out of the ark into a world so different that the existence of a rainbow is noted here for the first time as evidence of this extreme, fundamental change in the nature of reality.

Over and over again, for a thousand years or more, this group of people, or that one, has decided that the end is coming. They will sell all they own, move out to the woods or gather on a mountain, or huddle in jungle huts, waiting for God - or nowadays, the Ets - and when the sun finally rises on the glorious morn of redemption, well, some are so disappointed, or so determined to be right, that they will sink to any level to prove that their interpretation was the correct one. The Solar Cult and the Heaven's Gate group are just two cases of recent note. Such prognosticators obviously went wrong – terribly and disastrously wrong. And they were only the latest in a long line of similar groups. It is a pattern that repeats over and over again. So, again we ask, is there anything to any of it at all, and if so, what?

Carefully considered, the story of Noah is highly informative. The story does not tell us that some supernatural force prepared a place for Noah. On the contrary, Noah was told to perform certain tasks to ensure his survival as well as that of his family and certain animals. Assuming that the story is more than merely a metaphor for the Great Work, had Noah chosen not to exert these tremendous efforts, we would never have heard of him, whoever he might have been, in whatever culture or context he existed.

Do we have any way of knowing that we are presently in the so-called "End Times"? Of course, there is no way to say so with absolute certainty. However, we do have what I call the "Noah Syndrome" to guide us.

A "syndrome" is a constellation of signs and symptoms that, taken together, characterize or indicate a particular condition. "As it was in the days of Noah" can be interpreted on several levels. What, precisely, might have been meant by this clue? In Genesis, Chapter six, we read about the first "symptom".

> When men began to multiply on the face of the earth, the sons of God saw that the
> daughters of men were fair, and they took wives of all they desired and chose.

That is certainly a loaded statement! There have been endless speculations on the identity of these "sons of God", or "Nephilim". But before we even approach that, let's look at the first curious part of the statement is that referring to men "multiplying on the face of the earth", as though it was a *singularly significant factor*. "As it was in the days of Noah" seems to suggest a tremendous population growth. Could it be at all possible that a certain population figure – as suggested by this remark – was a sort of "critical mass" that precipitated the interaction with these "sons of God"? The Cassiopaeans - us in the future - have remarked that, at the time of the prior high civilization, the population of the world was right around the same figure we have on the planet at present: six billion.

The series of remarks in Genesis get even more impossible, I am sorry to say, because it goes on to declare:

> There were giants on the earth in those days, and also afterward, when the sons of
> God lived with the daughters of men, and they bore children to them. These were
> the mighty men who were of old, men of renown.

What in the world are we going to do with something like that if we claim to be rational thinkers? Nevertheless, it seems to be the crux of the matter. In the many myths and legends, it was *the offspring of these unions* mentioned above that *brought destruction* on the Earth. On the one hand, we can suppose that this was a commentary on the intermixing of the two races: Organic Portals and Souled humans. But it seems that such intermixing of the races led to a specific problem: the manipulation of individuals of great Creative power by the use of the Organic Portals. As we have already noted, at the present time, there seems to be a veritable invasion of hyperdimensional visitors masquerading as "aliens". This was recorded in the ancient legends as "invasion by the souls of the dead". There is a curious "sexual interest" in humanity expressed by these visitors concomitant with sexual excess of mankind at large. Could the two be related? And this leads us to the next symptom:

> The Lord saw that the wickedness of man was very great in the earth, and that every imagination and intention of all human thinking was only evil continually.

The passage comes back to this further on saying:

> The earth was depraved and putrid in God's sight, and the land was filled with violence (desecration, infringement, outrage, assault, and lust for power). And God looked upon the world and saw how degenerate, debased and vicious it was; for all humanity had corrupted their way upon the earth and lost their true direction.

Those are harsh words. Do they apply to us in this day and time? Fulcanelli writes:

> Already, because of the multiplicity of scientific acquisitions, man cannot live without tremendous energy and endurance, in an atmosphere of hectic, feverish and unhealthy activity. He created the machine that increased his means and his power of action a hundred fold, but he has become its slave and its victim. [...] [O]n the other hand, what does he know of himself, that is, of his origin, his essence, and his destiny? [...] Carried away by his passions, his desires, and his phobias, the horizon of his hopes recedes indefinitely. It is the frantic race towards the abyss. [...] Finally, we will reveal nothing by saying that the greatest part of discoveries, first oriented towards the increase of human well-being, were rapidly diverted from their goal and specifically applied to destruction. Instruments of peace are turned into machines of war and we already know too well the dominating role science played in modern cataclysms. Such is, unfortunately, the final goal, the outcome of scientific investigation; and such is also the reason why many who pursued it with criminal intent, called divine justice upon him and finds himself bound to be condemned by it. [88]

But *Noah found favor in God's eyes.* He was, undoubtedly, the one who was thought to be "sick" by all of the other people around him. He didn't fit, he was an anomaly – a man of discernment and circumspection in a time and place where everything that mankind had ever thought was good had been corrupted, perverted, turned upside down and twisted out of recognition. But Noah "found grace in the eyes of the Lord". We are told in the Pauline Letter to the Hebrews that:

> Prompted by faith Noah, being forewarned of God concerning events of which as yet there was no visible sign, took heed and diligently and reverently constructed and prepared an ark for the deliverance of his own family. By this he passed

---

[88] Fulcanelli, *Dwellings*, pp. 503-504.

judgment and sentence on the world's unbelief and became an heir and possessor of righteousness."[89]

That's an interesting clue: being *forewarned concerning events of which as yet there was no visible sign*. But isn't that the same thing as the many "doomsday cults" that have prophesied the end, only to discover that their prognostications failed? In considering this question, we find the point of the insertion of the "twist" in the story. Certainly, the tale has already given us "clues" that must have been apparent to Noah. But then, the story tells us that "God" warned Noah. Was that really the case? Or was there something else upon which Noah based his assessment of the situation? Let's return to consider the earlier remark: "There were giants on the earth in those days, and also afterward, when the sons of God lived with the daughters of men, and they bore children to them. These were the mighty men who were of old, men of renown." On the one hand, we could think that "giants" meant literally very large men. But considering the words that follow it: "mighty men, men of renown", it could also mean men who were "giant" in their deeds. Since the passage is, overall, discussing the great and oppressive evil of the day, what we suspect about this symptom of the syndrome was that there were wars and evil deeds in high places, scandalous wickedness perpetrated by political "giants" who were directly responsible for the conditions of the time. The fact that this little story is part of the story of Noah suggests to us that it was his observation of the conditions of the planet in specific terms that gave him the idea that something was up and he ought to "build an ark".

Looking at our idea of a Syndrome from another direction, acting in response to a consciousness of impending disaster might be seen as a form of mental aberration, a syndrome not common to all of humanity, but defining in very specific terms the "Noë of the Elect" and "the Chosen", those moved to see the End as a beginning of a new order. And, as in the time of Noah, those not afflicted with this particular cast of consciousness will react to it with derision and ridicule.

So we find that the Noah Syndrome describes both a condition of the planet in terms of its sickness-unto-death, as well as the condition of certain individuals who are sickened by the sickness. And just as an animal will sniff out the proper herb for its cure, such people begin to feel a restlessness, a questing spirit, and a drive to seek out and discover the thing that will bring relief to this nagging ache in their soul. Such a quest can only be undertaken with faith that is open and adventurous, following the nose, so to say, and finally, ingesting that which is of truth when it is finally discovered. Looking at our constellation of symptoms, it does seem to be that we are in a time period "as it was in the days of Noah". And so, many individuals, including yours truly, have embarked on quests for truth, for

---

[89] *The Bible*, Hebrews 11:7. All citations from *The Bible* are taken from the *Amplified* version published by Zondervan.

knowledge, and for understanding of the reality in which we live and why it is that the Terror of History still stalks us.

In the course of such a quest, the open-minded individual will, naturally, come across many anomalies that are inexplicable in terms of standard, uniformitarian science and history. Eventually, the question will be asked: could these things be evidence of an ancient, advanced civilization that perished? And once that question has been asked, the next question will be: how did it perish and could it happen again?

> Atlantis. Did this mysterious island, of which Plato left the enigmatic description, ever exist? A question difficult to solve, give the weakness of the means which science possesses to penetrate the secret of the abysses. Nevertheless, some observations seem to support the partisans of the existence of Atlantis. [...]

> Faith in the truthfulness of Plato's works results in believing the reality of the periodical upheavals of which the Mosaic Flood[90], we said it, remains the written symbol and the sacred prototype. To those who negate what the priests of Egypt entrusted to Solon, we would only ask to explain to us what Aristotle's master wanted to reveal by this fiction of a sinister nature. For we indeed believe that beyond doubt, Plato became the propagator of very ancient truths, and that consequently his books contain a set, a body of hidden knowledge. His *Geometric Number*, and *Cave* have their signification; why should the myth of Atlantis not have its own?

> Atlantis must have undergone the same fate as the others, and the catastrophe, which submerged it, falls obviously into the same cause as that which buried, forty-eight centuries later, under a profound sheet of water, Egypt, the Sahara, and the countries of Northern Africa. But more favored than the land of the Atlantean, Egypt gained from a raising of the bottom of the ocean and came back to the light of day, after a certain time of immersion. For Algeria and Tunisia with their dry "chotts" covered with a thick layer of salt, the Sahara and Egypt with their soils constituted for a large part of sea sand show that the waters invaded and covered vast expanses of the African continent. The columns of the Pharaohs' temples bear on them undeniable traces of immersion; in the hypostyle chambers, the slabs, still extant, which form the ceilings have been raised and moved by the oscillating motion of the waves; the disappearance of the outer coating of the pyramids and in general that of the stone joins (the Colosses of Memnon who used to sing) the evident traces of corrosion by water that can be noticed on the sphinx of Giza, as well as on many other works of Egyptian statuary have no other origin.[91]

---

[90] Indeed it is strange that Fulcanelli refers to the destruction of Atlantis as the "Mosaic Flood." Either he is referring to the book of Genesis as being written by Moses, or he is giving a clue.

[91] Fulcanelli, *Dwellings*, pp. 511-512.

WHAT PLATO TELLS US ABOUT ATLANTIS

One of the oft-reiterated themes of Fulcanelli is that the "ancient Greeks" — not the Egyptians — were the source of the Hermetic science.[92]

Timaeus and *Critias*, written by Plato some time around 360 BC[93] are the only existing written records which specifically refer to Atlantis. The dialogues are conversations between Socrates, Hermocrates, Timaeus, and Critias. Apparently in response to a prior talk by Socrates about ideal societies, Timaeus and Critias agree to entertain Socrates with a tale that is *"not a fiction but a true story"*.

The story is about the conflict between the ancient Athenians and the Atlanteans 9000 years before Plato's time. Knowledge of the ancient times was apparently forgotten by the Athenians of Plato's day, and the form the story of Atlantis took in Plato's account was that Egyptian priests conveyed it to Solon. Solon passed the tale to Dropides, the great-grandfather of Critias. Critias learned of it from his grandfather also named Critias, son of Dropides. Let's take a careful look at the main section of the story, omitting the introduction that describes Solon going to Egypt and chatting up the priests.

> Thereupon one of the priests, who was of a very great age, said: O Solon, Solon, you Hellenes are never anything but children, and there is not an old man among you. Solon in return asked him what he meant. I mean to say, he replied, that in mind you are all young; there is no old opinion handed down among you by ancient tradition, nor any science, which is hoary with age. And I will tell you why.

> There have been, and will be again, many destructions of mankind arising out of many causes; the greatest have been brought about by the agencies of fire and water, and other lesser ones by innumerable other causes. There is a story, which even you have preserved, that once upon a time Phaeton, the son of Helios, having yoked the steeds in his father's chariot, because he was not able to drive them in the path of his father, burnt up all that was upon the earth, and was himself destroyed by a thunderbolt. Now this has the form of a myth, but really signifies *a declination of the bodies moving in the heavens around the earth*, and a great conflagration of things upon the earth, which recurs after long intervals; at such times those who live upon the mountains and in dry and lofty places are more liable to destruction than those who dwell by rivers or on the seashore. And from this calamity the Nile, who is our never-failing saviour, delivers and preserves us.

> When, on the other hand, the gods purge the earth with a deluge of water, the survivors in your country are herdsmen and shepherds who dwell on the mountains, but those who, like you, live in cities are carried by the rivers into the sea. Whereas

---

[92] One of the threads we follow is that of these "ancient Greeks" and who they really were. We will cover this material partly in this discussion, but for full explication, the reader may wish to obtain copies of future volumes in this series as they become available.

[93] Translated by Benjamin Jowett.

in this land, neither then nor at any other time, does the water come down from above on the fields, having always a tendency to come up from below; for which reason the traditions preserved here are the most ancient. The fact is, that wherever the extremity of winter frost or of summer does not prevent, mankind exist, sometimes in greater, sometimes in lesser numbers. And whatever happened either in your country or in ours, or in any other region of which we are informed - if there were any actions noble or great or in any other way remarkable, they have all been written down by us of old, and are preserved in our temples.

We want to here make note of the fact that present day evidence suggests that it is true both that Egypt has been inundated and that it experienced a rainy climate. Fulcanelli even commented upon the inundation of Egypt. This leads us to question whether or not this story actually came from the mouth of a true Egyptian priest with the full knowledge of the ancient cataclysms. If so, he would have known of the period of heavy rain and shallow seas in Egypt, by which the Sphinx and other monuments were eroded, and which deposited a layer of salt on the interior of the pyramids and other structures. And so we suggest, to reconcile this difficulty, not that the story is false — because Fulcanelli has told us to "have faith in the account of Plato" — but rather that the speaker was not aware of certain ideas specifically relating to Egypt, and that the dialogue has been put into the mouth of an Egyptian priest in order to preserve it in the context of the then current "Egyptian craze". It might even be thought that this was a deliberate exoteric "blind".

> Whereas just when you and other nations are beginning to be provided with letters and the other requisites of civilized life, after the usual interval, the stream from heaven, like a pestilence, comes pouring down, and leaves only those of you who are destitute of letters and education; and so you have to begin all over again like children, and know nothing of what happened in ancient times, either among us or among yourselves. As for those genealogies of yours which you just now recounted to us, Solon, they are no better than the tales of children.

> In the first place you remember a single deluge only, but there were many previous ones; in the next place, you do not know that there formerly dwelt in your land the fairest and noblest race of men which ever lived, and that you and your whole city are descended from a small seed or remnant of them which survived. And this was unknown to you, because, for many generations, the survivors of that destruction died, leaving no written word. For there was a time, Solon, before the great deluge of all, when the city which now is Athens was first in war and in every way the best governed of all cities, is said to have performed the noblest deeds and to have had the fairest constitution of any of which tradition tells, under the face of heaven.

Again, let's interrupt the dialogue to point out that it is hardly likely that a priest of Egypt would have declared the Athenians to be "the fairest and noblest race of men", nor that they "performed the noblest deeds" and had the "fairest constitution … under the face of heaven"! Another clue that the speaker is giving us that it is NOT Egypt that is the source of this information - at least not Egypt as we know it now.

> Solon marveled at his words, and earnestly requested the priests to inform him exactly and in order about these former citizens. You are welcome to hear about them, Solon, said the priest, both for your own sake and for that of your city, and above all, for the sake of the goddess who is the common patron and parent and

educator of both our cities. She founded your city a thousand years before ours, receiving from the Earth and Hephaestus the seed of your race, and afterwards she founded ours, of which the constitution is recorded in our sacred registers to be eight thousand years old.

Yet again, the Egyptian priest is giving *greater antiquity to the Greeks than to the Egyptian*s! Another clue for the reader to understand that this is not an Egyptian story! What is being said is being put in the mouth of an Egyptian priest to "conceal". Indeed, the worship of the goddess, is the older form of worship in Egypt. But all of that came to an end, probably with the conquest of Narmer, the building of the temple to Hephaestus, the demoting of the goddess and the Moon calendar, and the instituting of the Solar worship and the solar calendar of 365 days.[94]

As touching your citizens of nine thousand years ago, I will briefly inform you of their laws and of their most famous action; the exact particulars of the whole we will hereafter go through at our leisure in the sacred registers themselves. If you compare these very laws with ours you will find that many of ours are the counterpart of yours as they were in the olden time.

Here, of course, we come to the idea that there was an ancient connection and communication between the truly "old Egyptians" and the Northern peoples. Georges Gurdjieff once remarked that Christianity was taken from Egypt, a statement that might suggest that he agreed with the Pan-Egyptian school. But no: Christianity, he hastened to explain, was not taken from the Egypt of history, but from a "far older Egypt" which is unrecorded.[95]

In the first place, there is the caste of priests, which is separated from all the others; next, there are the artificers, who ply their several crafts by themselves and do not intermix; and also there is the class of shepherds and of hunters, as well as that of husbandmen; and you will observe, too, that the warriors in Egypt are distinct from all the other classes, and are commanded by the law to devote themselves solely to military pursuits; moreover, the weapons which they carry are shields and spears, a style of equipment which the goddess taught of Asiatics first to us, as in your part of the world first to you.

The remark that the right function of society was "first taught to the Asiatics" is most interesting. The reference to "Asiatics" in this context from an historical "Egyptian Priest" is extremely questionable because, in the many Egyptian inscriptions of historical times, the Asiatics are always referred to as "Vile". Nevertheless, even in historical times, it is indeed true that the Egyptians borrowed their military equipment and war strategies from the Asiatics, but that was a much

---

[94] Which event may have been merely another of the cyclic events assimilated to an even earlier archetype.

[95] Ashe, Geoffrey, *The Ancient Wisdom,* (London: Sphere 1979) p. 8-9.

later development than the above story would suggest. The issue of who the "vile Asiatics" were is an ongoing debate, but it seems to devolve on such as the Hittites, Hyksos, and other Indo-European tribes that came down from the Steppes in various waves. We will discuss, further on, the evidence that the Steppe peoples were the worshippers of the goddess in the most ancient times, and that the war god, the weather god, the god of fire and the mountains, was introduced later from the South.

> Then as to wisdom, do you observe how our law from the very first made a study of the whole order of things, extending even to prophecy and medicine which gives health, out of these divine elements deriving what was needful for human life, and adding every sort of knowledge which was akin to them. All this order and arrangement the goddess first imparted to you when establishing your city; and *she chose the spot of earth in which you were born,* because she saw that the happy temperament of the seasons in that land would produce the wisest of men. Wherefore the goddess, who was a lover both of war and of wisdom, *selected and first of all settled that spot which was the most likely to produce men likest herself.* And there you dwelt, having such laws as these and still better ones, and excelled all mankind in all virtue, as became the children and disciples of the gods.

Again and again, this very strange "Egyptian" priest is saying things that completely contradict the more "historical" Egyptian view that they are the most "ancient and noble race". In the above remarks, he has said that the goddess imparted to the Greeks first all of the laws of health and those things needed to preserve and prolong life. The Greeks are pronounced to have been the "wisest of men", and those "most like the goddess" herself. And again "excelled all mankind in all virtue", which is not very likely to have been said by an Egyptian priest.

> Many great and wonderful deeds are recorded of your state in our histories. But one of them exceeds all the rest in greatness and valour. For these histories tell of a mighty power which unprovoked made an expedition against the whole of Europe and Asia, and to which your city put an end. This power came forth out of the Atlantic Ocean, for in those days the Atlantic was navigable; and there was an island situated in front of the straits which are by you called the Pillars of Heracles; the island was larger than Libya and Asia put together, and was the way to other islands, and from these you might pass to the whole of *the opposite continent* which surrounded the true ocean; for this sea which is within the Straits of Heracles is only a harbour, having a narrow entrance, but that other is a real sea, and the surrounding land may be most truly called a boundless continent.

> Now in this island of Atlantis there was a great and wonderful empire, which had rule over the whole island and several others, and over parts of the continent, and, furthermore, the men of Atlantis had subjected the parts of Libya within the columns of Heracles as far as Egypt, and of Europe as far as Tyrrhenia. This vast power, gathered into one, endeavoured to subdue at a blow our country and yours and the whole of the region within the straits; and then, Solon, your country shone forth, in the excellence of her virtue and strength, among all mankind. She was pre-eminent in courage and military skill, and was the leader of the Hellenes. And when the rest fell off from her, being compelled to stand alone, after having undergone the very extremity of danger, she defeated and triumphed over the invaders, and preserved from slavery those who were not yet subjugated, and generously liberated all the rest of us who dwell within the pillars.

Of all the things the "Egyptian priest" has said, the above is the most astonishing and the most telling. Again he is giving pre-eminence to the Greeks, that they performed the most heroic deed of all times, which was to *defeat the Atlantean Empire!* And this is the point that is so often just simply overlooked by all the Atlantis lovers! Atlantis was the original "evil empire of the Borg"! And what is more, in this passage, the clue is given that the ancient Egyptian civilization — the pyramids and other monumental architecture upon which so much of the current Egyptian craze is based, stemming from the work of Schwaller de Lubicz, and which is declared to be the offspring of Atlantis - the ancient Egypt *that is so admired by the current day flock of Egyptophiles* - was very likely an attempt to re-construct the EVIL EMPIRE OF ATLANTIS! In other words, the "priestly science" of the Egyptians, referred to by Fulcanelli, antedated the material so diligently studied and propagated by Schwaller and others for "clues" to alchemical secrets and methods of "ascension".

> But afterwards there occurred violent earthquakes and floods; and in a single day and night of misfortune all your warlike men in a body sank into the earth, and the island of Atlantis in like manner disappeared in the depths of the sea. For which reason the sea in those parts is impassable and impenetrable, because there is a shoal of mud in the way; and this was caused by the subsidence of the island.

> I have told you briefly, Socrates, what the aged Critias heard from Solon and related to us. And when you were speaking yesterday about your city and citizens, the tale which I have just been repeating to you came into my mind, and I remarked with astonishment how, by some mysterious coincidence, you agreed in almost every particular with the narrative of Solon; but I did not like to speak at the moment. For a long time had elapsed, and I had forgotten too much; I thought that I must first of all run over the narrative in my own mind, and then I would speak.

Here we find another interesting clue. Critias has just told us that Socrates was discussing the very things that are included in this story — that everything Socrates had been saying the previous day "agreed in almost every particular with the narrative of Solon". Apparently, this story had been handed down via another line of transmission.

> And so I readily assented to your request yesterday, considering that in all such cases the chief difficulty is *to find a tale suitable to our purpose*, and that with such a tale we should be fairly well provided. And therefore, as Hermocrates has told you, on my way home yesterday I at once communicated the tale to my companions as I remembered it; and after I left them, during the night by thinking I recovered nearly the whole it. Truly, as is often said, the lessons of our childhood make wonderful impression on our memories; for I am not sure that I could remember all the discourse of yesterday, but I should be much surprised if I forgot any of these things which I have heard very long ago. I listened at the time with childlike interest to the old man's narrative; he was very ready to teach me, and I asked him again and again to repeat his words, so that like an indelible picture they were branded into my mind.

> As soon as the day broke, I rehearsed them as he spoke them to my companions, that they, as well as myself, might have something to say. And now, Socrates, to make an end my preface, I am ready to tell you the whole tale. I will give you not only the general heads, but the particulars, as they were told to me.

The city and citizens, which you yesterday described to us in fiction, *we will now transfer to the world of reality*. It shall be the ancient city of Athens, and we will suppose that the citizens whom you imagined, were our veritable ancestors, of whom the priest spoke; they will perfectly harmonise, and there will be no inconsistency in saying that the citizens of your republic are these ancient Athenians. Let us divide the subject among us, and all endeavour according to our ability gracefully to *execute the task which you have imposed upon us*. Consider then, Socrates, if this narrative is suited to the purpose, or whether we should seek for some other instead.[96]

And we come to the final understanding that conveys to us the secret of the story of Atlantis: that it did not actually come from an Egyptian priest, but that this was a story that was created to "execute the task which you [Socrates] have imposed upon us", which was to veil in fiction something that was Truth. Does this mean that they were "making it up"? No, indeed. It means that they were attempting to find a vehicle for the history that would insure its preservation.

Thus we come to the conclusion that it is entirely possible that the story was *not* given to Solon by an Egyptian priest, but that it was attributed to same because at the time everyone was convinced of the antiquity of the Egyptians. It was as much a fad then as now, due to the presence of the pyramids and other monuments. If Fulcanelli is correct about the cult of the dead of the Egyptians being a distortion of this knowledge, and this cult was encouraged, supported, and furthered by the Egyptian elite of the past several thousand years, then it is almost a certainty that they were not in possession of the knowledge that was conveyed to Solon. But it seems apparent that he did, indeed, get it from somewhere. And he tells us that *the Greeks were instructed by the Arabs* which certainly makes us wonder who were the original "Arabs" since the time referred to was long before Abraham and his son Ishmael, the alleged "father of the Arabs".

Getting back to Fulcanelli and Hendaye and primitive Chiliasm, let us take the hint from some comments made by an old man in Florence who was speaking to Mark Hedsel, recorded in his book *The Zelator,* which will save us a lot of grief:

…[S]ometimes even Fulcanelli wraps his mysteries in mysteries, for he knows that some things may not be spoken, even today. […] Fulcanelli is far wiser than most of his readers know. He sets down less in words than he could, and delivers parables in parables. In this there is real wisdom. The alchemists insisted that one should *heat the retort many times before making the final distillation.* This is *an emblem of true thought*: one must *pass one's thinking through the furnace many times, to be sure.* One should *think with a hammer*, rather than with a brain, as one shapes our thought from dross matter.

As though imitating the hammer blows of Vulcan, he tapped his stick on top of the balustrade. "Iron, you see. Cast iron. Yet it looks like stone. That is the true

---

[96] Plato, *Timaeus*, translated by B. Jowett.

Philosopher's Stone, which never appears to be what it is. [...] There are deeper secrets in stone than in iron."[97]

The reader will be far more aware of what it means to "think with a hammer, rather than with a brain" by the time they are finished with this discussion. But for the moment, suffice it to say that the old master is pointing out that until a certain "initiation" has occurred in terms of achieving mental mastery over the tracks of emotional thinking (and nearly all thinking is emotional, no matter how logical it may seem), there is no possibility of understanding Fulcanelli. Further, this process of "rewiring" the brain by deliberate hammer blows of the will against the programmed circuits is the "heating of the crucible" of the alchemical transformation — the thing that produces the "stone", a particular "state" that comes to exist in the brain of the individual who has repeatedly "hammered" their thinking, producing what the ancients called the "magnetic center".

THE DOUBLE CATASTROPHE: THE BROTHERS HELIOPOLIS

Fulcanelli did not write about architecture, or even this particular monument at Hendaye, with the intent that the reader would find it necessary to go and see the items in question, to puzzle over them, to dissect them to extract a secret. That is the method of puffers. He wrote about the chosen subjects simply because *it was the platform of exposition of ideas.* Canseliet wrote in his introduction to *Le Mystere*, obviously written under instruction from Fulcanelli:

> Thanks to [Fulcanelli], the Gothic cathedral has yielded up its secret. And it is not without surprise and emotion that we learn how our ancestors fashioned the *first stone* of its foundations, that dazzling gem, more precious than gold itself, on which Jesus built his Church. All Truth, all Philosophy and all Religion rest on this *unique and sacred Stone.* Many people, inflated with presumption, believe themselves capable of fashioning it; yet how rare are the elect, those who are sufficiently simple, learned and skilful to complete the task!

> The hermeticists - those at least who are worthy of the name - will discover other things here. From *the clash of ideas, it is said, light bursts forth;* they will recognize here that is from the confrontation of the Book and the Building that the Spirit is released and the Letter dies.[98]

The "clash" of ideas is an expression of "thinking with a hammer". The cathedral, the "building" is the "temple"; in other words, the temporal lobes of the brain - the ability to think and later to see. The "Book" is what is accepted fact and history, not to mention the "book of our DNA", or programmed limitations.

---

[97] Mark Hedsel, The Zelator – A Modern Initiate Explores The Ancient Mysteries (York Beach: Samuel Weiser, Inc. 2000) p. 306

[98] Fulcanelli, *Mystery of the Cathedrals*, Introduction p. 6-7.

Fulcanelli says that one must be *"indifferent to theories, systems and hypotheses, which are generally accepted without question on the testimony of books"*. It is in the clash between that which is generally accepted, that which is published in books, which is accepted due to wishful thinking and lazy research, and the thinking processes that take effort, time and patience, that the light bursts forth in the magnetite that collects in the temporal lobes as a result of repeated "heating" of the crucible by thinking *with a hammer* and its consequent development of additional receptors and neuronal circuitry, not to mention production of specific ligands. One has to chisel away the barriers to truth, one hammer blow at a time. And it is a long, arduous, and difficult work.

For those who can see, I have just given away the fundamental secret of alchemy. And those who can see also see immediately how difficult a process it is. For those who can't see, it doesn't matter anyway. All else in alchemy follows from this process. It is "the *first stone* of its foundations", and *"All Truth, all Philosophy and all Religion rest on this unique and sacred Stone."* The stone of the mind, the *prima materia*, must be shaped by the hammer blows of thinking before anything else can proceed. This was the process that I led myself through from the future state of adeptship as the "Cassiopaeans".

In the Hendaye chapter, there is a mysterious inscription on the cross that Fulcanelli discusses, pointing out that the important thing about it is that the letter *S*, "which takes on the curving shape of a snake, corresponds to the Greek *khi* (X) and takes over its esoteric meaning". "It is the helicoidal track of the sun, having arrived at the zenith of its curve across space, at the time of the cyclic catastrophe. It is a theoretical image of the Beast of the Apocalypse, of the dragon, which on the days of Judgment, spews out fire and brimstone on macrocosmic creation."

Fulcanelli then gives the clue: "Thanks to the symbolic value of the letter S, displaced on purpose, we understand that the inscription must be translated in secret language, that is to say in the *language of the gods*, or the *language of the birds*, and that the meaning must be found with the help of the rules of *Diplomacy.*"

Fulcanelli discussed the subject of the "double catastrophe" much earlier than the second edition of *Le Mystere,* in which the Hendaye chapter first appeared. In his book *Dwellings of the Philosophers*, he launches his remarks on the platform of a mysterious obelisk located in the Crecy forest, that he describes as, *"the tangible, expressive image, absolutely conforming to tradition, of the double terrestrial calamity, of the conflagration and of the flood, on the terrible Judgment Day"*.

This suggests to me that someone - perhaps it was Fulcanelli himself - realized that the true message of *Dwellings of the Philosophers* was not getting through, and that a new mode of drawing attention to it had to be discovered.

So, let me ask the reader a question to contemplate: why are all of Fulcanelli's books dedicated to "The *Brothers* Heliopolis", and how does that relate to a *"Double* Catastrophe"? As Fulcanelli says, "Nature does not open the door of the sanctuary indiscriminately to everyone."

CYCLIC CATASTROPHES

In the present day and time, the causes of cosmic catastrophe are generally assigned by so-called "alternative researchers" and purveyors of esoteric wisdom to the idea of Pole Shift. The Pole Shift idea was described as the "ultimate disaster" by John White in his book appropriately entitled *Pole Shift*. White listed numerous psychic prophecies that are clearly describing a Pole Shift and attempted to relate them to scientific ideas. One source claims that the Hawaiian Islands will rise and become peaks of a great mountain chain on a new continent that will rise in the Pacific. Another source predicts that the Hawaiian Islands will sink beneath the sea. Such contradictions among psychics are often handily explained with the "branching universe" theory with a twist: both are true, they just refer to different periods of future history.

As it turned out, most of the psychic predictions analyzed by John White concerned the period right around the year 2,000. Well, it has come and gone, the pole didn't flip, and we are still here.

Naturally, many of the psychics and channels of the space brothers say that we ought to thank their guides or "guardians" for that fact, since they all pulled together to keep us from falling into the pit. Nice try, but, as the Cassiopaeans have said, "Tales are easy to sew/sow, when the past is yours only to know". And how true that is.

In the end, the chief problem of all the theories is that of the "trigger mechanism". What is driving the machine? What is changing in our solar system that we may not be told about? Why are the rumormongers and the theorists of such things as "Planet Nibiru" or "galactic alignment" or "precessional ages" allowed to promulgate their nonsense, while the real data is being so carefully hidden?

The fact that the Earth's magnetic poles have changed many times in history is now a well accepted scientific fact. But this actually says nothing at all about the planet itself "flipping". It just signifies a reversal of the magnetic field. As we now know, the Sun reverses its magnetic field regularly and cyclically with no apparent cataclysmic effects. So, a simple reversal of the magnetic field cannot be used in support of a physical and literal "Pole Shift".

In the end, the chief problem of all the "End of the World" theories is that of the "trigger mechanism". What is driving the machine?

The most popular theory of the present moment is that of Zecharia Sitchin who analyzed the myths of the Sumerians, concluding that they referred to a massive unseen planet, and further, that all of the stories point to a cyclical return at intervals of 3600 years.

For so many years we have heard about "End of the World" hoaxes and panics that it is becoming rather tiresome and tedious. When was the last time you heard about the Photon Belt nonsense? That one was pretty popular for awhile. Kept everybody going like crazy while dozens of folks made lots of money selling books and "ascension" courses to help people survive the "enlightening" of the planet.

Well, the "photon belt" apparently fizzled and then the Hale Bopp Frenzy cranked up leading to some mass suicides and a general air of paranoia all over.

What a lot of people didn't notice was that there were some extremely strange things going on here on the Big Blue Marble while Hale Bopp was decorating our skies - the weather was changing dramatically and Europe experienced what was called "The Flood of the Millennium". One has to wonder if the Hale Bopp affair was not just another form of distraction away from what was really going on - sort of a Cosmic O.J. Simpson trial?

After Hale Bopp Flopped, the Planet X Panic got its motor warmed up and Nancy Leider - deluded or a con artist, who can say? - may be facing some lawsuits for leading people astray with that one. Most certainly, our researches into secret government mind control projects suggest that Nancy and others are really not to blame for their lunacy: it is planned and deliberate.

Of course, all the while that was going on, the political world was going crazy and we are now sitting on a planet that is like a powder keg just waiting for somebody to casually light a cigarette...

In order to form any ideas about a "trigger", it is important to try to sort out the data that we can get and decide if a Pole Shift is even possible and if so, is it a gradual, Uniformitarian event, or if it is sudden and cataclysmic.

It is commonly accepted among scientists nowadays that there is a "cycle of extinction.". However, until recently, they continued to attempt to put it off so far into the past and future that it could not possibly concern our present civilization. It is only fairly recently that hints and clues have begun to emerge into public awareness - a sort of "testing the waters" - though, as usual, there is much back and forth debate. Generally, those who say that cyclic extinctions DO happen - and rather frequently - approach the subject from the point of view of collecting and presenting data. The naysayers generally approach the subject from the point of view of "explaining away" the data as being "faulty" or "misunderstood". They also tend to get emotional and attack the personalities of those who present data. Still, more and more facts, data, and confirmable information, keep coming to light.

The relative importance of an idea and the implications of the conclusions that can be drawn from that idea ought to determine the level of attention given to the idea. The fact is, the idea that something may be whacking through our solar system at periodic intervals is a concept of such importance that it simply cannot be overstated.

The Russians theorized in the 60s that there may be not one, but three planetary bodies existing in our solar system beyond Pluto. Aberrations in the orbital motion of Neptune and Uranus have convinced many other scientists that there is a strong likelihood that *some* kind of large body exists in solar space beyond Pluto and exerts strong gravitational attraction on the outermost planets. So we agree with Sitchin that, if a definite cycle exists, one of the most logical explanations for it is that it is caused by a planetary-like body making regular, predictable appearances. But we disagree that such a body travels into the inner solar system.

"If it does exist, and it does reappear cyclically, why doesn't science know about it?", the skeptical reader will ask.

This issue of the cycle of this purported "return" is of the utmost importance; we find ourselves facing the idea that the world is either due shortly for great geologic and meteorological events, *or it is not*. If we consider the remote possibility that this is going to happen, and if we are interested in human destiny, it behooves us to investigate whether or not there is a correlation between cyclical geologic changes in the earth's past and the future, and *what that cycle might be.* What is more, there is also compelling hard scientific evidence that our planet has relatively recently experienced cataclysmic geological changes. It has only been in recent years that some of the more convincing evidence of this kind, such as ice core samples and tree ring analysis, has been revealed.

If we, for one second, think that there is even a one-percent possibility that such events are cyclic, and that we may be approaching such an event, we ought to be putting the whole force of all our science and all the great minds of our civilization into researching the matter. But that does not seem to be the case. Are the leaders of our nations so stupid that they cannot think that far ahead? Or are they so greedy and power hungry that they don't care? Do they intend to "get while the getting's good", and then when - and IF - the final curtain comes down, they will think that they were the stars of the show? This poses a peculiar problem. How do we assess who really knows what?

Over and over again, as we have pushed deeper and deeper into our research, we find that investigating these matters is problematic for a lot of reasons. On the surface, what we see is that academic and professional geologists, glaciologists, geophysicists, paleontologists, oceanographers, astronomers, astrophysicists, physicists, mathematicians, archaeologists, and so on, do not take kindly to intrusions into their private little worlds. They have their gods of convention, whom they worship, and god forbid that anyone should criticize the acceptable protocols of the conventional interpretation. They are warm and safe and their career is protected by their covenant with the scientific Thought Police who are, in turn, high priests to the Control System.

And this is where we discover the problem. The Control System, via the offices of its high priests of science, ensures that glaciologists do not cross over into astrophysics and that geologists do not cross over into archaeology. In this way, there is no such thing as Comparative Science, and this is most especially true in the United States where the lines between disciplines are most strongly demarcated, patrolled, and enforced by the Scientific Thought Police.

These conditions bring our problem into sharp focus. As we have attempted to get to the very bottom of many of the claims of the experts in the various fields, we have discovered that there is much data that is completely suppressed by this system. There is also a great deal of data that falls under the control of government agencies, and access to it is severely limited. I discovered that there is, indeed, an effort on the part of various government agencies to investigate these cyclical returns and cometary impact matters, but that the results are generally unavailable to the public. They consist of technical papers, stored on microfiche, buried in research and special collections sections of university libraries. Some of it makes its way into print, but the volumes are so costly that the researcher in these fields must be well financed to be able to afford them. Those things that make it to print in technical journals are couched in such amazingly obtuse and opaque terminology that one must be as sharp as a Damascus sword to cut through the nonsense. And it is almost a given that only a trained scientist who knows the "hidden jargon" will be able to decipher the code.

I must also tell the reader that, for weeks on end, as we have ordered and read technical papers, books, files of data, reports and so forth, the enormity of the problem of suppression of information has become overwhelmingly evident. Every night, after a long day of analysis, calculations, plugging numbers into formulas and compiling results, we would prepare for bed, both of us shaking our heads and muttering over and over again: "lies, lies, lies; nothing but lies." COINTELPRO everywhere.

And so it is. Not only are the separate scientific disciplines most often unaware of developments in other fields which may have important data that would help their own studies, they are also conditioned — programmed — to consider it scientific blasphemy to compare their own conclusion with the data from other fields. And somebody is controlling this system of suppression.

The terrestrial axis is currently inclined at 23.5 degrees. The early Greek philosophers viewed this tilt as an "irregular condition", and not something that had been fixed since the beginning. Anaxagoras wrote:

> In the beginning the stars moved in the sky as in a revolving dome, so that the
> celestial pole, which is always visible, was vertically overhead; but subsequently
> the pole took its inclined position.

Hesiod discussed the cyclical conception of time in his *Works and Days*, saying that the human race had five ages: Gold, Silver, Bronze, Heroic, and Iron. The Heroic age is seen by many scholars as an addition to an earlier scheme meant to accommodate Greek history. During the *first* of these ages, mankind lived under the rule of Kronos, or Saturn, and was on friendly terms with the gods, and was free from hard work, pain, and old age. Plato wrote about a periodic reversal of the rotation of "the world", probably meaning the entire "cosmic machine", rather than just the planet, as being the cause of the end of one age and the beginning of another. He tells us that all the stories of the changes in the rising and setting of the sun and planets originate from the same event in cosmic history: the usurpation of the rule of Chronos by Zeus.

> When God was shepherd there were no political constitutions and no taking of
> wives and begetting of children. For all men rose up anew into life out of the earth,
> having no memory of the former things. Instead they had fruits without stint from
> trees and bushes; these needed no cultivation but sprang up of themselves out of the
> ground without man's toil. For the most part they disported themselves in the open
> needing neither clothing nor couch, for the seasons were blended evenly so as to
> work them no hurt, and the grass which sprang up out of the earth in abundance
> made a soft bed for them.[99]

---

[99] Plato, *The Statesman*, 272a, trans. J.B. Skemp.

But this age came to a close and the gods of that age gave up their benevolent governance, turning the rule of the world over to something "other". Plato describes the close of the era in terms of Pole Shift:

> The gods of the provinces, who had ruled under the greatest god, knew at once what was happening and relinquished the oversight of their regions. A shudder passed through the world at the reversing of its rotation, checked as it was between the old control and the new impulse which had turned end into beginning for it and beginning into end. This shock set up a great quaking, which caused — in this crisis of the world just as in the former one — destruction of living creatures of all kinds. Then, after the interval needed for its recovery, it gained relief at last from its clamors and confusion, and attaining quiet after great upheaval it returned to its ordered course and continued in it, having control and government of itself and of all within it.[100]

Herodotus seems to be quoting from the same source that Plato utilized when he reports:

> Thus in the period of eleven thousand three hundred and forty years they said that there had arisen no god in human form; nor even before that time or afterwards among the remaining kings who arose in Egypt, did they report that anything of that kind had come to pass. In this time they said that the sun had moved four times from his accustomed place of rising, and where he now sets he had thence twice had his rising, and in the place from whence he now rises he had twice had his setting; and in the meantime nothing in Egypt had been changed from its usual state, neither that which comes from the earth nor that which comes to them from the river nor that which concerns diseases or deaths.[101]

Both Herodotus and Plato are explicit in saying that the phenomenon is *dual natured*, that something happens "out there" in the Solar system and the results on the earth are cataclysmic. Herodotus says that it happened four times in an 11,500-year period, and Plato says that it is an ever-recurring phenomenon.

Modern interpreters of these passages generally divide into two groups: the catastrophists and the uniformitarians. The catastrophists suggest that the description is that of a literal 180-degree flip of the earth. The Uniformitarians like to talk in terms of "world ages" according to the "Precession of the Zodiac".

UNIFORMITARIANISM

In his *Principia Mathematica*, Isaac Newton demonstrated that the precession of the equinoxes is the result of the earth's oblate spheroidal shape, which causes it to spin in something less than a perfectly aligned motion. In short, it inscribes a very gradual circle in relation to the celestial axis and, according to Newton, the period

---

[100] Ibid.

[101] Herodutus, *The Histories*, Book II: 142.

in which this entire circle is completed is 26 thousand years. This means that not only does the sun rise in a slightly different location, but also the terrestrial axis points to a different area in the heavens as time goes by.

As it happens, the general area of the heavens pointed to by the terrestrial pole, does not have an abundance of visible stars to consistently have a pole star. So it is only occasionally that it really has one, and even then, the pole star is not quite "on the money".

Twelve thousand years ago, the time at which many occultists point out that one of the stars in Draco, Thuban, was the pole star, it was actually less of a pole star than the current one if we take into account the decreasing angle of the axis of the earth. That is assuming, of course, that present observations can be extrapolated backward.

Most of the occult or psychic speculations link the Pole Shift with Noah's Flood and the destruction of Atlantis, the fabled ancient high civilization. But, the uniformitarian view is also well represented in the occult literature. Sampson Arnold Mackey, a shoemaker in Norwich, England, formulated a grand theory of the ages of the world that is pretty much based on De Louville's gradual diminution of the angle of the terrestrial axis to the plane of the ecliptic, but also incorporating ideas based on the precession of the equinoxes. And here is where we find the first fully expounded idea that the precession itself is important as a clock that strikes the hours of world ages.

Mackey assumed the precessional cycle to be 25 thousand years. He also accepted the gradual diminution of the axial orientation at one degree every 6 thousand years. He assumed (from where, we don't know), that each completion of the precessional cycle diminished the angle of the earth axis by four degrees. Therefore, it will take four more precessional cycles to get to the "Golden Age". at which time the terrestrial axis is aligned with the celestial axis. Four more precessional cycles equals 150 thousand years from now. This is certainly an idea to make glad the heart of any scientist who projects catastrophe way into the distant past, or impossibly far in to the future.

Helena Blavatsky adopted some of Mackey's ideas during her short term of membership in a "secret society" called the Hermetic Brotherhood of Luxor, (H B of L) which taught Mackey's doctrine in an essay called *The Hermetic Key* composed by Thomas H. Burgoyne, secretary of that order. However, the H B of L made some "adjustments" to Mackey's ideas so they would better fit some other scheme of their own. They altered the degrees of change per cycle from 4 to $3°36''$ so that a complete cycle takes one hundred turns. They also changed the precessional period from 25 thousand years, to 25,920 years, coming closer to Newton's original figure.

Mackey believed that he had discovered the key to universal mythology in astrology. His entire scheme was based on certain mythological interpretations, and the H B of L claimed Mackey as a member, but of course, only after he was dead. This seems to be a common practice of many putative secret societies that seek to align themselves with certain ideas or people for one reason or another.

Nevertheless, the adoption of this precession idea by the H B of L, later taken up by the occultists Papus, Barlet, Guenon, Reuss, Kellner and Steiner, ensured that it would become a foundational philosophy among groups such as the *Ordo Templi*

Orientalis, the *Theosophical Society*, the *Golden Dawn*, and so on. Most of their ideas are founded on this uniformitarian, cosmic clock of precession and slow, spiraling movement of the earth's pole in a grand, shifting circle that reverses the polar directions every two million years or so.

There is another interesting motion of the earth's axis called the Chandler Wobble. The Chandler wobble, discovered by astronomer S. C. Chandler in 1891, is a variation in the earth's axis of rotation amounting to 0.7 seconds of arc over a period of 435 days, or about 14 months. This means that the earth's poles wander a bit as the planet spins, describing an irregular circle ranging from 10 to 50 feet in diameter. There's also *nutation*, an aggregation of sub-wobbles, the most significant of which has a period of 18.6 years and results from variations in the distance of the moon.

Scientists have been particularly intrigued by the Chandler wobble since its cause has remained a mystery, even though it has been under observation for over a century. Its period is only around 433 days, or just 1.2 years, meaning that it takes that amount of time to complete one wobble. The amplitude of the wobble amounts to about 20 feet at the North Pole. It has been calculated that the Chandler wobble would be damped down, or reduced to zero, in just 68 years, unless some force were constantly acting to reinvigorate it. But what is that force, or excitation mechanism? Over the years, various hypotheses have been put forward, such as atmospheric phenomena, continental water storage (changes in snow cover, river runoff, lake levels, or reservoir capacities), interaction at the boundary of Earth's core and its surrounding mantle, and earthquakes.

Researcher Michael Mandeville has charted and analyzed the Chandler Wobble and suggests that it is progressively shifting the location of the poles at an accelerating rate. His conclusion is that something is "driving" this change — possibly some interaction between the earth and the Sun and/or Moon. Whatever is driving it, it seems that the result is a heating up of the interior of the earth resulting in increased El Nino activity, and accelerating earthquake activity.

CATASTROPHISM

As I wrote above, in order to form any ideas about a "trigger", it is important to try to sort out the data that we can get and decide if a Pole Shift is a gradual, uniformitarian event, or if it is sudden and cataclysmic.

There are endless descriptions of possible scenarios, and none of them were ringing any bells in terms of the actual scientific data until I discovered the ideas of Immanuel Velikovsky. Indeed, John White devotes about 20 or so pages to Velikovsky's ideas, and in general, he merely used them to support the idea of past Pole Shifts, pointing out that Velikovsky made no predictions about future events of this type. We might also note that Velikovsky must have hit a real nerve to have been so viciously vilified. The Scientific Thought Police went into overdrive to suppress him! Velikovsky was condemned basically because he denied that the orbits in the solar system were stable.

When reading Velikovsky's blow-by-blow interpretation of the events of the Exodus as recorded in the Bible as the result of the close approach of a cometary Venus, I realized that these events mirrored, almost word for word, the events described in the book of Revelation. What is more interesting is that the book of Revelation was written long before the current craze of End Time Prophecies. It is sort of the Mother of all End Time Prophecies. While I didn't necessarily agree with all Velikovsky had to say, it certainly made me think of the descriptions of myth and legends in a new way.

As it happens, there are many individuals who have noted the evidence in ancient myths and legends. Sitchin is not the first. Theories of the earth encountering a comet did not originate with Velikovsky either.

In 1882, Ignatius Donnelly, a Minnesota congressman and scholar of all-things-Atlantean, wrote a book entitled *Ragnarok,* wherein he proposed that a giant comet had passed close to the earth in past ages. The intense heat from the comet had set off huge fires that raged across the face of the globe. He suggested that the comet had dumped vast amounts of dust on the earth, triggered earthquakes, leveled mountains, and initiated the ice age. He even explained some of the miracles of the Bible in terms of his comet, proposing that the standing-still of the sun at the command of Joshua was possibly a tale commemorating this event. Donnelly's readers were thrilled by his descriptions of the "glaring and burning monster" in the sky, scorching the planet with unearthly heat and shaking the land with "thunders beyond all thunders".

Possibly inspired by Donnelly, Camille Flammarion wrote *The End of the World* in 1893 in which he recounted a fictional collision between the earth and a comet fifty times its size. Flammarion's lurid prose ensured that his book was an immediate sensation!

For thousands of years, comets have been associated with disaster and misfortune. They are harbingers of plagues, earthquakes, floods, natural disasters and wars. In fact, the passing of a comet followed by war has been so frequent as to earn for comets the soubriquet "The Swords of Heaven". Tradition has assigned responsibility to comets for death and destructions, disease and decay, defeat and dissolution, the deaths of kings, and the fall of empires. It could be said that *no celestial phenomenon is so widely and generally feared*. Velikovsky believed that this fear had a foundation in fact: it was a sort of global subconscious memory of actual encounters between the earth and other cosmic bodies that were so devastating that the fearful reality of the event was suppressed into the collective subconscious, and only a "comet phobia" remained in evidence.

In 1857, an anonymous German astrologer predicted that a comet would strike the earth on June 13 of that year. The impending catastrophe became the talk of all of Europe. The French astronomer, Jacques Babinet, tried to reassure people by stating that a collision between the earth and a comet would do no harm. He compared the impact to "a railway train coming into contact with a fly". His words, apparently, had little effect. The Paris correspondent for the American journal, *Harper's Weekly*, wrote:

> Women have miscarried; crops have been neglected; wills have been made; comet-proof suits of clothing have been invented; a cometary life insurance company (premiums payable in advance) has been created… all because an almanac maker… thought proper to insert, under the week commencing June 13, 'About this time, expect a comet'.

Naturally, by the time of dawn on July 14, it was apparent that there wasn't going to be a comet. The point is: an astrologer's "prophecy" had terrified millions in the total absence of any evidence that there was a comet anywhere near the planet. And this type of scenario has occurred more than once, even down to our own day and time when the Heaven's Gate cult members committed mass suicide in response to rumors and prognostications regarding comet Hale Bopp.

Immanuel Velikovsky demonstrated rather convincingly that there was massive evidence of both a literary and scientific nature that great catastrophic earth changes had occurred during the second millennium BC due to cometary showers and the close passage of Venus. He settled on a date of 1450 BC, but more recent scientific evidence points to the date actually being between 1644 and 1600 BC. There is also evidence for a disruption circa 5200 BC, 8,800 BC, 12,400 BC, 16,000 BC, 19,600 BC, and by logical extension every 3,600 years previously for an indefinite and unknown period of time. What is more, if the last "return" was in 1600 BC, we are not just due, we are overdue for the next one.

Sitchin's theories about Nibiru do not take into account many of the literary reports from the ancients regarding these *great bombardments of comets*. Velikovsky tried to account for this by suggesting that a cometary Venus was hauling around a tail of rocks. It seems that Velikovsky and his supporters, and Sitchin and his supporters, although recognizing serious worldwide catastrophes, have failed to recognize the true nature of such events. Velikovsky proposed that Venus out of orbit was a more or less one-time event rather than a symptom of a long-term cycle. Sitchin came closer with his understanding of the cycle, but he failed to consider all the variables in his solution. What is more, once he settled on his idea as the one and only solution, his efforts to make the mythical elements fit the hypothesis became almost as absurd as the efforts of mainstream science to avoid them!

The confirmed linchpin for the fall of the late Bronze Age cultures, the Middle Eastern Civilizations, and other recorded disasters that are found to be "around that time", seems to be the period from 1644 BC to 1600 BC. The ice cores show the disturbances starting in 1644 (registering in 1645), and the tree rings show a big spike in 1628, though the entire period was disturbed.[102]

What is clear is that whatever comes at 3600 year intervals as shown by the ice cores is capable of setting off prolonged periods of earth changes that are above the levels of ordinary uniformitarian geologic and climatalogical changes. But what is important is that the mythical and archaeological evidence suggests that it is a shower of asteroids or comets that are NOT seen until it is TOO LATE.

---

[102] I am going to omit here the extensive evidence I have assembled which confirms this date of around 1600 BC. This will be treated in a future volume.

To ascribe all of the evidence of cyclic catastrophe to a "uniformitarian" idea that it just got cold and then got warm and got cold and warm... with such an evident cycle is sort of absurd. To ascribe it to a "galactic core explosion" is equally absurd.

I think that, based on the observations of the ancients that what we are looking for is a recurring shower of comets that cycles through the solar system regularly, on a 3,600-year orbit. What is more, it seems that this body of comets, clustered together, at some point, resembles a fiery serpent with a mouthful of devouring teeth in the blackness of space. For this reason, it was given the name *spdt*, *spdw*, and *spd-ibhw* (sharp toothed), in the Pyramid Texts. It undoubtedly is a terrifying spectacle!

We return again to the question: what is the "initiator" of these showers, and did they begin in some interaction with an "outside agent"?

According to scientific studies about the possibilities of our Sun having a companion, periodic comets were "bumped" into the solar system by a dark star, a "little brother" or "little sister" of our own Sun, which has a long, elliptical orbit measured, most likely, in millions of years.

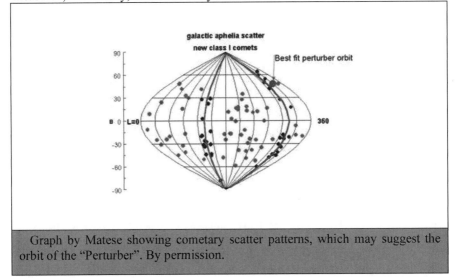

Graph by Matese showing cometary scatter patterns, which may suggest the orbit of the "Perturber". By permission.

If it is a companion star, present day science pretty clearly demonstrates that it must have a very long period; otherwise, we would notice it quite plainly in orbital perturbations of a certain type. In actual fact, the computer model that best fits the various dynamics is that of a 27 million year orbit.[103] And this, of course, leads us to a considerable difficulty: the period of return of the Dark Star, as opposed to the period of disasters. Obviously, a body with a 27 million year orbit isn't likely to be remembered. However, an ancient advanced science may have certainly figured it out exactly as it is being proposed in the present day, and it was remembered and passed down in what came to be seen as fantastic myths and legends.

The work by these experts suggests that the observations of other binary systems demonstrate the model for the projected separation they have given. Such paired stars are "physically connected systems", and these brown dwarfs are "burning", though non-nuclear. What is more, if it is out there, it never enters the Inner Solar system, though it may be seen from afar and may interact with our own Sun in dramatic ways. This is what Fulcanelli seems to be suggesting in his many allusions to the sun and to helicoidal tracks of the Sun, and to "doubles" and "diplomacy" and "mirrors", not to mention the dedication of his books to: The Brothers Heliopolis.

Thus, we understand that it is not this Twin sun that makes its "appearance" at *every* period of catastrophe. Nevertheless, the analyses of the periodic comets suggests that it does, at very long periods, again and again, crash through the Oort cloud like a bowling ball through rows of pins, sending a new collection of them spinning into a periodical orbit, and because they follow the the laws of celestial mechanics, they establish an orbit of 3,600 years. This idea has some support from scientific studies, which the theory of the Planet Nibiru as a visitor to the inner solar system does not.

When we look at the mythology of both Mesopotamia and Ancient Egypt, we suspect that these stories do not refer to a "Tenth Planet", but to the presence of the Sun's dark companion, a failed star classified as a "brown dwarf". It also seems to be the one hypothesis that encompasses all the "sub-hypotheses" of the many researchers who have attempted to deal with different aspects of the problems of the past and future of the earth.

Sitchin proposed that a "10th Planet" caroms through the inner solar system. Scientific evidence does not support a body, the size he suggests, entering into the inner solar system. However, science can support a cluster of comets spread out in space that returns at 3,600-year intervals. In the end, the potential for cataclysmic disruption of the earth is about as bad either way.

Sitchin suggests that his 10th planet is inhabited by the Annunaki/Nefilim. He claims that they are our creators and masters. His ideas are tremendously out of synch with the strong circumstantial evidence about the alien presence on this planet. Sitchin's ideas are also flawed for the other reasons we have already

---

[103] Matese, J.J., Whitman, P.G., Whitmore, D.P., "Cometary ecidence of a massive body in the outer Oort cloud", *Icarus* 141: 354-366. 1999.

mentioned, though he has certainly produced interesting work in his interpretations of the Sumerian texts as possibly referring to "alien interactions" and the periodic return of something!

Other theorists suggest that the Dark Companion of the Sun has its own habitable planetary system, home to the mythical 'gods' of the ancient world. This theory that a brown dwarf with its own planetary system is able to pass through the Oort cloud and the Kuiper belt, keeping its own mini-solar system *intact*, is obviously extremely problematical. In the same way that Sitchin simply passes right over the problems of Nibiru seeding life on earth, forgetting that evolutionary processes that are being postulated must apply to both bodies, the creator of the "Dark Star: Have Planets, Will Travel" theory also does not consider the fundamental problem of such an idea.

And so, I repeat: the two great themes of myth are the yearning for the golden age and a terror of a world-destroying catastrophe. The two ideas are inextricably linked to each other. In virtually all of the stories about the Fall from Eden and the Flood of Noah, the great celestial bodies in the heavens were said to have been out of control.

What seems to be a more "pristine" version of the story is that of Amlodhi, of Icelandic legend, who owned a mill, which, in his own time, "ground out peace and plenty". Later, in decaying times, it ground out salt. Finally, it fell to the bottom of the ocean and was grinding out rock and sand, creating a vast whirlpool, the Maelstrom. According to Giorgio De Santillana and Hertha Von Dechend, this myth was evidence for an astronomical process, the precession of the zodiac. As already discussed, this is the shifting of the sun through the signs of the zodiac, and, according to them, it determines "world ages". They write:

> Now it is time to locate the origin of the image of the Mill, and further, what its alleged breakup and the coming into being of Whirlpool can possibly mean.

> The starting place is in Greece. Cleomedes (c. AD 150), speaking of the northern latitudes, states: *"The heavens there turn around in the way a millstone does"*. Al-Farghani in the East takes up the same idea, and his colleagues will supply the details. They call the star Kochab, Beta Ursae Minoris, "mill peg", and the stars of the Little Bear, surrounding the North Pole, and Fas al-rahha (the hole of the mill peg), *"because they represent, as it were, a hole (the axle ring) in which the mill axle turns, since the axle of the equator (the polar axis) is to be found in this region, fairly close to the star Al-jadi…"* These are the words of the Arab Cosmographer al-Kazvini. Ideler comments: *"Koth, the common name of the Pole, means really the axle of the movable upper millstone which goes through the lower fixed on, what is called the 'mill-iron.'"*

> …The *Bhagavata Purana* tells us how the virtuous prince Dhruva was appointed as Pole star. The particular virtue of the prince, which alarmed even the gods, is worth

mentioning: *he stood on one leg for more than a month, motionless.* This is what was announced to him: "*The stars and their figures, and also the planets shall turn around you.*"[...]

There is a remark by Trimalchio in Petronius (*Satyricon* 39): "*Thus the orb of heaven turns around like a millstone, and ever does something bad.*" It was not a foreign idea to the ancients that the mills of the gods grind slowly, and that the result is usually pain.[104]

The nine grim goddesses who "once ground Amlodhi's meal", working now that "host-cruel skerry quern" *beyond the edge of the world,* are in Mundlfoeri, literally "*the mover of the handle*". The word "*mundil…is never used in the old Norse literature about any other object than the sweep or handle with which the movable millstone is turned*". Here we have a clue that refers directly to something that "turns the mill". The "nine grim goddesses", whom we may identify with the Egyptian Ennead, are located in the "handle".

The case is then established. But there is an ambiguity here, which discloses further depths to the idea. "*Moendull*" comes from Sanskrit "*Manthati*", says Rydberg, "it means to swing, twist, bore …Its direct application always refers to *the production of fire by friction*".[105]

And here we see the idea of a binary star system moving in tandem orbit with one another. A cosmic "machine", the "helicoidal track of the sun", as Fulcanelli put it. The authors of *Hamlet's Mill* struggle on, however, with their uniformitarian idea:

The identity of the Mill, in its many versions, with heaven is thus universally understood and accepted. But hitherto nobody seems to have wondered about the second part of the story, which also occurs in the many versions. How and why does it always happen that this Mill, the peg of which is Polaris, had to be wrecked or unhinged? Once the archaic mind had grasped the forever enduring rotation, what caused it to think that the axle jumps out of the hole? What memory of catastrophic events has created this story of destruction? Why should Vainamoinen … state explicitly that another Mill has to be constructed? Why had Dhruva to be appointed to play Pole star – and for a given cycle? For the story refers in no way to the creation of the world.[106]

The simple answer lies in the facts of the case. The Pole star does get out of place, and every few thousand years another star has to be chosen which best approximates that position. It is well known that the Great Pyramid, so carefully sighted, is not oriented at our Pole Star, but at alpha Draconis, which occupied the position at the pole 5,000 years ago. …It is the more difficult for moderns to

---

[104] De Santillana & Von Dechend, *Hamlet's Mill* (Boston: David R. Godine 1977) pp. 137-138.

[105] Ibid., p. 139.

[106] And here I beg to differ.

imagine that in those far-off ages men could keep track of such imperceptible shifting, as many of them are not aware of the mere facts.[107]

This remark about the Pyramid being oriented to Draconis is misleading. The fact is, the orientation of the pyramid to the terrestrial pole remains constant. It is only the pole stars that change by the shifting of the terrestrial axial orientation.

Most of these myths, however, come under a misleading name. They have been understood to deal with the end of the world. …What actually comes to an end is a world, in the sense of a world-age.

Coherence will be reestablished in this welter of traditions if it is realized that what is referred to is the grandest of heavenly phenomena, the Precession of the Equinoxes.[108]

Now, did you notice what these two authors have done here? Aside from their abysmally ignorant remark about the orientation of the pyramids to Draconis, they have resorted to Uniformitarianism to explain the great mystery of this worldwide myth of the "unhinging" of the Pole star. They, and many, many others, have followed this path, believing that all the clues from ancient monuments and myths have to do simply with *measuring time*, "World Ages", in more or less "cultural" and historical terms. The World Age of the Hebrews was the age of the Ram, symbolized by Abraham taking his son to sacrifice him, and a Ram appeared in the thicket, and such other allusions. The age of Pisces, the age of Christ, is symbolized by the fish, and numerous allusions are dredged up to support that one. Now, we are supposed to be entering (or have already done so, depending on your source), the Age of Aquarius. These more recent descriptions of "ages" directly contradict the ancient ideas of the Yugas and the decline of human morality. The New Age COINTELPRO has worked long and hard to promote the idea of the "Age of Aquarius" as a time of transcendent spiritual progress and "ascension" graded on the curve, of course.

I should also point out right here that if the Precession of the Zodiac was such a great way to *measure time* and world ages, there wouldn't be so many opinions about when one began and another ended. As a measure of time that is so "vastly elegant", it ought to at least work, right? Well, it doesn't. What is more, the zodiac has been created and altered within recorded history, having at various times ten signs, eleven, twelve and thirteen. So, what's the point? From this perspective, there isn't one except for an attempt to deny the possibility that the ancients meant exactly what they said, even if later interpreters have assured us that the tales were meant as allegories.

---

[107] It is far more difficult for me to comprehend how these two authors can be talking about the ancients grasping this concept, and then to wonder why anyone with the brains to do so would even care! That is, assuming it is just a "concept."

[108] De Santillana & Von Dechend, op. cit., p. 141.

But still, using this Precession as a giant clock, with some fantastic perambulations through archaic lore, a dozen or more authors have produced as many different versions of what a "world age" is, and "when" they begin and end, and how. They then try to link these ages to all sorts of weird theories from the opening of "stargates" to galactic core explosions to "monuments to the end of time".

The answer is a lot simpler than that. I think those things that point us to the idea that the pole comes "unhinged" do, indeed, point to the Precession. But the important thing about this Precession is that it points us to the fact that the Earth WOBBLES. And I think that the thing the ancients are trying most desperately to point out to us in these stories is that the Earth wobbles for a REASON, and we ought to notice this wobble and ask some questions about the "nine grim goddesses" who "turn the handle" and where and what that "handle" might be that increases friction to the point that fire is produced!

In Snorri's[109] *Gylfaginning*, there is a prediction for the future given in the *Song of the Sybyl*, followed by a dialogue between King Gylfi and the Aesir[110], disguised as men. King Gylfi asks, "What happens when the whole world has burned up, the gods are dead, and all of mankind is gone? You have said earlier that each human being would go on living in this or that world." The answer is that *there are several worlds for the good and the bad.* Then Gylfi asks, "Shall any gods be alive, and shall there be something of earth and heaven?" And the answer is:

> "The earth rises up from the sea again, and is green and beautiful and things grow without sowing. Vidar and Vali are alive, for neither the sea nor the flames of Surt have hurt them and they dwell on the Eddyfield, where once stood Asgard. There come also the sons of Thor, Modi, and Magni, and bring along his hammer. There come also Balder and Hoder from the other world. All sit down and converse together. They rehearse their runes and talk of events of old days. Then they find in the grass the golden tablets that the Aesir once played with. Two children of men will also be found safe from *the great flames of Surt.* Their names, Lif and Lifthrasir, and they feed on the morning dew and from this human pair will come a great population which will fill the earth. And strange to say, the sun, before being devoured by Fenrir, *will have borne a daughter, no less beautiful and going the same ways as her mother.*"

Again, the authors of *Hamlet's Mill* take a prosaic view of these matters, pronouncing sagely that it is "just a metaphor". And again, I have to disagree. I do not think that the point is to "measure time", in the sense of "world ages" of culture, civilizations, or even "psychic" or occult influences, except in that they

---

[109] Sturlson, Snorri, The Prose Edda – Tales From Norse Mythology, p. 90-92.

[110] Norse gods.

relate to something far more important: WHAT IS CAUSING THE WOBBLE AND WHAT CAN BE THE RESULT? And we have a clear answer in Snorri's tale: The sun will have borne a daughter - which can only occur via a "mating" or Hieros Gamos.

In this sense, the ancients might have supposed, and quite rightly, that if we ever noticed this fact, if we were pointed in this direction, if we were plainly told that there is a handle that turns the axis, that this handle gets hot, that the axis of the planet comes unhinged, that it started out spinning upright and then gradually wobbled out of place and finally FALLS OVER INTO THE SEA, that we would be clever enough to get it. The clue they are pointing out to us is that there is something OUT THERE that is the HANDLE and we ought to be able to figure out, by applying principles of physics to celestial mechanics, exactly what it is and what it does. The repeated references to the "dying and rebirth of the Sun", in some sort of cosmic hierogamy, and the Sun giving birth to a daughter, or having a Celestial Twin, ought to be pretty plain clues to anybody who is paying attention to these things.

In the third century BC, Berossus popularized the Chaldean doctrine of the "Great Year" in a form that spread through the entire Hellenic world. According to this teaching, the universe is eternal but it is periodically destroyed and reconstituted every "Great Year". What a Great Year is, exactly, varies from school to school. But, according to Berossus, when the seven planets assemble in Cancer, there will be a Great Winter; when they assemble in Capricorn, at the Summer solstice (clearly an astrological opposition to the Sun is implied here), the entire universe will be consumed by fire. Similar ideas are found in India and Iran as well as among the Maya and Aztec.

Now, what we need to remember about these postulations is the inherently *optimistic* character of them; the consciousness of the *normality of the cyclical catastrophe*, the certainty of its meaning, and, above all, that it is NEVER, EVER final! The ideas communicate to us that, just as three days of darkness preceding the rebirth of the Moon are necessary, so are the death of an individual and the periodic death of humanity necessary. Any material form, by the mere fact of its existence *in time*, loses vigor and becomes formless *if only for an instant*. It MUST return to chaos, to orgy, to darkness, to water; it must be reabsorbed into the primordial unity from which it issued to be reborn. The King is dead: long live the King!

Thus, the New Year celebrations and other initiations served to remind men that suffering is never final; that death is always followed by resurrection; that every defeat is annulled and transcended by the final victory of return to the Edenic state or the beginning of the new cycle.

In Eliade's opinion, the drama of Tammuz and other variations of the same archetype, including Jesus, reminded men of the sufferings of the just and thereby rendered them tolerable. Tammuz suffered without being guilty. He was humiliated, flogged until he bled, and then imprisoned in a pit, or Hell. It was there that the Great Goddess visited him, encouraged, and revived him. (In later corrupted versions, it was a "messenger" who visited, but the essential story has survived in Gnostic Manichaean and Mandaean prototypes, though with changes acquired during the period of Greco-Oriental syncretism.)

I would like to suggest that the drama of the dying god is not only the symbol of the literal "death of the Sun" in terms of its lengthy obscuration, but also includes the drama of the Cosmic Hieros Gamos between the Sun and its Companion. More than this, the "dying god" drama might also be the enacting of a certain technology that permits passage into other realms; the very technology that will be required to build the Ark and find the Holy Grail.

In the pit of Hell, during the descent into chaos, man is awakened by the Goddess who brings the good tidings of his salvation and imminent liberation and restoration to the Edenic state of innocence. As it was in the days of Noah, Noah *built* an Ark. The coming of the Goddess represents the coming of knowledge, of wisdom, of understanding the hyperdimensional realities by means of the symbols of our reality which are, ultimately, only shadows on the cave wall of Plato's allegory.

But something changed the world view. Somehow, the perception of the End of Time became a terrible punishment. Somehow, a god entered the world stage who destroyed the peace of Eden, and tempted man to place his trust in him, and him alone. "I am the Lord your God, and I am a jealous God!" And time became linear and with a prophesied end that was going to be final and complete. And woe to those who were not on the side of the "right god" who claimed to be the only one who could offer "salvation". The concept of the end being a precursor to a rebirth was lost with the introduction of monotheism. At that point, the End of Time became the End of the World – for everyone except those special chosen ones who were to be saved by a single, specific god to live in some mystical City of God with streets paved with gold, and almond-eyed houris serving dates and wine on every street corner. This single, specific god, has pretty much run the show ever since, in any number of disguises. Until this appearance of monotheism, a myth was annually enacted that described a condition of life that was accepted as the way things were: Time was cyclical. The world might end, but if it did, it was only because it had "run down" and needed to be "wound up" again. All of the elements of the story of Noah are found in these myths. "*As it was in the days of Noah.*"

CHAPTER 7
ANCIENT ENIGMAS

DINOSAURS

It is assumed that man is the product of slow and orderly evolution and his present hope for three-score and ten years is a great advancement, since recorded history indicates to us that during other periods of history, when more hostile conditions prevailed, man had a much reduced life-span. I would like to conjecture, however, that a fundamental reordering of things during several episodes in the earth's past might have appreciably altered conditions so that an original "Edenic condition" was lost. Must we assume that the ancients did not understand time as we know it when they claimed to live hundreds of years? Or must we assume that Time is always and forever the same thing?

Obviously many creatures have lived upon the earth that no longer live here. When they disappear or are all killed off, we say that they are "extinct". It occurred to me at some point that, perhaps, "extinction" is a *symptom* of the fact that the cosmos in which that species was able to flourish has lost its vigor. It doesn't matter how the species becomes extinct, because, in the end, it is only a symbol. What is more, the fact that a certain species does not reassert itself after such losses suggests that certain conditions have changed, and those changes are lethal.

When we begin to look at the South American cultures, the first thing we are told is how "recent" they are. Polish archaeologist Arthur Posnansky dated the Kalasasaya palace court at Tiahuanaco, near Lake Titicaca in Bolivia, to 15,000 to 10,000 BC. Mainstream experts assure us that this evidence simply cannot be considered because radiometric dating says otherwise. Well, we already know that radiometric dating is a lost cause, so we can set that aside for the moment and consider other factors.

This brings us back to the subject of Atlantis. According to Plato, "In those days the Atlantic was navigable; and there was an island situated in front of the straits which are by you called the Pillars of Hercules". We might want to ask what Plato could have meant by this remark since, based on all knowledge of the sea floor of the Atlantic, it has always been navigable. However, there is something about this that was pointed out to me by an individual in the shipping industry who wrote:

> I am intrigued by Plato's remarks that the Atlantic was "navigable" before. As ship equipment suppliers, when we say the water is navigable, it means not only that the water is deep enough (the Atlantic was deep when the Critias story was reconstructed, so how could it have been any more convenient before?), but

"navigable" also means, today, that on land there are sufficient radio direction or *lit* indicators and, that once a ship is out of sight of land, he has gyros, or echo sounders which, together with accurate charts means he can safely increment his way forward avoiding shipwreck. So "Navigable" on a deep ocean really means instruments are on land and on the ships and that accurate charts exist (with soundings) - all three.[111]

Since Ignatius Donnelly, scholars have produced a veritable shipload of books speculating on the location of Atlantis. I have a couple of shelves full of these books, and the theories range from the destruction of the island of Santorini by the eruption of Thera around 1600 BC[112] to Indonesia, to the Black Sea. More recently, Rand and Rose Flem-Ath have proposed that Antarctica was the "island of Atlantis" and that it "shifted" or "moved" South as a function of crustal displacement.

Plato described Atlantis as an "island empire" that, "in a single day... disappeared in the depths of the sea". But he also tells us that this "island" was bigger than Libya and Asia Minor combined. Right away we perceive that his terms are a bit different from what we would use. We might think that his term "island", meant simply that this body of land was not connected to Eurasia or Africa - that it was a distinct body of land surrounded by water - except for something else he added: Plato also told us that Atlantis was "the way to other islands, and from these you might pass to the whole of the opposite continent". This suggests to us an unusual land formation - an isthmus.

His expression that it "disappeared into the depths of the sea" may have beenmeant to suggest that it was swept by vast tsunamis as the result of some cataclysmic event. So, considering these clues - its vast size, the definition of the term "navigable", and the idea that "disappearing into the depths of the sea" very likely meant swept by terrifying walls of water, let take a peek through the Pillars of Hercules. What do we see? Well, we see the Americas. We see North and South America connected by an isthmus. We also see a lot of little islands in the Caribbean.

Another clue that Plato gives us is that Atlantis had a lot of elephants.

Something catastrophic happened to the large mammals roaming the world during the Pleistocene Epoch. Woolly mammoths, mastodons, toxodons, sabre-toothed tigers, woolly rhinos, giant ground sloths, and many other large Pleistocene animals are simply no longer with us. The fact is, more than 200 species of animals completely disappeared at the end of the Pleistocene

---

[111] Matthew Walker, private correspondence with the author.

[112] This approximate date is pretty well confirmed by Sturt Manning's *A Test of Time* which is devoted to the dating of the eruption of Thera which has been tree-ring calibrated.

approximately 12,000 years ago in what is known to Paleontologists as the "Pleistocene Extinction".

At the same time that the paleontologists are dealing with the unsettling notion of such a recent mass death, geologists are confronted with the evidence of terrifying geological changes which took place: extensive volcanism and earthquakes, tidal waves, glacial melting, rising sea levels, and so on. The Pleistocene Epoch didn't end with a whimper, for sure. It went out roaring and thundering.

We already know that Geologists and Paleontologists don't like catastrophism - it keeps them up at night. They fought long and hard against the Catastrophists. But in the present day, scientists in both fields have to face the fact that the Catastrophists were mostly right from the beginning - even if they might have gone overboard and explained *everything* in terms of catastrophe. It is evident that there *are* "gradual" changes, but that most of what happens on the Big Blue Marble in terms of significant changes is catastrophic.

One of the major facts that paleontologists and geologists and archaeologists have had to face is the stupendous number of frozen carcasses in Canada and Alaska in the western areas, and in Northern Russian and Siberia in the eastern areas - all dated to about 12000 years ago. This suggests, of course, that something dreadful happened on the planet, and its effect on the Northern hemisphere was more severe than on the Southern hemisphere.

Back in the 1940s Dr. Frank C. Hibben, Prof. of Archeology at the University of New Mexico led an expedition to Alaska to look for human remains. He didn't find human remains; he found miles and miles of icy muck just packed with mammoths, mastodons, and several kinds of bison, horses, wolves, bears and lions. Just north of Fairbanks, Alaska, the members of the expedition watched in horror as bulldozers pushed the half-melted muck into sluice boxes for the extraction of gold. Animal tusks and bones rolled up in front of the blades "like shavings before a giant plane". The carcasses were found in all attitudes of death, most of them "pulled apart by some unexplainable prehistoric catastrophic disturbance".[113]

The evident violence of the deaths of these masses of animals, combined with the stench of rotting flesh, was almost unendurable both in seeing it, and in considering what might have caused it. The killing fields stretched for literally hundreds of miles in every direction.[114] There were trees and animals, layers of peat and moss, twisted and tangled and mangled together as though some Cosmic

---

[113] Hibben, Frank, *The Lost Americans* (New York: Thomas & Crowell Co. 1946).

[114] Ibid.

mixmaster sucked them all in 12000 years ago, and then froze them instantly into a solid mass.[115]

Just north of Siberia *entire islands* are formed of the bones of Pleistocene animals swept *northward* from the continent into the freezing Arctic Ocean. One estimate suggests that some ten million animals may be buried along the rivers of northern Siberia. Thousands upon thousands of tusks created a massive ivory trade for the master carvers of China, all from the frozen mammoths and mastodons of Siberia. The famous Beresovka mammoth first drew attention to the preserving properties of being quick-frozen when buttercups were found in its mouth.

What kind of terrible event overtook these millions of creatures *in a single day*? Well, the evidence suggests an enormous tsunami raging across the land, tumbling animals and vegetation together, to be finally quick-frozen for the next 12000 years. But the extinction was not limited to the Arctic, even if the freezing at colder locations preserved the evidence of Nature's rage.

Paleontologist George G. Simpson considers the extinction of the Pleistocene horse in North America to be one of the most mysterious episodes in zoological history, confessing, "no one knows the answer". He is also honest enough to admit that there is the larger problem of the extinction of many other species in America at the same time.[116] The horse, giant tortoises living in the Caribbean, the giant sloth, the saber-toothed tiger, the glyptodont and toxodon. These were all tropical animals. These creatures didn't die because of the "gradual onset" of an ice age, "unless one is willing to postulate freezing temperatures across the equator, such an explanation clearly begs the question".[117]

Massive piles of mastodon and saber-toothed tiger bones were discovered in Florida.[118] Mastodons, toxodons, giant sloths and other animals were found in Venezuela quick-frozen in mountain glaciers. Woolly rhinoceros, giant armadillos, giant beavers, giant jaguars, ground sloths, antelopes and scores of other entire species were all totally wiped out at the same time, at the end of the Pleistocene, approximately 12000 years ago.

This event was global. The mammoths of Siberia became extinct at the same time as the giant rhinoceros of Europe; the mastodons of Alaska, the bison of Siberia, the Asian elephants and the American camels. It is obvious that the cause of these extinctions must be common to both hemispheres, and that it was not gradual. A "uniformitarian glaciation" would not have caused extinctions because

---

[115] Sanderson, Ivan T., "Riddle of the Frozen Giants", *Saturday Evening Post*, No. 39, January 16, 1960.

[116] Simpson, George G., *Horses,* New York: Oxford University Press) 1961.

[117] Martin, P. S. & Guilday, J. E., "Bestiary for Pleistocene Biologists", *Pleistocene Extinction,* Yale University, 1967.

[118] Valentine, quoted by Berlitz, Charles, *The Mystery of Atlantis* (New York, 1969).

the various animals would have simply migrated to better pasture. What is seen is a surprising event of uncontrolled violence.[119] In other words, 12000 years ago, a time we have met before and will come across again and again, something terrible happened - so terrible that life on earth was nearly wiped out in a single day.

Harold P. Lippman admits that the magnitude of fossils and tusks encased in the Siberian permafrost present an "insuperable difficulty" to the theory of uniformitarianism, since no gradual process can result in the preservation of tens of thousands of tusks and whole individuals, "even if they died in winter".[120] Especially when many of these individuals have undigested grasses and leaves in their belly. Pleistocene geologist William R. Farrand of the Lamont-Doherty Geological Observatory, who is opposed to catastrophism in any form, states, "Sudden death is indicated by the robust condition of the animals and their full stomachs ... the animals were robust and healthy when they died".[121] Unfortunately, in spite of this admission, this poor guy seems to have been incapable of facing the reality of worldwide catastrophe represented by the millions of bones deposited all over this planet right at the end of the Pleistocene. Hibben sums up the situation in a single statement: "The Pleistocene period ended in death. This was no ordinary extinction of a vague geological period, which fizzled to an uncertain end. This death was catastrophic and all inclusive."[122]

The conclusion is, again, that the end of the Ice Age, the Pleistocene extinction, the end of the Upper Paleolithic, Magdalenian, Perigordian, and so on, and the end of the "reign of the gods", all came to a global, catastrophic conclusion about 12,000 years ago. And, as it happens, even before this evidence was brought to light, this is the same approximate date that Plato gave for the sinking of Atlantis.

In recent years, a cartographer named J. M. Allen published a book entitled *Atlantis: The Andes Solution.* Allen focused on South America as Atlantis. He points to the fact that the Indian name for South America - before Columbus arrived - was "Atlanta". He informs us that this is related to the Quechua word for copper, "*antis.*" Allen believes he has found the plain of canals on the Altiplano of southern Peru and northern Bolivia. He suggests that the plain was very smooth and level, was surrounded by mountains on all sides, and was high above ocean level. This is, indeed, a close description of the Altiplano, supposedly the largest level plain in the world, containing the inland seas of Lake Titicaca and Lake Poopo. Allen found the remains of a channel of enormous dimensions in Bolivia,

---

[119] Leonard, R. Cedric, Appendix A in "A Geological Study of the Mid-Atlantic Ridge", Special Paper No. 1 (Bethany: Cowen Publishing 1979).

[120] Lippman, Harold E., *"Frozen Mammoths", Physical Geology*, (New York 1969).

[121] Farrand, William R., *"Frozen Mammoths and Modern Geology", Science*, Vol.133, No. 3455, March 17, 1961.

[122] Hibben, op. cit.

and was certain he had found the ancient city of Atlantis. Unfortunately, like William Farrand above, Allen is unable to let go of certain assumptions - such as reliance upon the chronologies established by uniformitarian believers. He suggests that the Andean/Atlantean civilization ended at the time of the eruption of Thera.

We already noted that Arthur Posnansky dated the Kalasasaya palace court at Tiahuanaco, near Lake Titicaca, in Bolivia to 15,000 to 10,000 BC. And Allen mentions that Lake Poopo is known to have flooded around 12000 years ago.

There are ancient terraced cornfields on the sides of the mountains rising above Lake Titicaca where corn no longer grows. Corn only grows at lower altitudes. The lower altitude terraces where corn still grows are still above Lake Titicaca. What this suggests is that peoples who constructed the terraces, and who were growing corn there, must have been doing so at a time when the land was lower.

There is a stone causeway leading "out" of Lake Titicaca to nowhere. This causeway is built like an ancient wharf, which has suggested that it was built *when the lake and the city were at sea level.*

The remains of Tiahuanaco, the site of a technologically advanced culture considered by many archaeologists (romantic, not orthodox) to be the oldest ruins in the world. Although some misguided scholars have attributed the buildings of Tiahuanaco to the Incas, it has now been established that the city was already in ruins when the first Incas came upon the scene.

> In 1540 the Spanish chronicler, Pedro Cieza de Leon, visited the area and his description of the statues and monoliths compares very closely to what we see today. The site is at an altitude of 13,300 feet, which places it some 800 feet above the present level of Lake Titicaca. Most archaeologists agree that in the distant past Tiahuanaco was a flourishing port at the edge of the lake, which means that the water *has receded almost 12 miles* and has *dropped about 800 feet* since then. All concur that the lake is shrinking, due mainly to evaporation, since *no rivers flow from it*

> In November 1980, the well known Bolivian author and scholar of pre-Columbian cultures, Hugo Boero Rojo, announced the finding of archaeological ruins beneath Lake Titicaca about 15 to 20 meters below the surface off the coast of Puerto Acosta, a Bolivian port village near the Peruvian frontier on the northeast edge of the lake.

> If, over the past 3 or 4000 years, Lake Titicaca has slowly receded, as appears to be the case - as all scientists agree, then how can we explain the existence of stone temples, stairways, and roads still under water'? The only answer is that they were built *before the lake materialized.* We must go back, then, to the remnants of Tiahuanaco and reexamine the more than 400 acres of ruins, only 10 percent of which have been excavated. We have pointed out that dirt covers the ancient civilization to a depth of at least 6 feet. The only explanation for this accumulation is water.

> A large amount of water had to have inundated the city; when it receded it left the silt covering all evidence of an advanced civilization, leaving only the largest statues and monoliths still exposed. It is logical to conclude, therefore, that Tiahuanaco was built *before the lake was created*, and not as a port on its shore. As the waters today continue to recede, we should be able to find more evidence of the city's remote peoples. Scientists theorize that the area at Lake Titicaca was at one

time at sea level, because of the profusion of fossilized marine life that can be found in the region. The area then *lifted with the Andean upheaval* and a basin was created which filled in to form the lake. No one has suggested the marine life might have been brought to the altiplano by seawaters that were at flood stage.

The Tiahuanacans could have been victims of worldwide flood, their civilization all but wiped out when their homes and structures were covered with seawater. Because of the basin-like geography of the area the floodwaters that became Lake Titicaca could not run off and have only gradually evaporated over the centuries. [...]

Professor Schindler-Bellamy as a disciple of Posnansky and Horbiger (who created the world famous Glacial-Cosmogony theory in the 1930's) has worked dozens of years in the Tiahuanaco area and has written books on the subject. According to him the large monolithic Sun Gate of Tiahuanaco was evidently originally the centerpiece of the most important part of the so-called Kalasasaya, the huge chief temple of Tiahuanaco. Its upper part is covered with a stupendously intricate sculpture in flat bas-relief. This has been described as a "calendar" almost as long as the monolithic gateway has been known to exist; thus the Sun Gate has also been called the Calendar Gate. This calendar sculpture, though it undoubtedly depicts a "solar year", cannot however be made to fit into the solar year as we divide it at present.

The "solar year" of the calendar's time had very practically the same length as our own, but, as shown symbolically by the sculpture, the earth revolved more quickly then, making the Tiahuanacan year only 290 days, divided into 12 "twelfths" of 24 days each, plus 2 intercalary days. These groupings (290, 24, 12, 2) are clearly and unmistakably shown in the sculpture.[...]

[According to Schindler-Bellamy], at the time Tiahuanaco flourished the present moon was not yet the companion of our earth but was still an independent exterior planet. There was another satellite moving around our earth then, rather close... Because of its closeness it moved around the earth more quickly than our planet rotated. Therefore it rose in the west and set in the east (like Mars' satellite Phobos), and so caused a great number of solar eclipses, 37 in one "twelfth," or 447 in one "solar year." These groupings (37, 447) are shown in the sculpture, with many Corroborating cross-references. Different symbols show when these solar eclipses, which were of some duration, occurred: at sunrise, at noon, at sunset.

These are only a small sample of the exact astronomical information the calendar gives. It also gives the beginning of the year, the days of the equinoxes and solstices, the incidence of the two intercalary days, information on the obliquity of the elliptic (then about 16.5 degrees; now 23.5) and on Tiahuanaco's latitude (then about 10 degrees; now 16.27), and many other astronomical and geographical references from which interesting and important data may be calculated or inferred by us. [...]

A few more facts revealed in the calendar are both interesting and surprising. As indicated by an arrangement of "geometrical" elements we can ascertain that the Tiahuanacans divided the circle factually astronomically, (but certainly mathematically} into 264 degrees (rather than 360). Also, they determined (ages before Archimedes and the Egyptians) the ratio of pi, the most important ratio between the circumference of the circle and its diameter, as 22/7, or, in our notation, 3.14+. They could calculate squares (and hence, square roots). They knew trigonometry and the measuring of angles (30, 60, 90 degrees) and their functions.

They could calculate and indicate fractions, but do not seem to have known the decimal system nor did they apparently ever employ the duodecimal system though they were aware of it. (For a still unknown reason, however, the number 11 and its multiples occur often.)

The most tantalizing fact of all is that the Tiahuanaco culture has no roots in that area. It did not grow there from humbler beginnings, nor is any other place of origin known. It seems to have appeared practically full-blown suddenly. Only a few "older" monuments, as can be inferred from the "calendrical inscriptions" they bear, have been found, but the difference in time cannot have been very great. The different, much lower cultures discovered at considerable distances from Tiahuanaco proper, addressed as "Decadent Tiahuacan" or as "Coastal Tiahuanaco", are only very indirectly related to the culture revealed by the Calendar Gate. [...]

When the satellite (the former moon) approached within a few thousand miles gravitational forces broke it up; according to the Roche formula each planetoid or asteroid disintegrates when approaching the critical distance of 50 to 60,000 kms. The fragments shattered down on earth; the oceans, released from the satellite's gravity, flowed back toward the continents, exposing tropical lands and submerging polar territories. [...]

Thus the approach of the "moon" caused a world-wide deluge, effecting changes of climate and provoking earthquakes accompanied by volcanic eruptions. The "ring" left by the satellite after breaking into fragments caused a sudden drop in temperature of at least 20 degrees... It is evident, for example, in the discovery of frozen mammoths in the Siberian tundra. Possibly gravity - and therefore physical weight - was also changed on earth, and with it biological growth: this would explain the widespread construction of huge megalithic monuments as well as the presence of giants - man and animal - in fossil strata, tombs, and myths. According to Horbiger four moons fell on earth, producing four Ice Ages; our present moon, the fifth one, will similarly be drawn into the critical configuration of one-fifth of its present distance (380,000 kms.) and will cause the fifth cataclysm.

Tiahuanaco apparently remained for only a very short period at its acme of perfection (evidenced by the Calendar Gate) and perished suddenly, perhaps through the cataclysmic happenings connected with the breakdown of the former "moon."

We have at present no means of determining when Tiahuanaco rose to supreme height, or when its culture was obliterated, as naturally, the calendar itself can tell us nothing about that. It will certainly not have been in the historical past but well back in the prehistoric. It must indeed have occurred before the planet Luna was captured as the earth's present moon, *about 12,000 years ago.* [123]

---

[123] Zettl, Helmut, *Catastrophism and Ancient History, Volume VI, Part 2,* A Journal Of Interdisciplinary Study, July 1984, Marvin Arnold Luckerman Executive Editor.

There are several fascinating items in the above material. One that interests me particularly is the speculation that the year was different prior to the deluge, and that the number 11 was significant in some mysterious way. The ideas about the capture of the moon, and a previous satellite which broke apart and rained destruction on the earth are interesting, but my guess is that this might just be interpretation of a swarm of comets or asteroids.

The theory of a falling moon has been discussed by Dr. John O'Keefe, a scientist at the Goddard Laboratory for Astronomy in Maryland. O'Keefe claims that the fragments of a moon's collision formed a ring around our planet that blocked the sun's rays, thus causing world-wide decline of temperatures. After a while the fragments disintegrated even further and showered down on earth, as tectites. These tectites O'Keefe suggests, were fragments of a fallen moon.

What is evident is that this world-wide cataclysm of 12,000 years ago appears in myths from every corner of the globe. The Egyptian Papyrus Ipuwer tells us that "The sun set where it rose" and an Egyptian tomb, (Senmut) shows Orion and Sirius painted in reverse position. The Finnish Kalevala says "the earth turned round like a potter's wheel" and the Popol Vuh describes a showering of *fiery hail from heaven*.

On the outskirts of Brno, Moravia, there is a quarry where workers uncovered the bones of a wooly mammoth. There, in the quarry, was discovered a 160 foot deep sequence of multiple soil cycles. Each climate cycle from warm to cold was expressed as a sequence of gradational soil types reflecting the change from a moist, deciduous forest to an arid, frozen tundra, cracked by deeply penetrating permafrost. Midway through each cycle, there are numerous bands of fine windblown dust delivered in what must have been *monstrous storms of continental scale*. Expert speculations suggest that this dust must have shrouded the earth for weeks or months at a time and must have produced a refrigerating effect on Europe's climate. In the colder part of each cycle, the environment had become so dry that even large rivers dried up.

It seems that the ice sheets that repeatedly advanced southward were accompanied by the development of vast, but temporary deserts throughout Russia and Ukraine, even extending into southeast Europe and to the shores of the Black Sea. Every passage back from freezing cold to warm was *abrupt in every cycle*.

Oceanographers from Turkey, Russia, Bulgaria and the United States teamed up to explore the Black Sea. Using sound waves and coring devices, they discovered that the Black Sea was once a vast freshwater lake. Glenn Jones of the Woods Hole Oceanographic Institution dated the samples from the bottom of the Black Sea and confirmed that around 7,500 years ago, the seas had burst through the Bosporus valley and the salt water of the Mediterranean poured into the lake with unimaginable force. What was evident was that it had happened suddenly and almost instantaneously. What was also noted was that the massive amounts of salt water pouring into the Black Sea had been deficient in Oxygen.[124]

While searching for the answers to this mysterious event, cores of coral were drilled from the ocean in order to determine the rates of growth on a year by year basis going back 20 thousand years. Apparently, ice melt affects the rate of coral growth. The results of these cores showed that there was a huge spurt of ice-melt around 12,000 years ago. The meltwater from this event was enormous. It filled up dozens of lakes that no longer exist - lakes formed by the sag in the Earth's crust caused by the weight of the huge ice dome. Immediately following this melt, the ice age returned for a brief period called the Younger Dryas.

> At 8 p.m. on June 5th, 8498 BC, the core parts of Asteroid A punched the first decisive hole in the fracture zone of the Atlantic Ridge. The forces of hell were let loose. Through these two newly formed vents the glowing red-hot magma shot up at terrific speed and mixed with the liquid above it - the waters of the Atlantic. This created all the conditions for a submarine volcanic eruption of the greatest possible violence. The fracture seam was torn apart. The bottom of the sea burst open. All existing volcanoes were activated and new vents formed. Terrestrial fire and ocean water became embroiled in ever-increasing volume. Magma mixed with steam. The chain of fire ran all the way between the two continents from the Beerenberg volcano on Jan Mayen in the north to Tristan de Cunha in the south.[125]

This rather dramatic description from the back of Otto Muck's book - *The Secret of Atlantis* - is based on his ideas about the causal relationship between isotherms and favorable climate in northwestern Europe, and the unobstructed flow of the Gulf Stream across the Atlantic. Muck attempts to use this flow to make a case for the prior existence of a large body of land in the Atlantic whose subsidence changed the ocean currents and warmed the British Isles about 10,500 years ago, give or take a day or two. Based on a varied and interesting collection of hard data, Muck suggests that the submarine massif of the Azores was once above water and could have blocked and deflected the Gulf Stream, preventing the circulation of the warmer waters, and thus contributing to the freezing temperatures of the British Isles. Muck writes:

> If we then date the transition from the Quaternary to the Quinternary Age at 12,000 years ago, or around 10,000 BC, we are doing so on the authority of contemporary geologists and paleontologists. We are at the same time fixing the date when Barrier Island X, which had hitherto prevented the Gulf Stream from reaching the coasts of Europe, sank beneath the Atlantic … a point in time … when the warm water and rain-bearing winds brought by the Gulf Stream were no longer deflected back to the west by the Atlantic island barrier, but flowed freely eastward because the barrier had sunk beneath the waves.

---

[124] Ryan, William, Pitman, Walter, *Noah's Flood* (New York: Simon and Schuster 1998).

[125] Muck, Otto, *The Secret of Atlantis* (New York: New York Times Books 1976) back cover blurb.

We have uncovered the traces of the greatest cataclysm on Earth that has been experienced by man. For there can be no doubt that this catastrophe of 12,000 years ago is the most terrible event that has ever taken place in all the dramatic history of mankind.[126]

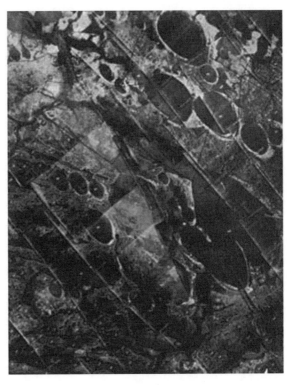

Essentially, what Muck did was to note that the geologically recorded isotherms moved significantly at this point in time. I still think his book is one of the better ones on the subject because he assembles a lot of interesting hard data, even if I don't necessarily agree that there was a big island that "sank beneath the Atlantic". There are other solutions to the problem of the isotherms, including current day research showing that this can result from global warming. While we don't deny that it's possible for such severe lithosphere disruption as Muck suggests to occur, and we aren't playing soft with the idea of mass destruction of species, it just seems that an event that would produce the sinking of so vast a body of land so completely would be an event from which absolutely nothing on the earth would survive.

Nevertheless, Otto Muck draws our attention to the meteor craters in the Carolinas. The Carolina bays are mysterious land features often filled with bay trees and other wetland vegetation. Because of their oval shape and consistent orientation, they are considered by some authorities to be the result of a vast meteor shower that occurred approximately 12,000 thousand years ago. What is most astonishing is the number of them. There are over *500,000 of these shallow basins* dotting the coastal plain from Georgia to Delaware. That is a frightening figure.

---

[126] Ibid., p. 84-85.

Unlike virtually any other bodies of water or changes in elevation, these topographical features follow a reliable and unmistakable pattern. Carolina Bays are circular, typically stretched, elliptical depressions in the ground, oriented along their long axis *from the Northwest to the Southeast*. [T]hey are further characterized by an elevated rim of fine sand surrounding the perimeter. [...]

The last twenty years have seen an explosion of evidence that earth has often encountered objects that profoundly alter our environment. For instance, it is now commonly accepted that an impact with a large object in the Gulf of Mexico caused the extinction of large dinosaurs - a theory considered bizarre and irresponsible at the time Kacrowski studied the Bays.

Robert Kobres, an independent researcher in Athens, Georgia, has studied Carolina Bays for nearly 20 years in conjunction with his larger interest in impact threats from space. His recent, self-published, investigations have profound consequences for Carolina Bay study and demand research by academia as serious, relevant and previously unexamined new information. The essence of Kobres' theory is that the search for "debris", and the comparison of Bays with "traditional" impact craters, falsely and naively assumes that circular craters with extraterrestrial material in them are the only terrestrial evidence of past encounters with objects entering earth's atmosphere.

Kobres goes a logical step further by assuming that forces associated with incoming bodies, principally intense heat, should also leave visible *signatures* on the earth. And, finally, that physics does not demand that a "collision" of the bodies need necessarily occur to produce enormous change on earth. To verify that such encounters are possible outside of the physics lab, we need look no further than the so-called "Tunguska event".

On June 30, 1908, in the vicinity of the Tunguska River deep in Siberia, a tremendous explosion instantly leveled 2000 sq. km. of tundra, felling trees by the millions, all left pointing outward from a central area. News accounts of the day told of Londoners being able to read newspapers from the glow of the night sky for days afterward. Seismographs worldwide recorded an apparent cataclysm in Siberia. Unfortunately (or fortunately as the case may be) the explosion had occurred in an area so remote, and during a time of such political turmoil, that no researcher pinpointed or even managed to travel to the suspected impact site for more than two decades. Not until pioneer Russian meteoritic researcher Leonard Kulik managed to gain entry to the inhospitable area in 1927, did anyone but local tribesmen view the devastation and its peculiar nature.

At the epicenter of the explosion lay not a large crater with a "rock" in it, as might be expected, but nothing more than a number of "neat oval bogs". The Tunguska literature generally mentions the bogs only in passing, since Kulik failed in digs there to locate any evidence of a meteorite and went on to examine other aspects of the explosion.[127]

What do we have so far? We have an event that seems to have affected Eastern Siberia and Northern North America more severely than other places, though whatever it was certainly amounted to a global event. We have already talked about the evidence of "nuclear bombardment" in the Great Lakes region provided by Firestone and Topping that tells us:

Radiocarbon dates for Pleistocene remains in northeastern North America are as much as 10,000 years younger than for those *in the western part of the country*.[…] Materials from the Gainey Paleoindian site in Michigan, radiocarbon dated at 2880 yr BC, are given an age by TL dating of 12,400 BC. It seems that there are so many anomalies reported in the upper US and in Canada of this type, that they cannot be explained by ancient aberrations in the atmosphere or other radiocarbon reservoirs, nor by contamination of data samples. […]

Our research indicates that the entire Great Lakes region (and beyond) was subjected to particle bombardment and a catastrophic nuclear irradiation that produced secondary thermal neutrons from cosmic ray interactions. The neutrons produced unusually large quantities of Pu239 and substantially altered the natural uranium abundance ratios […]

Sharp increases in C14 are apparent in the marine data at 4,000, 32,000-34,000, and 12,500 BC. These increases are coincident with geomagnetic excursions. […]

The enormous energy released by the catastrophe at 12,500 BC could have heated the atmosphere to over 1000 C over Michigan, and the neutron flux at more northern locations would have melted considerable glacial ice. Radiation effects on plants and animals exposed to the cosmic rays would have been lethal, comparable to being irradiated in a 5 megawatt reactor more than 100 seconds.

The overall pattern of the catastrophe matches the pattern of mass extinction before Holocene times. The *Western Hemisphere was more affected than the Eastern, North America more than South America, and eastern North America more than western North America.* Extinction in the Great lakes area was more rapid and pronounced than elsewhere. Larger animals were more affected than smaller ones, a pattern that conforms to the expectation that radiation exposure affects large bodies more than smaller ones.[128]

Firestone and Topping propose that this evidence of nuclear radiation is a result of "cosmic ray bombardment" from, perhaps, a supernova. D.S. Allan, a biologist at Cambridge, and J. B. Delair, coauthor of *Cataclysm!*, published in 1995 in the U.K, also like the supernova hypothesis. Evidence of a supernova explosion, in the

---

[127] Howard, George A., *The Carolina Bays*: http://www.georgehoward.net/cbays.htm

[128] Firestone, Richard B., Topping, William, *Terrestrial Evidence of a Nuclear Catastrophe in Paleoindian Times*, dissertation research, 1990 - 2001.

form of aluminium 22 (along with other scientific and mythological evidence), found in concentration at the edge of our solar system, helped Allan and Delair conclude that a stellar blast probably caused the massive destruction. Iron ore in the earth from about 11,000 years ago shows that its magnetic polarity violently reversed. This certainly suggests an extraterrestrial encounter with a magnetically powerful agent at that period. The supernova explanation, however, does not account for all the evidence, most particularly the mythic and geological evidence of massive bombardments of comets.

Dr. Paul LaViolette, author of *Earth Under Fire*, claims that he has discovered evidence of a different sort of cataclysm, a volley of cosmic waves resulting from an explosion in the galactic core. Entering our solar system, this galactic super wave (the most powerful energetic phenomenon in the galaxy) would have interrupted the solar wind's ability to repel most intruding cosmic dust particles.

LaViolette builds a mythological foundation for his scientific theory, the shakiest part of which is that he suggests that galactic core explosions are a cyclical event, recurring every 26,000-year cycles, a period that relates to the precession of the equinoxes. He claims that this is a great clock, and that the precessional cycle is the duration of one Great Year recognized by the ancient Greeks, Zoroastrians, and Chinese. La Violette's theory is weak because galactic core explosions, like other nuclear phenomena, are only statistically probable. Further, the record shows a frequency greater than every 26,000 years, and his attempts to introduce "mini-explosions" to account for this come across as so much prestidigitation of the data. Also his theory does not account for all of the evidence, most particularly the geological evidence of massive bombardments of cometary bodies. What is more, La Violette's claim that the precessional cycle is the "great clock", assumes that the current polar orientation has remained stable for eons, and the very mythic evidence he tries to use as his foundation contradicts this, most especially the decoded information from the Gate of the Sun at Tiahuanaco reported above.

In all of this searching high and low for Atlantis, and comparing the paleontogical records and geological records and archaeological records with the story of Plato, the one major thing that everybody seems to be forgetting is this: Plato's tale was about a WAR followed by cataclysm.

According to Plato's story, Atlantis was the center of a country of extreme economic wealth and military power that sought to enslave all of Europe. The Atlanteans were quite successful in defeating many European countries; however, the great civilization of Athens repelled their attacks and eventually succeeded in driving them back out of Europe. Unfortunately, almost all records of this great achievement were lost due to a very powerful flood that wiped out most of Athens and the whole continent of Atlantis in one day and one night.

Over and over again, what we see is the fact that something terrible happened on the earth around 12,000 years ago. This time period comes up over and over again in many disciplines having to do with the study of the past. And it just happens to be the period designated by Plato's characters as the time of the destruction of Atlantis, following a terrible war in which Atlantis was defeated after attempting to conquer the entire world, at the time of what is remembered as the greatest deluge in human history: The Flood of Noah.

In terms of human beings, the Bible tells us that after the Flood of Noah, man was no longer able to live the same lifespan that had originally been allotted to him. Symbolically, this suggests that something significant about the cosmos or the state of matter itself, had changed. Modern science, of course, completely dismisses such ideas with seeming good reason. But, we should like to ask: What if the shortening of man's lifespan actually happened? What if it happened more than once? What if such an event represents a loss of vigor or exhaustion of cosmic resources? Or, what if it represents the fact that mankind originally evolved in a different environment and the present one is no longer conducive to such long lives? In this regard, some observations about dinosaurs are pertinent.

There have been found dinosaur remains in "bone-yards" which had shoulder blades eleven feet long! The towering Brachiosaurus, an herbivore, stood up to fifty feet tall and weighed perhaps a hundred tons! How could it have sustained itself? One hundred tons is about *fifteen times* the weight of an adult African bull elephant - an animal that consumes 300 to 600 pounds of fodder every 24 hours and spends up to eighteen hours a day foraging for food! It seems totally out of the question to imagine this "Supersaurus" feeding itself.

If Brachiosaurus was warm-blooded like an elephant, it might have been unable to eat enough to keep itself alive! But, even as a cold-blooded animal, there is doubt that this gargantuan creature could have eaten enough with its small mouth and teeth. There is just no real solution to this problem if we assume that the earth has always been the same since life evolved on its surface.

We are taught by orthodox science that the dinosaurs were failures - colossal failures. There is a litany of "couldn'ts" recited about them. They couldn't walk on land because they were too heavy. They couldn't eat anything but mush because their heads were too small. They couldn't run fast because their joints were imperfect. They couldn't be warm-blooded because their brains were too small. They couldn't compete with smaller, warm-blooded animals.

Yet, when dinosaurs began to emerge as the dominant group, there were many other species which had equal opportunity to dominate, to win the race for king of the mountain. For five million years, the dinosaurs were on equal footing with the other inhabitants of the ecosystem. But then, the dinosaurs showed that they were the fittest and survived into absolute domination of the globe. During their rule, it is claimed that there was no non-dinosaur larger than a turkey! They don't call it the "age of reptiles" for no reason! The dinosaurs monopolized the planet for 130 million years. As they spread into every area of dominance, they drove out or destroyed other advanced clans which had also been evolving and adapting for tens of millions of years. During their long reign, there were other clans that could have threatened their survival, and each time the dinosaurs showed they were "firstest with the mostest" in terms of adaptive vigor.

It is posited that the class Mammalia emerged fully defined just as the dinosaurs began their expansion. But, obviously, *for some reason*, being a mammal *wasn't such an advantage* during that time. Dinosaurs evolved quickly, changed repeatedly, and maintained their dominance until some terrible event brought their rule to an abrupt end. Robert T. Bakker, author of *The Dinosaur Heresies,* writes:

> The sudden extinction of dinosaurs is one of the most popularized topics in
> paleontology. Why, after all, did the last dynasties finally end in total extinction? In

reality, however, the dinosaurs' history contains the drama of much more than a single death. They suffered *three or four major catastrophes* during their long predominance, each one thinning the ranks of the entire clan. And after each such fall, they recouped their evolutionary fortunes, rising again to fill the terrestrial system with yet another wave of new species and families of species. The final complete extermination did not come until sixty-five million years ago, at what geologists label the 'Time of Great Dying,' the greatest evolutionary disaster of all time... Our view of evolution must take into account the profoundly disorienting blows struck by the environment during these world-wide extinctions.[129]

There are many theories put forth to explain these problems but, as is the usual case with Darwinian thought, they are highly unsatisfactory and leave too many questions that require fantastic cerebral gymnastics to answer.

Using Occam's razor, might it not be more reasonable to assume that the earth was a different place at the time the dinosaurs walked? Just to speculate here, it might be that they obtained a portion of their nourishment from the act of breathing itself. Additionally, a different level of gravity would have greatly reduced the energy needs, and a more salubrious climate would have further eliminated the energy expenditure for heat regulation. At the same time, a soupier atmosphere would have shielded the inhabitants of the earth from the harmful radiation of the sun and would have been more conducive to extensive life spans, which may have been the means by which the dinosaurs grew to such fantastic sizes. Bakker also makes an excellent case for the warm-bloodedness of dinosaurs:

> No one, either in the nineteenth century or the twentieth, has ever built a persuasive case proving that dinosaurs as a whole were more like reptilian crocodiles than warm-blooded birds. No one has done this because it can't be done... So hundred-year-old dinosaur theories live on without being questioned, and too often they are assumed to be totally correct. Even when such a theory is caught in an error, it's likely to be excused. [...]

> Any attempt to analyze the events of the extinction of the dinosaurs runs into the fundamental difficulties that hinder the investigation of any of these mass murders of species. Most fossil bones *owe their preservation to quick burial by sediment* right after the death of their owner. But generally most spots in the terrestrial biosphere suffer erosion, not deposition.[130]

THE MYSTERY OF MALTA

I have on my desk a slim archaeological guidebook to Malta which proclaims on its first page that the first humans on the island arrived around seven thousand

[129] Bakker, Robert T., *The Dinosaur Heresies* (New York: William Morrow and Company 1986).
[130] Ibid.

years ago[131] from Sicily. The last page of the book mentions, in one paragraph, the enigmatic "cart ruts" that are "too obvious in the Maltese rocky landscape to be ignored". Well, a brief paragraph at the end of the book is about as close to being ignored as something can get that is declared to be so obvious in the landscape of the area under discussion. The author of the little guidebook informs us he believes they were intended for the transportation of construction blocks from the quarry in ancient times. He then makes a point of saying that he does not mean "prehistoric".

The temples of Malta are its main attraction. Anthony Bonanno[132], the author of the above mentioned booklet, declares in a news article[133] that the temples of Malta are "very reliably carbon-dated to the period 3,600 to 2,500 BC. In that space of time we have traced a regular evolution in style, from the small and rudimentary to the large and complex".

The first of these "Temples" was discovered in 1902 by a workman digging a trench for the foundations of a house. His digging activities broke through to a huge subterranean temple and cemetery, cut from solid rock. Twelve years later, a farmer kept hitting stones in his field as he ploughed, and this turned out to be a complex of temples. As time went by, more and more structures were revealed, and they have become known as the world's most impressive prehistoric monuments.

The first thing that I notice about this is that all of these things were buried for a very long time — so long that they were completely unknown to the inhabitants of the region. But uniformitarian science tells us that the surface of the earth is constantly being subjected to the processes of erosion unless, of course, we are talking about a river delta or a landslide or something. Apparently on Malta, things work backward. They get covered up by some conditions unknown to uniformitarian science, and then require millennia to be uncovered again.

As fascinating as they are, I don't want to discuss the "temples". There are numerous layers of them, and many of them are actually built on top of the thing that has my attention, the "cart ruts" which are so evident everywhere that they cannot be ignored. Yet, these "cart ruts" only receive a brief paragraph and most certainly are not being protected by the Maltese government, since they are of so little importance!

It's difficult to find a good set of photographs of the ruts, but with persistence, a photo here and another there, enough can be assembled to make some observations. The facts are that, for cart ruts, they follow strange rules. Very often,

---

[131] Curiously, this is the same time that the Black Sea was filled with water from the Mediterranean by overflowing the Bosporus valley. Connection?

[132] Museums Department, Department of Classics and Archaeology at the University of Malta.

[133] Old Temples Society, Second issue, November 1999.

indeed, there are two parallel furrows; but they differ not only from rut to rut, but a single parallel expanse can vary in width and depth from one end to the other. That's a strange cart that has an axle that expands and contracts. The ruts run through the valleys, up the hills, down the dales, and sometimes more than one set run side by side for awhile until they suddenly merge into a single set of ruts. What is more amazing is that they often just keep going — right into the Mediterranean — or right off the edge of a cliff.

Erich von Daniken paid a visit to the island to examine them and thoughtfully took his tape measure. It seems that the distance between a parallel series of ruts can range from 65 to 123 cm. What is more amazing is that some of them are up to 70 cm deep, going around sharp curves. Anyone who has ever played with toy cars and trucks in the sandbox, or driven a sulky, has some idea of the problem here. A wheel large enough to make a rut that deep could not possibly make such a curve. At one point near *San Pawl-Tat-Targa*, four pairs of ruts, with four different gauges, join up to make a single pair of ruts. Nearby, one set crosses another, each with different rut depths. Another rut that extends up to 60 cm deep is only 11 cm wide at its deepest point and 20 cm wide at its shallowest point.[134]

The ruts that run into the Mediterranean are most interesting. Divers have discovered that the ruts continue a long way below the sea level. What is more fascinating is that in July of 1999, amateur German archaeologist Hubert Zeitlmair discovered a megalithic temple on the sea-bed in Malta's territorial waters about 3 kilometers off the eastern coast. The problem with this is, in order for a temple to lie on the bed of the Mediterranean, it would have to date to the last ice age. The implication is that the Maltese temples are at least six thousand years older than Bonnano and his colleagues propose. Naturally, Bonnano was called upon to pronounce sage words regarding this discovery.

> If the underwater temple does prove authentic, it would have to be a contemporary of those built on the mainland. The only possibility that springs to mind is that of a separate island, or even part of the mainland, which sank because of a fault in the rock. It is highly unlikely, but it does remain a possibility. There are after all no written records of any kind dating back to that period.[135]

It, "sank because of a fault in the rock". It absolutely could NOT have been covered by rising water levels!

Malta's temples and tombs are unique in their construction: the massive piling of stone upon stone, and the deep excavations. According to the experts, they are a tremendous engineering feat, and they must have been the sole focus of the society that built them. All the people of Malta worked to build "temples" to the exclusion of all else, except for subsistence. According to the experts, the people of Malta

---

[134] Von Daniken, *Signs of the Gods.* pp. 82-135.

[135] Old Temples Society, Second Issue, November 1999.

neither built houses of stone nor learned how to write. They evolved all of their techniques for one reason and one reason only: to build "temples" to house their cult activities. How these people created a society that was ready, willing, and able to spend all their efforts and energy to labor incessantly in the work of tunneling and building, remains a great mystery.

The distribution of the "temples", plotted on a map, fall into clusters which command a major area of territory. The island seems to be divided into six major areas of this type. The problem arises when we consider the fact that the island, at its best, could never support more than 11,000 people divided up into these six areas, at no more than 2000 people per section. So, how could a group of about 2000 people at most, mobilize the labor to excavate all those caverns and build all those "temples" in each of the sections, particularly when you consider the fact that the evidence shows that the area could not have supported so many people in terms of food production. That leads to the problem of where they were getting their food and how were they getting their food, if all they were doing was building "temples" and performing cult activities? Colin Renfrew[136] has proposed the "Big Chief Theory" whereby the building of "temples" was instigated to awe the howling savages and keep them in line.

Why do I keep putting the word "temples" in quotes? Well, when I looked at the photographs of these structures, the ground plans drawn to scale, and the plaster models made of them, the only thing they reminded me of was simply houses - places where people lived. After all, why would there be so many "temples"? Of course! Because the natives devoted their energies to building temples while they, themselves, lived in grass or bearskin huts! That's it. Megalithic stone structures MUST be temples because what other reason could there be for such Herculean efforts to create them? That is, of course, assuming that the ability to manage large blocks of stone were unusual when they were built. It certainly would be for us today. So we cannot imagine that the ancient peoples might have done it as easily as we nail gypsum board on cheap two-by-fours to build our houses.

As noted, archaeologists explain the cart ruts by saying that they are evidence of the transporting of the blocks used to build the "temples". But, we see from our descriptions of the cart ruts above, that the idea that these grooves in the ground are really cart ruts runs into serious problems. Any effort to explain them in this way falls apart if an engineer instead of an archaeologist looks at them. In fact, in my humble opinion, archaeologists ought to be required to have a degree in engineering before they are allowed to say a word about anything. In the end, no one seems to have a single rational explanation for these "cart ruts". One of the great mysteries on the planet, and nobody seems to care. What a waste.

---

[136] Read his book *Before Civilization* for the details. The ideas are too puerile for me to waste any time on recounting them.

Do I have an idea to propose? I would like to suggest that these "ruts" look an awful lot like places where lightning has struck, and the electricity has blasted away the dirt and rock as it shoots along some sort of natural earth power grid conductor. The only difference is that the cart ruts are not random. Were the cart ruts some sort of networked energy conduction system? Could some sort of element have been placed in the ground by an ancient civilization; something that conducted power to their homes the way our vulgar power poles and lines criss-cross the landscape? And then, at some point in time, was the earth hit by such a surge of energy from some unknown source that these power "lines" melted the rock in which they were "strung"? Perhaps a surge of some kind of cosmic energy source? Maybe even the electromagnetic pulse of a nuclear explosion? Maybe it was neither of these, but merely a massive overheating of the surface of the earth so that the conduction element and its insulating covering melted and was swept away?

Among the artifacts discovered at Malta are a number of truly extraordinary "goddess" images. They are, without exception, extremely corpulent by today's standards. There are many representations of spirals and other "goddess" motifs, including waves of water. According to the experts, the very oldest form of religion that can be archaeologically identified anywhere was the worship of the Mother Goddess by wandering "hunter gatherers". It was thought, for a very long time, that such cultures were very primitive and narrow, but it has now been discovered that this is not the case. New archaeological sites are being excavated at the present time that show very advanced levels of art and culture among these "husbandmen" of the Earth. An example is the Japanese Jomon culture.

THE JOMON PUZZLE

The incipient Jomon culture is said to date between 11,000 and 7,500 BC. It is described as "one of the most affluent forager cultures to ever exist". Although the Japanese did not settle Japan until the third century BC, it seems that human beings have occupied the area from about 30,000 BC. During the Ice Ages, Japan was connected to the Korean peninsula by means of a land bridge. Additionally, all four main Japanese islands were connected, and the southern island of Kyushu was connected to the Korean peninsula while the northern island of Hokkaido was connected to Siberia.

As with all preliterate people, the only things we know about the Jomon is based on fragments of artifacts and the imaginative guessing of anthropologists and archaeologists. "Jomon" means "cord pattern", for these people put cord patterns on their pottery. Pottery is a characteristic of Neolithic peoples; the Jomon, however, were Mesolithic peoples (Middle Stone Age). The standard anthropological line on the development of human arts asserts that pottery-making developed *after* agriculture and is characteristic of a more sedentary culture. The Incipient Jomon, however, were hunter-gatherers who made pottery long before agriculture was introduced into Japan. In fact, the Incipient Jomon pottery-making dated to long before any human was introduced to agriculture. So, who were they? As in Malta, we have to go underwater again to find out.

In 1987, Kihachiro Arataka, a scuba instructor and diving guide, was exploring the southeast coast of Yonaguni Island, the last island of the Ryukyu chain. This string of islands in the East China Sea curves from Japan south and west toward China. Aratake was looking for interesting dive sites for tourist expeditions when he came across a submarine cliff that appeared to be cut in a series of immense geometric terraces.

Masaaki Kimura, a marine seismologist at the University of the Ryukyus in Okinawa, heard about the ruins in 1990 and went to check it out. For the next seven years, Kimura dived on the site repeatedly, taking his students with him on many occasions, and assembling a portfolio of drawings, maps and models. He became convinced that the Yonaguni formation was fashioned by human hands. Based on well-established studies of rises in the East China Sea during and after the last ice age, the Yonaguni Monument was last above sea level at around 6,000 to 8,000 BC. This means that it could represent an early, unknown civilization.

Geologist Dr. Robert Schoch went to investigate, made six dives, and noted several interesting things about the site

> Superficially the monument has the appearance of a platform or part of a step pyramid, something like the ancient Temple of the Sun near Trujillo in northern Peru. The top of the monument lies sixteen feet under the surface, the bottom at an approximate depth of eighty feet. Extending over 160 feet north to south, the asymmetrical monument has uneven stone steps ranging in height from a foot and a half to several feet, on its southern face. It looks like a great staircase up which only a giant could stride. The surfaces have a regular smooth surface, like dressed stone.[…]
>
> Much of the regularity of the surface was due not to a tooled smoothness of the rock but to a thick even coating of algae, corals, sponges, and similar organisms. […] In a number of spots I scraped the coating away, both to determine what kind of stone lay beneath and to look for tool scars or quarry marks. I found none. Even more telling, I couldn't find any evidence that Yonaguni consisted of separate pieces of stone. Stone blocks carved, set in place, and arranged in an order would clearly indicate a human-made structure. Rather, the monument is essentially a single piece of solid, "living" bedrock that is less precise than it appears at first. […] Still, Yonaguni posed a problem. If the monument was the result of a natural process, this natural process was unlike any I had seen before. What could it be?[137]

Dr. Schoch was faced with an interesting problem in his examination of the Japanese underwater "city". Since the sea level sequences were so well established, to state unequivocally that the structure was man-made would have been a terrible blow to the currently accepted chronology of human history. It would have been far worse than his claims that the Sphinx is older than Egyptologist claim because that issue can be debated from now until the cows

---

[137] Schoch, Robert, Ph.D., *The Voices of the Rocks*, (New York: Harmony Books 1999).

come home with no absolute resolution. Here, a declaration of human origin for these structures would be undeniable proof of an ancient civilization which built the monuments before the sea level rose.

I have a great deal of sympathy for Dr. Schoch's position. What did Dr. Schoch determine about the Underwater city? Well, after having noted that he had never before, as a trained geologist, seen anything like this in "natural structures", he went looking and found a "tentative answer". He noted that:

> The monument is composed predominantly of very fine sandstones and mudstones of the type we geologists call the Lower Miocene Yaeyama Group. Rocks of this type contain numerous, well-defined, parallel bedding planes that allow easy separation of the layers, and they are crisscrossed by many joints and fractures running parallel to one another and vertical to the bedding planes. Yaeyama Group sandstones lie exposed along the southeast and northeast coasts of Yonaguni Island, and I went there to see how the weather under current conditions above water. [...] I became convinced that the steplike and terrace like features of the underwater monument resulted from natural processes working on the stone, not from the activity of humans long ago.

> Possibly the choice between natural and human-made isn't simply either/or. Yonaguni Island contains a number of old tombs whose exact age is uncertain, but that are clearly very old. *Curiously, the architecture of the tombs is much like that of the monument.* It is possible that humans were imitating the monument in designing the tombs, and it is equally possible that the monument was itself somehow modified by human hands. [...] It is also possible that the monument served as a quarry from which blocks were cut, following the natural bedding, joint, and fracture planes of the rock, then removed to construct buildings that are now long gone. [...][138]

Thus Dr. Schoch determined that, even if the underwater structure can be explained by natural forces, he leaves the door open to an ancient civilization that existed on Yonaguni Island 12,000 years ago.

Coming at the problem from another direction, we discover that about ten thousand years ago, a group of people lived in the northern part of Japan who were ethnically distinct from the rest of the Japanese population. They were named "Ainu", meaning human being or *male* in their own language. This word is remarkably similar to the words "Manu" and "Anu", which we will encounter more than once. The Ainu were generally assumed to be descendants of an ancient people referred to as *Emishi* in the famous Japanese chronicles called *"Kojiki"* and *"Nihon-syoki"*. Today, the term Ainu is used to denote the indigenous people of Hokkaido, Japan's northernmost island, as a single, integrated population who are the descendants of the Ainu of ten thousand years ago.

---

[138] Ibid.

The traditional Ainu lifestyle was hunting, fishing and gathering. Ainu religious beliefs center around the existence of another world of spirit essences subject to the same forces that control the visible world. The people worship animal gods, *especially the bear*, with ritual, song and dance. Even the Ainu language is unusual in its Asian environment. Although they possessed no system of writing, they created a rich oral tradition of stories and poems expressed in formal prose and verse. We, of course, immediately think of the Bear cults of Europe, and the bear skulls found in the caves of France dating back in the tens of thousands of years.

The Ainu are a morphological problem. The characteristics that differentiate them from Asians are their hairiness and their hair "form". The explanation is that there is a strong admixture of Caucasoid genetics in the Ainu. Some experts consider them to be related to the Australian aborigines, and others think that they represent an independent grouping altogether. More recent studies have connected them genetically to Turkic populations of Central Asia, a combination of caucasoid and mongoloid genes.

So how are we to relate this "archaeology" of a "preliterate" culture to the fact that there is evidence of nearby remains of a former civilization far more advanced than the Jomon? I think that noting the dates might be important. It is as though the Jomon were survivors of a cataclysm. The infrastructure of their society may have been destroyed, along with many of the artifacts that might have been discovered by archaeologists of our day, and they began anew on a planet that had been swept clean - except for stone structures that survived the maelstrom.

GLOBAL EVIDENCE OF ANCIENT, PRE-HISTORIC HIGH CIVILIZATIONS

Over and over again we find these odd clues that point to an ancient civilization that existed something over 12,000 years ago. There has been a raging controversy for generations between pro-Atlanteans and anti-Atlanteans about this. There seem to be sufficient archaeological remains to justify a serious scientific study based on such a hypothesis but so far, there are no "takers" in the mainstream scientific community. Archaeology and ethnology, being observational sciences, and not experimental sciences, have built their entire framework upon the study of those remains. And when we look closely at the array of discoveries in those fields, we note bits and pieces of cultures of almost unspeakable age. The fact that uniformitarian science barely allows the idea of cataclysmic destruction to be part of the hypothesis cripples archaeologists and, in the end, may make fools of them all.

Without the algorithm of cyclic cataclysm, archaeologists cannot fully understand what they observe, nor can they explain the anomalies here and there, and the lack of other evidence that ought to be here and there (if one assumes great antiquity of civilization with no cataclysms). The fact seems to be that, what does continue to exist in terms of archaeological remains from times before 7,000 or more years ago, have been subjected to geological and cosmic cataclysms of almost incomprehensible violence and few major relics remain for perusal. Those few, however, are cast aside as the *anomalies* of archaeology and ethnology, and their very existence is buried or denied in efforts to avoid toppling the house of cards so laboriously established by those sciences.

Nevertheless, we find that all over the globe, with few exceptions, these studies break down almost completely right around 7,000 to 10,000 BC, at which point they meet with what mathematicians call a "discontinuity". Immediately after this discontinuity, all of the hot-spots of ancient civilization that archaeologists accept as valid suddenly appear with no indication of gradual, uniformitarian development. What is more, there seems to be considerable indication that these developments were degenerate remnants of something already lost in the mists of antiquity.

Entire libraries of books have been written demonstrating this antiquity of man and his civilizations, but it has not yet been accepted, even in principle, by any branch of modern science. The scientific thought police oppose any type of cataclysmic change in the structure of the earth and will go to any extremes to avoid coming to grips with its evidence. And yet, as we will see, science breaks down again when it is forced to contemplate the origin of man's intellectual development.

ANCIENT FLIGHT?

Is there any "hard" evidence for this ancient, worldwide, high civilization? I don't want to spend too much time going over all of it and attempting to reproduce the fine efforts of other writers. But, just to cover the subject briefly, one of the most telling pieces of hard evidence is included in Charles Hapgood's book, *Maps of the Ancient Sea Kings*. Hapgood, a Professor of Anthropology, included in his book a most interesting letter from a group of cartographers in the United States Air Force. The statements in this letter, to my knowledge, have never been challenged. In fact, the letter itself doesn't receive much attention, though Hapgood is certainly referred to as a crank often enough. The letter refers to a series of highly technical analyses of several maps that Dr. Hapgood presented to the cartographers. After their study, they wrote:

> It is not very often that we have the opportunity to evaluate maps of ancient origin. The Piri Reis (AD 1513) and the Oronteus Fineaus [sic] (AD 1531) maps sent to us by you, presented a delightful challenge for it was not readily conceivable that they could be so accurate without being forged. With added enthusiasm we accepted this challenge and have expended many off duty hours evaluating your manuscript and the above maps. I am sure you will be pleased to know that we have concluded that both of these maps were compiled from accurate original source maps, irrespective of dates. The following is a brief summary of our findings:

> The solution of the portolano projection used by Admiral Piri Reis, developed by your class in Anthropology must be very nearly correct; for when known geographical locations are checked in relationship to the grid computed by Mr. Richard W. Strachan (MIT), there, is remarkably close agreement. Piri Reis' use of the Portolano projection (centred on Syene, Egypt) is an excellent choice, for it is a developable surface that would permit the relative size and shape of the earth at that (latitude) to be retained. It is our opinion that those who compiled the original map had an excellent knowledge of the continents covered by this map.

As stated by Colonel Harold Z. Ohlmeyer in his letter (July 6, 1960) to you, the Princess Martha Coast of Queen Maud Land, Antarctica, appears to be truly represented on the southern sector of the Piri Reis Map. The agreement of the Piri Reis map with the seismic profile of this area made by the Norwegian-British - Swedish Expedition of 1949, supported by your solution of the grid, places beyond a reasonable doubt the conclusion that the original source maps must have been made before the present Antarctic ice cap covered Queen Maud Land coasts.

It is our opinion that the accuracy of the cartographic features shown in the Oronteus Fineaus [sic] Map (AD 1530) suggests, beyond a doubt, that it also was compiled from accurate source maps of Antarctica, but in this case of the entire continent. Close examination has proved the original source maps must have been compiled at a time when the land mass and inland waterways of the continent were relatively free of ice. This conclusion is further supported by a comparison of the Oronteus Finneaus [sic] Map with the results obtained by International Geophysical Year teams in their measurements of the subglacial topography. The comparison also suggests that the original source maps (compiled in remote antiquity) were prepared when Antarctica was presumably free of ice. The Cordiform projection used by Oronteus Fineaus [sic] suggests the use of advanced mathematics. Further, the shape given to the Antarctic continent suggests the possibility, if not the probability, that the original source maps were compiled on a stereographic or gnomonic type of projection (involving the use of spherical trigonometry).

We are convinced that the findings made by you and your associates are valid, and that they raise extremely important questions affecting geology and ancient history, questions which certainly require further investigation.

We thank you for extending us the opportunity to have participated in the study of these maps. The following officers and airmen volunteered their time to assist Captain Lorenzo W. Burroughs in this evaluation: Captain Richard E. Covault, CWO Howard D. Minor, MSgt Clifton M. Dover, MSgt David C. Carter, TSgt James H. Hood, SSgt James L. Carroll, and AIC Don R. Vance.

Lorenzo W. Burroughs, Captain,
USAF Chief, Cartographic Section
8th Reconnaissance Technical Sqdn
(SAC) Westover, Mass.[139]

The Antarctic ice cover is supposed to be millions of years old. Who could have made a map of Antarctica when it was not covered by ice, and when? Why is it that we believe this ice cover to be so old? And if it is not, how old is it really and why does it present the appearance of being millions of years old, assuming it does so to the trained scientist?

Charles Hapgood heard about these maps at a particular point in his life when he was studying the ice ages. A copy of an ancient map had been found in the

---

[139] Hapgood, Charles, *Maps of the Ancient Sea Kings* (London: Turnstone Press 1979).

Topkapi Palace in Istanbul in 1929, and a Turkish naval officer had presented a copy of it to the US Navy Hydrographic Office. It was examined by scholars who noted that the map represented Antarctica before it was covered with ice. Yet, the map was painted on parchment and was dated to 1513, over 300 years before Antarctica was officially "discovered". Core samples taken by the Byrd Antarctic Expedition showed that the last warm period in the Antarctic ended around 4,000 BC. It began about 9,000 years before that. The only conclusion that could be drawn was that someone had mapped Antarctica at least 6,000 years ago. Hapgood discovered that there were more of these ancient maps - portolans, as they are called - and that some of them strongly indicate that the mapmaker had an aerial view of what he was mapping! Hapgood himself writes:

> The evidence presented by the ancient maps appears to suggest the existence in remote times, before the rise of any known cultures, of a true civilisation, of an advanced kind, which either was localized in one area but had worldwide commerce, or was, in a real sense, a worldwide culture. This culture, at least in some respects, was more advanced than the civilizations of Greece and Rome. In geodesy, nautical science, and mapmaking it was more advanced than any known culture before the 18th century of the Christian Era. It was only in the 18th century that we developed a practical means of finding longitude. It was in the 18th century that we first accurately measured the circumference of the earth. Not until the 19th century did we begin to send out ships for exploration into the Arctic or Antarctic Seas and only then did we begin the exploration of the bottom of the Atlantic. The maps indicate that some ancient people did all these things.[...]

> When I was a youth I had a plain simple faith in progress. It seemed to me impossible that once man had passed a milestone of progress in one way that he could ever pass the same milestone again the other way. Once the telephone was invented, it would stay invented. If past civilizations had faded away it was just because they had not learned the secret of progress. But Science meant permanent progress, with no going back.[...] S.R.K. Glanville writes in *The Legacy of Egypt*: "It may be, as some indeed suspect, that the science we see as the dawn of recorded history was not science at its dawn, but represents the remnants of the science of some great and as yet untraced civilization."[140]

By a series of analyses, Hapgood and others came to the conclusion that there was an ancient civilization whose center or "home base" was Antarctica itself.[141] The fact that it was a global society, just as our own is, was also evident to these researchers from other clues. This was, to put it mildly, not an acceptable idea to the uniformitarian view of evolution.

---

[140] Ibid.

[141] Flem-Ath, Rand and Rose, *When the Sky Fell* (Canada: St. Martins 1995).

Dr. Hapgood never used the word "Atlantis" in his book. He knew the value of his academic reputation and that he just couldn't go there. But that was not a problem for Erich von Daniken.

Von Daniken's book *Chariots of the Gods?* came out in 1967 and proposed that the ancient portolans, side by side with other anomalies, suggested the presence and influence of extraterrestrial "gods" in ancient times. I find this to be a curious sort of "damage control" that attempts - in a left handed way - to support the uniformitarian hypothesis since it suggests strongly that mankind himself was incapable of creating an advanced civilization on his own.

The portolans studied by Charles Hapgood demonstrate that there have been very ancient cultures, or civilizations, which may have and could have developed methods of flight. The existence of the great megalithic structures further suggest that the energy sources of that time may have been much simpler and more effective than ours, and more directly associated with forces which we do not yet comprehend. Yes, we are dealing with indirect evidence, not always of the greatest clarity. Yet in support of such antiquity, we note that there is stonework carved out of the solid mountain of rock in South America, which certainly antedate the Andean glaciers, and almost as certainly predate the formation of the mountains themselves. This work is superior in technique to anything that can currently be produced by our mechanized civilization. It seems almost patently evident that the construction, sculpting and tunneling of our ancestors could only have been accomplished by forces different from those in use by us today. The problem can be solved by admitting to a levitating force developed and used by the same common denominator - space flight - which simplifies so many other puzzles for us. And it seems that these very things are what the myths of antiquity, including that most captivating story of all, the legend of the Holy Grail, are telling us.

On the basis of the evidence of an antiquity, we postulate the ancient development of some kind of science. In either case, it is of great importance to consider these matters in terms of the how's and why's and who's. Most books on these subjects approach the matter from one of these assumptions or the other, with little regard to what might be behind it all when considered in light of present day observations. For us, the most telling thing about this is that either angle is abhorrent to science and to most religions.

In the end, nothing but the existence of an extremely ancient high civilization answers all of the problems presented by observed and recorded facts. And that is what led us to ask the questions about what is the wellspring of our beliefs, what is the source of our denial and rejection of what is observable in favor of an imposed belief system? We will come to that issue soon enough.

THE NEANDERTHAL ENIGMA

Let's come back now to the idea that the earth may have been an entirely different place in terms of cosmic environment, thus enabling the dinosaurs to live and thrive, we can ask if other "different" environments might have existed at other times, specifically in relation to man himself? One example that might relate to such an idea is the extraordinarily strange disappearance of Neanderthal man.

Actually, the disappearance of a whole, distinct group of human type beings at such a relatively *recent* point in history, is scary as all get-out. Just think about it: Neanderthals were everywhere in the icy lands of Europe and Western Asia for over 150,000 years. They were enormously strong and manifestly intelligent. What went wrong?

It is also proposed that, at the same moment in time that Neanderthal man just went "poof!" homo sapiens sapiens (that's us), just dropped in for dinner, so to speak. Is there a connection between what went wrong for Neanderthal and what was "right" for modern man? That question is driving a lot of paleontologists batty.

Allan Wilson and Vincent Sarich of Berkeley undertook to determine the date of human origins via DNA analysis. They were looking at proteins because they knew that proteins evolve by accumulating mutations. They also knew that the proteins in related species are slightly different from one another because of the mutations that occur after a species splits off from the "common ancestor". Differences in proteins can be quantified.

Well, this wasn't so controversial a thing to be doing until Wilson and Sarich suggested that mutations occur across the millennia *at a steady rate*, like the ticks of a molecular clock. If this was true, it meant that the difference in a given protein in any two species would indicate not only how related they were, but also *how much time had elapsed since they shared a common ancestor*. In other words, Wilson and Sarich were going to analyze some proteins and tell us when we last were apes. Everyone was holding their breath for the answer to this one.

Wilson and Sarich's protein analysis suggested that the common ancestor of apes and humans had lived *only* five million years ago. Stretching it to accommodate errors, they could only give it eight million years. "*To put it as bluntly as possible*,", Sarich wrote, "*one no longer has the option of considering a fossil specimen older than about eight million years as a hominid no matter what it looks like*".

The idea that there was or was not any genetic connection between Cro-Magnon and Neanderthal led to many hot debates. A team of U.S. and German researchers extracted mitochondrial DNA from Neanderthal bone showing that the Neanderthal DNA sequence falls outside the normal variation of modern humans.

The researchers compared the Neanderthal sequence with 2,051 human sequences and 59 common chimpanzee sequences. They found that the differences in Neanderthal DNA occurred at sites where differences usually occur in both humans and chimps. In other words, Neanderthal was simply a different species.

When the researchers looked at the Neanderthal sequence with respect to 994 human mitochondrial DNA lineages including Africans, Europeans, Asians, Native Americans, Australians and Pacific Islanders, they found the number of base pair differences between the Neanderthal sequence and these groups was 27 or 28 *for all groups*.

There is a long and interesting case of some Neanderthal remains in a cave in Israel that some scientists were attempting to utilize as evidence that this was the region in which Neanderthal morphed into anatomically modern man. The interested reader may want to have a look at *The Neanderthal Enigma* by James Shreeve for a blow-by-blow account of this idea and how it was shot down. The end result is, just to save some time, the conclusion that it was another example of Darwinist wishful thinking.[142]

Naturally, since the idea that Neanderthal was not the precursor to modern man was now pretty well squashed, that meant that modern man evolved along another line. This opened the door to the acknowledgement of certain facts that had been rejected in earlier debates, while the Neanderthal hypothesis was still viable, but now looked like a reasonable way out of the dilemma. Suddenly, fossils of very old, modern humans, were acceptable, even if they existed long before the disappearance of Neanderthal.

The problem is, this little clue that a controversy exists is merely the end of a thread hanging out there in public view. When you take hold of this one, oh my! It does get deep and you do need hip-waders!

An interesting book was published a few years back entitled *Forbidden Archeology*. The authors, Michael Cremo and Richard L. Thompson, were savaged by the mainstream science critics for their "absurd ideas and ridiculous assertions". Most of all, it was suggested that, since they were not "experts", they simply could not understand the material they were assembling and, therefore, it had no validity. Sad to say, I delayed reading this book for a rather long time because of the negative reviews. However, as I pulled on this particular thread, one disturbing element leading to another, I finally gave in and ordered the volume and sat down to read it in a skeptical frame of mind. Just because it was well written did not resolve my skepticism. Just because there were hundreds of references to scientific papers did not persuade me that the authors had actually come to the correct conclusions about those papers. So, I undertook to go to the papers they cited myself.

As it turned out, I ended up reversing my opinion of Cremo and Thompson. A great many of these scientific papers that they have cited were written in rather plain terms that anyone could understand - even another non-expert like myself. What is more, the fact that they have been "buried", or marginalized, ignored, flamed and forgotten, suggests more about the experts who have done this, and who then adopt the jargon they use as a means of concealing that they really don't understand what they are doing, than it says about the authors who can clearly see that we have serious problems reconciling the observable and empirical facts with the "accepted theories". By the time the reader is finished with this book, they will be completely disgusted with the utter and absolute lies and fabrications of some of the most influential members of the mainstream scientific community, what I have come to call the Scientific Thought Police. When the masses of people come

---

[142] New data may change this. If it can be shown that Neaderthal did evolve into modern man, or was at least one of the sources for modern man, this opens intriguing possibilities for their relationship to what we have named the organic portal.

to the realization that the power structure of any given period creates the educational institutions that promulgate the lies and distortions that support the political structure, and that the majority of the scientific community only "follow the money" of the military-industrial complex, I tremble for those who have chosen the cozy lies over the truth. Again, that raises the question as to who or what ideology "controls" our world in such a way that science can - and is - manipulated to support a political agenda? What is that agenda? We will come to that.

EVIDENCE OF THE ICA STONES

Recently, some objects called the Ica Stones have become a subject of much discussion. These stones were brought to the attention of the scientific community in 1966 when a Dr. Javier Cabrera, a Peruvian physician, received a small, carved rock for his birthday from a poor native. The carving on the rock looked ancient to Dr. Cabrera, but intrigued him because it seemed to depict a primitive fish. It wasn't long before the locals were bringing the doctor scads more of these rocks gathered from a riverbank. He soon had a collection of more than 15,000 stones, many etched with impossible scenes that clearly depict such dinosaurs as triceratops, stegosaurus, apatosaurus, and human figures riding on the backs of flying pterodactyls! What's more, some of the scenes are of men hunting and killing dinosaurs! Others show men watching the heavens through what look like telescopes, performing open-heart surgery, and cesarean section births, and even some serious pornography.

Oh dear! How can this be? We have already been told that modern man is only about 2 million years old and dinosaurs are thought to have become extinct 65 million years ago.

Sophia Melewska, a geomorphologist, was commissioned to investigate the rocks, summarize their content, and comment on their authenticity. After studying the collection of Ica stones, Melewska said that she was in a state of "intellectual shock". Melewska is one of the scientists now trying to direct the attention of professional research toward this mystery with little success.

Part of the problem for mainstream science is the nature of artifacts themselves. Unlike clay figurines that have organic material (i.e., straw) in their composition, there are no organic materials that can be dated in plain old rock. The surface of these rocks has a varnish that is produced by bacteria and minute organisms over millennia. Such a varnish or patina will take thousands of years to discolor and coat each stone. The etching of the stones removed the existing varnish, revealing the lighter rock underneath. Since these rocks have developed additional varnish in the etched grooves, the evidence is that they were carved a very, very long time ago.

The BBC sent a team to investigate these stones, sending Neil Steede to examine them. Steede examined the varnish on the stones but was not able to guess at the date. Without recourse to radiometric dating, the strata in which an object is found can often give a clue to their age. However, these stones were revealed by accidental erosion, and their original resting place is not known.

Acting on a rumor, Steede traveled to a nearby village where he met a local farmer who, reportedly, was in the process of carving similar stones for tourists. The rumors of Dr. Cabrera's collection had brought tourists to the area, seeking what they are assured are the "real stones". Steede discovered that the artist was imitating the style on the Ica stones, but his technique was not as good. What was more telling, the *varnish was absent from his grooves*.

It is at this point that the Scientific Thought Police went into action, or so it seems. They pointed to these reproductions as proof of a hoax, and dismiss any serious study of the original collection which is still maintained by Dr. Cabrera.

Just to drive home the point and put an end to the controversy, after the broadcast of the BBC TV documentary, the farmer who had sold many of the stones to Dr. Cabrera, and who had been caught carving others, was arrested and interrogated. He was forced to admit that he had carved ALL of the stones himself to sell to tourists! So, the "hoax" was over.

However, we soon discover that under Peruvian law, if the stones were genuine, they belonged to the government, and if the farmer had been selling government property to anyone, he would have gone to prison. By claiming that he had created a hoax, the farmer was let off the hook and stayed out of jail. And rather than determine scientifically if the stones were authentic, the authorities were satisfied that they had dealt effectively with this troubling matter, and the farmer was released. German journalist Andreas Fischer visited the farmer later, at which time the poor traumatized guy revealed that he had admitted to perpetrating a hoax only to avoid going to prison.

Regarding the Ica stones, we have three possibilities: a human civilization existed during the age of the dinosaurs; dinosaurs survived to coexist with man; or the stones are an elaborate hoax. Considering all the other evidence of the Scientific Thought Police on the prowl, I vote against number three, but I can't claim any certainty about either of the other two solutions. I rather think that Time Loops could be added to the list.

OTHER ARTIFACTS

Now and again an anomalous artifact "pops up". One particular little item always fascinated me. It seems that, during mining operations in 1851, at Dorchester, Massachusetts, blasting threw out a bell shaped vessel from its bed in formerly solid rock. It was made of an unknown metal and was decorated with floral inlays of silver.[143]

When we consider ancient archaeological evidence, most of which consists of fragmentary bits and pieces of skeletons or stone tools, we do not get the idea of

---

[143] *Scientific American*, 7:298, June 5, 1852.

an ancient worldwide, advanced civilization. However, there is something about this that we need to consider before we discard such an idea.

The first thing to think about is the fact that our own "history" is a mere 5 thousand years old. When we talk about the possible existence of man on the earth for literally millions of years, many, many civilizations could have come and gone, leaving little more than fragmentary remains. If the reader will have a look at some books that show pictures of the ancient structures whose history we know, and think, for a moment, about what might remain of our own civilization after a period of ten thousand years, it becomes evident that even under the best of conditions, little would remain that would be recognizable as the works of man. I have tried to imagine what the structures of our civilization would look like after thousands of years of abandonment. I had to admit that we have not created a very substantial environment. The prospects of providing future archaeologists with such elegant ruins are indeed remote! And, to assume that societies which did leave sophisticated metropolitan centers were primitive in their technologies, and backward, compared to our own, seems to be the ultimate in absurd conceit.

In fact, in these terms, metal is the least substantial element of all. Many gravesites have been dug up after only a few hundred years, and metal objects, aside from precious metals, have tended to simply disintegrate into powder. So, as a matter of fact, the things that would be preserved the longest are objects of stone. So, just because the only remains we find are stone does not prove that technology of metals was not known. In fact, there is considerable evidence of metals mining all over the earth far into dim antiquity. Further, during those inter-civilizational periods when we might conjecture that man was forced to use whatever implements he could to survive, stone is always there, always handy, and always works. Thus it is that repeated periods wherein primitive stone tools are evidence, in no way contradicts the idea of other periods of high civilization.

There is another thing we need to consider about the possible survival of artifacts: cataclysm. The evidence that repeated worldwide cataclysms have occurred tells us that it is very likely that, during such events, the forces of the earth itself would grind up, pulverize, and bury the works of man so completely that the fact that we find any traces at all is practically a miracle. You could say that such artifacts have a very short "shelf life"!

It is generally agreed that agriculture first developed in the "Fertile Crescent" of the Middle East. In fact, the archaeological record supports this idea. It is also generally agreed that Pastoral Nomadism developed in the Central Asian Steppes. Archaeology also supports this idea. However, the archaeology of these two developments only go back to a certain relatively recent date which poses a problem when one considers the Nostratic language hypothesis. In other words, if an advanced civilization existed in the distant past, it was from the survivors of this civilization that the Shepherds and agriculturalists of our present world paradigm evolved.

About 35,000 years ago, at the same time that *homo sapiens sapiens* (Cro-Magnon) was supposed to have appeared on the stage of history, simultaneously with the mysterious disappearance of Neanderthal man, there also appeared *an explosion of representational art*. It is as if the birth of culture occurred from the primal continuum of the Paleolithic mind. Prominent among these first and most artistic creations are diverse representations of the creatrix goddess of fertility, complemented by sculptures and wall paintings of animals and the hunt of a more shamanic content. The consistency and the careful beauty of these figurines is consistent with the worship of the female as generator of the continued line of living existence.

The mainstream explanation for this event is that while primitive men were wandering hunters who had to remain silent in the shamanic meditation of the hunt, the women were collecting and recognizing a wide variety of plants, talking more and socializing and forming the foundation skills that underpinned the birth of civilization. The myths of diverse tribal cultures hint at a previous era when women were the founding influence in this way. The "Venuses" of Dolni Vestonice, Willendorff, Lespugue, and Laussel date from inter-Gravitean Solutrean 20,000-18,000 BC.

THE SUDDEN APPEARANCE OF CRO-MAGNON

As we have noted, it was formerly thought by paleontologists that Neanderthal morphed into Cro-Magnon, and that Cro-Magnon was the progenitor of human beings as we know them today. However, aside from the problems of the *Eve Hypothesis*, there are serious problems with the assumptions about when modern human types actually appeared on Earth. Even if we take the evolving scientific view of the present day, we find that Cro-Magnon man was something altogether different from other anatomically modern humans.

Over and over again we read in scientific studies that Cro-Magnon man was just an "anatomically modern human". The experts will say: *"The Cro-Magnons lived in Europe between 35,000 and 10,000 years ago. They are virtually identical to modern man, being tall and muscular and slightly more robust than most modern humans."*

Notice how they slip in that "slightly more robust" bit. The fact is, the Cro-Magnon man was, compared to the other "anatomically modern humans" around him, practically a superman. They were skilled hunters, toolmakers and artists famous for the cave art at places such as Lascaux, Chauvet, and Altamira. They had a high cranium, a broad and upright face, and cranial capacity *"about the same* as modern humans" (can we say larger?), but less than that of Neanderthals. The males were as tall as 6 feet. They appeared in Europe in the upper Pleistocene, about 40,000 years ago and "their geographic origin is still unknown". Their skeletal remains show a *"few small differences from modern humans"*.

Of course, the "out of Africa" theory advocates suggest that Cro-Magnon came from Sub Saharan Africa and a temperate climate and that, "they would eventually adapt to all extremes of heat and cold". In this way, the "slight differences" between Cro-Magnon and other forms of anatomically modern humans can be explained away as an adaptation to cold. But, as we will see, this idea doesn't hold water.

Cro-Magnon's tools are described as the Aurignacian technology, characterized by bone and antler tools, such as spear tips (the first) and harpoons. They also used animal traps, and bow and arrow. They invented shafts and handles for their knives, securing their blades with bitumen, a kind of tar, as long as 40 thousand years ago. Other improvements included the invention of the atlatl, a large bone or piece of wood with a hooked groove used for adding distance and speed to spears. They also invented more sophisticated spear points, such as those that detach after striking and cause greater damage to prey.[144]

The Cro-Magnon type man was also the "originator" of such abstract concepts as "time". They marked time by lunar phases, recording them with marks on a piece of bone, antler or stone. Some of these "calendars" contained a record of as many as 24 lunations.[145]

In the relatively recent past, tool industries diversified. The Gravettian industry (25 to 15 thousand years ago), characterized by ivory tools such as backed blades, is associated with mammoth hunters. One type of brief industry was Solutrean, occurring from 18 to 15 thousand years ago and *limited to Southwest France and Spain*. It is characterized by unique and finely crafted "laurel leaf" blades, made with a pressure technique requiring a great skill. *The industry is associated with horse hunters*. The tool industry of the *Clovis Culture* in North America (11 to 8 thousand years ago) is notable for its *remarkable similarity to Solutrean*. Some suggest that the Solutrean culture migrated to North America around 12,000 thousand years ago.[146]

Cro-Magnon people lived in tents and other man-made shelters in groups of several families. They were nomadic hunter-gatherers and had elaborate rituals for hunting, birth and death. Multiple burials are common in the areas where they were found. What is most interesting is that from 35 to 10 thousand years ago, there was *no differentiation by sex or age in burials*. They included special grave goods, as opposed to everyday, utilitarian objects, suggesting a very increased ritualization of death and burial..[147]

They were the first confirmed to have domesticated animals, starting by about 15 thousand years ago (though ancient sapiens may have domesticated the dog as much as 200 thousand years ago). They were the first to leave extensive works of art, such as cave paintings and carved figures of animals and pregnant women. Huge caves lavishly decorated with murals depicting animals of the time were at first rejected as fake for being too sophisticated. Then they were dismissed as being primitive, categorized as hunting, fertility or other types of sympathetic magic. Re-evaluations have put these great works of art in a more prominent place

---

[144] Eric Whitaker, Steve Stewart; Article Reviews; *Late Ice Age Hunting Technology* (Heidi Knecht) Scientific American, July 1994.

[145] Marshack, Alexander, *The Roots Of Civilization*—Moyer (Mt. Kisco, New York: Bell Limited 1991).

[146] Preston, Douglas, *"The Lost Man"*, New Yorker Magazine, June 16, 1997.

[147] Schirtzinger, Erin, The Evidence for Pleistocene Burials, Neanderthals versus Modern Humans, December 6, 1994.

in art history. They show evidence of motifs, of following their own stylistic tradition, of "impressionist" like style, perspective, and innovative use of the natural relief in the caves. Also possible, considering the new concepts of time reckoning practiced by Cro-Magnon, are abstract representations of the passage of time, such as spring plants in bloom, or pregnant bison that might represent summer.[148]

Aside from pregnant women and other goddess worship iconography,[149] representations of people, "anthropomorphs," are very few, and never show the accuracy or detail of the other animals. Humans are represented in simple outlines without features, sometimes with "masks", often without regard to proportion, being distorted and isolated. At the *Grottes des Enfants* in France are found four burials with red ocher, and associated with Aurignacian tools. At Lascaux, France, are the famous caves of upper Paleolithic cave art, dated to 17 thousand years ago, and even older, in some cases, by many thousands of years!

The modern human types that appeared in the Levant were, however, somewhat different from Cro-Magnon. They were the sub-Saharan type, less "robust" individuals than the Cro-Magnon "superman" of Europe.

What seems to be the truth of the matter is simply that the *modern humans of the Levant were "different" from the Cro-Magnon types that "appeared" in Europe.* Try as they would, there is simply was no way to prove that Cro-Magnon evolved in Africa or the Levant and then moved to Europe.

But then, how to explain what happened in any reasonable terms?

What the archaeological record seems to show is that in Europe, after millennia of almost no progress at all, even in the few areas where modern man *has* been found, suddenly human culture seems to take off like an explosion with the appearance of Cro-Magnon man. Not only does culture explode, but also new ways of doing things, new styles and innovations that were utterly unknown in the period immediately preceding them, suddenly appear, only to disappear again like an outdated fad. From Spain to the Urals, sites list the developments of sewing needles, barbed projectiles, fishhooks, ropes, meat drying racks, temperature controlled hearths, and complex dwellings.

The most amazing part of all of it is the art. Art suddenly springs onto the landscape, fully formed, with no period of gradual development; no signs of childish attempts preceding it. A piece of ivory carved 32,000 years ago is as

---

[148] Reeser, Ken, "*Earliest Art: Representative Art In The Upper Paleolithic Era*", 1994 (after: Marshack, 1991; Grand, 1967; Ucko, Peter J., and Rosenfeld, Andre, 1967; Brown, G. Baldwin, 1932; Breuil, Abbe H., date unknown) (unpublished).

[149] Stone, Merlin, *When God Was A Woman* (San Diego, New York, London: Harvest/Harcourt Brace Jovanovich 1976).

realistic as anything turned out by the most accomplished carver of the present day.

> The Upper Paleolithic signals the most fundamental change in human behavior that the archaeological record may ever reveal.[150]

The only explanation for this tremendous change is that *a new kind of human appeared on the earth stage.*

When we consider the difficulties of such an event, in terms of "evolution", we find that this presents a huge difficulty in our understanding. First of all, we still have the problem of a 60,000-year time lag between the appearance of the sub-Saharan modern type man who was on the scene with no "improvements" in his technology for that length of time. If Cro-Magnon evolved in Africa, why isn't there a continuous record of incremental developments? By the same reasoning, if he evolved only after crossing the Mediterranean to Europe, why isn't there a continuous record of incremental developments?

The most effective and popular way that science deals with this crisis is to ignore it, to deny it, or to seek to twist the facts to fit the theory. Many archaeologists continue to account for the cultural events of the Upper Paleolithic by tying them to the emergence of a more modern, intellectually superior form of human being from Africa. They propose a "second biological event" to explain this, never mind that it left no tracks in any skeletal shape.

Nowadays, the idea is to suggest that the other "modern men" of sub-Saharan Africa were not really fully modern. They were "near-modern". Thus, Africa is preserved as the origin of all mankind, and the only thing necessary was a breakthrough in the African lineage, a "neurological event" that allowed this "new man" to develop all these new cultural behaviors overnight, so to say.

What this amounts to is saying that the explosion of culture in the Upper Paleolithic times did not happen earlier because other modern men didn't have the brains to make it happen. Unfortunately, the support for this idea amounts only to circular logic. What's more, it seems that if it were a "neurological event", it would start in a small place and spread outward. But what seems to have happened is that it sort of exploded *in a lot of places at once*: from Spain to the Ural mountains in Russia! And in fact, the Middle East is the LAST place where art appears.

The earliest known Aurignacian sites are in the Balkans, and they are dated to around 43,000 years ago. Three thousand years later, the Aurignacian craze is all over Europe.

We ought to note that the Neanderthals did not have art. What's more, there was essentially no change in their stone tools *for 100,000 years*.

---

[150] Richard Klein, Stanford, quoted by Shreeve.

Some people suggest that the impetus for culture was the sudden development of speech. But that idea doesn't hold much water either. If we were to look at some of the aboriginal societies of Australia and New Guinea, they are certainly Neanderthal like in their stone tools. But they think and communicate in languages that are as rich as ours, and they construct myths, stories and cosmologies with these languages. They just don't seem to be much interested in technology.

There is another very strange thing about this explosion of *homo intellectualis technologicus*: it seems to have sort of "lost its steam" around 12,000 years ago.

We have already noted the pottery making of the Jomon. Even more startling is the fact that *twenty-six thousand years ago* the residents of Dolni Vestonice were firing ceramics in kilns. But you don't read that in archaeology textbooks. In the standard teachings, the emergence of ceramics is linked to the functional use of pottery which supposedly did not appear until the agricultural revolution in the Neolithic period some 12,000 years after the kilns at Dolni were last used.

Oh dear! Did we just stumble on something interesting? Didn't we just note that something happened to "cool" the steam of the cultural explosion of the Upper Paleolithic and that it happened about 12,000 years ago? And we noted that the Jomon culture "began" at about the same time. And here we note that the agricultural revolution occurred at about the same time as that "loss of creative vigor". Could the two have some connection?

In Bulgaria, a thousand miles to the east of Dolni Vestonice, there is a cave called Bacho Kiro. It is famous for containing the earliest known Aurignacian tool assemblages. They are 43,000 years old.

This brings us to another curious thing about Neanderthal man: he never seemed to go anywhere. He always made his tools out of what was locally available, and he never seemed to travel at all. What was made where it was made, stayed there. Nobody traded or shared among the Neanderthal groups. But it seems that right from the beginning, Cro-Magnon man was traveling and sharing and exchanging not only goods, but technology. If there was a better form of stone somewhere else, the word seemed to get around, and everybody had some of it. Distinctive flints from southern Poland are found at Dolni Vestonice, a hundred miles to the south. Slovakian radiolarite of red, yellow and olive is found a hundred miles to the east. Later in the Upper Paleolithic period, the famous "chocolate flint" of southern Poland is found over a radius of two hundred and fifty miles.[151] Naturally, these rocks didn't walk around on their own. Human legs carried them. And that leads us to our next little problem with Cro-Magnon man: You see, his legs were too long.

One of the sacred laws of evolutionary biology is called "Allen's Rule". This rule posits that legs, arms, ears, and other body extremities should be shorter in

---

[151] Shreeve, op. cit.

mammals that live in cold climates, and longer in mammals of the same period who live where it is hot. This is because having short arms and legs conserves heat. This is supposed to explain why Eskimos and Laplanders have short legs. It also is supposed to explain why Bantu people are leaner, and the Maasai are extremely long and lean in their tropical open country.

The only people who seem to be mocking Allen's rule are Cro-Magnon. They just refused to adapt. They all have much longer legs than they ought to. Of course, this is pounced upon as proof that they came from Africa. The only problem with this is that it is hard to imagine people from a warm climate migrating to a cold one by choice. Then, on top of that, to remain long-limbed for over a thousand generations? Keep in mind that, during that time, the thermometer kept going down and, at the glacial maximum, 18,000 years ago, it was like the North Pole in northern Europe! So how come they didn't adapt?

By whatever means they arrived in Europe, we ought to take note of the fact that their presence there may be related to the fact that Europe and other nearby locations are literally blanketed with megaliths. Indeed, it may be so that the megaliths came long after the appearance of Cro-Magnon man, but the connection ought not to be discarded without some consideration.

We have still another problem here, and it has to do with dating. Analyzing mitochondrial DNA data to reconstruct the demographic prehistory of Homo Sapiens reveals statistical evidence of explosive growth around 50,000 to 60,000 years ago. Is there a connection between this DNA evidence and the appearance of Cro-Magnon man? If so, it would mean that the DNA is dated to twice the age that archaeology confirms. Instead of assuming that the archaeological dates are correct, perhaps we ought to ask the question: could something be wrong with the dating? From a morphological point of view as well as judging by their industry and art, these highly evolved humans who coexisted with Neanderthal man represent a mutation so enormous and sudden as to be absurd in the context of evolutionary theory.

What in the world are we going to do with this problem? I could exhaustively describe the endless books and papers that seek to explain it away; to account for it, to marginalize it, and even ignore it. But at the end of it all, the fundamental problem still remains: a new kind of man appeared on the planet, seemingly from nowhere, and he was smart, artistic, and however he got here, he landed in a lot of places simultaneously.

Did I say "landed"?

Yes, I did. Am I suggesting that Cro-Magnon man was an alien? Not exactly. We still have to consider the mitochondrial DNA of Eve. I also haven't forgotten that annoying problem of the Asian vs. African origins of the "first mother" that has been so deftly dealt with by avoidance and non-answers. What do all of these factors, taken together, suggest? Well, any farmer can figure that one out: it suggests hybridization. But that would imply somebody doing the hybridizing.

Further, we might wish to make note of the range of this culture that suddenly dropped in on Europe: from Spain (and a small region of North Africa) to the Ural Mountains that are at the border of Central Asia.

The steppes of Central Asia, just north of Turkmenia, are a difficult environment for agriculture. Goats and sheep and cattle bones are found there that date to about

4000 BC. Later, the camel and horse came into use. These cultures spoke Indo-European languages and their members are believed to have been Caucasoid. There have been many theories that the Caucasoid nomads of the Central Asian steppes migrated to Europe. But, as we have seen, the initial migration *may have been from West to East*. The archaeological record is uncertain, and therefore the migrations of the Indo-Europeans (for so we may most assuredly call them) from the Asian steppes are no longer as clear in the minds of scholars as they once were.[152] The migrations into India and Pakistan, however, do seem to have some firmer foundation. These incursions were most likely from the Andronovo and Srubnaya cultures as the culture described in the oldest Aryan texts is very similar to that of the steppe nomads.

THE ROLE OF THE SHAMAN

With that idea, we come to some very interesting relationships that will go very far in providing clues to us in terms of asking some of the most interesting questions of all relating to our idea of the rites and myths of ancient man being the *disjecta membra* of a vanished civilization. Mircea Eliade writes:

> Recent researches have clearly brought out the "shamanic" elements in the religion of the Paleolithic hunters. Horst Kierchner has interpreted the celebrated relief at Lascaux as a representation of a shamanic trance.[...]

> Finally, Karl J. Narr has reconsidered the problem of the "origin" and chronology of shamanism in his important study.[153] He brings out the influence of notions of fertility (Venus statuettes) on the religious beliefs of the prehistoric North Asian hunters; but this influence did not disrupt the Paleolithic tradition.[...] it is in this "*Vorstellungswelt*" that the roots of the bear ceremonialism of Asia and North America lie. Soon afterward, probably about 25,000 BC, *Europe offers evidence for the earliest forms of shamanism* (Lascaux) with the plastic representations of the bird, the tutelary spirit, and ecstasy. [...]

> What appears to be certain is the antiquity of "shamanic" rituals and symbols. It remains to be determined whether these documents brought to light by prehistoric discoveries represent the first expressions of a shamanism *in statu nascendi* or are merely the earliest documents today available for *an earlier religious complex*, which, however, did not find "plastic" manifestations (drawings, ritual objects, etc) before the period of Lascaux.

> In accounting for the formation of the shamanic complex in Central and North Asia, we must keep in mind the two essential elements of the problem: on the one hand, the ecstatic experience as such, as a primary phenomenon; on the other, the

---

[152] Renfrew, 1973, 1987.

[153] Barenzeremoniell und Schauanismus in der Altern Steinzeit Europas.

historic-religious milieu into which this ecstatic experience was destined to be incorporated and the ideology that, in the last analysis, was to validate it. [...]

Everywhere in those lands, and from the earliest times, we find documents for the existence of a Supreme Being of *celestial structure*, who also corresponds morphologically to all the other Supreme Beings of the archaic religions. The symbolism of ascent, with all the rites and myths dependent on it, must be connected with celestial Supreme Beings; [...] This symbolism of ascent and "height" retains its value even after the "withdrawal" of the celestial Supreme Being — for, as is well known, Supreme Beings gradually lose their active place in the cult, giving way to religious forms that are more "dynamic" and "familiar" (the gods of storm[154] and fertility, demiurges, the souls of the dead, the Great Goddesses, etc.) [...]

The reduction or even the total loss in religious currency of Uranian Supreme Beings is sometimes indicated in myths concerning a primordial and paradisal time when *communications between heaven and earth were easy and accessible to everyone*; as the result of some happening, these communications were broken off and the Supreme Beings withdrew to the highest sky.[...]

The disappearance of the cult of the celestial Supreme Being did not nullify the symbolism of ascent with all its implication. [...]

The shamanic ecstasy could be considered a reactualization of the mythical *illud tempus* when men could communicate *in concreto* with the sky.

It is indubitable that the celestial ascent of the shaman is a survival, profoundly modified and sometimes degenerate, of this archaic religious ideology centered on *faith in a celestial Supreme Being and belief in concrete communications between heaven and earth.* [...]

The myths refer to more intimate relations between the Supreme Beings and shamans; in particular, they tell of a First Shaman, sent to earth by the Supreme Being or his surrogate to defend human beings against diseases and evil spirits.[155]

It was in the context of the "withdrawal" of the "Celestial Being" that the meaning of the shaman's ecstatic experience changed. Formerly, the activity was focused on *communing with the god and obtaining benefits for the tribe*. The shift of the function of the shaman associated with the withdrawal of the benevolent god/goddess was to "battling with evil spirits and disease". This is a sharp reminder of the work of Jesus, healing the sick and casting out demons - the shamanic exemplar "after the Fall".

There was, it seems, another consequence of this "shift". Increasingly, the descents into the "underworld" and the relations with "spirits" led to their

---

[154] Such as Yahweh.

[155] Eliade, Mircea, Shamanism, Archaic Techniques of Ecstasy, pp. 503-506.

"embodiment" or in the shaman's being "possessed" by "spirits". What is clear is that these were *innovations*, most of them recent. What is particularly striking in the research of the historiographers of myth, legend, shamanism, etc, is the discovery of the *"influences from the south, which appeared quite early and which altered both cosmology and the mythology and techniques of ecstasy"*. Among these southern influences were the contribution of Buddhism and Lamaism, added to the Iranian and, in the last analysis, Mesopotamian influences that preceded them.[156] Eliade writes:

> The initiatory schema of the shaman's ritual death and resurrection is likewise an innovation, but one that goes back to much earlier times; in any case, it cannot be ascribed to influences from the ancient Near East. But the innovations introduced by the ancestor cult particularly affected the structure of this initiatory schema. The very concept of *mystical death* was altered by the many and various religious changes effected by lunar mythologies, the cult of the dead, and the elaboration of magical ideologies.
>
> Hence we must conceive of Asiatic shamanism as an archaic technique of
>
> ecstasy whose *original underlying ideology* — belief in a celestial Supreme Being with whom it was possible to have *direct relations* by ascending into the sky — was constantly being transformed by an ongoing series of exotic contributions culminating in the invasion of Buddhism. [...]
>
> The phenomenology of the trance underwent many changes and corruptions, due in large part to *confusion as to the precise nature of ecstasy*. Yet all these innovations and corruptions did not succeed in eliminating the possibility of the true shamanic ecstasy.
>
> More than once we have discerned in the shamanic experience a "nostalgia for paradise" that suggests one of the oldest types of Christian mystical experience. As for the "inner light", which plays a part of the first importance in Indian mysticism and metaphysics as well as in Christian mystical theology, it is already documented in shamanism..[157]

What seems to be most important about Central Asian shamanism in the history of mysticism is the role the shaman plays in the *defense* of the psychic integrity of the community. Shamans are pre-eminently *the anti-demonic champions*; they combat not only demons and disease, but also the black magicians. The shaman is the tireless slayer of demons and dragons. And here we find explication of the "military" elements of the Grail Ensemble. The Sword in the Stone that can only be withdrawn by the "Heir", or the "Desired Knight", was represented in the

---

[156] For example, the co-opting and corruption of the Tree of Life symbolism by Judaism with complete loss of its true function.

[157] Ibid., pp. 506-508.

Steppe shamanic regalia as lance, cuirass, bow, sword, etc. These are accounted for in our study by virtue of the requirements of war against the demons, the true enemies of humanity. As Eliade points out, the shaman defends life, health, fertility, the world of "light", against death, diseases, sterility, disaster, and the world of "darkness". In short, the Shaman is a very early "type" of the Knight on the Quest for the Holy Grail - the Shamanic ascent to the Celestial Spheres.

We see that what is *fundamental and universal* to the shaman, to the heroes of myth, to the Quest for the Holy Grail, is the shaman's *struggle against what we could call "the powers of evil"*. The knight/shaman's essential role in the defense of the psychic integrity of the community depends above all on this: men are sure that one of them is able to help them in the critical circumstances produced by the *inhabitants of the invisible world.* Here we come to a crucial characteristic of the knight/shaman: he must be able to SEE *what is hidden and invisible* to the rest and to bring back direct and reliable information from the supernatural worlds. In short, in the accounts of shamanic ecstasies, we find correspondence to the themes of the great epics in oral literature. The knight/shaman's adventures in the other world, the ordeals and tests that he undergoes in his ecstatic descents below and ascents to the sky, describe in every detail the adventures of the figures in popular tales and the heroes of epic myths. This suggests that many epic "subjects" or motifs, as well as many characters, images, and clichés of these tales, are of ecstatic, or even other-worldly origin in the sense of interactions with hyper-dimensional realities.

TYING IT ALL TOGETHER

Here we may have found the essential key to the mystery of the Holy Grail, the Ark of the Covenant and Noah's Ark. We may even have, in a sense, found Arthur and Perceval of the Grail stories: the "Desired Knight" raised in obscurity, to discover that he is the "rightful heir" who can unlock DNA potential and achieve the shamanic ascent, or the Alchemical Transformation, and can remove the sword from the stone and defend the community against "sickness and demons" of an "otherworldly" nature.

Thus it is that we may find that our religious myths and rites are remnants of narratives – a message in a bottle - designed to explain these phenomena, and that the monotheistic versions, declaring a Final End, or a Judgment Day of a final end, are merely distortions of the myth designed to establish a Control System on our planet. These distortions are beneficial to those who seek power and wealth, who are under the control of archetypal forces of another realm of which our own reality is but a shadow or a reflection. Let me reiterate: I do not mean, here, to suggest that this other realm is "astral" or ephemeral or non-material. I am suggesting that it is an intermediate realm of para-physical, hyper-dimensional beings whose existence and nature has been carefully concealed from us for millennia – for a reason that is not to our benefit. And this leads us to another exemplar of the "primordial myth", Orion.

ORION, THE ARK AND THE HOLY GRAIL

The first question the reader might ask: What does Orion have to do with Noah's Ark and the Grail Quest? A great deal, I think. The similarities between the stories are many, the most evident being the theme of the prior "Golden Age" that was lost - as well as HOW it was lost. According to Edith Hamilton, the story of Orion goes like this:

> He was a young man of gigantic stature and great beauty, and a mighty hunter. He fell in love with the daughter of the King of Chios, and for love of her he cleared the island of wild beasts. The spoils of the chase he brought always home to his beloved, whose name is sometimes said to be Aero, sometimes Merope (one of the Pleiades). Her father, Oenopion, agreed to give her to Orion, but he kept putting the marriage off. One day when Orion was drunk he insulted the maiden, and Oenopion appealed to Dionysus to punish him. The god threw him into a deep sleep and Oenopion blinded him. An oracle told him, however, that he would be able to see again if he went to the east and let the rays of the rising sun fall on his eyes. He went as far east as Lemnos and there he recovered his sight.[158]

Other ancient sources suggest that the real reason for the attack upon Orion was due to the fact that his beloved's father, King Oenopion, a son of Ariadne and Dionysus, plotted against him. He was *tricked* into getting drunk, the same way Osiris (another variation on the story) was tricked into getting into a coffin, and as he slept, men fell upon him, put out his eyes, and then carried him to a beach and cast him there. Hephaestus - the Fire god - gave him his servant Cedalion to serve him as a guide. Orion set him on his shoulders and asked him to give directions to the sunrise, and when they arrived Orion was healed by the sun's rays.

The similarity to the story of Samson is evident. He, too, was deprived of his strength while sleeping, his eyes were put out, and he was put to work turning a millstone. In an encounter with the Pharisees, Jesus mentions the "strong man" who had been "bound" in an obvious allusion to the legend of Orion. What is interesting about it is the context in which this story was told:

> Then a blind and dumb man, *under the power of a demon*, was brought to Jesus, and He cured him, so that the blind and dumb man both spoke and saw. ... But the Pharisees hearing it said, This Man drives out demons only by and with the help of Beelzebub, the prince of demons. And knowing their thoughts, He said to them, Any kingdom that is divided against itself is being brought to desolation and laid waste, and no city or house divided against itself will last or continue to stand. And if Satan drives out Satan, he has become divided against himself and disunited; how then will his kingdom last or continue to stand? And if I drive out the demons by Beelzebub by whose help do your sons drive them out? ... Or how can a person go into a strong man's house and carry off his goods without first binding the strong man? Then indeed he may plunder his house. ... Either make the tree sound, and its

---

[158] Hamilton, Edith, *Mythology* (New York: New American Library 1942).

fruit sound, or make the tree rotten and its fruit rotten; for the tree is known and recognized and judged by its fruit.[159]

In the above story, being "blind and dumb" was compared to being a strong man who was bound, and who then was subjected to having all his goods stolen. As in the story of Orion (where he was tricked into becoming drunk), and in the story of Samson, (in which the sleeping man was deprived of his vigor represented by his hair), the condition of being "bound" or blind and dumb is attributed by Jesus to "demons".[160] Another interesting side reference in the New Testament is a remark Jesus made about the "blind leading the blind" and both of them falling into the ditch. This seems to be another reference to the story of Orion with Cedalion on his shoulders giving instructions. This event can also be related to the story of the Prodigal son who, when a famine came upon the land, asked a "resident of the far country" for help, who then sent him to live and eat with the pigs.

THE RELEVANCE OF ORION TO OUR SITUATION

The astute reader may note that it's a little bit curious that *deafness* was omitted from the condition of being bound. Being healed of deafness as a condition of becoming free is conspicuous by its absence in this story. The fact is, as we will discover in the course of our investigations, most of the distortions of our reality come to us by listening rather than observing. Deception and errors of perception would have far less influence on us, and we would have fewer illusions, if we would look at the face value of objects and see things for what they really are instead of allowing ourselves to be hypnotized by "experts" who have a vested interest in concealing the truth - the blind leading the blind. Most of mankind's illusions are the "children of the ear" and hearsay. My beloved grandmother always told me to, "believe none of what you hear and only half of what you see". This is very good advice. If we open our eyes and look at a problem as objectively as we can, forgetting all our beliefs and assumptions, and all the things we have been "told", we might be able to see *what is,* and if we then apply our minds to what we see, we might be able to draw some accurate conclusions.

It's easy to look back on history and see where this or that group was "misled" in their beliefs and this distorted their thinking, which then led them to perpetrate unspeakable horrors. We can point to the genocide advocated by the God of the Hebrews, whether it was actually committed or not, or the religious-zeal-run-amok

---

[159] *The Bible*, Matthew 12:22-33.

[160] The main point that Jesus was trying to make, of course, was that "If Satan drives out Satan, he has become divided against himself and disunited: how then will his kingdom last or continue to stand?" Jesus was pointing out to the Pharisees that it was completely illogical to accuse him of working in concert with darkness since the effect of his work was to free the man of his demonic attack which enabled him to both see and speak.

of the Catholic church when it instituted the Inquisition and the Crusades. We can see the twisted version of the desire to create a "genetic superman" that led to the holocaust. It's easy to discern these errors of the past, because we "know more now".

We *know* more now. How much more can we learn? Can we be certain that the current beliefs of our reality are not similar manipulations? How much more will we know in the future about our own present situation? Do we have any clues around us pointing out that something is dreadfully amiss as were present in the years preceding the Holocaust? How many people at that time ignored all the warning signs until it was too late? How many people didn't "get it" until they were bombed back to the Stone Age? Can we compare any of our present reality to such a scenario? After all, a smart man learns from his mistakes; a genius learns from the mistakes of others.

At the present time, there are, indeed, indicators that we are being maneuvered into a certain mind-set, a certain belief system. The "reality game" has just gotten more and more complex, but the same essential errors keep getting repeated. What is at the root? Will our descendants look back on our own time and shake their heads in dismay at how ignorant we were, how manipulated our thinking was, and how great an error we made because of our beliefs? As the reader will discover, it seems that we are presently facing just such a grand illusion; one that may be the grandest of them all, and if we do not find our way to the light whereby our eyes can be healed, we shall be, indeed, the householder who lost all he possessed because he was bound and blinded by "demons". And if we are blind, and follow the blind, we will most certainly all fall into a pit; one that we may not be able to get out of for a very long time.

We know that this question, "why is life the way it is?" is one that we don't like to face. But, when we awaken late at night, alone in our thoughts, with no distractions of daily life to fill the void, we are face to face with our existential dilemma. And it is a terrible silence. In those moments of cold clarity, the bleakness and futility of our existence in cosmic terms rises up to confront us as it has confronted all of humanity throughout millennia.

Looking back at history, we see that, to escape this monstrous "dark night of the soul", human beings will accept any answer—any religious belief or philosophy— that may be offered, because the cold, abyssal silence that follows the question must be filled at any cost. The sad fact is, there are plenty of people willing to try to convince us that they have "the answer to all our questions". These blind leading the blind can be found in the pulpits of nearly every church across the land, and in the seminars and lecture circuit of the New Age. But, these answers generally consist of confusing the discernment of reality with personal opinion which results in a judgment upon reality by refusing to acknowledge it as it really is. Those parts of reality that are not acknowledged have a way of biting us. "Those who do not learn from history are doomed to repeat it."

At the present moment in history, it seems that everybody and his brother are either looking for King Arthur and the Holy Grail, or are waiting for aliens to land on the White House lawn so they can kick the tires of the UFO Cadillac. I have hundreds of books on these subjects, and over two dozen recent books, all of which claim to have discovered that the two subjects overlap and that the Holy

Grail is really a bloodline, and that this bloodline of "special people" are offspring of alien beings, alternatively good guys or bad guys, depending on the orientation of the writer.

Most of the conclusions of the current raft of alternative researchers point to aliens from Mars having come to earth in the distant past, and that they are the real "Gods". The current fad of focus on the pyramids and the sphinx have led them all to conclude that the root of all of this is the great mysteries of Egypt - that the Egyptian gods are the original and true "gods". They declared to be advanced and superior beings from the "stars", i.e. Mars, and they originally had a great civilization there that was destroyed, and they came to earth and gave impetus to the formation of our own early civilizations.

The stories then sort of bifurcate between these gods being truly physical as humans are, or being "Neters" or principles, as in purely ethereal beings who occasionally deign to manifest on earth.

Meanwhile, the opposing parties often declare the "Serpent race" to be representative of a benevolent scaly gang of civilizers who have humanity's best interests at heart, as in Arthur C. Clarke's *Childhood's End*. This group promotes a reptilian bloodline of Christ, and proposes that a descendant of this line is going to come along, a New Christ, who will lead us all to true enlightenment if we prepare ourselves according to any number of bizarre proposals. This group tends to see the alleged hyperdimensional Reptilian race as physical like us and not, as we suggest, hyperdimensional creatures of variable physicality. Still other groups tell us that these reptilians are purely demonic, ethereal beings, who can "descend" into a person, or a human being can "host" a reptilian and "shape-shift" into this form (only if they have the genetics, mind you), and become temporarily reptilian themselves. The Queen of England and many of the leaders of the world have been listed as being of this latter type, with tales spun around them that pass the bounds of bizarre into lunacy.

There are any numbers of variations on these themes, with just about every preferred belief system from A to Z represented. In all cases, they have the chief feature of designation of this or that group of physical human beings as conspirators or guardians, (Masons, Rosicrucians, Templars, Illuminati, take your pick), or a strict ethereal conception of the conspirators or guardians. In the first case, humanity is divided into "good guys" and "bad guys". In the second case, people are encouraged to place their faith in the "ethereal good guys", in order to be saved from the "ethereal bad guys".

At the end of it all, as noted above, there is the strangest thing I have ever observed: they all seem to be focused, in one way or another, on "finding the Holy Grail". Just as Hitler was obsessed with discovery of some material object that would give him total and complete power over all the world, so do these different groups have a similar objective in mind: discover the Grail!

I thought about this for a long time. Why in the world is there this obsessive concentration on Reptilian beings and the Holy Grail? Is it a distraction, or is it an agenda? If it is either, what is driving it? I realized that the only way to come to any ideas about it would be to investigate the matter carefully.

The first thing we notice in undertaking such a study is that, in the minds of these individuals, identifying Arthur seems to be the prerequisite for discovering the grail itself. The theory seems to be that if you can figure out who Arthur really was, then you might be able to track his movements in history and discover the hiding place of this great object of power. In the numerous books I have on King Arthur, each one claims to have the one and only answer as to who he was and when he lived and where. Most of them are quite convincing with careful research and scholarship. And they all have a slightly different answer.

Does this mean that no actual object—such as the Holy Grail or the Ark of the Covenant, which, by the way, seem to often be confused as one and the same "item"—does not exist? My personal opinion is that, yes, it is possible that there is an "object of power". But based on the frantic searching going on, either it was lost, or it was hidden, and it seems that even the hyperdimensional beings are helpless to find it. Assuming, for the sake of the hypothesis we are playing with, that this is true, my theory is that they cannot SEE it because it is "occluded" by a frequency that is impenetrable to them for some reason. In fact, this idea seems to be another key element of the Grail Stories - the theme of the Sword in the Stone. Only the Heir can withdraw it and wield it. And so, the current craze for "finding the grail" seems to be promoted by those who are anxious to find this object in hopes that the "right person" will discover it and lead them to it.

FROM SCYTHIA TO CAMELOT

The important point at the moment regarding "Who is Arthur" is that it seems that the Arthur of the Grail Quest is not, in a certain sense, a real flesh and blood man, but is rather an archetypal complex of images. Arthur is other and more than the sum of his appearances in literature, and he is present in myths, stories and images that have NO direct mention of him. Arthur is present in the myths of all the sacrificial kings, dying saviors, and heroic slayers of dragons from time immemorial. His story grows with every episode we study, and after a time, we realize that Arthur, himself, is *only a clue*.

Orion, Arthur, Arca, Arcadia (Ark of God), Ark are all clues to the mythology of Fall and Redemption: The Once and Future King. He is the symbol of the Lost Eden and the New Jerusalem, the antediluvian world and the passage to the post-flood reality. His story has branches that reach out to embrace all the ideas of cyclical changes and all attempts to exert power over the environment as opposed to interacting *with* Nature.

There are two books out of this entire morass that I consider to be outstanding in terms of combining scholarship with thinking "out of the box". The first one is *From Scythia to Camelot: A Radical Reassessment of the Legends of King Arthur,* etc., by C. Scott Littleton and Linda A. Malcor, and *The Keys to Avalon: The True Location of Arthur's Kingdom Revealed*, by Steve Blake and Scott Lloyd.

Scott Littleton and Linda Malcor made the serendipitous discovery of the parallels between the stories of King Arthur and the Ossetian saga of Batraz which has enabled a major leap in understanding the origins of the themes, and we hope to develop it further here. According to Littleton and Malcor, a fellow scholar, J. P. Mallory, told them that at the end of the Marcomannian War in the year 175 AD, the Roman emperor Marcus Aurelius sent a contingent of 5,500 Sarmatian cataphracti[161] from Pannonia to Britain. Their descendants survived as an identifiable ethnic group into the fourth century and possibly longer. It was, as Littleton and Malcor put it, just an "interesting bit of trivia" gleaned from Tadeusz Sulimirski's book *The Sarmatians*.

Sarmatians are a sub-group of Scythians, and the term "Scythian" can mean either the ancient Scythian tribes described by Herodotus, or, in the larger sense, it can apply to all of the Northeast Iranian steppe peoples. The Scythians of antiquity, and their cousins, the Sarmatians and Alans, were nomads of the Central Asian steppes. At the time of their greatest manifestation on the stage of history, the tribes extended from Hungary to China. These Scythians were big, blond and blue-eyed, and based on the accounts that have come down to us, and archaeological findings, their nomadic culture has *sharp parallels with the most ancient occupants of Europe.*

At the end of the classical period, these steppe dwellers had been driven to the edges of their homeland by the Altaic speakers, the Huns and Turks. Some migrated to Afghanistan, eastern Iran, western India, and others invaded the Roman Empire as either conquerors or supporting mercenaries. Many of them migrated into Britain, Italy, France, Spain and North Africa. Others retreated into Poland, European Russia and the Caucasus. The assumption has been that the Scythians, the sub-tribes of Iazyge[162] Sarmatians, Alans, etc, vanished without a trace. But that is not, apparently, the case. It seems clear, upon reviewing the evidence, that the steppe dwellers became the aristocracy of Europe. According to Littleton and Malcor, another group of the Alani retreated into the Caucasus and survived as an ethnic group called the Ossetes, or Ossetians, in what is now known as the Republic of Georgia.

The Holy Grail was the chief concern of the Alans who settled in Gaul and Spain in the fifth century. They were tall, blonde and good looking, and lived a nomadic life in wagons. Their main claim to fame was their skill as horsemen. The Scythians (including the Alans) were referred to as Goths, and the one thing they all had in common was their extraordinary art. They assimilated into the territories they finally settled in, intermarrying with the Romans and other indigenous

---

[161] Cavalry, mounted soldiers.

[162] The name "Jadczyk" is a "Polish-ized" variation of Iazyge.

people. The name "Alan" and "Goar" are common among these groups, being passed down from generation to generation.

In addition to becoming the rootstock of most of the nobility of Europe, the Alans introduced the steppe pony and the Alan hunting dog. They introduced chain mail and the customs that were later to become Norman and Breton chivalry, and above all, let it be repeated, their natural home was on the back of a horse. Alienor of Aquitaine was undoubtedly a descendant of the Alani and the Nart sagas were a natural part of her heritage, becoming the foundation for the Grail stories written and promulgated through her "courts of love" after Geoffrey of Monmouth created the "history of Arthur".

> In the Latin chronicle *Draco Normannicus*, by Etienne de Rouen (1169); Arthur is still alive in the twelfth century. He exchanges letters with Henry II in which the monarchs discuss the sovereignty of Brittany, but he allows Henry to claim the feudal rights to the land *as his vassal*. This seems to reflect the Alanic attitude toward other rulers on the Continent from Gallo-Roman times on: allowing Roman, Merovingian, Carolingian, French and even British kings to rule over them while seeing themselves as having ultimate control *over the land*.[163]

In the Nart Sagas, the prototype of the grail cup is a large, magical vessel that appears at the banquets of the Narts, never runs dry, and magically rises to the lips of the hero who is without blemish. In other words, *it chose its own guardian.* The Grail legends tell of a special family that is intimately connected to the fertility of the land, from which is born a preeminent hero who becomes the sovereign of the Grail Castle and the guardian of the Grail. This grail cup of the Narts is also a "lie detector". It would magically float to the lips of the man who was telling the truth.

We see, of course, that there does not seem to be any particular "Christian" connection here, such as the Holy Grail being the cup of the Last Supper or whatnot. The *Nartamongae*, as it is called, is a purely pagan symbol. In the archaeological sites associated with the Sarmatians in southern Russia, cauldrons are found almost exclusively *in the graves of women*. In the Arthurian legends, the cup is almost always borne by a woman. In the Scythian origin myth, *a cup falls from the sky* and is recovered by Kolaxais, the youngest son of the primeval being Targitaos. *The cup is the prime symbol of sovereignty, and he who possesses it is established in his royal lineage.*

Following the connection between the saga of Batraz and the Narts and Arthur and the knights of the round table, Littleton remembered a passage in Dio Cassius's *Roman History,* written in 225 AD, where it is revealed that at the end of the Marcomannian war, 8,000 cataphracti from a Sarmatian tribe known as the Iazyges, were impressed into the Roman legions. Of these, 5,500 of them were sent to Britain. The Iazygian auxiliaries were posted in groups of five hundred to

---

[163] Littleton & Malcor, *From Scythia to Camelot* (New York: Garland 1994) p. 37.

the garrisons along Hadrian's Wall. When their period of service was up, they were settled into a veteran's colony at *Bremetennacum Veteranorum* near the modern village of Ribchester. What is most fascinating is that their first commander was a Roman officer named Lucius Artorius Castus, prefect of the VI legion Victrix. It seems that the Iazyges were conscripted into the Roman army, and riding under their own banner of the flying dragon, the Sarmatians must have been an impressive sight. Imagine 5,500 men with their thousands of horses and long baggage trains, making their way across Europe from the Hungarian plain to the shores of the Channel. Caesar himself had invaded with only 400 cavalry and word of the coming of the tall, fair horse warriors must have spread like wildfire across Britain.

As Littleton and Malcor demonstrate in their well-reasoned work, it seems that the 12 victories attributed to "Arthur" by Nennius and others, including the famous one at Badon Hill, which are conventionally dated to the early sixth century AD, may actually have belonged to Lucius Artorius Castus, won *between 183-185 AD in Northern Britain.*

There does not seem to be any evidence that the Iazyge women accompanied their men to Britain. There have been no traces found of Sarmatian jewelry, make-up, mirrors or anything of what could be considered evidence of Sarmatian femininity in the remains of Roman forts, settlements or graveyards in Britain. This means that it is very likely that they married local women and remained in Britain when their term of service was over.

By the beginning of the third century, with 5,500 Sarmatians having been stationed in northern England, it is certain that the skills, talents, ideas, beliefs and legends of the steppe peoples were being told and re-told, including their belief in the divine sword as war-god, worshiped by being thrust into and withdrawn from the ground. The divine sword was another potent and central symbol to the Sarmatians, so it is no surprise that it has come down to us as a central theme of the Arthurian saga - the "sword in the stone" motif. As the Sarmatians settled down and learned to speak the local Celtic dialect with their new womenfolk and children, it seems only natural that the great magical deeds of their own heroes, ancestors and deities would spread among this new hybrid population.

In 460 AD, Cunedda of the Votadini tribe was invited into North Wales to help expel the Irish. The Votadini came from the northeast of England; their capital was probably near Bamburgh, curiously close to the seat of the great Percy family, Alnwick, and in the region of the Parisi Celts - both interesting homonymic clues to the name Percival of Grail fame.

During the time Britain had been under Roman rule, the Votadini had acted as a police force for the Romans protecting their northern frontier. But they had suffered since the Roman withdrawal. From the north they were under threat from the Picts, from the west, the Irish, and from the east, the Angles. It is believed that they colonized northwest Wales. This theory is strengthened by the finding of distinctive Votadini pottery in Gwynedd dating from this period. It was at this point that the "dragon banner" became part of the Welsh culture, which suggests a blending of the Celtic Welsh and a Votadini-Sarmatian culture.

Thus we see a possible chain of evidence for the bringing of the stories to Wales at this point, along with heroic figures that were then assimilated to the mythical archetype, no matter what their actual deeds were. This must have been the moment in which the Welsh prototype, a blending of Celtic and Sarmatian imagery took place, during a period of turmoil and crisis.

Blake and Lloyd establish, with great clarity, that the *written* historical material drawn on by Geoffrey was, in fact, *a body of Welsh stories* - which were probably Sarmatian stories before they were Welsh - based upon real people whose histories and geography match the particulars so completely that there is little doubt left that Geoffrey was "reinventing Arthur" to suit contemporary agendas. In point of fact, as Blake and Lloyd show, Geoffrey's account was merely the first step in hijacking the Welsh prototype that has been followed ever since. The primary question asked by Blake and Lloyd is: where did Geoffrey get his materials? And they carefully and thoroughly demonstrate that they came from Wales, known originally as "Brittania".

> In the 12th century "Britannia" did not denote the whole of Great Britain, as we know it today but referred specifically to Wales. This raised a crucial question: if Britannia was the Latin name for Wales, what had been the original Latin name for England? ... We found the answer to this in the 12th century book of Llandaff, where the name of the land that bordered Britannia was given on more than one occasion: "The borders of Britannia and Anglia towards Hereford... From both parts of Anglia and Britannia... Anglia."[164]

Because of Geoffrey's spin on the stories, many researchers have come to the idea that a mysterious and shadowy "Riothamus" is *the* "Historical Arthur". Indeed, letters from Sidonius to Riothamus still survive and, according to Geoffrey of Monmouth, Arthur's antagonist during a continental invasion was "Leo, emperor of Rome". As it happens, the *eastern* Roman emperor at the time of Riothamus was Leo I, supported by the Alanic general Aspar. Leo appointed a *Byzantine* noble, Anthemius, to negotiate a British alliance in 467, which brought Riothamus, "king of the Britons", to Gaul in 468. Riothamus and his 12,000 troops fought a series of battles on the Continent, moving right into the region where the Lancelot legends are set. Sidonius' letter was an appeal to Riothamus to stop enticing away the slaves of a local landowner. Gaul's Imperial prefect called on Euric, King of the Visigoths, to crush Riothamus. The *Chronicles of Anjou* say that Arthur's betrayer was Morvandus, which is very likely a combination of the name of the traditional betrayer of Arthur, Mordred, and the real name of the prefect, Arvandus. There is no record of Riothamus's death, but the last mention of him has him moving toward a town called Avallon. Thus, Geoffrey Ashe proposes Riothamus as the "real" Arthur.

However, as Littleton and Malcor, Blake and Lloyd demonstrate, this Riothamus was a Johnny-come-lately to the archetypal assimilation process!

---

[164] Blake and Lloyd, *The Keys to Avalon*, (Shaftesbury, Dorset: Element Books 2000) p. 14.

Descendants of the Iazyges in Britain may have been among the troops of this Riothamus, and very likely, many of them never returned to Britain, and their legends of Arthur, assimilating their lost leader Riothamus, mixed with the variations on the Nart sagas brought to Gaul by the Alans, combined to form the corpus of the Arthurian tradition born in France.

What is of particular interest is the identity of the original Celtic Welsh, or Britons, who had earlier retreated defensively into Wales. As the Anglo-Saxons invaded and moved further west, many of the Britons fled the country to settle in Normandy.

Gildas, writing in the sixth century AD, is the first native British writer whose works have come down to us. Nennius, writing about 200 years later, refers to "the traditions of our elders". And Geoffrey of Monmouth praises the works of Gildas and Bede and wonders at the lack of other works about the early kings of Britain saying:

> "Yet the deeds of these men were such that they deserve to be praised for all time. What is more, these deeds were handed joyfully down in oral tradition, just as if they had been committed to writing, by many peoples who had only their memory to rely on."[165]

In describing the fifty or so years preceding his account of Arthur, Geoffrey of Monmouth tells us about Vortigern and the arrival of the Saxons under the leadership of Hengest and Horsa, an obvious assimilation of the earlier arrival of the Votadini and Sarmatians to Wales to drive out the Irish. Present throughout these events is the presence of Merlin - the British equivalent of Hiram Abiff - and Daedalus combined: the great architect of the temple.

What we are interested in is the fact that *Merlin was credited with building Stonehenge*. For some reason, based on the "oral tradition", Geoffrey of Monmouth connected the mysterious and legendary figure of Merlin to the prehistoric monument on the Salisbury plain. The question then is not about the accuracy of Geoffrey's history, but why he made this connection? Was it based on stories in the traditions that he had mentioned and considered to be reliable? *Traditions that predated the arrival of the Sarmatians?*

The Stonehenge story told by Geoffrey of Monmouth begins with a treacherous massacre of the Britons by Hengest and his Saxons, which took place at a peace conference. The Saxons hid their daggers in their shoes and, at a signal from their leader, drew them and killed all the assembled British nobles except the king. Geoffrey tells us that the meeting took place at the "Cloister of Ambrius, not far from Kaercaradduc, which is now called Salisbury". He later describes this as a monastery of three hundred brethren founded by Ambrius many years before.

---

[165] Geoffrey of Monmouth, *The History of the Kings of Britain*, translated by Lewis Thorpe, 1966, p. 1.

As it happens, there is a place called Amesbury about two and a half miles east of Stonehenge, which was originally called Ambresbyrig. This site in no way matches the description of the Cloister of Ambrius. The cloister is described as situated on Mount Ambrius, whereas Amesbury is in the valley of the river Avon. Geoffrey tells us that the victims of the massacre were buried in the cemetery beside the monastery, not two and a half miles away. What is more, since it seems that Geoffrey was acting under the pressure of the mythical norm of assimilating current events to the archetype, we then are left free to consider the possibility that this was the site of an ancient and famous massacre and that Stonehenge and the Cloister of Ambrius are one and the same.

The fact that Geoffrey called it a "cloister" is a curious choice of words since a cloister is "a covered arcade forming part of a religious or collegiate establishment". That certainly seems to describe Stonehenge very well. Geoffrey was obviously trying to "Christianize" Stonehenge in his references to monastery and monks. The Saxons gave Stonehenge the name by which we know it today. The Britons called it the *Giant's Dance*, and Geoffrey certainly had a tradition to draw on there if he had wanted to since he begins his history with the adventures of Brutus, a descendant of Aeneas, who, after much traveling and fighting, landed on Britain, which was uninhabited *except for a few giants*. Geoffrey had a reasonable context here in which to place Stonehenge, but he ignored it and instead attributed the building of Stonehenge to Merlin after the dreadful massacre by the Saxons. This enabled him to connect his Arthur to the great architect of the monument and all its glories. This suggests to us that there was a solid tradition behind this idea: that Stonehenge was the focal point of a people who had suffered a terrible, terminal disaster; after the disaster they had built Stonehenge, and the stones themselves had magical properties that could heal. In short, this tradition may reach back into the mists of antiquity.

In Geoffrey's story, Merlin suggests to Aurelius that he ought to send an expedition to Ireland to fetch the Giant's Ring from Mount Killaraus. The King begins to laugh and asks:

"How can such large stones be moved from so far-distant a country?" he asked. "It is hardly as if Britain itself is lacking in stones big enough for the job!"

"Try not to laugh in a foolish way, your Majesty," answered Merlin. "What I am suggesting has nothing ludicrous about it. These stones are connected with certain secret religious rites and they have various properties that are medicinally important. Many years ago the Giants transported them from the remotest confines of Africa and set them up in Ireland at a time when they inhabited that country. Their plan was that, whenever they felt ill, baths should be prepared at the foot of the stones; for they used to pour water over them and to run this water into baths in which their sick were cured. What is more, they mixed the water with herbal concoctions and so healed their wounds. There is not a single stone among them which hasn't some medicinal value."[166]

As W. A. Cummins, geologist and archaeologist remarks, all of this sounds like a pre-medieval tradition about Stonehenge, possibly even prehistoric. However, instead of coming from Africa, or even Ireland, the bluestones used in the construction of Stonehenge come from the Prescelly Mountains, or Mynydd Preselau. The so-called "altar stone", however, most likely came from somewhere in the Milford Haven area in Pembrokeshire. Cummins asks:

1. Why did the builders of Stonehenge go all the way to Mynydd Preselau for the bluestones, when there were perfectly satisfactory stones to be had much nearer home?

2. Why if their main source of bluestones was Mynydd Preselau, did they also bring a single huge block for micaceous sandstone (the Altar Stone), which quite certainly did not come from that area?[167]

Cummins remarks astutely that Geoffrey was eight and a half centuries closer to the event than we are, so maybe his account is correspondingly closer? In these few remarks by Geoffrey of Monmouth, referring to the Cloisters of Ambrius, and "baths" at the "foot of the stones", we find a possible hidden connection between the Cauldron of rebirth, the Holy Grail, and Stonehenge. Merlin's explanation of the importance of the stones as reported in Geoffrey's history, is that they were connected to "secret religious rites" that he further explains have to do with "magical healing properties", an interesting juxtaposition of "stones" and a sort of "elixir of life".

There is a very ancient Celtic tradition about cauldrons of rebirth, into which wounded, dead or dying soldiers were plunged, and came out healed, whole and reborn. The Holy Grail also bestowed health, healing of battle wounds, and curing of disease upon its bearers. The Celtic cauldrons were also sources of abundance, prophecy, inspiration, and knowledge. Cerridwen, the Welsh Moon Goddess, had a magic cauldron of inspiration. Welsh Bards called themselves Cerddorion (sons of Cerridwen). The Bard Taliesin, founder of their craft, was said to be born of Cerridwen and to have tasted her potion known as "greal", made from six plants for inspiration and knowledge. Branwen, the sister of Bran the Blessed, was the "Lady of the Cauldron", as well as the Lady of the Lake. In short, the "Lake" from which the famous Sword emerged, and to which it was returned, was a Cauldron, or the Holy Grail.

---

[166] Ibid., p. 139.

[167] Cummins, W. A., *King Arthur's Place in Pre-history*, (Surrey: Bramley Books 1992) p. 64.

CHAPTER 8
THE CULTURE OF STONES

MAGIC AND MEGALITHS

We want to turn back now to the many sculptures of female goddesses found in the most ancient archaeological levels. According to the experts, the discernible idea of the religion of the goddess is that of *an infinite bounty of the Great Mother*. It is proposed that such peoples didn't engage in agriculture because the idea of "owning land" may have been abhorrent to them. The idea of "forcing" the earth to yield, rather than accepting the natural abundance the Goddess provided was simply not a part of their philosophy. Their Goddess was a *Star Being,* and she was worshipped in outdoor Temples that were laid out along *Celestial Archetypes*.

But it may be that "worshipping the goddess" in the terms we understand worship was not precisely what was going on in these temples. Why do I say this? Well, because there was something else VERY mysterious about these ancient peoples - they seem to have had "super powers". In a previous chapter, we looked at Dr. Robert Schoch's work on the underwater pyramids off Japan known as the Yonaguni Monuments. Schoch noted the odd fact that there were no "quarry marks" on the stones of the underwater structure. From this, he concluded that they couldn't be manmade. But he ought to have considered other great stone cities where there is often a similar lack of evidence of our present quarrying technology. Morris Jessup wrote extensively about the megalithic structures in his book *The Case for the UFO*, concluding that, based on his own knowledge and experience, many of them seemed to have been fitted by a process of "grinding *in situ*". This, of course, would necessitate a means of handling stone that is completely outside the range of our present understanding. He then makes a remarkable observation:

> It may be that this tremendous power was limited in its application to articles of stone texture only, but this is a little doubtful. Or, perhaps it was limited to nonmagnetic materials in general. Such a limitation would have sidetracked the development of a mechanized culture such as ours of this day, and would partly

account for the strange fact that almost all relics of the profound past are non-metallic.[168]

It is a fact that the Earth is literally blanketed with megaliths from some ancient civilization. Tens of thousands of them! There are variations in placement and style, but the thing they all have in common is their incredible size and their undeniable antiquity. Many scholars attempt to place them within recorded history by digging around them and shouting "aha!", when they find something that can be dated within the current scheme of human history. It is now understood by the experts that the megalithic structures demanded complex architectural planning, and they propose that it was the labor of tens of thousands of men working for centuries.

No one has ever made a systematic count of the megaliths, but the estimate goes beyond 50,000. It is also admitted that this figure represents only a fraction, since many have been destroyed not only by the forces of nature, but also by the wanton destruction of man.

Even though there are megalithic monuments in locations around the world, there is nothing anywhere else like there is in Europe. The megaliths of Europe form an "enormous blanket of stone". Great mounds of green turf or gleaming white quartz pebbles formerly covered many of them. The quartz is, of course, electrically active. The megalithic mania of ancient Europe is:

> Unparalleled indeed in human history. For there has never been anything like this rage, almost mania, for megalith building, except perhaps during the centuries after AD 1000 when much the same part of Europe was covered with what a monk of the time called a 'white mantle of churches.' […]

> The megaliths, then, were raised by some of the earliest Europeans. The reason that this simple fact took so long to be accepted was the peculiar inferiority complex which western Europeans had about their past. Their religion, their laws, their cultural heritage, their very numerals, all come from the East. The inhabitants, before civilisation came flooding in from the Mediterranean, were illiterate; they kept no records, they built no cities. It was easy to assume that they were simply bands of howling half-naked savages who painted their bodies, put bear-grease on their hair and ate their cousins.[169]

The whys and wherefores of this "megalith mania" are still under debate. The fact is: you can't date stones. Yes, you can date things found around them, or near them, or under them, but you can't date the stones.

The interesting thing about the megalith builders is that the peoples who were able to perform these utterly amazing feats of engineering are still, in most circles, considered to be barbarians because *they did not build cities, engage in*

---

[168] Jessup, Morris K., *The Case For The UFO* (New York: Bantam Books 1955) p. 148.

[169] Reader's Digest, *The World's Last Mysteries*, 1977.

agriculture, develop the wheel, or writing. Yet, they did something that clearly cannot be, and was not, done by "civilized" peoples who did all of those "civilized" things. They had some sort of "power" that we cannot replicate and do not understand.

I would like to speculate here for a moment. The first thing that comes to my mind when I consider the problem of the megaliths is that of what I call "payoff". That is to say, nobody who is human ever does anything without a "payoff", or to put it more generally, *for a reason,* Colin Renfrew and his "Big Chief Theory" notwithstanding.[170] What could be the reason for the stones? There were clearly a great deal more of them than would be necessary for simple "monumental" or "worship" purposes, or even time keeping, as recent researchers have suggested. They appear to be arranged like the inner workings of some vast global machine whose purpose is an enigma to us. For example, at Carnac in Brittany, 3,000 menhirs formed thirteen parallel lines, sprawled across four miles of the French countryside.

At the same time, could the overabundant presence of these megaliths, their "machine-like" arrangement, have anything to do with the things that are observed to be "lacking" in these peoples, i.e. the signs of civilization: the wheel, agriculture, writing and cities? Might we suppose the reason for the stones and the reason for the absence of evidence of what we, today, call civilization, are identical? And since they are found in all the same areas as megaliths exist, might we also suppose that very corpulent women represented in the thousands of carvings had some relationship to these mystical powers as well?

I am just observing what is evident based on long periods of contemplating these structures and artifacts. If we sit down before them without any preconceived notions and try to imagine ourselves participating in the life of the people for whom they were a natural and necessary part of the landscape, and put that together with what we know about our own civilization, we come to some very startling ideas.

It is a matter of observation that cities developed in agricultural societies as a central place to manufacture and exchange goods. Agriculture is required to feed stable and static populations. Wheels are needed to both transport people and goods in cities and from agricultural zones to cities and back. Writing is needed to keep records of transactions, as is demonstrated by the clear evidence of the earliest forms of writing: endless lists and tallies of grain and cattle. And, writing was used for another reason: to record and promulgate the exploits of certain gods and goddesses as well as keeping track of all the goods tithed to the temple and priesthood.

---

[170] We discussed briefly Renfrew's theory in the last chapter.

So, suppose none of this was needed? Suppose a civilization existed that did not need cities, agriculture, wheels or writing? That is not to say that they did not produce goods en masse, nor that they did not produce food for large groups, or that they did not travel over vast distances or record their exploits. But, suppose they did not do it in the way we would expect? Suppose the STONES DID IT ALL?

What do I mean?

It may very well be that the "worship" of the ancients was not worship in the terms we understand it; it was a technology based on cosmic energy, having something to do with the stars as markers of periods of time in which cosmic rays could be collected, and utilizing stones in interaction with the human body, possibly very large women, to produce whatever the tribe needed. For those of you who are science fiction fans, simply think of a modified function of The Navigator in the book and movie *Dune*. It ought not to be lost on the reader that one of the titles of the goddess Isis, as well as other divine beings, is "The Navigator".

Another point about the goddess image of Isis is the odd construction on her head that is called the "throne". The term "seated" is regularly used in conjunction with goddess images, and in archaic times, kingship was bestowed by marriage to the representative of the goddess.

Worship of the moon is recorded in the oldest literatures of Egypt, Babylonia, India, and China—and is still practiced today in various parts of the world, particularly among certain African and Native American groups. The experts will tell us that Moon worship is founded on the belief that the phases of the moon and the growth and decline of plant, animal, and human life are related. In some societies food was laid out at night to absorb the rays of the moon, which were thought to have *power to cure disease and prolong life*. Among the Baganda of central Africa it was customary for a mother to bathe her newborn child by the light of the first full moon. The moon has also been associated with wisdom and justice, as in the worship of the Egyptian god Thoth and the Mesopotamian god Sin. The moon has also been the basis for many amorous legends and some superstitions (madmen were once considered to be moonstruck, hence the term *lunatic*). This is just the short version because entire libraries could be filled with books on the mythology of the Moon and related subjects.

The interesting points are that the rays of the moon were anciently thought to have the power to cure disease and prolong life and confer wisdom. These are motifs of both the Holy Grail and the Philosopher's Stone. And this brings us to another most interesting idea of Morris Jessup.

MORRIS JESSUP AND GRAVITATIONAL NODES

The reader familiar with Jessup's work will know that he died under very mysterious circumstances, and his death was the platform upon which the "legend" of the "Philadelphia Experiment" was founded. This story is about Secret Government experiments in radar invisibility that resulted in Time Travel/manipulation. It is too much to go into here and now, and not totally relevant to our subject, but we will say that, after much research and tracking of clues, we have concluded that Jessup was most likely murdered—but that it wasn't for the reasons that most people think. We believe that he was killed to give "substance" to the diversionary story of the Philadelphia Experiment, which is, in our opinion, designed to promulgate disinformation AND distract attention away from certain observations that he made in his book, cited above.

Jessup points out that UFOs have been sighted and recorded by human beings for thousands of years, and he cites these reports in detail. He informs us that some of the oldest and richest sources of such reports are records of Indian and Tibetan monasteries. He notes that records suggesting sightings 15,000 to 70,000 years ago are to be found there, and these, as well as a report from the court records of Thutmose III that has been, dated to approximately 1500 BC, are quite similar to the reports of the present day.

Jessup then moves to the many sightings made by skeptical astronomers, of which I have a collection myself. Their observations are quantitative and documented as to time and conditions of observation. The astronomers, though unable to explain what they were seeing, nevertheless faithfully recorded all details utilizing whatever equipment was available to them at the various periods when the observations were made. Simultaneous observations by two or more observers have at times established the approximate distances of the UFOs through the study of parallax calculations.[171] It was these observations, with certain specific data included, that provided the details upon which Jessup formulated his idea. He called it the "habitat of the UFOs".

> Refinements of Bode's law indicate *nodes in the gravitational field*, at which planets, asteroids, and possibly comets and meteors tend to locate themselves. An extension of the theory to the satellite systems of the major planets indicates a similar system of nodes on smaller scales, where planets, rather than the sun, are gravitational centers. ...it might well be that these *gravitational nodes* are occupied to some degree by navigable constructions.[...]

> We can, therefore, take it as highly probable that there are many zones of convenience around the planets, as well as around the sun, which are presently unoccupied by planets or satellites of any considerable size and which may well be used by enlightened space dwellers. Such zones, if they exist, are *in addition to the demonstrable earth-sun-moon neutral.*

> Since this system of nodes appears to be some function of the radius of the attracting body, it may be that there is a complete series of them in concentric circles starting at the surface of a parent body such as the earth, but their existence or true nature can hardly be known to us until we can in some way determine the nature of gravity itself. There may even be hints available to us regarding gravity. For instance, no final settlement has ever been made of the argument over the

---

[171] "Parallax" is the displacement, often measurable, caused by looking at an object from two different points; e.g. hold up a finger and view it with first one eye and then the other. The displacement against a distinct background is parallax.

opposed wave and corpuscular theories of the propagation of light. *An assumption that the ether, a necessary adjunct to the wave theory, is identical with the gravitational field, whatever that may be, would reconcile the opposing theories and a quantum of light would then be merely a pulsation or fluctuation in the gravitational field.* Intense studies of the movements of space-navigable UFOs might furnish vital clues to such problems.[...]

There is increasingly strong evidence that gravity is neither so continuous, so immaterial nor so obscure as to be completely unamenable to use, manipulation and control. [...] The lifting of the ancient megalithic structures, too, must surely have come through levitation.[...]

It is my belief that something of the sort was done in the antediluvian past, through either research or through some fortuitous discovery of physical forces and laws, which have not as yet been revealed to scientists of this second wave of civilization.[172]

Jessup next goes on to discuss the periodicity of events of celestial and spatial origin. As he stated, it is not particularly astonishing that such phenomena should be cyclic, for nearly everything astronomical IS periodic.

There are several important things in the comments of Jessup that are pertinent to our discussion here. Not only is he drawing very close to describing a para-physical, hyperdimensional state of existence which utilizes gravitational technology, he is also pointing out a certain "periodicity" to the activities of same in relationship to what might be considered points in time when "dimensional doorways" open and close naturally. This is the fundamental concept behind his idea of gravitational nodes in a three-body system, the Earth, Moon and Sun. Jessup came to these ideas by researching UFOs and other anomalous phenomena, and it is very interesting to speculate as to how this might connect to the ideas of Gurdjieff when he says we are "food for the Moon". In the latter case, Gurdjieff was repeating an ancient idea that may have been related to the concept of hyperdimensional beings using gravitational nodes as "portals" between dimensions.

Another important point about Jessup's comments is his connection between scientific observations and clues in ancient myths to the fact that the megalith builders had extraordinary abilities. In short, what could it mean to be "enthroned" in terms of the Goddess? How could this be a source of health, extended life, knowledge and other benefits? Where on earth did such ideas come from?

---

[172] Jessup, Morris K., *The Case for the UFO,* (New York: Bantum Books 1955) pp. 38-42.

THE DANCE OF THE HOURS

The *Book of Hours* of Jean de France, Duc de Berry, is considered to be one of the most magnificent of late medieval manuscripts that have survived into our time. A "Book of Hours" is a prayer book based on the religious calendar of saints and festivals throughout the year. The book commissioned by the Duke, undertaken by the brothers Limbourg, consists of twelve folios; one for each month. According to a lengthy analysis of these folios by Prof. Otto Neugebauer, this calendar encodes the traditions of ancient astronomy and mathematics from deepest antiquity. At the conclusion of a fascinating analysis, demonstrating the method of decoding the *Book of Hours*, Otto Neugebauer writes:

> The scheme ends where it began, with January 19, if we make the two last lunations
> 29 days long. This final exception to the rule of alternation was called *sallus lunae*,
> the "mump of the moon." In order to know which date is supposed to be a new
> moon, one need only know which number the present year has in the 19-year cycle.
> This number is called the "golden number" because, as a scholar of the 13th century
> expressed it, "this number excels all other lunar rations as gold excels all other
> metals."[173]

The 19-year cycle is called a "Metonic Cycle". It refers to the observational fact that 19 years (6939.689 days) is almost exactly the same length as 235 lunar months (6939.602 days) and that a 19-year cycle consisting of 12 years that were 12-lunar-months-long and 7 years that were 13-lunar-months-long would keep the lunar months in step with the seasons. In other words, the phases of the Moon start to reoccur, within about 2 hours, on the same days of the same months of the year.

Meton tried to sell the scheme to the Athenians, who weren't interested, it seems, and nevertheless they named the idea the "Metonic Cycle". This 19-year cycle is closely related to the 18.6 year precession of the moon's orbit about the earth which causes a corresponding wobble (nutation) on the earth's motion. This suggests that the megalith builders KNEW about the planetary wobble! In fact, the 18.6 year cycle seems to be a key concern of the megalith builders: it is also an observational fact that every 18.6 years, the moon reaches a major standstill point, which means that every 18.6 years, the rising or setting Moon reaches a northern extreme in rising and setting azimuth at summer solstice, and a southern extreme at winter solstice.

In 1897 at Coligny in Burgundy, fragments of a bronze tablet were discovered. Reassembled, this tablet is the longest known document in the Gallic language. Dating to around the 1st century BC, it contains forty different words written in Latin script, and it was a calendar. After it was deciphered, it became clear that the Celts worked in units of sixty-two lunar months, from one new moon to the next. One of these months would contain thirty days, the next twenty-nine, which gave

---

[173] Neugebauer, Otto, *The Exact Sciences in Antiquity*, (New York: Dover 1969).

half-months of fifteen days, or one fifteen-day period followed by a fourteen-day period. The days were counted from moon-rise to moon-rise. The year that emerged from all this was eleven days shorter than the 365-day solar year. They corrected this problem, however, by the simple expedient of alternating 12-month years with 13-month years, - 3 of the former and 2 of the latter in a complete cycle of 62 months.

Obviously, this was a rather ingenious solution to the problem but it begs the question: it's obvious that they had the mathematical skills to calculate the solar year rather accurately, so why didn't they use it as their calendar? Why were they not linking the passage of time to the Sun, the agricultural cycles? Why were they so obviously concerned with what the Moon was doing and having a precise way of keeping track of it? Why did they count their days from moon-rise to moon-rise? We note that this is a custom still reflected in the practices of the Jews and Moslems, who count a day as beginning when the Sun sets as a consequence of their interactions with the Indo-Europeans.

Well, of course the experts tell us it was because they "worshipped" the Moon. It was close and big and awesome to behold, so they naturally just created a whole slew of ignorant beliefs about it, and it became their "Goddess", or god, as the case may be. As I have already noted, by observing children, we may come to a better idea of how it would be unlikely for the ancients (assuming they were howling savages) to have come up with such ideas without some basis, without some "story" having been told to them. Children accept the natural world around them as it is until someone tells them a story. And even then, you have to work hard to convince them that the story is true because if you say that the moon is made of green cheese, the child will think you have gone nuts.

However, if we connect Jessup's idea of a gravitational node that lies somewhere between the earth and the moon, in a specific and cyclic relationship, to the strange marking of time by the ancients according to where the moon was, as well as the later "moon worship" as the transmission of an archaic knowledge of some secret source of power, then we come to the idea that the ancient technology was something quite extraordinary.

What seems to be evident is that the megalith builders were concerned enough with the "three body system" - that relates to the nutation of the Earth to the relative positions of the earth-moon-sun - that they based their calendrical system on this factor! This very well may suggest that they USED gravity. We want to emphasize that curious comment of a thirteenth century scholar quoted by Neugebauer who said, regarding the 19 year cycle: "*this number excels all other lunar rations as gold excels all other metals.*" If we then connect that remark to the quests of the alchemist to "transmute base metals into gold" via the "philosopher's stone", and the alchemical adage, "the right person, in the right place, at the right time, doing the right thing, can accomplish the work", we begin to realize that we are moving in the correct direction. Most particularly when we recall that curious story about Fulcanelli and Jacques Bergier:

> Certain geometrical arrangements of highly purified materials are enough to release atomic forces without having recourse to either electricity or vacuum techniques.[174]

This will become even more significant further on.

Are there any clues about stones themselves being part of an ancient technology? At present, there are many people who claim that the megaliths are arranged around the world on a grid, the structure of which is, according to them, 36 degrees of longitude apart. The assumption is that all of the megaliths belong to a single, pre-flood civilization. The assumption being made from this hypothesis is that the strange locations of these complexes implies that the purpose of the megaliths was not to derive power from a grid for local use, but rather, to do something *to* the earth grid by coordinating local actions on a global basis. In other words, the claim is that the megaliths appear to have been used to put energy into a global grid rather than to extract energy from it.

There are problems with this blanket assumption. First of all, while we do not think that the present scientific dating is reliable, we do think that some ball-park figures can be established if enough care is taken in observing individual situations and taking all the evidence into account. The undersea structures off Japan, Bimini, and Malta, as well as Tiahuanaco in South America, all suggest a civilization that belonged to a pre-cataclysmic environment. But many other megalithic structures clearly belong to an "eruption" of civilization in a post-cataclysmic environment, including the pyramids in Egypt, Central America, Stonehenge, and so on. What is striking is the difference between the pyramidal groups and the "circle making" groups, though many current researchers are trying to connect them to the same basic philosophical context. I think that may be a mistake.

It has been proposed by the advocates of so-called Sacred Geometry that the placing of the megaliths was a function of "Grid Engineering", and that this is mankind's oldest science. Such people further claim that precise geometrical spherical versions of the cube, such as the tetrahedron, octahedron, icosahedron, dodecahedron, and other compound and semi-regular solids, such as the cuboctahedron, are now recognized as evidence of Neolithic man's familiarity with the concepts of this putative sacred geometry. These folks then go on to propose that this was a "mystical" sort of practice that includes visualizing the earth's energy grid in certain ritualistic ways that will bring the individual in "tune" with the superior intelligence of the Earth by producing "resonance".

---

[174] Pauwels, L, and Bergier, J., *The Morning of the Magicians*, (New York: Stein and Day. 1964) p. 77.

I have to wonder about this interpretation. If, as we suspect, we have been under an "Hyperdimensional Raj"[175] for these many thousands of years, we might think that much of this material is designed to do one of two things: 1) to inform us about the "control system", or 2) to *perpetuate it*. What would be more natural than for the Matrix Control system to manipulate people to think that "visualizing" these grids will bring them into "harmony" with the earth and that this is a "good thing"? It may be, in fact, that it is designed to strengthen the prison and to make human beings into the "batteries" that keep it in place! However, that does not mean that discovering these things and knowing where these points are is not a useful exercise. But, to take this very scientific knowledge, ignore its possible correct applications, and fall into the trap of doing what amounts to "rituals" of visualization so as to bring oneself into "harmony" with the earth may be exactly what "they" want us to do. The very fact that it is being so widely promulgated in this way suggests to me that this is the case.

POSSIBLE ANTAGONISTIC POLARITIES IN ANCIENT CIVILIZATIONS

When one tracks back through all of the ancient "matters" and studies the different groups, trying to follow them as they moved from place to place, studying the genetic morphology in order to keep track of who is who, and comparing linguistics and myth and archaeology, one comes to the startling realization that there were significant polarities throughout space and time. I have tentatively identified these polarities as the Circle People and the Triangle - or Pyramid - People. In a general sense, one can see the broad brush of the triangle people in the Southern hemisphere, in the pyramids and related cultures and artifacts. For the most part, their art is primitive and stylistically rigid. In the northern hemisphere, one sees the circle makers, the spirals, the rough megaliths, the art of Lascaux and Chauvet and the many other caves. One can note a clear difference between the perceptions and the response to the environment between the two trends and groups. Of course, there are areas where there was obvious mixture of both cultures and styles, and ideological constructions, but overall, there is a very distinct difference.

There are many books on "alternative science" being published in the present time about the purported ancient civilizations. One assumption that they all seem to hold in common is that everything was all hunky dory, sweetness and light among all the people, and the only thing that happened was that a nasty cataclysm came along and brought it all to an end. They keep forgetting the issue of the *Vedas* and Plato's *Timaeus* where an ancient war was described, and it was at that point in time, or immediately after, that the cosmic catastrophe occurred. It would

---

[175] Thanks to C. Scott Littleton for this handy term.

then be only reasonable to suspect that the same differences between the warring parties would be carried over into the post cataclysmic world. And it seems to be a reasonable assumption that the "southern influence", including Egypt, was that of the "Atlanteans" of Plato, and that the "northern influence", including the builders of Stonehenge, were the "Athenians" of Plato, the "Sons of Boreas", or the North Wind, keeping in mind that these "Athenians" were obviously not from Athens as we know it today, though we are beginning to suspect that we know who they were.

We should also like to note that the so-called "civilizing influence" of the South, of the creators of agricultural civilizations, the instigation of writing and the wheel and so forth, is always connected in some way to "scaly" critters like Fish Gods or Serpents. *It isn't until fairly late that the Serpent makes his appearance among the archaeological finds of Europe and central Asia.* Before the serpent appeared there, there were only goddesses, birds, and wavy lines representing water and cosmic energy. I think that it is dangerous to confuse the issues. Again and again we see currents of two completely different processes, two factions, two ways of perceiving and interacting with the cosmos: one that wishes to conceal and one that wishes to reveal, one that wishes to dominate, one that wishes to share.

We notice that many megalithic sites are located a certain points that correspond with a certain geometry. But, if we look even closer, if we discard the current so-called "Sacred Geometry" and just look at the sites themselves and let them speak - all of them - instead of leaving this one or that one out because it doesn't quite fit, or only is "very close" to fitting, we may discover another relationship that is suggested by the sites, rather than working to fit the sites into an assumption.

So many bizarre ideas are being propagated at the present time, including the preposterous one about the megaliths being set up to absorb the energy of human sacrifices, and that the stones "drink blood,," that it is quite discouraging to realize how easily people are misled by nonsense. If such writers cannot figure out that the megaliths were demonized by the church because they were revered by the nature religions, which we theorize are carriers of ancient scientific knowledge, and the nature religions themselves were also demonized, then there isn't much chance that they will figure anything else out either. Such people also tend to be convinced that the Holy Grail is the cup from the Last Supper, too, and I won't even comment on that.

STONE TECHNOLOGY AND T.C. LETHBRIDGE

Getting back to our stones, and whether or not we can find even a hint that they were involved in some kind of technology, we note first of all that archaeologist T.C. Lethbridge once placed his hand on one of the stones and received a strong tingling sensation like an electric shock, and the huge, heavy stone felt as if it were rocking wildly. Many other people have received sensations of shock when placing their hands on certain stones, and photographs have occasionally shown inexplicable light radiations emanating from them. Upon examination, we find that many of the megaliths were engraved with "cup and ring" marks - concentric rings and channels. The first impression these designs give is that of a circuit board of a computer.

In Greek myth, the walls of Thebes were said to have been constructed by the skill of a musician called Amphion and his lyre. He played the lyre in such a way that *stones were made to move*. Phoenician myth speaks of the god Ouranus moving stones as if they had life of their own. This is one of *numerous* traditions from around the world that sound in various forms was used to levitate and move large stones.

Stones may have another interesting property that deserves serious research. In 1982, Tafter, the landlord at the Prince of Wales Inn at Kenfig in Mid-Glamorgan, Wales, complained of the sound of organ music and voices keeping him awake at night. To investigate, John Marke, an electrical engineer, and Allan Jenkins, an industrial chemist, connected electrodes to the wall of the pub after closing time one night. They fed 20,000 volts across the electrodes and locked tape recorders in the room for four hours. When the tapes were analyzed, they had succeeded in taping voices speaking in old Welsh, organ music, and a ticking clock. Interestingly, there was no clock in the room at the time. It has been suggested that the stones in the wall contained substances similar to those found in modern recording tape.

This last remark about "recordings" in stone brings us to another interesting item. Tom C. Lethbridge, the above mentioned archeologist (who became Director of Excavations for the Cambridge Antiquarian Society and Director of the University Museum of Archaeology and Ethnology), wrote a number of excellent books that form a collection that has been called one of the most fascinating records of paranormal research ever compiled. In recent years, Lethbridge is finally beginning to be fully appreciated. Combining the skills of a scientist with a completely open mind, he conducted a series of experiments that convinced him of the existence of hyperdimensional realms that interact dynamically with our own. Colin Wilson called him a man whose gifts were far ahead of his time and credited him with one of the most remarkable and original minds in parapsychology. We agree most heartily and highly recommend his work to the reader. Over the past ten years or more, Lethbridge's work has served us as a platform for many fruitful speculations and experiments about hyperdimensional realities.

Tom Lethbridge, the Cambridge don, took no interest in psychical research until after he had retired. But dowsing fascinated him. In the early 1930's, he and another archaeologist were looking for Viking graves on the Isle of Lundy in the Bristol Channel. After finding what they came for, they were just killing time while waiting for a ferry and decided to try some experiments with dowsing, which had been an interest of Lethbridge for some time. Lundy Island is crisscrossed with seams of volcanic rock that extrude through the slate, and Lethbridge wanted to see if dowsing would locate them. So, he had his friend blindfold him and lead him about with a forked hazel stick. Every time he passed over a volcanic seam, the hazel fork twisted violently in his hands. The friend was carrying a very sensitive magnetometer and was able to immediately verify that Lethbridge had accurately located the volcanic seams of rock.

Lethbridge realized that, like running water, volcanic rock has a faint magnetic field. He had written about dowsing earlier, "Most people can dowse, if they know how to do it. If they cannot do it, there is probably some fault in the electrical system of their bodies".

This remark makes us wonder if there are not people who have extremely powerful and well-developed electrical systems in their bodies, and if such conditions might not be a genetic inheritance? This question will come up again further on, so keep it in mind.

Lethbridge's success with finding volcanic rock started him off on his investigations into other realms. Hidden objects could not stay hidden when Lethbridge was wandering around with his rods, twigs or pendulum. There didn't seem to be any limits to what could be detected this way. He had proved to his complete satisfaction not only that dowsing worked, but that it was "mind stuff" — the rod or pendulum was connected to the mind of the person holding it in some way.

Tom Lethbridge's results proved to be not only accurate but also repeatable, and he found the responses appeared to be governed by vibrations of various wavelengths. The wavelength of water, for instance, was different to that of metal. His principal instrument became the pendulum, and he found a lot depended on the *length of the pendulum's cord*. He was able to test not only for minerals but abstract things and qualities like anger, death, deceit, sleep, colors, male, and female. In a lengthy series of trial and error experiments, he created a table of very precise measurements showing, for example, that a 22-inch length would reveal the existence of silver or lead, while iron demanded a 32-inch stretch, but sulphur a mere 7 inches. Stranger still, though, the pendulum would react to different emotions and attributes, with a different length for feminine (29") and masculine (24") objects, including human or animal remains. The details of his experiments are utterly fascinating. This open-minded and extremely literate man was aware that many people would regard his methods and findings with suspicion. He once wrote:

> "It is impossible for it to be imaginary. If you can use a pendulum to work out
> within an inch or two exactly where something lies hidden beneath undisturbed
> turf, and do this in front of witnesses, and then go to the spot which the pendulum
> has indicated and take off the turf, dig up the soil beneath and find the object. If you
> can do this same operation again and again and almost always succeed, this cannot
> be imagination, delusion, or any of those things. It is scientific experiment,
> however crude it may be."

Perhaps the reason why some still cannot accept dowsing is because it is so incredibly simple. At no cost at all you can produce an instrument no piece of expensive machinery can equal. But again, Lethbridge points out that *everything depends on the operator.*

Lethbridge found himself confronted with a very strange world — "far stranger I feel than anything produced by physics, botany or biology"—, and he wrote of millions of cones of force surrounding each of us in our homes and backyards which can be contacted instantly by something in our own "energy field". It was much more difficult to comprehend than molecules, atoms and electrons, he said, because we had been brought up to take these for granted.

As we have already noted, if the infrastructure of our civilization were to be destroyed, then if a person a hundred years later tried to explain the theory of radio and television, people would find it impossible to comprehend. It would sound like magic.

Where does the power to work a pendulum come from? Lethbridge thought that it might be something invisible and intangible, a part of us, which knows far more than we do. Is it mind or soul? Some sort of electromagnetic or psyche field? Something linked to a higher dimension? He agonized over this and admitted he wasn't wise enough to come to any definite conclusion, apart from the thought that ancient man knew far more about it than we do today.

Although, Lethbridge did a huge amount of experimental work in the field of dowsing, and his results deserve attention from any serious student of the deeper realities of our world, what we are interested in here is his work in another, though related, direction.

In 1957, Lethbridge left Cambridge in disgust at the narrow-minded attitudes of the scholars there. He moved into Hole House, an old Tudor mansion on the south coast of Devon. Next door to him lived a little old white-haired lady who assured Lethbridge that she could put spells on people who annoyed her and that she was able to travel out of her body at night and wander around the district. She explained that if she wanted to discourage unwanted visitors, she had only to visualize a five-pointed star in the path of the individual and they would stay away. Lethbridge, of course, was skeptical.

But, being an experimenter, Lethbridge was trying the visualization one evening while lying in bed. That night, his wife awakened with the feeling that somebody else was in the room. She could see a faint glow of light at the foot of the bed, which slowly faded. The next day the old lady came to see them and told them that she had come to "visit" them the previous night and had found the bed surrounded by *triangles of fire*.

Leaving aside whether or not we can prove this story to be anything more than a subjective experience, there are two important points we would like to make. The first one is that somehow, this practice of "visualizing pentagrams" seems to have a causal relationship to the *appearance* of the old woman in Lethbridge's bedroom. It was almost as though the practice "attracted" the visitor, possibly even inspiring the wish or compulsion to visit. The second is that the visualized pentagrams appeared as triangles of fire. Theories of how hyperdimensional objects might appear in fourth dimensional space-time, or how four dimensional objects might appear in three dimensional space time, in mathematical terms, lends a modicum of credibility to this story. If the old woman had seen fiery pentagrams, we would not take such notice of the event. That a pentagon in our world might appear as a triangle in another realm suggests something very mysterious here. I am also intrigued by the possible relationship to the differences of these hyper-dimensional solids and the difference between the perspectives of the "triangle people" and the "circle people". This is also a very important point related to the dangers of visualizing geometric shapes when we consider the susequent events that Lethbridge recounted.

Several years later, the old lady told Lethbridge that she was going to put a spell on the cattle of a farmer with whom she was quarreling. At this point, Lethbridge took her seriously and warned her about the dangers of practicing magic. She ignored him, and one day not long after declaring her intentions, she was found dead in her bed under mysterious circumstances. As it happened, the cattle of two other nearby farmers did get hoof and mouth disease, but the cattle of the farmer with whom the old lady was quarreling were unaffected. Lethbridge was convinced that the "spell" had rebounded on the old lady in some way. But, it was this event that led to an important insight for us here, which is why we have recounted the story.

Sometime after the old woman's death, Lethbridge was passing her cottage and suddenly experienced a "nasty feeling", a "suffocating sense of depression". His curiosity aroused, Lethbridge walked around the cottage and discovered a most interesting thing: he could step into and out of the "depression" just as if it were some kind of invisibly defined "locus".

This reminded Lethbridge of a similar experience he had had when walking with his mother as a teenager. It was in the Great Wood near Wokingham, on a nice morning, when suddenly the two of them experienced a "horrible feeling of gloom and depression, which crept upon us like a blanket of fog over the surface of the sea". They left in a hurry and only later discovered that the corpse of a suicide had been discovered lying just a few yards from where they had been standing.

Some years later, Lethbridge and his wife went to the seashore to collect seaweed for their garden. As he walked on the beach, he again experienced the sense of depression, gloom and fear descending on him. Resisting this influence, Lethbridge and his wife began to fill their sacks with seaweed. After a very short period of this activity, Lethbridge's wife, Mina, came running up to him demanding that they leave saying, "I can't stand this place a minute longer. There's something frightful here".

In a discussion about the phenomenon with Mina's brother the following day, the brother mentioned that he had experienced something very similar in a field near Avebury, in Wiltshire. When he said the word "field", it clicked in Lethbridge's mind and he remembered that field telephones often short circuit in warm, muggy weather. "What was the weather like?", he asked.

"Warm and damp", replied the brother.

Right there, the idea began to shape itself in Lethbridge's mind. Water. On the day he had been in the Great Wood, it had been warm and damp. When they had been at the beach gathering seaweed, it had likewise been warm and damp. Experiment was obviously in order!

The next weekend, Lethbridge and his wife again visited the bay. Again, as they stepped onto the beach, the same bank of depression and gloom enveloped them. Mina led him to the spot where she had experienced such an overwhelming sensation that she had insisted on leaving the place. At that spot, the sensation was so powerful that they actually felt dizzy. Lethbridge described it as being similar to having a high fever and full of drugs. As it happened, on either side of this spot were two streams of water.

Mina went off to the cliff to look at the scenery and suddenly walked into the "depression" again. She actually had the sensation that something or someone was urging her to jump off the cliff! When she had brought it to the attention of Lethbridge, he agreed that this spot was as "sinister" as the spot on the beach between the streams.

As it turned out, nine years later, a man did commit suicide from that exact spot. Lethbridge wondered if there was some sort of "timeless" sensation that had been "imprinted" on the area via some sort of "recording" principle. It seemed that, whether from the past or the future, feelings of despair were somehow recorded on the surroundings, in the very atmosphere, it seemed. The only question was, how? Lethbridge believed that the key was water.

A hint of what may be happening here is provided by the work of Y. Rocard of the Sorbonne, who had discovered that underground water produces changes in the earth's magnetic field, and this was proposed as the solution as to why dowsing works. The water does this because it has a field of its own which interacts with the earth's field. And most significantly to us here is that magnetic fields are the means by which sound is recorded on tape covered with iron oxide. This suggested to Lethbridge that the magnetic field produced by running water could record strong emotions that, as Lethbridge also noted, produce electrical activity in the human physiology. Such fields could be "played back" continuously, and amplified in damp and muggy weather.

This would explain why these "areas of depression" seem to form invisible walls. If you bring a magnet closer and closer to an iron object, you notice that at a certain point, the object is "seized" by the magnet as it enters the force field.

Lethbridge's experiments took a new turn at this point, and led to evidence that many things that are perceived as "hauntings" or "ghosts" are really just "recordings". At some point he thought about the fact that ghosts are often reported to reappear on certain "anniversaries" which suggests that there are other cyclical currents that turn such recordings on or off or simply amplify them.

To answer the question that is growing in the reader's mind, yes, it seems that some hauntings are the result of happy emotions, and strong happiness can also be recorded in the same way. It also seems that the type of material substance that the human "field" interacts with has an important role. For example, in the 1840s, a certain Bishop Polk told a Joseph Rhodes Buchanan that he could detect brass in the dark. He said that when he touched it, a distinctly unpleasant taste was produced in his mouth. Buchanan tested him and discovered that it was true, even if the metal was carefully and thickly wrapped in paper. Buchanan experimented with his students and found that some of them had a similar ability. In fact, it seemed that there were quite a number of substances that could be detected this way, and the only explanation that seemed reasonable was that the nerves of the human being produce some sort of field - he called it the nerve aura - which interacts with a similar "field" of the object. Buchanan and others called the ability to "read" these fields "psychometry", and it is popularly practiced today. What many people do not realize is that the principle of psychometry, that many take for granted - they can "feel the vibrations" - led Tom Lethbridge to some startling revelations.

As noted, Tom Lethbridge had concluded after a lot of experiments that a dowsing pendulum could somehow respond to different substances, and that lengthening or shortening the string was like tuning the pendulum to a particular wavelength. Lethbridge spent days testing all kinds of different substances. He discovered that the wavelength for silver is the same as lead: 22 inches. Truffles and beech wood both respond at 17 inches. This meant that there must be something further about such "paired" items to distinguish them. After some testing, Lethbridge discovered that it was not just the length of the string, but the number and direction of revolutions. For lead, the pendulum would gyrate 16 times and for silver it would gyrate 22 times. It was beginning to look like nature had a truly marvelous and foolproof code for identifying anything. It is also beginning to appear to us that the ancients knew this and that they may have attempted to transmit this knowledge to us via myth and legend and the "Green Language". (That magical mumbo jumbo might not be the solution to the mysteries is also becoming more and more apparent, but, let us continue into even more remarkable speculations of Tom Lethbridge.)

Through a variety of experiments, Lethbridge established the "frequency" for both death and violent anger: 40 inches. This also proved to be the frequency for cold and black. Indeed, colors have frequency. Grey is 22 inches— - not a surprise since it is the color of both lead and silver. Yellow is 29 and green is 30.

After months of experiments, Lethbridge had constructed his table of frequencies, and he had discovered that 40 inches was *some kind of limit*. Every single substance that he tested fell between zero and 40 inches. It was at this point that he discovered something curious: Sulphur reacts to a 7 inch pendulum; if he extended the pendulum to 47 inches, it would still react to sulphur, but not directly over it. It would only react a little to one side. He then discovered that this was true of everything else he tried beyond the number 40 — it would react, but only to one side. He noticed another odd thing: beyond 40 inches, there was *no rate for the concept of time*. The pendulum simply would not respond. Lethbridge realized that he was measuring a different dimension. However, when he lengthened the pendulum to 80 inches, there was a response to the idea of time. Lethbridge pondered this and finally theorized that in the realm beyond 40, the pendulum is *in time itself*, and that is why there is no reaction to the idea. But, beyond that, there are other "realms" where the *idea* of time exists in another world "beyond death".

Lethbridge discovered that if he lengthened the string again beyond 80 inches, he got the same result, as if there were still another dimension. Lethbridge realized that he had discovered worlds in other dimensions, outside the limits of space and time, and theorized that we cannot see it because our *physical bodies are limited detectors*.

Tom Lethbridge continued with his experiments and determined that the world of the "next" level beyond our own is one in which the energy vibrations are four times as fast as those of our world. The effect of encountering this reality is like a fast train passing a slow one. Even though they are both moving forward, the slow train seems to be moving backward. This hyperdimensional world is all around us, yet we are unable to see it because it is beyond the range of our senses. All the objects of our world are very likely just our limited perceptions of what is happening in this total reality.

His experiments with megaliths indicated that they were placed to mark places where the earth forces were most powerful, and to harness energy in some way now forgotten.

Unfortunately, Lethbridge died of a heart attack before he could complete his researches.

At this point we would like to note that Tom Lethbridge was not a spiritualist. He believed that magic, spiritualism, occultism and other forms of mumbo jumbo are merely crude attempts to understand the vast realm of hidden energies in which we live. We would like to add that expositions along the lines of most esoterica generally serve only to obscure, not to reveal; to disinform, rather than to produce real knowledge. Tom Lethbridge used logic and experiment and observation to come to the conclusion that there are other realms of reality beyond our world and that there are forms of energy that we do not even begin to understand.[176]

STONES AND "SACRED GEOMETRY"

Coming back now to our stones, and the questions about their placement, we realize that this matter is not as simple as the many "Sacred Geometry" specialists would have us believe. We need to do more investigating before we come to any solid conclusions about earth grids and what they may or may not do.

The temple at Baalbek, Lebanon, is probably one of the most astonishing structures on earth due to the sheer size of the stones used in its construction. In a quarry about a mile away from the actual temple is an abandoned stone that was never used. It is the biggest stone block *ever cut by man* and its measurements are 68 ft by 14 feet wide and 14 feet tall. In other words, it is a *single building block* that is as large as two complete modest homes put together. The block is estimated to weigh 1200 tons. From this single block, if cut into manageable pieces, stonemasons could build 15 houses, each 20 by 40 feet, with walls a foot thick.

The Egyptian obelisks were large; each being a single block, but the largest one standing today is less than half the size of this stone. The marble for the columns of Baalbek was obtained from a quarry far up the Nile, and then overland for 400 miles. The column drums themselves were cut in sections 20 feet long. The platform upon which Baalbek is built is composed of granite blocks and measures 900 feet by 600 feet. In this platform are positioned three stones that are each 63 feet long, 13 feet high, and 10 feet thick. The doorway of the "smaller" temple of Bacchus at Baalbek is fifty feet high and is said to be the most marvelous doorway in all of ancient architecture. Even as a ruin, having been damaged by wars and earthquakes, Baalbek is still one of the most awesome sights in the world. Curiously, most of those who write about ancient monuments seldom mention Baalbek except in passing. One has to wonder if it is because they simply prefer to not have to think about the cutting and moving of those stones?

THE CORAL CASTLE AND SPINNING AIRPLANE SEATS

In October of 1994, I asked the Cassiopaeans - myself in the future - how the stones of Baalbek were cut and moved. They replied that it was done by "sound wave focusing". Well, sure! But then they added that I was going to discover something about this myself, and they cryptically mentioned the "Coral Castle".

---

[176] Lethbridge, T.C., *The Power of the Pendulum* (Viking, Penguin, 1991); also see Wilson, Colin, *Mysteries* (Putnam Publishing Group, 1980).

Edward Leedskalnin was a 100-pound, unschooled wizard who single-handedly built an edifice known as the Coral Castle down in South Florida. Some of the stones Edward used in the construction of the Coral Castle weigh 28 tons. That is not in the same ballpark as the stones of Baalbek, but for the work of a single, little guy, it suggests to us that he certainly discovered something!

Leedskalnin also produced several pamphlets for sale during the mid-1940's dealing with magnetic currents. These pamphlets describe various experiments he undertook with home made magnets that he created using such things as welding rods, steel fishing line, and automobile batteries. It is thought that he was explicating the ideas that would lead the insightful reader to the same discovery he had made himself. So far, no one has figured it out except to propose that it had something to do with the so-called "earth grid", which, as we will see, is more nonsense.

As it happens, even though I lived my entire life in Florida, I had never been to see this purported marvel, and the only things I knew about it were what I had learned by watching a television program about it on *Unsolved Mysteries*, I believe.

The February following the Cassiopaean's remark about the Coral Castle, I was invited to give a talk to a study group in Orlando. After my little talk, a funny old man came up to me with a big grin on his face, grabbed my hand and shook it vigorously and said to me with a faint accent, "Ya know, I've been studying this UFO business for over 40 years—I talked with Hynek and Major Keyhoe and all that—and you are the first person I have ever heard who has gotten up in public and described it as it really is! I have some material you might be interested in. You should come and see me some time"!

Well, I thought he was just an old guy with a lot of time on his hands that needed company and might be using this as an excuse to get it. I thanked him, chatted a bit, and when he went off to get a snack, I "mingled" in the direction of the host of the event who was chatting with several other people, intending to make my adieus. He was apparently describing the Florida tourist attractions to a group of out-of-towners when he said, "And you might want to go down and have a look at this Coral Castle, too"!

"What is that?", one of them asked. The host proceeded to recap the *Unsolved Mysteries* presentation. Then he said: "You can ask Henry over there", pointing at my little old man who knew Hynek, "he was a close friend of the guy who built the Coral Castle".

Well, needless to say, after hearing this, I remembered the Cassiopaeans had said that I would "discover" something about this "sound-wave focusing". I decided that I wouldn't leave just yet, and went back to chat with the old man and said, "I hear you knew the guy who built the Coral Castle?"

"Ayup! Sure did! Knew him for years! I was stationed over there in Homestead area after the war and got to know him pretty well."

I asked, "Did he ever tell you how he did it?"

"Nope. He never would tell anybody. He would always say that he knew the secret of how the pyramids were built, but nobody ever saw him do it. I have some ideas about it, though, and I wrote a little book about him and my experiences and observations. You know, it's a shame that the television program didn't give the real story! All that nonsense about 'Sweet Sixteen' and a 'broken heart' and so on! What a lot of crap! Sure! If you come to visit, I can show you what I *do* know! Do 'ya know something? I am the only person ole Edward ever invited inside his private living quarters! Ayup! He was a real loner!"

I was already making plans for a visit!

I made the trip back over to the Orlando area within a couple of weeks. I was truly amazed at what I found. Henry hadn't been exaggerating when he said he had been interested in studying UFOs for forty years. His home was a veritable museum of UFOs! There were paintings, enlarged photographs on the walls, knick-knacks and memorabilia on the tables; and books! He had a HUGE collection of books in bookcases and papers in boxes all over his house.

Out of one of these boxes he pulled a loose-leaf notebook containing a typewritten manuscript. It had black and white photographs stuck in the appropriate places with corner tabs, and he said it was the only copy. I was appalled at that and offered to transcribe it onto the computer and give him a copy on diskette. He said he would like that very much, but he was not yet ready to let the only existing copy leave his possession. I certainly understood.

The manuscript was about his long friendship with Edward Leedskalnin and all their conversations. Henry wasn't one to pry, and that may be why he was accepted as a friend. The photographs were of Henry and Edward—Henry in his military uniform—and many others of his children playing among the great blocks of the Coral Castle.

I regret that I did not read the book carefully—because Henry died in 1996—but there was no time with all the other fascinating things to do and see. Henry took me on a tour of his memorabilia, his photographs, and his books. It was just too much to absorb at once! Finally, we sat down and I was able to ask about that most interesting of clues that Henry had let drop—that he had been inside the living quarters of Edward Leedskalnin while Edward was still living. I wanted to know what he had observed.

Henry described how Edward had done a lot of experiments and knew all kinds of secrets, but that he was very paranoid. That is why he told the crazy story about "Sweet Sixteen" and the phony broken heart. It was to put people off the trail, or so he thought. Edward had the idea that if he let it be known exactly what he knew, he would be picked up by some government officials and never seen again. Well, maybe he wasn't crazy!

Henry told me that, after much, or all, of the Coral Castle had been built, Edward had moved it from one location to another. Apparently there was some question of zoning and Edward was told he had to tear it down or move it. He moved it.

Certain "researchers" have claimed that it was moved because of some theory of earth grids relating to Sacred Geometry, but that does not seem to be true based on what Henry told me. It was simply a question of zoning and county regulations. And, since it was *built* in a different original location, that pretty much discounts the idea that the location was important to the act of building. It simply wasn't, and the evidence does not support the idea.

The mode of the moving of this pile of rocks was what was so interesting to me. Apparently, Edward hired a truck and driver; only he would have the driver park the truck overnight and send him home. The next morning, the truck would be loaded with the huge blocks of stone and would be driven to the new site. There was a block and tackle on tall poles prominently displayed and, apparently, Edward confided to Henry that this was his ruse to give the impression that this was what he was using to unload the blocks. He would send the driver off on an errand, leaving the truck there with the blocks on it, and when the driver would return, the truck would be unloaded. This was repeated over and over again until all the stones were moved to the new site. There are reports that say he placed his hands on the stones and "sang" to them.

Another peculiar thing was that Henry told me he had visited the quarry where the stones were cut and there were *no tailings*! Tailings are the stone equivalent of sawdust. When you saw wood, you have sawdust. When you cut stone or metal, you have tailings.[177] So, however Leedskalnin cut these stones, it was *not* a usual method!

The final and most interesting part of Henry's story was the description of the living quarters of Edward Leedskalnin. According to Henry, there were three pieces of ordinary furniture in the room: a cot type bed, a hand-made wooden table with a framed screen that fit over the top to keep insects off the food which was stored there since Edward had no refrigerator, and a hand-made wooden chair. What was *not* ordinary was an airplane seat suspended by chain from the ceiling— complete with seatbelt.

Now, for an extremely ascetic man, one who slept on a simple cot, and ate the simplest of diets, and who had absolutely no use for any kind of luxuries or comforts at all, what was he doing with an airplane seat suspended from the ceiling?

I thought about this for a while. I thought about swinging in such a seat. But if swinging was all that wanted, why not just build a wooden swing that would be in keeping with the other hand-made wooden items in the room.

But Edward did not do that. He had an airplane seat with a seatbelt. Why? Well, let's consider some of the things he has written in his little pamphlets. Edward writes about sphere or ball magnets, which can change the poles to any location on the sphere. He discusses *lengths* of magnetization (North vs. South) in a rod as varying by Earth's latitude. North and South are separate magnetic currents, running "against the other" in whirling, right-hand screw like fashion, i.e. dextrorotatory helices. He then says:

> Magnets they are the cosmic force, they hold together this earth and everything on it. [...] I have a generator that generates currents on a small scale *from the air* without using any magnets around it. [...] The natural path to the North Pole

---

[177] Remember Schoch's findings about the stones of the underwater monuments. They didn't appear to have been cut.

magnets in the Northern Hemisphere is to go down, and the South Pole magnets to go up. When the magnets are running out of the middle of the earth, as soon as they meet an object they attract it, on account of the fact that in any object there has both kinds of magnets in it.[178]

Now, one just has to wonder about his "generator" that generates currents "from the air", and whether or not it has anything to do with spinning in a right-hand, screw-like fashion? And then one gets the little light bulb lighting up over one's head that suggests that Edward Leedskalnin was using his airplane seat with the seatbelt to sit in and spin, and that he, himself, was the "generator". One also thinks immediately about the length of the chain in reference to Lethbridge's experiments.

Edward also mentioned another curious thing: "I have several lily pools where I keep water . I have watched the lily pools for sixteen years." This quote is interesting because of the connection in legend between the presence of water and "moving stones", as well as Lethbridge's connection of water to certain fields. Some ancient megaliths were said to go down to the nearest stream for a drink at certain astronomically propitious times of the year. And "astronomically propitious" may be another clue because, Edward also suggests that the experimenter "face the east". But, we still wonder about the mode of manifestation of this strange power that we seem to be approaching from several different directions. We may find a clue in the following:

> When a time-varying magnetic field is applied to a ferromagnetic, a rearrangement of local lattice strain fields due to the motion of non-magnetic domain walls occurs and emits elastic energy. The interaction between domain walls and lattice defects creates a discontinuity in the domain wall motion causing a burst of energy called Magneto-Acoustic Emission (MAE). The envelope of the time-averaged MAE bursts has a unique shape, which has been shown to be dependent upon the frequency and magnitude of the applied field and factors affecting lattice defects such as embrittlement. Although domain wall movement is a random process it does exhibit features of regularity which have been identified by studying phenomena such as $1/f$ flicker noise and self-organized criticality (the "domino effect"). Nevertheless, certain fundamental elements of the MAE characteristics remain unexplained.[179]

What the above is saying to us is that the application of a magnetic field causes motion of non-magnetic domain walls in the material and emits elastic energy. In other words, *it makes a sound in response to the magnetic field*. Was Edward

---

[178] Leedskalnin, Edward, *Magnetic Current* (Pomeroy, WA: Health Research 1998) p. 4. Other citations are from photocopies of a monograph published by Leedskalnin.

[179] J. P. Fulton, B. Wincheski and M. Namkung, *A Probabilistic Model for Simulating Magneto-Acoustic Emission Responses in Ferromagnets* M. Namkung, B. Wincheski, J. P. Fulton and R. G. Todhunter,

Leedskalnin spinning a precise number of times, at a precise frequency length, in order to produce an energy within him that connected him to another realm, which resulted in a "Magneto Acoustic Emission"? That is, did he produce a sound of a very special sort that enabled him to move massive blocks of stone, not because he was strengthened by what he did, but because this sound, emitted from a timeless dimension that he had tapped, directed at the stones, had an effect on gravity?

That's all fine and good for a single person to be able to utilize such a handy technique to manhandle some big chunks of rock like they were marshmallows. But now we want to inquire into how an entire civilization would utilize such a technology? What can it mean to suggest that in those areas where the megaliths march along the landscape, and where the megalithic temples are situated, that the peoples did not produce a civilization as we know it because they didn't need to? How does it all connect to Morris Jessup's remark that "*It may be that this tremendous power was limited in its application to articles of stone texture only...*[This would] *account for the strange fact that almost all relics of the profound past are non-metallic*"?

EGYPTIAN STONE VASES

Both Graham Hancock and Colin Wilson devote considerable time to describing the marvels of Egypt and the construction of the pyramid in terms of the possible techniques of cutting the stones with such amazing accuracy. They describe in some detail the event that led to the fraudulent dating of the pyramid, which date was taken up by mainstream archaeologists who cannot now repudiate it because they have too many other theories and dates hinged on this original error. What is interesting to us here about Egypt is a discovery made by Flinders Petrie in the village of Naqada in 1893. Naqada is 300 miles south of Cairo, and pottery and stone vases were discovered there that were produced by some technique that has created considerable controversy.

It seems that the pottery of Naqada had none of the striations that would indicate that it had been thrown on a wheel. But, without a pottery wheel, it is almost impossible to get pots to be "perfectly round". But this pottery was so perfectly rounded that it was absurd to think that it had been made by hand without a wheel! Petrie, of course, dated the pottery to the 11th dynasty, around 2000 BC, based on his observations of workmanship, rather than on any other criteria. The pottery was, however, so "un-Egyptian" that he called the creators "the New Race".

Petrie faced a certain difficulty when he later found some of these same types of stone vases in tombs of the First Dynasty dating from, according to Egyptologists, around 3000 BC. At this point, he dropped the Naqada vase from his chronology, preferring to ignore what he could not explain.

Did the Naqadans produce these artifacts?

The Naqada peoples were descended from Paleolithic farmers who began raising crops in North Africa around 5000 BC. They buried their dead facing West, and seemed to be your standard primitive culture. The only problem was: the vases. The most astonishing of them were, "tall vases with long, thin, elegant necks and finely flared interiors, often incorporating fully hollowed-out shoulders".[180] Even more amazing, it seems that more that 30,000 of these vases were found *beneath* the Step Pyramid of Zoser at Saqqara.

Christopher Dunn, a toolmaker, wrote an article entitled *Advanced Machining in Ancient Egypt*, where he notes:

> The millions of tons of rock that the Egyptians had quarried for their pyramids and temples—and cut with such superb accuracy—reveal glimpses of a civilization that was technically more advanced than is generally believed. Even though it is thought that millions of tons of rock were cut with simple primitive hand tools, such as copper chisels, adzes and wooden mallets, substantial evidence shows that this is simply not the case. Even discounting the argument that work-hardened copper would not be suitable for cutting igneous rock, the evidence forces us to look a little harder, and more objectively, when explaining the manufacturing marks scoured on ancient granite by ancient stone craftsmen.[…]

> Although the Egyptians are not given credit for the simple wheel, the machine marks they left on the granite found at Giza suggests a much higher degree of technical accomplishment. Petrie's conclusion regarding their mechanical abilities shows a proficiency with the straight saw, circular saw, tube-drill, and surprisingly, even the lathe.[181]

Naturally, Egyptologists do nothing but disparage and attack such views, but they are unable to produce any evidence to support their claims, while there is an ever-growing mountain of evidence to support the ancient technology. Again, I suggest that Egyptologists ought to be required to have engineering degrees, as well as broader educations in other terms. It is Egyptologists who seem to be the fundamental arbiters of our history, and over and over again, we will find that they are the blind leading the blind.

Getting back to Dunn, he examined blocks that had been hollowed out with some kind of drill in the Valley Temple at Giza. He noted that the drill marks left in the hole show that it was cutting into the rock at the rate of a tenth of an inch for every revolution of the drill![182]

What is so amazing about that? As it happens, such a rate cannot be achieved by hand without the application of over a ton of pressure. And that is patently absurd

---

[180] Hancock, Fingerprints of the Gods, op cit.

[181] See: *Technologies of Ancient Egypt* by Christopher P. Dunn (Bear and Co. 1998).

[182] Wilson, op. cit.

to consider in terms of hand drilling! Dunn inquired of specialists in drilling machinery and was informed that the best drills we have today, spinning at the rate of 900 revolutions per minute, can only cut into similar stone at the rate of one ten thousandth of an inch per revolution. Conclusion? The builders of the pyramids and the creators of the stone vases had drills that either worked 500 times as fast as those we have today, or they had a "secret". Colin Wilson tells us:

> Another aspect of the problem began to provide Dunn with a glimmer of a solution. A hole drilled into a rock that was a mixture of quartz and feldspar showed that the "drill" had cut faster through the quartz than the feldspar, although quartz is harder than feldspar. The solution that he suggests sounds almost beyond belief. He points out that modern ultrasonic machining uses a tool that depends on vibration.[...]

> Quartz crystals are used in the production of ultrasonic sound, and, conversely, respond to ultrasonic vibrations. This would explain why the "bit" cut faster through the quartz than the feldspar.

> What is being suggested sounds, admittedly, absurd: that the Egyptians had some force as powerful as our modern electricity, and that this force was based on sound.[183]

As Wilson and Hancock point out, this explanation goes a long way toward explaining the vases with swan necks that are hollowed out of such hard and brittle materials. He also notes how embarrassed Petrie would have been to know that similar vases have been removed from strata dated to 4000 BC when Egypt was supposed to have been occupied by nomads in tents.

But, we do still have the fact that there *were* nomads in tents at that point, and the only solution I can see is that these peoples were survivors of a cataclysmic event, and that they continued to use whatever they could find from their lost civilization. In this way, vases and other artifacts, scavenged from ruins, would be found in any number of "strata" laid down after such an event. It seems that these vases could be evidence that Petrie's "New Race" pre-dated pharonic Egypt by thousands of years.

We come back to Edward Leedskalnin who claimed to have discovered the secret of how the pyramids were built. And the theorists are having a field day!

PYTHAGORAS AND THE BARBARIANS

We have touched briefly in earlier sections on the issue of sacred geometry, which is often related to the secret significance of numbers. Most of the current craze for these ideas is usually traced back to Pythagoras. We believe Pythagoras has been maligned by these new age purveyors of sacred geometry and sacred numbers. Naturally, when one is considering the "secret significance" of numbers,

---

[183] Wilson, op. cit.

Pythagorean Mathematics will be among the earliest considerations. Manly Hall wrote that:

> The true key to philosophic mathematics is the famous Forty-seventh Proposition of Pythagoras, erroneously attributed to Euclid. The Forty-seventh Theorem is stated thus: In a right-angled triangle the square described on the hypotenuse is equal to the sum of the squares described on the other two sides.[184]

Everyone who has attended public school and paid the slightest attention in math class knows that one. The problem is: what does it really mean that it is the "true key to philosophic mathematics"? What does $C^2=A^2+B^2$ have to tell us?

Accounts of the travels and studies of Pythagoras differ, but most historians agree that he visited many countries and studied at the feet of many masters. Supposedly, after having been initiated into the Eleusinian mysteries, he went to Egypt and was initiated into the Mysteries of Isis. He then traveled to Phoenicia and Syria and was initiated into the Mysteries of Adonis. After that, he traveled to the valley of the Euphrates and learned all the secrets of the Chaldeans still living in the area of Babylon. Finally, he traveled to Media and Persia, then to India where he was a pupil and initiate of the Brahmins there. Sounds like he had all the bases covered.

Pythagoras was said to have invented the term "philosopher" in preference to the word "sage" since the former meant one who is attempting to find the truth, and the latter means one who knows the truth. Apparently Pythagoras didn't think he had the whole banana.

Pythagoras started a school at Crotona in Southern Italy and gathered students and disciples there whom he supposedly instructed in the principles of the secrets that had been revealed to him. He considered mathematics, music and astronomy to be the foundation of all the arts and sciences. When he was about sixty years old, he married one of his disciples and had seven children. I guess he was a pretty lively senior citizen! His wife was, apparently, quite a woman in her own right, and she carried on his work after he was assassinated by a band of murderers incited to violence by a student whom he refused to initiate. The accounts of Pythagoras' murder vary. Some say he and all his disciples were killed, others say that he may have escaped because some of his students protected him by sacrificing themselves and that he later died of a broken heart when he realized the apparent fruitlessness of his efforts to illuminate humanity.

The experts say that very little remains of the teachings of Pythagoras in the present time unless it has been handed down in secret schools or societies. Naturally, every secret society on the planet claims to have this "initiated" knowledge to one extent or another. It is possible that there exists some of the

---

[184] Hall, Manly P., *The Secret Teachings of All Ages* (Los Angeles: The Philosophical Research Society 1988) p. LXIX (facing page).

original secret numerical formulas of Pythagoras, but the sad fact is that there is no real evidence of it in the writings that have issued from these groups for the past millennium. Though everyone discusses Pythagoras, no one seems to know any more than the post-Pythagorean Greek speculators who, as Manley Hall put it, "talked much, wrote little, knew less, and concealed their ignorance under a series of mysterious hints and promises". There seems to be a lot of that going around these days! Even Plutarch did not pretend to be able to explain the significance of the geometrical diagrams of Pythagoras. However, he did make the most interesting suggestion that the relationship which Pythagoras established between the geometrical solids and the gods was the result of images seen in the Egyptian temples. The question we would ask is: what do geometrical solids have to do with "gods"?

Albert Pike, the great Masonic symbolist, also admitted that there were many things that he couldn't figure out. In his *Symbolism for the 32nd and 33rd degrees* he wrote:

> I do not understand why the 7 should be called Minerva, or the cube, Neptune. ...Undoubtedly the names given by the Pythagoreans to the different numbers were themselves enigmatical and symbolic—and there is little doubt that in the time of Plutarch the meanings these names concealed were lost. Pythagoras had succeeded too well in concealing his symbols with a veil that was from the first impenetrable, without his oral explanation.[185]

Manly Hall writes:

> This uncertainty shared by all true students of the subject proves conclusively that it is unwise to make definite statements founded on the indefinite and fragmentary information available concerning the Pythagorean system of mathematical philosophy.[186]

With what little we have examined thus far, we are beginning to realize how true this latter remark is. Of course, in the present time, there is a whole raft of folks who don't let such remarks stop them. Any number of modern gurus claim to have discovered the secrets of "Sacred Geometry"! Not only that, they don't seem to have even studied the matter deeply at all, missing many of the salient points that are evident in the fragments of Pythagorean teachings. Regarding this, there is a passage in *Foucault's Pendulum*, by Umberto Eco, that explicates the problem:

> Amid all the nonsense there are some unimpeachable truths... I invite you to go and measure [an arbitrarily selected] kiosk. You will see that the length of the counter is one hundred and forty-nine centimeters—in other words, one hundred-billionth of the distance between the earth and the sun. The height at the rear, one hundred and seventy-six centimeters, divided by the width of the window, fifty-six centimeters,

---

[185] Cited by Hall, ibid., p. LXIX.
[186] Ibid.

is 3.14. The height at the front is nineteen decimeters, equal, in other words, to the number of years of the Greek lunar cycle. The sum of the heights of the two front corners is one hundred and ninety times two plus one hundred and seventy-six times two, which equals seven hundred and thirty-two, the date of the victory at Poitiers. The thickness of the counter is 3.10 centimeters, and the width of the cornice of the window is 8.8 centimeters. Replacing the numbers before the decimals by the corresponding letters of the alphabet, we obtain C for ten and H for eight, or $C_{10}H_8$, which is the formula for naphthalene.

...With numbers you can do anything you like. Suppose I have the sacred number 9 and I want to get the number 1314, date of the execution of Jacques de Molay—a date dear to anyone who professes devotion to the Templar tradition of knighthood. ...Multiply nine by one hundred and forty-six, the fateful day of the destruction of Carthage. How did I arrive at this? I divided thirteen hundred and fourteen by two, by three, et cetera, until I found a satisfying date. I could also have divided thirteen hundred and fourteen by 6.28, the double of 3.14, and I would have got two hundred and nine. That is the year Attalus I, king of Pergamon, ascended the throne.

You see? ...The universe is a great symphony of numerical correspondences... numbers and their symbolisms provide a path to special knowledge. But if the world, below and above, is a system of correspondences where *tout se tient*, it's natural for the [lottery] kiosk and the pyramid, both works of man, to reproduce in their structure, unconsciously, the harmonies of the cosmos.[187]

The idea has been promoted with great vigor for over a thousand years that so-called Kabbalists and "interpreters of mysteries" can discover with their incredibly tortuous methods The Truth. This arrogance completely misses the point of a truth that is far more ancient: Mathematics is the language of Nature. The Pythagoreans declared arithmetic to be the mother of the mathematical sciences. This idea was based on the fact that geometry, music, and astronomy are dependent upon arithmetic, but arithmetic is not dependent upon them. In this sense, geometry may be removed but arithmetic will remain; but if arithmetic were removed, geometry will be eliminated. In the same way, music depends on arithmetic. Eliminating music affects arithmetic only by limiting one of its expressions.

The size, form, and motion of the celestial bodies are determined by the use of geometry and their harmony and rhythm by the use of music. If astronomy is taken away, neither geometry nor music is harmed; but if geometry and music are done away with, astronomy is destroyed. The priority of both geometry and music to astronomy is established and arithmetic is prior to all of them, being primary and fundamental. Playing endless games with numbers demonstrates only *that which*

---

[187] Eco, Umberto, *Foucault's Pendulum,* (San Diego, New York, London: Harcourt Brace Jovanovich 1988) pp. 288-289.

cannot be otherwise. The real secret seems to be much more profound and most, if not nearly all, "seekers" of truths never penetrate beyond the surface of the matter.

Nevertheless, we have now reached the point where we have some idea that there was an ancient technology that utilized simple arithmetic, and geometry, or spatial relationships, in conjunction with sound, to accomplish something of great import. We have also come to the idea that this ancient technology was the science of the mastery of space and time and gravity. This is the great secret of the Golden Age. This is why their civilization was based on different elements than our own. Aside from the fact that cataclysms may have washed away most of the evidence of this civilization, we have here an additional reason for the lack of metal and other such artifacts of the type we would consider to be evidence of "civilization".

THE DANCING GOD

Getting back to our spinning Edward Leedskalnin in his airplane seat, we realize that he must have stumbled onto this secret and was able to utilize it to some extent. But Leedskalnin didn't have a landscape covered with megaliths to collect and store energy. Edward had an airplane seat suspended from the ceiling by a chain. How can this possibly give us a hint about what the ancients were doing? Searching for clues as to how the ancients utilized this technology, we find the following most interesting item. Diodorus Siculus, writing in the first century BC, gives us a description of Britain based, in part, on the voyage of Pytheas of Massilia, who sailed around Britain in 300 BC.

> As for the inhabitants, they are simple and far removed from the shrewdness and vice which characterize our day. Their way of living is modest, since they are well clear of the luxury that is begotten of wealth. The island is also thickly populated and its climate is extremely cold, as one would expect, since it actually lies under the Great Bear. It is held by many kings and potentates, who for the most part live at peace among themselves.[188]

Diodorus then tells a fascinating story about the Hyperboreans that was obviously of legendary character already when he was writing:

> Of those who have written about the ancient myths, Hecateus and certain others say that in the regions beyond the land of the Celts (Gaul) there lies in the ocean an island no smaller than Sicily. This island, the account continues, is situated in the north, and is inhabited by the Hyperboreans, who are called by that name because their home is beyond the point whence the north wind blows; and the land is both

---

[188] *Diodorus of Sicily*, English translation by C. H. Oldfather, Loeb Classical Library, Volumes II and III. London, William Heinemann, and Cambridge, Mass., USA, Harvard University Press, 1935 and 1939.

fertile and productive of every crop, and since it has an unusually temperate climate it produces two harvests each year.[189]

Now, it seems that there is little doubt that Diodorus is describing the same location, but we notice that the climate is so vastly different in the two descriptions that we can hardly make the connection. However, let us just suppose that his description of Britain was based on the climate that prevailed at the time he was writing, and the legendary description of the Hyperboreans was based *on a previous climatic condition* that was preserved in the story. Diodorus stresses that he is recounting something very ancient as he goes on to say:

> The Hyperboreans also have a language, we are informed, which is peculiar to them, and are most friendly disposed towards the Greeks, and especially towards the Athenians and the Delians, who have inherited this goodwill from *most ancient times*. The myth also relates that certain Greeks visited the Hyperboreans and left behind them costly votive offerings bearing inscriptions in Greek letters. And in the same way Abaris, a Hyperborean, came to Greece in ancient times and renewed the goodwill and kinship of his people to the Delians.[190]

Diodorus remark about the relations between the Hyperboreans and the Athenians triggers in our minds the memory of the statement of Plato that the Atlanteans were at war with the Athenians, and we wonder if the Hyperboreans are the real "early Athenians". After all, the Greeks are said to be "Sons of the North Wind", Boreas. Herodotus expounds upon the relationship of the Hyperboreans to the Delians:

> Certain sacred offerings wrapped up in wheat straw come from the Hyperboreans into Scythia, whence they are taken over by the neighbouring peoples in succession until they get as far west as the Adriatic: from there they are sent south, and the first Greeks to receive them are the Dodonaeans. Then, continuing southward, they reach the Malian gulf, cross to Euboea, and are passed on from town to town as far as Carystus. Then they skip Andros, the Carystians take them to Tenos, and the Tenians to Delos. That is how these things are said to reach Delos at the present time.[191]

The legendary connection between the Hyperboreans and the Delians leads us to another interesting remark of Herodotus who tells us that Leto, the mother of Apollo, was born on the island of the Hyperboreans. That there was regular contact between the Greeks and the Hyperboreans over many centuries does not seem to be in doubt. The Hyperboreans were said to have introduced the Greeks to the worship of Apollo, but it is just as likely that the relationship goes much

---

[189] Ibid.

[190] Ibid.

[191] Herodotus, *The Histories, Book IV*, trans. Aubrey De Selincourt, revised John Marincola (London: Penguin 1972) p. 226

further back. Yes, this is contrary to the idea that culture flowed from south to north, but we are writing a contrary book; so don't let that bother you! Herodotus has another interesting thing to say about the Hyperboreans and their sending of sacred offerings to Delos:

> On the first occasion they were sent in charge of two girls, whose names the Delians say were Hyperoche and Laodice. To protect the girls on the journey, the Hyperboreans sent five men to accompany them ... the two Hyperborean girls died in Delos, and the boys and girls of the island still cut their hair as a sign of mourning for them... There is also a Delphic story that before the time of Hyperoche and Laodice, two other Hyperborean girls, Arge and Opis, came to Delos by the same route. ...Arge and Opis came to the island at the same time as Apollo and Artemis...[192]

Herodotus mentions at another point, when discussing the lands of the "barbarians", "*All these except the Hyperboreans, were continually encroaching upon one another's territory*". Without putting words in Herodotus' mouth, it seems to suggest that the Hyperboreans were not warlike at all.

A further clue about the religion of the Hyperboreans comes from the myths of Orpheus. It is said that when Dionysus invaded Thrace, Orpheus did not see fit to honor him but instead preached the evils of sacrificial murder to the men of Thrace. He taught "other sacred mysteries" having to do with Apollo, whom he believed to be the greatest of all gods. Dionysus became so enraged; he set the Maenads on Orpheus *at Apollo's temple* where Orpheus was a priest. They burst in, murdered their husbands who were assembled to hear Orpheus speak, tore Orpheus limb from limb, and threw his head into the river Hebrus where it floated downstream *still singing*. It was carried on the sea to the island of Lesbos. Another version of the story is that Zeus killed Orpheus with a thunderbolt for *divulging divine secrets*. He was responsible for instituting the Mysteries of Apollo in Thrace, Hecate in Aegina, and Subterrene Demeter at Sparta.[193] And this brings us to a further revelation of Diodorus regarding the Hyperboreans:

> And there is also on the island both a magnificent sacred precinct of Apollo and a notable temple, which is adorned with many votive offerings and is *spherical* in shape. Furthermore, a city is there which is sacred to this god, and the majority of its inhabitants are players on the cithara; and these *continually play on this instrument in the temple* and sing hymns of praise to the god, glorifying his deeds... They say also that the moon, as viewed from this island, appears to be but a little distance from the earth and to have upon it prominences, like those of the earth, which are visible to the eye. The account is also given that the god visits the island every <u>nineteen years,</u> *the period in which the return of the stars to the same place in the heavens is accomplished,* and for this reason the Greeks call the nineteen-year

---

[192] Herodotus, *The Histories*, pp. 226-227.

[193] See: Graves, Robert, *The Greek Myths* (London: Penguin, London) 1992

period the "year of Meton". At the time of this appearance of the god he both plays on the cithara and dances continuously the night through from the vernal equinox until the rising of the Pleiades, expressing in this manner his delight in his successes. And the kings of this city and the supervisors of the sacred precinct are called Boreades, since they are descendants of Boreas, and the succession to these positions is always *kept in their family.*[194]

I would like to note immediately how similar the above story of the Maenads murdering their husbands is to the story of the daughters of Danaus murdering their husbands on the wedding night connected to the story of the massacre at the Cloisters of Ambrius attributed much later to Hengist and Horsa. Keeping in mind that the Danaans were the family of the hero Perseus who cut off the head of Medusa, while comparing this to the beheading of Orpheus and his "singing" head floating down the river. The two themes, wives murdering husbands and a significant beheading are startling enough to give us pause. Was an original legend then later adapted to a different usage, assimilated to a different group or tribe? More than once?

In any event, we have discovered a most interesting little collection of things all in one place. First a "round temple" on an island that can only be Britain, may be describing Stonehenge and the way in which it was utilized by a group of people. Next we see that Diodorus is suggesting that the 19-year lunar calendar is a product of the Hyperboreans and that it relates to a period in which the "return of the stars" is accomplished. We realize immediately that these "stars" must refer to a geometric relationship between the Sun, Moon and Earth, rather than the "stars" in terms of real stars and the planets because they certainly do not "return" to any particular position every nineteen years. And we now suspect that this may have something to do with a gravitational node of a three-body system.

We begin to think that these ancient people really knew something!

In the Temple of Apollo, we also find that there are musicians whose job it is to continually play in the temple and sing, and the most famous of ancient singers and musicians is associated with the worship of Apollo. This suggests to us the possible use of sound for something; the utilization of gravitational nodes, perhaps?

There is an additional puzzle here. What did it mean that every nineteen years a god "dances" from the vernal equinox *until the rising of the Pleiades*? This suggests to us a very specific date is being recorded in this myth. The heliacal rising of the Pleiades does not happen every 19 years. So, aside from telling us about a regular event that occurred every nineteen years, the myth has recorded something else very significant, the date of which is internal to the myth. When did the Pleiades rise just before the sun on the vernal equinox?

---

[194] Diodorus, op. cit..

There are many who assume that a "heliacal rising" means that a star or constellation is in conjunction with the sun. But this is probably not correct. The ancients were practicing observational astronomy. Otto Neugebauer, in his many studies regarding what the ancients did or did not know about science and mathematics, noted the following:

> When we watch the stars rise over the eastern horizon, we see them appear night after night at the same spot on the horizon. But when we extend our observation into the period of twilight, fewer and fewer stars will be recognizable when they cross the horizon, and near sunrise all stars will have faded out altogether. Let us suppose that a certain star S was seen just rising at the beginning of dawn but vanished from sight within a very short time because of the rapid approach of daylight. We call this phenomenon the "heliacal rising" of S, using a term of Greek astronomy. Let us assume that we use this phenomenon as the indication of the end of "night" and consider S as *the star of the "last hour of night"*. [...] We may continue in the same way for several days, but during this time a definite change takes place. [...] Obviously, after some lapse of time, it no longer makes sense to take S as the indicator of the last hour of night. But there are new stars that can take the place of S. Thus year after year S may serve for some days as *the star of the last hour*, to be replaced in regular order by other stars.[195]

In order to observe a heliacal rising of a star or group of stars, they must rise long enough *before the sun* to be "observed", because as soon as the sun rises, the stars can no longer be seen. The heliacal rising of the Pleiades would have to occur *at least* 36 minutes before the sun comes up, in order to be *seen*. So, the real question seems to be: when did the Pleiades rise around half an hour before the sun, at the time of the equinox? When were the Pleiades the stars of the "last hour of the night", and what might have been the significance of this event?

Certain "standard" texts, written by individuals who have not taken into account the observational nature of a heliacal rising, have given 2300 BC as the date, because this was when the Pleiades were conjunct the Sun on the Vernal equinox. However, after careful calculations of our own, as well as assistance by expert astronomers, the date of the actual heliacal rising of the Pleiades, in the terms that Neugebauer has given us, occurred on April 16, 3100 BC. This date is most certainly correct as we will see further on.

There is an even greater mystery here regarding the Pleiades. In the cave of Lascaux, there is a prehistoric image of an Auroch, which is the largest picture in the whole assembly of images, and is painted almost entirely on the ceiling of the cave. Above the back of the Auroch, a strange figure of a cluster of six floating points can be seen. The distribution of the dots does not seem to be haphazard, but rather shows a clear structural element. It looks, in fact, like an exact portrayal of the constellation Taurus with the star cluster of the Pleiades placed precisely as

---

[195] Neugebauer, op. cit.

they actually relate to the constellation. The Navajo in America have also portrayed the Pleiades in exactly this same six-star arrangement in modern times, as handed down to them by their ancestors.[196]

The constellation Taurus was originally a complete image of a bull in the sky. The Babylonians called it the heavenly bull, and the Pleiades were recognized as the "bristle on the neck of the bull". At some point, the bull was cut in half to create Aries and Cetus, the whale.

So here we have a very interesting confluence of seemingly unrelated elements: We will pass from that subject for the moment to return to our matter of the dancing god who came every 19 years to Stonehenge, and how it may relate to spinning in airplane seats, producing sounds, and overcoming gravity - and perhaps even space and time and matter. What we find is that these elements are all connected in such a way that we suspect that they were elements of a technology that enabled an entire group of people to live in harmony, and to produce all they needed so that the artifacts of civilization, as we know them, were not required by these peoples. What is more, they seem to have been related to their ability to perform feats of which we are incapable with all our technology. These "wonders" that are the stuff of myth to us now, were, apparently, part of their daily reality.

In searching for additional clues in the nature religions associated with the symbols of the Holy Grail, we find that *dancing* was part of the archaic grail ensemble. The Sword Dances, Morris Dances, and Mumming Plays, for example, seem to be an inherited tradition of solemn ceremonial dances performed at stated seasons. And that is exactly what Diodorus has told us: The god danced all night every 19 years at the time of the Equinox.

Jessie Weston, among others, was moved to think of these dances and the entire Grail cycle ensemble as a ritual designed to *"preserve and promote the regular and ordered sequence of the processes of Nature"*. In other words, the *disjecta membra* of the advanced technology of a vanished civilization.

It seems to us, from looking at the evidence of the absolute reality of what these people were capable of doing, that the dances, the myths, and the rites, all point to an archaic technology that is preserved idealistically as "promoting the processes of Nature", but it was actually a *direct interaction with Nature* that resulted in the manifest production of all that was needed by the peoples in a literal and immediate sense.

The earliest recorded Sword Dancers are the Maruts, the attendants of the god Indra. They are a group of youths of equal age and identical parentage and are always dressed alike, and they are always dancers. Throughout the Rg-Veda the

---

[196] Chamberlain, Von Del, "Navajo Constellations in Literature, Art, Artifact and a New Mexico Rock Art Site", *Archaeoastronomy* 6 (1-4):48-58, 1983.

Maruts are referred to as, *"Gold bedecked dancers... with songs of praise they danced round the spring... When ye Maruts spear-armed dance, [the Heavens] stream together like waves of water"*.[197]

The image of the "spear armed" dancing of course has led people to think that they are dancing with spears, but what if it means something altogether different? Anyone who has watched traditional Celtic dances is immediately struck by the stiff armed posture of the dancers who only move the lower parts of their bodies. Dancing in perfect synchrony on a wooden platform produces a hypnotic and thrilling effect, and we find here a possible system of elevation of consciousness that might produce vibratory effects not only in stone, but also in the very cells of both the dancers and the audience. More than this, when we consider the immobility of the upper part of the body, and the stylized motion of the lower part of the body, we think of the "length of string" attached to a pendulum that accesses other realities. We may also consider the addition of a real "lance" as a "lengthener" of the "string", or something that was incorporated to connect the dancer to a specific frequency. Add to it very specific music, utilized to amplify the energetic effects, or sound that was a *result* of the dance, and we begin to see a very different picture of the dance of Apollo at Stonehenge every 19 years. In fact, we are reminded of that curious story where an alchemist supposedly told Jacques Bergier:

> Certain geometrical arrangements of highly purified materials are enough to release atomic forces without having recourse to either electricity or vacuum techniques.[198]

Most especially when we recall this:

> For it is by fire and in fire that our hemisphere will soon be tried. And just as by means of fire, gold is separated from impure metals, so, Scripture says, the good will be separated from the wicked, on the great Day of Judgment. [...][199]

The Maruts were the companions of Indra, his helpers in the fight against his adversaries, the evil gods who afflict mankind. But more than this, these dancers, (Dan-cers) were bringers of all necessities to the people in some magical, mysterious, and astonishing way:

> The adorable Maruts, armed with bright lances and cuirassed with golden breastplates, enjoy vigorous existence; *may the cars of the quick-moving Maruts arrive for our good.* ...Bringers of rain and fertility, shedding water, *augmenting food.* ...Givers of abundant food. ...Your milchkine are never dry. ...We invoke *the food-laden chariots* of the Maruts.[200]

---

[197] Von Schroeder, *Mysterium und Mimus*, quoted by Jessie Weston in *From Ritual to Romance*, p. 78.

[198] Pauwels and Bergier, op. cit.

[199] Fulcanelli, *Mystery*, op. cit. p. 149.

[200] Rg-Veda, Vol III.

We now begin to see the wild orgies of the New Year festivals, the Dionysian frenzies, and the Nature cults with parades of ecstatic men and women bordering on being in a state of madness, as *corruptions* of what was obviously an original, formalized series of dance type activities. And this makes us think of the Maze. The Labyrinth. Troy. Crete. Egypt?

THE LABYRINTH

Hundreds of mazes and labyrinths are found scattered across Europe, parts of Africa, Asia and the Americas. They are composed of turf, hedges, stone, brick, or tile work on floors. There are paintings and carvings of mazes on rocks that are incredibly ancient. One of the oldest representations that I have found is a 20,000-year-old bracelet carved from a single piece of mammoth ivory, found at Mezin, Ukraine. This piece has a magnificent "Greek Meander" or "maze" design which predates any other maze we are going to discuss here, but most definitely offers a clue since this area of the world is that hot-spot of Grail legends identified by Littleton and Malcor.

What most people know about the maze, or labyrinth, is due to the myth of Theseus and Ariadne. Briefly, the tale tells of King Minos of Crete, who demanded tribute from Athens, after defeating them in a war. The tribute was an annual shipment of seven youths and seven maidens who were sacrificed to the Minotaur by sending them into the maze, the specially constructed home of the beast, built by the great architect, Daedalus. The labyrinth was so cleverly constructed that even Daedalus had difficulty navigating in it. The Athenian young people would wander around in the maze, lost, until the Minotaur, half bull (top half) and half man (bottom half) caught up with them and devoured them. This, of course, reminds us of Herodotus' story of the Hyperborean girls sent to Delos bearing gifts, who died while there under what seem to be mysterious circumstances.

As a side note, we would like to draw attention to the fact that Daedalus, the "great architect", was connected to a king named Minos. Another king named Menes was the great unifier of Egypt, builder of the great city of Memphis, and a famous temple of Hephaestus there. This is dated to around 3100 BC, and we wonder if the image of the half bull, half man might not be a clue to a date such as the point at which the constellation Taurus was "cut in half" to make room for Aries, the ram, who represents Agni, god of fire. Hephaestus is, after all, the Greek version of the Smith God. Discovering a great architect connected, even indirectly, to a great unifier of two kingdoms and builder of a great Temple on the one side, and connected to another king with a similar name, and builder of a great labyrinth which is connected to a "power in the center", - the Minotaur, keeping in mind the legends of the building of Stonehenge, the "cloisters of Ambrius" where the god danced all night in the center around 3100 BC, makes us wonder if this is not all a clue to the manifestation of a certain power that has to do with sound and gravity and stones and so forth. We are naturally drawn to make connections between these matters and the myth of Solomon and Hiram Abiff and the Ark of the Covenant. When we think of the Temple of Solomon (about which we will learn a great deal further on), which was built to house the Ark, and we then think of the labyrinth which was built to house a monster, we naturally wonder just what is going on here? We also note that the victims of King Minos of Crete were "Athenians", and we remember what Plato said about the war between Atlantis and "Athens", even if we don't put any stock in it actually being the Athens we know today.

According to the myth, the labyrinth was built for one reason only: to hide the Minotaur, which was a source of horror and shame to Minos, whose wife had given birth to the monster after mating with a bull. This really doesn't follow logic since the victims were rounded up in public, and everyone apparently knew about the Minotaur.

In South Africa, a popular Zulu game is played where a maze is drawn on the ground, and the players take turns "finding the way to the king's hut" which is at the center. The game is played with toys carved in the shape of bulls. It seems that, thousands of miles from Crete, the same elements of the legend are played out from time immemorial: kingship, bulls, and conflict at the center of a labyrinth.

Excavations at Knossos have indeed uncovered evidence of a bull cult practiced in a maze like "palace" of hundreds of chambers and corridors. There were innumerable images of bulls in bas-reliefs, small sculptures, bull-shaped vessels, seals and imprints of seals, as well as stylized bulls' horns. All of these things linking the dynasty of Minos with bulls suggested that the vitality of the Minoan kings, like that of the pharaohs of ancient Egypt, was identified with the bull-god. What is more, ancient Greek writers came right out and said that the labyrinth of Minos was modeled on an original in northern Egypt. Very little survives of this Egyptian marvel except for a few brick courses. What Herodotus had to say about it is rather fascinating:

> Being set free after the reign of the priest of Hephaistos, the Egyptians, since they could not live any time without a king, set up over them twelve kings, having divided all Egypt into twelve parts. These made intermarriages with one another and reigned, making agreement that they would not put down one another by force, nor seek to get an advantage over one another, but would live in perfect friendship: and the reason why they made these agreements, guarding them very strongly from violation, was this, namely that an oracle had been given to them at first when they began to exercise their rule, that he of them who should pour a libation with a bronze cup in the temple of Hephaistos, should be king of all Egypt (for they used to assemble together in all the temples).

> Moreover they resolved to join all together and leave a memorial of themselves; and having so resolved they caused to be made a labyrinth situated a little above the lake of Moeris and nearly opposite to that which is called the City of Crocodiles. This I saw myself, and I found it greater than words can say. For if one should put together and reckon up all the buildings and all the great works produced by the Hellenes, they would prove to be inferior in labour and expense to this labyrinth, though it is true that both the temple at Ephesos and that at Samos are works worthy of note.

> The pyramids also were greater than words can say, and each one of them is equal to many works of the Hellenes, great as they may be; but the labyrinth surpasses even the pyramids. It has twelve courts covered in, with gates facing one another, six upon the North side and six upon the South, joining on one to another, and the same wall surrounds them all outside; and there are in it two kinds of chambers, the

one kind below the ground and the other above upon these, three thousand in number, of each kind fifteen hundred. The upper set of chambers we ourselves saw, going through them, and we tell of them having looked upon them with our own eyes; but the chambers under ground we heard about only; for the Egyptians who had charge of them were not willing on any account to show them, saying that here were the sepulchres of the kings who had first built this labyrinth and of the sacred crocodiles.

Accordingly we speak of the chambers below by what we received from hearsay, while those above we saw ourselves and found them to be works of more than human greatness. For the passages through the chambers, and the goings this way and that way through the courts, which were admirably adorned, afforded endless matter for marvel, as we went through from a court to the chambers beyond it, and from the chambers to colonnades, and from the colonnades to other rooms, and then from the chambers again to other courts. Over the whole of these is a roof made of stone like the walls; and the walls are covered with figures carved upon them, each court being surrounded with pillars of white stone fitted together most perfectly; and at the end of the labyrinth, by the corner of it, there is a pyramid of forty fathoms, upon which large figures are carved, and to this there is a way made under ground.[201]

What was Herodotus describing? He declared all the great architectural works of the Greeks and Egyptians, including the pyramids, to be "*inferior in labour and expense to this labyrinth*". We would also like to note that there were no references to bulls hidden in the Egyptian labyrinth; rather, in the hidden underground chambers were the "sepulchres of the kings who had first built this labyrinth and of the *sacred crocodiles*". Diodorus has a slightly different story about who built this famous labyrinth:

When the king died the government was recovered by Egyptians and they appointed a native king Mendes, whom some call Mares. Although he was responsible for no military achievements whatsoever, he did build himself what is called the Labyrinth as a tomb, an edifice which is wonderful *not so much for its size* as for the inimitable skill with which it was built; for once in, it is impossible to find one's way out again without difficulty, unless one lights upon a guide who is perfectly acquainted with it. It is even said by some that Daedalus crossed over to Egypt and, in wonder at the skill shown in the building, built for Minos, King of Crete, a labyrinth like that in Egypt, in which, so the tales goes, the creature called the Minotaur was kept. Be that as it may, the Cretan Labyrinth has completely disappeared, either through the destruction wrought by some ruler or through the ravages of time; but *the Egyptian Labyrinth remains absolutely perfect in its entire construction down to my time*. [...]

For they chose a site beside the channel leading into Lake Moeris in Libya and there constructed their tomb of the finest stone, laying down an oblong as the shape

---

[201] Herodutus, op. cit. Bk II:147.

and a stade as the size of each side, while in respect of carving and other works of craftsmanship they left no room for their successors to surpass them. For, when one had entered the sacred enclosure, one found a temple surrounded by columns, 40 to each side, and this building had a roof made of a single stone, carved with panels and richly adorned with excellent paintings. It contained memorials of the *homeland of each of the kings* as well as of the temples and sacrifices carried out in it, all skillfully worked in paintings of the greatest beauty. Generally it is said that the king conceived their tomb on such an expensive and prodigious scale that if they had not been deposed before its completion, they would not have been able to give their successors any opportunity to surpass them in architectural feats.[202]

Next there is the report of Strabo:

In addition to these things there is the edifice of the Labyrinth which is a building *quite equal to the Pyramids* and nearby the tomb of the king who built the Labyrinth. There is at the point where one first enters the channel, about 30 or 40 stades along the way, a flat trapezium-shaped site which contains both a village and a great palace made up of many palaces equal in number to that of the nomes in former times; for such is the number of peristyle courts which lie contiguous with one another, all in one row and backing on one wall, as though one had a long wall with the courts lying before it, and the passages into the courts lie opposite the wall. Before the entrances there lie what might be called hidden chambers which are long and many in number and have paths running through one another which twist and turn, so that no one can enter or leave any court without a guide. And the wonder of it is *the roofs of each chambers are made of single stones* and the width of the hidden chambers is spanned in the same way by monolithic beams of outstanding size; for *nowhere is wood or any other material included.* And if one mounts onto the roof, at no great height because the building has only one story, it is possible to get a view of a plain of masonry made of such stones, and, if one drops back down from there into the courts, it is possible to see them lying there in row each supported by 27 monolithic pillars; the walls too are made up in stones of no less a size.

At the end of this building, which occupies an area of more than a stade, stands the tomb, a pyramid on a oblong base, each side about 4 "plethora" in length and the height about the same; the name of the man buried there was Imandes. The reason for making the courts so many is said to be the fact that it was customary for all nomes to gather there according to rank with their own priests and priestesses, for the purpose of sacrifice, divine-offering, and judgment on the most important matters. And each of the nomes was lodged in the court appointed to it.

And above this city stands Abydos, in which there is the Memnonium, a palace wonderfully constructed of massive stonework in the same way as we have said the Labyrinth was built, though the Memnonium differs in being simple in structure.[203]

---

[202] Diodorus Siculus, op. cit., two passages in his history, Book I, 61 and 66.

[203] Strabo (ca. 64 BC - AD 19): Three passages in his geography, Book 17, I, 3 and 37 and 42.

Pliny tells us still another version of the stories about this amazing structure:

> Let us speak also of labyrinths, quite the most extraordinary works on which men
> have spent their money, but not, as may be thought, figments of the imagination.
> There still exists even now in Egypt in the Heracleopolite Nome the one which was
> built first, according to tradition *3,600 years ago by king Petesuchis* or Tithois,
> though Herodotus ascribes the whole work to Twelve Kings and Psammetichus, the
> latest of them. Various reasons are given for building it. Demoteles claims that it
> was the palace of Moteris, Lyceas the tomb of Moeris, but the *majority of writers*
> take the view that it was built as a temple to the Sun, and this is generally accepted.
> At any rate, that Daedalus used this as the model for the Labyrinth which he built in
> Crete is beyond doubt, but it is equally clear that he imitated only 100th part of it
> which contains twisting paths and passages which advance and retreat-all
> impossible to negotiate. The reason for this is not that within a small compass it
> involves one in mile upon mile of walking, as we see in tessellated floors or the
> displays given by boys on the Campus, but that frequently doors are buried in it to
> beguile the visitor into going forward and then force him to return into the same
> winding paths. This was the second to be built after the Egyptian Labyrinth, the
> third being in Lemnos and the fourth in Italy, all roofed with vaults of polished
> stone, though the Egyptian specimen, to my considerable astonishment, has its
> entrance and columns made of *Parian marble*, while the rest is of *Aswan granite*,
> *such masses being put together as time itself cannot dissolve even with the help of*
> *the Heracleopolitans; for they have regarded the building with extraordinary*
> *hatred.*
>
> It would be impossible to describe in detail the layout of that building and its
> individual parts, since it is divided into regions and administrative districts which
> are called nomes, each of the 21 nomes giving its names to one of the houses. A
> further reason is the fact that it also contains temples of all the gods of Egypt while,
> in addition, Nemesis placed in the building's 40 chapels many pyramids of 40 ells
> each covering an area of 6 arourae with their base. Men are already weary with
> traveling when they reach that bewildering maze of paths; indeed, there are also
> lofty upper rooms reached by ramps and porticoes from which one descends on
> stairways which have 90 steps each; inside are columns of imperial porphyry,
> images of the gods, statues of kings and representations of monsters. Certain of the
> halls are arranged in such way that as one throws open the door there arises within
> a fearful noise of thunder; moreover one passes through most of them in darkness.
> There are again other massive buildings outside the wall of the Labyrinth; they call
> them "the Wing". Then there are other subterranean chambers made by excavating
> galleries in the soil. One person only has done any repairs there-and they were few
> in number. He was Chaermon, the eunuch of king Necthebis, 500 years before
> Alexander the Great. A tradition is also current that he supported the roofs with
> beams of acacia wood boiled in oil, until squared stones could be raised up into the
> vaults.[204]

---

[204] Pliny (AD 23-79): One passage in his natural history, Book 36, 13.

We seem to have a bit of a problem here. Notice that Pliny assures us that Herodotus was wrong not only about who built the labyrinth, but also about when it was built. Pliny dates it to almost four thousand years before his own time. He also makes the most interesting remark that the building was regarded with extraordinary hatred. That would certainly be true of a structure that was utilized for dreadful sacrifices. Pliny mentions the mythical labyrinth of Crete, though it is a certainty that the temple at Knossos that was identified as the labyrinth by Arthur Evans was no longer available for view in the time of Pliny. It seems that Pliny, along with everyone else just took it for granted that the legends of the labyrinth on Crete were the truth.

So it is that we have found that the earliest known written account of the existence of labyrinths appears in the writings of the Greek historian Herodotus in approximately 450 BC. He describes a great labyrinth located in Egypt at the ancient site of Arsinoe on the eastern bank of a large body of water, Lake Moeris. The labyrinth was constructed in the style of a great compartmental palace with 3000 different chambers, 1500 of which were above ground and 1500 were below ground. The foundation was approximately 1000 feet long x 800 feet long. He claimed that it was built by Ammenemes III in the twelfth dynasty of the Old Kingdom in approximately 2300 BC. He further said that its primary purpose was for burial, and many kings were buried there. Pliny verified Herodotus' account in his writings on the four famous labyrinths of antiquity in approximately 50 AD. The remains of the city of Arsinoe have been excavated, but a great labyrinth to the extent of Herodotus' description has never been found.

Flinders Petrie did extensive excavation of the city of Arsinoe in 1888, but he never discovered the fantastic site that Herodotus described. Petrie found only a great bed of fragments which he believed was the labyrinth. The body of Ammenemes III was supposedly unearthed corroborating Herodotus. A sufficient quantity of the original foundation was unearthed which handily allowed it to be measured at 1000 feet X 800 feet which is exactly the dimension quoted by Herodotus! That it was definitely a labyrinth could not be determined.

More recently, Egyptologists have decided that the so-called "pyramid of Hawara" is the famous Egyptian labyrinth, but that makes no sense at all. Herodotus, Diodorus, Strabo and Pliny all describe so marvelous a structure that we are hard put to not think that there is truth behind what they were describing. The various propositions for what must be the "remains" of the structure simply do not fit the descriptions. And, while we can have some doubts about the accuracy of the history ascribed to the monument by the various ancient authors, depending on who gave them their information, it's difficult to doubt that they either saw it themselves, or had direct information.

Modern experts suggest that "Lake Moeris" is really Lake Qarun, the third largest lake in Egypt, which is located in Faiyyum. If so, we wonder why there are no remains of this labyrinth which Pliny tells us was constructed of, *"Parian marble*, while the rest is of *Aswan granite, such masses being put together as time itself cannot dissolve even with the help of the Heracleopolitans; for they have regarded the building with extraordinary hatred"*.

Of course, this last may provide a clue: if the building was so hated, it is altogether possible that it was deliberately destroyed, cut to pieces, and carried away block by block.

The bottom line seems to be that the legend of the labyrinth containing a horrible creature is based on the Egyptian labyrinth. The fact that the Cretans became "experts" in some sort of funerary cult, only created a fertile ground for transferring this legend to Crete. In fact, the Cretans may be closely related to the original Egyptians, the ones who were responsible for the building of the pyramids, the Sphinx, and other techno marvels. We notice a most peculiar series of events in regard to Egyptian "history", that may offer some clues:

The generally accepted sequence of Egyptian historical events tells us that a king from "upper Egypt" - that is, the arid highlands - named Narmer, Menes, or Aha, (who may have been separate individuals), defeated the King of Northern, or Lower Egypt, and thereby unified the two lands. This unification is commemorated in the famous Narmer Palette, which shows the ubiquitous "head smiting" scene, a euphemism for conquest.

According to Manetho, Menes/Narmer came from the Thinite province in Upper Egypt and, whether unification was achieved by military of peaceful means is uncertain, though head smiting seems to indicate the former.

According to tradition, Menes founded Memphis on an island in the Nile, conducted raids against the Nubians, and extended his power as far as the first cataract. He sent ambassadors to Canaan and Byblos in Phoenicia; he founded the city of Crocodilopolis and built the first temple to the god Ptah, who Herodotus and others say was Hephaestus, the volcano/fire god.

As a sidebar, skipping over the list and details of what is known via archaeology and conjectured via ignorance, we come to the reign of Peribsen in the so-called second dynasty. Peribsen was the fourth king of that line and some experts opine that he was actually not the legitimate heir of Nintejer, the king before him, but that he was an outsider who instigated a coup against Pharaoh Nintejer. Peribsen used the nomen "Seth" in his titles. Apparently, this signified sweeping political changes since the serekhs bearing the royal names are not surmounted by Horus anymore, but by his religious rival, Set, who became the primary royal patron deity of Peribsen.

Here we discover a most interesting point in history. Peribsen was claiming the title of the rival of Horus. Egyptologists admit that the events of the second dynasty are extremely uncertain, if not the most uncertain in Egyptian history. It just so happens that, right around the time of the Peribsen "rebellion", the Cretan civilization suddenly appeared in the Mediterranean. We also note the most curious fact that, based on the years assigned to the kings by Manetho, though we cannot be certain of the year in our own calendar system on which to affix these dates, the period between the unification by Narmer and the Peribsen rebellion happens to be right at 430 years - the period of slavery in Egypt claimed by the Jews. It is curious to find this "unification" of Egypt, the building of a great city and temple in Egypt, and a rebellion 430 years later. As it happens, it was precisely at this moment in time that a new group of people appeared on the island of Crete. Tacitus tells us:

> Some say that the Jews were fugitives from the island of Crete, who settled on the nearest coast of Africa about the time when Saturn was driven from his throne by the power of Jupiter. Evidence of this is sought in the name. There is a famous mountain in Crete called Ida; the neighboring tribe, the Idaei, came to be called Judaei by a barbarous lengthening of the national name.[205]

Is this an ancient tradition that was carried to Crete by refugees from Egypt, and then, at the time of the eruption of the volcano Santorini, was carried again to Palestine along with the terrifying images of death and destruction?

In the myths of the labyrinth, the most famous of Daedalus' architectural feats, it is said that King Minos imprisoned him in the labyrinth for helping Theseus escape. Daedalus and his son escaped by fashioning wings made of feathers and wax, though his son is killed by falling into the sea when the wax melts and the feathers begin to fall out. It was said that Daedalus fled to Sicily.

Again we make note of the curious similarity of the story of Minos and his great architect, Daedalus, and Solomon and his great architect Hiram Abiff. We see in the story of Menes/Narmer not merely a strong resemblance, but we see certain historical developments that, even though not specified, point us in the direction of thinking that the myth of Theseus, Ariadne, and Daedalus and the Minotaur in the labyrinth, actually relate to Menes and his labyrinth, and a rebellion 430 years after a "unification" and the building of a labyrinth.

It is most curious to find this ancient link between Crete and Egypt and the Jews, the purported possessors of the famous Ark of the Covenant, most especially when we consider the issue of the labyrinth and the Minotaur. Was the Labyrinth the real "Temple of Solomon"? We find another clue in the writings of our old gadabout recorder of all gossip, legends, and discombobulated history, Herodotus. Keep in mind that Herodotus was writing down what he was told and what he could get from inquiry. Indeed, the history had already been "mythicized", and different kings had been assimilated to the myth according to the pattern discovered by Eliade and friends, so keep that in mind as you read this passage:

> Apries having thus been overthrown, Amasis became king, being of the district of Saïs, and the name of the city whence he was is Siuph. Now at the first the Egyptians despised Amasis and held him in no great regard, because he had been *a man of the people* and was of no distinguished family; but afterwards Amasis won them over to himself by wisdom and not willfulness.

> First in Saïs he built and completed for Athene a temple-gateway which is a great marvel, and he far surpassed herein all who had done the like before, both in regard to height and greatness, so large are the stones and of such quality. Then secondly he dedicated great colossal statues and man-headed sphinxes very large, and for restoration he brought other stones of monstrous size. Some of these he caused to

---

[205] Herodotus, *The Histories*, Book V, c. 110 CE

be brought from the stone-quarries which are opposite Memphis, others of very great size from the city of Elephantine, distant a voyage of not less than twenty days from Saïs: and of them all I marvel most at this, namely a monolith chamber which he brought from the city of Elephantine; and they were three years engaged in bringing this, and two thousand men were appointed to convey it, who all were of the class of boatmen.

Moreover Amasis became a lover of the Hellenes; and besides other proofs of friendship which he gave to several among them, he also granted the city of Naucratis for those of them who came to Egypt to dwell in; and to those who did not desire to stay, but who made voyages thither, he granted portions of land to set up altars and make sacred enclosures for their gods.

Also with the people of Kyrene Amasis made an agreement for friendship and alliance; and he resolved too to marry a wife from thence, whether because he desired to have a wife of Hellenic race, or apart from that, on account of friendship for the people of Kyrene: however that may be, he married, some say the daughter of Battos, others of Arkesilaos, and others of Critobulos, a man of repute among the citizens; and her name was Ladike.[206]

We are suddenly reminded of the Hyperborean girls who brought offerings to Delos, one of whom was named Laodike. What is more, it brings to mind the journey of the great Queen of Sheba who heard of the fame of Solomon and came, bearing gifts, to see for herself.

THE SECRET OF CRETE

For centuries, bards in the marketplaces of the Mediterranean recited the stories of the Minotaur. Scholars of later centuries considered them to be fable and fantasy. The ideas of human sacrifice and grotesque creatures were reinterpreted as symbolic accounts of how higher Greek culture overcame the bloody bull cult of the ancient Cretans. And so the matter was interpreted until Arthur Evans discovered and excavated the "palace" at Knossos, a few miles south of the capital of Crete, Herakleion. (We note that Pliny mentions residents of an Egyptian city *Heracleopolis*.)

Nevertheless, Arthur Evans banished the myth of the Minotaur with his discovery. From the remains of twelve hundred deviously interconnected rooms, stairways, corridors, warehouses, colonnaded halls and cellars grouped around an interior court, and from the arrangements of wall paintings showing bull games, animal scenes, processions and portraits, Evans reconstructed the Minoan culture for the breathless world. Based upon Evan's analyses, the Greek bards who said such nasty things about the Cretans were all a bunch of frauds! The innumerable

---

[206] Herodotus, *The Histories*, Book II, 181.

battles between Theseus and the Minotaur portrayed on classical vases, murals, mosaics, reliefs, gems, and coins, were obviously based on pure imagination.

There were, of course, some criticisms of Evans' reconstruction, but by and large, no one really doubted that the excavated labyrinth at Knossos was, indeed, the home of the Cretan royal family - a palace. Not only that, but the world of Arthur Evans' time was amazed at the high culture of the Minoans. They had drainage systems, bathrooms, frescoes of women in striking toilettes that were actually similar to the styles at the time of the discovery - bared breasts and long skirts. The women of Knossos wore make-up and lived in country estates that were undefended - a sign of gracious living - as opposed to the gloomy citadels of the later Greeks. Clearly the Minoans lived in a land flowing with milk and honey and lived a carefree life devoted to sports, art, and love in the sunny kingdom of Minos, a veritable Solomon with his genius architect, Daedalus.

There was only one serious dissenter to the universal acceptance of the gay lifestyle of those amazing Minoans: Oswald Spengler. In his book *World History of the Second Millennium BC*, published in 1935, Spengler speculated on the archaeological finds of Crete. He noted the absence of any protecting walls around ancient Cretan palaces and country estates; he noted the pictures of bulls so reminiscent of the ancient Minotaur legend; he noted a very peculiar "king's throne" in the Palace of Knossos, which in his view, would have been more suitable "for a votive image of a priest's mummy". And then he asked, "were the 'palaces' of Knossos and Phaistos *temples of the dead*, sanctuaries of a powerful cult of the hereafter? I do not wish to make such an assertion, for I cannot prove it, but the question seems to me worthy of serious consideration".

But such a suggestion was ignored.

According to the experts, the position of Crete was particularly favorable for the purported Minoan domination of the sea, and for growth and development of their wonderful civilization. It was claimed to be the "crossroads", linking three continents, and all the racial and cultural elements of Europe, Asia and Africa met and mingled in the melting pot of Crete. It was this mingling that produced such a marvelous new way of life, a new philosophy, new art, and the "freshness, charm and variety" that enchanted the world.

The Minoan Kingdom was destroyed by the eruption of the terrible volcano of Santorini, which we will discuss further on in some detail, and after that, none of the Minoan "palaces" was ever re-inhabited. It seems that the original Minoans fled, never to return, and afterward, the purely Greek period of Crete began with the arrival of waves of Dorians.

According to Homer, Idomensus, grandson of the ruler of Knossos, fought side by side with the Achaeans against the Trojans. In the famous catalogue of ships in *The Iliad*, the Cretans are listed along with the rest of the Achaeans and not as foreign auxiliaries. There is absolutely no indication that the Cretans are anything other than Danaans, which means Achaeans or Greeks. Before the discoveries of Arthur Evans, there was no indication that the Minoans had not been Greeks. But after his excavations, such an idea could no longer hold sway. They were clearly not Greeks. The question in the minds of everyone is: who were these Minoans, really, and where did they go?

From the very beginning of his excavations, the finds at Knossos differed so fundamentally from the art and artifacts of classical Greece that there was simply no comparison. The russet skin color of the Minoan men on the frescoes in the Palace of Knossos was a distinct sign of their alien nature to the Greeks. They were not fair-haired Achaeans, but brown skinned, dark-haired tribes. Evans found no temples, no large sculpture, no amphitheaters with seats, and no inscriptions telling the deeds of the gods and great men, not even any familiar characters of the Greek pantheons.

Instead, Evans found strange columns that tapered toward the bottom, and architecture like no other in its shapes and arrangement of space. He found magazines full of gigantic jars - pithoi - deposits of clay tablets of endless statistical notations devoid of any historical character or mythological references. He found curious clay idols of women with bared breasts holding serpents.

The resemblances to finds at Mycenae and Tiryns in the Peloponnesus have prompted some experts to think that the lords of the citadels of Mycenae and Tiryns had visited Crete. The frescoes of women in Tiryns, with long black hair, exposed bosoms and slender waists; the dolphins, lotus blossoms and spiral motifs; and especially the characteristic Cretan double shields plainly showed the hand of a Cretan artist.

Knossos presented no clear parallel to other known cultures of the eastern Mediterranean. The Minoans were something quite "other". The only possible comparison in terms of elegance of lifestyle was either Greece or Egypt. But the people who lived at Knossos were quite different from either of them. Knossos had no mummies, no pyramids, no sphinxes or obelisks, no monumental statues of gods or pharaohs, no walls filled with hieroglyphs glorifying their rulers and their deeds.

Arthur Evans thought that something must have prevented a complete cultural and civilizational exchange. He came to believe that the inhabitants of Knossos had attained a height of civilization unique for the Middle to Late Bronze Age, with technical devices at their disposal that seemed strikingly modern. Again the question was asked: who were they and where did they go? What happened to the Minoans?

In 1974, Hans Georg Wunderlich, Professor of Geology and Paleontology at Stuttgart University, published *The Secret of Crete*. This book was the result of many observations he had made from a "geologists" point of view while visiting Crete. There were many puzzling facts about the strange 1200 room "palace". One thing his geologist's eye noticed immediately was that the steps of the "palace" were made of soft alabaster, but were not worn! There were many doorways, but stone slabs sealed them off. There were "bathtubs" equipped with drain holes, but no drainpipes! He found row after row of storage vessels, but no kitchen. The list goes on, and the reader is encouraged to read his book for the lengthy analysis. Wunderlich quotes the account of traveller Thomas Munster in Crete:

> What about the palace's access to light, air and sun? Where, for example, are the big windows without which we can scarcely imagine elegant living? When you look closer you see, to be sure, that the royal palace has open loggias, colonnaded halls, roofed over courts, but that there are scarcely any windows. A good many rooms are so completely boxed in within the complex structure that they do not

even border on an outside wall. There is something very odd about the idea of constructing a luxurious building in whose interior people would necessarily feel as if they were inside a cave. Yet they had the means to build in totally modern windows, *perhaps even glazed windows.*

In a state of devastation the place must have looked like a tangle of artificial caves in which nobody could find his way about… and the impression of mystery, vastness and confusion must have been complete.

No materials were carried away from Knossos to be used for peasant villages… The place was avoided with superstitious fear. What exactly happened, why Knossos was avoided like the site of a gallows or a witches' dancing floor, remains to be clarified.[207]

In the end, Wunderlich came to the realization, based on the objective evidence, that the "palace" of King Minos, so identified by Evans, was nothing but a necropolis. It had never been intended for the living, but was a place where a powerful cult of the dead practiced elaborate sacrifices, burial rites, and ritual games of death. He realized that the legend of Crete was essentially accurate, and that legend said that it was not a "home to a wise sovereign who fostered arts and sports", but that it was a sinister place belonging entirely to the underworld and a devouring god. In other words, it had the equivalent reputation among the civilizations of the Mediterranean that a graveyard and mausoleum have in our own society. Just as our society has a tendency to tell "ghost stories around the campfire", about terrifying apparitions of the dead in our own cemeteries, or "cities of the dead", so were similar tales told about Crete, where the only living inhabitants were the "resident undertakers", the "embalmers", and experts on death and the afterlife. Crete didn't need defensive walls because it was the place that the other cities and countries brought their dead for "cult care". It may also have been the site of human sacrifice for cult reasons as well. Wunderlich wrote his own observations:

I had visited the Minoan sites to explore the traces of early geological catastrophes, but what I found were curious contradictions. Were the excavated labyrinthine complexes really the palatial residences of glorious kings, of the legendary Minos and his brothers Sarpedon and Rhadamanthys? In fact, could these places be regarded as residences at all? My geological observations argued against any such assumption. Places of worship, shrines, sanctified earth, yes, but not places of human settlement. Comparison with other Mediterranean cultures suggested a cult of the dead […] that would mean, however, that Minoan culture, to the extent that we now know it, was almost entirely a funerary cult.[208]

---

[207] Munster, quoted by Wunderlich, *The Secret of Crete,* (New York: Macmillan 1974) p. 85.

[208] Ibid.

In dealing with the issue of what happened to the Minoans, Wunderlich points out that it is a mistake to think that just because an institution comes to an end, and the buildings of a civilization are destroyed, that it means an end to the peoples themselves. Institutions end when they no longer have a "living function". In light of the major destruction of the area by the cataclysmic eruption of Santorini, it is far more likely, as Wunderlich points out, that there was a "change in function", and an "abandonment of traditional ideas and modes of behavior". In other words, if a funerary cult is destroyed cataclysmically, it is entirely likely that the practitioners came to the conclusion that they needed a change of philosophy and were "born again" into a new and different cult that was considered to be less likely to evoke such disastrous responses from the "gods". And, in point of fact, that seems to be what happened.

Given all the evidence presented by Wunderlich, we can no longer think of Crete as an anomaly, an isolated civilization in the Mediterranean. Rather, we come to the rather startling realization that Crete did have an enormous role in the context of those times. Many connections are drawn between the Minoans and Etruria, Mesopotamia, Egypt and Greece. More than this, Wunderlich marshals a great body of evidence to show that the Cretan civilization was born from Egypt and interacted with Egypt in a long relationship.

> The Minoans were a dark, elegant people of mysterious origin. Even their ancient name is unknown; they were given the name Minoans by a modern-day British archaeologist, Arthur Evans, who derived it from Greek mythology. [...][209]

> About 3200 BC, a large number of newcomers reached southern Crete. Their religious symbols - the trident, the double axe, and the shield shaped like the numeral 8 - were those of the Delta tribes of Lower Egypt. The Libyan goddess, with her spear, snake, spindle, and goatskin bib, came with them, and she remained one of their chief deities. Other evidence of the newcomers' Egyptian or Libyan origin was the soldiers' custom of training their hair in a long lock curled over one shoulder and their use of a peculiarly shaped loincloth instead of a kilt. It seems likely that these people may have been fleeing from Menes' conquest of Lower Egypt. They mixed with the Neolithic Cretans of the mountains to form the Cretan civilization.[210]

Returning to our tracking of the story of the labyrinth, the hero of the story, Prince Theseus of Athens, volunteered to become one of the intended victims. However, the priestess Ariadne fell in love with him and helped him by giving him a ball of golden thread. He unraveled this as he penetrated to the heart of the maze, where he slew the Minotaur and was able to find his way out and escape. Afterwards, Theseus sailed away from Crete with Ariadne and the other Athenian

---

[209] Colon, Thuborn, *The Ancient Mariners,* (Alexandria, Virginia: Time-Life Books 1981) p. 12.
[210] Hayes, pp. 73-74.

youths and maidens who had been held captive in the labyrinth, and arrived at Delos. There he set up a shrine to Aphrodite, and he and his companions executed a dance which imitated the winding twists and turns of the labyrinth, which included weaving, turning movements to complex rhythms. It is known that locals performed a version of this dance until fairly recent times.

This connection of the myth of Theseus and Ariadne to the island of Delos brings us again back to the mysterious offerings that were sent from the Hyperboreans to the Delians, and the story of the four Hyperborean girls who never returned to their country, Hyperoche and Laodike, Opis and Arge, accompanied by five men who Herodotus tells us were later called "Pherpherëes". We see here a connection to the myth of the Athenian youths and maidens sent as tribute to Minos. We also see a connection to several other myths that all seem to be different versions of the same story that has received various treatments according to the "mythicization" principle. We are interested in the common elements so as to be able to determine the core event.

The majority of experts who write about the labyrinth, tell us that the plan and meaning of the maze clearly originated in Egypt, where it was the scene of the religious dramas involving killing the god-king in the form of a bull. They further tell us that the sacrifice was only token, and that a divine bull was substituted for the king in the culmination of several days of ritual dance, drama and combat performed in a labyrinth. A similar cult is said to be at the root of the Cretan labyrinth myth. The "bull of Minos" would be the representative of the kingship and power of Minos; and Theseus, by killing the bull and taking the king's daughter, was claiming the throne symbolically.

Indeed, such a solution would explain why bull, king and labyrinth occur together in both Crete and Egypt, but what it does not explain is the labyrinth itself and why the same design is found all over the world. Most scholars of ancient history and archaeology are powerfully influenced by the theories of Egyptology which posit that all civilizations diffused from ancient Egypt, or from Mesopotamia, at least. However, the sheer volume of physical evidence suggests that this is not the case.

The Egyptian labyrinths were always composed of straight lines, and the abstract mazes on seals were usually made up of square fret patterns. While Cretan coins from classical times often show labyrinths, some of which are of the Egyptian fretwork kind, most of them show a maze of a very different construction - the square or rounded spiral design - the Greek meander - of European tradition, which is never found in Egypt.

The spiraling maze consists of a series of interlocking concentric bands, usually seven in number, with a straight line of exit running from the center to the base. This is the form of nearly all the ancient mazes of Europe, including those known to have been focal points of nature religions and folk activity such as festivals, dancing, dramas and games. These designs are known as Troy towns. Spiral mazes with names that are obviously derived from the word "Troy" are found in Wales, Scotland, Ireland, England, Italy, Germany, Sweden, Norway and Russia.

In short, there is absolutely nothing Egyptian about the Troy mazes, and there is every reason to believe that they are indigenous to the megalithic cultures, which were independent developments from the civilizations of the Near East.

But in the stories of the Hyperborean girls, the myths of Theseus, as well as several other myths we are going to examine, we find two independent aspects of the maze puzzle meeting and interacting, and what they have in common is, in our opinion, ancient technology - a device that may have been at the center of the dance of the god at Stonehenge, utilized to manipulate gravity, space and time. That similar powers were available to the Egyptians seems to be evident, but it is also clear that their perception of the world, their reaction to it, and their utilization of this technology was quite different.

In the stories of the Egyptian labyrinth, the object at the center was a terrible, devouring power. In the story of the Hyperboreans, the dance of the god was a celebration of life, of bounty, of victory over the serpent. The "spear-armed Maruts" danced and brought forth baskets of bountiful blessings, materializing from the waves of the great Star Goddess, the Enthroned Queen.

Something happened. Something terrible, and whether or not we discover that any sort of "object" was at the center of the labyrinth, we believe that our investigations will lead us to the knowledge of the Ark. And so far, even if it left Egypt, it does not seem to have made it to Crete.

CHAPTER 9
PERCY-ING THE VEIL

RETURN TO CAMELOT

Littleton and Malcor discovered the link between the stories of Arthur and the Sword in the Stone and the Sarmatian sagas of Batraz and the Narts. But their research did not end there. They point out that the earlier opinions of scholars that there may have been ancient contact between the ancestors of the Ossetians and the ancestors of the Celts does not answer all of the issues of the Scythian origin of the Grail stories. For example, it does not explain the Lancelot problem. Many Arthurian scholars accept tacitly that Lancelot is derived from Lance a Lot, or Lanz a Lot, and refers to the spear or lance of the Celtic god Lug. Some of the present day "alternative scholars" have bizarre etymologies, including references to Lazarus, the man raised from the dead by Jesus (a function of the Cauldron of regeneration if ever there was one!), most of which are more silly than serious. As Littleton and Malcor demonstrate, Lancelot comes from "Alanus-a-Lot", or "The Alan of Lot", a reference to their lands in the Lot River Valley.

The Alans were first cousins to the Iazyges who, along with the Visigoths, Vandals, and other Germanic tribes, had settled in small enclaves in Gaul and the Iberian Peninsula in the early years of the fifth century. It seems that the Alans had brought with them a variation on the Grail stories that had evolved after the Iazyges had left the region. In short, Lancelot was also derived from the same prototype as Arthur and Batraz. He was the local variation of the original prototype, and when the stories were combined, since it was not known to the scribes that they were talking about the same individual who had been given a different name relating to some favored hero or ancestor of the particular tribe, they wrote the two individuals into the same story, and rearranged the relationships to accommodate this maneuver. Again and again we will see this treatment of ancient legends in action.

One of the items Littleton and Malcor discussed stuck in my mind as significant: it was that one of Lancelot's early magic items was a *mirror*. This is a Sarmatian element in the story with Alanic correspondences. Many experts discuss the Sarmatian practice of carrying mirrors, and many Sarmatians, especially the warrior women, were buried with mirrors. Littleton and Malcor note that Sulimirski argues for the Sarmatian rather than Visigothic ethnicity of an occupant of a grave based on whether or not a mirror is found there. Sulimirski feels that many brooches found from Troyes to Carthage, including the Saone Valley, the

Department of the Aube, and Albaci, Spain, that are currently identified as Gothic *may actually be Alanic*. If that is the case, then *we cannot understand Gothic in any way at all without understanding the Sarmatian-Scythian origins in the Northeast Iranian traditions that constitute its foundation.*

One of the more fascinating discoveries of this intrepid team of Grail questors was Linda Malcor's elucidation of the fact that one group of Alanic Sarmatians allied with Alaric's Visigoths, seems to have been responsible for a famous theft of some vessels of great value from the Basilica of St. Peter's during the sack of Rome in 410 AD. Whether or not one of these vessels was a sacred chalice associated with the Last Supper is not definitively known, but the fact is that the pagan marauders carried the treasure to southern Gaul, to the very region traditionally associated with the Grail legends. The treasure disappeared shortly thereafter, and it seems that the stories of these stolen "holy vessels" were combined with the stories of the Holy Cup of the Narts, the Nartamongae, which was hidden from all but the bravest and purest warriors. And so, a cup stolen from a church became the object of a sacred quest, obscuring the true history and meaning of the stories.

The genealogies given for the Grail knights, Perceval, Galahad, and Bors, are extensive, and they are all related to Lancelot - Alanus-a-Lot - a specific tribe or family of Alans from the region around the Lot river in France. In the *Perlesvaus*, Perceval's father is Alain le Gros de la Vales. Littleton and Malcor present a fascinating etymology of many of the names involved in the stories, showing their connection to the Nart Sagas, and the reader is encouraged to dig more deeply into these matters there. For the moment, let us just mention that the prenomen "Pant", as in "Pantdragon", evolving to "Pendragon", in what now seems to be the most likely Scythian-Steppe culture etymology, was a word meaning "king" or "ruler over" whatever followed. Thus, the family of "Pendragon", rather than being "sons of the dragon", become *"rulers over the dragon"*, or *Dragon Slayers*. The title Ban, Pant, and Pen was very likely an original Scythian word, carried to Britain by the Iazyges and to Gaul by the Alans. Thus, the banners of the Sarmatians emblazoned with dragons signify their function as rulers over, and slayers of dragons, in the same way that warriors collect trophies of their victories to display and advertise their prowess in a particular famous battle. This subtle difference will be very important as we go along.

Perceval was the best known of the Grail heroes, but he was not the original one. There are also many medieval stories about this Perceval that have nothing to do with the Grail. He was so popular that he was depicted on wall frescoes, carvings on assorted items, tapestries, and so on. You could say that he was a "Star" in the Medieval Hollywood. The question is: was this just propaganda, or was it, as is suggested by experts on esotericism, conveyance of a symbolic meaning?

Perceval was also known as Parsifal, Percival, Persevelle, Peredur, Perlesvaus, Paladrhir, and so on. His name has been generally interpreted as meaning "Pierce the valley", implying a tantric connotation, or general balance in a person's life, as in Taoist teachings. He has been called the "Spearman with a Long Shaft", relating him to Osiris, who was the "Mummy with a Long Member", which would be literally "he who Pierces the valley" in sexual terms - a sexual reference that probably did not originally relate to sex.

The Celtic story of Peredur has been explained as an allegory of Druidic initiation, and the adventures were "staged" in order to describe the levels of initiation. Peredur spent twenty-one days in the castle of the witches of Caer Loyw as opposed to Perceval in the castle of the Fisher King. In the women's "great court", he witnessed the Cauldron of Regeneration performing resurrections of the Sons of the King of Suffering, near a sacred cave with a phallic pillar at its entrance. Two women who closely resembled the functional relationships of the Biblical Mary and Martha to Jesus, gave Peredur bread and wine to serve at a banquet that was obviously not a *copy* of the Last supper, but must have been derived from an older source, which suggests that the Biblical Last Supper may have originated from the same inspiration. A Shakti-like Lady Love who wore the colors of the Triple Goddess guided Peredur through his initiations. At her departure, she told him *"When thou seekest for me, seek in the direction of India"*.[211]

A similar Shakti figure instructs Perceval in the twelfth century *Roman de Perceval*, where the Welsh hero metamorphoses into the Desired Knight sent to cure the world's ills. It was claimed that Perceval would heal the lame Fisher King and restore the Waste Land to Fertility.

Like many "Divine Children", Perceval was born under mysterious circumstances; he was hidden and brought up in poverty and secrecy by his mother, a "widow". His instructress, Blancehflor, or White Flower, revealed to him the secret meanings of chivalry and the mysticism of love. Spiritual union with Blanceflor, achieved through sexual union, made Perceval invincible in battle.

The Christian church took hold at this point, and reformed Perceval into a saintly, abstinent hero who was strengthened by his virginity. Monks worked on the unfinished *Roman de Perceval* for about thirty years, Christianizing the poor guy until he discovered that the true meaning of chivalry was not what his Love taught him at all, but the doctrines of the church. The monks vilified Blancheflor as a "Jewess named Blanchefleure" who fornicated with Satan at the Witches' Sabbath and gave birth to the Antichrist. This "evolved" Perceval was no longer the champion of women, but the champion of the Church. He then castrated himself so as to become one of the pure knights. With this final shift of the original stories, manipulated by the church, interest in the subject declined and Grail legends fell in popularity until their later discovery in more modern times.

At present, the legends of the Quest for the Grail have the ability to grip the imagination and trigger our unconscious minds into transforming the muddled and confusing story into anything we want it to be. "Muddled and confusing?" Indeed. Very few "believers" in the Holy Grail have actually read any of the dozen or so

---

[211] Goodrich., pp. 63-69.

original Grail romances. Even fewer are fully apprised of the pagan and apocryphal models upon which the legends are framed. Yet most believers will sagely nod their heads and agree that the Quest for the Holy Grail is the greatest of all spiritual endeavors, most likely related to the cup or platter of the Last Supper of Christ. They will then point to this or that "True Grail" in the possession of any of several families for many centuries as proof that the Grail is a "Christian Matter".

Chretien de Troyes, who is, in the end, the one individual who was mostly responsible for the subsequent popularity of the Arthurian legends of the period, wrote one of his early romances under the strict guidance of Marie de Champagne, daughter of Eleanor of Aquitaine, wife of Henry II of England. Eleanor (Alienor - the "other Alan-Elen-Helen") was descended from the great Alanic bloodlines and traditions.

One of the earliest contemporary *Christian* references to the Grail appears in a passage from the *Chronicle of Helinandus*, a monk of Froidmont, right at the turn of the twelfth century. Helinandus writes about a hermit living in eighth century Britain who had a vision of Joseph of Arimathea, keeper of the bowl used by Christ at the last Supper. This theme was expounded in a work called the *Lancelot Grail*, which gives the precise date of the vision as Good Friday evening in 717 AD. Supposedly, Christ appeared to the hermit and announced: *"This is the book of thy descent, Here begins the Book of the Holy Grail, Here begin the terrors, Here begin the marvels".*

Yet, even though Chretien was supposed to be writing a Christian work, he never actually mentions any connection with Christ in his final romance, *Le Conte del Graal*. For Chretien, the Grail is a costly and magical dish whose function is never quite revealed because the work is unfinished. Whether Chretien died before finishing, or just put it aside at the time is unknown. But, it was so popular that the next twenty-five years saw a spate of continuations and imitations.

At this point, we have a very good idea where Chretien got the inspiration for his story, and the reader will soon see how fruitful this discovery of Littleton and Malcor will turn out to be. But what we notice is that the later writers of sequels and prequels, and alternative versions, all claimed to have access to some original, secret documents, described variously as direct transcriptions *from Christ himself*, from an angel, from a mysterious alchemical work that came either from Britain, Spain or the Far East. We then look back at Chretien's story, and see that his imagery has obvious and traceable elements with precedents in Celtic-Scythian traditions, and we realize that what we are observing, *post facto*, is *a huge cover-up going into operation*. The astonishing variations of the *later* Christian and alchemical versions, written by individuals who were practiced in the art of Jewish Kabbala, seem to exactly fit the criteria for disinformation.

Wolfram von Eschenbach created the German version of the Grail story with his *Parzival*. In this rendering, he saw the Quest as the individual struggle toward wholeness expressed in the Grail. For Wolfram, the quest *occurs between the two extremes of black and white*, or the Eastern Way of Tao. His primary message was that the individual ought to take the path of allowing the natural flow of life to guide one's actions.

We don't wish to go into all the versions and variation, as there are many fine books that undertake such a task with excellent scholarship. The point we wish to make here is that the grail legends are composed by different authors, at different times, coming from different backgrounds, with different agendas, and for the most part, the central mystery is obscured in alternating historicizations and mythicization processes. The essential story is that of a hero who is destined to achieve the quest for an otherworldly object with particular themes that repeat whether the action is set in Britain, Wales, Scotland, Brittany, Southern France, India, Egypt or the Near East.

Different authors, at different times, have set the story in any of these places, giving a wealth of detail which lures the researcher to believe that there is a real, physical object called the Holy Grail, waiting somewhere to be found, which will bring the discoverer unlimited power and glory, or will "heal" the land, in any of a dozen various ways.

The conception and birth of the hero, who is variously named Arthur, Gawain, Peredur, Perlesvaus, Parzival, Perceval, Galahad, or Bors, is generally the result of the mysterious conjunction of parents who possess unusual potency in some respect that varies from story to story, but generally includes courage and purity.

The hero is reared under conditions of extreme restriction in some way. He often lacks worldly comprehension, and is thus called a Fool. He is usually distinctive in some respect, but not quite "acceptable" in polite company because he is a sort of geek, or dork as they called them when I was young. There is always something prodigious about him in terms of strength or intellect, and he always has an impeccable pedigree. At some point, by some divine bestowal of gifts, he is marked as the "Chosen one", or "The Heir".

The adventure of the Grail Quest has a number of elements that repeat often enough to be considered an ensemble. The initiate-hero has to ask the "right" question, avenge a wrong, win the Grail, remain pure even after his achievement, and finally capture a castle. Through all of these actions, he is transformed, and the environment is changed as well. A "wounded king" is healed, and the world becomes a paradise.

After considering all of these issues, we still come back again to that most annoying of simple-minded questions: Why Perceval? Why was the hero named Perceval in Chretien's original story, and was this based on some particular meaning *known to those who guided his hand* in the construction of the tale?

As Littleton and Malcor point out, the notion that the figure of Perceval was derived from an Iranian source was discussed amongst Arthurian scholars in the early part of the 20th century. It was even suggested that Wolfram's *Parzival* was a free translation from the Persian stories. Unfortunately, most of this scholarship has been ignored in favor of the Celtic hypothesis advanced by Loomis. It is proposed by some of those who follow the Celtic formation, that all of the Grail manuscripts ultimately drew upon Robert de Boron's *Joseph* as their source. Littleton notes:

> Although Perceval was well known in the continental Grail tradition, the British Sir Perceval of Galles (ca. 1300-1340) makes no mention of the Grail, even though images that employed the motif of the Chalice at the Cross were already known in Britain at this time. This makes it unlikely that the Perceval branch of the Grail

tradition developed out of the Welsh Pryderi or Peredur tales, as Loomis has suggested. [...] The presence of large numbers of Sarmatians and Alans in Britain and Gaul during the period in which the Arthurian tradition was formed has once again made the eastern-origin hypothesis attractive.[212]

There is a tradition of "Peronnik l'idiot" found in the region of Vannes. These are folktales about a hero who fights the Devil, and they bear a strong resemblance to the stories of Perceval. It is likely that these are among the earliest survivals of legends of Batraz carried to the region by Alans in the fifth century.

As it happens, the very name "Perceval" does connect us to these Eastern sources. The Iranian words *gohr*, *gohar* and *djauhar*, which form the root of the Alanic name Goar, translate into German as *Perle*, with, as Littleton notes, the semantic field of *a jewel, gem, or stone*. When we consider the etymology for Perlesvaux, we find that *vaux* is well established as "valley", and thus "Perles-vaux" is Perle's valley, or "Gohar's valley" or "Valley of the Stone-gem". We find in this etymology the subtext of the association of Perceval with a grail that is a "stone" as opposed to a chalice or cauldron. The fifteenth century German poem *Lorengel* describes the grail as a "stone of victory" with which Parsifal drove back Attila and his troops at the moment they were going to destroy Christianity. In this clue, we find a curious shadow of the Ark of the Covenant, which ensured military might, and victory for its possessors. The most interesting fact of this matter is that it *was* the Alans of Orleans who, in 451 AD, actually held the line against Attila. The fifth-century leader Goar originally commanded these Alans.

The reader who is familiar with the literature of both the scholars of the Grail, as well as the many "alternative" theory books being published in the present time, will have no difficulty in identifying the cross-correspondences between the Grail stories and the stories of Jesus in the New Testament that seem to be highly sanitized versions of the same general schemes. For example, in addition to the reference made above to a "Last Supper," there are also the stories of the multiplying loaves and fishes juxtaposed against the head of John the Baptist on a *platter*. We note that the Head of Bran the Blessed and other "talking heads" on platters were associated with multiplying loaves and fishes, prophecy, and abundance in general. It is fairly simple to see how present day researchers have been misled to associate the Grail stories with the myths of Jesus (with a lot of disinformation produced by the church at the time, it must be admitted), and to assume that the "bloodline of Jesus" is the primary issue of the so-called "Sang Real", or "Holy Bloodline". However, with this firm connection to an older Ossetian story, a Scythian cycle of sagas, we find that we must look much further into the past for the origin of our Perceval/Christ. We note in passing also, the

---

[212] Littleton and Malcor, op. cit., 130.

curious story in the Bible of the "Pearl of Great Price", and the casting of "Pearls before Swine" as hints of these relationships.

At this point we would like to make note of a curious series of remarks by the Master Fulcanelli in the first pages of his book *Dwellings of the Philosophers*. He tells us in his first sentences that there is a gross misconception about the Middle Ages common among scholars and laymen, produced by a written history that is not supported by the evidence. History tells us that the Dark Ages were a time of invasions, wars, famines, epidemics, and a host of disruptions to life and culture; yet the very same period was the time of the building of great cathedrals, monuments, houses, cities, and so forth; none of which bear the marks of such scourges. He then goes on to point out that art is entirely reflective of a culture, and generally only thrives during times of peace. The Gothic buildings - cathedrals and others - all undeniably reflect peace, serenity, prosperity, and a flourishing, happy society. The statuary, obviously having used live models, shows us plump, well-fed people, with jovial expressions, fond of good living and satire. Even gargoyles are more comical than frightening, and the suffering Christs are generally depicted as "resting" rather than actually in torment. As Fulcanelli points out, if that period of history had been as "dark" as it is depicted, had the people been suffering and moaning in misery of human affliction, the art would have depicted it. But it didn't. Something is, indeed, inexplicably amiss here. And, as Fulcanelli points out:

> *it is easy to fabricate texts and documents out of nothing. [...]* Falsification and counterfeiting are as old as the hills, and history, which abhors chronological vacuums, sometimes had to call [counterfeiters] to the rescue.[213]

In the seventeenth century, a Jesuit Father, Jean Hardouin, uncovered a fraud wherein locals were creating ancient Greek and Roman coins and medals and burying them about the countryside to "fill in the gaps" of history as well as make money by selling such "finds". In 1639, a certain Jacques de Bie published *The Families of France, Illustrated by the Monuments of Ancient and Modern Medals*, which, according to Anatole de Montaiglon contained more "invented medals than real ones".[214] Fulcanelli goes on to cite more instances in which the possibility - probability - that our history has been largely fabricated looms as an ever-growing specter of confusion. We will discover, as we go along, that this problem of falsification of history is not just an idea, but also a *fact*.

As it happens, there are some eminent experts in the present day who have smelled the rat and who propose the exact same thing that Fulcanelli has suggested. When we investigate the matter, we discover that the chronology of

---

[213] Fulcanelli, *Dwellings*, pp. 25, 26.

[214] Anatole Montaiglon. Preface of *Curiositiez de Paris*, reprinted after the original edition of 1716, Paris 1883.

ancient and medieval history in its present form was created and completed to a considerable extent in a series of works during the 16th and 18th centuries, beginning with J. Scaliger (1540-1609), the "founder of modern chronological science". and D. Petavius (1583-1652). Chronology is what tells us how much time has elapsed between some historical event and the present. To determine real chronology, one must be able to translate the data in the ancient documents into the terminology and units of modern time reckoning. Many historical conclusions and interpretations depend upon what dates we ascribe to the events in a given ancient document.

The accepted traditional chronology of the ancient and medieval world rests on a foundation of quicksand. For example, between different versions of the dating of such an important event as the foundation of Rome, there exists a divergence of 500 years. What is more, falsification of numbers was carried out down even to contemporary history. Alexander Polyhistor took the first steps towards filling up the five hundred years, which were wanting to bring the destruction of Troy and the origin of Rome into the chronological connection. But, was he helping, or further confusing the matter? As it happens, according to another chronology, Troy had fallen at the same time as the foundation of Rome, and not 500 years before it.

Isaac Newton, as we will see, devoted many years to historical and chronological studies. He made up his own tables that came to be the generally accepted timeline. A lot of people are not aware that some of the important events of Greek history were arbitrarily moved forward by him as much as 300 years, and those of the Egyptian were moved forward up to a thousand years. Naturally, penetrating minds were able to discern the problems and as early as the sixteenth century. A.D., Professor of Salamanca University de Arcilla published two papers in which he stated that the whole of history earlier than the fourth century AD, had been falsified.

In more modern times, the first serious attempt to systematize the considerable critical material, and to analyze historical paradoxes and duplicates from the standpoint of natural science was undertaken by a Russian scientist and academician, N. A. Morozov (1854-1946). In 1994, A. T. Fomenko, a Russian Mathematician, published *Empirico-statistical analysis of narrative materials and its applications to historical dating*. The abstract of this book says:

> These two volumes represent a major, unique work, which is the first of its kind published in the English language. A comprehensive set of new statistical techniques is presented for the analysis of historical and chronological data. These techniques constitute a new important trend in applied statistics.
>
> The first volume concentrates mainly on the development of mathematical statistical tools and their applications to astronomical data: dating of ancient eclipses, dating of *Almagest* etc. The problems of correct dating for ancient and medieval events are discussed.
>
> The second volume concentrates on the analysis of ancient and medieval chronicles and records (such as Egyptian, Byzantine, Roman, Greek, Babylonian, European etc.). An astonishing wealth of historical data is considered.

The conclusions, which are drawn concerning the accepted chronological dating of events in ancient history, will certainly provoke controversy and serious debate. The author suggested a new chronology, which is dramatically different from the traditional one. [...]

The book provides the necessary background and material for intelligent participation in such debates.[215]

Fomenko's work deserves far more discussion than I can devote to it here. I would like to note that mainstream historians and archaeologists are crying "Foul!" about it, despite the fact that the work has drawn some extraordinary conclusions and presents a thorough analyses with logical arguments and a sincere desire to get at the Truth. As we have already noted, it is increasingly clear that the "status quo" is more important to some people than the Truth. Regarding the medieval period with which we are presently concerned, Fomenko points out that

We have discovered that there exists a strong parallelism between durations of reigns for English history of 640-1327 A.D. from one side and Byzantine history of 378-830 A.D. continued by Byzantine history of 1143-1453 A.D. from another side.

[This parallelism] suggests that Byzantine is an original in above parallelism, and England before 1327 A.D. - a reflection. It could be seen [...] how English history before 1327 A.D. was constructed from several reflections of the Byzantine Empire of 1143-1453 A.D. [...]

The reader asks: How could the Byzantine chronicles be inserted into medieval English history (of the island Anglia)? The answer will be extremely simple if we will erase from our minds the picture, which is imposed by traditional Scaliger's chronology.

Starting from 11th century, several crusades stormed the Byzantine Empire. Several feudal crusaders' states were founded on the territory of Byzantine empire in 11-14th cc. In these states many nations were mixed: local population, the crusaders from England, France, Germany, Italy etc. In these crusaders' regions and in Byzantine Empire the new culture was created, in particular, were written a historical chronicle. Among Byzantine inhabitants were a lot of people from Europe, in particular, from some island, which later will be called England. In 1453 AD Turks conquered Constantinople. Byzantine empire was ruined and the crowds of its inhabitants left the country. Many of them returned to Europe, to their old homeland. In particular - in the island Anglia.

These descendants of crusaders took with them their Byzantine historical chronicle, because these texts describe their own real history in Byzantine Empire (during many years - one or two hundreds years). Several decades passed. On the island

---

[215] Kluwer Academic Publishers, 1994. P.O.Box 17, 3300 AA Dordrecht, The Netherlands. ISBN 0-7923-2604-0 (Volume 1) ISBN 0-7923-2605-9 (Volume 2).

Anglia starts the writing its history (i.e., the history of the people living on the island). In 16-17th centuries some qualified historians appear and start to create the general history of the whole land Anglia ("from the beginning"). They search for ancient documents. Suddenly they find several old trunks with "very old" documents. The documents are dusty, the paper is very fragile, and the old books fall to pieces. These chronicles were transported from Byzantine Empire. But now (in 16-17th cc.) nobody knew this. Unfortunately, the prehistory of these trunks is forgotten. And, unfortunately, is forgotten that these chronicles describe the history of ANOTHER LAND.

The English historians of 16-17th centuries carefully analyze these texts as the history "of island England" and put them into the basis of "old British-island history, which started many centuries ago." In some strong sense they were right because, really, the authors of the chronicles were closely connected with island Anglia (but, let us repeat, described ANOTHER LAND - Byzantine empire). This process is quite natural and does not suggest any special falsification of the history. Such natural errors were inevitable at the first steps of creating of the general history. As a result, appeared such chronicles as *Anglo-Saxon Chronicle*, the Nennius' chronicle etc.

After some time this wrong version of an old English history standing stock-still, becomes a "monument". Further historians simply modify (only a little) the initial scheme of the history, add some new documents. And only today, using some statistical and other methods we start to discover some strange regularities inside the "history textbook" and start to realize that the real history was possibly sufficiently shorter and that today we need to remove from the "old English history" its "Byzantine part" and return this piece to its right place (in time and in the geographical sense). This procedure is very painful. We realize this because we discovered the same problem in the old Russian history, when we also found several chronological duplicates.

It is possible, that this process of "insertion of an old Byzantine chronicle" in the beginning of a "local history" is presented for *several different regions*, which were closely connected with Byzantine Empire. In particular, it is true for Russia, for England, for Rome, for Greece. [...].[216]

And what are those corollaries? Well, if Fomenko is correct, the ancient histories of Byzantium were carried to Europe, and because many of the local legends also arrived from that region of the world, i.e. the Nart sagas, it was assumed that this was the real history of Britain and even Europe. In short, Fomenko's idea connects events from the time of Jesus, and the area of the world in which Jesus was said to live, to the general area of the world from which the Nart Sagas originated, the roots of the Grail Legends, and they may all be a

---

[216] A.T.Fomenko, G.V.Nosovskij, New Hypothetical Chronology and Concept of the English History British Empire as a Direct Successor of Byzantine-Roman Empire.

mythicized history, and historicized myth of actual seed events of real history that has been, until the present time, incompletely understood.

Again and again we are finding the threads leading off to the east - to Russia, Siberia - which happens to be the general area of the land of *Colchis.* Apollodorus tells us about Hercules:

> When the labours had been performed in eight years and a month, Eurystheus ordered Hercules, as an *eleventh* labour, to fetch *golden apples from the Hesperides*, for he did not acknowledge the labour of the cattle of Augeas nor that of the hydra.

> These apples were not, as some have said, in Libya, but on Atlas *among the Hyperboreans.* They were presented (by Earth) to Zeus after his marriage with Hera, and guarded by an *immortal dragon* with a hundred heads, offspring of Typhon and Echidna, which spoke with many and diverse sorts of voices. With it the Hesperides also were on guard, to wit, Aegle, Erythia, Hesperia, and Arethusa. [...]

> Now Prometheus had told Hercules not to go himself after the apples but to send Atlas, first relieving him of the burden of the sphere; so when he was come to Atlas *in the land of the Hyperboreans,* he took the advice and relieved Atlas. But when Atlas had received three apples from the Hesperides, he came to Hercules, and not wishing to support the sphere, he said that he would himself carry the apples to Eurystheus, and bade Hercules hold up the sky in his stead. Hercules promised to do so, but succeeded by craft in putting it on Atlas instead. For at the advice of Prometheus he begged Atlas to hold up the sky till he should, put a pad on his head. When Atlas heard that, he laid the apples down on the ground and took the sphere from Hercules. And so Hercules picked up the apples and departed. But some say that he did not get them from Atlas, but that he plucked the apples himself after killing the *guardian snake.* And having brought the apples he gave them to Eurystheus. But he, on receiving them, bestowed them on Hercules, from whom Athena got them and conveyed them back again; for it was not lawful that they should be laid down anywhere.[217]

It is extremely interesting to note the similarity between the hydra - a hundred headed snake - and the gorgon slain by Perseus. We also note the connections to the Hyperboreans, and the fact that the Golden Apples were given to Athena, who was also gifted with the head of Medusa by Perseus. Another interesting note is that the area where these apples were located was the Hesperides which is said, in the account above, to be in the Land of the Hyperboreans. We also want to note that the same general story is told about the Quest for the Golden Fleece:

> No sooner did Pelias hear that than he bade him go in quest of the fleece. Now it was at Colchis in a grove of Ares, hanging on an oak and guarded by a *sleepless dragon.*

---

[217] Apollodorus, Book II:5.11. cited by Graves, *The Greek Myths*, pp. 509-11.

Medea guided Jason to the fleece by night and used her drugs to send the guardian dragon to sleep, and then, carrying the fleece with her, made her way back to the *Argos* with Jason.

Curiously, the name "Pelleas" occurs in a number of Grail Stories. The important thing is, however, that we have a sneaking suspicion that this Colchis is also the Hesperides - the Land of the Hyperboreans. We also wonder about the possible relationship between "Arcadia" and Colchis. If the ancient "Athenians" of Plato's tale were not actually from Athens, as we know it, then it is also possible that a far more ancient "Arcadia" existed as well.

WHY PERCEVAL?

At this point we are brought back to face the puzzle of "Why Perceval"? Was it indeed, a hint from the hand of Eleanor of Aquitaine and her daughter Marie de Champagne, to embody something that was generally known at the time, into a corpus of stories by giving the hero of those stories the name "Perceval"?

As it happens so often, a series of funny synchronous events brought the issue into sharp focus and gave me the key. I had been pondering the question for weeks on end, searching through etymologies, mythologies, genealogies, and a host of other references, none of which truly dealt with what I felt to be the central issue of the name. Yes, I read endless esoteric interpretations, and most of it is nonsense. I read books about the "Pierced Eye" of Dagobert, the "Merovingian Marvels", and the Sinclair Solipsisms, and other absurd notions, and it was all piling to heaven with wishful thinking of every would-be "savior" or claimant to the role of the "Desired Knight". At the end of the day, none of these things really answered the question: Why Perceval?

So, there I sat, at the end of the line. No more books, no more references to search, no more hope for the answer to my question: Why Perceval? At that very moment a tremendous blast of lighting struck nearby, followed almost immediately by thunder that shook my house and nearly made me jump out of my skin. My first thought was for my dog who was terrified of thunder, "Poor Percy!", I thought. And as I thought the thought, I received the answer. You see, we call him "Percy", but his name (given to him by my children some years earlier when they were avidly reading Greek mythology), is Perseus. With that one realization, the biggest part of the puzzle fell into place.

Perseus Pen Dragon - the dragon slayer par-excellence! The beheader of the Gorgon; the slayer of the sea monster, the rescuer of Andromeda the "Ruler of Men"; the child of a widow, impregnated by a god; brought up in isolation, hidden away from his birthright, gauche and simple, sent to do an impossible task in hopes that it would kill him; Perseus, the babe fished out of the ocean with his mother, by a fisherman, brother to a king - a "fisher king"; Perseus, gifted with the initiations of the "witches", of the Hyperboreans, who obtains the "eye of Horus", of the Graea; Perseus, aided by Athena, to whom he presents the head of the Gorgon, from whose blood sprang the winged horse Pegasus, with all the elements of the Scythian story, right down to the Scythian mirror, and like the Urim and Thummim of the Levites, Athena places the head of the Gorgon, the prophesying Head of Bran or John the Baptist, on her breastplate. Perseus uses the head of the

Gorgon like the Ark of the Covenant to achieve victory over his enemies, turning them to stone. Finally, a thousand connections made sense: the grail hero is called Perceval because he must be of the royal bloodline of Dragon Slayers, the semi-legendary Perseids. Perseus is David, a semi-divine being, the founder of a line of kings, "semites" because of his marriage to Andromeda, the "ruler of men".

There are two main royal figures in the Grail tradition: the Maimed King and the Fisher King. At some point, they merge, but in the earliest traditions, they are still separate. The Maimed King has suffered a wound that leaves him impotent. It is described as being "wounded in the thigh" and is the result of some sort of sin on the part of the wounded king. The emphasis is usually a sickly king, rather than a wounded one. In any event, this is known as the Dolorous Stroke. It gets all twisted around and elaborated in the many Christianized versions of the story that we won't go into here. What we are interested in is the figure from the Nart Sagas who not only most closely resembles the Maimed-Sickly king, but also gives us insight into the issue of the Golden Fleece.

Uryzmaeg, the husband of the Goddess Satana (nothing to do with Satan, trust me!), is an aged man who is depicted sitting on a hill near the sea, watching the sheep or horses because he is too old to do anything else. In a variation, he is named Uaerxtaenaeg, and he sits in the village square waiting for his son to return, but he is the same figure. His chief claim to fame is the fact that he has a shirt of golden mail that he wears as he sits and waits in his aged condition. As he sits wherever it is, three sons of an evil sorcerer take the shirt away from him, as well as two *strips of flesh from his back*, and they retreat to the mountains and hide in a cave. When the son, Sybaelc comes home from his adventures, his mother tells him that he can't come in the house until he brings back the golden shirt and heals his father's back.

Sybaelc, with the help of his maternal grandfather, goes off on a quest for the golden shirt and the skin from his father's back. He finds the sons of the evil magicians, kills them, recovers his father's skin and shirt, and returns to the house to restore the skin to his father's back, and gives him back his golden shirt.

Besides the obvious relationship to the theme of the Golden Fleece (and it sure gives new meaning to "the shirt off his back"!), we find the detail that his maternal grandfather aided Sybaelc. In several of the Grail stories, Perceval's maternal grandfather is the Fisher King who helps him in his quest. This is a curious reference to a matrilineal transfer. The title of Fisher King was hereditary; being transferred from Uncle to nephew, a *son of a sister*.

We begin to suspect that when we speak of Theseus, Jason and the Argonauts, and Perseus, we are talking about variations on a single core event or archetypal occurrence. And we will discover that this archetype has a very far-reaching influence as we go along. The evidence that the answer to my question, "Why Perceval", is that the original story of all these variations was the story of Perseus, receives curious support in the Stars. You see, the myth of Perseus is the only one to be fully depicted in the heavens, with all its main players present. We find the players all arranged around a Ram that was inserted into the zodiac at a certain point in history. There they are, Perseus the hero holding aloft the great magical sword and the severed head of the serpent-haired gorgon, with his mirrored shield and helmet of invisibility; Andromeda, the woman in chains, Cassiopeia her mother, the seated, or enthroned Queen, Cepheus her father, and Cetus the sea serpent. No other myth of all the fascinating stories in mythology is so fully displayed to our senses as the answer to "Why Perceval?".

If the reader will recall, the story of Perseus has many of the motifs found in the story of Theseus. Prince Theseus of Athens volunteered to become one of the intended victims of the Minotaur, the devouring power at the center of the Labyrinth. However, the priestess Ariadne fell in love with him and helped him by giving him a ball of golden thread. He unraveled this as he penetrated to the heart of the maze, where he slew the Minotaur and was able to find his way out and escape. Afterwards, Theseus sailed away from Crete with Ariadne and the other Athenian youths and maidens who had been held captive in the labyrinth, and arrived at Delos. There he set up a shrine to Aphrodite and he and his companions executed a dance, which imitated the winding twists and turns of the labyrinth.

We also recall that, in our survey of labyrinths, we found that the majority of experts tell us that the plan and meaning of the maze originated in Egypt, where it was the scene of the religious dramas involved in killing the god-king in the form of a bull. They further tell us that the sacrifice was only token, and that a divine bull was substituted for the king in the culmination of several days of ritual dance, drama and combat performed in a labyrinth. Most scholars of ancient history and archaeology are powerfully influenced by the theories of Egyptology, which posits that all civilizations diffused from ancient Egypt, or from Mesopotamia, at least. However, the sheer volume of physical evidence suggests that this is not the case.

We also wish to recall that there are two types of mazes. The Egyptian labyrinths were always composed of straight lines, and the abstract mazes on seals were usually made up of square fret patterns. Cretan coins from classical times often show labyrinths, some of which are of the Egyptian fretwork kind, but most of them show a maze of a very different construction - *the square or rounded spiral design* - the Greek meander - of European tradition, *which is never found in Egypt.* It seems that Crete was the meeting ground of two completely separate traditions.

ARCADIA?

The Ukraine is a fascinating and mysterious place. Most of it is a vast, flat plain extending East from the base of the legendary Carpathian Mountains. The soil is rich and black in the central and southern areas, and the temperature ranges from temperate Continental to sub-tropical on the Black Sea coast. It is easy to understand why this area may have been the cradle of the great Celtic tribes that settled Europe and created one of the most mysterious civilizations on Earth.

The oldest house in the world has been found in Ukraine. It is a 15 000 year old assemblage of mammoth bones which was probably covered with mammoth hides. A Ukrainian farmer who was digging a new cellar six feet below his home found this house. It formed part of a village and was so strongly built, it was obviously intended to last for several generations. In Kostienki, Ukraine, there was a huge house from the same period, which measured 115 feet by 50 feet with eleven hearths for cooking, warmth and light! And, speaking of cooking, the oldest known primitive, but identifiable, ovens were also found in Ukraine and date from

20 000 BC! There were probably a lot of mammoths in the neighborhood because, not only the oldest house, but the oldest map in the world was also inscribed on a mammoth tusk and discovered in Ukraine in 1966, dated to about 10 000 BC.

According to accepted historical research, the first horseman rode in Ukraine about 6 000 years ago. Trousers may also have been invented about the same time and were the typical clothing of the Scythian warriors documented to 2, 600 years ago. It is interesting that Herodotus, 2 500 years ago also described the Celts of Europe as wearing trousers and being extraordinary horsemen.

The gold work of the Scythians is legendary and bespeaks a culture far finer than is generally supposed by current scholars. The jewelry of the region of Ukraine is so similar to the work of the European Celts that it is hard not to see the connection. But, even older than many of the specimens of metal and stonework jewelry is a 20 000 year old bracelet carved from a single piece of mammoth ivory, found at Mezin, Ukraine. This piece has a magnificent design which can be found to this day in the embroidery of Ukrainian costumes. This pattern is also similar to, but predates the famous Greek "meander" pattern, or "maze".

These materials indicate to us that there is absolutely nothing Egyptian about the Troy mazes, and there is every reason to believe that they are indigenous to the megalithic cultures, which were *independent developments* from the civilizations of the Near East.

In the stories of the Hyperborean girls, the myths of Theseus, as well as several other myths, we find two independent aspects of the maze puzzle meeting and interacting, and what they have in common is, in our opinion, ancient technology - a device that may have been at the center of the dance of the god at Stonehenge, utilized to manipulate gravity, space and time. That similar powers were much later available to the Egyptians seems to be evident, but it is also clear that their perception of the world, their reaction to it, and their utilization of this technology was quite different.

In the stories of the Egyptian labyrinth, *the object at the center was a terrible, devouring power*. In the story of the Hyperboreans, the dance of the god was a celebration of life, of bounty, of victory over the serpent. The "spear-armed Maruts" danced and brought forth baskets of bountiful blessings, materializing from the waves of the great Star Goddess, the Enthroned Queen, Cassiopeia.

We remember at this point that Fulcanelli has told us that we would derive great benefit from his little book on the Cathedrals, providing he did not despise the works of the *Old Philosophers*, and if he would study with care and penetration the classical text so as to understand the obscure points of the practice. Naturally, we cannot possibly include a page-by-page examination of *Le Mystère* in this volume, but there are a number of important points to be made here.

In the first edition, Canseliet tells us right at the end of his preface:

> The key to the major Arcanum is given quite openly in one of the figures
> illustrating the present work. And this key consists quite simply in a color revealed
> to the artisan right from the first work. No Philosopher, to my knowledge, has
> emphasized the importance of this essential point. In revealing it, I am obeying the
> last wishes of Fulcanelli and my conscience is clear.[218]

Most of the preface to the second edition is taken up discussing a, "star shining on the mystic virgin - who is at one and the same time our mother (mere) and the hermetic sea (mer) - announces the conception".[219] Canseliet tells us, "the star is the great sign of the Work". Naturally, this is wrapped in parables, with a sufficient amount of diversion to occupy the puffers. But, having said all that, Canseliet tells us even more. He comments that the reader might wonder that he has spent so much time *discussing the star*, but the reason is that *it leads us straight into Fulcanelli's text*. He next tells us:

> Indeed, right from the beginning my Master has dwelt on the primary role of the
> star, this mineral Theophany, which announces with certainty the tangible solution
> of the great secret concealed in religious buildings. This is the *Mystère des
> Cathédrales*, the very title of the work.[220]

The only problem is, for the puffer, these remarks are nonsense. Fulcanelli begins *Le Mystère* talking about cathedrals in general, the feast of fools, and wanders all over the place. He most certainly does not begin by talking about "the primary role of the star", this "great *sign* of the work", or does he?

Yes, he does.

Remember what Canseliet said?

> The key to the major Arcanum is given quite openly in <u>one of the figures</u>
> <u>illustrating</u> the present work. And this key consists quite simply in a colour
> revealed to the artisan <u>right from the first work</u>. No Philosopher, to my knowledge,
> has emphasized the importance of this essential point.

Well, for a mind that thinks in terms of Kabbala, there is no way to understand this. But, for a mind that thinks in *cabala,* the language of the gods, the birds, the mother tongue, the solution is easy. If one opens to the very first "work of the artisan", or *sentence of the book*, there is a "figure" given - figure = number also! - and that figure that is the key to the Major Arcanum is the number seven.

In the first sentence of the book, "the work of the artisan", Fulcanelli writes...

---

[218] Fulcanelli, *Mysteries*, p. 7.

[219] Ibid., p. 13.

[220] Ibid., p. 17.

The strongest impression of my early childhood - I was SEVEN years old...[221]

...and we have the "key to the major Arcanum".

How to interpret the number seven? Well, there are several ways to think about it, but the simplest is just to find chapter seven in the book to see what it says. So, we turn the pages over and begin to read:

> Varro, in his *Antiquitates rerum humanorum*, recalls the legend of Aeneas saving his father and his household gods from the flames of Troy and, after long wanderings, arriving at the fields of Laurentum, (Laurente- Laurentium is cabalistically *l'or ente*, or grafted gold) the goal of his journey. He gives the following explanation: "After his departure from Troy, *he saw every day and ruling the day the Star of Venus*, until he arrived at the fields of Laurentum, where he ceased to see it. This fact made him realize that these were the lands allotted by destiny."[222]

Indeed we have found a star that is the "great sign of the work", leading to a color: *Gold*. We have the *figure* seven which takes us to a color and then, to confirm that we have made the correct interpretation, we find that a star, which was the major part of the discussion of the second preface, is the guide to the "fields of Laurentum", or gold. This paragraph is, as Canseliet said, *The Key to the Major Arcanum*. And the Major Arcanum is not, as the puffer Kabbalists would like to think, referring to the Tarot. It refers to the "Great Work". That's cabala, not Kabbala. And part of that key is related to the legend of Aeneas, the burning of Troy, and the fields of Laurentum - the Dwellings of the Mystics, all of which takes us to the North, to the "Athenians", who stood against Atlantis, the archetypal myth of the Trojan wars, the Perseids, the Scythians living in the Hesperides, Laurentum, the original Arcadia.

But, Fulcanelli is busy wrapping his parable in a parable, and it is absolutely delightful to dive into the sea (mer) of his mind. After giving us this huge welcome, a reassurance that we have discovered his intent, he now begins to give us many more "keys" that we ought to keep in mind while reading all else he has written, as these are the themes that indicate to us whether what we are reading is a false turn in the labyrinth, or whether it is an idea that will lead to understanding.

First of all, Fulcanelli has identified for us a Trojan connection and the name of Aeneas as being significant. We also find that whatever it is we are looking for left Troy and traveled to Laurentum - gold -*East*. This is both a literal and symbolic meaning. He then connects us to the name of Seth - or Scyth - and tells us, "A race existed in the Far East on the shores of the Ocean, who *possessed a book attributed to Seth*, which spoke of the *future appearance of this star* ... which

---

[221] Ibid., p. 35.

[222] Ibid., pp. 51-2.

prediction was given as transmitted from father to son by generations of the wise men". [223]

In this remark, Fulcanelli has established the route of transmission. We then think of the Central Asian shamanic tradition.

Fulcanelli incorporates this information into the legends of the birth of Jesus, which produces a number of interesting connections. First he mentions Judaea, which suggests to us that the original teachings of the man around whom the Jesus legend formed, and then he connects this to Persia and inserts a most curious remark:

> Chalcidius... taught that the gods of Greece, the gods of Rome and the gods of foreigners should be adored, has preserved a record of the Star of the Magi and the explanation for it given by the wise. After having spoken of a star called *Ahc* by the Egyptians, which announces bad fortune, he adds: "There is another and more venerable story, which attests that the rising of a certain star announced not sickness or death, but the descent of a venerable God, for the grace of conversation with man and for the advantage of mortal affairs." [224]

Fulcanelli has here indicated to us, oh so subtly, that the Egyptian "star", or following the Egyptian trail, is the path to "bad fortune". And so, the reader has been warned that when Egyptian matters are brought into the discussion, they are following of the star of *Ahc*. He then clearly identifies the knowledge of the "descent of a venerable God" as being transmitted by the *Magi*, and further explicates that Diodorus was on the right track when he said, "this star was not one of those which people the heavens, but *a certain virtue or urano-diurnal force,* having assumed the form of a star in order to announce the birth of the Lord among us". [225]

The English word *magic* is derived through the Latin, Greek, Persian, Assyrian from the *Sumerian* or Turanian word *imga* or *emga* ("deep", "profound"), a designation for the Proto-Chaldean priests or wizards. *Magi* became a standard term for the later Zoroastrian, or Persian, priesthood through whom *Eastern* occult arts were made known to the Greeks; hence, *magos* (as also the kindred words *magikos*, *mageia*, a magician or a person endowed with secret knowledge and power like a Persian *magus*.)

Herodotus said that the Magi were the sacred caste of the Medes. They provided priests for Persia, and, regardless of dynastic changes, retained their religious influence.

Media was an ancient country of Asia. The Hebrew and Assyrian form of the word Media is *mdy* (*Madai*) which corresponds to the *Mada* by which the land is

---

[223] Ibid., p. 52.

[224] Ibid., p. 54.

[225] Ibid.

designated in the earliest Persian cuneiform texts. The origin and significance of the word are unknown

The earliest information concerning the territory occupied by the Medes, and later in part by the Persians, is derived from the Babylonian and Assyrian texts. In these it is called *Anshan*, and comprised probably a vast region bounded on the north-west by Armenia, on the north by the Caspian Sea, on the east by the great desert, and on the south by Elam. It included much more than the territory originally known as Persia. Later, however, when the Persian supremacy eclipsed that of the Medes, the name of Persia was extended to the whole Median territory.

Ethnological authorities are agreed that the peoples who, under the general name of Medes, occupied this vast region in historic times, were not the original inhabitants. They were the successors of a prehistoric population about whom little or nothing is known. The Medes appeared *at the dawn of history* and, if they did have a written language, no fragments of it have survived, so nothing is directly known concerning their language. Judging, however, from the proper names that have come down to us, there is reason to believe that it was similar to Old Persian. They would thus be of Aryan stock.

The first recorded mention of these people is in the cuneiform inscription of Shalmaneser II, King of Assyria, who claims to have vanquished the Madai in his twenty-fourth campaign, about 836 BC. The records of the succeeding reigns down to that of Asshurbanipal (668-625), constantly refers to the "dangerous Medes" (inscriptions of Tiglath-Pileser IV, 747-727), in terms which show that they were an ever-increasing menace to the power of the Assyrians. During that period, the power of Anshan was gradually strengthened by the accession and assimilation of new peoples of Aryan stock, who established themselves in the territory once held by the Assyrians east of the Tigris.

By virtue of the rising influence of another branch of the Aryan race, there came about the transition from the Median to the Persian rule. Cyrus first appeared as King of Anshan, and later became King of Persia. In 549 B. C. he defeated Astyages, becoming master of the kingdoms of Anshan, Persia, and Media.

Cyrus is known as a great and brilliant conqueror, and his fame is memorialized in the fantastic legends associated with his name by the Greek and Roman writers. His power was a menace to all western Asia, and Nabonidus, King of Babylonia, Amasis, King of Egypt, and Crœsus, King of Lydia, joined together to fight Cyrus. But even such a formidable alliance was unable to stop Cyrus who, after having subjected the whole of the Median empire, marched into Asia Minor. Crœsus was defeated and taken prisoner in 546, and within a year the entire peninsula of Asia Minor was annexed to the new Persian empire.

The west being fully subdued, Cyrus led his victorious armies against Babylonia. Belshazzar, the son of the still reigning Nabonidus, was sent as general in chief to defend the country against Cyrus, but he met with disastrous defeat. After this Cyrus entered Babylon, where he was received as a liberator, in 539 BC. The following year he issued the famous decree permitting the Hebrew captives to return to Palestine and "rebuild" the temple. It is interesting to note in this connection that Cyrus is often alluded to in Isaiah as the Lord's anointed.

In addition to sending the Hebrews back to Jerusalem to build a temple - which event will be even more interesting further on - Cyrus conquered the sacred caste of the Magi. His son Cambyses further suppressed the Magi, who then revolted and set up Gaumata, their chief, as King of Persia under the name of Smerdis. He was, however, murdered in 521 BC, and Darius became king. According to Herodotus, this downfall of the Magi was celebrated by a national Persian holiday called *magophonia* . Still the religious influence of this priestly caste continued and, at the time of the birth of Christ it was still flourishing under the Parthians. Strabo says that the Magian priests formed one of the two councils of the Parthian Empire and there is a legend that the Magi represented the three families decending from Noah.

Regarding the Parthians among whom the Magi continued to exist up to the time of Christ, we find that there was a district named Partukka or Partakka which was known to the Assyrians as early as the seventh century BC. The origins of the Parthian people are obscure, but we find that Strabo[226] says the first king, Arsaces, was a Scythian man who, with the semi-nomadic Parni tribe, invaded and conquered Parthia. Strabo also mentions those who claim Arsaces was a Bactrian who escaped from Diodotus after a failed revolt. Other ancient sources agree that Arsaces was a Scythian.

In 53 B.C. Crassus and over 40,000 Roman troops were annihilated by the Parthian forces of Orodes II and the peoples from the Mediterranean to the Indus were made acutely aware of the strength of Parthia. By 40 BC, Rome had to acknowledge Parthia whose forces had penetrated into the heart of the Roman East and captured the provinces of Asia, Pamphylia, Cilicia, and Syria, and as far south as Petra. The western border between Rome's dominions and Parthia was finally established on the banks of the Euphrates. Major campaigns by the Romans were seen in AD 116, 161, 195, 217 and 232, but Parthia was never conquered.

In AD 224, Ardashir, Parthian governor in the Achaemenid home province of Persis (Fars), overthrew Artabanus IV and established the Sasanid dynasty. The Sasanians would rule Iran until the Islamic conquest in AD 641. The Sasanians were ardent Zoroastrians in conflict with their Armenian subjects who originally were Zoroastrians but subsequently embraced Christianity.

The ancient Iranian religion of fire, light, and Wisdom was founded by the Prophet Zarathustra over 3000 years ago. The powerful influence of Zoroastrianism on Judeo-Christianity and all of western civilization is not generally known, but the fact is that the twisting of Zarathustra's words changed the nature of civilization in the west.

Hardly anything is known about Zarathustra's life and it is not even certain when he lived. The ancient Greeks speculated that he lived *six thousand years* before the philosopher Plato though several scholars have argued for a date at the beginning of the sixth century BC. Modern scholars believe that Zarathustra is the

---

[226] xi, 515

author of the *Gâthâ*'s (a part of the *Avesta*), which they date - on linguistic grounds- to the fourteenth or thirteenth century BC. This corroborates the date given by Diogenes Laertius, who states that, "Zoroaster lived six hundred years before Xerxes' invasion of Greece", that is 1080 BC[227].

It is unclear where Zarathustra was born and where he spent the first half of his life. Following the "assimilation of the hero to the myth" model, every tribe that converted to Zoroastrianism made up new legends about his life, and nearly all of them claimed that the prophet was "one of them". On linguistic grounds, we may argue that the author of the *Gâthâ*'s belonged to a tribe that lived in the eastern part of Iran, in Afghanistan or Turkmenistan. This fits with a tradition that connects Zarathustra with the ancient country named Bactria and a cypress at Kâshmar but it doesn't really prove Zarathustra's origins. It is interesting that the same mythical model is in place for both Zarathustra and the first king of the Parthians, Arsaces.

The *Gâthâ*'s do contain some personal information, but not enough to complete a biography. The *Denkard*, a late Avestic text, does contain a summary of an older biography consisting of legends that are questionable as to reliability.

According to what is pieced together from these sketchy sources, Zarathustra was born in Bactria or Aria, now known as Western Afghanistan. The Arians (The name means "noblemen"), were nomads from central Asia, who settled in Iran at the end of the second millennium. As the son of a lesser nobleman named Purushaspa and a woman named Dughdhova. Zarathustra was the third of five brothers. He became a priest and seems to have showed a remarkable sympathy for all living creatures.

Zarathustra's life changed when the god Ahuramazda granted him a vision. A spirit named *Good Thought* appeared and told Zarathustra to oppose the bloody sacrifices of the traditional Iranian cults and to give aid to the poor.

Zarathustra started to preach that there was a supreme god, the "wise lord" Ahuramazda, who had created the world, mankind and all good things in it through his holy spirit, *Spenta Mainyu*. The rest of the universe was created by six other spirits, the *Amesha Spentas* ("holy immortals"). However, the order of this *sevenfold creation* was threatened by The Lie. Good and evil spirits were fighting and mankind had to support the good spirits in order to accelerate the inevitable victory of the good.

Zarathustra used words to describe the demons which are remarkably similar to words from the Indian *Rig veda*. Now it is reasonably certain that the language of the *Rig veda* was spoken in *eastern Iran* at some stage in the history of the second millennium BC and it is reasonable to assume that Zarathustra opposed the old religion, which was to flourish in the Punjab.

---

[227] Lives and opinions of the philosophers 1.2

According to Zarathustra, it was the duty of the believer to align himself with Ahuramazda, which was possible by avoiding lies, supporting the poor, several kinds of sacrifices, the cult of fire, and so on. Additionally, Zarathustra warned the people that there would be a Last Judgment, where the friends of The Lie were to be condemned to Hell and the pious allowed to enter Heaven.

Yasna 30.1-6, 8-9

Truly for seekers I shall speak of those things to be pondered, even by one who already knows, with praise and worship for the Lord of Good Purpose, the excellent Wise One, and for Truth. [...]

Hear with your ears the best things. Reflect with clear purpose, each man for himself, on the two choices for decision, being alert indeed to declare yourselves for Him before the great requital.

Truly, there are two primal Spirits, twins renowned to be in conflict. In thought and word, in act they are two: the better and the bad. And *those who act well have chosen rightly* between these two, not so the evildoers. And when these two Spirits first came together they created life and not-life, and how at the end Worst Existence shall be for the wicked, but the House of Best Purpose shall be for the just man.

Of these two Spirits the Wicked One chose achieving the worst things. The Most Holy Spirit, who is clad in the hardest stone, chose right, and so do those who shall satisfy Ahuramazda continually with rightful acts.

The daevas indeed did not choose rightly between these two, for the Deceiver approached them as they conferred. Because they chose worst purpose, they then rushed to Fury, with whom they have afflicted the world and mankind.

Then when retribution comes for these sinners, then, Mazda, Power shall be present for Thee with Good Purpose, to declare himself for those, Lord, who shall deliver The Lie into the hands of Truth. And then may we be those who shall transfigure this world. O Mazda and you other Lords, be present with support and truth, so that thoughts may be concentrated where understanding falters. [228]

There seem to have been some conflicts between Zarathustra and the followers of the religions of sacrifice. Zarathustra was forced to flee his country since not even his family would help him.

Finally, Zarathustra obtained asylum from a king named Hystaspes who may have ruled in Chorasmia (modern Uzbekistan) or Aria. At his court, the prophet debated with the priests of Mithra; on an official gathering, they discussed *thirty three questions*, and Zarathustra's opinions prevailed.

---

[228] Translated by Mary Boyce.

Many noblemen followed the example of Hystaspes and converted to Zarathustra's new religion. From then on, Zarathustra lived at the court of Hystaspes, until he was killed at the age of *seventy-seven* by invading nomads. Some locate his death at Bactra (Balkh, near modern Mazâr-e Sharîf), in Afghanistan.

Zarathustra's teachings are strongly dualistic; the believer *has to make a choice* between good and evil thus making Zoroastrianism one of first world religions to make ethical demands on the believers

Western civilization owes mainly to Zarathustra its fundamental concept of linear time, as opposed to the cyclical and essentially static concept of ancient times. This concept, which was implicit in Zarathustra's doctrines, makes the notion of progress, reform, and improvement possible. For the most part, ancient civilizations, were profoundly static, believing that the ideal order had been handed down to them by the gods in some mythical Golden Age and they saw their religious task as a necessity to adhere to the established traditions as closely as possible. To reform or modify them in any way would have been a deviation from and diminution of the ideal.

Zarathustra gave to Persian and Greek thought the idea that there was a purpose and goal to history. All people, he declared, were participants in a supernatural battle between Good and Evil, the battleground for which was the Earth, and the very body of individual Man. This essential dualism was adopted by the Jews, who only after exposure to Zoroastrianism incorporated a demonology and angelology into their religion with a twist: instead of ethical conduct that depended on wisdom, it was Yahweh who was going to save them if they obeyed his rules, adhering to the established traditions as closely as possible. You could say that, in a way, the adoption and twisting of the ideas of Zoroaster just provided more ammunition in the arsenal of Yahweh for absolute control of his "chosen people". From Zoroastrianism, belief in demonic possession came to be a cultural obsession, as is reflected in the Gospels where Jesus was the savior and redeemer rather than Yahweh and his endless rules. Nevertheless, in terms of hyperdimensional realities, we find Zarathustras' teachings to be of great interest.

Zarathustra claimed special divine revelation and had attempted to establish the worship of one supreme God, Ahura Mazda, but after his death, the earlier Aryan polytheism reemerged. Many other features of his theology, however, have endured to the present time, through the religions that eventually superseded and twisted them.

The Babylonian captivity of the 6th century BC transformed nascent Judaism in a profound way, exposing the Jews to Zoroastrianism, which was virtually the state religion of Babylon at the time. Until then, the Jewish conception of the afterlife was inherited from their Sumerian origins, a vague shadowy existence in *Sheol*, the underworld, land of the dead (not to be confused with Hell). Zarathustra, however, preached the bodily resurrection of the dead, who would face a last judgment (both individual and general) to determine their ultimate fate in the next life: either Paradise or torment. Daniel - an advisor to King Darius - was the first Jewish prophet to refer to resurrection, judgment, and reward or punishment.

The new doctrine of resurrection was not widely accepted by the Jews and remained a point of contention for centuries until its ultimate acceptance and twisting to mean that only Jews, the Chosen People of Yahweh, would participate in this earthly kingdom of Yahweh. The Gospel of Matthew, Chapter 22:23, records that the dispute was still going on at the time of its writing, with the Sadducees denying resurrection and the Pharisees affirming it. We might also wish to note the similarity between the names *Pharisee* and *Farsi* or *Parsee*, the Persians from whom the doctrine of resurrection was borrowed.

In addition to incorporating the doctrines of resurrection and judgment, exposure to Zoroastrianism substantially altered Jewish Messianism as well. Zarathustra predicted the imminent arrival of a World Savior who would be born of a virgin and who would lead humanity in the final battle against Evil. Jewish Messianism merged these conceptions with their preexisting expectations of an earthly Davidic king who would save the Jewish nation from oppression.

It was at this time, as a response to their captivity, that apocalyptic literature appeared in Judaism, based on Babylonian models and patterned after their symbology. This was to have a strong influence on later Christian theology. With the key elements of resurrection, judgment, reward or punishment, a Savior, apocalypse, and ultimate destruction of the forces of Evil, it can be concluded that Jewish and Christian eschatology is Zoroastrian from start to finish. This suggests that Zoroastrianism may be the source of Primitive Chiliasm as referenced by Fulcanelli.

The similarities don't end with eschatology either. A lot of the tradition and sacramental ritual of Christianity, particularly Catholicism, traces back to Zoroastrian precursors. The Zoroastrian faithful would mark their foreheads with ash before approaching the sacred fire, a gesture that resembles Ash Wednesday tradition. Part of their purification before participating in ritual was the confession of sins, categorized into three types: thought, word, or deed.

Zoroastrians also had a Eucharistic ritual, the Haoma ritual, in which the god Haoma, or rather his presence, was sacrificed in a plant. The worshipers would drink the juice in expectation of eventual immortality. There is a curious connection here to the *Epic of Gilgamesh* where he was told that a plant could give him immortality. One wonders, of course, if this wasn't a later addition utilizing consciousness altering substances to imitate mystical states of ecstasy.

Finally, Zoroastrians celebrated All Souls' Day, reflecting, like the Catholics, a belief in intercession by and for the dead. We should also note that the story of the Magi, who were said to have visited the newborn Jesus, resembles an earlier story of Magi who looked for a star foretelling the birth of a Savior, in this case Mithras. Magi were not kings but Zoroastrian astrologers, and the birthday of Mithras - and other "dying and resurrecting gods" - on December 25th was appropriated by the church.

Christianity also seems to have borrowed the story of the temptation in the desert from Zoroastrianism, since an earlier legend placed Zarathustra himself in that situation. The principal demon, Ahriman, promised Zarathustra earthly power if he would forsake the worship of the supreme God. Ahriman, like Satan when tempting Jesus, failed.

A final interesting parallel is the three days that Jesus was said to have spent in the grave. This concept may have been derived from a Zoroastrian belief that the soul remains in the body for three days before departing. Three days would have established death yet left his soul in a position to reanimate his body. As a Messiah, Jesus functioned purely along Zoroastrian lines. While purportedly of the Davidic line, he offered only redemption from sin, rather than national salvation for the Jews. He was a world savior rather than a Jewish Messiah. The Jews did not recognize him as their Messiah, and in a real sense he wasn't and isn't. Their Messianic expectations, which preceded any foreign influence, went unfulfilled; in fact, their nation was ultimately destroyed once and looks to be heading in the same direction at present. Neither did Jesus effect a final triumph over Evil. This has been reserved for a second coming in conjunction with the last judgment and the rewards and punishments of either Heaven or Hell.

The Magi who were featured in the story of Jesus were probably not completely Zoroastrian. As the Zoroastrian faith, and the Persian empire, expanded westward into the territory of Media, the priests of an extremely ancient religion, the Magi, adopted themselves into Zoroastrianism, though not without major social upheavals. The general scholarly opinion is that these priests of the old Indo-Iranian faith, which Zarathushtra preached *against* in the *Gathas*, re-adapted many practices of the old religion back into the faith - such as reverence for subordinate divinities, the haoma - sacrifice, and purity rituals.

"The teachings of Zarathushtra were intermingled with the old religion, and the Magi's position was transformed into the priests of the new religion...", writes Dariush Jahanian. Many of the Magian practices were themselves adapted from far more ancient sources.

What, then, were the Magi searching for in the story of the birth of Jesus recounted by Fulcanelli as a clue to the alchemical transformation?

When we look into the matter of Zoroastrian mysticism - the Magian influence from the more ancient sources - we find that it posits individuals who have had a direct experience of the Deity, or God. Such individuals live their lives in the presence of God, a God to which the mystic relates as a Beloved as well as a Source of Wisdom. This Zoroastrian mysticism is *rationally tested* but transcends any rational explanation.

Some of the basic results of such a mystical life are: a powerful sense of a divine Presence, with which one can engage in inner dialogue and prayer, the loving and friendly quality of that Presence, the *increase in intelligence and alertness* it brings - which is often related to a concept of God as Divine Wisdom - a feeling of happiness and peace, and, as a sign, the inner perception of brilliant light - a *star*.

These experiences certainly can be counterfeited, by various mind- altering techniques or drugs, but the true experience can be measured by its power to bring about personal and moral transformation towards what is good and constructive - what Zoroastrians call the path of *Asha*, or Righteousness.

The Gathas of Zarathushtra show that their author, is speaking from just such an authentic mystical experience. These mystical experiences are easily describable in Zoroastrian terms. The mystical perception of God in the "inner eye" or "imagination", the mystical Light, the sense of divine Wisdom, the love between God and human, the infusion of virtue, courage, and perseverence - all these basic factors clearly exist in the Gathas. In the Gathas (and other texts) mysticism is hidden in plain sight.

In Zarathushtra's Gathas, Yasna 28, the first Song of the Gathas, verse 28,2 Zarathustra. speaks of the mystical means of that relationship, how it comes about, "Wise God, I approach you through *good mind...*".[229]

The simple phrase "through good mind", speaks of a high level of mystical experience. S. Insler, another modern translator of the Gathas, translates *vohu manah*, the original Avestan, as "Good Thinking"; but this misses the point of the Prophet's mystical way. Good Thinking is a human virtue, and approaching God through good thinking is something a non-mystical liberal Protestant or rationalist humanist would say. It is far more than "good thinking" to Zarathushtra. Good Mind is a living emanation of the Wise Lord. To approach ("be encircled by" in literal translation) Good Mind is to achieve communion, *through the mind*, with the Divine Mind, or Divine Intelligence. It is a sharing of the divine Mind through the cooperation of human mind and Divine communication. Through this union of minds comes *perception of divine information*, the laws of humanity and nature - perception of *Asha*.

Eugene Canseliet writes in his Preface to the second edition of Fulcanelli's Alchemical Masterpiece, *The Dwellings of the Philosophers:*

> According to the meaning of the Latin word adeptus, the alchemist has then received the Gift of God, or even better, the Present, a cabalistic pun on the double meaning of the word, underlining that he thus enjoys the infinite duration of the Now.[...] 'In the Kingdom of Sulpur there exists a Mirror in which the entire World can be seen. Whosoever looks into this Mirror can see and learn the three parts of Wisdom of the entire World.

This is what Fulcanelli means by the Star that heralds the birth of the Christ within. Another point of interest to us is the fact that, after the division of the Catholic Church into East and West, the Catholic Church started referring to its "Nestorian" converts as "Chaldeans" to distinguish them from their brothers and sisters in the mother church who continued to be referred to by Rome as "Nestorians" (followers of Nestorius, Patriarch of Constantinople in 428 AD whose teachings were declared heretical by the Catholic Church in 431 AD). This leads us in a circle back to the Ancient Eastern Esoteric Tradition revealed by Boris Mouravieff.

Regarding Fulcanelli's reference to Troy, Apollodorus tells us that Libya owed its name to a daughter of Epaphus, a king of Tyre (or Sidon) and a son of Io and Zeus, born after Io, under the form of a white heifer, had fled Argos and *reached the coast of Syria* in the area that was to become the country of the Phoenicians. Poseidon, from whom she had two sons, Agenor, the mythical hero of Phoenicia,

---

[229] Jafarey translation

and Belus, the mythical hero of Egypt, loved this daughter named Libya. Agenor in turn was the father of Europa and her brothers Cadmus the founder of the Greek Thebes, Phoenix (the eponym of Phoenicia), Cilix (the eponym of Cilicia), and Thasus (the eponym of the island of Thasos), all of whom founded settlements and cities during their quest for their sister after she had been loved and abducted by Zeus taking the guise of a bull to become the mother of the Cretan king Minos. Belus, for his part, gave birth to Danaus and Egyptus, whose offspring returned to Argos.

Now, looking at the Biblical version of the same myths, Abraham was the father of Ishmael who was the 'father of the Arabs', according to the Hebrew texts. Hermes was supposed to have been the father of Arabus who was also called the 'father of the Arabs'. This Arabus was the legendary father of Cassiopeia, which is almost a parallel development with just some name changes. It seems as though Arabus and Ishmael were comparatively the same in type and function and there are further comparisons to be made. But, the essential thing here is that Cassiopeia would then have been a granddaughter of Hermes/Abraham and a daughter of Ishmael. This would mean that the granddaughter of Ishmael was "Andromeda", the bride of Perseus, the son of Danae, the daughter of the king of Argos. We note also that the mother of Ishmael was "Hagar the Egyptian". Cassiopeia was said to have been married to Cepheus, the King of either "Joppa" or Ethiopia. Most sources say Ethiopia.

As it happens, this Ethiopia of which Cepheus was king, is not the land we know of as Ethiopia today.[230] We notice that Eusebius tells us, "In the reign of Amenophis III a body of Ethiopians migrated from *the country about the Indus, and settled in the valley of the Nile*". We might toss this aside as mere fable except for the fact that a similar statement is made by Apollonius of Tyana: "The Ethiopians are colonists sent from India". This is a very important clue, particularly the "time of Amenophis III", but we will not pursue it here. We will pause, however, to comment on the fact that Memnon, the son of Aurora and Tithonus, was also said to be the King of the Ethiopians to the "extreme East". Memnon was related to Priam, King of Troy, and came to fight in the Trojan War. Perhaps Cepheus and Memnon were the same individual since both the two names are related to "head" etymologies.

Returning to the remarks of Fulcanelli in describing the transmission of the knowledge of the "descent of a venerable God", further explicating the matter by telling us that Diodorus was on the right track when he said, "this star was not one of those which people the heavens, but *a certain virtue or urano-diurnal force,* having assumed the form of a star in order to announce the birth of the Lord among us", we find that we are dealing with matters having to do with the "inner

---

[230] "The Road to Meluhha" in *Journal of Near Eastern Studies,* 41, 1982, pp. 279-288.

work" of the alchemist which will result in the appearance of a "star", or a light in the "sea", or mind; as well as a more or less hyperdimensional energy, force, or level of reality that can interact with our own, according to certain "urano-diurnal" time-tables as we have already discussed in terms of the dances of the Maruts, the dancing god at Stonehenge, and the technology for the mastery of space and time. Fulcanelli explicates that this is clearly what he is referring to:

> Speaking of such strange happenings and faced with the impossibility of attributing the cause of them to any celestial phenomenon, A. Bonnetty, struck by the mystery which envelops these narratives, asks, "Who are these Magi and what is one to think of this star? That is what rational critics and others are wondering at this moment. It is difficult to reply to these questions, because ancient and modern Rationalism and Ontologism, drawing all their knowledge from their own resources, have made one forget all the *means by which the ancient peoples of the East preserved their primitive traditions*".[231]

We thus come to the idea that the stories of the birth of Jesus, the appearance of a star, and all of the related ideas and stories are descriptions of a *technology* of interaction with this hyperdimensional reality. That this technology clearly includes, or is predicated upon, certain development of potentials within the alchemist is also certain.

Fulcanelli then connects us to The Assyrians, and Balaam, who he identifies as one of the Mages. He then tells us that, "there shall come a Star out of Jacob, and a Sceptre shall rise out of Israel...". We find that we have traveled from the Far East, across Asia, to Chaldea, to Assyria, to Judaea. Then what does Fulcanelli tell us? He connects us again to the fields of Laurentum - Gold - the East:

> G.J. Witkowski describes for us a very curious stained glass window, which used to be near the sacristy in the old church of Saint-Jean at Rouen, now destroyed. This window showed the Conception of St. Romain. His father, Benoit, Counselor of Clothair II, and his mother, Felicite...[232]

Now, lest the reader think that Fulcanelli is talking about the St. Romain, archbishop of Rouen, (631-641) former chancellor of Clotaire II, about whom legend tells that he delivered the environs of Rouen from a monster called Gargouille, let me just suggest a cabalistic meaning: *Holy Roman* dragon slayer. Immediately, we are reminded of the theories of Fomenko, that the true histories of England and Europe were confused with the histories of Byzantium, and that the real history of Europe and England are lost, and we wonder how it all connects?

One explanation that offers itself is that there is a particular family, or "bloodline" of dragon slayers. That is a very popular line of thinking at present,

---

[231] Fulcanelli, op. cit., p. 55.

[232] Ibid., p. 56.

and if the material we have uncovered is correct, then it means that everyone has been looking in the wrong places for the wrong things, for the wrong reasons.

The deeper explanation is that the story of Jesus, as we have received it in the gospels, is a historicized and *glossed* myth that contains within it the clues to a certain "preparation" of the initiate for the function of the "descent" of the benevolent God, or, as Diodorus has put it, "*a certain virtue or urano-diurnal force having assumed the form of a star*". In short, we find ourselves again thinking of Edward Leedskalnin and his spinning airplane seat, and the dance of the god of the Hyperboreans every nineteen years, according to some "scheduled" interaction between the three body system of the Sun, Moon and Earth, that facilitates a gravitational node as described by Jessup.

Going back to Fulcanelli, we find that his discussion of the origins of the Gothic cathedrals is most interesting. He tells us that the term "gothic", which imposed its rules on all the productions of the Middle Ages, from the twelfth to the fifteenth century, was not an inheritance of ancient Germanic peoples as many "experts" suppose, but was rather a production of the descendants of the Argotiers, or Argonauts. He then speaks of the journey to Colchos, the land of the Golden Fleece, and that *art got* is really *art cot*, or the art of light of the spirit. Fulcanelli then makes a most amazing remark:

> The fact is that there is neither chance nor coincidence nor accidental
> correspondence here below. All is foreseen, preordained, regulated; and it is not for
> us to bend to our pleasure the inscrutable will of Destiny.[233]

Again and again we find Fulcanelli suggesting the existence of a hyperdimensional reality in which our own world is "embedded", and from which our reality takes its form as a shadow cast upon the cave wall described by Plato. As we continue to think in these terms, it becomes more and more apparent that this Great Work of the alchemists was essentially the process of becoming "free of the Matrix", described in alchemical and allegorical terms.

Fulcanelli then takes us through several remarks about the symbolism of the *art cot*, until he brings us to the ornamentation of the floors of cathedrals. Here, he connects us to Fomenko's ideas by remarking that the art of ceramics had reached perfection, and the use of multi-colored marble, *in the manner of the Byzantine mosaics,* was also utilized. The Labyrinth at Chartres designated by Fulcanelli as *La Lieue* (the league) and *Le Lieu* (the place) is described, and finally he tells us that there used to be a scene of the combat of Theseus and the Minotaur at the center. He then remarks that the point is to make a connection between the mytho-hermetic meanings rather than to establish any connection to the famous constructions of antiquity, *the labyrinths of Greece and Rome.*

---

[233] Ibid., p. 43.

Right here we notice a strange thing: the famous labyrinths of antiquity were *not* those of Greece and Rome, they were those of Egypt and Crete! But we already know that there was a significant difference between the Egyptian/Cretan Labyrinths and the labyrinths of the Northern peoples. So, immediately, we realize that Fulcanelli has dropped a "double clue" in our lap.

Fulcanelli then, immediately, jumps to the subject of the Labyrinth of Solomon! The only problem is: there was no famous labyrinth of Solomon; at least not unless Fulcanelli is telling us in this way that the famed "Temple of Solomon" was really a maze, and the object placed in the "temple of Solomon" was the same as the object at the center of the maze. He then tells us that this labyrinth/temple of Solomon is:

> ...a series of concentric circles, interrupted at certain points, so as to form a bizarre
> and inextricable path. The picture of the labyrinth is thus offered to us as
> emblematic of the whole labour of the Work, with its two major difficulties, one the
> path which must be taken in order to reach the center - where the bitter combat of
> the two natures takes place - the other the way which the artist must follow in order
> to emerge. It is there that the thread of Ariadne becomes necessary for him, if he is
> not to wander among the winding paths of the task, unable to extricate himself.
>
> My intention is not to write, as Batsdorff did, a special treatise on what this thread
> of Ariadne is, *which enabled Perseus to fulfill his purpose.* But in laying stress on
> the *cabala*, I hope to furnish shrewd investigators with some precise information on
> the symbolical value of the famous myth.[234]

We are first of all struck by the terms "bitter combat of the two natures", in terms of Zarathustra's claim that the battle between the forces of good and evil take place within the human being. We are also puzzled: what does Ariadne have to do with Perseus[235]? What do the Argonauts have to do with Aeneas? What is the relation between the Fields of Laurentum and Colchos? What is the connection between the Golden Fleece and the Holy Grail? What about the Temple of Solomon and the Labyrinth and the Ark of the Covenant and the Minotaur? And what is the "symbolical value" of the famous myth?

---

[234] Ibid., p. 48.

[235] This may be a misprint or the translator's error. I have checked the French version of the Second Edition against the English translation, and the error only exists in the English. I am unable to locate a first edition of Fulcanelli to check if the error exists in the original which it may have done, then could have been corrected by the editor of the French version. The translator of the English version may have worked from a first edition. In any event, it was a fortuitous error for me as I was working with the "mythicization" concept, and the similarities of the heros of so many myths were already obvious, so the confusion of Perseus with Theseus seemed to be "confirmation."

NEO, NOAH, NOË = PERSEUS

At this point, let's think about these stories as metaphors for the Great Work of Alchemy. As we have surmised, this "work" consists in becoming aware of, and possibly interacting with, a hyperdimensional reality in which our own is embedded. At the present time, we have a very good modern example of this process in the movie *The Matrix*. On the surface, this movie was a presentation of possibilities inherent in technological manipulation of society and individual reality. What many people do not realize is that it is a metaphor for the True Reality - a Matrix that is even more mysterious and subtle than anything suggested in the movie – a Matrix of which speculations and formulae relating to hyperdimensional physics and modern studies in consciousness have only revealed the tip of the iceberg.

The true Matrix of human experience on Earth is only a shadow of a reality that exists beyond our human conceptions of society, religion, belief systems, technology, and even alien paradigms promulgated at the present time in such volume and variety. Many scientific speculations of recent times have begun to unravel the puzzle of our existence in troubling ways. One of these threads seems to suggest – in definitely hard science – that not only is Time cyclical, but that our present human race and technological society may not be the pinnacle of Darwinian evolution. In fact, the possibility of races and civilizations before us, of even greater sophistication and achievement, is becoming more likely every day, as we have already discussed.

In considering this and the Matrix nature of our reality, the questions that we have brought forward are: if time is cyclical, if greater civilizations than ours existed in the "past", how did they perish? And, if they perished, did some elements of their knowledge survive in myths and folk tales? If so, what can we, today, learn from them about our own Matrix?

In terms of the myths and stories of the search for the Holy Grail, or, in our modern metaphor – the escape from the Matrix - most of the figures appearing in the Greek constellations were said to have been placed there by one of the gods to honor and perpetuate their memory. As we have noted, the constellation figures of Cepheus and Cassiopeia are unusual in that they were not granted their positions as an honor, but were placed there to complement the story of Perseus, Andromeda and Cetus. This is a group of five constellations that is unusual in that it is *the only classical myth to be so fully depicted.* And this happens to be the myth which Fulcanelli has emphasized by his funny little "mistake" about Ariadne giving the clue to Perseus, and all the other strange connections he has drawn between this myth and the "birth of the Christ child", leading up to the depiction of the conception of St. Romain. Just what is it that Fulcanelli is trying to tell us? Is he suggesting that a certain family, the family of the Perseids, is the dragon slaying bloodline of Jesus?

More even than this, can it be that this is a "track", a clue that this myth is a sort of "message in a bottle" to mankind? Does the story of Perseus represent our potential for discovering the truth? Do the elements of the story represent the actions we must undertake in order to symbolically "take the red pill", or "Cut off the Head of Medusa"?

Of all the ancient heroes of myth and legend, Perseus stands out as being supremely successful - so many others started out with good intentions, had numerous successes, but then fell from glory due to hubris or trickery or temptation. Was it because of his ultimate success that Perseus became the archetype of the Grail Quest hero – Perceval - an archetype in which all can participate as Neo did in the movie, *The Matrix*? Joseph Campbell writes:

> The figure of the tyrant-monster is known to the mythologies, folk traditions, legends, and even nightmares, of the world; and his characteristics are everywhere essentially the same. He is the hoarder of the general benefit. He is the monster avid for the greedy rights of 'my and mine'. The havoc wrought by him is described in mythology and fairy tale as being universal throughout his domain.[236]

In the present time, it seems that this "monster tyrant" is being manifested from hyperdimensional realities in the form of such as George Bush and Ariel Sharon, and the monster is becoming more and more evident and overtly active. We seem to be at a point in the cycle of time where it is manifesting in our world in very real and frightening ways. There is an increase of chaos, a loss of vigor of what is good and noble and clean, a decline of virtue of cosmic resources. We are, it seems, living "As it was in the days of Noah". In this sense, we think the homophony of the name of the hero of the movie, Neo, to Noah, is more than coincidental.

In *The Matrix*, this realization that there was something dreadfully wrong with reality is what drove Neo to search, night and day, for some clue to – what? He did not know. But Morpheus explains to him what the sickness in his soul really is:

> You have the look of a man who accepts what he sees because he is expecting to wake up. You're here because you know something. What you know, you can't explain, but you feel it. You've felt it your entire life – that there's something wrong with the world. You don't know what it is, but it's there, like a splinter in your mind, driving you mad.[237]

Joseph Campbell asks,

> The hero is the man of self-achieved submission. But submission to what? The first work of the hero is to retreat from the world scene of secondary effects *to those causal zones of the psyche where the difficulties really reside,* and there to clarify the difficulties, eradicate them in his own case, and break through to the undistorted, direct experience and assimilation of the archetypal images. This is the process known to Hindu and Buddhist philosophy as Viveka, "discrimination".

The Sufis call this process of learning discrimination "acquiring perspicacity". Zarathustra described it as a war between good and evil *within our reality*, and within individual human beings. We have described it as choosing and aligning

---

[236] Campbell, Joseph, *The Hero With A Thousand Faces* (New York: MJF 1949) p. 15.

[237] Morpheus to Neo, *The Matrix*.

with Thought Centers of either Being or Non-being. It is also the *first stage* of the Great Work of the Alchemists. The most basic way of putting it is that one must first *choose*.

Neo chose: he took the Red Pill and it was then that the struggle for his True Being began, the battle between the "metals" or "beasts" described by the alchemists. After a long period of "reconditioning", and "training", Neo was, finally, himself.

> The hero, therefore, is the man or woman who has been able to battle past his personal and local historical limitations to the generally valid, normally human forms. Such a one's visions, ideas, and inspirations come pristine from the primary springs of human life and thought. They are eloquent of the unquenched source through which society is reborn. The hero has died as a modern man; but as eternal man - he has been reborn. His second solemn task and deed, therefore, is to return then - transfigured, and teach the lesson he has learned of life renewed.[238]

In the end, we have the three-fold formula: Separation - Initiation - Return. The adventure of the hero follows the pattern of separation from the world, penetration to some source of power or knowledge which Zarathustra called "Good Mind", and a life-enhancing return. Campbell says, "The really creative acts are represented as those deriving from some sort of dying to the world....". This is the giving up of the limiting self-perception and choosing alignment. This is being unplugged from *The Matrix*. This is the first calcination of the Magistery of the alchemists.

> The matrix is everywhere – it is all around us – even now in this very room. You can see it when you look out your window or when you turn on your television. You can feel it when you go to work; when you go to church; when you pay your taxes. It is the world that has been pulled over your eyes to blind you from the truth – that you are a slave. Like everyone else, you were born into bondage – born into a prison that you cannot smell or taste or touch – a prison for your mind.[239]

Joseph Campbell suggests that one of the problems of the "failed hero" is that there is a dangerous temptation to *not* return and recycle the energy to mankind. The problems of making known a way of illumination to people still wrapped in worldliness may seem too great to solve. There is also the danger of those who have, like Prometheus, darted to the goal by violence, manipulation or "selling their souls", and who then present their view of the "boon for mankind" which is an unbalanced gift that will react sharply, and they will end up being "blasted from within and without like Prometheus on the rock of his own violated consciousness". There is a lot of that going around nowadays in the guise of New Age teachings, and even from the hyperdimensional reality itself - those beings of

---

[238] Campbell, op.cit., pp. 19-20.

[239] Morpheus to Neo, *The Matrix*.

darkness that create and maintain the Matrix and have a strong vested interest in seeing to it that their "food/power source" is not lost.

It is in this problem that the greatest danger lays. Since those forces that create and maintain the Matrix have so much to lose, they exert a great deal of energy to keep the Matrix of lies and false beliefs in place. And doing it from a state of hyperdimensional reality enables them to work from a state of timelessness, so as to be able to produce all the perceived effects that support their agenda; the Evil Magician of Gurdjieff; the "Flyer" of Castaneda; the Shaitans of the Sufis. And the reality has been manipulated for so long that it seems natural. It has become a comfortable prison in which Stockholm Syndrome reigns supreme, and the inmates love their captors. The result of this is that when a hero returns with true knowledge of the Matrix, he or she meets with such blank misunderstanding and disregard from those he wishes most of all to help, that he gives up in despair. Morpheus warned Neo about this:

> The Matrix is a system, Neo. That system is our enemy. When you are inside you look around – what do you see? Businessmen, teachers, lawyers, and carpenters – the very minds of the people we are trying to save. But, until we do, these people are still part of that system and *that makes them our enemy.*

> You have to understand: most of these people are not ready to be unplugged – and many of them are so inert, so inured – hopelessly dependent on the system – that *they will fight to protect it.*[240]

The hero is generally described as one who begins life as the "youngest" or "despised" child. There is some serious "rejection" of his being from his very birth. But it is the triumphing over these personal oppressions that gives him the means of regeneration of humanity as a whole.

> The cosmogonic cycle is presented with astonishing consistency in the sacred writings of all the continents, and it gives to the adventure of the hero a new and interesting turn; for now it appears that the perilous journey was a labor not of attainment but of *reattainment*, not discovery but *rediscovery*. The godly powers sought and dangerously won are revealed to have been within the heart of the hero all the time. He is 'the king's son' who has come to know who he is and therewith has entered into the exercise of his proper power – 'God's son', who has learned to know how much that title means. ...The hero is symbolical of that divine creative and redemptive image which is hidden within us all, only waiting to be known and rendered into life.

> The effect of the successful adventure of the hero is the unlocking and release again of the flow of life into the body of the world. The miracle of this flow may be represented in physical terms as a circulation of food substance, dynamically as a streaming of energy, or spiritually as a manifestation of grace. Such varieties of

---

[240] Morpheus to Neo, *The Matrix* (emphasis ours).

> image alternate easily, representing three degrees of condensation of the one life force. ...Grace, food substance, energy: these pour into the living world, and wherever they fail, life decomposes into death.
>
> The torrent pours from an invisible source, the point of entry being the center of the symbolic circle of the universe...[241]

We witnessed this streaming energy pouring into the world through Neo in *The Matrix*. In terms of understanding the comparable roles of the myth of Perseus and Andromeda, we find that each person who is part of this archetype, who is "colinear" with it, at different times must enact the different parts in the personal as well as the universal plane. That means that the hero, Perseus, is in all, both male and female. He represents the obscure and oppressed and abandoned "child of the king" who is partly human and partly divine. He is Neo in the Matrix, raised in a pod as a "battery", and finally waking up.

Neo-Perseus is there, seemingly forgotten and obscure and with all kinds of odds against him. For a long time he is even under the powers of those who would wish to see him dead, but cannot just kill him without incurring great consequences to themselves. The oracle told Acrisius, father of Danae, mother of Perseus, "you will have no sons, and your grandson must kill you". To forestall this fate, Acrisius imprisoned Danae in a dungeon ... Zeus came upon her in a shower of gold, and she bore him a son named Perseus. When Acrisius learned of Danae's condition, he would not believe that Zeus was the father... but, not daring to kill his own daughter, locked her and the infant Perseus in a wooden ark, which he cast into the sea. A fisherman found them and turned them over to his brother, King Polydectys who wanted to marry Danae and get rid of Perseus. So, there are traps all around.

We see these traps in *The Matrix* in the actions of the "Agents". In the present time, we see these traps as the vast Cosmic COINTELPRO operation that has been in operation for millennia.

Polydectys sets another trap for Perseus: he pretends that he wants to marry someone else, only he needs a special gift – the head of Medusa. Perseus, thinking that by helping Polydectys marry someone else, he will be helping his mother avoid having a marriage forced on her, readily agrees to go after Medusa.

Medusa symbolizes the Matrix control over our minds. Medusa is the monster that must be "beheaded" in the Great Work of Alchemy.

Polydectys is sure that Perseus will fail, that he will not be able to unplug himself from the Matrix by cutting off the gorgon's head, or overcoming his own limitations. But, since Perseus is the child of Zeus, there are beings at higher levels that are interested in helping. Athene gives him a brightly polished shield and

---

[241] Campbell, op. cit., p. 40.

warns him to never look directly at Medusa, but only at the reflection, and this will be the guide to cutting off the head.

This is represented in our world as "reading the signs" of the activation of the Matrix mind by observing our reality – its synchronicities and experiences of déjà vu and other things that do not "fit" - and thereby being aware of when there is interaction between our reality and the hyperdimensional reality so as to be able to take those actions that will serve to protect and free us.

Hermes gave Perseus a sickle—the power of the mind/frontal cortex in its unemotional confrontation of Truth: we cut through lies to the truth.

Perseus also needed to collect a pair of winged sandals, a wallet to hold the head in, and a helmet of invisibility. But these had to be obtained from the Stygian Nymphs: and the only ones who knew where they were, were the Graea who had a single eye and tooth between three of them. Perseus is clever and steals the eye and tooth while it is being passed and refuses to return it until they tell him what he needs to know. We find it interesting that this "single eye" is often used as "occult" symbols such as the Eye of Horus and the eye at the top of the pyramid on the U.S. paper money system.

Gaining control of the Eye represents the gaining of knowledge and awareness of the Matrix mind - the crypto-geographic Overlords of Entropy - and the Control System, without which the mission cannot succeed. You must know the enemy. You must be as wise as serpents and as gentle as doves, as it is put in the wisdom literature.

Armed with all these gifts, Perseus finds the Gorgon and is able to successfully cut off her head. And from her blood springs the winged steed, Pegasus. This symbolizes his "knighting". He has broken through to the streams of creative force locked up by the control system.

On his way back to rescue his mother, he spies Andromeda.

Now, Andromeda is chained to a rock because *her* mother boasted of her beauty. This brought a whole host of troubles down on the heads of her people and her father was told that the only way to solve this problem was to sacrifice Andromeda. She was chained to a rock for the devouring sea serpent to come and eat.

The much-maligned Cassiopeia represents knowing one's "beauty". This seems to be a very dangerous stance to take because knowing one's own power gets a person into hot water. This is why the alchemists described the process in such veiled and difficult terminology. To speak about these things plainly is to court all the wrath of the Matrix Control System. According to many commentators, Cassiopeia and Danae are actually one and the same just as Perseus and Andromeda can both be aspects of one being.

We can see the role of Cassiopeia in *The Matrix* as The Oracle – the cookie baking lady whose cryptic words are just what Neo needs to hear – even if they seem to be negative at the beginning, and do seem to get him into some very hot water!

In the same terms, Cassiopeia may have known what she was doing when she caused her daughter to become bait for the Sea Serpent, Cetus. As an "Oracle", she would have known that Perseus, like Neo, could overcome all obstacles to save others – and that this was the extra motivation needed to ensure success. The result was, of course, that Perseus killed the sea serpent and married Andromeda. They set off together as a team: righting wrongs, freeing the oppressed, turning the bad guys into stone, and lived, as far as is known, happily ever after.

Thus, as a symbol of gaining Freedom from the Matrix, we find Perseus to be the Hero of choice, and the dynamics of the only myth that is fully represented in the Sky over our very heads, to be that which suggests to us our path of "tracking" the clues that will enable each participant to not only cut off the head of their own Medusa, thus releasing the Truth in the form of the Winged Horse, Pegasus, and with the aid of this Truth, to participate in the Freeing of Andromeda - the accomplishment of the Great Work of the Alchemists, the accessing the rightful powers and abilities of the "child of the king".

When we consider our dancing Maruts and our spinning Edward Leedskalnin, we think that we ought to follow the path of the dancers to attempt to discover something about this most interesting idea. Going from the early Aryan forms to the classical Greek, we come across the Kouretes, whose function so closely parallels that of the Maruts that we cannot doubt the identity of origin.

The Kouretes were a band of armed youths of semi-divine origin whose home was in Crete where they were associated with the worship of the goddess Rhea. Their dance was supposed to have been taught to them by Athene, and a text discovered among the ruins of a temple in Crete, *The Hymn of the Kouretes*, demonstrates that the dance was designed to *bring increase in the reproductive energies of Nature*. What is more interesting is that the God is not being worshipped in a subservient way, but is being invited to join in the dance as the act that will produce the results!

Thus we find that there is evidence that the classic Greeks carried a tradition from their Aryan forefathers that a group of special people, of semi-mythical origin, represented as armed youths, who were notable dancers, were closely associated with the abundance of Nature in a very specific relationship.

As we track such things, again and again we see that such matters always have two faces. The dance of the Phrygian Korybantes is a case in point. This dance was distinguished from that of the Kouretes by its orgiastic character. It was wild and whirling, similar to that of the modern dervishes, and was often accompanied by self-mutilation, wild cries, and un-rhythmic clashing of weapons. Some think that this latter characteristic was included to drown out the cries of the victims. In short, the dance of the Korybantes was sacrificial in nature; that of the Kouretes initiatory and interactive with the cosmos for purposes of praise and abundance.

As we have noted, this dance was not of a warlike nature. In the Roman Salii, we find a connection between the modern Morris and Mummers dances and an archaic ceremony utilizing certain elements of the Grail Legends that have since been separated to a great extent. The Salii was a college of twelve priests dedicated to Mars in his primitive growth and vegetation aspect: Ares. Long before he was the god of war, Mars was the spring deity whose name is memorialized in the month March. It was only in later times that he became associated with warlike elements.

The first of March was the traditional birthday of Mars and during the whole month, the Salii offered sacrifices and performed dances in his honor. They wore *pointed caps* or helmets, swords at their sides, and carried on their left arms a shield that was purported to be modeled on a fabled "shield" that fell from heaven. In this, we see an early reference to the grail as platter. In their right hand the Salii carried an object that has been described as a short lance, but it seems that certain bas-reliefs have shown that these objects actually resemble the Wands of the Tarot deck. It is suggested that they were drumsticks used to beat on the shields, which may have been made of skin stretched on a frame. In this case, the shield as a representation of the feminine being rhythmically struck by the wands as phallic symbols would have been utilized as a sound accompaniment to the dance. The suggestion by many is that this is a Tantric reference, but we think that many of the "sexual" implications do not refer to sex at all, but rather to a far more fundamental thing about procreation: DNA. And, like everything else, it has been corrupted.

At the conclusion of their songs the Salii invoked *Mamurius Veturius*, the fabled smith who was supposed to have made the copies of the original shield that fell from heaven. On the 14th of March, a man dressed in skins, representing the smith, was led through the streets, beaten by the Salii with rods, and thrust out of the city. The following day, the 15th, the Salii celebrated the feast of Anna Perenna.

The most famous form of the Sword Dance that survives today is that of *Papa Stour*, on one of the Shetland Islands. The dance is performed at Christmas by seven dancers who represent the "seven champions of Christendom". Their leader, playing the part of St. George, gives a speech, after which he dances solo, followed by a presentation of each of his companions who each give a performance, followed by an elaborate dance in unison.

In both the Sword Dance and the Mumming Play, the chief character is St. George, the *dragon slayer*. This connects us back to Indra and the Maruts, Perseus and St. Romain. The English Morris dance has lost the dramatic elements, but has retained other elements, including the skin-draped clown, that the Sword Dance and the Mumming Play no longer have.

At the end of some of the Sword Dances, the dancers form a pentagon and cry, "A Nut! A Nut!". Jessie Weston notes that this is similar to the game of "Nuts", or breast-knots, which are nosegays affixed to the chest at Mayday celebrations. This naturally reminds us of the head of Medusa with it's knotted serpent hair that was affixed to the breastplate of Athene, and its relation to the Head of Bran that was both oracular as well as the source of endless bounty. The reader might also want to note the story of the head of John the Baptist on the platter is juxtaposed against the miracle of the loaves and fishes, and the head of Bran was known to specialize in loaves and fishes!

In *Gawain and the Green Knight*, the hero's badge is the Pentacle, explained there as the "Endless Knot". In some Tarot decks, the pentacles replace the dish, so we find another connection. In one form of the Morris dance, the lead dancer actually carries a chalice at the same time he carries a sword and a bull's head on the end of a long pole![242]

These ancient cults that we suspect to be representations of an archaic technology consistently refer to the same symbols, or objects of cultic value. These mysterious objects form the central theme of the action of the story of the quest, and it seems that a true understanding of these objects is as essential to the hero himself as it is to the modern day "seeker of mysteries". The objects, the cup or dish, the lance or sword, and the stone, when reassembled, bring us to some idea of the rites of the Temple of Apollo where the god "danced all night" until the heliacal rising of the Pleiades.

We see that the symbols of the ancient technology are often separated from each other - some in a rather haphazard way. They no longer form a complete ensemble, and even the dates of the performance of the action have shifted. But careful research shows that they were all originally part of a whole, and at some point, whatever they represent was all utilized in a single process.

At the same time, we see in the dancers the original formation of the Grail Knights - warrior priests whose duty was to not only protect society, but to ensure abundance. And so we move from Maruts to Kouretes to Salii to Templars - and Gothic architecture.

Chartres Cathedral, begun in 1194, is the epitome of Gothic architecture. Prior to the cathedral, a Christian church had stood on the same site since at least the 4th century. Long before, by hundreds of years, an oak grove stood on the same site where Druids held their ceremonies..[243] Speculation on the origins of Gothic architecture has produced many references to the Gothic cathedral as being a simulation of *a forest glade* with the nave, transepts and choir, with their ribbed vaults, likened to trees. It is a compelling image and in the 18th and 19th centuries much was written about the sylvan origins of Gothic architecture. In 1792, Sir James Hall, using posts of ash and pliant willow rods, demonstrated to his own satisfaction the timber construction foundation of Gothic architectural forms.[244] Today these ideas are generally dismissed, but they are important to us here because it was from the forests of the North that the original ideas of the Ark and the Grail originate, though it was in the South, in Mesopotamia, that it was last "seen".

---

[242] Weston, op. cit.

[243] Charpentier, Louis, *The Mysteries of Chartres Cathedral*, translated from the French by Ronald Fraser (New York: Avon Books, 1975) (first published 1966; English translation first published 1972).

[244] Hall, Sir James, Essays on the Origins, History and Principles of Gothic Architecture, London, 1813.

CHAPTER 10
WHO WROTE THE BIBLE AND WHY?

THE ARK OF THE COVENANT AND THE TEMPLE OF SOLOMON

When considering the idea of the god "dancing all night" in the round temple of the Hyperboreans, our mind naturally turns to that most remarkable of incidents in the Bible where David danced before the Ark of the Covenant - in his underwear, no less! Another curious item is the fact that there is a tableaux on one of the porches of the Chartres Cathedral of Melchizedek, the "king-priest of Salem", and the Queen of Sheba. Equidistant between them is the Ark of the Covenant in a cart. Melchizedek is holding a cup that is supposed to be the Holy Grail. Inside this cup is a cylindrical object of stone. Of course, one wonders what Melchizedek is doing with the Queen of Sheba who is supposed to be contemporary with Solomon, but there are many mysteries here.

The Ark of the Covenant: that most mysterious and powerful object that we are led to believe was the object of the Templars sojourn and searches in Jerusalem. What do we really know about the Ark?

In order to come to any idea about the Ark, we will naturally have to make a careful examination of the religious structure in which it is situated: Judaism. When I began to study the issues that concerned me: religious questions, philosophical problems, and so on, I really had no idea that I would uncover something so horrific and far reaching as what I came to realize about religions in general and monotheism in particular. Please don't misunderstand me or think that I am promoting paganism or any other form of worship of "gods" or images of god. I am quite convinced that the source of all existence is consciousness, and that this consciousness is, at its root, what we would call God, or Divine Mind. What we are concerned about here is the imposition of monotheism in the form of *any one group claiming that their version of who or what god is or is not is the only correct one.* And the further result of this is that Judeo-Christian monotheism prevailed with its twisted conception of linear time borrowed from Zoroastrianism.

People have been reading the Bible for ages. It has achieved a status in our culture assigned to no other single body of text. There are more copies of the Bible on the face of the planet than any other single book. It is quoted (and misquoted) more often than any other book. It is translated into more languages than any other book ever written as well. More people in recorded history have read it, studied it, taught it, admired it, argued about it, loved it, lived by it, and killed and died for it. It is the singular document at the heart of Judaism and Christianity, and yet the common man doesn't really seem to ever ask: Who wrote it, really? They think they know: it is divinely dictated, revealed or inspired.

In spite of what the average person believes about it, many investigators – mostly theologians - have been working on this question for about a thousand years – when they aren't being burned at the stake for even asking it. What is ironic is the fact that most of them have only been seeking closer communion with God by trying to get closer to the original text "from the Hand of God", so to say.

When one studies literature in a classroom setting, it is important to also study the life of the author, even if only through the clues of the literary works under examination. One is enabled to see significant connections between the life of the author and the world that the author is depicting. In terms of the Bible, these things become crucial. Nevertheless, the fact is, when we are talking about such "fuzzy" things as religion and history, we immediately come up against a certain problem.

Historians, when writing about history, not only discuss the theoretical facts that are being proposed as the timeline, but also the means by which they arrived at their ideas. Generally, they draw their conclusions about history by reading "sources", or earlier accounts of the matter at hand. In some cases these are eye-witness accounts, in others, accounts told to a scribe by a witness, and so on.

Historians try to make a distinction between sources as "primary" and "secondary". A primary source is not necessarily an eye-witness account - though it would be nice if it was - but is defined by historians as one that cannot be traced back any further and does not seem to depend on someone else's account. Secondary sources are those that are essentially copies or "re-worked" primary sources. Often, they consist of material from several sources assembled together with commentary or additional data.

Well, obviously this could present a problem if the primary source is completely falsified.

Primary sources can legitimately require interpretation and assessment; this is the role of a good secondary source, providing the distinction between source and interpretation is made clear. Indeed secondary sources - analyses - are vital to the average reader who may not have the necessary linguistic, historical and cultural background to assess the primary sources. But, all too often, historians deal with their sources exactly as J. K. Huysmans has described:

> Events are for a man of talent nothing but a spring-board of ideas and style, since they are all mitigated or aggravated *according to the needs of a cause* or according to the temperament of the writer who handles them.

> As far as documents which support them are concerned, it is even worse, since none of them is irreducible and all are reviewable. If they are not just apocryphal, other no less certain documents *can be unearthed later which contradict them,* waiting in turn to be devalued by the unearthing of yet other no less certain archives. [Huysmans, 1891, Ch II].

In the early years of the 20th century, M. M. Mangasarian, a former Congregationalist and Presbyterian Minister, who studied at Princeton Theological Seminary, and very early in his life renounced his Christian affiliation to pursue a remarkable career as a proponent of Free Thought wrote:

The Bible is an Extraordinary Book: A book which claims infallibility; which aspires to absolute authority over mind and body; which demands *unconditional surrender* to all its pretensions upon *penalty of eternal damnation*, is an extraordinary book and should, therefore, be *subjected to extraordinary tests.*

But it isn't.

Neither Christian priests nor Jewish rabbis approve of applying to the bible the same tests by which other books are tried.

Why?

Because it will help the bible? It cannot be that.

Because it might hurt the bible? We can think of no other reason.

The Truth is that The Bible is: A Collection of Writings of Unknown Date and Authorship Rendered into English From Supposed Copies of Supposed Originals unfortunately Lost.[245]

Recently, Richard Dawkins, author of the *Blind Watchmaker*, suggested that religion was a virus.

Dawkins argued that the widespread presence of religion —despite its lack of obvious benefits—suggests that it was not an evolutionary adaptation. [...] Society provides a breeding ground for the "virus" of religion by labeling children with the religion of their parents. Children, in turn, absorb these beliefs because they are *conditioned to do so*.

Though it is universal, Dawkins said, religion is not widely beneficial. Rejecting the theory of many of his contemporaries, Dawkins argued that religion has *not* helped people to adapt or to survive. Beyond acting as a source of solace, religion provides no protection against diseases or physical threats.

"A person who is faced with a lion is not put at ease when he's told that it's a rabbit", Dawkins said. Religion, in Dawkins' view, not only provides false comfort—it is actively divisive and harmful. Designated as Christians or Muslims by their parents, children are apt to face the discrimination associated with these labels, Dawkins said. Dawkins pointed to the example of Protestant fundamentalists in Belfast spitting at young Catholic girls merely because their parents labeled them Catholic.[246]

Dawkins is right in many respects. Even if I do not agree with his ideas that promote existence as solely the consequence of the "accidental mechanicalness of the universe", I have to say that he has zeroed in on the crucial element of religion - or cult - as it is known in our day: that it is a virus, and a *deadly* one at that. One thing that Dawkins said that I disagree with is, "A person who is faced with a lion

---

[245] *The Bible Unveiled*, M.M. Mangasarian, 1911; Chicago: Independent Religious Society

[246] ASYA TROYCHANSKY, Harvard Crimson, Thursday, November 20, 2003

is not put at ease when he's told that it's a rabbit". As it happens, that is exactly the problem we face when we consider our reality. Many people *are* "put at ease" by being told that the lion is a rabbit. It doesn't help them to survive, or to solve the problems of humanity, but it distracts their attention away from asking uncomfortable questions about our reality that the Powers That Be do not want them to ask. As to why people believe the lies of the Monotheistic Cults, Dawkins points out rather succinctly that religion is a societal norm that stems from children's psychological tendencies. "It is their *unique obedience* that makes them vulnerable to viruses and worms", Dawkins said.

Their unique obedience. Religion is a form of coercing obedience a la Machiavelli.

As the reader might know,[247] I spent a number of years as a hypnotherapist as part of my search for answers in the "realm of mind". That work gave me a unique perspective on just about every other branch of study I have followed since. The main thing I learned from this is that most, if not *all, human perspective is rooted in emotional thinking.* Emotions have a curious tendency to "frame" and "color" what we see, experience and remember so that what we *think* becomes, very often, a matter of "wishful thinking".

The problem with the subject of the Bible and History is that there are so many fields that can contribute data - archaeology, paleontology, geology, linguistics, and so forth - these types of things provide DATA, which are discarded in favor of "wishful thinking". On the other side we have mythology and history. They are, unfortunately, quite similar because, as it is well known, the "victors write history". And people are prone to do many evil deeds in difficult situations, which they later wish to cover up in order to present themselves in a more positive light for posterity.

The oldest extant texts of the Old Testament in Hebrew are those found at Qumran which date only to two or three centuries before Christ. The oldest version before the Qumran texts were discovered was a *Greek* translation from about the same period! The earliest complete *Hebrew* text dates *only from the tenth century AD*! Something is wrong with this picture.

It is generally believed from textual analysis, that a very small part of the Old Testament was written about 1000 BC and the remainder about 600 BC. The Bible, as we know it, is the result of many changes throughout centuries and is contradictory in so many ways we don't have space to catalog them all! There are entire libraries of books devoted to this subject, and I recommend that the reader have a look at the material in order to have some foundation upon which to judge the things I am going to say.

---

[247] See: St. Petersburg Times Magazine section on February 13, 2000 for a 20-page article on my work as a hypnotherapist and exorcist, written by Pulitzer Prize winner, Thomas French.

Biblical scholars generally date Abraham to about 1800 - 1700 BC. The same scholars date Moses to 1300 or 1250 BC. However, if we track the generations as listed in the Bible, we find that there are only seven generations between and including these two patriarchal figures! Four hundred years is a bit long for seven generations. Allowing 35 to 40 years per generation, places Abraham at about 1550 BC and Moses at about 1300 BC. This obviously means that there are a few hundred years not accounted for in the text. Tracking back to Noah, using the generations listed in the Bible, one arrives at a date of about 2000 to 1900 BC - about the time of the arrival of the Indo-Europeans into the Near East. The geological and archaeological records do not support a cataclysm at that time, though what could be described as a global discontinuity of cataclysmic elements is supported right around 12,000 years ago. In this case, we have lost 8,000 years, give or take a day.

In a more general sense, using the Bible as historical source material presents a number of very serious problems, most particularly when we consider the "mythicization" factor. There are many contradictions in the text that cannot be reconciled by standard theological mental contortionism. In some places, events are described as happening in a certain order, and later the Bible will say that those events happened in a different order. In one place, the Bible will say that there is two of something, and in another it will say that there were 14 of the same thing. On one page, the Bible will say that the Moabites did something, and then a few pages later; it will say that the Midianites did exactly the same thing. There is even an instance in which Moses is described as going to the Tabernacle before Moses built the Tabernacle! (I guess Moses was a time traveler!)

There are things in the Pentateuch that pose other problems: it includes things that Moses could not have known if he lived when he is claimed to have lived. And, there is one case in which Moses said something he could not have said: the text gives an account of Moses' death, which it is hardly likely that Moses described. The text also states that Moses was the humblest man on earth! Well, as one commentator noted, it is not likely that the humblest man on earth would point out that he is the humblest man on earth!

All of these problems were taken care of for most of the past two thousand years by the Inquisition, which also took care of the Cathars and anybody else who did not follow the Party Line of Judao-Christianity.

For the Jews, the contradictions were not contradictions; they were only "apparent contradictions"! They could all be explained by "interpretation"! (Usually, these interpretations were more fantastic than the problems, I might add.) Moses was able to "know things he couldn't have known" because he was a prophet! The medieval biblical commentators, such as Rashi and Nachmanides, were *very* skillful in reconciling the irreconcilable!

In the 11th century, a real troublemaker, Isaac ibn Yashush, a Jewish court physician in Muslim Spain, mentioned the distressing fact that a list of Edomite kings that appears in Genesis 36 named a few kings who lived long after Moses was already dead. Ibn Yashush suggested the obvious, that someone who lived after Moses wrote the list. He became known as "Isaac the Blunderer".

The guy who memorialized clever Isaac this way was a fellow named Abraham ibn Ezra, a 12th century rabbi in Spain. But Ibn Ezra presents us with a paradox because he also wrote about problems in the text of the Torah. He alluded to several passages that appeared not to be from Moses' own hand because they referred to Moses in the third person, used terms Moses would not have known, described places that Moses had never been, and used language that belonged to an altogether different time and place than the milieu of Moses. He wrote, very mysteriously, *"And if you understand, then you will recognize the truth. And he who understands will keep silent"*.

So, why did he call Ibn Yashush a "Blunderer"? Obviously because the guy had to open his big mouth and give away the secret that the Torah was not what it was cracked up to be, and if the truth got out, lots of folks who were totally "into" the Jewish mysticism business would lose interest. And keeping the interest of the students and seekers after power was a pretty big business in that day and time. More than that, however, we would like to note that *the entire Christian mythos was predicated upon the validity of Judaism,* being its "New Covenant", and even if there was apparent conflict between Jews and Christians, the *Christians most desperately needed to validate Judaism and its claim to be the revelation to the "chosen people" of the One True God.* It was on that basis that Jesus was the Son of God, after all. In short, it could even be said that Christianity created Judaism in the sense that it would have faded to obscurity long ago if there had not been the infusion of validating energy during the Dark Ages.

In 14th century Damascus, a scholar by the name of Bonfils wrote a work in which he said, *"And this is evidence that this verse was written in the Torah later, and Moses did not write it"*. He wasn't even denying the "revealed" character of the Torah, just making a reasonable comment. Three hundred years later, his work was reprinted with this comment edited out!

In the 15th century, Tostatus, Bishop of Avila, also pointed out that Moses couldn't have written the passages about the death of Moses. In an effort to soften the blow, he added that there was an "old tradition" that Joshua, Moses successor, wrote this part of the account. A hundred years later, Luther Carlstadt commented that this was difficult to believe because the account of Moses' death is written *in the same style as the text that precedes it.*

Well, of course, things were beginning to be examined more critically with the arrival of Protestantism on the world stage and the demand for wider availability of the text itself. The Inquisition and assorted "Catholic Majesties" tried, but failed, to keep a complete grip on the matter. But, it's funny what belief will do. In this case, with the increase in literacy and new and better translations of the text, "critical examination" led to the decision that the problem was solvable by claiming that, yes, Moses wrote the Torah, but editors went over them later and added an occasional word or phrase of their own!

Wow. Glad we solved that one!

A really funny thing is that the Catholic Index blacklisted one of the proponents of this idea of editorial insertions, who was only trying to preserve the *textus receptus* status of the Bible. His work was put on the list of "prohibited books"! Those guys just kept shooting themselves in the foot.

Well, finally, after hundreds of years of tiptoeing around this issue, some scholars came right out and said that Moses didn't write the majority of the Pentateuch. The first to say it was Thomas Hobbes. He pointed out that the text sometimes states that this or that is so *to this day*. The problem with this is that a writer describing a contemporary situation would not describe it as something that has endured for a very long time, "to this day".

Isaac de la Peyrère, a French Calvinist, noted that the first verse of the book of Deuteronomy says, "*These are the words that Moses spoke to the children of Israel across the Jordan...*". The problem was that *the words meant to refer to someone who is on the other side of the Jordan from the writer*. This means that the verse amounts to the words of *someone who is* west *of the Jordan at the time of writing, who is describing what Moses said to the children of Israel on the* east *of the Jordan*. The problem is exacerbated because Moses himself was never supposed to have been in Israel in his life.

De la Peyrère's book was banned and burned. He was arrested and told that the conditions of his release were conversion to Catholicism and recanting his views. Apparently he perceived discretion as the better part of valor. Considering how often this sort of thing occurred, we have to wonder about the "sanctity" of a text which is preserved by threat and torture and bloodshed.

Not too long after this, Baruch Spinoza, the famous philosopher, published what amounted to a real rabble rousing critical analysis. He claimed that the problem passages in the Bible were not isolated cases that could be solved one by one as "editorial insertions". but were rather a pervasive evidence of a third person account. He also pointed out that the text says in Deuteronomy 34 "*There never arose another prophet in Israel like Moses....*". Spinoza suggested, quite rightly, that these were the words of a person who lived a long time after Moses and had had the opportunity to make comparisons. One commentator points out that they also don't sound like the words of the "humblest man on earth"![248]

Spinoza was really living dangerously because he wrote, "*It is [...] clearer than the sun at noon that the Pentateuch was not written by Moses, but by someone who lived long after Moses*".[249] Spinoza had already been excommunicated from Judaism; now, he was in pretty hot water with the Catholics and Protestants! Naturally, his book was placed on the "prohibited books" list, and a whole slew of edicts were issued against it. What is even more interesting is that an attempt was made to assassinate him! The lengths to which people will go to preserve their belief in lies are astonishing.

A converted Protestant who had become a Catholic priest, Richard Simon, undertook to refute Spinoza and wrote a book saying that Moses wrote the core of the Pentateuch, but there were "some additions". Nevertheless, these additions were clearly done by scribes who were *under the guidance of God or the Holy*

---

[248] Friedman, Richard Elliot, *Who Wrote the Bible*, (New York: Harper & Row 1987).

[249] Quoted by Friedman.

Spirit, so it was okay for them to collect, arrange and elaborate on the text. It was still God in charge here.

Well, you'd think the Church would know when it was ahead. But, nope! Simon was attacked and expelled from his order by his fellow Catholics. *Forty refutations* of his work were written by Protestants. Only six copies of his book survived burning. John Hampden translated one of these, getting himself into pretty hot water. He, "repudiated the opinions he had held in common with Simon [...] in 1688, probably shortly before his release from the tower".[250]

In the 18th century, three independent scholars were dealing with the problem of "doublets", or stories that are told two or more times in the Bible. There are two different stories of the creation of the world. There are two stories of the covenant between God and Abraham. There are two stories of the naming of Abraham's son Isaac, two stories of Abraham's claiming to a foreign king that his wife is his sister, two stories of Isaac's son Jacob making a journey to Mesopotamia, two stories of a revelation to Jacob at Beth-El, two stories of God changing Jacob's name to Israel, two stories of Moses' getting water from a rock at Meribah, and on and on.

Those who simply could not let go of the *a priori* belief that Moses wrote the Pentateuch, tried to claim that these doublets were always complimentary, not repetitive nor contradictory. Sometimes they had to really stretch this idea to say that they were supposed to "teach" us something by their contradictions that are "not really contradictions".

This explanation, however, didn't hold up against another fact: in most cases one of the two versions of a doublet would refer to the deity by the divine name, Yahweh, and the other would refer to the deity simply as "God", or "El". What this meant was that there were two groups of parallel versions of the same stories, and each group was almost always consistent about the name of the deity it used. Not only that, there were various other terms and characteristics that regularly appeared in one or the other line of stories, and what this demonstrated was that *someone had taken two different old source documents and had done a cut and paste job on them to make a "continuous" narrative.*

Well, of course, at first it was thought that one of the two source documents must be one that Moses had used as a source for the story of creation and the rest was Moses himself writing! But, it was ultimately to be concluded that both of the two sources had to be from writers who lived *after* Moses. By degrees, Moses was being eliminated almost entirely from the authorship of the Pentateuch!

Simon's idea that scribes had collected, arranged and elaborated on the *textus receptus* was, finally, going in the right direction.

---

[250] Ibid.

I would like to note right here that this was not happening because somebody came along and said, "hey, let's trash the Bible"! Nope. It was happening because there were *glaring problems,* and each and every researcher working on this throughout the centuries was struggling mightily to *retain* the *textus receptus* status of the Bible! The only exception to this that I have mentioned in this whole chain of events is our curious guy Abraham ibn Ezra, who KNEW about problems in the text of the Torah in the 12th century and enjoined others to silence! Remember what he said? *"And if you understand, then you will recognize the truth. And he who understands will keep silent."* What do we see as the result of this silence? Over eight hundred years of Crusades, the Inquisition, and general suppression, and in our present day, the wars between the Israelis and Palestinians based on the claim that Israel is the Promised Land, and that it "belongs" to the Jews. Which brings us to another startling bit of information.

The great Jewish scholar, Rashi de Troyes, (1040-1105), makes the astonishingly frank statement that the Genesis narrative, going back to the creation of the world, *was written to justify what we might now call genocide.* The God of Israel, who gave his people the Promised Land, had to be unequivocally supreme so that neither the dispossessed Canaanites nor anyone else could ever appeal against his decrees.[251] Rashi's precise words were that God told us the creation story and included it in the Torah, *"to tell his people that they can answer those who claim that the Jews stole the land from its original inhabitants. The reply should be; God made it and gave it to them but then took it and gave it to us. As he made it and it's his, he can give it to whoever he chooses".*

The fact is, the Jews are still saying this, with the support of many Christian Fundamentalists whose beliefs are being pandered to by George Bush and his purported Christian cronies for their own imperialist and economic motives.

This leads us to another interesting point: the establishing of "one god" over and above any and all other gods, is an act of violence no matter how you look at it. In *The Curse of Cain*, Regina Schwartz writes about the relationship between Monotheism and Violence, positing that *Monotheism itself is the root of violence*:

> Collective Identity, which is a result of a covenant of Monotheism, is explicitly
> narrated in the Bible as an invention, *a radical break with Nature.* A transcendent
> deity breaks into history with the demand that the people he constitutes obey the
> law he institutes, and first and foremost among those laws is, of course, that they
> *pledge allegiance to him, and him alone*, and that *this is what makes them a unified
> people* as *opposed* to the 'other',as in *all other people,* which leads to violence. In
> the Old Testament, vast numbers of 'other' people are obliterated, while in the New

---

[251] Ashe, Geoffrey, *The Book of Prophecy*, (Blandford, London 1999) p. 27.

Testament, vast numbers are colonized and converted for the sake of such covenants.[252]

Schwartz also writes about the idea of the "provisional" nature of a covenant: *that it is conditional.* "Believe in me and obey me or else I will destroy you." Doesn't sound like there is any choice, does there? And we find ourselves in the face of a pure and simple Nazi Theophany.

In the 19th century, Biblical scholars figured out that there were not just two major sources in the Pentateuch; there were, in fact, *four*. It was realized that the first four books were not just doublets, but there were also triplets that converged with other characteristics and contradictions leading to the identification of another source. Then, it was realized that *Deuteronomy was a separate source altogether*. More than that, there was not just the problem of the original source documents, there was the problem of the work of the "mysterious editor".

Thus, after years of suffering, bloodshed and death over the matter, it was realized that somebody had "created" what Westerners know as the Old Testament by assembling four different source documents in an attempt to create a "continuous" history, designated at different times as Torah, as well as additional "edited" documents. After much further analysis, it was concluded that most of the laws and much of the narrative of the Pentateuch were not even part of the time of Moses. And, that meant that *it couldn't have been written by Moses at all*. More than that, the writing of the different sources was not even that of persons who lived during the days of the kings and prophets, but were evidentially products of writers who lived toward the end of the biblical period!

Many scholars just couldn't bear the results of their own work. A German scholar who had identified the Deuteronomy source exclaimed that such a view, *"suspended the beginnings of Hebrew history not upon the grand creations of Moses, but upon airy nothings"*. Other scholars realized that what this meant was that *the picture of biblical Israel as a nation governed by laws based on the Abrahamic and Mosaic covenants was completely false.* I expect that such a realization may have contributed to a suicide or two; it most definitely led to a number of individuals leaving the field of Theology and textual criticism altogether.

Another way of putting their conclusions was that the Bible claimed a history for the first 600 years of Israel that probably never existed. It was all a lie.[253]

---

[252] Schwartz, Regina M., *The Curse of Cain*, (Chicago: The University of Chicago Press 1997).

[253] Of course, by now the reader has realized that it is not really a "lie," properly speaking. It is just a highly mythicized account of the doings of some people in a certain historical context. But after the mythicization, and the imposition of the belief in the myth as the reality, as well as the passage of a couple of thousand years, figuring out who is who and who really did what is problematical at best.

Well, they couldn't handle this. After years of being conditioned to believe in an upcoming "End of the World", with Jehovah or Christ as saviors of the chosen during this dreaded event, the terror of their condition, *that there might not be a "savior"*, was just too awful to bear. So along came the cavalry – Julius Wellhausen (1844-1918) - to the rescue.

Wellhausen synthesized all of the discoveries so as to *preserve the belief systems of the religious scholars.* He amalgamated the view that the religion of Israel had developed in three stages with the view that the documents were also written in three stages, and then he defined these stages based on the content of the "stage." He tracked the characteristics of each stage, examining the way in which the different documents expressed religion, the clergy, the sacrifices and places of worship as well as the religious holidays. He considered the legal and narrative sections and the other books of the Bible. In the end, he provided a "believable framework" for the development of Jewish history and religion. The first stage was the "nature/fertility" period; the second was "spiritual/ethical" period; and the last was the "priestly/legal" period. As Friedman notes, *"To this day, if you want to disagree, you disagree with Wellhausen. If you want to pose a new model, you compare its merits with those of Wellhausen's model".*[254]

I should also note at this point, that even though Wellhausen was trying to save the buns of Judaism and Christianity from the fire, he was not appreciated in his own time. A professor of Old Testament, William Robertson Smith, who taught at the Free Church of Scotland College at Aberdeen, and who was the editor of the *Encyclopedia Britannica*, was *put on trial* before the church on the charge of *heresy* for promoting the work of Wellhausen. He was cleared, but the tag "the wicked bishop" followed him to his grave.

Nevertheless, analysis of the Bible has proceeded. The book of Isaiah was traditionally thought to have been written by the prophet Isaiah who lived in the eighth century BC. As it happens, most of the first half of this book fits such a model. But, chapters 40 through 66 are apparently written by someone who lived about 200 years later! This means that, in terms of "prophecy", it was written *after the fact*.

New tools and methods of our modern time have made it possible to do some really fine work in the areas of linguistic analysis and relative chronology of the material. Additionally, there has been a veritable archaeological frenzy since Wellhausen! This archaeological work has produced an enormous amount of information about Egypt, Mesopotamia, and other regions surrounding Israel, which includes clay tablets, inscriptions on the walls of tombs, temples and habitations, and even papyri. Here we find another problem: in all the collected sources, both Egyptian and west Asian, there are virtually *no* references to Israel,

---

[254] Friedman, op. cit., pp. 26-7.

its "famous people" and founders, its Biblical associates, or anything else *prior to the 12th century BC.* And the fact is, for 400 years after that, *no more than half a dozen allusions can be deduced.* And they are questionable in context. Yet the fundamentalist Orthodox Jews cling to these tattered references like straws in the hands of a drowning man. Oddly, the Fundamentalist Christians just simply close off any awareness to the entire matter by the simple expedient of the execution of the 11th commandment: thou shalt not ask questions!

The problem of the lack of outside validation of the existence of Israel as a sovereign nation in the area of Palestine finds correspondence in the Bible itself. The Bible displays absolutely no knowledge of Egypt or the Levant during the 2nd millennium BC. The Bible says nothing about the Egyptian empire spreading over the entire eastern Mediterranean (which it did); there is no mention of the great Egyptian armies on the march (which they were); and no mention of marching Hittites moving against the Egyptians (which they did); and especially no mention of Egyptianized kinglets ruling Canaanite cities (which was the case).

The great and disastrous invasion of the Sea Peoples during the second millennium is not even mentioned in the Bible. In fact, Genesis described the Philistines *as already settled in the land of Canaan at the time of Abraham!*

The names of the great Egyptian kings are completely absent from the Bible. In other places, historical figures that were not heroic have been transformed by the Bible into heroes as in the case of the Hyksos Sheshy (Num. 13:22). In another case, the sobriquet of Ramesses II is given to a Canaanite general in error. The Egyptian king who was supposed to assist Hosea in his rebellion of 2 Kings 17:4 has "suffered the indignity" of having his city given as his name. The Pharaoh Shabtaka turns up in the Table of Nations in Genesis 10:7 as a Nubian tribe!

The errors of confirmed history and archaeology pile higher and higher the more one learns about the actual times and places, so that the idea that comes to mind again and again is that *the writers of the Bible must have lived in the 7th and 6th centuries BC, or later*, and knew almost nothing about the events of only a few generations before them. Donald B. Redford, Professor of Near Eastern Studies at the University of Toronto, has published extensively on archaeology and Egyptology. Regarding the use of the Bible as a historical source, he writes:

> For the standard scholarly approach to the history of Israel during the United Monarchy amounts to nothing more than *a bad attack of academic 'wishful thinking'*. We have these glorious narratives in the books of Samuel and 1st Kings, so well written and ostensibly factual. What a pity if rigorous historical criticism forces us to discard them and not use them. Let us, then, press them into service – what else have we? – and let the burden of proof fall on others.[…]

> While one might be unwise to impute crypto-fundamentalist motives, the current fashion of treating the sources at face value as documents written up in large part in the court of Solomon, arises from an equally misplaced *desire to rehabilitate the faith and undergird it with any arguments, however fallacious.*[…]

> Such ignorance is puzzling if one has felt inclined to be impressed by the traditional claims of inerrancy made by conservative Christianity on behalf of the Bible. And indeed *the Pentateuch and the historical books boldly present a precise chronology that would carry the Biblical narrative through the very period when the ignorance and discrepancy prove most embarrassing. […]*

Such manhandling of the evidence smacks of prestidigitation and numerology; yet it has produced the shaky foundations on which a lamentable number of "histories" of Israel have been written. Most are characterized by a somewhat naive acceptance of sources at face value coupled with failure to assess the evidence as to its origin and reliability. The result was the reduction of all data to a common level, any or all being grist for a wide variety of mills.

Scholars expended substantial effort on questions that they had failed to prove were valid questions at all. Under what dynasty did Joseph rise to power? Who was the Pharaoh of the Oppression? Of the Exodus? Can we identify the princess who drew Moses out of the river? Where did the Israelites make their exit from Egypt: via the Wady Tumilat or by a more northerly point?

One can appreciate the pointlessness of these questions if one poses similar questions of the Arthurian stories, without first submitting the text to a critical evaluation. Who were the consuls of Rome when Arthur drew the sword from the stone? Where was Merlin born?

Can one seriously envisage a classical historian pondering whether it was Iarbas or Aeneas that was responsible for Dido's suicide, where exactly did Remus leap over the wall, what really happened to Romulus in the thunderstorm, and so forth?

In all these imagined cases none of the material initially prompting the questions has in any way undergone a prior evaluation as to how historical it is! *And any scholar who exempts any part of his sources from critical evaluation runs the risk of invalidating some or all of his conclusions.*[...]

Too often "Biblical" in this context has had *the limiting effect on scholarship by implying the validity of studying Hebrew culture and history in isolation.* What is needed rather is a view of ancient Israel within its true Near Eastern context, and one that will neither exaggerate nor denigrate Israel's actual place within that setting.[255]

Please take careful note of Redford's comment: "any scholar who exempts any part of his sources from critical evaluation runs the risk of invalidating some or all of his conclusions". The seriousness of this cannot be understated. You see, people have died by the millions because of this book called The Bible and the beliefs of those who study it. And they are dying today in astonishing numbers for the same reasons!

In the end, *if* those who read and/or analyze this book and come to some particular belief about it are wrong, and they then impose this belief upon millions of other people, who are then influenced to create a culture and a reality based upon a false belief, and in the end, it is wrong, what in the name of God is going on? (No pun intended!)

---

[255] Redford, Donald B., *Egypt, Canaan, and Israel in Ancient Times*, (Princeton: Princeton University Press 1992), pp. 301, 258, 260-1, 263. (Italics ours)

The problem with using the Bible as history is the lack of secondary sources. There is considerable material from the various ancient libraries prior to the 10th century BC, "grist for the historian's mill", but these sources fall silent almost completely at the close of the 20th dynasty in Egypt. Thus, the Bible, being pretty much the only source that claims to cover this particular period, becomes quite seductive; never mind that the archaeology doesn't really "fit", or can only be made to fit with a large helping of assumption or closing of the mind to other possibilities.

But, might there be a *reason* for this silence of other sources? That's one good question about "what is".

The person who is using the Bible as history is forced, when all emotion is taken out of the picture, to admit that he has no means of checking the historical veracity of the Biblical texts. As Donald Redford noted above, the scholars who admit, when pressed, that rigorous historical criticism forces us to discard the Biblical narratives, *nevertheless will use them* saying "what else do we have"?

Again, I ask: why?

In older times, we know that the many books written about the Bible as history were inspired from a fundamentalist motivation to *confirm the religious "rightness" of Western Civilization*. In the present time, there is less of this factor involved in Biblical Historical studies. Nevertheless, there is still a tendency to treat these sources at "face value" by folks who ought to know better!

I could go on about this in some detail, but I think everyone reading this is with me here in having a clue about what I am saying, even if they don't agree. But, the point is, again, "Who wrote the Bible and *why*?".

We come back to that curious assertion of Rashi's that *the Genesis narrative was written to justify genocide.* If we put that together with Umberto Eco's implication in his book, *The Search for The Perfect Language*, that validation of the Hebrew Bible was supported by early Christian scholars primarily to validate Judaism, which was necessary in order to then "validate" Christianity as the "one true religion", we begin to get the uneasy feeling that we have been "had". What this amounts to is that we are all "Christian" so that the "rights" of the Jews, the unappealable decrees of Jehovah/Yahweh, could be "inherited" by the Christian Church as instituted for political reasons by Constantine! Nevertheless, by the very act of validating Judaism, and "creating" Christianity in the form of the Egyptian religion, the Western world, in its greed for power, may very well have taken a tiger by the tail.

During this very period when the New Testament came into being, (incorporating some older texts, based on internal evidence, but highly edited and mostly a "cut and paste" job), we find the Western world in the midst of the dark ages from which, again, very few secondary sources survived.

Isn't that strange?! The Old Testament is written about a Dark Age, though a few hundred years after it, and the New Testament is written about a Dark Age, also a few hundred years after it. Both of them incorporate some probably valid stories though mostly they are edited, cut and pasted, with a lot of glossing and interpolation from the perspective of a definite "political" agenda.

Do we see a pattern here? Could there be a reason?

At the end of it all, what we observe is a basically *Draconian, monotheistic system in place over most of the globe*. It is the wellspring from which nearly every aspect of our society is drawn. It has been the justification for the greatest series of bloodbaths in "recorded" history. Could there be a reason for this?

Considering this, one would think that the knowledge of who wrote the Bible, and when they probably did it, would be considered crucial to anyone who wishes to be better equipped to make decisions of faith and belief *upon which every aspect of their lives may depend.*

As we have already discovered, what began as a search for answers about the puzzling contradictory passages in the Pentateuch led to the idea that Moses didn't write them. This then led to the discovery that several widely divergent sources were combined into one, and that even this was done at different times, in different ways. Each of the sources is clearly identifiable by characteristics of language and content. New breakthroughs in archaeology and our understanding of the social and political world of the time have helped enormously in our understanding of the milieu in which this document was created. Because, in the end, the Bible's history is really the history of the Jews.

The Old Testament is a book that is a combination of several sources, J (Yahweh), E (lohim), D(euteronomy), P(riestly) and the final editor who combined all of these and added his own touches.

It is theorized, based on the evidence, that the E version was written by a Levite priest advocate of the Mosaic line of priests at Shiloh, and J was written by an advocate of the Aaronic line of priests and the Davidic royal house at Jerusalem. The conclusion is that they were each written down from oral sources of myth and legend with some history mixed in *after* the purported split of the two kingdoms, and then recombined after the Syrian conquest during the reign of Hezekiah. However, it is also entirely likely that there never was a united kingdom of Israel in Palestine, but that these stories of a great kingdom were tribal memories of something else altogether. The author of J is estimated to have lived between 848 and 722 BC and the author of E between 922 and 722 BC. Thus it is that E is probably the older document and J represented either a different perspective, or changes that were added.

In the Bible, the story of the unification of the tribes of Israel under David, followed by the great reign of Solomon, followed by schism in the reign of Solomon's son Rehoboam, is the central theme. The "hope of Israel" is based on the idea of reunification of Judah and Israel under a Davidic king. Of course, all of this is based on the giving of the land to the Children of Israel when they were "brought out of Egypt" by the hand of God during the Exodus to begin with. Moses represents the divinely inspired leader who revealed the god of the patriarchs to the nation as the "Universal Deity". Does the testimony of the spade support the Exodus on either side of the story?

The Exodus story describes how a nation enslaved grows great in exile and then, with the help of the Universal God, claims its freedom from what was then the greatest nation on earth: Egypt.

Powerful imagery, yes? Indeed! So important is this story of liberation that fully four-fifths of the central scriptures of Israel are devoted to it.

The fact is: two hundred years of intensive excavations and study of the remains of ancient Egypt and Palestine have failed to support the Exodus story in the context in which it is presented.[256]

THE HOUSE OF DAVID

From the earliest times, Israel was composed of a poorly distinguished and variable number of "city-states" (more like tribal towns) whose population was a melting pot from all areas of the Mediterranean. The specific location that is identified as Israel proper was a more or less backward, rural buffer zone between the civilized Syrians and the nomads of Arabia. The "culture" of this region was a mixture of the advanced cultures surrounding: Egyptian, Assyrian and Babylonian. These "city states" rose and fell, fighting each other incessantly. A retrospective view seems to suggest that acquiring plunder was seen as more productive than agriculture. In another sense, these petty wars were seen as the conflict between the gods of one tribe against the gods of another. As we will discover, this concept may not have been too far from the truth.

What about the Kingdom of David and Solomon?

The books of Samuel tell us that the anointing of David, son of Jesse, as king over all the tribes of Israel was the culmination of the promises that had begun with the covenant between Abraham and "God". Never mind that the first choice for king had been the heroic and dashing Saul from the tribe of Benjamin, it was David who became the "folk hero" of early Israelite history.

The endless stories in praise of King David were claimed by the Bible to be so widespread that it passes understanding how they were not known in the "external world" of Egypt, Greece, Assyria and Babylon - if they were true. But, as we will discover, perhaps they were - under a different name and title. The only question is: which versions are the most accurate? Did the Hebrews co-opt these stories to their own "history", or was there something about their history that was borrowed by the later sources? And in either case, what is the actual historical setting of these stories? Were they an overlay of myth on an actual historical series of events? Or was a historical series of events manufactured out of myth?

In any event, just as Perseus slew the Gorgon and cut off her head, David slew the giant, Goliath. They both had "wallets" and "stones" were important elements of both stories. David was "adopted" into the royal court because he was a famous harpist and singer in the manner of Orpheus. Like Hercules and other Greek heroes, David was a rebel and freebooter, and like Paris stole Helen, he stole another man's wife - Bathsheba. He also conquered the great citadel of Jerusalem and a vast empire beyond.

---

[256] Ibid.

The stories of David's son and heir (from Bathsheba), Solomon, tell us that he was the wisest of all kings. He was also the greatest of all builders. The stories tell how he was so brilliant and how his judgments stand as a model for all time. What is more, his wealth was beyond anything else in the known world, and most particularly, he constructed the great Temple in Jerusalem.

For millennia, readers of the Bible have discussed the days of David and Solomon in Israel as though they actually occurred exactly as described. Even people who are not Christian accept that the Temple of Solomon existed, and the plan of this temple has been developed and discussed endlessly by esotericists for centuries. Endless books and legends and secret doctrines have been based on the stories of the Temple of Solomon. Pilgrims, Crusaders, visionaries and even many modern-day books about human origins and the origins of Christianity, have all spread fabulous stories about the magnificence of David's city and Solomon's Temple and the supposed treasures contained within. Our entire Western culture has a heavy, vested interest in these stories being true. What are we going to do with this vast body of literature, including such things as Masonic and Magical lore if it turns out that there never was a "Temple of Solomon"?

But, the fact is, that seems to be the case. At least, there was no Temple of Solomon in the terms described in the Bible.

One of the first quests of archaeologists in Palestine was the search for the remains of Solomon's Temple and the great empire of David. It would be tedious to go through all the descriptions of the many excavations, the results, the assumptions, the wild claims of "I've found something that proves it!", which were then followed by sober science demonstrating that it wasn't so. The reader who is interested in deeper knowledge in this area can certainly read both sides of the argument, and then look at the scientific evidence and come to the same conclusion we have: The Kingdom of David and the Temple of Solomon in Jerusalem never existed as described by the Bible.

Even though there were remains of some sort of "kingdom" found at Megiddo, Gezer and Hazor, it was later determined that this "empire" was actually something altogether different than might initially be supposed as we shall soon see.[257] What is important, however, is the fact that the area that was *specifically* claimed as the "homeland" of David and Solomon - Judah - was "conspicuously undeveloped" during the time of the purported empire of Solomon. The facts are that the culture of this region was extremely simple. Based on the evidence of the spade, the land was rural - with no trace of written documents, inscriptions, or even any signs of the kind of widespread literacy that would be necessary for a functioning monarchy. What is more, the area was not even homogeneous. There

---

[257] Finkelstein, Israel, and Silberstein, Neil Asher; *The Bible Unearthed*, (New York: The Free Press 2001).

is no evidence of any kind of unified culture, nor of any sort of central administration. The area from Jerusalem to the north was densely settled, and the area from Jerusalem to the south, the land "in question", was very sparsely settled in the time that David and Solomon were supposed to have lived. In fact, Jerusalem itself was little more than a typical highland village. Archaeologically, nothing can be said about David and Solomon. Yet the legend endured. Why?

The important thing to remember at this point is the fact that the evidence supports only a gradual emergence of a distinct group in Canaan at the end of the thirteenth century BC, not a sudden arrival of a vast number of Israelite settlers. And, as noted, the ones who were present in the land were not very organized or "civilized" in the area that was claimed as the great kingdom of David and Solomon.

AHAB AND JEZEBEL: SOLOMON AND SHEBA?

Biblical historians and biblical archaeologists have long attempted to take the biblical account of the rise and fall of the united monarchy at face value. They have assumed an original ethnic unity and distinctiveness of the Hebrew people reaching into the primeval past. They took for granted that the united monarchy of David and Solomon, and its tragic collapse, were *facts* belonging to Israel in terms of the land of Palestine at a particular period in time. Further, it was assumed that, since Judah and Israel, the two kingdoms, had originally been one, when they split, they both inherited fully formed institutions of church and state. At that point, they were believed to have engaged in competition with one another on a more or less equal footing.

However, intensive archaeological work in the hill country of Israel in the 1980s put those ideas to rest. Curiously, what the archaeologists found was that there had been three waves of settlement activity. The first was between 3500-2200 BC. The second was around 2000-1550 BC. The third was 1150-900 BC. We recognize these time windows as being previously related to possible cataclysms.[258]

In any event, during these three periods of settlement activity - periods when new people arrived and left evidence of a distinct cultural norm, the northern and southern "kingdoms" always seemed to be separate in these terms. The northern settlement system was always dense and possessed evidence of complex hierarchy of large, medium, and small sites. These sites were heavily dependent on settled agriculture.

The southern "kingdom", on the other hand, was sparsely settled in small sites, with only evidence of a population of migratory pastoral groups. We have, then, a division between agriculturalists and shepherds right from the beginning.

---

[258] Baillie, Mike, *Exodus to Arthur* (London: B.T. Batsford 1999).

During the early period of settlement, these northern and southern regions were each dominated by a single center that was probably the focus of regional politics, economics, and most likely, cultic activity. In the north, it was the area that was later occupied by a city that the Bible calls Tirzah. This became the first capital of the northern kingdom. In the south, the main center was Ai, located northeast of Jerusalem.

In the Middle Bronze Age, there was the second wave of settlement, again, the north was dense and agricultural and the south was sparse - with tiny settlements - and a lot of evidence of wandering pastoralists. But, by now, the central site of cult and economy was Jerusalem - a heavily fortified city that gives evidence of being part of the Hyksos Empire. This matches Manetho's account of the Hyksos leaving Egypt and building a city and temple in Jerusalem. The only problem is: it's the wrong date to have been built *after* the Hyksos left Egypt, so most archaeologists just assume that there was a Hyksos presence in Canaan that was contemporary to the Hyksos in Egypt. Nearby was Hebron; also heavily fortified. In the north, the center of activity had moved to Shechem. Apparently, Shechem possessed significant fortifications and a *massive temple*.

Regarding this particular period of history, there is also external evidence from Egypt as to who was who and what was what. These consist of what are called the "Execration Texts", the Egyptian version of voodoo. The Egyptians would write curses on clay figures of their enemies and then smash them and ceremonially bury them. The idea was, of course, to symbolically smash the object of the curse. What is important about the Execration Texts is that they give us a clue as to who the Egyptians felt to be most threatening. The Execration Texts mention a large number of coastal and lowland cities of Canaan, but only two highland centers: Shechem and Jerusalem. Keeping in mind the probable link between the Hyksos in Egypt and the Canaanites in Palestine, we can conjecture why the Egyptians were feeling so hostile toward Shechem and Jerusalem. The important thing is that the execration texts, which purportedly date back to at least 1630 BC, mention Jerusalem, Shechem, and Hazor, but none of them ever mention Israel.

Another Egyptian inscription, which records the adventures of a general named Khu-Sebek who led an expedition into the Canaanite highlands, purportedly in the 19th century BC, refers to the "land of Shechem", and compares Shechem to *Retenu* which is one of the Egyptian names for all of Canaan. Interestingly, the Egyptians also referred to the Hyksos as *"princes of Retenu"*. This indicates that as early as 1800 BC there was *a territorial entity in northern Canaan* and that an important center of this territory was Shechem; further, that it did indeed have a close relationship, at some point, to the Hyksos in Avaris, and it wasn't Israel.

The Tell el-Amarna letters confirm that there is, at some point late in this period, a *southern* territory of some significance to Egypt, with the city of Jerusalem as an important center. A number of these letters refer to the rulers of these two city-states - a king named Abdi-Heba who reigned in Jerusalem; and a king named Labayu who reigned in Shechem. Each of them controlled a territory of about a thousand square miles. This was the largest area held by a single local ruler since all the rest of Canaan was divided up into small city-states. It is also curious to note the similarity of these names to "Abraham" and "Laban."

The problem is, as Redford notes, that "one has the sinking feeling in approaching this period that a most significant page is missing in the record". And indeed there is.

The bottom line is: archaeological evidence suggests that despite the biblical claims of richness and glory, Jerusalem was little more than a village *in the time assigned to David and Solomon*. In the interim, during the "missing page period", the former fortified city had long since disappeared. In other words, the northern kingdom that was supposed to have "broken away" from the rule of Jerusalem was well on its way to major state status while Judah had been returned to a condition not unlike a backwater sheep station.

At the same time that the northern highlands were outpacing the southern highlands during all the three periods of settlement, the coastal city-states were leaving both of them in the dust. They were busy, thriving, cosmopolitan, and wealthy. Archaeologists think that what made possible the initial independence of the highlands was the fact that the city-state system of Canaan suffered *a series of catastrophically destructive upheavals* at the end of the Late Bronze Age. The archaeologists are uncertain as to the cause of this "cataclysm", suggesting it to be the invasion of the Sea Peoples or other such propositions. We have an idea already that it was probably more than that.

What seems to have happened is that the coastal city-states recovered from the "cataclysms", had been rebuilt and were thriving, when suddenly they were *destroyed a second time in a rather short period,* this time - supposedly - by military onslaught and fire. Whatever it was, the destruction was so complete that the Canaanite cities of the plain and the coast never recovered. The source of this destruction is thought to have been the military campaign of Shishak, founder of the twenty-second Dynasty. This invasion is mentioned in the Bible where it says that, *"In the fifth year of Rehoboam, Shishak king of Egypt came up against Jerusalem; he took away the treasures of the house of the Lord and the treasures of the king's house; he took away everything. He also took away the shields of gold that Solomon had made"*.

Shishak/Sheshonq commissioned a triumphal inscription to commemorate the event on the temple walls at Karnak. This inscription lists about one hundred fifty towns and villages he wiped out in his "march to the sea", so to speak. The targets of the Egyptians seem to have been the great Canaanite cities of Rehov, Beth-shean, Taanach, and Megiddo. A fragment of a victory stele bearing the name of Shishak was found at Megiddo.[259] Thick layers of ash and the evidence of the collapse of buildings bear mute testimony to the rage of Pharaoh, which led to the sudden death of the Canaanite territory in the late tenth century BC. There is very

---

[259] Unfortunately, it had been dumped in the trash at the archaeological site so its precise provenance is unknown.

little evidence of this assault in the hill country, the main campaign being directed at the cities of the Jezreel valley. If there was a "Temple" that was plundered by Shishak, it wasn't in Jerusalem.

Nevertheless, it is suggested that this raid of Shishak's created an opportunity for the people of the highland to expand into the lowlands at the beginning of the ninth century. Meanwhile, the archaeological records show that, far to the south, Jerusalem continued along as a regime of dispersed villages and pastoral shepherds.

This is the evidence of the spade at the time of the supposed end of the united monarchy around 900 BC.

In the northern kingdom, regional administrative centers were built in the early ninth century. They were heavily fortified and complete with elaborate, luxurious palaces. These cities include Megiddo, Jezreel, and Samaria. Similar constructions appear in the southern territory *only in the seventh century*. Yet, even when the construction methods moved south, the buildings were smaller and the construction was of a poorer quality.

In short, it can be said that the northern kingdom of Israel, supposed to have been the "bad boy breakaway" from the great united kingdom of David and Solomon in the south, was actually a fully developed state while Judah was still a country cousin.

Yahweh was present in both kingdoms, however - among many other cult gods. And it is certain that peoples of both kingdoms shared similar stories about their origins, though in different versions, and they most certainly spoke a similar language. By the 8th century BC, they also both wrote in the same script. The chief thing about them, however, is that the two kingdoms had *a different experience of the world around them*. Their demographics were different. Their economy was different. Their material culture was different. How they related to their neighbors was different. In short, they actually had quite different histories and cultures.

The question we should like to ask is: why does the Bible tell the story of the schism and secession of Israel from Judah when that is clearly not supported by the evidence of either archaeology or history as known to external sources? Why were the two kingdoms systematically portrayed as twin offspring of a single great empire that was headquartered in Jerusalem? There was a reason, as we will soon see.

In actual fact, the first great king of Israel was Omri. The Bible gives a very sketchy and confused history of the first period of the Northern kingdom after its supposed defection from unity. The sordid tale of violence and treachery culminates in the suicide of a usurper, Zimri, in the flames of the royal palace at Tirzah. Omri, the commander of the army is invited by the people to become king, and he naturally obliges. It was a good choice. Not only that, the story bears some resemblance to the selection of David - a military commander - for kingship over the heirs of Saul.

Omri built a new capital for himself at Samaria and laid the foundations of his dynasty. After twelve years, his son Ahab came to the throne. Ahab made a brilliant marriage to the daughter of the Phoenician king Ethbaal, King of Tyre, so we have again a curious reflection of the Bible story of Solomon and his friendship with "Hiram, King of Tyre". Was this Ethbaal the real "Hiram"? In any event, Ahab built magnificent cities and established one of the most powerful armies in the region. He conquered extensive territory to the north and in the Transjordan, and Israel enjoyed wealth and extensive trade connections. The kingdom of Israel was finally something to notice! However, the character of this kingdom was markedly different from the tiny kingdom of Judah.

Ahab was about the most hated individual in all the Biblical texts. What Ahab did that caused him to be so viciously vilified, according to the editor of the Bible, was that he committed the greatest of Biblical sins: he introduced foreign gods into the land of Israel and caused the priests and prophets of Yahweh to be put to death. What's more, he did it because of the influence of that wicked Phoenician princess he had married: Jezebel.

The Bible dwells long and pruriently upon the sins of this famous couple. Nevertheless, we ought to note that *these very same sins were attributed to Solomon,* who was, however, transmogrified into a southern kingdom monarch, and was, therefore, forgiven even if Yahweh was determined to punish his family. One gets the disorienting feeling that the stories of Omri and Ahab and David and Solomon are, essentially, the same. Jezebel was most especially hated because she tossed the prophets and priests of Yahweh out on their ears. Solomon was also recorded to have ejected the priests of Shiloh, so again, we have a cross connection.

In the Bible, the heroes of the story of Omri and Ahab are the prophets Elijah and Elisha - no doubt priests of Shiloh (which will become quite significant rather soon) - since it was recorded as the home of the prophet Ahijah in 1 Kings, 14:2. A great demonstration of the power of Yahweh is said to have been engineered by Elijah in his confrontation with Ahab, and the result was that the people seized the prophets of the foreign god, Baal, and slaughtered them at the brook Kishon.

Jezebel, naturally, went on a rampage, and Elijah felt it was time to get out of Dodge. He headed for the hills in the wilderness and talked to God on Mount Horeb just like Moses was supposed to have done. Yahweh pronounced a dire prophecy against Ahab, but curiously gave him a few more chances to redeem himself as evidenced by his victories against Ben-Hadad, king of Aram-Damascus. Yahweh, apparently, was willing to relent if Ahab would kill Ben-Hadad. However, Ahab decided to make peace instead, and a treaty was arranged. On and on the account goes, vilifying Ahab and Jezebel. After his death, Elisha anointed another general in the army to be king, Jehu. This guy was more to Yahweh's liking, apparently, and Yahweh saw to it that Jezebel suffered a terrible death, thrown from a window and devoured by dogs. Jehu then sent for all of Ahab's sons, (there were reportedly 70 of them), by any number of wives or concubines, and had them all slaughtered and their heads piled up in a mound at the gate of the city to inspire awe and confidence in the new king, not to mention Yahweh.

The Bible says that Jehu brought down the Omrides, yet there is evidence that this is probably not true.

In 1993, an inscription was found that is believed to have been produced by Hazael, king of Aram-Damascus. From the inscription, it seems that Hazael captured the city of Dan around 835 BC and refers to the "House of David". Hazael's invasion was clearly the one that weakened the power of the northern kingdom. The text of the Dan inscription links the death of Jehoram, the son of Ahab and Jezebel, to an Aramaean victory. Hazael boasts:

> [I killed Jeho]ram son of [Ahab] king of Israel and [I]killed [Ahaz]iahu son of
> [Jehoram kin]g of the House of David. And I set [their towns into ruins and turned
> [their land into[desolation].

Thus it is that the likelihood that the violent destruction of the "Solomonic" palaces that was long ascribed to the Egyptian raid led by Pharaoh Shishak in the late 10th century BC, actually took place around 835, and was due to Hazael and not Jehu. Thus ended the Omride dynasty.

Let me emphasize that the Omride dynasty is referred to by Hazael as the "*House of David*". Why? Was Omri, in fact, the "Beloved" of Yahweh? Or was the House of the Beloved originally the Beloved of another "god"?

Nevertheless, we begin to see how Elijah's terrible prophecy on the fate of Ahab was fulfilled: by twisting the facts *after* the fact. Of course, as we will see, an awful lot of Yahweh's other prophecies were "fulfilled", after the fact and *only* during the writing of the Bible. The invasion of Ben-hadad, who Ahab was supposed to kill and didn't, and thus angered Yahweh, actually took place much later in the history of the northern kingdom.

So we find, again and again, when the anachronisms and historical inaccuracies are removed from the story, there is really nothing left of the Bible proper except a tedious tale of threats by Yahweh and fulfillment of those threats all designed to establish Yahweh as the Universal God. Never mind that this process includes twisting and distorting the facts all out of recognition. What the record of the spade shows about the Omrides is a great kingdom and a time of general prosperity for all. It provides, in fact, a model of the Davidic and Solomonic kingdom of Israel *in all respects except for the worship of Yahweh*. That is why it was damned by the writers of the Bible and retold in a "new version" that promoted Yahweh as the god who had made Israel great, and whose abandonment had brought it to its knees.

The facts are exactly the opposite. Israel never achieved anything under the rule of the priests of Yahweh except constant suffering and exile because of rulers who kept shooting themselves in the foot with their two-faced politics and religio-cultural isolationist policies.

The Omrides were a militarily powerful family of rulers reigning over one of the strongest states of the Near East during that period of time. It was only then that the rest of the world began to sit up and take notice of Israel. A stele from this time says that, "Omri was king of Israel, and he oppressed Moab." Moab was a vassal state of Israel. The stele continues by telling us how Mesha, the king of Moab responsible for the stele, expanded his territory in rebellion against Israel. We learn from Mesha that the kingdom of Israel reached far to the east and south of its earlier domain in the central hill country.

The Bible stresses the Omride's military embarrassments repeatedly, but it seems that they were sufficiently competent that they could assemble a force that impressed the heck out of the great Assyrian king Shalmaneser III, and sent him home in a hurry. Naturally, Shalmaneser boasted of his victory in what is called the Monolith inscription. But it was found in Nimrud, *not* Israel, which testifies to who really prevailed! The Bible mentions an "Aramaean army" besieging Samaria; it is clear that it was the Assyrian army and that Israel held their own.

The many archaeological finds in Palestine that were at first loudly proclaimed to have been evidence of the reigns of David and Solomon, actually turned out to be the building projects of Omri and Ahab. Thus it is that if there was a David and Solomon of Israel, it was Omri and Ahab, the dynasty that established the first fully developed monarchy in Israel.

It is evident that the building projects of Omri employed sophisticated earthmoving operations to turn small hilltop settlements into significant fortresses. Where did the power and wealth come from? What occurred to enable the northern kingdom to grow into the Omride state? With the limited resources of the hill country being only sufficient to maintain relatively small towns and villages, what happened to nurture expansion?

Well, as noted, there was a wave of destruction of the cities of the lowlands at the end of the 10th century BC, prior to the destruction of the "Solomonic palaces", of the Omrides and it is now thought that this opened the way for a strong man with brains and ambition to grab the reins and create an empire. Apparently Omri was such a man. He wasn't responsible for the destruction of the "Philistines", as the Bible claimed about David, but he was certainly the man of the hour who knew when his star was on the ascendant. He expanded from the original hill country into the heart of the former Canaanite territory at Megiddo, Hazor, and Gezer. He enveloped the territories of southern Syria and Transjordan. He established a vast and diverse territorial state that controlled rich agricultural land and held sway over a busy international trade route. What was even more significant: his territory was a multi-ethnic society. This was another reason the authors of the Bible demonized him.

When the northern kingdom of Israel united the Samarian highlands with the northern valleys, it amounted to the integration of several ecosystems including the heterogeneous population. It is very likely that the core territory in the highlands would have identified themselves as Israelites, but the peoples of the lowlands, the valleys, were the indigenous Canaanite population. Farther to the north were those whose ethnicity was Aramaean. Toward the coast, Omri ruled over peoples who were Phoenician in origin. The archaeology shows that the cultural roots of each group were consistent through this period, and thus were apparently not disturbed by Omri. The evidence shows stability in the settlement patterns such that it is evident that Omri did not try to force anything on anybody; not even religious beliefs. He truly "united the tribes of Palestine", even if they weren't, as the Bible suggests, the "sons of Jacob" united under the divine guidance of Yahweh; they were a diverse and unique mix. And it is very likely this gathering together of different ethnic groups was the real, historical event that was later falsified in the myth of the 12 tribes as actual "families" of sons descended from Abraham. It seems that this very diversity was the most important factor contributing to the growth and expansion of the Omride dynasty. According to estimates, Israel may have been the most densely populated state in the Levant. Its only rival was Aram-Damascus in southern Syria.

The rise to power of Omri coincided with the general revival of eastern Mediterranean trade. The harbor cities of Greece, Cyprus, and the Phoenician coast were busily involved in trade and commerce, and thanks to Omri, Israel participated. There was a strong Phoenician artistic influence on the Israelite culture, and a great many Cypro-Phoenician style vessels appear in the archaeological strata. This isn't terribly unusual considering the fact that Ahab married a Phoenician princess.

Conceptually and functionally, the Omride citadels resemble the great Canaanite city-states of the Late Bronze Age. A similar cultural continuity is evident in places like Taanach, where a decorated cult-stand from the 9th century BC displays elaborate motifs of the Canaanite traditions of that time. All of this is interesting, however it creates a problem. From the archaeological perspective, *there is nothing particularly Israelite about the northern kingdom at all.* In fact, it is only from the Bible that we learn - or are told - that it was an Israelite kingdom, broken away from the Solomonic empire. The true character of the Omride dynasty is that of military might, architectural achievement, governmental sophistication, and cosmopolitan *tolerance*. But all we learn from the Bible was how much Omri and Ahab were hated.

The Biblical author obviously had to tell the "real" stories about Omri, even if they had already been "mythicized", but he twisted and distorted every word. He diminished their military might with ridicule and recitations of failures. He omitted the many victories and successes that must have occurred or the dynasty would not have achieved such expansion. The Biblical author also linked the opulence of the dynasty with idolatry and social injustice; he connected the Phoenician princess to evil practices and whoring after false gods. The Biblical author historicized what had already been mythicized, only he put his own negative spin on it. In short, he wanted to show that the entire history of the northern kingdom had been one of sin and degradation piled to heaven.

Yet, the evidence of the spade says otherwise.

The Biblical author then tells the tales of the "House of David" as though it were the exclusive possession of the Southern kingdom. And we are beginning to understand why: it was to justify Yahweh as the Only God: the god of Israel.

THE TEN LOST TRIBES

As it turned out, the kingdom Omri built actually fell because he succeeded too well. As an independent kingdom sitting in the shadow of the great Assyrian empire, northern Israel was a tempting treasure just asking to be plundered.

In the reigns of the several kings that followed Ahab, Yahweh is typically hypocritical in his judgments. Or rather, he is written into the narrative as being behind the successes or failures of the kings. If they succeeded at anything while remaining idolatrous, it was because Yahweh had pity on the people. If the kings were faithful to Yahweh, but were political failures causing the people to suffer, it was because of some sin attributed to their forebears. Divine blessings seemed to be singularly arbitrary. It never seemed to occur to any of the priests of Yahweh that maybe he wasn't such a hot choice for the national god after all.

In any event, after a string of kingly failures, or failures of Yahweh to come through on his promises, a truly idiotic king came to the throne: Hoshea.

At the same point in time, the late 8th century BC, Shalmaneser V came to the throne of Assyria. Hoshea gave his word to be a vassal to Shalmaneser, but went behind his back to form an alliance with Egypt. He must have been a lousy judge of on which side his bread was buttered, as well as not too ethically inclined since he made one promise and then immediately reneged on it. Remember how much Egypt is supposed to be hated because of the slavery of the Jews there? Well, we will notice repeatedly that this factor never seemed to have entered the minds of the Israelites during this early period. What Hoshea wanted from Egypt was support for a revolution against Assyria. When Shalmaneser heard about it, he took Hoshea captive, invaded what was left of Israel, laid siege to Samaria for three years, and when he captured it, he "carried the Israelites away to Assyria.." Well, at least those who could not buy their freedom.

After exiling the Israelites, Assyria brought in people from Babylon, Cuthah, Avva, Hamath, and Sepharvaim, and settled them in the cities of Samaria to replace the people of Israel. None of the original inhabitants were ever reported to have returned, and the legend of the Ten Lost Tribes of Israel was created from this event.

These lost tribes have been reported at: Great Zimbabwe in Africa; Mexico, North America; Persia; Central Asia; China (the Chiang-Min of Sichuan), and Japan.[260] The *Book of Mormon* discusses at great length this matter of the "lost tribes" in America. The problem is, of course, the assumption that there ever was 12 *real tribes* to begin with *as described in the Bible;* that is, begun by the sons of a single father, Jacob. I think that, by this time, the reader may be coming to the realization that there could not be ten lost tribes because there were no "tribes" to begin with – at least *not in the terms explicated in the Bible.*

The story of Joseph in Egypt - Genesis 37 to 50 - is so different in style and excellence that scholars believe it to be a literary composition rather than a record. It shares many features with many other Egyptian and Near Eastern stories of the same genre. The change in style in passing from the short and disjointed sections dealing with Abraham, Isaac, and Jacob is unusual in other ways. The story of Joseph demonstrates no interest at all in the covenant, promises, and precedents of the rights of Israel or any of the other matters that concern the authors of the earlier tales. There are no meetings with Yahweh/Jehovah, no angels, no cities being blown up; in short, nothing Jewish at all.

According to Genesis 45:11, the journey of Jacob and his family to Egypt was an emergency measure to help them survive a famine. Another version suggests that their clear intent was to *settle in Egypt permanently.* This suggests the story is

---

[260] In Japanese, *koru* means to freeze, and in Hebrew, *kor* means cold. This is taken as proof that the "lost tribes" went to Japan, rather than the obvious solution that there was, at one time, a proto-Nostratic language from which all others descend.

a borrowed piece of Middle Eastern Literature, inserted into the Biblical narrative as history, and, most especially, as a "genealogical placeholder". The popular and obviously well known story of Joseph was claimed as the origin of the diverse tribes that were later assimilated as "one people". The Joseph story brings all the "sons of Jacob" to Egypt where they live out their lives. This directly and emphatically contradicts the traditions of the individual tribes. For example, in Genesis 38, Judah marries, settles, and raises his family in Canaan; Simeon marries a Canaanite in Genesis 46:21; Ephraim dies in Palestine in I Chronicles 6:20; Manasseh married an Aramaean in I Chronicles 7:14, and his son, Machir, was at home in Gilead in both Numbers 32:40 and I Chronicles 2:21-22.

Another discordant element in the Joseph story is that the Egyptian names it mentions, Saphnathpane'ah, Asenath, Potiphar, and Potipherah, are names that belong to the 21st Egyptian dynasty, and were common in the 9th through 7th centuries BC - the Kushite-Saite period. Also, in Genesis 42:34, an Aramaic title - *saris* from the Akkadian *sa resi* - is a title found in the Persian administration of Egypt. In short, a strong case for a 7th or 6th century origin of the story can be made, and the parallels to the story of Daniel in exile in Babylon are numerous.

So, again, it seems that the "twelve sons of Jacob", as the progenitors of the twelve tribes of Israel, were originally just simply loosely associated tribes with no specific familial connection, and the story of Jacob as their father was developed as a genealogical placeholder/connector.

THE FIRST "TORAH" AND THE FIRST "TEMPLE"

At the time of fall of the Northern kingdom in 722 BC, many of the refugees from Israel (who could be considered members of the other "ten tribes" if one wishes to look at it that way), fled south into the rural hill country of Judah. Apparently, among them, were the priest-prophets of Shiloh - the enemies of Jezebel who felt that their king had been corrupted by a woman - bringing their E document with them. It was at this point that E was joined to J – probably by a member of the Aaronic priesthood in Jerusalem, as part of King Hezekiah's program to consolidate his power.

Taking advantage of the situation presented to him – the destruction of Israel, the acquiring of some of the population and its priests - Hezekiah decided he wanted to unify the population and centralize everything. He was going to be the new "David". He was going to unite all the people into one, and part of his unification plan obviously included the *psychological unity of religion*. The lesson of Omri's tolerance for different groups and their beliefs was obviously lost on Hezekiah. Either that, or he was well and truly under the control of the priesthood.

This was the important moment in which the P document was created and the division of priestly status was established, with the Aaronite priests taking the higher position and the Shiloh priests - the alleged descendants of Moses - reduced to a servile status, which they did not like one bit. The P document was the Aaronic priesthood's editorial gloss of the combined JE document. Even though they were unable to dispose of the stories in J and E (the common property of the people), which reflected a hostile view of Yahweh, history, and particularly of Aaron, they utilized them in clever ways that laid the foundation for the later full and final imposition of the controls of Yahweh. The P document sought to glorify Yahweh over the other gods that were an integral part of the original stories, and it would naturally have edited out any praiseworthy mention of them, though, as noted, the stories themselves could not be dispensed with.

The writer of P was someone who knew the texts of J and E. The P text was not just similar to J and E, nor was it just a lot of doublets from J and E, it was written *following* J and E to *stand, as it's own version of those stories.* It was clearly written to be presented *in place of* J and E, and that it is likely that J and E were *suppressed* at the time of the presentation of P.

Not only did P open with a creation story and a flood story like J and E, it went on to the major matters of the Abrahamic covenant, the exodus from Egypt, and the covenant at Sinai. It refers to all kinds of specific things that appear in the J/E text. There are more than twenty-five cases of parallel accounts that were obviously *not intended to have been combined with J and E,* as was done by a later redactor. What's more, though the similarities are blatant, the *differences* are even more telling. The question we need to ask is this: why did the author of P think that it was necessary to write a new version when he obviously had J and E in hand?

First of all, we need to consider what is said in J and E that is significantly different from P. The peoples of the northern kingdom had a long tradition of descent from Moses himself. Their documents cast Aaron in a very bad light as the priest of the Golden Calf and whose sister, Miriam, was stricken with disease because she criticized the wife of Moses. The northern kingdom, apparently, did not worship a god who demanded sacrifices. The northern kingdom beliefs emphasized prophets chosen by the gods, rather than a bloodline priesthood.

In the purest sense, the creation of this part of the text was primarily political just as the creation of the Christian theology was primarily political. Both were designed to emphasize those things that would make the subjects of the kingdom amenable to control and domination.

Hezekiah undertook the elimination of all forms of religious practice other than sanctioned worship at the Temple in Jerusalem. Rigid religious control was instituted which meant that all the places of worship of other gods, and even Yahweh, outside of the Temple had to be destroyed. These worship sites were called "high places". They were eliminated and centralized religion under the control of the Levites in Jerusalem became the law in secular terms. In fact, the law of Yahweh became the law of the land. As noted, the Levites in charge at that time were the Aaronid Levites.

In order to understand the implications of this, one needs to understand what was being done at these "high places" and why. The function of sacrifice in the Middle Eastern world was not just the senseless killing of an animal; it was, for the most part, a ritual killing of the animal *for food,* and part of it was offered to any of a number of gods. The point was, if man wanted to eat meat, he had to understand it as a taking of life, and such an act was sacred, to be performed in a prescribed manner by an appointed person, a priest, who also received a portion.

Thus, the effect of this ruling was that, if people wanted to have lamb for dinner, you could no longer perform the sacrifice at home or in a local "high place". You had to haul your sheep to Jerusalem where there was a conclave of Levites. This, of course, meant putting a lot of economic control and power into the hands of a very few people. At the same time, the Aaronid Levites who were writing the text of this new Torah made sure to add in specific sacrifices to Yahweh over and above the simple ritualized killing of their dinner. This ensured the enrichment of the priesthood at the expense of the people.

Nevertheless, this very point of seeking to centralize religion at that moment in time, and the writing of the P document, leads to one of the important clues regarding the alleged existence of the Temple of Solomon in Jerusalem.

You see, one of the central controversies about the Bible in terms of researching the internal evidence of the documents in order to determine who wrote what and when, has been the period from which the P document originated. It has been long accepted that J and E came from the earlier period - from the two kingdoms of Judah and Israel (8th and 9th centuries BC). It is almost universally accepted that D was written in the time of Josiah (mid to late 5th century BC), as we will see further on. But, figuring out who wrote the P document has been a very difficult job. And, the fact is, P is the largest of the sources, being the size of the other three put together.

The P document includes the creation story in the first chapter of Genesis. It includes the cosmic version of the flood story, the version in which the windows of the heavens and the fountains of the deep are opened to flood the world. It has the stories of Abraham, Jacob, the exodus, and the journey through the wilderness, most of which are doublets of stories in J and E. It also contains a tremendous body of law, covering about thirty chapters of Exodus and Numbers and *all* of the book of Leviticus. So, this is a significant question here that we cannot gloss over lightly!

In 1833, Eduard Reuss gave a lecture to his students in Strassburg. In this lecture, he stated that the biblical prophets do not refer to the Priestly law; they do not quote the P part of the Bible, nor do they give any impression that they are even familiar with it. From this observation, Reuss concluded that the law was later than the prophets.[261] Of course, Reuss was afraid to say this in public and waited forty-six years before publishing a monograph on the subject in 1879. At this point, one of his braver students had already taken the idea even further, publishing his own paper on the matter.

This student was Karl Graf. Being convinced by Reuss that the law was later than the prophets, he began to search the text for clues. It was already accepted that D was written after J and E, and that this was in the time of Josiah, so Graf assumed a priori that P must have been written after that time, during the period of the Second Temple. This was part of the view that was synthesized later by Wellhausen, claiming that the elaborate legal and ritual system, the centralization

---

[261] Friedman, op. cit., p. 162.

of the priesthood, were later developments in the lives of the Israelites at the end of the biblical period.

There was one serious problem with this view that P was written by a member of the post exile priesthood: a Temple is never mentioned *once* in the P document. In P, Yahweh *never* commands Moses to tell the people to build a Temple. There is not one law in P that requires the presence of a Temple. What is more, even though P talks about the Ark of the Covenant, an altar, cherubs, the Urim and Thummim, and other sacred accoutrements of worship, there is not a single solitary reference to a Temple.[262]

Graf's solution to the problem of the missing Temple was that the Temple *was* mentioned repeatedly *as the Tabernacle*. The Tabernacle was the tent of meeting that Moses erected in the desert to house the Ark of the Covenant. It is mentioned in the E document only three times and in J and D it is not mentioned at all. P, on the other hand, mentions it over two hundred times! What is more, P gives elaborate details on its materials and construction and the laws relating to it. It is a regular feature of the stories in P; all assemblies of the people take place at the Tabernacle. In short, the Tabernacle is essential to P.

So, Graf's solution was that the Tabernacle *never existed*, that it was a fiction made up during the Second Temple period because the writer wanted to establish a law code that was in the interests of the Temple priests and needed the antiquity and authority of Moses to validate the Temple as a replacement of the Tabernacle.

Thus, Graf decided that the Tabernacle must have been deliberately - falsely - created so as to pass its authority to the Temple being rebuilt in the Second Temple period after that Babylonian captivity, and the transfer of the ark from the Tabernacle to the Temple and the laws that required the presence of the Tabernacle would now require the presence of the Temple. Thus he proposed that the Priestly Tabernacle was a literary and legal fiction created by the post-exile author of P to support the rebuilt temple of the Second Temple period.

So, again we notice that along came Wellhausen. Once he had accepted Reuss' theory that the law was later than the prophets, and Graf's theory that the Tabernacle was nothing more than the symbol for the Temple, he was able to suggest that, in the P document, centralization of religion was not being demanded, as it was during the time of D, but was *understood* to already exist. He stated that the laws and stories of P *take centralization for granted*.

In the P list of different kinds of sacrifices there is one called a "sin offering" and one called a "guilt offering". Such sacrifices are not mentioned in J, E, or D. Wellhausen reasoned that it was only logical that sin and guilt offerings should be established *after* the exile when the people felt guilty, believing that their exile was punishment for their sins.

---

[262] Ibid., p. 163.

In the P list of holidays, there is a holiday that is known now as the Fall New Year, or Feast of Tabernacles, followed ten days later by a Day of Atonement. *These holidays are not mentioned in J, E, or D.* And, since these two holidays involve atonement for sin, Wellhausen said that this proved that they were part of the Second Temple period when Israel was loaded with guilt that their faithlessness to Yahweh had led to the destruction of the kingdom and their exile to Babylon.

Another "proof" that was accepted by Wellhausen as demonstration that P was written after the exile was the "Ezekiel matter". Ezekiel was an Aaronid priest who was exiled to Babylon (which we will shortly discuss), and it was there that he wrote his book that bears his name. The book of Ezekiel is written in a style and language that is remarkably similar to that of the P document. There are whole passages in Ezekiel that are nearly word-for word extracts from P. In Ezekiel, the writer declares that in the future only certain Levites may be priests. All others are disqualified from the priesthood because of their past sins. The only Levites who may function as priests are those who are descendants of Zadok. Zadok was David's Aaronid priest. And so, according to Ezekiel, only Zadokian Aaronid priests are legitimate; all others are excluded.

It is also quite clear in the P document that only Aaronids are priests in any context. P simply *does not recognize the descendants of Moses* (the Shiloh priests) as legitimate. So, Wellhausen decided that P had to have been written during the days of the Second Temple, when the Aaronid priests came to power, taking Ezekiel's prophecy as their inspiration. At that point in time, the competition between the priestly families was over. The Aaronids had won and one of them wrote a "Torah of Moses" that reflected their victory.

It was a good argument. But as Friedman says, "*it was logical, coherent, persuasive - and wrong*".[263]

Reuss was wrong from the beginning of the argument because it is clear that the prophets *do* quote P, most notable among them being Jeremiah. The fact is, Jeremiah seemed to fiendishly enjoy playing with the P document and reversing its language in clever ways. Jeremiah also can be found to *reject the Ark of the Covenant* in a "twist" of the language of the P document. Ezekiel also seems to know the P document quite well. The reader may wish to refer to Friedman for the list of comparisons.

In 1982, Avi Hurvitz of the Hebrew University in Jerusalem demonstrated that P is *written in an earlier form of Hebrew* than Ezekiel's work, so Wellhausen's idea that it had been written *after* Ezekiel was dealt another blow. Five other scholars in recent years have uncovered additional linguistic evidence that *most* of P is written in the biblical Hebrew of the days *before* the exile to Babylon.

---

[263] Ibid., p. 167.

The bottom line is: Reuss was wrong, Graf was wrong, and Wellhausen was wrong. But, by being wrong, they ended up highlighting a crucial bit of evidence for *something else altogether:* the issue of the Tabernacle. This Tabernacle brings us face to face with the question: *when was the "first temple"- the famed Temple of Solomon - in Jerusalem really built, if one was built at all?*

> Jerusalem has been excavated time and again - and with a particularly intense period of investigation of Bronze and Iron Age remains in the 1970s and 1980s under the direction of Yigal Shiloh, of the Hebrew University, at the city of David, the original urban core of Jerusalem. Surprisingly, as Tel Aviv University archaeologist David Ussishkin pointed out, fieldwork there and in other parts of biblical Jerusalem *failed to provide significant evidence for a tenth century occupation.* Not only was any sign of monumental architecture missing, but also, so were even simple pottery shards. Some scholars have argued that later, massive building activities in Jerusalem wiped out all signs of the earlier city. Yet excavations in the city of David revealed impressive finds from the Middle Bronze Age and from later centuries of the Iron Age - just *not from the tenth century BC.* The most optimistic assessment of this negative evidence is that tenth century Jerusalem was rather limited in extent, perhaps *not more than a typical hill country village.* This ... meshes well with the ... pattern of the rest of Judah in the same period, which was composed of only about *twenty small villages* and a *few thousand inhabitants*, many of them wandering pastoralists.[264]

By the 7th century BC, Jerusalem had finally become a relatively large city, dominated by a Temple to the God of Israel that served as the single national shrine. But this was the Second Temple, which was built as a result of the vision of the "captives" who had returned from exile in Babylon.

The priesthood that returned from Babylon developed the Bible AS history in order to bring scattered, war weary people together, to prove to them that they had experienced a stirring history under the direct intervention of God. The glorious epic of the united monarchy was - like the stories of the patriarchs and the sagas of the Exodus and conquest - a brilliant composition that wove together ancient heroic tales and legends into a coherent and persuasive prophecy for the people of Israel in the seventh century BC.

An elaborate theology had been developed in order to validate the connection between the heirs of the Davidic line and the destiny of the entire people of Israel. According to this manufactured history, David was the first to stamp out the abominable influence of "other gods". David, being devoted and faithful to Yahweh, was assigned the task of completing the unfinished job of Joshua, which was to conquer the rest of the Promised Land and establish a glorious empire over all the vast territories that had been promised to Abraham! These were, in fact, the *political ambitions* of the priests in charge, not accurate history. And so, the

---

[264] Finkelstein, op. cit., p. 2001,

glorious tale of David and Solomon and their marvelous Ark were created to inspire the masses. We do, of course, think that these stories were based on more ancient models, but what is clear is that the Great King Solomon - whoever he might have been originally - was not a king of Israel or a worshipper of Yahweh.

In searching for a single, clear mention of the existence of a major temple in Jerusalem during the period in question, that can be verified archaeologically, I have come up empty handed. Even Finkelstein, quoted above, sort of skips over the issue. He says that in the 7th century BC, Jerusalem was a "relatively large city dominated by a Temple to Yahweh". If that were the case, then there would not have been so much focus in the P document *on the Tabernacle*. It seems to have been fairly easy to put words in Moses' mouth retroactively; that problem hadn't stumped the priests so far; so why the big deal about the Tabernacle? They could have slid right over the Tabernacle problem altogether by having Moses say, "when you get there, fold up the tent and build a Temple". For some reason, that was *not* an option. This "Tent of Meeting" was clearly something that the P Document sought to establish as an item of great significance to the people. For some reason, it had to be emphasized, and its historical status as the only Tabernacle *that was legitimate* obviously needed to be established over and above all other such "tents". We find several new things in the P document that were obviously a new spin being put on something that was so commonly known and accepted by the people that it required specific "shaping" to the purposes of the priests.

First of all, we have a new *Fall Holiday* that was formerly known as the *Feast of Tabernacles*. Next, we have a very specific Tabernacle itself. Finally, we have the ostensible reason for this tabernacle being the one and only legitimate tabernacle: an object that goes *inside* the tabernacle: the Ark of the Covenant!

All the references to the Tabernacle in the P document suggest that this was an object with tremendous historical value because it was assembled *under the direction of Moses himself.* The P document describes it as the sacred shrine that housed the Ark of the Covenant, the tablets, the Urim and Thummim, and the cherubs. The P document tells us that the Tabernacle itself was constructed of precious wood, gold, brass, wool and linen woven with gold, scarlet, and purple, with a covering of red leather.

Even though the Tabernacle was supposed to have resided at Shiloh with the Ark inside it, (according to the P text), the E document of the northern kingdom, the domain of the Shiloh priests, *never mentions the ark!* According to the E texts, the "Tent of Meeting" was the most important sign of god's presence. God was *in the tent*, not the ark. And clearly there were *many* "Tents of Meeting".

The J document, on the other hand, mentions that the Ark was very important to the children of Israel as they journeyed to the Promised Land. In the book of Numbers, the Ark was said to have been carried in front of the people as they traveled. Another J text emphasizes the Ark as a military "weapon"; the idea being that it was impossible to be successful in military matters without it. And then, of course, in the J text remarks about the Temple of Solomon, we find that the Ark was the most important object in it. It should come as no surprise that the Tent of Meeting is never mentioned in the J document!

Of course, this leads us to a bit of a problem. If the kingdom of Omri was the mythicized/historicized Jewish Kingdom of Solomon, and yet they knew of no "ark", and there is clear evidence that no Temple of Solomon ever existed in the kingdom of Judah wherein an ark could have been lodged prior to the time of Hezekiah, then were did the idea of the ark come from? What was the "real" Temple of Solomon? Well, we will come back to this. For now, we only need to understand that, via mythicization of history and historicization of myth, some serious prestidigitation is going on here. Tents that were formerly used for a particular purpose are now being eliminated, and the centralization process is beginning by the focus on one tent, and one tent only. The legitimization of that tent is based on its use as the "home of the ark", and a "historical background" for this use of the tent is being created in the P text.

Whatever the Tent of Meeting was used for in ancient times, and whatever the ark of the covenant might have been, it is interesting to note that the overall tenor of the J document - the ark people - is more balanced in its attitude toward women. The E document, from the Northern kingdom priests - the tent people - was quite male in perspective and concentrated on male characters with, essentially no heroines, such as Tamar in Genesis 38. No wonder Jezebel kicked them out!

Speaking of Jezebel, the second to the last mention of the ark in the Bible is in 2 Chronicles, 8:11[265], where it is mentioned in relation to Solomon and his wife, the daughter of Pharaoh.

> Solomon brought the daughter of Pharaoh out of the city of David into the house he had built for her, for he said, My wife shall not dwell in the house of David king of Israel, because the places are holy to which the ark of the Lord has come.

The next to the last mention of the ark is also in 2 Chronicles, 35:3:

> To the Levites who taught all Israel and were holy to the Lord, he said, Put the holy ark in the house which Solomon son of David, king of Israel built; it shall no longer be a burden carried on your shoulders. Now serve the Lord your God and His people Israel.

We will shortly discuss the authorship of the books of Kings, but let us just say here that the authorship of Chronicles reflects the language and interests of the Aaronid priests. Most especially, they extol Hezekiah, which indicates that this was the point in time when the P text was produced.

The *last* mention of the ark in the Bible is a sneering "I told you so" kind of comment by Jeremiah who writes:

> And it shall be that when you have multiplied and increased in the land in those days, says the Lord, they shall no more say, The ark of the covenant of the Lord. It shall not come to mind, nor shall they remember it, nor shall they miss or visit it, nor shall it be repaired or made again.

---

[265] Nice numbers for all the esotericists!

That is certainly a bizarre dismissal of simply the most important item in Jewish history! (At least, according to the Bible.) We will soon see why Jeremiah had this attitude toward the ark. But, the point is, he is clearly talking about it in terms that indicate it had been broken or needed to be "made again". Almost certainly, this suggests that the Babylonians destroyed the ark that existed at the time of the kingdom of Judah along with everything else. What is strange is the implication that it was not of sufficient value for them to even cart it off or it would have been mentioned in the objects that were specifically named as having been taken from the temple. And for those who might wish to think that the lack of mention indicates some major secret or conspiracy, allow me to point out all the many confabulations that exist in the Bible have one single objective: to inflate the importance of Yahweh. They do this by using anything and everything as lessons to whip Yahweh's people into line. If there was any way whatsoever that the loss of the ark could have been used to induce guilt, I think it would have been. What seems clear is that a substitute ark was all that existed in Judah from some point in history. Thus, at the time of the exile, the loss of this substitute ark was no big deal.

It seems that when the ark was no longer needed as a major item to legitimize only one Tabernacle, to change the perceptions of the people, it was dropped as an issue. The idea that it was taken with the fleeing Jews to Egypt and then to Ethiopia is another red herring. There are several Arks that claim to be the legitimate "original". One of them is at Axxum, in Ethiopia. This item has been venerated for centuries, housed in a special chapel, and cared for by a priest whose life is devoted to maintaining the chapel and its grounds. It seems fairly self-evident that if the Axxum Ark were the real thing, the Israeli Authorities would stop at nothing to claim it and retrieve it. Despite many rumors, nothing like this has ever occurred.

But again, let us remember that even if the ark that was present at the time of the Babylonian destruction was merely a "representative" object, it was still based on some real object that existed at some other point in time and space, and the history had been mythicized, and then re-historicized. Nevertheless, this deals another blow to the seekers of the Ark of the Covenant under the Temple of Solomon in Jerusalem!

Getting back to a First Temple, we note that Finkelstein mentions that the evidence of the destruction of Jerusalem, as a whole, is clearly present in the archaeological layers, and it definitely reveals the violence and thoroughness with which the city was obliterated from the landscape; but no specific mention of a Temple. That does not mean that one was not built in Jerusalem somewhere along the way, Solomon just didn't build it, and it wasn't built in the 10th century BC. Also, the issue of whether or not a Temple of Yahweh existed in a precise context at the time of Hezekiah, when the P text was being produced, is problematical.

A temple most certainly seems to have existed at the time of the destruction of the northern kingdom. One clue to this is the references to Hezekiah "repairing" the Temple as part of his reforms. Rather than "repairing" the Temple of Yahweh", he might have been repairing and refurbishing a Temple of another god in Jerusalem, and claiming that it was the "Temple of Solomon", when in fact it wasn't. So, legitimizing the Tabernacle as the temporary home of the ark, and then transferring that home to a "cleansed" Temple would have made sense.

The writer of the P document talks about the "Temple of Solomon" and the items that were kept there, but none of those things were present in the Second Temple, nor were they considered to be important. This is another point favoring the writing of the P document before the Second Temple period. Why would the writer talk about things that no longer existed as though they did, even if we have some idea that their claimed existence was a deliberate displacing of one idea for another? What is more, we have already noted the astonishing silence of the Bible as to the fate of the Ark except for that brief and telling remark by Jeremiah.

The Ark had a deadly reputation. Touching it was supposed to have been lethal. After a battle, 50,000 Philistine soldiers rashly pitched their camp with the Ark gaping open, and all died in their sleep. Their King promptly ordered it to be sealed and sent back to the Israelites. A bearer of the Ark tripped and touched it, and was instantly killed. Two of Moses' men peeked inside it and were struck dead. Moses made sure they were buried in the desert far away from the camp. Some have argued that this indicated that the Ark was radioactive or was some sort of technological device. It is a certainty that, if it had been so powerful an object in military terms, it would have been mentioned as being used against the Babylonians. The failure of the ark to prevail against Nebuchadnezzar, or the carrying away of the ark, mentioned in the older tales as bringing devastation upon those who dared to touch it, would have been recounted, if such events had happened. They didn't, and weren't. And that may have been the reason for the silence about the object afterward. In the final analysis, the only stories we have of the actual use or presence of a significant ark-in-action are in the historicized myths or mythicized history that lead us back to a time long before the exile imposed by the Assyrians, or the carrying away of the people to Babylon. One is even compelled to wonder about the destruction of the Northern Kingdom by Hazael. Surely if the Ark had been present there, it would have made the Omrides invincible militarily. Also, certainly, if Hazael had taken the Ark, it would have been mentioned somewhere. So much build-up had been given to the ark, and then destruction fell in spite of the presence of the ark. What were the priests to say? It didn't work, and better to just forget it than have all the people asking why.

At this point, the writers of the bible, so close in time to the events, simply could not get away with that sort of nonsense, and they didn't even try. What's more, it's clear that they no longer needed the ark at the time of the Second Temple, so it was simply allowed to fade into oblivion as a nice story of the grand and glorious ancestors. Again, I suggest that this was based on some seed of ancient truth, but figuring out what it was - or is - is not going to be as simple as the many Ark chasers of the present day would have us think. One thing seems to be clear: there was no Temple of Solomon in Jerusalem, and no Ark of the Covenant inside whatever temple did exist there. So we can discard the tales of the Ark in Axxum or the Ark under the Temple being retrieved by the Templars or the Roman Emperor, Titus.

Nevertheless, the person who wrote P placed a specific Tabernacle, the Tent of Meeting, with Yahweh embodied in the ark, at the center of Israel's religious life back as far as Moses, and forever into the future, leading to the conclusion: P had to be written before D, since the laws *all through P* say that sacrifices and other ceremonies must take place *at the entrance to the Tabernacle* and nowhere else and that this is the law "forever". It also demonstrates that the Tabernacle was at the center of worship in Jerusalem until a temple of some sort was either built or cleansed, and that this probably occurred at the time of Hezekiah.

Friedman suggests that the Tabernacle was later placed in the Holy of Holies of *a* Temple in Jerusalem, under the spread wings of the "cherubs". But, as we have seen by now, there is no archaeological evidence for the existence of a temple of the dimensions of the Temple of Solomon in Jerusalem. So, we are left with the conclusion that either a smaller temple was was used, or that the Tabernacle, a tent, was all that there ever was until the Second Temple period.

In the stories of a specifically Jewish King Solomon, who we now suspect to be Ahab assimilated to an even older archetype, it is said:

> And they brought up the ark of Yahweh and the Tent of Meeting and all of the holy implements that were in the Tent.[266]

Josephus, the Jewish historian, also wrote that the Tabernacle was *brought into the Temple*, but he is also noted to have obtained his "mystical interpretation" of the Tabernacle from Philo of Alexandria. In any event, all of this leads us to ask the question: what was the activity that transpired in the Tent of Meeting before it was deliberately designated as the lodging of the ark? Why would a tent need to be brought into a Temple except for the purpose of *changing its function*?

As to the destruction of the "Temple" in Jerusalem, Psalm 74:7 is quoted to refer to this event saying:

> They cast your sanctuary into the fire; they profaned your name's Tabernacle to the ground.

However, it is suggested by textual analysis[267] that Psalms 50, and 73 through 83 were composed between 730 and 720 BC for festal worship at the northern sanctuary in Bethel, and accepted with marginal amendments in Jerusalem thereafter. Thus, either this verse about the Tabernacle being burned and profaned refers to a *prior event,* before the fall of the northern kingdom, or it was added after the Fall of Jerusalem to the celebratory hymn. In the first case, it suggests that the Tabernacle that was set up as *the* Tabernacle in Jerusalem was merely a creation of that time, or - again - that there never was a Temple at all prior to the Second Temple period.

---

[266] *The Bible*, 1 Kings 8:4; 2 Chronicles 5:5.

[267] Goulder, Michael D., *The Psalms of Asaph and the Pentateuch* (Sheffield Academic Press 1997).

THE TRIBE OF DAN

An analysis of the genealogies in the Bible is very illuminating. According to the book of Chronicles there is no genealogy for the tribe of Dan. It has been observed by numerous scholars that many of the names occurring in the genealogies themselves are either blatantly geographical or connected with place-names; while others are definitely personal names.[268] But the case of the Tribe of Dan is special, and holds a clue for us in this matter of the Temple and the Tabernacle and the Ark of the Covenant. In II Chronicles 2:11-14 the D historian writes:

> Then Hiram the king of Tyre answered in writing, which he sent to Solomon, Because the Lord hath loved his people, he has made you king over them. Hiram said moreover, Blessed be the Lord God of Israel, that made heaven and earth, who has given to David the king a wise son, endued with prudence and understanding, who should build a house for the Lord, and a palace for his kingdom. And now I have sent a skilled man, endued with understanding, even *Huram-abi*, my trusted counselor, the son of a woman of the daughters of DAN; his father was a man of Tyre. He is a trained worker in gold, silver, brass, iron, stone, and wood, in purple, blue, and crimson colors, and in fine linen; also to engrave any manner of engraving, and to carry out any design which shall be given to him, with your skilled men, and with the skilled men of my lord David your father.

The above is supposed to be a letter from Hiram of Tyre to Solomon, discussing the attributes of a particular man, the trusted counselor of the great Hiram, who is being sent to help the son of David as a great favor. This man is presented as a great designer and architect. He is named, and his mother is designated as being of the tribe of Dan. He is going to be the architect of the Temple of Solomon. In other words, he is the model for the archetypal "great architect" Hiram Abiff of Masonic lore.

So, what is the problem?

Look at this next excerpt from Exodus 31:1-7:

> And the LORD spake unto Moses, saying, See, I have called by name Bezalel the son of Uri, the son of Hur, of the tribe of Judah: And I have filled him with the spirit of God, in wisdom, and in understanding, and in knowledge, and in all manner of workmanship, To devise skillful works, to work in gold, and in silver, and in bronze, and in cutting of stones for setting, and in carving of wood, to work in all manner of craftsmanship. And behold, I have appointed with him Aholiab, the son of Ahisamach, of the tribe of DAN; and to all who are wise hearted I have given wisdom and ability to make all that I have commanded you: The tent of meeting, and the ark of the testimony, and the mercy seat that is on it, and all the furniture of the tent...

---

[268] De Geus, Cornelis, "Of Tribes and Towns: The Historical Development of the Isaelite City." *Eretz-Israel* 24, 1993.

The above description of the command to build the Tent of Meeting and the Ark sounds almost identical to the purported letter from Hiram to Solomon, even including strong similarities in the names of the principal worker: Huram-abi of the tribe of Dan has become Hur of the tribe of Judah:

> And Bezalel the son Uri, the son of Hur, of the tribe of Judah, made all that the LORD commanded Moses. And with him was Aholiab, son of Ahisamach, of the tribe of Dan an engraver, and a skillful craftsman, and an embroiderer in blue, and in purple, and in scarlet, and fine linen.

The next problem arises when we find in I Kings, chapter 7:13-21, the following most confusing information about Hiram:

> And King Solomon sent and fetched Hiram out of Tyre. He was *a widow's son of the tribe of Naphtali,* and his father was a man of Tyre, a worker in brass: and he was filled with wisdom, and understanding, and skill to work all works in brass.
>
> And he came to king Solomon, and wrought all his work. For he cast two pillars of brass, of eighteen cubits high apiece: and a line of twelve cubits did compass either of them about. And he made two chapiters of molten brass, to set upon the tops of the pillars: the height of the one chapiter was five cubits, and the height of the other chapiter was five cubits: And nets of checker work, and wreaths of chain work, for the chapiters which were upon the top of the pillars; seven for the one chapiter, and seven for the other chapiter. And he made the pillars, and two rows round about upon the one network, to cover the chapiters that were upon the top, with pomegranates: and so did he for the other chapiter. And the chapiters that were upon the top of the pillars were of lily work in the porch, four cubits. And the chapiters upon the two pillars had pomegranates also above, over against the belly which was by the network: and the pomegranates were two hundred in rows round about upon the other chapiter. And he set up the pillars in the porch of the temple: and he set up the right pillar, and called the name thereof Jachin: and he set up the left pillar, and called the name thereof Boaz.

We see without too much difficulty that these passages are taken from the same source, though one refers to the building of a Temple and the other refers to the construction of a tent and an ark. One of the problems is, of course, that according to the Bible, the two events are separated by a very long period of time. We also note the curious name similarities between Huram-abi of the passage in II Chronicles, and Hur, the father of Bezalel, connected to Aholiab of the tribe of Dan. Also curious is the name of Bezalel, which is so similar to Jezebel, who we have tentatively identified as the Phoenician princess, daughter of Ethbaal, king of Tyre. More curious still is the claim of the Dan inscription that, in the destruction of the *City of Dan,* the House of David was destroyed. What was the connection of the Tribe of Dan to the House of the Beloved? Were they, as it seems from these clues, one and the same?

In the Exodus passage, we find an interesting substitution taking place: the tribe of Judah has been connected with the tribe of Dan, even taking precedence. The architect sent by Hiram whose mother was of the tribe of Dan, and whose father was a man of Tyre, is now relegated to a subservient position to Bezalel, of the tribe of Judah, who is now the "son of Hur". Importantly, we see that a member of the tribe of Dan was the builder of the Ark! We are entitled to ask: is the tribe of Dan the true "house of the beloved" or Davidic line? And if so, who are they?

When we search for the source of this tribe, we find many interesting things as well as things that are conspicuous by their absence. In Genesis 30:1-6, we discover that Dan was the child of Rachel's maid, Bilhah:

> And when Rachel saw that she bare Jacob no children, Rachel envied her sister; and said unto Jacob, Give me children, or else I die. And Jacob's anger was kindled against Rachel: and he said, Am I in God's stead, who hath withheld from thee the fruit of the womb? And she said, Behold my maid Bilhah, go in unto her; and she shall bear upon my knees, that I may also have children by her. And she gave him Bilhah her handmaid to wife: and Jacob went in unto her. And Bilhah conceived, and bare Jacob a son. And Rachel said, <u>God hath judged me</u>, and hath also heard my voice, and hath given me a son: therefore called she his name Dan.

This story is remarkably similar to the story of Sarai and Hagar in Genesis 16:1-5

> Now Sarai Abram's wife bare him no children: and she had a handmaid, an Egyptian, whose name was Hagar. And Sarai said unto Abram, Behold now, the Lord has restrained me from bearing: I ask you, have intercourse with my maid; it may be that I may obtain children by her. And Abram listened to Sarai. And Sarai Abram's wife took Hagar her maid the Egyptian, after Abram had dwelt ten years in the land of Canaan, and gave her to her husband Abram to be his wife. And he had intercourse with Hagar and she conceived: and when she saw that she had conceived, her mistress was despised in her eyes. And Sarai said unto Abram, My wrong be upon thee: I have given my maid into thy bosom; and when she saw that she had conceived, I was despised in her eyes: *the Lord judge between me and thee.*

The last lines of both passages, dealing with "judgment", indicate that *they are, in fact, the same story.*

Another interesting connection pops up when we consider the identification of Hiram as a member of the tribe of Naphtali in the passage describing the creation of the pillars Jachin and Boaz. From I Chronicles, chapter 7:13:

> The sons of Naphtali; Jahziel, and Guni, and Jezer, and Shallum, *the sons of Bilhah.*

Keep the name "Shallum" in mind because we will encounter it again later in the chapter.

We next come to another clue. In Genesis 49, the patriarch Jacob has called all his children to gather around his deathbed so that he can pronounce their destiny upon them. When he gets to Dan, in verses16 -18, he says:

> Dan shall <u>judge</u> his people, *as one of the tribes of Israel.* Dan shall be a serpent by the way, a horned snake in the path, that bites at the horse's heels, so that his rider shall fall backward. I wait for thy salvation, O Lord.

This is said almost as though the activity of Dan that is negative toward Israel, *is* the salvation. In Deuteronomy 33:22, Moses blesses the tribe of Dan by saying, "*And of Dan he said, Dan is a* lion's whelp: *he shall leap from Bashan*". But in the blessing of Jacob, in Genesis 49:8-9 the *attribute of the Lion* is given to Judah:

> Judah, you are the one whom your brothers shall praise. Your hand shall be on the neck of your enemies; your father's sons shall bow down to you. Judah, a *lion's cub*! With the prey, my son, you have gone high up the mountain; he stooped down, he crouched as a lion, and as a lioness; who dares provoke and rouse him?

Let's compare that to two additional items: the destiny prescribed by God when he appears to Hagar at the well when she ran away after Sarai was cruel to her during her pregnancy, and the blessing given by Isaac to his beloved son Esau after Jacob had defrauded his father with the help of his mother, Rebekah. There are interesting resonances to the remarks made about Judah. The first event is recounted in Genesis 16:11-12, and the second in Genesis 27:39-40:

> 1) And the angel of the Lord said unto her, Behold, you are with child and shall bear a son, and shalt call his name Ishmael, or God hears, because the Lord has heard and paid attention to your affliction. And [Ishmael] will be as a wild man; his hand will be against every man, and every man's hand against him; and he shall live to the east and on the borders of all his kinsmen.

> 2) And Isaac his father answered and said unto [Esau], Behold, Your dwelling shall all come from the fruitfulness of the earth, and from the dew of heaven from above; And by your sword shalt you live, and serve your brother. But the time will come when you will have the dominion, and you will break his yoke from off your neck.

One of the more interesting things we discover when we dig into this subject is that Samson was of the tribe of Dan. Robert Graves remarks:

> Hercules first appears in legend as a pastoral sacred king and, perhaps because shepherds welcome the birth of twin lambs, is a twin himself. His characteristics and history can be deduced from a mass of legends, folk-customs and megalithic monuments. He is the rainmaker of his tribe and a sort of human thunderstorm. Legends connect him with Libya and the Atlas Mountains; he may well have originated thereabouts in Paleolithic times. The priests of Egyptian Thebes, who called him "Shu", dated his origin as, "17,000 years before the reign of King Amasis". His symbols are the acorn; the rock dove, which nests in oaks as well as in clefts of rock; the mistletoe, and the serpent. All of these are sexual emblems. The dove was sacred to the Love-goddess of Greece and Syria the serpent was the most ancient of phallic totem-beasts; the cupped acorn stood for the glans penis in both Greek and Latin; the mistletoe was an all-heal and its names *viscus* and *ixias* are connected with vis and ischus (strength) probably because of the spermal viscosity of its berries, sperm being the vehicle of life.[…]

> The manner of his death can be reconstructed from a variety of legends, folk customs and other religious survivals. At mid-summer, at the end of a half-year reign, Hercules is made drunk with mead and led into the middle of a circle of twelve stones arranged around an oak, in front of which stands an altar-stone; the oak has been lopped until is it T-shaped. He is bound to it with willow thongs in the "five-fold bond" which joins wrists, neck, and ankles together, beaten by his comrades till he faints, then flayed, blinded, castrated, impaled with a mistletoe stake, and finally hacked into joints on the altar stone.[269] His blood is caught in a basin and used for sprinkling the whole tribe to make them vigorous and fruitful. The joints are roasted at twin fires of oak-loppings, kindled with sacred fire

---

[269] The five-fold bond was reported from China by the Arab merchant Suleyman in 851 AD. He writes that "when the man condemned to death has been trussed up in this fashion, and beaten with a fixed number of blows, his body, still faintly breathing, is given over to those who must devour it."

preserved from lightning blasted oak or made by twirling an alder or cornel-wood fire drill in an oak log. [...]

The twelve merry men rush in a wild figure-of-eight dance around the fires, singing ecstatically and tearing at the flesh with their teeth. The bloody remains are burnt in the fire, all except the genitals and the head. These are put into an alder-wood boat and floated down a river to an islet; though the head is sometimes cured with smoke and preserved for oracular use. [...]

To this type of Hercules belong such diverse characters as Hercules of Oeta, Orion the Hunter of Crete, Polyphemus the Cyclops, Samson the Danite, Cuchulain of Muirthemne the Irish Sun-Hero, Ision the Lapth - who is always depicted stretched in a "five-fold bond" around a Sun-wheel - Agag the Amalekite, Romulus of Rome, Zeus, Janus, Anchises, the Dagda and Hermes. [...]

In the classical myth which authorized his sovereignty he is a miraculous child born in a shower of gold; strangles a serpent in his cradle, which is also a boat, and is credited with causing the spurt of milk that made the Milky Way; as a young man he is the undefeated monster-slayer of his age; kills and dismembers a monstrous boar; [...] his other self ... succeeds him for the second half of the year; having acquired royal virtue by marriage with the queen, the representative of the White Goddess, and by eating some royal part of the dead man's body - heart, shoulder or thigh-flesh.[270]

We see in the above all the elements of the Jesus myth, realizing that Jesus was said to have been of the Davidic line, the house of Judah, the Tribe of Dan.

To finish off this little diversion, we find another curious remark about the tribe of Dan in Judges 5:17:

Gilead abode beyond Jordan: and why did Dan remain in ships?

That's a strange thing; an allusion to a sea-faring people? The prophet Amos seems to have some conviction that this tribe of Dan is a serious threat to Yahweh. He writes in 8:14-15:

They that swear by the sin of Samaria, and say, Thy god, Oh Dan, liveth; and, the manner of Beersheba liveth; even they shall fall, and never rise up again.

Amos seems to be suggesting that the "sin of Samaria" is directly connected to the tribe of Dan. And we have some idea already that the "sin of Samaria" was also the sin of Ahab and Jezebel, the House of the Beloved. Which brings us back to the question: just what was the tribe of Dan, and why was it changed to the tribe of Judah? If the tribe of Judah is really the tribe of Dan, then that means that *the House of David is the tribe of Dan.* And following the clues, we discover that this lineage *belonged to Ishmael and Esau,* not to Isaac and Jacob. We further discover that the lineage is that of the "architect of the temple of Solomon", the designer

---

[270] Graves, Robert, *The White Goddess,* (New York: The Noonday Press 1948) pp. 125-6,.

and builder of the Ark of the Covenant, the right hand man of the legendary King Hiram of Tyre.

THE FESTIVAL OF TABERNACLES

This matter of the Tabernacle leads us into some additional interesting speculations. Many scholars believe that the psalms were literary creations for the central festival of the Canaanites: The Festival of Tabernacles, or "booths". The Feast of Tabernacles is a weeklong autumn harvest festival. It is also known as the Feast of the Ingathering, Feast of the Booths, Sukkoth, Succoth, or Sukkot (variations in spellings occur because these words are transliterations of the Hebrew word pronounced "Sue-coat"). The two days following the festival are separate holidays, Shemini Atzeret and Simkhat Torah, but are commonly thought of as part of the Feast of Tabernacles.

One of the more interesting references to what may have been an early celebration of the Feast of Tabernacles occurs in Genesis 33. We discover from our exegetes that verses 1 through 17 are from the E source of the northern kingdom. The incident in question follows a peculiar event in the previous chapter where Jacob sends his family away and remains alone to wrestle with a "man" all night. This "man" is later identified as an angel of God, and the angel "wounds" Jacob in the thigh.

What does it mean to say that Jacob was wounded in the thigh? According to some commentators, he apparently sustained an injury common to wrestlers, the inward displacement of the hip that is produced by *forcing the legs too widely apart*. The injured person finds his leg flexed, abducted and externally rotated. He can only walk with a lurching or swaggering gait, and on his toes. The affected leg is lengthened and this tightens the tendons in the thigh and the muscles go into spasm.

Since the story of Jacob comes to us from the age when women were the transmitters of the right to rule, and since Jacob won his sacred name and inheritance which could only be granted by a woman on this same occasion, it seems that something is wrong with this picture. The element that stands out is that of a transition from the hieros gamos to the ritual combat, with residual sexual overtones.

In the myth of combat between Set and Horus, Set tries to *mate sexually* with Horus. This is usually interpreted as being an insult, but there is something deeper here.

It was a formal principle of Greek myth and literature that love and death were two aspects of the same power. In Homer, there are as many ways to kill as to love, if not more. The language and images are disturbingly interchangeable.

> The verb *damazō* (as also its equivalent *damnēmi*) spans a range of meanings from subjugation to slaughter to rape to seduction, and the "mingling" conveyed by *meignymi* may be that of lovers or that of warriors.

> Both kinds of couples grapple and cling and know a desperate, intense intimacy with few if any parallels anywhere else in human experience. Furthermore, both the love-act and the death-act are accompanied by "small talk" and preceded by a form

of play, a not-yet-violent contest soon to be raised to a higher power and decided or consummated on another plane.[271]

In his *Poetics*, Aristotle traced the origin of poetry to the pleasure human beings derive in mimesis, or "imaging" that which is delightful *or* disturbing. He tells us that, very early, poetry divided into two currents: a poetry of praise and a poetry of assault.

In the Greek war of wars and its subsequent Song of Songs, the *Iliad*, the violation of the city of Troy and the violation of its women became, in the minds of the Bronze Age thinkers, one. The metaphor is linguistically embedded in the word *krēdemna* which means both a city's battlements and women's veils. In the tale of the Trojan war, the shining object of desire was not gold or horses or jewels or even power: it was a woman, Helen.

Outside of the Greek tradition, in the cultural milieu of the Eastern Mediterranean world of the Bronze Age, there was the same convergence of *eros* and *eris*. The theme of violence or the threat of violence provoked by rivalry over a beautiful women which was absent from older literature of the ancient Near East, is evident in the story of Abram, the husband of a remarkably beautiful woman. Fearing that his wife's beauty and desirability might put him at risk, he passes himself off as her brother. In the end, the Pharaoh who takes Abram's wife to his bed is described as anxious to see her go since she brought nothing but plague and disaster to him and his house.

When we peer deeper into this connection between *eros* and *eris*, erotic love and deadly conflict, we find an even older layer preserved in the poetic tradition and enacted in rituals such as that of Jacob and the Angel. In ancient cities, it was the king in his priestly or divine capacity who, with his temple consort, reenacted the hieros gamos, the sacred mating of Heaven and Earth.

The story of Helen of Troy - her great beauty that provoked such grief - is a key to the shift in the perception of women in the ancient world. Hesiod explicated this shift in his story of the first woman, Pandora.

Supposedly Hesiod composed his *Theogony* and *Works and Days* sometime around the 8th or early 7th century BC. It is thought that the works of Hesiod, like the works of Homer, represented the terminus of a vast oral tradition of anonymous voices of uncertain origin and age.

The *Theogony* is an account of origins of those divine beings who created and preside over the cosmos. It is a Divine history, tracing a succession of regimes culminating in the reign of Olympian Zeus. The narratives are undoubtedly rooted in an array of succession myths that circulated throughout the ancient Near East, and which, due to the cosmopolitan nature of the Omride kingdom, were familiar

---

[271] Meagher, Robert Emmet, *Helen: Myth, Legend and the Culture of Misogyny*, 1995, Continuum, New York, chapter 3.

to the nascent Jews. And this is where it becomes very interesting. The likeliest principal influence on Hesiod's account would seem to be the Hittite versions of the Hurrian Kumarbi and Ullikummi myths as well as the Babylonian *Enuma Elish*. It is suggested that such Oriental material reached Hesiod via Crete and Delphi.

The *Theogony* - like the Bible - is not metaphysics; it is, plainly and simply, a political tool. In the *Theogony*, the regime of Zeus and the reign of Olympian justice are celebrated as the achievement of the aeons just as Yahweh is celebrated in the *Torah*. In the *Theogony*, Hesiod recounts his new version of the beginnings of Creation, making certain to regularly propagandize in favor of Zeus who is as "just as he is terrible". Many passages in the *Theogony* can be compared to the hymns to Yahweh supposedly composed by David, or to the *Enuma Elish* which sings the praises of the warrior king, Marduk. In each case, there is a fusion of military might with absolute authority, glory and promised justice to the exiled and enslaved. And clearly, in each instance there is the complete subordination of the female to the male, presented as a philosophical achievement, an evolution from the old, savage, order to the new, glorious world of male theriomorphism.

In the *Theogony*, the first woman is the "*kalon kakon*". *Kalon* means "beautiful" and *kakon* means "evil". In other words, the first woman is a living oxymoron. Now, of course, this term could mean either "beautiful evil" or "evil beauty". That is to say, is woman essentially beautiful and qualifiedly evil, or essentially evil though qualifiedly beautiful, or both essentially evil and beautiful?

Hesiod doesn't leave us in suspense because he clarifies this point for us by telling us that it is *kakon* that defines the substance, or essence or woman. Woman is revealed as unambiguously evil. "Thunderous Zeus made women to be a *kakon* for mortal men [...] he fashioned this *kakon* for men to make them pay for the theft of fire."

Prometheus was provoked by Zeus' withdrawal of fire from mankind in retaliation for Prometheus' earlier theft of the finest sacrificial portions. Prometheus had proven himself more clever than Zeus, outwitting the king of the gods. In the first instance, Prometheus wrapped the meat and fatty portions of the sacrificial ox in the victim's inedible hide and stomach and then wrapped the bare bones in glistening fat, knowing that Zeus would mistakenly insist on the latter as his prerogative. In the second instance, Prometheus concealed living embers in a hollow fennel stalk, enabling him to elude Zeus' embargo and to return fire to mankind.

The theme is "skill" or "craft" that is used to create a "ruse" or *dolon*. The words *techne*, *dolie*, and *dolon* occur repeatedly in Hesiod's account of Prometheus's offenses which lead up to Zeus's retaliation in kind.

It is the word *dolon* that describes woman: once she is dressed, veiled and crowned, she is called a dolon, a trick, a baited trap. Woman, fashioned and dressed up by the gods is a fitting retort for the glistening bag of bones foisted on Zeus by Prometheus.

According to Hesiod, the difference between woman's beauty and her evil is the difference between surface appearances and reality. Decked out in flowers and gold, woman is a *thauma*, a "wonder to behold", and men and gods alike are filled with awe at the sight of her. However, it is only men who are defenseless against her charms. Woman is a "lure" and men have no "resistance" and it was designed that way by the gods. A man is unable to resist the irresistible bride who, after they get her home and exhaust her superficial charms, will find that they are stuck with a great misery, a bottomless pit into which they will pour all their goods and efforts and life force.

And so it is, the moment of woman's creation is the moment of man's destruction. In other words, the sacrifice to the gods that went wrong - a brief insubordination - ends in humanity's endless misery with a vengeance.

However, what is not initially seen is that the issue is actually sovereignty. Prometheus has issued two stunning challenges to Zeus' wit and rule in the name of humankind. The fact is, the four sons of Iapetus[272] and Clymene - Atlas, Menoetius, Prometheus, and Epimetheus - were trouble to Zeus from the start because they represent a *rival line of descent* from Ouranos and Gaia, which, if allied with unruly mankind, could mean trouble for the gods! The most troublesome of the four was Prometheus. His name means "forethought," and his knowledge of what was to come is what inspired him to try to help mankind. He was an arch-rebel and champion of mankind who was determined to elevate the status of humanity by giving them creative imagination, defiant wit, and divine fire - all that is needed to make them like gods.

The story suggests to us a "contest" between humankind and the gods that was to be decided in the act of animal sacrifice.[273] The humiliation of Zeus prompted him to take the extreme measure of withholding fire from mankind, without which they would soon be little more than animals. Humiliated the second time, Zeus formulated the Final Solution: Woman.

In Hesiod's *Works and Days*, Four ages of man have now come and gone, each one worse than the one before. Strife defines every relationship, virtue (as well as everything else) is rewarded with misery, and Hesiod recounts with great longing how men once lived without toil and without pain. Why so much pain and suffering? Hesiod's account of the Fall of man answers that question with one word: Woman.

The "first woman" in *Works and Days*, Pandora, is again, bait set by the gods to trap men. She is given the appearance of a goddess, the character of a hyena, and the heart and mind of a jackal. Woman, adorned by the gods, brings to man all that is hideous and devouring. Woman, who takes all that is bright and beautiful from

---

[272] A Titan, son of Gaia and Uranus. Clymene, and Ocianid, bore him the Titans Prometheus, Epimetheus, Atlas, and Menoetius. In the war between gods and Titans, he was imprisoned by Zeus in Tartarus.

[273] There are curious reflections in this story of the sacrifice challenge of Prometheus to the story of the challenge made by Elisha against the priests of Baal, following which fire came down from heaven to consume Elisha's sacrifice.

man, gives back only that which is dark and filthy. Her name, Pandora, means both "All Giver" and "All Gifted". Hesiod tells us that she is called Pandora because, "all those who dwell on Olympos gave each one to her a gift, a grief for men who strive and toil". She has only one reason for her existence: to produce human misery.

The gifts Pandora receives from the gods - the contents of Pandora's Jar - are intended to produce endless torment for man. It is only in later centuries that a "box" was substituted for a "jar". This change of imagery was attributed to the sixteenth century monk Erasmus who mistranslated the original Greek word *pithos* with the Latin *pyxis*. A pithos is a jar that is womb-like in shape and is a symbol for the earth, the mother of all.

The implications of the pithos to the story of Pandora are obvious. Pandora's gifts are released from her own womb. Her fault lies not in her curiosity, but in her being. She is constitutionally deceptive and lethal because she draws men into her pithos, and brings new men forth for a life of misery. She further perpetuates the misery of man by bringing forth female babies.

The image of Woman as a pithos is extremely ancient. In many ancient Helladic burials, the pithos was used as a coffin. The deceased was placed inside in a fetal position, covered with honey, and buried in the hope of new life and regeneration. Hesiod records for us ideas that were, apparently, spreading like wildfire in his time: the profound estrangement of one half of humanity from the other. We should like to know why?

In Hesiod's re-writing of the ancient myths, man has somehow come into being without being born of woman and contrary to the most ancient depictions, it is woman who is derivative. Certainly, the emergence of the first human being presents a challenge to any thinking person; the existence of women before men is a mystery, but the existence of men before women is absurd.

Hesiod presents the view that woman is a disruption to nature. Because of woman, man can no longer *appear and disappear by his own will*. Because of woman, man must be born in suffering, and then man must die in suffering. What Hesiod fails to notice is that, if men were suffering in that time, women were suffering also - and probably a lot more.

Hesiod's account of woman is a conscious denial and a deliberate misogynistic propaganda. We see Hesiod's line of argument reflected in the J Document account of creation. In Genesis, man is created and lives in a deathless, god-like existence, and woman is the "second" creation, the "afterthought". She soon brings death and destruction on mankind by "eating of the fruit of the tree of good and evil".

In these accounts, we perceive a common thread of woman as an "interloper" into the original scheme of things, bringing sex, strife, misery and death. Hesiod works with the ancient images of the all-giving mother, twisting and disfiguring them until they reflect only the shame and degradation of the creatress of life. Woman, created from clay according to Hesiod, is not only not semi-divine as is man, she is something less than human.

Zeus, with timely advice from Ouranos and Gaia, appropriates his own wife's powers. He marries and swallows Metis and is thus able to give birth to his daughter, Athena. In swallowing Metis, he reverses the succession and the primacy of female fecundity, and thus becomes sovereignty itself. Hesiod's insistence that Zeus does so with the consent of both Ouranos and Gaia sounds like the ritual charade in which consent is elicited from sacrificial animals just prior to their deaths. This claim to the agreement of the older gods is designed to give this most radical of reversions a certain "legitimacy" and "continuity" with the past. With the parthenogenetic birth of Athena from the head of Zeus, history has a new beginning in which woman will play no role.

The entire theme of *Theogony* is - as Hesiod would have it - a triumphal ascent from the female womb of Gaia to the male womb of Zeus, from savage nature, to Olympian civilization. These were the ideas making their way around the Eastern Mediterranean during the time in which the Bible was being written. It's difficult to even suggest the source. Yahweh, like Marduk and Zeus sweeps the field of rivals, making his power incontestable. This brings us back to the Theophany of Jacob, wrestling with the Angel, during which incident he apparently sustained an injury common to wrestlers, the inward displacement of the hip that is produced by *forcing the legs too widely apart.*

> The dream of a purely paternal heredity never ceased to haunt the Greek imagination. Greek poetry is resonant with the voices of men who long for a world exorcised of women, a world in which men by themselves are capable of producing their own sons. [...]
>
> Here, Mysogyny may be seen to conspire with the love of men for men; for when men make love to men, their seed often finds its way to the head and to the thighs, the would-be wombs of Zeus.[274]

The fact is that there was organized sodomy in many temples of the late Bronze Age where male devotees sought to "become women". We note that circumcision is a symbolic castration, and many male devotees attempted to become a woman, to receive the seed of the god directly.

Immediately after this wrestling match, the "angel" then changed Jacob's name from Jacob, meaning "supplanter, schemer, trickster and swindler", to *Israel.* This certainly mirrors Hesiod's depiction of woman as schemers and tricksters. In fact, Jacob was noted as being "feminine" and completely unlike his brother, the rough and ready Esau, so much so that his father disdained him.

The name changing incident after a meeting with a "divine being" reminds us of the name-changing incident of Abraham which followed an appearance of Yahweh and the making of the famous "covenant" which was immediately followed by the circumcision of both Abraham and Ishmael[275], which leads to another odd "doublet" in terms of essential events: Moses. Immediately after the

---

[274] Meagher, Robert Emmet, *Helen: Myth, Legend and the Culture of Misogyny*, 1995, Continuum, New York, chapter 3.

[275] *The Bible*, Genesis 17:22-26.

"burning bush" incident in which God talked to Moses telling him to go back to Egypt and free his people, the following happens:

> 4:24 And it came to pass by the way in the inn, that the LORD met him, and sought to kill him.
>
> 4:25 Then Zipporah took a sharp stone, and cut off the foreskin of her son, and cast it at his feet, and said, Surely a bloody husband art thou to me.
>
> 4:26 So he let him go: then she said, A bloody husband thou art, because of the circumcision.

This incident is like a "connecting link" between the story of Abraham and the covenant of circumcision, the story of Jacob wrestling with the Angel, *and* the story of Moses. We begin to suspect that, at the root of all the Bible stories is a single story that was mythicized in different tribal groups, and then later the different stories were reassembled and "historicized". Names were changed within each tribe by assimilating their own ancestors to the primary story, so it was only necessary to insert genealogies to make the different variations on the same story look "vertical" in time, when in fact, they were horizontal in time.

Getting back to the story of Jacob, while he was still in the womb, Jacob supplanted his twin, Esau, by catching hold of his heel, draining him of royal virtue. The Greek word *pternizein*, used by the Septuagint in this context, means to "trip up someone's heel". This brings us around again to the issue of Dan. We recall that Dan was the child of Rachel's maid, Bilhah:

> Bilhah conceived, and bare Jacob a son. And Rachel said, *God hath judged me*, and hath also heard my voice, and hath given me a son: therefore called she his name Dan.

...which is similar to the story of Sarai and Hagar in Genesis 16:1-5

> And he had intercourse with Hagar and she conceived: and when she saw that she had conceived, her mistress was despised in her eyes. And Sarai said unto Abram, My wrong be upon thee: I have given my maid into thy bosom; and when she saw that she had conceived, I was despised in her eyes: *the Lord judge between me and thee.*

...compared to Genesis 49, where the patriarch Jacob has called all his children to gather around his deathbed so that he can pronounce their destiny upon them. When he gets to Dan, in verses 16 -18, he says:

> Dan shall *judge* his people, *as one of the tribes of Israel*. Dan shall be a serpent by the way, a horned snake in the path, that *bites at the horse's heels*, so that his rider shall fall backward. I wait for thy salvation, O Lord."

...compared to Deuteronomy 33:22, where Moses blesses the tribe of Dan by saying, "*And of Dan he said, Dan is a* lion's whelp" ... But in the blessing of Jacob, in Genesis 49:8-9 the *attribute of the Lion* is given to Judah:

> Judah, you are the one whom your brothers shall praise. Your hand shall be on the neck of your enemies; your father's sons shall bow down to you. Judah, a *lion's cub!*

...compared to the destiny prescribed by God when he appears to Hagar at the well when she ran away after Sarai was cruel to her during her pregnancy, and finally, the blessing given by Isaac to his beloved son Esau after Jacob had defrauded his father with the help of his mother, Rebekah.

There are interesting resonances to the remarks made about Judah. The first event is recounted in Genesis 16:11-12, and the second in Genesis 27:39-40:

> 1) And the angel of the Lord said unto her, Behold, you are with child and shall bear a son, and shalt call his name Ishmael, or God hears, because the Lord has heard and paid attention to your affliction. And [Ishmael] will be as a wild man; his hand will be against every man, and every man's hand against him; and he shall live to the east and on the borders of all his kinsmen.
>
> 2) And Isaac his father answered and said unto [Esau], Behold, Your dwelling shall all come from the fruitfulness of the earth, and from the dew of heaven from above; And by your sword shalt you live, and serve your brother. But the time will come when you will have the dominion, and you will break his yoke from off your neck.

To look at this a bit more deeply, let's see the story of Jacob's birth from Genesis:

> 25:21 And Isaac intreated the LORD for his wife, because she was barren: and the LORD was intreated of him, and Rebekah his wife conceived.
>
> 25:22 And the children struggled together within her; and she said, If it be so, why am I thus? And she went to enquire of the LORD.
>
> 25:23 And the LORD said unto her, Two nations are in thy womb, and two manner of people shall be separated from thy bowels; and the one people shall be stronger than the other people; and the elder shall serve the younger.
>
> 25:24 And when her days to be delivered were fulfilled, behold, there were twins in her womb.
>
> 25:25 And the first came out red, all over like an hairy garment; and they called his name Esau.
>
> 25:26 And after that came his brother out, and his hand took hold on *Esau's heel*; and his name was called Jacob: and Isaac was threescore years old when she bare them.

Again we have a barren wife, only in this case, instead of having a maid to give birth to the "other brother", Rebekah has twins, and one of them is "red". The story that connects this back to Judah and Dan is the story of Tamar.

> 38:6 And Judah took a wife for Er his firstborn, whose name was Tamar.
>
> 38:7 And Er, Judah's firstborn, was wicked in the sight of the LORD; and the LORD slew him.
>
> 38:8 And Judah said unto Onan, Go in unto thy brother's wife, and marry her, and raise up seed to thy brother.
>
> 38:9 And Onan knew that the seed should not be his; and it came to pass, when he went in unto his brother's wife, that he spilled it on the ground, lest that he should give seed to his brother.
>
> 38:10 And the thing which he did displeased the LORD: wherefore he slew him also.
>
> 38:11 Then said Judah to Tamar his daughter in law, Remain a widow at thy father's house, till Shelah my son be grown: for he said, Lest peradventure he die also, as his brethren did. And Tamar went and dwelt in her father's house.
>
> 38:12 And in process of time the daughter of Shuah Judah's wife died; and Judah was comforted, and went up unto his sheepshearers to Timnath, he and his friend Hirah the Adullamite.
>
> 38:13 And it was told Tamar, saying, Behold thy father in law goeth up to Timnath to shear his sheep.
>
> 38:14 And she put her widow's garments off from her, and covered her with a vail,

and wrapped herself, and sat in an open place, which is by the way to Timnath; for she saw that Shelah was grown, and she was not given unto him to wife.

38:15 When Judah saw her, he thought her to be an harlot; because she had covered her face.

38:16 And he turned unto her by the way, and said, Go to, I pray thee, let me come in unto thee; (for he knew not that she was his daughter in law.) And she said, What wilt thou give me, that thou mayest come in unto me?

38:17 And he said, I will send thee a kid from the flock. And she said, Wilt thou give me a pledge, till thou send it?

38:18 And he said, What pledge shall I give thee? And she said, Thy signet, and thy bracelets, and thy staff that is in thine hand. And he gave it her, and came in unto her, and she conceived by him.

38:19 And she arose, and went away, and laid by her vail from her, and put on the garments of her widowhood.

38:20 And Judah sent the kid by the hand of his friend the Adullamite, to receive his pledge from the woman's hand: but he found her not.

38:21 Then he asked the men of that place, saying, Where is the harlot, that was openly by the way side? And they said, There was no harlot in this place.

38:22 And he returned to Judah, and said, I cannot find her; and also the men of the place said, that there was no harlot in this place.

38:23 And Judah said, Let her take it to her, lest we be shamed: behold, I sent this kid, and thou hast not found her.

38:24 And it came to pass about three months after, that it was told Judah, saying, Tamar thy daughter in law hath played the harlot; and also, behold, she is with child by whoredom. And Judah said, Bring her forth, and let her be burnt.

38:25 When she was brought forth, she sent to her father in law, saying, By the man, whose these are, am I with child: and she said, Discern, I pray thee, whose are these, the signet, and bracelets, and staff.

38:26 And Judah acknowledged them, and said, She hath been more righteous than I; because that I gave her not to Shelah my son. And he knew her again no more.

38:27 And it came to pass in the time of her travail, that, behold, twins were in her womb.

38:28 And it came to pass, when she travailed, that the one put out his hand: and the midwife took and bound upon his hand a *scarlet thread*, saying, This came out first.

38:29 And it came to pass, as he drew back his hand, that, behold, his brother came out: and she said, How hast thou broken forth? this breach be upon thee: therefore his name was called Pharez.

38:30 And afterward came out his brother, that had the scarlet thread upon his hand: and his name was called Zarah.

Notice that the story of the birth is told in identical terms except that instead of a "red man", we have a "scarlet thread". The important thing about Pharez is that he was the purported ancestor of King David. Pharez had another son, Hezron about whom it was said:

2:18 And Caleb the son of Hezron begat [...] took unto him Ephrath, which bare him Hur.

2:20 And Hur begat Uri, and Uri begat Bezaleel.

Remember Hur and Uri and Bezaleel who were supposed to have lived at the time of Moses? We found a descriptive hint of them in the story about the architect sent by Hiram of Tyre. In II Kings we find this:

> 4:7 And Solomon had twelve officers over all Israel, which provided victuals for the king and his household: each man his month in a year made provision.
> 4:8 And these are their names: The son of Hur, in mount Ephraim: ...

This Hur is a most mysterious individual. He appears at Moses' side:

> 17:10 So Joshua did as Moses had said to him, and fought with Amalek: and Moses, Aaron, and Hur went up to the top of the hill.
> 17:11 And it came to pass, when Moses held up his hand, that Israel prevailed: and when he let down his hand, Amalek prevailed.
> 17:12 But Moses hands were heavy; and they took a stone, and put it under him, and he sat thereon; and Aaron and Hur stayed up his hands, the one on the one side, and the other on the other side; and his hands were steady until the going down of the sun.

It all becomes even more mysterious when we consider the names of Terah's other sons: Nahor, and Haran which remind us homophonically of Hur and Aaron...

Getting back to Jacob, after his wrestling match, he becomes the sacred king in a new way: instead of marrying the representative of the goddess, he has usurped that role and has succeeded to his office by becoming like a woman. In I Kings, 18:26, where the priests of Baal dance at the altar and cry out, "Baal, hear us!", they leaped up and down, according to the Authorized Version. The original Hebrew word is formed from the root *psch*, which means "to dance with a limp", and from which Pesach, the name of the Passover Feast, is derived.

The Passover seems to have been a Canaanite Spring festival which the creators of the Bible adapted to their own use as commemoration of the Exodus from Egypt. At Carmel, the dance with a limp may have been a form of sympathetic magic to encourage the appearance of the God with a bull's foot who was armed, like Dionysus, with a torch. The writer of the Bible refrains from mentioning his real name, but since those particular priests of Baal (and Baal merely means "lord") were Israelites, it is likely to have been "Jah Aceb" of "Jacob", the Heel God. Jah Aceb seems to have been also worshipped at Beth-Hoglah, the Shrine of the Hobbler, between Jericho and the Jordan south of Gilgal. This has been identified as the threshing floor of Atad where Joseph mourned for Jacob.

After his "wounding in the thigh" incident, Jacob travels on to meet his estranged brother, Esau, whom he swindled many years before, and being afraid of Esau's wrath, he put his children and wives in the front of the cavalcade in hopes that they would soften his brother's heart so Esau wouldn't kill him.[276]

But Esau was long past any rancor, and he embraced Jacob and *accepted his gifts of livestock and possibly even slaves.* The story then takes a truly bizarre twist. Apparently Esau thought that Jacob/Israel was going to travel with him to

---

[276] In other words, he was hiding behind the womens' skirts.

Seir. But Jacob hemmed and hawed and finally told Esau to go on ahead. Then, after Esau had left, Jacob went in a completely different direction where it is said he, "*built himself a house, and made booths or places of shelter for his livestock; so the name of the place is called Succoth*". (v. 17)

When we investigate this word, we discover that the archaic meaning of it was that of a small cubicle set up by a "temple prostitute" along the side of the road as in the story of Judah and Tamar in Genesis 38:14, from the J document!

This brings us back to the question of what was the Canaanite Festival of Tabernacles?

The ancient Greek civilization dedicated one of their harvest festivals to the goddess of the earth and all grain, Demeter. The festival, known as the *Thesmosphoria,* was celebrated for three days and featured the building of shelters by married women, fasting and offerings to Demeter. The connection between married women and the festival may point to a belief that childbearing and healthy crops were interconnected. The word *Mete* is, of course, related to mother, and *De* is the delta, or triangle, a female genital sign. This letter in the ancient alphabets originally represented the Door of birth, death, or sexual paradise. Thus, the "booth" or Tabernacle, was little more than a structure set up to manifest a "doorway". Doorways in general were considered sacred to the Goddesses, and in Sumeria they were painted red to represent the female "blood of life". In Egypt, doorways were smeared with real blood for the religious rites of the goddess. Where have we heard of that before?

The cult of Demeter which celebrated the *Eleusinian rites* was well established in Mycenae in the 13th century BC, and it is more than likely that the Feast of Tabernacles in Canaan was an offshoot of this activity. Our sources of information regarding the Eleusinian Mysteries include the ruins of the sanctuary there, numerous statues, bas reliefs, and pottery. We also have reports from ancient writers such as Aeschylos, Sophocles, Herodotus, Aristophanes, Plutarch, and Pausanias - *all of whom were initiates* - as well as the accounts of Christian commentators like Clement of Alexandria, Hippolytus, Tertullian, and Astorias, who were critics and not initiates. Yet for all this evidence, the true nature of the Mysteries remains shrouded in uncertainty because the participants were remarkably steadfast in honoring their pledge not to reveal what took place in the Telesterion, or inner sanctum of the Temple of Demeter. To violate that oath of secrecy was a capital offense.[277] For these reasons, scholars today must make use of circumstantial evidence and inferences, with the result that there is still no consensus as to what did or did not take place.

---

[277] Aeschylos, for example, once had to fear for his life on account of coming too close to revealing forbidden truths.

Foucart and his followers concluded that the Mysteries at Eleusis originally must have come from Egypt. The fact is, the sanctuary ruins in Eleusis evidently go back centuries earlier than the Egyptian *Hymn to Demeter* recited by Homer that is often cited as the proof that the origin was Egyptian. What is more, the excavations have unearthed no Egyptian artifacts there from that period.

Many scholars today favor the view that the cult of Demeter probably derived from Thessaly or Thrace. They base this conclusion partly on references in Homer and other ancient authors to some evidently pre-Dorian temples to Demeter in the Thessalian towns of Thermopylae, Pyrasos, and Pherai; partly on certain etymological links connecting key words in the rites of Demeter to pre-Hellenic dialects from the north. Other scholars point out that Demeter may be the same as a goddess "Dameter", who is mentioned briefly in Linear B tablets from Pylos dating from approximately 1200 BC. This evidence suggests that the cult of Demeter may, after all, have originated in the southern Peleponnesus.

In any case, whether the specific cult of Demeter at Eleusis originated in northern or southern Greece, the undeniable parallels with worship of grain goddesses in other parts of the eastern Mediterranean region point to frequent contacts and the cross-fertilization of religious ideas. And while we certainly think that the Canaanite Feast of Tabernacles was a corrupted version of some more ancient form, we also think that there is something very mysterious going on behind this deliberate establishing of the Tabernacle as the place where the laws of Yahweh were kept, so as to convert it from some other, prior function.

As it happens, the term "Thesmophoria" is derived from *thesmoi,* meaning, "laws", and *phoria*, "carrying", in reference to the goddess as "*law-bearer*". But the symbolism of the ark of the covenant with Yahweh as the "law bearer" in the "tent of meeting", or the "Mother-Delta", the "doorway to the higher realms", replaced the original meaning and the role of women in the process.

Entire books are written that are full of speculations about the Eleusinian rites. I may write one some day myself, but, let me cut to the chase here: The closest we can come to understanding the goal of these rites is to suggest that they had to do with "ascent" or "descent" to other realms in order to perform the archetypal act of creation of the New Year.

We already have some idea what these rites and celebrations represented since they show clear parallels to the Grail ensemble we examined briefly in the earlier chapters of this book. The New Year festivals of the ancients included rites that symbolized the cyclical nature of time, the exhaustion of cosmic resources resulting in chaos, followed by the *hieros gamos*, or sacred marriage. This was, effectively, the "planting of the seed" into the new universe, or the "passage" through the waters of the flood, in an ark, into the new world. It may also represent, in its most original form, a utilization of the knowledge of Time Loops - a Time Machine.

In this sense, it seems only reasonable to suggest that the ascent or descent may have been the *function or goal* of the hieros gamos itself and that perhaps the sacred intercourse that symbolized union with the Goddess, also indicated in act, if not in fact, the meeting of man with the divinity, and the receiving of the "laws" or "destinies" for the entire group during the coming year. Taking this imagery even further into the past - the hypothesized ancient science - it may be that the hieros gamos was only another symbol of the "dissolving into time" of a Time Machine.

It was during the hieros gamos that the lights were extinguished, the hierogamy took place under the direction of the hierophant, *in a tent erected for privacy*, and when the lights were re-lit, it was a symbol that the old year had died, and the seed had been planted for the new year to be born. It is said that, "*the ultimate mystery was revealed at Eleusis in the words, 'an ear of corn reaped in silence'* - a sacred fetish that the Jews called *shibboleth*".[278]

This business of the "shibboleth" is an interesting clue here. The word itself is derived from an unused Hebrew root, *shebel*, which means, "to flow" as a lady's train, or something that *trails after a woman or flows out of her*. Thus, the "ear of corn" is seen as something that grows "out of a woman", or that grain "flows from her", as grain is the gift of the goddess. We have here an image of just exactly what bio-electronic energy may have been required to transduce cosmic energy to bring down the cars full of baskets of grain as described in the *Rg Veda*:

> The adorable Maruts, armed with bright lances and cuirassed with golden breastplates, enjoy vigorous existence; *may the cars of the quick-moving Maruts arrive for our good.* ...Bringers of rain and fertility, shedding water, *augmenting food.* ...Givers of abundant food. ...Your milchkine are never dry. ...We invoke *the food-laden chariots* of the Maruts."[279]

The word "shibboleth" occurs only one place in the Bible, in a truly tragic story in the book of Judges, chapters 11 and 12. It seems that there was a man named Jephthah who was the son of a harlot. He was kicked out of the family home by the legitimate sons of his father, Gilead, and went off and became a sort of leader of other dispossessed persons. Sounds rather like Robin Hood so far. Also sounds like David during his outlaw days.

As it happened, his brothers who had kicked him out, the "elders of Gilead", were being attacked by the "children of Ammon". They desperately needed help, and they knew that Jephthah had a reputation as a fierce warrior with a well-trained band of "merry men". So, they went to ask Jephthah for help.

Jephthah pointed out that they had a lot of nerve asking him to help them fight their battles, but they persuaded him by saying "if you help us now, we will make you head of the family". That was more than Jephthah could resist, so he agreed. Not only that, but he swore a public oath to Yahweh that if Yahweh made him successful in this enterprise, he would give as a burnt offering "*whatsoever cometh forth of the doors of my house to meet me, when I return*". I'm sure the reader sees what is coming now. Jephthah was, indeed, successful in his battle.

---

[278] D'Alviella, Count Goblet, *The Migration of Symbols*, (New York: University Books 1956).

[279] *Rg-Veda*, Vol III.

And Jephthah came to Mizpeh unto his house, and, behold, *his daughter came out to meet him* with timbrels and with dances: and she was his only child; beside her he had neither son nor daughter.

And it came to pass, when he saw her, that he rent his clothes, and said, Alas, my daughter! thou hast brought me very low, and thou art one of them that trouble me: for I have opened my mouth unto the LORD, and I cannot go back.

And she said unto him, My father, if thou hast opened thy mouth unto the Lord, do to me according to that which hath proceeded out of thy mouth; forasmuch as the Lord hath taken vengeance for thee of thine enemies, even of the children of Ammon.

And she said unto her father, Let this thing be done for me: let me alone two months, that I may go up and down upon the mountains, and bewail my virginity, I and my fellows. And he said, Go. And he sent her away for two months: and she went with her companions, and bewailed her virginity upon the mountains.

And it came to pass at the end of two months, that she returned unto her father, who did with her according to his vow which he had vowed: and she knew no man. And it was a custom in Israel, That the daughters of Israel went yearly to lament the daughter of Jephthah the Gileadite four days in a year.

Well, aside from the fact that if we are to take the Bible literally, we have here a definite indication that Yahweh was originally a God who may have *demanded* human sacrifice, we most definitely have an indication that Yahweh at least *accepted* human sacrifice upon occasion! But, in another sense, this is merely another version of the story where Abraham almost sacrificed his son Isaac, which is almost identical to a Vedic story of Manu. These acts were based on what was called *sraddha* which is related to the words *fides*, *credo*, faith, believe and so on.[280]

The word *sraddha* was, according to Dumezil and Levi, too hastily understood as "faith" in the Christian sense. Correctly understood, it means something like the trust a workman has in his tools and techniques as acts of magic! It is, therefore, part of a "covenant" wherein the sacrificer knows how to perform a prescribed sacrifice correctly, and who also knows that if he performs the sacrifice correctly, it *must* produce its effect.

In short, it is an act that is designed to gain control over the forces of life that reside in the god with whom one has made the covenant. Gods such as these, who make covenants are not "literary ornaments" or abstractions. They are active partners with intelligence, strength, passion, and a tendency to get out of control if the sacrifices are not performed correctly. In this sense, the sacrifice is simply magic.

---

[280] Meillet, Antoine, Memoires de la Society de Linguistique de Paris, XXII, 1992.

In another sense, the ascetic or "self-sacrificer", is a person who is striving for release from the bondage and order of nature by the act of attempting to mortify the self, the flesh; testing and increasing the will *for the purpose of winning tyrannical powers while still in the world*. He seeks mastery of himself, other men, and even the gods themselves.

In the story of Manu from India, we find that he has a mania for sacrifice just as the ascetics and saints have a mania for self-sacrifice. The most famous of the stories depicts Manu, enslaved to his *sraddha*, giving up everything of value in his life to the demonic "Asura brahmans, Trsta and Varutri". To get something from Manu, all these demons need to do is say "Manu, you are a sacrificer, your god is sraddha". So, one thing after another is demanded of him, and finally even his wife, Manavi. Indra, however, intervenes at this point to save Manavi and appears to Manu and uses the same words, *"Manu, you are a sacrificer, your god is sraddha"*. To foil the plot of the demonic Brahmins who have produced in Manu the state of *sraddha*, or the *belief in the necessity of sacrifice*, Indra demands the sacrifice of the two demonic Brahmins themselves! Manu, being a devotee of *sraddha*, hands them over without any difficulty, and Indra beheads them with the water of the sacrifice.

Acts of sacrifice are, effectively, *acts of trade* - an execution of a contract of exchange between man and divinity. "I give that you may give." In the story in the Bible where Cain's sacrifice of grain was rejected, we find a reflection of the idea that a god *evaluates* the greater or lesser worth of a proposed offering.

Manu, deprived of his victim by the merciful intervention of Indra, did not like his "rights" to be infringed. "Finish my sacrifice!", he said to Indra. Indra gives him a pledge: *"The desire you had in taking your wife for your victim, let that desire be granted you; but let that woman be!"*[281]

In the story of Abraham's sacrifice of his son, Isaac, and the appearance of the ram in the thicket, we have a most interesting variation on this theme. Agni is equated with Vasishtha, "lotus born", or "of the goddess".

In the story of Jephthah's daughter, we find that the editor of the biblical texts felt that the story could not be removed, but had to disguise the true nature of the sacrifice. The matter becomes clearer with the following:

> Llew Llaw Gyffes (the Lion with the Steady Hand), a type of Dionysus or Celestial Hercules worshipped in ancient Britain, is generally identified with Lugh, the Goidelic Sun-god... 'Would that it were no more than the Sun! It is the glowing face of Lugh the Long-handed - which nobody could gaze upon without being dazzled.'

---

[281] Sylvain Levi, quoted by Dumezil, Georges, *Mitra-Varuna: An Essay on Two Indo-European Representations of Sovereignty* (Zone Books; reprint edition 1988) p. 63.

His death on the first Sunday in August - called Lugh nasadh, later altered to Lugh-mass or Lammas - was until recently observed in Ireland with Good Friday-like mourning and kept as a feast of dead kinsfolk, the mourning procession being always led by a young man carrying a hooped wreath. Lammas was also observed as a mourning feast in most parts of England in mediaeval times...

In some parts of Wales, Lammas is still kept as a fair. Sir John Rhys records that in the 1850's the hills of Fan Fach and South Barrule in Carmarthenshire were crowded with mourners for Llew Llaw on the first Sunday in August, their excuse being that they were 'going up to bewail Jephthah's daughter on the mountain'. This, oddly enough, was the very same excuse that the post-Exilic Jewish girls had used, after the Deuteronomic reforms, to disguise their mourning for Tammuz, Llew Llaw's Palestinian counterpart.[282]

The sacrifice of Jephthah's daughter is, thus, another instance where the new view of women as explicated by Hesiod and his Bible writing counterparts was being imposed on the Eastern Mediterranean world. It's interesting to think about Pandora's "pithoi" from which troubles flowed with the clue of the shibboleth that is included in the story of Jephthah:

12:4 Then Jephthah gathered together all the men of Gilead, and fought with Ephraim: and the men of Gilead smote Ephraim, because they said, Ye Gileadites are fugitives of Ephraim among the Ephraimites, and among the Manassites.
12:5 And the Gileadites took the passages of Jordan before the Ephraimites: and it was so, that when those Ephraimites which were escaped said, Let me go over; that the men of Gilead said unto him, Art thou an Ephraimite? If he said, Nay;
12:6 Then said they unto him, Say now *Shibboleth*: and he said Sibboleth: for he could not frame to pronounce it right. Then they took him, and slew him at the passages of Jordan: and there fell at that time of the Ephraimites forty and two thousand.

Another clue to the Eleusinian rites is that they were said to be celebrated by *women only* throughout all Greece in the month of *Pyanepsion* (late October), their characteristic feature being a *pig sacrifice*, the usual sacrifice to chthonic[283] deities.

The Greeks attributed special powers to pigs on account of their fertility, the potency and abundance of their blood, and perhaps because of their uncanny ability to unearth underground tubers and shoots. Experts suggest that it was believed that mingling pig flesh with the seeds of grain would increase the abundance of next year's harvest. The scholars also tell us that the ceremonies comprised fasting and purification, a *ritualized descent into the underworld*, and the use of sympathetic magic to bring renewed life back out of the jaws of death.

---

[282] Robert Graves, *The White Goddess*, (New York: Noonday Press 1948) pp. 302, 303.
[283] "Dark, primitive and mysterious."

Thus we see that the participants in the Themosphoria revered swine, and their rituals featured the washing and sacrificing of young pigs sacred to Demeter (although this took place on the beaches at Pireas near Athens rather than at Eleusis itself). And somehow we find this to be a Canaanite practice that is now very strangely juxtaposed against a religion that is known for its ban on pork. Was that because the sacred animal of the rival religion was the pig, or was it because, in some deep inner core of the founding of the religion of Judaism, the pig is actually protected from being eaten because of reverence? And if so, why would that be the case? Was the pig ever an embodiment of a god? Well, let's look at this for a moment. In Genesis 12:6-7 we find Abraham making a covenant with God.

> And Abram passed through the land unto the place of Sichem, unto the plain of Moreh And the Canaanite was then in the land. And the LORD appeared unto Abram, and said, Unto thy seed will I give this land: and there builded he an altar unto the LORD, who appeared unto him.

Next we find God telling Abraham in Genesis 22:2-3

> And he said, Take now thy son, thine only son Isaac, whom thou lovest, and get thee into the land of Moriah; and offer him there for a burnt offering upon one of the mountains which I will tell thee of. And Abraham rose up early in the morning, and saddled his ass, and took two of his young men with him, and Isaac his son, and clave the wood for the burnt offering, and rose up, and went unto the place of which God had told him.

And in II Chronicles 3:1 we find:

> Then Solomon began to build the house of the LORD at Jerusalem in mount Moriah, where the Lord appeared unto David his father, in the place that David had prepared in the threshing floor of Ornan the Jebusite.

Another name for Moriah is Mount Zion. Isaiah tells us that Mount Zion is the Throne of the Lord of Hosts who, "scatters, distributes and treads underfoot". The "Temple" was built on the "threshing floor" of Ornan (Araunah in another version), symbolic of the harvest god Tammuz, who demanded the "first fruits" of the grain. However, Jehovah wasn't terribly interested in grain. He wanted blood:

> Exodus 34:19 All that openeth the womb is mine; and every firstling among thy cattle, whether ox or sheep, that is male. 34:20 But the firstling of an ass thou shalt redeem with a lamb: and if thou redeem him not, then shalt thou break his neck. All the firstborn of thy sons thou shalt redeem. And none shall appear before me empty. 34:21 Six days thou shalt work, but on the seventh day thou shalt rest: in plowing time and in harvest thou shalt rest.

Jehovah's claim to the Seventh day as sacred to himself identifies him with Cronos or Saturn. The Phrygian Adonis is said to have been metamorphosed into a fir by the Goddess Cybele who loved him, *when he lay dying from a wound dealt him by a boar sent by Zeus.*

Set, the Egyptian Sun-god, *disguised as a boar*, killed Osiris. Apollo the Greek Sun-god, *disguised as a boar*, killed Adonis, or Tammuz, the Syrian, the lover of the Goddess Aphrodite. Finn Mac Cool, *disguised as a boar*, killed Diarmuid, the lover of the Irish Goddess Grainne. An unknown god *disguised as a boar* killed Ancaeus the Arcadian King, a devotee of Artemis, in his vineyard at Tegea, and according to the Nestorian *Gannat Busame*, Cretan Zeus was similarly killed. October was the boar-hunting season, as it was also the revelry season of the ivy-wreathed Bassarids. The boar is the beast of death and the "fall" of the year begins in the month of the boar.

In Egypt, the year was counted as 360 days divided into three 120-day seasons each containing five periods of equal length, 24 days, with five days left over. The Egyptians said that the five days were those which the God Thoth (Hermes) won at draughts from the Moon goddess Isis, composed of the seventy-second parts of every day in the year. The birthdays of Osiris, Horus, Set, Isis and Nephthys were celebrated on them in that order. It seems that, based on the myth, *a change in religion necessitated a change in the calendar*. The old year of 364 days with one day left over was succeeded by a year of 360 days with five left over. Under later Assyrian influence, the three seasons were divided into four periods of thirty days each rather than five periods of 24 each. The 72 day season occurs in the Egypto-Byblian myth that the Goddess Isis hid her child Horus, or Harpocrates, from the rage of the ass-eared Sun-god Set during the 72 hottest days of the year, that third of the five seasons ruled by the Dog star Sirius and the two Asses.

The Greek legend that the God Dionysus placed the Asses in the Sign of Cancer suggests that the Dionysus who visited Egypt and was entertained by Proteus, King of Pharos, was Osiris, brother of the Hyksos god Typhon, alias Set.

According to the Homeric legend of King Proteus, the earliest settlers in the Delta used Pharos, the lighthouse island off what later became Alexandria, as their sacred oracular island. Proteus, king of Pharos, lived in a cave where Menelaus consulted him. He had the power of changing his shape. Apuleius connects the sistrum of Osiris, used to frighten away the god Set, with Pharos. This suggests that Proteus and Osiris were regarded there as the same person. Another Proteus, or Proetus, was an Arcadian.

The wide landing-quay at the entrance to the port of Pharos consisted of rough blocks, some of them sixteen feet long, deeply grooved with a checkerboard pattern of pentagons. Since pentagons are inconvenient figures for such constructions, some researchers think that the number five must have had some important religious significance. Robert Graves asks: "Was Pharos the center of a five-season calendar system?"

The island had been otherwise oddly connected to the numbers five and seventy-two at the beginning of the Christian era. The Jews of Alexandria used to visit the island for an annual festival, the excuse for which was that the Five Books of Moses had been miraculously translated there into Greek by seventy-two doctors of the Law who had worked for seventy-two days each.

What is behind this story?

Festivals in ancient times generally commemorated some sort of treaty or act of unification. What happened here?

Aeschylus calls the Nile Ogygian, and Eustathius the Byzantine grammarian said that Ogygia was the earliest name for Egypt. When the Byblians first brought their Syrian Tempest-god to Egypt, the one who, *disguised as a boar*, yearly killed his brother Adonis, the god always born under a fir-tree, they identified him with Set, the ancient Egyptian god of the desert whose sacred beast was the wild ass, and who yearly destroyed his brother Osiris, the god of the Nile vegetation. Sanchthoniatho the Phoenician, quoted by Philo, says, "the mysteries of Phoenicia were brought to Egypt". He said that the two first inventors of the human race,

Upsouranios and his brother Ousous consecrated two pillars, one to fire and one to wind. These are the earliest forms of the Jachin and Boaz pillars representing Adonis, god of the waxing year and the newborn sun, and Typhon, god of the waning year and of destructive winds. The Hyksos Kings under Byblian influence similarly converted their Tempest-god into Set.

In pre-dynastic times, Set may have been the chief of all the gods of Egypt, since the sign of royalty which all the dynastic gods carried was Set's ass-eared reed scepter. The Egyptians also identified him with the long-eared constellation Orion, "Lord of the Chambers of the South", and the "breath of Set" was the South wind from the deserts which, then as now, causes a wave of criminal violence in Egypt, Libya and Southern Europe whenever it blows. The ass appears in many of the anecdotes of Genesis and the early historical books of the Bible.

Egyptian texts and pictorial records are notorious for their suppression or distortion of fact. It seems that the aristocratic priests of the "Establishment Church of Egypt" had begun to tamper with the popular stories *as early as 2800 BC*. For example: in the *Book of the Dead*, at the Twelfth Hour of Darkness, when Osiris' sun-boat approaches the last gateway of the Other world before his reemergence into the light of day, he is pictured bent backwards in the form of a hoop with his hands raised and his toes touching the back of his head. This is explained as "Osiris whose circuit is the other world". It is supposed to suggest that by adopting this absurd acrobatic posture, Osiris is defining the other world as a circular region thus making the Twelve Hours analogous with the Twelve Signs of the Zodiac. It is clear that a priestly corruption has been imposed on a more archaic understanding. This posture represents Osiris who has been captured by Set, and has been tied, like Ixion or Cuchulain, in the five-fold bond that joined wrists, neck and ankles together. In other words, Osiris in this posture is an economical way of describing the effects on him by the activity of the god of the underworld, the serpent, Set who also appears as a Boar and an Ass.

We now have many more clues about the early formation of the religion of Yahweh, including the description of the construction of the Pillars Jachin and Boaz, historicized myths of the Bible, attributed to Solomon. We also see a connection to the Peribsen rebellion followed by the emergence of the Cretan civilization which was later linked to Judaism.

In the present day, the Jews celebrate their New Year in September of the year around the time of the harvest. This is followed by the Feast of Tabernacles, which is supposed to commemorate the fact that the children of Israel built "temporary shelters" while wandering in the desert, the domain of Set. It is said that it was "in the tent that God first tabernacled with man" during the Exodus. The Tabernacle was a place for the meeting of God with man. The comparisons are so obvious I don't even need to point them out.

Now, returning to our most peculiar story of Jacob wrestling with the "man", following which he went *south* and did the whole "Tabernacles" thing, it is clear that *an ancient ritual drama has been historicized.*

Certain ancient myths tell us that a battle takes place either between two brothers, or between father and son. The battle ends when the elder king is "wounded in the thigh", or ritually castrated to symbolize his loss of potency. The kingdom, represented by the queen, is then given over to the winning brother, or from father to son because the queen symbolizes the land. It is interesting that this drama was enacted between Jacob, and an "angel of Yahweh", playing the role of Set. In this way, the people understood that the kingship had been handed to Yahweh personally because he "Tabernacled with Jacob" playing the role of the goddess. Yahweh, the Boar god.

We need to understand here that these ritual combats, dying kings, cannibalistic and sacrificial activities are only the *extreme* corruptions of an original, core idea that can be seen to represent an ancient technology. Indeed, the technology aspect emerges from time to time, but is often so disguised that it is difficult to sort out the many twists and turns in the threads of transmission. Among the most archaic representations of these ideas - even though we can consider it to still be a corruption of the truly ancient knowledge - are the rites of the Shamans of central Asia.

When we look to the function of the shaman, we discover: the shaman either descends to the underworld to save man, or he ascends to the heavens to intercede with the gods on behalf of his people. He is, in effect, the divinely chosen "knight" who has the "right stuff" to be able to make this journey. The symbolism of the stairs on which the shaman ascends and descends are typically shamanic. The "Tree of Life", the symbol of the birth goddess, is a symbol of the shamanic ascent to the celestial spheres to receive the communication from god concerning the fate of the tribe. In this sense, the cosmic axis and the heavenly book have become joined in terms of symbolism. One can clearly see these elements in the story of Jacob's ladder and his wrestling with the "angel". Unfortunately, Jacob lost the match.

What is most fascinating in terms of shamanic studies is a mysterious "female sickness" that male shamans often suffered. One of the reported (and variable) symptoms of becoming a shaman is that the individual begins to dress as a woman, to act as a woman, and to generally begin a process of feminization. We see a hint of this factor in Jacob's journey south to "build booths" which was a strictly female activity!

This feminization of the shaman directs us to consider the fact that the original shamanic/grail function was most likely *fulfilled by women only*, and at some point, men attempted to dispense with the function of the female and to acquire her attributes and natural shamanic capabilities. It seems that, at the same point in time, the place of the woman in the rites, who was present to "embody" the goddess in the sacred marriage, was replaced by other items, including stairs, celestial trees, and even horses. The rhythmic function of ritual intercourse, which was merely a corruption of the act of "dissolving" into space/time, was replaced by drumming and other trance inducing methods.

The clues to these transitions are held in the very words themselves: knight and mare. Knight is derived from the same root as yogi, or juga, which means "to join together", and the word "mare" for "mer" or Sea of the mother is obvious. In order to get us a bit closer to some idea of how the transitions occur, Eliade remarks on the shamanic role in funerary rites, which have been described and observed. It is thought that these sorts of rites are very similar to the "secret rites" or functions that are hidden by vows of secrecy.

Herodotus has left us a good description of the funerary customs of the Scythians. The funeral was followed by purifications. Hemp was thrown on heated stones and all inhaled the smoke; "the Scythians howl in joy for the vapour-bath." [...] The howls compose a specific religious ensemble, the purpose of which could only be ecstasy. In this connection Meuli cites the Altaic séance described by Radlov, in which the shaman guided to the underworld the soul of a woman who had been dead forty days. The shaman-psychopomp is not found in Herodotus' description; he speaks only of the purifications following a funeral. But among a number of Turko-Tatar peoples such purifications coincide with the shaman's escorting the deceased to his new home, the nether regions.[...]

The use of hemp for ecstatic purposes is also attested among the Iranians, and it is the Iranian word for hemp that is employed to designate mystical intoxication in Central and North Asia.

It is known that the Caucasian peoples, and especially the Osset, have preserved a number of the mythological and religious traditions of the Scythians.

Now, the conceptions of the afterlife held by certain Caucasian peoples are close to those of the Iranians, particularly in regard to the deceased crossing a bridge as narrow as a hair, the myth of a Cosmic Tree whose top touches the sky and at whose root there is a miraculous spring, and so on. Then, too, diviners, seers, and necromancer-psychopomps play a certain role among the mountain Georgian tribes. The most important of these sorcerers are the *messulethe*; their ranks are filled for the most part from among *the women and girls. Their chief office is to escort the dead to the other world, but they can also incarnate them.* [...] The *messulethe* performs her task by falling into trance.[284]

At this point, allow me to interject the comment that we see a curious parallel to the fact that the Themosphoria was celebrated "only by women". In other words, it was very likely an archaic custom of what has been called "sacred prostitution" but the sacred prostitution was clearly derived from archaic techniques of ecstasy which we have surmised were actually *disjecta membra* of an ancient technology that effectively modified DNA. Over millennia of transmission, the terminology describing this DNA factor was corrupted to refer to sexual elements. We shall also later see that what was once a "spiritual idea" was given a literal, physical meaning. The role and participation of women is indeed important, but not at all the way many occultists have interpreted it.

What is clear is that the very ancient idea of women as priestesses, or as so-called "temple prostitutes", was merely derived from the fact of the natural role of the woman as true shaman. When women were extirpated from their role as natural psychopomp for their tribes, a host of other items had to be invented to take their place: trees, bridges (which is a word strikingly similar to "bride" and

---

[284] Eliade, Shamanism, *Archaic Techniques of Ecstasy*, pp. 394-6.

"bridle" as is used for a horse!), ladders, stairs, drums, rattles, chants, dances, and so on; and most especially ritual combat instead of unification.

> We have observed the striking resemblance between the other world ideas of the Caucasians and of the Iranians. For one thing, the *Cinvat bridge* plays an essential role in Iranian funerary mythology; crossing it largely determines the destiny of the soul; and the crossing is a difficult ordeal, equivalent in structure, to initiatory ordeals. [...]

> The Cinvat bridge is at the "Center", at the "middle of the world" and "the height of a hundred men". [...] The bridge connects earth and heaven at the "Center". Under the Cinvat bridge is the pit of hell.

> Here we find a "classic" cosmological schema of the three cosmic regions connected by a central axis (pillar, tree, bridge, etc.) The shamans travel freely among the three zones; the dead must cross a bridge on their journey to the beyond. [...] The important feature of the Iranian tradition is (at least as it survived after Zarathustra's reform) is that, at the crossing of the bridge, there is a sort of struggle between the demons, who try to cast the soul down to hell, and the tutelary spirits who resist them.

> The Gathas[285] make three references to this crossing of the Cinvat bridge. In the first two passages Zarathustra, according to H.S. Nyberg's interpretation, *refers to himself as a psychopomp*. Those who have been *united to him in ecstasy will cross the bridge with ease.*[286] [...]

> The bridge, then, is not only the way for the dead; *it is the road of ecstatics.* [...] The Gathic term *maga* is proof that Zarathustra and his disciples induced an ecstatic experience by ritual songs intoned in chorus *in a closed, consecrated space*. In this sacred space (maga) communication between heaven and earth became possible. [...] The sacred space became a "Center".[...]

> Shamanic ecstasy induced by hemp smoke was known in ancient Iran. [...] In the Videvdat *hemp is demonized*. This seems to us to prove complete hostility to shamanic intoxication. [...] The imagery of the Central Asian shamans would seem to have undergone the influence of Oriental, and principally Iranian, ideas. But this does not mean that the shamanic descent to the underworld derives from an exotic influence. The Oriental contribution only amplified and added color to the dramatic scenarios of punishments; it was the narratives of ecstatic journeys to the underworld that were enriched under Oriental influences; the ecstasy long preceded them. [....]

> We ... have found the technique of ecstasy in archaic cultures where it is impossible to suspect any influence from the ancient East. [...]

---

[285] Zarathustra's hymns.

[286] Here I will comment that the influence of Zoroastrianism on the creation of the Bible may have been profound.

The magico-religious value of intoxication for achieving ecstasy is of Iranian origin. [...]

Concerning the original shamanic experience ... *narcotics are only a vulgar substitute for "pure" trance.*

The use of intoxicants is a recent innovation and points to a decadence in shamanic technique. Narcotic intoxication is called on to provide an *imitation* of a state that the shaman is no longer capable of attaining otherwise. Decadence or vulgarization of a mystical technique - in ancient and modern India, and indeed all through the East, we constantly find this strange mixture of "difficult ways" and "easy ways" of realizing mystical ecstasy or some other decisive experience.[287]

With this very small series of hints, we can deduce that Jacob's dream of the ladder and his ritual combat with the "man" who was an "angel of Yahweh", are simply glosses of the true activities of Jacob as a shaman. Whether or not there was ever a historical Jacob, we can't say. What does seem to be true is that somebody did something at that point in time and was "assimilated" to the myth of the "Heel God". We think again of the encounters between Abraham and God, and Moses and God, resulting in circumcision. In any event, the three events: wrestling with the angel, the name changing, the circumcision of Abraham and the son of Moses, were very likely originally a single event, separated in time and context by the redactor of the Bible who we will soon encounter.

Nevertheless, Jacob lost the battle, failing to fulfill the function of the shaman, and the following day, met his brother, knowing that he had been "mortally wounded", and transferred to him the "blessing" or kingship. My own question is this: was this meeting also a record of the *transferring of some vital item to Esau as a result of his shamanic failure*?

Here, of course, is a stupendously key element that I must explain. As it happens, there is one significant story in the Bible that is claimed as "history" that DOES have external verification in the records of Egypt in the form of the "rest of the story". This story is that of Abram and Sarai in Egypt. And in fact, this is one of the very problematical "triplets". The story goes:

12:10 And there was a famine in the land: and Abram went down into Egypt to sojourn there; for the famine was grievous in the land.
12:11 And it came to pass, when he was come near to enter into Egypt, that he said unto Sarai his wife, Behold now, I know that thou art a fair woman to look upon:
12:12 Therefore it shall come to pass, when the Egyptians shall see thee, that they shall say, This is his wife: and they will kill me, but they will save thee alive.
12:13 Say, I pray thee, thou art my sister: that it may be well with me for thy sake; and my soul shall live because of thee.
12:14 And it came to pass, that, when Abram was come into Egypt, the Egyptians

---

[287] Eliade, Shamanism, Archaic Techniques of Ecstasy, pp. 396-401.

beheld the woman that she was very fair.

12:15 The princes also of Pharaoh saw her, and commended her before Pharaoh: and the woman was taken into Pharaoh's house.

12:16 And he entreated Abram well for her sake: and he had sheep, and oxen, and he asses, and menservants, and maidservants, and she asses, and camels.

12:17 And the LORD *plagued Pharaoh and his house with great plagues* because of Sarai Abram's wife.

12:18 And Pharaoh called Abram and said, What is this that thou hast done unto me? why didst thou not tell me that she was thy wife?

12:19 Why saidst thou, She is my sister? so I might have taken her to me to wife: now therefore behold thy wife, take her, and go thy way.

12:20 And Pharaoh commanded his men concerning him: and they sent him away, and his wife, and all that he had.

13:1 And Abram went up out of Egypt, he, and his wife, and all that he had, and Lot with him, into the south.

13:2 And Abram was very rich in cattle, in silver, and in gold.

I'M MY OWN GRANDPA

In all of Egyptian history, nothing is as mysterious as the strange life of Akhenaten and the odd appearance and equally mysterious disappearance of his queen, Nefertiti, whose name means "a beautiful woman has come". We notice in the above account that the "the Lord plagued Pharaoh and his house with great plagues because of Sarai". This reminds us of the plagues at the time of the Exodus. We also notice that the pharaoh told Abraham, "take your wife and go". This strangely mirrors the demand of Moses, "Let my people go".

The timing of this event is also important, and I think that we can nail it down to the time of the eruption of Thera on the island of Santorini around 1600 BC, which happens to be the time that the entire Earth experienced a disruption recorded in ice cores, and brought the Bronze Age world to an end. It was very likely also the time when many refugees from many areas of the Mediterranean all showed up in Palestine - including Danaan Greeks - to form the mixed ethnic groups from which the later Jewish state evolved.

There is evidence that the eruption of Thera coincided generally with the ejection of the Hyksos from the Nile Delta. There is also evidence that many of the king list segments that are currently arranged in a linear way may have represented different dynasties in different locations, *some of which ruled simultaneously* exactly as Manetho has told us. In particular, there is evidence that the 18th dynasty overlapped the Hyksos kings to some considerable extent. This is important to us at present because of the fact that the story of Abraham and Sarai in Egypt is mirrored by the story of Akhenaten and his Queen, Nefertiti. The earliest document that describes the time of the Hyksos is from the Temple of Hatshepsut at Speos Artemidos which says:

> Hear ye, all people and the folk as many as they may be, I have done these things
> through the counsel of my heart. I have not slept forgetfully, (but) I have restored
> that which had been ruined. I have raised up that which had gone to pieces
> formerly, since the Asiatics were in the midst of Avaris of the Northland, and
> *vagabonds* were in the midst of them, *overthrowing that which had been made.*

They ruled without Re, and he did not act by divine command down to (the reign of) my majesty.[288]

The expulsion of the Hyksos was a *series* of campaigns which supposedly started with Kamose who was king in Thebes. He unsuccessfully rebelled against the Hyksos. His son Ahmose was finally successful in pushing the Hyksos out. An army commander named Ah-mose records in his tomb the victory over the Hyksos. He says:

> When the town of Avaris was besieged, then I showed valor on foot in the presence of his majesty. Thereupon I was appointed to the ship, 'Appearing in Memphis'.
> Then there was fighting on the water in the canal Pa-Djedku of Avaris. Thereupon I made a capture, and I carried away a hand. It was reported to the king's herald.
> Then the Gold of Valor was given to me. Thereupon there was fighting again in this place....Then Avaris was despoiled. Then I carried off spoil from there: one man, three woman, a total of four persons. Then his majesty gave them to me to be slaves. Then Sharuhen was besieged for three years. Then his majesty despoiled it.[289]

Note that Avaris was besieged, there is no mention of how Avaris was taken, and there is no burning of Avaris claimed. What is more, the archaeological evidence shows that Avaris was not destroyed in a military engagement. The likelihood is that, after years of unstable relations with the Southern Egyptian dynasty, Avaris was abandoned due to the eruption of Thera.

This exodus from Egypt by the Hyksos, many of whom fled to Canaan, was part of their history. In fact, there were probably many refugees arriving in the Levant from many places affected by the eruption and the following famine. When the descendants of the refugees were later incorporated into a tribal confederation known as Israel, the story became one of the single events they all agreed upon. In this respect, they all did, indeed, share a history.

The fact is, other than the expulsion of the Hyksos, there is no other record of any mass exit from Egypt. Avaris was on the coast, and thus closer to the effects of the volcano. Naturally, the Egyptians of Thebes saw the expulsion of the Hyksos as a great military victory, while the Hyksos themselves, in the retelling of the story, viewed their survival as a great salvation victory. This seems similar to other events recorded in ancient history where both sides claim a great victory. Nevertheless, that there was something very unusual going on during this time comes down to us from the *Rhind Mathematical Papyrus*. There is a little diary

---

[288] ANET 1969, p. 231; Breasted, James, *Ancient Records of Egypt*, 1906-7, rpt. 1988, 5 Vols.(London: Histories & Mysteries of Man Ltd. 1988) pp. 122-26; Shanks, Hershel, "The Exodus and the Crossing of the Red Sea, According to Hans Goedicke." Biblical Archaeology Review 7:5 (September/October 1981). p. 49.

[289] ANET 1969, p. 233.

preserved on the reverse of this work that records the events leading up to the fall of Avaris.

> Regnal year 11, second month of shomu - Heliopolis was entered. First month of akhet, day 23 - the Bull of the South gores his way as far as Tjaru. Day 25 - it was heard tell that Tjaru had been entered. Regnal year 11, first month of akhet, the birthday of Seth - a roar was emitted by the Majesty of this god. The birthday of Isis - the sky poured rain.

Recorded on a stela of King Ahmose from the same period:

> The sky came on with a torrent of rain, and [dark]ness covered the western heavens while the storm raged without cessation...[the rain thundered] on the mountains (louder) than the noise at the Cavern that is in Abydos. Then every house and barn where they might have sought refuge [was swept away ... and they] were drenched with water like reed canoes ... and for a period of [...] days no light shone in the Two Lands.[290]

The *Rhind Mathematical Papyrus* is named after the Scottish Egyptologist Henry Rhind, who purchased it in Luxor in 1858. The papyrus, a scroll about 6 metres long and 1/3 of a metre wide, includes certain information about who wrote it and when it was written. The scribe identifies himself as Ahmes, and says that he is copying the scroll for the Hyksos king Apophis, in the year 33 of his reign. Ahmes then tells us that he is copying the text from an older version. It is here that we find some disagreement. Some experts think that the original of the mathematical problems, which is what the papyrus consists of, was written during the reign of Amenemht III, from the 12th dynasty. Egyptologist Anthony Spalinger does not, however, entirely agree. In a lengthy, detailed analysis of the papyrus, the mathematics, the arrangement of the problems, and every observable detail about it, he asks:

> One might query at this point the source or sources of Rhind. Did the original exemplar contain the opening table as well as the subsequent problems, or, to complicate the case further, was that treatise itself derived from various unknown works now lost? That this is not idle speculation can be seen by [Egyptologist] Griffith's remarks concerning the grain measures employed. He stressed the presence of the quadruple hekat in this papyrus, a measure which was unknown to him as a standard in the Middle Kingdom. [...]

> In Rhind the quadruple hekat occurs in Books II and III but not in Book I, in which only the single hekat occurs. [...] In the Middle Kingdom (Dynasty 12), only the single and double hekat have been found; one has to wait for Rhind to note the presence of its four-fold companion. [...]

---

[290] Vandersleyen, C. RdE 19 (1968), pls. 8, 9; W. Helck, *Historisch-biographische Texte der 2. Zwischenzeit* (Wiesbaden, 1975), pp. 106-7.

Can we therefore assume that Book I represents the copy mentioned at the beginning, and Book II (as well as the problems on the verso) another source or sources? […]

I am of the belief that the sources of Book II (and III, but this needs more clarification) was either different from that of Book I or else a reworked series of problems having their origins in the copy that Scribe Ahmose employed.[…]

Significantly, the relationship of one deben of weight to 12 "pieces" can also be found *at the end of the 18th dynasty*, a point that Gardner stressed in his important breakthrough of the Kahun Papyri.[…]

After the papyrus had been completed, and undoubtedly after some use as a teaching manual, later remarks were written on the verso in the great blank following problem 84. […] Upside down, in a different (and thicker) hand than that of the original scribe, it presents *an early case of cryptographic writing*. Gunn, in his review of Peet, was the first to attempt a concise evaluation of the meaning, and he observed the presence of such writing from Dynasty 19 on, citing examples from Theban tombs, as well as other monuments from that capital. […]

Following Gunn, I feel that the *presence of cryptography at this point* ought to predicate a date *within Dynasty 18*, and the eventual location of Rhind at Thebes just may supply some support for this supposition. After all, it is from that city that we know the most about this so-called enigmatic writing, and such texts are dated to the New Kingdom and not earlier.

With no 87, located […] roughly in the center, Rhind presents the famous and highly-debated jottings concerning the taking of Avaris by Ahmose. I feel that it was added to the middle of the verso, and right side up, so to speak, soon before the entire roll was transported to Thebes from the north. […]

The brief remarks provide not merely a terminus a quo for the presence of Rhind later than year 33 of the Hyksos ruler Apophis, they also indicated that *a major historical event was purposively written down* on a mathematical tractate, itself being of high importance and value.

Soon after, Rhind was, I believe, transported back by someone in the victorious Theban army to the new capital and later used there as a treatise, only to have a further addition entered (no. 87). […]

I feel that the regnal dates do *not* refer to the reign of Ahmose but rather to that of the last Hyksos ruler in Egypt, a position that I am well aware is open to question; however, the historical event is at least clear: the end of Hyksos control in the eastern delta (Heliopolis and Sile are noted as having fallen). If we follow Moller, then the possessor of Rhind at that time felt these major events worthy of a remark on one of his prized treasures. [...] The scribe was identical to the copyist of Rhind itself.[291]

I hope that the reader caught the term *"cryptographic writing"* in reference to the account of the events leading to the fall of Avaris. It actually took me awhile to realize what these guys were talking about when I read these references to "cryptographic writing" in the 18th and 19th dynasties. Finally, I understood that they were not suggesting that something was being written in a secret code for military purposes. What this term actually means to Egyptologists is that, "since we cannot possibly give up our chronology to allow these matters to coincide with a certifiable cataclysm going on in the region, we must therefore say that the writers do not mean what they say, but rather they are using metaphors. What's more, we will call it 'cryptographic writing'."

Egyptologist R. Weill was the first to insist on this distortion being a type of literary fiction. It then became the convention for interpreting Egyptian historical writing. In this way, a period of desolation and anarchy would be described in exaggeratedly lurid terms of catastrophe and climatological cataclysm, usually for the glorification of a monarch to whom the salvation of the country is ascribed.[292]

Well, that's pretty bizarre! Handy, too. A bunch of guys spend their lives trying to validate the history and chronology of these people, and when it doesn't agree with what they want to believe about it, it can be consigned to "literary fiction". And of course, this means that what is or is not "literary fiction" can be completely arbitrary according to the needs of the Egyptologist!

Based on this "cryptographic" interpretation, Sturt Manning contends that the text on the verso of the Rhind papyrus is not about a "real storm" or climatological event, but that it is about "the restoration of the Egyptian state to the order and station of the Middle Kingdom - after the dislocation (all-wrecking storm) of the Hyksos era, and the destruction of Middle Kingdom shrines...One might even argue that the whole Theban text is a symbolic encoding of Ahmose's defeat of the Hyksos..."[293]

I must say that I was rather astonished to read such a remark.

Part of Manning's (and others') arguments have to do with keeping the 18th dynasty cleanly separated from the time of the Hyksos. No overlapping is to be allowed here despite the fact that Manetho clearly said that the Hyksos dynasties were concurrent with the Theban dynasties. We can't have Ahmose experiencing something that has been dated by the experts to well before Ahmose was born!

---

[291] Spalinger, Anthony, (1990), *The Rhind Mathematical Papyrus As A Historical Document,* Studien zur altagyptischen Kultur; 17, p. 295-338.

[292] cf. Redford, op. cit.

[293] Manning, Sturt, *A Test of Time* (Oxbow: Oxford) p. 1999.

Let's have a look at how famed Egyptologist Gardner has described the problem of the dynasties in question.

> Since the passage of Time shows no break in continuity, nothing but some momentous event or sequence of events can justify a particular reign being regarded as inaugurating an era. What caused Sobeknofru, or Sobeknofrure' as later sources call her, to be taken as closing Dyn. XII will doubtless never be known. But the Turin Canon, the Saqqara king-list, and Manetho are unanimous on the point.
>
> The Abydos list jumps straight from Ammenemes IV to the first king of Dyn.XVIII. The date of Amosis I, the founder of Dyn. XVIII, being fixed with some accuracy, the interval from 1786 to 1575 BC must be accepted as the duration of the Second Intermediate Period. This is an age the problems of which are even more intractable than those of the First. Before entering upon details, it will be well to note that the general pattern of these two dark periods is roughly the same. Both begin with a chaotic series of insignificant native rulers. In both, intruders from Palestine cast their shadow over the Delta and even into the Valley. Also in both, relief comes at last from a hardy race of Theban princes, who after quelling internal dissension expel the foreigner and usher in a new epoch of immense power and prosperity.
>
> Some account has already been given of the formidable difficulties here confronting us, but these must now be discussed at length. As usual we start with Manetho. The Thirteenth Dynasty according to him, was Diospolite (Theban) and consisted of sixty kings who reigned for 453 years. The Fourteenth Dynasty counted seventy-six kings from Xois, the modern Sakha in the central Delta, with a total of 184 or, as an alternative reading, 484 years. For Dyns. XV to XVII there is divergence between Africanus and Eusebius, while a much simpler account is preserved by the Jewish historian Josephus in what purports to be a verbatim extract from Manetho's own writing.
>
> For our present purpose the data supplied by Africanus must suffice. His Fifteenth Dynasty consists of six foreign so-called 'Shepherd' or Hyksos kings, whose domination lasted 284 years. The Sixteenth Dynasty consisted of Shepherd kings again, thirty-two in number totaling 518 years. Lastly, in the Seventeenth Dynasty Shepherd kings and Theban kings reigned concurrently, forty-three of each line altogether 151 years. Adding these figures, but adopting the lower number of years given for Dyn. XIV, we obtain 217 kings covering a stretch of 1590 years, over seven times the duration to which acceptance of the *Sothic date* in the El-Lahun papyrus has committed us.
>
> To abandon 1786 BC as the year when Dyn. XII ended would be to cast adrift from our only firm anchor, a course that would have serious consequences for the history, not of Egypt alone, but of the entire Middle East.[294]

---

[294] Gardiner, Sir Alan, Egypt of the Pharaohs.

Gardner's problem, as he states it above, is that the numbers of kings and years of reign given by the sources of Manetho result in, "a stretch of 1590 years, over seven times the duration to which acceptance of the *Sothic date* in the El-Lahun papyrus has committed us".

Remember what we said about scientific hypotheses in an earlier chapter? In doing good "science", a researcher must be aware of this tendency to be fooled by his own mind - his own wishes. And, a good scientist, because he is aware of this, must scrutinize things he wishes to accept as fact in a more or less "unemotional" state, as far as is possible. Things *must be challenged,* taken apart, compared, tested for their ability to explain other things of a like nature, and *if a flaw is found, no matter how small, if it is firmly established as a flaw, the hypothesis must be killed.* That does not mean, of course, that the next hypothesis we make has to be radically different; it may just need a slight expansion of parameters. As Thomas Edison pointed out, before he invented the light bulb, he discovered 99 ways how *not* to make a light bulb. Hypotheses ought to be the same. If the observations or facts don't fit, it's not the end of the world. One just has to be flexible and try to think of ways that the hypothesis can be adjusted.

The problem is that Egyptologists do not adjust the hypothesis except by shedding of blood. They prefer to twist the facts so that square pegs are pounded into round holes. In fact, Egyptologists did not start out with a hypothesis; they started with a "convention". This means that they decided what would be firmly accepted and anything that did not fit, had to be either discarded, or forced to fit the convention.

It strikes me that Gardner didn't even notice the clues to the solution of the problem: the two "intermediate periods" in question, being almost identical in so many respects, might very well be the same, single period! That would mean that the Abydos list was, essentially, correct when it, "jumps straight from Ammenemes IV to the first king of Dyn.XVIII". Perhaps Sobeknofrure was identical to Hatshepsut?

Egypt's Middle Kingdom has conventionally been dated to some 4000 years ago, largely on the basis of documents that are interpreted to indicate a heliacal rising of Sirius on Pharmuthi 16 in Year 7 of Sesostris III (1871 BC). Sesostris was also known as Senuseret.

The 12th Dynasty was a family of kings typically given dates in the mid-20th to mid-18th century BC and consisted of 8 rulers: Amenemhat I, Senuseret I, Amenemhat II, Senuseret II, Senuseret III, Amenemhat III, Amenemhat IV, Neferusobek, or Sobeknofrure, a woman who, in one of the few depictions of her in statuary, is shown with normal breasts, and without a false beard as Hatshepsut was depicted.

Regarding Hatshepsut, we discover that she was said to be the fifth ruler of the 18th Dynasty, and was the daughter of Thutmose I and Queen Ahmose. Hatshepsut disappeared, supposedly, when Thutmose III, wishing to reclaim the throne, led a revolt. Thutmose had her shrines, statues and reliefs mutilated.

When we consider the careers of both Sesostris III and Thutmose I, we find them to be remarkably similar, right down to being succeeded by a daughter. I suggest that they were one and the same person.

One of the many problems of sorting out Egyptian chronology is the fact that the individuals in question used many names for many reasons. In fact, it seems as though many of the names were actually titles, such as Thutmosis, which would be "son of Thoth". There is also Ramesses, which is "son of Ra". It is hardly likely that the chief god would change with each king as often as these titles suggest. It is far more likely that each king was a "Thutmosis" and a "Ramesses". Of course, in a certain sense, that complicates things a bit. But, in another sense, it simplifies them.

Just to give a specific example: in conventional chronology, we find that King Ahmose married his sister, Ahmose-Nefertari, daughter of Sekenenre II and Queen Ahotep. His son, Amenhotep I, co-reigned with Nefertari, though he supposedly married a Queen Senseneb. Their son, Thutmosis I ALSO married Princess Ahmose, daughter of Queen Ahotep, which, of course, means that Queen Ahotep must have also been married to his father, Amenhotep I, who was said to have been the son of Ahmose-Nefertari, making Queen Ahotep his grandmother.

Well, I'm my own grandpa!

It's a bit simpler to consider the idea that Ahmose and Thutmosis I were one and the same individual.

The original reason for the identification of Kamose and Ahmose as brothers is a statue of a prince who is the son of King Tao and a certain Ahhotep. It is generally assumed that the king is Tao II and the queen is King Ahmose's mother Ahhotep who is well-attested elsewhere. The problem is that Kamose came between Tao and Ahmose, therefore it seems logical to assign Kamose as the older brother. But here we come to the problem with Ahhotep. The exact relationship of Kamose to the royal family is also a bit problematic. Vandersleyen suggests that Kamose might have been the uncle rather than the brother of Ahmose.[295]

Other evidence from the cranio-facial studies by Wente and Harris[296] shows that Ahmose is not close enough to the skeletal forms of Sekenenre Tao or Amenhotep I to be the son of the one or the father of the other. The remains of Kamose were destroyed upon their discovery in 1857, so they could not be included in the study. Finally, we come to a most interesting fact. Donald B. Redford notes that the tying of Kamose to the royal family of Sekenenre Tao was a Ramesside development.[297] Why would the Ramesside rulers even care unless they had a vested interest? And what could their interest be except to validate their own progenitor: Horemheb?

We note that King Amosis asserts his own parents to have been the children of the same mother and father, a classical example of brother and sister marriage. As

[295] Egypt et la vallee du Nil volume II.

[296] X-ray atlas of the Royal Mummies, pp, 122-30 and in C.N. Reeves, After Tutankhamun: Research and Excavation in the Royal Necropolis at Thebes, p. 6.

[297] History and Chronology of the Eighteenth Dynasty, p. 37.

we have noted above, these parents are assumed to be Ahhotep and Sekenenre Ta'o II. Ahhotep, Ta'o II's queen, supposedly attained to even greater celebrity than her mother. A great stela found at Karnak, after heaping eulogies upon her son Amosis I, its dedicator, goes on to exhort all his subjects to do her reverence. In this curious passage she is praised as *having rallied the soldiery of Egypt*, and as having *put a stop to rebellion*. One thinks, of course, of Hatshepsut and Sobeknofrure.

Kamose's tomb was the last of the row inspected by the Ramesside officials, but later the mummy was removed in its coffin to a spot just south of the entrance of the Wady leading to the Tombs of the Kings, where it was found by Mariette's workmen in 1857. The coffin was not gilded, but of the feathered rishi type employed for non-royal personages of the period.

Horemheb's tomb was discovered in 1907/08 by Theodore Davis. Bones were found in the tomb, some still in the sarcophagus, but others had been thrown into other rooms. The mummies belonging to Horemheb and his queen had not been recovered in the cache of kings, and so it seems likely that these pathetic remains are all that is left of this particular pharaoh and his queen (although there exist some inspection graffiti on a door jamb within the tomb that cast a little uncertainty on this assumption). If a correct and proper excavation had been undertaken at the time, perhaps more questions might be answered, but Davis and his team were true to form of the early "egyptologists" - greedy and careless and determined to prove their theories more than to find out facts - and much of the evidence has been lost.

We can note that the mummy of Amenhotep III - father of Amenhotep IV, also known as Akhenaten - was actually "found" in the tomb of Amenhotep II. It was supposedly moved there for protection, which is a reasonable explanation. The point is, the provenance of so many things Egyptian cannot be firmly established and that means one must be even more aware of the tendency to muddle things up by adopting wrong hypotheses.

Part of the problem of sorting out the different kings and dynasties is, I think, that we have the problem of what, exactly, constituted a "king" during those times. It is beginning to seem likely that many of the kings whose tombs have been found, who memorialized themselves, or were memorialized by their families, were little more than local rulers, or even just glorified puppets of a still higher king.

Another interesting item is the fact that a proposal to extract DNA samples from different mummies to see what the familial relationships really might have been was halted by the Egyptian government.

> Egypt has indefinitely postponed DNA tests designed to throw light on questions that have intrigued archaeologists for years: Who was Tutankhamun's father, and was he of royal blood? The head of Egypt's Supreme Council of Antiquities, Gaballah Ali Gaballah, said Tuesday that plans for DNA tests on the mummies of Tutankhamun and his presumed grandfather, Amenhotep III, had been canceled. "There will be no test now and we have to see if there will be one later," Gaballah told The Associated Press. He declined to give a reason. [...]

> The announcement of the planned tests had sparked a controversy among Egyptian archaeologists. Some said they were an unnecessary risk that might harm the

mummies. Others said the results might be used to *rewrite Egyptian history*. "I have refused in the past to allow foreign teams to carry out such tests on the bones of the Pyramids builders because there are some people who try to tamper with Egyptian history," the chief archaeologist of the Giza pyramids, Zahi Hawass , told the Akhbar Al-Yom weekly.[298]

The above news release is more interesting and mysterious than might be initially thought since Tutankhamen was undoubtedly the son of the Heretic king, Akhenaten and Nefertiti who may, indeed, have been Abraham's Sarai which would mean that she was also the putative mother of "Isaac", the patriarch of the Jews.

> The tomb of Tutankhamun was undoubtedly the greatest archaeological discovery of all time, yet everyone knows this remarkable find was beset by troubles. The untimely death of Lord Carnarvon just after the opening of the tomb, and his appetite for the occult, swiftly gave rise to rumours of a curse. Also, the presence of certain art treasures in museums across the United States provides evidence that Howard Carter and his aristocratic patron *removed pricelss objects from the tomb* [illegally].
>
> What is not so well known is that among the wonderful treasures Carter and Carnarvon unearthed were also rumoured to be papyri that held *the true account of the biblical Exodus* of the Israelites from Egypt.
>
> Why did Carter threaten to reveal this volatile information to the public at a meeting with a British official in Cairo shortly after the discovery of the tomb? At a time when Arab hostility towards Britain's support for the establishment of a Jewish homeland in Palestine was spilling onto the streets of Jerusalem and Jaffa, such actions on the part of the hot-headed Englishman could have caused untold chaos across the Middle East.[299]

The only thing I can think of that would make it imperative to conceal the "true story of the Exodus" by the British government would be because in some way, such information would have put a period to the Jewish claim to the "Promised Land". It may also have put a period to Judaism and Christianity altogether.

The fact is that most of the early Egyptologists came to their subject as committed, if not fanatical, Christians. They sought to use Egypt as a means of expanding and supporting the Biblical narrative. Many of them saw Akhenaten as the inspired founder of a pre-Christian monotheistic religion, and his faith in one god made him a figure of admiration.

To the early scholars in the field, Akhenaten was "The first individual in History", [Breasted]; to Toynbee his sun-cult was a prototype of the Roman

---

[298] The Associated Press, Cairo, Egypt, Dec. 13, 2000.

[299] Jacket blurb from: Collins, Andrew and Ogilvie-Herald, Chris, *Tutankhamun: The Exodus Conspiracy*, 2002, Virgin Books, London.

imperial Sol Invictus; to Freud, he became a mentor of the Hebrew lawgiver, Moses. To some, Akhenaten was a forerunner of Christ or otherwise a great mystic.

Such ideas took shape and moved farther and farther away from the primary sources and it keeps growing like a fungus. As Donald Redford says, "one must constantly return to the original sources [...] in order to avoid distortion".

Our knowledge of Egypt has to be gleaned from a random assortment of archaeological remains, a great deal of religious and mortuary art and architecture, supplemented by a small collection of historical documents. The Amarna period, the time of Akhenaten, is particularly difficult because it seems that all of Egypt sought to erase the memory of Akhenaten from the individual and collective consciousness. Akhenaten was hated, and apparently, so was Nefertiti.

The first five years of Akhenaten's reign actually represents a startling discontinuity in historical knowledge. So thoroughly were the memorials of this period eradicated - whether temple reliefs, steles, or tombs - that little remains to tell the story. In other words, historically speaking, no connected narrative is even possible. So complete was the destruction of the Amarna remains by the pharaoh Horemheb, that quite literally, no stone was left standing upon another.

Horemheb was the fourteenth king of the 18th Dynasty. He was chief of the army during Tutankhamun's reign. When Tutankhamun died, Ay apparently usurped the throne. Ay favored Horemheb and kept him on as a military leader. When Ay died without an heir, Horemheb was made king. Restoring order was his main objective. Once accomplished, Horemheb moved to Memphis and began work on internal affairs. He returned properties of the temples to the rightful priests and lands to the rightful owners. He had restoration projects and building additions in Karnak. He erected shrines and a temple to Ptah. He built tombs at Thebes, in the Valley of the Kings, and Memphis. He was noted for admonishing high-ranking officials against cheating the poor and misappropriating the use of slaves and properties. He promised the death penalty for such offenses.

> Nothing tears the mask from the Amarna Age like the Edict of Reform. The picture conjured up is not like the beautiful relief scenes at Karnak or Akhetaten. Gone are the elegant ladies and gentlemen, bowing low before a benign monarch beneath the Sun-disc, his father; in their place emerge starkly an army allowed to run riot, a destitute peasantry, and corrupt judges. It may be maintained that these conditions could only have prevailed at the close of the period of heresy, but the evidence opposes any such defense. The withdrawal and the subsequent isolation of the head of state and his court, which clearly brought on the anarchy, must be laid to the charge of Akhenaten himself.[300]

---

[300] Redford, Donald B., *Akhenaten: The Heretic King*, 1984, Princeton University Press, Princeton, p. 225.

Horemheb had no heir so he appointed a military leader to succeed him. That leader was Ramesses I and that was when the "sorting of the mummies" began. One can only wonder if some of the confusion that exists today isn't due to the deliberate attempt on the part of Horemheb and his Ramesside heirs to simply create a new history?

One interesting fact to note about the 18th dynasty is that, artistically and in every other way, it appears to be the continuation of the 12th dynasty. If we consider the idea that the Hyksos kings ruled concurrently with a Southern Egyptian dynasty, this factor then begins to make sense.

Manetho, quoted by Eusebius, Africanus, and Josephus, presents a very messy history of the Second Intermediate Period, with impossibly long lengths of reign for Dynasties XIII-XVII, and a confusing picture of which group of kings belonged to which dynasty. I think that it is entirely possible that a misunderstanding of what he wrote led to errors among those who quoted him; i.e. Eusebius, Africanus, and Josephus; all of whom had an axe to grind. And, for all we know, Manetho had an agenda as well.

The problem seems to lie in the fact that, in its original form, Manetho's Second Intermediate Period consisted of five dynasties, three Theban and two Hyksos which were *not sequential*, but rather concurrent. Manetho said this, but it has been rejected. It seems that, in order to indicate which dynasties served concurrently, and which dynasties served consecutively, a series of subtotals was used and this practice was misunderstood by those who quoted Manetho. They thought they were looking at a sequential list of kings interspersed with summaries and subtotals. They thought that the summaries were additional groups of kings. As a result, Africanus, Eusebius, and Josephus committed grave errors in their citations of Manetho. This led to a number of errors, such as Africanus's mixing together Hyksos and Theban kings into one dynasty, and Africanus and Eusebius disagreeing as to whether a dynasty was Hyksos or Theban, or how many years it reigned.

Getting back to our problem, it seems that what we are dealing with is a rather restricted time frame in which the Middle Bronze age came to a cataclysmic end, the Hyksos were ejected from Egypt, and these events did not occur in the middle of the 15th century BC, but rather over 200 years earlier. We also find that the curious "cryptographic writing" of the 18th dynasty fits a model that includes the end of the Middle Bronze Age and extraordinary climatological events.

The archaeological excavations of the Islands of Santorini and Crete demonstrate that the destruction of the Middle Bronze Age civilization occurred in *two phases* which would account for the turmoil in the time of Hatshepsut, followed by a second period of disruption at the time of Akhenaten. This coincides with the fact that there were indications of climatological anomalies as early as 1644 BC, leading up to the final disaster of the eruption of Thera in 1628 BC, followed by climatological disruption for the following forty years or so. The evidence on Santorini and Crete show that there was initial volcanic activity - earthquakes - followed by rebuilding and habitation for some time before the final, decisive eruption of Thera at least one or two generations later! That there was some warning of the impending eruption is verified by the fact that no bodies were found in the several meters thick layer of pumice that buried the town of Akrotiri.

Also, since portable precious items were missing, it seems safe to assume, therefore, that the population abandoned the town in haste.

The Dilmun civilization of Bahrain is said to have existed from 3200 BC until 1600 BC. The Indus Valley civilization is said to have ended around 1700 to 1600 BC. The Great Babylonian Empire ended around 1600 BC. The Middle Kingdom in Egypt is said to have ended around 1600 BC (though we now think that the 18th dynasty was the last of the Middle Kingdom dynasties). The Xia Dynasty in China ended in 1600 BC. The use of Stonehenge ended around 1600 BC. In nearly every case, the end of the civilization and the mass destruction read in the record unearthed by the spade is ascribed to war and rampaging Sea Peoples or tribes of barbarians on the march.

Two of the most influential German scholars, von Rad and Noth, have argued that, "The Exodus and Sinai traditions and the events behind them were originally unrelated to one another".[301] Von Rad pointed out that the Sinai covenant in the Feast of Tabernacles was celebrated at Shechem while the settlement tradition was celebrated at Gilgal with the Feast of Weeks. Von Rad also noted that the salvation history was strikingly silent about the Sinai events in Deuteronomy 26. It was then proposed that early Israel was actually a tribal league more or less like city-state confederations later attested in Greece and Italy and known to the Greeks as "amphictyonies".[302] If such tribal groups were later amalgamated during the reign of Hezekiah, it would then be necessary to "create" a national history, utilizing the available oral traditions. And this is, of course, where it becomes most interesting because it seems that at least one small group - Abraham and his wife Sarai - had a series of experiences during these times that was utterly extraordinary.

There are various suggestions as to where Mt. Sinai really was. Jewish tradition seems to place Mt. Sinai in Arabia. Demetrius stated that Dedan was Jethro's ancestor which is identified with the oasis of el-'Ela, and when Moses went to Midian he stayed in Arabia.[303]

In 1954 Mendenhall put forth the idea that the Sinai covenant is similar to the Hittite suzerainty treaties. There does seem to be clear parallels between the Sinai covenant and ancient suzerainty treaties, and ancient tribal leagues did exist.

In Josephus' book *Antiquities of the Jews* he placed Sinai where the city of Madiane was.[304] In the *Babylonian Talmud*[305] R. Huna and R. Hisda say, "the Holy

---

[301] Nicholson, E.W., *Exodus and Sinai in History and Tradition* (Richmond: John Knox Press 1973).

[302] Ibid.

[303] De Vaux, Roland, *The Early History of Israel* translation by David Smith. (Philadelphia: Westminster Press 1978) p. 435.

[304] Antiquities, II.264; III.76.

[305] Sotah 5a, Freedman and Simon 1935, pp. 18-19.

One, blessed be He, ignored all the mountains and heights and caused His *Shechinah* to abide upon Mount Sinai".

According to Old Testament passages Mt. Sinai is identified with Seir and Mt. Paran. Deuteronomy 33:2 says, "The Lord came from Sinai, and rose up from Seir unto them; he shined forth from mount Paran".[306] It seems that the itinerary that was followed in Numbers 33:18-36 locates Sinai in northern Arabia. Midian was also located here where Moses lived with Jethro, priest of Midian, for forty years.[307] De Vaux believed that the theophany of Sinai was a description of a volcanic eruption in northern Arabia because Exodus 19:18 describes the mountain like a furnace of smoke. From a distance it would look like a pillar of cloud in the day, and a pillar of fire at night. Following this cloud of smoke would lead them right to the volcano.

The only problem is, *there are no volcanoes in Sinai*. There are several in northern Arabia, but we come back again to the fact that the only known large eruption around this time is Santorini on the Greek island of Thera. On this point, we discover an intriguing passage in *The Histories* of Tacitus:

> The Jews are said to have been refugees from the island of Crete who settled in the remotest corner of Libya in the days when, according to the story, Saturn was driven from his throne by the aggression of Jupiter. This is a deduction from the name Judaei by which they became known: the word is to be regarded as a barbarous lengthening of Idaei, the name of the people dwelling around the famous Mount Ida in Crete.

> A few authorities hold that in the reign of Isis the surplus population of Egypt was evacuated to neighboring lands under the leadership of Hierosolymus and Judas.[308] Many assure us that the Jews are descended from those Ethiopians who were driven by fear and hatred to emigrate from their home country when Cepheus was king.[309] There are some who say that a motley collection of landless Assyrians occupied a part of Egypt, and then built cities of their own, inhabiting the lands of the Hebrews and the nearer parts of Syria.[310] Others again find a famous ancestry for the Jews in

---

[306] KJV, see also Judges 5:4-5, Hab. 3:3,7.

[307] *The Bible*, I Kings 11:18; Exodus 2:15, 3:1.

[308] "Hierosolymus" and "Judas" are the Greek renderings of the Hebrew words for Jerusalem and Jew.

[309] According to Greek legend, Cepheus was king of Ethiopia. His daughter Andromeda was married to the hero Perseus. The main question about this is: where was ancient "Ethiopia"?

[310] This theory is plausible. In Greek and Latin, the word 'Assyrian' can indicate everyone living in modern Iraq or Syria. Aramaeans, a tribe to which the Hebrews seem to have been related, also fit within the definition of an Assyrian. We also note that Abraham's family referred to relatives as "Syrians." There is also the fact that the genetic studies show the Jews to be very closely related to Syrians, both Jewish and non-Jewish.

the Solymi who are mentioned with respect in the epics of Homer:[311] this tribe is supposed have founded Jerusalem and named it after themselves.

Most authorities, however, agree on the following account. The whole of Egypt was once plagued by a wasting disease which caused bodily disfigurement. So Pharaoh Bocchoris [312] went to the oracle of Hammon to ask for a cure, and was told to purify his kingdom by expelling the victims to other lands, as they lay under a divine curse. Thus a multitude of sufferers was rounded up, herded together, and abandoned in the wilderness. Here the exiles tearfully resigned themselves to their fate. But one of them, who was called Moses, urged his companions not to wait passively for help from god or man, for both had deserted them: they should trust to their own initiative and to whatever guidance first helped them to extricate themselves from their present plight. They agreed, and started off at random into the unknown.

But exhaustion set in, chiefly through lack of water, and the level plain was already strewn with the bodies of those who had collapsed and were at their last gasp when a herd of wild asses left their pasture and made for the spade of a wooded crag. Moses followed them and was able to bring to light a number of abundant channels of water whose presence he had deduced from a grassy patch of ground. This relieved their thirst. They traveled on for six days without a break, and on the seventh they expelled the previous inhabitants of Canaan, took over their lands and in them built a holy city and temple.

In order to secure the allegiance of his people in the future, Moses prescribed for them a novel religion quite different from those of the rest of mankind. Among the Jews all things are profane that we hold sacred; on the other hand they regard as permissible what seems to us immoral. In the innermost part of the Temple, they consecrated an image of the animal which had delivered them from their wandering and thirst, choosing a ram as beast of sacrifice to demonstrate, so it seems, their contempt for Hammon.[313] The bull is also offered up, because the Egyptians worship it as Apis. They avoid eating pork in memory of their tribulations, as they themselves were once infected with the disease to which this creature is subject.[314]

They still fast frequently as an admission of the hunger they once endured so long, and to symbolize their hurried meal the bread eaten by the Jews is unleavened. We are told that the seventh day was set aside for rest because this marked the end of their toils. [...] Others say that this is a mark of respect to Saturn, either because they owe the basic principles of their religion to the Idaei, who, we are told, were

---

[311] The Solymi are mentioned by Homer in *The Iliad* 6.184 and 204 and in *The Odyssey* 5.283. They were brave warriors from Lycia. The word Jerusalem was read as "Hiero-Solyma" or "holy place of the Solymi."

[312] Josephus, Africanus and Eusebius all list a King Orus who the "experts" agree is Amenhotep III.

[313] The Egyptians represented Ammon with a ram's head. However, there is more to this than Tacitus suspects.

[314] Leprosy.

expelled in the company of Saturn and became the founders of the Jewish race, or because, among the seven stars that rule mankind, the one that describes the highest orbit and exerts the greatest influence is Saturn. A further argument is that most of the heavenly bodies complete their path and revolutions in multiples of seven. [...]

Rather than cremate their dead, they prefer to bury them in imitation of the Egyptian fashion, and they have the same concern and beliefs about the world below. But their conception of heavenly things is quite different. The Egyptians worship a variety of animals and half-human, half-bestial forms, whereas the Jewish religion is a purely spiritual monotheism. They hold it to be impious to make idols of perishable materials in the likeness of man: for them, the Most High and Eternal cannot be portrayed by human hands and will never pass away. For this reason they erect no images in their cities, still less in their temples. Their kings are not so flattered, the Roman emperors not so honored. However, their priests used to perform their chants to the flute and drums, crowned with ivy, and a golden vine was discovered in the Temple; and this has led some to imagine that the god thus worshipped was Prince Liber [315], the conqueror of the East. But the two cults are diametrically opposed. Liber founded a festive and happy cult: the Jewish belief is paradoxical and degraded.[316]

Regarding the "hearsay" recitation of Tacitus is that he states quite clearly that the nation of Israel was an amalgamation of tribes, including people who had once lived on Crete, who brought a volcano story with them, and another most unusual group that had been expelled from Egypt under very peculiar circumstances, bringing an altogether different story to the mix. Tacitus' record of this group, its expulsion, and the fact that he has connected them to King Bocchoris is an important clue.

The pagan story of the flood of Ogyges and its relationship to the story of Noah was a problem for biblical commentators, as was that of the later flood of Deucalion, which Deucalion survived with his wife by floating in a large chest. Eusebius tells us that Ogyges "lived at the same time of the Exodus from Egypt".[317]

In the past, scholars concluded that Ahmose must have caused the destruction of the Middle Bronze Age, but Redford has shown that Ahmoses' campaign was restricted to Sharuhen and its neighborhood to punish the Hyksos.[318] The first

---

[315] A common title for Dionysus, the god of wine, intoxication and ecstasy.

[316] Tacitus, *The Histories*, Book V: 2-5. Translation by Kenneth Wellesley.

[317] Eusebius, Pamphilus, *Preparation of the Gospel*. Translation by Edwin Gifford. (Grand Rapids: Baker Book House 1981) p. 524.

[318] Redford, Donald "A Gate Inscription From Karnak and Egyptian Involement in Western Asia During the Early 18th Dynasty." *Journal of the American Oriental Society* 99:2. 1979 p. 274; Bietak, Manfred 1991. "Egypt and Canaan During the Middle Bronze Age." *Bulletin of the American School of Oriental Research* 281 1991 p. 58; Weinstein 1981, pp. 1-28.

substantial campaign against inland Palestine was by Thutmose III.[319] From a survey of the central hill country Finkelstein does *not* connect the Egyptian conquest with the end of the Middle Bronze Age. He states, "There is no solid archaeological evidence that many sites across the country were destroyed simultaneously, and such campaigns would fail to explain the wholesale abandonment of hundreds of small rural settlements in the remote parts of the land".[320]

Again, what I am suggesting is that the 18th dynasty of Egypt was not only the continuation of the 12th dynasty in Southern Egypt, but that it ran concurrently with the last Hyksos dynasty, the 15th dynasty, that it ended simultaneously with the expulsion of the Hyksos.

Now, I am not even going to attempt to sort out all the assumed or presumably confirmed family relationships of the Egyptian dynasties. For our present purposes, the Egyptian chronology is only important insofar as it enables us to sort out those matters that might lead to the identification of the Ark of the Covenant and its possible wherabouts during certain periods of the past. This period of time is that surrounding the eruption of Thera, the fall of Avaris and the *end* of the 18th dynasty.

I want to remind the reader of the problem defined by Gardner which was that the numbers of kings and years of reign given by the sources of Manetho result in "a stretch of 1590 years, over seven times the duration to which acceptance of the *Sothic date* in the *El-Lahun papyrus* has committed us."

Gardner tells us why this just can't be:

> To abandon 1786 BC as the year when Dyn. XII ended would be to cast adrift from our only firm anchor, a course that would have serious consequences for the history, not of Egypt alone, but of the entire Middle East.[321]

SOTHIS: THE SHARP TOOTHED

As it happens, all the archaeological dating in the Mediterranean has been suspended upon Egyptian chronology under the influence of foundations laid by believers in the Biblical chronology. What is more, all of their dates rely upon two major assumptions: the *Sothic Cycle* and the identification of the Egyptian King Shoshenq I with the Biblical King Shishak, the Egyptian ruler who came against Rehoboam and took "all" the treasures of Solomon's Temple and "Solomon's house".

---

[319] Bietak, op. cit., p. 59.

[320] Hoffmeier, James K., "Some Thoughts on William G. Dever's 'Hyksos, Egyptian Destructions, and the End of the Palestinain Middle Bronze Age.'" *Levant* 22. 1990, p.87.

[321] Gardiner, Sir Alan, Egypt of the Pharaohs.

It is understood that Manetho only included 30 dynasties, the 31st being added later for the sake of completeness. However, the fact is, there are no original copies of *The Egyptian History* by Manetho. All we have of his work are excerpts cited by Josephus, the Jewish historian of the first century AD, and by two important Christian chronographers, Sextus Julius Africanus (3rd century AD), and Eusebius (4th century AD). George the Monk, Syncellus, used both Africanus and Eusebius extensively as his sources in his history of the world written in 800 AD. It is fairly easy to realize that *all three of these men had agendas.* We also note, once again, the period of time in which they were writing, and the fruits of their efforts in terms of the imposition of Christianity based on the platform of Judaism, the ultimate arbiter of the "you are doomed" linear view of Time.

It is regularly claimed that Egyptian chronology is based on "astronomical dating". What does this mean? It actually means that *Egyptian dating is based on a theory that the Egyptians used astronomical dating.* But many people do not realize this and believe that Egyptian chronology is actually based on astronomy. The fact is there *are* astronomically fixed Near Eastern dates, but they are not Egyptian dates. Two Babylonian cuneiform tablets have been found, each one filled with an entire year of data on the sun, planets, and eclipses. These dates fix two years: part of 568 / 567 B.C. and part of 523 / 522 B.C. *Those are our oldest astronomically fixed dates.* There is one other older Near Eastern eclipse, noted by the Assyrians, which has enough partial data to fix it at one of two years: it applies either to 763 BC or 791 BC. But experts do not agree on which date this eclipse occurred.

When we dig even deeper into these dating assumptions, we find that the main peg upon which the assumptions are hung is called the "Sothic cycle".

What is the Sothic cycle?

The experts tell us that the Egyptian civil year had 365 days - 3 seasons, (Akhet, Peret, Shemu), 4 months each with 30 days per month. To this, they added 5 additional epagomenal days. Since the actual orbit of the earth around the sun takes 365 and about a quarter days, this calendar falls behind by one day every four years. Nowadays, we correct this by adding an extra day every four years in a "leap year". However, if no calendar corrections are made, such a year would soon create significant problems (the experts say). How the Egyptians dealt with this was a matter of some conjecture, and it was finally decided that they corrected their calendar every 1460 years at the time of the heliacal rising of Sirius.

Where did this idea come from?

Our information on the alleged Sothic cycle depends largely on the late classical writers Censorinus (ca. 238 AD) and Theon (379-395 AD). Sir William Flinders Petrie writes, referring to a table of purported observations of Sirius:

> Now in going backward the first great datum that we meet is that on the back of the medical Ebers papyrus, where it is stated that Sirius rose on the 9th of Epiphi in the 9th year of Amenhotep I. As the 9th of Epiphi is 56 days before the 1st of Thoth, Sirius rose on that day at 4 X 56 years (224) before the dates at the head of the first column. As only 1322 B.C. can be the epoch here, so 1322 + 224 = 1546 B.C. for the 9th year of Amenhotep I, or 1554 B.C. for his accession. And as Aahmes I reigned 25 years, we reach 1579 B.C. for the accession of Aahmes and the beginning of the XVIIIth dynasty. This is not defined within a few years owing to four years being the equivalent of only one day's shift; owing to the rising being

perhaps observed in a different part of Egypt at different times; owing to various minor astronomical details. But this gives us 1580 B.C. as the approximate date for the great epoch of the rise of the XVIIIth dynasty. [322]

We will soon discover that there is significant reason to discard the above dates, but for now, we can just notice that even with such a great system, Petrie - as did Gardner - is still having some problems here.

Before that we next find another Sirius rising and two seasonal dates in the XIIth dynasty, and an indication of a season in the VIth dynasty. The most exact of these early dates is a rising of Sirius on the 17th of Pharmuthi in the 7th year of Senusert III, on a papyrus from Kahun. This is now in Berlin, and was published by BORCHARDT in Zeits. Aeg. Spr., xxxvii, 99-101. This shows that the 17th of Pharmuthi then fell on July 21st, which gives the 7th year of Senusert III at 1874 or 3334 B.C. As he reigned probably to his 38th year, he died 1843 or 3303 B.C. Amenemhat III reigned 44 years by his monuments, Amenemhat IV 9 years, and Sebekneferu 4 years by the Turin papyrus; these reigns bring the close of the XIIth dynasty to 1786 or 3246 B.C. We have, then, to decide by the internal evidence of the monuments of the kings which of these dates is probable, by seeing whether the interval of the XIIIth to XVIIth dynasties was 1,786 - 1,580 = 206 years, or else 1,666 years. This question has been merely ignored hitherto, and it has been assumed by all the Berlin school that the later date is the only one possible, and that the interval was only 206 years. [323]

Please notice that this only other "Sirius rising" is dated to either 1874 or 3334 BC. That's quite a jump. You would think that in all those thousands of years, if they observed this every year, they would write it down more often. But Petrie struggles on mightily to fit the square peg in the round hole:

Setting aside altogether for the present the details of the list of Manetho, let us look only to the monuments, and the Turin papyrus of kings, which was written with full materials concerning this age, with a long list of kings, and only two or three centuries later than the period in question. On the monuments we have the names of 17 kings of the XIIth dynasty. In the Turin papyrus there are the lengths of reigns of 9 kings, amounting to 67 years, or 7 years each on an average. If we apply this average length of reign to only the 17 kings whose reigns are proved by monuments, we must allow them 120 years; leaving out of account entirely about 40 kings in the Turin papyrus, as being not yet known on monuments. Of the Hyksos kings we know of the monuments of three certainly; and without here adopting the long reigns stated by Manetho, we must yet allow at least 30 years for these kings. And in the XVIIth dynasty there are at least the reigns of Kames and Sekhent.neb.ra, which cover probably 10 years. […]This leaves us but 46 years, out of the 206 years, to contain 120 kings named by the Turin papyrus, and all the Hyksos conquest and domination, excepting 30 years named above.

---

[322] Petrie, Flinders, *Researches in Sinai* (London: John Murray 1906).
[323] Ibid.

This is apparently an impossible state of affairs; and those who advocate this shorter interval are even compelled to throw over the Turin papyrus altogether, and to say that within two or three centuries of the events an entirely false account of the period was adopted as the state history of the Egyptians.

This difficulty has been so great that many scholars in Germany, and every one in the rest of Europe, have declined to accept this view. If, however, the Sirius datum is to be respected, we should be obliged to allow either 206 or else 1,666 years between the XIIth and XVIIIth dynasties. As neither of these seemed probable courses, *it has been thought that the Sirius datum itself was possibly in error,* and here the matter has rested awaiting fresh evidence. [324]

At this point, Petrie has almost fallen on his face on the very clue that would lead him out of the dilemma. To see him state it so clearly, and then just stumble on in the dark is almost painful.

What do I mean? I mean that *perhaps Sothis is not Sirius.* And perhaps the "Sothic Cycle" was something altogether different.

To be clear, let's look at these assumptions. First, it is assumed that a Sothic calendar was used in Egypt. We do not know that for a fact. We only know it *because Censorinus said so.* Censorinus wrote his idea rather late to be considered so great an authority. He was a Roman living in the *third century AD* who wrote *de Die Natali,* a work on ancient methods of computing time. What is more, Censorinus was highly praised by Cassiodorus, a converted Christian of about two centuries later, so we discover here that *Censorinus' work was very likely preserved because it was "approved", while other works that may have contradicted his ideas may be lost to us.*

The next big problem is the assumption of the beginning date of the Sothic cycle of 1,460-years. Again, Censorinus' word was accepted despite the endless problems this assumption has created. As it happens, when one begins to investigate the issue more thoroughly, it is found that the dates based on this theoretical Sothic calendar do not agree with one another. [325]

In the end, we find that the most fundamental problem of all is that it is an *assumption* of modern Egyptologists that the word they have translated in the observations listed above - *spd.t* - is even Sirius at all! A lot of people are sure that this is exactly what the Egyptians meant, but the fact is, no one really knows this for sure! The word that is translated as Sothis could have been something else! Another point is that, in the context above, it is not even certain what "rising"

---

[324] Ibid.

[325] It is known that a lunar calendar was used in ancient Egypt, but not much is known about it. The end result of the use of this calendar is that every date on any monument would have to tell us which calendar was being used, but the Egyptians didn't do that.

means. It could mean a star, or it could mean the rising of the river. It could also mean a ceremony that was to be conducted called the "Raising of Sothis".

As we discussed in a previous chapter regarding observational astronomy, Sirius rises in the sky from any given vantage point once every 24 hours, but it cannot be seen during those times when the sun is in the sky. The so-called heliacal rising of Sirius would have to occur at least 36 minutes before the sun comes up in order to be *seen*, which presupposes a rather accurate time keeping method, which *obviates the entire argument about a Sothic cycle to begin with.*

Although it has been made the keystone of the absolute dating of ancient history, the chronology of ancient Egypt rests on a host of unproven assumptions. The whole structure is rendered even more shaky by the lateness and the fragmentary nature of most of the literary sources which are crucial for providing a skeleton for Egyptian chronology.

As noted, the basic organization of Egyptian history around 31 dynasties begins from the work of Manetho compiled in the 3rd century BC. Manetho's records are supplemented and corrected by records recovered from the ancient monuments and archeological excavations of Egypt. Manetho's work survives only in quotation. John Brug writes in *The Astronomical Dating of Ancient History before 700 AD*:

> The use of astronomical calculations to decipher references to this Sothic cycle in ancient Egyptian records forms the foundation of all ancient chronology. Censorinus says:
>
> 'The moon is not relevant to the "great year" of the Egyptians which we call the "Year of the Dog" in Greek and the "Year of the Little-Dog" in Latin, because it begins when the constellation or star "Little-Dog" [allegedly the modern Canis Major or Sirius] rises on the first day of the month which the Egyptians call "Thouth". For their civil year has only 365 days without any intercalation. Thus a quadrennium among them is about one day shorter than the natural quadrennium, thus it is 1461 years before this "year" returns to the same beginning point. This "year" is called "heliacal" by some and "the divine year" by others.' (Censorinus, *De Die Natali*, ch. 18, my translation).
>
> Censorinus' statement certainly is not exhaustive. It gives us little information about how this "great year" was used or when it came into use. It is certainly open to debate how applicable this description of the Egyptian calendar and astronomy is to the 2nd and 3rd millennia BC. It does not address the issue of changes in the nature of the Egyptian calendar which may have occurred over the millennia. We have no definite proof that the Egyptians were aware of dating long eras by the Sothic cycle in the 2nd millennium BC. Even if we grant that they did, we have no certain knowledge of the date when any Sothic cycle began.
>
> Most historians presently accept the claim that Censorinus places the beginning of a Sothic cycle in about 140 AD and by extension in 1320 BC, 2780 BC and perhaps 4240 B.C. Censorinus says:
>
> 'As among us so also among the Egyptians a number of "eras" are referred to in their literature, such as that which they call "of Nabonnasar" which began from the first year of his reign, which was 986 years ago. Another is called "of Philip" which is counted from the death of Alexander the Great which was 562 years ago. But the beginning of these is always from the first day of the month which the Egyptians

call Thoth, which this year fell on the 7th day before the Calends of July [June 25], 100 years ago when Emperor Antoninus Pius was consul for the second time, and Bruttius Praesens was the other consul, the same day fell on the 12th [corrected to the 13th] day before the Calends of August [July 21, corrected to July 20] at which time the "Little-Dog" usually rises in Egypt. Therefore it is possible to know that of that great year, which as I wrote above is called "solar" or "of the Little-Dog" or the "divine year", now the hundredth year has passed. I have noted the beginnings of these years lest anyone think that they begin from January 1 or some other time, since the starting points chosen by the originators of these years are no less diverse than the opinions of philosophers. For that reason the natural year is said to begin by some at the new sun, that is the winter solstice, by others at the summer solstice, by others at the vernal equinox and by others at the autumnal equinox, by some at the rising of the Pleiades and by some at their setting, by many at the rising of "the Dog".' (Censorinus, Ch. 21, my translation).

Again it is noteworthy how little Censorinus actually says and how much is deduced from his statement. Censorinus is writing not to establish a system of chronology, but *to discuss various dates for New Years Day in different cultures.* He gives no specific date as the starting point for a Sothic Cycle as he does for the other eras which he mentions. All he does is give the date of the Julian calendar on which the first of Thoth fell in the year of his writing, which is well established as 238 or 239 AD and one hundred years earlier in 139 AD. In 238 AD the first of Thoth fell on about June 25 Julian. One hundred years earlier it fell on about July 20, which is the date The Little-Dog (supposedly Sothis) usually rises in Egypt. He seems to be referring to a conventional method of dating more than to an actual observation of the rising of Sothis on that date. […]

Besides lack of agreement of the time when a Sothic cycle began, this theory also faces other uncertainties. It is not certain how long a Sothic cycle lasts since there are other astronomic variables involved besides the precise length of the solar year. Calculations of the Sothic cycle have ranged from 1423 to 1506 years.

We do not know for sure with which star or constellation Sothis should be identified for all periods of Egyptian history. It is generally accepted that Sothis is the star which we call Sirius, although none of the sources gave any evidence for this from before classical times. Porphry in *De Antro Nym harum* says, "*Near Cancer is Sothis which the Greeks call the Dog*". *Solinus Polyhistor* says that this star rises between July 19-21.

In Chapter 21 of his work, concerning Isis and Osiris, Plutarch says, "*The soul of Isis is called 'Dog' by the Greeks and the soul of Horus is called Orion*". Since Sothis is identified with Isis in other Egyptian texts, and Sirius is called the Dog in Greek, we conclude that Sothis is the star which we-call Sirius. However there are a number of difficulties. At least the second half of Plutarch's statement appears to be in error, because Orion is usually associated with Osiris not Horus. According to some Egyptologists Egyptian astronomical names did not always remain attached to the same celestial object. Osiris was first associated with Venus; later Osiris was associated with Jupiter. The planet Venus, which was first identified with Osiris, was later identified with Isis. Sometimes "right eye" is a title of Isis-Hathor, sometimes it is a title of the sun.

Plutarch also identifies Osiris with the constellation which the Greeks call Argo. The hieroglyphic triangle which represents Sothis also appears to represent the zodiacal light, and the Egyptians apparently knew both an Isis-Sothis and a Horus-

Sothis. The term *wp rnpt* which refers to the rising of Sothis, also refers to the beginning of the civil year and the birthday of the king. *Even the Greek word "Sirius" is not always attached to the same celestial object.* Similar shifts and uncertainties apply to the identification of ancient astronomical names in general, for example, the constellations in Job.

According to the English astronomer Poole, Sirius was not on the horizon coincident with the rising of the sun on the Egyptian New Year's Day in 140 BC, *the date specified by Censorinus* and those who follow him. Macnaughton set up a chronology based on the supposition that Sothis was Spica, not Sirius, as a way around this difficulty. Canopus and Venus are other candidates that have been suggested, perhaps less plausibly. Kenneth Brecher has revived the doubts about identifying the bright star referred to in records as Sothis/the Dog/Sirius with the star we call Sirius today. Babylonian and Roman sources as late as Ptolemy all call "Sirius" a red star. Seneca says it is redder than Mars. In his star catalog Ptolemy refers to the bright red star in the face of the Dog. He links Sirius with red stars like Aldebaran and Arcturus.

The star which we presently call Sirius is not a red star. No theory of stellar evolution offers any explanation for how a red star could become white in 2000 years, although much speculation has centered around possible changes in the companion star which is part of Sirius. There is a flaw either in our identification of Sothis as our Sirius, in the ancients' observations, in our translation of their texts, or in present theories of stellar evolution, which must be based more on computer analysis than on observation.

One explanation which has been offered is that the red color refers to the star only as observed in heliacal rising near the horizon. Perhaps "red" simply means "bright" or "beautiful" as it does in Akkadian or Russian. *At any rate, we can say that there is at least some question about the identification of Sothis as our star Sirius, and a thorough re-study of the pertinent Egyptian and Greek astronomical terms would be valuable.*[326]

Despite all of the problems and reasons to discard the entire chronology based on the Sothic dating in conjunction with the Biblical chronology, all of Egyptian chronology is based on this Sothic cycle inferred from Censorinus, even if there has been much argument about when said cycle is supposed to have begun. In the absence of any real evidence, the experts decided on one set of dates (1320 BC to AD141) as the cycle, and proclaimed it as the standard for the setting of ancient dates.

Quite a number of Egyptologists have rejected the theory of the Sothic cycle entirely. What is more, the theoretical sothic cycle does not agree with radiocarbon dating, even if we already have an idea that radiometric dating methods have their

---

[326] Brug, John, The Astronomical Dating of Ancient History before 700 AD. 1988.

own problems. For dates within certain ranges, these problems have been adjusted with tree-ring calibration.

Another controversial item of Sothic dating is the so-called "era of Menophres". This discussion is based on a statement in the late classical writer, Theon who says:

> On the 100th year of the era of Diocletian, concerning the rising of the Dog,
> because of the pattern we received from the era of Menophres to the end of the age
> of Augustus the total of the elapsed years was 1605.

Many attempts have been made to identify Theon's Menophres. Menophres has been identified as the city Memphis or one of a number of pharaohs. Merneptah, Seti I, Harmhab, and Ramses I are among the candidates that have been suggested. There is simply not enough evidence to draw any firm conclusions about the meaning of this text.

Otto Neugebauer began the ten-page section on Egypt in his later *History of Ancient Mathematical Astronomy* with the provocative sentence, "Egypt has no place in a work on the history of mathematical astronomy".[327]

Did you catch that? Neugebauer is telling us that *the Egyptians were scientifically illiterate.* He read and examined everything. All the Egyptologists who were inculcated into the belief of the superiority of Egyptian science were sending him their papyri and inscriptions from tombs and monuments. All the things that are so difficult to get hold of nowadays were sent to Neugebauer. And what did Neugebauer say?

> Mathematics and astronomy played a uniformly *insignificant* role in all periods of
> Egyptian history. [...] The fact that Egyptian mathematics has preserved a
> relatively primitive level makes it possible to investigate a stage of development
> which is no longer available in so simple a form, *except* in the Egyptian documents.

> To some extent Egyptian mathematics has had some, though rather *negative,
> influence* on later periods. Its arithmetic was widely based on the use of unit
> fractions, a practice which probably influenced the Hellenistic and Roman
> administrative offices and thus spread further into other regions of the Roman
> empire. [...]The influence of this practice is visible even in works of the stature of
> the Almagest, where final results are often expressed with unit fractions in spite of
> the fact that the computations themselves were carried out with sexagesimal
> fractions. [...] And this old tradition doubtless contributed much to restricting the
> sexagesimal place value notation to a purely scientific use.

> It would be quite out of proportion to describe Egyptian geometry here at length. It
> suffices to say that we find in Egypt about the same elementary level we observed
> in contemporary Mesopotamia.

---

[327] Neugebauer, Otto, *The Exact Sciences in Antiquity* (New York: Dover 1969).

The role of Egyptian mathematics is probably best described as *a retarding force* upon numerical procedures. Egyptian astronomy had much less influence on the outside world for the very simple reason that it remained through all its history on an *exceedingly crude level* which had practically no relations to the rapidly growing mathematical astronomy of the Hellenistic age. Only in one point does the Egyptian tradition show a very beneficial influence, that is, in the use of the Egyptian calendar by the Hellenistic astronomers. This calendar is, indeed, the only intelligent calendar which ever existed in human history. A year consists of 12 months of 30 days each and five additional days at the end of each year.

A second Egyptian contribution to astronomy is the division of the day into 24 hours, through these hours were originally not of even length, but were dependent on the seasons. [...]

Lunar calendars played a role since early times side by side with the schematic civil calendar of the 365-day year. An inscription of the Middle Kingdom mentions "great" and "small" years, and we know now that the "great" years were civil years which contained 13 new moon festivals in contrast to the ordinary "small" years with only 12 new moons. The way these intercalations were regulated, at least in the latest period, is shown by the Demotic text.

This Demotic text contains a simple periodic scheme which is based on the fact that 25 Egyptian civil years (which contain 9125 days) are very nearly equal to 309 mean lunar months. These 309 months are grouped by our text into 16 ordinary years of 12 lunar months, and 9 "great" years of 13 months. Ordinarily two consecutive lunar months are given 59 days by our scheme, obviously because of the fact that one lunar month is close to 29 ½ days long. But every 5th year the two last months are made 60 days long. This gives for the whole 25 year cycle the correct total of 9125 days.

Since at this period all astronomical computations were carried out in the sexagesimal system, at least as far as fractions are concerned, the equinoctial hours were divided sexagesimally. Thus our present division of the day into 24 hours of 60 minutes each is the result of a Hellenistic modification of an Egyptian practice combined with Babylonian numerical procedures.

Finally, we have to mention the decans. [...] The decans *are the actual reason for the 12 division of the night* and hence, in the last analysis, of the 24 hour system. Again, in Hellenistic times the Egyptian decans were brought into a fixed relation to the Babylonian zodiac which is attested in Egypt only *since the reign of Alexander's successors*. In this final version the 36 decans are simply the thirds of the zodiacal signs, each decan representing 10 degrees of the ecliptic. Since the same period witnesses the rapid development of astrology, the decans assumed an important position in astrological lore and in kindred fields such as alchemy, the magic of stones and plants and their use in medicine. In this disguise the decans reached India, only to be returned in still more fantastic form to the Muslims and the West. [...]

[In the decans] *we have not a calendar but a star clock.* The user of this list would *know the hour of night* by the rising of the decan which is listed in the proper decade of the month. [...]

We call this phenomenon the "heliacal rising" of S, using a term of Greek astronomy. [...]

It is this sequence of phenomena which led the Egyptians to *measure the time of night by means of stars,* which we now call decans. This was intended to devise some method of indicating the times of office for the nightly service in the temples, (and other practical reasons.) Just as the months were divided into decades, so were the services of the hour-stars. For 10 days, S indicated the last hour of night, then the next star for the next ten days, and so on. [...]

All this was, in fact, taken into account by the inventors of the decanal hours, as can be demonstrated by the terminal section of the "diagonal calendars" on the coffin lids. [...]

By the time of the New Kingdom, the usefulness of the decans as indicators of hours had ceased. [...] The decans held a secure position as representatives of the decades of the year in the decoration of astronomical ceilings, as in the tomb of Senmut or in the cenotaph of Seti I. In this form, they continued to exist until their association with the zodiac of the Hellenistic period revived them and made them powerful elements of astrological doctrine.

The coffins with the "diagonal calendars" belong roughly to the period from 2100 BC to 1800 BC. [...] Astronomical accuracy was nowhere seriously attempted in these documents. [...]

In summary, from the almost three millennia of Egyptian writing, the only texts which have come down to us and deal with a numerical prediction of astronomical phenomena *belong to the Hellenistic or Roman period.* None of the earlier astronomical documents contains mathematical elements; they are crude observational schemes, partly religious, partly practical in purpose.

Ancient science was the product of a very few men; and these few happened *not* to be Egyptians.[328]

It seems that we have learned several things from Neugebauer's examination of the texts of the various papyri, tomb inscriptions, monuments, calendars, and so forth. One of the most important things we have learned is that the Egyptians did, indeed, correct their calendar every five years, similar to what we do every four years with our leap year. This naturally makes the idea of the Sothic cycle irrelevant in terms of calendrical reconciliation. We also begin to understand some of the totally incomprehensible sayings of the *Pyramid Texts.* They were recitations of prayers and magical spells that had to be performed at a certain "moment" in the night, and the only way to determine time at night was by the stars. According to Neugebauer, there are sufficient numbers of these star clocks in tombs to confirm this idea.

Next we note that Neugebauer tells us that the only texts which have come down to us and deal with a numerical prediction of astronomical phenomena *belong to*

---

[328] Neugebauer, ibid., pp. 71-2, 78, 80-1, 90, 81-4, 86-9, 91.

the Hellenistic or Roman period and in Hellenistic times the Egyptian decans were brought into a fixed relation to the Babylonian zodiac, which is attested in Egypt only *since the reign of Alexander's successors.*

In other words, the "occult secrets" generally attributed to the Egyptians, must actually belong to the Greeks.

However, there is something just a little bit deeper here that I would like to point out. As Neugebauer says, the Egyptians of historical times were really scientifically illiterate. So much so that their influence was inhibiting upon mathematics and science. But we still have that most astonishing fact that they came up with what Neugebauer declares to be the most sensible calendar ever devised. Even the Babylonians, whose mathematics sends Neugebauer into raptures, did not have so clever a calendar. We find ourselves asking: *where did the Egyptians get this calendar?*

In an attempt to come to some understanding of this matter of Sothis, (which actually is the Greek name for Sirius, and it is an assumption that the word transliterated from the Egyptian texts is, actually, Sothis or Sirius), I undertook a comparative reading of Faulkner's translation of the *Ancient Egyptian Pyramid Texts.* Indeed, I am not an Egyptologist nor an expert in these matters, but I wondered if I would notice anything at all with my "beginner's mind", assuming that the translator dealt honestly with his text. Reading every reference to the word transliterated into English as "*spdt*", that is then translated as Sothis, brought me face to face with a number of interesting problems.

If we remember that Sirius is also supposed to represent Isis, we notice first of all that the Egyptians had no problem specifying Isis when they wanted to, sometimes *in the same passage where Sothis is mentioned.* In Utterance 216 of the Pyramid Texts, it is translated, "*Sothis is swallowed up by the Netherworld, Pure and living in the horizon*". However, there is a footnote that says: "Despite the lack of correct gender ... in a triple repetition of the phrase, the scribe has ignored the discrepancy of gender in the case of Sothis".[329]

In other words... Sothis is described in words of male gender and the translator is having to deal with this problem.

Apparently this gender issue pops up several more times, and the footnote directs us to a paper in the *Journal of Near Eastern Studies,* volume 25, p. 159. Repeatedly the word *spdt* is translated as "my sister is Sothis..." after which, we are again referred to the above paper, p. 153, which suggests that in each of these instances, the problem with that pesky male gender keeps popping up.

In Utterance 366, we find Isis and Sothis mentioned together in a strange way: [Osiris is being addressed]

---

[329] Faulkner, *The Ancient Egyptian Pyramid Texts,* (Aris and Phillips. 1969)

"Your sister Isis comes to you rejoicing for love of you. You have placed her on your phallus and your seed issues into her, she being ready as Sothis, and Har-Sopd has come forth from you as Horus who is in Sothis."

Isis is described as being "ready like Sothis". This readiness is described in overtly sexual terms as though some dynamic interaction between bodies of the cosmos is being described sexually - an exchange takes place between them. We then read that, as a result of this cosmic interaction of impregnation, "*sopd*" is supposed to be "born from Isis as Horus comes forth from Sothis".

What is this "*sopd*"?

In utterance 412 the following lines:

> "The Great One falls upon his side, He who is in Nedit quivers, his head is lifted by Re; he detests sleep, he hates inertness. O flesh of the King, do not decay, do not rot, do not smell unpleasant. Your foot will not be overpassed, your stride will not be overstridden, you shall not tread on the corruption of Osiris. You shall reach the sky as Orion your soul shall be as effective as Sothis; have power, having power; be strong, having strength; may your soul stand among the gods as Horus who dwells in Irs. May the terror of you come into being in the hearts of the gods like the Nt-crown..."

In this passage, it seems as though Sothis is compared to something that is "effective and powerful" and having strength like Horus.

In utterance 472, we find this:

> "I go up on this eastern side of the sky where the gods were born, and I am born as Horus, as Him of the horizon; I am vindicated and my double is vindicated; Sothis is my sister, the Morning Star is my offspring."

First the writer says I am "as Horus", followed by an allusion to Horus being his "double" followed by an immediate mention of Sothis as this double, though the allusion to a "double" is given as a "sister".

In Utterance 1074:

> "Sothis goes forth clad in her brightness, she censes the bright ones who are among them. The striking powers of the city are quiet, the region is content. I have prepared a road that I may pass on it, namely what Meref foretold in On."

This passage is, apparently, very problematical because Faulkner has footnoted almost every term. In particular, the word "brightness" above is noted to be a word that means "sharpness".

This brings us to our strange word that is transliterated as *spd*, or *Soped*. Regarding the above mention of "sharpness" related to Sothis going forth, we find that *spd-ibhw* means "sharp toothed". Sharp toothed occurs repeatedly in a certain context illustrated by Utterance 222:

> "I have come to you, my father, I have come to you, O great Wild Bull. ...I have come to you, my father, I have come to you, O *Sopd*."

Now, this "*Sopd*" is transliterated as "*spdw*" being very similar to "*spdt*" that is translated as "sothis". It is obvious that the translators have a problem with this "*spdw*", and just translate it as "*Sopd*". In the end, we have three very similar words: *spdt*, *spdw*, and *spd-ibhw* (sharp toothed), and my guess is that this "sharp toothed" business may relate to something that is visually similar to a mouth full of gleaming, sharp teeth. Also, sharp toothed can mean that something is radiating clearly defined "rays", that are "sharp" like "teeth".

The word *sp* occurs by itself in one reference:

> "O god; your third is he who orders offerings. The perfume of Iht-wtt is on this King, a bnbn-loaf is in the Mansion of Sokar, a foreleg is in the House of Anubis. This King is hale, the Herdsman stands up, the month is born, Sp lives."

The more I read these texts, the more I think that these are rote repetitions of something that once really meant something, but through the centuries, with the changes in language and semantics, they had long ago lost their meaning and were simply being recited as magical texts. Either that, or the experts in Egyptian language have a long way to go! An important point is, however, that *every single reference* to *spdw* occurs in a passage about the "great wild bull" and both Osiris and Seth were referred to as bulls though bulls aren't generally thought of in the context of sharp teeth. Seth was the "*Bull of the South*". Utterance 580 is a text to be recited at the sacrifice of a Red Bull. This bull is supposed to represent Seth being sacrificed by Horus. Addressed to Seth the bull:

> "O you who smote my father, who killed one greater than you, you have smitten my father, you have killed one greater than you."

This is followed by a passage addressed to the dead king/Osiris:

> "O my father Osiris this King, I have smitten for you him who smote you as an ox; I have killed for you him who killed you as a wild bull; I have broken for you him who broke you ...[he lists all the parts he has cut off]. Its upper foreleg is on Khopr, its lower foreleg belongs to Atum, father of the gods, its haunches belong to Shu and Tefenet, its shanks belong to Hnt-irty and Kherty, its back belongs to Neith and Selket, its heart belongs to Sakhmet the Great, the contents of its udder belong to these four gods, the children of Horus, Hapy, Imsety, Duamutef, Kebhsenuf. Its head, its tail, its arms, and its legs belong to Anubis...[330]

Now, of course, we wonder how an ox has an udder... and of course, Faulkner has an explanation that the scribe "forgot" that he was writing about a bull! Nevertheless, the reference to Sakhmet brings up a very interesting remark in Utterance 704:

> "This King is the [...] which went forth from Re, this King has come forth from between the thighs of the Two Enneads; he was conceived by Sakhmet, the King was borne by Shezmetet. This King is the falcon..."

The footnote tells us that where it says "he was conceived", that, regarding the word "he", the scribe "for once employs the feminine suffix". So, we think that certain other translations of "he" may have been "she" or vice versa.

---

[330] Faulkner, ibid.

Remembering that *"Sopd"* is supposed to be "born from Isis as Horus comes forth from Sothis", we find the curious relationship above to "two Enneads" and they are there described as Sakhmet and Shezmetet. Utterance 248:

> "The King is a great one, the King has issued from between the thighs of the Ennead. The king was conceived by Sakhmet, and it was Shezmetet who bore the king, *a star brilliant and FAR TRAVELLING*, who brings distant products to Re daily."

We naturally have questions about the many references to the "sisters" the "Two Enneads", the "double" and the "twins" that are repeatedly mentioned.

Sekhmet is the patroness of divine retribution, vengeance, and conquest. She is represented with the head of a lion to suggest the "mane" or "coma" of brightness. Sekhmet means "The Mighty One", and she was one of the most powerful of the gods and goddesses. She was the goddess who meted out divine punishment to the enemies of the gods and of the pharaoh. In this capacity she was called the "Eye of Ra". She also accompanied the pharaoh into battle, launching fiery arrows into battle ahead of him. Sekhmet could send plagues and disease against her enemies, and for this reason, as a preventative, was sometimes invoked to avoid plague and cure disease.

Sekhmet's capacity for destruction is well documented. In one story, Ra sent her to punish those mortals who had forgotten him, and she ended up nearly destroying the entire human race. Only the cleverness of Ra stopped her rampage before it consumed every living thing.

Sekhmet's breath was the hot desert wind, and her body took on the glare of the midday sun. She represented the *destructive force of the sun*. According to the legends, she came into being when Hathor was sent to earth by Ra to take vengeance on man. She was the one who slaughtered mankind and drank their blood, only being stopped by trickery. She was said to be the *destructive side of the sun*, and a solar goddess given the title Eye of Ra. Since several of these attributes also belonged to Set, the "Bull of the South" whose breath was the hot desert wind that brings crime and destruction, we wonder if Sekhmet is not a different "model"? If so, considering the descriptions of Sekhmet, put together with the "sharp toothed" appelation and the "far travelling star", then we might suggest that the term Sothis simply refers to a comet? In such a case, we can have no idea of which comet it might be, whether or not it is a periodic body, and even if it is, what its period might have been.

In any event, in a general sense, we discover that the great astronomical and scientific knowledge attributed to the Egyptians falls far short of that which has been promoted by many "alternative researchers" as well as mainstream Egyptologists. No wonder Neugebauer's results aren't popularly known. They pretty much put a period to the idea that the Egyptians were observing Sirius and precession, or that they had a calendar based on a Sothic cycle of 1460 years. Real Science was applied to the subject of Egyptology, and the Egyptophiles just couldn't stand it. They withdrew into their private little world of dreams and illusions of Egyptian grandeur, clinging desperately to the rags and tatters of their occult beliefs like a drowning man clutches at straws.

It is only in recent years that the disruptions of civilization have been scientifically related to celestial phenomena by serious researchers, and even their observations have not moved the Egyptologist one inch from their firm adherence to their chronology. After corresponding with a few of them, reading their books and technical papers, I found that not one of them was capable of answering a single question directly, though one of them did suggest to me in a roundabout way that he had a few mildly radical ideas. Obviously, he didn't want to say it too loudly for fear of being run out of Dodge.

MOSES AND AARON

Returning to the matter of Biblical chronology and its imposition upon our world even down to the present day, we need to consider several things. The redactor and editor of the Bible selected the order of the stories in the new "history" to fulfill the function of tribal unification for purposes of political and religious control. This has resulted in many problems for those who have sought to find real "history" in the Biblical history.

We have seen that the Priestly source that amalgamated the stories of the loose tribal groups of Iron Age Canaan was constrained by the need to include several variations of the same story. His audience would have rejected any "history" that did not include oral traditions they actually knew. Also, the evidence suggests he assembled these stories in a certain order that was designed to create the illusion of a long history of "chosenness". This is exactly the thing that Isaac Newton accused other ancient authors of doing, yet he did not consider it possible in regards to the Bible.

Nevertheless Newton outlined for us the process by which it was done. The editors of the Bible created their history by inserting segments of the *Book of Generations*, so that retellings of stories that occurred during the same time period suddenly looked like they'd happened over many hundreds or even thousands of years. In other words, the stories *"horizontal" arrangement in time became a vertical arrangement.* What happened to many peoples suddenly happened to the "chosen" people. What is more, the stories that were passed from group to group about a single individual and series of activities, were often "personalized" to that specific group according to the idea of mythicization we have already discussed.

The way we need to think about these matters is to consider first the facts as we can discover them, and then see if *any* of the stories of the Bible fit to those facts in any way, *disregarding entirely the manufactured genealogies and "historical timeline" of the Bible* as it is presented in the Bible.

The Bible is supposed to be the history of a long series of eponymous founders. The different versions of the stories, assembled from the different tribes, were arranged in a vertical timeline across centuries, with the insertion of genealogies, most of which were uncertain and repetitious if not actually invented for the purpose. Even so, I have suggested, there is one story of a series of interactions situated in one frame of time reference that can be extracted from these stories that IS recorded in both Egyptian history and the Bible so accurately that the two sides of the story fit together like a hand in a glove. What is more, as I have suggested, understanding this event, this connection of a real historical event that is reported both in the Bible, and in Egyptian records, is the key to unlocking the entire puzzle of the Ark of the Covenant.

Returning to the reforms of Hezekiah after the fall of the northern kingdom, what is a descendant of Aaron to do in the southern kingdom, upon the arrival of all the northern refugees, carrying their stories and histories and genealogies? What are you going to do when your own role, as a priest of the Aaronic line is denigrated by these stories, and your role as the arbiter of the laws of Yahweh, and your income as the only group that can perform the sacrifice is being threatened?

Well, you write another Torah! What else? The P text was written as an *alternative* to J and E. In P, *Aaron* is introduced as *the* authority. In JE, miracles are performed in Egypt using Moses' staff. But the author of P made it Aaron's staff. In JE, Aaron is introduced as Moses' "Levite brother", which could mean only that they are members of the same tribe, and not necessarily actually brothers as has been thought. But now, the author of P states categorically that Moses and Aaron were literal brothers, sons of the same mother and father. What's more, P states that Aaron was the firstborn!

In P, there are no sacrifices *until the sacrifice made on the day that Aaron is consecrated as High priest*. The author of P clearly didn't want anybody to have any ideas whatsoever that anyone other than an Aaronid priest could offer a sacrifice! The author of P deliberately omitted the sacrifices offered by Cain, Abel, Noah, Abraham, Isaac, and Jacob. When he couldn't omit the sacrifice from the story, he omitted the entire story.

For example: in the J version of the flood story, Noah took seven pairs of all the animals that were fit for sacrifice. P says he took only two of every kind. In J, at the end of the story, Noah offers a sacrifice. He needed the extra animals so he wouldn't wipe out a species! But in the P story, there is no sacrifice.

To the author of P, the issue of *bloodline priests* as the only intermediaries between man and god looms very large. There were no angels, no talking animals, no prophetic dreams, and most definitely *anyone who oversteps such boundaries is to be put to death*. In P, Yahweh is a universal, abstract god who created the "heavens and the earth" and brought punishment on mankind due to a cosmic crisis at the time of the flood. In J and E, god created the earth and the heavens - *in that order* - and god is personal and talks to man on intimate terms. The story of the flood was a cyclical great rain, not a cosmic disaster of guilt and revenge.

So it is that, throughout P we read about a cosmic god of order and control with whom man can communicate *only* via the offices of an ordained, bloodline priest, using the ordered rituals provided to the priest by Yahweh. Over and over again P reiterates that the Aaronid priest at the altar is the *only access to god*. These priests have become the psychopomp, the feminized participants in a bizarre hieros gamos with a male deity in which their role is symbolized by ritual castration - circumcision.

In Plutarch's *Convivial Questions*, one of the guests claims to be able to prove that the god of the Jews is really Dionysus Sabazius, the Barley-god of Thrace and Phrygia; and Tacitus similarly records in his History (v. 5) that, "*some maintain that the rites of the Jews were founded in honour of Dionysus*". The historian Valerius Maximus says that in the year 139 BC, the praetor of Foreigners, C. Cornelius Hispallus, expelled from Rome certain Jews who were, "trying to corrupt Roman morals by a *pretended cult* of Sabazian Jove". The inference is that the praetor did not expel them for a *legitimate* worship of this god, but because they were foisting a bizarre new rite on the Thracian religion - circumcision! It is curious that later followers of this perversion soon began to resort to full castration in adoration of their god, even after their god had transmogrified from Jehovah to Jesus! St. Augustine was one such, and it is conjectured that St. Paul was also a self-mutilated eunuch, though I disagree. In later times, this practice was modified to the idea of celibacy and monasticism which further obscured and distorted the "Fire of Prometheus".

In the P text, there is not a single reference to god as merciful. The words mercy, grace, faithfulness and repent *never* occur. The writer intends for the reader to understand that forgiveness cannot be had just because one is sorry or has learned a lesson. Forgiveness can only, *only,* be had by sacrifice through an approved priest who then, because he is unable to fulfill the true function of the ecstatic ascent, makes a blood sacrifice to his god as a substitution.

The person who wrote the P document was not just changing a few stories: *he was developing a complete concept of god* - and his motivation was theological, political, and economic control. He also intended to establish one group as the legitimate authority on earth: the Aaronid Levites. The writer of P could not establish his authority just by defending Aaron or placing him in a better light. He also felt it necessary to deal with Moses and his descendants in a very careful way. This suggests that he realized that he was in a very precarious position.

With the arrival of the refugees from the northern kingdom, the Shiloh priests who were the descendants of Moses, the author of P couldn't just trash Moses outright. Moses was the national hero of the northern kingdom, the kingdom of the Omride dynasty, even if they had been displaced by Jezebel and her gods. Moses was, in fact, the *founder* of the northern kingdom.

So the creator of the P document couldn't just make up lies about any of it. But he could present the stories with a particular spin. He could make up certain details that could be claimed as "inside" or "prior knowledge" or "revelation from god", if need be, to bolster his claims and position.

Being concerned with the idea that the people would accept the new Torah, the author of the P document had to consider what the people already knew and accepted. He had to artfully produce an account of the past that the audience would accept. So, for the most part, he accepted the place of Moses in the tradition, but he minimized his character and even completely twisted a couple of the stories to place Moses in a very bad light.[331]

The author of P also tells his own version of the revelation at Mount Sinai. P adds a detail at the end of the story that is, up to that point, very similar to the original. This detail is that there was something very unusual about Moses' face when he came down from the mountain. When people looked at him, they were

---

[331] See the differences in the "water from the rock" stories in Exodus 17:2-7 and Numbers 20:2-13.

afraid to come near him, and he was forced to wear a veil. According to P, whenever we think of Moses for the last 40 years of his life, we are supposed to think of him wearing a veil.

What is it about Moses' face? The meaning of the Hebrew term is uncertain, and for a long time, people thought that it meant that Moses had acquired horns. This resulted in many depictions of Moses with horns in Medieval art. Another interpretation was that something was wrong with Moses' skin - that light beamed out from his skin. So many translations and interpretations go along with this idea and teach that there was "glory" shining from Moses' face that hurt the eyes of the beholders. I was taught this version myself.

In more recent times, biblical scholar, William Popp, has assembled an array of evidence that suggests that the writer of P was telling his audience that Moses was disfigured in the sense that he is so horrible to look upon that the people cannot bear to see him. The text does tell us that the "glory of Yahweh" is like a "consuming fire" and this suggests that the flesh of Moses' face has been eaten away making him a specter out of your worst nightmare. If this was an understood colloquialism of the time, then it is a masterly touch of manipulation by the author of P. He hasn't denigrated Moses, but he has created an image of horror that no one will want to contemplate!

However, I believe that there is a different reason for this allusion. Going back to our Sun-god allusion, we find that one of the early efforts to demonize the goddess was the symbolism of the Old Babylonian god *Huwawa* (Humbaba). Huwawa appears in the Gilgamesh stories as Enlil's *guardian of the Cedar Forest*, and we have some idea that cedar wood was very important to the god of Moses as presented in the P text. We also know the earlier importance of the fir tree to the birth goddess, so we find this Huwawa assimilating the goddess' prerogatives as well. We also note that most interesting name: Huwawa. Sounds close to Yahweh to me!

The use of cedar in the sacrifices, and the demand to build the temple of cedar wood are indeed, most curious connections to this god Huwawa. In 2 Samuel, chapter 7:7, Yahweh is reported as saying to David via his prophet, Nathan,

> In all places where I have moved with all the Israelites, did I speak a word to any from the tribes of Israel whom I commanded to be shepherd of My people Israel, asking, Why do you not build Me a house of cedar?

And then, in verse 13 Yahweh tells David that his son shall be the one to build this house. "*He shall build a house for My name and I will establish the throne of his kingdom for ever.*" In 1 Kings, 5:6, Solomon is recorded as requesting cedars from Lebanon to build the Temple of Solomon. Curiously, in the Bible story, Solomon raised a levy of forced labor for the cutting of the trees and building of the temple, quite similar to the stories of bondage in Egypt. The foundations of the temple were "great costly stones" which, of course, have never been found in Jerusalem.

Was the relationship of the terrible face of Moses, in comparison to the terrible visage of Huwawa, the guardian of the cedar forest, understood by the people? Huwawa was described as a giant protected by *seven layers of terrifying radiance*. He was killed by Gilgamesh and Enkidu in a story that is quite similar to the slaying of Goliath by David and Medusa by Perseus. In those stories, the Osirian hero prevails over the Setian serpent.

Melam and *ni* are two Sumerian words which are often linked. Strictly speaking *ni* seems to denote the effect on human beings of the divine power *melam*. The Babylonians used various words to capture the idea of *ni*, including *puluhtu*, "fear". The exact connotation of *melam* is difficult to grasp. It is a brilliant, visible glamour which is exuded by gods, heroes, sometimes by kings, and also by temples of great holiness. While it is in some ways a phenomenon of light, *melam* is at the same time terrifying and awe-inspiring. *Ni* can be experienced as a physical creeping of the flesh. Gods are sometimes said to "wear" their *melam* like a garment or a crown, and like a garment or a crown, *melam* can be "taken off". While it is always a mark of the supernatural, *melam* carries no connotation of moral value since demons and terrifying giants can "wear" it too.[332]

So, it seems that this is very likely the point that the writer of P was trying to make about Moses. Moses was being compared to Huwawa/Humbaba, the horrible guardian of the cedar forest, a variation on the sun-god whose face is so brilliant that it must be "veiled"; following which Huwawa/Yahweh demanded that his sacrifices contain cedar, and his house be built of cedar!

The author of P was not only eliminating things that he specifically rejected for theological or political reasons, he was also eliminating the long tales of the J and E texts. Retelling the wonderful stories of the people was not his intent; his intent was the business of establishing Yahweh and his agents: the Aaronid priesthood. He shows no interest whatsoever in the literary interests of the people, alluding to them only in short lines or paragraphs where they are mostly dismissed as pagan nonsense. In all of P there are only three stories of any length that are similar to JE: the creation, the flood and the covenant with Noah (excluding the sacrifice after the flood), the covenant with Abraham, (excluding his almost sacrifice of Isaac). He also added a story that is not present in the older documents: the story of the death of Aaron's sons Nadab and Abihu which is presented to instruct the people that the sacrifice must only be performed as commanded by god, even if it is performed by bloodline Levites! He was leaving no angle uncovered! The repeated emphasis on this point tells us that he was trying to change something that had existed for a long time: that anybody could enter the Tent of Meeting. But now, with a fake ark of the covenant in there, only the priests could enter. In this way, only they were able to see that the replacement ark was not the original. Clever, yes? The P writer seems overwhelmingly concerned with Sinai and the giving of the law, since half of Exodus, half of Numbers, nearly all of Leviticus, is concerned with the *Levite law*.

---

[332] Black, Jeremy, and Green, Anthony, *Gods, Demons and Symbols of Ancient Mesopotamia* (Austin: University of Texas Press 1992).

There is another story that P presents that has no parallel in the older accounts, so is thought to be entirely made up: the story of the cave of Machpelah. This story gives a lengthy description of the negotiations between Abraham and a Hittite over a piece of land with a cave on it which Abraham buys as a burial place for his family. Why does the P source, which leaves out so many fun facts and stories, divert to mention this mundane piece of business? Friedman believes that it is to establish a legal claim to Hebron, an Aaronid priestly city. But if that were the case, it could have been done any number of other ways. My thought is that maybe the story is not made up. Perhaps, since it was an Aaronid city, there was a certain tradition about it that was only now being added to the "history". And maybe this tradition of Abraham being a "Great Prince" of the Hittites wasn't just blowing smoke because it does, indeed, indirectly point us in the direction of Huwawa! But what I think is more important is the fact that it points us away from something else that the author of the P text does not want us to consider.

At any event, we now have a pretty good idea of what was going on at the time of the Hezekiah reforms in the southern kingdom of Judah, after the fall of the northern kingdom. We don't know if Hezekiah went along with this plan because he was promised that he would benefit from the gifts to the priesthood, or if he was just simply convinced that it would assist his consolidation of power and expansionist aims. Whatever forces were behind the activity, we see that Hezekiah was casting himself in the role of a new Omri-David with his plans to rebel against the Assyrian empire. He organized the Phoenician and Philistine cities against Assyria, and he managed to get Egypt as an ally.

Assyria's Sennacherib launched a massive military response and captured the Judaean's fortress of Lachish in an assault that prefigured the Roman capture of Masada eight hundred years later. The excavations at Lachish tell part of the story. The rest of the story is at the palace of Nineveh, the capital of the Assyrian empire. There, depicted on the walls, is one of the few known representations of what Jews looked like in Biblical times. These panels are now in the British museum, with casts of them in the Israel Museum.

The story is that the Assyrians failed to bring Judah to her knees. When Sennacherib appeared on the horizon, the call went out for, "the kings of Egypt and the archers, chariotry and cavalry of the king of Kush, an army beyond counting", to come to fight the mighty Assyrian army. Egypt, under Shabaka, had a large standing army poised in the Delta, apparently waiting for the signal to march. In the end, we have contemporary evidence of this campaign in the Assyrian records, as well as Egyptian reliefs. These latter are rather general, employing the standard "head smiting" scene with some text.

There is no doubt that this battle was a serious reverse for Sennacherib, and he ultimately permanently withdrew from the Levant. However, the Bible tells us: "*And it was, that night, that an angel of Yahweh went out and struck one hundred eighty-five thousand in the Assyrian camp, and they rose in the morning and here they were all dead corpses. And Sennacherib traveled and went and returned, and he lived in Nineveh.*" Curious how the Egyptian army was transmogrified into an "angel of Yahweh".

Nevertheless, this was the turning point in Judah's history. Though Sennacherib had laid waste to the outlying districts, Jerusalem had not fallen. And Jerusalem began to grow into the "Holy City". The population increased because, obviously, it was more convenient to be close to the source of meat preparation. And the Levites grew in power.

THE SIN OF MANASSEH: EXILE IN BABYLON

After Hezekiah died, his son, Manasseh came to the throne. During his reign, the Assyrians returned, and he must not have been very friendly to them because he was sent into exile in Babylon where the Assyrian king's brother was ruler. It is not known whether it was because the people demanded it, or because the Assyrian's put pressure on him, but Manasseh's exile ended after he and his son reinstituted pagan worship, including putting pagan statues in the Temple. They also rebuilt the sacrificial locations outside of Jerusalem. Manasseh was succeeded by his son, Amon, who was assassinated after only two years after which Amon's eight year old son, Josiah, became king. (At least according to one version!)

> Josiah was eight years old when he began to reign, and he reigned in Jerusalem one and thirty years. And he did that which was right in the sight of the LORD, and walked in the ways of David his father, and declined neither to the right hand, nor to the left. For in the eighth year of his reign, while he was yet young, he began to seek after the God of David his father: and in the twelfth year he began to purge Judah and Jerusalem from the high places, and the groves, and the carved images, and the molten images. [...]

> Now in the eighteenth year of his reign, when he had purged the land, and the house, he sent Shaphan the son of Azaliah, and Maaseiah the governor of the city, and Joah the son of Joahaz the recorder, to repair the house of the LORD his God. [...] And when they brought out the money that was brought into the house of the LORD, Hilkiah the priest *found a book of the law of the Lord* given by Moses. And Hilkiah answered and said to Shaphan the scribe, I have found the book of the law in the house of the LORD. And Hilkiah delivered the book to Shaphan.

> And Shaphan carried the book to the king, and brought the king word back again, saying, All that was committed to thy servants, they do it. And they have gathered together the money that was found in the house of the LORD, and have delivered it into the hand of the overseers, and to the hand of the workmen. Then Shaphan the scribe told the king, saying, Hilkiah the priest hath given me a book. And Shaphan read it before the king. And it came to pass, when the king had heard the words of the law, that he rent his clothes. [...]

> And Hilkiah, and they that the king had appointed, *went to Huldah the prophetess*, the wife of Shallum the son of Tikvath, the son of Hasrah, keeper of the wardrobe; (now she dwelt in Jerusalem in the college) and they spake to her to that effect. And she answered them, Thus saith the Lord God of Israel, Tell ye the man that sent you to me, Thus saith the Lord, Behold, I will bring evil upon this place, and upon the

> inhabitants thereof, even all the curses that are written in the book which they have
> read before the king of Judah.[…]

> And Josiah took away all the abominations out of all the countries that pertained to
> the children of Israel, and made all that were present in Israel to serve, even to
> serve the LORD their God. And all his days they departed not from following the
> LORD, the God of their fathers.[333]

Someone had created a document called The Law Code, that was different from the ritualistic laws of the P source, and this was then, "suddenly discovered" and officially endorsed as the Torah. This code was thus going to be woven into a new version of the official history.

As we see in the above account, in the eighteenth year of Josiah's reign, 622 BC, Josiah received word from his scribe, *Shaphan*, that the priest *Hilkiah* had found a "scroll of the Torah" in the Temple of Yahweh. When Shaphan read the text of this book that Hilkiah had brought to the king, Josiah tore his clothes, (a sign of anguish), and *consulted a prophetess* concerning its meaning. After this consultation, he held a giant national ceremony of renewal of the covenant between God and the people. The book that the priest Hilkiah said he found in the Temple in 622 BC was Deuteronomy.

So it was that Josiah, instituted another "cleansing of Judah" and centralization of religion after the manner of Hezekiah, overturning his father's and grandfather's more lenient practices. What was more, in addition to smashing the idols, cleansing the Temple, and destroying the high places, Josiah also extended his sphere of influence into the old kingdom of Israel in the highlands. Once again, everyone was required to bring all their sacrifices to Jerusalem, and the outlying priests were given menial jobs in the Temple.

The fact that the Assyrian empire was weakening and that there were tensions between it and Babylon at that time is probably what allowed Josiah to get away with what he was doing. As it happened, Egypt had now switched sides and was becoming friendly with Assyria; they both had designs on Babylon. Josiah, like Hezekiah, was definitely anti-Assyrian and throwing off the Assyrian yoke had been the goal of Judah for some time. Previously, when Egypt had been after Assyria, Judah had sided with Egypt. But now, Egypt was on the side of Assyria, and Babylon was against Assyria, so Josiah turned against the Egyptians who had helped Hezekiah, and went out to fight them on the side of Babylon. He met the Egyptian army at Megiddo and not terribly unexpectedly, he was killed.

Josiah's early death meant an end to political independence and religious reform. The high places were rebuilt yet again (!), and three of his sons and one grandson ruled for the next twenty-two years. Or so it is thought. The reader may think that the history in the Bible was a little confused over the Omri-Ahab time.

---

[333] *The Bible*, 2 Chronicles 34.

You are about to witness almost the most awful mess of historical writing skullduggery ever committed.

According to the accepted timeline, the first of Josiah's sons to ascend the throne was Jehoahaz, who ruled for three months until the Egyptian king dethroned him and hauled him off to Egypt, placing his brother on the throne. The brother, Jehoiakim ruled as an Egyptian vassal and managed to keep his seat for eleven years. Meanwhile, the Babylonians finally subdued the Assyrians, and cast their eyes on Egypt. Judah was more or less in the way and Johoiakim died in battle against the Babylonians.

Jehoiakim's son, Jehoiachin (yeah, I know, all these "Jehoia's" are getting tedious, but bear with me here) ruled for three months, but was captured by the Babylonians. Nebuchadnezzar exiled him to Babylon along with thousands of other Judaeans. Nebuchadnezzar hauled back to Babylon everybody who was educated, professional, or could cause trouble in Judea behind his back, plus anyone who might be useful in Babylon. Nebuchadnezzar put another of Josiah's sons on the throne: Zedekiah.

Zedekiah managed to do all right for eleven years before he got stupid and rebelled against Nebuchadnezzar. That was the living end, and it was not a joke. Nebuchadnezzar and the Babylonian army came back and destroyed Jerusalem and exiled the rest of the population. Nebuchadnezzar brutally murdered the children of Zedekiah right before his eyes – and then blinded him. It was the last thing he ever saw. Or so the story goes.

Thus ended the rule of the "Davidic" line.[334]

Nebuchadnezzar was tired of playing games so he appointed a Jewish governor, Gedaliah, son of Ahikam, son of Shaphan, the scribe who had reported the finding of the Deuteronomy scroll.

Now, as we noted, Josiah had been pro-Babylonian, and the Shaphan family was also pro-Babylonian. In fact, the prophet Jeremiah was pro-Babylonian. Nevertheless, having a pro-Babylonian governor from a family of scribes placed over them, purportedly so infuriated the house of David that, two months later, a relative of that family assassinated Gedaliah.

That was a very bad idea. The people of Judah already knew that Nebuzzy had a notoriously bad temper and it was said that virtually the entire population fled to Egypt, although that was not exactly the case. Probably just the family and connections of the assassin left.

Now, before we attend the razing of Jerusalem, let's examine this new "Torah" that was presented in the reign of Josiah a bit more carefully.

---

[334] Even if we have very strong suspicions that the "Davidic Line" was so manipulated and/or falsified that to try to sort it out would be like cleaning the Augean stables.

The book of Deuteronomy, which is the item in question, is presented as Moses' farewell speech before his death. It is set in the plains of Moab.[335] There is a special relationship between the person who wrote this text and the *next six books of the Bible*[336]. It can be shown that this set of books is a thoughtfully arranged work that tells a continuous story – the history of the people in their land. It was not by a single author because it was evident that there were accounts written by a different hand (the court history of David and the stories of Samuel). But it was clear that the finished product was the work of a single editor.

What emerges from the textual analysis is that this writer had selected from a group of stories available to him and had arranged the texts, either shortening or lengthening them as needed, adding occasional comments of his own. All of this can be detected by linguistic analysis. It is as clear as identifying fingerprints, and in this case, we can ironically refer to it as the "fingerprints of God". In effect, *this writer created the history of Israel* extending from Moses to the destruction of the kingdom of Judah by the Babylonians. And he most definitely had an agenda.

For this man, Deuteronomy was *the* book – the Torah. He constructed everything that followed to support this idea. Deuteronomy was to be the *foundation* of the history. The book of Joshua picks up where Deuteronomy leaves off, thanks to this writer. Joshua develops the themes of Deuteronomy and refers to Deuteronomy. Many of the key passages of Joshua, Judges, Samuel and Kings use the same linguistic expressions that are present in Deuteronomy. It became clear to the scholars that *the author of Deuteronomy was the producer of the next six books of the Bible: the Deuteronomistic history.*

But there is a particular little difficulty: this writer occasionally speaks of things existing "to this day", when the things in question actually only existed while the kingdom was standing. This begs the question: why would someone writing a history in, say 560 BC refer to something as existing "to this day", when that something had ended back in 587?

In Kings 8:8 there is a reference to the poles that were used for hoisting and carrying the ark. It states that the poles were placed inside the Temple of Solomon on the day it was dedicated and that "they have been there unto this day". Why would someone write these words after the Temple had burned down? This suggests to us that this is the writer who created the history of the Temple of Solomon as being in Jerusalem and applying this history to a temple that was most likely built during the reign of Hezekiah or even a temple that had been built for another god, but was taken over by Hezekiah in his "repair and cleansing" of the temple. But, more than that, why would he talk about a Temple that had items in it

---

[335] Remember that Moab was "Hell city" to the Aaronid priesthood.

[336] *The Bible*, Joshua, Judges, Ruth, 1 & 2 Samuel; 1 Kings.

that had existed "to this day" when that temple and those items had all been destroyed?

The obvious solution is that there were two editions of the Deuteronomistic history. The original was by someone living *during the reign of King Josiah*. It was a positive, optimistic account of the people's history. It emphasized the importance of the Davidic covenant and made certain that the people realized that the Temple was the Temple of Solomon. This writer believed that the kingdom would thrive under Josiah and survive. But after Josiah's death, his sons' disastrous reigns, and the fall of the kingdom, this original version of the national history was not only out of date, the tragic events had made its view completely foolish. So, someone wrote a new edition of the history after the destruction in 587.

This second edition was about 95 percent the same as the first edition. The main difference was *the addition of the last chapters* of the story – the last two chapters of the book of 2 Kings – which give the account of the reigns of Judah's last four kings. The updated history ends with the fall of Judah.

In the first version of the history, the "editor" referred to things as existing "to this day" because in Josiah's time they really still existed. The editor of the second edition did not bother to edit them out because that was not his concern. He was not rewriting the whole history or looking for contradictions to eliminate. He was simply *adding the end of the story*, with a little preface at the beginning.

There is another interesting thing that suggests that the author of Deuteronomy lived during the reign of Josiah. It has been pointed out that the length of the text dealing with Josiah is all out of proportion to his importance and achievements. There are other kings who lived longer and supposedly did more things. Josiah's reform was very short-lived. Not only that, the books of Jeremiah, Ezekiel, 2 Kings, and 2 Chronicles all suggest that Josiah's innovations were discarded after his death. So why was there so much emphasis on this one, minor and relatively unsuccessful king?

We have examples of similar writings in other times and places: Josiah was obviously the king when the history was written, and it was written to flatter him and to culminate in him by someone who was currying favor or seeking control.

There is another funny thing about this. The book of 1 Kings, chapter 13, tells a story about King Jeroboam. He set up the golden calves at Dan and Beth-El to celebrate a festival. When he came to the altar to burn incense, something very strange happened:

> And here was a man of God coming from Judah by the word of Yahweh to Beth-El as Jeroboam was standing on the altar to burn incense. And he called out upon the altar by the word of Yahweh, and he said, "Altar, altar. Thus says Yahweh: 'Here a son will be born to the house of David, Josiah by name, and he will sacrifice on you the priests of the high places who burn incense on you. He will burn human bones on you.'"

Now, the point is that this story about Jeroboam is supposed to be set *three hundred years* before the birth of Josiah! The fact is, there is no other case of such explicit prediction of a person by name so far in advance in any of the biblical narratives! What is more, later in the text, the Deuteronomistic writer of Kings and Chronicles made a special point of this story. He *created the fulfillment of the prophecy* by writing an account of how Josiah went to Beth-El to destroy the high place that has been there, "since Jeroboam's days". Just to make sure that the reader is sufficiently impressed, he describes how, while at Beth-El, Josiah sees some graves nearby and digs up the bones in them to burn on the altar to defile it, "*according to the word of Yahweh*". If, by this time, we are not sufficiently staggered at the predictive powers of the prophets of Yahweh, the writer drives home the point by describing how Josiah next notices the grave of the prophet who, purportedly three hundred years before, had predicted each of these specific actions! Upon finding out whose grave it is, Josiah tells everyone not to disturb the bones of such a great guy.

Actually, it is not just that there was a prediction of the birth of Josiah at the beginning of the history, and the fulfillment of the prediction later on that raises questions. The fact is, the writer of this history rates every single other king in between – both of Israel and Judah – below Josiah in significance and holiness and all other praiseworthy virtues! Josiah is just the cat's miaou! Most of the kings are rated as "bad", and those that are rated as "good" are still not as good as Josiah. Even the great and heroic King David is criticized for adultery with Bathsheba. In other words, the writer of the Deuteronomistic history rates Josiah, and Josiah alone, as *the unqualified model of kingly virtue*. But history shows that Josiah did absolutely nothing except to make very bad political decisions and managed to get himself killed thereby. Whoever wrote this history wrote it at the beginning of what was hoped to be a new and wonderful dynasty, coordinated with a centralized religion, beginning with Josiah. And the author obviously saw his own place in this dynasty as significant.

Thus we come to the idea that the person responsible for seven books of the Bible was someone from Josiah's reign. This individual designed his history of the Jews to culminate in Josiah, who was, effectively, compared to Moses. In all the Bible, the words "None arose like him" are applied *only to Moses and Josiah*. The final words of Deuteronomy are, "And there did not arise a prophet again in Israel like Moses". The final comment on Josiah was, "*...and none arose like him after him*".

Here is another curious fact: the book of the Torah is mentioned only in Deuteronomy, in Joshua, and then never again in the Hebrew bible except in one story: Josiah. Moses supposedly writes it, gives it to the priests, who place it beside the ark, and it ceases to be an issue until we find the story of its discovery by the priest Hilkiah.

The writer of the Deuteronomistic history describes Josiah as the culmination of Moses. Everything he did was modeled on Moses. The covenant with Moses is to be fulfilled in Josiah. And then: *full stop*, as Friedman notes. The story resumes after the death of Josiah from a radically different point of view.[337]

We also note that this writer's agenda is centralization of religion. All the kings who are rated as "bad" are those who restored the "high places" where the sacrifice could be made locally. The one consistent criterion applied to every king is based on this centralization of religion. But after Josiah, this criterion vanishes from sight. This suggests to us that religion was not centralized in the time of Josiah, but when the Bible itself was finally assembled during or at the end of the exile in Babylon, that was no longer an issue, it was a *fait accompli;* accomplished by the Persians, I should add..

King David also figures powerfully in the writings of the Deuteronomist. Half of the book of 1 Samuel, all of 2 Samuel, and the first chapters of 1 Kings deal with his life. The writer states explicitly that because of David's merit even a bad king of Judah cannot lose the throne as long as he is descended from David. He compares Josiah to David. The name David occurs about *five hundred times* in the Deuteronomistic history. Then, suddenly, it stops. The text stops referring to the Davidic covenant, no one is compared to David anymore, and it does not explain how this covenant failed to save the throne. What is more, we have already seen that the "House of David" was the Omride dynasty, and it was utterly destroyed by the Assyrians when they massacred the sons of Ahab. So, what is the deal here?

Someone created the book of Deuteronomy and the following six books of the Bible as one continuous work. The original edition told the story from Moses to Josiah. One of the primary features of this work was what is known as the "law code". This law code takes up half of Deuteronomy – chapters 12 through 26. And the first law is the centralization of worship. The second law is that *the king must be chosen by Yahweh* – which, of course, means that a king reigns only by virtue of being approved by the priests. The further law codes include prohibitions against pagan religions, false prophets, rules covering charity, justice, family and community law, holidays and dietary laws, laws about war and slaves and agriculture and magic. Most especially, it refers repeatedly to the sustaining of the well-being of the Levites; *all Levites*, not just the Aaronid family.

So, clearly, the author of this series of books was not *merely* a scribe or someone from the royal court seeking to garner favor from Josiah. It strictly proscribes the power of the king, and gives the power firmly and fully into the hands of the Levites – including the power of summoning the tribes to battle.

The fact that the writer of Deuteronomy favors Levites in general, with no specific mention of Aaron, indicates that this writer was of the lineage of the Shiloh priesthood of the Northern Kingdom who has been indoctrinated into the Yawist religion. Deuteronomy also never makes mention of the ark, the cherubs,

---

[337] Cf. Friedman, p 136 ff.

or any other religious implements that were housed in the Jerusalem Temple. It also never refers to the office of High Priest – an office of the Aaronid priesthood.

The law code does not reflect the views of the priests of Beth-El during the two hundred years between Jeroboam and the fall of Israel in 722. Those priests were not Levites. Deuteronomy only favors Levites. They are the only legitimate priests.

The conclusion is that the author of the Deuteronomistic history is a person who wanted to centralize religion, but who was *not tied to the ark or to the Jerusalem priesthood itself.* Yes, they cared about the Levites in general, but the focus was on a group of central Levites *descended from Moses.* This writer accepted a king as a necessity, but sought to insure that the king was controlled by this central group of Mushite Levites. And, most of all, this individual wanted to establish and maintain control over military actions. He wanted the power to wage war.

Well, as we noted, it started with Moses "writing the Torah" and then ended with the triumphant recovery of the scroll, discovered by the priest Hilkiah, who then read it to Josiah, and Josiah (probably believing every word of it, because it prophesied his own birth) implemented the whole deal.

Why do the experts think it was a priest of Shiloh? Because it minimizes the Aaronid priesthood – mentioning Aaron only twice: once to say that he died, and once to say the God was mad enough to destroy him over the golden calf episode.

Further, this history actually presents Solomon in the worst light possible, giving him bad habits and a bad end. Then, of course, Josiah comes along and destroys all the sinful works of "Solomon" in terms of the setting up of the "high places". It even specifies that these things that Josiah was destroying were built by Solomon. The Shiloh priests had an axe to grind because, three centuries earlier, or so their tradition said, Solomon – or a reasonable facsimile - had tossed them all out on their ears and had instituted the Aaronid priesthood. Or so it was claimed. And we know already who it was that tossed the Shiloh priests of Yahweh out - it was Ahab and Jezebel.

Now, remember that Hilkiah the priest was the one who discovered the scroll, and Shaphan the scribe carried it to King Josiah and read it to him. As it happens, when Jeremiah later, after the fall of Jerusalem and the exile to Babylon, sent a letter to the exiles in Babylon, it was delivered for him by Gemariah, *son of Hilkiah,* and by Elasah, *son of Shaphan.*[338]

My my! Doesn't the plot thicken?! But hang on, it gets better.

Jeremiah was closely connected to Josiah's counselors who were involved with "the book of the Torah". Gemariah and Ahikam, sons of Shaphan stood by Jeremiah at several critical moments; once even saving Jeremiah from being stoned. It was Gedaliah, son of Ahikam, who was appointed governor of Judah by

---

[338] *The Bible*, Jeremiah, 29: 1-3.

Nebuchadnezzar. It could be said that Jeremiah was associated with the pro-Babylonian party and was probably the one who gave Josiah the bad advice to side with Babylon against Egypt and Assyria. So much for the divine inspiration and superior advice of a priest of Yahweh. Seems to be so that every time his advice is taken, it leads to death and destruction for Israel. Maybe they ought to notice this.

More than this, Jeremiah is the one prophet in the Bible to refer to Shiloh. He calls Shiloh, *"The place where I [God] caused my name to dwell"*. This was, essentially, the *central place of worship*.

As we mentioned above, Solomon-Ahab had not been very nice to the Shiloh priests. Their leader, Abiathar, had been one of Omri-David's two chief priests. They were expelled from Jerusalem by Solomon, banished to their family estate in the town of Anathoth. This was a town of the Aaronid priests, and presumably Abiathar could be kept under house arrest there.

So, how do we connect things here? The first verses of the book of Jeremiah say, "The words of Jeremiah, *son of Hilkiah*, of the priests who were in *Anathoth*".

And now we know how this "Torah" was "discovered" so conveniently at just the "right moment". It was created just for that purpose. And we know who created it.

Jeremiah is a priest who never sacrifices, which is consistent with the position of the priests at Shiloh. He is also the only prophet to allude to a story of Moses' bronze snake.[339] That story comes from the E source, the Shiloh source. King Hezekiah had smashed that snake. His destruction of an ancient relic that was associated with Moses himself is astonishing in and of itself. But, the fact is, it was powerfully associated with the Shiloh priesthood. They were the ones who told the story of this serpent. They were the ones who held Moses in higher esteem than anyone, and *they were, most probably, Moses descendants* – whoever Moses might have been. The term in Hebrew for the bronze snake was "Nehushtan". *Josiah married his son to a woman named Nehushta.*[340]

Now we must ask another question: if such a document was written by the priests of the Northern kingdom, how did it find its way into the Temple in Judah since we know that the Aaronid priests had a pretty firm grip on things there? How did it become the law of the land?

Here we come to a very strange thing that I have alluded to above in terms of the confused genealogies.

In I Chronicles 3:15 we read:

> "And the sons of Josiah were, the firstborn Johanan, the second Jehoiakim, the third Zedekiah, the fourth Shallum." In verse 16 we read: "And the sons of Jehoiakim: Jeconiah his son, Zedekiah his son.".

---

[339] *The Bible,* Jeremiah, 8: 17-22.

[340] *The Bible,* 2 Kings, 24:8.

This means that there are two Zedekiahs. In any event, remember the fourth son of Josiah, "Shallum".

In 2 Kings 23, the death of Josiah is recounted. Verses 30 and 31 tell us:

> "And his servants carried him in a chariot dead from Megiddo, and brought him to Jerusalem, and buried him in his own sepulchre. And the people of the land took Jehoahaz the son of Josiah, and anointed him, and made him king in his father's stead. Jehoahaz was twenty and three years old when he began to reign; and he reigned three months in Jerusalem. And his mother's name was Hamutal, the *daughter of Jeremiah of Libnah*."

The only problem at this point is that in the first passage from I Chronicles above, the four sons of Josiah are listed and none of them are named Jehoahaz. But, we do notice that the mother of the new king is named as a daughter of someone named Jeremiah who hails from the town of Libnah. This would mean that the new king is this Jeremiah's grandson, and that the dead king, Josiah was his son-in-law. In other words, Hamutal is the wife of Josiah.

Next we find in the book of Jeremiah, chapter 1:3

> It [the word of the Lord] came also in the days of Jehoiakim the son of Josiah king of Judah, unto the end of the eleventh year of Zedekiah the son of Josiah king of Judah, unto the carrying away of Jerusalem captive in the fifth month.

Very clearly here, Zedekiah, is the son of Josiah and Hamutal, and is the guy who is taken captive to Babylon.

Chapter 52 verse 1, tells us the following:

> "Zedekiah was one and twenty years old when he began to reign, and he reigned eleven years in Jerusalem. And his mother's name was Hamutal the daughter of Jeremiah of Libnah."

Remember what the chronology is supposed to be: The first son of Josiah, Jehoahaz. He is 23 years old when he came to the throne and he ruled for three months until the Egyptian king dethroned him and hauled him off to Egypt, placing his brother on the throne. The brother, Jehoiakim ruled as an Egyptian vassal for eleven years. He died in Battle against the Babylonians.

Jehoiakim's son, Jehoiachin, ruled for three months, but was captured by the Babylonians and exiled with everybody who was anybody. The Bible says in 2 Chronicles:

> "Jehoiachin was eight years old when he began to reign, and he reigned three months and ten days in Jerusalem: and he did that which was evil in the sight of the Lord."

I can hardly imagine what an eight year old can do that is evil in only three months. This is, however, directly contradicted by 2 Kings where it says:

"So Jehoiakim slept with his fathers: and Jehoiachin his son reigned in his stead.[...] Jehoiachin was *eighteen years old* when he began to reign, and he reigned in Jerusalem three months. And his mother's name was Nehushta, the daughter of Elnathan of Jerusalem. And he did that which was evil in the sight of the Lord, according to all that his father had done.[...] And Jehoiachin the king of Judah went out to the king of Babylon, he, and his mother, and his servants, and his princes, and his officers: and the king of Babylon took him in the eighth year of his reign.[341]

At this point, the mysterious Zedekiah comes to the throne. He is a twenty-one year old son of Josiah and he reigned for eleven years before he was hauled off by the Babylonians.

Well, aside from the most interesting fact that we have a sort of doublet here in terms of the lengths of the reigns, there is the totally bizarre fact that in both "sets", the three month reign ends in *being taken hostage*: Jehoahaz to Egypt, and Jehoiachin to Babylon. Not only that, but Jehoiakim's eleven year reign ends in him being killed in battle against the Babylonians, and Zedekiah's children are slain, his eyes are put out and he is taken in chains to Babylon.

All of that is confusing enough. But, we notice that after Jehoahaz is taken to Egypt, Pharaoh Necho supposedly put his brother on the throne. Once again, we have a double header. But this one has a twist: The second book of Kings, chapter 24, vs. 17 says:

> "And the king of Babylon made Mattaniah, Jehoiachin's uncle, king in his stead, and changed his name to Zedekiah."

But the second book of Chronicles tells us, in chapter 35, vs. 10:

> "In the spring, King Nebuchadnezzar sent and brought him to Babylon, with the precious vessels of the house of the Lord, and made Zedekiah the brother [of Jehoiachin] king over Judah and Jerusalem."

This means that we have now used up three of Josiah's four sons. And if the Bible can be specific enough to name an uncle in one place, and a brother in another, I don't think that the argument that a "brother" can mean just a kinsman holds up. What is more, only one of the names of these brothers is the same as given in the genealogy: Johanan, Jehoiakim, Zedekiah, Shallum as opposed to: Jehoahaz, Jehoikim, Mattaniah. We also know that Jehoiachin is the only one of this little group of kings at this period of time whose existence has been confirmed by external evidence. Within the corpus of administrative documents found in the excavations of Babylon are some dating to the reign of Nebuchadnezzar. One broken document mentions providing rations to Jehoiachin, specifically named as the king of Judah, and to his sons. This same Babylonian document also mentions

---

[341] *The Bible*, 2 Kings, 24:6.

provisions for the Philistine king of Ashkelon, as well as for other kings. A second document, also broken, mentions the kings of Gaza and Ashdod performing duties for Nebuchadnezzar

So, who the heck is Shallum?

Well, first of all we remember that earlier in this chapter, we recounted the story of the finding of the book of Deuteronomy in the temple. It was found by the priest Hilkiah, apparently the father of Jeremiah, and it was turned over the royal scribe, Shaphan. The king then ordered Shaphan to do something: he sent Hilkiah to a prophetess!

> "And Hilkiah, and they that the king had appointed, went to Huldah the prophetess,
> the wife of Shallum the son of Tikvath, the son of Hasrah, keeper of the wardrobe;
> (now she dwelt in Jerusalem in the college)."

So we find a possible strange connection here, even if the genealogy of the individual is given as being different from the Shallum with whom we are concerned.

In Jeremiah chapter 32, King Zedekiah, the last of Josiah's sons to reign, a purported brother of a son of Josiah named Shallum, has locked Jeremiah up in prison because Jeremiah keeps telling him that the Babylonians are going to get him. Jeremiah is ranting about this dreadful situation and tells us about a business transaction that he, Jeremiah, was instructed to undertake.

> And Jeremiah said, The word of the Lord came unto me, saying, Behold, Hanameel
> the son of *Shallum thine uncle* shall come unto thee saying, Buy thee my field that
> is in Anathoth: for the right of redemption is thine to buy it. So Hanameel mine
> uncle's son came to me in the court of the guard in accordance with the word of the
> Lord, and he said to me, I pray you buy my field that is in Anathoth, which is in the
> land of Benjamin; for the right of inheritance is yours and the redemption is yours;
> buy it for yourself. Then I knew that this was the word of the Lord. And I bought
> the field that was in Anathoth of Hanameel my uncle's son...

This suggests that the Shallum in question is dead, the son has inherited, and that Jeremiah is the next of kin, giving him the first right of refusal to buy this field that the son of Shallum wants to sell. Of course, if Zedekiah were really a son of Josiah and a brother of the Shallum in question, he would have the right of redemption. So obviously we have either two Shallums, or just one Shallum.

Again, who is Shallum, listed as a "son" of Josiah? Is it the same Shallum who is listed as the uncle of Jeremiah? And who is the Jeremiah who is the father of the wife of Josiah, and therefore the grandfather of Zedekiah? Well, we can't be sure, but my personal opinion is that the genealogy has been doubled more than once and that a few people have been inserted here who may never actually have existed at that particular point in time and that there was only one Shallum whose name was added as a son of Josiah in order to establish a claim or a connection.

So, even if there is no way possible to determine the relationships or even the precise times, or to determine how these names all came to be maneuvered into a timeline that obviously either did not exist, or was so confused as to make any attempts to sort it out futile, we still have a very powerful impression that Jeremiah, author of at least seven books of the Bible, had a definite agenda in his prestidigitation of the putative "history of Israel". He was also of the Davidic line himself, whatever that was supposed to mean, and that he was also connected somehow to the Aaronid line of priests. His exact personal relationship we cannot determine with any certainty, but he may actually have been a cousin of king Zedekiah, or father-in-law to Josiah. In either case, this is what gave him his "in" with the royal family.

Getting back to the content of Deuteronomy, the final result of the analysis of the documents tells us that D and E complement each other. Both traditions refer to the mountain of Moses as Horeb. J and P call it Sinai. These traditions regard Moses as a superluminary individual. He is at the turning point of history, and is, in fact, the crucial element of history. His life and times are carefully and thoroughly developed with nothing comparable in the J and P sources. The Deuteronomistic books also give great emphasis to prophets. The word *prophet* occurs only once in P and never in the J source. The Deuteronomistic historian also gives great favor and support to the Levites. In J, however, the Levites are dispersed for having massacred the people of Shechem. In P, the Levites are separate from, and lower than, the Aaronid priests. And finally, D and E both regard Aaron as bad, referring to the golden calf event and the leprosy of Miriam. Neither of these is mentioned in either J or P.

If we take a close look at this history, we find a curious thing: all of the passages that mention the Davidic covenant divide into two categories: conditional and unconditional. In the first case, a representative of the line of David on the throne of Israel is conditional on the obedience of the people. In the event of the destruction of Israel, the Davidic covenant refers simply to "holding the throne". Why is this? It is obviously because the writer had to finally re-edit his work. He had told the story of how the house of David began ruling the whole united kingdom of Israel, but that they had lost all of it except their own tribe of Judah which would be theirs forever. And then, he had to deal with the fact of the death of the sons of Zedekiah and the exile in Babylon.

Some have called this a "pious fraud". Some would suggest that he made up the Davidic covenant. But it does seem, indeed, that the writer was only writing about what the people of this tribe believed. The Davidic covenant tradition appears in some of the psalms that were composed before the Deuteronomist ever wrote his history. So, he wasn't making the story up out of thin air; if he had tried to do that, who would have believed him? Nobody. He had to deal with accepted "stories" of the people around him. And this was one of them. He merely transferred the history he knew from the northern kingdom and placed it in the setting of the southern kingdom and appropriated it to those to whom it did not belong. In this way, he could write the prophecy in the early part of the book that would make Josiah out to be the messiah, and then all he had to do was work on Josiah to make it all come true.

The Deuteronomistic historian based his interpretation of the traditions and his additions to the work on four things: faithfulness to Yahweh; the Davidic covenant; the centralization of religion at the Temple in Jerusalem; and the Torah – as Deuteronomy, that is. His interpretations of what happened were that: the kingdom split because Solomon had forsaken Yahweh and the Torah. David's descendants retained Jerusalem because they had an unconditional covenant. The northern kingdom fell because the people and their kings did not follow the Torah. And now, at the time of the writing, all was going to be smooth sailing because the

Torah had been rediscovered and Josiah, the descendant of David, was going to make everything right again!

And then Josiah took an Egyptian arrow, and the game was lost.

So, twenty-two years after the writing of this history, it all looked pretty sad and silly. The great "eternal kingdom" had ended ignominiously. The family that would never be "cut off from the throne" had not only been cut off, but had almost virtually ceased to exist. The great place that Yahweh had "caused his name to dwell" was in ashes and all the things that were said to exist "to this day" no longer existed.

So someone had to go back through the whole work and insert some changes that would explain this mess. He couldn't just add a few lines describing the later events; he had to save Yahweh's buns from the fire and make it comprehensible why the great dream of the followers of Yahweh had failed – which ended up making Yahweh look like a half-wit himself. And the evidence shows that this is what was done. The evidence shows grammatical breaks such as shifts from singular to plural, special terms, themes, syntax and literary structure – all designed to explain everything that had happened in terms of the breaking of the covenant so that Yahweh, above all, would stand forth as the only god. Never mind that all the advance planning that was supposed to have been attributed to Yahweh had fallen flat. Yahweh's face had to be saved. It was a dirty job, but somebody had to do it.

One of the most amazing things was the way Jeremiah dealt with the death of the "chosen one", Josiah, at the hands of the Egyptians. What he inserted into the text was a "prophecy" of Yahweh from the mouth of the Egyptian king that was ignored by Josiah, resulting in his death.

> But [Necho] sent ambassadors to [Josiah], saying, What have I to do with you, you king of Judah? I come not against you this day, but against the house with which I am at war; and God has commanded me to make haste. *Refrain from opposing God*, Who is with me, lest He destroy you. Yet Josiah would not turn away from him, but disguised himself in order to fight with him. He did not heed the words of Necho from the mouth of God, but came to fight with him in the valley of Megiddo.[342]

Aside from the fact that the story of a king's disguise leading to his death in battle actually belongs to Ahab, as told in the 18th chapter of II Chronicles, it seems that this individual did not rewrite the whole thing; he only added occasional paragraphs here and there to the "After the death of Josiah edition". He added passages that predicted exile, and it is noticeable when such "prophecies" break the context and shift the grammar.

Finally, to finish the whole thing off, the writer added in the reason for the exile: the people had followed after other gods. On this point, he only had to emphasize

---

[342] *The Bible*, 2 Chronicles, 35:21-22.

what was already written in Deuteronomy, that the worship of Yahweh alone was the first commandment. So, the exiled writer of this new edition added ten more references to the command against apostasy and *tied every one of them to a reference to exile* if this was not obeyed.

He then added this point to the last prophecy of God's that Moses hears. God tells Moses that after he is dead:

> "This people rise and whore after alien gods of the land into which they are coming, and they will leave me and break my covenant which I have made with them. And my anger will burn against them in that day, and I shall leave them, and I shall hide my face from them, and they will be devoured, and many evils and troubles will find them…"[343]

The Deuteronomist then had to find a plausible guilt hook for the whole thing, and the textual analysis reveals this, as well. It was obvious he couldn't blame Josiah after all the praises heaped on him, despite the fact that Josiah wasn't a very convincing hero in terms of the actual events of his life. Thus, his silly wasted life was played so as not to contradict his position as a hero. A reason for the death and destruction and exile had to be found that kept Josiah in the exalted position he had been assigned, and the only way to do it was to make his exalted position a grand and noble - but futile - attempt to right the most terrible of all wrongs, but – as wonderful as Josiah was – he was unable to balance the evil of...

Manasseh.

Yes, indeed Josiah's grandfather. According to the first version of the Deuteronomistic history, Manasseh had undone all the religious reforms of his father, Hezekiah. He had set up a statue of the goddess Asherah and built altars to pagan gods in the temple precincts. This had set the stage for the story of Josiah and his great reforms that were even more holy and complete than those of Hezekiah.

But, the *revision* of the D history elaborates on Manasseh's crimes and adds in the consequences of those crimes. Again, this is clearly evident in the textual analysis. Here is what was added:

> Manasseh instigated them to do wrong, more than the nations that Yahweh had destroyed before the children of Israel. And Yahweh said by the hand of his servants the prophets,

> Because Manasseh King of Judah has done these abominations … he has caused Judah to sin by his idols. Therefore I am bringing such evil on Jerusalem and Judah that the ears of whoever hears about it will tingle… I shall wipe Jerusalem the way one wipes a plate and turns it over on its face. And I shall reject the remnant of my possession and put them in their enemies' hand, and they will be a spoil and booty

---

[343] *The Bible*, Deut 31: 16-18.

for all their enemies, because they have done wrong in my eyes and have been angering me from the day their fathers went out of Egypt to this day.[344]

Heavy-duty guilt trip! Manasseh is so bad, and the people are so bad by following along with him, that it is now prophesied that the kingdom will fall. And then, the writer jumps to the end of the scroll and, where it says *"no king ever arose like Josiah"*, he added, *"But Yahweh did not turn back from his great fury which burned against Judah over all the things in which Manasseh had angered him".*[345]

There is a question with all this, however, because when we read the texts in question, we find that the shoe does not fit. For example, in 2 Chronicles, starting with chapter 32, vs.33, we read the following story:

And Hezekiah slept with his fathers, and they buried him in the chiefest of the sepulchres of the sons of David: and all Judah and the inhabitants of Jerusalem did him honour at his death. And Manasseh his son reigned in his stead. Manasseh was twelve years old when he began to reign, and he reigned fifty and five years in Jerusalem, but did that which was evil in the sight of the Lord, like unto the abominations of the heathen, whom the Lord had cast out before the children of Israel.

And the Lord spake to Manasseh, and to his people: but they would not hearken. Wherefore the LORD brought upon them the captains of the host of the king of Assyria, which took Manasseh among the thorns, and bound him with fetters, and carried him to Babylon.

And when he was in affliction, he besought the Lord his God, and humbled himself greatly before the God of his fathers, and prayed unto him: and he was entreated of him, and heard his supplication, and brought him again to Jerusalem into his kingdom. Then Manasseh knew that the Lord he was God.

Now after this he built a wall without the city of David, on the west side of Gihon, in the valley, even to the entering in at the fish gate, and compassed about Ophel, and raised it up a very great height, and put captains of war in all the fenced cities of Judah. And he took away the strange gods, and the idol out of the house of the Lord, and all the altars that he had built in the mount of the house of the LORD, and in Jerusalem, and cast them out of the city.

And he repaired the altar of the Lord, and sacrificed thereon peace offerings and thank offerings, and commanded Judah to serve the Lord God of Israel.

Nevertheless the people did sacrifice still in the high places, yet unto the Lord their God only.

---

[344] *The Bible*, 2 Kings 21:8-15.

[345] Well, it almost seems like Manasseh is really Zedekiah. But no point in going off on another series of speculations on that point

Now the rest of the acts of Manasseh, and his prayer unto his God, and the words of the seers that spake to him in the name of the Lord God of Israel, behold, they are written in the book of the kings of Israel.

His prayer also, and how God was entreated of him, and all his sins, and his trespass, and the places wherein he built high places, and set up groves and graven images, before he was humbled: behold, they are written among the *sayings of the seers*.

So Manasseh slept with his fathers, and they buried him in his own house: and Amon his son reigned in his stead.

Amon was two and twenty years old when he began to reign, and reigned two years in Jerusalem.

But he did that which was evil in the sight of the LORD, as did Manasseh his father: for Amon sacrificed unto all the carved images which Manasseh his father had made, and served them; and humbled not himself before the LORD, as Manasseh his father had humbled himself; but Amon trespassed more and more.

And his servants conspired against him, and slew him in his own house. But the people of the land slew all them that had conspired against king Amon; and the people of the land made Josiah his son king in his stead.

First of all, something very fishy is going on here. Now we have *another guy* who was hauled off to Babylon by the Assyrians. Only this one was miraculously returned without a single raised eyebrow. He did a few rotten things, was punished, prayed some sort of wonderful prayer that is nowhere to be found in the Bible, even though it is said that Manasseh's prayer is recorded in the book of Kings and in a book called the "sayings of the seers". What is the "sayings of the seers"? They aren't there. What is there is the following:

Manasseh was twelve years old when he began to reign, and reigned fifty and five years in Jerusalem. And his mother's name was Hephzibah. And he did that which was evil in the sight of the Lord, after the abominations of the heathen, whom the LORD cast out before the children of Israel. For he built up again the high places which Hezekiah his father had destroyed; and he reared up *altars for Baal*, and made a grove, *as did Ahab* king of Israel; and worshipped *all the host of heaven*, and served them.

And he built altars in the house of the LORD, of which the LORD said, In Jerusalem will I put my name. And he built altars for all the *host of heaven* in the two courts of the house of the LORD. And he *made his son pass through the fire*, and observed times, and used enchantments, and dealt with familiar spirits and wizards: he wrought much wickedness in the sight of the Lord, to provoke him to anger.

And he set a graven image of the grove that he had made in the house, of which the Lord said to David, and to Solomon his son, In this house, and in Jerusalem, which I have chosen out of all tribes of Israel, will I put my name for ever: Neither will I make the feet of Israel move any more out of the land which I gave their fathers; only if they will observe to do according to all that I have commanded them, and according to all the law that my servant Moses commanded them.

But they hearkened not: and Manasseh seduced them to do more evil than did the nations whom the LORD destroyed before the children of Israel. And the Lord

spake by his servants the prophets, saying, Because Manasseh king of Judah hath
done these abominations, and hath done wickedly above all that the Amorites did,
which were before him, and hath made Judah also to sin with his idols: Therefore
thus saith the Lord God of Israel, Behold, I am bringing such evil upon Jerusalem
and Judah, that whosoever heareth of it, both his ears shall tingle. And I will stretch
over Jerusalem the line of Samaria, and the plummet of the house of Ahab: and I
will wipe Jerusalem as a man wipeth a dish, wiping it, and turning it upside down.
And I will forsake the remnant of mine inheritance, and deliver them into the hand
of their enemies; and they shall become a prey and a spoil to all their enemies;
because they have done that which was evil in my sight, and have provoked me to
anger, since the day their fathers came forth out of Egypt, even unto this day.

Moreover Manasseh shed innocent blood very much, till he had filled Jerusalem
from one end to another; beside his sin wherewith he made Judah to sin, in doing
that which was evil in the sight of the Lord.

Now the rest of the acts of Manasseh, and all that he did, and his sin that he sinned,
are they not written in the book of the chronicles of the kings of Judah? And
Manasseh slept with his fathers, and was buried in the garden of his own house, in
the garden of Uzza: and Amon his son reigned in his stead.[346]

Will the real Manasseh please stand up? It sounds like two completely different
people! Not only that, but the mention of the captivity of Manasseh in Babylon is
missing, as well as his repentance and his repairs of the Temple that are recited in
Chronicles. Just what is going on here?

Speaking of repairs to the temple, it was actually during repairs to the Temple
that the purported scroll of the Torah of the Levites was discovered during the
reign of Hezekiah, Manasseh's father. Again, one has the sensation of loss of
balance here; a page has been torn out. Is it possible that Hezekiah and Manasseh
were one and the same person? In fact, we find a strange resonance between the
"humbling event" of Manasseh and something that humbled Hezekiah, but which
is not elaborated:

In those days Hezekiah was sick to the death, and prayed unto the Lord: and he
spake unto him, and he gave him a sign. But Hezekiah rendered not again
according to the benefit done unto him; for his heart was lifted up: therefore there
was wrath upon him, and upon Judah and Jerusalem. Notwithstanding Hezekiah
humbled himself for the pride of his heart, both he and the inhabitants of Jerusalem,
so that the wrath of the Lord came not upon them in the days of Hezekiah.[347]

Somehow it sounds like Hezekiah wasn't the great guy he was portrayed to be
and Manasseh was not as wicked as he was depicted. What's more, it is
increasingly evident that some sort of cover-up is going on here. What and why?

---

[346] *The Bible*, 2 Kings: 21.

[347] *The Bible*, 2 Chronicles 32.

We may never know, but such questions need to be asked, and such texts need to be considered when one is deciding whether or not to believe that the Bible is the divinely inspired word of God. My thought is that the story of Hezekiah and Manasseh is just another doublet of the story of Omri and Ahab. One begins to wonder if the exile of the Jews really began with the fall of the Northern Kingdom and if everything that was added after that, the whole history of the Southern Kingdom and its kings and so on, wasn't just simply made up by priests in exile?

Another problem that the writer of this history had to deal with was the promise of Yahweh that King Solomon's Temple would last forever. He had already written, obviously under some kind of "guidance",[348] that God said:

> "I have sanctified this house that you have built to set my name there forever, and my eyes and my heart will be there all the days."[349]

Well, that's pretty definite! But now, the writer was facing the fact that everything was gone, ashes, destroyed. What to do? He obviously wasn't ready to give up the idea that this had been promised to Israel. So, he enfolded the promise in the conditional nature of the Mosaic covenant. He added four sentences wherein God tells the people that if they do not keep the commandments he has given them, he will exile them and reject the Temple.

He then did something else: a long list of curses was added to the text of Deuteronomy proper. This list of curses that would fall on the people if they did not keep the covenant is still about the most awful passage in the text. It included diseases, madness, blindness, military defeats, destruction of crops and livestock; starvation and cannibalism and then, the clincher: the last curse of Deuteronomy is *"And Yahweh will send you back to Egypt"*.

The last sentence of 2 Kings is: "And the entire people, from the smallest to the biggest, and the officers of the soldiers, arose and came to Egypt, because they were afraid of the Babylonians".

And so, until the return of the exiles, the biblical texts warred with each other as the weapons of the battle of the priests for the control of the peoples' minds. It was the final editor in Babylon who put it all together, blending and combining the four documents, cutting and pasting, adding and subtracting, glossing and enhancing in so marvelous a way that most people read the text and get the feeling that it is one continuous story. Only occasionally did he slip and make it obvious to even the untrained eye that something was wrong. But for the trained eye, for the seeker of the deeper truths of the Bible, the winding and turning of the text, first this way and then that, becomes evident. It finally reveals itself as a maze with something at

---

[348] We will deal in a future volume with the possible "source" of this guidance.

[349] *The Bible*, 1 Kings, 9:7.

the center that some think is God. And, perhaps it is. The only question is: What God?

Another question at this point in the discussion is this: if there was no Ark of the Covenant, and no Temple of Solomon, as the Bible tells us, then what about the now famous story of the Templars and their "doings" in the Temple? What about the claims of many occult and secret societies - most of whom stake claims on "Egyptian Secrets" transmitted through Moses to Judaism? Is it possible that these stories were made up after the fact as Fulcanelli has suggested? If that is the case, who were the Templars really and what were they doing and where?

That brings us back to our problem of Abram and Sarai in Egypt. This entire story will require a further volume to explicate adequately, but allow me to just propose here that Sarai and Nefertiti were one and the same person; that Abraham and Moses were one and the same person; that they may have been in possession of some sort of "object of cultic value", if not an ancient techno-marvel; and that they took it away from Egypt when they fled, during the eruption of Thera, which caused the mad Pharaoh, Akhenaten, to come after them in a fury. If the real story was: "give me back my wife", rather than: "Let my people go", and the drama played out in the midst of a geological and atmospheric catastrophe leading to the collapse of the Bronze Age, then we have a useful lynchpin upon which to evaluate the rest of the chronology. Moreover, if, in fact, there were concurrent Hyksos and Theban dynasties, and Abram was possibly connected to the Hyksos, then we also have a framework in which to understand the mythicization.

Reassembling the original story from its scattered pieces, given as stories of different characters, (Abraham, Isaac, Ishmael, Jacob, Esau, Moses and Aaron, and even the exploits of the great King David), we have some hope of coming close to what really may have happened and who was who. As mentioned, I plan to devote another volume to comparison and analysis of these individuals, but for the moment, I believe that the creative thinker can go to the original texts, extract the elements of these stories, arrange them in columns, and see for themselves that there are so many correspondences that it is extremely likely that it was all about a single individual, or small group, who lived at a single period of history, and that period was the time of the eruption of Thera. One thing that strikes me as particularly important is this: if Abram and Moses were one and the same person; if Sarai and Nefertiti were one and the same person, "A beautiful woman has come", then we must think about the fact that the one thing that these men all had in common - including Akhenaten - was Monotheism, and this may have had more to do with the woman in question - who was shared among them - than anyone might think.

And that takes us back to that odd event recorded in Genesis 33:11, where something was transferred from Jacob to Esau.

Perhaps it was the Ark of the Covenant? The "Blessing"?

And if that is the case, and it was taken *East*, which is a most intriguing idea when considering the grail stories and certain remarks of Fulcanelli, (that we are to have faith in the story of Plato, in which we are told that *the Greeks were instructed by the Arabs),* it certainly makes us wonder who were these original "Arabs" who seem to be the Tribe of Dan. And we note, of course, the name similarity to Danae, the mother of Perseus. And of course, Perseus had the gorgon's head which was so similar in function to the Ark of the Covenant, and the stories belong to the ancient Scythians.

CHAPTER 11
TIME

THE CULT OF THE HEAD

Coming back to our Grail ensemble: We understand that the lance and the cup are two ark/grail symbols that "go together" in terms of being part of the ensemble of the Grail stories. As far back as we can track them, we find them as symbols of gender, penetration and planting the seed, and gestation followed by birth. Found in juxtaposition, the spear upright in the vase, their signification is admitted by all familiar with "life symbolism". They form part of a function that deals with the processes of life and vitality and, as we have said, we do not think that it is Tantra, but rather symbolic of a more basic reproductive concept, i.e. DNA. We also note the odd fact that the letters can be rearranged to form the name "DAN". Green language and Time Loops?

Nevertheless, we wish to note that Perseus, who was the founder of the Perseid Dynasty, was said to have also founded and built the Citadel of Mycenae. For a very long time, the name of Mycenae puzzled me because it is translated to mean "Place of the Mushroom". This, of course, has led to many expositions on the value of "magic mushrooms" in initiatory rites, and we do, indeed, realize that the use of drugs in many of the ancient rites can be documented. But, when looking at the image of Melchizedek on Chartres cathedral, holding that funny cup with the cylindrical object inside, I couldn't help but think of an upside down mushroom. And suddenly, it became clear what the connection might be: a mushroom is a natural symbol for sexual union with the female dominant. In other words, it may express the fecundity of Nature as the Goddess and giver of all gifts. And in more specific terms, it may express the function of the mitochondrial DNA over of the paternal ancestry. In short, it may well be a symbol of DNA, not sex, and not drugs. In another sense, understanding the complex of "centers" as explicated by Mouravieff, another layer of explanation is the union of the lower centers of man with the higher centers, and thus gaining access to hyperdimensional states of being. In other words, this little symbol expresses to us the Great Work of Alchemy which is often expressed in "sexual" terms which many "puffers" interpret as "Tantric".

In the legends of the Grail, we discover by careful reading that there is a specific task that the hero must accomplish that is, somehow, not of a nature that would accrue benefits to himself, but it is rather a battle against evil forces to "free a ruler" and his land from disastrous consequences. The close relationship between the illness of the king and the condition of the wasteland is not a literary invention of the Middle Ages. It is, in fact, a deeply rooted element from immemorial antiquity. As we have seen, connected to the legends of the grail are a complex of "ceremonial practices" which hold to a certain form no matter what variation of the story one encounters. But we also see that something happened to bring to an end the dances of Apollo and the lifestyle of the megalith people.

Tied in to all of this is the ancient alchemical lore about the "philosopher's stone", the Holy Grail, the head of Bran the Blessed, the head called "Baphomet" of the disappearing Templars, and Noah's Ark. All are connected to the idea of certain powers that have to do with the stopping or manipulating of time, a source of endless abundance (multiplying loaves and fishes), passage to a new life with a load of animals, eternal life or the "elixir of life", and so forth. And, most importantly, we perceive the idea of "cycles" and astronomical placements being necessary to the "work". And it is not entirely out of the question that if such was the case, the megaliths could have just simply "translated" the Stone Movers into another Quantum Future at some point when astronomical alignments were right: the "Big Payoff of going home", so to speak.

In general terms, it seems likely that they understood the utilization of cosmic energy - designated in the Bible as the "hosts of heaven" - and that these stone "machines" were designed to collect and focus this energy. Their careful record keeping in such funny ways (the 19 year moon cycle, for example; and the 19th day as a special day of rest for the Assyrians) had to do with the moments in space/time when certain activities were most easily accomplished. Maybe they weren't a bunch of silly, superstitious savages hauling stones around and sweating like crazy just to dance around in the moonlight and discover when to plant the corn?

And this brings us to another kind of "stone": The Cult of the Head. Everywhere we look when we investigate these matters, we come across those ubiquitous talking heads, or heads of plenty, or heads that prophesy, or heads that turn people into stone. The most contemporary traces of the Cult of the Head are from the records of the trials of the Templars where they were accused of worshipping a head called "Baphomet". We also find the interesting references to something called a "Merkaba", or "celestial chariot".

In ancient literature, something called a Merkaba is talked about, but the definition of this extremely mysterious thing has been lost down through the centuries. There have been many "explanations" from such sources as the Midrash - Jewish commentaries - but there is even argument there. It seems that, even then, nobody knew what it was. But now, we have all these New Age folks coming along who have decided that they know what it is, and it is described as "rotating double tetrahedrons"!

Well, it's a curious word because it is composed of two words: *mer kaba*. *Kaaba* is Arabic for cube, and it is the square stone building in which the fabled Black Stone that fell from heaven is housed in Mecca. It was supposed to have been built by Ishmael and Abraham. So we have *mer*, which means sea and mother, combined with *kaaba*, which is stone, or cube, and we come to Soul stone? Mother stone? Magnetic center, indeed!

Baphomet has been variously identified as a "bisexual idol or talking head". Several derivations of the name Baphomet have been suggested. Some say it was Arabic *abu-fihamet*, or "Father of Wisdom". Some have said it is a corruption of the word Mohammed. There are several other ideas bruited about this Baphomet including that it was Pope Sylvester's Armillary Sphere. Some say it is *Baphe Meteos*, or the baptism of Metis. Metis was a Gnostic Goddess of Wisdom. However, in thinking about it in terms of cabala, we come to a different idea. Fulcanelli said it was a, "complete emblem of the secret traditions of the Order". He then says that this is "fire enclosed in water". That already refers us back to Merkaba, a "fiery stone in the sea". Baphomet includes the syllable "*pho*", which is derived from roots that mean "breath" or breathing, and from the movement of air, comes sound. In fact, a phoneme is a unit of distinctive sound in the description of any given language. In the end, we have a different idea of the "talking head" of Baphomet, and it doesn't look like it is Pope Sylvester's Armillary Sphere at all.

There is also the interesting connection of blood relationship of the Maruts. They were all of the "same parentage", and this suggests that a certain genetic inheritance was necessary in order to be able to produce the necessary energies for this very important work on behalf of the tribe or civilization. But we would like to suggest that it is not necessarily a "family line" in terms of genetics (though we cannot exclude that), but rather that the reference points out to us that the Great Work is work on the DNA! In this sense, the "Child of the King" was anyone who achieved the Alchemical Transformation!

So, we have a curious series of factors to contend with that all seem to point in the direction of DNA being far more interesting and mysterious than we might have supposed. On the one hand we have such naturally transmitted "powers", and on the other hand we have folks who can engage in some activity that either temporarily or permanently changes something in their physiology - and the apparent result is psi phenomena and/or "supernatural abilities" that may not be supernatural at all - they may be the accessing of hyperdimensional states of being via some change in the neurons of the brain as a result of turning on latent genes. After all, we note the similarity of the words "shaman" and "sarmoung" or "sarman", and the latter has been traditionally translated as "those whose heads have been purified". A much later corruption of the idea of "purification of the head" may have come down as trephination. Once the real technology was lost, they attempted to do it by brute force.

BACK TO ATLANTIS

According to Plato's story, Atlantis was the center of a country of extreme economic wealth and military power that sought to enslave all of Europe. The Atlanteans were quite successful in defeating many European countries; however, the great civilization of Athens repelled their attacks and eventually succeeded in driving them back out of Europe. Unfortunately, almost all records of this great achievement were lost due to a very powerful flood that wiped out most of Athens and the whole continent of Atlantis in one day and one night. Let's look at an even more interesting item from Frank Joseph's book: *The Lost Pyramids of Rock Lake.*

While reading, keep in mind our dating problem that was identified since Joseph wrote his book, so we very likely will have to push the early dates way back.

Someone took an awful lot of raw copper from North America a very long time ago. Who was responsible for this and what they did with it represent an enigma of vast proportions that investigators have been puzzling over for more than a century, although most Americans are unaware of the story.

Beginning around 3,000 BC, in excess of 500,000 tons of copper were mined in Michigan's Upper Peninsula, with most activity taking place at Isle Royale, an island in Lake Superior on the Canadian border. The mines abruptly and inexplicably shut down in 1200 BC, reopening no less mysteriously 2,300 years later . Until 1320 AD, some additional 2,000 tons were removed, destination unknown. As before, operations were suddenly suspended for no apparent cause. Tools - mauls, picks, hammers, shovels and levers - were left by their owners in place. Octave Du'Temple, a foremost authority on early Michigan, asks, "Why did these miners leave their operations and implements as though planning on taking up their labors the next day, and yet mysteriously never returned."

William P.F. Ferguson writes, "The work is of a colossal nature," and "amounted to the turning over of the whole formation to their depth and moving many cubic acres - it would NOT be extravagant to say cubic MILES - of rock."

The prehistoric mines were NOT crude holes in the ground, but incredibly efficacious operations to extract staggering masses of raw material as quickly as possible. An average of 1,000 to 1,200 tons of ore were excavated per pit, yielding about 100,000 pounds of copper each. […]

The ancient enterprise was a mind-boggling affair, including about 5,000 mines mostly along the Keweenaw Peninsula and the eastern end of Lake Superior above the St. Mary's river. On the northern shore, the diggings extended 150 miles, varying in width from four to seven miles... The pits ran in practically a contiguous line for 30 miles through the Rockland regions...

Estimates of 10,000 men working the mines for 1,000 years seem credible, as does the conclusion that they were not slaves, because the miners carried away their dead. No ancient graves nor evidence of cremations have been found in the Upper Peninsula. Indeed, virtually all they left behind were their tools, literally *millions of them*. As far back as the 1840s, 10 wagonloads of *stone hammers* were taken from a single location near Rockland. The mauls appeared to be mass produced in various sizes and types to serve different tasks.

W.H. Holmes succinctly writes, "It is unlikely, however, that any considerable amount of the shaping work was conducted on the island. It seems to me more likely that the pieces of metal obtained were carried away to *distant centers of population* to be worked by skilled artisans and we may justly assume that a considerable trade existed in the raw material." Those "distant centers of population" were Rock Lake and *Aztalan*, which were connected to the Great Lakes mining areas by a belt of similar mounds. One upper Peninsula temple-mound was 10 feet tall, 15 feet long at the sides and virtually identical to Aztalan's Pyramid of the Moon. As we shall see, the ancient copper miners and the inhabitants of Rock Lake-Aztalan were one and the same people.

America's ancient copper mines represent the key to unlocking Rock Lake's deepest secrets. The grandiose mining enterprise began suddenly around 3,000 BC and terminated just as abruptly 1,800 years later. [...] When prehistoric America's copper mining ceased all at once in 1200 BC, the Michigan pits were abandoned for the next 21 centuries. They were suddenly opened in 900 AD, an event that can only mean that, despite the virtual abandonment of the Rock Lake area for thousands of years... [somebody KNEW about it - and came back]. [...] Alliance with another mound building people at Spiro, Oklahoma, near the Arkansas River, provided portage to Mesoamerica Trade Centers. [...] Roy Ward Drier writes, "That the copper from which tools, scattered over such a vast area of country, were manufactured, came from the ancient mines of Lake Superior, does not admit of doubt. Although large and numerous deposits of copper ore are scattered through Arizona, New Mexico, Mexico and Central and South America, there is no evidence that the aborigines had sufficient metallurgical knowledge or skill to reduce the ores to refined copper. The shores of Lake Superior have the only known workable deposits of native copper in the world. The term virgin copper is well used to denote its purity. In this latter day, it outranks all others in the markets of the world." [...]

Archaeological excavations in the 1930s at Aztalan discovered the remains of a large rectangular building containing an abundance of unworked copper, establishing the site's identity as a mining town. [...]

Frank Joseph found some very strange pyramidal type structures in Rock Lake, Wisconsin. They were different from other pyramidal structures - being conical - and he was astounded some years later to see identical, unusual, pyramidal structures in the Canary Islands.

The original inhabitants of the Canary Islanders referred to themselves as "Canari" long before the Romans arrived. The name appears to have had a similar meaning in both Latin and the native speech, which was a mixed Indo-European language with at least several Latin cognates.

Previous to the 1st century AD, the Atlantic group was known throughout the Mediterranean World as the Blessed Isles, the Fortunate Isles, the Hesperides, or the Isles of the Blessed. Forgotten for all of classical civilization, they were isolated from outside contact for almost 1,000 years until their rediscovery by Portuguese sailors in the 14th century. The Canari more commonly referred to themselves as Guanches (men) a once civilized race that had slowly degenerated over millennia of interbreeding, while their level of society slid back, quite literally, into the caves...

Before their virtual elimination, some studies were made of the Guanches, a white people, fair complected and with red, auburn, and occasionally blond hair. Despite their genetically debased condition, they preserved traditions from long gone ages of civilized greatness and still gathered at the ruined stone monuments of their ancestors for special events. Some of these cyclopean walls, called tagora, survive as crumbling rectangular enclosures, circles, and even pyramids.

At Santa Cruz, capital of Tenerife, largest of the islands, I was surprised to learn that regular, ancient contacts between the Canaries and North America were generally acknowledged by the academic community. Talk of possible pre-Columbian visitors from Europe is taboo throughout professional circles in the United States, but Tenerife's leading historical scholar, Professor Lopez Herrera, writes: "One fact about which we may be certain is that there existed a relation in ancient times between the people of Canarian origin and the inhabitants of America." [...]

From Tenerife I took a ferry to Lanzarote, which is 125 miles closer to North Africa than any of the rest of the seven islands. After docking at the capital port of Arrecefe and checking into my hotel, I walked through the ocean-front park, intent only on some casual sightseeing, when I was thunderstruck to confront the very object that had been sought in the depths of Rock Lake for more than 50 years: a 20 foot conical pyramid. It exactly matched the sunken structure seen in the lake in 1937. [...]

In all my travels throughout Europe and studies of classical and preclassical societies, I had never found so much as a reference to a conical stone pyramid such as this one, and, as far as I knew, nothing of the kind existed anywhere else except under the waters of Rock Lake, Wisconsin.[350]

Are Rock Lake and the copper mines remnants of the civilization known by Plato as Atlantis? Adding 10,000 years to Joseph's dates, as suggested by Firestone and Topping, would put these sites into the timeframe indicated by Plato.

The evidence that Firestone and Topping discovered is puzzling for a lot of reasons. But, the fact is, there are reports of similar evidence of possible Nuclear War from such widely spread regions as India, Ireland, Scotland, France, and Turkey; ancient cities whose brick and stone walls have literally been vitrified - fused together like glass. There is also evidence of vitrification of stone forts and cities. It seems that the only reasonable explanation for such anomalies - taken in conjunction with the rest of the evidence - is an atomic blast. This fits with Plato's story of a war between the Atlanteans and "Athens".

If the Americas were "Atlantis", and if there was a war going on prior to the cataclysm, it seems that - fitting the descriptions together - North America was the hardest hit. There is not only the evidence of the nuclear activity, but the massive bombardments of exploding cometary bodies which blasted away nearly all traces of civilization. We recall that the animal carcasses found in the ice seem to have been swept northward, and this may have been the result of a sudden seven degree shift of the terrestrial axis - from 16.5 degrees to the current 23.5 - initiating tectonic shifts that not only raised the mountains of South America, but changed the face of North America, raising parts of it from under water, submerging other parts under water, and destroying nearly every living thing. The evidence of the Bimini megalithic structures under water, as well as the recently discovered underwater city near Cuba, testify to this inundation. Prior to the cataclysm, according to the information from the Gateway of the Sun at Tiahuanaco, the earth revolved about the sun in a period of 290 days.

The question is, of course, who was who? Who was on first?

---

[350] Joseph, Frank, *The Lost Pyramids of Rock Lake* (Lakeville, MN: Galde Press, Inc. 1992).

We have looked at the Americas as the possible ancient empire of Atlantis. It is now time to reiterate certain observations. We have noted earlier that the practice of human sacrifice seems to have originated and spread in the Southern Hemisphere. We have also noted that human sacrifice was most closely associated with Solar deities. The further north you go, the less importance the Sun had, the more importance the Moon was given, and the incidence of human sacrifice diminished. At certain points, where the two "types" mingled, it was not uncommon to find Moon worship associated with human sacrifice, or Sun worship divorced from Human Sacrifice. But what is evident from tracking the myths and folktales and artifacts, is that Human Sacrifice was primarily a Southern Hemisphere production. It would be almost impossible to track the ancient peoples with firm accuracy, but the point is that there is evidence that the religion of the Jews came from South America via India to the Middle East, bringing its bloodthirsty, flesh flaying, genital mutilating god along.

At the same time, we find megalithic structures on Malta that predate the deluge, and the conical pyramids of Rock Lake, Wisconsin, connected to similar structures on the Canary Islands. We have tracked our long-legged Cro-magnon types across Europe to Central Asia and back again. And we most certainly suspect that they were inhabitants of North America as well. We have found the shamanic goddess worshipping peoples of Central Asia, shepherds and horsemen and husbandmen of the land.

What happened to the peoples of North and South America? Where was "Athens"? How did the "Athenians" defeat the evil empire of Atlantis?

When we contemplate these questions, what comes to mind is that amazing, ancient tale of the Ark, represented in a hundred tales down through the millennia as any number of things from five smooth stones picked up from a stream flung by a young lad at a giant, after which he cut off his head, to the head of a Gorgon held up as a weapon to turn the wicked into stone. We find a reflection of the idea of being "turned to stone" in the story of Lot's escape from the wicked cities of Sodom and Gomorrah where, when his wife hesitated and *looked* back, she was turned to a pillar of salt. In the legend of Perseus, just *looking* at Medusa would turn one to stone.

As we review the myths and legends, we find that strange story of the Sumerians about the theft of the "tablet of destinies", which connects us to the golden tablets of the Aesir of Snorri Sturlson, and the Emerald tablets of Hermes, from which we move on to the tablets of the law in the Ark. Then we come in a circle to the idea of the "law bearer" or Ark, as the Thesmophoria of the Eleusinian mysteries celebrated only by women - and the woman was represented as a doorway, a delta - a *cross* even - from which the hanged man, Odin, hung for nine days to receive the secrets of the Goddess, the runes, and for which he sacrificed his eye to drink from the spring of wisdom. What a tangled web.

Speaking of webs, when we consider the possibility that all of our dating methods might be useless if the earth has been repeatedly subjected to cataclysmic - including nuclear- events, we are then free to consider Tiahuanaco as possibly being a surviving Atlantean city. We have only Plato's discussions upon which to speculate about the Atlanteans, and we will come to that soon enough. For the moment, we certainly wish we could query the silent stones about the past. The

only thing we know about Tiahuanaco in a more direct way, is from the myths and legends of the Inca.

Chavín is claimed to be the Mother Civilization of the Andes. The term Chavín has been applied to a developmental stage of Andean history, to an archaeological period, to an art style and to a hypothetical empire. Chavín has been interpreted as a culture, a civilization and a religion. The Chavín culture was one of agriculture and fishing and seafaring. It's earliest manifestation is in the Ica area, and we have already noted the Ica stone artifacts which suggest far greater antiquity for this culture than mainstream science even considers.

The Moche culture developed in the same area which had previously belonged to the Chavín culture, so we may assume that it was formed of survivors. Expert opinions suggest that one can easily see the influence of the oldest civilisation of Peru, the Chavín, on the Moche. Chavín was a well-developed class society, which was divided into nobility, farmers and slaves. The Moche people were developed in agriculture, fishing, handicraft, trade, sea-faring and metallurgy. The anthropomorphic pottery of the Mochicans is thought to express the mythological and social themes which were the peak of this art genre in the whole civilisation of Peru.

This raises an interesting issue because the human-shaped pottery shows that the typology of the Mochicans includes Mongoloid as well as Negroid features.

The earliest "god" image, the one carved on the Gate of the Sun, is a godlike creature holding *staves or sticks* in both of its hands. It is thought that the deity with staves was a celestial supreme being, a god of the heavens, who in the course of time was attributed the characteristic features of a thunder-god. The worship of the deity with staves spread from Chavín all over Peru, more particularly so in the Tiahuanaco culture on the Altiplano Plateau in South-Peru, where he was called Viracocha.[351]

Several versions of Andean Genesis at Tiahuanaco were recorded by Juan de Betanzos in 1551, and Cristobal de Molina in 1553. In the early version preserved by Betanzos, the world creator is named *Contiti Viracocha*, and he emerges from Lake Titicaca to create, "the sun and the day, and the moon and the stars". Viracocha orders "the sun to move in its path" and so the time of mankind begins. After calling the people out from caves, rivers, and springs scattered through the mythical landscape of creation time, Contiti Viracocha furiously *turns some of them into stone for sacrilegious behavior*. Then, he starts creation all over again! Only this time, he creates the people from stone instead of turning them into stone.

Of course we wonder about the "staves" in the hands of Viracocha? Were these the "tools" he used to "turn people into stone" or call flesh forth from stone? Are they the origins of the pillars Jachin and Boaz? How do these staves relate to the staves Jacob drove into the ground in the story about the magical increase of his flocks?

These questions bring us to consider the Semites and Sargon.

SARGON THE GREAT

According to "experts", Sargon of Akkad reigned approximately 2,334-2,279 BC, and was one of the earliest of the world's great empire builders, conquering all of southern Mesopotamia as well as parts of Syria, Anatolia, and Elam (western Iran). He established the region's first *Semitic dynasty* and was considered the founder of the Mesopotamian military tradition.

Sargon is known almost entirely from the legends and tales that followed his reputation through 2000 years of cuneiform Mesopotamian history, and not from any documents that were written during his lifetime. The lack of contemporary record is explained by the fact that the capital city of Agade, (note the homophonic similarity to Arcadia) which he built, has *never been located and excavated*. It was destroyed at the end of the dynasty that Sargon founded and was never again inhabited, at least under the name of Agade.

According to a folktale, Sargon was a self-made man of humble origins; a *gardener* (think "gardens of the Hesperides"), having found him as a baby floating in a basket on the river, brought him up in his own calling. His father is unknown; his mother is said to have been a priestess in a town on the middle Euphrates.

---

[351] Berezkin, Juri 1983. Mochica. Tsivilizatsia indeitsev Severnogo poberzhia Peru v I-VII vv. Leningrad.

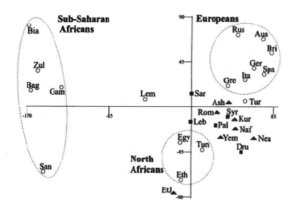

(Note all the similarities to the story of Moses *as well as* Perseus.) Rising, therefore, without the help of influential relations, he attained the post of *cupbearer* to the ruler of the city of Kish, in the north of the ancient land of Sumer. (Notice the clue of the cup here.)

The event that brought him to supremacy was the defeat of Lugalzaggisi of Uruk (biblical Erech, in central Sumer). Lugalzaggisi had already united the city-states of Sumer by defeating each in turn and claimed to rule the lands not only of the Sumerian city-states but also those as far west as the Mediterranean. Sargon became king over all of southern Mesopotamia, the first great ruler for whom *the Semitic tongue* known as Akkadian, rather than Sumerian, was natural from birth.

Sargon wished to secure favorable trade with Agade throughout the known world and this, along with what was obviously a very energetic temperament, led Sargon to conquer cities along the middle Euphrates to northern Syria and the silver-mining mountains of southern Anatolia. He also took Susa, *capital city of the Elamites,* in the Zagros Mountains of western Iran, where the only truly contemporary record of his reign has been uncovered.

As the result of Sargon's military prowess and ability to organize, as well as of the legacy of the Sumerian city-states that he had inherited by conquest, and of previously existing trade of the old Sumerian city-states with other countries, commercial connections flourished *with the Indus Valley*, the coast of Oman, the islands and shores of the Persian Gulf, the lapis lazuli mines of Badakhshan, the cedars of Lebanon, the silver-rich Taurus Mountains, Cappadocia, Crete, and perhaps even Greece.

During Sargon's rule, his Akkadian language became adapted to the script that previously had been used in the Sumerian language, and there arose new spirit of writing evident in the clay tablets and cylinder seals of this dynasty. There are beautifully arranged and executed scenes of mythology and festive life. It could be suggested that this new artistic feeling is attributable directly to the Semitic influence of Sargon and his compatriots upon the rather dull Sumerians. In contrast to the Sumerian civilization, in Sargon's new capital, military and economic values were *not* the only things that were important.

The latter part of his reign was troubled with rebellions, which later literature ascribes, predictably enough, to sacrilegious acts that he - like Solomon - is supposed to have committed; but this can be discounted as the standard cause assigned to all disasters by Sumerians and Akkadians alike. The troubles, in fact, were probably caused by the inability of one man, however energetic, to control so vast an empire. There is no evidence to suggest that he was particularly harsh, nor that the Sumerians disliked him for being a Semite. What's more, the empire did not collapse totally, for Sargon's successors were able to control their legacy, and later generations thought of him as being perhaps the greatest name in their history. What is most interesting is that Sargon attributed his success to the patronage of the goddess Ishtar, in whose honor Agade was erected.

Sargon's story sounds a lot like a combination of the Biblical stories of Moses, David and Solomon and certainly, there is evidence of infusion of Semitic traditions into the culture of the Sumerians. We also wish to consider the the the fact that Sargon was the first "semite". Nowadays "Semitic peoples" are generally understood to be, more or less, individuals of Middle Eastern origins: Jews and Arabs predominantly. That is to say, to be an Arab or a Jew is to be "Semitic".

In recent years the idea has taken hold that the Ashkenazi Jews are really Turkish and not Jews at all. Recent genetic studies place the Ashkenazi as closest in kinship to Roman Jews on one side, who are just a small step away from Lebanese non-Jews, and Syrian non-Jews on the other. The Syrian non-Jews are very close to the Kurdish Jews and the Palestinian non-Jews - i.e. the "Palestinians".

What actually seems to have happened is that when the Khazar kingdom "converted" to Judaism, they invited Jewish rabbis to come and teach them how to be proper Jews. These rabbis, being "proper Jews", took Khazar wives, mixing with the Khazar population in this way. Additionally, after the fall of the Khazar kingdom, Yiddish-speaking "Jewish" immigrants from the west (especially Germany, Bohemia, and other areas of Central Europe) - which would include Roman Jewish lines - began to flood into Eastern Europe, and it is believed that these newer immigrants intermarried with the Khazars. Thus, Eastern European Jews have a mix of ancestors who came from Central Europe and from the Khazar kingdom. The two groups (eastern and western Jews) intermarried over the centuries.

In this sense, the Ashkenazi Jews are, indeed, descendants of the Israelites through the male line.[352]

---

[352] Jews are represented by triangles: Ashkenazim = Ash, Roman Jews = Rom, North African Jews = Naf; Near Eastern Jews = Nea; Kurdish Jews = Kur, Yemenite Jews = Yem; Ethiopian Jews = EtJ; non-Jewish Middle Easterners = Pal, non-Jewish Syrians = Syr, non-Jewish Lebanes = Leb, Israeli Druze = Dru, non-Jewish Saudi Arabians = Sar; Non-Jewish Europeans: Rus = Russians, Bri = British, Ger = Germans, Aus = Austrians, Ita = Italians, Spa = Spanish, Gre = Greeks, Tun = North Africans and Tunisians; Egy = Egyptians, Eth = Ethiopians, Gam = Gambians, Bia = Giaka, Bag = Bagandans, San = San, Zul = Zulu. Tur = non Jewish Turks, Lem = Lemba from south Africa.

Analysis of the Y chromosome has already yielded interesting results. Dr. Ariella Oppenheim of the Hebrew University in Jerusalem said she had found considerable similarity between Jews and Israeli and Palestinian Arabs, as if the Y chromosomes of both groups had been drawn from a common population that began to expand 7,800 years ago.[353]

About two-thirds of Israeli Arabs and Arabs in the territories and a similar proportion of Israeli Jews are the descendents of at least three common prehistoric ancestors who lived in the Middle East in the Neolithic period, about 8,000 years ago. This is the finding of a new study conducted by an international team of scholars headed by Prof. Ariella Oppenheim, a senior geneticist in the Hebrew University's hematology department and at Hadassah Hospital in Jerusalem. In the study, soon to be published in the scientific journal 'Human Genetics,' the researchers probed the history of Jewish and Arab men by analyzing the genetic changes in the Y chromosome.[...]

The results of the study, says Prof. Oppenheim, 'support the historical documentation according to which the Arabs are descendents of an ancient population of the country and that a large proportion of them were Jews who converted to Islam after Islam reached Eretz Israel in the seventh century CE.' [...]

They [...] discovered that Jews and Arabs have common prehistoric ancestors who lived here until just the last few thousand years..[...] In view of the small geographical area of Israel and the Palestinian Authority, the researchers were surprised to discover that some Palestinians on the West Bank have a unique genetic trait that is reflected in a relatively high frequency of certain genetic signs. This fact indicates that they are the descendents of people who have lived here for a few hundred years at least. [...] Dr. Filon says that the unique genetic trait is characteristic of a population that has lived in the same place for many generations." [354]

Data on the Y chromosome indicates that the males originated in the Middle East, while the mothers' mitochondrial DNA seems to indicate a local Diaspora origin in the female community founders.[355]

We have analyzed the maternally inherited mitochondrial DNA from each of nine geographically separated Jewish groups, eight non-Jewish host populations, and an Israeli Arab/Palestinian population, and we have compared the differences found in Jews and non-Jews with those found using Y-chromosome data that were obtained, in most cases, from the same population samples. The results suggest that most

---

[353] Nicholas Wade. "Scientists Rough Out Humanity's 50,000-Year-Old Story." *The New York Times* (November 14, 2000)

[354] Tamara Traubman. "A new study shows that the genetic makeup of Jews and Arabs is almost identical, and that both groups share common prehistoric ancestors." *Ha'aretz* (2000).

[355] Judy Siegel-Itzkovich. "Dad was out and about, while Mom stayed home." *Jerusalem Post* (June 16, 2002).

Jewish communities were founded by relatively few women, that the founding process was independent in different geographic areas, and that subsequent genetic input from surrounding populations was limited on the female side. In sharp contrast to this, the paternally inherited Y chromosome shows diversity similar to that of neighboring populations and shows no evidence of founder effects. These sex-specific differences demonstrate an important role for culture in shaping patterns of genetic variation and are likely to have significant epidemiological implications for studies involving these populations. We illustrate this by presenting data from a panel of X-chromosome microsatellites, which indicates that, in the case of the Georgian Jews, the female-specific founder event appears to have resulted in elevated levels of linkage disequilibrium.[356]

The emerging genetic picture is based largely on two studies, [...] that together show that the men and women who founded the Jewish communities had surprisingly different genetic histories.[...]

A new study now shows that the women in nine Jewish communities from Georgia, the former Soviet republic, to Morocco have vastly different genetic histories from the men. [...] The women's identities, however, are a mystery, because, unlike the case with the men, their genetic signatures are *not related* to one another or *to those of present-day Middle Eastern populations*.[...]

The new study, by Dr. David Goldstein, Dr. Mark Thomas and Dr. Neil Bradman of University College in London and other colleagues, appears in The *American Journal of Human Genetics* this month.... His [Goldstein's] own speculation, he said, is that most Jewish communities were formed by unions between Jewish men and local women, though he notes that the women's origins cannot be genetically determined.[...]

Like the other Jewish communities in the study, the Ashkenazic community of Northern and Central Europe, from which most American Jews are descended, shows less diversity than expected in its mitochondrial DNA, perhaps reflecting the maternal definition of Jewishness. But *unlike the other Jewish populations*, it does *not* show signs of having had *very few female founders*. It is possible, Dr. Goldstein said, that the Ashkenazic community is a mosaic of separate populations formed the same way as the others.[...]

'The authors are correct in saying the historical origins of most Jewish communities are unknown,' Dr. [Shaye] Cohen [of Harvard University] said. 'Not only the little ones like in India, but even the mainstream Ashkenazic culture from which most American Jews descend.'[...] If the founding mothers of most Jewish communities were local, that could explain why Jews in each country tend to resemble their host

---

[356] Mark G. Thomas, Michael E. Weale, Abigail L. Jones, Martin Richards, Alice Smith, Nicola Redhead, Antonio Torroni, Rosaria Scozzari, Fiona Gratrix, Ayele Tarekegn, James F. Wilson, Cristian Capelli, Neil Bradman, and David B. Goldstein. "Founding Mothers of Jewish Communities: Geographically Separated Jewish Groups Were Independently Founded by Very Few Female Ancestors." *The American Journal of Human Genetics* 70:6 (June 2002): 1411-1420.

community physically while the origins of their Jewish founding fathers may explain the aspects the communities have in common, Dr. Cohen said.[…]

The Y chromosome and mitochondrial DNA's in today's Jewish communities reflect the ancestry of their male and female founders but say little about the rest of the genome... Noting that the Y chromosome points to a Middle Eastern origin of Jewish communities and the mitochondrial DNA to a possibly local origin, Dr. Goldstein said that the composition of ordinary chromosomes, which carry most of the genes, was impossible to assess.[357]

These studies suggests the idea that some of the early ancestors of the ancient Levant and Mesopotamian civilizations originated in the region of Armenia and moved southwards - that they were "Semitic" the same way Sargon was. Further, the Tanach records extensive evidence of intermarriage between Jews and ancient peoples who originated in eastern Anatolia, such as the Hittites and Hurrians (including the Jebusites of Jerusalem). The Edomites who were of mixed Hebrew and Hurrian ancestry were also absorbed into the Jewish people. The Armenians and Kurds are the descendants of people who remained in Eastern Anatolia, Armenia and Kurdistan, subsequently intermarrying with the Turks and neighboring peoples. So, we see the idea of the "Ten Lost Tribes", or even the "Thirteenth Tribe" to be myths exploded by the science of genetics.

The problem is, of course, that all existing studies fail to compare modern Jewish populations' DNA to ancient Judean DNA. The question remains: If Sargon was the "original Semitic ruler", was he a Semite as we understand Semites today? The next question that occurs to us is: Did Sargon, as a conqueror, impose a language and cultural expression on a genetically different people, the Sumerians, who had already imposed their own language and culture on the indigenous population of the Fertile Crescent?

What we notice most particularly is that Sargon was said to have come "from the North" and that he worshipped the Goddess Ishtar. Also, when we think of the word "Semitic" in terms of the Green language, we naturally wonder if it doesn't imply something that was "half" of one thing and "half" of another?

The question then becomes: Who were the Sumerians that absorbed and adopted the Semitic language and cultural expressions, adapting them to their own use?

The Sumerians were a *non-Semitic* people who, judging by archaeological remains, were generally short and stocky, with high, straight noses and downward sloping eyes. Many wore beards, but some were clean-shaven. These people apparently migrated to the Fertile Crescent - they suddenly appeared in the area - and immediately established what was, for a long time, considered to be the first *real* 'Civilization'. They built cities, *step-pyramid-temples*, large residences and

---

[357] Nicholas Wade. "DNA, New Clues to Jewish Roots." *The New York Times* (May 14, 2002): F1 (col. 1)

economic facilities. They referred to themselves as the "black-headed people" as if to emphasize their difference from the indigenous population who, one might assume, were not black-headed.

The picture painted by the archaeological record of the Sumerian City-State civilization before Sargon is one of constant strife between these cities, especially the most prominent ones: Kish, Erech, Ur, Adab, and later Lagash and Umma. Constant warring weakened the Sumerians until, "the kingship was carried away by *foreigners*", such as the king of Awan, Sargon of Akkad, the Gutians, the Elamites, and eventually Hammurabi. Sargon of Akkad, the first Semite, was then, a "foreigner" to the Sumerians who had (as we will see) a rather "lengthy" history prior to the Semitic influence.

It is quite curious that despite their sense of nationalism and the sharing of a common identity, the "black-headed people" were unable to unite in order to resist the conquerors. What is even more ironic is the fact that, even though they were unable to resist being conquered and ruled - in fact - by foreigners, the Sumerian culture was, to a great extent, *assimilated by the conquerors* by the adoption of their customs, script, and literature, including many of their religious myths.

The cultural "soul" of a people can be found in their stories, myths, and rituals. The stories of Sumer, as inscribed on its clay tablets, allow us to reconstruct, at least partially, a process of dynamic development that took place over many centuries. *Some experts* propose that Sumerian storytelling was indebted to the *wandering Semitic tribes*, who, being allegedly "illiterate", had the narrative memory capacity of "illiterate peoples". It is suggested by such experts that these Semites often entertained their more "civilized" Sumerian hosts by "telling tales around the campfire" or in the market place. It is then suggested that these stories were then written down by Sumerian scribes, who attempted to categorize the material into orderly groups of continuous narrative. Obviously, the "wandering, illiterate Semites" weren't quite so backward since they conquered the Sumerians and their influence actually gave the Sumerian civilization a cultural boost. What is more likely is that the writing of the Sumerians was developed for economic and military purposes, which was the purview of the "god" and his priests. It was only after the incursions of the Semites that a literary tradition began, and the development of writing proceeded in such a way that it could be utilized for literature.

The experts tell us that the Sumerians themselves had no real "sense of history", even though they had invented writing. This opinion is arrived at due to the fact that the Sumerians had recorded a sort of "history", in the form of a King list that was, to understate the matter, astonishing.

The Sumerians' relationship with their gods was *the* driving force in the rise of their civilization. The very reason for the existence of Sumer and her people seemed to lie with these strange and *mortal* 'deities'. The very reason for being was to *serve* the appropriate deity.

The Sumerian religion was more like a feudal covenental relationship with an overlord than the mystical *worship* of a god as we would understand religion today. For the Sumerian, worship of the gods meant *complete* servitude - the very purpose for which mankind was, (according to the Sumerians), created by the Sumerian gods.

According to the Sumerians, the city-states had been founded by the gods far back in time and it was the gods who had given the Sumerians, "the black-headed people", all the tools and weapons and marvelous inventions of their culture. For the Sumerians, everything that they had - cities, fields, herds, tools, institutions - had always existed because the gods had created all of it before they had created the black headed people to run things as their slaves. This immediately makes one think of the only people who claim an origin as slaves: the Jews.

This "slave-master" Religion was the central organizing principle of the city-states, each city *belonging* to a different deity who was worshipped in a large temple. According to the Sumerians, even if the gods might prefer to be just and merciful, they had also created evil and misfortune and there was nothing that the black-headed people could do about it. Judging from the *Sumerian Lamentation texts*, the best one could do in times of trouble would be to, "plead, lament and wail, tearfully confessing his sins and failings". Their family god or city god *might* intervene on their behalf, but that would not necessarily happen even if the rules were carefully followed. After all, man was created as a broken, labor saving, tool for the use of the gods and at the end of everyone's life, lay the underworld, a dreary place like the Sheol of the early Hebrews.

According to the Sumerians, their gods were very intelligent, extremely long-lived and yet, very *mortal* beings. This is evident in their king lists. According to the Sumerians, the time *before the flood* was said to be a period of 432,000 years. Two kings from after the flood that are listed were Gilgamesh and Tammuz. The legends of Tammuz were so well-liked that they were assimilated to the pantheon of Babylon and later became the model for Adonis to the Greeks. Gilgamesh became the hero of the Babylonian epic poem which bears his name, and which also contains an account of the flood.

Until recently, these king lists and the names in them were thought to be purely mythic, but in the 1930's, Sir Leonard Woolley, while excavating a building at Ur on the Ubaid level, found an inscription indicating that the structure had been erected by the son of the founder of the First Dynasty of Ur, a person up till that time regarded as fiction. Gilgamesh, too, has inscriptions telling of the buildings he built.

The "King-List" is divided into dynastic periods that are city-state oriented as apparently regards the seat of central power. The most startling of these sections is the list dealing with the pre-deluge Kings . Eight *Annunaki Kings* are listed, as are five city-states where centralized rule apparently was seated. Length of rule is given in what is known as a "sar". All of the remaining King-List sections have the length of rule measured by years. The "sar" was equivalent in length to 3,600 years.

Length of Rule

King	City of Rule	Sars	Years
A-lu-lim	NUN	8	28,800
A-la(l)-gar	NUN	10	36,000
En-me-en-lu-an-na	Bad-tabira	12	43,200
En-me-en-gal-an-na	Bad-tabira	8	28,800

Dumuzi	Bad-tabira	10	36,000
En-Sib-zi-an-na	Larak	8	28,800
En-me-en-dur-an-na	Sippar	5 (5 ner)	21,000
(?) du-du	Suruppak	5 (1 ner)	18,600

And here ends the Kingship of the Annunaki.

Now it is important to note that during this astonishing length of time recorded as "history" by the Sumerians, only two *Annunaki* held overall reign. First was Enki (later known as Ea) and the second was Enlil, a half-brother of Enki. The event that ended this first list was the legendary deluge. It was also during the latter part of this first period of the King-List that human beings appeared.

Calculating the length of time back to the arrival of these "Annunaki", brings us to about 450,000 years ago. That puts it well before the *accepted date* of the appearance of modern man.

The numbering system of the Sumerians is actually quite fascinating. The Sumerian civilization can be more or less divided into three periods of cultural manifestation. The first included the development of glyptics where cylinder seals were engraved with parades of animals or scenes of a religious nature. This was followed by the development of sculpture, and finally, the emergence of writing.

During the first period of cultural manifestation, archaeology indicates that there were no palaces for such as what we would consider a real king. The "king" was actually a priest who lived in the temple. The priest-king was titled "EN", or "Lord". It was only later, in the second cultural period that the title of king, or Lugal, came into use. At the same time, palaces became evident, witnessing a separation of the State - and its military forces - and the priesthood.

At the beginning of the second millennium BC, the Sumerians came back to dominance for a period, but after Hammurabi, Sumer disappeared entirely as a political entity. Nevertheless, the Sumerian language remained a language of priests.

Around 3,200 BC, the Sumerians devised their numerical notation system, giving special graphical symbols to the units 1, 10, 60, 600, 3,600. That is to say, we find that the Sumerians did not count in tens, hundreds and thousands, but rather adopted base 60, grouping things into sixties, and multiplying by powers of sixty.

Our own civilization utilizes vestiges of base 60 in the ways we count time in hours, minutes and seconds, and in the degrees of the circle.

Sixty is a large number to use as a base for a numbering system. It is taxing to the memory because it necessitates knowing sixty different signs (words) that stand for the numbers from 1 to 60. The Sumerians handled this by using 10 as an intermediary between the different sexagesimal orders of magnitude: 1, 60, 60^2, 60^3, etc. The word for 60, *geš, is the same as the word for unity.* The number 60 represented a certain level, above which, mutiples of 60 up to 600 were expressed by using 60 as a new unit. When they reached 600, the next level was treated as still another unit, with multiples up to 3,000. The number 3,600, or sixty sixties, was given a new name: šàr, and this, in turn, became yet another new unit.

The Sumerian numbering system often required excessive repetitions of identical marks, placing symbols side by side to represent addition of their values. The number 3,599 required a total of twenty-six symbols. For this reason, the Sumerians would often use a "subtractive convention" with a little symbol that meant "take this number away from that number to get the number that is being indicated".

In the pre-Sargon era, certain irregularities started to appear in the cuneiform representations of numbers. In addition to the subtractive convention, entirely new symbols were being created for multiples of 36,000. This means that instead of repeating 36,000 however many times it was to be indicated, the numbers 72,000, 108,000, 144,000, 180,000 and 216,000 had their own symbols assigned to them.

In all of human history, the Sumerians are the only ones we know of who invented and used a sexagesimal system. This can be seen as a "triumph" of their civilization, and a great mystery as well. Many people have tried to understand why they did this and numerous hypotheses were offered from Theon of Alexandria to Otto Neugebauer. These hypotheses range from "It was the easiest to use" and the "lowest of numbers that had the greatest number of divisors", to "it was natural" because the number of days in a Solar year rounded down to 360, and so on. Daniel Boorstin suggested that the Sumerians used base 60 because they multiplied the number of planets known to them (5) times the number of months in the year. It was pointed out by the Assyriologist, G. Kewitsch in 1904 that neither astronomy nor geometry can really explain the origin of a number system, presupposing that abstract considerations preceded concrete applications. Kewitsch speculated that the sexagesimal system actually resulted from the *fusion of two civilisations*, one of which used a decimal number-system, and the other used base 6 derived from a special form of finger-counting. This was not easily accepted since there is no historical record of a base 6 numbering system anywhere in the world.

However, duodecimal systems, or base 12 numbering systems ARE widely attested, *especially in Western Europe*. It is still used for counting eggs and oysters. We regularly use the words "dozen" and "gross" and measurements based on 12 were used in France right up to the Revolution, and are still used in Britain and the U.S.

The Romans had a unit of weight, money and arithmetic called the *as*, divided into 12 ounces. One of the monetary units of pre-Revolutionary France was the *sol*, divided into 12 deniers. The Sumerians, Assyrians, and Babylonians used base 12 and its multiples and divisors vary widely as well. The Mesopotamian day was divided into twelve equal parts, and they divided the circle, the ecliptic, and the zodiac into twleve equal sectors of 30 degrees. This means that base 12 could very well have played a major part in shaping the Sumerian number system.

The major role of 10 in the base 60 system is well attested as well, since it was used as an auxiliary unit to circumvent the main difficulty of the sexagesimal system. This leads us to an important clue: the Sumerian word for "ten" also means "fingers" suggesting an earlier counting system.

Taking this back to a variation on Kewitsch's hypothesis, Georges Ifrah proposes that base 60 was a "learned solution" to the union between two peoples, one of which used a decimal system derived from a *vigesimal system* and the other a system using base 12. As it happens, 60 is the lowest common multiple of 10 and 12 as well as the lowest number of which all the first six integers are divisors and, 5 X 12 is 60.

What is interesting to note is that the French words for 80 and 90 (quatre-vingts, quatre-vingt-dix) carry the traces of a *vanished vigesimal arithemetic* in Ancient Europe.

Ifrah's hypothesis is that the Sumerian society had both decimal and duodecimal number systems, and its mathematicians subsequently devised a system that combined the two bases.

Of course, this hypothesis fails on the ground that it pressupposes way too much intellectual sophistication. Unless, of course, we consider the *disjecta membra* of a vanished high civilization.

It is evident that the Mesopotamian basin had one or more indigenous populations prior to the arrival of the Sumerians. The Sumerians were "immigrants" who came from somewhere else about which we know nothing since they seem to have broken all ties with their previous environment.

Coming back to the question: "Who were the Semites?", we understand that the term itself derives from the Old Testament where the tribes of Eber (the Hebrews), Elam, Asshur, Aram, Arphasad, and Lud are said to be the descendants of Shem, one of Noah's three sons. However, this claim makes the Elamites, who spoke an Asianic language, *first cousins* to the Hebrews, Assyrians, and Aramaeans, whose languages belong to the Semitic group.

"Asianic" is the term used for the earlier inhabitants of the Asian mainland whose languages, mostly of the agglutinative-kind, were neither Indo-European nor Semitic. It is generally believed that Mesopotamia was originally inhabited by Asianic peoples prior to the arrival of the Sumerians. It is thought that the Semitic-speaking population came in a later wave and that Sargon was the first Semitic king of a "Semitic nation". Of course, that still doesn't explain the Sumerians and their language.

Significant Semitic elements are to be found in the cultures of Mari and Kis at the beginning of the third millennium BC, and it has even been proposed that the El Obeid peoples were the original Semites, though they were absorbed and assimilated by the Sumerians. The discovery of the Ebla tablets reveal the existence of a Semitic language in the mid-third millennium BC.

When Sargon founded the first Semitic state by defeating the Sumerians, Akkadian became the language of Mesopotamia and pushed aside the unrelated language of Sumer. When the Sumerian cuneiform writing was adapted by the Akkadians, the writing system was already several centuries old. The Akkadians found an ideographic writing system that was already drifting toward a phonetic system and accelerated this drift while still retaining some of the ideographic meanings. The Akkadian and Sumerian cultural heritages merged, creating a true literary tradition. When Akkadian speech and writing finally supplanted their Sumerian counterparts in Mesopotamia, a strictly decimal numbering became the norm in daily use. The ancient signs for 60, 600, 3,600 and so on, progressively disappeared. In the hands of the Semites, cuneiform numerals and Mesopotamian arithmetic were gradually adapted into a system with a different base working on different principles. Nevertheless, base 60 did not disappear entirely, as we have already mentioned.

We should note, however, that it was with the sudden appearance of the Sumerian civilization - as early as the 5th millennium BC - that the long era of the tribal, egalitarian society of the Neolithic came to an end between 4,000 and 3,000 B.C. Archaeologists and anthropologists have documented that the early society of Mesopotamia had been *guided by women* and had a Goddess as deity. The end of female leadership can be deducted from the following quote in "*In the Wake of the Goddesses*" by Frymer-Kenski:

> The dynasty of Kish was founded by Enmebaragesi, a contemporary of Gilgamesh.
> The name breaks down as follows: *enetik - eme - ebakin - aragikor - ageriko - ezi*
> which can be transliterated to "from that time on - female - harvest - lustful -
> notorious - to domesticate" or "From that time on the lustful, notorious harvest
> female was domesticated."

This "name" tells us in no uncertain terms that the time of the Goddess was on the decline, because male domination had arrived with the Sumerians. Sargon, conversely, attributed all of his successes to the Goddess.

Now, let's come back to the clues that the French words for 80 and 90 (quatre-vingts, quatre-vingt-dix) carry the traces of a vanished ancient European vigesimal arithmetic, put together with the fact that the first Semitic king came from the "North" and that the "Semitic influence" of the Goddess worshipping Sargon accelerated the development of the Sumerian culture toward something more than being economic slaves to the gods. Considering these factors, we might wish to reconsider the term "Semitic".

Indeed, the religion of the ancient Sumerians has left its mark on the entire Middle East. Not only are its temples and ziggurats scattered about the region, but the literature, cosmogony and rituals influenced their neighbors to such an extent that we can see echoes of Sumer in the Judeo-Christian-Islamic tradition today. In other words, most of what we consider to be Semitic is actually Sumerian written in the Semitic Akkadian language. Undoubtedly, those peoples who today are called Semitic by virtue of having had a name assigned to them from the Bible, are actually descendants of the Sumerians, and their "Semitic language" was imposed on them by Sargon of Akkad who was clearly *not* one of the "black-headed people".

The linguistic affinity of Sumerian has not yet been successfully established. Ural-Altaic (which includes Turkish), Dravidian, Brahui, Bantu, and many other groups of languages have been compared with Sumerian, but no theory has gained common acceptance. [358]

---

[358] Arno Poebel, *Grundzüge der sumerischen Grammatik* (1923), partly out of date, but still the only full grammar of Sumerian in all its stages; Adam Falkenstein, *Grammatik der Sprache Gudeas von*

SARGON REPRISE

Sargon became king over all of southern Mesopotamia, the first great ruler for whom *the Semitic tongue* - not Sumerian - known as Akkadian was natural from birth. This suggests to us that Sargon was not Sumerian, but that he was the bringer of a new language to Mesopotamia, imposing it on the peoples there in the same way that Spanish was imposed on South and Central America, and English has been adopted all over the world as a result of American domination of trade.

The language issue is our clue as to who relates to whom. The Afro-Asiatic language phylum has six distinct branches including Ancient Egyptian, which was known in its last years as Coptic, and which became extinct in the seventeenth century. The other five branches are Berber, Chadic, Cushitic, and Omotic. The Semitic language group is subdivided into an extinct Eastern branch, Akkadian, spoken by Sargon, and a Western branch with two sub-branches, Central and South. The Central group consists of Aramaic, Canaanite, and Arabic. The Southern group consists of South Arabian and Ethiopic. And here is the curiosity: one of the other branches of the Afro-Asiatic language tree is Berber, with sub-branches of *Guanche* - spoken by the original Canary Islanders; East Numidian, which is Old Libyan, and Berber proper.

Now, you ask, what is the oddity?

THE GUANCHE LANGUAGE.

Some experts tell us that the Guanches must have come from the neighboring African coast long ages before the Black and Arab "invaders" overran it. We are sagely informed that Mauritania was formerly inhabited by the, "same ancient Iberian race which once covered all *Western Europe*: a people tall, fair and strong". Spain invaded, and most of the Guanches were wiped out by diseases to which they had no resistance due to their long isolation. It was over a hundred years before anyone attempted to record their language, customs, and what could be remembered of their history. Friar Alonso de Espinosa of the Augustine Order of Preachers, writing in 1580, tells us:

> ...It is generally believed that these are the Elysian Fields of which Homer sings.
> The poet Virgil, in the 4th book of the *Aeneid*, mentions the great peak of this
> island, when he makes Mercury, sent by Jupiter, go to Carthage to undeceive
> Aeneas, and to encourage him so that he might not abandon the voyage to Italy
> which he had undertaken.

Lagas, 2 vol. (1949-50), a very thorough grammar of the New Sumerian dialect, and *Das Sumerische* (1959), a very brief but comprehensive survey of the Sumerian language; Cyril J. Gadd, *Sumerian Reading Book* (1924), outdated but the only grammatical tool in English; Samuel N. Kramer, *The Sumerians* (1963), provides a general introduction to Sumerian civilization.

It has not been possible to ascertain the origin of the Guanches, or whence they came, for as the natives had no letters, they had no account of their origin or descent, although some tradition may have come down from father to son. [...]

The old Guanches say that they have an immemorial tradition that sixty people came to this island, but they know not whence they came. They gave their settlement the name, "The place of union of the son of the great one".

Although they knew of God, and called Him by various names, they had no rites nor ceremonies nor words with which they might venerate Him. [...] When the rains failed, they got together the sheep in certain places, where it was the custom to invoke the guardian of the sheep. Here they *stuck a wand or lance in the ground*, then they separated the lambs from the sheep, and placed the mothers round the lance, where they bleated. They believed that God was appeased by this ceremony, that he heard the bleating of the sheep and would send down the rain.

...They knew that there was a hell, and they held that it was in the peak of Teyde [the volcanic mountain}, and the devil was Guayota.

They were accustomed when a child was born, to call a woman whose duty it was, and she poured water over its head; and this woman thus contracted a relationship with the child's parents, so that it was not lawful to marry her, or to treat her dishonestly. They know not whence they derived this custom or ceremony, only that it existed. It could not be a sacrament, for it was not performed as one, nor had the evangelic law been preached to them.[...]

The inviolable law was that if a warrior meeting a woman by chance in the road, or in any solitary place, who spoke to her or looked at her, unless she spoke first and asked for something, or who, in an inhabited place, used any dishonest words which could be proved, he should suffer death for it without appeal. Such was their discipline. [...]

This people had very good and perfect features, and well-shaped bodies. They were of tall stature, with proportionate limbs. *There were giants among them of incredible size...*

They only possessed and sowed barley and beans. ... If they once had wheat, the seed had been lost... They also ate the flesh of sheep, goats, and pigs, and they fed on it by itself, without any other relish whatever... The flesh had to be half roasted because, as they said, it contained more substance in that way than if it was well roasted.

They *counted the year by lunations*... The lord did not marry with anyone of the lower orders, and if there was no one he could marry without staining the lineage, brothers were married to sisters.

They were wonderfully clever with counting. Although a flock was very numerous and came out of the yard or fold at a rush, they counted the sheep without opening their mouths or noting with their hands, and never made a mistake. [359]

I'm sure that the reader can see that even though we have very little to go on, there are a couple of suggestive indicators recorded by the good friar. The first thing we note is the custom of driving a lance into the ground for the sheep to "call the god". A memory of ante-diluvian technology, perhaps?

But more than this, the clues seem to indicate that what we call the "Semitic language" may actually have been a northern tongue, an Aryan language, adopted by peoples we think of as ethnically "Semitic" in modern terms but who, in ancient terms, were not Semitic at all.

THE RISE OF SACRIFICE

Returning to Viracocha, what we learn about him was that he was a *carver and shaper of humanity*. He was a god of action, a creator and destroyer of worlds: the Shiva of the Andes. Before successfully creating the world of humans, Viracocha had annihilated previous worlds; first by fire and then again by flood. In short, for the Andeans, humanity emerged not from a utopian Garden of Eden - which is a Northern concept - but from the hard, living rock and water of the natural world: clay. Viracocha had two faithful servants who he sent in opposite directions to generate a new race of humans.

In Cristobal de Molina's version of the same myth, these two culture heroes are the Andean Adam and Eve: the primeval male-female pair who were the children of Viracocha. Unlike the theme of a prior Golden Age, the events of the myth begin only *after* a universal flood. The Spanish cleric Bernabe Cobo informs us that the original name for Tiahuanaco was Taypi Kala. Taypi Kala meant "the stone in the center"; the natives ascribed this name to the site because they considered the city to be in, "the center of the world, and that from there the world was repopulated after the flood".

The peoples of the Andes had no known form of indigenous writing, so the evidence for their activities must come from other sources. The early Spanish chroniclers recorded what had been described to them about life in Inca times; their accounts include frequent references to "sacrifice" and "offering". Some doubt has been expressed about these accounts, however, accusing the Europeans of a negative, Catholic point of view, suggesting that the chroniclers did not ask the right questions. However, pictorial evidence for sacrifice has long been known. The Incas made little in the way of figurative art, but existing *pre-Inca depictions* give *visual evidence for sacrifice*. Examples of archaeological evidence are now

---

[359] De Espinosa, Alonso, *The Guanches of Tenerife*, trans. by Sir Clements Markham (Nendeln/Liechtenstein: Kraus Repring 1972).

accumulating in the data from recent excavations in a number of places. Most of the archaeological evidence for human sacrifice in the Andes - most clearly among the Inca and the Moche - has been discovered only recently.

For many people in the modern Western world, making a sacrifice means either giving without receiving or giving up something valuable for a cause that may benefit others. What seems to be evident about the process of sacrifice in primitive belief systems is that sacrifices of animals and humans were done for the greater good of the group - to appease the anger of the god and prevent disaster. Blood was the symbol of life, of animation, of nourishment, the most important offering that could be given to the natural and supernatural beings. It was thought that the sacrificial nourishing of the "sacred beings" made life possible. It was also thought that the cosmos "ran" on this "nourishment". It has been suggested that the number and violence of the sacrifices increased as the desperate Moche priests tried to appease the Gods. Unfortunately, such speculations do not fully answer the question as to why *any* human being *ever* thought that the death of another human being would satisfy the gods in some way.

In artistic depictions, the Moche are seen to cut the throats of prisoners of war and then *drink their blood*. Afterwards, the bodies were dismembered. It's hard to say what the purpose of these endless sacrifices might be. Perhaps the priests thought that they obtained power from drinking the blood. We are reminded of the Biblical injunction that "the blood is the life", and the Hebrews were forbidden to drink it or to eat meat that had not been thoroughly bled. Perhaps this was because the blood - and the life in it - was supposed to be reserved for the god exclusively. Child sacrifice is a recurrent theme not only in the Andes but also in much of the world.

Returning now to our problem: Yahweh. It seems that, like the Moche and the Aztecs, the Jewish priesthood began with terrifying cannibalistic rituals and sacrifices. Just picture the priest - kohane - standing before the worshippers spattered with dripping, stringy clots of blood, throwing basins of blood on the congregation to "cleanse" them, all the while the subliminal message being conveyed that, "if you don't obey Yahweh, this is what he will do to you"! This may have been what was taking place in the great Temple of Solomon which was very likely a displaced memory of a place so hated, the Temple of Hephaestus - the labyrinth - in Memphis, and was later transferred to the "labyrinth" at Crete. It was then brought to Palestine by the refugees from the eruption of Thera, and combined later with other tales of the cataclysm to produce some of the Old Testament and the rites of Judaism. We begin to understand why the labyrinth of Egypt was, according to Pliny, regarded with "extraordinary hatred" and why so many myths of a human eating Minotaur at the center circulated in the ancient world.

The idea of the ritual sacrifice of the king instead of thousands of virgins, children, or warriors, seems to be the result of the mingling of the Southern Sun god worship with the influence of the Northern Moon worshippers. This seems to be a distortion of the idea that the king was ruler by virtue of his "marriage" to the goddess, or her representative, and that this "marriage" involved a shamanic death in order to be able to transduce the cosmic energies of benevolence and prosperity to the tribe or to defend the tribe against evil spirits.

The northern custom of a king who had lost his vigor voluntarily abdicating and being replaced by the "right heir" who could "marry the goddess" was mixed with the sacrifice customs, and the result was that the priesthood had a weapon to wield over the monarch to keep him in line. Thus arose the idea of the "scape goat" king who was sacrificed in the labyrinth instead of maidens and warriors.

Herodotus tells us what seems to be an already garbled version of this mixing of the two ideas:

> Being set free after the reign of the priest of Hephaistos, the Egyptians, since they could not live any time without a king, set up over them twelve kings, having divided all Egypt into twelve parts.

This may be the original story of Jacob and Esau and the 12 tribes.

This shift was also recorded in the myth of Theseus.

What seems to be so is that there was some sort of "object of power" at the center of the myth of the Sons of Aegyptus and the daughters of Danaus. It was a descendant of this "union" - Perseus - who "cleansed the temple" and restored the Goddess to her rightful place as depicted in the story of the slaying of Medusa, the freeing of Pegasus, and the rescue of Andromeda. But again, this is merely the assimilation of later events to the primal myth of Atlantis.

When we examine the evidence, we find many clues, but with the passage of time, the movements of people in migration and/or conquest, it is impossible to say with certainty just "who is on first". There is, of course, much more to this than the little bit I am able to include here. This will be dealt with in a future volume.

In the Bible the "wise king Solomon" is portrayed as "whoring after" the Tyrian fire and sun god Moloch/Molech. One has to wonder what this means considering the fact that there is no difference between Moloch and Yahweh when one digs beneath the surface. Some "experts" suggest that the priest Melchizedek - who was the purported teacher of Abraham - was a priest of "Moloch", and that the name means, "Righteous Moloch". However, that is a cross-conceptualization, and a somewhat sly way to trick the reader. If you are going to translate one word into English, you ought to translate the other. *Malkiy*, or *Malak*, means simply "king". *Tsedeq* means "right" or "just" or benevolent. It carries the abstract suggestion of "prosperity".

What seems to have happened, once again, is that a possible revelation of truth about our reality was co-opted and diverted by the denizens of hyperdimensional realities who do not wish their nature and agenda to be discerned. In the standard method of disinformation, truth was mixed with lies in order to mislead and divert. Those who wish that everything was either clearly black or clearly white, do not take the time to patiently pick through the threads and separate them so as to discern the truth. My suggestion on this point is that the ancient Priesthood of Melchizedek was designated thus for the express purpose of distinguishing it from the worship of Moloch, the Fire god.

The apparent co-opting of names and terms and symbolism throughout the ages continues. In the present day, there are many who claim to be "of the Order of Melchizedek" who are in fact, not.

Some experts quote Paul's remark from Hebrews 9:22 where it says: "under the Law almost everything is purified by means of blood, and without the shedding of blood there is neither release from sin and its guilt nor the remission of the due and merited punishment for sins." What such experts fail to mention - again a sly twisting - is what follows in that particular passage, which is an argument against such practices.

The religion of the Great Mother Goddess existed and flourished for many thousands of years in the Near and Middle East before the arrival of the patriarch Abraham who is depicted as the first prophet of the dominator male deity, Yahweh. Archaeologists have traced the worship of the Goddess back to the Neolithic communities of about 7000 BC, some to the Upper Paleolithic cultures of about 25,000 BC. From Neolithic times, at least, its existence has been repeatedly attested to well into Roman Times. Yet, Bible scholars tell us that Abraham lived in Canaan as late as between 1800 and 1550 BC, a veritable Johnny-come-lately! How in the world has such a recent appearance on the world scene managed to push itself into such prominence and domination?

Over and over again in the studies of the ancient religions it is noted that, in place after place, the goddess was debased and replaced by a male deity - the worship of a young warrior god and a supreme father god. It has been assumed that this was the Indo-European invasion from the north. But when the cultural connections are considered, it is clear that this ideation moved northward from the South. Perhaps we ought to call it the "Indo-Incan" invasion since we have suggested a connection to the cultures of South America. Archaeology reveals that, after these incursions, the worship of the Mother Goddess fluctuated from city to city. As the invaders gained more and more territory over the next two thousand years, the male began to appear as the dominant husband or even the murderer of the Goddess! The transition was accomplished by brutally violent massacres and territorial acquisition throughout the Near and Middle East. The same is true regarding the conversion of the western world to Christianity. Something is definitely strange about this picture.

This corruption drifted north, as Eliade has noted, changing the shamanic cultures from goddess worshippers to male dominated societies. In studying the legends about the Golden Age, the Antediluvian world, we realize over and over again that these stories talk about a garden where woman and man lived in harmony with each other and nature. That is, until a dominator male god decided that woman had been a very bad girl and must now and forever be subservient to man.

The Chinese *Tao Te Ching* describes a time when the *yin*, or feminine principle, was not yet ruled by *yang*, the male principle, a time when the wisdom of the mother was still honored and followed above all. To many people, references to these times are no more than mere fantasy.

It seems that there were ancient societies organized very differently from ours, and chief among the finds in such digs are the many images of the Deity as female. Thus we are better able to interpret the references to the Great Goddess in ancient art, myth, and even historical writings.

The chief idea of these people was that the Universe was an all-giving mother. Indeed, this idea has survived into our time. In China, the female deities Ma Tsu and Kuan Yin are still widely worshiped as beneficent and compassionate goddesses. Similarly, the veneration of Mary, the Mother of God, is widespread.

Even if in Catholic theology she is demoted to non-divine status, her divinity is implicitly recognized by her appellation "Mother of God", as well as by the prayers of millions who daily seek her compassionate protection and solace. In fact, the story of Jesus' birth, death and resurrection seems to be little more than a reworking of those of earlier 'mystery cults' revolving around a Divine Mother and her son or, as in the worship of Demeter and Kore, her daughter.

It is, of course, reasonable that the deepest understanding of divine power in human form should be female rather than male. After all, life emerges from the body of a woman, and if we are to understand the macrocosm by means of the microcosm, it is only natural to think of the universe as an all-giving Mother from whose womb all life emerges and to which, like the cycles of vegetation, it returns after death to be again reborn.

What is more important to us here is the idea that societies that view the universe as a Mother would also have very different social structures from our own. We might also conjecture that women in such a society would not be seen as subservient. Caring, nurturing, growth and creation would have been valued. At the same time, it does not make sense to think that such societies were "matriarchal" in the sense that women dominated men. They were, instead, by all the evidence, societies in which differences were valued and not equated as evidence of either superiority or inferiority.

What we do know is that "Venus" figurines have been found by the thousands, all over Eurasia, from the Balkans to Lake Baikal in Siberia, across to Willendorf in Austria, and the *Grotte du Pappe* in France. Some scholars (clearly with their minds where they ought not to be) have described them as "erotic art" of the stone-age and have proposed that they were used in obscene fertility rites!

But is that really so?

Can these ubiquitous female images found from Britain to Malta even be described accurately as erotic "Venus" figures? Most of them are broad-hipped, sometimes pregnant, stylized and frequently faceless. They look like pithoi and are clearly symbolic, just as the cross with the crucified man is a symbol. Future archaeologists who might dig in the remains of our civilization would find equally ubiquitous and symbolic crosses!

The worship of a female creator goddess appears, literally, in every area of the world. What is significant is that the most tangible line of evidence is drawn from the numerous sculptures of women found in the Gravettian-Aurignacian cultures of the Upper Paleolithic Age. Some of these date back to 25,000 BC, as noted above, and are frequently made of bone or clay. They were often found lying close to the remains of the sunken walls of what are probably the earliest known human-made dwellings on earth. Researchers say that niches or depressions were made in the walls to hold the figures. Such finds have been noted in Spain, France, Germany, Austria, Czechoslovakia and Russia. These sites span a period of at least ten thousand years!

It appears highly probable that the female figurines were idols of a "great mother" cult, practiced by the nomadic Aurignacian mammoth hunters who inhabited the immense Eurasian territories that extended from southern France to Lake Baikal in Siberia.

In the oldest archaeological finds, the Goddess was represented by birds and wavy symbols that indicated water and/or energy. These same wavy lines are retained as the symbol of the Astrological sign of Aquarius which may be the oldest extant symbol of the Great Mother Goddess.

But suddenly, at a certain point, around 5000 years ago, serpents became associated with the goddess, and the wavy lines of water/energy were transmogrified to snakes. What happened to bring about this association? By 4000 BC, Goddess figures appeared at Ur and Uruk, both on the southern end of the Euphrates river, not far from the Persian Gulf. At about this same period, the Neolithic Badarian and Amaratian cultures of Egypt first appeared. It is at these sites that agriculture first emerged in Egypt.

From that point on, with the invention of writing, history as we know it, emerged in both Sumer and Egypt - about 3000 BC. (5000 years ago!) In every area of the Near and Middle East, the Goddess was known in historic times. It seems clear that many changes must have taken place in both the forms and modes of worship, but, in various ways, the worship of the Goddess survived into classical Greece and Rome. It was not totally suppressed until the time of the Christian emperors of Rome and Byzantium, who closed the last Goddess Temples about 500 AD.

It appears that the Goddess ruled alone in the beginning, though she was "married" to the king via a human female representative. Thus, the son or brother who was also her lover and consort was part of the goddess religion in much earlier times. This individual was also truly "Semitic" in the sense of being half human and half divine.

Later, as the corruption crept in - seemingly after some dramatic, cataclysmic event - it was this youth - known in various languages as Damuzi, Tammuz, Attis, Adonis, Osiris or Baal - who died in his youth causing an annual period of grief and lamentation among those who paid homage to the Goddess.

For a very long time, this myth was annually enacted representing the fact that time was cyclical the same way the seasons were. It was the passing down of the knowledge of cyclical catastrophes connected to cyclical time. The world might end, but if it did, it was only because it had "run down" and needed to be "wound up" again.

But something changed all that. Somehow, the perception of the End of the World became a terrible punishment that might be prevented by savage sacrifices. And the sub-text of this idea was that time was linear and would end, finally and completely. This idea was brought with the invaders from the South, the murderers of the Goddess, the rapers of the Maidens of the Wells: the dominator religion that drove the sword into the stone.

Part of the cover-up seems to involve blaming this corruption on "northern invaders" or Aryan Indo-Europeans. The invasions of the Aryans took place in waves over a period of up to three thousand years according to standard teachings. They are called invasions because it seems that the arrival of masses of new people was always related, in some way, to evidence of destruction which may or may not have been related to wars of conquest. It may just as well have been related to atmospheric or geologic disruption. Those incursions of prehistoric times are suggested by speculative etymological connections. I propose that there

were also invasions from the South, and these invasions brought the corruption that spread like a disease all over the globe, corrupting even the Northern worshippers of the Moon and the Goddess.

What is most significant is that the coming of the "Northern invaders" revolutionized not only war, but also art and culture. They introduced the horse-drawn chariot, and the charioteer became a new aristocracy. Since the ancient steppe peoples used carts for traveling and carrying their goods, it seems logical to suggest that it was only after the mixing with the war-like Southern peoples that such vehicles were converted to the use of war and destruction.

Many "experts" tell us that it was these northern people who brought with them the concepts of light as good and dark as evil and of *a supreme male deity.* However, the archaeological and mythographic record suggests otherwise. If, indeed, they later assimilated the supreme male deity to their pantheon, it is clear that these ideas came from the mixing of cultures in Mesopotamia. The interweaving of the two theologies are recorded mythologically in the cultures of this region, and for too long, the blame has been cast in the wrong direction. But most of these ideas were formed before the knowledge of the Southern, American cultures was available. It is in the myths of South America that we discover the origins of the attitude that led to the destruction of the Goddess. It is also in these stories that we find the beginning of the concept of time as linear, with a beginning and an end for human beings, at least.

When we were in Mexico in 1997, I noticed an odd sculpture from one of the ancient temples that had been placed in the museum of anthropology. It was of a man whose skull, elbow joint, and thigh had been flayed, while the rest of his flesh was intact. This was a clear representation of not only the components of the skull and crossed thigh bones, but also the ubiquitous "joint" symbol of certain occult secret societies - societies that worship the flaying, blood drinking, male god.

I photographed the carving, and you will note that it also includes a rattlesnake entwined around the body of the flayed man.

The theme of flaying is also present in India in the dance of Shiva on the elephant god. After the elephant is flayed, Shiva dons the skin as a symbol of *acquiring the power of the god.* The same flaying and donning of the skin of the sacrificial victims was practiced by the South American sun worshippers, by the Egyptians, and also - so it seems - by the early Jewish priesthood.

Viracocha was the supreme Inca god, a synthesis of sun god and storm god. One version of the story says that the Creator God Viracocha, "rose from Lake Titicaca during the time of darkness to bring forth light". Viracocha was represented as wearing the sun for a crown, with *thunderbolts in his hands,* and tears descending from his eyes as rain. Viracocha made the earth, the stars, the sky and mankind, but his first creation displeased him, so he destroyed it with a flood and made a new, better one, taking to his wanderings - disappearing across the ocean, walking on water - as the Christianized version goes - as a beggar, teaching his new creations the rudiments of civilization, as well as working numerous miracles.

Another version of the story tells us that the Viracocha were *so hated that the people rose up against them and massacred them*, but that *a couple of them escaped across the ocean*. This is the most likely scenario considering all of the evidence. It also reminds us of the hatred of the Egyptian labyrinth. We should note that there are significant artistic representations in both South America and Egypt of "black headed" peoples sacrificing blond or red-headed men.

The term "viracocha" also refers to a group of men named the *suncasapa* or bearded ones - they were the mythic soldiers of Viracocha, also called the "angelic warriors of Viracocha". Later one of the Inca Kings (the eighth Inca ruler) took the name of Viracocha. But in all cases, we see the "hint" that they were Aryans was provided by the Spanish friars, and is not supported by the archaeological evidence.

On the Gateway of the Sun, the famous carved figure on the decorated archway in the ancient (pre-Incan) city of Tiahuanaco most likely represents Viracocha, flanked by 48 winged effigies, 32 with human faces and 16 with condor's heads.

What seems to be evident is that there were people who rose to power in South America known as the Viracocha. After the Spaniards destroyed all of the records of the natives of the Americas, they wrote their own versions, which included stories of the Viracocha being blond, Aryan types. This was due to the fact that the Spaniards noted a certain similarity between the myths of the Incan civilizing gods and their own religious beliefs. This was later taken up by Thor Heyerdahl, but a careful examination of the records gives no firm evidence that these individuals were Aryans. The evidence of Aryan types on Easter Island has been convincingly explained as the result of the survivors of a shipwreck taking up residence and has nothing to do with the "travels of the Incas". However, the links between certain scripts found on Easter Island, and the script of the Indus Valley, and certain mythical motifs, strongly suggest a connection between South America, Easter Island, India, Mesopotamia, Egypt, and the religion of the Jews. Of course, it *is* possible that such civilizing influence was transmitted by "big, blond, sailor" types who rose to power in South America and were destroyed in revolutions by the enslaved, native masses. Images of red headed men being sacrificed are known in South America, so perhaps they were viewed as "gods" and the indigenous population sought to acquire their powers by "flaying" them and donning their skins. We realize that skin color has been an issue throughout human history, so it would be reasonable to think that the primitive mind might see the white skin as a transmitter of power. Of course, that doesn't even address the question as to why light skinned individuals were perceived as "higher caste" and worthy of emulation to begin with, but that's another issue.

So we suggest "Viracocha" left the lands of the Inca and traveled across the Pacific. In India, we find the most interesting Indus Valley civilization which - upon visual inspection of the ruins - presents a striking resemblance to the ruins of the ancient cities of South America. The only difference was that the ability to shape megaliths seems to have been lost, and the Indus valley cities, while *stylistically* similar, are built of brick. As mentioned, we can note the similarity of certain writings found on Easter Island to the Indus Valley script.

At a later point in time, the movement was north to Mesopotamia where again, certain sigils found on cylinder seals are similar to the Indus Valley script. The rigid caste system of the Incas is found also in India.

Another item of considerable interest that connects Egypt to South America is the Ica skulls compared to the representations of elongated skulls among the Egyptian royalty. This is a subject I will cover more thoroughly in another volume. The point at the moment is to make clear the obvious connection between some very strange things in South America, and other strange things in Egypt and the

Middle East, all connected in mysterious ways to the creation of three monotheistic religions, and the present day struggle among the three.

And so we find the Viracocha types from across the Pacific, making their way up the Indian peninsula, to meet with a group of big blond nomadic herdsmen from the Altai Mountains, probably in Mesopotamia. And so, the Southern male god was adopted by the Altai Aryans in their mingling with the Southerners that invaded India from across the Sea.[360] "And the sons of God looked upon the daughters of men and saw that they were fair and took wives…"

This new "Aryan" god was frequently depicted as a storm god, high on a mountain, blazing with the light of fire or lightning from the thunderbolts he held in his hand. In many of these transposed myths, the goddess is depicted as a serpent or dragon, associated with darkness and evil. Sometimes the dragon is neuter or even male, but in such cases, is closely associated with the goddess, usually as her son.

The Goddess religion seems to have assimilated the male deities into the older forms of worship, and survived as the popular religion of the people for thousands of years after the initial Southern Sumerian invasions. But her position had been greatly lowered and continued to decline. In the form of Judaism and eventually Christianity, the male sun god finally suppressed the religion of the goddess.

And here we come to the most interesting thing of all: it is in the accounts of these mixed Aryans that we find the original religious ideas of the Hebrews. It is also from this mixing - the region from which Zarathustra emerged - that we get the original ideas of the End of the World. In the mixing of the two idealogies,

---

[360] See *Gods of the Cataclysm* for the evidence of this route of transfer of ideas.

there is the mountain-top god who blazes with light; there is the duality between light and darkness symbolized as good and evil; there is the myth of the male deity defeating the serpent; and there is the supreme leadership of a ruling class: the priestly Levites; all of these are to be found in both the Indo-Incan and Hebrew religious concepts and politics!

In India, we suggest that there is another way to interpret the evidence. We propose a "Southern Sumerian" invasion from across the sea, meeting and mingling with the Aryan invasion from the North which resulted in the assimilation of the Goddess worshippers and the emerging dominance of the Southern male god. The books known as the *Vedas* were a record of the Aryans in India. They were written between 1500 and 1200 B.C. in Sanskrit using scripts possibly borrowed from the Akkadians.

The "Southern" attitude toward women is made clear in two sentences attributed to Indra in the *Rg Veda:* "*The mind of woman brooks not discipline. Her intellect has little weight.*" And orthodox Jewish males daily thank god that they were not born women! This leads us to the obvious idea: The Indo-Incan patterns were either adopted by the Jews, or the Sumerian/Jewish priests were Indo-Incans from the start.

The Indo-Aryan *Rg Veda* says that "in the very beginning there was only '*asura*', or 'living power'." The *asura* broke down into two cosmic groups. One was the enemies of the Danavas, or Dityas, whose mother was the Goddess Danu or Diti; the other group, were known as the A-Dityas. Aside from the fact that this clearly depicts exactly what we are discussing here, the title betrays the fact that this mythical structure was created in reaction to the presence of the worshippers of Diti, since A-Ditya literally means "not Dityas", or "not people of Diti".

> [M]many sociologists believe that some kind of a hierarchical social order, in terms of an individual's occupation and duties, was in place perhaps *ahead of the arrival of the Aryans*. Its evolution into the caste or the *varna* system as we know today - with the four distinct castes of Brahmin, Kshatriya, Vaisya and Sudra in the order of social standing - probably occurred with the settling of the Aryans who sanctified and legitimised the social order in their own terms which had a distinct religious underpinning. Some sociologists hold that the societal stratification in terms of rights and duties of the individual was a creation of the Aryans in their bid to exercise power over the indigenous proto-Asian populations of North India. [...]

> In recent times, with the rise of strident nationalism in the form of "Hindutva" ideology, which rejects the premise that Aryans were outsiders and views them as part of the continuum from the Indus valley civilisation, an unequivocal answer to this may have political implications. While material evidence of ancient history has not been able to resolve this issue, modern population genetics, based on analyses of the variations in the DNA in population sets, has tools to provide a more authoritative answer. Certain inherited genes carry the imprint of this information through the ages. [...]

> An international study led by Michale J. Bamshad of the Eccles Institute of Human Genetics of the University of Utah of caste origins has found (the findings have been reported in a recent issue of the journal *Genome Research*) that members of the upper castes are genetically more similar to Europeans, *Western Eurasians* to be specific, whereas the lower castes are more similar to Asians. This finding is in tune with the expectations based on historical reasoning and the prevalent views of

many social historians. In exercising their superiority over native proto-Asian populations, the Aryans would have appointed themselves to higher rank castes. [...]

Interestingly, an analysis of the genetic variations in the markers associated with the maternally inherited mtDNA and paternally inherited Y-chromosome show strikingly different trends. Maternally inherited DNA was overall found to be more similar to Asians than to Europeans, though the similarity to Europeans increases as we go up the caste ladder. Paternally inherited DNA, on the other hand, was overall more similar to Europeans than to Asians but, unlike in the case of maternal inheritance, with no significant variation in affinity across the castes. This is intriguing, but there is a plausible explanation. Migrating Eurasian populations are likely to have been mostly males who integrated into the upper castes and took native women. Inter-caste marriage practices, while generally taboo, are occasionally allowed, in which women can marry into an upper caste and move up in the social hierarchy. However, such upward mobility is not permissible for men. The caste labels of men are thus permanent, while women, by means of their limited mobility, cause a gene flow across caste barriers. This is the reason, according to the researchers, for the differing affinities of gender-specific genes among castes to continental populations. [361]

One of the major Indo-Aryan gods was known as Indra, Lord of the Mountains, "he who overthrows cities". Upon obtaining the promise of supremacy if he succeeded in *killing Danu and Her son Vrtra*, he does accomplish the act, thus achieving kingship among the *A-Dityas*. This reminds us of the early Sumerian text reported above:

The was founded by Enmebaragesi, a contemporary of Gilgamesh. The name breaks down as follows: *enetik - eme - ebakin - aragikor - ageriko - ezi* which can be transliterated to, "rom that time on - female - harvest - lustful - notorious - to domesticate" or "From that time on the lustful, notorious harvest female was domesticated".

This "name" tells us in no uncertain terms that the time of the Goddess was on the decline, because male domination had arrived with the Sumerians.

In a hymn to Indra in the *Rg Veda* which describes the event, Danu and Her son are first described as serpent demons; later, as they lie dead, they are symbolized as cow and calf. After the murders, "the cosmic waters flowed and were pregnant". They in turn gave birth to the sun. This concept of the sun god emerging from the primeval waters appears in other Indo-Sumerian-Incan myths and also occurs in connection with two of the prehistoric invasions. We suggest that all of this connects such events to times of cataclysm wherein the sun is "darkened" or concealed by dust and clouds.

---

[361] Ramachandran, R., *The Genetics of Caste*, Frontline, Volume 18 - Issue 12, Jun. 09 - 22, 2001; India's National Magazine, from the publishers of THE HINDU.

The *Rg Veda* also refers to an ancestral father god known both as Prajapati and Dyaus Pitar. Dyaus Pitar is known as the "supreme father of all". The spread of the Indo-Sumerian culture mixed with the Aryan incursions brought with it the origins of the Hindu religion and the concept of light-colored skin being perceived as better or more "pure" than darker skins. (The Sanskrit word for caste, "varna" actually means color.)

The Indo-Sumerian-Aryan beliefs are found in Iran, though the records are very late - dating back only as far as 600 B.C. What the experts suggest is that the Indians and early Iranians - prior to the arrival of the Sumerians - were derived from the same ethnic group and had been established on the Iranian plateau from about 4000 BC speaking a Vedic Sanskrit dialect.

Though there is a considerable change from the *Rg Veda* to the Iranian *Avesta*, we still find the great father who represents light, with a new name: Ahura Mazda. He is the Lord of Light and his abode is on a mountaintop glowing with golden light. The duality of light and dark is inherent in Iranian religious thought. Ahura Mazda is on high in goodness, and the devil figure, Ahriman is "deep down in darkness". We note in this the mixing of the Shamanic concepts with the Inca-Sumerian idea of a anthropomorphized god.

In the Iranian texts of 200 AD known as *Manichean*, we again find good and evil equated with light and dark. However, we are told in these writings that the problems of humanity are *caused by a mixture of the two*. And here, Mithra appears as the one who defeats the "demons of darkness".

There is another clue that deserves note: the name of the Guanche Devil, *Guayota*. In the Iranian texts there is a character named *Gayo Mareta* who is the "first man". He seems to relate to Indra in the Indian versions. *Gauee* or *gavee* in Sanskrit means cow. *Mrityu* in Sanskrit means death or murder, surviving in the Indo-Aryan German language as *mord*, meaning murder, and in the Indo-European English language as the word murder itself. Thus *Gavo Mareta* appears to be named "Cow Murderer". Danu was symbolized as the cow Goddess, whose worship is best known from Egypt before Narmer. Gayo Mareta may once have held a similar position in Iran to Indra, the murderer of Danu, the cow Goddess.

In the *Pahlavi Books* of about 400 BC. it was written, "From Gayo Mareta, Ahura fashioned the family of the Aryan lands, the seed of the Aryan lands". We notice right away that this is an inversion. It is pretty clear that in the most ancient times, the Goddess was worshipped, and Gayo Mareta - Guayota, the Devil, murdered her.

In any event, we are certainly entitled to speculate on the fact that the Guanches, Aryans, a group isolated for possibly thousands of years, spoke a near cousin to the language of Sargon, a worshipper of the Goddess, and that the name of the "evil" in their language, was almost identical to the name of the hero in the *Pahlavi books*. Due to the fact that the Guanches were isolated for a very long, unknown period of time, one begins to suspect that they retained their original language from very ancient times. Perhaps there was a global, antediluvian language. And perhaps this gives us a clue as to who was really "on first"?

When we consider the "ancient Egyptian language", we realize that it developed after the conquest of Narmer, and there is a very strong suggestion that Narmer had close ties with Sumeria. The famous Narmer Palette has distinctive Sumerian motifs, and also includes a row of men - sacrificial victims - with their heads cut off and placed between their thighs. Skull and Crossbones?

THE SHELL GAME

As early as the fourth millennium BC, a group entered the Tigris-Euphrates area. They were described as "newcomers from the east". The statement derives a certain support from tradition; "as they jouneyed from the east they found a plain in the land of Shinar [Babylon] and they dwelt there" [*Genesis* XI, 2]; but it is based on the material evidence of the pottery of al Ubaid and of Susa respectively, and on that evidence it is generally agreed that these people were related, culturally and presumably ethnically, to the early inhabitants of Elam.

Some scholars suggest that the Ubaid people brought the *Sumerian* language, which is neither Semitic nor Indo-European. Aratta is a place name often mentioned in Sumerian texts.

The Ubaid people established a major settlement in the place later known as Eridu. They broke up the Halaf culture, and wreaked devastation upon them. These Ubaids spread as far north as Lake Urmia and Lake Van, close to the Iranian-Russian border. This section was later known as Ararat or Urartu which could be corruptions of Aratta. The name "Eridu" could also be a corruption of Aratta, suggesting the original homeland.

In about 4000 BC, the Ubaid people built a temple at Eridu which appears to be the first built on a high platform. At this temple, *not a single goddess figurine was found.* Interestingly, a statue found in graves of the Ubaid people depicted a mother and baby with *lizard-like features.*

It is noteworthy that the Sumerians and present day "Semites" only differ in language, not religion, culture or politics.

The deity worshipped at Eridu in historic times was the god Enki. Before this, the god of the shrine seems to have been a fish or water god who rose up out of the water exactly like Viracocha, had scales, and was a civilizer-teacher of language and culture. Enki was thought of later as the god of the waters and was described as riding around in his boat. He was also described as "he who rides". This concept of the fish or water god is similar to one found in a fragment of an Indo-Aryan Hittite tablet which tells of a sun god who rose from the water with fish on his head. It is also similar to the idea of the sun god who was born from the cosmic waters released by Indra by the deaths of Danu and Vrtra. Though Enki is not generally designated as a sun god, in the myth of Marduk he is named as Marduk's father and Marduk is called the "son of the sun".

The Ubaid people are credited with developing irrigation canals in Eridu which could hint at their origin in places that were along rivers and streams and where fish were common. Another clue to the identity of these people is the institution of kingship, and the mention of the name Alalu as the very first king of Sumer in the king lists of the earliest part of the second millennium. According to these tablets which refer to a prehistoric period, it was in Eridu that, "kingship was first lowered from heaven". Sounds rather like the Inca myth of Viracocha.

Now, let's think about this for a moment. We have a god with a fish on his head, thereby associated with scales, and who is described as "he who rides". This scaly

god not only rides, he rose from the water like the sun! Also, he was born from the
deaths of the Mother goddess and her son. Mountains of fire are involved, gold,
and kingship being "lowered from heaven". It rather sounds like UFOs coming up
out of the water as they have so often been reported to do in more modern times,
or descending on mountain tops.

A third male deity - An or Anu - comes onto the Sumerian stage sometime after
the beginning of the second millenium - the same period that the Hurrians are
known to have entered the area, so they may well have brought this Anu with
them.

In the early Sumerian period the name Anu is relatively obscure, and his name
does not appear on any of the eighteen lists belonging to this period.

Anu appears as the successor to Alalu in the Hurrian and Hittite Kumarbi myth.
But most interesting is his appearance in the later myth of Marduk, "the son of the
sun". Here we learn that Enki was first asked to subdue the Creatress-Goddess,
whom they call Tiamat, and was not able, though he did manage to kill her
husband Apsu, thus becoming Lord of the Abzu (primeval waters) himself. Anu
was then asked to subdue Tiamat, but according to the legend when he confronted
Her, he cringed in fear and refused to complete his mission. Finally Marduk, son
of Enki, was willing, though only upon the promise of the supreme position among
all other deities if he succeeded. This previously secured promise brings to mind
the one Indra requested before murdering Danu and Her son Vrtra; both of these
myths were probably written down at about the same period (1600-1400 BC)
though they are undoubtedly far older. In passing, I would like to note that the
name *Tiamat* is similar to some of the earliest known names of male deities
including Tiu, Tyr, Thor, etc, plus *Mat* which reminds us of Egyptian Maat, which
was a goddess who represented truth, law and universal order.

This legend, known as the *Enuma Elish*, which explains the supremacy of
Marduk, has long been designated as Babylonian and therefore Akkadian and
Semitic. But more recent research suggests that, though Marduk was known in the
Hammurabi period, the myth claiming his supremacy did not actually appear until
after the Kassites, another tribe, had conquered Babylon. Saggs points out that
"none of the extant texts belonging to it is earlier than the first millennium", and
that "it has been suggested that in fact this work arose only in the Kassite period, a
time now known to have been one of intense literary activity". Gurney tells us
that, "The *names of Indian deities* are found to form an element in the names of
the Kassite rulers of Babylonia".[362]

In about 2100 BC a *Sumerian* king named Ur Nammu declared that he would
establish justice in the land. He did away with the heavy duties and taxes that were
burdening the people at that time and, "rid the land of the *big sailors* who seized

---

[362] Gurney, O.R., *The Hittites* (London, New York: Penguin revised edition 1991).

oxen, sheep and donkeys". [363] One suspects that they were Aryan types corrupted by the worship of the male storm god.

Now, after all this invading, conquering and demolishing of the Goddess Worship over in the Tigris-Euphrates area, the same thing happened later on in Egypt with Narmer-Menes!

There is considerable evidence for contact between Egypt and Sumer. "Abundant evidence of Mesopotamian cultural influence is found at this time in Egypt." Significant is the fact that cylinder seals (a specifically Mesopotamian invention) occur there, together with methods of building in brick foreign to Egypt but typical of the *Jemdet Nasr* culture of Mesopotamia and the Indus Valley civilization. Mesopotamian motifs and objects also begin to be represented in Egyptian art, such as boats of Mesopotamian type. The idea of writing, though it was expressed quite differently in Egypt, seems to have developed more or less coevally with Mesopotamia. Paintings in early dynastic tombs portray a conical basket type of fish trap, nearly identical to those of the Ertebolle people of northern Europe who were descended from the Maglemosians, a European Mesolithic culture, which links us back to the Akkadians as being from the North. The male deity of Egypt arrived with the invaders, and was portrayed as the sun riding in a boat!

Professor Walter Emery spent some forty-five years excavating the ancient tombs and pyramids of Egypt. Discussing the arrival of these people, he writes:

> Whether this incursion took the form of gradual infiltration or horde invasion is uncertain but the balance of evidence... strongly suggests the latter. ...we see a style of art which some think may be Mesopotamian, or even Syrian in origin, and a scene which may represent a battle at sea against invaders... [in these] representations we have typical native ships of Egypt and strange vessels with high prow and stem of unmistakable Mesopotamian origin...

> At any rate, towards the close of the fourth millennium BC we find the people known traditionally as the "Followers of Horus" apparently forming an aristocracy or master race ruling over the whole of Egypt. The theory of the existence of this master race is supported by the discovery that graves of the late pre-dynastic period in the northern part of Upper Egypt were found to contain the anatomical remains of a people whose *skulls are of greater size* and whose bodies were larger than those of the natives, the difference being *so marked* that any suggestion that these people derived from the earlier stock is impossible. [364]

These invaders were known to the Egyptians as the "*Shemsu Hor*", or people of Hor. And, of course, they brought with them their male god, *Hor-Wer* or Great

---

[363] Hawkes, Jacquetta, The first great civilizations; life in Mesopotamia, the Indus Valley and Egypt (New York: Knopf 1973).

[364] Quoted by Stone, op. cit.

Hor. By 2900 BC, pictures of this sun god show him riding in his "boat of heaven".

It certainly makes one wonder if a brilliant UFO rising up out of the water would cause the ancient peoples to connect a boat (that goes on water) with flying through the air while looking like the sun! And, over and over again we are finding this image or juxtaposition of images.

According to Emery, the name of the first king of the First Dynasty, known as Narmer or Menes in Manetho's history of 270 BC, was actually Hor-Aha. Later, the name of Hor appears to have been incorporated into the more ancient goddess religion as the "son who dies". This has led to a lot of confusion between the two "Hors", Horus the Elder, god of light of the invaders, and Horus the Younger, the son of the goddess Isis.

Hor later was transmogrified into Horus by the Greeks, and is depicted as fighting a ritual combat with another male deity known as Set. Set is supposed to be his uncle, the brother of his mother Isis and father Osiris. The combat was supposed to symbolize the overcoming of darkness or Set, by light, symbolized by Hor.

In Sanskrit the word '*sat*' means to *destroy by hewing into pieces*. In the myth of Osiris, it was Set who killed Osiris and cut his body into fourteen pieces which naturally reminds us of the sacrifices of the Moche. However, the word "*set*" is also defined as "queen" or "princess" in Egyptian! "*Au Set*", known as Isis by the Greeks, means, "exceeding queen"!

In the myth of this ritual combat, Set tried to mate sexually with Horus; this is usually interpreted to have been an extreme insult. But the most primitive identity of the figure Set, before the wavy lines of water or energy became serpents, may be found in the goddess religion, and this combat, just as with the combat of Marduk with Tiamat, may have represented the suppression and destruction of the Goddess religion. Of course, the conquering invaders presented themselves as "saviors" and their conquest as a triumph of light over darkness!

So it has always been.

Nevertheless, the followers of Hor established the institution of kingship in Egypt. And, again, marrying the representative of the goddess in order to "steal her power" was an important part of the assumption of kingship as was recorded in the story of Solomon - he married an Egyptian Princess. We may justifiably compare the name of "Hor" to the Hurrians or Horites who came from India to Sumer.

Around the time of the Second Dynasty, the town of Heliopolis (known to the Egyptians as Annu!) became the home of a school of scribal priests who also worshipped a sun god who rode in a boat. In this town they used the name Ra. In Sanskrit, *Ra* means royal or exalted on high. This prefix is found in the Sanskrit word for king, *raja* and queen, *rani*. It survives in the German word *ragen*, to reach up, in French as *roi*, meaning king, as well as in the English words royal, reign and regal.

In the pyramid texts of the Fifth Dynasty, Horus was equated with Ra. Both Horus and Ra were closely connected, at times competitively, with the right to kingship. As Ra-Harakhty, Ra is identical with Horus of the Horizon, both meaning the sun at rising. Ra too is portrayed as the sun who rides across the heavens sitting in his sacred boat. Again, why a boat in the heavens?

Ra's boat was said to emerge out of the primeval waters, much as Enki was said to ride his boat in the deep waters of the Abzu of Eridu, or as the Indo-Aryan sun god was said to have emerged from the cosmic waters, as in the myth of the sun god in the water who rises from the sea with fish on his head, so too Ra rose from the waters each morning.

As the name of Horus was assimilated into the Goddess religion, as the son of Isis, the priests of Memphis proposed another concept of the great father god. This time his name was Ptah, curiously like the Sanskrit *Pitar*. The texts concerning him describe the creation of all existence, suggesting that Ptah was there first. This time we are told that it was through an act of masturbation that Ptah caused all the other gods to come into being, thus totally eliminating the need for a divine Mother!

This idea of the masturbating god is not new. One of the Sumerian gods, Enki, was supposed to have masturbated and thereby caused the Tigris and Euphrates rivers to flow!

Even though these conquering Indo-Incans came in wave after wave, bringing their gods who ride in shining boats in the sky, the goddess religion still survived. This very fact may indicate the presence of another group who worked quietly to preserve the ancient truths in the face of almost overwhelming opposition. The new male gods were assimilated and synthesized, creating an almost impossible to sort mish-mash of gods and goddesses.

With the knowledge that the worship of the Goddess was violently overturned by invading Indo-Incans who were descendants of the Incan Sun worshippers, whose objective was to forestall another "end of the world" with the sacrifice of enormous numbers of human beings, we may better understand the transitions and inversions that have occurred in our myths and legends as well as our concepts of time. With this understanding, we are free to pursue a more open and reasonable series of speculations as to what the End of the World, and all the prophecies related to it, might be about.

Just as there was a Dark Age surrounding the period of time in which the Old Testament came into being, during which time Monotheistic Judaism - the parent of Christianity and Islam whose validity is established only by the Old Testament - was imposed forcibly on the Canaanites, there was also a similar period of Dark Ages enveloping the development and codification of the New Testament and the imposition of Monotheistic Christianity on the Western World, and Islam on those who were susceptible to neither of the former two.

Don't you find that curious?

THE END OF TIME

The god of the Jews is a personality who purportedly ceaselessly intervenes in history and who reveals his will through events. Historical facts thus acquired a religious value in the fact that they were specific situations between man and god, transforming history into the epiphany of god. This conception was continued and magnified by Christianity. We can see the seeds of the original myths here, but we can also see the major distortions.

In monotheism, *every event is definitely situated in time* - a given time and no other - and is not *reversible;* it is a historical event with weight and value in and of itself, and that weight is upon the shoulders of mankind, individually and collectively.

In Judaism's daughter, Christianity, the Messianic hope, the victory over the forces of darkness, is projected indefinitely into the future and will only happen *once* in terms of linear time. Further, there is only *one* who can accomplish this conquest of darkness, and man's only hope is to give up his will to this one who has been crucified and resurrected to symbolize his verity, despite having really done nothing to change the state of the world in *real* time. When the Messiah comes again, (never mind that he was supposed to have already been here and global conditions did not improve), the world will be saved once and for all, and history will cease to exist - and most of humanity along with it, not to mention a "third of the angels", and so on.

This idea of irreversible, linear time, was imposed upon mankind through violence and exclusion, serving as the basis for the philosophy of history that Christianity, from St. Augustine on, has labored to construct.

In case you didn't notice what just happened here, let me make it a little clearer. The concept of linear time gives value to the "future" as an *end* to everything. That's it; there is nothing more. Further, the arbiter of that future is *one* god, who, I might add, is his own surety because he has helpfully announced at the beginning that he *is* the *one* god. This one god has a select group of servants who will be preserved to the exclusion of all others in some way if they obey him, and destroyed if they disobey him. But, of course, it is "free will choice" as to whether to believe this or not. It doesn't sound like a choice; it sounds like an ultimatum!

We begin to smell a rat here, a hint that the introduction of the concept of linear time was the *raison d'être* for the introduction of monotheism. In this way, all of humanity can be trapped in a condition of believing lies instead of truth, and "binding" spiritual drugs, preventing any possibility of "ascension".

For the most part, our modern world is predicated upon linear time. Thus, the reason for the *raison d'être* can be dimly seen by those who have been tracking with me here: it is that linear time is a supreme weapon to use against the mind of man in terms of *control and domination!* Monotheism is a myth that establishes a particular identity as an antithesis, against another - actually, just about all Others! The ultimate club of elitists!

We come back to the fact that most of the Old Testament is a chronicle of genocide and horrendous practices of human and animal sacrifice. In the New Testament, we find that the work of a remarkable man who lived two thousand years ago in the Middle East, whose teachings gave birth to Christianity, has been replaced by a "story" based a human sacrifice ritual which was an already ages old corruption - the ubiquitous solar/fertility cult. At about the same time this was done, Judaism was revived, the Cathars were destroyed, and the Crusades were begun to discover some mysterious object in the "Holy Land".

Curious, eh?

In any event, the concept of the barbaric custom of blood sacrifice passed into Christianity. It is, in fact, the heart of Christianity as it is understood by Christians today. However, making Christ the "once for all atonement" for everyone had curious consequences. With such an event as an "example", it became quite easy to manipulate the populace to willingly emulate this self-sacrifice, and thus, the motivation for the Crusades, and endless wars and genocide by "civilized" peoples was made "normal".

Fiendishly clever, I say.

There appears to be a group that has existed from the time of the Dark Ages, and this group is, effectively, the "new vehicle" for the Machiavellian machinations of these beings who may also be the Elohim who originally "fenced in" the Semitic peoples, in order to utilize them in various ways including the creation of an "army" for hyperdimensional manipulations with the seeming objective of dividing and conquering humanity.

Considering a "group" that may be behind the machinations of history, we must consider the term "fifth column", defined as "A clandestine subversive organization working within a given country to further an invading enemy's military and political aims" (*American Heritage Dictionary*, 1976).

There are certain self-proclaimed "experts" who tell us that Jews and Germans collaborated against the Catholic Church in the 9th century, forming a group of elitists that engaged in "sickening sacrificial rituals". When I first read this claim, my immediate reaction was to snort in disgust and declare it to be nonsense. I am very sensitive to anything Anti-Semitic. However, after reviewing the history of the creation of the Bible, and putting it all together, I have come to the idea that such a claim is not *too* far off - except that it probably wasn't Jews, but rather "occultists" behind such activity. When I say "occult", I don't necessarily mean "black magic" or similar such nonsense, though such things are certainly not excluded. Generally, however, when such things as "occultism" are brought into the mixture, after careful investigation, one usually discovers the presence and activity of hyperdimensional beings masquerading as "angels" or "demons" as well as about anything in between.

Nearly all experts of "esoterica", after years and years of searching and studying, eventually come to the idea that there is some sort of major conspiracy that has been running the show on planet earth for a very long time. The problem is, there are any number of conclusions as to "who is on first" in this trans-millennial, multi-national, global ballgame. The thing that raises red flags, however, is that just about *any* of the many conclusions can be supported by *reams* of "evidence". At the same time, there is a concerted effort on the part of the official culture to persuade everyone that "conspiracy" theories are a sign of mental instability.

There is a little known fact about hypnosis that is illustrated by the following story:

A subject was told under hypnosis that when he was awakened he would be unable to see a third man in the room who, it was suggested to him, would have become invisible. All the "proper" suggestions to make this "true" were given, such as "you will *not* see so- and-so", etc... When the subject was awakened, lo and behold!, the suggestions did *not* work.

Why? Because they went against his belief system. He did *not* believe that a person could become invisible.

So, another trial was made. The subject was hypnotized again and was told that the third man was *leaving the room*... that he had been called away on urgent business, and the scene of him getting on his coat and hat was described in great detail with sound effects: the door was opened and shut, etc., and then the subject was brought out of the trance.

Guess what happened?

He was *unable to see* the Third Man.

Why? Because his perceptions were modified *according to his beliefs*. Certain "censors" in his brain were "activated" in a manner that was "acceptable" to his "ego survival"[365] instincts.

The Third Man went about the room picking things up and setting them down and doing all sorts of things to test the subject's awareness of his presence, and the subject became utterly hysterical at this "anomalous" activity! He could see objects moving through the air, doors opening and closing, but he could *not see* the source of these movements because *he did not believe* that there was another man in the room.

So, what are the implications of this factor of human consciousness? (By the way, this is also the reason why most therapy to stop bad habits does not work - they attempt to operate against a "belief system" that is imprinted in the subconscious that this or that habit is essential to survival.)

One of the first things we might observe is that everyone has a different set of beliefs based upon their social and familial conditioning, and that these beliefs determine how much of the *objective reality* anyone is able to access. Again, considering the issue of ligands, we notice how belief can act as a drug to blind the individual to objective reality.

Realities, objective, subjective, or otherwise, are a touchy subject to scientists, especially physicists, so I don't want to get bogged down there just now. Suffice it to say that years of work inside the minds of all kinds of people has taught me that human beings almost *never* perceive reality as it truly *is*. Let me just say that, in the above story, the *objective reality is what it is*, whether it is truly objective, or only a consensus reality. Yet, in this story, there is clearly a big part of that reality that is inaccessible to the "subject" due to a perception censor which was activated by the suggestions of the hypnotist. That is to say, the subject has a strong belief, based upon his *choice* as to who or what to believe. In this case, he has chosen to

---

[365] The survival of the ego is established pretty early in life by our parental and societal programming as to what *is* or is *not* possible; what we are "allowed" to believe in order to be accepted. We learn this first by learning what pleases our parents and then later we modify our belief based on what pleases our society - our peers - to believe.

believe the hypnotist and not what he might be able to observe if he dispensed with the perception censor put in place by the hypnotist. Again, we draw a relation between synthetic and natural ligands.

And so it is with nearly all human beings: we believe the hypnotist - the "official culture" - and we are able, with preternatural cunning, to deny what is often right in front of our faces. In the case of the hypnosis subject, he is entirely at the mercy of the "Invisible Man" because he chooses not to see him. The same is true in our reality regarding hyperdimensional realities.

Let's face it: we are all taught to avoid uncomfortable realities. Human beings - faced with unpleasant truths about themselves or their reality - react like alcoholics who refuse to admit their condition, or the cuckolded husband who is the "last to know", or the wife who does not notice that her husband is abusing her daughter.

In *States of Denial: Knowing about Atrocities and Suffering*, [366] Stanley Cohen discusses the subject of denial which may shed some light on the context in which I have speculated about hyperdimensional realities. I am not surprised at the state of denial of scientists and those who might be best able to figure out what is really going on in our world. It is the cultural norm. I am also not surprised at the projection of this discomfort onto "conspiracy theorists".

Denial is a complex "unconscious defence mechanism for coping with guilt, anxiety and other disturbing emotions aroused by reality". Denial can be both deliberate and intentional, as well as completely subconscious. An individual who is deliberately and intentionally denying something is lying. I don't think that we are dealing with this in the denial of "conspiracy theories". What we are dealing with is denial that is subconscious and therefore organized and "institutional". This implies propaganda, misinformation, whitewash, manipulation, spin, disinformation, etc.

Believing anything that comes down the pike is not the opposite of denial. Acknowledgement of the probability of a high level of Truth about a given matter is what should happen when people are actively aroused by *certain* information. This information can be, 1) factual or forensic truth; that is to say, legal or scientific information which is factual, accurate and objective; it is obtained by impartial procedures; 2) personal and narrative truth including "witness testimonies".

I should add here that skepticism and solipsistic arguments - including epistemological relativism - about the existence of objective truth, are generally a social construction and might be considered in the terms of the hypnotized man who has been programmed to think that there "is no truth".

Denial occurs for a variety of reasons. There are truths that are "clearly known", but for many reasons - personal or political, justifiable or unjustifiable - are

---

[366] Cambridge: Polity Press; Malden, MA: Blackwell Publishers, 2001

concealed, or it is agreed that they will not be acknowledged "out loud". There are "unpleasant truths" and there are truths that make us tired because if we acknowledge them - if we do more than give them a tacit nod - we may find it necessary to make changes in our lives.

Cohen points out that, "All counter-claims about the denied reality are themselves only manoeuvres in endless truth-games. And *truth, as we know, is inseparable from power*".

Denial of truth is taking synthetic spiritual drugs and is, effectively, giving away your power.

There are different kinds of denial. First, there is literal denial which is the type that fits the dictionary definition, the assertion that something did not happen or does not exist. This most often occurs in very painful situations where there are conflicts of love: the wife would say that the husband could not have molested his daughter, therefore the child must be making it up, or something equally traumatic and threatening to safety. This also seems to apply to denial of the state of our manipulated reality. Our love for our parents, our need for their approval, is often transferred to our peers, our employers, and the State. To think about stepping outside of the belief system that makes us "belong" is just too frightening. It assaults our deepest sense of security.

The second kind of denial is "interpretative". In this kind of denial, the raw facts that something actually happened are not really denied - they are just "interpreted". If a person is reasonably intelligent, and is faced with evidence of phenomena that do not fit into the belief system of one's family, culture, or peer group, there is nothing to do but to interpret - to rationalize it away. "Swamp gas" and the Planet Venus given as an explanation for UFOs are good examples. Another is Bill Clinton's "But I didn't *inhale*" interpretation of his marijuana use, as well as the famous, "I didnot have sexual relations with that woman" interpretation.

The third kind of denial is termed by Cohen as implicatory denial where there is no attempt to deny either the facts or their conventional interpretation; what is ultimately denied are the psychological, political and moral implications that follow from deep acknowledgement. For example, the idea that America is being run by a madman with designs on the entire planet, or that Zionists are obviously behind this activity is recognized as a fact, but it is not seen as psychologically disturbing or as carrying any moral imperative to act.

The deeper implication of the denial of conspiracy theories is more unsettling: that *true* progress in science is being hampered by a "system" that may serve to exclude innovative thinking - and *real* science - by a far-reaching network where:

> Too much research is in "safe" areas - producing nothing but "papers". The truth is that, Physicists, to make their living, must produce papers, must be "quoted"; and so they quote each other; colleagues quote colleagues and produce graduate students who quote their masters, after which they become masters, quoting each other, and producing graduate students who quote them, in an endless cycle of life in the ivory towers.

> And this is not something unique in physics. Not at all! It is true in other fields of study, too. But in physics the results are really bad: there has been no apparent progress in our understanding of Nature for seventy long years.... And nature *really*

needs to be understood, because things are getting a little out of hand out there in the "real" world.

> Don't misunderstand me: there *are* many very *good* physicists - real experts - but they generally don't get prime-time play in either books or journals because they are so busy working on trying to *really* understand what is going on, that they have little time to play the political games that get them the cushy jobs in the "stables" of physics, run by "big bosses" who are the interface with the government "approvers" of funding. And it seems that getting to the Truth of our reality is the *last* thing the funding sources wish to see happen in the hallowed halls of academia. [367]

Science operates on funding just like everything else. We personally know many excellent scientists who are toiling away in hot little cubicles, underpaid and overworked, never using their potential - for what? Just to be able to live, to hope that one day they will have a little time to breathe, to work on their own ideas, to make real progress in science. There are also gifted amateurs - those who work in science for the sheer love of it - and who are excluded from the "good ole boy network" because they don't happen to love the politics and aren't willing to sell their souls.

And finally, there *are* those who are masters quoting masters - just because they can - because they admire themselves and their "master status". And many of them discover which masters must be quoted and *how* to quote them in order to get the most money for the least amount of work, all the while being considered the "highest master".

So it is in any profession; physics is no different.

But that is the "official culture" explanation. We can go back to sleep and get some rest with this explanation.

The fact is, science is controlled by money. Scientists, for the most part, *have* to work on those things that get funding. There is nothing terribly unusual about that since that is a general rule for everyone. If you don't get money for your work, you starve and then you don't do any work at all. Yes, that's somewhat simplistic, but still relevant to the subject here.

The question is: what gets funded? Who decides? What is the context in which *all* science is being done?

Bear with me a moment here and let's apply a little logic to the problem.

The first thing we want to think about is the fact that the word "conspiracy" evokes such a strong reaction in all of us: nobody wants to be branded as a "conspiracy theorist". It just isn't "acceptable". It's "un-scientific" or it's evidence of mental instability. Right?

In fact, I bet that even the very reading of the word produces certain physiological reactions: a slight acceleration of the heartbeat, and perhaps a quick

---

[367] Jadczyk, Arkadiusz, *Physic and the Mysterious*, 1997, www.cassiopaea.org

glance around to make sure that no one was watching while you simply read the word silently.

Have you ever asked yourself *why* the word evokes such an instantaneous emotional reaction? Have you ever wondered why it stimulates such a strong "recoil"? After all, it is only a word. It only describes the idea of people in "high places" thinking about things and doing things that manipulate other people to produce benefits for themselves which is generally accepted as the way things work, right?

Richard Dolan has written about "conspiracy" in the following way:

> Some will dismiss this as one of the many conspiracy theories dotting America's landscape. The very label serves as an automatic dismissal, as though no one ever acts in secret. Let us bring some perspective and common sense to this issue.

> The United States comprises large organizations - corporations, bureaucracies, "interest groups", and the like - which are conspiratorial by nature. That is, they are hierarchical, their important decisions are made in secret by a few key decision-makers, and they are not above lying about their activities. Such is the nature of organizational behavior. "Conspiracy", in this key sense, is a way of life around the globe.

> Within the world's military and intelligence apparatuses, this tendency is magnified to the greatest extreme. During the 1940s, [...] the military and its scientists developed the world's most awesome weapons in complete secrecy... [...]

> Anyone who has lived in a repressive society knows that official manipulation of the truth occurs daily. But societies have their many and their few. In all times and all places, it is the few who rule, and the few who exert dominant influence over what we may call *official culture.* - All elites take care to manipulate public information to maintain existing structures of power. It's an old game.

> America is nominally a republic and free society, but in reality an empire and oligarchy, vaguely aware of its own oppression, within and without. I have used the term "national security state" to describe its structures of power. It is a convenient way to express the military and intelligence communities, as well as the worlds that feed upon them, such as defense contractors and other underground, nebulous entities. Its fundamental traits are secrecy, wealth, independence, power, and duplicity.

> Nearly everything of significance undertaken by America's military and intelligence community in the past half-century has occured in secrecy. The undertaking to build an atomic weapon, better known as the Manhattan Project, remains the great model for all subsequent activities. For more than two years, not a single member of Congress even knew about it although its final cost exceeded two billion dollars.

> During and after the Second World War, other important projects, such as the development of biological weapons, the importation of Nazi scientists, terminal mind-control experiments, nationwide interception of mail and cable transmissions of an unwitting populace, infiltration of the media and universities, secret coups, secret wars, and assassinations all took place far removed not only from the American public, but from most members of Congress and a few presidents. Indeed, several of the most powerful intelligence agencies were themselves established in secrecy, unknown by the public or Congress for many years.

Since the 1940s, the US Defense and Intelligence establishment has had more money at its disposal than most nations. In addition to official dollars, much of the money is undocumented. From its beginning, the CIA was engaged in a variety of off-the-record "business" activities that generated large sums of cash. The connections of the CIA with global organized crime (and thus de facto with the international narcotics trade) has been well established and documented for many years. Much of the original money to run the American intelligence community came from very wealthy and established American families, who have long maintained an interest in funding national security operations important to their interests.

In theory, civilian oversight exists over the US national security establishment. The president is the military commander-in-chief. Congress has official oversight over the CIA. The FBI must answer to the Justice Department. In practice, little of this applies. One reason has to do with secrecy. [...]

A chilling example of such independence occurred during the 1950s, when President Eisenhower effectively lost control of the US nuclear arsenal. The situation deteriorated so much that during his final two years in office, Eisenhower asked repeatedly for an audience with the head of Strategic Air Command to learn what America's nuclear retaliatory plan was. What he finally learned in 1960, his final year in office, horrified him: half of the Northern Hemisphere would be obliterated.

If a revered military hero such as Eisenhower could not control America's nuclear arsenal, nor get a straight answer from the Pentagon, how on earth could Presidents Truman, Kennedy, Johnson, or Nixon regarding comparable matters?

Secrecy, wealth and independence add up to power. Through the years, the national security state has gained access to the wrorld's most sophisticated technology sealed off millions of acres of land from public access or scrutiny, acquired unlimited snooping ability within US borders and beyond, conducted overt or clandestine actions against other nations, and prosecuted wars without serious media scrutiny. Domestically, it maintains influence over elected officials and communities hoping for some of the billions of defense dollars. [including scientists, universities, etc.]

Deception is the key element of warfare, and when winning is all that matters, the conventional morality held by ordinary people becomes an impediment. When taken together, the examples of official duplicity form a nearly single totality. They include such choice morsels as the phony war crisis of 1948, the fabricated missile gap claimed by the air force during the 1950s, the carefully managed events leading to the Gulf of Tonkin resolution... [...]

The secrecy stems from a pervasive and fundamental element of life in our world, that those who are at the top of the heap will always take whatever steps are necessary to maintain the status quo.

[S]keptics often ask, "Do you really think the government could hide [anything] for so long"? The question itself reflects ignorance of the reality that secrecy is a way of life in the National Security State. Actually though, the answer is yes, and no.

Yes, in that cover-ups are standard operating procedure, frequently unknown to the public for decades, becoming public knowledge by a mere roll of the dice. But also no, in that ... information has leaked out from the very beginning. It is impossible to shut the lid completely. The key lies in neutralizing and discrediting unwelcomed information, sometimes through official denial, other times through proxies in the media.

[E]vidence [of conspiracy] derived from a grass roots level is unlikely to survive its inevitable conflict with official culture. And acknowledgement about the reality of [conspiracies] will only occur when the official culture deems it worthwhile or necessary to make it. [Don't hold your breath.]

This is a widespread phenomenon affecting many people, generating high levels of interest, taking place in near-complete secrecy, for purposes unknown, by agencies unknown, with access to incredible resources and technology. A sobering thought and cause for reflection.[368]

Consider this: even if Dolan is writing specifically about America, in a world dominated by the United States, it must be considered that pressures are applied elsewhere from within this "national security state" to comply with the demands of the US.

In an earlier chapter, I pointed out that part of the nature of COINTELPRO is to create *bogus organizations and to promote bogus ideas.* In the scientific community, this can work in any number of ways, the most common being "proprietary organizations" that fund research that leads nowhere in order to keep someone with promising ideas busy. It is not stretching things to consider that "exciting new ideas" or areas of research might be promoted for the express purpose of vectoring scientists into following false and time-wasting research so as to prevent them making significant breakthroughs. What we do not know is how far and wide the practice extends, though we can certainly guess.

There exists in our world today a powerful and dangerous secret cult.

So wrote Victor Marchetti, a former high-ranking CIA official, in his book *The CIA and the Cult of Intelligence.* This is the first book the U.S. Government ever went to court to censor before publication. In this book, Marchetti tells us that there IS a "Cabal" that rules the world and that its holy men are the clandestine professionals of the Central Intelligence Agency. In our opinion, the CIA is but one "arm" of the cult, just as Benedictines were but one order of the Catholic Church. To borrow from, and paraphrasing, Marchetti:

This cult is patronized and protected by the highest level government officials in the world. It's membership is composed of those in the power centers of government, industry, commerce, finance, and labor. It manipulates individuals in areas of important public influence - including the academic world and the mass media. The Secret Cult is a global fraternity of a political aristocracy whose purpose is to further the political policies of persons or agencies unknown. It acts covertly and illegally.

---

[368] Dolan, op. cit.

And we see it happen before our very eyes and most people refuse to acknowledge it! What is more frightening is the fact that Woodrow Wilson, a president of the United States wrote in *The New Freedom* (1913):

> Some of the biggest men in the United States, in the field of commerce and manufacture, are afraid of something. They know that there is a power somewhere so organized, so subtle, so watchful, so interlocked, so complete, so pervasive, that they better not speak above their breath when they speak in condemnation of it.

Remember: those who are at the top of the heap will always take whatever steps are necessary to maintain the status quo, and maintaining the "status quo" in science *has* to be one of the main objectives of the Power Elite.

And how do they do that? By "official culture". And official culture, understood this way, from the perspective of elite groups wishing to maintain the status quo of their power, means COINTELPRO.

The most effective weapon of COINTELPRO is Ridicule and Debunking. Notice that Marchetti points out that this is done via manipulation of individuals in areas of important public influence - including the *academic world* and the *mass media*. This is how the official culture is maintained, most particularly in the Scientific Community.

Bottom line is: if you have bought into the emotionally manipulated consensus of "official culture", that there are no conspiracies, that there is no "Third Man", it is very likely that you are being manipulated by fear of ridicule. You are in denial. You have been hypnotized by the suggestions of the holy men of the Secret Cult and you have chosen to believe them over your own possible observations and senses.

Now, think about the word "conspiracy" one more time and allow me to emphasize the key points of Dolan's remarks: From a historical point of view, the *only* reality is that of conspiracy. Secrecy, wealth and independence add up to power. ...Deception is the key element of warfare, (the tool of power elites), and when winning is all that matters, the conventional morality held by ordinary people becomes an impediment. Secrecy stems from a pervasive and fundamental element of life in our world, that those who are at the top of the heap will always take whatever steps are necessary to maintain the status quo. If we consider the attack on the World Trade Center in this context, we have a much better chance of figuring out "whodunit"?

When I first began my own research in a serious and dedicated way, I was quite distressed by the *confusion* factor. The only thing that I did different from most researchers was to take this confusion as a "given" fact that was *intended*. There were two things that had been burned into my mind very early on, and I found both of them to be very useful when applied to the present problem. The first was a remark attributed to Franklin Roosevelt[369]: "Nothing in politics happens by accident. If it happens, you can bet it was planned." The other idea was a remark made to me by a friend who had been trained in Army Intelligence. He said that the first rule of Intelligence is to just observe what IS and understand that it is very likely the way it is for a reason. Once you have settled that firmly in your mind, you can then begin to form hypotheses about who might benefit the most from a given situation, and once such hypotheses are formed, you can then begin to test them. You may have to discard any number of ideas when you find some flaw, but unless you begin with this process, you will be duped over and over again.

In considering the problem before us, we can see that there exist "tracks" throughout history of some pretty mysterious goings on that do, indeed, suggest a "conspiracy". If we take that as an observation of what IS, we immediately face the second big question: is it a conspiracy? If we decide that the evidence supports a conspiracy, then we have to move to the next question: is it a conspiracy of "good guys" or "bad guys"? It is at this point that all the various conspiracy experts begin to diverge into their assorted rants about Zionists or Masons, and all the many variations thereof.

But what if, instead of asking that question and beginning to argue, we just settle back and observe what is and try to find the answer based on observation?

The single biggest argument against historical conspiracy is the relatively short lifespan of human beings, combined with the observable psychological make-up of man. A corollary objection is the fact that, very often, the domino effect of events that "change history" are of such a nature that it would be impossible for ordinary human beings to engineer them. In other words, Time and Space are barriers to the idea of human beings being engaged in a global conspiracy.

Well, of course the diligent researcher has by now tried every other way to make the puzzle pieces fit ending in repeated failures to account for everything, including the numerous views that oppose and contradict one another. So, when we stop for a moment to think about this initial, observable fact of the barrier of Time and Space, we then think of an idea: what if the conspirators are *not* constrained by Time or Space? Our initial reaction to this thought is to dismiss it out of hand. But as we pursue our researches, as we come across repeated "anomalies" and "glitches" and "tracks" throughout space and time - what we call "history" - we begin to get the uneasy feeling that we ought to take another look at this idea.

As it happens, once the possibility of manipulation of space and time has been added to our hypothesis, things finally begin to "fall into place". When we begin to look at history from this trans-millennial, trans-spatial perspective, the character

---

[369] I've never been able to confirm this attribution, but the idea, as a hypothesis, seems to be quite useful in predicting.

of the "conspiracy" begins to emerge, and only the most gullible - or negative intentioned - occultist could hold onto, or continue to promote, any idea that this conspiracy is benevolent. In fact, it becomes abundantly clear that many, if not most, religions and systems of philosophy, have been created and introduced by the conspirators in order to conceal the conspiracy itself. When you are considering hyperdimensional realities and beings with mastery over space and time, the thousands of years needed to develop any given aspect of the overall plan is negligible; human beings, no matter how important they believe themselves to be, are merely useful idiots who have been manipulated. In consideration of such beings, we come again to the idea of hyperdimensional space - known as "4th density" - and its denizens.

As it happens, precisely at the time I was struggling to understand the bizarre nature of the 10th -12th centuries, the C's - myself in the future - used the opportunity to give me a "lesson in history".

> Q: Next question: is there any relationship between the fact that Roger de Mortimer, the carrier of the last of the line of the Welsh kings, was the lover of Isabella of France, who was the daughter of Philip the Fair, the destroyer of the Templars, and the murder of Edward II, the first of the English Prince of Wales?
> A: Templars are a setup, insofar as persecution is concerned. Remember your "historical records" can be distorted, in order to throw off future inquiries, such as your own.
> Q: I know that. I have already figured that one out! But, it seems that no one else has made this connection. I mean, the bloodlines that converge in the Percys and the Mortimers are incredible!
> A: You should know that these bloodlines become parasitically infected, harassed and tinkered with whenever a quantum leap of awareness is imminent. : Such as "now".
>
> Here is something for you to digest: Why is it that your scientists have overlooked the obvious when they insist that alien beings cannot travel to earth from a distant system??? Even if speed of light travel, or "faster", were not possible, and it is, of course, there is no reason why an alien race could not construct a space "ark", living for many generations on it. They could travel great distances through time and space, looking for a suitable world for conquest. Upon finding such, they could then install this ark in a distant orbit, build bases upon various solid planes in that solar system, and proceed to patiently manipulate the chosen civilizations to develop a suitable technological infrastructure. And then, after the instituting of a long, slow, and grand mind programming project, simply step in and take it over once the situation was suitable.
> Q: Is this, in fact, what has happened, or is happening?
> A: It could well be, and maybe now it is the time for you to learn about the details.
> Q: Well, would such a race be 3rd or 4th density in orientation?
> A: Why not elements of both?
> Q: What is the most likely place that such a race would have originated from?
> A: Oh, maybe Orion, for example?
> Q: Okay. If such a race did, in fact, travel to this location in space/time, how many generations have come and gone on their space ark during this period of travel, assuming, of course, that such a thing has happened?
> A: Maybe 12.
> Q: Okay, that implies that they have rather extended life spans...
> A: Yes...

Q: Assuming this to be the case, what are their life-spans?

A: 2,000 of your years. When in space, that is...

Q: And what is the span when on terra firma?

A: 800 years.

Q: Well, has it not occurred to them that staying in space might not be better?

A: No. Planets are much more "comfortable".

Q: Okay... imagining that such a group has traveled here...

A: We told you of upcoming conflicts... Maybe we meant the same as your Bible, and other references. Speak of... The "final" battle between "good and evil..." Sounds a bit cosmic, when you think of it, does it not?

Q: Does this mean that there is more than one group that has traveled here in their space arks?

A: Could well be another approaching, as well as "reinforcements" for either/or, as well as non-involved, but interested observers of various types who appreciate history from the sidelines.

Q: Well, SWELL! There goes my peaceful life!

A: You never had one! You chose to be incarnated now, with some foreknowledge of what was to come. Reference your dreams of space attack.

Q: Okay, what racial types are we talking about relating to these hypothetical aliens?

A: Three basic constructs. Nordic, Reptilian, and Greys. Many variations of type 3, and 3 variations of type 1 and 2.

Q: Well, what racial types are the 'good guys'?

A: Nordics, in affiliation with 6th density "guides".

Q: And that's the only good guys?

A: That's all you need.

Q: Wonderful! So, if it is a Grey or Lizzie, you know they aren't the nice guys. But, if it is tall and blond, you need to ask questions!

A: All is subjective when it comes to nice and not nice. Some on 2nd density would think of you as "not nice", to say the least!!!

Q: That's for sure! Especially the roaches! Maybe we ought to get in touch with some of these good guys...

A: When the "time" is right. Just pay attention to the signs, please!

Q: There is a lot being said about the [UFO] sightings out in the Southwest area. They are saying that this is the "new" imminent invasion or mass landing. Can you comment on this activity?

A: Prelude to the biggest "flap" ever.

Q: And where will this flap be located?

A: Earth. Invasion happens when programming is complete...

Q: What programming?

A: See Bible, "Lucid" book, Matrix Material, "Bringers of the Dawn", and many other sources, then cross reference...

Q: Well, we better get moving! We don't have time to mess around!

A: You will proceed as needed, you cannot force these events or alter the Grand Destiny.

Q: I do NOT like the sound of that! I want to go home!

A: The alternative is less appetizing. Reincarnation on a 3rd density earth as a "cave person" amidst rubble and a glowing red sky, as the perpetual cold wind whistles...

Q: Why is the sky glowing red?

A: Contemplate.

Q: Of course! Comet dust!

[...]

Q: (L) I read the new book by Dr. David Jacobs, professor of History at Temple University, concerning his extensive research into the alien abduction phenomenon. [Dr. Jacobs wrote his Ph.D. thesis on the history of the UFOs.] Dr. Jacobs says that now, after all of these years of somewhat rigorous research, that he KNOWS what the aliens are here for and he is afraid. David Jacobs says that producing offspring is the primary objective behind the abduction phenomenon. Is this, in fact, the case?

A: Part, but not "the whole thing".

Q: (L) Is there another dominant reason?

A: Replacement.

Q: (L) Replacement of what?

A: You.

Q: (L) How do you mean? Creating a race to replace human beings, or abducting specific humans to replace them with a clone or whatever?

A: Mainly the former. You see, if one desires to create a new race, what better way than to mass hybridize, then mass reincarnate. Especially when the host species is so forever ignorant, controlled, and anthropocentric. What a lovely environment for total destruction and conquest and replacement... see?

Q: (L) Well, that answered my other question about the objective. Well, here in the book, Dr. Jacobs says that there is ongoing abductions through particular families. I quote:

"Beyond protecting the fetus, there are other reasons for secrecy. If abductions are, as all the evidence clearly indicates, an intergenerational phenomenon in which the children of abductees are themselves abductees, then one of the aliens' goals is the generation of more abductees. [...]

To protect the intergenerational nature of the breeding program, it must be kept secret from the abductees so that they will continue to have children. If the abductees KNEW that the program was intergenerational, they might elect not to have children. This would bring a critical part of the program to a halt, which the aliens cannot allow. The final reason for secrecy is to expand the breeding program, to integrate laterally in society, the aliens must make sure that abductees mate with non-abductees and produce abductee children."[370]

Now, this seems to suggest that there is a particular bloodline that is susceptible to...

A: We have told you before: the Nazi experience was a "trial run", and by now you see the similarities, do you not? Now, we have also told you that the experience of the "Native Americans" vis a vis the Europeans may be a precursor in microcosm. Also, what Earthian 3rd density does to Terran 2nd density should offer "food for thought". In other words, thou art not so special, despite thy perspective, eh? And we have also warned that after conversion of Earth humans to 4th density, the Orion 4th density and their allies hope to control you "there". Now put this all

---

[370] From David Jacobs book, *The Threat;* 1999, Simon and Schuster, **ISBN:** 0684848139

together and what have you? At least you should by now know that it is the soul
that matters, not the body. Others have genetically, spiritually and psychically
manipulated/engineered you to be body-centric. Interesting, as despite all efforts by
4th through 6th density STO, this "veil" remains unbroken.

There are many items in the above excerpts of extreme interest considering
current events. One thing is the issue of "mind programming". Contrary to what
many conspiracy theorists claim, the main "mind programming" project on Earth
has been - and continues to be - *religious and cultural.*

The second most predominant method of mind control is via the media and
controlling the flow of information. It might even be possible that beings with
mastery of space/time could travel back in to the past and destroy documents and
plant their own "version of history". The C's commented on this as well:

Q: Who burned the library at Alexandria, since I have heard two stories: one that
the Christians did it and the other that the Arabs did it. Which?
A: Neither.
Q: Who DID burn it?
A: Sword keepers of "the lock".
Q: Who are the Sword Keepers of the Lock?
A: Has to do with Illuminati.
Q: What was their purpose in burning this library?
A: What is the purpose in burning ANY library?
Q: To destroy knowledge. Prevent other people from having access to it.

Again we find a "track" that suggests to us that somebody wanted to keep
human beings in the dark. We can, of course, ascribe this to just ordinary human
activities of greed and ignorance as many materialist interpreters do. If that is the
approach one chooses, the approach of religion, then, when one begins to add up
all of the similar types of events throughout history, the indictment against man
cries to heaven for an end to his existence. And yet, as a hypnotherapist, I have
never found this assessment to be satisfactory. On the many occasions when I have
peered into the inner recesses of the human mind, what I have found most often is
that most human beings just want to have a better life for themselves and for their
children. Human beings are not intrinsically evil and there is no such thing as
"original sin" unless one considers the first individual who wanted to put one over
on someone else (Cain vs Abel is the mythical representation of this idea) as being
the "original sin". Clearly, in order to have the idea structure that there might be
some reward for deception and murder, such an idea must exist in the idea content
continuum of that individual. And that is how hyperdimensional realities interface
with our own: via ideas and the emotion required to bring them to fruition.

Let's now look again at the issue of the Jews. At the point in time that I was
really struggling to come to some understanding of this terrible event in our
history wherein 60 *million* or more people lost their lives, of which one tenth of
them were Jewish. I initiated a dialogue with "myself in the future".

Q: (L) Is there some karmic element that was fulfilled by the Holocaust?
A: Of course.
Q: (L) Could you tell us what karma was being expunged in that activity, and what
group the Jews represented?
A: This is not germane, but it was Atlantean overseers "expunging" guilt from that
life experience.

Q: (L) Now, you have said that the Jews were Atlantean descendants, and that Noah was an Atlantean...

A: Most of them.

Q: (L) What is the significance of this relating to their religion and their experiences and the current state of the Jews?

A: No special karmic significance to being "Jewish", special significance is experiencing holocaust for purpose of purging extraordinary karmic debt.

The answer that "most" of the Jews were Atlantean descendants was not really noticed by me at the time it was given. It was only much later that I realized that this was a significant clue. I continued to research the history and myths and archaeology that led off in endless trails from the central issue, and again and again I kept coming up against what I called "The Scottish Question" in terms of so-called conspiracies. What this term was intended to designate was the fact that whenever I tracked a series of clues, I always hit a closed door that was connected in some way to Scotland - including Scottish Rite Masonry.

Q: (L) I would like to know what is the origin of the Freemasons?

A: Osirians.

Q: (L) Can you tell us when the original Freemasons formed as a society?

A: 5633 BC.

Q: (L) Is Freemasonry as it is practiced today the same?

A: 33rd degree, yes.

Q: (L) So, there is a continuing tradition for over seven thousand years?

A: Yes.

Q: (L) Is this organization with a plan to take over and rule the world?

A: Not exactly.

Q: (L) What is their focus?

A: Overseers.

Q: (L) Of what?

A: The status of Quorum.

Q: (L) What is the Quorum?

A: Deeper knowledge organization. Totally secret to your kind as of yet. Very important with regard to your future.

Q: (L) In what way?

A: Changes.

Q: (L) Can you get more specific? Is that changes to us personally?

A: Partly.

Q: (L) Earth changes?

A: Also.

Q: (L) What is the relationship between this Quorum and the Cassiopaeans [myself in the future?]

A: They communicate with us regularly.

Q: (L) Do they do this knowing you are Cassiopaeans or do they do it thinking...

A: Yes.

Q: (L) Has there been an ongoing relationship between the Cassiopaeans and this Quorum for these thousands of years?

A: For some time as you measure it.

Q: (L) Who was Hermes Trismegistus?

A: Traitor to court of Pharoah Rana.

Q: (L) Who was Pharoah Rana? [Notice that the word "pharoah" simply means "house of" and Rana is the feminine of Raja, Ra, etc. So the term would mean the "house of the Queen".

A: Egyptian leader of spiritual covenant.

Q: (L) In what way was Hermes a traitor?

A: Broke covenant of spiritual unity of all peoples in area now known as Middle East.

Q: (L) Who did Hermes betray?

A: Himself; was power hungry.

Q: (L) What acts did he do?

A: Broke covenant; he inspired divisions within ranks of Egyptians, Essenes, Aryans, and Persians et cetera.

Q: (L) What was his purpose in doing this?

A: Divide and conquer as inspired by those referred to as The Brotherhood in the Bramley book you have read. [*The Gods of Eden.*]

Q: (L) Is this the Brotherhood of the snake Hermes formed in rejection of unity?

A: Hermes did not form it; it was long since in existence.

Q: (L) Who was the originator of the Brotherhood of the Serpent as described in the Bramley book?

A: Lizard Beings.

Q: (L) I would like to know the approximate year of the life of Hermes Trismegistus.

A: 5211 approx.

If this date for the formation of the society later to become the Freemasons - 5633 BC - is correct, it means that it was in existence for about 2,400 years before the Hermes rebellion, which took place 5211 years ago. The C's said that Hermes was a "Traitor to court of Pharaoh Rana" who was the Egyptian leader of a spiritual covenant of spiritual unity of all the peoples in area now known as Middle East.

What we find to be most interesting is the use of the dates as clues here - the 33 representing the Osirians - the early Freemasonic society - and the 11 representing Hermes and the Brotherhood of the Serpent. We notice also that the story about Jacob wrestling with the angel is in *chapter 33* of Genesis, and the verse that tells us that Jacob passed something to Esau is *verse 11*. Esau was, of course, the legendary father of the Arabs.

Q: One thing I do want to understand, since it is involved in all of this, is the idea of the 'Shepherd'. All of the ancient legends and stories and myths lead, ultimately, to something about the 'shepherd', or the 'Shepherd King'.

A: Shepherd is most likely to be struck by lightning, due to staff, and thus "enlightened", or "illumened"!!

Q: Funny spelling! But, what is the contrast between the concept of the shepherd and the agriculturalist? This goes back to the very roots of everything? There is Cain and Abel, Jacob and Esau, Isaac and Ishmael...

A: Are not you "able" to figure this out?

Q: I noticed in Genesis Chapter 33, verse 11, it says that Jacob, who wrestled with the angel the previous night and was on his way to see his brother Esau, who he had tricked into giving up his blessing years before, gave Esau the blessing. What was this? The birthright from his father or the blessing Jacob received from the angel?

A: Trampled leaves of wrath.

Q: This is what Jacob gave to Esau?

A: Yes, and what is the "core" meaning there?

Q: I don't know. What is the core meaning?

A: Leaves are of the Tree of Apples, from whence we get the proverbial "grapes of wrath", the Blue Apples incarnate!

Q: Why are these leaves 'trampled'?

A: Removes chlorophyll.

Q: What is the significance of the chlorophyll?

A: When the chlorophyll dies, the autumnal equinox is at hand.

Q: Did this signify something about the autumnal equinox?

A: Discover what the significance is, my Dear!

Q: Why did Jacob then deceive his brother again? He was to travel and meet him in Edom, but then went in the other direction as soon as Esau was on his way.

A: Refer to last answer, and cross reference.

Q: After wrestling with the 'angel', Jacob was renamed 'Israel', which means 'he will rule as a god'. This tends to make me think that this angel whom Jacob seems to have conjured, did something. What was this being that Jacob wrestled with?

A: Elohim provides the conventional response.

Q: (L) Well, okay. Who were the Elohim of the Bible?

A: Transdefinitive. And variable entities.

Q: (L) Were the Elohim 'good guys'?

A: First manifestation was human, then non-human.

Q: (L) Well, what brought about their transformation from human to non-human?

A: Pact or covenant.

Q: (L) They made a pact or covenant with each other?

A: No, with 4th density STS. [Overlords of Entropy]

Q: (L) Well, that is not good! Are you saying that the Elohim are STS? Who were these STS beings they made a pact with?

A: Rosteem, now manifests as Rosicrucians.

Q: (L) We have the brother issue to deal with. We have Abraham and his nephew, Lot. Then we have Moses and Aaron, Jacob and Esau, Isaac and Ishmael. Were all of these sets of brothers just different aspects or views on the same stories, a set of singular individuals, whether brothers or not?

A: Pretty much though with added elements from other stories blended in.

Q: (L) Was it a brother/brother relationship as in actual brothers?

A: No. The "brother" relationship was created to legitimize a "false" line of transmission.

Q: (L) So there wasn't a brother, or Aaronic relationship present, assuming any part of that story was true. Is that it?

A: Yes.

Q: (L) One aspect of the variation on the story was that Jacob gave his brother, Esau, the 'blessing' and some 'gift'. Does this reflect an accurate part of the story that Abraham/Moses, in his "mythical incarnation" as Jacob , passed something on to someone elses - something that was important?

A: Yes.

Q: (L) Was it Moses/Abraham who was doing this?

A: Yes.

Q: (L) Who did he pass it on to?

A: It was finally understood by "Moses" that the danger of the object was greater than the ability of descendants to resist corruption. He handed it over to those who had created it.

Q: (H) Was it STS or STO forces that created it?

A: STS.

Q: (H) So, the Ark was an object created by STS. Did this amount to some sort of realization on Moses' part? Did he start to wake up?

A: Yes. The story of the "contending with the angel" was the significant turning point as well as the moment of return.

Q: (L) What was the blessing he gave to quote Esau, if giving the object to the "angel" was the event of returning the ark? What was the story there?

A: Two separate events.

Q: (L) So, he returned the ark to the so-called angel. And then, he gave something to someone else. Previously, when I asked about this, you said that what he gave to Esau was "trampled leaves of wrath, the blue apples incarnate", and remarked that I should inquire into the "core meaning",

A: And who was "Kore"?

Q: (L) Was this Abraham's daughter?

A: It was the last living member of the Perseid family.

Q: (L) Was it a male or female?

A: Female.

Q: (L) And how did Abraham come to be in possession of this female?

A: Search the text and you will see.

The C's described this item - the "blessing" - as "trampled leaves of wrath", and mentioned cycles and the ends of cycles.[371] At a later point in time, the C's connected the number 11 to "Medusa", and we have recently seen this element in action on 9-11.

But let's look a little bit closer at the Hermes affair. The generally accepted sequence of Egyptian historical events tell us that a king from "upper Egypt" - that is, the arid highlands - named Narmer, Menes, or Aha, defeated the King of Northern, or Lower Egypt, and thereby unified the two lands. This unification is commemorated in the famous Narmer Palette, which shows a "head smiting" scene, a euphemism for conquest. The "expert" estimates for the date of this event is in the vicinity of 3100 BC which is in the same ballpark as the date given by the C's. In other words, the great "unifier" of Egypt may have been this Hermes, and this may have been an act of rebellion against a covenant of peace that existed up to that time.

Here we discover a most interesting item in history. Prior to this point, the pharaohs from the time of Narmer/Menes, were affiliated with Horus - the "son of Osiris". This means that apparently Horus - the Shemsu Hor - were the Hermes rebellion gang.

Q: (L) Who were the "Followers of Horus"?

A: Those who held the 3rd "insight".

---

[371] As we pick up the clues, again and again we are disturbed by the niggling thought that the Bible was assembled by individuals who had "foreknowledge," and that this information was not favorable to the Jews. It is almost as though someone traveled into the past to "plant" the Bible for nefarious purposes intended to come to fruition in the present time.

Q: (L) What was the third insight?
A: There are 10. *The 3rd involves transcendental existence.*

That certainly sounds very positive, but we have to be careful about our assumptions considering that similar terms were used to describe the mysterious Elohim who cut the deal with Jacob prior to the passage of the Ark to the East - and we realize that everything is not always as it appears: "Rosteem now manifests as Rosicrucians". What begins to glimmer through the darkness is that the Sons of Horus and the Elohim must have been one and the same: the Hermes gang that rebelled against the spiritual covenant of the Osirians. The myth of Isis and Osiris and Set and Horus takes on a whole new meaning - and we see how it has been given a slight twist to obscure the truth. We also begin to suspect a strange link between this group - with their Mesopotamian connections - and the "creation" of Judaism via a conglomeration of Egyptian elements, as well as the conversion of Christianity to a similar Egyptian myth. Egypt, Egypt, everywhere!

CHAPTER 12
OUT OF TIME

ONCE UPON A TIME

It is in the sense outlined in this book that I propose that the myths and rites of the ancients are a dim reflection of ancient science, and that it is only due to the advances of modern science that we have any hope of deciphering this technology, this "science of the soul", this Great Work of Alchemy. It does no one any good for these matters to be consigned to the realms of magic and mysticism and mumbo jumbo artists of all forms and sorts who only manage to embarrass themselves, and drive legitimate scientists away with their nonsense, their silly "sacred geometry" and Kabbalistic rants.

Fulcanelli tells us that the Gothic Cathedrals are an expression of the initiatory power of a learned and transcendent philosophy. He points out that they are "severe and austere productions, not the light, graceful, and pleasing motifs", such as the emotional art of the Renaissance. In saying this, he is making an important point. And he drives his point home by remarking that:

> While the latter aspire only to flatter the eye or to charm the senses, the artistic and literary works of the Middle Ages are founded on higher thought, true and concrete, the cornerstone of an immutable science, the indestructible basis of religion.[372]

Right in these words, Fulcanelli has given us more evidence that our view of the key is correct. He has said that "higher thought" is the "cornerstone". And in many other places, this "stone" is the same one that is described as the "first stone" of the work. So we understand that "higher thought" is the means of achieving the Stone. He then asks us playfully if we would like an example?

Well, sure!

Fulcanelli then directs us to look at a figure from a tympanum from the 12th century. The figure is of a master teaching a pupil, pointing a finger to the pages of an open book. Beneath these figures there is a vigorous athlete strangling a

---

[372] Fulcanelli, *Dwellings*, p. 35.

monster, a dragon. This is next to an embracing couple symbolizing emotion. Fulcanelli pronounces for us the meaning of this set of symbols, the cabalistic interpretation: *Science is the ruler of Strength and Love; one must oppose the superiority of mind to the physical manifestations of power and feeling!*

And even though these ideas are in direct opposition to the current New Age ideas based on the teachings of Helena Blavatsky, Schwaller de Lubicz and others, we have to point out that it seems to be apparent, despite the attempts of the COINTELPRO operation to destroy his work, his reputation, his achievements, Fulcanelli was a Master who had achieved the Great Work and was *given the Present*: that he did, indeed, escape the Matrix. He became the Child of the King, he became Perseus, and he cut off the head of the Gorgon. And that is the secret and the answer to the question: Why Perceval?

TIME IS ON MY SIDE

Knowing what we do now about the literature of the Holy Grail, we think that there is more to the legend's enduring fascination than just the fad of the Middle Ages. The story has appeared in different forms and times long before Geoffrey's *Historia* began the craze. As noted, Arthur represents something else, something other than just a British *Dux Bellorum,* he represents a long ago Golden Age, a time of social harmony and wise government, a time of ethics and morality, a time of the "Way of Former Kings", *a time when there was no Time.*

The theme of the "lost Golden Age" is so potent that when Geoffrey made Arthur a sort of Messiah, combining Welsh myth and tradition with genuine history, he touched something so deep in the human psyche that the Medieval Soul took flight in hopes of the restoration of the Kingdom on Earth *which could only be restored by the discovery of the Grail;* or, in other terms, the "building of the Ark" and *the abolishing of Time.* Again, the focus may have been shifted from a process to an object, and I don't mean a mystical process either, but a literal scientific procedure or technology as well as a different state of being, quantumly speaking, in relation to the environment. Part of this state of being may have been an essentially different view of time.

In the present day, within the framework of the three dominant religions of our time: Islam, Judaism, and Christianity, there is the linear concept of a *limiting of the cosmos* to some specific number of millennia at which point it will all grind to a screeching halt, and the saved will go to "Nirvana/Heaven" and the damned will fry eternally. For Christianity, time is real because it has a meaning - the *redemption* at the END*end*.

> A straight line traces the course of humanity from the initial Fall to final
> redemption. And the meaning of this history is unique, because the Incarnation is a

unique fact. Consequently, the destiny of each one of us, are both likewise played out once, once for all, in a concrete and irreplaceable time which is that of history and life.[373]

The linear conception of time is intimately connected to the idea of evolution. The events of history are a continuing unfoldment of new and more perfect manifestations of both man, man's works, and thus the spirit of God.

> But despite the reaction of the orthodox Fathers, the theories of cycles and of astral influence on human destiny and historical events were accepted, at least in part, by other Fathers [of the church] and ecclesiastical writers, such as Clement of Alexandria, Minucius Felix, Arnobius, and Theodoret, the conflict between these two fundamental conceptions of time and history continued into the seventeenth century.

> We must remind the reader that, at the height of the Middle Ages, cyclical and astral theories begin to dominate historiological and eschatological speculation. Already popular in the twelfth century, they undergo systematic elaboration in the next, especially after the appearance of translations from Arabic writers. ...Albertus Magnus, St. Thomas, Roger Bacon, Dante, and many others believe[d] that the cycles and periodicities of the world's history are *governed by the influence of the stars*, whether this influence obeys the will of God and is his instrument in history or whether it is regarded as a force immanent in the cosmos.[374]

In short, the time of the creation of the Grail legends was precisely the moment when eschatological conceptions were combined with and complemented by the theory of the cyclic return of events. In spite of the Crusades and Inquisition, these ideas dominated down to the seventeenth century. And it was then that the Control System began a mop-up operation to eradicate these ideas. Because, it is also at this precise time that the linear progress of history began to assert itself, most particularly through the influence of Isaac Newton.

> From the seventeenth century on, linearism and the progressivistic conception of history assert themselves more and more, inaugurating faith in an infinite progress, a faith already proclaimed by Leibniz... popularized in the nineteenth century by the triumph of the ideas of the evolutionists.[375]

Karl Marx, in an extremity of materialism, proposed that all of the suffering of humanity is not arbitrary; it is designed to lead man to a definite and coherent end - a final elimination of the Terror of History via a material salvation which constituted an "age of gold", or Heaven on Earth of Marxism. This, of course, justified the *exacerbation of evil to hasten the final deliverance* - an idea not unknown to Judaism and Christianity as evidenced in the Crusades, Inquisition,

---

[373] Puech, Henri-Charles, *Gnosis and Time*, quoted by Eliade, 1954, 143.

[374] Eliade, op. cit., 143-144.

[375] Ibid., pp. 145-146.

and, frighteningly, in the present day regression into fundamentalism in America and Israel. It is also a fundamental concept of the many secret societies currently promoting Egyptian mysticism and the return of the Egyptian Gods and the Divine Theocracy.

An important question now is: how does free will enter in here?

It seems, on the surface, that modern man has affirmed his "autonomy" by rejecting concepts of periodicity and cycles and archetypes. The modern "historical man" or Christian, views archaic man's view of history as endlessly repeating archetypal gestures as a symptom of a fear of movement and spontaneity - or having no free will or courage.

> On the other hand, the more modern and "mechanistic" man becomes, the less able he is to "make" history himself. As a "cog" in a vast, mechanized society, history is made by an increasingly *small number of men* who not only prohibit the mass of their contemporaries from directly or indirectly intervening in the history they are making, but in addition, have at their disposal means sufficient to force each individual to endure, for his own part, the consequences of this history, that is, to live immediately and continuously in dread of history. Modern man's boasted freedom to make history is illusory for nearly the whole of the human race. At most, man is left free to choose between two positions:
>
> (1) to oppose the history that is being made by the very small minority (and, in this case, he is free to choose between suicide and deportation);
>
> (2) to take refuge in a subhuman existence or flight.
>
> Marxism and Fascism must lead to the establishment of two types of historical existence: that of the leader (the only really "free" man) and that of the followers, who find, in the historical existence of the leader, not an archetype of their own existence, but the lawgiver of the gestures that are provisionally permitted to them.[376]

Thus, modern man in his linear time, is *neither free nor a creator of history*. And worse, he is trapped in this horror house with a prophesied *end* to it *all* looming on the horizon, with all the guilt of endless millennia of human suffering on his shoulders!

So we see that, even if only in a certain psychological sense, the ancients, in their cyclical existence, were free! They were free to annul their history, to abolish time, to regenerate themselves - even if only symbolically. And, in the very most ancient times, *perhaps they were free to do this literally.* And, if not this time, another time! No eternal blame, no arbitrary guilt, no everlasting Hell-fire and damnation. The King is dead; long live the King.

---

[376] Ibid., pp. 156-157.

THE HOPE OF THE WORLD

Returning finally to our images of the maze, the crane dance of Theseus/Perseus, the dancing Maruts, Perseus/Theseus with the thread of Ariadne escaping the Egyptian maze; cutting off the head of the Gorgon, the Ark of the Covenant, the Hyperboreans and their dancing god at nineteen year intervals, and a whole host of related clues, we come to the idea of a group of people who understood that the biophysical energies of certain individuals, moving in a *specific geometric relationship to one another*, in specific geometric relationship to an arrangement of megaliths set up for the purpose, become an effective "machine" which has the ability to transduce cosmic energies. *"When ye Maruts spear-armed dance, [the Heavens] stream together like waves of water."* And we find in this idea, an explanation for the origin of the representations of the Mother Goddess as wavy lines representing the confluence of Cosmic Energies in response to an activity of ecstatic "ascent". We also begin to understand what Pythagoras may have meant by his references to geometry, astronomy, and sound - things he was supposed to have learned from the Northern Barbarians. The idea that movement, *especially group movement*, as a stimulant to the production of certain energies seems to have been a part of the archaic technology. But it was only participated in by a group of adepts: those who had achieved freedom from the maze, or who had cut off the head of Medusa, and who therefore had the power of the "Ark"; those who could combine the functions of diviner, medicine man and mediator between the worlds of humans and transcendental powers in an ecstatic manner: Shamans.

Tearing the veil away, the actual "art cot" or Art of Light, is the Quest for the Holy Grail, the building of the Ark, through which the human being may "pass through the conflagration" at the End of Time. Fulcanelli tells us:

> The obelisk of Dommartin-sur-Tigeaus is the tangible, expressive image, absolutely conforming to tradition, of the double terrestrial calamity, of the conflagration and of the flood, on the terrible Judgment Day. [...] This monument seems to be erected on the plane of the ancient hexagram; a figure composed of the water and fire triangles, which is used as the signature of the *physical* Great Work and of its result, the Philosopher's Stone. [...]

> Two sides of the pyramid are exactly aligned on the highway's North-South axis. On the Southern side, one can notice the image of an old oak sculpted in bas-relief. [...] If we question the oak of stone, it can answer us that times are near, because it is its figurative foreboding. It is the revealing symbol of our times of decadence and perversion; and the initiate to whom we owe the obelisk, carefully chose the oak tree as a frontispiece for his work, in the fashion of a cabalistic prologue, in charge of *pinpointing in time* the ill-omened period of the end of the world. The characteristics of this period, which is ours, are clearly indicated in the twenty-fourth chapter of the Gospel of St. Matthew. [...]

> These frequent geological tremors, accompanied with unexplained climatic changes [...] are symbolically expressed by the oak. This word, whose French pronunciation ("chêne") is lisped, phonetically corresponds to the Greek word (Khen), and designates the common goose. The old oak tree, because of this fact, takes on the same value as the expression the old goose and the secret meaning of the old law, heralding the return of the Ancient Covenant or the Reign of God [...] Saturnalia, Paradise and of the Golden Age.

Here, we encounter the so-called Da Vinci Code discussed in the section of comments on the cover of this book. We recall here what. Sir John Rhys wrote about Cassiopeia:

> We have to look for help to enable us to identify the great 'SHE' persistently eluding our search in the syntax of the Welsh language. Only two feminine names suggest themselves to me as in any way appropriate: One is Tynghed, 'fate or fortune', and the other is Don, mother of some of the most nebulous personages in Celtic literature.

> It is from Don that Gwydion, the bard and arch-magician, and Gofannon the smith his brother, are called sons of Don; and so, in the case of Arianrhod, daughter of Don, mother of Ilew, and owner of the sea-laved castle of Caer Arianrhod, not far distant from the prehistoric mound of Dinas Dinlle...

> In Irish legend, we detect Don under the Irish form of her name, Danu or Donu, genitive Danaan or Donaan, and she is almost singular there in always being styled Divinity. From her the great mythical personages of Irish legend are called Tuatha De Danaan, or 'the Goddess Danu's Tribes', and sometimes Fir Dea, or 'the Men of the Divinity'.

> The last stage in the Welsh history of Don consists of her translation to the skies, where the constellation of Cassiopeia is supposed to constitute Ilys Don, or Don's Court.[377]

The word "casse" means *oak*, and Cassiopeia, the great celestial W/M means, literally, the "Voice of the Oak", the Sibyl, the Great Mother, the Virgin, the object at the end of the Milky Way, the pilgrimage route of St. Jacques. Returning now to Fulcanelli's comments:

> In the time of the Golden Age, the regenerated man knows no religion. [...] He respects, honors and venerates God in this radiating globe which is the heart and brain of Nature and the dispenser of earthly goods. [...] In the midst of the radiating celestial body, under the pure sky of a rejuvenated earth, man admires the divine works, without outer manifestations, without rites, without veils. [...]

> The Golden Age, a solar age par excellence, has for cyclic symbol the very image of the celestial body, the hieroglyph that has always been used by the old alchemists, in order to express the metallic gold or mineral sun. On the spiritual level, the Golden Age is personified by the evangelist Saint-Luke. The Greek (Luchas, from (Luchnos), light, lamp, torch, (lux, lucis in Latin), brings us to consider the Gospel according to Luke, as the Gospel according to the Light. It is the Solar Gospel esoterically conveying the journey of the celestial body and that of its rays, *back to their primary state of splendor*. It marks the dawn of a new era, the exaltation of the radiating power over the regenerated earth and the return of the yearly and cyclical orb. [...]

---

[377] John Rhys, Celtic Folklore

[W]e consider accurate all the descriptions that have been made of the earthly Paradise, or, if you prefer, of the golden age; but we are not going to dwell on the various theses aimed at proving that the refuge, inhabited by our ancestors, was located in one well defined country. If we deliberately don't specify where it was located, it is only because, during each cyclic revolution, there is only one thin belt left, that is respected and which remains fit for habitation on its earthly soil. However we emphasize it, the zone of salvation and mercifulness is located sometimes in the Northern Hemisphere, in the beginning of the cycle, sometimes in the Southern hemisphere at the beginning of the next cycle.[378]

And in the mysterious Hendaye chapter of *Le Mystere des Cathedrales*, Fulcanelli further says:

[W]e learn that a country exists, where death cannot reach man at the terrible time of the double cataclysm. As for the geographical location of this promised land, from which the elite will take part in the return of the golden age, it is up to us to find it. For the elite, the children of Elias, will be saved according to the word of Scripture, because their profound faith, their untiring perseverance in effort, will have earned for them the right to be promoted to the rank of disciples of the Christ-Light. They will bear his sign and will receive from him the mission of renewing for regenerated humanity the chain of tradition of the humanity which has disappeared. [...] For it is by fire and in fire that our hemisphere will soon be tried. [...]

The age of iron has no other seal than that of Death. Its hieroglyph is the skeleton, bearing the attributes of Saturn: the empty hour-glass, symbol of time run out, and the scythe, reproduced in the *figure seven*, which is the number of transformation, of destruction, of annihilation. The Gospel of this fatal age is the one written under the inspiration of St. Matthew. [...] Matthaeus [...] means science. This word has given study, knowledge, to learn. It is the Gospel according to Science, the last of all, but for us the first, because it teaches us that, save for a small number of the elite, we must all perish. For this reason the angel was made the attribute of St. Matthew, because science, which alone is capable of penetrating the mystery of things, of beings and their destiny, can give man wings to raise him to knowledge of the highest truths and finally to God.[379]

On June 6, 1996, the following exchange took place between me and Myself in the Future while looking into the *mirror of the world*:

Q: (L) As you know, I have been studying the Sufi teachings, and I am discovering so many similarities in these Sufi "unveilings" to what we have been receiving through this source, that I am really quite amazed, to say the least.   So, my question is: could what we are doing here be considered an ongoing, incremental, "unveiling", as they call it?

A: Yes.

---

[378] Fulcanelli, *Dwellings*, pp. 519-521.

[379] Fulcanelli, *Le Mystere*, pp. 168, 169, 171.

Q: (L) Now, from what I am reading, in the process of unveiling, at certain points, when the knowledge base has been sufficiently expanded, inner unveilings then begin to occur. Is this part of the present process?

A: Maybe.

Q: (L) My experience has been, over the past couple of years, that whenever there is a significant increase in knowledge, that it is sort of cyclical - I go through a depression before I can assimilate - and it is like an inner transformation from one level to another. Is there something we can do, and if so, is it desirable, to increase or facilitate this process in some way?

A: It is a natural process, let it be.

Q: (L) One of the things that Al-Arabi writes about is the ontological level of being. Concentric circles, so to speak, of states of being. And, each state merely defines relationships. At each higher level you are closer to a direct relationship with the core of existence, and on the outer edges, you are in closer relationship with matter. This accurately explicates the 7 densities you have described for us. [...]

Q: (L) Al-Arabi presents a very complex analysis and he probably didn't know it all either... Nevertheless, it almost word-for-word reflects things that have been given directly to us through this source.

A: Now, learn, read, research all you can about unstable gravity waves... Meditate too! ... We mean for you, Laura, to meditate about unstable gravity waves as part of research. ...Unstable gravity waves unlock as yet unknown secrets of quantum physics to make the picture crystal clear.

Twenty days later, as a result of sharing this information on the internet, I met my husband, a theoretical-mathematical physicist who was researching gravity waves. At almost the same time as the above exchange occurred, he was sitting on a megalith in Italy, writing about gravity waves in his research notebook. When I asked about the fact that the C's were constantly urging me in the direction of "science", the following exchange took place:

Q: (L) At one point you mentioned that I needed to learn mathematics, which can be a years long effort. And now, Ark is a mathematician. Was this a clue that Ark was to be part of this?

A: Ark was coming into the picture all along. All is eternal, time is selective. We can see the entire jukebox menu selection at all "times".

In more recent times, as we discussed the identity of Fulcanelli as Jules Violle with Patrick Riviere, the subject of the Hendaye chapter came up. The reader who is familiar with this chapter will notice that the above quoted excerpt from *Dwellings* is startlingly similar to the material of the Hendaye chapter. This was the first time I had ever heard the word "Hendaye" pronounced by a native French speaker and I was startled to hear it, realizing that it was quite similar in sound to the French word for wave, which is onde. With sudden clarity, I realized the reason for the Hendaye chapter: not only had the C's urged me to study "gravity waves", but their central focus was on "waves" in general. On June 21, 1997, a rather startling exchange took place:

A: Alfalfa fields in Rhineland yield as of yet undreamed of treasures.
Q: Where are these alfalfa fields?
A: Near tracks well worn.

Q: Another clue, please?

A: Nope, that is enough for now!!

Q: You guys are gonna drive me crazy! Do you mean Rhineland as in Germany proper?

A: We do not mean Rhinelander, Wisconsin... Or do we?!? Who is to tell?

Q: Who?

A: The searcher, the sepulcher, the one who carries the staff in constant search for greener pastures.

Q: Is there anything that can be expanded, or any additional clues for me or Ark?

A: Last clue for tonight: Look for the vibratory frequency light.

Which brings us to the work of Jules Violle. Remember that the "violle" is a unit of light intensity equal to a square centimeter of platinum, glowing at its melting temperature of 1769 °C (3216 °F). It was the first unit of light intensity that did not depend on the properties of a particular lamp. Obviously, the reference to "Rhineland" does not refer to Germany, but in Green language, refers to France, the land of a thousand cheeses, all of which have a "rhind". This clue is explicated in the reference to the pilgrimage route of St. Jacques, "the searcher, the sepulcher, the one who carries the staff in constant search for *greener* pastures". What are the "undreamed of treasures"? Certainly, Auch Cathedral is part of it. From July 27, 1997:

Q: You previously talked about "undreamed of treasure in alfalfa fields of Rhineland." Is this a physical, spiritual or knowledge based treasure?

A: It is all three.

Q: Who put this treasure in the alfalfa fields of Rhineland?

A: Discover.

Let me now reiterate our hypothesis, formed after all these years of collecting data and noting a certain pattern: that religious myths might be the narratives of an ancient technology and knowledge of the cosmos that far surpasses our present day understanding, as well as a warning to us about some perilous state in which we are living, and some future event toward which we are heading. We have also hypothesized that the myths, rituals and ceremonies of the ancient religions are but surviving fragments of this technology from which the true significance has vanished. What I would like to suggest at this point is that it is in discovering the secrets of this "technology" - The Holy Grail - that mankind has a chance to become free of the Terror of History, to construct an Ark, and survive the coming Deluge.

Over and over again we have seen our tracks of the Grail/Ark lead us to Russia, to Central Asia, to the Scythians, the Tribe of Dan. It is interesting to note at this point a prophecy of Edgar Cayce about Russia and China. In 1944, he prophesied that China would one day be, "the cradle of Christianity as applied in the lives of men". "Through Russia", he said "comes the hope of the world. Not in respect to what is sometimes termed Communism or Bolshevism - no! But freedom - freedom! That each man will live for his fellow man. The *principle has been born there.* It will take years for it to be crystallized; yet out of Russia comes again the hope of the world." In reference to this, and the many other "Russian references", Geoffrey Ashe writes in *The Ancient Wisdom:*

From Greece to the Indus Valley, we find people holding Ursa Major in reverence almost as far back as we can document... In various ways they introduce the Bear into beliefs that connect the centers Above and Below. [...] We have enough to reconstruct a common myth that might underlie all primary versions of the seven-mystique [...] from which the rest follow.

In the far north there is a high and paradisal place, peopled by an assembly of beings of superhuman longevity and wisdom. *They have associates and contacts at lower levels.* [...]

[B]iblical editing never quite censored out the northern mountain and Zion's mystical identity with it. [...] The prophet's imagery is baffling, and rabbis in later ages claimed that it concealed a great secret, an occult wisdom. Only the wisest and holiest could expound the Work of the Chariot. Robert Graves has maintained that the God of the Chariot actually is Apollo.[...]

Is there reason to believe that the northern Something was literally there [...] that a cosmic system was actually taught by the Rishis on a real Meru, and carried south and west along several routes? [...] The inquiry has [...] led to what no one ever identified before - an arguable locale, to which the search can be narrowed down.

[W]e are justified in reverting to Guthrie's theory of Apollo. If this god was brought to Asia Minor and thence to Greece from a Siberian birthplace, a real Land of the Hyperboreans, then he implies a northern Something which actually was there: a center of an influential species of shamanism, with Hyperborean Apollo as one of its gods. [...] If Apollo did make this journey from Siberia, the bear-goddess Artemis was probably paired with him at an early stage.[380]

The story of Apollo and his twin sister Artemis is interesting and connects us back to Orion. Some sources say that Artemis fell in love with Orion and was going to give up her avowed virginity to marry him. Apollo, her brother, did not approve and tricked Artemis into shooting Orion who was swimming in the sea. In her grief, Artemis placed Orion in the sky to honor him.

Other sources say that Orion had raped one of Artemis' female followers, and so Artemis killed him as punishment. She sent a scorpion after him, which stung him and poisoned him. When Orion and the scorpion were placed among the stars, they were given places opposite each other, so that Orion would be out of danger. When Scorpius is just rising, chasing after Orion, the hunter is just starting to disappear behind the western horizon.

The veneration of the bear is so ancient that we even find it in the French cave remains of almost unspeakable antiquity. The symbolism is deep here. A bear is supposedly born as a tiny shapeless lump and "licked into shape". His winter sleep symbolizes death-and-rebirth - or, more significantly, "survival in an Ark". The bear stands on his legs and is an omnivore, like humans.

---

[380] I would like to suggest that the constellaton Orion may have originally been representative of Artemis the huntress.

The point is that the bear, Arca, Arthur, takes us back to his origins in Northern and Western Europe and Siberia. The Siberian shamans tell that in former ages all men had access to the gods, whereas now, only shamans have it and that Shamanism itself has been degraded. Shamanism presents itself as the remnant of an Ancient Wisdom teaching which once flourished across the Northern Hemisphere. The main feature of the Shaman's universe is the cosmic center, an axis connecting earth with both heaven and hell. It is often represented as a tree, a ladder, or a pole. The shaman can utilize this tree to travel upward to commune with the gods, or downward to battle demons. Numbers are important: there are a fixed number of steps, or celestial stages. The cosmic tree can also be represented as a mountain with seven stories. The mountain is made of gold and the name "Altai" itself actually means "gold". We note that the Scythians were famous goldsmiths. What is more, even the most untrained eye can see that the art of the Scythians is identical to the art of the French caves and the art of the Celts of Europe.

It is clear that shamanism, as it is known, has declined from its original unified and coherent system. One reason for thinking so is that, while there are many local terms for a male shaman, there is only one for a female shaman. Shamanism, it seems, was formerly a woman's activity. In one Tartar dialect, *utygan*, the word for a woman-shaman, also means "bear".

There is a place called Mal'ta, fifty-five miles north-west of Irkutsk, in country where the remnants of Altaic shamanism are still active. Carvings have been discovered there which include an oblong panel of mammoth ivory with designs on it. The dominant design is a spiral of dots which goes around *seven times*, and winds into or out of a central hole - a spiral maze. This is the oldest known heptad in the world - almost 30,000 years old.

There are claims that the Ancient Wisdom survives in Central Asia to this very day. We cannot confirm that. The only thing we do know is that out of Russia came the work of Georges Gurdjieff mainly through the efforts of another Russian, P. D. Ouspensky. The Third Man, Boris Mouravieff, has expounded on the Fourth Way material of Gurdjieff in significant ways that relate directly to the Grail Issue. Gurdjieff and Mouravieff have called this Tradition, "Esoteric Christianity, suggesting that it was the true teachings of the man we know as Jesus". But we now suspect that what was originally taught by an obscure man in the area of the Middle East over 2000 years ago was a revival of *a far more ancient Tradition* - a Tradition that extends back into the mists of pre-history to a time when man interacted with his environment in an altogether different way - a Way that seems magical and mysterious to us in our present state of reduced capacities. Let's look at what has survived of this tradition first, and then let's see if we can't put it in more scientific terms.

> Boris Mouravieff's *Gnosis* is an attempt to recover and describe, in terms
> understandable to modern man, a particular Tradition handed down over the
> centuries, in a sometimes perhaps broken line but one that still exists today in the
> Orthodox Church. [..] This tradition could be said to be the Christian equivalent of
> Yoga, Zen and the other inner traditions of the far Eastern religions, disciplines
> which have each existed as specializations within the religion of which they are

part. [...] It's later form can be traced particularly in the Russian Church [and] clearly relates to the oral tradition known as the Royal Way. [...]

Mouravieff himself admits that the survival of this tradition within the church is tenuous, that the doctrine does not appear to survive in full or has not been collected together in full. [...] Monks on Athos admit the existence of the Tradition but say that it has never been fully spelled out in writing.[381]

In carefully studying the work of Mouravieff, we discover that we have found many of the missing pieces of our puzzle. What is more significant is that these pieces relate directly to the *hidden meanings* of the Quest for the Holy Grail and the Great Work of the Alchemists.

Again and again, Seekers have sought to interpret the process of "Ascension" in terms of their external experiences. As Fulcanelli has told us, it is in the clash of ideas that the letter dies and the spirit is born. That is to say: the knowledge is in the meaning, not in the words.

Again and again the esoteric Tradition is misunderstood in this way and so it dies. Then, when the time is ripe, it must be either restored or rephrased. In the meantime the meaning is kept alive in communities or schools symbolized by the name "ark", of which Noah's ark was one. Mouravieff writes:

With time, the revealed Word, sometimes handed down from extinct civilizations, is subject to damage due to human forgetfulness: it becomes fragmentary. Then it receives arbitrary additions from purely human sources. With time, those conjectures are generally taken as realities.

Apart from these mutilations, we should not lose sight of a phenomenon of a totally different order. Divine Revelation, the source of all true Tradition, does not crystallize into immobility through the course of millennia. Revelation is given in stages: metered out each time in a necessary and sufficient way in answer to the needs of the epoch and of the Cause.[382]

Mouravieff's words echo those of Fulcanelli:

Every prudent mind must first acquire the Science if he can; that is to say, the principles and the means to operate. Otherwise he should stop there, without foolishly using his time and his wealth. And so, I beg those who will read this little book to credit my words. I say to them once more, that THEY WILL NEVER LEARN THIS SUBLIME SCIENCE BY MEANS OF BOOKS, AND THAT IT CAN ONLY BE LEARNED THROUGH DIVINE REVELATION, HENCE IT IS CALLED DIVINE ART, or through the means of a good and faithful master; and

---

[381] Amis, Robin, translator and editor: *Gnosis II, Study and Commentaries on the Esoteric Tradition of Eastern Orthodoxy* by Boris Mouravieff (Robertsbridge, UK: Praxis Institute Press 1992) pp. xiii, xiv.

[382] Ibid, p. 96.

since **there are very few of them to whom God has granted this grace**, there are also very few who teach it.[383]

When we turn back for a moment to consider the problems of the many and varied teachings of "Ascension" that we noted in the introduction, we find that this issue of "works vs. faith" has always been the condition confronting the Seeker. It is part of the Haunted Forest through which he must pass even before he is faced with his true tests of stamina, courage, and discernment. Mouravieff discusses this also:

A very ancient maxim quoted in Saint Luke's Gospel places the problem [of Ascension] in its proper context. He writes: *"the labourer is worthy of his hire."* This maxim is given in the context of sending the seventy disciples "as lambs among wolves' to announce to the people that 'The kingdom of God is come nigh unto you."

This means that in the esoteric field, as in everyday life, man earns a salary for the service he provides. [...]

In the esoteric field we can gain nothing pure or true and thus nothing beautiful *without making efforts whose sum and importance are equivalent to the result to which the worker aspires.* Conversely, the value of the results we obtain is always equivalent, quantitatively and qualitatively, *to the measure of the services rendered on the esoteric level.*

It is possible to obtain so-called esoteric results that are *impure*, but they are *false* and thus *transitory*.

Here we refer to the vast realm of occultism, where the children of this century, more capable than the children of light, seek to apply their abilities beyond the visible world. This occurs in what we call mysticism of phenomena. [...]

If the seeker [...] approaches the esoteric domain driven by the desire to find in it personal and thus *impure* satisfaction for himself, he will not be able to advance very far along this way. If he persists, he will meet with failure. The error of conception made at the start will imperceptibly lead him towards this "mysticism of phenomena".

The attentive reader will draw a practical conclusion from the above: one must find a genuine esoteric task being carried out in the world, make oneself useful in that work, and take an active part in it. [...]

[We are in the heart of this period] we will call the Time of Transition. [...] All the signs show that the necessary conditions for the End are emerging before our very eyes. [...]

---

[383] Fulcanelli, *Dwellings*, p. 94.

The preparatory task fundamental to the Time of Transition can and must be accomplished [...] for human beings and by human beings. This is, therefore, a question of the New Man. [...]

In practice, this problem can be reduced to the need to form a new elite [the Children of Elias, as Fulcanelli states]. In the time of transition between our civilization which has now reached its end and the new era into which humanity is now moving in its historical evolution, success depends on the emergence in the near future of a sufficient number of people belonging to this new human type. [...][384]

So, let us briefly describe what the Ancient Secret Science of Ascension is *really* about according to research, what we have learned from the Cassiopaeans.

Organic life on Earth serves as a "transmitter station". As such a transmitter, during times of Transition, as it is in the case of a quantum wave collapse, what is being "transmitted/observed" determines the "measurement". There are approximately 6 billion human beings on the planet at this moment of transition, most of them contributing to the *quantitative* transmission. But what is missing is the *qualitative frequency resonance vibration* that will create the template for the New World.

The *quality* of humanity has changed little in the past many millennia. Most human beings are still ruled by fear, hunger and sex in states of misery and chaos.

In short, although the global intensity of transmission has grown exponentially with the increase of the population of the planet, the spectrum of energies transmitted is incomplete. It lacks *massive* amounts of the finest energies of the psyche. Only human beings on the verge of *true spiritual* ascension are capable of ensuring the transmission of these energies in sufficient quality and quantity.

The energies needed are the Three Currents of Objective Love: Spiritual, Emotional/Mental, and physical love. And we emphasize that these currents must be *pure*.

Man alone has the ability to capture and live all three. But to grasp and fully experience the Soul Love, the giving love, the courteous Love demonstrated and taught by Chivalry and the Knights of the Grail stories, the Seeker must develop a magnetic center within himself.

Human beings are penetrated through and through by the two currents of mental/emotional and physical love, but these currents are not pure; without a fully developed magnetic center, the individual has no capacity to capture them. It is only by actualizing these three currents in his or her life, either in the mode of the Alchemist, or in the Model of the Grail Quest, both of which exemplify the Shamanic Ecstatic Ascent, that a person has the *real* possibility of Ascension, the return to the Golden Age.

---

[384] Mouravieff, *Gnosis II*, pp. xxvii-xxxiii.

We have seen in our survey of the history and the evidence, what the potentials are: a Return to the Edenic State in the literal terms of Primitive Chiliasm - a New Heaven and a New Earth.

Again, this depends upon capturing and holding stable - possibly in the face of extraordinary events - massive quantities of what the tradition refers to as purified Objective Love.

It is clear to those who have been paying attention to what is going on in the world that there are forces that do *not* wish for this possibility to manifest! They do not want to lose their supply of negative energy food! And with this end in mind, they propagate endless lies and deceptions upon humanity - so as to deceive even the very elect!

How to achieve this anchoring of the frequency - the three currents of Objective Love? Let's look first at what the tradition teaches utilizing the commentary of Mouravieff with editorial clarification.

The attitude a person takes toward Love reflects his level of being. The splendor of the Love of God/Creation is generally inconceivable to human beings; it would burn out all their circuits with a mere glimpse. However, a human being *can* glimpse and survive the spiritual Love of Objective Knowledge. But, in order to do this, the individual must pass to a higher level of BEing and become a *true* individuality. Only those beings who have achieved the level of Individuality, who obey the imperatives of the Divine within, the real "I", have the possibility of holding this frequency and radiating it at the Time of Transition.

The "Elect", the Children of Elias as Fulcanelli terms them, are human beings who have crossed the Second Threshold and who have achieved the Second Birth. They will be "gathered from the four winds, from one end of heaven to the other", to pass through the Transition and form the seed of humanity in the New World. This means that they will be humans of all colors and types - the only criteria being that they have crossed the Second Threshold. Each of them will be Fully Conscious through a direct and indissoluble union of the Personality with his Higher Emotional/Intellectual Center. This direct contact of the new humanity with the higher planes explains why the Second Coming will not require a "new incarnation of Christ." This is why we were warned: "If any man shall say unto you, Lo, here is Christ or there; believe it not. For there shall arise false Christs and false prophets and shall show great prodigies and miracles; insomuch that, if it were possible, they shall seduce the very elect."

The path that must be followed is that which is exemplified in the Quest for the Holy Grail. Human beings must travel from the residue of Celestial Love that we experience in our ordinary lives, to the Love of the Spirit. This is the general requirement for "Salvation".

This path is the way to the Second Birth. But to be reborn, a human being must pass the test of True Love. Only he who has mastered his personality and *burns* with this True Love can cross the Second Threshold. And before he can even reach this point, the Seeker, will pass through intermediate stages. These stages include challenges that test Sincerity and Strength. These challenges cannot be met without discernment, and discernment can only be acquired by first attaining Knowledge.

Knowledge acquired through study and work is only a temporary - but essential - stage. Only Higher Love can reveal the Divine Nature. But if there is no vessel built by Knowledge to receive Gnosis, there is no possibility of anchoring the Forerunner Spirit - creating the magnetic center - which will open the gates to the Holy Spirit. The Gatekeeper is Knowledge.

But for this to occur, the sign of Knowledge, that is, the Sign of St. Matthew-Science as Fulcanelli describes it, must be correctly oriented. And this means that the Seeker must be liberated from lying and believing in lies. Without this, there is no possible access to the Era of the Holy Spirit. No matter how well-meaning the individual, if they are following practices or teachings that are based on lies, they will not achieve the Grail. And so, we see why knowledge and discernment is essential. Again, I refer the reader to the section of this book that discusses neurochemistry.

Access to knowledge *requires courage*, as it demands a special psychological effort from the Seeker: he has to accept the postulate that, "the truth is out there, but it is very difficult to find", while at the same time disregarding his own ideas and personal beliefs to which he is emotionally attached.

With the approach of the era of the Holy Spirit, everything must be gradually brought to the light of day, not only the secrets of the laboratory, but the deepest meaning of esotericism. The same must happen with illusions, errors and lies, which must be revealed so that they can be rectified. This process, including the Revelation of the deepest esoteric Knowledge that has been promised and prophesied, will fully reveal the many deviations of man's fundamentally inquiring spirit. Initiation, in the esoteric meaning of the word, is not simply a "ceremony". In fact, the "initiation ceremony" does not occur on the human plane with human rituals. True initiation occurs on the super-sensory plane. It confirms the Initiate in a new dignity *earned by his Work*, and carries him towards the *Divine Grace*.

To solve the problem of anchoring the Three Currents of Objective Love, we must concentrate on a positive and practical solution to the problems of individual human beings. A practical application of esoteric knowledge should help those who are Seekers and who burn with the desire to reach the Second Birth.

The Seeker of the Holy Grail, burning for Truth, just as depicted in the stories, must first assimilate all he can learn exoterically and mesoterically. And he must then be ready to serve the Cause joyfully.

To Burn and to Serve is the motto of the new Knight.

The Tradition teaches - and this knowledge can be discerned in the Grail Legends as well as in the fragments of the Catharist teachings - that at the End of Time, the Children of Elias will consist of Polar Couples and their affiliated groups and helpers.

The evolutionary path of love from the Fall has traveled from polygamy, with other human beings (mostly women) considered as "chattel", to the Free Choice of partners based on spiritual love as exemplified in the Grail stories. It now is a decaying form, leading to over-emphasis on the physical expression and, in some cases, is even regressing to a form of "polygamy", or multiple partners. Mouravieff writes:

A revolution is occurring silently which will replace the free romance, distinctive mark of the Christian era, with the singular romance characteristic of the Holy Spirit. Liberated from servitude to procreation, this romance of tomorrow is called on to cement the indissoluble union between two strictly polar beings, a union which will assure their integration in the bosom of the Absolute. As St. Paul says:

"Nevertheless, neither is the woman without the man, nor man without the woman in the Lord."

The vision of such a romance has haunted the highest minds for thousands of years. We find it in platonic love[385], the basis of the singular romance in the myths of Androgyny man; of Orpheus and Euridice; of Pygmalion and Galatea... This is the aspiration of the human heart, which cries in secrecy because of its great loneliness. This romance forms the essential aim of esoteric work. Here is that love which will unite man to that being who is unique for him, the Sister-Wife, the glory of man, as he will be the glory of God. Having entered into the light of Tabor, no longer two, but one drinking at the fount of true Love, the transfigurer: the conqueror of Death.

The principle of Woman's intervention is found in ALL crucial periods of history.

Periods where the ennobling role of the woman in the life of human society has faded are marked by a triviality of morals and manners, expressed in particular by a taste for realism carried to its utmost limits.

Today, human relations suffer from a real distortion in the innate role that woman is destined to play at the side of man: instead of being the active force in these relations, the inspiring and fruitful complement to the man, the woman tends to follow a parallel path, which no longer permits her to exercise her own creative vocation. [...]

Man and woman once formed a single spiritual being - even if in separate bodies - endowed with the unique consciousness of the real Self; the Being described in the myth of the Androgyne.

The incomplete "I" of the Personality, unfinished and powerless, wanders in life with no faith and no true affection. It goes from error to error, from weakness to weakness, and from lie to lie. A prisoner - perhaps voluntarily - but nevertheless a prisoner - man does not do what he wants to do in life, but does what he hates, blindly obeying a diabolical mechanicalness which, under its three aspects: fear, hunger and sexuality, rules his life.

This purely factitious existence has nothing real except the possibility of evolution - which remains latent, and forms the objective of esoteric studies and work. Apart from this seed, everything in exterior life is based on lies.

---

[385] Though Plato missed the point and thought that polarity on the physical plane could be minimized or excluded.

If the Fall is a direct consequence of identifying with the "I" of personality [the predator's mind, the degraded DNA state], and the solitude of polar beings separated by the Fall is the source of weakness in humans who have in this way become mortal, the return of Unity appears to be an inexhaustible source of new energies. These energies are necessary to man, and to restore the dangerously disturbed equilibrium of today's public and private life, he must seek them out.

However, this return to the perfect unity of polar beings is not given freely. It is the exclusive privilege of those who have crossed, or are ready to cross, the Second Threshold of the Way.

It is through realization of the totally indivisible unity of their real "I", by two polar Individualities arrived at the Second Birth, that the original sin can and must be redeemed.[386]

The next step of the evolution of Love is the Alchemical Androgyne. This is *not to be understood in the physical sense*, but rather in the Spiritual meaning. *The Divine Androgyne is the highest condition of Human Consciousness* which crowns the efforts of the Seeker and which Union results in the Second Birth.

Mouravieff interpreted the Tradition to mean a relation between two people, but it is actually more simple than that. Objective Love can only be attained here, in human existence, by its complete and vivifying manifestation at the time of the Second Birth.

The practice of Courtly Love demands sacrifices and exploits. These are tests. For those who surmount them, the salutary effect of Gnosis is doubled.[387]

The courtly Love of the Knight and his Lady is a metaphor that describes the proper relation between matter - *mother* - and spirit - *logos*.

THE TREE OF LIFE

"In the beginning was the Word, and the Word was with God, and the Word was God Himself. He was present originally with God. All things were made and came into existence through Him; and without Him was not even one thing made that has come into being. In Him was Life and the Life was the Light of Men. And the Light shines on in the darkness, for the darkness has never overpowered it, and is unreceptive to it." [John 1: 1-5, *Amplified*, Zondervan]

The word "Logos", in Greek, means "word". When it was used in archaic, esoteric terms, it had a more specific meaning which was that "Divine Essence" was concentrated in its *Name*. This theory of creation was passed from Tantrism to Neoplatonic philosophy, and was later adopted into Christianity and from there, it was suggested to apply only to Jesus. The Christian enthusiasm for this idea may

---

[386] Mouravieff, *Gnosis I*, pp. xxv-xxvi, 225-227.

[387] Mouravieff, *Gnosis III*, Author's Introduction p. xx.

have been related to the fact that it provided exclusively male gods the means by which to give birth! They could just "speak the word" and that was that! Thus, it has become a widely known and popular theological construct.

However, the ability to create and destroy with words was originally the domain of the Goddess in all her many manifestations. She created alphabets, languages and secret words of power, or Mantras. Every manifestation of life was brought into being by the, "supreme syllable and mother of all sounds, Ohm".

The Logos idea is actually almost identical to the Oriental concept of the Oversoul, which was supposed to be the essence of the Great Mother. *Origen*, one of the early fathers of the Christian church wrote:

> As our body while consisting of human members is yet held together by one soul,
> so the universe is to be thought of as an immense living being which is held
> together by one soul, the power of the Logos.

The doctrine of the Logos was so widespread in the ancient world that it would have been impossible for Christians to ignore it. However, not only did they appropriate its use to their own ends, they also destroyed the ancient *Logoi*, or sacred writings of the Orphics, mentioned by Plato and other philosophers. This was a large portion of the Wisdom Literature which survived in part in the Bible, and was also preserved in fragments in certain Gnostic writings discovered at Nag Hammadi in 1945. The Gospel of Truth says:

> "When the Word appeared, the Word which is in the hearts of those who
> pronounced It... It was not only a sound, but It had taken on a body as well."[388]

Christians gave the idea very simplistic interpretation, assuming the "body" was Christ's. The more perceptive of the ancient writers intended to say that man, the nomothete, creates all his gods out of his Word.

And here we find ourselves back in the domain of the Names of God, or Thought Centers.

Q: (L) Is there only one ultimate creator of the universe

A: All is one. And one is all.

Q: (L) How does thought become matter?

A: Bilaterally.

Q: (L) What do you mean by "bilaterally"?

A: Dual emergence.

Q: (L) Emergence into what and what?

A: Not "into what and what," but rather, "from what and to what."

Q: (L) What emerges from what?

---

[388] The Gnostic Gospels

A: The beginning emerges from the end, and vice versa.

Q: (L) And what is the beginning and what is the end?

A: Union with the One.

Q: (L) What is the One?

A: 7th density, i.e.: all that is, and is not.

Q: (L) In terms of major STS, this may or may not be related, could you tell us the nature of a Black Hole?

A: Grand Scale STS. Black Holes are a natural force reflection of Free Will consciousness pattern of STS. Notice that Black Holes are located at center of spiral energy forces, all else radiates outward. All in creation is just that: a radiating wave.

Q: (L) Where does the energy go that gets sucked into a black hole?

A: Inward to total nonexistence. Universe is all encompassing. Black holes are final destination of all STS energy. Total nonexistence balances total existence. Guess what is total existence? "God." Prime Creator. As long as you exist, you are of the Prime Creator.

Q: (L) Now, this stuff that goes into Black Holes, that goes into nonexistence, is that, then, not part of the Prime Creator?

A: Correct.

Q: (L) How can Prime Creator lose any part of him or itself?

A: Prime Creator does not "lose" anything.

Q: (L) Well, then, how would you describe this energy that was in existence and then is no longer in existence because it has become or gone into a Black Hole?

A: *Reflection is regenerated at level 1 as primal atoms.* 1st density includes all physical matter below the level of consciousness. Seventh density is union with the one... it is timeless in every sense of the word, as its "essence" radiates through all that exists in all possible awareness realms. And, remember, there is only one "God", and that the creator includes all that is created and vice versa!

Q: (L) Okay, who created the Cassiopaeans?

A: Your super ancient spiritual ancestors.

Q: (L) Do these beings have a name?

A: No. They are Transient passengers.

Q: (L) What is the meaning of this term and who are these beings?

A: Transient passengers are not beings. Transient Passengers are unified thought form.

Q: (L) Why are they called Transient Passengers?

A: Because they transit all forms of reality. And they spring forth from the Unified form of existence.

Q: (L) Well, are these Transient Passengers Realms?

A: Yes. So are you.

Q: (L) Are the 6th density Orions, also known as Transient Passengers, are they the same Transient Passengers that have been referred to as the ones who genetically engineered us or put us here?

A: Close. They are Wave riders.

Q: (L) Is "riding the wave" part of the definition of Transient Passengers?

A: Yes.

Q: (L) Do they like to ride this wave?

A: Is it "fun" for you to live on earth?

Q: (L) Well, I like living on earth a great deal, but I don't like pain and suffering, and I don't like man's inhumanity to man and I don't like to see other people suffer.

A: Do you live on earth for amusement?

Q: (L) I would like to live on Earth for amusement but I haven't had a whole heck of a lot of laughs since I have been here this time. I would like to have a life on the planet where things were pleasant...

A: You misunderstood.

Q: (L) I see what you are saying. That's where they live because that's where they live.

A: Yes.

Q: (L) Are there Service to Self beings at 6th density that some call the 6th density Orions?

A: These are only reflections of individuals, not unified entities. These reflections exist for balance. They are not whole entities, just *thought forms*.

Q: (L) Are these 6th density beings what the Bible describes as a "gathering" of angels as in the story of Job where "Lucifer" came in before the Lord...

A: Yes.

Q: (L) So, in addition to STO, there are STS at 6th density which balance? And they are just there, they exist?

A: Reflection for balance.

Q: (L) Is there any kind of hierarchy to this thing? Do these beings come before some kind of "Grand Council" and make plans and discuss things, and make decisions and implement them?

A: No.

Q: (L) Well, how do things happen? Do things just sort of happen as a natural interaction of things and energies?

A: Yes.

***

Q: (L) You say that you are unified thought forms in the realm of knowledge.

A: Yes.

Q: (L) Ibn Al-'Arabi describes unified thought forms as being the 'Names of God.' His explication seems to be so identical to things you tell us that I wonder...

A: We are all the names of God. Remember, this is a conduit. This means that both termination/origination points are of equal value, importance.

Q: (L) What do you mean? Does this mean that we are a part of this?

A: Yes. Don't deify us. And, be sure all others with which you communicate understand this too! Remember: 1st density includes all physical matter below the level of consciousness. 6th density is uniform in the level pattern of lightness, as there is complete balance on this density level, and the lightness is represented as knowledge. 7th density is union with the one... it is timeless in every sense of the word, as its "essence" radiates through all that exists in all possible awareness realms. The light one sees at the termination of each conscious physical manifestation is the Union, itself. Remember, 4th density is the first that includes variable physicality!! Ponder this carefully!!! And, remember, there is only one "God", and that the creator includes all that is created and vice versa!

Now, let's form a little hypothesis here - a working model. Let's say that Unified Thought Form at 6th density are the Names of God. This is a level of pure consciousness; the Platonic level of ideas, or essences or Noumena.

The 6th density level of Knowledge-of-All would be just "below" the *One* at 7th density. We would call this The Name of Knowledge; it is the "Logos" or "Word" that engenders *all* existence. It could be symbolized by the ancient yin-yang symbol since it includes *all* the names. It could also be symbolized as the "Universal Hermaphrodite/Androgyne". It is the "Two in One" where the work of generation begins. It is the first manifestation of the Eternal Parent and is a "Bi-sexual Universal Being". It combines within itself the elements and principles of both Masculinity and Femininity.

However, we have to make a distinction of the Knowledge of *all* as opposed to the "Names of Wrath" and the "Most Beautiful Names".

Now, in trying to think through this idea, I wanted to have a visual image. I struggled for months to think of a way to present it with little success. Finally, it occurred to me that the Cabalistic Tree of Life might be a useful form to work with. I found an image in a book, and it didn't seem quite the thing, but I thought I could play with it a bit, modify it, and get it to do what I wanted, so I put it on the scanner to make an image. When I did, the way the scanner was sitting forced me to have to place the book upside down. When the image came up on the screen, reversed, I immediately recognized that this WAS useful! So here is my little modification of the Tree of Life that represents the Cosmos, or "Body of God". [See Plate 1.]

Now, I want you to notice, first of all, that the vertical axis has 7th Density "Union with the One" at the top, and 1st density matter at the bottom. If I were able to present this in a hyperdimensional way, the position at the top would include Being and Non-being that serves as a sort of mobius connection between 1st density and 7th. In other words, they are not really separate - they connect in an endless cycle. "The beginning emerges from the end and vice versa". It might be useful to refer back to the *tesseract* idea to be able to realize that this is a 3 dimensional representation of something that is not 3 dimensional!

Now, the next thing we want to consider about this vertical axis is the placement of the sixth density level of Knowledge on the vertical axis *as a "mirror image" of the placement of 2nd density as the realm of Nature.* That is, Flora and Fauna. There is an important key here that we must realize. If sixth density is, "uniform in the level pattern of lightness, as there is complete balance on this density level, and the lightness is represented as knowledge", then we must think of the realm of

Nature as being the physical *reflection* of this principle. That is to say, "nature" - *all* of creation - is a reflection of *all* of consciousness!

We also notice that second density is only able to recycle through 5th density in order to "graduate" to any of the other densities, and this is reflected in our observations of Nature. We do not ever see any creatures from the animal kingdom suddenly developing self-consciousness in the sense of the nature of human consciousness.

Actually, we don't necessarily have any hard evidence that it is possible for humans to graduate to the higher densities which might be indicated by the lateral axes in the figure which show direct channels between 3rd, 4th and 6th densities, but we have been told that it is possible; there is circumstantial evidence in esoteric literature that it has happened; and we do have some idea that certain "divine beings" who have appeared throughout history have a more or less "human" form. So, we might assume that, generally speaking, there is not so great a barrier between our 3rd density state and the higher densities, as there is between 2nd density and the densities that are reflected in human self-consciousness and awareness.

So, 2nd density is shown without a direct conduit to the higher densities except through 5th, the "recycling zone".

One thing that occurs to me as I look at this little modification of the Tree of Life is that it seems to model and define in pretty simple and precise terms the relationships we are coming to understand about our reality, as well as the *potentials* for moving from one point on the Tree to another.

It should be understood, again, that the conduits of connection are really "hyperdimensional" in nature and not really separated as they appear on the model. Not only that, but the two lateral axes identified as STS and STO - or creation and entropy - represent literally infinite dimensions, or potential ideas, in number. These dimensions can represent different Names of God and their "extensions" down through the densities either as single individuals or as groups of individuals, or simply potentials. However, there is always balance, so for every STO-Creation axis, there is an equal and corresponding STS-Entropy axis.

Another thing that occurs to me as I examine the relationships is that, from any of the lateral axes, by accessing the Nature/Knowledge relationship, one is also aligning with the vertical axis of Being which could be defined as the *axis of gravity* within each of us. Perhaps by aligning with this axis, one could theoretically, "open a doorway" into this axis. Once one was in the axis, one could then open a doorway into any of the other positions of either the lateral or vertical axes. Of course, talking about it and *doing* it are two different things! Apparently this is one of the aspects of the "Great Work" of Alchemy. And in studying alchemy we find some warnings that it would do us well to heed.

The alchemists wrote that the study and contemplation of the metaphorical "Philosopher's Stone" along with the chemical work was a necessary component to elevate the mind and prepare the soul for transmutation.

> "By invigorating the Organs the Soul uses for communicating with exterior objects,
> the Soul must acquire greater powers not only for conception but also for retention,
> and therefore if we wish to obtain still more knowledge, the organs and secret

springs of physical life must be wonderfully strengthened and invigorated. The Soul must acquire new powers for conceiving and retaining... That this has not been the case with all possessors was their own fault.

.... Those who study only the material elements can at best discover only half the mystery... *alchemy is a mystery in three worlds - the divine, the human and the elemental...* alchemy in the hands of the profane becomes perverted...

Man's quest for gold is often his undoing, for he mistakes the alchemical processes, believing them to be purely material. He does not realize that the Philosopher's Gold, the Philosopher's Stone, and the Philosopher''s Medicine *exist in each of the four worlds* and that the consummation of the experiment cannot be realized until it is successfully carried on in four worlds simultaneously according to one formula.

Furthermore, one of the constituents of the alchemical formula exists only within the nature of man himself, without which his chemicals will not combine, and though he spend his life and fortune in chemical experimentation, he will not produce the desired end [which is] the subtle element which comes out of the nature of the illuminated and regenerated alchemist. *He must have the magnetic power to attract and coagulate invisible astral elements.*"[389]

The alchemical literature includes stories of alchemists who blew themselves up, who suffered horrible diseases, who came under the power of demonic influences because their technical abilities surpassed their spiritual development, or who shot to "stardom" like a meteor, and then crashed and burned in ignominy

But, we are gathering more clues here. We have a remark that, "Alchemy is a mystery in *three* worlds", and that the work takes place in *four* worlds simultaneously. The three worlds are defined as "divine, human and elemental". The Cassiopaeans have also talked about these "three worlds" as:

"Each soul has its own patterning, which is held in place by the *three bodies of existence* 'thought center, spirit center and physical center,' there are specific methodologies for adjusting these, and traveling into or out of other planes of existence. When one does not properly utilize these, one tears the fabric of their trilateral continuum when they seek to travel. This can be very problematic, and may lead to the soul being unable to reconnect with the body, thus causing the physical center to perish!!!" [Cassiopaeans, 10-05-96]

The Cassiopaeans have also talked about the "four worlds".

"And remember, *your consciousness operates on four levels*, not just one! [They are] Physical body, genetic body, spirit-etheric body, and consciousness. [These are] the four composites of the human manifestation in 3rd and 4th densities." [Cassiopaeans, 10-10-98]

Now, as I pondered these things, it occurred to me that this modified Tree of Life could be used to represent each individual human being since, as the

---

[389] Eugenius Philalethes, quoted by Manly Hall, *The Secret Teachings of All Ages*, emphases, mine.

Cassiopaeans have pointed out, all of creation exists within each and every one of us! When we align with the central axis, we are aligned with 7th density, which is the origin of all other "engendered beings", and we thereby have access to all of Creation in very literal terms.

However, since man is a "mirror image" of God, we now need to reverse the image as the Cabalists constructed it with, again, my little modifications.

Now, look at this Tree. [See Plate 2.] Note that, on the vertical axis, below the level of Union with the One, or 7th density, there are 4 positions. If this is the relationship we are looking for, then we see that the physical body relates to 1st density matter, the genetic body relates to 2nd density, the spirit-etheric body relates to 5th density, and consciousness relates to 6th density knowledge. At the same time, we always retain our connection to 7th density, so that must be considered the "pivot" or "true dimension".

Q: (L) Physicists talk about multi-dimensional universes. The idea is that our 3 dimensional space and 1 dimensional time is an illusion of plane beings, while the true universe has more dimensions perpendicular to the above ones. Physicists have different guesses here: 5, 6, 7, 11, 256. How many dimensions does the true universe have?

A: Not correct concept. Should be: How many universes does the "true" dimension have?

Q: (L) All right, then. I think that from a previous session we were told that the number of universes was not countable. Is that correct?

A: Infinite, maybe, but more to the point: **variable and selective.**

Q: (L) Explain variable and selective, please?

A: For those who know how, universes can be created at will in order to transmodify reality merge.

Q: (L) What is a reality merge?

A: What does it sound like?

Q: (T) Merging of realities from one universe into another? A creating of a new reality which is then merged with the old to create a new universe. (L) Maybe it means the realities of different people merge to create a sort of "mutual universe"? Like the idea "you create your own reality"?

A: T is closer; Laura is playing "left field."

Q: (T) A structure of the universe that holds the levels together... everything is connected. The consciousness of 6th density is perfectly bonded and balanced with 3rd density, and the quasi-physical level of 4th density, and the totally physical levels 3 through 1, and the total ONE of 7th, and whatever 5th is. (L) We have four levels of physical expression, so to speak, going from the really solid, minimal consciousness level 1 to....

A: Yes, but the Terran scientists have been programmed to believe that nothing can exist unless it can be measured, estimated, calculated and represented in some way in the physical material plane. Not true!!!!!!! For example: We are in NO WAY physical.

Q: (L) Well, I also want to know why you refer to a technological device that supposedly transports someone from one density to another, as a 'Trans Dimensional Atomic Remolecularizer'?

A: In order to reconstruct 3rd density into 4th density physical, other dimensions must be utilized in the process. Remember, we are talking about exact duplicates which are merged.

Q: (L) But, a little while ago you said there was a single dimension and many universes, and now you are saying utilizing another dimension, so the terminology is getting to be a little bit confusing... (T) It is like a program loading onto a computer. Some programs just load straight in. Others need to create a space on the hard drive to put files that they need to LOAD the program, but are not PART of the program, and when it is finished loading, it erases all the "loading instructions." The hard drive is still the hard drive, but for a time, the program used a sector of the hard drive, and created a temporary dimension, let's say. (L) Is this what we are looking at here?

A: Close. And remember, we said "true" dimension!

Q: (L) So, it is like one hard drive, many programs, loading instructions for new programs that are then erased, etc. If there is one "true dimension", and infinite universes within it, does one particular universe exist, of and by itself, at any given time, until it is merged into a new one, or **is there within this one true dimension, multiple universes as real as ours is, to which we could go, and could be there alongside ours, so to speak?**

A: Yes to the latter.

Q: (L) And, can infinite numbers of "dimensions" exist within each level of density, even if temporary?

A: Yes. If you want to go back and change "history," either for individuals or for universal perception, you must first create an alternate universe to do it. Your 4th density STS "friends" have been doing this a lot.

Q: (L) If you, being a general term, create an alternate universe, does the former one continue to exist, or does the former one merge into the new one?

A: Both.

Q: (L) If the former one continues to exist, does it exist and evolve on its own, disassociated with the second one, or this offshoot?

A: Clarify.

Q: (T) The universe you are in: you are going along and say, "I think I will create a new Universe". You do it, and move to it, and you bring your universe with you. That is the merging of realities. But, when you move to the new universe, you are no longer in the original one, which continues along on its own. The pattern of the old universe, you bring **into** the new one, and when you become part of the new universe you have just created, you are no longer part of the old one you just left which just goes along with everybody else there, only without you. Is this possible?

A: Sort of... remember, one can create all ranges of types of alternate possibilities.

Q: (L) So you could create a new universe with a new "past", even?

A: Yes.

Q: (L) So, in that way, both actually occur and you can change the whole thing?

A: When merged, the former never existed.

Q: (T) Not for the person creating the new universe, but the former will continue for everybody else.

A: Close.

Q: (L) So, for the person creating a new universe, the former never existed, but the other beings who are satisfied with that old universe, and "go" with it, are still continuing along as though...

A: Your 3rd density mind restrictions limit the scope of your comprehension in this area.

Q: (L) If you decide you don't like your present universe, and you work like crazy to learn how to create a new one, and you do it, do you, essentially, forget that you did this? And why you did this? And forget the other universe?

A: If you wish.

Q: (L) So you can or you can't... (T) Going by what you just said: "an unhappy universe", exists maybe because you're perceiving the universe you are in as being unhappy because that is the way **you** are and **where you are** at, in terms of learning, and by creating a new universe, you are simply wishing to change the way the universe is around you, and really it's not the universe that has a problem, but you...

A: Off track. [So much for **that** version of "you create your own reality"!]

Q: (L) So, the universe you are in, is what it is, and you are in it for some reason... (T) You're in it to learn lessons... just to change the universe because you don't want to learn the lessons you've chosen to learn... (L) Or, you have learned them and thereby CAN change the universe... (T) When you learn, you just move on automatically, you don't have to change the universe. The universe will change for you.

A: Déjà vu comes to you compliments of 4th density STS.

Q: (L) Is déjà vu a result of some sensation of the universe having changed?

A: Or... some sensation of reality bridging.

Q: (L) What is reality bridging?

A: What does it sound like?

Q: (T) A bridge is something you put between two things...

A: You wish to limit, wait till 4th density, when the word will be obsolete!

Q: (L) That still doesn't help me to understand déjà vu as a "sensation of reality bridging". Is déjà vu because something comes into our reality from another?

A: One possibility.

Q: (T) Didn't we talk about this? That it is a bleed through from other dimensions... that when we think we have been someplace before, it is because in another dimension we have...

A: Yes.

Q: (L) If you are now in a particular universe that has been created and merged by 4th density STS, and there is still the old universe existing, and you feel a connection, or a bridging, because some alternate self is in that alternate universe, living through some experience... or a similar thing?

A: No limits of possibilities.

Q: (L) So it can be any and all of those things, and bridging realities of "past" and "future", as well. Is it possible to change the past within a discrete universe, or does every change imply a new or alternate universe?

A: Discrete does not get it.

Q: (L) Well, within a particular, selected one of the universes, can you go back in time, within that universe, change the past, and have it change everything forward, still within that selected universe, like a domino effect?

A: In such a case, yes.

Q: (L) But, you said that if you want to change the past, you have to create an alternate universe... (T) No, you asked about changing the past, and they said you have to create a temporary place to work from, a position from which you can manipulate the reality...

A: That is for specialized activities. What was described is not the same as an "alternate universe".

Q: (L) It is a temporary file that will go away when you are finished loading the program. And that is not creating an alternate universe, but rather a temporary dimension...

A: Close.

Q: (L) In our particular universe, what is the primary mode? Are we constantly shifting and merging universe to universe, or is our past being changed and reacting like the domino effect... at least in the past few years... (T) But, we wouldn't know if the past has been changed because we wouldn't see it...

A: Measurements are inadequate.

Q: (L) Is it that any and all possibilities will and do take place?

A: Closer.

Q: (L) Are the words "universe" and "dimension" synonymous?

A: Yes and no. For you, these are "gray" areas, and no matter how hard you try, until your perception shifts fundamentally, you ain't gonna get it!

Q: (L) Okay, there are 4 physical densities...

A: No, three.

Q: (L) Okay, there are 3 physical densities, and the 4th is...

A: One is variable. Three Ethereal.

Q: (L) Okay, three that are physical, three ethereal, and one in between that is both.

A: Close.

Q: (L) Is awareness the only thing that determines what density one exists in?

A: No. Awareness is the bond that unites the reality.

Q: (L) You have said that gravity is the binder of all reality.

A: Yes.

Q: And now you talk about perception bonding.

A: Yes. Now, try to picture how gravity is the binder of all reality!!!

Q: (L) If gravity is the binder, is gravity consciousness?

A: Not exactly. Did you know that there is no "right" or "left" in 4th density through 7th density? If you can picture this exactly, then you may be able to understand the responses to all the questions you are asking. If not, best "give it a rest". Because it will only be productive learning when you ponder and reflect/review "later".

Regarding the three worlds, "divine, human and elemental", or, as the Cassiopaeans put it: [The] soul has three bodies of existence "thought center, spirit center, and physical center", we look again at the tree and note that each of the lateral axes has three positions: 6th density, 4th density, and 3rd density. In other words, our physical third density body is directly connected to our "spirit center" at 4th density, which emerges from the 6th density *Thought* center, which is the level of the Names of God.

However, in keeping with our "mirror image" of the Cosmic tree, we have designated the two axes as STS - or entropic - and STO - or creative. On the STS axis, beings that "graduate" become more and more "encapsulated" until, at 5th density, they exist completely in entropic thought with no activity whatsoever. At some point, these contractile energies "gain sufficient weight" to "graduate" to 6th density, at which point, in contact with All Knowledge, they perceive their true function which is to "regenerate at level One as primal atoms". They become "matter". This occurs at the same "instant" that STO energies have "gained weight" on an opposing axis, and rise to Union with the One. In short, a constant cycling.

Q: (T) Now, another force in what we term as the past, defeated you and used the power of the light in order to alter us in different ways, is this correct?

A: Yes. Now understand this: It is all part of natural grand cycle.

Q: (L) You say it is a natural thing or part of a natural grand cycle. Is this natural grand cycle just part of the interaction between light and darkness, which just simply must be?

A: Yes. We are at "front line" of universe's natural system of balance. That is where one rises to before reaching total union of "The One". 6th level.

Q: (T) Now, the battle you had with the other side...

A: Are having.

Q: (T) This battle goes on... do you have the light power back?

A: Never lost it, you did.

Q: (T) Okay, I guess that for us the Lizzies are the main force even though they have others on their side...

A: Yes.

Q: (T) They took our light, not yours?

A: Not against you. Currently in union with you.

Q: (T) So we are but one battle in the universe in an overall, ongoing struggle?

A: Yes. Balance is natural. Remember, it's all just lessons in the grand cycle.

Q: (T) When we put out energy as positive or negative energy, there are beings on other levels that feed on this energy. Is this true?

A: Yes.

Q: (T) Okay, and you said that the Lizzies feed on the negative energy?

A: Yes.

Q: (T) Who feeds on the positive energy?

A: You do.

Q: (T) How do we feed on the positive energy?

A: Progression toward union with the one, i.e. level 7.

Q: (L) In other words, you fuel your own generator instead of fueling someone else's. (T) You are at level 6, what do you feed on?

A: You have the wrong concept. We give to others and receive from others of the STO. We feed each other.

Q: (L) So, by feeding each other you move forward and grow but those of the STS path do not feed each other so must feed off of others. (T) Now, you are talking to us now. This is considered STO?

A: Yes.

Q: (T) We are providing energy for the channel also, does that provide you with energy?

A: No.

Q: (L) What do you want from us?

A: We don't want when pure STO. We came because YOU wanted. But that is STS until you share with others. [...]

Q: (B) What is the purpose of this contact?

A: To help you to learn, thus gain knowledge, thus gain protection, thus progress.

Q: (B) What do the Cassiopaeans gain from this contact?

A: By helping you, we are moving toward fulfilling of our destiny of union with you and all else, thus completing the Grand cycle.

Q: (B) Is this the only probability open to you or is this the best probability open to you?

A: Both.

Q: (B) Are you a great distance from us in light years?

A: Distance is a 3rd density idea.

Q: (B) Light years is 3rd density?

A: Yes.

Q: (B) What do you mean by traveling on the wave?

A: Traveling on thoughts.

Q: (L) Whose thoughts are they?

A: Thoughts unify all reality in existence and are all shared.

Q: (S) You travel on a wave of energy created by all thought forms?

A: Thought forms are all that exists!

Q: (B) Have those that are STS acknowledged that those that are STO are going to win in this race or conflict?

A: No, absolutely not! In fact, the STS cannot conceive of "losing" but instinctively feel pressure building upon them, that is the reason for the impending turmoil.[390]

Q: (B) What happens to them when they lose, does this mean that they are degaussed, or does that mean that they have to go back and do the whole evolutionary process all over again on the other polarity?

A: Latter.

Q: (B) So, there is a nexus point coming up?

A: Close. When we said "close" we meant concept was "close" to reality. Not close in terms of time or distance.

Q: (B) At that point do they experience the pain that they have caused?

A: No, that is what happens on 5th level only.

When considering "thought centers", a particular remark of the Cassiopaeans may give us another clue for our quest:

"Remember, most all power necessary for altering reality and physicality is contained within the belief center of the mind. This is something you will understand more closely when you reach 4th density reality where physicality is no longer a prison, but is instead, your home, for you to alter as you please. In your current state, you have the misinterpretation of believing that reality is finite and therein lies your difficulty with finite physical existence. We are surprised that you are still not able to completely grasp this concept." [Cassiopaeans, 08-12-95]

This suggests to us that the way to "change our reality" is to access something called a "thought center" or "belief" center. The only problem is, it seems that by "aligning" ourselves with the 4th density Service to Self reality, we have also come under the domination of the STS "thought center" or "control center". Let's have a look at some of the references to Thought Centers to determine if we can sort out the matter:

Q: (L) Who created the Lizzies?

A: Ormethion.

Q: (L) And who is this individual?

A: Thought center.

Q: (L) Located where?

A: Everywhere.

Q: (L) Can you give us a little more of a clue?

A: Another sector of reality.

Q: (L) Is this a sentient, self-aware being that created the Lizzies?

---

[390] Note that this session, predicting world conditions following 9-11, was dated January 11, 1995.

A: Yes and no.

Q: (L) And who created this Ormethion?

A: Not being. Thought center.

One thing we notice is that "Thought Centers" are slightly different from "Unified Thought Forms" that are identified as Transient Passengers. This is another clue that our Tree of Life model is set up correctly, since the *Unified* thought forms would exist at the 6th density level of knowledge, which contains the "thought" of STS for balance, but no STS Unified Thought "beings", so to say. But, the Thought Center realm is, apparently, a 6th density level of being. The difference is easily identified by looking at the tree. The 6th density Thought Center for STS does *not* Transit all densities and realities - it is restricted to the STS realm. The same is true for the purely STO Thought Center level - it is restricted to the STO realm. However, the 6th density Unified Consciousness level is located on the central, vertical axis as the Logoic "offspring" of 7th density.

Q: (L) Where does gravity emanate from?

A: Thought center.

Q: (L) You have mentioned thought centers on many occasions. Is there more than one?

A: All are one and all.

Q: (L) If you have a thought center, how do thought centers relate to 7th density, the One?

A: Exactly!

Q: (L) Are thought centers 7th density?

A: All is.

Q: (L) All is thought centers?

A: No. All is 7th density. We have told you before that gravity is the foundational force of absolutely everything!!! This means at all density levels, all dimensions... It is the "stuff" of all existence. Without it, nothing would exist. Your thoughts are based in gravity, too!!

Looking at this from a slightly different angle, there is the incident that is included in a chapter of my book *The Wave*. The session was one in which a guest had brought an "aura camera" and a couple of strange photos resulted. In the following excerpt, "AM" is the guest with the camera.

Q: (AM) Take a deep breath and hold... [aura photo of L is taken]

We waited a few minutes for the photo to develop and when it did, it was totally unlike the "aura photos" taken of all the other participants at this session. [See Plate 3.] Since the camera is essentially taking a photo and superimposing another image on it, it should at least show the physical outlines of the subject. It didn't.

Q: (L) [looking at aura photo of self] This is very strange, guys. How come I am not in this picture and F shows up in his? Why have I physically disappeared?

A: Learning builds spiritual growth, and awareness "solidifies" knowledge.

Q: (L) Okay, guys, smile for the camera! [Aura photo of board is taken with L's and F's fingers on planchette.] (L) Okay, but that does not explain why I disappeared.

A: Because the energy field enclosure was unifying you with the conduit, as is usual during channeling sessions between 3rd and 6th density level communications.

Q: [Photo of board develops, and geometric figure appears to sounds of amazement from group] (L) What is this geometric figure?

A: Was a visual representation of the conduit, indeed!!! The reason for such clear luminescence is that thought centers were clear and open in you at the moment of the photograph. In other words, there was an imbalance of energy coming from 6th density transmission point. So, what you are viewing is 100 per cent pure light energy of uncorrupted knowledge transmitted through you. This has never been seen in 3rd density ever before. You do not completely realize the ramifications of this yet, but you will. We have made history here tonight folks!!!!!

In Plate 3, you can see my hand at the right and F***'s hand at the left with our fingers resting lightly on the little plastic planchette.

I began writing the Wave Series and other articles as a way of collecting excerpts together in general subjects. As I published them, more and more readers asked questions. In my attempts to *give* answers to them, as the Cassiopaeans had given to me, I found that a truly extraordinary thing began to happen.

The Cassiopaean Experiment had resulted in transmissions from myself "in the future", and I realized that by doing the suggested research, by digging for the answers based on the clues given me, I was *becoming* myself in the future - a cosmic self. I began to see what I had been trying to convey to myself from this superconscious state. The years of experimental work had created a new circuit wherein it was possible to simply ask a question in my mind about the subject at hand, and the answer would flow through my fingers onto the keyboard. I was often as amazed at what came out as anyone.

I asked the C's about it in the September 23rd, 2000 session, and here was what they said:

Q: I have to say that the writing of this [Wave] series has been one of the most educational projects I have ever undertaken. Because, in the writing, I have had to comb through the transcripts and have had to explain it to other people and before I can do that, I have to explain it to myself. It has become a profound mind expansion thing...

A: Good.

Q: It's almost as much fun to be learning the things I am having to assemble as if I were reading it. And I'm the one writing it. It's really quite amazing.

A: In part you are [writing].

I finally understood what the Cassiopaeans meant when they said:

Q: (L) Al-Arabi describes unified thought forms as being the 'names of God'. His explication seems to be so identical to things you tell us that I wonder...

A: We are all the names of God. Remember, this is a conduit. This means that both termination/origination points are of equal value, importance.

So it seems that, by this time, I was truly merging with "Myself in the Future", and I had direct access to this awareness through my writing, showing me how to assemble and edit the material together after I had made such a mess of it in the original question and answer phase. It was as though the long period of working with the board had developed a circuit that bypassed my conscious mind and worked directly through my hands.

The idea of the "Names of God" as explicated by Ibn Al'Arabi also assists us in understanding what the Cassiopaens meant when they said, "We are *where* we are".

Certainly, this process of working with the material creatively has come under a great deal of attack from those who would like to "deify" the Cassiopaeans and declare that the material "belongs to humanity", and that I have no right to research it, examine it, correct it, or otherwise refine it according to the principles of alchemy. I find that attitude to be quite disturbing.

In any event, this discussion indicates to us, perhaps, something of a foretaste of the effect of the wave upon mankind - or at least portions of mankind. Perhaps these experiences give us an inkling of what 4th density might be like?

I can verify that there were many physical experiences that I passed through in my interaction with the Cassiopaeans. I have alternately burned and shivered many times as a consequence of certain meditative exercises, not to mention participation in the channeling process. And of course, there were numerous "visionary" states that included bi-location.

The important thing to note is that initiation denotes a "change from one situation to another", and is described as "self transmutation". I suspect that The Wave is an energy source that will interact with every individual according to his or her frequency resonance. To some, it may indeed be the End of the World. But for others...

> "Meantime, the world in which we exist has other aims. But it will pass away,
> burned up in the fire of its hot passions: and from its ashes will spring a new and
> younger world, full of fresh hope, with the light of morning in its eyes." Bertrand
> Russell

This suggests that I was in a state of total "non-anticipation" at the moment of the photograph, which allowed a sort of "zero-point energy" function to activate in a psychic way. But, more importantly, it suggests the idea that we are connected via some sort of "conduit" to these archetypal Thought Centers as depicted in our Tree of Life image.

Another remark about Thought Centers demonstrates again that our Tree of Life figure is going to take us somewhere:

> First of all, confusion abounds here due to incorrect interpretations of the last
> subject discussed. Dimensions are not densities!!!! Dimensions are strictly the result
> of the universal consciousness as manifested in the imagination sector of thought.
> *Density means level of development* as measured in terms of closeness to union with
> the one...

We might think, then, that the lateral axes represent dimensions resulting from various thought centers which are infinite even if they do fall under the general "categories" of STS-Entropy and STO-Creation or the Wrathful and Beautiful Names of God.

In trying to understand the relationships of our given position at the 3rd density level to the vertical lateral axes, or the densities 3, 4, and 6, to which we are connected in a direct way, we might look at this bit of information as a clue:

Q: (A) Which part of a human extends into 4th density?

A: That which is effected by pituitary gland.

Q: (L) And what is that?

A: Psychic.

Q: (A) Are there some particular DNA sequences that facilitate transmission between densities?

A: Addition of strands.

Q: (L) How do you get added strands?

A: You don't get; you receive.

Q: (L) Where are they received from?

A: Interaction with upcoming wave, if vibration is aligned.

Q: (L) How do you know if this is happening?

A: Psycho-physiological changes manifest.

Q: (A) When you speak of an upcoming wave, it is a wave of what?

A: Think of it as a wave of reflection from the beginning and end point.

Q: (A) But what vibrates? Energy? Aether?

A: Energy and aether are directly symbiotic. "Aether" is Terran material science's attempt to address ether. The trouble is, there is simply no way to physicalize a plane of existence, which is composed entirely of consciousness. It is the union of perfect balance between the two "states" or planes that is the foundation and essence of all creation/reality. You cannot have one without the other!

Q: (L) When you say the two states or planes, you are saying the physical state and the state of consciousness...

A: Yes.

Q: (L) And you can't have one without the other. And the state of consciousness and the state of material existence are so completely connected, that both are infinite? One cannot exist without the other...

A: Yes, connected, intertwined, bonded... Merged.

Q: (A) When this aether-energy-matter vibrates, then in which dimension does it do this?

A: The densities 3 and 4 at transition junction.

Q: (A) If not in linear time, then in what?

A: Cyclical "time".

Q: (A) What measures the distance between one crest and another?

A: Ending/beginning of cycle.

Q: (A) Is DNA acting as a superconductor?

A: Yes!!! But variably.

Q: (A) I am trying to understand the universe in terms of a triad: matter - geometry - information. Is it the right idea?

A: If one thinks of matter as "living" rather than "dead". And now, when you merge densities, or traverse densities, what you have is the merging of physical reality and ethereal reality, which involves thought form versus physicality. When you can merge those perfectly, what you realize then, is that the reason there is no beginning and no end is merely because there is no need for you to contemplate a beginning or an end after you have completed your development. When you are at union with the One at Seventh density, that is when you have accomplished this and then there is no longer any need for difference between physical and ethereal forms.

This brings us back, in a curious way, to the study of Nature - all of Creation - as a means of drawing closer in alignment with the central, vertical axis.

By invigorating the Organs the Soul uses for communicating with exterior objects, the Soul must a acquire greater powers not only for conception but also for retention, and therefore if we wish to obtain still more knowledge, the organs and secret springs of physical life must be wonderfully strengthened and invigorated.

The pituitary connection was mentioned. It would take too long to describe the function of this gland and the numerous hormones it produces, but let me suggest that the reader do some research on their own in order to discover exactly how, when properly "connected", the pituitary may, indeed, be the gland that can initiate the processes of physical transmutation.

Cassiopaeans: "Stones were once utilized to provide for all needs, as the energies transmitted connected directly with the pituitary gland to connect spiritual realities with the material realms of 3rd and 4th densities. So you see, the "stone" was viewed as Matriarchal indeed!"

And the alchemists say:

The study and contemplation of the metaphorical "Philosopher's Stone" along with the chemical work was a necessary component to elevate the mind and prepare the soul for transmutation.

The Cassiopaeans relate the alchemical transmutation to 4th density:

Q: (L) Were the beings involved in this type of activity 3rd density, 4th density or bi-density?

A: Originally 4th when home was in other locators.

Q: (L) Could it be said that the pituitary gland itself is the body's own "mother stone"?

A: If you prefer.

Q: (J) What exactly is the function of the pituitary gland in your references to Stonehenge?

A: This gland is your uplink.

Q: (L) Is it possible that the pituitary can be stimulated by external sources such as radio waves, waves from a supernova, or other frequencies in the environment?

A: Yes and experiments have ensued.

Q: (L) Would it be beneficial for us to experiment with such things?

A: Not wise. You could fry yourself in your zeal.

Regarding the strictly physical aspects of our being, we look again at our Tree of Life and note specifically the arrangement of third, 4th and 6th densities on the lateral axes. The third density position is directly connected with 5th density contemplation zone, as are all the other densities. The Cassiopaeans once remarked about the chakras that:

A: First of all, "chakras" are a little understood and nonproven phenomenon. Now, it just so happens they do exist, but in different form than reported by many in the so-called "psychic" community.

Q: (L) What, exactly, is a chakra?

A: An energy field that merges density one, two, three or four with five. You are all connected with level five when you are on a short wave cycle. Chakras are the connection with physical imprint locator.

***

Q: (A) Now, I was reading in the transcripts that sleep is necessary for human beings because it was a period of rest and recharging. You also said that the SOUL rests while the body is sleeping. So, the question is: what source of energy is tapped to recharge both the body and the soul?

A: The question needs to be separated. What happens to a souled individual is different from an organic portal unit.

Q: (L) I guess that means that the life force energy that is embodied in Organic Portals is something like the soul pool that is theorized to exist for flora and fauna. This would, of course, explain the striking and inexplicable similarity of psychopaths, that is so well defined that they only differ from one another in the way that different species of trees are different in the overall class of Tree-ness. So, if they don't have souls, where does the energy come from that recharges Organic Portals?

A: The pool you have described.

Q: Does the recharging of the souled being come from a similar pool, only maybe the "human" pool?

A: No - it recharges from the so-called sexual center which is a higher center of creative energy. During sleep, the emotional center, not being blocked by the lower intellectual cener and the moving center, transduces the energy from the sexual center. It is also the time during which the higher emotional and intellectual centers can rest from the "drain" of the lower centers' interaction with those pesky organic portals so much loved by the lower centers. This respite alone is sufficient to make a difference. But, more than that, the energy of the sexual center is also more available to the other higher centers.

Q: (L) Well, the next logical question was: where does the so-called "sexual center" get ITS energy?

A: The sexual center is in direct contact with 7th density in its "feminine" creative thought of "Thou, I Love". The "outbreath" of "God" in the relief of constriction. Pulsation. Unstable Gravity Waves.

Q: Do the "enters" as described by Mouravieff relate at all to the idea of "chakras"?

A: Quite closely. In an individual of the organic variety, the so-called higher chakras are "produced in effect" by stealing that energy from souled beings. This is what gives them the ability to emulate souled beings. The souled being is, in effect, perceiving a mirror of their own soul when they ascribe "soul qualities" to such beings.

Q: Is this a correspondence that starts at the basal chakra which relates to the sexual center as described by Mouravieff?

A: No. The "sexual center" corresponds to the solar plexus.

Lower moving center - basal chakra
Lower emotional - sexual chakra
Lower intellectual - throat chakra
Higher emotional - heart chakra
Higher intellectual - crown chakra

Q: (L) What about the so-called seventh, or "third eye" chakra?

A: Seer. The union of the heart and intellectual higher centers.

[Laura's note: This would "close the circuit" in the "shepherd's crook" configuration and certainly relates to the pituitary.]

Q: (V) What about the many ideas about 12 chakras, and so forth, that are currently being taught by many new age sources?

A: There are no such. This is a corrupted conceptualization based on the false belief that the activation of the physical endocrine system is the same as the creation and fusion of the magnetic center. The higher centers are only "seated" by being "magnetized". And this more or less "External" condition [location of the higher centers] has been perceived by some individuals and later joined to the perceived "seating" locations, in potential. This has led to "cross conceptualization" based on assumption!

Q: Are the levels of initiation and levels of the staircase as presented by Mouravieff fairly accurate?

A: Yes, but different levels accessed in other so-called lives can relieve the intensity of some levels in "another" life.

Q: (L) So work on the self in different incarnations - assuming one is not an organic portal - can be cumulative? You can pick up where you left off if you screw up?

A: Yes. To some extent.

Getting back to our hypothesis about Archetypes and/or Names of God, let me propose that 4th density is a realm where the Archetypes are "embodied" in Group souls. These group souls then have "extensions" of themselves into the third density reality in the same way a hand has five fingers. Only in these "projections", each finger is a different lifetime of an individual soul, which lifetimes are *not* limited to sequential experience; and we cannot limit the number of hands or fingers! In this sense, it could be said that 3rd density is a "projection" of 6th density through the "lens" of 4th density.

Q: (D) When 4th density beings communicate it's telepathic, right?

A: Yes.

Q: (D) Okay, since time doesn't exist, how do you communicate about happenings? If you're communicating telepathically on 4th density, and time doesn't exist, how do you communicate about events as one happens now, as opposed to later, and the next thing happens, and the next thing happens? (J) How is it sequential?

A: Translate.

Q: (D) Okay, let me explain what I mean. I mean, we talk about 1907 something happened...

A: That is how it is done.

Q: (T) You translate the experience?

A: From 4th density to 3rd density. And vice versa.

Q: (L) So, in other words, it's almost like making movies. So, in other words, if you're a 4th density being, everything is more or less happening, excuse the term happening, everything is simultaneous, and if you wish to discuss or communicate or have any focus upon any particular aspect of this unified dimension, then what you do is you kind of extract it out, project it into 3d density like a movie...

A: Close. But you will not understand fully until you get there.

Now, each of these archetypal "Qualities" or "Names" of God manifest on 4th density in "Archetypal Dramas". This relates us back to Mircea Eliade's concept of the Archetypal Gesture - *illud tempus* - from the beginning.

Every hero repeated the archetypal gesture, every war rehearsed the struggle between good and evil, every fresh social injustice was identified with the passion of a divine messenger, each new massacre repeated the glorious end of the martyrs. ... All religious acts are held to have been founded by gods, civilizing heroes, or mythical ancestors. ...Not only do rituals have their mythical models, but any human act whatever acquires effectiveness to the extent to which it exactly repeats an act performed at the beginning of time by a god, a hero, or an ancestor.[391]

This expresses the idea that the world in which we live is a "form", or reflection or "double" of another cosmic world that exists on a higher level. These were Celestial Archetypes.

Q: (L) Earlier Eva and I were talking on the phone about mythological figures possibly representing group souls. That is, on our level of 3rd density, groups of individuals who are separated by flesh, might be extensions of group souls at a higher level...

A: Whom does Zeus represent?

Q: (F) The father of the gods?

A: And the implication is...?

Q: (L) Does Zeus represent 7th density?

A: Or does Zeus represent the grasping for 7th density?

Q: (L) Are we saying grasping in ways that are not suitable?

A: No grasping is "not suitable".

---

[391] Eliade, *The Myth of the Eternal Return*, 1954; emphasis, mine

Q: (L) Okay. Are we all pieces of ... are there groups and groups and groups that are pieces of a larger whole, or larger wholes, and they can only graduate when they assemble?

A: More to the point would be that that makes the progress speed up for most of those involved in such a process.

Q: (C) Are we part of a group soul or group entity?

A: What do you think?

Q: (C) Yes.

A: And...

Q: (C) I think that we are part of a group soul... whatever that means, we have a purpose; I think we have a similar interest, and that is to discover the truth. And it is also to advance us.

A: And...

Q: (C) When one group advances, then it filters down to others...

A: How does it "filter down"?

Q: (C) Because I believe that all are connected.

A: How so?

Q: (L) I get it! The Zeus thing. The whole Zeus thing, the bearing of children, the moving out in all these various ways, manifestations or patterns as defined by the 'children of the gods' through all the various levels, so that it eventually all comes back around to 7th density.

A: And what does it mean when it "comes back around"?

Q: (L) Union with the One. And it all just keeps going around and around.

A: And C___ says...

Q: (C) If we are patterned after the myths of Zeus, and we have gone forth, and there are lots of smatterings of fragments upon the earth having many experiences, and as we grow and advance, we come to the truth and the full meaning, we merge back together again with all of the wisdom of all of these experiences.

A: Yes, but is not just the "Earth".

Q: (C) They are in the same process.

A: Yes.

Q: (C) Do they have different myths?

A: They have different everything... But, in the final analysis, it is really just the same!

Q: (C) Then I would say that when everyone graduates from their finite, physical existence, then they occupy the same space at a different vibration, and go onto other lessons and experiences and advances that I cannot conceive of at the moment.

A: But what is "the moment"?

Q: (C) The moment? I haven't thought that far ahead yet!

A: Or have you, but you simply do not perceive it as such?

Q: (C) Probably so. How many people are in this particular group that Laura and I are in, for the purpose of this work?

A: Up to you to discover.

Q: (C) Well, I thought I'd give it a shot! Thinking is electrical. Does a person leave an electrical echo and can certain combinations produce harmony which is cumulative and exponential, thereby certain groups thinking can produce more than others, or individually?

A: Close. Now, Suggestion: Combine frequencies to witness the development of a directed wave effect; packs a potent "punch".

Q: (LC) I'm really curious. I feel like all of us here have been drawn together for a reason. We had a hell of a time getting here, every one of us, but we did, and I'm just wondering what is this all about? Why did all of us feel so drawn that we just HAD to be here?

A: You are not wondering so much as you are seeking confirmation.

Q: (LC) I don't know. I just feel something powerful.

A: Every one here thinks on more than one level. This already puts everyone into a different category than the status quo. You all have quite well developed senses, a more difficult task is learning to trust the messages. Remember, you all have received negative programming at the third density level, which is designed to derail your higher psychic awareness. You by now know that this is false programming, but we realize that **the subconscious centers are more difficult for you to overcome.** Patience will pay off for you big time!!!

Q: (P) This is my feeling about the whole thing: us coming together, the energy created by each of us being in each other's presence is a key; it's unlocking something that we agreed to come together at this time, though it may not be apparent now, it's going to be. That's the way I have felt about this whole thing. (LC) Okay, another question, and this is a kind of selfish one I am thinking about...

A: Wait a minute, remember, your plane of existence is STS by its very nature and that is okay, because you're all where you are for a reason... Now L__, fire away and be just as selfish as you please, dear. [Laughter]

Q: (LC) Well, if that's the case! I want to ask about past life relations between us. I'm sure there is. Are there any specific past life connections between any of the women in this room?

A: Before we answer that, we wish to hear from you what you perceive a past life circumstance to be. How do you perceive the reincarnation process to be?

Q: (LC) I perceive it as you come back with people you choose to come back with, and that you choose people that you are karmically connected to. (I) I see it a little bit differently than that...

A: Aha! We have a variance!

Q: (I) I think that when we die and go to 5th density, that we make pacts with people in each incarnation, so when you come back, it is coming back to fulfill that pact. (LC) Yes, that is the way my line of thinking is going. But, when they asked that question, I was thinking that you have people you come back with because of closeness. Somebody may be your mother in one life, and there is a love bond, and then there are other people that you come back with because you have to resolve something to let go of that person rather than to get closer.

A: This is partially correct. But, there is more to it than this. For example, one can incarnate on various planes of existence, not just the one you perceive currently. And, one may actually reincarnate on more than one plane concurrently, if one is advanced enough to do this.

Q: (L) Are you suggesting that that we are all part of the same soul unit here?

A: Yes, we are! To an extent, but you may not yet understand what exactly a "soul unit" is in that sense. And of course, there is more than one sense for this as well. The "trick" that 3rd density STS life forms will learn, either prior to transition to 4th density, or at the exact juncture, is to think in absolutely limitless terms. The first and most solid step in this process is to not anticipate at all. This is most difficult for you. We understand this, but this as also why we keep reiterating this point. For example, imagine if one of your past lives is also a future life?

Q: (P) Now, I just want to say that I think that we have all of us here traveled back in time to change the way things are now. We inserted ourselves into this time period to wake up and see what is really happening. This is 3rd density thinking, I know, but it is the only way I can describe it. We looked back on the way things happened, the way the world is now, and we have come back to change things. We have come from the future, to wake up now, because we didn't wake up before. Because the world is going in this direction, and *something* had to be done. That's what I see. Not just that, things happen to keep us from waking up period! We've all been bombarded with stuff all our lives.

A: That is surprisingly close to the truth. Now just a moment... reflect please.

Q: (L) P___ was saying that we have come back from the future and inserted ourselves into this timeline...

A: Yes. That is close to being totally correct!

Q: (L) In terms of reincarnation, which we were talking about a few minutes before that, we are possibly incarnations of ourselves incarnated at different levels. This just happens to be one of the levels of reality that we are occupying, but there are other selves at other levels thinking and doing other level stuff, and these other levels are perceived by us as the future...

A: Maybe for some of you, but let us not get ahead of ourselves.

Q: (P) The C's say that they are US in the future. So, we, being THEM in the future, some of who they are in the future, have come back as us, to do what we are doing, to undo what is happening on Earth...

A: Close, but more complex than that. It would be difficult for you to completely understand at this point, but let us just say that you are close. You should reflect upon all that is in the reflection!

Q: (L) What is the reason for the use of the term "reflection"?

A: "Alice through the looking glass."

Q: (L) When she went through the mirror, she was in an alternate reality. (I) Are we in an alternate reality?

A: Yup. But then again, are not all realities "alternate"?

Q: (P) I think we are creating a possibility that would not have existed if we had NOT come together here.

A: Yes, but that is generally true in most similar circumstances. The question is the degree to which there is significance.

We encounter in myths the idea that man only repeats the acts of the gods; his calendar commemorates, in the period of a year or other longer cycles, all the cosmogonic phases which took place in the beginning or which take place repeatedly at another level of reality.

Myths are only a much later formulation of an archaic content that presuppose an absolute reality, or levels of reality that are extrahuman. If we begin to think that our reality is but a sort of slide show projected from a hyperdimensional realm, we have to begin to think about the archetypal dramas themselves. If we come to the idea that we are extensions of our higher selves, fulfilling the purposes of the great Cosmic Dramas, we come up against a couple of important concepts.

The first of these concepts is Free Will.

Going back to what the Shaykh Ibn al-'Arabi had to say about it:

> You should know that the divine call includes believer and unbeliever, obedient and disobedient... This call derives only from the divine names.

> One divine name calls to someone who is governed by the property of a second divine name when it knows that the term of the second name's property within the person has come to an end.

> Then this name which calls to him takes over. So it continues in this world and the next.

> Hence everything other than God is called by a divine name to come to an engendered state to which that name seeks to attach it.

> If the object of the call responds, he is named "obedient" and becomes "felicitous".
> If he does not respond, he is named "disobedient" and becomes "wretched". [392]

This gives us a clue as to the true extent of our so-called Free Will. Basically, it amounts to the fact that we can identify *which* archetypal drama we are living and acknowledge it, witness it in our mind, and accelerate or extend the concluding of it. We accelerate by our "obedience" to the "call" or we extend it by our rejection and "disobedience". In the first case, the outcome can be felicitous if we are careful to "finish the drama" within the archetype, even if only symbolically (which is often the wisest choice in the event of being caught in a drama of great negative potential); and in the second case, we can refuse to acknowledge the drama, continue to struggle against it like a bug striking a window over and over again, and be wretched as a result.

Of course, the problem many people have is in understanding that they don't *have* to remember their past lives in order to "learn". The soul has a memory of its own.

---

[392] *Futuhat*, II 592.32

Q: (L) OK, let me ask this question. In talking about time, I would like to ask, in relation to time, what is memory? Some understanding of time refers to it as the 'now', the ever-present now. Well, a lot of people remember a lot of other 'nows', some people don't remember any 'nows' at all, and it seems like memory is almost like a reverse function of anticipation. Anticipation being almost like a memory of the 'future' and memory being like a reverse anticipation into the past. So, what I would like to know is if time is merely a 'now', what is memory?

A: Conscious and subconscious record of perceptions.

Q: (L) OK. If memory is subconscious or conscious recording of perceptions, when one accumulates a sufficient amount of memory, does one then become 'timeless'?

A: One is always timeless.

Q: (L) OK, but does one then become aware of one's timelessness?

A: In 4th density.

Q: (L) OK. Does an electron have a memory?

A: Electron is borrowed unit of 7th density.

Q: (L) All right, in the picture of the crop circle you designated as being 'Atomic Structure', there was the concentric circles and then these three things on the outside corners of the triangle, one being zigzag, one being plain and round, and the other one kind of like a wheel, it had like little divisions. Would the zig-zaggy one be the electron?

A: Not correct concept atomic structure unifies elemental atoms.

Q: (L) What is an elemental atom, as opposed to an ordinary atom?

A: Elemental defines singular body of structure. Within, as in: "element of". Electron is element of atomic structure.

Q: (L) Is there anything about an atom that holds memory?

A: Memory is subjective, atom is not.

Q: (L) Well, some atoms seem to be somewhat subjective.

A: No, it is your interpretation.

Q: If memory is conscious and subconscious record of perception, as you have stated, and there occurs a "reality merge", as you also described previously, some sort of time manipulation, does this automatically change individual perceptions?

A: Perceptions "leap" into place according to markers in the eternally present continuum.

Q: What are these markers?

A: Experiential breaks in the perceptual realm of continuance.

Q: Markers are experiential breaks. So, one experiences breaks and they become markers... perceptions leap into place... is this saying that, when there is a perception of a break, that some part of the psyche seeks to bridge this break by leaping into some sort of...

A: The definition of the previous responses will become clear for you only after some reflection, my dear!

Q: Okay, you said that memory is subjective and an atom is not. If memory is subjective, what you have just been describing means that each and every person has a slightly different perspective, even if they are involved with the same incident or the same time sequence.

A: Of course! That is the treasury of learning.

Q: Who is the treasurer?

A: The learner.

Q: But still, what you said still implies that an atom has an objective existence. Is this correct?

A: Yes.

Q: Would you please tell us what constitutes objectivity?

A: The effort on the part of the observer to leave prejudice "at the door".

Q: How does the effort on the part of the observer to leave prejudice at the door relate to the objective existence of an atom?

A: An atom, as with absolutely everything else, cannot exist without an observer.

Q: So, in the case of the objectivity of an atom, if the human observers are not objective, where is the observer who makes the atom objective, or **does the atom not exist if there is no observer?**

A: Yes to the latter comment.

Q: So there must be an observer. Must the observer be human?

A: The observer must be a consciousness.

Q: If you say that an atom has an objective existence, yet it only exists if it is perceived by a consciousness, then an atom does not have an objective existence, correct?

A: No.

Q: Okay, what is the distinction? You say that objectivity is the *attempt* on the part of the observer to leave prejudice at the door.

A: Without consciousness, there is neither objective nor subjective!!

Q: So the crux is the attempt to leave prejudice at the door in the same manner as one would be non-anticipatory in order to create?

A: Yes.

Q: Well, that is a *very* tricky... (A) Is consciousness objective?

A: Consciousness is objective, until it has the capacity to choose to be otherwise.

Q: What is the stimulus for the change, for the giving of the capacity to choose?

A: The introduction of prejudice.

Q: In a cosmic sense, cosmic consciousness, in the sense of The One Unified Consciousness, what is the stimulus there for the ability to choose?

A: When the journey has reached union with The One, all such lessons have been completed.

Q: But, that doesn't answer the question.

A: Yes, it does!

And this is where the study of nature comes in. There is a passage from Psalms about Nature as a source of knowledge:

The heavens declare the glory of God, and the firmament shows and proclaims His handiwork.

Day after day pours forth speech, and night after night shows forth knowledge.

There is no speech nor spoken word; their voice is not heard yet their voice goes out through all the earth, their sayings to the end of the world.[393]

The Alchemists tell us:

In order to respect the principle of hermetism adopted by the Tradition, we must understand that esoteric teachings are given in a sibylline form.

St Isaac the Syrian points out that: The Holy Scriptures say many things by using words in a different sense from their original meaning. Sometimes bodily attributes are applied to the soul, and conversely, attributes of the soul are applied to the body. The Scriptures do not make any distinction here. However, enlightened men understand.

This is the point at which we begin to understand our reality. The Celestial myths are the archaic representations of the Archetypes. In studying these stories and their characters we can have access to very deep knowledge about any human situation or drama in which we may find ourselves. We can also identify which character, or part, we are being activated to "play". Once we have identified the drama of the moment (which may extend over years or even an entire lifetime, or merely be a "mini-drama" of a few minutes, hours or days' duration), we can fully activate our participation *with some degree of control*.

By recognizing the play, by acknowledging our "part", we have formed a link between ourselves and the director, producer and writer of the production at the higher densities! We are psychically "linked" to them in a real and symbiotic way. And, by being linked, we can have access to a Free Will that is not ordinarily accessible.

Joseph Chilton Pearce was aware that there was something deeper and more involved in our reality than many suppose, and he called it the "Cosmic Egg". Well, he may have been more right about this than he ever suspected. If Thought Centers are Cosmic Eggs laid from 6th density into 4th density via 5th density, and hatched into 3rd density, then we have only one issue to deal with at *this* density, and that is *WHICH EGG IS OURS?*

More than that, if we don't like the present egg, can we "crack it", and get out?

Well, here we come up against the ever-present problem of the "Catch 22".

Q: (L) When we are talking about dimensional curtains, we are talking about divisions at the same level of density, is that correct?

A: Maybe.

---

[393] Psalm 19: 1-4, *Amplified*, Zondervan

Q: (L) Can dimensional curtains be between dimensions at the same level of density?

A: Yes.

Q: (L) Are dimensional curtains also something that occurs between levels of density?

A: Yes.

Q: (L) So, a dimensional curtain is a point at which some sort of change takes place... what causes this change?

A: Nature.

Q: (L) What defines this change?

A: Experience.

Q: (L) Is it in any way related to atomic or quantum physics or the movement of atoms?

A: Yes.

Q: (L) Okay. An atom is in 3rd density. What distinguishes it from an atom in 4th density?

A: Reality.

Q: (L) What distinguishes one realm from another?

A: Assumptions.

Q: (L) Okay, what you assume or expect is what you perceive about that atom depending upon which reality you are in, is that correct?

A: Close.

Q: (L) What determines your assumptions?

A: Experience. Every thing that exists is merely a lesson.

Q: (L) Okay, so once we have learned certain lessons, as in experience of certain things, then our assumptions change?

A: Yes.

Q: (L) Okay, is this wave that is coming our direction going to give us an experience that is going to change our assumptions?

A: Catch 22: One half is that you have to change your assumptions in order to experience the wave in a positive way. All is merely a lesson, and nothing, repeat nothing, more.

How do we get the experiences that will change our assumptions?

Well, let's look at our Tree of Life again. We notice that in both versions, the Cosmic and the Human mirror, the different levels of the different densities "recycle" through 5th density on the Central axis. There does exist a sort of "conduit" between the Centers, but these conduits do not have an "exchange point" on the Central axis that would facilitate a "shift" of Thought Centers or "assumptions". From this we can conjecture that it is somewhat difficult to "change polarity" without some sort of facilitator. This is why the way of the Monk, the Yogi and the Fakir are so difficult. They attempt to bridge the gap without a facilitator on the Central axis.

We notice that, on the Cosmic Tree, the position of Knowledge is a facilitator for the cycling of 6th density energies to move into Union with the one which is, in effect, an instantaneous (or timeless) to Being and Non-being which then initiates a new cycle of consciousness that regenerates as dense matter and consciousness that emerges bilaterally into the Beautiful Names and Wrathful Names of God to initiate the drama all over again.

When we look at the Human Tree of Life, which is the mirror image, we see that the position of Knowledge is now held by the genetic body, which is ON the Central axis. We then realize that *this* is our facilitator.

The genetic body is the control center for the physical body since it transduces the Central axis energies, so whichever Thought Center is dominant will control the physical experience. Not only that, but we can see another possibility - namely, that knowledge and genetics are *directly interactive*. At the 3rd density level, *genes* are the *Logos*!

> In the beginning was the Word, and the Word was with God, and the Word was
> God Himself. He was present originally with God. All things were made and came
> into existence through Him; and without Him was not even one thing made that has
> come into being.

Sounds like Cosmic Chromosomes! It is through our genetics that we have the potential of aligning with the Central vertical axis and "changing Thought Centers". And, just as 2nd density Nature is a reflection of 6th density Knowledge in the Cosmic Tree, so is our genetic code the 2nd density reflection of all that exists as potential within US as human beings.

It could even be said that *all* of nature exists within US.

Gurdjieff addressed the issues of this chapter as well, showing that the source of his information was very similar to the "Q source" of Alchemical teachings. This is evident in the answer he gave to Ouspensky when the latter asked, "Can it be said that man possesses immortality?", Gurdjieff replied:

> "Immortality is one of the qualities we ascribe to people without having a sufficient
> understanding of their meaning. Other qualities of this kind are 'individuality', in
> the sense of an inner unity, a 'permanent and unchangeable I', 'consciousness', and
> 'will'. All these qualities can belong to man, but this certainly does not mean that
> they do belong to him or belong to each and every one."

> "In order to understand what man is at the present time, that is, at the present level
> of development, it is necessary to imagine to a certain extent what he can be, that is,
> what he can attain. Only by understanding the correct sequence of development
> possible will people cease to ascribe to themselves what, at present, they do not
> possess, and what, perhaps, they can only acquire after great effort and great labor."

> "According to an ancient teaching, traces of which may be found in many systems,
> old and new, a man who has attained the full development possible for man, a man
> in the full sense of the word, consists of four bodies. These four bodies are
> composed of substances which gradually become finer and finer, mutually
> interpenetrate one another, and form four independent organisms, standing in a
> definite relationship to one another but capable of independent action."

Gurdjieff's idea was that it was possible for these four bodies to exist because the physical human body has such a complex organization that, under certain favorable conditions, a new and independent organism actually can develop and grow within it. This new system of organs of perception can afford a more convenient and responsive instrument for the activity of an awakened consciousness.

"The consciousness manifested in this new body is capable of governing it, and it has full power and full control over the physical body.

"In this second body, under certain conditions, a third body can grow, again having characteristics of its own. The consciousness manifested in this third body has full power and control over the first two bodies; and the third body possesses the possibility of acquiring knowledge inaccessible either to the first or to the second body.

"In the third body, under certain conditions, a fourth can grow, which differs as much from the third as the third differs from the second, and the second from the first. The consciousness manifested in the fourth body has full control over the first three bodies and itself.

"These four bodies are defined in different teachings in various ways. The first is the physical body, in Christian terminology the 'carnal' body; the second, in Christian terminology, is the 'natural' body; the third is the 'spiritual' body; and the fourth, in the terminology of esoteric Christianity, is the 'divine body'. In theosophical terminology the first is the 'physical' body, the second is the 'astral', the third is the 'mental', and the fourth the 'causal'.

"In the terminology of certain Eastern teachings the first body is the 'carriage', (the body), the second is the 'horse' (feelings, desires), the third the 'driver' (mind), and the fourth the 'master' (I, consciousness, will).

"Such comparisons and parallels may be found in most systems and teachings which recognize something more in man than the physical body. But almost all these teachings, while repeating in a more or less familiar form the definitions and divisions of the ancient teaching, have forgotten or omitted its most important feature, which is: that man is not born with the finer bodies. They can only be artificially cultivated in him, provided favorable conditions both internal and external are present.

"The 'astral body' is not an indispensable implement for man. It is a great luxury which only a few can afford. A man can live quite well without an 'astral body'. His physical body possesses all the functions necessary for life. *A man without 'astral body' may even produce the impression of being a very intellectual or even spiritual man, and may deceive not only others but also himself.*

"When the third body has been formed and has acquired all the properties, powers, and knowledge possible for it, there remains the problem of fixing this knowledge and these powers. Because, having been imparted to it by influences of a certain kind, they may be taken away by these same influences or by others. By means of a special kind of work for all three bodies the acquired properties may be made the permanent and inalienable possession of the third body."

"The process of fixing these acquired properties corresponds to the process of the formation of the fourth body."

"And only the man who possesses four fully developed bodies can be called a 'man' in the full sense of the word. This man possesses many properties which ordinary man does not possess. One of these properties is immortality. All religions and all ancient teachings contain the idea that, by acquiring the fourth body, man acquires immortality; and they all contain indications of the ways to acquire the fourth body, that is, immortality."[394]

In a general sense, to almost everyone, including yours truly, the very idea of time traveling, mind marauding, hyperdimensional beings with full powers to create and maintain a reality of illusion and restriction in which we are confined like sheep, waiting daily to see which of our number will be "taken" for their wool, skins, or flesh, is so horrifying a concept that accepting it as a real possibility, is tantamount to being stripped of all hopes, dreams and comfort.

Like many of you, I began this work full of frustration with teachings that don't work or don't make sense when compared with honest observation of reality and experience. There was such a labyrinth of contradictions everywhere I searched, and I *knew* it was necessary to go beyond everything hitherto known or tried. I did have the idea that this knowledge had been available in ancient times, judging by the evidence of the megaliths and other incomprehensible structures all over the globe, but whether or not it would be possible to rediscover this path was uncertain.

It was *very* clear that there was a serious discrepancy between the observable reality and some "deeper reality" from which, presumably, ours derives something of its form and structure, but I knew there was something that separated "us" from "them". And again, when searching for answers, it always ended in a maze of insupportable assumptions and irreconcilable facts. Yes, to all of you who have written to ask me if I have checked "this" source or "that" source, it is very likely I have, and more. And I repeat, when you read *all* of them, you find, as Blaise Pascal said:

> "I reject equally the religion of Mahomet, of the Chinese, of the Romans, and of the Egyptians, for this simple reason that since one has no greater marks of truth than another, my reason cannot be disposed to receive any one in preference to the rest." [*Pensees*, Chapter XI]

You can add a hundred other "sources" to Pascal's list on my behalf. They all end in a maze of assumptions and irreconcilable "facts".

But when the Cassiopaeans began to communicate, to say things that *did* explain the problems I was finding in science, religions and philosophies, and those things they told us were *not* part of my expectations, I became furious and railed at such a bleak picture of our existence.

I had already gone through some of this process in earlier years while reading Gurdjieff and Ouspensky, but I found that what the Cassiopaeans were saying was far more dispiriting than I was prepared to receive.

---

[394] Gurdjieff, quoted by Ouspensky, *In Search of the Miraculous*, op. cit.

I rejected ideas that suggested our "fairy tale" beliefs just *might* be imposed on us to keep us asleep and unaware because I didn't like them either! As time went by and evidence from other sources mounted, I raged at lessons that drove home these points in my personal life; and I have wept oceans for the loss of my innocence. So, believe me when I say to those of you who write to me struggling to grasp this, trying to reason and rationalize some way to hang on to the old, false belief systems - I *do* understand!

But, when all is said and done, I think I wept even more for all the years wasted in stupidity and blindness. After a time, I realized that we are only stupid and blind exactly as long as we *need* to be stupid and blind, and not one second longer. I am enormously grateful for all those experiences because they *did* teach me in a very deep way.

Now, a curious thing about the teachings of both Gurdjieff and Castaneda, both of which claim that man is "food" for something "other", is the lack of really specific information about this "other". Yes, Castaneda goes further than Gurdjieff in telling us some of the history of the "flyer", or the "predator", but it is still somewhat vague and amorphous.

We have often speculated as to whether Gurdjieff knew the "truth" the way the Cassiopaeans have explicated it and just simply could not bring himself to tell anyone; or if he *did* tell some of his students, was this something that only those on the "inside" knew, and held back?

Ark met with Henri Tracol, one of Gurdjieff's students, in Marseilles back in July of 1986. It was a brief meeting in an airport restaurant, lasting about two hours at most. His interest was in determining if joining with such a school as the Gurdjieff Foundation in Paris would be helpful to his own awakening. He asked many questions, most particularly relating to this idea of "being eaten" by "something". His assessment, (which is highly developed from many years as both a scientist and an instructor), of Mr. Tracol's reaction to this question was that the man was *afraid to answer*.

As he recalls it, Mr. Tracol glanced about nervously as though he might be overheard, though there was clearly no one to overhear, and made a somewhat vague allusion to something like "interdimensional beings" of some sort.

Since it is almost twenty years since this meeting, it is hard for Ark to remember exactly what was said, but the entries in his journal in the days following the meeting reflect his state of mind at the time:

Marseilles, July 21, 1986

I am an energy transformer and a converter. That is the essence of my existence. That is my only possible goal. I can choose to serve this goal or not. I can serve only as an energy transformer. So it seems to not make much difference what I do. The result will be the same.

Or, I can serve as a channel. This is the choice between self-will and discipline. What "I" do, that is "I-Personality", is self-will. What acts through me is not self-will. Thus I wish to allow, "that which can act through me" that is not self-will. For this end I need to eliminate self-will. But, God forbid, not to eliminate control!

So I wish to eliminate self-will. I wish to eliminate identification. Eliminating identification is most important. I wish to self-remember. I wish to plan to account for each and every hour. I wish to get rid of my hump. To cease being a camel.

How? Through elimination of identification. I want to listen. And to consider internally.

July 23, 1996 1986

All this world is vanity. A vanity which will pass. The sky will pass, earth will pass, trees will pass, and people will pass too. Human aspirations will pass. Science will pass. All that keeps me together - will pass. A goal - at this level - does not exist. To set a goal - at this level - is to lie to oneself.

Humanity, truth, knowledge - these are empty words. Words surrounded by suffering which is meaningless. When I say I want to "help humanity" - these are empty words. When I say "science", "knowledge", "truth", "cognizance" - these are phantom words.

I am an energy transformer, and I need to serve as such. And that is what I can do.

Where is the way out?

Nothing will remain of what I am doing. I might as well not exist at all. To think that I am "different"? That I am "exceptional"? That I can accomplish things that no one has succeeded in accomplishing - but I will because I will have the luck? Oh Lord, that it is possible to believe these vain illusions! I will die and nothing will be left. Nothing will succeed. Nothing will remain. No goal will be reached. Only one goal seems possible - that when the end is near, suffering will be so great that I will pass with relief.

Where is the way out? What purpose do humans serve? This is an experiment! What originates in me does not count. The only thing I can do is to allow something more powerful to speak through me. To allow something more knowledgeable to talk to me and through me. To allow something more powerful to act through me. To allow something more powerful to use me. I am just a shell, I am a machine. I am a device. I am a means to an end. I am a possibility for something more powerful to be in me and to act through me. I am a place that waits to be filled. I am a carriage without a driver and without a master. True, there is brain, there are body members, there are senses. But I am just a carriage. With no driver and no master. A personality that pretends to have rights. Which play the roles - sometimes of a driver, sometimes of a master - which says "I" continuously. Yet I am just a carriage, which goes nowhere, and is doomed to crash in some ditch.

My aspirations, my ambitions, my wants - all these belong to an empty carriage and horse that is left without control. All that I am doing means nothing. All that I am doing is personality. And that comes from personality is ballast. All that comes from personality is a camel's hump.

How to pass through a needle's eye while carrying a hump? Personality must be left aside. Aspirations and whims - that is not me. Blessed are those who are meek. To be meek - that is what I need. Nonattachment. Eliminating unnecessary things. And also being conscious of the fact that *every moment is a branching of the universe.*

So, this was his state of mind after a two-hour talk with Henri Tracol.

But what it is that "acts through" or controls mankind or creates the conditions of this sleep as Gurdjieff taught? We have discussed this between us, combing through the available resources, trying to determine if this was one of the big "secrets" of the Gurdjieff work, but with little result.

If it is true that humans are being bred and raised like cattle in a global stockyard and fed upon both psychically and sometimes even physically, we have a truly serious situation going on here, to put it mildly. As I have explained before, I have *never* seen a Drachomonoid being except in dreamlike states or almost hypnopompic semi-sleep states. So, when the Cassiopaeans began to talk about them, it was truly "Twilight Zone" time, in my opinion!

I have also stated that, whenever the Cassiopaeans have told us anything, I work very hard to discover if there is any form of what I call vertical or lateral corroboration. Vertical data is that which is located in history at any point different from the present. Lateral data consists of collecting reports, witness information, and other data that amounts to circumstantial evidence from the present time. It is always better if the two types of data "cross" or intersect. But it is still not the same as having a "smoking gun". But, when you are dealing with hyperdimensional realities, "smoking guns" are not very likely to be found.

In the case of the idea of man being "food" for hyperdimensional beings, there is an enormous amount of both vertical and lateral corroboration of *all* kinds. So much so that, in fact, it is almost impossible to understand why it is not generally known. Clearly, there have been deliberate efforts to "hide this fact". And, the fact that it is hidden may itself tell us something.

The point is, when Don Juan and Gurdjieff and the Cassiopaeans (and others) tell us that our religions, our social structure, our values, our beliefs about our spiritual nature and condition have been deliberately created to perpetuate the illusion that we are free; that we are (or can be) "special and adored children of a loving God"; that we are or can be "co-creators" with God, that we can *do* anything at all of a positive and powerful nature, we need to carefully examine this issue!

But it is *work* to examine it objectively. It is *hard work* because it consists of long and difficult self-examination in order to be able to overcome the emotions that prevent us from discovering what illusions we are hanging onto, what illusions are preventing us from seeing and acting in such a way as to *become free*.

Gurdjieff's teachings became known as the *Fourth Way* as opposed to the three ways that had, as far as we can tell, existed within, and utilized, the very religious and social structures that we may think are in place for the purpose of keeping us imprisoned. This is what Gurdjieff meant when he said that many are hypnotized into believing they are Men or Magicians. The problem with these three ways, as we have already discussed, is that they concentrate on only one of the three centers in man: bodily discipline, mental development or the "way of the heart" - Love. Gurdjieff's way incorporated all of these through a form of *Conscious Labor and Intentional suffering.*

What did Gurdjieff mean by these things? No two of his students have ever given the same answer. The only thing we can think about this fact is that the understanding of his students was based upon their effort, experience and *level of being.*

Conscious labor quite obviously does *not* refer to digging ditches or breaking rocks, though it *could*. It must refer to efforts we are not accustomed to making in our ordinary lives. Intentional suffering obviously cannot be present if a person is asleep because it depends on conscience and, according to Gurdjieff, until an individual is awake, they are neither conscious nor do they have a *real* conscience. For Gurdjieff, conscience and consciousness cannot be separated.

There are now many "Fourth Way" methods scattered around the world, all of them partial and incomplete, it seems. But, the point is: Gurdjieff made a big step, he cut away a great deal of the obstructions in the path of finding ways to bring the technology back to the awareness of the group mind, and because he did, those who came after him were able to go even further in this effort.

Unfortunately, the Control System immediately put "damage control" into operation to patch the holes of revelation, and fences of secrecy and restriction were erected so that IF anybody in the organization had the deeper knowledge, it became so hidden that it is likely that the process of distortion and corruption will proceed on its normal course there as well.

Even so, we have to see each of these things as "steps". We can't leave out Sufism, Alchemy, Catharism, and other persecuted systems of knowledge that were the stepping-stones before Gurdjieff. By looking at the overall picture, we can pretty safely say that when a revelation is seen to be useful, that it helps the people who are involved in it to lead fuller, more meaningful lives, the forces that be will immediately go into overdrive to destroy or conceal it. And, if they cannot do that, they will ensure that it is distorted and corrupted by putting their own "agents" in place on the "inside" to see the job done. Witness the development of Christianity via the Catholic Church.

Yes, Gurdjieff may have achieved the level of a True Sage himself, leaving us a legacy of process and application, but our job at present is to go further. And, as we do we must *expect* a continuous effort to counteract, to obfuscate, to corrupt and co-opt the concepts from all quarters. Gurdjieff addressed these very problems:

> "The humanity to which we belong, namely, the whole of historic and prehistoric humanity known to science and civilization, in reality constitutes only the *outer circle of humanity,* within which there are several other circles." [...]

> "The inner circle is called the 'esoteric'; this circle consists of people who have attained the highest development possible for man, each one of whom possesses individuality in the fullest degree, that is to say, an indivisible 'I', all forms of consciousness possible for man, full control over these states of consciousness, the whole of knowledge possible for man, and a free and independent will."

> "They cannot perform actions opposed to their understanding or have an understanding which is not expressed by actions."

> "At the same time there can be no discords among them, no differences of understanding. Therefore their activity is entirely co-ordinated and leads to one common aim without any kind of compulsion because it is based upon a common and identical understanding."

> "The next circle is called the 'mesoteric', that is to say, the middle."

"People who belong to this circle possess all the qualities possessed by the members of the esoteric circle with the sole difference that their knowledge is of a more theoretical character."

"This refers, of course, to knowledge of a cosmic character. They know and understand many things which have not yet found expression in their actions. They know more than they do. But their understanding is precisely as exact as, and therefore precisely identical with, the understanding of the people of the esoteric circle."

"Between them there can be, no discord, there can be no misunderstanding. One understands in the way they all understand, and all understand in the way one understands. But as was said before, this understanding compared with the understanding of the esoteric circle is somewhat more theoretical."

"The third circle is called the 'exoteric,' that is, the outer, because it is the outer circle of the inner part of humanity."

"The people who belong to this circle possess much of that which belongs to people of the esoteric and mesoteric circles but their cosmic knowledge is of a more philosophical character, that is to say, it is more abstract than the knowledge of the mesoteric circle."

"A member of the *mesoteric* circle *calculates,* a member of the exoteric circle *contemplates.* Their understanding may not be expressed in actions. But there cannot be differences in understanding between them.. What one understands all the others understand."

"In literature which acknowledges the existence of esotericism humanity is usually divided into two circles only and the 'exoteric circle' as opposed to the 'esoteric', is called ordinary life."

"In reality, as we see, the 'exoteric circle' is something very far from us and very high. For ordinary man this is already 'esotericism'."

"'The outer circle' is the circle of mechanical humanity to which we belong and which alone we know."

"The first sign of this circle is that among people who belong to it there is not and there cannot be a common understanding. Everybody understands in his own way and all differently."

"This circle is sometimes called the circle of the 'confusion of tongues', that is, the circle in which each one speaks in his own particular language, where no one understands another and takes no trouble to be understood."

"In this circle mutual understanding between people is impossible excepting in rare exceptional moments or in matters having no great significance, and which are confined to the limits of the given *being. "*

"If people belonging to this circle become conscious *of this general lack of understanding* and acquire a desire to understand and to be understood, then it means they have an unconscious tendency towards the inner circle because mutual understanding begins only in the exoteric circle and is possible only there."

"But the consciousness of the lack of understanding usually comes to people in an altogether different form."

"So that the possibility for people to understand depends on the possibility of penetrating into the exoteric circle where understanding begins."

"If we imagine humanity in the form of four concentric circles we can imagine four gates on the circumference of the third inner circle, that is, the exoteric circle, through which people of the mechanical circle can penetrate."

"These four gates correspond to the four ways described before."

"The first way is the way of the fakir, the way of people number one, of people of the physical body, instinctive-moving-sensory people without much mind and without much heart."

"The second way is the way of the monk, the religious way, the way of people number two, that is, of emotional people. The mind and the body should not be too strong."

"The third way is the way of the yogi. This is the way of the mind, the way of people number three. The heart and the body must not be particularly strong, otherwise they may be a hindrance on this way."

"Besides these three ways yet a fourth way exists by which can go those who cannot go by any of the first three ways."

"The fundamental difference between the first three ways, that is, the way of the fakir, the way of the monk, and the way of the yogi, and the fourth way consists in the fact that they are tied to permanent forms which have existed throughout long periods of history almost without change. At the basis of these institutions is religion. Where schools of yogis exist they differ little outwardly from religious schools. And in different periods of history various societies or orders of fakirs have existed in different countries and they still exist. These three traditional ways are *permanent* ways within the limits of our historical period."

"Two or three thousand years ago there were yet other ways which no longer exist and the ways now in existence were not so divided, they stood much closer to one another."

"The fourth way differs from the old and the new ways by the fact that it is never a permanent way. It has no definite forms and there are no institutions connected with it. It appears and disappears governed by some particular laws of its own."[395]

"The fourth way is never without some *work* of a definite significance, is never without some *undertaking* around which and in connection with which it can alone exist."

"When this work is finished, that is to say, when the aim set before it has been accomplished, the fourth way disappears, that is, it disappears from the given place, disappears in its given form, continuing perhaps in another place in another form."

---

[395] In my opinion, the ancient ways that Gurdjieff claimed no longer exist were, in fact, the "Fourth Way" as he described it, though more "permanent."

"Schools of the fourth way exist for the needs of the work which is being carried out in connection with the proposed undertaking. They never exist by themselves as schools for the purpose of education and instruction."

"Mechanical help cannot be required in any work of the fourth way. Only conscious work can be useful in all the undertakings of the fourth way. Mechanical man cannot give conscious work so that the first task of the people who begin such a work is to create conscious assistants."

"The work itself of schools of the fourth way can have very many forms and many meanings. In the midst of the ordinary conditions of life the only chance a man has of finding a 'way' is in the possibility of meeting with the beginning of work of this kind. But the chance of meeting with such work as well as the possibility of profiting by this chance depends upon many circumstances and conditions."

"The quicker a man grasps the aim of the work which is being executed, the quicker can he become useful to it and the more will he be able to get from it for himself."

"But no matter what the fundamental aim of the work is, the schools continue to exist only while this work is going on. When the work is done the schools close. The people who began the work leave the stage. Those who have learned from them what was possible to learn and have reached the possibility of continuing on the way independently begin in one form or another their own personal work."

"But it happens sometimes that when the school closes a number of people are left who were *round about* the work, who saw the outward aspect of it, *and saw the whole of the work in this outward aspect.*"

"Having no doubts whatever of themselves or in the correctness of their conclusions and understanding they decide to continue the work. To continue this work they form new schools, teach people what they have themselves learned, and give them the same promises that they themselves received. All this naturally can only be outward imitation." [396]

"But when we look back on history it is almost impossible for us to distinguish where the real ends and where the imitation begins. Strictly speaking almost everything we know about various kinds of occult, masonic, and alchemical schools refers to such imitation. We know practically nothing about real schools excepting the results of their work and even that only if we are able to distinguish the results of real work from counterfeits and imitations."

"But such pseudo-esoteric systems also play their part in the work and activities of esoteric circles. Namely, they are the intermediaries between humanity which is entirely immersed in the materialistic life and schools which are interested in the education of a certain number of people, as much for the purposes of their own existences as for the purposes of the work of a *cosmic* character which they may be carrying out. The very idea of esotericism, the idea of initiation, reaches people in most cases through pseudo-esoteric systems and schools; and if there

---

[396] This is certainly what happened to Gurdjieff's work.

were not these pseudo-esoteric schools the vast majority of humanity would have no possibility whatever of hearing and learning of the existence of anything greater than life because the truth in its pure form would be inaccessible for them."

"By reason of the many characteristics of man's being, particularly of the contemporary being, truth can only come to people *in the form of a lie*— only in this form are they able to accept it; only in this form are they able to digest and assimilate it. Truth undefiled would be, for them, indigestible food."

"Besides, a grain of truth in an unaltered form is sometimes found in pseudo-esoteric movements, in church religions, in occult and theosophical schools. It may be preserved in their writings, their rituals, their traditions, their conceptions of the hierarchy, their dogmas, and their rules."[397]

As I have written previously, circumstantial evidence points to the existence of a secret fraternity unknown in its entirety to the human race. Other so-called "Secret" groups (Rosicrucians, Illuminati, Freemasons, Modern day Templars, Priory of Zion, etc.) are generally red-herrings to distract and divert the seeker. Gurdjieff points out that these groups do serve a useful function because the very idea of esotericism reaches people through the pseudo-esoteric systems that such groups promote. And so it is that I say, most, if not all, of the great religions of antiquity were symbolic representations of the alchemical work.

This brings us to the most interesting remark that Gurdjieff made above about the inner circle:

"The inner circle ... consists of people who have attained the highest development possible for man, each one of whom possesses individuality in the fullest degree, that is to say, an indivisible 'I', all forms of consciousness possible for man, full control over these states of consciousness, the whole of knowledge possible for man, and a free and independent will."

"They cannot perform actions opposed to their understanding or have an understanding which is not expressed by actions."

"At the same time there can be no discords among them, no differences of understanding. Therefore their activity is entirely co-ordinated and leads to one common aim without any kind of compulsion because it is based upon a common and identical understanding."

And we are reminded again of the alchemical maxim: "Like attracts like."

"When a candidate has developed virtue and integrity acceptable to the adepts, they will appear to him and reveal those parts of the secret processes which cannot be discovered without such help."

---

[397] Gurdjieff, quoted by Ouspensky, *In Search of The Miraculous,* op. cit.

"Those who cannot progress to a certain point with their own intelligence are not qualified to be entrusted with the secrets which can subject to their will the elemental forces of Nature."

So, certainly some process must be followed to achieve the requisite level for "attracting" help.

When we dig as deeply into all of these matters as possible, over and over again we come upon the idea that Self-knowledge is the key. It is NOT the end, but it is the means; the first stage in self-development and the beginning of awakening from sleep is to be able to know the self in an objective way so that the "predator's mind" can be controlled. Note very clearly that I say "controlled" and *not* merged.

Gurdjieff said that we have many "I's" and at the same time, we have an animal nature and a spiritual nature. Self-observation and other disciplined efforts were taught as the means of "crystallization" of a "single I". William Baldwin thought that the real source of these many "I's" was the spirit attachment problem. In working with this, he found that his techniques could assist the person in eliminating this barrier manifesting the true self, in the effort to "grow the will".

The downside of it is the failure to encourage the assimilation of other knowledge as a means of having a context in which to place the discoveries that the self makes in the processes.

But what good is this knowledge when it seems that all the Cassiopaeans have to say is that we are "helpless" in the face of so great a deception? The fact is, they have said or suggested a lot more than that. More importantly, if we understand the Cassiopaean communication properly, we see that it is truly a Fourth Way Work, and that the Cassiopaeans are the teacher that appeared to reveal the parts of the Secret Processes which cannot be discovered without help.

What is that big secret?

Gurdjieff refers to the Evil Magicians. The alchemists said the same thing:

Eugene Canseliet, in his preface to the Second Edition of Fulcanelli's *Dwellings of the Philosophers*, writes:

"Philippe de Mallery engraved with a delicate touch: 'Image of the World, in which Calamities and Perils are emblematically presented along with the opposition in feeling between the Love of God and that of man.'"

"The first emblem straightforwardly points to the original, if not unique, source of all ills of our Humanity. It is also underlined by the Latin inscription which, in the parenthesis, is another pun of phonetic cabala: *'Totus mundus in maligno positus est'*; the whole world is established inside of the devil."[398]

---

[398] Fulcanelli, Dwellings of The Philosophers, op. cit.

What is this world inside the Devil? It is the world of lies and confusion. How did Gurdjieff described it?

> 'The outer circle' is the circle of mechanical humanity to which we belong and which alone we know.

> The first sign of this circle is that among people who belong to it there is not and there cannot be a common understanding. Everybody understands in his own way and all differently.

> This circle is sometimes called the circle of the 'confusion of tongues,' that is, the circle in which each one speaks in his own particular language, where no one understands another and takes no trouble to be understood.

> In this circle mutual understanding between people is impossible excepting in rare exceptional moments or in matters having no great significance, and which are confined to the limits of the given *being*. [399]

Gurdjieff seemed to have the idea that a "will" could be "nurtured" in a man and accelerated, so to say.

Clearly Gurdjieff was aware of the very "damage control" factor of the Control System and how quickly it moves in to damp down any rips in the fabric of the illusion. His idea that we must continually invent *new alarm clocks* is a clear indication that he knew that his method would have to be reworked, revised, added to and expanded. His hope to accelerate the awakening of man seems to have been the driving force behind everything he did, and he was aware of what might happen to his work. It wasn't just the idea of distortion; he knew that it *had* to be constantly reinvented to keep pace with the evolving Control System.

Can we accelerate the awakening?

The Cassiopaeans have indicated that, yes it is possible:

> Q: (L) Is there a tool that enhances free will?

> A: No tool is needed because all there is is lessons. The learning cycle is variable, and progress along it is determined by events and circumstances as they unfold.

> Q: (L) So, when a person is being hypnotized and controlled from outside, because that is the matter of concern we were discussing earlier, they are hypnotized and controlled until they learn to stop it?

> A: Yes.

> Q: (L) So, using the analogy of the pigsty, they just have to wallow in it and suffer until they have had enough?

> A: Using your analogy of the bicycle: Is there a tool, which makes it unnecessary for the child to learn how to ride the bicycle, in order to know how to ride it?!?

> Q: (MM) Don't you get more free will by assimilating knowledge?

---

[399] Ouspensky, op. cit.

A: Yes!! Yes!!

Q: (L) So, in other words, knowledge and awareness makes you aware that you have free will, and also makes you aware of what actions actually ARE acts of free will, and therefore, when you know or suspect the difference between the lies and deception and truth, then you are in a position to be in control of your life?

A: Yes. Remember, *you learn on an exponential curve, once you have become "tuned in"*. This means that you become increasingly able to access the universal consciousness. Please learn to trust your increasing awareness. All who are present here are at one point or another on that cycle of progression, some further along than others. If you properly network without prejudice, you may all wind up at the same point on this cycle.

What does it mean to be "tuned in"? We return again to the issue of "Like attracts like."

When a candidate has developed virtue and integrity acceptable to the adepts, they will appear to him and reveal those parts of the secret processes which cannot be discovered without such help.

Those who cannot progress to a certain point with their own intelligence are not qualified to be entrusted with the secrets which can subject to their will the elemental forces of Nature.

The Cassiopaean Transmissions are just such an "appearance". The process is best described by Eugene Canseliet in his Preface to the second edition of Fulcanelli's Alchemical Masterpiece, *The Dwellings of the Philosophers:*

According to the meaning of the Latin word *adeptus*, the alchemist has then received the Gift of God, or even better, the Present, a cabalistic pun on the double meaning of the word, underlining that he thus enjoys the infinite duration of the Now.[...]

'In the Kingdom of Sulpur there exists a Mirror in which the entire World can be seen. Whosoever looks into this Mirror can see and learn the three parts of Wisdom of the entire World.'

After thirty years of study and two years of dedicated experimentation, detailed in my autobiography, *Amazing Grace*, the Cassiopaean communications began.

"We are you in the Future", they said. "We transmit 'through' the opening that is presented in the locator that you represent as Cassiopaea, due to the strong radio pulses aligned from Cassiopaea, which are due to a pulsar from a neutron star 300 light years behind it, as seen from your locator. This facilitates a clear channel transmission from 6th density to 3rd density."

Through this "Gift of God", - the Present - I have been enabled to look into the "Mirror in which the entire World can be seen" from my own omnipresent self, in a state of full awareness. In short, based on all the details, the Cassiopaean Transmissions are a true Fourth Way work, and exactly as Gurdjieff described, the first order of business of such a work is to network, to teach and train assistants.

"Schools of the fourth way exist for the needs of the work which is being carried out in connection with the proposed undertaking. They never exist by themselves as schools for the purpose of education and instruction."

"Mechanical help cannot be required in any work of the fourth way. Only conscious work can be useful in all the undertakings of the fourth way. Mechanical man cannot give conscious work so that the first task of the people who begin such a work is to create conscious assistants."[400]

So, learning, networking with others who are further along on the cycle of progression, and doing this without prejudice *can* make a difference, it seems.

What is the specific purpose of the Cassiopaean work? Let's stop and consider that: At the beginning of World War I, Ouspensky's speculated to Gurdjieff that the war was a consequence of life in the industrial age, wherein humans were becoming more "mechanized" and had stopped thinking for themselves because they had things too easy. Gurdjieff replied:

> "There is another kind of mechanization which is much more dangerous: being a machine oneself. Have you ever thought about the fact that all people themselves are machines? ...Look, all those people you see are simply machines - nothing more. ...You think there is something that chooses its own path, something that can stand against mechanization; you think that not everything is equally mechanical."

At this point, Ouspensky raised what would seem to be a most logical objection:

> "Why of course not! ...Art, poetry, thought, are phenomena of quite a different order."

Gurdjieff replied: "Of exactly the same order. These activities are just as mechanical as everything else. Men are machines and nothing but mechanical actions can be expected of machines." He then continued:

> "[Western civilization] armed with 'exact knowledge' and all the latest methods of investigation, has no chance whatever and is moving in a circle from which there is no escape."

> "That is because people believe in progress and culture. There is no progress whatever. Everything is just the same as it was thousands, and tens of thousands, of years ago. The outward form changes. The essence does not change. Man remains just the same. 'Civilized' and 'cultured' people live with exactly the same interests as the most ignorant savages. Modern civilization is based on violence and slavery and fine words."

> "...What do you expect? People are machines. Machines have to be blind and unconscious, they cannot be otherwise, and all their actions have to correspond to their nature. Everything happens. No one does anything. 'Progress' and 'civilization', in the real meaning of these words, can appear only as the result of conscious efforts. They cannot appear as the result of unconscious mechanical actions. And what conscious effort can there be in machines? And if one machine is unconscious, then a hundred machines are unconscious, and so are a thousand machines, or a hundred thousand, or a million. And the unconscious activity of a million machines must necessarily result in destruction and extermination."

---

[400] Ouspensky, op. cit.

"It is precisely in unconscious involuntary manifestations that all evil lies. You do not yet understand and cannot imagine all the results of this evil. But the time will come when you will understand."

Again we note: Gurdjieff was speaking at the beginning of the First World War, in the opening rounds of a century of unprecedented warfare. And now, almost a hundred years later, humanity is on the edge of a precipice and no one knows what feather will plunge us all into the abyss.

Wilhelm Reich wrote about the same problems that concerned Gurdjieff and Ouspensky:

Why did man, through thousands of years, wherever he built scientific, philosophic, or religious systems, go astray with such persistence and *with such catastrophic consequences?* [...]

Is human erring necessary? Is it rational? Is all error rationally explainable and necessary? If we examine the sources of human error, we find that they fall into several groups:

Gaps in the knowledge of nature form a wide sector of human erring. Medical errors prior to the knowledge of anatomy and infectious diseases were necessary errors. But we must ask if the mortal threat to the first investigators of animal anatomy was a necessary error too.

The belief that the earth was fixed in space was a necessary error, rooted in the ignorance of natural laws. But was it an equally necessary error to burn Giordano Bruno at the stake and to incarcerate Galileo?[...]

We understand that human thinking can penetrate only to a given limit at a given time. What we fail to understand is why the human intellect does not stop at this point and say: "this is the present limit of my understanding. Let us wait until new vistas open up." This would be rational, comprehensible, purposeful thinking. [...]

What amazes us is the *sudden turn from the rational beginning to the irrational illusion.* Irrationality and illusion are revealed by the *intolerance and cruelty* with which they are expressed. We observe that human thought systems show tolerance as long as they adhere to reality. The more the thought process is removed from reality, the more intolerance and cruelty are needed to guarantee its continued existence.[401]

Who or what is responsible for this state of mankind is a major issue, most particularly if we assume a benevolent God and a hierarchy of benevolent beings guiding the destiny of mankind. Gurdjieff commented on this in the following way (edited for clarity):

"We must remember that the ray of creation... is like a branch of a tree. ... Growth depends on organic life on earth. ...If organic life is arrested in its development, in

---

[401] Ether, God and Devil, Wilhelm Reich]

its evolution, and fails to respond to the demands made upon it, the branch may wither. This must be remembered."

"To this ray of creation, exactly the same possibility of development and growth has been given as is given to each separate branch of a big tree. But the accomplishment of this growth is not at all guaranteed. It depends upon the harmonious and right action of its own tissues."

Organic life on earth is a complex phenomenon in which the separate parts depend upon one another. General growth is possible only on the condition that the 'end of the branch' grows. Or, speaking more precisely, there are in organic life tissues which are evolving, and there are tissues which serve as food and medium for those which are evolving. Then there are evolving cells within the evolving tissues, and cells which serve as food and medium for those which are evolving. In each separate evolving cell there are evolving parts and there are parts which serve as food for those which are evolving. But always and in everything it must be remembered that evolution is never guaranteed, it is possible only and it can stop at any moment and in any place."

"The evolving part of organic life on earth is humanity. If humanity does not evolve it means that the evolution of organic life will stop and this, in its turn will cause the growth of our ray of creation to stop."

"At the same time if humanity ceases to evolve it becomes useless from the point of view of the aims for which it was created and as such it may be destroyed. In this way the cessation of evolution may mean the destruction of humanity."

"We have no clues from which we are able to tell in what period of planetary evolution we exist. We cannot know this but we should bear in mind that the number of possibilities is never infinite."

"At the same time in examining the life of humanity as we know it historically we are bound to acknowledge that humanity is moving in a circle. It one century it destroys everything it creates in another and the progress in mechanical things of the past hundred years has proceeded at the cost of losing many other things which perhaps were much more important for it."

"Speaking in general there is every reason to think and to assert that humanity is at a standstill, and from a standstill there is a straight path to downfall and degeneration."

"A standstill means that a process has become balanced. The appearance of any one quality immediately evokes the appearance of another quality opposed to it. The growth of knowledge in one domain evokes the growth of ignorance in another; refinement on the one hand evokes vulgarity on the other; freedom in one connection evokes slavery in another; the disappearance of some superstitions evokes the appearance and growth of others; and so on."

"A balanced process proceeding in a certain way cannot be changed at any moment it is desired. It can be changed and set on a new path only at certain 'crossroads'. In between the crossroads nothing can be done."

"At the same time if a process passes by a crossroad and nothing happens, nothing is done, then nothing can be done afterwards and the process will continue and develop according to mechanical laws; and even if the people taking part in this process foresee the inevitable destruction of everything, they will be unable to do anything."

"I repeat that something can be done only at certain moments which I have just called 'crossroads' and which in octaves, we have called the 'intervals'."

"The process of evolution, of that evolution which is possible for humanity as a whole, is completely analogous to the process of evolution possible for the individual man. And it begins with the same thing, namely, a certain group of cells gradually becomes conscious; then it attracts to itself other cells, subordinates others, and gradually makes the whole organism serve its aims and not merely eat, drink and sleep."

"In humanity as in individual man everything begins with the *formation of a conscious nucleus*. All the mechanical forces of life fight against the formation of this conscious nucleus in humanity, in just the same way as all mechanical habits, tastes, and weaknesses fight against conscious awareness in man."

"Can it be said that there is a conscious force which fights against the evolution of humanity?", Ouspensky asked.

"From a certain point of view it can be said", said G.

"Where can this force come from?", Ouspensky asked.

"There are two processes which are sometimes called 'involutionary' and 'evolutionary'. The difference between them is the following: An involutionary process begins consciously in the absolute but at the next step it already becomes mechanical - and it becomes more and more mechanical as it develops; an evolutionary process begins half-consciously but it becomes more and more conscious as it develops."

"But consciousness and conscious opposition to the evolutionary process can also appear at certain moments in the involutionary process."

"From where does this consciousness come?"

"From the evolutionary process of course. The evolutionary process must proceed without interruption. Any stop causes a separation from the fundamental process. Such separate fragments of consciousnesses which have been stopped in their development can also unite and at any rate for a certain time can live by struggling against the evolutionary process. After all, it merely makes the evolutionary process more interesting."

"Instead of struggling against mechanical forces there may, at certain moments, be a struggle against the intentional opposition of fairly powerful forces though they are not of course comparable with those which direct the evolutionary process."

"These opposing forces may somethimes even conquer."

"The reason for this consists in the fact that the forces guiding evolution have a more limited choice of means; in other words, they can only make use of certain means and certain methods. The opposing forces are not limited in their choice of means and they are able to make use of every means, even those which only give rise to a temporary success, and in the final result they destory both evolution and involution at the point in question."

"Are we able to say for instance that life is governed by a group of conscious people? Where are they? Who are they?"

"We see exactly the opposite: that life is governed by those who are the least conscious, by those who are most asleep."

"Are we able to say that we observe in life a preponderance of the best, the strongest, and the most courageous elements?"

"Nothing of the sort. On the contrary we see a preponderance of vulgarity and stupidity of all kinds."

"Are we able to say that aspirations towards unity, towards unification, can be observed in life?"

"Nothing of the kind of course. We only see new divisions, new hostility, new misunderstanndings."

"So that in the actual situation of humanity there is nothing that points to evolution proceeding."

"On the contrary, when we compare humanity with a man we quite clearly see a growth of personality at the cost of essence, that is, a growth of the artificial, the unreal, and what is foreign, at the cost of the natural, the real, and what is one's own."

"Together with this we see a growth of automatism."

"Contemporary culture requires automatons. And people are undoubtedly losing their acquired habits of independence and turning into automatons, into parts of machines."

"It is impossible to say where is the end of all this and where the way out - or whether there is an end and a way out. One thing alone is certain, that man's slavery grows and increases. Man is becoming a willing slave. He no longer needs chains. He begins to grow fond of his slavery, to be proud of it. And this is the most terrible thing that can happen to a man."[402]

Carlos Castaneda puts the problem another way in the words of don Juan:

"You have arrived, by your effort alone, to what the shamans of ancient Mexico called *the topic of topics.* I have been beating around the bush all this time, insinuating to you that *something is holding us prisoner.* Indeed we are held prisoner! This was an energetic fact for the sorcerers of ancient Mexico. [...] They took over because *we are food for them*, and they squeeze us mercilessly because we are their sustenance. Just as we rear chickens in chicken coops, the predators rear us in human coops. Therefore, their food is always available to them."[...]

"I want to appeal to your analytical mind," don Juan said. "Think for a moment, and tell me how you would explain the contradiction between the intelligence of man the engineer and the stupidity of his systems of beliefs, or the stupidity of his contradictory behavior. Sorcerers believe that the predators have given us our systems of beliefs, our ideas of good and evil, our social mores. They are the ones who set up our hopes and expectations and dreams of success or failure. They have given us covetousness, greed and cowardice. It is the predators who make us complacent, routinary, and egomaniacal."[...]

---

[402] Gurdjieff quoted by Ouspensky, op. cit, 1949

"In order to keep us obedient and meek and weak, the predators engaged themselves in a stupendous maneuver - stupendous, of course, from the point of view of a fighting strategist. A horrendous maneuver from the point of view of those who suffer it. *They gave us their mind!* Do you hear me? The predators give us their mind, which becomes our mind. The predators' mind is *baroque, contradictory, morose, filled with the fear of being discovered any minute now.*" [...]

"Through the mind, which, after all, is their mind, the predators inject into the lives of human beings whatever is convenient for them."[403]

This, of course, takes us to Gurdjieff's story of the Evil Magician which we have already discussed. We should pay particular attention to this remark made by Gurdjieff:

The evolving part of organic life on earth is humanity. If humanity does not evolve it means that the evolution of organic life will stop and this, in its turn will cause the growth of our ray of creation to stop.

At the same time if humanity ceases to evolve it becomes useless from the point of view of the aims for which it was created and as such it may be destroyed. In this way the cessation of evolution may mean the destruction of humanity.

In short, based on an objective assessment of the world around us, we are in deep trouble. In another place, Gurdjieff makes a rather spooky remark:

"There is a definite period", he said, "for a certain thing to be done. If, by a certain time, what ought to be done has not been done, the earth may perish without having attained what it could have attained."

"Is this period known?", I asked.

"It is known", said G. "But it would be no advantage whatever for people to know it. It would even be worse. Some would believe it, others would not believe it, yet others would demand proofs. Afterwards they would begin to break one another's heads. Everything ends this way with people."

Gurdjieff gave other hints about this, though I expect that he didn't fully know the details since his own work was that of one who prepares the ground and plants the seeds that are crucial to us now when considering the Cassiopaean "Mission". In this passage, Gurdjieff returns again to the subject of evolution which, as he pointed out, has stopped in humanity.

"Everything I have said till now I have said about the whole of humanity. But as I pointed out before, the evolution of humanity can proceed only through the evolution of a certain group, which, in its turn, will influence and lead the rest of humanity."

"Are we able to say that such a group exists? Perhaps we can on the basis of certain signs, but in any event we have to acknowledge that it is a very small group,

---

[403] Castaneda, *The Active Side of Infinity,* 1998, pp. 213-220.

quite insufficient, at any rate, to subjugate the rest of humanity. Or, looking at it from another point of view, we can say that humanity is in such a state that it is unable to accept the guidance of a conscious group."

"How many people could there be in this conscious group?", someone asked.

"Only they themselves know this", said G.

"Does it mean that they all know each other?", asked the same person again.

"How could it be otherwise?", asked G.

"Imagine that there are two or three people who are awake in the midst of a multitude of sleeping people. They will certainly know each other. But those who are asleep cannot know them. How many are they? We do not know and we cannot know until we become like them."

"It has been clearly said before that each man can only see on the level of his own being. But *two hundred conscious people,* if they existed and if they found it necessary and legitimate, could change the whole of life on the earth. But either there are not enough of them, or they do not want to, or perhaps the time has not yet come, or perhaps other people are sleeping too soundly."[Emphasis added.][404]

Gurdjieff was right that it was not the right time then. Based on observation and research, it is apparent that humanity has now reached a great historical crossroads. We have come to the end of a two thousand year history of intolerance, cruelty and stupidity, which has created our present state of global, collective madness. Humanity, as a collective whole, is arriving at a state of collective Spiritual Bankruptcy, or "death". And yet, we cannot assume that this is meaningless.

Those who understand the principles of electricity will comprehend when I say that this present global estate is the way nature works and is the establishing of sufficient Contact Potential Difference for the inflow of energy of Cosmic Light. But just as it is in the case of the individual, when that point is reached - that Dark Night of the Soul - there is a "choice" that becomes apparent: the soul is offered the way "up" or the way "down". In order for this coming inflow of energy to act in positive ways, to create a new reality of Free Will and Balance, there must be a point of contact that can conduct the energy. There must be human "micro-chips" or "circuits" sufficient to sustain this energy or all of humanity will perish. This means that only the development of human beings of a certain sort - with a certain "wiring", so to say - will result in the global capacity to confront the energies of the Crossroads.

The only other Turning Point in history that can be compared with the present one is that of the "Great Flood". And so, we come to the idea that the search for

---

[404] Ouspensky, op. cit.

the Holy Grail and the alchemical work of distillation of the Philosopher's Stone is ALSO the "building of an Ark" in order to pass over into the New World.

That is the Fourth Way Work of the Cassiopaeans.

How can anybody be sure of anything in this day and time when the world seems to have gone mad and we find ourselves collectively in the position of the hero/heroine of the horror movie who hears a noise but can't see its source. Indeed, the audience can see that the monster is lurking in the bushes (no pun intended) just outside the door, the soundtrack is heavy with ominous portent, and with innocent naivete and a handy flashlight, the star of the movie puts his or her hand on the doorknob. The audience groans with the agony of knowing and collectively shouts, "DON'T OPEN THE DOOR"! But, unfortunately, the movie world is not connected to the world of the audience, and no warning can cross that divide.

In the old days, movie heroes and heroines generally always survived such mistakes by dint of clever scripting. In more recent years, you can never be sure anymore: the hero or heroine is likely to die - reflecting real life - because of their stupidity.

Admittedly, when I was much younger, I only liked the kind of movies where the hero or heroine triumphed in the end. I was always upset and angry - I felt cheated - if the movie ended as real life often does: no haven, no help, no hope. Only later did I realize the usefulness of such movies; that they could be teaching tools that help us to analyze our hopes, our beliefs, our wishful thinking that "right will prevail" no matter what, so that, if - indeed - we ever found ourselves in similar situations, we could circumvent the "failures of intelligence" that led to failures in awareness and strategy. In short, observing how wishful thinking most often leads to disaster in real life, could teach us how to think rationally, how to analyze and predict, and thus, formulate an adequate response to any situation of danger.

It's a useful concept.

But it still doesn't bridge the divide between the actors in the movie and the audience that can *see*.

In order to share our knowledge, to complete the loop and give to those others who are asking for the Truth, we began a daily news page in 2002 called *Signs of the Times*.[405] Our job is to report the state of the world *as it is*. We get a lot of letters from readers and entries in our forum by people who complain that the Signs Team sounds like they are "frustrated" or "insulting" or "repetitious", or they don't understand that it is all just a cosmic game and we can go home at the end and have a party with all the bad guys. These readers aren't aware, of course,

---

[405] http://www.signs-of-the-times.org/

of the many discussions we have trying to figure out what may or may not work to get the attention of the reader in a way that will truly serve to galvanize them to wake up. One day we may try one thing, and another day, we will try something else.

At the present time, it seems that much of the outside world is watching America in the same way an audience watches a horror movie. The audience, of course, has the benefit of a "bird's eye view", and all the clues of music and privileged perspective granted by the movie maker. The actors are in a state of "fantasy", or "wishful thinking", if you like. They have agreed, individually and collectively, to engage in acting out the drama. They have agreed to "forget" all they know about the script so as to more effectively "get into" their roles. When the movie making is over, they all have a cast party, toast each other for how well they managed to fool the audience, and agree that it was a great movie and go home to read another script.

The audience, on the other hand, if they are knowledgable, will agree that their favorite actors sure had them going there for a bit! They will declare sagely how good the monster was, and how evil the villian was because the actor or actress was such a master of their craft.

Such analogies as audience and movie are often used by philosophers as a way of suggesting that all that happens on earth is exactly that: a grand play and everybody is all the same when the show is over: actors and audience are simply two sides that have agreed to play "parts" in the life of humanity. Certainly, at some ultimate "level" of reality, this may be true in a certain way, but we suspect that it is not at all exactly that simple.

Sure, in the ultimate Grand Scheme of things, everything goes back to source. The difference is that those with the BEing nature of Creativity don''t like the idea of Entropy and they reserve the right to make a choice.

It is easier to resist evil at the begining than at the end.

And it is oh, so easy to excuse yourself from resisting by just saying, "Oh, it's just a movie! We can all go home at the end and know that everyone played their parts well...".

There is more than a little scientific support for the above ideas that consciousness - the root of existence and *being* - has two fundamental states: on, or off. In the final analysis, it seems that the metaphor of humanity and its collective "higher selves" being a movie and an audience, may be simply anthropomorphizing creative and entropic forces of the universe for the purposes of "self-calming". The stakes, it seems, are a lot higher and more real.

This brings us to the issue of subjectivity vs. objectivity.

As the C's have said, and this is echoed in the most ancient traditions: "It's not where you are, but *who* you are and *what you see* that counts." This "who" and "what you see" have been somewhat problematical as research subjects, and it has only been in the last three years that clear understanding of these concepts have been articulated.

About two hundred years ago, the French mathematician and physicist Pierre Laplace wrote:

> We must regard the present state of the universe as the effect of its past and the
> cause of its future. Consider an intelligence which, at any instant, could have a
> knowledge of all forces controlling nature together with the momentary conditions
> of all the entities of which nature consists. If this intelligence were powerful enough
> to submit all this data to analysis it would be able to embrace in a single formula the
> movements of the largest bodies in the universe and those of the lightest atoms; for
> it, nothing would be uncertain; the future and the past would be equally present to
> its eyes.

Certainly, such an intelligence as Laplace describes would be "Godlike", you
agree? And certainly, no one of us human beings is capable of such "seeing", you
will also agree. However, what does seem to be true is that this is a significant clue
to the solutions to the pressing issues of our day: knowledge that leads to
awareness.

Here I will refer the reader back to the section on neurochemicals. As the brain
interacts with its environment, synaptic circuits combine to form synaptic maps of
the world perceived by the senses. These maps describe small segments of that
world - shape, color, movement - and these maps are scattered throughout the
brain. As the brain's synaptic network evolves, beginning at birth - or even before
- these maps process information simultaneously and in parallel. Based on our
synaptic maps of the world, we are enabled to have a more or less objective view
of reality.

Classical physics asserts that the future already exists, as do the present and past.
Everything that ever will happen has already happened. But for some unknown
reason our minds can only experience the future a piece at a time in what we call
the present.

Quantum physics says that we can never predict the future with absolute
certainty. The future does not yet exist in a single definite state. Quantum
uncertainty does not deny us all knowledge about the future. It gives us the tools to
make predictions, but only in terms of probabilities.

Bohr and other leading physicists of the Copenhagen School say that objective
reality is an ambiguous concept at the quantum level. In physics, our knowledge
comes only when we actually measure something, and even then the way we
decide to perform the measurement affects the results we obtain.

Asking the same question in different ways may give seemingly contradictory
answers, but no single experiment will itself provide contradictory information.
Some experiments will show electrons as waves, and others will show them as
particles. In no single experiment do electrons display wavelike and particlelike
behavior simultaneously. Bohr called this complementarity.

Quantum mechanics leaves the observer uncertain about the actual nature of
reality. Are they really waves or particles? We don't know and no experiment will
tell us. Detecting one of the attributes automatically excludes knowledge about the
other.

There is a striking similarity between life and thought. Just as there are more
potential life forms than the planet can hold, there are more potential ideas than
our minds can possibly absorb and remember.

Just as evolutionary natural selection may generate change by choosing from among the many potential forms of life, so may thought be able to generate evolutionary change by choosing among many potential thoughts.

The master evolutionary mechanism is found in the wave function of the universe. The observer guides the selection from an infinite number of potential arrangements that the universe may assume from moment to moment.

The universe has many possible future states or potentialities represented by the wave function. The wave function is constantly collapsing into the present as the many possible states become a single state as the present unfolds and possibilities become actualities.

Many individuals have decided that this Quantum Uncertainty means that you can "create your own reality" by what you believe, or depending upon what you give your attention to. This is a popular idea among many New Age types, and is actually the foundation of most religions whether they realize it or not.

Chris Floyd wrote in the *Moscow Times* on October 22, 2004:

> Now we come at last to the heart of darkness. Now we know, from their own words, that the Bush Regime is a cult -- a cult whose god is Power, whose adherents believe that they alone control reality, that indeed they create the world anew with each act of their iron will. And the goal of this will -- undergirded by the cult's supreme virtues of war, fury and blind faith -- is likewise openly declared: "Empire".

> You think this is an exaggeration? Then heed the words of the White House itself: a "senior adviser" to the president, who, as *The New York Times* reports, explained the cult to author Ron Suskind in the heady pre-war days of 2002.

> First, the top Bush insider mocked the journalist and all those "in what we call the reality-based community", i.e., people who "believe that solutions emerge from your judicious study of discernible reality". Suskind's attempt to defend the principles of reason and enlightenment cut no ice with the Bush-man.

> "That's not the way the world really works anymore. We're an empire now, and when we act, we create our own reality", he said. "And while you're studying that reality, we'll act again, creating other new realities, which you can study too, and that's how things will sort out. We're history's actors ... and you, all of you, will be left to just study what we do."

> Anyone with any knowledge of 20th-century history will know that this same megalomaniacal outburst could have been made by a "senior adviser" to Hitler, Stalin, Mussolini or Mao. Indeed, as scholar Juan Cole points out, the dogma of the Bush Cult is identical with the "reality-creating" declaration of Mao's "Little Red Book": "It is possible to accomplish any task whatsoever." For Bush, as for Mao, "discernible reality" has no meaning: Political, cultural, economic, scientific truth -- even the fundamental processes of nature, even human nature itself -- must give way to the faith-statements of ideology, ruthlessly applied by unbending zealots.

The view of the Bush Reich is, as it happens, diametrically opposed to the view we promote at *Signs of the Times*. This view has been stated quite economically by the Cassiopaeans:

> Life is religion. Life experiences reflect how one interacts with God. Those who are asleep are those of little faith in terms of their interaction with the creation. Some people think that the world exists for them to overcome or ignore or shut out. For

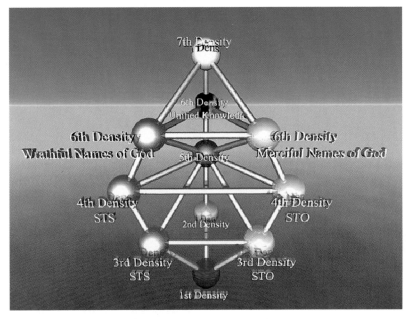

Plate 1. *The Tree of Life*

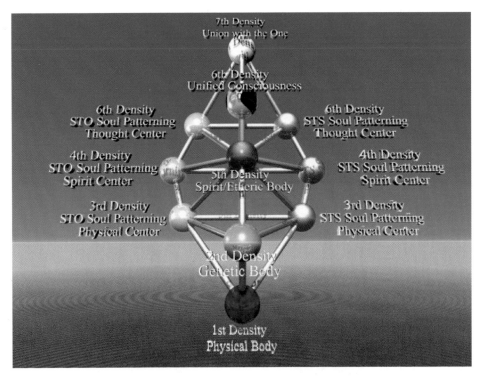

Plate 2. *The reworked Tree of Life*

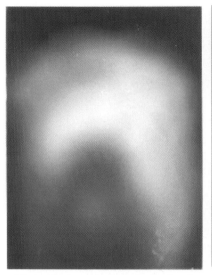

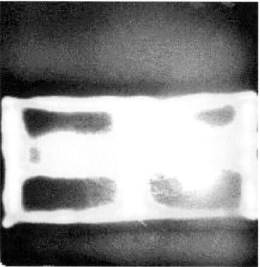

Plate 3. *Aural photograph of Laura.*

Plate 4. *Aural photograph of Laura and Fred's hands while using the board.*

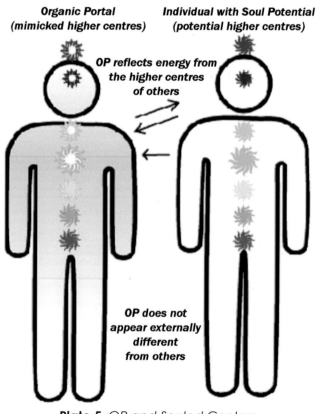

Plate 5. *OP and Souled Centers*

Plate 6. *Burial of Christ – Auch Cathedral*

Plate 7. *The Sibyl Samos – Auch Cathedral*

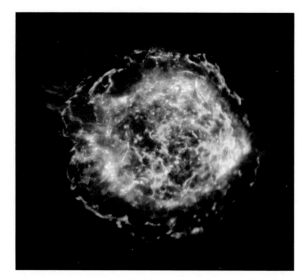

Plate 8. *The Prototype of the Great Rose Windows?*

Plate 9. *Tomb of Pierre-Henri Gerault de Langalerie – Auch Cathedral*

Plate 10. *Mary Magdalene – Auch Cathedral*

Plate 11. *The Family of Christ – Auch Cathedral*

Plate 12. *The Wife of Christ – Auch Cathedral*

Plate 13. *Sibyl – Auch Cathedral*

Plate 14. *The Gifts of the Magi – Auch Cathedral*

Plate 15. *Thinking With A Hammer – Auch Cathedral*

Plate 16. *Initiation – Auch Cathedral*

Plate 17. *Skull & Crossbones – Auch Cathedral*

Plate 18. *The Last Judgment
– Leonardo da Vinci*

Plate 19. *The Last Judgment
– Leonardo da Vinci*

Plate 20. *St. John*

St. John. Louvre. It is said to be the most disquieting of Leonardo's work. Leonardo has transformed John, the alleged precursor of Christ, from a gaunt ascetic to what can only be said to be almost a hermaprhodite with soft, womanly flesh, glancing out of the painting with a look that is not renunciation, but sly mystery and devious invitation with finger pointing heavenward.

From Leonardo's notebooks:

"The limbs which are used for labour must be muscular and those which are not much used you must make without muscles and softly rounded. Represent your figures in such action as may be fitted to express what purpose is in the mind of each; otherwise your art will not be admirable."

"Therefore it is here represented with a reed in his right hand which is useless and without strength, and the wounds it inflicts are poisoned. [...] And for these reasons the reed is held as their support. Evil-thinking is Envy or Ingratitude."

"Envy must be represented with a contemptuous motion of the hand towards heaven, because if she could she would use her strength against God..."

What, exactly, was Leonardo trying to tell us about St. John?

Plate 21. *Virgin of The Rocks, Version One, Louvre,* 1483 Notice the pointing
finger of contempt from the Angel to John the Baptist

Plate 22. *Virgin of the Rocks, Second Version,* 1506
Notice the reed in the right hand of John the Baptist.

Plate 23. *The Last Supper – Leonardo da Vinci*

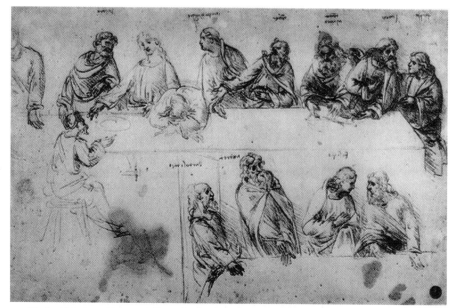

Plate 24. *Looking at the study for The Last Supper, we realize that Leonardo began with the "standard" ideas, but somewhere along the way he decided to do something remarkably different.*

Plate 25. *Pleasure and Pain. Jesus and the mystery woman.*

Plate 26. *Placement of Hands in The Last Supper - One*
I have placed question marks over the "questionable" hands, the one hold-ing the knife, which seems to belong to the man whispering in the woman's ear. Also, I would suggest that his other hand, making the "head cutting" motion at the woman's neck is not altogether anatomically impossible, but it is certainly awkward. But perhaps "awkwardness", or "twisted-ness" is what Leonardo intended to convey about St. Peter?

Plate 27. *Placement of Hands in The Last Supper - Two*
Above, you see the one person with only one hand in view, his upraised finger pointing insolently to heaven as in the portrait of St. John, Leonardo's last painting.

Plate 28. *Peter's Hand,*
The Last Supper (detail)

Plate 29. *Study for Peter's Arm*

Plate 30. *The Real Da Vinci Code?*

Plate 31. *The
Constellation
Cassiopeia.*

those individuals, the worlds will cease. *They will become exactly what they give to life.* They will become merely a dream in the "past". People who pay strict attention to objective reality right and left, become the reality of the "Future".

Human beings are both fascinated and repelled by what is called "evil". The fascination stems from the fact that "good" people find it difficult to comprehend how evil can exist in a world that is allegedly overseen by a benevolent and loving creator. And so, they struggle to identify it, quantify it and understand it.

Throughout history, different individuals or groups of individuals have been labeled "evil" by the "authorities" of the time. In our own period, we often find that the mass media will display photographs of murderers with the caption, "The face of evil". The viewer shudders with fear and thanks his lucky stars that such an individual is not a part of *his* of *her* life!

At the top of the list of the 20th-century's most evil people, we find an ordinary looking guy named Adolf Hitler. Like George Bush, he was more comical and absurd than frightening. There are many surviving photographs that show him dandling babies and fondling pets.

Nevertheless, when we gaze upon these old photos of Hitler, our perceptions are automatically conditioned to produce that frission of fear: this is HITLER, the *Face of Evil*. We see, in retrospect, that the dandling of babies and scratching the dog's ears were undoubtedly the propaganda of the time. We know that because we know the history of what Hitler did.

What we all tend to forget is that Hitler could not have come to power and committed Germany to its policies of war and genocide without the tacit consent of the German people and without the rest of the world turning a blind eye to what was going on in Germany. In a certain sense, this makes the entire world responsible for the crimes committed in Germany.

Would the German people have been so susceptible to Nazi rule if there had been a concerted effort on the part of other peoples to assist them in waking up, in seeing their folly?

Why did everyone think "it's not my business", most particularly those governments that could have acted more strongly to curtail the rising power of Hitler? How much responsibility do they hold for the 65 million deaths of the Global Holocaust that was World War II?

Knowing that the German people were the foundation on which Hitler stood, his soldiers and workers and assistant killers, is one thing; understanding how it came to be is another.

If other countries did not forcefully object, surely the German people thought that the direction Hitler was taking them was at least their own solution to their particular problems, even if not exactly the solution other countries would have chosen.

There was no real concensus of rejection of the Nazi ideals conveyed to Germany in an effective way and, certainly, the German people were suffering a variety of serious internal problems to which Hitler's answers seemed to be good ones.

There was no single moment in time when the German people - as a whole - suddenly "became evil". The Germans - the people susceptible to Adolf Hitler - were a people desperate for identity and economic prosperity. Germany was a country torn apart by overwhelming economic, political and social blows: World War I, the treaty of Versailles, hyperinflation and the Great Depression, were all blows that ruined or diminished the admirable qualities of Germany as a whole. These disasters left the way open for a truly horrifying ideology.

Hitler tapped into this desperation, whipping the people of Germany into a religious, messianic fervor. Little by little, they were induced to close off their consciences as the price that had to be paid for their dreams; they were induced by clever fear tactics and propaganda to incrementally realign their collective morality so that, in the end, the Face of Evil was the face of every supporter of Hitler.

The story of the rise of Adolf Hitler is the single most important story of the 20th century. With this event, in less than a single lifetime, one of the most civilized countries in Europe was reduced to moral, physical, and cultural ruin. The rest of the world was nearly gobbled into this black hole of evil. This should give everyone something to think about - and think about it long and hard.

At present, the model of what transpired in Germany can quite easily be seen by many people as unfolding in the United States today. There were other ways that the history of Germany could have unfolded in that time. There are other ways the history of the United States can unfold.

Complicity does not mean that you have to support evil, it simply means that the only thing necessary for the triumph of evil is for good men to do nothing.

In my work, I am not in the business of telling anyone what to do. The work, as with *Signs of the Times*, stands as a lighthouse, a constant sweeping illumination that goes around and around to shine light on the terror of the situation. The goal is provide knowledge of the objective reality in which we live, a reality that appears to be veering out of control. This brings us back to the issue of how does Knowledge Protect?

We were recently approached by representatives of two different "consortiums of power" of a global scale. Both of these groups asked about our interest in becoming part of a "network" approach to current global issues that we all understand well: that is, we are living in a powder keg and giving off sparks.

Now, as best we can understand it, these proposed networks have the stated goal of "exposing the lies" of the U.S. administration with a view to waking Americans up "politically".

The conditions that would be imposed on us would be that we would have to distance ourselves from our own stated goal of waking people up to the hyperdimensional nature of the control system. One of the above mentioned "agents"[406] wrote to me as follows:

> My interest in US politics is not so much concerned with trying to change (or save, or preserve) the US, which is tightly under the control of / committed to business interests, but in attracting attention to my ultimate objective of saving the planet's environment (e.g., stopping the mass species extinction, stopping global warming), with primary emphasis on what to do after the current system of global industrialization collapses. [...]

Well, well, well.... It looks like the folks at the top are beginning to worry a bit about their plans not working quite the way they want them to.

Well, to make a long story short, we declined these invitations even though the carrot of large scale funding was dangled. It seemed to us that, even if it was legitimate, it was the wrong approach designed just to serve someone else's agenda rather than the agenda of truth which suggests that all this "good cop, bad cop" routine is just a smoke and mirrors show controlled by hyperdimensional factors.

It occurred to me that both of the above contacts, coming so close together, amounted to a sort of "pincer movement" designed to try to contain and suppress the information we are desseminating about the root issues: hyperdimensional realities.

To the gentleman who represented one of the "consortiums" of power, I responded as follows:

> "It seems that you perceive that we here at cass may, indeed, have a pretty good track record of seeing and predicting, even if we point out that prediction can only be statistical, and attaching dates is a fool's game."

> "It also seems that what you are seeking to do is a sort of 'let's tell people as much as we have to in order to make this or that adjustment to the dynamic, since our own ideas don't seem to be panning out so well, but we can't tell them everything...' approach."

> "It's already way too late for that."

> "For example, just the other night we had a couple questions about the recent earthquake and tsunami. Here is the exchange with the C's:"

Session date: Jan 9, 2005

---

[406] I know of this individual because of the research I did on game theory. He was closely associated with Wheeler and did studies on using game theory as a means of killing the most people with the least expenditure of energy as a means of reducing the planet's population significantly.

Q: Regarding the recent earthquake and tsunami, there is a huge buzz on the net that this was not a natural phenomenon. Some say it could have been a meteor; others say it was a US nuke; others say it was India and Israel playing around in the undersea trenches. Then there is the speculation on an EM weapon of some description. The New agers are saying it was the start of the final 'Earth Changes'. So what really caused this earthquake that happened one year minus one hour after the earthquake in Iran?

A: Pressure in earth. Not any of the preferred suggestions. But remember that the human cycle mirrors the cycle of catastrophe and human mass consciousness plays a part.

Q: In what way does mass consciousness play a part?

A: When those with higher centers are blocked from full manifestation of creative energy, that energy must go somewhere. If you cannot create "without" you create "within".

In the past three years, we have made some considerable progress on our mandate of discovering what really makes reality tick and how does humanity fit into it. Much of this work is pure science - physics and mathematics - but I'm not going to give you the formulas or the computer simulation codes, I'm going to explain it to you in simple terms.'

Our universe seems to be made up of matter/energy and of consciousness.

Matter/energy by itself "prefers", as it seems, a chaotic state.

Matter/energy by itself doesn't even have a concept of "creation" or "organization". It is the consciousness that brings to life these concepts and by its interaction with matter pushes the universe towards chaos and decay or towards order and creation.

This phenomenon can modeled mathematically and simulated on a computer using EEQT (Event Enhanced Quantum Theory[407]). Whether EEQT faithfully models the interaction of consciousness with matter, we do not know. But chances are that it does because it seems to describe correctly physical phenomena better than just the orthodox quantum mechanics or its rival theories. (Bohmian mechanics, GRW etc.)

What we learn from EEQT can be described in simple terms as follows:

Let us call our material universe "the system". The system is characterized by a certain "state". It is useful to represent the state of the system as a point on a disc. The central point of the disk, its origin, is the state of chaos. We could also describe it as "Infinite Potential". The points on the boundary represent "pure states" of being, that is states with "pure, non-fuzzy, knowledge". In between there are mixed states. The closer the state is to the boundary, the more pure, more "organized" it is.

Now, an external "observer", a "consciousness unit", has some idea - maybe accurate, maybe false or anywhere in between - about the "real state" of the system, and observes the system with this "belief" about the state. Observation, if

---

[407] http://quantumfuture.net/quantum_future/papers/petruc/petruc.html

prolonged, causes the state of the system to "jump". In this sense, you DO "create your own reality", but the devil, as always, is in the details.

The details are that the resulting state of the system under observation can be more pure, or more chaotic depending on the "direction" of the jump. The direction of the jump depends on how objective - how close to the reality of the actual state - the observation is.

According to EEQT if the expectations of the observer are close to the actual state of the system, the system jumps, more often than not, into *more organized*, less chaotic state.

If, on the other hand, the expectation of the observer is close to the negation of the actual state (that is when the observer's beliefs are closer to being false than to being true according to the *actual* state - the objective reality), then the state of the system, typically, will jump into a state that is more chaotic, less organized. Moreover, it will take, as a rule, much longer time to accomplish such a jump.

In other words, if the observer's knowledge of the actual state is close to the *truth*, then the very act of observation and verification causes a jump quickly, and the resulting state is more organized. If the observer's knowledge of the actual state is false, then it takes usually a long time to cause a change in the state of the system, and the resulting state is more chaotic.

What this means is that order can be brought out of chaos by observing chaos as it IS and not pretending that it is otherwise.

In short, everyone who "believes" in an attempt to "create reality" that is different from what IS, increases the chaos and entropy. If your beliefs are orthogonal to the truth, no matter how strongly you believe them, you are essentially coming into conflict with how the Universe views itself, and I can assure you, you ain't gonna win that contest. You are inviting destruction upon yourself and all who engage in this "staring down the universe" exercise with you.

On the other hand, if you are able to view the Universe as it views itself, objectively, without blinking, and with acceptance, you then become more "aligned" with the Creative energy of the universe and your very consciousness becomes a transducer of order. Your energy of observation, given unconditionally, can bring order to chaos, can create out of infinite potential.

In the *Adventure Series*[408], I concentrated to a great extent on the problem of psychopathy in our world today. I was motivated to do this by the fact that we had been victimized by a psychopath whose behavior was utterly incomprehensible. As a consequence of this research, I was much better prepared to understand George Bush and his Reich and that served to "inoculate" me against the fear tactics that are utilized by the psychopath to paralyze their victims. I realize that Americans who are "stupid" are that way by design. In a sense, it is not their fault. They are no more

---

[408] http://www.cassiopaea.com/cassiopaea/adventureindex.htm

capable of thinking on their own than the mouse is capable of escaping the claws of the cat determined to eat it.

But not everyone is a mouse. It is for those who are evolving that we continue to keep the lighthouse going. But be aware, the day may come - and sooner than you might expect - when the storm is so violent that the keepers of the flame will abandon the task, knowing that no light can be seen in such Stygian darkness.

In the *Adventure Series*, I wrote the following:

Could it ever be an evolutionarily stable strategy for people to be innately unselfish?

On the whole, a capacity to cheat, to compete and to lie has proven to be a stupendously successful adaptation. Thus the idea that selection pressure could ever cause saintliness to spread in a society looks implausible in practice. It doesn't seem feasible to outcompete genes which promote competitiveness. "Nice guys" get eaten or outbred. Happy people who are unaware get eaten or outbred. Happiness and niceness today is vanishingly rare, and the misery and suffering of those who are able to truly feel, who are empathic toward other human beings, who have a conscience, is all too common.

Nevertheless, a predisposition to, conscience, ethics, can prevail if and when it is also able to implement the deepest level of altruism: making the object of its empathy the higher ideal of enhancing free will in the abstract sense, for the sake of others, including our descendants.

In short, our "self-interest" ought to be vested in collectively ensuring that all others are happy and well-disposed too; and in ensuring that children we bring into the world have the option of being constitutionally happy and benevolent toward one another.

In short, if psychopathy threatens the well-being of the group future, then it can be only be dealt with by refusing to allow the self to be dominated by it on an individual, personal basis.

Preserving free will for the self in the practical sense, ultimately preserves free will for others.

Protection of our own rights AS the rights of others, underwrites the free will position and potential for happiness of all.

If mutant psychopaths pose a potential danger then true empathy, true ethics, true conscience, dictates using prophylactic therapy against psychopaths.

It seems certain from the evidence that a positive transformation of human nature isn't going to come about through a great spiritual awakening, socio-economic reforms, or a spontaneous desire among the peoples of the world to be nice to each other. But it's quite possible that, in the long run, the psychopathic program of suffering will lose out because misery is not a stable strategy.

In a state of increasing misery, victims will seek to escape it; and this seeking will ultimately lead them to inquire into the true state of their misery, and that may lead to a society of intelligent people who will have the collective capacity to do so.

And so it is that identifying the psychopath, ceasing our interaction with them, cutting them off from our society, making ourselves unavailable to them as "food" or objects to be conned and used, is the single most effective strategy that we can play. [...]

To allow oneself to be conned, or used by a psychopath is to effectively become part of his "hierarchy" of feeding. To believe the lies of the psychopath is to submit to his "bidding" (he bids you to believe a lie, and you acquiesce), and thus, to relinquish your free will.

In strictly material terms, this doesn't seem to be much of an issue, right? After all, somebody lies to us and who really cares? Is it going to hurt us to just let them lie? Is it going to hurt us to just go along with them for the sake of peace, even if we know or suspect they are lying? After all, checking the facts and facing the psychopath with truth, and telling them "no" is generally very unpleasant. Remember, the game is set up so that we pay a lot for being ethical in dealing with the psychopath. In material terms, it really doesn't seem to be worth it because we suffer all kinds of attack - verbal, psychological, and even physical abuse - so it's just easier to let sleeping dogs lie, right? [...]

At best, we can only really penetrate to the level of the psychological reality, observed behavior that is discordant, or self-destructive. And we are thoroughly programmed to help by giving until it hurts, or trying to fix, or to make nice. All of these things, all of these accommodations of psychopathy, on just a practical level, can be seen to "select for psychopathy" in terms of the gene pool.

But on another level, considering the great amount of evidence we have that there is something very mysterious going on that has to do with "controlling the minds of humanity", and covering up something that may affect every single human being on this planet, we find that the issue is crucial. Refusing to accommodate the manipulations and maneuvers of the psychopath may, indeed, be critical to the positive transformation of our planet. [...]

And we see that the ultimate aim of the psychopath, as living representatives of the Universal forces of Entropy, of Non-Being, is to *master* creative energy. To assimilate it to the self, to deprive others of it by inducing them to believe lies.

Because, when you believe the lie of the psychopath, you have given him control of your Free Will - the essence of Creativity. [...]

The first Divine Command is *Be*! And that includes Being and Non-being instantaneously. Therefore, the second law is "follow Being or Non-being according to your choice and your inherent nature".

All creation is a result of the engendering command. So, in this respect, there is no Evil. But the second, prescriptive law determines to which "Face of God" one will return: Life or Death.

There *are* such things as "evil planets", and dark stars. And the real question at this time is: Is Mother Earth about to become one?

Now, you are a smart guy - no question in my mind about that - so I am sure you can do a bit of extrapolating from the above and understand that there is one, and *only* one way to "save the earth". Since humanity - as a whole - is an "organ for transducing cosmic energies onto our planet", the condition of humanity - as a whole - is reflected by the planet. The suffering of humanity, the lies that humans believe, all have a profound effect on the planet.

VERY IMPORTANT: it is not whether or not one "believes" in good things or bad things that makes good things or bad things happen. It is the factual observation of reality and whether or not it leads to a true assessment or lies.

The effort to view the universe *as it views itself* with love and acceptance even in the face of what might be termed "horror" can actually lead to amelioration of that horror. To view the universe and to deny the truth and to insist that one can believe whatever one wants and thereby make it so, is to deny reality and contributes to the chaos, the destruction, the suffering.

And so, what is the solution? The *truth* - as close to it as we can objectively get - *must* be propagated as widely and as soon as possible.

That is the only thing that will "save the planet". Because it is in the creative centers of humanity - both kinds, those with souls and those without - that the fate of the earth lies.

We come now to the specifics. We have seen what Mouravieff has said about "Courtly Love", what Gurdjieff has said about Esoteric circles, what all three of them have said about the so-called "End of the World", so what, exactly, do we do? If the Grail Consciousness is Objectivity, how do we learn to see the universe objectively, as it sees itself? Another way of putting it is: how do we overcome our own subjectivity? The answer is by mastering the impermanent parts of our personality and bringing them under the control of that part of us which is permanent, that part of us that has a link with the Creative force. And in this struggle, we discover that not only do we bind with truth spiritually, but this process also induces a change in our brain chemistry which can literally lead to a physical transmutation.

TRANSMUTATION OF THE PERSONALITY

Anyone who has done a bit of introspection will have noticed how our personality appears to be divided. One minute we are promising ourselves to give up sweets with all of the will-power we can muster, and the next minute we have our hand back in the box of chocolates. We set out on a diet only to "forget" the next time we see something tempting on our list of forbidden foods. We promise ourselves to get to those bills next, only to decide to make a coffee first, followed by reading a magazine. How many times have we done something that we know is harmful to us, in spite of the interior voice telling us that we will have to pay the consequences? Gurdjieff tells us that the whole work consists in the struggle between "yes" and "no".

The first thing, then, that we notice about ourselves is that there appear to be many different "I's" pushing and pulling us in many different directions. They come and go so subtly that we think that we have a permanent 'self' when in fact we are a bundle of conflicting and contradictory urges and impulses. We might identify each of these little voices as a different aspect of our subjectivity or our personality, but we have also discussed these as "programs" inculcated into us from childhood, generally with significant emotional effect. The Tradition refers to these programmed thought loops, ideas, opinioins, as impermanent parts of ourselves. Certainly, to some extent, our tastes, desires, and needs change as we grow, but there are many of these circuits that are laid in our brains during our infancy, and are thus "pre-verbal", and extremely deep. If we are to arrive at an objective view of reality, these voices of subjectivity must be recognized for what they are and then aligned and brought under the control of that essential part of oneself that might be termed "soul". This essence is the part of the self that - in the individual who is of an intrinsic creative nature - has the possibility of truly *See*ing, or that at least wishes to see, the world as it really is. But how is this done?

In our normal state of running on auto-pilot, we generally just seek a comfortable, conflict free existence. Our momentum carries us along a certain path, and it is only when we hit impediments or even unforeseen attractions that we are forced to change direction. These are shocks. It is through shocks to the system that we are aroused from our state of sleep. Because we are conditioned to seek a conflict free life, we generally seek to move past these shocks with as little disturbance to the system as possible. In short, we seek to go back on auto-pilot as quickly as possible. As a result, if we are forced to turn off our autopilot and deal with the world in real-time, we try to find the quickest and easiest way to accommodate the shock with as little disturbance to our way of life as possible.

However, when things do not go as we would like them to, when the world does not act or react according to our desires, our wishes, our predictions, our anticipation, we then receive an even greater shock. It is in such conditions that human beings become aware of the false assumptions that get us into situations that our programming can't handle. In short, it is during these moments of shock that all the different parts within are momentarily aligned while we seek to create a "new program" that will, in future, manage such situations. This means that, for that period of time that we are seeking a solution, we face a choice: to "take a drug" for the pain, or to fully experience it so that the body itself (and here we refer to the spiritual body) will produce its own "chemical" that will properly "heal" the wound. In other words, in those moments of such shock, we have the opportunity to break our habits, eliminate the assumptions we have acquired by rote, and stop the mechanical ways in which we do things. In other words, the key to fusing the self consists in using these shocks, these moments of self-awareness, as aids in becoming less mechanical. The shock can make us aware for a brief instant of where we are, how we got there, what our assumptions were, or, in other words, of the program that we were running, if we seize it during the brief instant it exists. However, the moment during which we can override the autopilot is narrow because we have back-up systems in place that can kick-in, programs for dealing with shocks, (spiritual drugs, beliefs, etc), and these programs are every bit as mechanical as the others. So one must learn to discern the moment when the transfer of the programs takes place and *consciously* step in before the new program.

As we are mechanical in all aspects of our lives, the shocks that can awaken us can also be found in all areas of our lives: at work, at home with our spouses, children, or parents, in reports about the day's news, or even at the movies. But we must know how to put them to work. One must be able to stop when one is shocked and properly observe our reactions as they take place. This process is referred to in the Tradition as "The Doctrine of the Present".

In the process of applying certain aspects of the Doctrine of the Present, the seeker can observe the physiological changes brought on by the shock: a quickening of the pulse, a shortening of the breath, perhaps a tightness in the chest. It happens in an instant. The physiological changes are always accompanied by an emotion, perhaps fear, the sense that one is being attacked. Fear can lead to a response of attack or flight, either physical or simply mental, closing oneself off or letting off a string of angry words.

In time and with practice, we can watch all of this happen as if it is not happening to us. We can become more and more objective about ourselves. Of course it takes time to develop, to be able to separate oneself from the physical manifestations, the emotional reaction, and the subsequent intellectual justifications that we elaborate to explain our reaction to the shock. In this respect, a network or a group proves invaluable because we can easily fall into extremely subtle intellectual rationalizations, fuelled by "colored" emotional energy.

As we gain practice, through proper utilization of a network of like-minded seekers, an esoteric group, we can begin to identify the different small "I's" as they react. Some of these are physical, some are emotional, and others are intellectual. They are the myriad manifestations of the three bodies we discussed earlier in respect to the Tree of Life. In the terms of esoteric Christianity, they are defined as the motor center (the physical and instinctive aspects), the emotional center, and the intellectual center. The work of aligning these centers is the work of understanding them, stepping outside of them to watch them work, and then, eventually, changing the habitual and mechanical responses they engender to something controlled by the essence - the objective observer. Rather than reacting to shocks as the chemicals race through the system and carry us away, we are in control, and can, for once, begin to truly act instead of merely reacting to stimuli.

This is what Gurdjieff means when he says that as we are we are incapable of *action*. We are merely *reacting* mechanically until we "crystallize" or "grow" that spiritual body that can control our programs.

Through this work of self observation and self-mastery, we are in a sense rewiring ourselves, creating new circuits, physiologically. And it isn't easy. It hurts. You will suffer. You will suffer physically, emotionally, and mentally. To grab control of the emotions while the chemicals are pumping through the body is going to hurt, but this is the necessary and unavoidable part of the process. It is the body that is the alchemical crucible, and the proper use of mental and emotional and physical energies is the process that transmutes lead into gold.

By seeking objectivity about ourselves and the world around us, as opposed to what we are programmed to think or what appeals to us via emotion, the brain is forced to produce a different chemical mix and binding of Truth takes place on two initial levels: as above, so below. This activity can be cumulative, and can unlock DNA potentials as described in the section on neurochemicals. With this understanding, read again the following:

> By invigorating the Organs the Soul uses for communicating with exterior objects,
> the Soul must acquire greater powers not only for conception but also for retention,
> and therefore if we wish to obtain still more knowledge, the organs and secret
> springs of physical life must be wonderfully strengthened and invigorated. The Soul

must acquire new powers for conceiving and retaining... That this has not been the case with all possessors was their own fault.

.... Those who study only the material elements can at best discover only half the mystery... *alchemy is a mystery in three worlds - the divine, the human and the elemental...* alchemy in the hands of the profane becomes perverted...

Man's quest for gold is often his undoing, for he mistakes the alchemical processes, believing them to be purely material. He does not realize that the Philosopher's Gold, the Philosopher's Stone, and the Philosopher's Medicine *exist in each of the four worlds* and that the consummation of the experiment cannot be realized until it is successfully carried on in four worlds simultaneously according to one formula.

Furthermore, one of the constituents of the alchemical formula exists only within the nature of man himself, without which his chemicals will not combine, and though he spend his life and fortune in chemical experimentation, he will not produce the desired end [which is] the subtle element which comes out of the nature of the illuminated and regenerated alchemist. *He must have the magnetic power to attract and coagulate invisible astral elements.*[409]

Gurdjieff spoke of *intentional suffering*. We see now how suffering can be used, if one is conscious and has made the choice, for transmutation. Using the model of the many small "I's", we can say that the heat of the crucible, the fire engendered through our suffering, becomes the fuel needed to fuse together the many small "I's" to one purpose: Truth. This activity is mirrored in the chemicals in the body that affect DNA. The word "fuse" is used to good purpose because the self becomes a furnace in which the repetitive process of heating and cooling the personality is analogous to the heating and cooling used to forge and temper iron. If it is done all in one blow, the iron becomes brittle and will crack, the seeker will go mad, but if it is done slowly and carefully, heating and cooling over and over again, the iron becomes stronger, able to resist ever stronger shocks.

And so it goes with the inner work on the self.

You may have to go through the process for each of the small "I's" - each thought loop of reactions learned from society, family, experience - as each kicks and screams when it does not get its way, a process that will occur and reoccur as each is aligned and fused with your overriding will for the Truth that will set you free; true liberation: the mastery of the Self.

This process is the Quest that leads to the   Holy Grail of the self transmuted both psychically, and physically via DNA. These battles with the self are the tests of the Knight, tests of his commitment, designed to fell the Knight, either through force or distraction or seduction. Each choice we make is a test. Do we continue to live in the old way, or are we beginning to live in a new way? Do we continue to react to the shocks as we have always reacted? Or do we move on, understanding

---

[409] Eugenius Philalethes, quoted by Manly Hall, *The Secret Teachings of All Ages*, emphases, mine.

why we have always reacted thusly (under the illusion that we were in fact *acting*) and working to change, to no longer be mechanical, dependent upon our chemistry? Do we fall into confluence with the world, slipping out of awareness and into patterns of habit or mechanical activity? When we are walking into a trap, can we identify it in time or are we caught? If we are caught in a trap, do we recognized we are caught, or do we find excuses to justify to ourselves that we are free?

These choices will of necessity be difficult and painful. I know in my life there were times that I felt as if my heart was being crushed with the pain of facing the truth, of accepting it, and acting on it! And all the while the pain was unleashed and running wild through my system, a little voice was telling me that nothing was worth this pain, that the whole quest was nothing but an illusion, begging me to stop, to change course, to return to the comfort of the old life.

But the old life was never comfortable. The old life had driven me to the desperation of being willing to do anything to get out, so in the midst of the pain one must continue to see through the illusion, must hold onto the ultimate aim, the objective truth.

That is the thought that I needed to keep in mind when my body and my emotions were telling me to quit, when my mind was using my emotions to elaborate stories on how my old situation wasn't that bad after all, on how things could be different if I would just make a teeny change, a miniscule compromise of what was right. It took enormous will to remain connected to that part of me that knew the truth, that knew I could not continue on in the old ways, the part that knew compromise was just another lie.

That continual barrage of shocks is the fuel for the work, and the emotions are the fire that heats the crucible. That fire must be stoked over and over. Just because one has passed one test is no guarantee that one will pass the next. In fact, it is easy to become overconfident and complacent and forget that we are not in control of our own minds.

In our work with the Quantum Future School we have seen students who, full of energy and drive, have made enormous progress, dealing with many issues until the day comes when they face that one point, that one sacred cow, that they refuse to abandon. Quite often these are individuals who have previously made accurate assessments of the very same subjective state in others. However, even if they were able to see the dynamic playing out in others, as soon as it comes home, as soon as the fire is burning within them, they find excuses, rationalizations and justifications to explain why their case is special, unique, different, and why they should be excused from staring the truth in the face. Self-importance followed by self-pity.

And here we see the truth of the scripture when it says "Many are called but few are chosen."

Conscious suffering, the ability to sit in the fire while it burns and look at it objectively, that is, to see it for what it is without trying to put it out, to damp it, to cover it over, is the means by which we fuse our small "I's".

The magnetic center in the esoteric Christian tradition is the fourth body. It does not exist and must be created as the bridge to the higher self, the so-called soul. Let us look more closely at the structure of these centers.

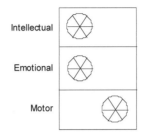

This is a diagram of the three lower centers, the motor center, the emotional center, and the intellectual center. Each center is composed of two halves, the positive and negative; each half is divided into three regions representing the three lower centers. Boris Mouravieff defines the three centers as follows:

The Intellectual Centre registers, thinks, calculates, combines, researches etc.;

The Emotional Centre has for its domain the feelings as well as refined sensations and passions;

The Motor Centre directs the five physical senses, accumulates energy in the organism through its instinctive functions, and with its motor functions governs the consumption of this energy. [410]

He further elaborates on the positive and negative parts of the centers:

Persistent introspection will later allow us to constate that each one of the three centres is divided into two parts: positive and negative. Normally these two parts act in conjunction with one another: for they are in fact polarized as are the double organs of the body, which duplicate the same function or participate in the same work at the same time; our arms for example. That division of the centres, a reflection of the universal polarization, allows them to establish *comparisons:* to consider both sides of problems posed to them. The positive part of each centre looks -one might say-to the head, and the negative part to the tail of these problems. The centre as a whole constructs an appropriate synthesis and draws its conclusions, inspired by the constatations made by each of the two parts.

An example is the process of critical analysis. It is therefore totally erroneous to consider that the names of these parts indicate a beneficent or harmful role depending on whether they are positive or negative. These terms do not imply any

---

[410] Mouravieff, Boris, *Gnosis*, Vol I, p. 11.

value judgement-any more than the constatation of positive and negative charges upon elementary particles.

If we consider the functioning of the motor centre, we can perceive that these parts are inseparable one from the other, in their structure as well as in their action. [...]

This symmetry-this polarity-is to be found in the two other centres. Constructive and creative ideas are born in the positive part of the intellectual centre. But it is the negative part that evaluates an idea, that takes its measure, so to speak. It is on the basis of this functional polarity that this centre, as a whole, judges.

It is the same with the emotional centre, the action of the negative part opposes the positive part, which at the same time completes it, for example permitting the centre as a whole to distinguish the agreeable from the disagreeable.

We can nevertheless misuse the faculties of the negative parts. This negative abuse is a real danger. The case is obvious as far as the motor centre is concerned, yet here physical exhaustion acts as a control, intervening to stop excessive consumption of energy. When it comes to the other centres, the misuse of the negative parts takes much more insidious forms, which entail more serious consequences for our minds as well as our bodies. [...]

In every centre there is therefore as much on the positive side as on the negative; one sector of each possesses the characteristics of that centre in a pure state. In the intellectual centre are sectors which are purely intellectual-positive and negative; in the emotional centre sectors which are purely emotional- positive and negative; in the motor centre sectors which are purely motor -positive and negative. Beside the pure sectors we find composite sectors which are, so to speak, the representatives of the two other centres. .[411]

We do not have the space in this book to go into any more detail about the centers and their functioning. This topic is dealt in great detail both in Mouravieff's work as well as in *In Search of the Miraculous* by P.D. Ouspensky who gives us Gurdjieff's ideas. We wish to give a brief overview of what happens to the centers as one undertakes the work described above.

In "souled" individuals, those characterized by Mouravieff as belonging to the Adamic race which has been discussed in an earlier section of this volume, there are three other centers - two higher and one "lower" - that constitute the "body" of the "higher self". As mentioned, a bridge has to be built to unite the higher and lower self. The two higher centers are the Higher Emotional center and the Higher Intellectual center. The lower center - which is, relatively speaking, still a "higher" center - is the sexual center. The diagram of the six centers looks like this:

The two higher centers are independent of our physical body and our Personality. They represent our Soul, the Logos. Although the higher centers are

[411] Ibid., pp. 24-25.

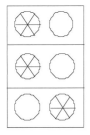

working at full capacity, the lack of balance - the bridge - in our three lower centers prevents us from receiving the messages they send. The work of the lower centers has as its goal to bring them into balance and purify them, that is, rid ourselves of our programs so that the energy from the higher centers can be received without distortion, interference and noise. As we achieve this balance, we begin to form what we have referred to as the fourth body above, our magnetic center.

At right, we see the magnetic center as it begins to form its connections to the other centers. It is still small, a black dot of "essence" that, little by little, can grow until it is able to balance and regulate the energy between all the centers. Eventually the magnetic center becomes strong enough to draw the lower emotional center and the higher emotional center together to form a single unit. This then results in what is called the "Knowledge of the Heart". Unfortunately, most expositions of this subject commonly available today are woefully misguided. At the start of this process, the diagram would look like the figure at left. Mouravieff describes the process as follows:

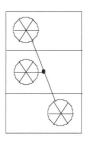

> When the *magnetic centre* finally takes shape, it establishes an undisputed authority over the three centres of the Personality. [...] This is how the *magnetic centre's* growth is perfected and how its development commences. The latter is a function of conscious efforts to develop the lower centres up to their limits. The further this development is continued, the more the *magnetic centre* absorbs the lower emotional centre, at the same time identifying itself more and more with the higher emotional centre. Once the three lower centres are fully developed and equilibrated, the magnetic centre once and for all identifies itself with the higher emotional centre, dragging with it the lower emotional centre which it finally absorbs. From now on the lower emotional centre, with the magnetic centre, will form an integral part of the higher emotional centre.[412]

When the merging of the centers is complete, the higher emotional center takes

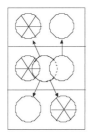   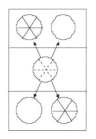

the place of the lower emotional center and we are left with the figure at right which those acquainted with esoteric work will recognize as the true esoteric representation of the Pentagram: the "Ascended Being".

At this point, the false personality is replaced by true Individuality which has, itself, a long series of stages of growth and development to undergo.

In Chapter 5 we spoke about the pre-Adamic race, what we also call the Organic Portal. The OP does not have the higher centers. They can and do however mimic them, reflecting back to the individual who has them in potential an image which can become a trap. The potentially souled individual can take the reflection, the illusion, for the real thing. Plate 4 models how this works. [See Plate 5.]

We have learned that a major part of our esoteric work is to learn to extricate ourselves from the energy feeding dynamic inherent in relationships with Organic Portals. Moreover, because those who have the higher centers in potential are subject to the same programming and are mechanical, reaction units until they undertake the work to develop their higher centers, the same thing holds true in our interactions and dynamics with them. We are all feeders until we learn to stop our feeding off of others and how to stop others from feeding off of us. Esoteric work demands enormous amounts of energy, and this energy is the energy off of which others feed.

In order to progress in esoteric work, it is fundamental to understand this underlying dynamic of feeding; it is pointless and dangerous to attempt to identify and to classify individuals as organic portals because we are all OPs until we choose to be otherwise. To turn a tool for understanding the true terror of our situation in this world of the fallen into a weapon against individuals is to empty it of its spiritual importance and render it a tool of our enslavement in the material world, the same process that has occured to all of the world's religions during the course of our unhappy history.

A true understanding of the organic portal and the world in which we live gives us the knowledge necessary for getting out "alive", whether that is literally or whether it is just being alive to our true nature as souls locked in material bodies in order to learn important lessons that only this world can teach. We can no more hate those who have no access to the higher truths because of who they are than we can hate the cat who plays with the mouse prior to killing and eating it.

Let me quote again the C's comment on the matter of Organic Portals in their relations with human beings who have the higher centers:

Q: (A) Now, I was reading in the transcripts that sleep is necessary for human
beings because it was a period of rest and recharging. You also said that the SOUL

---

[412] Ibid., pp. 59-60.

rests while the body is sleeping. So, the question is: what source of energy is tapped to recharge both the body and the soul?

A: The question needs to be separated. What happens to a souled individual is different from an organic portal unit.

Q: (L) I guess that means that the life force energy that is embodied in Organic Portals is something like the soul pool that is theorized to exist for flora and fauna. This would, of course, explain the striking and inexplicable similarity of psychopaths, that is so well defined that they only differ from one another in the way that different species of trees are different in the overall class of Tree-ness. So, if they don't have souls, where does the energy come from that recharges Organic Portals?

A: The pool you have described.

Q: Does the recharging of the souled being come from a similar pool, only maybe the "human" pool?

A: No - it recharges from the so-called sexual center which is a higher center of creative energy. During sleep, the emotional center, not being blocked by the lower intellectual center and the moving center, transduces the energy from the sexual center. It is also the time during which the higher emotional and intellectual centers can rest from the "drain" of the lower centers' interaction with those pesky organic portals so much loved by the lower centers. This respite alone is sufficient to make a difference. But, more than that, the energy of the sexual center is also more available to the other higher centers.

Q: (L) Well, the next logical question was: where does the so-called "sexual center" get ITS energy?

A: The sexual center is in direct contact with 7th density in its "feminine" creative thought of "Thou, I Love". The "outbreath" of "God" in the relief of constriction. Pulsation. Unstable Gravity Waves.

In this last remark, we begin to understand how the hyperdimensional Lords of Entropy utilize Organic Portals to steal the creative energy of the Mother, Mater, Mer.

Ibn al-'Arabi discusses the Universal Reality or Reality of Realities, i.e. Nature. In his cosmology, Nature alludes to the feminine side of a male/female, active/receptive, or yang/yin relationship. The words he uses in his discussion bring to mind receptivity toward an activity "coming from above," so to say. Nature is receptive to the Word, or "sign". Even though Nature is described as "receptive", it can be active or receptive according to the "forms" that are "impressed" into it via the Logos. Nature, the higher Sexual Center in Esoteric Christianity, is the Virgin of the World.

Nature is also the Black Virgin because, relatively speaking, Nature is "dark" and "unformed" without the Logos, or Light. At the same time, Nature is also Light because only absolute non-being is true Darkness since it is neither perceived, nor does perception take place through it. Thus, Nature, though it may be called the Black Virgin in relation to the Spirit which infuses it with life, is light in relation to absolute nothingness.

Nature is envisaged by al-'Arabi as receptive toward the Divine Names, or Thought Centers as we refer to them. In this sense, it is the Breath of God, the "highest and greatest Mother", who gives birth to all things, though she herself is never seen". The Black Virgin is the receptivity that allows the existent things to be manifest.

The specific properties of Nature are "heat, cold, wetness, and dryness". Two of them are active and two receptive. Heat is the root of dryness and cold is the root of wetness. But all four are receptive in relation to the Divine Command. Heat and cold, as well as wetness and dryness, display opposition and mutual aversion. As a result, everything that displays the properties of Nature reflects this opposition and conflict. But, like Nature, these properties cannot be assigned a category of "good" or "evil" without context, the third force.

> The root of the Breath is the property of love. Love has a movement within the lover, while "breath" is a movement of yearning toward the object of love, and through that breathing enjoyment is experienced. And God has said, as has been reported, "I was a Treasure but was not known, so I loved to be known". Through this love, breathing takes place, so the Breath becomes manifest, and the Cloud comes into being.

The Cloud is Nature.

The Divine Marriage, or sexual union of the Cosmos occurs when the Logos "penetrates" Nature to produce the possible entity of the endless potential of being. However, the Cosmic Union has a deeper and more important meaning for us. Al-'Arabi tells us:

> That which is desired from marriage may be reproduction - I mean the birth of offspring - or it may simply be enjoyment. The Divine Marriage is the attentiveness of the Real toward the possible thing in the presence of possibility through the desire of love, so that there may be bliss along with desire. When the Real turns His attentiveness toward the possible thing as mentioned, He makes manifest the coming to be of this possible thing. Hence, that which is born from this coming together is the existence of the possible thing.

> The entity of the possible thing is named "wife", the attentiveness through desire and love is called "marriage", and the production of the offspring is called a "bestowal of existence" upon the entity of that possible thing or, if you prefer, an "existence".

> The Beloved keeps Himself absent from the lover for the sake of imparting knowledge and teaching courtesy in love. For if the lover is truthful in his claim, while God tests him by the absence of his Beloved, then there will appear from the lover a movement of yearning to witness Him. Through this yearning he shows the truth of his claim; thereby his station is increased, and his reward through bliss in his Beloved is multiplied. For the pleasure which he finds at encounter is greater than the pleasure of unceasing companionship. This is similar to the frightened

person who finds the sweetness of reaching security: the sweetness of unceasing security is not nearly as intense.[...][413]

To love God objectively, in all His states, is to be attentive toward reality and to prove that love by the inward "movement of yearning to witness" the Beloved.

> Life is religion. Life experiences reflect how one interacts with God. Those who are asleep are those of little faith in terms of their interaction with the creation. Some people think that the world exists for them to overcome or ignore or shut out. For those individuals, the worlds will cease. *They will become exactly what they give to life.* They will become merely a dream in the "past". People who pay strict attention to objective reality right and left, become the reality of the "Future".

The world is as it is for a reason. When we have learned our lessons and have aligned ourselves with one or another of the two fundamental universal principles, Creation or Entropy, we are permitted to leave by one of two doors, either up or down, the ascending or descending path. The choice is ours. That is the great cosmic economy and the great secret of the world.

Truth comes from Knowledge. Knowledge leads to Love. To achieve Love in the Higher Realms, one must hold that Love here in the Lower Realm, but not the love that seeks to overcome or ignore or shut out the truth of the nature or the world within which we live, the objectivity of Nature as it is viewed, with love, by the Logos - unconditionally.

Today, as in the time of the emergence of the Grail Stories, Courtly Love remains, by definition, the indispensable condition for the success of the vivifying objective Love of the Higher Realms, the transducing of the energies of Creation, the objective of the Quest for the Holy Grail. It is only by achieving this state of objectivity, true unconditional love that SEES and KNOWS and yet LOVES, can the Seeker gain access to the Ancient Secret Technology which includes mastery of Space and Time and Matter: The Philosopher's Stone: Ascension.

The Alchemical Androgyne: I have become One: Creator of worlds.

---

[413] *Futuhat* , translated by William Chittick, op. cit.

AFTERWORD

At the present time, when millions of people have read *The Da Vinci Code*, by Dan Brown, it seems that the *awareness that man's true history has been hidden is growing apace* with the thirst for the truth. In this book, *The Secret History of the World*, I have dealt with many tributaries of the "hidden stream" of knowledge that have periodically emerged into the world during recorded history. These traditions include the Eleusinian Mysteries, the Orphic Tradition, Gnosticism, Gurdjieff's Fourth Way or "Esoteric Christianity",Catharism, which went underground as the stories of the Holy Grail emerged, and Alchemy, linking them to the most ancient traditions from pre-history, including Siberian Shamanism, the "Archaic Techniques of Ecstasy", as Mircea Eliade refers to the matter.

Thus, it is only fair that I warn the reader that this series of remarks will be comprehensible only to individuals well versed in studies of esoteric history and comparative religions, including *Gnosticism*, *Sufism*, the *Holy Grail*, *Alchemy*, (particularly the mysteries surrounding the French alchemist known as Fulcanelli), and *hermeticism* in general. This article plunges directly and immediately into the great mystery. Those who are immersed in Fourth Way Work and who have actually begun to "see" may also recognize the deeper implications of Gurdjieff's work.

Plate 6 - The Burial of Christ - is from a photograph I made in Auch Cathedral (Gers – 32). This Cathedral is dedicated to the *Black Virgin*.

These two words, suggesting initiation, hide a spiritual reality that is very much alive in the world today. The "Black Virgin" is a hidden presence that can guide the seeker to rebirth. The inscription of dedication of Auch Cathedral is engraved in black marble over the central door, and reads, *"To Mary, the Virgin who is to give birth to God"*.

Significantly, it reads "who is to...", not "who did...".

There are two representations of the Black Virgin in the Cathedral, suggested by certain details. In chapel 13, as the Sibyl of Samos, (below right) her costume and her face are brown, she is pregnant, and she holds a cradle in her hands.

The other representation is found in the choir stalls, in the canopies, immediately after the panel representing Adam and Eve. It is named Charity. There are two children standing at her feet, waiting and stretching their hands towards her.

A retired priest, Raymond Montané, who has spent his life studying the remarkable esoteric art in Auch Cathedral has written as follows:

> It is above all the windows of *Arnaud de Moles* that deserve our attention. Produced between 1507 and 1513, *they are esteemed as the finest of the Renaissance*. The

famous art critic Emile Male wrote: *"For the breadth of thought, no work of this period equals the windows of Auch."*

This extraordinary set includes a series of 18 windows. They are presented as a rich decoration, in which a crowd of characters of every origin meet each other. Most come from the Bible, but some of them, like the *Sibyls*, come from pagan religions. The themes of these story windows have been chosen with the greatest care. To discover the themes, we need to *find the golden thread creating an invisible link* between heterogeneous characters, apparently strangers to each other.

The visit of these windows must be made from the left to the right, going from the transept, beginning with *chapel 11*.[…] [See Plate 7.]

An idea brings them together. What is it? *The key to this mystery is in the <u>hands</u> of the Sibyl*. The object she carries gives us the key to the enigma. This symbolic biblical object concerns each of the characters in a window in some way. It brings them together for a single idea. The artist provoked these encounters to clarify a theme, to illustrate a story...

These windows are not a gallery of merely famous characters. *Among the most illustrious, some of them are not there, but some lesser known characters occupy a place of choice.* What counts first of all is not the character itself, but the story it evokes, *the destiny it attempts to direct.* Like the sibyls, each is dedicated to serving a story. They find themselves at the heart, the very *crucible* [...]

They come from everywhere, they are from all classes, from every origin. They come willingly like celebrity artists, finding themselves in a gigantic gala, not for their own benefit, but *for the benefit of a social and humanitarian task.*

These celebrity characters of Arnaud de Moles' windows contribute, in their own way, to the illustration of the greatest epic, *the unfolding of a HISTORY.*

Now, a question is asked: *What was the real role of Arnaud de Moles*, the master glazier, in the realization of the opus that bears his signature?

Arnaud de Moles showed himself truly as a master for the realisation of the kind of **screenplay** entrusted to him. He was a clever workman formed at the school of the Compagnons - a school that was marked by the techniques of the Middle Ages and the Gothic period. His companions were like him, earnest, available, and applied to their task.

The 18 windows of Arnaud de Moles are therefore an exceptional piece of work. What is truly unique - in this ensemble as well as the choir stalls - is the message that is revealed. *Arnaud de Moles was the artist, not the inspiration. The thought was given by unknown patrons.* […]

What first strikes the attentive mind is the wealth and variety of details. The source of this inspiration draws not only on the Bible and the lives of the Saints, but on nature, mythology, pagan religions, the Holy Grail and chivalry. […]

This remarkable set is not mere art! Like the windows, it contains thought, a message.

When we carefully observe the details, in the stalls, something immediately appears to our eyes: *Demons and snakes, malevolent animals and monsters* of all species swarm there. This *invasion* contributes to give to this whole *a tragic aspect that also agrees very well with the profound movement of history that is narrated to us.*

This tragic aspect is complementary and has to be placed in relationship to the windows of Arnaud de Moles. The windows and stalls constitute a whole. The two masterpieces were designed at the same time. The same story is told. Its theme was proposed to the glaziers and the sculptors. This theme evokes the same reality: *the reality of man in general.*

One would almost think about Dante's Inferno. *But this obvious tragedy is not hell - it is the history of humanity on earth.* Charity - empty handed - walks right before the monsters and demons, sustained by one same hope, going alone, but courageous, to face evil, the malevolent snake. *At the end of the cycle, she becomes triumphant Strength.* Her mission is accomplished because we see all malevolent snakes crushed under her feet or finally mastered in her hands.

Since this history is told and relived in retrospect, our artists knew in advance that this dramatic adventure had to bring us to Life.

What breadth! What perspective comes forth from the woodwork of the choir of Auch! Some connoisseurs are not afraid to compare the extraordinary work of these stalls with the frescoes of Michelangelo. [Raymond Montané]

I would like to make a note of the fact that, after spending some time trying to find out who *Arnaud de Moles* actually was, the information I was able to obtain suggests that it was a name given to a group, *The Companions Devoted to Liberty*,[414] or, perhaps an anagram. In terms of Green Language clues, the name "De Moles" is rich with meaning, ranging from the possibility of homophonic pronunciation "de Molay", as in the last Grand Master of the Templars, as well as the meaning of "mole", which, in French means *"stone"*, or a jetty: a breakwater. In English, the Green Language leads us to a creature that lives underground, or the "going underground" of a tradition. And then, of course, it can also say "Mea Deus Leonard". A reader may find a better solution. There is more, but I don't want to divert onto that subject at the moment because I have a story to tell.

In 2003, we decided for various reasons to re-locate to France. Having previously worked in France at a number of research centers with a number of French scientists who were enthusiastic about the possibility of Ark's return to Europe, we decided to pursue these mutual research interests.

We longed very much for a peaceful, country life, where we could work, continue our research, and feel safe from the intensifying pressures of various sources that threatened not only our peace of mind, but our very lives.[415] After

---

[414] http://www.cassiopaea.org/cass/Laura-Knight-Jadczyk/column-lkj-28-07-03.htm

[415] In my partial autobiography, *Amazing Grace*, I have discussed, at some length, many of the surpassingly strange events that began shortly after I was born, and which have continued to the present day, that give evidence of the fact that there is, indeed, within mysterious groups, some sort of extraordinary interest in my existence and work. It is clear from the objective evidence that some of these groups do not wish to kill me, but most definitely wish to control me, while others wish to protect

weeks of studying detailed maps of France, demographics, and so forth, I decided that the area around Auch was where I wanted to be, mainly because it was rural and agricultural. And so, we informed our friends in France of this choice and the search for a house was begun.

When we arrived in France, numb with fatigue and anxiety over so great a change in our lives, I made a mental note of the cathedral next to the real estate agency where we signed the lease for the new place. I was casually pleased to see such an interesting old church would be so close, but I didn't bother to go inside and look at it. After all, I had been to Notre Dame in Paris! Wasn't Fulcanelli's book, *Le Mystère de Cathedrales* focused on the edifices in Paris, Amiens, and Bourges? What could a cathedral in Auch have to offer?

However, after a question by a visitor from the U.S. (thank you Charlotte), made me curious to see "the famous statues" that I had never heard of, I took the time to go and look. Once I had seen the windows by Arnaud de Moles and the choir, I was so stunned by the clear esoteric import of Auch Cathedral that *I could not understand why Fulcanelli had failed to mention it.*

It was a puzzle, and it was only over time, as more clues were revealed, as I will explain here, that I realized that it must have been omitted *intentionally* for the simple reason that it was quite obviously the cathedral with the keys. Fulcanelli was hardly going to give away the keys to the greatest secrets of reality so cheaply that they could be figured out in a year or two by a dilettante. Additionally, according to Fulcanelli, *without divine assistance* - which we most certainly had via the Cassiopaean transmissions - there could be no hope of solving the mystery. This is one of the precepts of esoteric work that is often overlooked by those who promote themselves as esotericists. The Great Sufi Shaykh, Ibn al-'Arabi points out that one seeker may stand at the door and knock his entire life, and it will never open to him, and another may be admitted with a single request.

In studying the matter we learn that, among the rules that must direct the process of understanding, are the following, each of which leads, in a natural progression, to the next:

> 1) The Soul must acquire greater powers not only for conception but also for retention, and therefore if we wish to obtain still more knowledge, the organs and secret springs of physical life must be wonderfully strengthened and invigorated. "The Soul must acquire new powers for conceiving and retaining..."

> 2) In order to respect the principle of hermetism adopted by the Tradition, we must understand that esoteric teachings are given in a *sibylline* form.

> St Isaac the Syrian points out that: The Holy Scriptures state many things by using words in a different sense from their original meaning. Sometimes bodily attributes

---

me and ensure that I succeed in some "mission" of which I have very little conscious awareness, but apparently, am discovering in a satisfactory way "one step at a time."

are applied to the soul, and conversely, attributes of the soul are applied to the body. The Scriptures do not make any distinction here. However, enlightened men understand.

3) "Like attracts like." When a candidate has developed virtue and integrity acceptable to the adepts, *they will appear to him* and reveal those parts of the secret processes *which cannot be discovered without such help.* Those who cannot progress to a certain point with their own intelligence are not qualified to be entrusted with the secrets which can subject to their will the elemental forces of Nature.

As I continued to marvel at Auch Cathedral, I began to realize fully, for the first time, that the Cassiopaean Transmissions was just such an "appearance of the adepts",It finally began to dawn on me that the process I had followed, instinctively, had been quite accurately described by Eugene Canseliet in his Preface to the second edition of Fulcanelli's *The Dwellings of the Philosophers:*

According to the meaning of the Latin word *adeptus*, the alchemist has then received the Gift of God, or even better, *the Present*, a cabalistic pun on the double meaning of the word, underlining that he thus enjoys **the infinite duration of the Now**.[...]

In the **Kingdom of Sulpur** (cabalistically: Soul Fire) there exists a Mirror in which the entire World can be seen. Whosoever looks into this Mirror can see and learn the three parts of Wisdom of the entire World.

July 14, 1996

Q: (L) In other words, as long as we are in the pigstye, we are in the pigstye, and until we get *out* of it, we are *in* it?

A: Until you reach that point on the learning cycle. [...] "Passion" does not set one "free", quite the opposite!

Q: (L) But what if your passion is for knowledge?

A: That is not passion, it is soul questing.

Q: (L) What is it that gives some people this drive, this steamroller effect that they are determined to get to the absolute bottom of everything and strip away every lie until there is nothing left but the naked truth? What is the source of this desire?

A: Wrong concept. It is simply that one is at that point on the learning cycle. At that point, no drive is needed.

Q: (L) So, you more or less are there because some critical mass has been reached that 'jumps' you to the point where seeking truth is simply who you are? It defines the parameters of your being.

After thirty years of study and two years of dedicated experimentation, detailed in my autobiography, *Amazing Grace*, the Cassiopaean communications began: I began to look into the Mirror in which the entire world can be seen.

"We are you in the Future", they said. "We transmit 'through' the opening that is presented in the locator that you represent as Cassiopaea, due to the strong radio pulses aligned from Cassiopaea, which are due to a pulsar from a neutron star 300 light years behind it, as seen from your locator. This facilitates a clear channel transmission from 6th density to 3rd density... [in] "Zero" time [utilizing Electromagnetics and gravity which are interconnected, or you could say "unified".

Space and time are selective and flexible. ... You see, when one utilizes zero time, there is zero space as well."

In short, the Cassiopaean Transmission was initiation preparatory to receiving the "Gift of the Present".

After living in the Gers for 11 months, we found a more permanent - and safer - house with all the features we needed for our work. We moved in and shortly discovered that one of our neighbors was *Patrick Rivière*, a noted historian of religions and author of many books on the subject of comparative religions, alchemy and the Holy Grail. He is also an expert on the "Rennes-le-Chateau" phenomenon. Patrick, as an alchemist (*Adeptus*) also happened to be a student of *Eugene Canseliet, the disciple of Fulcanelli.* We dispatched a note to him and were very happy to receive a call a couple of days later suggesting a meeting. It seems that Patrick had been "waiting" for us. His own studies and lifelong work had brought him to the point where, as an adept, he knew that, "The Sybil Would Appear when the time was right". This was the beginning of our collaborations.

I was very anxious to query Patrick about any clues to the true identity of Fulcanelli. I had read many theories about this, but due to a particular clue that was dropped almost casually by Eugene Canseliet in his description of his visit to the "enclave of the alchemists" in Spain, I was convinced that Fulcanelli was a single individual, not a "committee" as some materially-minded thinkers propose, and that he had, indeed, achieved the "Great Work". Patrick agreed and responded that he knew the identity of Fulcanelli, and that he had written a small book on the subject in French that was not yet available to English speaking audiences, *Fulcanelli* in the "Qui suis-je?" series. [Red Pill Press will be bringing out Patrick's work in English soon.]

We spent many pleasant hours with Patrick at a table going over his process of discovery, his reasoning, and looking at the documentation he had collected over the years. This man has truly devoted his entire life to this work. In the end, I was convinced that Patrick is quite right: the true identity of Fulcanelli was *Jules Violle*, a famous French physicist of the 19th century. As noted, Patrick's own work on this subject is being translated and I will leave it to him to describe his process of discovery. It was what we discovered together, after receiving this clue, that is most important to discuss here. It is, in fact, I believe, the solution to the "Da Vinci Code".

Jules Violle was a graduate of the École Normale Supérieure at Paris, he taught at the University of Lyon (1883), then at the École and, from 1891, at the Conservatoire des Arts et Métiers, Paris. He made the first high-altitude determination of the solar constant on Mont Blanc in 1875. The "violle" is a unit of light intensity equal to a square centimeter of platinum, glowing at its melting temperature of 1769 °C (3216 °F). *It was the first unit of light intensity that did not depend on the properties of a particular lamp.*

When I read this, my mind immediately went back to an excerpt from the Cassiopaean Transmissions:

June 21, 1997

A: Alfalfa fields in Rhineland yield as of yet undreamed of treasures.

Q: Where are these alfalfa fields?

A: Near tracks well worn.

Q: [...] Do you mean Rhineland as in Germany proper?

A: We do not mean Rhinelander, Wisconsin... Or do we?!? Who is to tell?

Q: Who?

A: The searcher, the sepulcher, the one who carries the staff in constant search for greener pastures.

Q: Oh my! You are being *very* obscure tonight! [...] any additional clues for me or Ark?

A: Last clue for tonight: Look for the vibratory frequency light. Good Night.

I suddenly realized that the funny remark about "Rhinelander, Wisconsin" pointed directly at France - the land of a Thousand Cheeses - because, to the American mind, Wisconsin is "the land of Cheese". I later learned that the Garonne River was referred to as "The Rhine of France". And then, of course, there are "rhinds" on cheeses. But the icing on the cake was, of course, "look for the vibratory frequency of light", and the Violle: *the first unit of light intensity that did not depend on the properties of a particular lamp.*

As I began to dig into the background of Jules Violle, I discovered another significant clue: he was closely associated with *Camille Flammarion*, French astronomer and popular author. Flammarion was the founder of the French Astronomy Society, and he served for many years at the Paris Observatory and the Bureau of Longitudes. Flammarion set up a private observatory at Juvisy (near Paris) in 1883 and his studies were particularly focused on *double and multiple stars* - a particular focus of the Cassiopaean Transmissions - and of the moon and Mars. It is easy to see that Violle and Flammarion had a lot in common, particularly their interest in stars. Double and multiple Stars gives Fulcanelli's dedication *"To The Brothers of Heliopolis"* an all new level of meaning!

When examining the life and associations of Camille Flammarion, additional clues began to finally fit together: he was an associate of, and greatly influenced by, *Allan Kardec*, the French Pedagogue, medical student, linguist and researcher of "spirit communications".

In the spring of 1858, Kardec founded the *Societe Parisienne des Etudes Spirites*. In the late 1850s and early 1860s, small Spiritist groups began to proliferate throughout France, especially in Paris, Lyon and Bordeaux.

Camille Flammarion remarked: "I have no hesitation in saying that he who states that spiritist phenomena are contrary to science does not know what he is talking about. Indeed, there is nothing super-natural in nature. There is only the unknown: but what was unknown yesterday becomes the truth of tomorrow".

Victor Hugo, another advocate of scientific spiritualism said: "Turning a blind eye to the spiritist phenomena is turning a blind eye to the truth".

The Societe Parisienne was similar to the Society for Psychical Research in London, a body devoted to unbiased inquiry. Kardec's efforts were largely focused on promoting *the impartial and rational study of spiritual matters. The Spiritist views of Kardec were scientific, not mystical*; and *he promoted objective discovery over intuitive insight,* just as the Cassiopaean Transmissions and our own work does.

Turning now to the comments on millenarialism in the works of Fulcanelli, it is interesting to note that Kardec's final book, *La Gazette selon le Spiritisme*, appearing in 1868, *strongly reflected the millenialist view*. The work closed with a series of communications and commentaries declaring that "the time chosen by God has come", stating that a new generation of highly-evolved souls was in the process of being incarnated on Earth.

This is precisely what Fulcanelli stated in the mysterious *Hendaye chapter* of *Mystery of the Cathedrals* as well as in the final chapters of *Dwellings of the Philosophers*. We also note that *Fulcanelli emphasized the role of science in the so-called "End Times" as being crucial. Not only was Jules Violle a scientist, but my husband, Ark is a scientist: an expert in Hyperdimensional Physics, Nonlinear Dynamics and Complex Systems.*

Finding a well established link between Flammarion and Jules Violle, followed by a well established link between Flammarion and Kardec, gives an entirely new perspective on the work of *Violle as Fulcanelli*. It also leads us to the very important question: *Is it possible that Fulcanelli made use of "superluminal communication techniques" as I had myself?* Was this why Fulcanelli insisted as follows:

> "Furthermore, in our opinion, it seems insufficient to know how to recognize and classify facts exactly; one must still question nature and learn from her in what conditions and under the control of what will her manifold productions take place. Indeed, the philosophical mind will not be content with the mere possibility of identifying bodies. It demands the knowledge of the secret of their elaborations. To open ajar the door of the laboratory where nature mixes the elements is good; *to discover the occult force*, under whose influences her work is accomplished, is better."[...]

> "Alchemy is obscure only because it is hidden. The philosophers who wanted to transmit the exposition of their doctrine and the fruit of their labors to posterity took great care not to divulge the art by presenting it under a common form so that the layman could not misuse it. Thus because of the difficulty one has of understanding it, because of the mystery of its enigmas and of the opacity of its parables, *the science has come to be shut up among reveries, illusions and chimeras.*" [...]

> "With their confused texts, sprinkled with cabalistic expressions, the books remain the efficient and genuine cause of the gross mistake that we indicate. For, in spite of the warnings... students persisted in reading them according to the meanings that they hold in ordinary language. *They do not know that these texts are reserved for initiates, and that it is essential, in order to understand them, to be in possession of their secret key. One must first work at discovering this key."*

> "Most certainly these old treatises contain, if not the entire science, at least its philosophy, its principles, and the art of applying them in conformity with natural laws. But if we are unaware of the hidden meaning of the terms - for example, the meaning of Ares, which is different from Aries - strange qualifications purposely used in the composition of such works, we will understand nothing of them or we will be infallibly led into error."

"We must not forget that it is *an esoteric science*. Consequently, a keen intelligence, an excellent memory, work, and attention aided by a strong will are NOT sufficient qualities to hope to become learned in this subject."

"Nicolas Grosparmy writes: 'Such people truly delude themselves who think that we have only made our books for them, but we have made them to keep out all those who are not of our sect.'"

"Batsdorff, in the beginning of his treatise, charitably warns the reader in these terms: 'Every prudent mind must first acquire the Science if he can; that is to say, the principles and the means to operate. Otherwise he should stop there, without foolishly using his time and his wealth. And so, I beg those who will read this little book to credit my words. I say to them once more, that THEY WILL NEVER LEARN THIS SUBLIME SCIENCE BY MEANS OF BOOKS, AND THAT IT CAN ONLY BE LEARNED THROUGH DIVINE REVELATION, HENCE IT IS CALLED DIVINE ART, or through the means of a good and faithful master; and since there are very few of them to whom God has granted this grace, there are also very few who teach it.'" [Fulcanelli, *The Dwellings of the Philosophers,* Boulder: Archive Press 1999, pp. 49, 65, 84]

In view of this question, it might be useful to look at excerpts from an article written by Camille Flammarion, the friend and associate of Jules Violle and Allan Kardec which reflects our views exactly:

Spiritism is, in general, in bad repute, and *deserves to be.* Most of its disciples are unmethodical; they are often lacking in mental poise, are often dupes of illusions. *They prefer a belief and a religion which merely console, to the impartial and critical investigation without which we can be sure of nothing.* These are bad conditions for research; adequate safeguards are lacking.

In Allan Kardec's time (in the course of the speech which I made at his grave on April 2, 1869) I believed it helpful and even necessary to proclaim, at this very grave, that *"spiritism is not a religion but a science"*, and to add that *"we are now at the dawn of an undiscovered science"*. During the fifty years which followed the utterance of these words, *the continued progress of our research* has lent them greater and greater emphasis, confirmed them more and more fully.

It is by the scientific method alone that we may make progress in the search for truth. Religious belief must not take the place of *impartial analysis*. We must be constantly on our guard against illusions.

Apart from deliberate deception, dishonest and inexcusable, there is *autosuggestion leading to involuntary deception.* [...]

There are also dishonest exploiters of credulity, who give "séances", promising apparitions and posthumous manifestations to the simpletons who listen to them. Those who have been gulled then complain, laughably, of having been robbed! The human race, supposedly intelligent, is truly strange. *One must have a great deal of*

courage to work perseveringly, surrounded by these impostors; one must be
sustained by the conviction that there are truths to be discovered. [...][416]

Flammarion makes a profound distinction between "spiritualism" and
"spiritism". By "spiritualism" he means the general doctrine that departed spirits
hold intercourse with mortals. By "spiritism" he means *mediumistic research.*

As we continued to examine and discuss the documents Patrick Riviere had
collected, including many that he only reveals in his book on the identity of
Fulcanelli, the talk naturally turned to *the third book of Fulcanelli* that was
withdrawn: *Finis Gloria Mundi.* This book has been the subject of much
speculation, and I hear that someone has actually published a volume claiming to
be the "real deal". It's clear from the evidence that this is not the case, that the
book in question is a fraud.

The title of this Third Book of Fulcanelli, *Finis Gloria Mundi (The End of the
Glory of the World),* certainly *reflects the millennialist perspective,* which I
discuss at some length in *The Secret History of The World.* As we went over the
notes and outline that were in the possession of Eugene Canseliet at his death, we
came to the realization that my own book, *The Secret History of The World,* may
be quite close in content and structure to the actual *Finis Gloria Mundi* though it is
certainly, again, a strange coincidence. Certainly, all of the chapter headings of
that book cover the subjects in *Secret History,* only I believe I have actually gone
further given the new data available in the intervening years. I would like to
highlight a portion of the Preface that Patrick has written for this volume:

> This book of revolutionary importance is essential reading. [...]
>
> Throughout her exposé, Laura Knight-Jadczyk refers to two powerful works of the
> scientist-alchemist Fulcanelli: The Mystery of the Cathedrals and Dwellings of the
> Philosophers. She applies her vast knowledge to the continuation of his work.
>
> Thus, following in the footsteps of Fulcanelli (citing Huysmans) when he
> denounces the constant lies and omissions from official History over the course of
> time, Laura Knight-Jadczyk, citing numerous examples, exposes the manipulations
> in the official history of ancient civilizations of which humanity is the victim. She
> strives to re-establish the truth, and her answers are often enlightening.
>
> According to Laura Knight-Jadczyk, the mysteries of the Holy Grail and the Ark of
> the Temple refer to a particular, very advanced "technology" - with the aim, for
> example, of teleportation and changing between space-time dimensions - a secret
> and sacred science of which only a few great "Initiates" have remained custodians.
> Christ Jesus was the surest guarantor of this precious legacy, and, although it might

---

[416] Camille Flammarion's *Death and Its Mystery - After Death. Manifestations and Apparitions of the
Dead; The Soul After Death* Translated by Latrobe Carroll (1923, T. Fisher Unwin, Ltd. London:
Adelphi Terrace.

displease Dan Brown (author of The DaVinci Code), the genealogical lineage of the "Sangréal" (the "Sang Royal" or "Holy Blood"), is not at all as he believes it to be!

The reader of this important work by Laura Knight-Jadczyk will realize that there are completely different conclusions to that mystery. Her erudition cannot but impress the reader during the course of an assiduous reading of this quite astonishing book.

As to her inspiration, what can we say, and, from whence could it come, if not the Light of the stars?

Rivière has hypothesized in our conversations that Fulcanelli withdrew the book because he did not have proof of certain scientific elements concerning the pole shift and, as a scientist, did not wish to promote ideas for which there was no evidence at the time. While I consider this to be a valid argument, with the hyperdimensional perspective factored in, we both agreed that *Fulcanelli withdrew the book because he knew it was not yet time*. Those who have received the *Gift of God*, the Present, can certainly "see the unseen" including future probabilities.

Another interesting clue was discussed among us. At one point, we were discussing Canseliet's visit to Seville where he encountered Fulcanelli as a *young girl*. The issue of our discussion was: what was the meaning of this event and was it intended to convey a message? And if so, to whom? It certainly was the one thing that conveyed to *me* reams of information about the nature of the Great Work. In 1995, the Cassiopaeans had described some of the effects of a "4th density bleedthrough" on 3rd density humans in the following way:

4th density frees one from the illusion of "time" as you WILL to perceive it. Picture driving down a highway, suddenly you notice auras surrounding everything.... Being able to see around corners, going inside little cottages which become mansions, when viewed from inside... Going inside a building in Albuquerque and going out the back door into Las Vegas, *going to sleep as a female, and waking up male...* Flying in a plane for half an hour and landing at the same place 5 weeks later... Picture driving to reach New Mexico by car and "skipping" over and arriving in San Diego instead, or... driving to the grocery store in Santa Fe, and winding up in Moscow, instead.

As we examined every aspect of the event, it came out that the incident occurred when I was 2 years old, exactly at the time that, as I have described in my autobiography, I disappeared and then reappeared in a very strange manner that is still inexplicable to this day. Then, of course, there is the mysterious "Hendaye Chapter", which was included in the Second Edition of *Mystery of the Cathedrals* concomitant with the withdrawal of *Finis Gloria Mundi.*

One evening, as we discussed Fulcanelli around the fire in Patrick's charming farm-house, alchemical laboratory, warming our glasses of amber Armagnac in our hands, Patrick mentioned "Hendaye". My brain suddenly snapped to attention.

"What did you say?" He repeated the word, and I suddenly understood something quite profound. You see, the word "Hendaye", pronounced by a native French speaker, sounds very much like "Onde", which is French for "Wave". I had begun *The Wave Series*[417] in 1999 and worked on it well into 2000 before an offer was made to translate it into French, at which time I learned the French word "Onde". But I had never heard it properly pronounced before.

So, with this sudden realization, put together with the other clues that were, one by one, revealing themselves to us, we began to speculate on the real reason for Fulcanelli to have written this piece which, essentially replicates most of the same information he includes in his final chapters of *Dwellings of the Philosophers*. Could the reason have been purely "Green Language", to relate The Wave to Onde via Hendaye? Was it a clue specifically for us, at that moment in space/time, when the "right people" with the right keys were all brought together in the peaceful French countryside overlooking the Garonne River, the "Rhine of France"?

Undreamed of Treasures indeed!

In any event, the title of Fulcanelli's Third Book was taken from a painting that is found in *Seville*. We began to discuss a proposed trip to Seville to visit the place where Canseliet had this meeting with Fulcanelli and to view the painting. It was at this point that I noted the interesting fact that, following the rules of language changes, the word "Seville" was very similar to Sibyl. Another "Green Language clue" just for us? That brings us back to Auch Cathedral and its many Sibyls which led to even more discoveries - even, in fact, the True "Da Vinci Code".

A single Sibyl is first mentioned about 500 B.C. by Heraclitus: "The Sibyl, with frenzied mouth uttering things not to be laughed at, unadorned and rough, yet reaches to a thousand years with her voice by aid of the god".

Later, there were more Sibyls; Christians in the late middle ages recognized as many as twelve. The most famous sibyls were the Erythraean and the Cumaean. There is some confusion as to whether they were always young and virginal, or old hags. The Cumaean sibyl was alleged to have lived for nearly a thousand years, at the end of which, all that was left of her was her voice, *kept in an empty jar*. One has to wonder about this in terms of the images of Mary Magdalene and her "alabaster jar" and the possible Green Language clues there. In any event, the fame of the Cumaean sibyl was due to Virgil's use of her in the *Fourth Eclogue* to foretell the birth of a saviour (40 B.C.) and as Aeneas' guide to the underworld in Book Six of the *Aeneid*. This, curiously, leads us back to Fulcanelli.

Canseliet writes in his first preface to *Mystery of the Cathedrals*:

> I know, not from having discovered it myself, but because I was assured of it by the
> author more than ten years ago, that the key to the major arcanum is given quite

---

[417] http://www.cassiopaea.org/cass/waveindex.htm. Also available from Red Pill Press as a multi-volume set.

openly in one of the figures, illustrating the present work. And this key consists quite simply in a colour revealed to the artisan right from the first work.

In his introduction to the Second Edition, Canseliet tells us that Basil Valentine was Fulcanelli's initiator - and makes the point of distinction between "first initiator", and "true initiator". That could certainly indicate the difference between a "human" teacher" and a "hyperdimensional" teacher. He then discusses a letter that was left by Fulcanelli after he "died", and which he says was obviously received by Fulcanelli's master from some unknown individual, and which Canseliet said was the "written proof of the triumph of his *true initiator*", which provides a "powerful and correct idea of the sublime level at which the Great Work takes place". This letter has a number of remarkable references which suggest to me that it may not be a letter to Fulcanelli's master, but was to Fulcanelli himself, and may have referred to his attempts to communicate with Basil Valentine directly via techniques learned from Kardec via Flammarion. The references that suggest this to me are:

> This time you have really had the Gift of God; it is a great blessing and, for the first time, I understand how rare this favour is.[…]

> When my wife told me the good news… I was only briefly informed about the matter…[…]

> You have extended generosity to the point of associating us with this high and occult knowledge, to which you have full right and which is entirely personal to you. […]

> My wife, with the inexplicable *intuition of sensitives*…

> One can almost say that he, who has greeted the morning star, has forever lost the use of his sight and his reason, because he is fascinated by this false light and cast into the abyss… *Unless, as in your case, a great stroke of fate comes to pull him unexpectedly from the edge of the precipice.*

For me, this "great stroke of luck" that pulled me from the precipice[418] was the Cassiopaean Transmissions. They have done it more than once! I would like to point out that the "familiarity" of the remark, *"You have extended generosity to the point of associating us with this high and occult knowledge, to which you have full right and which is entirely personal to you"*, struck me in a profound way in regard to this. The reader might wish to read Ark's comments on "Reductio ad Absurdum"[419] to understand exactly what this phrase can refer to, not to mention

---

[418] http://www.cassiopaea.org/cass/mirror.htm

[419] http://www.cassiopaea.org/cass/swerdlow.htm

The Adventures Series[420] which describes a period in which I was perilously close to being entrapped in a pit.

Returning to Canseliet's preface to the second edition of *Mystery of the Cathedrals*, we find that he continues on with a discussion of the "star" in question asking:

> Does not this phrase apparently contradict what I stated twenty years ago… namely that the star is the great sign of the Work; that it sets its seal on the philosophic matter; that it teaches the alchemist that he has found not the light of fools but the light of the wise; that it is the crown of wisdom; and that it is called the *morning star*? […]

> It may have been noted that I specified briefly that the hermetic star is admired first of all in the *mirror of the art* or *mercury*, before being discovered in the *chemical sky*…

> **Our star is single and yet it is double.** Know how to distinguish its true imprint from its image and you will observe that it shines with more intensity in the light of day than in the darkness of night.

> This statement corroborates and completes the no less categorical and solemn one made by Basil Valentine (*Douze Clefs*):

> 'Two stars have been granted to man by the Gods, in order to lead him to the great Wisdom; observe them. Oh man! And follow their light with constancy, because it is Wisdom.'[…]

> There are, then, two stars which, improbable as it may seem, are really only one star. The star shining on the mystic Virgin - who is at one and the same time *our mother (mère)* and the *hermetic sea (mer)* - announces the conception and is but the reflection of that other, which precedes the miraculous advent of the Son. For though the celestial Virgin is also called *stella matutina*, the *morning star*; it is possible to see on her the splendour of a divine mark; though the recognition of this source of blessings brings joy to the heart of the artist; *it is no more than a simple image, reflected by the mirror of Wisdom.*

Canseliet continues to give clues for the seeker to figure out what he is talking about, followed by a story designed to confuse those who are more materially minded. In short, he introduces a deliberate obfuscation. Canseliet then says:

> The reader may be surprised that I have spent so much time on a single point of the Doctrine… However, it must be obvious how logical it was for me to dilate on this subject which, I maintain, *leads us straight into Fulcanelli's text*. Indeed, *right from the beginning my Master has dwelt on the primary role of the star*, this *mineral Theophany, which announces with certainty the tangible solution of the great secret concealed in religious buildings…*

---

[420] http://www.cassiopaea.com/cassiopaea/adventureindex.htm

The remark: "Mineral Theophany" struck another spark with the Cassiopaean Transmissions where I had asked a few brief questions about a dream I had. But first, let me recount the dream from my journal:

> There was a "high priest" who appeared in my dream wearing a skirt like the Cretan depictions of the goddess with the many tiered skirt... only this was a man. He showed me how the different tiers could be "rotated" so that certain "symbols" aligned which then gave a message. The symbols were zodiacal and the *star names* were of great significance. The trick was, to align them properly.
>
> The same dream then morphed. I was holding a vase that appeared to be onyx or something like that. Others had tossed it on a junk heap, and I picked it up and was examining a lot of "scratch" marks all over it. I could see that it was engraved all over, but that all the grooves were filled with dirt and it was coated with grime. I began to clean it with Q-tips and water very carefully going into all the little cracks and tracing out all the lines. As I did so and the dirt came away, I was awestruck at the beauty of this thing. It was not only cunningly worked with some great mythical scene being enacted, but it was inlaid with amazing veneers of various colored stones... and, it was also translucent so that the "blackness" turned out to be really a deep, translucent purple as though there was a light within.
>
> The dream morphed again: Ark and I were walking and it seemed to be a sort of "park" or "recreation" area of some sort with mountains and cliffs and so forth. We were walking about looking at rock formations and shrubbery - it was very dry and needed water - and he was walking along a path and I decided to hide in a bush and see how long it took for him to notice I was missing... just playing... but I suddenly found myself standing on the path *ahead* of him... and he asked "how did you do that?". So, I said... well, I ducked into this bush and there was a cleft in the rock, and I started to squeeze into it and something happened and here I am!
>
> He insisted that I go back and show it to him. So, we went back, and there was a small cave entrance... looking rather like the broken cleft of the tomb in the Arcadian Shepherd's painting. He said that it was impossible... too small ... I told him "try it".
>
> So, he stooped down and entered the cave... meanwhile, I decided to stay busy by cleaning all the cracks in the rocks around the cave entrance... there was a trickle of water, and I was using some sort of cloth... and as I did, the water kept increasing its flow until it was a veritable fountain! At this point, Ark came stumbling out of the cave, holding his eyes, crying tears and laughing at the same time saying "I believe! I believe! I've seen it with my own eyes!", and that sort of thing.
>
> So, we started to leave the park and as we were walking out the entrance, I glanced up at the cliff face, and there was a *huge* mosaic set in the rock... on the right were seven sharks... the bottom one was pale, and they got darker as they went up... stacked, exact same images... and on the left was a *huge* whale depicted in the act of "whipping around" with his mouth opening, his eye on the sharks and preparing (by implication of the frozen posture) to devour them all at one bite. I told myself that I needed to remember this dream and woke up.

> July 19, 1997
>
> Q: I had a dream the other night. As Ark and I were leaving [a large park area] in my dream, I looked up and saw a mosaic on the side of the mountain. It had seven sharks, one above the other, the lowest being pale almost to the point of transparency, and the highest being very dark and intense in color. There was a

huge sperm whale to the upper left, he was in the posture of whipping around, his eye had caught the sharks, and his mouth was open and he was going to swallow them all in a single gulp. What was the meaning of the whale and the sharks?

A: Logic.

Q: Are you telling me to use logic, or that the meaning *is* logic?

A: Logic says to you: examine!

Q: The other part of the dream was that I disappeared and reemerged from a cleft in a rock. I was cleaning... [Ark] went to investigate [the cleft which was just a slit and impossible to enter or exit from]... [while he was gone, I continued to clean out all the little cracks and crevices in the rocks on the ground] and he returned and was crying and all this water was flowing out of there like a spring that seemed to have resulted from my cleaning efforts... What was the significance of this?

A: Trace minerals interact with deeply held secrets.

Q: The other night you said something about what I had found as being one leg of the table. How many legs does the table have?

A: Search for answer. When found in literature, profound meanings enclose compartment.

I hope that this contributes to the reader's understanding of Canseliet's remark: "this *mineral Theophany,* which announces with certainty the tangible solution of *the great secret concealed in religious buildings...*"

Feb 19, 2000

Q: Diodorus Siculus, writing in the 1st century B.C., said that "certain sacred offerings wrapped in wheat straw come from the Hyperboreans into Scythia, whence they are taken over by the neighboring peoples in succession until they get as far west as the Adriatic. From there they are sent south, and the first Greeks to receive them are the Dodonaeans. Then, continuing southward, they reach the Malian gulf, cross to Euboea, and are passed on from town to town as far as Carystus. Then they skip Andros, the Carystians take them to Tenos, and the Tenians to Delos. That is how these things are said to reach Delos at the present time."

So, from very ancient times, there was this practice of the Hyperboreans sending sacred offerings to the Island of Delos. Now, the Island of Delos is supposedly the birthplace of Phoebus Apollo, whose mother was Leto. Supposedly he was born on Mt. Cynthus. This is a very curious thing. This is contrary to the old view that the cultural flow was from the Mediterranean to the North, that civilization began in the Near East. It implies a cultural flow from the North to the South. What were these ancient Hyperboreans sending to the Island of Delos?

A: Leaves bearing cryptic codes.

Q: What was the connection between the Hyperboreans, including the Celts of Britain, I believe, and the people of Delos?

A: Northern peoples were responsible for civilizing the Mediterranean/Adriatic peoples with the encoded secrets contained within their superior extra-terrestrially based genetic arrangement. Practice of which you speak was multi-trans-generational habit.

Q: Is it the case that some of them communicated with higher density beings via Stonehenge, and that these communications they received...

A: Stonehenge used to resonate with tonal rill, teaching the other wise unteachable with wisdoms entered psychically through crown chakra transceiving system.

This brings us back in a curious way to my profound understanding of the previously mentioned comment made in the letter left by Fulcanelli: *"You have extended generosity to the point of associating us with this high and occult knowledge, to which you have full right and which is entirely personal to you"*. If the reader has had a look at "Reductio ad Absurdum" and related links, then this exchange will not only fill in a few blanks, it will reveal the terrible struggle that must be sustained by one seeking truth. "Frank" is a pseudonym for the individual who embarked with me on the experiment that led to the Cassiopaean Transmissions. He was present at nearly every session (but not all, and certainly, the experiment has continued with even greater clarity and more profound discoveries for the past five years), and the experiences we had with him and subsequent events, only clarified Fulcanelli's tactics for us.

Jan 10, 2002

Q: As you know, we have become aware this evening of Frank's extraordinary conversion to the dark side. Is that an accurate way of perceiving it?

A: Close enough.

Q: Quite a few years ago, there were several remarks made on two or three occasions regarding Frank's battle with the Dark Forces, and the issue of whether or not he would be able to resist their domination. Was it always known that he would fail?

A: He is not a failure.

Q: What do you mean?

A: From the perspective of [the forces of Entropy] he is a success.

Q: Why was it that we were able to [receive creative] material, with Frank being so borderline regarding this ultimate choice between [Entropy and Creation]?

A: *He was programmed for the specific purpose of "downloading" from you secrets coded into you before birth of your present body.* He failed because you were incorruptible. He is now charged with the mission, in concert with Vincent Bridges, of destroying your ability to accomplish your mission.

Q: Well, that means that there is a strong possibility that the material that came through while Frank was a participant was very likely corrupted. Is that why you gave the figure of 72 percent purity of the material regarding those sessions?

A: Yes. Q: So, are you saying that Frank's presence produced that 30 percent corruption?

A: Yes.

Q: What was the form that most of that corruption took? Can we identify it?

A: Predictions and terror tactics.

It was certainly only *after* the exit of Frank, and after the exposure of Vincent Bridges[421] as an "esoteric poseur", to understate the matter, that the Work moved to it's present level of intense work and gathering of support from around the world.

So, let me return now to the remarks about stars made by Canseliet made 20 years apart, that, juxtaposed, reveal something quite marvelous:

> **From the FIRST edition:** I know, not from having discovered it myself, but because I was assured of it by the author more than ten years ago, that *the key to the major arcanum is given quite openly in one of the figures, illustrating the present work*. And *this key consists quite simply in a colour* revealed to the artisan right from the first work.

I suspect that the reader has, by now, figured out that Canseliet and Fulcanelli were very tricky. And so, we look at this clue and try to think of what Canseliet is saying. He says that the clue is in a *"figure illustrating the present work"*, that it is revealed *"right from the first work"* and *in the preface to the second edition*, adds the clue that *the subject of the star "leads us straight into Fulcanelli's text" saying that "right from the beginning my Master has dwelt on the primary role of the star…".*

We turn to the very beginning of Fulcanelli's text where he writes:

> The strongest impression of my early childhood - **I was *seven* years old** - an impression of which I still retain a vivid memory, was the emotion aroused in my young heart by the sight of a gothic cathedral. I was immediately **enraptured** by it. I was *in an ecstasy*, struck with wonder, unable to tear myself away from the attraction of the marvellous, from the magic of such splendour, such immensity, such *intoxication* expressed by this more divine than human work.

Never does he mention a star. He mentions no color. He makes no reference to an illustration.

Or does he?

What he does talk about is his *emotional state*, his ecstasy, *and his age*: Seven. It occurred to me as I meditated upon this matter, that a *number is also a figure*, and that the use of an *"impression of childhood"* is certainly an "illustration". So, there is, indeed, a "figure illustrating" something that might be a "key" to the "major arcanum." *Seven* and *Ecstasy*.

What to do with the number Seven?

I simply turned to chapter Seven and began to read.

> Varro, in his *Antiquitates rerum humanorum*, recalls the legend of Aeneas saving his father and his household gods from the flames of Troy and, after long wanderings, arriving at the *fields of Laurentum*, the goal of his journey.

---

[421] http://www.cassiopaea.com/archive/most.htm

Fulcanelli inserted a footnote to the word *Laurentum*, at the beginning of chapter Seven of *Le Mystere* telling us that *"Laurente* (Laurentium) is cabalistically *l'or enté* (grafted gold)". And so indeed, we have been led to a *color*! Not only that, but a color that reflects my very name. There is another interesting reference to the number seven in the Cassiopaean Transmissions:

July 26, 1997

Q: ... Now, when the Templars were arrested, they were accused of worshipping a head, or skull, and also the god Baphomet. Were these spurious accusations designed to defame them?

A: Skull was of pure crystal.

Q: What is the definition of the god 'Baphomet', if they did, indeed, worship such?

A: The holder of the Trent.

Q: What is THAT?

A: Seek.

Q: What is the meaning of 'The Widow's Son?' The implication?

A: Stalks path of wisdom incarnate.

Q: Why is this described as a Widow's son? This was the appellation of Perceval...

A: Perceval was knighted in the court of seven.

Q: The court of seven what?

A: Swords points signify crystal transmitter of truth beholden.

August 22, 1998

Q: (L) ... You once said that Perceval was 'knighted in the Court of Seven' and that the sword's points signify 'crystal transmitter of truth beholden'. Do these seven sages relate to this 'Court of Seven' that you mentioned?

A: Close.

Q: (L) When you said 'swords points signify crystal transmitter of truth beholden,' could you elaborate on that remark?

A: Has celestial meaning.

And, as I mentioned, it was only when we arrived at Auch, in the clear skies of the French Countryside, that I SAW Cassiopaea as if for the first time: right at the end of the Milky Way, the Chemin de St. Jacques de Compostela.

July 12, 1997

Q: Okay, what is this P-S related to that appears on the stone slab from the Rennes le Chateau churchyard? Everybody is talking about the "Priory of Sion". But, what does this P-S mean? Is that it?

A: Look into ancient tongues...

Q: Ancient tongues? Get me a little closer to it!

A: Swords, daggers pierce...

Q: Is this P-S something about "Percy?" Swords, daggers, pierce... Damascus? Damascus steel?

A: Search for learning. [...]

Q: ... we have this Prae-cum which is above the spider image. Why is the arrow pointing from the P-S down to the spider? What is the spider?

A: You know of the spider!

Q: Well, yes, but I know what I know, but I don't know if I am getting anywhere!

A: You will when you connect "the dots."

Q: Connect the dots... My God! Swords, daggers.... I GET IT!

A: It is the "destiny!" [...]

[Ark had written to me that day:

Some thoughts:

Before I go on to study all these Celts and Cathers and Templars and grails and bloodlines and dna and gold and mercury and oaks and ...

Before all this let me try to formulate my present view of the situation. It will be a kind of a bird's eye view; from a distance when details are unimportant. So I will pick up SOME themes that seem to me important. There will be several of these themes and they will be discussed separately.

1. I take it as a hypothesis which perhaps is true and perhaps not, but I take it to be true unless proven otherwise: that for you and for me nothing happens by mere accident. All that happens has a meaning and purpose. It is hard work for us to find out what is this purpose exactly and to an extent we are also the creators of this purpose.

Thus it is not an accident that you are who you are. It is not an accident that I am a physicist. It is not an accident that we are separated for a while. It is not an accident that we have had our lives the way we had. It could be little bit different, or it is a little bit different in some parallel realities, but we are now concerned about our reality, our present and our future.

2. Thus every book that you ever read was not an accident and every conversation that you ever had; even those silly books and conversations were lessons. The same with me.

3. We are both searching for something and it was clear that we would never find it in this lifetime while alone. There was ONE who you saw somehow in your imagination. There was also my thoroughly repressed idea of having an "American wife". Somehow it was coming to my head, but I was instantly repelling it as a completely silly thought. But it was knocking. This way I was being "prepared" because otherwise I was/am very conservative.

Anyhow we have found each other and there is purpose in that. I take it as possible that you/me -we are connected to the Creator and are distant parts of it so that we are His tools and we are responsible for something, this something being the whole universe and its fate. This is not a crazy idea. It can be explained in completely plain terms. You/me - we can discover something, a formula or an idea that will change the future development of humanity - even if a little, it will magnify after years and years so that world will be "saved" by it. This is what we learned from the concepts of chaotic mechanics. There are systems, if sufficiently complex, such that a little change now leads to a dramatic change after a time.

Now the universe is not only a complex system but also it has intelligence in it. It may well be that an "intelligent" change that we do now will change completely the fate of the universe. Instead of dying a thermal death it will flourish forever....

My whole life I have lived with this feeling of responsibility. It was a recurring theme in my journal. If we accept the hypothesis that nothing happens to US by chance then there is a purpose in this feeling too.

4. So we you/me are responsible. We accept it. That is clear. Now, from C's we know you have "all the keys". In a sense we find it in Pleiadians or in the Bible that everybody has the keys. But in too many these keys are broken, destroyed, desynchronized, detuned and hard or impossible to make them work. We do not know how many people there are on this earth who have keys and how many of them are already using these keys or assisting other people in using them. And for a while it does not matter. All is lesson - we accept it - and we have our homework. Neither you nor me have a wish "to be told".

5. So you have the keys and we were brought together. Now, I am a physicist and know the math which is the universal language. On the other hand you know and like all these funny stories that merge history/alchemy/whatever. These are all words while math is all logic. While physics is testable and helps us to build technologies, this stuff of grail and Templars and Rennes is somewhat unsharp and for those who have no math, can lead nowhere...

But NO! If nothing with us happens accidentally, then the fact that you are interested in what you are interested is also not an accident. So what can be a purpose of all that? A purpose can be that the KNOWLEDGE is not just math and equations but it is also intelligence and consciousness and mind and idea. Because equations DO NOTHING alone. So we need both. There were many that perhaps followed the path of technology and are working underground doing "great physics" or "great math". But this is not what we are about. We do not want to sell our souls like Faustus. We do not serve to the dark. Therefore we need knowledge. And the more knowledge we have the more protected we are. This point is again easily understood in plain terms. Once we play not only with TDARM's and time machines and gold making but also with ouija boards and history and templars and Arcadian shepherds and all this funny stuff - we are not considered as dangerous because we clearly are not after power. Neither do we want to take power FROM somebody.

Our goal is all different. We have our personal mission to fulfill: External dark forces being dispersed by multiplicity of our frequencies - so to say.

6. But why ARE all these Templars and Rosicrucians important? Because it is all knowledge. Pieces of knowledge from here and there. We are not gonna use or try to use this knowledge. But somehow it is necessary for us to know this so as to find out the best possible use of this knowledge.

7. I think this IS true that the only limits that we find are those imposed by our own minds and thinking habits. Thus we must be more and more bold in our thinking. On the other hand we need always to go step by step. Otherwise there is danger.

8. Is the life sufficiently long? We take it as a working hypothesis that yes, it is. Because it depends only on us how long it is gonna be. There is a great work that is in front of us and this work includes rethinking and rearranging our cellular structure. We believe it can be done even with the presently known (secret)

technology. The fountain of youth, and such things, but also what we know from C's and Pleiadians and alchemical texts etc. all point to it. It is possible. But the point is of course what purpose one is using it for. If just for prolonging one's own life - well.... But we have something different in mind because we are service-men here for the Creator, to whom we return.

8. So we continue. I do my math but also I have to learn a lot of stuff. Not only I NEED TO LEARN, BUT ALSO I NEED TO HELP YOU AND WE ARE SUPPOSED TO ACT TOGETHER!]

Returning now to the session in question with the clue that later proved to be so important, I asked about Ark's message quoted above.

Q: Okay, here is Ark's first question: if the general view of the situation that I wrote you, "bird's eye view" is correct?

A: Why not? The thought would not be so "nagging" if were not so!

Q: (L for Ark) Or, perhaps, I am missing some important point(s), and if so what is(are) this point(s)?

A: When one is on a quest for true learning and higher knowledge, there are no "missing points," only those not yet discovered!

Q: (L for Ark) How "long" will they still be able to use the **Cassiopaean transmitter**, should we start to take some steps thinking of the future when the transmission point will have to be moved? Or, perhaps, this is not something we have to worry about in advance? I would like to know.... I do not like to be taken by surprise....

A: No need to worry! ... "If one has the will of a Lion, one does not have the fate of a mouse!"

Q: Very cute! I liked that one! But, now, you took the wind out of my sails with the answer about the destiny. But, in my perception of this arrangement on this stone, is it that the two sides need to be united, is that correct? Or is the Arrow from the P-S pointing at the spider a divider of two opposing groups?

A: Open for your discovery!

Q: Oh, you guys are BAD to me tonight!

A: No, we be berry berry goood to Lawra!

Of all the many odd things that have come through the Cassiopaean Experiment in "code", this last was one of the strangest. "We be berry berry goood to Lawra." And it was transcribed exactly as they gave it, with the extra "o" in the word "good" and the peculiar spelling of my name.

One of the first things that we noted when the temporary house was found for us near Auch was that the name of the domaine was "En Laurenc". That's close and interesting, but there was to be much, much more. In fact, the "more" actually came via the Rennes-le-Chateau link.

I have read and studied this "mystery" for some time and have written a series about it that can be read on the web[422]. The careful reader will realize that I do agree that there is a mystery at Rennes-le-Chateau, but it is not at all what the dozens of theorists may suppose. *The greatest mystery of Rennes-le-Chateau was that of Abbe Boudet's book, "The True Celtic Language".*[423]

It was on our visit to Alet-les-Bains, where Berengar Sauniere had formerly been the cure, that we learned that this was the *true* birthplace of Nostradamus, not St. Remy. As you will see, this may be significant.

Getting back to "*we be berry berry goood to Lawra!*" coming from a discussion of Rennes-le-Chateau, along with Canseliet's "key from *the key to the major arcanum is given quite openly in one of the figures, illustrating the present work.* And *this key consists quite simply in a colour* revealed to the artisan right from the first work. The first words of Mystery of the Cathedrals, lead us to chapter SEVEN, where we read: "Varro, in his *Antiquitates rerum humanorum*, recalls the legend of Aeneas saving his father and his household gods from the flames of Troy and, after long wanderings, arriving at the *fields of Laurentum*, the goal of his journey", Fulcanelli's footnote: "*Laurente* (Laurentium) is cabalistically *l'or enté* (grafted gold)", and En Laurenc near Auch Cathedral, I knew I was being given a complex puzzle to solve. Knowing that Abbe Boudet, the most interesting figure in the whole Rennes-le-Chateau phenomenon, had written quite a strange book about the "True Celtic Language", giving something like Green Language clues about places and names in France, I decided to see what he had to say about Auch.

THE GASCONS - THE OCCITANIANS. THE AUQITAINS AND THEIR TRIBES. - AUCH. BORDEAUX

The Celts imposed upon the descendants of the Tubal certain designations wherein are revealed customs that the centuries have been unable to wipe away. ... It is not a question of considering the names of all the Iberian tribes; we must, however, make an exception for the Vascons or Gascons.

"According to history, the **Basques** had the privilege of forming the avant-garde of the Carthaginian armies, and to measure themselves first against the enemy. Their reputation of indomitable courage was so well establish that Caesar didn't dare cross **Vaconia,** so much did he dread them, going instead to Spain to avoid meeting them by the Aspe valley in the Bearn."

---

[422] http://www.cassiopaea.org/cass/grail.htm

[423] The reader may enjoy my expose of Rennes-le-Chateau published on the web at:http://www.cassiopaea.org/cass/grail_5f.htm. For our own photos of the place and commentary, see: The Quantum Future Group Goes to Rennes-le-Chateau: http://www.cassiopaea.org/Rennes-le-Chateau/

The Gascons gave their name to our French Gascony. We can hardly say that their establishment in Aquitaine was an invasion because **the Aquitains were their brothers,** and the Gascons had come to their aid to fight the yoke of domination that Clovis sought to impose upon them. We see them first under the children of Clovis, established on the right bank of the Adour, and, later, around 626 AD, occupying the entire Novempopulanie that from then on was called Gascony. They received their strange name from the unique shoe they had adopted and that their descendants have hardly abandoned. Gaskins, in the Celtic language, means large, ancient shoe. It is the sandal that in Languedoc we call spardillo, in Catalan, spadrilla, and that the Basques call spartinac.

The word spartinac is far from meaningless: it is composed of the verb to spare, the prelude to combat, and the adjective thin (thinn), délié, clair-semé, peu nombreux. This light shoe permitted the Basques to engage in fighting by ambushes: with rare agility, we might even say elusive agility, they advanced in small groups, beginning the combat with deadly and isolated strikes that must have singularly surprised their enemies. This term spartinac shows us the genius, warrior character of the Basques: they were long ago what we call today guerrillas.

After giving us the meaning of the names of the Iberian tribes, the Celtic language explains just as easily those of the Aquitain tribes. In this part of Gaul, the Celtic family left larger and stronger traces than in its mix with the Iberian family. All authors have recounted the different character traits that separate the Iberians and the Celts: the Celts were gay, light, ardent, loved to fight and were quick to attack; the Iberians, on the contrary, were grave, serious, almost somber, loved war as well and defended it with an invincible stubbornness. When the two people met, the shock must have been terrible.

After having fought for the possession of their country, reports Diodorus of Sicily, the Celts and the Iberians lived there together, by virtue of a peace treaty, and they mixed through alliances. From this mix came the Celtiberian nation in which Iberian blood remains predominant. The Aquitains, who, according to their traditions, were not issued from the Celts, belong to the Celtiberian family, because if they were very close to the Iberians by their traits and their customs, they nonetheless adopted the habits and institutions of the Celts. We offer as proof the institution of the soldures, which appear to us to be absolutely Celtic, although one generally attributes it to the Iberian nation.

"An institution that is particular to (Aquitaine), and that is a stranger to the Gauls," says the highly esteemed author of the History of Gasconny, Abbé Monlezun, "is that of the solduriens, or, rather, saldunes (of Escualdunal, zaldi or saldi, horse; salduna, one who has a horse, horseman, l'eques romain); one names in this way soldiers who make a vow to a chief, to forever share their destiny or rather to identify so strongly with him that there is no example of one who ever survived. As soon as the chief succumbed, we saw them looking for a glorious death in battle, and if they could find it, they came back and pierced themselves on the bodies of one who had their faith."

We can observe that in the account of the war against the Aquitains, Ceasar speaks only of the institution of the soldurii, without affirming elsewhere that the soldures existed in the other parts of Gaul. The term soldures, that in the Basque language brings no idea to mind, presents, on the contrary, in the language of the Technosages, a meaning perfectly in accord with the institution itself. It is the soldier devoted to his chief, and the accidents of war will not separate them; the life of the soldura will not outlast that of his chief. - Soul (sôl), life, âme. - to dure (dioure), durer. - In our day, are not they called soldiers in the Anglo-Saxon ? From whence comes this soldier, if not from soldure (soldioure), and how would this term exist in the Anglo-Saxon if the institution of the soldurii was unique to the Iberians? **This institution that, it seems to us, is common to the Celts and the Celtiberians, indicates to us how, on Aquitain soil, the fusion operated between the two families. The name of Occitania was used to designate Aquitain. [...]**

The author of the *Mémoires de l'Hitoire du Languedoc* wishes, because of the first syllable of Occitania, to apply this term to the Languedoc, but this expression, broken down and interpreted by the Celtic language, demonstrates with the latest evidence that the Occitani were the inhabitants of the maritime coasts that surrounded the Gulf of Gascony, that is to say, the Aquitains and the Cantabrians. The reputation of the Basques and the Cantabarians as intrepid mariners has never been contested, and it is not without reason that they attribute to themselves the honour of being the first to hunt whales. For the rest, if the whales fell rarely under their blows, it wasn't the same for the porpoise, and this regular hunting of porpoises earned them their name of Occitani - hog-sea (hogsi), porpoise, - to hit, frapper, - hand, la main - *hogsihithand*. - The term Occitani was thus the general name designating the fishermen of the Gulf of Gascony.

The Celtiberians of the interior of the country **between the Ocean, the Pyrénées, and the Garonne,** received another designation, general as well, the Aquitains. It is said the Basques called their language Escualdunac: it is the *language of horse-tamers*, tamers with a somber and cool face - scowl (skaoul), somber air, cool, - to down (daoun), tame - hack, horse. -

The title of horse-tamers does not only belong to the Basques, it was shared with the Aquitainians, and this commonality of tastes and customs seems to us a remarkable trait of affinity that one should not neglect. It was difficult for the Aquitains to be poor horsemen because their country was rich with famous horses. The Benedictine savant, Dom Martin, from whom modern authors borrowed the most curious details on the morals, the government, and the religion of the Celts, understood that this production of magnificent horses had a great influence on the name given to Aquitaine. He also puts forward that this country was first called Equitaine, from the Latin, equus, horse. The remarkable shrewdness of the religious scholar was hardly in fault, because they were still hardy tamers of horses, these Aquitaini. - hack, horse, -- to cow (kaou), intimidate, - to hit, frapper, - hand, main, -hackcowhithand. - Aquitaine.

Has the passion for horses disappeared from the heart of modern Aquitains? It is certain that, in spite of the changes brought on by the centuries to their habits, it still retains the same vivacity: the horse exercises of any circus suffice, in effect, to excite in the soul of the Aquitains and the Gascons an interest and an enthusiasm that cannot be reined in.

There were about forty tribes living in the Aquitaine, of which the nine main ones inspired the Romans to call the country *Novempopulanie*. We will examine the names of some of these tribes with those of several cities, and it will be notice that they all belong to the Celtic language. [...]

The Auscii formed the most powerful tribe in Aquitaine. Ancient geographers gave their principal city the name of Climberris. We think it was an error on their part; they did not correctly capture the exact meaning of this term, distinctive to the entire country, because Auch has never seen its name vary, a name taken from the

Auscii. For the rest, it seems to us that we can discover the truth by the meaning of Climberris, which should apply to the entire country, the city of Auch as well as that of Eluse. All of this country produces berries and grain - clime, region, country, -- berry, berry, grain, -- Climeberry --.

Why would they have attributed to one city the production of grain and grapes, when it is the production of the entire region? And we shouldn't be surprised to see **the berries of the vine, grapes,** enter into the composition of Climberris because vines existed in the Gauls in a wild state. A considerable time may have passed without thinking of its cultivation, and history seems to honour the Greeks with having taught the Celts how to make wine, a fact that seems highly dubious to us, as the Celts were as advanced as the Greeks in material civilization, and superior to the sons of Javan in philosophical and religious sciences.

We have already said that Auch took its name from the Auscii and was their main city. In looking to give Auch a Celtic pronunciation, we are forced to say Aouch, and it is probably the real name of this town, written in Anglo-Saxon as *Ouch*, et pronounced Aoutch.

Ouch signifies a golden necklace, a setting for a precious stone, and Auscii designates skillful workers, applied to working with precious metals and making these magnificent golden necklaces with which the warriors decorated their breasts on the joyous days which were, for them, the days of combat - ouch (aoutch), necklace of gold, - hew (hiou), to cut.

The Auscii easily became skillful in working in gold; *this metal was almost like a weed in their region*, and diverse historians say that the avid Greek and Phoenician merchants, coming back to their countries, used the gold gathered in the Pyrénées for ballast in their vessels. [...] [424]

"We be berry, berry goood to Lawra" indeed!

Varro, in his *Antiquitates rerum humanorum*, recalls the legend of Aeneas saving his father and his household gods from the flames of Troy and, after long wanderings, arriving at the **fields of Laurentum**, the goal of his journey. [...] "*Laurente* (Laurentium) is cabalistically *l'or enté* (grafted gold)".

I will let this passage along with the other clues I have revealed stand here for the reader to contemplate Auch Cathedral as *the* Cathedral of the Mysteries of Fulcanelli.

This brings us back to the subject of the Sibyls. (Fulcanelli warned his readers that having a good classical education was essential to read his subtextual meaning.) As already noted, the Cumaean sibyl was made famous by Virgil to foretell the birth of a saviour and as *Aeneas'* guide to the underworld. As we continue to read chapter seven, we see that Fulcanelli is discussing this very matter and we note again his particular reference to Varro.

---

[424] Translation, Henry See

The best known and most quoted catalogue of the sibyls (although the original is lost) is that of the Roman scholar cited by Fulcanelli, Varro (116-27 B.C.), whose ten named sibyls are known from the *Divinae Institutiones* written by Lactantius (ca. 250 – after 317). It was the first book printed in Italy (Subaico, 1465). *The Sibyl remained for the Christians who were, at heart, still attached to their pagan roots, a direct witness to the* gesta Dei*, or signs of God.*

In the Hellenistic period Jewish forgeries appearing in Alexandria were passed off as Sibylline oracles and used as propaganda. Supposedly genuine Sibylline oracles located in the temple of Capitoline Jupiter in Rome were extant in Rome until the end of the empire. The collection we know now is a rather chaotic compilation called the *Oracula Sibyllina* and is full of religious propaganda and apocalyptic predictions. The Greek text was recovered from antiquity and published in 1545 in Basel.

The Sibyls were popular figures in medieval and Renaissance art, the most famous occurrence being Michelangelo's Sistine Chapel. We are reminded that Raymond Montané compares the work at Auch with the work of Michelangelo. The subject of Sibyls disappeared almost entirely in Christian art after the Council of Trent concluded in *1563*. The dedication of Auch Cathedral took place on February 12th, 1548, at which time the 18 windows of Arnaud de Moles and the 113 stalls in the choir were completed and which feature the Sibyls prominently. So, the fact that these Sibyls appear there at all is an oddity in itself.

The Sibyls uttered their prophecies *in a state of ecstasy*, which the reader of this volume has learned is related to the function of the ecstatic ascent or descent of the Shaman, originally a *function of women* exclusively - Sibyls. This takes us right back to Fulcanelli's description of his own state of ecstasy upon viewing his first Gothic cathedral and certainly leads us to his appearance near Seville as "a woman" and a "young girl" at the very time I disappeared.

As the reader can tell by this time, solving the greatest mystery of our world is, on the one hand, quite simple and in plain sight, and on the other hand, circuitous, like a maze. The end of chapter seven of *Mystery of the Cathedrals* brings us to the subject of the Virgin saying:

> In symbolic iconography, **the star is used to indicate conception, as well as birth**. The Virgin is often represented with a nimbus of stars. The Virgin at Larmor (Morbihan) forms part of a fine triptych, representing *the death of Christ* and the suffering of Mary (Mater dolorosa). In the sky of the central composition can be seen the sun, moon and stars and the scarf of Iris. **The Virgin holds in her right hand a large star** - *maris stella* - an epithet given to her in a Catholic hymn.

This small passage is pregnant with meaning and clues that lead in several directions at once. First, it suggests that we consider the relation of the Virgin to the subject of stars, which leads us to the *Camino de Santiago Compostela*, known in France as the Chemin de St. Jacques de Compostella.

The word *Compostela* is most obviously interpreted "campus stellae" or *field of the star*. The whole Camino de Santiago, from San Juan pied de port until Compostela, is populated with villages, places and mountain passes that are named after stars, as if to suggest that the whole Camino is a stellar route, the Milky Way, a route that leads to a special point: the field of *the star*. We are again reminded of the clue given in the Cassiopaean Transmissions:

A: Alfalfa fields in Rhineland yield as of yet undreamed of treasures.

Q: Where are these alfalfa fields?

A: Near tracks well worn.

Q: ... Do you mean Rhineland as in Germany proper?

A: We do not mean Rhinelander, Wisconsin... Or do we?!? Who is to tell?

Q: Who?

A: The searcher, the sepulcher, the one who carries the staff in constant search for greener pastures. ... Last clue for tonight: Look for the vibratory frequency light. Good Night.

"Near tracks well worn" can certainly be considered to be a reference to the Camino de Santiago Compostela.

Fulcanelli gives us a clue:

> **The Route of Saint James is also called the *Milky Way*.** Greek mythology tells us that the gods followed this route *to go to the palace of Zeus* and the heroes as well followed it to *enter Olympus*. The Route of Saint James is the stellar route, **accessible to the *chosen ones*,** to the courageous, persevering and wise mortals.

Another interpretation comes from an alchemical term: *compost*. This refers to the subject of Canseliet's prefaces: the appearance of a white star indicating the accomplishment of the first part of the Great Work. Fulcanelli notes:

> Pure Matter, of which the hermetic star consecrates the perfection: it is now our compost, the blessed water of Compostela (from the Latin *albastrum* a contraction of *alabastrum*, white star). And it is also **the vase filled with perfume, the vase of alabaster** (Latin *alabastrus*) and the bud that comes out from the flower of knowledge, the hermetic rose.

> The operation is achieved when there appears on the surface a shining star formed by the rays coming from one center, the prototype of the great rose windows of our gothic cathedrals. This is the sure sign that the pilgrim has happily reached the end of his first journey. He has received the mystical blessing of Saint James, confirmed by the luminous imprint that shone, they say, over the tomb of the apostle. The humble and common shell that he wore on his hat has become a shining star, in a halo of light.

It was only after I moved to France that I was able to understand the importance of the relationship of the Virgin, the star, the Chemin or Camino, the Milky Way, and my own path. It had been years since I was able to clearly see the stars from our home in Florida. There is so much light pollution that only the brightest stars can be seen on a clear night. I hadn't seen the Milky Way since I was a child.

In rural France, the skies are a delight for star gazing. We went out one night and the Milky Way was so clear and shimmering that it was like fingers of light plucking the strings of some great atmospheric harp. And there, *right at the very end of the Milky Way*, nestled like the final destination, the Palace of Zeus, Olympus, the "luminous imprint that shone over the tomb", was Cassiopeia: a gigantic letter M or W depending on the season of the year. Certainly, Cassiopaea is similar in configuration to the Shell of St. Jacques. The Shell is a star, and the star is the vase of alabaster, the hermetic rose, the Star in the *hand* of the Virgin.

Cassiopeia is an enthroned woman, at whose right hand is a star-crowned King Cepheus holding his sceptre toward her. Ancient writings describe her as his wife, and she is also referred to in other ancient sources as, *"The Bride, the Lamb's wife"*.

Cassiopeia was the daughter of Arabus (whose name was given to Arabia), a son of Hermes. Supposedly, according to the "Stalinized" myths of the Greeks, Cassiopeia was prideful and willful, and it was because of this that her daughter was made to suffer. It was said that Poseidon put Cassiopeia in the heavens as a punishment - yet, this is an honor that is generally a "reward". How do we explain this confusing element?

Cassiopeia is seated in a chair that turns upside down in each twenty-four hours and this is supposed to be the "punishment". However, *all* the constellations are "upside-down" from one perspective or another within every 24 hour period.

When considering the concepts of the "Triple Goddess", Cassiopeia could be viewed as the maternal element of the triad with Andromeda, the virgin, and Medusa, the crone or destructive element of the story. Cassiopeia is often represented *holding a palm frond*, a symbol of fertility which compares her to Demeter giving grain to Triptolemus. We note that the Sibyl of Samos, depicted in the windows of Arnaud de Moles, *held a palm frond.*

Julius Schiller (1627) *saw Cassiopeia as Mary Magdalene*, and some have seen a parallel between Cassiopeia and Bathsheba.

The Celts called this constellation *Ilys Don*, or the "house of Don", known as "Tuatha de Danaan". In this role of Danae, she was the mother of Perseus. Thus we may see the combining of the two women, and the *hieros gamos* (sacred marriage) of Perseus to his sister, Andromeda as an expression of the androgyne of alchemy, achieving the "Great Work".

In terms of the myths and stories of the search for the Holy Grail, or, in our modern metaphor - the escape from the Matrix - most of the figures appearing in the Greek constellations were said to have been placed there by one of the gods to honor and perpetuate their memory. The constellation figures of Cepheus and Cassiopeia are unusual in that they were not granted their positions as an honor, but *are there to complete the story of Perseus, Andromeda and Cetus*. This is a group of *five* constellations that is unusual in that *it is the only classical myth to be so fully depicted.*

Can it be that this is a clue that this myth - including the important role of Cassiopaea - is a sort of "message in a bottle" to mankind? Cassiopaea, the field of the Stars:

> The operation is achieved when there appears on the surface a shining star formed by the rays coming from one center, the prototype of the great rose windows of our gothic cathedrals. [See Plate 8.] This is the sure sign that the pilgrim has happily reached the end of his first journey. He has received the mystical blessing of Saint James, confirmed by the luminous imprint that shone, they say, over the tomb of the apostle. The humble and common shell that he wore on his hat has become a shining star, in a halo of light.

> Cassiopaea: the shining star formed by the rays coming from one center... the sure sign that the pilgrim has happily reached the end of his first journey. He has received the mystical blessing of Saint James...

> "We are you in the Future", they said. "We transmit 'through' the opening that is presented in the locator that you represent as Cassiopaea, due to the strong radio

pulses aligned from Cassiopaea, which are due to a pulsar from a neutron star 300 light years behind it, as seen from your locator. This facilitates a clear channel transmission from 6th density to 3rd density... [in] "Zero" time. [utilizing Electromagnetics and gravity which are interconnected, or you could say "unified". Space and time are selective and flexible. ... You see, when one utilizes zero time, there is zero space as well."]

Julius Schiller, who reinterpreted the constellations in Christian terms, called Andromeda "*Sepulchrum Christi*", or "the tomb of Christ". There is also the Freudian analogy which associates a cask with the female. The fertility implications are obvious: Christ was in a tomb, waiting to rise again - the seed ready to emerge in Spring. This connects us back, of course, to what Fulcanelli has said: "He has received the mystical blessing of Saint James, confirmed by the luminous imprint that shone, they say, "*over the tomb of the apostle*"," together with the clue from Cassiopaea: "Who is to tell? ... The searcher, the sepulcher, the one who carries the staff in constant search for greener pastures."

The Phoenicians saw a "threshing floor" in the constellation of Andromeda which is an interesting connotation when one thinks of the ideas of "reaping" and "separating the wheat from the tares". Also, the word "tribulation" is connected to "threshing", or the separating of the grain from the chaff.

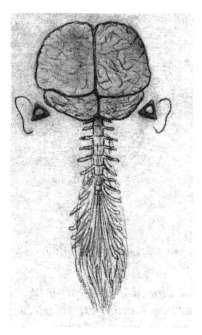

The horse, mare, mer, mere, sea, mother - the Virgin where the star appears - the Prima Materia

Sirrah, the star that flashes from Andromeda's head, is also one of the four stars that make up the square in the constellation of Pegasus - the steed of Perseus - who was born from the spurting blood of the decapitated gorgon, Medusa. This star *in the head of Andromeda* is also known as the "navel" of Pegasus - the horse, mare, mer, mere, sea, mother.

Pegasus was the offspring of Poseidon, with whom Medusa mated in Athena's temple, violating the Goddess' sacred space. This violation was a grievous offense, since Athena prided herself on being a virgin, and "Parthenon" means, "the place of the virgin".

Pegasus' name may come from the Greek "*pege*", or "spring", and is thereby another connection to the idea that the beheading of the Gorgon is also a *restoration of the waters* of the virgins of the wells of Grail myths, thereby being operative in healing the wasteland.

There are many winged horses in Middle Eastern art, and these all may be related to this myth. Some say that the early Aryans claimed that this constellation represented *Asva*, the sun, and it was actually Chiron's daughter, Thea. She was a companion of Artemis and was seduced by Aeolus, the god of the wind. Poseidon helped her by turning her into a *horse*. The long and well known association of horses with the Celts and with the Perseids should be considered here also.

The Egyptians identified this constellation as "The Servant", and some of its stars as a jackal. The Arabs called its quadrangle *Al Dalw*, or "water bucket", which has also been identified as the urn in the zodiacal constellation Aquarius, my own birth sign.

I think that the picture above will make it clear. The brain is the "horse of God" which the seeker "schools" in order to arrive at his destination, and we note the striking resemblance to the Omega symbol.

The Greeks identified the four stars in Pegasus as the *gate to paradise*. The Hebrews called it "Nimrod's horse". Christians saw it as the ass that carried Christ into Jerusalem which suggests hidden worship of the Goddess as the true rite expressed allegorically as the crucifixion. We must not forget that there is the image of the Templars - two men on a horse. What could this represent but a duality, spirit and matter, unified via "riding the horse"? Certain alchemical symbols depict either two men, or a two-headed man, mounted on a horse which climbs a ladder, or tree.

Whatever variation of the story we find, the essential element seems to be that of a hero who accomplishes some impossible deed and thereby obtains a "flying horse", and who then rides the horse and accomplishes more impossible tasks having to do with "freeing" others. In the course of all this, he wins the maiden of his choosing, and - in the case of Perseus - lives happily ever after.

In Freudian terms, the winged horse is associated with the potent phallus with which it is possible for the hero to overcome all obstacles. There are many representations of winged *phalloi* in ancient Greek art. This element of sexuality may refer to both actual genetic principles as well as the subject of "polar opposites" that is discussed in this book, an ancient Gnostic tradition revealed by Boris Mouravieff.

One story tells us that Perseus built a ship called Pegasus that was said to sail as swiftly as the horse that flies. This is the prototype of the story of the Argonauts which is also related by virtue of the "flying ram" which later becomes the Golden Fleece, keeping in mind that *the constellations under discussion are all found in the sign of the Ram*. In this story, the brother and sister are rescued by the flying ram, but the sister falls into the sea. Did she then become Andromeda? Do we begin to see the difference between Ares and Aries?

We should also note that the subject of the Argonauts was a particular theme of Fulcanelli's, and that he referred to this as a Green Language way of saying: "*Art cot*", or the art of light. We find ourselves again considering Jules Violle and the measure of light, the "violle". Fulcanelli also associated Perseus with Jason of the Argonauts, and I am convinced that this was a deliberate "mistake".

Another important point: of all the ancient heroes of myth and legend, Perseus stands out as being supremely successful; so many others started out with good intentions, had numerous successes, but then fell from glory due to hubris or trickery or temptation.

We find an interesting relationship between Cassiopeia and Danae in that they both are the "root" of the problem that leads to the main action of the story.

Perseus is exposed to great danger in his efforts to "rescue" his mother, and Andromeda is similarly exposed to great danger as a "sacrifice" for her mother. For some reason, Danae cannot tell Polydectys "no" - he has power over her - and the much maligned Cassiopeia speaks for her daughter and the daughter's beauty and this gets them both into hot water.

In the same terms, Cassiopeia may have known what she was doing when she caused her daughter to become bait for the Sea Serpent, Cetus. As an "Oracle", she would have known that Perseus, like Neo, could overcome all obstacles *to save others;* and that this was the extra 'something', the proper perspective of serving others that was needed to ensure success.

The result was, of course, that Perseus killed the sea serpent and married Andromeda. They set off together as a team: righting wrongs, freeing the oppressed, turning the bad guys into stone, and lived, as far as is known, happily ever after.

Thus, as a symbol of gaining Freedom from the Matrix, we find, first, that Perseus is the Hero of choice, and, second, that the dynamics of the only myth that is fully represented in the Sky over our very heads are those which suggest to us our path of "tracking" the clues that will enable each participant to not only cut off the head of their own Medusa, thus releasing the Truth in the form of the Winged Horse, Pegasus, but also, with the aid of this Truth, to participate in the Freeing of Andromeda. We believe that no more important task is before us on the Earth today.

Getting back to the present, when we moved to our current house, we found that we lived now in a village that is called "Belcassé". This name interested me because it reminded me of "Beautiful Cassiopaea". We learned that the name meant "Beautiful Oaks". I began tracking words and meanings and finally came to the realization that Cassiopeia can mean, literally, the "Voice of the Oak", the Sibyl, the Great Mother, the Virgin. Things became a bit more interesting when I learned that the oldest name of the village was "Lampe Adagio", or "Slow Light". Hmmm.. "Look for the Frequency of light."

This region, only a short distance from Agen where Nostradamus spent many years of his life (we will come to that), was quite a center of Catharism, as was Alet-les-Bains, the birthplace of Nostradamus. The interesting thing was that even the Catholic monks were "infected with the heresy", so to say, and there are stories of Cathars being protected in local religious houses. The Abbey Belleperche, for example, sited right on the Garonne river, and which I can view from my office window, used to own all the land leading right up to our Chateau. They were famous for their horses. Many fields that now produce wheat, rapeseed, sunflowers, etc, were used to pasture horses... "Alfalfa fields in Rhineland"?

At the beginning of this article is an image of the Burial of Christ. It is found in Chapel 17 in Auch Cathedral which formerly was called the "royal chapel" and is also known as the chapel of the *Trinity*. It is on this site that the foundation stone of the cathedral was laid on July 4th, 1489. (I found this to be synchronous also since it was on July 4th that Ark first wrote to me from Florence where Leonardo da Vinci spent so much of his life.) It is also in the crypt directly under Chapel 17 where the burial, or "sepulcher" stands, that another strange coincidence was noted. On my first visit (I'm now such a regular that the caretaker just gives me the key instead of taking me down himself), as I stood under the burial of Christ just looking around in an unfocused way to see if there was anything that caught my eye, I finally looked at the floor under my feet. There was a grave there, an Archbishop, and the dates of his appointment and death - one date at the toes of each of my feet - were my birthday and my husband's (Ark) birthday. The Cathedral was also dedicated on my birthday: February 12.

We discussed the strange date synchronicities with mathematician Robert Coquereaux[425], and he admitted that our more or less "random choice" for the area of our new home having a cathedral dedicated on my birthday, with the foundation stone laid on the anniversary of the date Ark first wrote to me, and then including a grave stone in the crypt above the foundation stone with both our birthdays on it was stretching "coincidence" a bit. But, being a true scientist, he proposed that we should have to do many "trials" to be "scientific" about drawing any conclusions.

Returning to the burial of Christ, which is in the chapel over the grave of Pierre-Henri Gerault de Langalerie [See Plate 9.], we find an excellent description of the piece in the writings of Raymond Montané:

> The Burial assembles eight traditional characters together in a very unusual way. There is Jesus laid out on a cloth and, arranged behind him, Mary the mother of Jesus, two additional women, St. John the Apostle, and *Mary Magdalene standing at Jesus' feet* with her alabaster jar. Joseph of Arimathea and Nicodemus hold the shroud at each end.

Each character in the tableau is identifiable by attitude, details of costume, position in relation to Jesus, or by the object in his or her hand. *The woman standing next to Jesus' mother is shown in a very special way: she actually occupies the central place of honor, and holds the crown of thorns - a "star", perhaps?* She is wearing the head covering of a married woman, and her place of honor depicts her as *the wife of Jesus*. But, this wife *is not Mary Magdalene* who is clearly positioned at the feet. Mary Magdalene is depicted in such a way that you cannot mistake who she is with her long hair on display and holding the alabaster jar. Her headdress, in fact, is that of an unmarried girl. In fact, if you look at Mary Magdalene up close, she looks more like a daughter of the family gathered about the body. [See Plate10.]

Father Raymond Montané tells us:

> The canopy, of flamboyant style, is decorated with an original Trinity. It is the "showing" of Christ on the Cross, by God the Father himself. The Holy Spirit, symbolised by a dove, is placed between the Father and the Son. *This theophany is truly in relation with the Burial of Christ*, and even more with the *theological basis* of the Passion, but *not with the text properly said to be of the Gospels.*

---

[425] See "The Cave Beneath the Sea": http://www.cassiopaea.org/cass/Laura-Knight-Jadczyk/article-lkj-18-10-03.htm

He notes in passing that the monument was inspired by *Margaret of Austria*. Margaret's husband, *Philibert de Savoie* was a cousin of one of the bishops that was involved in the commissioning of the work of the cathedral, *Francois de Savoie, and this was the family in possession of the Shroud of Turin.*

It is also noted in the history of Auch that *Marguerite of Navarre*, the second cousin of Margaret of Austria, was closely associated with Auch Cathedral. We will be delving further into the people associated with the Cathedral Ste-Marie at Auch in another book dedicated to its mysteries, but allow me to give the reader some clues.

Marguerite of Navarre takes us right back to Fulcanelli.

In the early 1520s, Marguerite became involved in the movement for the reform of the church, meeting and corresponding with the leading reformers of the period. In 1527, apparently by her own choice, (rare in those days), Marguerite married Henri d'Albret, King of Navarre (though most of his kingdom was in Spanish hands). Henri d'Albret was the son of *Catherine de Foix*, descended from a famous Cathar family.

Around 1531, Marguerite allowed a poem she had written to be published, *Miroir de l'ame pecheresse* (Mirror of the sinful soul). Marguerite gave a copy of *Miroir* to one of her ladies in waiting, *Anne Boleyn*, and it was later translated into English by Anne's 12 year old daughter, *Elizabeth*, later to become the greatest monarch England has ever known. As it happens, Anne Boleyn had previously been the lady in waiting to *Margaret of Austria*, so the two ladies undoubtedly communicated with one another and shared a Lady in Waiting. It also makes one wonder about the possibility that there was a great mystery surrounding Anne Boleyn?

A fascinating article entitled *The Holbein Code* has recently been published in *Fortean Times* (FT 202), written by David Hambling, a well respected journalist. He suggests that the painting *The Ambassadors* by Holbein was intended to deliver a specific message. He writes:

> There is no contemporary record of the painting, and the two sitters were not identified for centuries. In 1890, Sir Sidney Colvin suggested that the man on the left was Jean de Dinteville, French ambassador to the court of Henry VIII, because of the presence of Polisy, Dinteville's chateau, on the terrestrial globe visible in the painting. In 1900, Mary Hervey did some historical detective work, visiting Polisy and sifting through 17th century documents, including a 1653 inventory of possessions. She confirmed that the painting had originally hung there, and identified the second sitter as George de Selve, bishop of Lavour and sometime French ambassador to the Holy Roman Empire.

> The picture, then, shows French ambassadors on a mission to London at a crucial point in history. Henry VIII was about to discard the Spanish Catherine of Aragon and declare Anne Boleyn his new queen. Anne had spent her formative years at the French court...

> The driving force of the Renaissance was the new concept of Humanism, "the spirit of intellectual freedom by which man asserted his independence from the authority of the Church"." In the mediaeval view, the Church could pronounce on everything, from the nature of God to the motion of the stars and the shape of the Earth. Humanism challenged the existing order.

There were new sources of information available from outside the Christian world: pagan Greek philosophers... Humanists tried to integrate all this into a single whole. A new spirit of inquiry was stirring. Copernicus had just published his theory that the Earth was not the centre of the Universe, and Martin Luther nailed his 95 theses to the door of the church...

The Church resisted, sometimes violently. Luther's proposed reforms were seen as heretical; so was Copernicus's theory. And anyone experimenting with Alchemy, Astrology, Cabalism or novel religious views learned to keep quiet or face burning.

We know Anne Boleyn supported the Evangelical cause. The writings of poet Nicholas Bourbon, who fled to England under her protection, give us an indiscreet glimpse of the group surrounding her. There were Thomas Cromwell and Thomas Cranmer, as well as Evangelical Bishop Hugh Latimer, Nicholas Kratzer, William Butts - and the painter Hans Holbein. [...]

The members of this small, close-knit cabal that engineered Anne Boleyn's rise had two things in common: they were self-made men rather than aristocrats, and they held views which could be dangerous. Hence, their actions to turn England down a new road and make it safe for those threatened by the established church, kickstarting the Reformation in the process.

Dinteville was an ally of Anne Boleyn. He was a patron of the humanist Jacques Lefevre, and Mary Hervey notes that he was also rumoured to be an enthusiast for the "secret sciences" of alchemy and astrology. Holbein's painting might indicate religious sympathies...

The most detailed study of the painting has been carried out by Professor John North, emeritus professor of the History of Philosophy and the Exact Sciences at the University of Groningen in the Netherlands. His book, The Ambassadors' Secret, contains a wealth of detail... [426]

As it happens, the instruments depicted in the painting indicate an exact time and date: 4 p.m. on 11 April 1533. This date was Good Friday, the day and hour of the alleged death of Jesus *if* he had actually been crucified 1,500 years earlier in AD 1.

North is not given to theorising without a solid base of evidence. Like others, he considers the possible influence of the great Renaissance magus Cornelius Agrippa of Nettesheim, a figure at the French court who may have been an acquaintance of Dinteville, Holbein or Kratzer, but he finds the sheer volume and complexity of symbolism used by Agrippa makes it impossible to be certain of correspondences. [...]

---

[426] David Hambling, Fortean Time, FT 202

The Ambassadors is not just a portrait of two French dignitaries, but was intended as an instrument to - quite literally -change history. [427]

Here, I will give the "other side of the story" that may suggest an entirely different explanation for the "Holbein Code", and how it may very well mesh with the so-called "Da Vinci Code". What does seem to be true is that a desperate attempt was being made to transmit knowledge, to propagate Gnosis, but it failed when the headsman came to remove the head of Anne Boleyn because she could not produce a male heir for Henry.

But then, perhaps it did *not* fail after all? Perhaps it was just not yet time?

Getting back to *Marguerite of Navarre*, the mistress and teacher of Anne Boleyn, Sorbonne theologians condemned her poem, *Miroir*, as heresy. A monk said Marguerite should be sewn into a sack and thrown into the river Seine, and students at the College of Navarre satirized her in a play as "a fury from Hell". But her brother, Francis I, King of France, forced the dropping of the charge and an apology from the Sorbonne.

Marguerite was one of the most influential women in France. Her salon became famously known as the "New Parnassus". The writer, Pierre Brantôme, said of her: "She was a great princess. But in addition to all that, she was very kind, gentle, gracious, charitable, a great dispenser of alms and friendly to all",

The Dutch humanist, Erasmus, wrote to her, "For a long time I have cherished all the many excellent gifts that God bestowed upon you; prudence worthy of a philosopher; chastity; moderation; piety; an invincible strength of soul, and a marvelous contempt for all the vanities of this world. Who could keep from admiring, in a great King's sister, such qualities as these, so rare even among the priests and monks?"

As a generous patron of the arts, Marguerite befriended and protected many artists and writers, among them *François Rabelais*.

Fulcanelli refers us frequently to Francois Rabelais. As it happens, his Gargantua-Pantagruel series, *Le Tiers Livre des faicts et dicts héroïques du bon Pantagruel* (1546), was dedicated to *Marguerite of Navarre*.

Another of Marguerite's associates and correspondents was *Jules Cesar Scaliger* who was a close friend and associate of Nostradamus. Nostradamus, as mentioned, was born in Alet-le-Bains, in *Foix* lands - Cathar country. *Nostradamus also attended school with Rabelais.*

In 1525 Nostradamus settled in *Agen*, not far from Toulouse and Auch. In 1534, it is said he married a woman of "High Estate", who gave him two children. This woman has never been identified, but considering his highly probable association with Marguerite of Navarre, it is likely that there was some connection there. It is

---

[427] Ibid.

said that, in 1538, his wife and children died of the plague. Around the same time, he had a falling out with Scaliger, and *he was accused of heresy by the Inquisition* because of a statement made in earlier years.

Nostradamus' biographers tell us that he left Agen and "wandered around Southern France". It was only in 1546, two years before the consecration of Auch Cathedral, that Nostradamus settled in the village of Salon de Craux which has laid claim to his glory for all these many years. To sum up the mystery we find here, Nostradamus lived in Agen for 13 years, and there are 8 years that *no one knows exactly where he was or what he was doing*. It is quite likely that he took refuge with Marguerite of Navarre who was the patron and protector of such as Nostradamus. One wonders what influence Nostradamus may have had on the history depicted in Auch Cathedral?

Scaliger, we should note, is the "author" of the *accepted historical chronology* that is coming more and more into question in the present day. It is possible that the falling out between him and Nostradamus related, in part, to disagreements regarding how history should be viewed and taught.

In 1550, one year after Marguerite's death, a tributary poem, *Annae, Margaritae, Ianae, sororum virginum heroidum Anglarum, in mortem Diuae Margaritae Valesiae, Nauarrorum Reginae, Hecatodistichon,* (yes, long title!) was published in England. It was written by the nieces of Jane Seymour (1505-37), third wife of *King Henry VIII*. So, certainly, all these ladies were in contact with one another, and it is likely that secrets were shared among them.

Thus we see, in the person of *Marguerite of Navarre*, an individual who is central to the mystery of Auch Cathedral, whose associations suggest to us that she was well acquainted with esotericism and possibly even secrets passed down from the time of the Crusades against the Cathars - and more. Fulcanelli points us to Rabelais, and Rabelais leads us to Marguerite, and so we arrive at Auch Cathedral where the great mystery awaits the attentive seeker.

The next photograph is a close-up of the Burial of Christ said to have been inspired by Margaret of Austria, kinswoman of Marguerite of Navarre, showing the four women of the eight figures. [See Plate 11.] Notice the headdresses of the four women. That of the woman in the position of wife is distinctively different from those of Mary, the mother, and the woman to the right of the "wife".

Plate 12 is a close-up of the woman standing in the place of honor of the wife of the deceased, holding the crown of thorns. In Plate 13 you will see a Sibyl from the windows of Arnaud de Moles holding a palm branch of Hope/Fertility. Note carefully the spiral insignia over their breasts. Note also the unusual turban of the wife, identical to the turban of the Sibyl.

Now, let's take a look at one of the carvings in the Choir of Auch Cathedral that depicts the Gifts of the Magi to the Infant Christ. [See Plate 14.] Notice, in particular, the hats of the "Three Kings". The one at far right still has his on, the one kneeling has laid his on the ground, and the one in the center of the tableau has lifted his in such a way that it seems it covered the chalice he holds in his other hand. Again, we note the similarity of the head coverings: turbans that are associated today with the Arabs. We wonder what relationship the "wife" of Jesus had to the "Magi"?

There are two other images I would like to show the reader because they are typical of the esoterica displayed in this marvelous Cathedral. [See Plate 15 and 16.] Both of them represent a similar theme that will be easy to discern in imagery, but requires some interpretation to bring the symbol to understanding.

Now, what are these figures trying to tell us? In Plate 16, something is being done to the head of the central figure. It looks as though the attendants are trying to dislodge something from the head of the seated man by force. In Plate 15, we see an individual being held down with his (or her) head placed on an anvil while the three associated figures are depicted as hammering the head!

Is this some terrible Medieval torture being depicted?

No, it is a depiction of *initiation*. And, in fact, in one of the windows of Arnaud de Moles, Jesus is depicted as the central figure - identical to the carving at left - having something done to his head. The figure is meant to indicate Jesus because the head is shown with a "crown of thorns".

A Shaman is, as Historian of Religion, Mircea Eliade describes, a *Technician of Ecstasy*. This is an essential qualification and/or result of contact with the Divine. More than that, in order to be in direct contact with the Divine, the human being must be able to "see the unseen". This Seeing is the capacity of human beings to enlarge their perceptual field until they are capable of assessing not only outer appearances, but also the essence of everything in order to access the level of being that enables them to make choices that are capable of initiating a new causal series in the world. It has nothing at all to do with "hallucinations" or mechanical means of altering brain perceptions: it is a "soul" thing, so to say.

The word "shaman" comes to us through Russian from the Tungusic *saman*. The word is derived from the Pali *samana*, (Sanskrit *sramana*), through the Chinese *sha-men* (a transcription of the Pali word).

The word shaman, may be related to Sarman. According to John G. Bennett , Sarmoung or Sarman:

> "The pronunciation is the same for either spelling and the word can be assigned to old Persian. It does, in fact, appear in some of the Pahlawi texts...

> "The word can be interpreted in three ways. It is the word for bee, which has always been a symbol of those who collect the precious 'honey' of traditional wisdom and preserve it for further generations.

> "A collection of legends, well known in Armenian and Syrian circles with the title of *The Bees*, was revised by Mar Salamon, a Nestorian Archimandrite in the thirteenth century. The Bees refers to a mysterious power transmitted from the time of Zoroaster and made manifest in the time of Christ."

> "'Man' in Persian means the quality transmitted by heredity and hence a distinguished family or race. It can be the repository of an heirloom or tradition.

The word sar means head, both literally and in the sense of principal or chief. The combination sarman would thus mean the chief repository of the tradition..."

"And still another possible meaning of the word sarman is... literally, those whose heads have been purified."[428]

Those whose heads have been purified! What an interesting idea!

The central theme of Shamanism is the "ascent to the sky" and/or the "descent" to the underworld. In the former, the practitioner experiences Ecstasy, in the latter, he battles demons that threaten the well being of humanity. There are studies that suggest evidence of the earliest practices is in the cave paintings of Lascaux with the many representations of the bird, the tutelary spirits, and the ecstatic experience (ca. 25,000 BC). Animal skulls and bones found in the sites of the European Paleolithic period (before 50,000 - ca. 30,000 BC) have been interpreted as evidence of Shamanic practice.

The "ecstatic experience" is the primary phenomenon of Shamanism, and it is this ecstasy that can be seen as the act of merging with the celestial beings. Merging results in Forced Oscillation that changes Frequency. Continued interaction with Celestial beings is a form of Frequency Resonance Vibration.

January 14, 1995

Q: (L) We have some questions and the first one is: You have told us in the past that you are us in the future and that you are moving this way to merge with us.

A: Yes.

Q: (L) As we measure time, how far in the future are you us?

A: Indeterminate as you measure time. [...] What is "future", anyway?

Q: (L) The future is simultaneous events, just different locales in space/time, just a different focus of consciousness, is that correct?

A: Yes, so if that is true, why try to apply linear thinking here, you see, we are merging with you right now!

The idea that there was a time when man was directly in contact with the Celestial Beings is at the root of the myths of the Golden Age that have been redacted to the Grail stories of the 11th and 12th centuries. During this paradisiacal time, it is suggested that communications between heaven and earth were easy and accessible to everyone. Myths tell us of a time when the "gods withdrew" from mankind. As a result of some "happening", i.e. "The Fall", the communications were broken off and the Celestial Beings withdrew to the highest heavens.

But, the myths also tell us that there were still those certain people who were able to "ascend" and commune with the gods on the behalf of their tribe or family. Through them, contact was maintained with the "guiding spirits" of the group. The

---

[428] John G. Bennett, *Gurdjieff: Making of A New World*]

beliefs and practices of the present day shamans are a survival of a profoundly modified and even corrupted and degenerated remnant of this archaic technology of concrete communications between heaven and earth such as the Cassiopaean Transmissions.

The shaman, in his ability to achieve the ecstatic state inaccessible to the rest of mankind, due to the fusion of his emotional center via suffering, generally, (witness the metaphor of the Crucifixion), was regarded as a privileged being. More than this, the myths tell us of the First Shamans who were sent to earth by the Celestial Beings to *defend* human beings against the "negative gods" who had taken over the rule of mankind. It was the task of the First Shamans to activate, in their own bodies, a sort of "transducer" of cosmic energy for the benefit of their tribe. This was expressed as the concept of the "world tree", which became the "axis" or the Pole of the World and later the "royal bloodlines".

It does seem to be true that there is a specific relationship between this function and certain "bloodlines". But, as with everything that has been provided to help mankind, this concept has been co-opted by the forces seeking to keep mankind in darkness and ignorance. The true and ancient bloodlines of the First Shamans have been obscured and hidden by the false trail of the invented genealogies of the Hebrew Old Testament supposedly leading to certain branches of present day European royal and/or noble families, which seek to establish a counterfeit "kingship" that has garnered a great deal of attention in recent times. I devote some attention to this subject in The Secret History of the World.

As we have already noted, *before* the Fall, every human being had access to communication with the higher densities via the "Maidens of the Wells" of ancient Celtic legend.

After the Fall, it seems that a specific genetic variation was somatically induced by the incarnation of certain higher density beings who "gave their blood" for the "redemption of man". That is to say that they changed the body and DNA by Forced Oscillation. It is likely that this was done through the female incarnations because of the role of the mitochondrial DNA, but I don't want to get ahead of myself here, so we will leave that for the moment.

Nevertheless, the presence of this DNA, depending upon the terms of recombination, makes it very likely that there are many carriers of this bloodline/Shamanic ability on the earth today, though very few of them are carrying the "convergent" bloodlines.

The Sufis have kept the "Technician of Ecstasy" concept alive in their tradition of the "Poles of the World". The *kutub* or *q'tub* (pole of his time) is an appointed being, entirely spiritual of nature, who acts as a divine agent of a sphere at a certain period in time. Each *kutub* has under him four *awtads* (supports) and a number of *abdals* (substitutes), who aid him in his work of preserving and maintaining the world. The interesting thing about this idea is that the individual who occupies the position does not even have to be aware of it! His life, his existence, even his very physiology, is a function of higher realities extruded into the realm of man. That this has a very great deal to do with "bloodlines", as promulgated in recent times is true, but not necessarily in the ways suggested.

In the present time, it seems that those with the "bloodline" are awakening. It is no longer feasible to be a "Pole of the World" who is asleep, because there are some very serious matters of choice and action that may be incumbent upon the awakened Shaman. The first order of business seems to be to awaken and accumulate strength of polarity.

Shamans are born *and* made. That is to say, they are born to be made, but the making is their choice. And, from what I have been able to determine, the choice may be one that is made at a different level than the conscious, 3rd density linear experience. Those who have made the choice at the higher levels, and then have negated the choice at this level because they are not able to relinquish their ordinary life, pay a very high price, indeed.

A shaman stands out because of certain characteristics of "religious crisis". They are different from other people because of the intensity of their religious experiences. In ancient times, it was the task of the Shamanic elite to be the "Specialist of the Soul", to guard the soul of the tribe because only he could see the unseen and know the form and destiny of the Group Soul. But, before he acquired his ability, he was often an ordinary citizen, or even the offspring of a shaman with no seeming vocation (considering that the ability is reputed to be inherited, though not necessarily represented in each generation.)

At some point in his life, however, the shaman has an experience that separates him from the rest of humanity. The Native American "vision quest" is a survival of the archaic understanding of the natural initiation of the shaman who is "called" to his vocation by the gods.

A deep study of the matter reveals that those who seek the magico-religious powers via the vision quest when they have not been called spontaneously from within by their own questing nature and feeling of responsibility for humanity, generally become the Dark Shamans, or sorcerers; those who, through a systematic study, obtain the powers deliberately for their own advantage.

The true Shamanic initiation comes by dreams, ecstatic trances combined with extensive study and hard work: intentional suffering. A shaman is expected to not only pass through certain initiatory ordeals, but he/she must also be deeply educated in order to be able to fully evaluate the experiences and challenges that he/she will face. Unfortunately, until now, there have been precious few who have traveled the path of the Shaman, including the practice of the attendant skills of "battling demons", who could teach or advise a course of study for the Awakening Shaman. In my own case, over thirty years of study, twenty years of work as a hypnotherapist and exorcist, and the years of "calling to the universe" that constitute the Cassiopaean Experiment stand as an example of how the process might manifest in the present day.

The future shaman is traditionally thought to exhibit certain exceptional traits from childhood. He is often very nervous and even sickly in some ways. (In some cultures, epilepsy is considered a "mark" of the shaman, though this is a later corrupt perception of the ecstatic state.) It has been noted that shamans, as children, are often morbidly sensitive, have weak hearts, disordered digestion, and are subject to vertigo. There are those who would consider such symptoms to be incipient mental illness, but the fact is that extensive studies have shown that the so-called hallucinations or visions consist of elements that follow a particular model that is consistent from culture to culture, from age to age, and is composed of an amazingly rich theoretical content. It could even be said that persons who "go mad", are "failed shamans" who have failed either because of a flaw in the transmission of the genetics, or because of environmental factors. At the same time, there are many more myths of failed Shamanic heroes than of successful ones, so the warnings of what can happen have long been in place. Mircea Eliade remarks that:

> "... The mentally ill patient proves to be an unsuccessful mystic or, better, the caricature of a mystic. His experience is without religious content, even if it appears to resemble a religious experience, just as an act of autoeroticism arrives at the same physiological result as a sexual act properly speaking (seminal emission), yet at the same time is but a caricature of the latter because it is without the concrete presence of the partner."

Well, that's a pretty interesting analogy! It even suggests to us the idea that one who attempts to activate a Shamanic inheritance within the STS framework of Wishful Thinking, has an "illusory" partner as in the above-described activity, with similar results. In other words, Sorcery is like masturbation: the practitioner satisfies himself, but his act does no one else any good. And, by the same token, a Shaman who operates without knowledge is like the proverbial "three minute egg": he gets everybody all excited, and then leaves them hanging! In both cases, such an individual has satisfied only themselves, and it could be said that, in the latter case, it is actually worse because another individual has been used for that satisfaction.

But, such amusing vulgarities aside, (even if they DO make the point remarkably well) the thing about the shaman is that he/she is not just a sick person, he/she is a sick person who has been *cured*, or who has succeeded in curing himself, at least spiritually!! The possibility of achieving the Shamanic powers for Service to Self also exists, so great care has to be used in trying to "see the unseen".

In many cases, the "election" of the shaman manifests through a fairly serious illness which can only be cured by the "ascent to the sky". After the ecstatic vision of initiation, the shaman feels *much* better! After the response to the calling of the gods, the shaman shows a more than normally healthy constitution; they are able to achieve immense concentration beyond the capacity of ordinary men; they can sustain exhausting efforts and, most importantly, they are able to "keep a cool head" in the face of experiences that would terrify and break an ordinary person.

Another point that should be emphasized is that the Shaman must be able to be in full control of himself even when in the ecstatic state! (Trance channeling with no memory of what transpired is *not* the activity of a Shaman!) This ability to "walk in two worlds simultaneously" demonstrates an extraordinary nervous constitution. It has been said that the Siberian shamans show no sign of mental disintegration well into old age; their memories and powers of self-control are *well* above average.

Castaneda's Don Juan calls this state being "impeccable". This idea is also reflected in the archaic systems of the *Yakut*, where the shaman must be "serious, possess tact, be able to communicate effectively with all people; above all, he must not be presumptuous, proud, ill-tempered". The true shaman emanates an inner force that is conscious, yet never offensive. *At the same time, it should be noted that a true shaman might evoke very negative responses from those who are under the domination of the Entropic forces.* I have certainly experienced this more times than I care to mention.

Getting back to the infirmities, nervous disorders, illness of crisis and so forth that are the "signs of election", it is also noted that, sometimes an accident, a fall, a blow on the head, or being hit by lightning are the signs from the environment that the shaman has been elected. But, being "called" is not the same as being "chosen", or, more precisely, choosing. "Many are called; few choose to respond."

This choosing is a process, and it is a process of struggle and pain and suffering because, in the end, what is being killed is the ego.

The pathology of the Shamanic path seems to be part of the means of reaching the "condition" to be initiated. But, at the same time, they are often the means of the initiation itself. They have a physiological effect that amounts to a transformation of the ordinary individual into a technician of the sacred.

(But, if such an experience is not followed by a period of theoretical and practical instruction, the shaman becomes a tool for those forces that would use the Shamanic function to further enslave mankind as we have already noted.)

Now, the experience that transforms the shaman is constituted of the well-known religious elements of *suffering, death and resurrection.* One of the earliest representations of these elements is in the Sumerian story of the descent of Ishtar/Inanna into the Underworld to save her son-lover, Tammuz. She had to pass through Seven "gates of Hell" and, at each door or gate, she was stripped of another article of her attire because she could only enter the Underworld Naked. While she was in the underworld, the earth and its inhabitants suffered loss of creative vigor. After she had accomplished her mission, fertility was restored.

The most well known variation of this story is the myth of Persephone/Kore, the daughter of Demeter, who was kidnapped by Hades/Pluto.

The Shamanic visions represent the descent as *dismemberment of the body, flaying of the flesh* from the bones, *being boiled in a cauldron*, and then being reassembled by the gods and/or goddesses. This, too, is well represented in myth and legend, including the myth of Jesus: Suffering, death, and resurrection. In short, the crucifixion - the Burial of Christ - is a symbol of the Shamanic Transformation:

> A Yakut shaman, Sofron Zateyev, states that during this visionary initiation, the
> future shaman "dies" and lies in the yurt for three days without eating or drinking.
> ...
>
> Pyotr Ivanov gives further details. In the vision, the candidate's limbs are removed
> and disjointed with an iron hook; the bones are cleaned, the flesh scraped, the body
> fluids thrown away, and the eyes torn from their sockets. After this operation all the
> bones are gathered up and fastened together with iron.

According to a third shaman, Timofei Romanov, the visionary dismemberment lasts from three to seven days; during all that time the candidate remains like a dead man, scarcely breathing, in a solitary place.[429]

According to another Yakut account, the evil spirits carry the future shaman's soul to the underworld and there shut it up in a house for three years (only one year for those who will become lesser shamans). Here the shaman undergoes his initiation. The spirits cut off his head, which they set aside (for the candidate must watch his dismemberment with his own eyes), and cut him into small pieces, which are then distributed to the spirits of the various diseases. Only by undergoing such an ordeal will the future shaman gain the power to cure. His bones are then covered with new flesh, and in some cases he is also given new blood.

According to another account, the "devils" keep the candidate's soul until he has learned all of their wisdom. During all this time the candidate lies sick. *There is also a recurring motif of a giant bird that "hatches shamans" in the branches of the World Tree which is an allusion to an "Avian bloodline" that is opposed to a Reptilian heritage.* The following excerpts are from the available accounts obtained in field research and should be read with the awareness that we have now entered a world of pure symbolism:

"...The candidate ...came upon a naked man working a bellows. On the fire was a caldron "as big as half the earth." The naked man saw him and caught him with a huge pair of tongs. The novice had time to think, "I am dead!" The man cut off his head, chopped his body into bits, and put everything in the caldron. There he boiled his body for three years.

There were also three anvils, and the naked man forged the candidate's head on the third, which was the one on which the best shamans were forged. ...

The blacksmith then fished the candidate's bones out of a river in which they were floating, put them together, and covered them with flesh again. ...

He forged his head and taught him how to read the letters that are inside it. He changed his eyes; and that is why, when he shamanizes, he does not see with his bodily eyes but with his mystical eyes. He pierced his ears, making him able to understand the language of plants.

...The Tungus shaman Ivan Cholko states that a future shaman must fall ill and have his body cut in pieces and his blood drunk by the evil spirits. These throw his head into a caldron where it is melted with certain metal pieces that will later form part of his ritual costume.

...Before becoming a shaman the candidate must be sick for a long time; the souls of his shaman ancestors then surround him, torture him, strike him, cut his body

---

[429] Eliade, 1964, op. cit.

with knives, and so on. During this operation the future shaman remains inanimate; his face and hands are blue, his heart scarcely beats.

...A Teleut woman became a shamaness after having a vision in which unknown men cut her body to bits and cooked it in a pot. According to the traditions of the Altain shamans, the spirits of their ancestors eat their flesh, drink their blood, open their bellies and so on.

...In South America as in Australia or Siberia both spontaneous vocation and the quest for initiation involve either a mysterious illness or a more or less symbolic ritual of mystical death, sometimes suggested by a dismemberment of the body and renewal of the organs.

...They *cut his head open, take out his brains, wash and restore them*, to give him a clear mind to penetrate into the mysteries of evil spirits, and the intricacies of disease; they insert gold dust into his eyes to give him keenness and strength of sight powerful enough to see the soul wherever it may have wandered; they plant barbed hooks on the tips of his fingers to enable him to seize the soul and hold it fast; and lastly they pierce his heart with an arrow to make him tenderhearted, and full of sympathy with the sick and suffering.

...If the alleged reason for the renewal of the organs (conferring better sight, tenderheartedness, etc.) is authentic, it indicates that the original meaning of the rite has been forgotten.

...Then the master obtains the disciple's "lighting" or "enlightenment", for [this] consists of a *mysterious light* which the shaman suddenly feels in his body, *inside his head*, within the brain, an inexplicable searchlight, a *luminous fire*, which enables him to see in the dark, both literally and metaphorically speaking, for he can now, even with closed eyes, see through darkness and perceive things and coming events which are hidden from others...

The candidate obtains this mystical light after long hours of waiting, sitting on a bench in his hut... When he experiences it for the first time, "it is as if the house in which he is suddenly rises; he sees far ahead of him, through mountains, exactly as if the earth were one great plain, and his eyes could reach to the end of the earth. Nothing is hidden from him any longer; not only can he see things far, far away, but he can also discover souls, stolen souls, which are either kept concealed in far, strange lands or have been taken up or down to the Land of the Dead.

...The experience of *inner light* that determines the career of the Iglulik shaman is familiar to a number of higher mysticisms. In the *Upanishads*, the "inner light" defines the essence of the atman. In yogic techniques, especially those of the Buddhist schools, *light of different colors* indicates the success of particular meditations. Similarly, the *Tibetan Book of the Dead* accords great importance to the light in which, it appears, the dying man's soul is bathed during his mortal throes and immediately after death; a man's destiny after death (deliverance or reincarnation) depends on the firmness with which he chooses the immaculate light.

...The essential elements of this mystical vision are the *being divested of flesh*. ...In all these cases *reduction to the skeleton* indicates a passing beyond the profane human condition and, hence, a deliverance from it.

...*Bone represents the very source of life*. To reduce oneself to the skeleton condition is equivalent to reentering the womb for a complete renewal, a mystical rebirth. ...It is an expression of the will to transcend the profane, individual condition, and to attain a transtemporal perspective.

...The myth of renewal by fire, cooking, or dismemberment has continued to haunt men even outside the spiritual horizon of shamanism. ...

The myth of rejuvenation by dismemberment and cooking has been handed down in Siberian, Central Asian, and European folklore, the *role of the blacksmith* being played by Jesus or other saints.[430]

The reader may now have a better idea of what the strange images of work being done on the initiate's head, including the hammering of the head on an anvil, must mean: the Shamanic Initiation, the Alchemical Transmutation via Techniques of Ecstasy. We now better understand what Fulcanelli was trying to tell us:

The strongest impression of my early childhood - I was *seven* years old - an impression of which I still retain a vivid memory, was the emotion aroused in my young heart by the sight of a gothic cathedral. I was immediately enraptured by it. I was *in an ecstasy*, struck with wonder, unable to tear myself away from the attraction of the marvelous, from the magic of such splendour, such immensity, such *intoxication* expressed by this more divine than human work.

These same ideas of death and re-birth are well represented in Alchemical literature as the various processes of "chemical transmutation". As we have quoted already:

In order to respect the principle of hermetism adopted by the Tradition, we must understand that esoteric teachings are given in a sibylline form.

St Isaac the Syrian points out that: The Holy Scriptures say many things by using words in a different sense from their original meaning. *Sometimes bodily attributes are applied to the soul, and conversely, attributes of the soul are applied to the body.* The Scriptures do not make any distinction here. However, enlightened men understand.

We also now have a better understanding of the ancient image of the *skull and crossbones* surrounded by little tongues of fire that is prominently displayed in Auch Cathedral as shown in Plate 17.

Years ago I read the story promoted in the book *Holy Blood, Holy Grail*, that Jesus had a wife and that she was Mary Magdalene. I immediately consulted with friends in France who live in Marseille about this so-called "well-known" legend. What I learned is that yes, it was said that Mary Magdalene came to France accompanied by other individuals. She was closely associated with St. Maximin, but never, until the raft of books following *Holy Blood, Holy Grail*, was she thought to have been the wife of Jesus.

---

[430] Ibid.

Clearly, in 1548, and much, much earlier, it was known that Jesus had a wife as is depicted in the statues of Auch Cathedral, but it clearly wasn't Mary Magdalene. We cannot even be certain that the depiction of a "wife" means that literally, that it does not indicate to us a process rather than an actual state of physical marriage.

So, the question is: who was the wife of Jesus and does this depiction suggests a "physical" wife, or does it depict an Initiatory process?

I will deal with that question in a future volume, but for now, let me share with the reader additional clues.

We come now to the intriguing link between Marguerite of Navarre and **Leonardo da Vinci** who died in 1519, *while he was a guest of Marguerite and her brother Francis*. A Venetian ambassador of the time praised Marguerite as "knowing all the secrets of diplomatic art", and thus, a person to be treated with deference and circumspection. We see here a definite clue since Fulcanelli repeatedly referred to the Green Language as "The Language of Diplomacy".

By 1508, Leonardo's career was drawing to a close though it would yet be ten years before his death. Only two paintings survive from that period; the Louvre's Virgin and Child with St. Anne and St. John.

Leonardo had made Milan, ruled by the French, his home for some time. In 1512, an alliance of Swiss, Spaniards, Venetians and papal forces drove the French out of Milan which was a minor issue of history for France, but a major disaster for Leonardo. He was about 60 years old and had been treated by the French with understanding and compassion. Now, he suddenly found himself without patronage or income, verging on total poverty. His fame had faded and, while the new rulers of Milan were not openly hostile toward him, he was certainly not accorded any honor or comfort.

In February of 1513, Pope Julius II died and was succeeded by Leo X - made famous by saying "It has served us well, this myth of Christ" - a Medici. The Medici had never shown Leonardo any special favor, but he apparently decided to throw himself on their mercy since they were, after all, patrons of the arts.

In September of 1513, the aging Leonardo set off for Rome. Pope Leo X was persuaded to give Leonardo a small commission - subject unknown - but the result was a disaster. When Leonardo started the project by compounding a special preservative varnixh, the Pope reportedly threw up his hands saying, "This man will never accomplish anything! He thinks about the end before the beginning!". Leonardo's notebooks record, around this time: "We should not desire the impossible", and "Tell me if anything was ever done..."

Not surprisingly, Leonardo became ill. The nature of his illness is unknown, but it is thought from other clues that he suffered a mild stroke affecting his right side. (He was left handed, fortunately.) Leonardo's self-portrait was apparently made during this time. His last painting was completed in Rome, noted to have been done without commission, but due to some inner compulsion. It is in the Louvre: *St John*.

Sick and forgotten in Rome, Leonardo was not forgotten by the French. Francis I, brother of Marguerite of Navarre, offered Leonardo a manor house in France near the royal chateau of Amboise, and any funds he might require for his needs, wants, and any project he might, on his own, wish to undertake. Francis only wished the pleasure of Leonardo's company.

Leonardo set off for France taking with him his notes, his drawings, his last two paintings: The *St. John*, *The Virgin and Child with St. Anne*, and a portrait described as "a certain Florentine Lady".

When Leonardo arrived at the royal castle at Amboise, he was given the title: "Premier peinctre et ingenieur et architecte du Roy" not for anything he was expected to do, but for what he had done already. Francis always went to see Leonardo, taking the view that it was easier for a vigorous 22 year-old king to make a call on an aging artist than vice versa.

Leonardo must have made quite an impression on Francis because, 24 years later, Benvenuto Cellini, then in the French service also, wrote:

> King Francis being violently enamored of his great talents took so great a pleasure
> in hearing him discourse that there were few days in the year when he was
> separated from him... He said that he did not believe that there had ever been
> another man born into the world who had known as much as Leonardo, and this not
> only matters concerning sculpture, Painting and Architecture, but because he was a
> great Philosopher.

It was in 1517, while Leonardo was at Amboise, that Martin Luther nailed his 95 theses to the door of the church at Wittenberg. Most of his activities in France are unknown. He died on May 2, 1519.

Vasari, Leonardo's biographer, raised a smoke screen around Leonardo's religious beliefs (or lack of them). In the first edition of his "*Lives of the Painters*", published in 1550, he wrote that "Leonardo was of such a heretical frame of mind that he did not adhere to any kind of religion, believing that it is perhaps better to be a philosopher than a Christian." In the second edition (1568), he omitted the sentence, writing instead: "He desired to occupy himself with the truths of the Catholic faith and the holy Christian religion. Then, having confessed and shown his penitence with much lamentation, he devoutly took the Sacrament."

Leonardo himself had written about Christian funerals: "Of the dead who are taken to be buried: The simple folk will carry a great number of lights to illuminate the journeys of all those who have wholly lost the power of sight. O human folly! O madness of mankind!"

But it seems that Leonardo was not an atheist either. The name of the Creator appears often enough in his writings and indicates that he had an extraordinary conception of a divine power. Certainly, if he had wished to be explicit about it in words, he was quite capable. But he didn't explain - except perhaps, in his art. Before his death he wrote:

> "See: one's hopes and wishes to return to one's homeland and origin - they are just
> as moths trying to reach the light. And the man who is looking forward with joyful
> curiosity to the new spring, and the new summer, and always new months and new
> years - and even if the time he is longing forever comes, it will always seem to him
> to be too late - he does not notice that his longing carries within it the germs of his
> own death."

> "But this longing is the quintessence, the spirit of the elements, which through the
> soul is enclosed in the human body and which craves for return to its source. You
> must know that this very yearning is the quintessence of life, the handmaid of
> Nature, and that Man is a model of the world."

As he aged, Leonardo's dark view of mankind and his general pessimism grew. He was reported to erupt into fury liberally laced with scatological phrases that remind us of the diatribe about man penned by Jonathan Swift: "Men who can call themselves nothing more than a passage for food, producers of dung, fillers up of privies, for of them nothing else appears in the world, nor is there any virtue in them, for nothing of them remains but full privies."

Francis I had such great respect for Leonardo that he required nothing of him at all - he just wanted to be able to drop in as often as possible and talk to the Master. It was in France, an "alien land", that Leonardo gave his final trumpet blast in an apocalyptic series of drawings called "The Deluge" which he predicted would one day inundate the earth and end the world of Man.

These drawings, almost abstract in their abandonment of traditional artistic styles, were obviously vivid exercises of his imagination. His scientific knowledge is applied here with devastating effect, showing how puny are the means of man when pitted against nature.

> "Ah, what dreadful tumults one heard resounding through the gloomy air!", he wrote in the commentary to these drawings; "Ah me, how many lamentations!"

His depictions of the deluge were terrifying:

> "Let the dark, gloomy air be seen beaten by the rush of opposing winds wreathed in perpetual rain mingled with hail... All around let there be seen ancient trees uprooted and torn in pieces by the fury of the winds... And let the fragments of some of the mountains be fallen down into the depths of one of the valleys, and there form a barrier to the swollen waters of its rivers, which having already burst the barrier rushes on with immense waves..."

This was Leonardo's Last Judgment on the World, his last message to mankind. [See Plates 18 and 19.] Strange that it is the message of Auch Cathedral, the message of Fulcanelli, Kardec, Nostradamus, etc. And strange that they are all tied together via their connections to Marguerite of Navarre.

Recall that the burial scene of Christ in Auch Cathedral was inspired by **Margaret of Austria**, who married into the family that was in possession of the Shroud of Turin. Margaret's husband, **Philibert de Savoie** was a *cousin of one of the bishops that was involved in the commissioning of the work of the cathedral*, Francois de Savoie, and that **Marguerite of Navarre**, the second cousin of Margaret of Austria, was closely associated with Auch Cathedral.

Remember: Marguerite of Navarre takes us right back to Fulcanelli via François Rabelais whose series, *Le Tiers Livre des faicts et dicts héroïques du bon Pantagruel* (1546), was dedicated to **her.**

It was after the death of Leonardo that Marguerite became involved in the movement for the reform of the church, meeting and corresponding with the leading reformers of the period. In 1527, Marguerite married Henri d'Albret, King of Navarre. Henri d'Albret was the son of **Catherine de Foix**, descended from a famous Cathar family.

Recall also that another of Marguerite's associates and correspondents was **Jules Cesar Scaliger** who was a close friend and associate of **Nostradamus,** that Nostradamus, as mentioned, was born in Alet-le-Bains, in **Foix** lands, and that *Nostradamus also attended school with Rabelais.*

Recall: It was around 1531, Marguerite allowed a poem she had written to be published, *Miroir de l'ame pecheresse* (Mirror of the sinful soul). Marguerite gave a copy of *Miroir* to one of her ladies in waiting, **Anne Boleyn**, and it was later translated into English by Anne's 12 year old daughter, **Elizabeth** I. Recall as well that Anne Boleyn had previously been the lady in waiting to **Margaret of Austria before she went to serve Marguerite of Navarre.**

The connections are just simply too much to ignore, too much to consider "coincidence" in my opinion. Therefore I believe it is only in the brief context I have been able to present in this book, that we can truly come to some understanding of the *real* "Da Vinci Code".

After his death, Leonardo left his notebooks and manuscripts to his companion, Francesco Melzi. He took them all to his home near Milan where he guarded that "as though they were religious relics". Until Melzi's death, they were in safe hands. On his death, he left them to his son, a lawyer, trusting that he would honor them as well. Apparently not. The progress of dispersal began, and the manuscripts and unbound sheets were sold, stolen, given away, and scattered over half the planet. In more recent years, attempts have been made to assemble at least facsimiles, but no one knows how much was lost. In the late 19th century, a great number of pages in the possession of the British Crown somehow disappeared, and the guess is that they were hidden, not destroyed. One has to, of course, wonder why?

In any event, as mentioned, there are portions of his notebooks that have been collected together, and a close study of his available writings give us many clues as to what he wished to "speak" about in his art. For example:

> The mind of the painter must resemble a mirror, which always takes the colour of the object it reflects and is completely occupied by the images of as many objects as are in front of it. Therefore you must know, Oh Painter! that you cannot be a good one if you are not the universal master of representing by your art every kind of form produced by nature. And this you will not know how to do if you do not see them, and retain them in your mind.

> We know very well that errors are better recognised in the works of others than in our own; and that often, while reproving little faults in others, you may ignore great ones in yourself. To avoid such ignorance in the first place make yourself a master of perspective, then acquire perfect knowledge of the proportions of men and other animals, and also, study good architecture, that is so far as concerns the forms of buildings and other objects which are on the face of the earth; these forms are infinite and the better you know them the more admirable will your work be.

> The universal practice which painters adopt on the walls of chapels is greatly and reasonably to be condemned. Inasmuch as they represent an historical subject on one level with a landscape and buildings, and then go up a step and paint another, varying the point [of sight], and then a third and a fourth, in such a way as that on one wall there are 4 points of sight, which is supreme folly in such painters. We know that the point of sight is opposite the eye of the spectator of the scene; and if you would [have me] tell you how to represent the life of a saint divided into several pictures on one and the same wall, I answer that you must set out the foreground with its point of sight on a level with the eye of the spectator of the scene, and upon this plane represent the more important part of the story large and then, diminishing by degrees the figures, and the buildings on various hills and

open spaces, and can represent all the events of the history. And on the remainder of the wall up to the top, put trees, large as compared with the figures, or angels if they are appropriate to the story, or birds or clouds or similar objects; otherwise do not trouble yourself with it for your whole work will be wrong.

When you have well learnt perspective and have by heart the parts and forms of objects, you must go about, and constantly, as you go, observe, note and consider the circumstances and behaviour of men in talking, quarrelling or laughing or fighting together: the action of the men themselves and the actions of the bystanders, who separate them or who look on.

When you compose a historical picture take two points, one the point of sight, and the other the source of light; and make this as distant as possible.

Historical pictures ought not to be crowded and confused with too many figures.

Of composing historical pictures. Of not considering the limbs in the figures in historical pictures; as many do who, in the wish to represent the whole of a figure, spoil their compositions. And when you place one figure behind another take care to draw the whole of it so that the limbs which come in front of the nearer figures may stand out in their natural size and place.

The figure is most admirable which by its actions best expresses the passion that animates it.

You must show a man in despair with a knife, having already torn open his garments, and with one hand tearing open the wound...

A picture or representation of human figures, ought to be done in such a way as that the spectator may easily recognise, by means of their attitudes, the purpose in their minds. Thus, if you have to represent a man of noble character in the act of speaking, let his gestures be such as naturally accompany good words; and, in the same way, if you wish to depict a man of a brutal nature, give him fierce movements; as with his arms flung out towards the listener, and his head and breast thrust forward beyond his feet, as if following the speaker's hands.

Thus it is with a deaf and dumb person who, when he sees two men in conversation - although he is deprived of hearing - can nevertheless understand from the attitudes and gestures of the speakers, the nature of their discussion.

When you wish to represent a man speaking to a number of people, consider the matter of which he has to treat and adapt his action to the subject. Thus, if he speaks persuasively, let his action be appropriate to it. If the matter in hand be to set forth an argument, let the speaker, with the fingers of the right hand hold one finger of the left hand, having the two smaller ones closed; and his face alert, and turned towards the people with mouth a little open, to look as though he spoke. And if he is sitting, let him appear as though about to rise, with his head forward. If you represent him standing make him leaning slightly forward with head towards the people. These you must represent as silent and attentive, all looking at the orator's face with gestures of admiration; and make some old men in astonishment at the things they hear, with the corners of their mouths pulled down and drawn in, their cheeks full of furrows, and their eyebrows raised...

The motions of men must be such as suggest their dignity or their baseness.

Make your work carry out your purpose and meaning. That is when you draw a figure consider well who it is and what you wish it to be doing.

The limbs which are used for labour must be muscular and those which are not much used you must make without muscles and softly rounded. Represent your figures in such action as may be fitted to express what purpose is in the mind of each; otherwise your art will not be admirable.

Fame should be depicted as covered all over with tongues instead of feathers, and in the figure of a bird.

Pleasure and Pain represent as twins, since there never is one without the other; and as if they were united back to back, since they are contrary to each other.

This represents Pleasure together with Pain, and show them as twins because one is never apart from the other. They are back to back because they are opposed to each other; and they exist as contraries in the same body, because they have the same basis, inasmuch as the origin of pleasure is labour and pain, and the various forms of evil pleasure are the origin of pain. Therefore it is here represented with a reed in his right hand which is useless and without strength and the wounds it inflicts are poisoned. In Tuscany they are put to support beds, to signify that it is here that vain dreams come, and here a great part of life is consumed. It is here that much precious time is wasted, that is, in the morning, when the mind is composed and rested, and the body is made fit to begin new labours; there again many vain pleasures are enjoyed; both by the mind in imagining impossible things, and by the body in taking those pleasures that are often the cause of the failing of life. And for these reasons the reed is held as their support. Evil-thinking is Envy or Ingratitude.

Envy must be represented with a contemptuous motion of the hand towards heaven [See Plate 20.], because if she could she would use her strength against God; make her with her face covered by a mask of fair seeming; show her as wounded in the eye by a palm branch and by an olive-branch, and wounded in the ear by laurel and myrtle, to signify that victory and truth are odious to her. [431]

It is thus strongly suggested that, in every painting he ever executed, Leonardo da Vinci was conveying messages. Not only that, the messages were somewhat codified. We can extract general principles from his writings and utilize them in examining his works.

As time passed after the death of Leonardo, critics began to come forward declaiming loudly that, "after all, Leonardo was only a man and his paintings, like those of other artists, consisted simply of colors applied to a surface". This was John Ruskin's general opinion paraphrased, and he made it clear that he thought the Master was greatly overrated. Renoir said: "Leonardo da Vinci bores me."

The most dramatic attacks on Leonardo's image came via Sigmund Freud. Working with what he mistakenly thought were historical facts, he produced an

---

[431] Leonardo's quotes from: *The Notebooks of Leonardo Da Vinci* compiled and edited from the original manuscripts by Jean Paul Richter, Dover Edition, 1970, first published in 1883 by Sampson Low, Marston, Searle & Rivington under the title *The Literary Works of Leonardo da Vinci.* Dover Publications, New York

essay, *"Leonardo da Vinci, and a Memory of His Childhood"*. He suggested that Leonardo, lacking a father in the first years of his life, had abnormally erotic relations with his mother and later, when his father brought him into his household, that his stepmother was "too affectionate", perhaps even erotically so.

Freud's biggest blunder, however, was the emphasis he placed on a childhood dream of fantasy recorded by the artist himself of a large bird alighting on his shoulder. Freud coupled this with a remark made by Leonardo, to wit: "The act of procreation and everything that has any relation to it is so disgusting that human beings would soon die out if there were no pretty faces and sensuous dispositions", and concluded that Leonardo was a latent homosexual. That smear has stuck pretty well though there is absolutely *no* evidence that it is true.

Freud placed his reliance on a largely fictional work by Dimitri Merejkowski, *The Romance of Leonardo da Vinci*, which included the passage by Leonardo about the bird encounter. Unfortunately, the word had been rendered "vulture" which sent Freud off into raptures of humorless psychoanalysis based on ancient Egyptian mythology and sexual-religious beliefs concerning the vulture-headed goddess named *Mut*. Freud solemnly declaimed, "We may question whether the sound similarity to our word 'mother' is only coincidental?".

The actual word that Leonardo used in describing his dream/fantasy was "kite", a bird of the hawk family common in Europe. In short, Freud's dissertation on Leonardo was irrelevant. But then, in my opinion, Freud himself is irrelevant.

Nevertheless, the word "kite" caught my attention. Here's why:

> June 20, 1998
>
> Q: ... Okay, let me ask this, these guys who have researched this Holy Bloodline business have sort of focused all the attention on a particular line, purportedly the line of Jesus going into the Merovingian kings... This guy, Pierre Plantard, seems to have more or less created a geneology with their own validations... sort of like describing x in terms of y and y in terms of x. Now, is this Pierre Plantard a genuine carrier of the bloodline that we are concerned with?
>
> A: Partially.
>
> Q: Then, that makes me think that the significant thing that we are looking for is a convergence of the blood lines... These lines are symbolized by the god figures, the children of Odin, and what we are looking for is a place where these lines converge?
>
> A: Yes.
>
> Q: Well, what characteristics might an individual have who is a product of this convergence?
>
> A: Fair skinned and cleft chin.
>
> Q: Well, Ark and F*** both have cleft chins, but C** and I don't! Does this mean...
>
> A: We aren't saying that all with these features are of that blood line!
>
> Q: So, you can have the bloodline and look quite different?
>
> A: Yes.
>
> Q: How many persons on the planet contain these 'convergant' bloodlines?
>
> A: 7367. Kites were used for cross communication between bloodline members.

Q: Kites?! What do kites have to do with it? What the heck... you guys are driving me NUTS! Do you mean kites as in paper and string or kites as in the bird?

A: Yes, paper wood and string.

Q: ... (C) This is implying that such people know they have the bloodline and keep in touch with each other? (L) Or, is this something for the future when those of the bloodline wake up?

A: Yes. [to the] Latter.

Q: So, we need to go fly a kite... (C) With a particular shape and symbol...

A: Research kites.

Q: (C) The Japanese fly kites... and there are a lot of people who hang banners outside their houses all the time...

A: Want revelations? Prepare for "Treasure" Hunt.

Q: Thanks a lot!

A: These quests energize you, Laura!

Q: Yes, they do. When I start finding things that connect, it is like having little explosions of energy in the brain... (A) Well, I don't understand these kites. They don't fly by themselves, they are on a string. You cannot see them at great distances... only a few miles... what is the point of communicating this way with someone who is only a few miles away?

A: Kites can be released, or left behind too!

Q: (A) When you release a kite, it falls down! Well, maybe we ought to wait and see where this clue goes before we get stuck on the technical aspects. Maybe it is just sort of a marker... We don't know if it will relate to a literal kite, or a reference to a kite, a drawing of a kite... a carving... something will appear that will connect, I am sure. It always does.

Indeed, it did. Leonardo da Vinci's *The Kite and the Treatise upon the Flight of Birds* includes the following:

> "*This writing distinctly about the kite seems to be my destiny*, because among the first recollections of my infancy, it seemed to me that, as I was in my cradle, a kite came to me and opened my mouth with its tail, and struck me several times with its tail inside my lips." (Codex Atlanticus)

> The kite is a bird with a large wingspan, which uses air currents to stay aloft while gliding. He studied the kite and other birds, trying to learn how they flew so that he could successfully imitate nature. Little is known about da Vinci's private life, because he usually never wrote about it in his journal. However, this is an interesting exception because we see that *Leonardo wrote that it was his destiny to write about and study the kite,* and also means that he thought it was his destiny to build flying machines, and enable men to fly.

> When once you have tasted flight, you will forever walk the earth with your eyes turned skyward, for there you have been, and there you will always long to return. [Leonardo]

Now, having assembled so many interesting clues, let's go in a slightly different direction. In 1483, Leonardo da Vinci painted *The Madonna of the Rocks*. (Full title: *The Virgin of the Rocks (The Virgin with the Infant Saint John adoring the Infant Christ accompanied by an Angel)*) (Louvre) [See Plate 21.]. Between 1506 and 1508, he produced the second, or "London version", of the *Madonna of the Rocks* [See Plate 22.]. It is believed that the first was done to fulfill a contract with the Milanese Confraternity of the Immaculate Conception. Apparently, they didn't like it, and it passed into the hands of the French. The Confraternity commissioned a second version in which Ambrogio da Predis was to have a share of the work. Arguments and lawsuits between him and Leonardo and the Confraternity followed, and twenty-five years passed before the Confraternity finally got the version they wanted.

It is in comparing the two paintings that one gets the feeling that the first version must have conveyed a message that the Confraternity wanted to suppress, and in the second version, apparently acceptable to them, Leonardo managed to deliver his message anyway. Either that, or he had little to do with the second version.

The Louvre version is generally accepted as Leonardo's, but there is continuing doubt about the National Gallery version.

In any event, the compositional changes reveal to us, apparently, what the Confraternity objected to. They obviously objected to the angel, seated beside the infant Jesus, pointing at the infant John the Baptist. They probably asked for halos to be included, but I think Leonardo added the "reedy cross" across the shoulder of John on his own initiative.

The paintings are about equal in size, but the figures in the second version are brought closer to the viewer and made "heavier" and "more idealized" as though they are made of stone. The colors of the second version have been subdued to the point of actually looking as though they are dead bodies - a corpselike pallor seems to deliberately emphasize that the "message" of the painting is "death".

The item in the first painting that has received the most comment is the strange, almost threatening hand of the Virgin. Let's look at the hands from the two versions side by side, keeping in mind all of Leonardo's comments about "telling a story" with his paintings, the gestures of the hands, and so on. I don't think the hand is threatening at all, as we will soon discover.

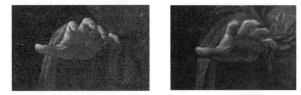

Now, let's take a look at another of Da Vinci's works: *The Last Supper*... [See Plate 23.]

The Last Supper is said to be the "freezing of a moment in time", the moment when Christ has just spoken the words, "One of you shall betray me", and the disciples all react to the words with magnificent displays of poses and gestures, "revealing the intentions of their souls". Leonardo undoubtedly made many studies before he began to paint, but only two of them are left to us today. One of them is hastily - even roughly - drawn and shows *all* of the figures, even if they are not lined up in a row behind the table. Unable to place all of them at the table because of the small size of the page he was drawing on, he placed four of them at the bottom. However, his intention was clear because he placed a repeated shoulder/arm of one of the disciples at the left of the upper row. In the sketch, Leonardo was keeping to the standard iconographic style, leaving Judas sitting alone on the near side of the table.

What seems to be the case is that, beyond freezing this moment in time, Leonardo also intended other, deeper meanings, as we can well surmise from his commentaries on painting quoted above, compared with the study [Plate 24] and the finished painting.

Many individuals have made much of the fact that this painting is supposed to depict Jesus dining with his "wife", Mary Magdalene next to him. I certainly agree that the figure next to Jesus is obviously a woman - a woman who is missing from the preliminary study unless she is the one who has all but collapsed face down next to Jesus. But is it Mary Magdalene? Or is it someone else? Or is the clue meant to point to something else altogether?

But, before I go further, let me suggest, from Leonardo's own words, a possible meaning of the two figures, appearing almost as twins, facing somewhat away from each other, yet joined by the proximity of their draped arms resting side by side on the table, forming the "M" that may take us one step deeper:

> Pleasure and Pain represent as twins, since there never is one without the other; and
> as if they were united back to back, since they are contrary to each other. [...] This
> represents Pleasure together with Pain, and show them as twins because one is
> never apart from the other. They are back to back because they are opposed to each
> other; and they exist as contraries in the same body... [See Plate 25.]

Leonardo also had formulas for the hands that were to "match" the nature of the discourse of the subject of the painting:

> When you wish to represent a man speaking to a number of people, consider the
> matter of which he has to treat and adapt his action to the subject. Thus, if he
> speaks persuasively, let his action be appropriate to it. If the matter in hand be to set
> forth an argument, let the speaker, with the fingers of the right hand hold one finger
> of the left hand, having the two smaller ones closed; and his face alert, and turned
> towards the people with mouth a little open, to look as though he spoke.

Considering the announcement that Jesus is supposed to have just made in the Last Supper, the aspect of his hands is most interesting. We notice the supplicating gesture of the left hand, but the right hand is truly curious. It was only after I had looked at it for a bit that I realized what it reminded me of: The Virgin of the Rocks. Let's look at the hands side by side:

Jesus hand, Last Supper   Mary's hand, Louvre   Mary's hand, London

We actually see that the right hand of Jesus in the Last Supper matches almost exactly the left hand of Mary in the Virgin of the Rocks. In other words, whatever was being "said" by the hands in both paintings was the same thing. But, of course, in the Last Supper, according to the "plot" of the story, Jesus was about to take up a piece of bread and dip it in the bowl together with Judas whose hand is also reaching in a strange way. Is the implication that John the Baptist, in the Virgin of the rocks, was a sort of "Judas"?

Another controversy about the Last Supper has to do with the two "anomalous hands" in the painting. In the following image, I have taken a high resolution scan of a professional photograph purchased on site in Milan by a member of the Quantum Future Group. (No photos are allowed to be taken by tourists.) I enlarged the photo and circled each evident or partly evident hand in the painting. I have placed a number above the head of each individual showing how many hands THAT particular individual has showing. I then cut the image so that I could fit it on the page in two parts. [See Plates 26 and 27.]

There are thirteen people at the table and, if we count the hands, we have 25, because one hand is hidden: the one belonging to the man with the upward pointing finger.

The figure whispering in the ear of the woman has been identified as St. Peter. One of the hands that must belong to him is found making a "cutting motion" at the throat of the woman seated next to Jesus.

It is obvious that Leonardo intended to convey a message because he spoke clearly enough about completing bodies that are to be behind other bodies so that the anatomy might be accurate. Plate 29 is the only other study from the Last Supper known to be extant, next to the arm of St. Peter from the painting:

It is clear that the hand with the knife [Plate 28] and the hand making the cutting motion at the neck of the woman both belong to St. Peter.

Let's look again at what Leonardo wrote:

> The figure is most admirable which by its actions best expresses the passion that animates it.

> ...when you place one figure behind another take care to draw the whole of it so that the limbs which come in front of the nearer figures may stand out in their natural size and place.

> You must show a man in despair with a knife.... A picture or representation of human figures, ought to be done in such a way as that the spectator may easily recognise, by means of their attitudes, the purpose in their minds. ...The motions of men must be such as suggest their dignity or their baseness.

> Make your work carry out your purpose and meaning. That is when you draw a figure consider well who it is and what you wish it to be doing.... Represent your figures in such action as may be fitted to express what purpose is in the mind of each... Envy must be represented with a contemptuous motion of the hand towards heaven, because if she could she would use her strength against God...

So, most certainly, not only might we have "Twin Representations" in the figures of Jesus and the woman to his right as the "Pleasure, Pain Principle", but also the hand holding the knife that emerges *from behind Judas* Iscariot is holding a knife: "You must show a man in despair with a knife...", and, if we suppose that the bread, the Eucharist, is to represent "the body of Christ", then the action of the knife over the bread might very well be Envy making a "contemptuous motion of the hand towards heaven". Put that together with the head cutting motion and the whispering in the ear, *conspiring*, and a rather unpleasant picture of St. Peter emerges. It seems that *Peter is hiding his actions behind Judas.*

Curious.

As I continued to study this painting, I noted something else that seems to be quite remarkable:

If you use the hand with the knife, the hand making the cutting motion, the right hand of Jesus, his forehead, and the palm of his left hand as "points", you have exactly traced the constellation of Cassiopeia *mirrored*. [See Plates 30 and 31.]

Now, in order to understand the possible implications of this strange figure that is clearly evident in the painting, let me repeat again the somewhat obscure information about this famous Star group cited earlier in this article.

> "The star's name comes from a star picture envisioned by the Arabic peoples that is very different from the Greek conception of the constellation", Teske explains. "Despite this, its **Arabic name** was inserted into the Greek conception of Cassiopeia *around 400 years ago.*"

That would put the insertion of the Arabic names right around the time of Da Vinci and the circle connected to Auch Cathedral. So, certainly they were aware of the following:

The Arabic names of the main stars of Cassiopeia give some clues to the esoteric meaning of the constellation, among them being "breast",(schedir-seder?) "hand", "hump of the camel", "knee", and "elbow", all of which are esoteric symbols found in many arcane works. The Arabs called the entire constellation the *seder tree*. Earlier Arabs thought that this constellation was "*the large hand stained with henna*", the brightest stars being the fingertips.

Which reminds us again of the strange, large hand of the Virgin of the Rocks, the hand that is the mirror image of the right hand of Jesus in the painting of the Last Supper.

Cassiopeia is a beautiful constellation at the end of the Milky Way Galaxy and is associated with what is known as the *Perseus Constellation Family*. It is in the zodiacal sign of the Ram wherein one finds the stars *Shedir*, "The Breast", (the star on the forehead of Jesus), *Ruckbah*, (knee) "The Enthroned", (the star on the hand making the cutting motion at the throat of the woman next to Jesus), and *Dat al-Cursa*, "The Seated". The Chinese called Cassiopeia *Ko Taou*, or a *"doorway"*. Some saw this constellation in the shape of a *key*.

> Hanging nearly overhead in November's mid-evening sky is the W-shaped constellation we know as Cassiopeia... Observers who face north will see the star called "Caph", meaning *the palm of a hand*, on the left end of Cassiopeia's upside-down "W".

Interesting that there is the "palm of the hand" and the "palm branch", located at the upturned palm of Jesus? Also strange that Cassiopeia is referred to as being an "upside down W" rather than the more obvious M - an attempt to "hide" a relationship?

In 1893, E. W. Bullinger wrote about Cassiopeia:

> The captive delivered, and preparing for her Husband, the Redeemer. In the last chapter we saw the woman bound (Andromeda); here we see the same woman freed, delivered, and enthroned.

ULUGH BEY says its Arabic name is *El Seder*, which means the freed.

With the hands of the woman in *The Last Supper* clasped together as though "bound," and the cutting motion being made by St. Peter, concealing his knife, we certainly can see a relationship here.

In the Denderah Zodiac (Egyptian) her name is Au-Set - Isis - which means set up as Queen. ALBUMAZER says this constellation was anciently called "the *daughter of splendour*." This appears to be *the meaning of the word Cassiopeia*, the enthroned, the beautiful. The Arabic name is Ruchba, the enthroned. This is also the meaning of its Chaldee name, *Dat al cursa*. There are 55 stars in this constellation, of which five are of the 3rd magnitude, five of the 4th, etc.

This beautiful constellation passes vertically over Great Britain every day, and is easily distinguished by its five brightest stars, forming an irregular "W." *This brilliant constellation contains one binary star, a triple star, a double star, a quadruple star, and a large number of nebulae.* In the year 1572 Tycho Brahe discovered in this constellation, and very near the star k (under the arm of the chair), *a new star, which shone more brightly than Venus. It was observed for nearly two years, and disappeared entirely in 1574.*

The brightest star, a (in the left breast), is named *Schedir* (Hebrew), which means the freed. The next, b (in the top of the chair), likewise bears a Hebrew name - *Caph*, which means the branch; it is evidently given on account of *the branch of victory which she bears in her hand.* She is indeed highly exalted, and making herself ready. Her *hands, no longer bound,* are engaged in this happy work. With her right hand she is arranging her robes, while with her left she is adorning her hair. She is seated upon the Arctic circle, and close by the side of Cepheus, the King. *This is "the Bride, the Lamb's wife, the heavenly city, the new Jerusalem", the, "partakers of the heavenly calling".*

Cassiopeia is *visible all night and all year and neither rises or sets*, but instead circles endlessly around our northern Pole star [Polaris]. The Big Dipper is located on the opposite side of the pole to Cassiopeia.

The Lithuanians refer to the stars in Cassiopeia as "Rider", "Justandis" or "food carrier" - breast? - or "Abakukas" Star' and *"Mary's stars"*. This brings us to what Sir John Rhys wrote about Cassiopeia:

We have to look for help to enable us to identify the great 'SHE' persistently eluding our search in the syntax of the Welsh language. Only two feminine names suggest themselves to me as in any way appropriate: One is Tynghed, 'fate or fortune', and the other is Don, mother of some of the most nebulous personages in Celtic literature.

It is from Don that Gwydion, the bard and arch-magician, and Gofannon the smith his brother, are called sons of Don; and so, in the case of Arianrhod, daughter of Don, mother of Ilew, and owner of the sea-laved castle of Caer Arianrhod, not far distant from the prehistoric mound of Dinas Dinlle...

In Irish legend, we detect Don under the Irish form of her name, Danu or Donu, genitive Danaan or Donaan, and *she is almost singular there in always being styled Divinity.* From her the great mythical personages of Irish legend are called Tuatha De Danaan, or 'the Goddess Danu's Tribes', and sometimes Fir Dea, or 'the Men of the Divinity'.

The last stage in the Welsh history of Don consists of her translation to the skies, where the constellation of Cassiopeia is supposed to constitute Ilys Don, or Don's Court.[432]

Was Leonardo da Vinci indicating Cassiopeia in his painting of *The Last Supper*? Were Marguerite of Navarre, Rabelais, Nostradamus, Francis I, Anne Boleyn, and others, part of a group in contact with "Us in the Future"?

So, let me return now to the remarks about stars made by Canseliet made 20 years apart, that, juxtaposed, reveal something quite marvelous:

> From the FIRST edition: I know, not from having discovered it myself, but because I was assured of it by the author more than ten years ago, that *the key* **to the major arcanum is given quite openly in one of the figures, illustrating the present work**. And **this key consists quite simply in a colour** revealed to the artisan right from the first work.

I suspect that the reader has, by now, figured out that Canseliet and Fulcanelli were very tricky. And so, we look at this clue and try to think of what Canseliet is saying. He says that the clue is in a *"figure illustrating the present work"*, that it is revealed *"right from the first work"* and in the preface to the second edition, adds the clue that **the subject of the star** *"leads us straight into Fulcanelli's text"* **saying that "right from the beginning my Master has dwelt on the primary role of the star..."**

We turn again to the very beginning of Fulcanelli's text:

> The strongest impression of my early childhood - **I was *seven* years old** - an impression of which I still retain a vivid memory, was the emotion aroused in my young heart by the sight of a gothic cathedral. I was immediately enraptured by it. I was *in an ecstasy*, struck with wonder, unable to tear myself away from the attraction of the marvelous, from the magic of such splendour, such immensity, such *intoxication* expressed by this more divine than human work.

> Varro, in his *Antiquitates rerum humanorum*, recalls the legend of Aeneas saving his father and his household gods from the flames of Troy and, after long wanderings, arriving at the **fields of Laurentum**, the goal of his journey. **"Laurente** (Laurentium) is cabalistically *l'or enté* (grafted gold)". And so indeed, we have been led to a *color*!

Abbe Boudet:

> The Auscii easily became skillful in working in gold; *this metal was almost like a weed in their region*, and diverse historians say that the avid Greek and Phoenician merchants, coming back to their countries, used the gold gathered in the Pyrénées for ballast in their vessels.

Is the Da Vinci Code also the Mystery of the Cathedrals we have been led to by Fulcanelli? Do they both point to the work of the Cassiopaeans?

---

[432] John Rhys, *Celtic Folklore*

Patrick Rivière, alchemist, student of Eugene Canseliet, disciple of Fulcanelli:

Throughout her exposé, Laura Knight-Jadczyk refers to two powerful works of the scientist-alchemist Fulcanelli: *The Mystery of the Cathedrals* and *Dwellings of the Philosophers*. **She applies her vast knowledge to the continuation of his work.** [...]

As to her inspiration, what can we say, and, from whence could it come, if not the Light of the stars?

BIBLIOGRAPHY

Aaboe, Asger, "Remarks on Theoretical Treatment Of Eclipses In Antiquity", *JFHA* 3 June 1972.

———. "Babylonian Planetary Theories", Brown University Dissertation, 1957, 58-4346. in *Centauris* V, 1958.

Aardsma, Gerald. 1993. *A New Approach to the Chronology of Biblical History from Abraham to Samuel.* El Cajon: Institute for Creation Research.

Abehsera, Abraham A. 1991. *Babel: The Language of the 21st Century.* Jerusalem: EQEV Publishing House

Adolf, Helen. 1960. *Visio Pacis/ Holy City and Grail: An Attempt at an Inner History of the Grail Legend.* State College: Pennsylvania State U.P..

Aharoni, Yohanan. 1979. *The Land of the Bible. Revised.*Translated by A.F. Rainey. Philadelphia: Westminster Press.

Ahituv, S. 1984. *Canaanite Toponyms in Ancient Egyptian Documents.* Leiden.

Ahlstrom, Gosta. 1993. *The History of Ancient Palestine from the Palaeolithic Period to Alexander's Conquest.*Sheffield: JSOT Press.

Al-Biruni The Chronology of Ancient Nations. C. E. Sachau (trans.)t *Oriental Translation Fund*, Vol. 73, London: Willaim H. Allan, 1879.

Albright, W.F 1935. "The Names Shaddai and Abram." *Journal of Biblical Literature* 54.

———. 1943a. "Two Little Understood Amarna Letters From the Middle Jordan Valley." *Bulletin of the American School of Oriental Research* 89.

———. 1943b. "An Archaic Hebrew Proverb in an Amarna Letter From Central Palestine." *Bulletin of the American School of Oriental Research* 89.

———. 1955. "Northwest-Semitic Names in a List of Egyptian Slaves From the Eighteenth Century B.C." *Journal of the American Oriental Society* 74.

———. 1961. "Abram the Hebrew: A New Archaeological Interpretation." *Bulletin of the American School of Oriental Research* 163.

———. 1934. *The Vocalization of the Egyptian Syllabic Orthography.* New Haven: American Oriental Society.

———. 1957. *From Stone Age to Christianity.* Garden City: Doubleday & Company.

Alcock, L.. 1971. *Arthur's Britain.* London: Allan Lane

Alexander, Joseph A. 1953. *Commentary on the Prophecies of Isaiah.* rpt. 1846-7. Grand Rapids: Zondervan.

Aling, Charles 1986. *Har Karkom: The Mountain of God.* New York: Rizzoli.

———. 1995. "Some Remarks on the Historicity of the Joseph Story." *Near East Archaeological Society Bulletin* 39-40

Aling, Charles. 1981. *Egypt and Bible History.* Grand Rapids:Baker Book House.

Allegro, John. *The Sacred Mushroom and the Cross*, Abacus

Amis, Robin. *A Different Christianity: Early Christian Esotericism and Modern Thought.* Albany: SUNY Press, 1995.

Anati, Emmanuel. 1963. *Palestine Before the Hebrews.* New York: Alfred A. Knope.

Andreae, Johann Valentin. 1459. *The Chymical Wedding of Christian Rosenkreutz*, Minerva Books, London

Andrews, Richard & Schellenberger, Paul. 1996. *The Tomb of God: The Body of Jesus and the Solution to a 2,000-year-old Mystery* New York: Little, Brown.

Ante-Nicene Fathers. 1975. 10 Vols. ed by Roberts and Donaldson. Grand Rapids: Eerdmans.

Arthurian Tradition & Chrétien de Troyes, Columbia University Press, NY (1949),

Ashe, Geoffrey. 1990. *King Arthur The Dream of a Golden Age.* London: Thames and Hudson.

———. 1982. *Kings and Queens of Early Britain.* London: Methuen.

————. 1979. *The Ancient Wisdom*. London: Sphere.

————. 1999. *The Book of Prophecy,*. London: Blandford.

————. 1985. *The Discovery of King Arthur*. London: Guild.

————. 1975. *Camelot and the Vision of Albion*. Panther.

————. 1979. *The Ancient Wisdom*. London: Sphere.

————. 1999. *The Book of Prophecy*. London: Blandford.

Astour, M. 1975. "Place Names." Ras Shamra *Parallels*. Vol. 2, ed by Loren R. Fisher. Rome: Pontificium Institutum Biblicum.

————. 1979. "Yahweh in Egyptian Topographical Lists." *Festschrift Elmar Edel* 12. ed. by Gorg and Pusch.

Atkinson, R. J. C. 1979. *Stonehenge Archaeology and Interpretation*. Penguin Harmondsworth.

Aubrey, John. 1718. *Natural History and Antiquities of the County of Surrey*, 5 Vols. London: Curll.

Augstein, Rudolf. 1999. *Jesus Menschensohn*, Hamburg: Hoffmann and Campe.

Baigent, M., Leigh, R., & Lincoln, H. 1982. *The Holy Blood and the Holy Grail*. London: Jonathan Cape.

Baigent, Michael & Leigh, Richard 1990 [1989] *The Temple and the Lodge*. London: Corgi Books.

Baigent, Michael, et.al. 1986. *The Messianic Legacy*. New York: Dell.Publ.Co.

Baillie, Mike. 1999. *Exodus to Arthur*. London: B.T. Batsford. 1999.

Baker, Robert. 1961. *Introduction to Astronomy*. Princeton, N.J.: D. Van Norstrandt

Bakker, Robert T. 1986. *The Dinosaur Heresies.*; New York: William Morrow and Company.

Balfour, Michael. 1992. *Megalithic Mysteries*. Limpsfield, Surrey: Dragon's World.

Barber, Chris. 1987. *Mysterious Wales*. London Paladin.

Barber, Richard. 1993. *The Arthurian Legends: An Illustrated Anthology*. New York: Barnes & Noble Books.

Barrett, C.K. 1994. *A Critical and Exegetical Commentary on the Acts of the Apostles*. Vol. 1. Edinburg: T&T Clark.

Bartar W. "Die Chronologie der 1. bis 5. Dynastie nach den Angaben des rekonstruierten Annalensteins" *ZAS* 108(1981).

Bartholomew, Robert E., and Howard, George S. 1998. *UFOs and Alien Contact: Two Centuries of Mystery*. Amherst (NY): Prometheus.

Beaumont, Comyns. 1945. *The Riddle of Prehistoric Britain*. London: Rider & Co.

Bell, Barbara. 1975. "Climate and the History of Egypt." *American Journal of Archaeology* 79.

Bellingham, David. 1990. *Celtic Mythology*, London: Apple Press.

Bennett, J. A. W., ed. 1963. *Essays on Malory: Walter Oakeshott, C. S. Lewis, E. Vinaver, D. S. Brewer, P. E. Tucker, F. Whitehead, et. al.* Oxford: Clarendon Press.

Berezkin, Juri. 1983. *Mochica. Tsivilizatsia indeitsev Severnogo poberzhia Peru* v I-VII vv. Leningrad. Berlin 1945.

Berlitz, Charles. 1969. *The Mystery of Atlantis*. New York: Avon.

Bevent, Edwyn. 1927. *A History of Egypt Under the-Ptolemaic Dynasty*. London: Methuen & Co.

Bickerman, E.J. 1968. *Chronology of the Ancient World*. London:Thames & Hudson.

Bierling, Neal. 1992. *Giving Goliath His Due*. Grand Rapids: Baker Book House.

Bietak, Manfred. 1987. "Comments on the Exodus." *Egypt, Israel, Sinai: Archaeological and Historical Relationships in the Biblical Period*. Tel Aviv: Tel Aviv University.

————. 1988. "Contra Bimson, Bietak Says Late Bronze Age Cannot Begin as Late as 1400 B.C." *Biblical Archaeology Review* 15:4 (July/August).

————. 1991. "Egypt and Canaan During the Middle Bronze Age." *Bulletin of the American School of Oriental Research* 281.

Bimson and Livingston. 1987. "Redating the Exodus." *Biblical Archaeology Review* 13:5 (September/October).

Bimson, John J. 1980. "Archaeological Data and the Dating of the Patriarchs." *Essays on the Patriarchal Narratives*. ed. by Millard and Wiseman. Winona Lake: Eisenbrauns.

————. 1981. *Redating the Exodus and Conquest*. 2nd ed.Sheffield: The Almond Press.

Black, Jeremy, and Green, Anthony. 1992. *Gods, Demons and Symbols of Ancient Mesopotamia*. Austin: University of Texas Press.

Blake and Lloyd. 2000. *The Keys to Avalon*. Shaftesbury, Dorset: Element Books.

Blavatsky, H.P. 1980. *The Esoteric Writings of Helena Petrovna Blavatsky*. Wheaton, IL: Theosophical Publishing House. Originally published in 1897 as the third volume to The Secret Doctrine.

Boeckhr, August. *Menetho und die Hundsternperiode*.

Bogdanow, Fanni. 1973. "The Transformation of the Role of Perceval in Some Thirteenth Century Prose Romances." *Studies in Medieval Literature and Languages in Memory of Frederick Whitehead.* Manchester: Manchester University Press.

Bonanno, Anthony. 1999. Article in *Old Temples Society* 2. November.

Borchardt, Ludwig. "Der zweite Papyrusfund von Kahunp" *Zeitschrift futr Aeawtische--§grache* 37 (1M)r p. 89-103. Die Annalen und die zeitliche Festleguna des alten Reighen der aeqwtischen Geschichte. Quellen und Forschungen zu Zeitbestimmung der ASMMtischen Geschichte. Berlin 1917.

Bord, Janet and Colin. 1974. *Mysterious Britain.* Paladin.

Bosroff, Marie (trans). 1967. *Sir Gawain and the Green Knight.* New York: WW Norton & Co.

Bower, B. 1996. "Ancient World Gets Precise Chronology." *Science News* 149 (June 29th).

Bramley, William. 1990. *The Gods Of Eden.* New York: Avon.

Branston, B. 1957. *Lost Gods of England.* London: Thames and Hudson.

———. 1978. *Gods and Heroes From Viking Mythology.* London: Peter Loewe.

———. 1980. *Gods of the North.* London: Thames and Hudson.

Breasted, James. 1988 rpt. *Ancient Records of Egypt* 1906-7, 5 Vols. London: Histories & Mysteries of Man Ltd.

Brecher, Kenneth. 1979. "Sirius Enigmas" *Astronomy Of The Ancients.* Cambridge, Mass.: MIT Press.

Brewer, E. Cobham, Rev. Dr. 1885. *Dictionary of Phrase and Fable.* London: Cassell & Company.

Britton, John. *On the Quality of Solar and Lunar Observations and Parameters In Ptolemys Almagest.* Yale Dissertation, 67-6997.

Brown, A. C. L. 1940. "Arthur's Loss of Queen and Kingdom," *Speculum,* XV (January).

Bruce, J. D. 1928. *The Evolution of Arthurian Romance.* Peter Smith Pub. 2nd edition (July 1983).

Brug, John. 1988. *The Astronomical Dating of Ancient History before 700 AD.* Wisconsin Lut1983heran Seminary.

Brugsch, K.H. 1968. *Thesaurus Inscriptionum Aeavaticarum,* I-IV. Graz v Austria: Akademische Druck.

———. 1870. "Ein neues Sothis-Datum" *Zeitschrift der Aegyptische Sprache* 8.

Bruins and Plicht. 1996. "The Exodus enigma." *Nature* 382 (July 18).

Bryant, Nigel. 2001. *Merlin and the Grail.* Cambridge UK: D.S.Brewer.

———. (trans.). 1978. *The High Book of the Holy Grail.* NJ: Brewer, Rowman and Littlefield.

Buccellati, Giorgio. 1977."Apiru and Munnabtutu--The Statelessof the First Cosmopolitan Age." *Journal of Near Eastern Studies* 36.

Budge, E.A.W. 1904. (1976).*The Decree of Memphis and Canopus.* London: Kegan Paul. AMS Reprint N.Y.

Bulgakov, Fr. Sergius. 1993. *Sophia: The Wisdom of God.* Hudson NY: Lidisfarne.

———. 1997. *The Holy Grail and the Eucharist.* Hudson NY: Lidisfarne.

Bullinger, E.W. 1968. *Figures of Speech used in the Bible.* rpt.Grand Rapids: Baker Book House.

Burland, C. A. 1972. *Echoes of Magic: A Study of Seasonal Festivals through the Ages.* Totowa, NJ: Rowman and Littlefield.

Burnham, Terry and Jay Phelan. 2000. *Mean Genes.* Cambridge, Massachusetts: Perseus Publishing.

Byron, Cyril. 1931. *The Papyrus Ebers.* N.Y.: D. Appleton.

———. 1970. Cambridge Ancient History. 3rd Edition. I:1-2.

Campbell, Bruce F. 1980. *Ancient Wisdom Revived: A History of the Theosophical Movement.* Los Angeles:Univ. of California Press.

Campbell, Joseph. 1949. *The Hero With A Thousand Faces.* New York: MJF.

Campion, Nicholas. 1994. *The Great Year: Astrology, Millenarianism and History in the Western Tradition.* London: Arkana.

Capon, Robert Farrar. 1971. *The Third Peacock: The Goodness of God and the Badness of the World.* 1st ed. Garden City, N.Y.: Doubleday.

Carroll, Michael P. 1986. *The Cult of the Virgin Mary: Psychological Origins.* Princeton: Princeton University Press.

Casperson, L.W. 1986. "The Lunar Dates of Thutmose III," *JNES* 45.

Castaneda, Carlos. 1998. *The Active Side o Infinity.* New York: Harper Collins.

———. 1984. *The Fire From Within.* New York: Pocket Books.

Loomis, Roger Sherman. 1927. *Celtic Myth and Arthurian Romance.* New York: Columbia University Press.

Censorinus, (ed. Otto Jahn). 1900. *De Die Natali, Berolini.* 1845. New York: Wm. Maude.

Ceram, C.E. 1956. *The Secret of The Hittites*. trans. Richard and Clara Winston. New York: Alfred A. Knopf.

Chamberlain, Von Del. 1983. "Navajo Constellations in Literature, Art, Artifact and a New Mexico Rock Art Site." *Archaeoastronomy* 6 (1-4).

Chambers, E. K. 1947. *English Literature at the Close of the Middle Ages*. New York: Oxford University Press.

Chambers, Henry. 1983. "Ancient Amphictyonies, Sic Et Non." *Scriptures in Context* II. ed. by Hallo, Moyer, and Perdue. Winona Lake: Eisenbrauns.

Chari, C.T.K. 1972. "Precognition, Probability and Quantum Mechanics." *Journal of the ASPR*, 66.

Charlesworth, James. 1983. *The Old Testament Pseudepigrapha*. Vol. 1. Garden City: Doubleday & Comapny.

Charpentier, Louis, and Ronald Fraser, trans. 1975. *The Mysteries of Chartres Cathedral*. New York: Avon Books.

Chaucer, Geoffrey. 1982. *The Caterbury Tales.* Hieatt, trans., ed. New York: Banta.

Chittick, William. 1989. *The Sufi Path of Knowledge*. Albany: State University of New York.

Chretien de Troyes. 1957. "Perceval, or the Story of the Grail." *Medieval Romances.* Loomis, Roger & Laura, ed. New York: Random House.

Cohn, Norman. 1970. *The Pursuit of the Millenium: Revolutionary Millenarians and Mystical Anarchists of the Middle Ages*. London: Pimlico.

———. 1996. *Warrant for Genocide: The Myth of the Jewish World Conspiracy and the Protocols of the Elders of Zion*. London: Serif.

Colon Thuborn. 1981. *The Ancient Mariners* Alexandria, Virginia: Time-Life Books.

Conway, Flo, Siegelman, Jim. 1978. *Snapping: America's Epidemic of Sudden Personality Change*. Lippincott, Williams and Wilkins.

Cooper, Alan. 1981. "Divine Names and Epithets in the Ugaritic Texts." *Ras Shamra Parallels* Vol. 3. ed. by Stan Rummel. Rome: Pontificium Institutum Biblicum.

Cooper-Oakley, Isabel. 1970 [1912]. *The Count of Saint-Germain.* New York: Steiner Publications.

———. 1977 [1900]. *Masonry & Medieval Mysticism: Traces of a Hidden Tradition.* London: Theosophical Publishing House.

Copenhaver, Brian P. 1992. *Hermetica: The Greek Corpus Hermeticum and the Latin Asclepius* in a new English translation with notes and introduction. Cambridge, New York and Melbourne: Cambridge University Press.

Corny J. 1961. "Note On The Supposed Beginning Of A Sothic Cycle Under Seti I" *JEA* 17.

Courville, Donovan. 1971. *The Exodus Problem and its Ramifications*. Loma Linda: Challenge Books.

Craigie, Adrian. 1985. *Cities of the Biblical World: Ugarit.*Grand Rapids: Eerdmans.

Cremo, Michael A., Thompson, Richard L. 1993. *Forbidden Archaeology*. Bhaktivedanta Institute.

Cretien de Troyes. 1991. *Arthurian Romances*. Trans. William W. Kibler. New York: Penguin Books.

Cross, Frank. 1973. *Canaanite Myths and Hebrew Epic*. Cambridge:Harvard University Press.

Cruse, Christian. 1955. *Eusebius, Pamphilus. The Ecclesiastical History of Eusebius Pamphilus*. Grand Rapids: Baker Book House.

Cummins, W. A. 1992. *King Arthur's Place in Pre-history*. Surrey: Bramley Books.

Curott, D.R. 1966. "Earth's Deceleration From Ancient Solar Eclipses." *Astronomy Journal* 71.

Curtis, Peter. 1983. *Ugaritic and the Old Testament*. Grand Rapids: Eerdmans.

D'Alviella, 1956. Count Goblet. *The Migration of Symbols*. New York: University Books.

De Boron, Robert, ed. W.A.Nitze, *Joseph d'Arimithie* published as *Le Roman de l'Estoire dou Saint Graal*, 1927, Les Classiques français du moyen-âge, Paris. Parts of the text were translated by M. Schlauch and published in *Medieval Narrative*, 1928, NY. The Modena-manuscript prose versions of de Boron's *Joseph and Merlin*, together with the Modena *Perceval* have recently been translated into English in Bryant, N. 2001.

de Camp, L. Sprague. 1970 (1954). *Lost Continents: The Atlantis Theme in History, Science and Literature*. New York: Dover.

De Espinosa, Alonso. 1972. *The Guanches of Tenerife* trans. by Sir Clements Markham. Nendeln/Liechtenstein: Kraus Repring.

De Geus, Cornelis. 1993. "Of Tribes and Towns: The Historical Development of the Isaelite City." *Eretz-Israel* 24.

De Moor, Johannes. 1990. *The Rise of Yahwism*. Leuven: Leuven University Press.

De Santillana & Von Dechend. 1977. *Hamlet's Mill*. Boston: David R. Godine.

De Troyes, Chrétien, tr. Nigel Bryant, D.S. Brewer, 1982. *Perceval: The Story of the Grail (Perceval ou il Conte du Graal* or *Perceval li Gallois).* Cambridge UK. Bryant's slightly abridged edition incorporates large parts of the Continuations, in which various authors (or editors) attempted to complete Chrétien's unfinished romance.

De Vaux, Roland. 1978. *The Early History of Israel.* Translation by David Smith. Philadelphia: Westminster Press.

Deimelt Anton. 1935. *Die Altbabylanische Koenigsliste und ihre Bedeutung fuer die Chronoligie Rome.*

Dever, William G. 1990. "'Hyksos', Egyptian Destructions, and the End of the Palestinian Middle Bronze Age." *Levant* 22.

Devereux, Paul, and Brookesmith, Peter. 1998. *UFOs and Ufology: The First Fifty Years.* New York: Facts on File.

Dicks, D.R. I954. "Ancient Astronomical Instruments" *Journal of British Astronomical Society* 64.

———. 1970. *Early Greek Astronomy to Aristotle.* Ithaca N.Y: Cornell University Press.

Die Mittel-zur zoitliche Festl2gung von Punkten der aewptilghen Seschichte und ihre Answenduna Cairo 1935.

Dijkstra, Meindert. 1995. "El, YHWH and their Asherah" in *ALASP* 7:43-73. Munster: Ugarit-Verlag.

Diodorus of Sicily. 1935, 1937. *Library of History.* English translation by C.H. Oldfather, Loeb Classical Library, 12 Vols. London: William Heinemann. Cambridge, Mass, USA: Harvard University Press, 1935 and 1939.

Discoveries in the Judaean Desert XII: Qumran Cave 4. 1994.Vol. VII. Oxford: Clarendon Press.

Dobbs, Adrian. 1967. "The Feasibility of a Physical Theory of ESP," in Smythies, *Science And ESP.* New York: Humanities Press.

Dolan, Richard. 2002. *UFOs and the National Security State.* Charlottesville: Hampton Roads.

Dothan, Trude and Moshe. 1992. *People of the Sea: The Search for the Philistines.* New York: Macmillan.

Doyle, Arthur Conan. *Sherlock Holmes in The Boscombe Valley Mystery.*

Dumezil, Georges. 1988. *Mitra-Varuna: An Essay on Two Indo-European Representations of Sovereignty.* Zone Books; reprint edition.

Dundes, Alan. "The Father, the Son, and the Holy Grail," *Literature and Psychology,* XII (1962), 101112.

Dunn, Christopher P. 1998. *Technologies of Ancient Egypt.* Bear and Co.

Eamon, William. 1994. *Science and the Secrets of Nature: Books of Secrets in Medieval and Early Modern Culture.* Princeton: Princeton University Press.

Ebers, G. "Papyrus Ebers" *Zeitschrift fuer egyptische Sprache* 11 1873 and *ZAS* 12, 1874.

Eco, Umberto. 1988. *Foucault's Pendulum.* San Diego, New York, London: Harcourt, Brace Jovanowich.

———. 1995. *The Search For The Perfect Language.* Oxford: Blackwell.

Edd, Rhys, J. and Evans, J. Gwenogvryn. 1887–90. *Mabinogion and the Bruts from the Red Book of Hergest.* 2 vols. Oxford.

Edgerton, W.F. 1942. "Chronology of the 12 th Dynasty" *JNES* 1.

Ehrich, Robert, ed. 1965. *Chronologies of Old World Archeology .* Chicago: University of Chicago.

Einstein, Albert and P. Bergmann. 1938. "Annals of Mathematics." Vol. 38, No. 3, July.

Eisenlohr, A. 1870. "Das doppelte Kalendar des Herrn Smith," *Zeitschrift fuer Aegyptische Sprache*

Eliade, Mircea. 1954. *The Myth of The Eternal Return.* New York: Bollingen Foundation, Princeton University Press

———. 1972. *Shamanism:Archaic Techniques of Ecstasy.* Princeton: Princeton University Press.

Ellerbe, Helen. 1995. *The Dark Side of Christian History.* Orlando: Morningstar and Lark.

Epstein, Isidore. ed. 1935. *The Babylonian Talmud.* 35 Vols. London: Soncino Press.

Eric Whitaker, Steve Stewart. *Article Reviews: Late Ice Age Hunting Technology (Heidi Knecht).* Scientific American, July 1994

Eusebius, Pamphilus 1956. *Eusebius Werke: Die Chronik Des Hieronymus.* ed. by Rudolf Helm. Berlin: Akademie-Verlag.

———. 1955. *The Ecclesiastical History of Eusebius Pamphilus.* Translation by Christian Cruse.Grand Rapids: Baker Book House.

———. 1981. *Preparation of the Gospel.* Translation by Edwin Gifford. Grand Rapids: Baker Book House.

Evans, Sebastian, trans. *The High History of the Holy Grail.* Everyman.

Farrand, William R. 1961. "Frozen Mammoths and Modern Geology," *Science*, Vol.133, No. 3455, March 17.

Faulkner. 1969. *The Ancient Egyptian Pyramid Texts*. Aris and Phillips.

Fenster, Mark. 2001. *Conspiracy Theories: Secrecy and Power in American Culture* Minneapolis: University of Minnesota Press.

Ferguson, Arthur B. 1960. *The Indian Summer of English Chivalry: Studies in the Decline and Transformation of Chivalric Idealism*. Durham, N. C.: Duke University Press.

Finegan, Jack. 1964. *Handbook of Biblical Chronology*. Princeton: Princeton University Press.

Finkelstein, Israel, and Silberstein, Neil Asher. 2001. *The Bible Unearthed*. New York : The Free Press.

Firestone, Richard B., Topping, William. 2001. "Terrestrial Evidence of a Nuclear Catastrophe in Paleoindian Times," dissertation research, 1990 - 2001.

Fitzmer, Joseph. 1971. *The Genesis Apocryphon of Qumran Cave I*. Rome: Biblical Institute Press.

Flem-Ath, Rand and Rose. 1995. *When the Sky Fell*. Canada: St. Martins.

Fleming, Stuart. 1976. *Dating in Archeology*. N.Y: St. Martin's Press.

Fomenko, A.T, Nosovskij, G.V. *New Hypothetical Chronology and Concept of the English History British Empire as a Direct Successor of Byzantine-Roman Empire.*

Fomenko, A.T. 1994. *Empirico-Statistical Analysis of Narrative Materials and its Applications to Historical Dating*. Dordrecht, The Netherlands: Kluwer Academic Publishers.

Forwald, Haakon. 1969. "Mind, Matter and Gravitation: A Theoretical and Experimental Approach." *Parapsychology Monographs*, Number 11. New York: Parapsychology Foundation.

Fotheringham, J.K. et. al. 1921. "Historical Eclipses," *Oxford Lectures on History*. Oxford.

———. 1928. *The Venus tablets of Ammizaduga*. Oxford,

Fox, Hugh. 1976. *Gods of the Cataclysm*. New York: Dorset/Harper and Row.

Frank, Edgar. 1956. *Talmudic and Rabbinical Chronology*. Jerusalem: Feldheim Publishers.

Freedman and Graf. 1983. *Palestine in Transition*. Sheffield: Almond Press.

Freedman, H. and Simon, M. eds. 1939. *Midrash Rabbah*. 10 Vols. London: Soncino Press.

French, Thomas. 2000. "The Exorcist in Love." *St. Petersburg Times Magazine* section on February 13, 2000.

Frerichs, E. and Lesko, L. eds. 1997. *Exodus: The Egyptian Evidence*. Winona Lake: Eisenbrauns.

Friedman, Richard Elliot. 1987. *Who Wrote the Bible*. New York: Harper & Row.

Fulcanelli. 1984. *The Mystery of the Cathedrals*. Las Vegas: Brotherhood of Life,.

———. 1999. *The Dwellings of the Philosophers*. Boulder: Archive Press.

Fulton, J. P., Wincheski, B. and Namkung, M., A *Probabilistic Model for Simulating Magneto-Acoustic Emission Responses in Ferromagnets* M. Namkung, B. Wincheski, J. P. Fulton and R. G. Todhunter.

Gandz, Sol. 1970. *Studies in Hebrew Mathematics and Astronomy* N.Y.: KTAV.

Gantz, Jeffrey, tr. 1976. *Mabinogion or The Four Branches of the Mabinogi*. unknown. Harmondsworth UK: Penguin Books Ltd.

Gardiner, Alan H. 1916. *Notes on the Story of Sinuhe*. rpt.Recueil de travaux, Vols. 32-36, Paris.

———. 1947. *Ancient Egyptian Onomastica*. Oxford: Oxford University Press.

———. 1961. *Egypt of the Pharaohs*. Oxford: Oxford University Press.

Gardner, Martin. 1957. *Fads and Fallacies in the Name of Science*. New York, Dover.

Gaskell, G.A. 1960. *Dictionary of All Symbols and Myths*. The Julian Press, Inc.

Geoffrey of Monmouth. 1966. *History of the High Kings of Britain*, translated by Lewis Thorpe. Harmondsworth UK: Penguin Books Ltd.

Gershom, Yonassan, Rabbi. 1992. *Beyond the Ashes*. Virginia Beach: A.R.E. Press.

Gildas. 1978. *De Excidio Britanniae*. ed. and trans. by Michael Winterbottom as *The Ruin of Britain*. In History from the sources. Vol. 7. Chichester: Phillimore.

Ginzburg, Carlo. 1992. *Ecstasies: Deciphering the Witches' Sabbath*. Harmondsworth, Penguin.

Ginzel, F.K. 1911. *Handbuch der mathematischen-und technischen Chronologie II*, Leipzig.

Godwin, Jocelyn. 1991. *The Mystery of the Seven Vowels*. Phanes Press.

———. 1994. *The Theosophical Enlightenment*. New York: SUNY.

———. 1995. *Harmonies of Heaven and Earth : Mysticism in Music from Antiquity to the Avant-Garde* . Inner Traditions.

———. 1996. *Arktos: The Polar Myth in Science, Symbolism, and Nazi Survival*. Kempton, Illinois: Adventures Unlimited Press.

Godwin, Joscelyn, Chanel, Christian, Deveney, John P. 1995. *The Hermetic Brotherhood of Luxor*. York Beach: Samuel Weiser.

Godwin, Malcolm. 1994. *The Holy Grail: Its Origins, Secrets, and Meaning Revealed*. New York: Viking Studio Books.

Goodrich, Norma Lorre. 1986. *King Arthur*. New York: F. Watts.

Goodrick-Clarke, Nicholas. 1985. *The Occult Roots of Nazism: Secret Aryan Cults and their Influence on Nazi Ideology*. New York: New York Univ. Pr.

Goodwin, C.N. 1873. "Notes on the calendar in Mr. Smith's papyrus," *Zeitschrift fuer Aegyptische Sprache11*

Goulder, Michael D. 1997. *The Psalms of Asaph and the Pentateuch*. Sheffield Academic Press.

Graves, Robert. 1948. *The White Goddess*. New York: The Noonday Press.

———. 1992. *The Greek Myths*. London: Penguin.

Gray, H. J. B. 1928. "The Mystical Doctrine of the Queste del Sainte Graal," *Arthuriana*, I, 4957.

Gregory of Nyssa. 1994. "On the Soul and Resurrection." In *Nicene and Post-Nicene Fathers*, Second Series, ed. Philip Schaff and Henry Wace, Volume 5, 428 - 470. Peabody, MA: Hendrickson, 1994. BR60 .N66

Gross, Paul R., Levitt, Norman, and Lewis, Martin W., eds. 1996. *The Flight from Science and Reason*. New York: New York Academy of Sciences.

Guirdham, Arthur. 1977. *The Great Heresy: The history and Beliefs of the Cathars*. Saffron Walden UK: C.W.Daniel.

———. 1978. *The Cathars and Reincarnation: The Record of a Past Life in 13th Century France*. Wheaton,Ill.: Theos. Publ. House.

Gurney, O.R. 1991. *The Hittites*. Harmondsworth UK: Penguin. Revised edition.

Haich, Elisabeth. 1974. *Initiation*. Palo Alto: Seed Center.

Hall, Manly P. 1944. *The Secret Destiny of America.* Los Angeles: Philosophical Research Society.

———. 1999. *The Secret Teachings of All Ages*. Los Angeles: Philosophical Research Society.

Hall, Sir James. 1813. *Essays on the Origins, History and Principles of Gothic Architecture*. London.

Halpern, Baruch. 1983. *The Emergence of Israel in Canaan*. Chico: Scholars Press.

———. 1987. "Radical Exodus Redating Fatally Flawed."*Biblical Archaeology Review* 13:6 (November/December).

———. 1992. "The Exodus from Egypt: Myth or Reality?" *The Rise of Ancient Israel*. Washington D.C.: Biblical Archaeology Society.

———. 1993. "The Exodus and the Israelite Historians." *Eretz-Israel* 24.

Hamilton, Edith. 1942. *Mythology*. New York: New American Library.

Hamilton, Victor. 1990. *The Book of Genesis:* Chapters 1-17. Grand Rapids: Eerdmans.

Hancock, Graham. 1992. *The Sign and the Seal: The Quest for the Lost Ark of the Covenant* New York: Crown.

———. 1996. *Fingerprints of the Gods*. Crown Publishing. Reissue Ed.

Hapgood, Charles. 1979. *Maps of the Ancient Sea Kings*. London: Turnstone Press.

Hartner, Willy. 1968. "The Earliest History of the Constellations," *Oriens Occidens*, Hildesheim: Georg Olms Verlagsbuchhandlung.

———. 1977. "The Role of Observation in Ancient and Medieval Astronomy" *JFHA* 8

Hawkes, Jacquetta. 1973. *The First Great Civilizations; life in Mesopotamia, the Indus Valley and Egypt*. New York: Knopf.

Heath, Thomas. 1913. *A History of Greek Astronomy To Aristarchus*. Oxford.

Heironimus, John Paul, trans. 1952. "Selected Letters of the Younger Pliny," in MacKendrick, Paul and Herbert M. Howe, *Classics in Translation*, Vol. II.- Latin Literature, C. Madison: The University of Wisconsin Press.

Heline, Corinne. 1973. *Mysteries of the Holy Grail*. New Age Press.

———. 1991. *Sacred Science of Numbers.* DeVorss & Company.

Herdner, Andree. 1963. *Corpus Des Tablettes En Cuneiformes Alphabetiques*. Paris.

Herm, Gerhard. 1976. *The Celts: the people who came out of the darkness.* London: Weidenfeld and Nicolson.

Herodotus. 1920. *The Histories*: Books I-II. Translation by A. D. Godley. Cambridge: Harvard University Press.

———. 1972. *The Histories*, Book II, IV, V. De Selincourt, trans., and Marincola, ed. . London: Penguin.

Hess, Richard. 1993. "Early Israel in Canaan: A Survey of Recent Evidence and Interpretations." *Palestine Exploration Quarterly* 125.

————. 1994. "Asking Historical Questions of Joshua 13-19:Recent Discussion Concerning the Date of the Boundary Lists." *Faith Tradition & History*. ed. by Millard, Hoffmeier, and Baker. Winona Lake: Eisenbrauns.

————. 1996. "A Typology of West Semitic Place Name Lists With Special Reference to Joshua 13-21." *Biblical Archaeology* 59:3.

Hibben, Frank. 1946. *The Lost Americans*. New York: Thomas & Crowell Co.

Hippolytus Werke: Die Chronik. 1929. ed. by Rudolf Helm.Leipzig: J. C. Hinrichs'sche Buchhandlung.

Hodson, F.R. ed. 1974. "The Place of Astronomy in the Ancient World," *Philosophical Transactions of the Royal Society of London* 276.

Hoffmeier, James K. 1989. "Reconsidering Egypt's Part in the Termination of the Middle Bronze Age in Palestine." *Levant* 21:181-93.

————. 1990. "Some Thoughts on William G. Dever's "'Hyksos', Egyptian Destructions, and the End of the Palestinain Middle Bronze Age." *Levant* 22.

————. 1994. "The Structure of Joshua 1-11 and the Annals of Thutmose III." *Faith Tradition & History*. ed. by Millard, Hoffmeier, and Baker. Winona Lake: Eisenbrauns.

————. 1997. *Israel in Egypt: Evidence for the Authenticity of the Exodus Tradition*. Oxford: University Press.

Homer. 1924. *The Iliad*. 2 Vols. Translation by A.T. Murray.Cambridge: Harvard University Press.

————. 1951. *The Iliad of Homer*. Translation by Richmond Lattimore. Chicago: University of Chicago Press.

Horn, S.H. 1953. "Jericho in a Topographical List of Ramesses II." *Journal of Near Eastern Studies* 12.

Hornung, Erik. 1964. "Untersuchungen zur Chronologie und Geschichte des Neuen Reiches," *Aegyptologische Abhandlungen*, IV.

Horowitz, W. and Shaffer, A. 1992. "A Fragment of a Letter from Hazor." *Israel Exploration Journal* 42.

Howard, George A. *The Carolina Bays*: http://www.georgehoward.net/cbays.htm

Huber, Peter. 1974. "Early Cuneiform Evidence -for the Planet-Venus3 *AAAS Annual Meeting*, San Francisco. Reprint in Yale Babylonian Collection.

————. 1982. "Astronomical Dating of Babylon I and Ur III" , *Occasional Papers on the Near East*. Udena.

Huffmon, Herbert. 1971. "Yahweh and Mari" in *Near Eastern Studies in Honor of William Foxwell Albright*. ed. by Hans Goedicke. Baltimore: John Hopkins Press.

Humboldt, Alexander von. 1851. *Cosmos* III, N.Y.:Harper.

Idler, Ludwig. 1825. *Handbuch der Chronologie* I & II , Berlin: August Rucker.

Ingham, M.F. 1969. "The Length of the Sothic Cycle," *Journal of Egyptian Archeology* 55, p. 36-40.

Jackson and Lake. 1979. *The Acts of the Apostles*. Vol. 4.Grand Rapids: Baker Book House.

James, Peter. 1993. *Centuries of Darkness*. New Brunswick:Rutgers University Press.

Jackson, Kenneth. 1945. "Once Again King Arthur's Battles," *MP*, XLIII, 4457.

Jenkins, Elizabeth. 1975. *The Mystery of King Arthur*. New York: Dorset Press.

Jessup, Morris K. 1955. *The Case For The UFO*. New York: Bantam Books.

Johnson, Kenneth and Marguerite Elsbeth. 1995. *The Grail Castle: Male Myths and Mysteries in the Celtic Tradition*. Minneapolis: Llewellyn.

Jones, Wilbur. 1982. *Venus and Sothis: How the Ancient Near East Was Discovered*. Chicago: Nelson and Hall.

Joseph, Frank. 1992. *The Lost Pyramids of Rock Lake*. Lakeville, MN: Galde Press.

Josephus, Flavius. 1830. *The Works of Flavius Josephus*.Translation by William Whiston. Baltimore: Armstrong and Plaskitt.

————. 1926. *Josephus*. Translation by H. ST. J. Thackeray. Vol. 1. Cambridge: Harvard University Press.

Kempe, Dorothy. 1905. *The Legend of the Holy Grail*. London: Dorothy Kempe.

Kempinski, Aaron. 1985. "Some Observations on the Hyksos (XVth)Dynasty and Its Canaanite Origins." in *Pharaonic Egypt* Jerusalem: Magnes Press.

King James Version of the Bible (KJV). 1979. Philadelphia: A.J. Holman Company.

Kingsley, Peter. *In the Dark Places of Wisdom*. Parmenides and the Hesychast Movement among the Ancient Philosophers.

Kitchen, K.A. 1965. "Theban Topographical lists, Old and New." *Orientalia* 34.

————. 1967. *Ancient Orient and Old Testament*. Chicago:Inter-Varsity Press.

Kline, Meredith. 1957. "The Ha-BI-ru - Kin or Foe of Israel?" *Westminster Theological Journal* 19-20.

Knight, Christopher and Lomas, Robert. 1997. *The Hiram Key: Pharaohs, Freemasons and the Discovery of the Secret Scrolls of Jesus* Rockport, MA: Element Books.

Kraus, Rolf K. 1981. *Probleme des altaegyptischen Kalendars-und der Chronologie des mittelern and neuen Reiches in Aegypten*. Dissertation, Berlin.

Krupp, E.C. 1977. *In Search of Ancient Astronomies*. Garden City, N.J.: Doubleday.

Kudlek, Manfred and Mickler, Erich. 1971. *Solar and Lunar Eclipses From. 3000. BC to 0 With Maps* Neu Kirchen Vluyn: Verlag Butzon & Bercher.

Kugler, F.X. 1907-1912. Sternkunde und Sterndienst in *Babel*, I-III, Muenster.

Kuniholm P.I. et al. 1996. "Anatolian tree rings and the absolute chronology of the eastern Mediterranean, 2220-718 BC." *Nature* 381 (June 27).

Lauth, A. "Die Schaltage des Ptolemaeus Euergetes I und des Augustus," *Sitzunaberichte der Muench Akademie*, I 1874

Leadbeater, Charles W. 1986. *Ancient Mystic Rites* Wheaton, IL: TPH. [1926], original title: *Glimpses of Masonic History*.

Lee, Rupert. 1996. "Exodus enigma." *Nature* 383 (September 5).

Leedskalnin, Edward. 1998. *Magnetic Current*. Pomeroy, WA: Health Research.

Lello, Glenn. 1948. "Thutmose III's First Lunar Date" *JNES* 7 p. 327-331.

Lemche, Niels Peter. 1991. *The Canaanites and Their Land*. Sheffield: JSOT Press.

Leon, Harry J., trans., "Selections from Tacitus" in MacKendrick, Paul and Herbert M. Howe. 1952. *Classics in Translation*, Vol. II: Latin Literature, C. Madison: The University of Wisconsin Press.

Leonard, R. Cedric. 1979. *A Geological Study of the Mid-Atlantic Ridge*, Special Paper No. 1, Bethany: Cowen Publ.

Lepsius, R. 1859. "Ueber einige Beruehrungspunkte der Aegyptische, Griechischen und Roemischen Chronologie". Berlin.

———. 1870. "Einige Bemerkungen ueber denselben Papyrus Smith." *Zeitschrift fuer Aegyptische Sprache* 8.

———. 1949. *Chronologie der Aegypter*, Berlin: Nicolaische Buchhandlung.

Lethbridge, T.C. 1991. *The Power of the Pendulum*. Viking, Penguin.

Lewis, James R. 1995. *The Gods have Landed: New Religions from Other Worlds*. Albany, State University of New York Press.

Lichtheim, Miriam. 1975. *Ancient Egyptian Literature*. Vol. 1.Berkeley: University of California Press.

Lightfoot, John. 1979. *A Commentary on the New Testament from the Talmud and Hebraica: Matthew-I Corinthians*. rpt.1859. 4 Vols. Grand Rapids: Baker Book House.

Lincoln, Henry. 1991. *The Holy Place*. New York: Little, Brown.

Lippman, Harold E. 1969. "Frozen Mammoths," *Physical Geology*. New York.

Littleton and Malcor. 1994. *From Scythia to Camelot*. New York: Garland.

Lloyd, G.E.R. 1972. *Greek Science After Aristotle*. N.Y.: W.W. Norton.

Lloyd-Morgan, Ceridwen. 1986. "Perceval in Wales: Late Medieval Welsh Grail Traditions." In *The Changing Face of Arthurian Romance: Essays on Arthurian Prose Romances in Memory of Cedric E. Pickford*. Arthurian Studies XVI. Ed. Alison Adams, Armel H. Diverres, Karen Stern and Kenneth Varty. Cambridge: D. S. Brewer. pp. 78-91.

Lockyer, J. Norman. 1964. *The Dawn of Astronomy*. Cambridge, Mass.: MIT Press.

Long, Ronald. 1974. "A Reexamination of the Sothic Chronology of Egypt," *Orientalia* 43 n.s., p. 261-274.

———. 1976. "Ancient Egyptian Chronology: Radio-carbon Dating and Calibration," *Zeitschrift fuer Aegyptische Sprache* 103. pp. 30-48.

Loomis, L. H. 1926. "Arthur's Round Table." *PMLA*, XLI, 771784.

Luckenbill, Daniel. 1927. *Ancient Records of Assyria and Babylonia II*. Chicago: University of Chicago.

Luckert, Karl W. 1991. *Egyptian Light and Hebrew Fire: Theological and Philosophical Roots of Christendom in Evolutionary Perspective*. New York: SUNY Press.

Macaulay, David. 1979. *Motel of the Mysteries*. Boston: Houghton Mifflin.

Mackay, Charles. 1980. *Extraordinary Popular Delusions and the Madness of Crowds*. New York: Crown. originally 1841.

Macnaughton, Duncan. 1930. *A Scheme of Babylonian Chronology*. London: Luzac and Co.

Mahler, E. 1889. "Koenig Thutmosis III" *Zeitschrift fuer Aegyptische Sprache* 27, p. 98.

Maitland, S.R., trans, Raynaldus, 1832. "Annales," in *History of the Albigenses and Waldenses*, London: C. J. G. and F. Rivington. pp. 392-4.

Malory, Sir Thomas. 1970. *Le Morte d'Arthur*. Penguin UK.

Maltwood, K E. 1964. *A Guide to Glastonbury's Temple of the Stars*. James Clarke.

Manetho of Sebennytos, *History of Egypt and Book of Sothis*, W.C. Waddell, ed, Loeb Volume 350.

Manetho. 1940. *Manetho*. Translation by W. G. Waddell. Cambridge: Harvard University Press.

Manning, Sturt. 1999. *A Test of Time*. Oxford: Oxbow.

Markale, Jean. 1999. *The Grail: The Celtic Origins of the Sacred Icon*. Rochester, VT: Inner Traditions.

Marrs, Jim. 2000. *Rule by Secrecy: The Hidden History that Connects the Trilateral Commission, the Freemasons, and the Great Pyramids*. New York: HarperCollins.

Marshack, Alexander. 1991. *The Roots Of Civilization*. Mt Kisco, New York: Moyer Bell Limited.

Martin, P. S. & Guilday, J. E. 1967. *Bestiary for Pleistocene Biologists, Pleistocene Extinction*. New Haven: Yale University.

Martinez, Florentino 1986. *The Early Biblical Period*. ed. by Ahituv and Levine. Jerusalem: Israel Exploration Society.

———. 1996. *The Dead Sea Scrolls Translated*.2nd ed. Grand Rapids: Eerdmans.

Matarasso, P.M. trans. 1969. *The Quest of the Holy Grail*. Penguin.

Matese, J.J., Whitman, P.G., Whitmore, D.P. 1999. "Cometary ecidence of a massive body in the outer Oort cloud." *Icarus* 141: 354-366.

Mazar, Benjamin. 1963. "The Military Elite of King David." *Vetus Testamentum* 13:310-20.

McCarter, P. Kyle. 1992. "The Origins of Israelite Religion." in *The Rise of Ancient Israel*. Washington D.C.:Biblical Archaeology Society.

Meillet, Antoine. 1992. Memoires de la Society de Linguistique de Paris. XXII,

Mellaart, James. 1979. "Egyptian and Near-Eastern Chronology-A Dilemma." *Antiquity* 53/207. pp. 6-18. C-14.

Mendenhall, G.E. 1958. "The Census Lists of Numbers 1 and 26." *Journal of Biblical Literature* 77.

Mendenhall, G.E. 1962. "The Hebrew Conquest of Palestine." *Biblical Archaeology* 25.

———. 1973. *The Tenth Generation: The Origins of the Biblical Traditions*. Baltimore: Johns Hopkins University Press.

Meyer, Eduard. 1904. *Aegyptische Chronologie Abhandlungen der koeniglich preussischen Akademie der Wissenschaften*. Phil.-hist. Klasse. Berlin, p. 1-212, "Nachtraege zur Aegyptischen Chronologie" 1907 p. 1-46.

Meyer, Marvin W. 1984. *The Secret Teachings of Jesus: Four Gnostic Gospels*. New York, Random House.

Meyers, Eric M. ed. 1997. *The Oxford Encyclopedia of Archaeology in the Near East*. 5 Vols. Oxford: Oxford University Press.

Michael D. Goulder. 1997. *The Psalms of Asaph and the Pentateuch*, Sheffield Academic Press.

Miller, Timothy (ed). 1995. *America's Alternative Religions*. SUNY.

Montaiglon, Anatole. 1994. *Preface of Curiositiez de Paris*, Volume II, reprinted after the original edition of 1716, Paris 1883. Kluwer Academic Publishers, Dordrecht.

Moran, William. ed. 1992. *The Amarna Letters*. Baltimore: Johns Hopkins University Press.

Motz, Lloyd and Duveen, Anetta. 1977. *Essentials of Astronomy*. N.Y.: Columbia University Press.

Mouravieff, Boris. 1993. *Gnosis*, Volume III, edited by Robin Amis. MA: Praxis Institue.

———. 1992. *Gnosis: Study and Commentaries on the Esoteric Tradition of Eastern Orthodoxy*. Robertsbridge, UK: Praxis Institute Press.

Muck, Otto. 1976. *The Secret of Atlantis*. New York: New York Times Books.

Muller, Richard. 1988. *Nemesis*. Univ of Arizona Press.

Murtonen, A. 1951. *The Appearance of the Name YHWH Outside of Israel*. Helsinki: Studia Orientalia.

Na'aman and Aviv. 1988. "Biryawaza of Damascus and the Date of the Kamid El-Loz 'Apiru Letters." *Ugarit-Forschungen* 20.

———. 1992. "Canaanite Jerusalem and its Central Hill Country Neighbours in the Second Millennium B.C.E." *Ugarit-Forschungen* 24.

———. 1994. "The Canaanites and Their Land: A Rejoinder." *Ugarit-Forschungen* 26.

Na'aman, Nadav. 1979-1981. "Hebron was Built Seven Years Before Zoan in Egypt." *Vetus Testamentum* 31.

Na'aman, Nadav. 1979-1984. "Statement of Time-Spans by Babylonian and Assyrian Kings and Mesopotamian Chronology" *IRAQ* 46.

———. 1979-1986. "Habiru and Hebrew: The Transfer of a Social Term to the Literary Sphere." *Journal of Near Eastern Studies* 45.

———. 1979. "The Origin and Historical Background of Several Amarna Letters." *Ugarit-Forschungen* 11.

———. 1984. "Statements of Time-Spans by Babylonian and Assuyrian Kings and Mesopotamian Chronology" *Iraq* 46.

Narr, Karl J. *Barenzeremoniell und Schauanismus in der Altern Steinzeit Europas.*

Needleman, Jacob. 1990. *Lost Christianity; A Journey of Rediscovery to the Centre of Christian Experience.* Rockport, MA: Element.

Nennius. 1980. *Annales Cambriae.* trans. by John Morris as *British History and the Welsh Annals.* In *History from the sources.* Vol. 8. Chichester: Phillimore.

Neugebauer, Otto. 1938. "Die Bedeutunglosigkeiten der Sothisperiode fuer die aeltere aegyptische Chronologie", *Acta Orientalia* 17, pp. 169-195.

Neugebauer, Otto. 1941. "The Chronology of the Hammurabi Age", *JAOS* 61, pp. 58-61.

———. 1942. "The Origin of the Egyptian Calendar" *JNES* 1, pp. 396-403

———. 1945. "The History of Ancient Astronomy" *JNES* 4, pp. 1-38.

———. 1953. *Astronomical Cuneiform Texts, I-III*, Princeton: Institute for Advanced Study.

———. 1962. *Exact Sciences in Antiquity.* N.Y.: Harper.

———. 1969. *The Exact Sciences in Antiquity.* New York: Dover.

———. 1975. *A History of Ancient Mathematical Astronomy* I-III Berlin: Springer Verlag.

Neugebauer, Paul. 1929. *Astronomische Chronologie, I-II* Berlin-Leipzig: De Gruyter.

Neusner, Jacob. 1985. *Genesis Rabbah.* 3 Vols. Atlanta: Scholars Press.

Newman, Robert. 1973. "The Astrophysics of Worlds in Collision" *Journal of the American Scientific Affiliation* 25:4.

Newstead, Helaine. 1939. *Bran the Blessed in Arthurian Romance.* New York: Columbia University Press.

Newton, R.R. 1970. *Ancient Astronomical Observations.* Baltimore: Johns Hopkins.

———. 1974. "Two Uses of Ancient Astronomy" *Royal Society of London* 276, pp . 99-117.

———. 1976. *Ancient Planetary Observations and the Validity of Ephemeris Time.* Baltimore: Johns Hopkins.

———. 1977. *The Crime of Claudius Ptolemy.* Baltimore: Johns Hopkins.

———. 1979. *The Moon's Acceleration and its Physical Origins As Deduced From Solar Eclipses.* Baltimore: Johns Hopkins.

Nicholson, E.W. 1973. *Exodus and Sinai in History and Tradition.* Richmond: John Knox Press.

Nutt, Alfred. 1888. *Studies on the Legend of the Holy Grail with Especial Reference to the Hypothesis of its Celtic Origin.* London: David Nutt.

Nutt, David. 1903. *Sir Gawain at the Grail Castle.* London.

———. 1909. *The Legend of Sir Perceval.* London: David Nutt.

Nutt, W.A. 1888. *Studies on the Legend of the Grail.* London.

Old Temples Society, Publication of the Museums Department, Department of Classics and Archaeology at the University of Malta, Second issue, November 1999.

Oldfather, C.H., trans., 1935 and 1939. *Library of History.* Diodorus of Sicily, Loeb Classical Library, Volumes II and III. London, William Heinemann, and Cambridge, Mass., USA, Harvard University Press.

Olsson, Ingrid, (ed.). 1970. *Radiocarbon Variations and Absolute Chronology* 12th Nobel Symposiums Stockholm: Almsquist and Wiksell Forlag.

O'Mara P.F. 1962. *The Chronology of the Palermo and Turin Canons* . N.A. Oppolzer, Theodor von, Canon der Finsternisse, Denkschriften der kaiserlichen Akademie der Wissenschaften Math-Maturwissensch. Klasse, LII, Vienna, 1887. English: New York, Dover, 1962.

Oren, Eliezer. 1981. "How Not to Create a History of the Exodus-A Critique of Professor Goedicke's Theories." *Biblical Archaeology Review* 7:6 (November/December).

Origen of Alexandria. 1994. "On First Principles." In *Ante-Nicene Fathers*, ed. Alexander Roberts, 1826-1901 and James Donaldson, Sir, 1831-1915, 4, 239 - 384. Peabody, MA: Hendrickson. BR60 A56 1994

O'Shea, Stephen. *The Perfect Heresy: The Revolutionary Life and Death of the Medieval Cathars.* Walker & Company.

Ouspensky, P.D. 1920. *Tertium Organum.* New York: Vintage Books.

Pagels, Elaine. 1985. *The Gnostic Gospels* New York: Vintage Books.

Panati, Charles. 1996. *Sacred Origins of Profound Things: The Stories Behind The Rites and Rituals of The World's Religions.* New York, NY: Penguin Arkana.

Parker, Richard and Neugebauer, 0. 1960. *Egyptian Astronomical Texts I-II* , Providence, RI: Brown University.

Parker, Richard. 1950. "The Calendars of Ancient Egypt," *Studies in Ancient Oriental Civilizations* 26, Chicago: University of Chicago.

———. 1957. "Lunar Dates of Tutmose III and Ramesses II," *JNES* 16, pp. 39-40.

———. 1974. "Ancient Egyptian Astronomy," *Royal Society of London* 276, pp. 51-66.

———. 1976 "The Sothic Dating of the 12th and 18th Dynasties," *Studies in Ancient Oriental Civilization* 39, Chicago: University of Chicago, p. 177-189.

Parker, Richard, and Dubberstein, Waldo. 1946. Babylonian Chronology-625 BC-AD 45, Chicago: University of Chicago.

Paton, Lewis. 1913. "Israel's Conquest of Canaan." *Journal of Biblical Literature* 32.

Patton, Guy and Mackness, Robin. 2000. *Web of Gold: the Secret Power of a Sacred Treasure.* London: Macmillan.

Pauwels, L., and Bergier, J. 1964. *The Morning of the Magicians.* New York: Stein and Day.

Pederson, Olaf. 1974. *A Survey of the Almagest.* Odenske U Press.

Petrie, Flinders. 1906. *Researches in Sinai.* London: John Murray.

Pettinato, Giovanni. 1981. *The Archives of Ebla.* Garden City: Doubleday & Company.

———. 1991. *Ebla: A New Look at History.* Trans. by C. Faith Richardson. Baltimore: John Hopkins Press.

Pfeiffer, Charles. 1963. *Tell El Amarna and the Bible.* Grand Rapids: Baker Book House.

Phillips, Graham & Keatman, Martin. 1983. *The Green Stone.* Jersey: Neville Spearman.

Pike, Albert. *Morals and Dogma, Ancient and Accepted Scottish Rite, Symbolism for the 32nd and 33rd degrees.*

Pipes, Daniel. 1997. *Conspiracy: How the Paranoid Style Flourishes and Where It Comes From.* New York: The Free Press.

Plato, and Benjamin Jowett, trans. *Critias.*

———. *Republic*, Book VII.

———. *Timaeus.*

Pliny (AD 23-79) *Natural history.* Book 36.

Plutarch, De Iside et Osiride Loeb Classical Library, Moralia V, 1962

Pooler, R.S. 1851. *The Chronology of Ancient Egypt*, London: John Murray.

Pope, Marvin. 1955. *El in the Ugaritic Texts.* Leiden: Brill.

Potts, Daniel Thomas. 1982. "The Road to Meluhha," in *Journal of Near Eastern Studies*, 41, pp. 279-288.

Potvin, Ch. 1866-71. *Perceval le Gallois*, compilation, tr. , Société des Bibliophiles de Mons. Seven volumes. Modern French text of *Perceval and the Continuations*, with Perlesvaus.

Powell, T.G.E. 1980. *The Celts.* London: Thames and Hudson.

Preston, Douglas. 1997. "The Lost Man." *New Yorker Magazine*, June 16.

Pritchard, James (ed). 1969. *Ancient Near Eastern Pictures Relating to the Old Testament.* (ANEP) Princeton: Princeton University Press.

Quigley, Carroll. 1966. *Tragedy and Hope: A History of the World in our Time.* New York: Macmillan.

Rabinovich, Abraham. 1996. "How the Israelites took Israel." *The Jerusalem Post*: International Edition. (August 10).

Rainey, Anson F. 1963. "A Canaanite at Ugarit." *Israel Exploration Journal* 13.

———. 1972. "The World of Sinuhe." *Israel Oriental Studies* 2:369-408.

———. 1982. "Linguistic Notes on Thutmose III's Topographical List." *Egyptological Studies* vol. 28 ed. by Sarah Israelit-Groll. Jerusalem: Magnes Press.

———. 1991. "Rainey's Challenge." *Biblical Archaeology Review* 17:6 (November/December).

———. 1992. "Anson F. Rainey Replies." *Biblical Archaeology Review* 18:2 (March/April).

Rappoport, Angelo. 1966. *Myth and Legend of Ancient Israel.* 3 Vols. New York: Ktav Publishing House.

Ravenscroft, Trevor. 1973. *The Spear of Destiny: The Occult Power behind the Spear that Pierced the Side of Christ.* New York: Bantam Bks.

Raynaldus. "Annales." *History of the Albigenses and Waldenses*, S. R. Maitland, trans. London: C.J.G. and F. Rivington, 1832.

Read, John. 1970. "Early 18th Dynasty Chronology," *JNES* 29, pp. 1-12.

Reader's Digest. 1977. *The World's Last Mysteries.*

Redford, Donald. 1966. "On The Chronology Of The 18th Dynasty," *JNES* 25, pp.113-124.

———. 1970. *A Study of the Biblical Story of Joseph.*Leiden: E.J. Brill.

———. 1979. "A Gate Inscription From Karnak and Egyptian Involement in Western Asia During the Early 18th Dynasty." *Journal of the American Oriental Society* 99:2.

————. 1982. "A Bronze Age Itinerary in Transjordan (Nos. 89-101 of Thutmose III's List of Asiatic Toponyms)." *Journal of the Society for the Study of Egyptian Antiquities* 12:55-74.

————. 1987. "Perspective on the Exodus." *Egypt, Israel, Sinai: Archaeological and Historical Relationships in the Biblical Period*. Tel Aviv: Tel Aviv University.

————. 1992. *Egypt, Canaan, and Israel in Ancient Times*. Princeton: Princeton University Press.

Reeser, Ken, 1994; "Earliest Art: Representative Art In The Upper Paleolithic Era" (after: Marshack, 1991; Grand, 1967; Ucko, Peter J., and Rosenfeld, Andre, 1967; Brown, G. Baldwin, 1932; Breuil, Abbe H., date unknown) (unpublished).

Reeves, C.N. 1992. *After Tutankhamun: Research and Excavation in the Royal Necropolis at Thebes*. New York: Columbia University Press.

Reiner, Erica & Pingree, David. 1975. *The Venus Tablets of Ammisaduga*, Malibu, Ca: Udena.

Renfrew, Colin. 1996. "Kings, tree rings and the Old World." *Nature* 381 (June 27).

Rg-Veda, Vol III.

Rhys, J. 1901. *Celtic Folklore*. 2 vols. Oxford.

Richardson, Robert. 1999. "The Priory of Sion Hoax" *Gnosis*, No. 51, Spring.

Riel, Carl. 1875. *Die Sonnen- und Siriusjahr der Ramessiden mit Geheimnis der Schaltung und des jahr des Julius Caesar*. Leipzig: F.A. Brockhaust.

Roberts and Donaldson, eds. 1975. *Ante-Nicene Fathers*. 10 Vols. Grand Rapids: Eerdmans.

Robertson, C.C. 1990. *On the Tracks of the Exodus*. rpt. 1936. Thousand Oaks: Artisan Sales.

Robinson, James M., ed. 1988. *The Nag Hammadi Library*. New York: Harper & Row.

Rohl, David M. 1995. *Pharaohs and Kings: A Biblical Quest*.New York: Crown Publishers.

Roux, Georges. 1964. *Ancient Iraq*. 3rd ed. New York: Penguin Books.

Rowton, M.B. 1946. "Mesopotamian Chronology and the Age of Hammurabi" *Iraq* 8, pp. 94-110.

————. 1950. "The Date of the Founding of Solomon's Temple." *Bulletin of the Society of Oriental Research* 119 (October).

————. 1958. "Date of Hammurabi" *JNES* 17, p. 97.

————. 1976. "Dimorphic Structures and the Problem of the 'Apiru-'Ibrim." *Journal of Near Eastern Studies* 35.

Rudgley, Richard. 1999. *The Lost Civilizations of the Stone Age*. New York: The Free Press.

Ryan, William, Pitman, Walter. 1998. *Noah's Flood*. New York: Simon and Schuster.

Sachs, A. 1971. "Absolute Dating From Mesopotamian Records" Royal Society of London 269, pp. 19-23.

————. 1974. "Babylonian Observational Astronomy", Royal Society of London 276, pp. 43-51.

Salvini, Mirjo. 1996. *The Habiru Prism of King Tunip-Tessup of Tikunani*. Rome: Istituti Editoriali e Poligrafici Internazionali.

Sanderson, Ivan T. 1960. "Riddle of the Frozen Giants," *Saturday Evening Post*, No. 39, January 16.

Schaff, Philip. 1910. *History of the Christian Church*. Vol. 2.Grand Rapids: Eerdmans.

Scharpe, S. 1870. *The Decree of Canopus*.

Schirtzinger, Erin. 1994. "The Evidence for Pleistocene Burials, Neanderthals versus Modern Humans," *New Yorker Magazine* December 6.

Schnabel, Jim. 1994. *Round in Circles: Poltergeists, Pranksters and the Secret History of Cropwatchers*. Amherst (NY): Prometheus.

————. 1997. *Remote Viewers: The Secret History of America's Psychic Spies*. New York: Dell.

Schoch, C. 1928. *Die Neubeartbeitung der Syzygientafln von Oppolzer*. Mit des. Astr. Reicheninstitutes. Berlin: Dahlem, 7, 2, Kiel.

Schoch, Robert, Ph.D. 1999. *The Voices of the Rocks*. New York: Harmony Books.

Schwartz, Regina M.. 1997. *The Curse of Cain*. Chicago: The University of Chicago Press.

Scientific American. 1852. 7:298, June 5.

Scudder, Vida D. 1921. *Le Morte D'arthur of Sir Thomas Malory and Its Sources*. New York: E. P. Dutton.

Septuagint Version of the Old Testament, with an English Translation. 1970. Grand Rapids: Eerdmans.

Septuaginta. 1935. ed. by Alfred Rahlfs. Germany: Deutsche Bibelgesellschaft Stuttgart.

Shanks, Hershel. 1981. "The Exodus and the Crossing of the Red Sea, According to Hans Goedicke." *Biblical Archaeology Review* 7:5 (September/October).

Shea, William H. 1979. "The Conquests of Sharuhen and Megiddo Reconsidered." *Israel Exploration Journal* 29:1.

Shermer, Michael. 1997. *Why People Believe Strange Things: Pseudoscience, Superstition and Other Confusions of Our Time*. New York, W. H. Freeman.

Showalter, Elaine. 1997. *Hystories: Hysterical Epidemics and Modern Culture*. London, Picador.

Shuker, Karl P. N. 1995. *In Search Of Prehistoric Survivors: Do Giant "Extinct" Creatures Still Exist?* London: Cassell.

Simons, J. 1937. *Handbook for the Study of Egyptian Topographical Lists Relating to Western Asia.* Leiden.

Simpson, George G. 1961. *Horses: The Story of the Horse Family in the Modern World and Through Sixty Million Years of History.* Oxford University Press

Skeels, D. 1961. *Didot Perceval also known as Perceval le Gallois* tr. as *The Romance of Perceval in Prose.* DC.: Univ. of Washington Press,

Sklar, Elizabeth Sherr, and Donald L. Hoffman, eds. 2002. *King Arthur in Popular Culture.* Jefferson, N.C.: McFarland. DA152.5.A7 K57 Dewey: 942.01/4 21.

Soggin, J. Alberto. 1993. "Prolegomena on the Approach to Historical Texts in the Hebrew Bible and the Ancient Near East." *Eretz-Israel* 24.

Spalinger, Anthony. 1990. "The Rhind Mathematical Papyrus As A Historical Document," *Studien zur altagyptischen Kultur*; 17, 295-338.

Stager, Lawrence. 1985. "Merenptah, Israel and Sea People: New Light on an Old Relief." *Eretz-Israel* 18.

Starbird, Margaret. 1998. *The Woman with the Alabaster Jar: Mary Magdalen and the Holy Grail.* Santa Fe: Bear & Company.

Steiner, Rudolf. 1905. *The Fourth Dimension, Sacred Geometry, Alchemy, and Mathematics*, A six-lecture series held in Berlin from March 24 to June 7. Anthroposophic Press.

Stephanson, F.R. 1975. "Astronomical Verification and Dating of Old Testament References Referring to Solar Eclipses" *PEQ*, July-Dec., pp.107-120.

Stephanson, S.K. and Sawyer, J.F.A. "Literary and Astronomical Evidence for a Total Eclipse of the Sun Observed at Ancient Ugarit," London University: *Bulletin of the Schools of Oriental and African Studies* 33 (1970), p. 467-489.

Stern, Ephraim. ed. 1993. *The New Encyclopedia of Archaeological Excavations in the Holy Land.* Jerusalem: Israel Exploration Society & Carta.

Stone, Merlin. 1976. *When God Was A Woman.* San Diego, New York, London: Harvest/Harcourt Brace Jovanovich.

Strabo. Geography, Book 17, I, 3 and 37 and 42.

Sturlson, Snorri. *Gylfaginning.*

Sufi Shaykh, Ibn Al-'Arabi, in *Futuhat* (Unveiling) III 38.23, translated and quoted by William Chittick in *The Sufi Path of Knowledge.*

Sutton, Antony C. 1986. *America's Secret Establishment: An Introduction to the Order of Skull & Bones.* Billings, Montana: Liberty House Press.

Swerdlow, Noel "Ptolemy On Trial" *American Scholar* no date, p.525-531.

Tacitus. 1925. *Histories and Annals.* 4 Vols. Translated by C. H. Moore and J. Jackson. Cambridge: Harvard University Press.

————. 1964. *The Histories.* Translation by Kenneth Wellesley. London: Penguin Books.

Targum Pseudo-Jonathan. 1992. *Genesis.* Translation by Michael Maher. Collegeville: Liturgical Press.

Targum Pseudo-Neofiti I. 1994. *Exodus.* Translation by Martin McNamara. Collegeville: Liturgical Press.

The Anglo-Saxon chronicles.

The Mabinogion. 1838. Trans. by Lady Charlotte Guest. 3 vols. Ed. Nutt, A. 1902.

The Matrix. The Wachowski Brothers, Joel Silver. VHS, DVD. Warner Bros, 1999.

The Vulgate Version of the Arthurian Romances. 1909. The Carnegie Institute.

Thiele, Edwin. 1965. *The Mysterious Numbers of the Hebrew Kings.* Grand Rapids, Mich.: We. B. Eerdmans.

————. 1983. *The Mysterious Numbers of the Hebrew Kings.* Grand Rapids: Zondervan.

Thuborn, Colon. 1981. *The Ancient Mariners.* Alexandria, Virginia: Time-Life Books.

Tiller, William A., Ph.D., Dibble, Walter E., Ph.D., Kohane, Michael J., Ph.D., 2001, Pavior, Walnut Creek (www.pavior.com).

Toombs, Lawrence. 1985. "Shechem." *Harper's Bible Dictionary.* San Francisco: HarperCollins Publishers.

Treharne, R. F. 1975. *The Glastonbury Legends.* Abacus.

Unknown, tr. P.M. Matarasson. 1969. *The Quest of the Holy Grail* (Queste del Saint Graal). Harmondsworth UK: Penguin Books Ltd.

Unknown, tr. S. Evans. 1969. *Perlesvaus, Le Haut Livre du Graal or The High History of the Grail.* 1903. 1969 reprint. Cambridge UK: James Clarke.

Vallee, Jacques. 1979. *Messengers Of Deception* And/Or Press.

———. 1991. *Revelations, Alien Contact And Human Deception.* Ballantine.

Van Buren, Elizabeth. 1986. *Refuge of the Apocalypse : Doorway into Other Dimensions. Rennes-Le-Château, The Key.* England: CW Daniel Co.

Van der Broek, Roelof & Wouter J. Hanegraaff. 1998. *Gnosis and Hermeticism from Antiquity to Modern Times.* SUNY.

Van der Waerden, B.L. 1949. "Babylonian Astronomy II, The 36 Stars," *JNES* 8, pp.6-26.

———. 1945-1948. "The Venus Tablets of Ammizaduga" *Ex Oriente Lux* , No. 10, pp. 414-424.

Van Seters, John. 1966. *The Hyksos.* New Haven: Yale University Press.

Vandersleyen, C. 1968. RdE 19, pls. 8, 9; W. Helck, *Historisch-biographische Texte* der 2. Zwischenzeit (Wiesbaden, 1975), 106-7.

Vankin, Jonathan, and Whalen, John. 1995. *50 Greatest Conspiracies of All Time: History's Biggest Mysteries, Coverups and Scandals.* New York, Citadel.

Velikovshy, Immanuel. 1950. *Worlds in Collision.* New York: Dell Publishing.

———. 1952. *Ages in Chaos.* Garden City: Doubleday.

———. *Peoples of the Sea*, N.Y.: Doubleday.

Von Däniken, Erich. 1979. *Signs of the Gods.* London: Souvenir Press.

von Eschenbach, Wolfram. 1980. *Parzival*, Translated by A. T. Hatto. New York: Penguin.

———. 1961. *Parzifal.* Mustard, Passage, trans. New York: Random House)

Waite, A. E. 1961. *The Holy Grail: The Galahad Quest in the Arthurian Literature.* New York: University Books.

Wallace, I. and Wallechinsky, D. *The People's Almanac.* New York: Doubleday.

Ward, William A. 1976. "Some Personal Names of the Hyksos Rulers and notes on the Epigraphy of Their Scarabs." *Ugarit-Forschungen* 8.

Washington, Peter. 1993. *Madame Blavatsky's Baboon: A History of the Mystics, Mediums, and Misfits Who Brought Spiritualism to America.* New York: Shocken.

Weinstein, James M. 1981. "The Egyptian Empire in Palestine:A Reassessment." *Bullentin of the Society of Oriental Research* 241.

Weippert, M. 1962. "Canaan, Conquest and Settlement of." *The Interpreter's Dictionary of the Bible Supplementary Volume.* Nashville: Abingdon Press.

Weir, John D. 1982. "The Venus Tablets, A Fresh Approach," *Journal for the History of Astronomy* 13, pp. 23-50.

Weir, W. 1972. *Venus Tablets of Ammizaduga*, Leiden and Istanbul: Nederland Institut voor het Nabye Oosten.

Wells, G.A. 1988. *The Historical Evidence for Jesus.* Buffalo, N.Y.: Prometheus.

Wente and Harris. 1980. *X-ray atlas of the Royal Mummies.* Chicago: University of Chicago Press.

Weston, Jessie. 1906, 1909. *The Legend of Sir Perceval: Studies upon Its Origin, Development, and Position in the Arthurian Cycle* . 2 vols. (Vol. 1: Chrétien de Troyes and Wauchier de Denain; Vol. 2: The Prose Perceval according to the Modena MS.) London: David Nutt.

———. 1920. *From Ritual to Romance.* London: Cambridge University Press.

———. trans 1995. *Sir Gawain at the Grail Castle.* Llanerch Publishers.

Whitaker, Eric and Steve Stewart. 1994. Article Reviews; "Late Ice Age Hunting Technology" (Heidi Knecht) *Scientific American.* July.

Whiteman, J.H.M. 1977. "Parapsychology and Physics," in Wolman, *Handbook.*

Wilgus, Neal. 1978. *The Illuminoids: Secret Societies and Political Paranoia* Albuquerque NM: Sun Books.

Wilson, Colin. 1980. *Mysteries.* Putnam Publishing Group.

Wilson, Robert. 1977. *Genealogy and History in the Biblical World.* New Haven: Yale University Press.

Wise, Abegg, and Cook. 1996. *The Dead Sea Scrolls.* San Franciso: HarperSanFranciso.

Wood, Bryant. 1993. "One Thousand Years Missing From Biblical History? A Review of a New Theory." *Bible and Spade* 6:4 (Autumn).

Wood, Lynn. 1945. "The Kahun Papyrus and the Date of the 12th Dynasty" *BASOR* 99, pp.5-9.

Wright, G.E. 1962. *Shechem: The Biography of a Biblical City.* New York: Doubleday.

Wunderlich. 1974. *The Secret of Crete.* New York: Macmillan.

Yadin, Yigael. 1963. *The Art of Warfare in Biblical Lands.* London: Weidenfeld and Nicolson.

Yamauchi, Edwin. 1973. "Immanuel Velikovshy's Catastropic History." *Journal of the American Scientific Affiliation* 25:4 (December).

Yamauchi, Edwin. 1994. "The Current State of Old Testament Historiography." *Faith, Tradition, and History* ed. by Millard, Hoffmeier, and Baker. Winona Lake: Eisenbrauns.

Yates, Frances. 1972. *The Rosicrucian Enlightenment.* London: Routledge & Kegan Paul.

————. 1983. *The Occult Philosophy in Elizabethan England.* London: Ark. [1979]

Yeivin, S. 1971. *The Israelite Conquest of Canaan.* Istanbul:Nederlands Historisch-Archaeologisch Instituut in HetNabije Oosten.

Young, Edward J. 1969. *The Book of Isaiah.* 3 Vols. Grand Rapids: Eerdmans.

Younger, K. Lawson. 1990. "Ancient Conquest Accounts: A Study in Ancient Near Eastern and Biblical History Writing." *JSOT Sup* 98. Sheffield: JSOT Press.

Yurco, F.J. 1990. "3,200-Year-Old Picture of Israelites Found in Egypt." *Biblical Archaeology Review* 16/5.

Zettl, Helmut. 1984. "Catastrophism and Ancient History," Volume VI Part 2 July 1984 *A Journal Of Interdisciplinary Study* Marvin Arnold Luckerman Executive Editor

Zevit, Ziony 1985. "The Problem of Ai." *Biblical Archaeology Review* 11:2 (March/April).

Zobel, Hans-Jurgen. 1990. "Jacob," and "Israel." *Theological Dictionary of the Old Testament.* Vol. 6 ed. by Botterweck and Ringgren. Grand Rapids: Eerdmans.

INDEX

B

C

H

I

J

N

O

P

V

W

The Wave (4 Volume Set)

Laura Knight-Jadczyk

With a new introduction by the author and never before published, UNEDITED sessions and extensive previously unpublished details, at long last, Laura Knight-Jadczyk's vastly popular series *The Wave* is available as a Deluxe four book set. Each of the three volumes include all of the original illustrations and many NEW illustrations with each copy comprising approximately 300 pages.

The Wave is an exquisitely written first-person account of Laura's initiation at the hands of the Cassiopaeans and demonstrates the unique nature of the Cassiopaean Experiment.

Laura writes:

I began writing the Wave Series and other articles as a way of collecting excerpts together in general subjects. As I did this, a truly extraordinary thing began to happen. The Cassiopaean Experiment had resulted in transmissions from myself "in the future", and I realized that by doing the suggested research, by digging for the answers based on the clues given me, I was BECOMING myself in the future - a cosmic self. I began to see what I had been trying to convey to myself from this superconscious state. The years of experimental work had created a new circuit wherein it was possible to simply ask a question in my mind about the subject at hand, and the answer would flow through my fingers onto the keyboard. I was often as amazed at what came out as anyone.

The Wave is a term used to describe a Macro-Cosmic Quantum Wave Collapse that produces both a physical and a "metaphysical" change to the Earth and all those residing upon it. It is theorized to be statistically probable sometime in the early 21st century.

Few will deny that at present humanity appears to be perched on the edge of an ever-widening abyss. The Bush administration's "war on terror" seems set to spread further death and destruction around the planet, polarizing and entrenching humanity along religious lines as it does so. The world economy is long past its sell by date, meteorites are raining down across the globe, increasingly frequent and ferocious earthquakes and hurricanes allow no one the comfort of feeling safe. As more and more people begin to awaken to these facts, the need for the truth to be shared as widely as possible grows significantly.

The concept of *The Wave* is vital for anyone wishing to understand the deeper meaning and reality of the human experience and what our very near future may have in store for us. By skillfully collecting and arranging the pieces of the puzzle as provided by the Cassiopaean transmissions and coupling them with in depth research and insights from hard-won personal experiences, Laura presents the reader with a compelling and provocative picture of the cognitive, biological, historical and ontological nature of humanity. In *The Wave* books, Laura presents what the Cassiopaeans -We are YOU in the future - have to say about the eventuality of *The Wave* - FROM the future.

We all have a responsibility to equip ourselves with the necessary knowledge to weather the approaching storm – *The Wave* will provide you with that knowledge.

The High Strangeness of Dimensions, Densities and the Process of Alien Abduction

Laura Knight-Jadczyk

Anyone who wants to understand the hyperdimensional reality which is the "home" of alleged aliens, should pick up Laura Knight-Jadczyk's latest book, *The High Strangeness of Dimensions, Densities and the Process of Alien Abduction*. With diligent research and a relentless drive for the facts, Laura strips away the facade of alien abductions masquerading as mind control and mind control masquerading as alien abductions. She then goes on to show how the Evil Elite rulers of the planet have merged, at the highest levels, with the Overlords of the Matrix Control System that underlies the structure of our reality.

Now, after 9-11, the fusion of the two worlds is almost complete. We have little time left, and the Controllers know it and they have made plans...

Those who prefer the nourishment of truth over the poison of New Age myths, those who want a real peek at what is behind the Stargate Conspiracy, should get this book. Today. Read it -- and weep.

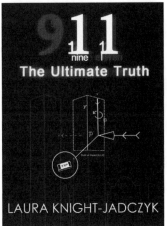

9-11: The Ultimate Truth

Laura Knight-Jadczyk with Joe Quinn, Henry See, and Scott Ogrin

Preface by Darren Williams, author of *Pentagon Strike*, the flash animation seen by 500 million people around the world

This hard-hitting book presents new and ground-breaking insights into just how the 9/11 attacks played out, answering the fundamental question of "why?".

911: The Ultimate Truth makes a strong case for the idea that September 11, 2001 marked the moment when our planet entered the final phase of a diabolical plan that has been many, many years in the making. It is a plan developed and nurtured by successive generations of ruthless individuals who relentlessly exploit the negative aspects of basic human nature to entrap humanity as a whole in endless wars and suffering in order to keep us confused and distracted to the reality of the man behind the curtain.

Drawing on historical and genealogical sources, Knight-Jadczyk eloquently links the 9/11 event to the modern-day Israeli-Palestinian conflict. She also cites the clear evidence that our planet undergoes periodic natural cataclysms, a cycle that has arguably brought humanity to the brink of destruction in the present day.

For its no nonsense style in cutting to the core of the issue and its sheer audacity in refusing to be swayed or distracted by the morass of disinformation employed by the Powers that Be to cover their tracks, 911: The Ultimate Truth can rightly claim to be THE definitive book on 9/11 - and what that fateful day's true implications are for the future of mankind.